Steinrötter / Heinze / Denga

EU Platform Law

EU Platform Law

A Handbook

edited by

Björn Steinrötter
Christian Heinze
Michael Denga

2025

BECK • HART • NOMOS

Published by
Nomos Verlagsgesellschaft mbH & Co. KG, Waldseestraße 3-5, 76530 Baden-Baden, Germany,
email: vertrieb@nomos.de

Co-published by
Verlag C.H.Beck oHG, Wilhelmstraße 9, 80801 München, Germany,
email: bestellung@beck.de

and

Hart Publishing, Kemp House, Chawley Park, Cumnor Hill, Oxford, OX2 9PH, United Kingdom,
online at: www.hartpub.co.uk

Published in North America by Hart Publishing,
An Imprint of Bloomsbury Publishing 1385 Broadway, New York, NY 10018, USA
email: mail@hartpub.co.uk

ISBN 978 3 8487 8891 0 (NOMOS Print)
ISBN 978 3 7489 2946 8 (NOMOS ePDF)
ISBN 978 3 406 78997 7 (C.H.BECK)
ISBN 978 1 5099 5979 2 (HART)

First Edition 2025

Foreword

In recent years, the European Union has demonstrated remarkable legislative energy in addressing the complex digital landscape spanning data, artificial intelligence (AI), and digital platforms. The EU legislature has been extremely prolific in framing regulations within this digital triad. However, the inherent complexity of these fields, coupled with the EU's multi-layered governance structure, poses substantial challenges for stakeholders navigating this evolving regulatory landscape.

Platform regulation has been a central focus, with recent legislative milestones including the Digital Services Act (DSA), the Digital Markets Act (DMA), and, more recently, the European Media Freedom Act (EMFA). While these regulations target platform governance, they also have significant implications for data and AI regulation. Conversely, platform operators must also consider a wider array of EU rules impacting data and AI to ensure comprehensive compliance.

This handbook aims to clarify and organize the EU's supranational requirements, identify pertinent legal issues, and suggest possible solutions. It strives to answer pressing practical questions with careful legal analysis, and we are deeply grateful to the authors for their expert contributions, which are indispensable to this work. We also extend our sincere thanks to Dr. Marco Ganzhorn of Nomos, whose committed, skilled, and constructive guidance was invaluable throughout the creation of this book.

Potsdam/Heidelberg/Halle, November 2024 — The Editors

Contents

List of Authors

Ranjana Andrea Achleitner holds a doctoral degree in law and a Master's degree in political science. She is a Postdoctoral Research Fellow at the Department of European Law at the Johannes Kepler University Linz, where she works on her post-doctoral thesis (Habilitation). Her doctoral thesis on the Digital Single Market (Geoblocking) was recognized with awards, and her research has received additional recognition. In 2023, she had the opportunity to present her research and gain new insights on online platforms and freedom of speech at the Information Law Institute at the New York University. Additionally, she serves as the Academic Coordinator of the European Documentation Centre of the European Commission at the Johannes Kepler University.

Dominik Arncken has worked as a lawyer with several digital platforms and is now a legal policy officer with Germany's Federal Ministry of Economic Affairs and Climate Action.

Dr. *Malek Barudi*, M.Jur. (Oxford) is a German-qualified attorney (Rechtsanwalt) and partner at international law firm Taylor Wessing. He acts for his clients from tech, media, entertainment, and science sectors in complex copyright disputes and other technology related litigation, frequently involving the legal framework for Internet service providers.

Hannes Bastians is a PhD candidate at the University of Potsdam (Prof. Dr. Björn Steinrötter) and a LL.M. candidate at the University of Cambridge. His research particulary focuses on the civil law aspects of digitalisation, contracts on digital products and tokens as well as the regulation of artificial intelligence.

Dr. *Matthias Berberich*, LL.M. (Cambridge), is lawyer in the IT, IP, and TMT practice group at Hengeler Mueller's Berlin office. He advises and represents companies and business associations, predominantly from the IT, technology, infrastructure, communication and media sectors. His practice focuses on technology-related M&A transactions, complex outsourcing, IT infrastructure and joint venture projects, litigation and regulatory advice, inter alia, for internet, telecommunications, media, fintech, e-commerce and data-driven business models. He regularly publishes on digital regulation and data economy topics and holds visiting lectures.

Dr. *Albrecht Conrad*, LL.M. (Columbia University) is a partner of Hengeler Mueller in London. He represents clients in matters of copyright and IP as well as technology and media regulation before German and European courts.

PD Dr. *Michael Denga* completed his PhD in the field of collective IP-rights management in 2014 at the Faculty of Law of the Humboldt University of Berlin (Germany). There he also received his habilitation in the subjects of European and German private and business law as well as in IT- and IP law in 2022. Since then, he has been an interim professor for private and business law at the Martin Luther University Halle-Wittenberg (Germany). He holds an LL.M. of King's College London and a Maîtrise en Droit of Paris II (Assas). He also has been a research fellow at the Weizenbaum Institute and the European New School of Digital Studies. His research focus lies at the junction of corporate- and technology law, taking a special interest in the corporate governance of digital business.

Ak. Rat Dr. *Max Dregelies* is a senior research assistant at the chair of Prof. Dr. Benjamin Raue (Trier) and research fellow at the Institut für Recht und Digitalisierung Trier (IRDT, Institute for Law and Digitalisation Trier). He researches and teaches mainly on platform regulation (DSA), intellectual property, media and personality rights.

Prof. Dr. *Christian Heinze*, LL.M. (Cambridge), is Professor of Civil Law, Commercial Law, EU Law and Comparative Law at Ruprecht Karls University of Heidelberg (Germany).

Prof. Dr. *Veronica Hoch-Loy* is a Junior Professor of Civil Law, Intellectual Property Law and Digitalization Law at the University of Bayreuth. Her research focuses on digitalization-related issues of civil law and commercial law.

Tom Kettler is a PhD candidate and researcher at Ruprecht Karls University of Heidelberg (Prof. Dr. Christian Heinze).

Carsten König is a postdoctoral researcher and senior lecturer at the University of Cologne. He has been a visiting lecturer at the Goethe University Frankfurt and the University of Würzburg, a postdoctoral fellow at the Harvard Law School Program on Corporate Governance and a visiting researcher at the Max Planck Institute for International, European and Regulatory Procedural Law in Luxembourg. His research interests include competition law and regulation (especially digital markets and energy markets), corporate law, private law, law and economics, and comparative law.

Sarah Legner is a Professor of Civil Law, Competition and Intellectual Property Law, European Private Law at the EBS University of Business and Law, Oestrich-Winkel. Her research focuses on the protection of competition in digital markets.

Sebastian Louven is a competition and regulatory lawyer, as well as a certified specialist in international business law, at Louven Rechtsanwälte PartGmbB in Detmold (Germany). His practice and research focus on competition law in the digital economy and telecommunications law. He also advises clients on European state aid law.

Prof. Dr. *Juliane Mendelsohn* is Junior-Professor of Law and Economics of Digitization and the Technical University of Ilmenau. She wrote her PhD thesis on systemic risk and banking crises under the supervision of Prof. Dr. Heike Schweitzer and currently focusses on competition and regulatory policy, in particular the regulation of Big Tech.

Dr. *Sarah Milde* is a competition partner at Hengeler Mueller's Munich office and advises in all areas of European and German competition law, covering merger control proceedings, antitrust litigation and compliance trainings/audits. In antitrust litigation, her focus is on dominance and cartel investigations (including the digital sector) and follow-on damages litigation. With her long-standing experience on the economic side of follow-on damages litigation, Dr. Sarah Milde has a strong focus on the crucial economic parameters of a case. She represents clients before the European Commission, the German Federal Cartel Office, and the European and German courts.

Philipp Richter, LL.M. (University College London), is a PhD scholar and researcher in the field of Data Governance and Law and Economics of Digitization and affiliated with the MPI Bonn (Collective Goods) and the Technical University of Ilmenau.

Dr. *Fiona Savary* is an attorney admitted to the bar in both Germany and Switzerland. Her practice focuses on IT law and digital regulation. Dr. Savary is a counsel at law firm CMS in Munich and has extensive experience in advising international clients on complex IT projects, including on contentious matters. She regularly publishes on digital regulation and data economy topics.

Dr. *Lina Marie Schauer* is a research assistant at law firm Nordemann Czychowski & Partner. Previously, she conducted research in the field of competition law and platform regulation at the University of Potsdam, Germany.

Sebastian Schwamberger is Assistant Professor for Civil Law, Commercial Law and the Law of Digitalization at the University of Rostock.

Prof. Dr. *Björn Steinrötter* is a Junior Professor in the field of IT law and Media law (tenure track) and Co-Director of the research centre 'Intellectual Property - Digitalisation - Competition' at the University of Potsdam, Germany.

Alexander Tribess is a founding partner of GreenGate Partners. He is a legal advisor to both start-up/scale-up and established technology companies. His focus is on integrating new technological developments into contracts and corporate compliance structures and processes. Alexander Tribess has published several articles on technology law and data protection issues in Germany and has contributed to international publications on the development of a legal framework for AI. He chairs the AI Substantive Law Committee of the ITechLaw Association.

Lennard Ullrich is writing his doctoral thesis on the Data Act with Prof. Dr. Björn Steinrötter and works as a research assistant at A&O Shearman in Hamburg.

Bibliography

Auer-Reinsdorff/Conrad IT- und DatenschutzR-HdB	Auer-Reinsdorff/Conrad, Handbuch IT- und Datenschutzrecht, 3. Ed. 2019
BeckOK DatenschutzR	Wolff/Brink/von Ungern-Sternberg, BeckOK Datenschutzrecht, 44. Ed. 2023
BeckOK InfoMedienR	Gersdorf/Paal, BeckOK Informations- und Medienrecht, 39. Ed. 2023
BeckOK UWG	Fritzsche/Münker/Stollwerck, BeckOK UWG, 20. Ed. 2023
Busch	Busch, P2B-VO, 2022
Calliess/Ruffert	Calliess/Ruffert, EUV/AEUV, 6. Ed. 2022
Dauses/Ludwigs EU-WirtschaftsR-HdB	Dauses/Ludwigs, Handbuch des EU-Wirtschaftsrechts, 57. Ed. 2022
Dreier/Schulze	Dreier/Schulze, Urheberrechtsgesetz, 7. Ed. 2022
Fezer/Büscher/Obergfell	Fezer/Büscher/Obergfell, UWG, Volumes 1 and 2, 3. Ed. 2016
Gola/Heckmann DS-GVO/BDSG	Gola/Heckmann, DS-GVO – BDSG, 3. Ed. 2022
Grabitz/Hilf/Nettesheim	Grabitz/Hilf/Nettesheim, Das Recht der Europäischen Union, 78. Ed. 2023
Graf v. Westphalen/Thüsing VertrR/AGB-Klauselwerke	Graf von Westphalen/Thüsing, Vertragsrecht und AGB-Klauselwerke, 48. Ed. 2022
Harte-Bavendamm/Henning-Bodewig	Harte-Bavendamm/Henning-Bodewig, UWG, 5. Ed. 2021
Hoeren/Sieber/Holznagel MMR-HdB	Hoeren/Sieber/Holznagel, Handbuch Multimedia-Recht, 58. Ed. 2022
Immenga/Mestmäcker	Immenga/Mestmäcker, Wettbewerbsrecht, Volumes 1–5, 6. Ed. 2019
Köhler/Bornkamm/Feddersen	Köhler/Bornkamm/Feddersen, UWG, 41. Ed. 2023
Kraul Der neue DSA	Kraul, Das neue Recht der digitalen Dienste, 2023
Kühling/Buchner	Kühling/Buchner, DS-GVO BDSG, 3. Ed. 2020
Loewenheim/Meessen/Riesenkampff/Kersting/Meyer-Lindemann	Loewenheim/Meessen/Riesenkampff/Kersting/Meyer-Lindemann, Kartellrecht, 4. Ed. 2020
MüKoStGB	Erb/Schäfer, Münchener Kommentar zum Strafgesetzbuch, Bände 1–9, 4. Ed. 2020
MüKoUWG	Heermann/Schlingloff, Münchener Kommentar zum Lauterkeitsrecht, Volumes 1 and 2, 3. Ed. 2019
MüKoWettbR	Bien/Meier-Beck/Montag/Säcker, Münchener Kommentar zum Wettbewerbsrecht, Volumes 2–5, 4. Ed. 2021
MüKoZPO	Krüger/Rauscher, Münchener Kommentar zur ZPO, Volumes 1 1–3, 6. Ed. 2020

Oxford HdB Online Intermediary Liability	Frosio, The Oxford Handbook of Online Intermediary Liability, 2020
Paal/Pauly	Paal/Pauly, DS-GVO BDSG, 3. Ed. 2021
Podszun HK-DMA	Podszun, Digital Markets Act, 2023
Schmidt/Hübener Der neue DMA	Schmidt/Hübener, Das neue Recht der digitalen Märkte, 2023
Schricker/Loewenheim	Schricker/Loewenheim, Urheberrecht, 6. Ed. 2020
Schröter	Schröter/Jakob/Klotz/Mederer, Europäisches Wettbewerbsrecht, 2. Ed. 2014
Simitis/Hornung/Spiecker gen. Döhmann	Simitis/Hornung/Spiecker gen. Döhmann, Datenschutzrecht, 2019
Spindler/Schmitz	Spindler/Schmitz, TMG, 2. Ed. 2018
Spindler/Schuster	Spindler/Schuster, Recht der elektronischen Medien, 4. Ed. 2019
Streinz	Streinz, EUV/AEUV, 3. Ed. 2018
Sydow/Marsch DS-GVO/BDSG	Sydow/Marsch, DS-GVO - BDSG, 3. Ed. 2022
von der Groeben/Schwarze/Hatje	von der Groeben/Schwarze/Hatje, Europäisches Unionsrecht, 7. Ed. 2015
Wandtke/Bullinger	Wandtke/Bullinger, Urheberrecht, 6. Ed. 2022
Wiedemann KartellR-HdB	Wiedemann, Handbuch des Kartellrechts, 4. Ed. 2020

Abbreviations

ACM	Autoriteit Consument & Markt (Netherlands)
AEUV	Vertrag über die Arbeitsweise der Europäischen Union (TFEU)
AfP	Zeitschrift für das gesamte Medienrecht / Archiv für Presserecht (journal)
AG	Advocate General
AGCM	Italian Competition Authority
AI	Artificial Intelligence
alt.	alternative
API	application programming interface
ARC	Act against restraints of competition (Gesetz Gegen gegen Wettbewerbsbeschränkungen)
Art.	Article(s)
BB	Betriebs-Berater (journal)
BeckRS	beck-online.RECHTSPRECHUNG (database)
BEREC	Body of European Regulators for Electronic Communications
BGB	Bürgerliches Gesetzbuch (German Civil Code)
BGH	Bundesgerichtshof (German Federal Court of Justice)
BKartA	Bundeskartellamt
BMWK	Bundesministerium für Wirtschaft und Klimaschutz (German Federal Ministry for Economic Affairs and Climate Action)
BR-Drs.	Bundesratsdrucksache (documents of the German Federal Council)
BT	Bundestag (German Federal Parliament)
BT-Drs.	Bundestags-Drucksache (German Federal Parliament Document)
CDSM	Directive (EU) 2019/790 of the European Parliament and of the Council of 17 April 2019 on copyright and related rights in the Digital Single Market and amending Directives 96/9/EC and 2001/29/EC
CEPR	Centre for Economic Policy Research
CERRE	Centre on Regulation in Europe
cf.	confer/compare
CFR	Charter of Fundamental Rights of the European Union
CJEU	Court of Justice of the European Union
CMA	Competition and Markets Authority (UK)
CMLR	Common Market Law Review
Concurrences	Antitrust law journal
CPC	Cost per click
CPI	Código da Propriedade Industrial (Portuguese Industrial Property Code)
CPS	core platform service
CR	Computer und Recht (journal)
DB	Der Betrieb (journal)
DCDS	Discrete and Continuous Dynamical Systems
DCS	Digital Services Coordinator
DG COMP	Directorate-General Competition
Dir.	Directive

DMA	Digital Markets Act
DSA	Digital Services Act
DS-GVO	Datenschutzgrundordnung (General Data Protection Regulation)
DStR	Deutsches Steuerrecht
e.g.	for example
E.L. Rev.	European Law Review (journal)
EBDS	European Board for Digital Services
EC	European Community
ECJ	European Court of Justice
ECLI	European Case Law Identifier
ECLR	European Competition Law Review
ECN	European Competition Network
ECR	European Conservatives and Reformists (political group)
ECtHR	European Court of Human Rights
edn	edition
eds	editors
eIDAS	Electronic Identification, Authentication, and trust services
EMFA	European Media Freedom Act
EP	European Parliament
et al.	and others
et seq./et seqq.	following
etc.	and so forth
ETSI	European Telecommunications Standards Institute
EU	European Union
EuCML	Journal of European Consumer and Market Law
EuGRZ	Europäische Grundrechte-Zeitschrift (journal)
EUR	Euro
EuR	Europarecht (journal)
EuZW	Europäische Zeitschrift für Wirtschaftsrecht (journal)
FCO	Foreign, Commonwealth and Development Office
fn	footnote
FRAND	Fair, reasonable and non-discriminatory terms
FS	Festschrift (jubilee publication)
GAFMA/GAFAM	Google, Apple, Facebook, Microsoft and Amazon
GDPR	General Data Protection Regulation
GPR	Zeitschrift für das Privatrecht der Europäischen Union (journal)
GREDEG	Groupe de Recherche en Droit, Economie et Gestion
GRUR	Gewerblicher Rechtsschutz und Urheberrecht (journal)
GRUR-Int	Gewerblicher Rechtsschutz und Urheberrecht – International (journal)
GWB	Gesetz gegen Wettbewerbsbeschränkungen (German Competition Act)
GWR	Gesellschafts- und Wirtschaftsrecht (journal)
i.e.	id est (that is)
ID	Identity and Democracy (political group)
IIC	International Review of Intellectual Property and Competition Law
IJLTP	Illinois Journal of Law, Technology & Policy
IoT	Internet of Things

ISO	International Organization für Standardization
ITRB	IT-Rechtsberater (journal)
IWRZ	Journal of International Business Law
JAE	Journal of Accounting and Economics (journal)
JCLE	Journal of Competition Law & Economics
JECLAP	Journal of European Competition Law & Practice
JFTC	Japan Fair Trade Commission
JIPITEC	Journal of Intellectual Property, Information Technology and Electronic Commerce Law
JREG	Yale Journal on Regulation
JZ	Juristenzeitung (journal)
KCC	Korean Telecommunications Commission
KFTC	Korea Fair Trade Commission (South Korea)
Ltd	Limited
M&A	Mergers & Acquisitions
MEP	Member of the European Parliament
MFN	most favoured nation
MMR	Multimedia und Recht (journal)
mn.	margin number(s)
MüKoWettbR	Münchener Kommentar zum Wettbewerbsrecht
MüKoZPO	Münchener Kommentar zur Zivilprozessordnung
NFC	near field communication
NGO	Non-governmental organization
NIICS	Number-independent interpersonal communications services
NJW	Neue Juristische Wochenschrift (journal)
no.	number(s)
NVwZ	Neue Zeitschrift für Verwaltungsrecht (journal)
NZKart	Neue Zeitschrift für Kartellrecht (journal)
NZWiSt	Neue Zeitschrift für Wirtschafts-, Steuer- und Unternehmensstrafrecht (journal)
OECD	Organisation für Economic Co-operation and Development
OFT	Office of Fair Trading
OJ	Official Journal
OLG	Oberlandesgericht (German Higher Regional Court)
OS	Operating System
OTA	Over-the-Air
ÖZK	Österreichische Zeitschrift für Kartellrecht (journal)
p.	page(s)
P2B	Platform to Business
PAR	Regulation on the Transparency and Targeting of Political Advertising
para.	paragraph(s)
PIMS	personal information management system
RDi	Recht Digital (journal)
rec.	recital(s)
Reg.	Regulation(s)
RFI	request for information
SDK	Software Development Kit
sent.	sentence
SNIA	Storage Networking Industry Association

SSRN	Social Science Research Network
subpara.	subparagraph(s)
SWD	Staff working document
TEU	Treaty on European Union
TFEU	Treaty on the Functioning of the European Union
TILEC	Tilburg Law and Economics Center
TMG	Telemediengesetz (Telemedia Act)
UK	United Kingdom
UOKiK	Office of Competition and Consumer Protection
US	United States
UWG	Gesetz gegen den unlauteren Wettbewerb (German Act against Unfair Competition)
v	versus
VAT	Valued Added Tax
VBER	Vertical Block Exemption Regulation
VerfVO	Verfahrensordnung
VLOP(s)	Very large online platform(s)
VLOSE(s)	Very large online search engines
VO	Verordnung (Regulation)
VR	Virtual Reality
VuR	Verbraucher und Recht (journal)
WuW	Wirtschaft und Wettbewerb (journal)
ZAG	Zahlungsdiensteaufsichtsgesetz (German Payment Services Oversight Act)
ZD	Zeitschrift für Datenschutz (journal)
ZEuP	Zeitschrift für Europäisches Privatrecht (journal)
ZfDR	Zeitschrift für Digitalisierung und Recht (journal)
ZG	Zeitschrift für Gesetzgebung (journal)
ZGE	Zeitschrift für Geistiges Eigentum (journal)
ZPO	Zivilprozessordnung (German Code of Civil Procedure)
ZUM	Zeitschrift für Urheber- und Medienrecht (journal)
ZWeR	Zeitschrift für Wettbewerbsrecht (journal)

CHAPTER 1:
DSA

§ 1
Introduction

Literature: *Achleitner*, 'Der Digital Services Act als risikobasierte Regulierung', MR-Int 2022, 114; *Beaujean/Oelke/Wierny*, 'Immer mehr Verordnungen aus Brüssel und ihre Auswirkungen auf die Medienregulierung', MMR 2023, 11; *Beck*, 'Der Entwurf des Digital Services Act – Hintergrund, Ziele und Grundsätze künftiger Regulierung des virtuellen Raumes in der EU', DVBl 2021, 1000; *Berberich/Seip*, 'Der Entwurf des Digital Services Act', GRUR-Prax 2021, 4; *Busch*, 'Der Digital Services Act: Ein neuer Rechtsrahmen für den Online-Handel?', ZdiW 2021, 88; *Busch/Mak*, 'Putting the Digital Services Act in Context: Bridging the Gap Between EU Consumer Law and Platform Regulation', EuCML 2021, 109; *Denga*, 'Plattformregulierung durch europäische Werte: Zur Bindung von Meinungsplattformen an EU-Grundrechte', EuR 2021, 569; *Dregelies*, 'Der Schutz vor Dark Patterns im DSA, MMR 2023, 243'; *Dregelies*, 'Digital Services Act. Überblick über den neuen Rechtsrahmen für das Internet', MMR 2022, 1033; *Dregelies*, 'Verbraucherschutz im Digital Services Act, VuR 2023, 175; *Duivenvoorde*, 'The Liability of Online Marketplaces under the Unfair Commercial Practices Directive, the E-commerce Directive and the Digital Services Act', EuCML 2022, 43; *Eisenreich*, 'Digital Services Act – ein wirksames Instrument gegen Hass und Hetze im Netz?', RDi 2021, 289; *Frank*, 'Inhaltemoderation, Erfahrungsbericht: Wie YouTube als digitale Plattform Verantwortung übernimmt', MMR 2022, 1026; *Gerdemann/Spindler*, 'Das Gesetz über digitale Dienste (Digital Services Act) (Teil 1). Grundlegende Strukturen und Regelungen für Vermittlungsdienste und Host-Provider', GRUR 2023, 3; *Gerdemann/Spindler*, 'Das Gesetz über digitale Dienste (Digital Services Act) (Teil 2). Die Regelungen für Online-Plattformen sowie sehr große Online-Plattformen und -Suchmaschinen', GRUR 2023, 115; *Gerpott*, 'Das Gesetz über digitale Dienste nach den Trilog-Verhandlungen', CR 2022, 516; *Gerpott*, 'Neue europäische Regeln für digitale Plattformen. Vergleichender Überblick zu den Vorschlägen der EU-Kommission für Gesetze über digitale Märkte und über digitale Dienste', CR 2021, 255; *Gertz/Martini/Seeliger/Timko*, 'Dark Patterns – eine interdisziplinäre Analyse', LTZ 2023, 3; *Gielen/Uphues*, 'Digital Markets Act und Digital Services Act. Regulierung von Markt- und Meinungsmacht durch die Europäische Union', EuZW 2021, 627; *Grünwald/Nüßing*, 'Vom NetzDG zum DSA: Wachablösung beim Kampf gegen Hate Speech? Diskussionsstand zu beiden Gesetzesvorhaben und deren Vereinbarkeit', MMR 2021, 283; *Härting/Adamek*, 'Digital Services Act, (Compliance-)Verpflichtungen für Online-Provider', IPRB 2021, 100; *Härting/Adamek*, 'Digital Services Act – ein Überblick', CR 2021, 165; *Härting/Adamek*, 'Lässt der Digital Services Act Raum für ein "Gesetz gegen digitale Gewalt"? ', CR 2023, 316; *Holznagel*, 'Chapter II des Vorschlags der EU-Kommission für einen Digital Services Act. Versteckte Weichenstellungen und ausstehende Reparaturen bei den Regelungen zu Privilegierung, Haftung & Herkunftslandprinzip für Provider und Online-Plattformen', CR 2021, 123; *Holznagel*, 'Zu starke Nutzerrechte in Art. 17 und 18 DSA', CR 2022, 594; *Janal*, 'Der Entwurf eines Digital Services Acts: Neue Perspektiven der Verantwortung von Diensteanbietern der Informationsgesellschaft', K&R supplement 1 to Issue 6/2021, 6; *Janal*, 'Friendly Fire? Das Urheberrechts-Diensteanbieter-Gesetz und sein Verhältnis zum künftigen Digital Services Act', GRUR 2022, 211; *Janal*, 'Haftung und Verantwortung im Entwurf des Digital Services Acts', ZEuP 2021, 227; *Janka/Kuß/Waletzko*, 'Die "Digital Acts" – Verschärfte Spielregeln für die digitale Welt', ZdiW 2021, 44; *Kaesling*, 'Evolution statt Revolution der Plattformregulierung', ZUM 2021, 177; *Kalbhenn/Hemmert-Halswick*, 'EU-weite Vorgaben für die Content-Moderation in sozialen Netzwerken', ZUM 2021, 184; *Keber*, 'Der Konstruktionsfehler im Krisenreaktionsmechanismus nach Art. 36 Digital Services Act', CR 2022, 660; *Kettemann/Schulz/Fertmann*, 'Anspruch und Wirklichkeit der Plattformregulierung. Kommissionsentwürfe der Rechtsakte zu digitalen Diensten und Märkten', ZRP 2021, 138; *Kühling*, '»Fake News« und »Hate Speech« – Die Verantwortung der Medienintermediäre zwischen neuen NetzDG, MStV und Digital Services Act', ZUM 2021, 461; *Kühling/Sauerborn*, '"Dark patterns" unter der DS-GVO und dem DSA – Neue Herausforderung für die digitale Rechtsordnung', CR 2022, 226; *Kuhlmann*, 'Der Digital Services Act und seine Folgen für das nationale Medienrecht', ZUM 2023, 170; *Kuhlmann/Trute*, 'Die Regulierung von Desinformationen und rechtswidrigen Inhalten nach dem neuen Digital Services Act', GSZ 2022, 115; *Kuß/Lehmann*, 'Digital Services Act – Entwurf eines einheitlichen Rechtsrahmens für die EU-Digitalwirtschaft', DB 2021, 605; *Lobigs*, Qualitätsrisiken der Plattformökonomie für die Wissenschaftskommunikation, Berlin 2021; *Lutzi*, 'The Scope of the Digital Services Act and Digital Markets Act: Thoughts on the Conflict of Laws', Dalloz IP/IT 2023, 278; *Mendelsohn*, 'Die "normative Macht" der Plattformen – Gegenstand der zukünftigen Digitalregulierung?', MMR 2021, 857; *Müller*, 'Künftige Plattformregulierung und effektive Durchsetzung in Deutschland', MMR 2022, 1007; *Peguera*, 'The Platform Neutrality Conundrum and the Digital Services Act', IIC 2022, 681; *Peukert*, 'Zu Risiken und Nebenwirkungen des Gesetzes über digitale Dienste (Digital Services Act)', KritV 2022, 57; *Picht/Richter*, 'The Proposed EU Digital Services Regulation 2020: Data Desiderata', Max Planck Institute for Innovation and Competition Research Paper No. 21–21, 1; *Raue*, 'Die Regulierung von Hate Speech mit Mitteln des Zivilrechts', JZ 2022, 232; *Raue*, '"Unberührt" – das Verhältnis von DAS zur DSM-RL und zum UrhDaG', ZUM 2023, 160; *Raue/Heesen*, 'Der Digital Services Act', NJW 2022, 3537; *Rohrßen*,

'Digitale Distribution in der EU – Digital Single Market: Neue Regeln im E-Commerce ab 2022', ZVertriebsR 2021, 71; *Rössel*, 'Digital Services Act. Vorschlag zur Harmonisierung der Verantwortlichkeit von Onlineplattformen', ITRB 2021, 35; *Savary*, 'Der Digital Services Act steht vor der Tür: ein Meilenstein in der Regulierung von Online-Plattformen?', BB Issue 10/2022, Die erste Seite; *Savova/Mikes/Cannon*, 'The Proposal for an EU Digital Services Act. A closer look from a European and three national perspectives: France, UK and Germany', CRi 2021, 38; *Schäufele/Krück*, 'Der Digital Services Act – Revolution für Vermittlungsdienste?', GRUR-Prax 2023, 120; *Schmid/Grewe*, 'Digital Services Act: Neues "Grundgesetz für Onlinedienste"?', MMR 2021, 279; *Sesing-Wagenpfeil*, 'Suchmaschinen im Digital Services Act', CR 2023, 113; *Spindler*, 'Der Vorschlag für ein neues Haftungsregime für Internetprovider – der EU-Digital Services Act (Teil 1)', GRUR 2021, 545; *Spindler*, 'Der Vorschlag für ein neues Haftungsregime für Internetprovider – der EU-Digital Services Act. Teil 2: Große und besonders große Plattformen', GRUR 2021, 653; *Spindler*, 'Haftung von Infrastrukturbetreibern, insbesondere DNS-Resolver nach TMG und geplantem Digital Service Act', CR 2022, 318; *Spindler*, 'Die Zukunft des europäischen Haftungsrechts für Internet-Provider – der Digital Services Act', MMR 2023, 73; *Stark*, Law for Sale: A Philosophical Critique of Regulatory Competition, Oxford 2019; *Steinrötter*, 'EU-Plattformregulierung und der Wettbewerb der Regelsetzer', EWS 5/2022, Die erste Seite; *Steinrötter*, 'Obacht, Online-Plattformen: Der Digital Services Act kommt, EWS 6/2020, Die erste Seite; *Tschorr*, 'Meldepflicht von illegalen Inhalten an staatliche Stellen. Digital Services Act versus Netzwerkdurchsetzungsgesetz', MMR 2022, 1053; *Voigt/Bastians*, 'Pflicht zur Benennung von EU-Vertretern im europäischem Digitalrecht', MMR 2022, 930; *von Lewinski/Klink*, 'Compliance-Pflichten nach dem DSA – ein umfassender Überblick', RDi 2023, 183; *Wampfler*, 'Empörungsengagement und Desinformation – politische Kommunikation und die Dynamik digitaler Plattformen' in Klein/Schmidt (eds), Was macht die Digitalisierung mit der Politik?, Oldenburg 2022, p. 111; *Wehde*, 'Datenzugang über Art. 31 Abs. 2 DSA-E', MMR 2022, 827.

A. Preliminary remarks

1 With the Digital Services Act (DSA)[1], the supranational legislator has created **specific liability privilege rules and special due-diligence obligations for online intermediary services,** which fully apply since 17 February 2024. In terms of both the scope and depth of the regulation, this is a globally unprecedented step towards regulating intermediary services, in particular online platforms.[2] The regulation does not follow a sector-specific approach, but rather **applies horizontally** to a broad range of services.[3]

2 Initially, the **legislative project** went **largely unnoticed.**[4] However, once the public realised what fundamental and substantial regulations were to be created for online intermediary services, **the number and intensity of reports and opinions accompanying the legislative process swelled steadily**. Superlatives and buzzwords were not spared in the discussions that arose from that point. The various 'interest groups' or lobby groups had a lot at stake, of course. Some claimed an attack on the platforms' business models, some warned that the freedom of the internet was endangered, and others demanded

[1] Digital Services Act – Regulation (EU) 2022/2065 of the European Parliament and of the Council of 19 October 2022 on a Single Market for Digital Services and amending Directive 2000/31/EC, OJ 2022 L 277, 1.

[2] Gerdemann/Spindler GRUR 2023, 115 (124).

[3] Janka/Kuß/Waletzko ZdiW 2021, 44 (46).

[4] Thus, at the end of December 2020, one could still read articles such as "Watch out, online platforms: The Digital Services Act is coming"; cf. Steinrötter EWS 6/2020, Die erste Seite.

the containment of rights violations or hate and incitement tirades, or have spoken in favour of the stronger regulation of (maybe too) potent platforms. In spite of the uproar, **the DSA was passed remarkably quickly**, less than two years after the European Commission's draft was made available.[5] It aims to bridge the gap between the conflicting positions outlined above and – in its own words – ensure a 'safe, predictable and trusted online environment that facilitates innovation and in which fundamental rights enshrined in the Charter, including the principle of consumer protection, are effectively protected' and 'contribute to the proper functioning of the internal market for intermediary services' (Art. 1(1) DSA).

With **156 recitals, 93 articles, and altogether more text than the** GDPR[6] – which, however, has 173 recitals and 99 articles – the DSA comes across as extremely opulent. 3
If one adds the (expected) delegated acts[7], along with the implementing acts and guidelines of the European Commission, it quickly becomes clear from the quantitative results alone that the addressed platforms can expect to put forth **considerable additional efforts obtaining legal advice.**[8] This applies all the more since – as the contents of this handbook demonstrate – other recent EU and accompanying legislation must also be taken into account. Furthermore, **the DSA is brimming with indeterminate legal terms.** This allows for future changes to the platform regulations, as they are open to development and guided by fundamental rights, in which the interests of users and the general public can be adequately accounted for.[9] Here, the ECJ will have to gradually make adjustments / concretisations to the law, which will be difficult for platform operators to anticipate. For the time being, it will therefore be a matter of complying with the requirements as best as possible, whereby the recommendation is to opt for the 'stricter' handling of the regulatory requirements in case of doubt, in view of the quite consumer-friendly tendencies of the ECJ case law.

The EU legislator **bases its legislative competence to issue the DSA 'in particular'** 4
on Art. 114 TFEU, which it states even before the recitals in the official document. **However,** the internal market harmonisation clause, which refers solely to economic regulatory aspects, does **not apply to media and content regulation**. Rather, these areas remain within the competence of the Member States.[10] Nevertheless, the DSA also deals with the handling of media content, insofar as it is distributed by online intermediary services, especially since various platforms have a serious influence on the formation of individual and public opinion.[11]

---

[5] European Commission, 'Proposal for a regulation of the European Parliament and of the Council on a Single Market For Digital Services (Digital Services Act) and amending Directive 2000/31/ECCOM(2020)', 15.12.2020, COM(2020) 825 final; on this, for example, Beck DVBl 2021, 1000; Berberich/Seip GRUR-Prax 2021, 4; Busch/Mak EuCML 2021, 109; Härting/Adamek CR 2021, 165; Holznagel CR 2021, 123; Janal K&R supplement 1 to Issue 6/2021, 6; Kaesling ZUM 2021, 177; Kalbhenn/Hemmert-Halswick ZUM 2021, 184; Savova/Mikes/Cannon CRi 2021, 38; Schmid/Grewe MMR 2021, 279; Spindler GRUR 2021, 545; Spindler GRUR 2021, 653.

[6] General Data Protection Regulation – Regulation (EU) 2016/679 of the European Parliament and of the Council of 27 April 2016 on the protection of natural persons with regard to the processing of personal data and on the free movement of such data, and repealing Directive 95/46/EC (General Data Protection Regulation), OJ 2016 L 119, 1.

[7] Cf., e.g., C(2023) 6807 final.

[8] Systematic preparation of compliance obligations under the DSA in v. Lewinski/Klink RDi 2023, 183.

[9] Cf. also Raue/Heesen NJW 2022, 3537 (3543).

[10] Beaujean/Oelke/Wierny MMR 2023, 11 (13).

[11] Beaujean/Oelke/Wierny MMR 2023, 11 (13).

B. From the E-Commerce Directive to the Digital Services Act

5 Without doubt, the E-Commerce Directive 2000/31/EC[12] has its merits, which the DSA legislator also acknowledges in rec. 16(1)(1) DSA, according to which the legal framework at that time contributed to legal certainty for intermediary services, which in turn promoted their expansion and rapid development.[13] The DSA therefore intends to preserve this legal framework,[14] which is why, **according to Art. 2(3) DSA,** it has **no effect on the application of the E-Commerce Directive 2000/31/EC.** Pursuant to Art. 89(1) DSA the Directive is only amended to the extent that **Art. 12–15 E-Commerce Directive** and thus the liability privileges for intermediary services as well as the prohibition of general monitoring obligations are **deleted.** They are replaced by **Art. 4–6, 8 DSA.** These provisions largely have the same content as the respective provisions of the Directive, with certain concretisations concerning the participation of the parties concerned in the case of blocking or deletion of content. However, there is still no general obligation to monitor intermediary services. References in other legal acts to Art. 12–15 E-Commerce are deemed to be references to Art. 4–6, 8 DSA in accordance with Art. 89(2) DSA. The **country-of-origin principle** from Art. 3 E-Commerce Directive 2000/31/EC **remains in force** (→ § 2 mn. 67 et seqq.). Accordingly, the formal replacement of the liability provisions as the 'cornerstone of the internet economy'[15] did not take place because their contents were excessively outdated (→ § 3 mn. 7 et seqq.). The fear in parts of the digital economy that this could lead to a substantial softening of Art. 14 E-Commerce Directive has thus ultimately proven to be unfounded. Rather, the EU legislator was primarily concerned with presenting a **Europe-wide regulation solution that is directly binding** (Art. 288(2) TFEU), which – in contrast to directive requirements that have to be transposed into national law (Art. 288(3) TFEU) – is completely detached from national peculiarities (→ § 3 mn. 19 et seqq.).

6 Although an EU regulation is now in force and thus the direct applicability of its provisions is ensured, it will still primarily be **the Member States that determine what content** is **illegal.**[16] Thus, **a central reference point of numerous DSA provisions remains unharmonised.** For example, Art. 3(h) DSA defines the term 'illegal content' as 'any information that, in itself or in relation to an activity, including the sale of products or the provision of services, is not in compliance with Union law or the law of any Member State which is in compliance with Union law, irrespective of the precise subject matter or nature of that law'. Further refinement is provided by rec. 12 DSA, which states that the term 'should broadly reflect the existing rules in the offline environment'. Furthermore, 'that concept should be understood to refer to information, irrespective of its form, that under the applicable law is either itself illegal, such as illegal hate speech or terrorist content and unlawful discriminatory content, or that the applicable rules render illegal in view of the fact that it relates to illegal activities'. As specific examples, the recital then mentions 'the sharing of images depicting child sexual abuse, the unlawful non-consensual sharing of private images, online stalking, the sale of non-compliant or counterfeit products, the sale of products or the provision of services in infringement of consumer

---

12 Directive 2000/31/EC of 8 June 2000 on certain legal aspects of information society services, in particular electronic commerce, in the Internal Market ('Directive on electronic commerce'), OJ 2000 L 178, 1.

13 Rec. 16 sent 1. DSA. This is likely to apply in particular to the liability privileges; Gielen/Uphues EuZW 2021, 627 (632).

14 Rec. 16(1)(2) DSA.

15 Berberich/Seip GRUR-Prax 2021, 4 (6).

16 This is criticised by Dregelies MMR 2022, 1033 (1038).

protection law, the unauthorised use of copyright-protected material, the illegal offer of accommodation services or the illegal sale of live animals'. The **term 'hate speech'** has been incorporated into the recital from the **'marketing language' of the COM**, which has probably also caught on in the journalistic reporting of the legislative process. It is not a legal term,[17] but a term originating from the political discourse in the USA.[18] Ultimately, in the respective legal systems of the Member States, it refers to criminal offences such as incitement to violence and/or hatred based on racist or xenophobic motives.[19] Not least at this point, there are likely to be **discrepancies among the individual Member States.**

The fact that a Regulation replaces a Directive (albeit only partially due to the continued existence of the E-Commerce Directive) is a trend in recent EU legislation. However, the differences between the objectives of the E-Commerce Directive and those of the DSA are not insignificant. Whereas pursuant to its Art. 1(1)(2) the E-Commerce Directive was intended 'to contribute to the proper functioning of the internal market by ensuring the free movement of information society services between the Member States' and 'without prejudice to the level of protection for, in particular, public health and consumer interests, as established by Community acts and national legislation implementing them in so far as this does not restrict the freedom to provide information society services', **the DSA significantly broadens its teleological fundament compared to the E-Commerce Directive.** The smooth functioning of the internal market for intermediary services is no longer to be found exclusively in the enumeration of Art. 1(1) DSA. Rather, the aim is 'a safe, predictable and trusted online environment that facilitates innovation and in which fundamental rights enshrined in the Charter, including the principle of consumer protection, are effectively protected'. Ultimately, it is about nothing less than giving the digital space a new and modern framework.[20] However, the DSA also introduces entirely new obligations (especially for very large online platforms, VLOPs). 7

C. Legal policy background

The relevance of intermediary services, both for the EU economy and for the everyday life of citizens, who often use these services on a daily basis, is already prominently emphasised in rec. 1(1)(1) and (3). DSA. Online platforms are therefore by no means to be fundamentally called into question. However, the legislator wants to **address the new risks and challenges** that are emerging as a result of the digital transformation and the increased use of such online platforms – namely, 'for individual recipients of the relevant service, companies and society as a whole'.[21] In particular, these are problems related to taking action against illegal content and online disinformation. **Scientific studies** have long since identified the connection between procedures of disinformation or attention economy and the logic of platforms.[22] To put it briefly, it is usually the most adventurous statements that experience the greatest dissemination, which is why **social media** 8

17 Critically, already Steinrötter, 'Digital Services Act zur Regulierung großer Digitalkonzerne' (science media center germany, 25.04.2022) <www.sciencemediacenter.de/alle-angebote/rapid-reaction/details/news/digital-services-act-zur-regulierung-grosser-digitalkonzerne/> (last accessed: 23.7.2024).

18 Gerdemann/Spindler GRUR 2023, 3 (4) are correct, pointing out that this is why the addition 'unlawful' was therefore ultimately added.

19 Gerdemann/Spindler GRUR 2023, 3 (4).

20 Dregelies MMR 2022, 1033.

21 Rec. 1(1)(4) DSA.

22 Wampfler in Klein/Schmidt, p. 111; Lobigs, p. 37 et passim.

platforms in particular resemble a megaphone – not only, but also – for advocates of extreme opinions.[23] Disinformation campaigns within (also algorithmically compiled) filter bubbles can virtually become a **propagandistic weapon.**[24] At the same time, they are difficult to combat in a liberal democracy.[25]

D. Goals

9 As already mentioned, Art. 1(1) DSA states: 'The aim of this Regulation is to contribute to the proper functioning of the internal market for intermediary services by setting out harmonised rules for a safe, predictable and trusted online environment that facilitates innovation and in which fundamental rights enshrined in the Charter, including the principle of consumer protection, are effectively protected'. It is worth noting that **consumer protection** plays an even more central role than under the aegis of the E-Commerce Directive, which can be seen, inter alia, in the adaptation of the liability privilege in Art. 6(3) DSA as well as the newly stipulated due-diligence obligations of Chapter 3, Section 4.[26] From the beginning it was also a concern of the draft regulation to **level out existing fragmentation within the digital single market**[27] **or to counteract its development.**[28] The legislative coherence was indeed threatened by various laws or legislative initiatives within the Member States, which, incidentally, regularly faced allegations of being unconstitutional and/or contrary to EU law. This applied, for example, to the German 'NetzDG',[29] the Austrian Communications Platforms Act, and the French 'Loi Avia',[30] which has been rejected as partly unconstitutional. The reason for these national legislative efforts was that the E-Commerce Directive seemed to be 'outdated'', i.e. it was no longer considered capable of adequately dealing with the **new economic and social dangers** posed by the modern **platform economy** (in addition to numerous advantages), e.g. criminal offences that are difficult to prosecute, dangers to informational self-determination, copyright infringements, market concentration and the abuse made possible by this, as well as a flood of hate, agitation, and fake news.[31] The reason for the national legislative projects is probably also the previous restraint at the EU level, which at best issued vague and non-binding codes of conduct, recommendations or communications.[32]

---

[23] Gielen/Uphues EuZW 2021, 627 (632).

[24] Gielen/Uphues EuZW 2021, 627 (632).

[25] Ladeur, 'Schutz vor Verletzung von Persönlichkeitsrechten und "Desinformation" in sozialen Medien unter Bedingungen der politischen Polarisierung' (Verfassungsblog, 13.12.2022) <verfassungsblog.de/personlichkeitsrecht-soziale-medien/> (last accessed: 23.7.2024).

[26] Dregelies VuR 2023, 175 (176): 'nothing less than a paradigm shift'.

[27] On legal fragmentation in the Digital Single Market: Janal K&R Supplement 1 to Issue 6/2021, 6 mn. 1 with further evidence.

[28] Rec. 2(1)(3) and (4) DSA; BT Wissenschaftliche Dienste No. 10/20 of 15.9.2020, 1; Raue/Heesen NJW 2022, 3537; Steinrötter EWS 6/2020, Die erste Seite; Wilman, 'The Digital Services Act (DSA) – An Overview' (Social Science Research Network, 16.12.2022) <ssrn.com/abstract=4304586> or <dx.doi.org/10.2139/ssrn.4304586> (last accessed: 23.7.2024).

[29] Guggenberger NJW 2017, 2577 (2581 et seq.), for example, sees an incompatibility with the country-of-origin principle; Spindler ZUM 2017, 473 (474 et seqq.), in detail; Kalscheuer/Hornung NVwZ 2017, 1721, for example, assume an unconstitutionality.

[30] Conseil Constitutionel, Décision n° 2020–801 DC du 18 juin 2020; cf. Heldt, 'Loi Avia: Frankreichs Verfassungsrat kippt Gesetz gegen Hass im Netz' (JuWissBlog No. 96/2020, 23.6.2020) <www.juwiss.de/96-2020/> (last accessed: 23.7.2024).

[31] Dregelies MMR 2022, 1033.

[32] Gielen/Uphues EuZW 2021, 627 (632); on the traditional reluctance of the EU to regulate digital processes: Beck DVBl 2021, 1000.

10 **Legal harmonisation** via EU regulation is intended to 'provide businesses with access to new markets and opportunities to exploit the benefits of the internal market, while allowing consumers and other recipients of the services to have increased choice'.[33] At the same time, it should increase legal certainty (especially for developers) and drive interoperability.[34] The technology-neutral designs aim to promote innovation.[35]

11 Responsible and diligent conduct on the part of the providers of intermediary services appears to be a basic prerequisite for ensuring that natural persons may exercise in particular their right to the freedom of expression and information, the freedom to conduct a business, the right to non-discrimination, and that the achievement of a high level of consumer protection is guaranteed.[36] Various other recitals (e.g. rec. 9 et seq., 40 DSA) make it clear at the same time that the DSA does not only pursue **economic** but also **democratic and socially relevant concerns**, freedom of expression and information, including freedom of the media and media pluralism.[37]

E. Overarching regulatory concept

12 The DSA establishes specific liability exemption rules and special due-diligence obligations for online intermediary services that offer their products to users in the EU (Art. 1(2)(a)(b) DSA), whereby the **procedural enforcement architecture** (Art. 1(2)(c) DSA) is reminiscent of the GDPR mechanisms,[38] but takes them a step further.[39] The continuation of the liability privilege for service providers for the user content they provide in Chapter II is a core aspect of the DSA. In addition, there are numerous due diligence and transparency obligations (Chapter III). These primarily concern content moderation and (other) restrictions on user content and will entail a noticeable additional organisational effort.[40] As an overarching conceptual rule of thumb, it can be stated that the duties of online intermediary services vary depending on their role, size, and impact in the online environment, which is **a risk-based approach**[41] (for more details, see → § 2 mn. 2, 19 et seqq., → § 5 mn. 7 et seqq.). An increasingly smaller group of norm addressees must fulfil **increasingly stricter requirements** (four-level regulation; Figure 1).[42]

---

[33] Rec. 2(1)(3) DSA.
[34] Rec. 4(1)(3) DSA.
[35] Rec. 4(1)(4) DSA.
[36] Cf. Rec. 3 DSA.
[37] Beaujean/Oelke/Wierny MMR 2023, 11 (12).
[38] The same is true regarding the territorial scope of application via a unilateral conflict-of-laws rule; see Lutzi Dalloz IP/IT 2023, 278.
[39] Janal K&R Supplement 1 to Issue 6/2021, 6; Raue/Heesen NJW 2022, 3537.
[40] Schäufele/Krück GRUR-Prax 2023, 120.
[41] Achleitner MR-Int 2022, 114 (116 et seqq.).
[42] Gerdemann/Spindler GRUR 2023, 3.

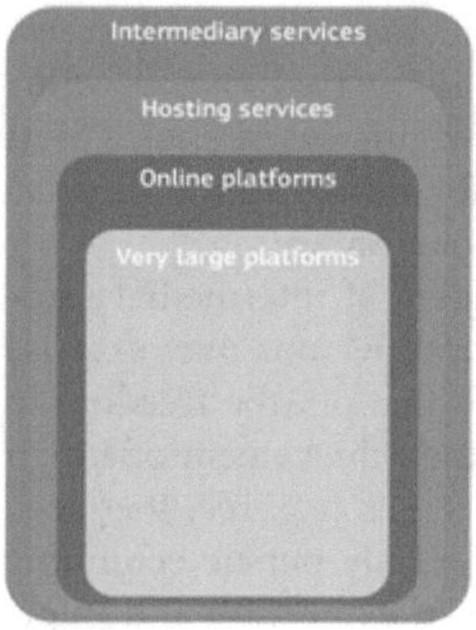

- Intermediary services, Art. 3(g) DSA
- Hosting services, Art. 3(g)(iii) DSA
- Online platforms, Art. 3(i) DSA
- Very large online platforms, Art. 33(1) DSA

Figure 1[43]

13 The general provisions (Art. 1–3 DSA) are followed by provisions on the lowest level of regulation, which applies to all intermediary service providers (Art. 4–15 DSA).[44] Then, some further requirements apply specifically to hosting service providers, including online platforms (Art. 16–18 DSA). An additional increase or tightening of the set of obligations then arises for online platforms (Art. 19–32 DSA), before the last and most obligation-intensive level regulating providers of very large online platforms and very large online search engines (Art. 33–48 DSA).[45] These last two stages appear groundbreaking, as the EU legislator is venturing for the first time to comprehensively regulate online platforms as central information intermediaries of Web 2.0.[46] Remarkable novelties result from, among other things, the provisions on dark patterns in Art. 25 DSA (→ § 9 mn. 87 et seqq.).[47]

14 Chapter IV then deals with supervision and enforcement (Art. 49 et seqq. DSA). The supervisory structure is not exactly clear. The **COM** plays **a strong role** within the legal act, especially in the supervision and enforcement of the DSA requirements vis-à-vis the very large online platforms or search engines (Art. 64 et seqq. DSA). This indeed suggests a more vigorous enforcement than that of the GDPR in some parts of Europe,[48] but may at the same time leave a somewhat **insipid aftertaste** in light of the requirement of institutional balance ("Konzept der Staatsferne").[49] The fact that the EU COM has initiated the DSA itself, i.e. has granted itself at least some of the authority, is also quite remarkable. Apart from that, however, it remains with the **competent national authorities**. Probably because digitisation is blurring the traditional market boundaries and EU legislation has recently tended to regulate horizontally rather than sector-specifically, it is by no means clear who the competent authority might be.

15 In addition, the DSA provides the central figure of the **'Digital Services Coordinator'**, who, according to Art. 49(2)(2) DSA, is in principle 'responsible for all matters relating to supervision and enforcement of this Regulation in that Member State, unless the Member State concerned has assigned certain specific tasks or sectors to other competent authorities'. The authority that fills this role must have **competence in media and**

---

[43] According to European Commission, 'The Digital Services Act' <commission.europa.eu/strategy-and-policy/priorities-20192024/europe-fit-digital-age/digital-services-act-ensuring-safe-and-accountable-online-environment_de> (last accessed: 23.7.2024).

[44] On the effects on online marketplaces and comparison platforms: Busch ZdiW 2021, 88.

[45] On search engines in the DSA: Sesing-Wagenpfeil CR 2023, 113.

[46] Gerdemann/Spindler GRUR 2023, 115 (124): 'the two heart chambers of the DSA'.

[47] Dregelies MMR 2023, 243; in general on the phenomenon: Gertz/Martini/Seeliger/Timko LTZ 2023, 3.

[48] Raue/Heesen NJW 2022, 3537 (3543).

[49] Cf. Beaujean/Oelke/Wierny MMR 2023, 11 (13).

data law, even antitrust and consumer protection law.[50] There are already differing approaches among the individual EU member states, e.g. Italy (Autorità Garante per le Garanzie nelle Comunicazioni), France (Autorité de régulation de la communication audiovisuelle et numérique), Germany (Bundesnetzagentur für Elektrizität, Gas, Telekommunikation, Post und Eisenbahnen) and Ireland (Coimisiún na Meán).[51]

Finally, the **European Board for Digital Services** is to coordinate the different super- **16**
visory bodies to a certain extent and thus ultimately ensure uniform application of the law and public administration practices throughout the Union (Art. 61–63 DSA).

The **sanction mechanisms** in the form of fines (Art. 74 DSA) and periodic penalty **17**
payments (Art. 76 DSA) are likely to prove effective.[52] The DSA does not contain any provisions on **private enforcement** (cf., however, Art. 54 DSA), but this does not mean that private enforcement is inadmissible. This is rather a matter for the respective Member State law.[53]

F. Outlook

Whether and to what extent the DSA will prove itself for the internal market remains **18**
to be seen. It also remains to be seen whether there will be a **Brussels Effect**, similar to the GDPR, i.e. whether other regions of the world will follow the EU approach in terms of regulatory law. Such **competition between legal systems in the sense of a race to the top** would certainly seem desirable.[54] Since those considerations are based on the assumption that regulations, just like products, are subject to the economic mechanism of supply (by the legislator) and demand (by those subject to the law), it would, however, also remain conceivable that those subject to the law, in their search for the most attractive regulatory framework, might initiate a race to the bottom in the form of a damaging deregulation spiral.[55]

Finally, it is worth noting that few regulatory areas so forcefully demonstrate the **19**
urgent need for a **supranational interpretation doctrine** within the EU multi-level system as is increasingly the case in IT law.[56] The reason is that, despite the supposed clarity of this regulation, difficult questions of demarcation are likely to arise in the future.[57]

---

[50] On the topic: Schumacher, 'Deutschland sucht den Digital Services Koordinator – Zur nationalen Umsetzung des Digital Services Act' (JuWissBlog No. 50/2022, 18.8.2022) <www.juwiss.de/50-2022/> (last accessed: 23.7.2024); for a reorganisation of the existing supervisory structure in the area of platforms and the creation of a new 'strong digital agency': Busch ZdiW 2022, 275 (276).

[51] van Cleynenbreugel/Mattioli, 'Digital Services Coordinators and other competent authorities in the Digital Services Act: streamlined enforcement coordination lost?' (European Law Blog 49/2023, 30.11.2023) <https://europeanlawblog.eu/2023/11/30/digital-services-coordinators-and-other-competent-authorities-in-the-digital-services-act-streamlined-enforcement-coordination-lost/> (last accessed: 23.7.2024); see the current status on: <https://digital-strategy.ec.europa.eu/en/policies/dsa-dscs> (last accessed: 23.7.2024).

[52] This is also the assessment of Savary BB 2022, Die erste Seite.

[53] Gerdemann/Spindler GRUR 2023, 3 (4).

[54] Steinrötter EWS 5/2022, Die erste Seite.

[55] On the different levels of competition between rule makers: Steinrötter EWS 5/2022, Die erste Seite.

[56] Steinrötter GRUR 2023, 216; cf. on the DSA also Schmid/Grewe MMR 2021, 279 (282); in detail Raue ZUM 2023, 160.

[57] Schmid/Grewe MMR 2021, 279 (282).

§ 2
Scope of application

Literature: *Berger/Janal*, 'Eine Untersuchung zur Störerhaftung von Online-Auktionshäusern', CR 2004, 917; *Berger*, 'Rechtliche Rahmenbedingungen anwaltlicher Dienstleistungen über das Internet', NJW 2001, 1530; *Bräutigam/Leupold*, Online-Handel: Betriebswirtschaftliche und rechtliche Grundlagen, Munich 2003; *Brönneke/Föhlisch/Tonner* (eds.), Das neue Schuldrecht, Baden-Baden 2021; *Dauses/Ludwig* (eds), Handbuch des EU-Wirtschaftsrechts, Munich 2023; *Dreier/Schulze* (eds), Urheberrechtsgesetz, 7th edn, Munich 2022; *Dregelies*, 'Digital Services Act', MMR 2022, 1033; *Dregelies*, 'Verbraucherschutz im Digital Services Act', VuR 2023, 175; *Eisenreich*, 'Digital Services Act – ein wirksames Instrument gegen Hass und Hetze im Netz?', RDi 2021, 289; *Engel*, 'Anmerkung zu: BGH, Urteil vom 9.8.2022 – VI ZR 1244/20 – OLG Köln', ZUM 2022, 907; *Erb/Schäfer* (eds), Münchener Kommentar zum Strafgesetzbuch VIII, 4th edn, Munich 2023; *Finger/Conraths*, 'Anmerkung zu: BGH, Urteil vom 26.11.2015 – I ZR 174/14 (OLG Köln, LG Köln)', MMR 2016, 180; *Frank*, 'Inhaltemoderation – Erfahrungsbericht: Wie YouTube als digitale Plattform Verantwortung übernimmt', MMR 2022, 1026; *Frey*, Die Haftung von Host-Providern für Immaterialgüterrechtsverletzungen, Baden-Baden 2018; *Freytag*, '(K)ein deutscher Sonderweg – Haftung für "zueigengemachte" Inhalte nach deutschem und europäischem Recht', GRUR-Prax 2010, 355; *Gerdemann/Spindler*, 'Das Gesetz über digitale Dienste (Digital Services Act) (Teil 1)', GRUR 2023, 3; *Gerdemann/Spindler*, 'Das Gesetz über digitale Dienste (Digital Services Act) (Teil 2)', GRUR 2023, 115; *Gersdorf/Paal* (eds), Beck'scher Onlinekommentar Informartions- und Medienrecht, 42nd edn, Munich 2023; *Grabitz/Hilf/Nettesheim* (eds), Das Recht der Europäischen Union I, Munich 2023; *Hacker*, 'Daten als Gegenleistung: Rechtsgeschäfte im Spannungsfeld von DS-GVO und allgemeinem Vertragsrecht', ZfPW 2019, 148; *Hamann*, 'Der Entwurf einer E-Commerce-Richtlinie unter rundfunkrechtlichen Gesichtspunkten', ZUM 2000, 290; *Harte-Bavendamm/Henning-Bodewig/Goldmann/Tolkmitt* (eds), Gesetz gegen den unlauteren Wettbewerb (UWG), 5th edn; Munich 2021; *Heckmann/Paschke (eds)*, jurisPK-Internetrecht, 7th edn, 2021; *Heinze*, 'Der internationale Anwendungsbereich des digitalen Binnenmarkts. Eine Skizze' in: Kubis/Peifer/Raue/Stieper (eds), Ius Vivum: Kunst – Internationales – Persönlichkeit. Festschrift für Haimo Schack zum 70. Geburtstag, Tübingen 2022, p. 440; *Hoffmann*, 'Zivilrechtliche Haftung im Internet', MMR 2002, 284; *Holznagel*, 'Chapter II des Vorschlags der EU-Kommission für einen Digital Services Act', CR 2021, 123; *Holznagel*, 'Zum Stand des Herkunftslandprinzips der E-Commerce-RL', CR 2023, 321; *Hoeren/Sieben/Holznagel* (eds), Handbuch Multimedia-Recht, Munich 2023; *Janal*, 'Haftung und Verantwortung im Entwurf des Digital Services Acts', ZEuP 2021, 227; *Limperg/Oetker/Rixecker/Säcker* (eds), Münchener Kommentar zum Bürgerlichen Gesetzbuch III, 9th edn, Munich 2022; *Lányi/Swiatek*, 'Caching', cms-journal 2009 no. 31, 23; *Lutzi*, 'The Scope of the Digital Services Act and Digital Markets Act. Thoughts on the Conflict of Laws', Dalloz IP/IT 2023, 278; *Müller*, 'Künftige Plattformregulierung und effektive Durchsetzung in Deutschland', MMR 2022, 1007; *Paal/Kumkar*, 'Die digitale Zukunft Europas', ZfDR 2021, 97; *Paal/Pauly* (eds), Datenschutzgrundverordnung. Bundesdatenschutzgesetz, 3rd edn, Munich 2021; *Raue/Heesen*, 'Der Digital Services Act', NJW 2022, 3537; *Redeker*, IT-Recht, 8th edn, Munich 2023; *Sack*, 'Herkunftslandprinzip und internationales Lauterkeitsrecht', WRP 2019, 1095; *Simitis/Hornung/Spiecker called Döhmann* (eds), Datenschutzrecht, Baden-Baden 2019; *Schauer*, Reputation auf Online-Plattformen, Baden-Baden 2024; *Spindler*, 'Der Vorschlag für ein neues Haftungsregime für Internetprovider – der EU-Digital Services Act (Teil 1)', GRUR 2021, 545; *Spindler*, 'Die Verantwortlichkeit der Provider für "Sich-zu-Eigen-gemachte" Inhalte und für beaufsichtigte Nutzer', MMR 2004, 440; *Spindler*, 'Die Verantwortlichkeit der Provider für "Sich-zu-Eigen-gemachte" Inhalte und für beaufsichtigte Nutzer', MMR 2004, 440; *Spindler/Schmitz* (eds), Telemediengesetz, 2nd edn, Munich 2018; *Spindler/Schuster* (eds), Recht der elektronischen Medien, 4th edn, Munich 2019; *Streinz* (ed), EUV/AEUV, 3rd edn, Munich 2018; *Wagner*, 'Streaming aus der Sicht des Endnutzers – noch Graubereich oder bereits tiefschwarz?', GRUR 2016, 874; *Wandtke/Bullinger* (eds), Praxiskommentar Urheberrecht, 6th edn, Munich 2022, *Wandtke/von Gerlach*, 'Die urheberrechtliche Rechtmäßigkeit der Nutzung von Audio-Video Streaminginhalten im Internet', GRUR 2013, 676; *Weiden*, 'DSA-Verordnungsentwurf: Neue Grundregeln für die Digitalwirtschaft' in: Baumgärtel/Hoppen (eds), DGRI-Jahrbuch 2019/2020, Cologne 2021, p. 79.

A. Overview

1 The Digital Services Act (DSA)[1] applies according to Art. 2(1) DSA 'to intermediary services offered to recipients of the service that have their place of establishment or are located in the Union, irrespective of where the providers of those intermediary services have their place of establishment'. Accordingly, the scope of application is to be determined primarily **on the basis of a material-personal element** (offer of intermediary services → mn. 3 et seq.) **and a personal-territorial element** (recipient with place of establishment or located in the Union → mn. 61 et seq.). Structurally, the material scope of application is divided into four levels of increasingly regulatory-intensive provisions whose applicability is linked to 'personal' requirements of the intermediary services (→ mn. 19 et seqq.). The classification into the different regulatory levels is based on the type and scope of the respective activity as well as the size of the service providers. The broad scope of application delimited in this way aims to create a safe, predictable, and trustworthy online environment and to **counteract the spread of disinformation and illegal content** associated with intermediary services.[2]

2 With this step-wise increase in regulation, the legislator takes into account the fact that the influence of intermediary services and the risks emanating from their use depend significantly on their type, importance, and reach, which is why specifications of varying intensity seem to be necessary.[3] **The legal framework** for online intermediary services, which **has so far been determined by the E-Commerce Directive,**[4] is thus being **modernised** and supplemented in line with the **digital change.**

B. Material-personal scope of application: intermediary services

3 Pursuant to Art. 2(1) DSA, the regulation is applicable to intermediary services in the sense of Art. 3(g) DSA, i.e. to elementary **information society services,** namely **mere**

[1] Digital Services Act – Regulation (EU) 2022/2065 of the European Parliament and of the Council of 19 October 2022 on a Single Market for Digital Services and amending Directive 2000/31/EC, OJ 2022 L 277, 1.

[2] Rec. 3, 4, 9(1)(1) DSA.

[3] Rec. 13 subpara. 1 sent. 1, 48(1)(1), 75(1)(1) DSA.

[4] Directive 2000/31/EC of the European Parliament and of the Council of 8 June 2000 on certain legal aspects of information society services, in particular electronic commerce, in the Internal Market ('Directive on electronic commerce'), OJ 2000 L 178, 1.

conduit services, caching services, and hosting services. These online intermediaries form an important part of the European Union's economy and the everyday life of EU citizens.[5] They serve to ensure better availability, efficiency, speed, and security of systems that transmit, store, access, and help to 'find' data/digital information online.[6] Intermediary services are thus significantly contributing to the creation and development of an increasingly complex digital ecosystem.[7]

4 From the legislator's perspective, the use of intermediary services is primarily for legitimate and socially beneficial purposes; however, at the same time, they carry the **risk of disseminating illegal and otherwise harmful information.**[8] The dangers they pose have grown with the development of new and innovative business models and services such as social media and e-commerce platforms and their increasing use by EU citizens. Therefore, the concept of intermediary services is broadly defined in order to subject as many as possible to the provisions of the DSA and thus create a uniform regulatory regime for platforms operating in the internal market.[9]

I. Information society services

5 Pursuant to Art. 3(a) DSA, the Regulation uses – just like Art. 2(a) E-Commerce Directive[10] – the definition of 'information society services' from Art. 1(1)(b) of Directive (EU) 2015/1535[11]. According to this definition, the term refers to **'any service normally provided for remuneration, at a distance, by electronic means and at the individual request of a recipient of services'.**[12] It follows from the requirement of uniform application of Union law in all Member States and the principle of equality that the concept of information society services is to be **interpreted autonomously under Union law.**[13]

6 The **concept of services** corresponds to that of the fundamental freedoms in Art. 56 and Art. 57 TFEU.[14] It is thus to be understood extensively and extends to all self-employed activities, usually provided for remuneration, which are not merely incidental to activities that fall primarily within the scope of other fundamental freedoms.[15] In particular, these include industrial, commercial, craft, and freelance activities, Art. 57(1)(2) TFEU.

---

5 Rec. 1(1)(1) DSA.

6 Rec. 28(1)(1) DSA.

7 Rec. 28(1)(1) DSA.

8 Rec. 1(1)(4) and (5) DSA.

9 Cf. rec. 9(1)(1) DSA.

10 Art. 2(a) E-Commerce Directive explicitly refers to Art. 1 no. 2 Directive 98/34/EC as amended by 98/48/EC, which has expired. However, the references to the repealed Directive are deemed to be references to Directive (EU) 2015/1535 pursuant to Art. 10(1)(2) of Directive (EU) 2015/1535 (OJ L 241, 1).

11 Directive (EU) 2015/1535 of the European Parliament and of the Council of 9 September 2015 laying down a procedure for the provision of information in the field of technical regulations and of rules on Information Society services (codification), OJ 2015 L 241, 1.

12 Rec. 5(1)(1) DSA.

13 ECJ 11.1.2000 – case C-287/98, ECLI:EU:C:2000:468 = NVwZ 2001, 421 mn. 43 – Grand Duchy of Luxemburg v Berthe Linster, Aloyse Linster and Yvonne Linster; ECJ 29.7.2019 – case C-516/1, ECLI:EU:C:2019:625 = GRUR 2019, 940 mn. 62 – Spiegel Online GmbH v. Volker Beck; ECJ 21.10.2010 – case C-467/08, ECLI:EU:C:2010:620 = GRUR 2011, 50 mn. 32 – Padawan SL v Sociedad General de Autores y Editores de España (SGAE).

14 ECJ 3.12.2020 – case C-62/19, ECLI:EU:C:2020:980 = MMR 2021, 309 mn. 43 – Star Taxi App SRL v Unitatea Administrativ Teritorială Municipiul Bucureşti prin Primar General and Consiliul General al Municipiului Bucureşti.

15 Müller-Graf in Streinz AEUV Art. 56 mn. 15; Randelzhofer/Forsthoff in Grabitz/Hilf/Nettesheim AEUV Art. 56, 57 mn. 34.

a) The first prerequisite for the classification of a service as an information society service is that it is **usually** provided **against payment.** The EU law does not provide for a more detailed definition. However, a largely consistent and broad understanding of the term has developed in ECJ case law. According to this, the requirement of remuneration does not presuppose direct remuneration of the service by the recipient who benefits from it.[16] **Any economically oriented or at least cost-covering, not purely altruistic activity** of the service provider is covered.[17] It is sufficient if the provider pursues commercial interests and finances the services, for example, through advertising revenue.[18] 7
The same must apply to business models that do not demand direct monetary remuneration and provide their services supposedly 'free of charge', but allow themselves to be **'paid' with the (personal) data of their recipients.**[19] In view of the **economic value of these data,** such offerings are also to be classified as remunerated.[20] This finding is confirmed by a look at Article 3(1)(2) of the Digital Content Directive 2019/770.[21] According to this, the digital goods regime applies, inter alia, 'where the trader supplies or undertakes to supply digital content or a digital service to the consumer, and the consumer provides or undertakes to provide personal data to the trader'. Although it is debatable what the subject matter of the consumer's performance is and how it is linked to the performance of the trader,[22] it seems plausible that (at least personal) data can be regarded as a tradable economic good under private law.[23]

b) Furthermore, the supplier must provide the service **'at a distance'**, i.e. according to Art. 1(1)(b)(2)(i) of Directive (EU) 2015/1535 **without the simultaneous physical presence** of the supplier and the recipient. Accordingly, offerings in which both contracting parties are physically present are not covered. This applies even if electronic devices are used for the conclusion of the contract, such as the online booking of a flight ticket in a travel agency or the consultation of an electronic catalogue in a shop, in each case in the presence of the customer.[24] 8

c) According to Art. 1(1)(b)(2)(ii) of Directive (EU) 2015/1535, the requirement **'by electronic means'** presupposes 'that the service is sent initially and received at its destination by means of electronic equipment for the processing (including digital compression) and storage of data, and entirely transmitted, conveyed and received 9

[16] ECJ 11.9.2014 – case C-291/13, ECLI:EU:C:2014:2209 = MMR 2016, 63 mn. 28 et seq. – Sotiris Papasavvas v O Fileleftheros Dimosia Etaireia Ltd and Others; ECJ 15.9.2016 – case C-484/14, ECLI:EU:C:2016:689 = GRUR 2016, 1146 mn. 42 – Tobias Mc Fadden v Sony Music Entertainment Germany GmbH; ECJ 4.5.2017 – case C-339/15, ECLI:EU:C:2017:335 = GRUR 2017, 627 mn. 36 – Criminal proceedings against Luc Vanderborght(→ § 3 mn. 52); cf. rec. 18(1)(4) E-Commerce Directive.

[17] Rec. 18(1)(3) E-Commerce Directive; Raue in Dreier/Schulze UrhDaG § 2 mn. 6; Klement in Simitis/Hornung/Spiecker gen. Döhmann DS-GVO Art. 4 no. 25 mn. 9.

[18] ECJ 11.9.2014 – case C-291/13, ECLI:EU:C:2014:2209 = GRUR 2016, 1146 (1148) – Sotiris Papasavvas v O Fileleftheros Dimosia Etaireia Ltd and Others; Janal ZEuP 2021, 227 (233 et seq.); cf. ECJ 26.4.1988 – case C-352/85, ECLI:EU:C:1988:196 = NJW 1989, 2189 mn. 16 – Bond van Adverteerders and others v The Netherlands State; ECJ 15.9.2016 – case C-484/14, ECLI:EU:C:2016:689 – Tobias Mc Fadden v Sony Music Entertainment Germany GmbH; Gerdemann/Spindler GRUR 2023, 3 (4).

[19] On data as consideration: Hacker ZfPW 2019, 148 (153 et seqq.).

[20] Rauer in Wandtke/Bullinger UrhDaG § 2 mn. 11; Gerdemann/Spindler GRUR 2023, 115.

[21] Directive (EU) 2019/770 of the European Parliament and of the Council of 20 May 2019 on certain aspects concerning contracts for the supply of digital content and digital services, OJ 2019 L 136, 1.

[22] In detail, Steinrötter in Staudinger BGB § 327 mn. 64 et seqq.

[23] Metzger in Limperg/Oetker/Rixecker/Säcker BGB preliminary remarks § 327 mn. 17; Tamm/Tonner in Brönnecke/Föhlisch/Tonner § 2 mn. 38.

[24] Annex I no. 1 lit. b, c Directive (EU) 2015/1535.

by wire, by radio, by optical means or by other electromagnetic means'. In other words, it requires **performance over an electronic communications network.**

10 This does not include services that are only provided with the help of electronic devices, as is the case, for example, in telemedicine by telephone or fax.[25] The same applies to ordering terminals in restaurants (e.g. McDonald's 'easy-order terminals'), which enable users to place food and beverage orders independently without the intervention of staff and either collect it themselves or have it delivered to the table (→ § 15 mn. 21).

11 d) 'At the individual request of a recipient of services' means 'that the service is provided through the transmission of data on individual request', Art. 1(1)(b)(2)(iii) Directive (EU) 2015/1535. For this reason, classic linear media such as television and radio services and teletext are not to be classified as information society services, as they address an unlimited number of recipients simultaneously without a request.[26]

12 The same applies **to real-time transmissions in livestreams** via providers such as YouNow or Twitch, whose transmission is also independent of an individual query by the recipient. In the case of platforms such as Facebook or Instagram, which allow both permanent storage and retrievability of content as well as its real-time transmission, a differentiation between the different offerings is necessary.

13 The understanding of 'information society services' thus encompasses a wide range of providers of diverse digital services such as social networks, booking portals,[27] e-commerce platforms, taxi apps,[28] search engines, rating platforms,[29] and internet access providers.[30]

14 However, according to Art. 2(2) DSA, services that are not classified as intermediary services are not covered. This also applies if the service is provided using intermediary services, as is the case with transport, accommodation or delivery services.[31]

15 If the offering extends to various services, the material scope of application only encompasses the services to be qualified as information society services.[32]

II. Information provided by a recipient

16 The common point of reference for the intermediary services of 'mere conduit', 'caching', and 'hosting' mentioned in Art. 3(g) DSA is that the **recipient provides information.**

17 As for the question of whether this requirement is fulfilled, a **technical-functional consideration** is therefore necessary in accordance with the understanding of the E-Commerce Directive.[33] **The recipient of the service**, i.e. according to the understand-

---

[25] Annex II Directive (EU) 2015/1535.

[26] Annex I no. 3 Directive (EU) 2015/1535.

[27] ECJ 19.12.2019 – case C-390/18, ECLI:EU:C:2019:1112 = = MMR 2020, 171 mn. 39 et seq. – Airbnb Ireland.

[28] ECJ 3.12.2020 – case C-62/19, ECLI:EU:C:2020:980 = MMR 2021, 309 mn. 48 – Star Taxi App SRL v Unitatea Administrativ Teritorială Municipiul Bucureşti prin Primar General and Consiliul General al Municipiului Bucureşti.

[29] Schauer Reputation auf Online-Plattformen, p. 228 et seq.

[30] Müller MMR 2022, 1007 (1008).

[31] Rec. 6 DSA.

[32] Rec. 15 DSA.

[33] Rec. 18, 23(1)(5), 24(1)(3) DSA; cf. Frey, p. 177; Sobola in Auer-Reinsdorff/Conrad § 42 mn. 13; Spindler in Spindler/Schmitz TMG § 7 mn. 8.

ing of Art. 3(b) DSA 'any natural or legal person who uses an intermediary service, in particular for the purposes of seeking information or making it accessible',[34] must have **sole power over the selection and uploading** of the content.[35] This is the case if he or she decides of his or her own accord whether and how content is made available.

Whether the activity of the service provider is limited to the mere technical and automatic processing of the information provided[36] or whether the service provider actively takes note of, influences or modifies the information is not decisive for including it under the material scope of application. The question is, however, relevant for the applicability of the exclusions of liability under Art. 4 et seq. DSA (→ § 3 mn. 66 et seqq.). 18

III. Intermediary services in the sense of Art. 3(g) DSA

The DSA is based on a **principle of graduated regulation intensity**.[37] According to this principle, the scope of application implies a cascade of increasingly regulatory-intensive provisions that apply to increasingly smaller groups of norm addressees.[38] 19

- **Level I** 20
  The first and at the same time the **weakest regulatory level of Art. 4–15 DSA addresses all intermediary services in the sense of Art. 3(g) DSA**, i.e. mere conduit services as well as caching and hosting services. Its central provisions include the liability exclusions of Art. 4–6 DSA, which are largely based on Art. 12–15 E-Commerce Directive, and incorporate these rules into the DSA with minor adjustments.[39] In doing so, the European legislator also retains the differentiation between mere conduit services (Art. 4 DSA), caching services (Art. 5 DSA), and hosting services (Art. 6 DSA) and exempts them from liability for the information of their recipients, in principle (→ § 3 mn. 93 et seqq.).
- **Level II** 21
  The scope of application of **Art. 16–18 DSA** refers to intermediary services that fulfil the personal requirements for **hosting services** (→ mn. 36 et seqq.) pursuant to Art. 3(g)(iii), Art. 6(1) DSA **including online platforms**. The differentiation between the various categories of intermediary services is thus relevant beyond the liability privileges.
- **Level III** 22
  The provisions of **Art. 19–32 DSA** are directed at the **intermediary services that qualify as online platforms** and represent a sub-category of hosting services (→ mn. 40 et seqq.).[40]
- **Level IV** 23
  The **most regulatory-intensive** 'Level IV' addresses **online platforms or online search engines that exceed certain thresholds** and are therefore classified by the

[34] Rec. 2(1)(4) DSA.

[35] On Art. 12–15 E-Commerce Directive: Sobola in Auer-Reinsdorff/Conrad § 42 mn. 13; Spindler in Spindler/Schmitz TMG § 7 mn. 8; Altenhain in Erb/Schäfer TMG preliminary remarks § 7 mn. 24; Hennemann in Gersdorf/Paal TMG § 7 mn. 33; Freytag GRUR-Prax 2010, 355 (357); already on §§ 9–11 TDG: Spindler MMR 2004, 440 (441); Berger/Janal CR 2004, 917 (918 et seq.).

[36] Rec. 18(1)(1) DSA.

[37] Gerdemann/Spindler GRUR 2023, 3; Paal/Kumkar ZfDR 2021, 97 (110): 'pyramid model'.

[38] Gerdemann/Spindler GRUR 2023, 3.

[39] Critically, Eisenreich RDi 2021, 289 (290).

[40] Art. 24(2)–(4) DSA also concerns online search engines, cf. rec. 65(1)(2) DSA.

European Commission as very large online platforms (**VLOPs**) or **very large online search engines** (**VLOSEs** → mn. 55 et seqq.). Art. 33–48 DSA contain, among other things, regulations regarding risk assessments and mitigations, crisis response mechanisms, and increased transparency obligations. It should be noted, however, that 'very large online search engines' are not necessarily hosting services. Unlike online platforms, the European legislator has refrained from explicitly classifying online search engines as intermediary services. Furthermore, they are not always to be classified as online platforms either, which is already clear from the fact that they are explicitly addressed in some provisions which would otherwise only apply to online platforms, e.g. Art. 24(2)(4) DSA. As a rule, however, they are to be classified as hosting services and online platforms.[41]

24 The individual stages of regulation can be summarised as follows:

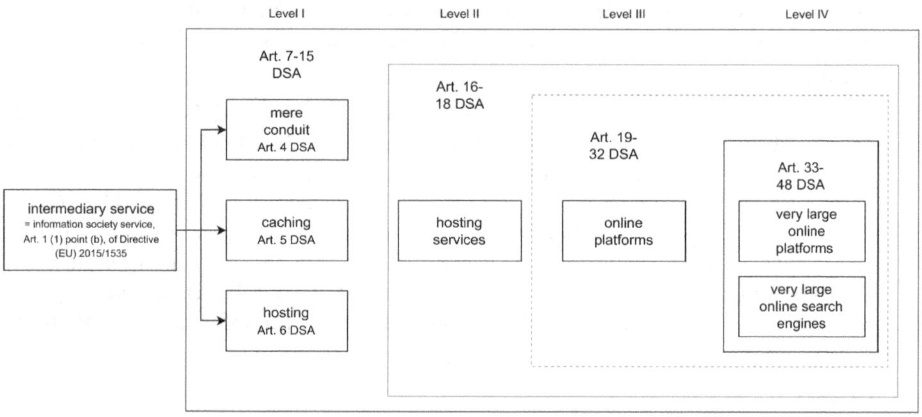

Figure 2

25 Whether the intermediary service is a mere conduit, a caching service or a hosting service depends exclusively on its **technical functions** and is to be determined on a **case-by-case basis.**[42] The classification may change with modification of the service's functions, such as if the service expands or reduces its range of services.[43]

1. Mere conduit services, Art. 3(g)(i), 4(1) DSA

26 According to Art. 3(g)(i), 4(1) DSA[44] the service of acting as a '**mere conduit**' consists of transmitting the information provided by a recipient into a communications network or providing access to such a network. The regulation thus covers two different types of transit.

27 The transmission of information provided by a recipient means the online transfer of data packets without the intermediary service exerting any influence on the selection or the actual content (so-called '**routing**').[45] It is therefore a purely technical process of

[41] Raue/Heesen NJW 2022, 3537 (3538).
[42] Rec. 29(1)(4) DSA.
[43] Rec. 29(1)(4) DSA.
[44] Cf. Art. 12 E-Commerce Directive.
[45] Cf. on § 8 TMG: Roggenkamp/Stadler in Heckmann/Paschke jurisPK Internetrecht ch. 1.4. mn. 188 et seqq.; Hoffmann/Volkmann in Spindler/Schuster TMG § 8 mn. 16; Hoffmann MMR 2002, 284 (286).

transmitting information without storing it permanently (short-term temporary storage in the RAM is irrelevant in this case).[46]

The provision of access to communication networks concerns services that enable third parties to access electronic communication networks, such as the internet, in a wireless or wired manner (so-called '**access providers**').[47] 28

According to rec. 29 subpara. 1 sent. 2 DSA, mere conduit services include, in particular, internet exchange points, wireless access points, virtual private networks, DNS services and DNS resolvers,[48] top-level domain name registries, certification authorities for digital certificates, and internet voice telephony and other interpersonal communication services. Telephone service providers or telecommunications companies such as Vodafone, AOL or Deutsche Telekom are also included. 29

According to Art. 4(2) DSA, the activities of a mere conduit service also include the 'automatic, intermediate and transient storage of the information transmitted'. The prerequisite for this is that 'this takes place for the sole purpose of carrying out the transmission in the communication network, and provided that the information is not stored for any period longer than is reasonably necessary for the transmission'.[49] It has only a **supporting function for the transmission of the content** until its completion.[50] An example of this is the intermediate storage of an e-mail.[51] 30

Pursuant to Art. 4(1) DSA, the services are in **principle not liable for the transmitted content**. However, under Art. 4(3) DSA, the possibility of judicial and administrative orders remains unaffected. The exclusion of liability does not apply if the intermediary service has initiated the transmission, selects the addressee of the information or actively influences the selection and content of the transmission, Art. 4(1) DSA (→ § 3 mn. 94 et seqq.). 31

2. Caching services, Art. 3(g)(ii), Art. 5(1) DSA

According to Art. 3(g)(ii), Art. 5(1) DSA,[52] the intermediary activity of a caching service consists of 'the transmission in a communication network of information provided by a recipient of the service, involving the automatic, intermediate and temporary storage of that information, performed for the sole purpose of making more efficient the information's onward transmission to other recipients upon their request'. Caching thus describes the technical **process of intermediate storage** that providers perform to enable accelerated access to the requested information from the internet.[53] 32

---

[46] Cf. on § 8 TMG: Hennemann in Gersdorf/Paal TMG § 8 mn. 14; Hoffmann/Volkmann in Spindler/Schuster TMG § 8 mn. 16.

[47] Cf. on § 8 TMG: Hoffmann/Volkmann in Spindler/Schuster TMG § 8 mn. 17; Spindler in Spindler/Schmitz TMG § 8 mn. 39; Goldmann in Harte-Bavendamm/Henning-Bodewig/Goldmann/Tolkmit UWG § 8 mn. 636; Hennemann in Gersdorf/Paal TMG § 8 mn. 15; Roggenkamp/Stadler in Heckmann/Paschke jurisPK Internetrecht ch. 1.4. mn. 188 et seqq.; Finger/Conraths MMR 2016, 186; Hoffmann MMR 2002, 284 (286).

[48] Against a classification of DNS resolver providers as access providers in the sense of § 8 TMG: OLG Köln 9.10.2020 – 6 U 32/20, GRUR 2021, 70.(75 et seqq.); LG Hamburg 12.5.2021 – 310 O 99/21, GRUR-RS 2021, 26845.

[49] Cf. on § 8(2) TMG: Roggenkamp/Stadler in Heckmann/Paschke jurisPK Internetrecht ch. 1.4. mn. 265; Hoffmann/Volkmann in Spindler/Schuster TMG § 8 mn. 38 et seqq.; Spindler in Spindler/Schmitz TMG § 8 mn. 25, § 9 mn. 3.

[50] Spindler in Spindler/Schmitz TMG § 8 mn. 24.

[51] Cf. on § 8 TMG: Spindler in Spindler/Schmitz TMG § 9 mn. 3.

[52] Cf. Art. 13 E-Commerce Directive.

[53] Sieber/Höfinger in Hoeren/Sieber/Holznagel Multimedia-Recht part 18.1 mn. 70; Martens/Schwarz-Gondek in Bräutigam/Leupold Online-Handel p. 1069; Lányi/Swiatek cms-journal 2009 no. 31, 23; Wagner GRUR 2016, 874 (875).

33 A caching service is initially the **operation of proxy cache servers** (French: caché = to hide) on which the information provided by the recipients is temporarily stored.[54] If the recipient requests the content again, it is immediately available from the proxy cache, so that no further data transmission is required.[55] This makes it possible to speed up the transmission of the requested content to the recipients.[56]

34 In distinction to the automatic caching for mere conduit services under Art. 4(2) DSA, caching beyond the transmission is not technically necessary, but aims at increasing the efficiency of the transmission.[57]

35 For caching services, the regulation lists as examples 'the sole provision of content delivery networks, reverse proxies or content adaptation proxies'.[58] Furthermore, the operation of automatic **mirror servers,**[59] which 'mirror' copies of frequently accessed content, is also covered.[60] Caching services are exempted from liability for the information provided by recipients under Art. 5(1) DSA in order to limit the liability risks of intermediary services and thus prevent a slowdown of the technical communication process.

3. Hosting services, Art. 3(g)(iii), Art. 6(1) DSA

36 According to Art. 3(g)(iii), Art. 6(1) DSA,[61] a hosting service consists 'of the **storage of information provided by, and at the request of, a recipient of the service**'. This is usually based on a contractual obligation between the service provider and the recipient; however, it does not prevent the classification as a hosting service if the contract is ineffective.[62]

37 These intermediary services are **characterised by the supply of storage and computing capacities,** with which they offer a technical infrastructure for the storage, exchange, and retrievability of data.[63]

38 The broad understanding of the term covers a wide range of online services such as **cloud computing services** (e.g. Apple iCloud, Google Drive, Microsoft OneDrive), **web hosting services** (e.g. IONOS, dogado, HostEurope), and **referencing services against payment.**[64] Also covered are services that enable the online exchange of information and content, including the exchange and storage of files.[65] This includes **social networks**

---

[54] Sieber/Höfinger in Hoeren/Sieber/Holznagel Multimedia-Recht part 18.1 mn. 70; cf. Wagner GRUR 2016, 874 (875).

[55] Wandtke/Gerlach GRUR 2013, 676 (677); Wagner GRUR 2016, 874 (875).

[56] Sieber/Höfinger in Hoeren/Sieber/Holznagel Multimedia-Recht 18.1 mn. 70.

[57] Sieber/Höfinger in Hoeren/Sieber/Holznagel Multimedia-Recht part 18.1 mn. 71; Roggenkamp/Stadler in Heckmann/Paschke jurisPK Internetrecht ch. 1.4. mn. 217; Spindler in Spindler/Schmitz TMG § 9 mn. 3.

[58] Rec. 29 sent. 2 half-sentence 2 DSA.

[59] On the understanding of the term: Roggenkamp/Stadler in Heckmann/Paschke jurisPK Internetrecht ch. 1.4. mn. 263.

[60] OLG Köln 9.10.2020 – 6 U 32/20, GRUR 2021, 70 (72 et seq.); OLG Düsseldorf 15.1.2008 – I-20 U 95/07, ZUM 2008, 332 (334 et seq.); Sieber/Höfinger in Hoeren/Sieber/Holznagel Multimedia-Recht part 18.1 mn. 70; Spindler in Spindler/Schmitz/ TMG § 9 mn. 8; v. Welser in Wandtke/Bullinger UrhG § 44a mn. 6; Roggenkamp/Stadler in Heckmann/Paschke Multimedia-Recht ch. 1.4. mn. 265; different view by Altenhain in Erb/Schäfer TMG § 9 mn. 10; cf. on § 10 German TDG: Pelz in Bräutigam/Leupold Online-Handel p. 271.

[61] Cf. Art. 14 E-Commerce Directive.

[62] Cf. on § 10 TMG: Spindler in Spindler/Schmitz TMG § 10 mn. 15; Hennemann in Gersdorf/Paal TMG § 10 mn. 21; Hoffmann/Volkmann in Spindler/Schuster TMG § 10 mn. 15.

[63] Roggenkamp/Stadler in Heckmann/Paschke jurisPK Internetrecht ch. 1.4. mn. 67; Redeker IT Recht mn. 1257.

[64] Rec. 29(1)(4) DSA; on referencing services: ECJ 23.3.2010 – joined cases C-236/08 and C-237/08 and C-238/08, ECLI:EU:C:2010:159 = MMR 2010, 315 mn. 106 et seqq., 120 – Google France and Google.

[65] Rec. 29(1)(4) DSA.

such as Facebook,[66] **file hosting services,**[67] and **rating platforms,**[68] as well as **online trading platforms** such as eBay.[69]

Art. 6(1) DSA exempts hosting services from liability for the content stored (temporarily or even permanently[70]) on behalf of recipients (→ § 3 mn. 120 et seqq.). The DSA thus aims to limit the responsibility of service providers for the information of their recipients and thus protect them from excessive liability. **39**

4. Special categories of intermediary services

a) *Online platforms*

aa) *Dissemination of information to the public*

With the provisions of Art. 19–32 DSA, the regulation addresses intermediary services that are to be qualified as 'online platforms'. This is a **sub-category of hosting services** that not only store the information provided by the recipient but also disseminate it to the public on behalf of the recipient (Art. 3(i) DSA).[71] **40**

The DSA understands the concept of 'dissemination to the public' in line with Regulation (EU) 2021/784[72] as **making the information available to** a **potentially unlimited number of people.**[73] This refers to the **platform-side creation of easy access** for a general audience **without** the need for action by the recipient commissioning the storage of the information.[74] Whether there is actual access to the information is irrelevant for the classification as an online platform.[75] The term 'online platforms' covers **e-commerce platforms** such as Amazon, which enable consumers to conclude distance contracts with traders, as well as **social media platforms** such as Facebook and Instagram.[76] **41**

If the **group of addressees** for the information is not unlimited, as is often the case with short messages (instant messaging) or e-mail services, the **information is not disseminated to the public**. Therefore, interpersonal communication services in the sense of Directive (EU) 2018/1972[77] such as WhatsApp or Signal are generally not to be classified as online platforms.[78] This is not the case if they enable the provision of information to a potentially unlimited number of recipients over which the sender has no influence. Examples of this are public groups or open channels without access restrictions, such as those commonly used for the instant messaging service Telegram. **42**

---

[66] ECJ 3.10.2019 – case C-18/18, ECLI:EU:C:2019:821 = NJW 2019, 3287 mn. 22 – Eva Glawischnig-Piesczek v Facebook Ireland Limited.

[67] BGH 12.7.2012 – I ZR 18/11, GRUR 2013, 370 – Alone in the Dark; BGH 15.8.2013 – I ZR 80/12, GRUR 2013, 1030 (1032) – File Hosting Service.

[68] Schauer Reputation auf Online-Plattformen, p. 228 et seqq.; Engel ZUM 2022, 911 (913); cf. on Art. 14 Directive 2000/31/EC and § 10 TMG: BGH 19.3.2015 – I ZR 94/13, NJW 2015, 3443 (3345) – Hotelbewertungsportal; OLG Hamburg 30.6.2016 – 5 U 58/13, MMR 2017, 120 (123); OLG Stuttgart 11.9.2013 – 4 U 88/13, MMR 2014, 203 (204); Spindler/Schmitz/Spindler TMG § 10 mn. 93.

[69] ECJ 12.7.2011 – case C-324/09, ECLI:EU:C:2011:474 = GRUR 2011, 1025 mn. 107 et seq. – L'Oréal SA and Others v eBay International AG and Others.

[70] Cf. on § 10 German TMG: Hoffmann/Volkmann in Spindler/Schuster TMG § 10 mn. 1.

[71] Rec. 13 subpara. 1, 2; 14 5(1)(5) DSA.

[72] Regulation (EU) 2021/784 of the European Parliament and of the Council of 29 April 2021 on addressing the dissemination of terrorist content online, OJ 2021 L 172, 79.

[73] Rec. 14(1)(1) DSA, cf. Art. 2 no. 3, rec. 14(1)(1) Regulation (EU) 2021/784.

[74] Rec. 14(1)(1) DSA.

[75] Rec. 14(1)(1) DSA.

[76] Rec. 13 subpara. 1 sent. 2 DSA; Raue/Heesen NJW 2022, 3537 et seq.

[77] Directive (EU) 2018/1972 of the European Parliament and of the Council of 11 December 2018 establishing the European Electronic Communications Code, OJ 2018 L 321, 36.

[78] Cf. rec. 14(1)(3) DSA.

43 If the service provider designs **access restrictions**, such as registration or inclusion in a user group, dissemination of information to the public is only deemed to exist if these restrictions are automatically overcome.[79] In particular, no human decision or selection of who is granted access may be required for this.[80]

bb) No real or insignificant secondary work activity

44 In order to avoid excessive use, hosting service providers are not to be classified as online platforms if the activity of dissemination to the public is **insignificant and inseparable from another service** or an insignificant **function of the main service which**, for objective and technical reasons, cannot be used without the other service.[81]

45 The DSA cites **as an example the commentary field of an online magazine**, which is a mere secondary function to its main function, which is to publish news under the editorial responsibility of the publisher.[82]

46 By contrast, the **storage of comments on social networks** such as Instagram, Facebook, and YouTube is to **be understood as an online platform service** insofar as it is clear that an essential feature of the service is involved.[83] The fact that it is a secondary service to the publication of content by the recipients does not preclude this classification.[84] However, platforms are prevented from evading the specific obligations by outsourcing dissemination to the public to other services, Art. 3(i) half-sentence 3 DSA.

47 **Cloud computing and web hosting services,** furthermore, are generally not to be classified as means for disseminating information to the public insofar as they serve as infrastructure, i.e. insofar as they function, for example, as the underlying infrastructural storage and computing service of an internet-based application, website or online platform.[85]

cc) Exemption for micro- and small enterprises

48 With the exception of Art. 24(3) DSA, the additional provisions of the online platform providers under Art. 19–28 DSA do not apply to online platform providers that are to be classified as **micro- or small entrepreneurs**, Art. 19(1)(1) DSA. With this exemption, the DSA creates opportunities for market debutants and start-ups to flourish without subjecting them to the additional requirements of regulatory level III for online platforms.[86]

49 The classification as a micro- or small enterprise is based on Recommendation 2003/361/EC.[87] According to Art. 2(2) of Recommendation 2003/361/EC, an enterprise is to be classified as a **small enterprise** if it employs fewer than 50 persons and its annual turnover or annual balance sheet does not exceed 10 million EUR. Article 2(3) of Recommendation 2003/361/EC classifies enterprises as **microenterprises** if they employ fewer than 10 persons and have an annual turnover or annual balance sheet not exceeding 2 million EUR.

---

79 Rec. 14(1)(2) DSA.
80 Rec. 14(1)(2) DSA.
81 Rec. 13 subpara. 1 sent. 3 DSA.
82 Rec. 13 subpara. 1 sent. 4 DSA.
83 Rec. 13 subpara. 1 sent. 5 DSA.
84 Rec. 13 subpara. 1 sent. 5 DSA.
85 Rec. 13 subpara. 2 DSA.
86 Weiden in Baumgärtel/Hoppen p. 79 et seqq. mn. 9.
87 Commission Recommendation 2003/361/EC of 6 May 2003 concerning the definition of micro-, small, and medium-sized enterprises, C (2003) 1422, OJ 2003 L 124, 36.

As soon as the online platforms that were previously micro-sized or small exceed the respective size categories,[88] the provisions of Art. 19 et seqq. DSA, except Art. 24(3) DSA, only apply after an interim period of 12 months, unless they already exceed the threshold of very large online platforms beforehand, Art. 19(1)(2) DSA. Service providers are not covered by the scope exception from the outset if they have been classified as very large online platforms in the sense of Art. 33 DSA, Art. 19(2) DSA. The reason for this is their greater reach and the associated influence on the public information exchange and communication process.[89] 50

dd) Online platforms allowing consumers to conclude distance contracts with traders

Chapter 3 Section 4 of the DSA dictates specific provisions for **B2C online platforms**. The concept of 'online platforms allowing consumers to conclude distance contracts with traders' is similar to that of an 'online marketplace' from Art. 2(n) UCP Directive 2005/29/EC.[90] However, the latter also covers platforms on which consumers conclude distance contracts with consumers. The DSA, on the other hand, restricts the term to B2C platforms and thus excludes pure C2C platforms such as Vinted from the scope of Art. 29–32 DSA. Platforms such as AllTrippers, Gumtree or Facebook Marketplace, which cover both the B2C and C2C sectors, on the other hand, are subject to the additional requirements of Chapter 3 Section 4 DSA.[91] 51

Article 29(1) of the DSA provides an exemption for small and microenterprises as defined in Recommendation 2003/361/EC (→ mn. 48 et seqq.). According to Art. 29(2) DSA, this does not apply to providers of B2C platforms that have been classified as VLOPs.

b) Online search engines

Online search engines play a **key role in the accessibility, discoverability, retrievability,** and thus also the **visibility of online content**, which is why they are subject to the strict requirements of Art. 33–48 DSA if they are classified as very large online search engines. 52

The DSA defines the term 'online search engines' in its Art. 3(j). According to this, it is 'an intermediary service that allows recipients to input queries in order to perform searches of, in principle, all websites, or all websites in a particular language, on the basis of a query on any subject in the form of a keyword, voice request, phrase or other input, and returns results in any format in which information related to the requested content can be found'.[92] **Google, Ecosia, and Duckduckgo** are prominent examples. 53

Unlike online platforms, **online search engines are not explicitly assigned to any of the categories of intermediary services** from Art. 3(g) DSA. Therefore, it must be de- 54

---

[88] Art. 4(2) Recommendation 2003/361/EC: 'Where, at the date of closure of the accounts, an enterprise finds that, on an annual basis, it has exceeded or fallen below the headcount or financial ceilings stated in Article 2, this will not result in the loss or acquisition of the status of medium-sized, small or microenterprise unless those ceilings are exceeded over two consecutive accounting periods.'

[89] Rec. 57(1)(4) DSA.

[90] Directive 2005/29/EC of the European Parliament and of the Council of 11 May 2005 concerning unfair business-to-consumer commercial practices in the internal market and amending Council Directive 84/450/EEC, Directives 97/7/EC, 98/27/EC and 2002/65/EC of the European Parliament and of the Council and Regulation (EC) No 2006/2004 of the European Parliament and of the Council (Unfair Commercial Practices Directive), OJ 2005 L 149, 22 as consolidated on 25 May 2022.

[91] Dregelies VuR 2023, 175 (178).

[92] Cf. Art. 2 no. 5 P2B Regulation (EU) 2019/1150 of the European Parliament and of the Council of 20 June 2019 on promoting fairness and transparency for business users of online intermediation services, OJ 2019 L 186, 57.

cided on a case-by-case basis according to their respective activity or on the basis of their technical functions whether they are to be classified as mere conduit, caching or hosting services.[93]

c) Very large online platforms and very large online search engines

55 The larger an online platform or search engine is, the greater its potential reach and thus its influence on the perception and communication of information by recipients. In order to take these facts into account, the DSA assigns special obligations to **very large online platforms** ('VLOPs') and **very large online search engines** ('VLOSEs') with the provisions of Art. 33–48 DSA.[94] The imposition of those obligations is justified by the fact that reach-efficient service providers have a significant influence over the public communication process and the acquisition and dissemination of information beyond the mere provision of the infrastructure, and that the societal risks associated with them are wider and more pronounced than small platforms.[95] In order to prevent over-regulation, the DSA aims to design the obligations in a reasonable proportion to the social power of the service providers.[96]

56 Whether the specific service provider is a very large online platform or a very large search engine is to be determined **on a case-by-case basis** and depends largely on the **average number of active recipients** of the service per month within the territory of the EU, Article 33(4) DSA.[97] In doing so, the legislator assumes that the systematic risks associated with online platforms and online search engines have a disproportionate impact if the services reach a significant proportion of the EU's population.[98] According to Art. 33(1) DSA, such a reach exists if the number of active recipients exceeds an operational threshold of 45 million and thus around 10 % of the approximately 448.4 million people[99] currently living in the EU.[100] In view of the need to continuously update the level of the operational threshold, the Commission is authorised under Article 33(2) DSA to supplement the regulation by means of delegated acts.[101]

57 In order to determine the actual reach of the respective service providers, it is **necessary to determine the average number of active recipients**, which does not necessarily correspond to the number of registered recipients.[102] The regulation only sets out in its recitals what requirements must be imposed on the activities of the recipients in order to be considered as being reached by the platform and empowers the Commission, in accordance with Article 33(3) DSA to adopt delegated acts to define specific demarcation criteria and methods.[103]

58 According to rec. 77 DSA, **active recipients** of online platforms are those who have used the services at least once within a certain period of time.[104] This includes any use

---

[93] Rec. 29(1)(5) DSA; Dregelies MMR 2022, 1033 (1034); Raue/Heesen NJW 2022, 3537 (3538).

[94] In the Commission's draft regulation, online search engines were not yet considered separately, cf. European Commission, 'Proposal for a regulation of the European Parliament and of the Council on a Single Market For Digital Services (Digital Services Act) and amending Directive 2000/31/EC', 15.12.2020, COM (2020) 825 final.

[95] Rec. 75(1)(1) and (2); 76 sent. 1 DSA.

[96] Rec. 76(1)(2) DSA.

[97] Rec. 65 DSA.

[98] Rec. 76(1)(4) DSA.

[99] Eurostat, 'Facts and figures on life in the European Union', <european-union.europa.eu/principles-countries-history/key-facts-and-figures/life-eu_de> (last accessed: 15.07.2024).

[100] Rec. 76(1)(4) DSA.

[101] Rec. 76(1)(5) DSA.

[102] Rec. 77 subpara. 2 sent. 2 DSA.

[103] Critical on this: Gerdemann/Spindler GRUR 2023, 115 (121).

[104] Rec. 77 subpara. 1 sent. 2 DSA.

that exposes recipients to the information disseminated by the services, for example by viewing or listening to published content or providing information themselves.[105] Any further interaction with the information by clicking, commenting, linking or carrying out transactions is not necessary.[106]

According to rec. 77 DSA, active recipients of an online search engine are those who **actively view the information at least once on the online interface.**[107] The owners of the websites indexed in the search results, on the other hand, are not included due to the lack of active use.[108] **59**

According to Art. 24(2) DSA, the providers of online platforms and online search engines are/were obliged to release information on the average number of active recipients per month in a publicly accessible area of their online interface by 17.2.2023 and at least every six months thereafter. At the request of the Commission, this information must be transmitted to the Commission and to the coordinator for digital services at the place of establishment, Art. 24(3)(1) DSA. On the basis of these figures, the switching services are classified as VLOPs or VLOSEs by a decision of the Commission, Art. 33(4)(1) DSA. **60**

The COM has **already classified VLOPs and VLOSEs.**[109] The VLOPs include, for example, Amazon,[110] Apple AppStore, Instagram, LinkedIn, TikTok, X (formerly Twitter), Wikipedia, YouTube, and Zalando,[111] as well as Pornhub, Xvideos, and Stripchat. The VLOSEs include Google Search and Bing. The COM has **initiated formal proceedings against X** for the first time under the DSA. It is investigating whether X has violated the DSA in the areas of risk management, content moderation, dark patterns, advertising transparency, and access to data for researchers.[112]

C. Territorial-personal scope of application

From a territorial-personal perspective, the applicability of the DSA requires, according to Art. 2(1) DSA, that the **intermediary services are offered 'to recipients** of the service that have their place of establishment or are **located in the Union**, irrespective of where the providers of those intermediary services have their place of establishment'. According to Art. 3(b) DSA, a recipient of the service is 'any natural or legal person who uses an intermediary service, in particular for the purposes of seeking information or making it accessible'. It is noteworthy that the DSA **separately and uniformly defines the international scope of application** for the limitation of liability of intermediaries **by means of a unilateral conflict-of-laws rule.**[113] The E-Commerce Directive did not have any conflict-of-law rules so far, which is why the general rules of private international law (in particular the Rome II Regulation;[114] cf. its Art. 15(b)) applied. Only at the level **61**

---

[105] Rec. 77 subpara. 1 sent. 2 DSA.

[106] Rec. 77 subpara. 1 sent. 2 DSA.

[107] Rec. 77 subpara. 2 sent. 3 and 4 DSA.

[108] Rec. 77 subpara. 2 sent. 3 DSA.

[109] The current status is available on the following website: <https://digital-strategy.ec.europa.eu/en/policies/list-designated-vlops-and-vloses> (last accessed: 15.07.2024).

[110] Amazon has filed a lawsuit against the EU regarding its classification as a VLOP; see GC 27.9.2023 – case T-367/23 R, ECLI:EU:T:2023:589 – Amazon Services Europe v Commission.

[111] Zalando has also filed a lawsuit against the EU regarding its classification as a VLOP.

[112] European Commission, 'Commission opens formal proceedings against X under the Digital Services Act' (European Commission's Press Release, 18.12.2023) <ec.europa.eu/commission/presscorner/detail/en/ip_23_6709> (last accessed: 15.07.2024).

[113] See Lutzi Dalloz IP/IT 2023, 278.

[114] Regulation (EC) No 864/2007 of the European Parliament and of the Council of 11 July 2007 on the law applicable to non-contractual obligations (Rome II), OJ 2007 L 199, 40.

of substantive law did the liability limitations take effect via the EU country of origin law of the service.[115] Unfortunately, the DSA approach does not solve the conflict-of-laws problems in their entirety. Instead, there is now a complex interplay between the unilateral DSA rules and legal questions that continue to be answered according to the general multilateral rules of private international law.[116] To give just one example,[117] the question of the liability of intermediary services under the DSA may require clarification of whether certain content is illegal. However, this question is not answered by the DSA, but by national law. Since violations of personal rights are not covered by the Rome II Regulation,[118] the national conflict of laws is responsible for determining the applicable substantive law. The basic rule is that every court with international jurisdiction applies its own private international law. However, it may also come to the conclusion that the law of another country must answer the question of whether content is illegal. In short, such questions are highly complex and will remain so.[119]

I. Marketplace principle

62 The DSA, like other European legal acts,[120] e.g. the GDPR,[121] opts for the **marketplace principle** in order to ensure the effectiveness of the regulatory requirements and fair conditions of competition (at least) throughout the European internal market.[122] Accordingly, pursuant to Art. 2(1) DSA the provisions of the DSA also apply to **intermediary services that are located in non-Member States** but whose offer is directed at recipients with their place of establishment or who are located in the territory of the EU. This means that non-EU platforms that provide their services within the EU are also covered by the scope of application. This is to be welcomed in order to avoid competitive disadvantages and the possible migration of companies established on the territory of the Union.[123]

1. Place of establishment or recipients located in the European Union

63 The territorial scope covers firstly offerings to **recipients who have their domicile in a Member State**. If the offer of intermediary services is directed at commercial recipients, they must be established within the Union. The concept of **establishment** is to be interpreted autonomously under EU law, so that no recourse to the respective national understanding is possible. However, as a point of reference, rec. 22(1)(2) and (3) GDPR may be used as a starting point. According to this, an establishment requires

[115] Cf. ECJ 25.10.2011 – joined cases C-509/09 and C-161/10, ECLI:EU:C:2011:685 = NJW 2012, 137 mn. 58 et seq. – eDate Advertising GmbH and Others v X and Société MGN LIMITED.

[116] Lutzi Dalloz IP/IT 2023, 278.

[117] Lutzi Dalloz IP/IT 2023, 278 (280).

[118] Art. 1(2)(g) Rome II Regulation.

[119] Lutzi Dalloz IP/IT 2023, 278 (280): 'the relevant legal regime for this kind of questions will inevitably consist of a mosaic of national laws and European Regulations, only one of which will be the DSA [...]. Thus, the DSA [...] has not made identifying the relevant legal framework easier; if anything, it has added yet another layer of complexity to the puzzle'.

[120] In-depth on the international scope of application of the legal acts of the Digital Single Market: Heinze in Kubis/Peifer/Raue/Stieper Ius Vivum – FS Schack p. 440.

[121] General Data Protection Regulation – Regulation (EU) 2016/679 of the European Parliament and of the Council of 27 April 2016 on the protection of natural persons with regard to the processing of personal data and on the free movement of such data, and repealing Directive 95/46/EC (General Data Protection Regulation), OJ 2016 L 119, 1.

[122] Rec. 7 DSA.

[123] German Federal Council BR-Drs. 96/21B, 6.

the 'effective and real exercise of activity through stable arrangements'.[124] The legal form of the establishment, which can be a branch or subsidiary, and the nature of the activity are not decisive in this respect.[125] Following the previous case law of the ECJ, there are no high requirements for the existence of an establishment, so that even activities on an insignificant scale,[126] such as the maintenance of small offices, are sufficient.[127]

2. Offerings for recipients

Pursuant to Art. 3(d) DSA, the **offering of intermediary services to recipients within the territory of the Union** requires 'enabling natural or legal persons in one or more Member States to use the services of a provider of intermediary services that has a substantial connection to the Union'. 64

A service provider has a substantial connection to the Union pursuant to Article 3(e) half-sentence 1 DSA if it is **established in the EU.** If this is not the case, a substantial connection can be established on the basis of special factual criteria such as the **number of recipients in the Union** (Art. 3(e) half-sentence 2 indent 1 DSA) or the **targeted orientation of activities towards Member States** (Art. 3(e) sentence 2 indent 2 DSA). However, the cumulative fulfilment of these criteria is not a prerequisite; rather, it is sufficient if either one or the other condition is met. Accordingly, service providers are covered by the scope of application even if a significant number of recipients from one or more Member States in relation to the respective population utilise the offering, despite the fact that the offering is not directed at them. Accordingly, it is difficult for service providers to 'escape' the DSA. 65

According to rec. 8(1)(2) DSA, it is to be determined whether activities are targeted towards one or more Member States, taking into account all the circumstances of the specific individual case. For example, the language in which the offering is presented to the recipients, in which currency the payment is to be made or which top-level domain is used are all to be considered.[128] In this way, the DSA is based on the criteria already developed by the ECJ in connection with other European legislation, in particular international EU civil procedure law.[129] 66

---

[124] Cf. also rec. 19(1)(1) E-Commerce Directive; rec. 19(1)(1) Directive 95/46/EC of the European Parliament and of the Council of 24 October 1995 on the protection of individuals with regard to the processing of personal data and on the free movement of such data, OJ 1995 L 281, 31.

[125] ECJ 1.10.2015 – case C-230/14, ECLI:EU:C:2015:639 = NJW 2015, 3636 mn. 28 et seq. – Weltimmo s.r.o. v Nemzeti Adatvédelmi és Információszabadság Hatóság; ECJ 13.5.2014 – case C-131/12, ECLI:EU:C:2014:317 = NJW 2014, 2257 mn. 48 et seqq. – Google Spain SL and Google Inc. v Agencia Española de Protección de Datos (AEPD) and Mario Costeja González; rec. 22(1)(3) GDPR.

[126] ECJ 1.10.2015 – case C-230/14, ECLI:EU:C:2015:639 = NJW 2015, 3636 mn. 31 – Weltimmo s.r.o. v Nemzeti Adatvédelmi és Információszabadság Hatóság: 'any real and effective activity — even a minimal one — exercised through stable arrangements'; ECJ 28.7.2016 – case C-191/15, ECLI:EU:C:2016:612 = NJW 2016, 2727 mn. 75 – Verein für Konsumenteninformation v Amazon EU Sàrl.

[127] Ernst in Paal/Pauly DS-GVO Art. 3 mn. 8.

[128] Rec. 8(1)(2) DSA.

[129] See in particular: ECJ 7.12.2010 – joined cases C-585/08 and C-144/09, ECLI:EU:C:2010:740 = NJW 2011, 505 mn. 55 et seq. – Peter Pammer v Reederei Karl Schlüter GmbH & Co. KG and Hotel Alpenhof GesmbH v Oliver Heller; ECJ 6.9.2012 – case C-190/11, ECLI:EU:C:2012:542 = NJW 2012, 3225 – Daniela Mühlleitner v Ahmad Yusufi and Wadat Yusufi; ECJ 17.10.2013 – case C-218/12, ECLI:EU:C:2013:666 = NJW 2013, 3504 mn. 27 et seq. – Lokman Emrek v Vlado Sabranovic; ECJ 23.12.2015 – case C-297/14, ECLI:EU:C:2015:844 = NJW 2016, 697 mn. 27 et seq. – Rüdiger Hobohm v Benedikt Kampik Ltd & Co. KG and Others.

II. Continuation of the country-of-origin principle

67 The entry into force of the DSA does not affect the provisions of the E-Commerce Directive with the exception of Art. 12–15 according to Art. 2(3) DSA. For this reason, the **country-of-origin principle**[130] from Art. 3 E-Commerce Directive continues to apply.[131] According to this principle, only the **law of the country of residence determines the legal responsibility of the service provider.**[132] The country-of-origin principle thus fundamentally **sets considerable limits on the responsibility of providers**: according to Art. 3(2) E-Commerce Directive, Member States may not restrict the free movement of information society services from another Member State for reasons that fall within the **coordinated field.**[133]

68 Subject to the exceptions of Art. 3(4) E-Commerce Directive, the country-of-origin principle prohibits the service provider from being subject to stricter legal requirements than those resulting from the applicable substantive law of its country of establishment.[134] Accordingly, the **respective Member State must ensure that the application of national law does not lead to stricter regulation than that provided for by the country of origin** – which is often Ireland. Art. 3(4) E-Commerce Directive loses some of its significance in that national law no longer applies if and to the extent that the DSA itself provides exhaustive requirements.[135] However, since the DSA does not regulate many legal requirements for intermediary services, the country-of-origin principle remains of interest.[136]

69 From the perspective of the claimant, the country-of-origin principle is often not an attractive solution, since the protection afforded is based solely on the Member State law of the providers's country of residence.[137] However, rec. 38 DSA provides for an **exception to the country-of-origin principle** for orders to take action against illegal content and to provide information:[138] the orders must relate to specific illegal content or specific information, so that they do not in principle restrict the freedom of providers to provide their services across borders.[139] Accordingly, the provisions of Art. 3 E-Commerce Directive do not apply to these orders.[140]

70 The orders covered include both court and official decisions such as titles and administrative acts.[141]

---

[130] Cf. Hamann ZUM 2000, 290 (291); Berger NJW 2001, 1530 (1531); Micklitz/Rott in Dauses/Ludwigs H. V. mn. 39.

[131] Dregelies MMR 2022, 1033 (1035); Dregelies VuR 2023, 175 (176); Spindler GRUR 2021, 545 (546); Frank MMR 2022, 1026 (1028).

[132] Sack WRP 2019, 1095; Holznagel CR 2021, 123.

[133] On the term 'coordinated field' see Art. 2(h) E-Commerce Directive.

[134] ECJ 25.10.2011 – joined cases C-509/09 and C-161/10, ECLI:EU:C:2011:685 = NJW 2012, 137 (141) – eDate Advertising GmbH and Others v X and Société MGN LIMITED.

[135] Holznagel CR 2023, 321 (322).

[136] Holznagel CR 2023, 321 (322 et seq.).

[137] Holznagel CR 2021, 123 (130).

[138] In-depth on this: Holznagel CR 2021, 123 (130 et seqq.).

[139] Rec. 38(1)(2) DSA.

[140] Rec. 38(1)(3) DSA.

[141] Dregelies MMR 2022, 1033 (1035).

D. Intertemporal scope of application

The DSA entered into force on 16.11.2022, 20 days after its publication in the Official Journal of the EU (Art. 93(1) DSA; cf. Art. 297(1) subpara. 3 sent. 2 TFEU). By virtue of Art. 93(2) DSA, it applies in full since 17.2.2024. 71

If a service provider is designated as a very large online platform or very large online search engine, the **Commission shall immediately notify the companies concerned of the classification** pursuant to Article 33(6) subpara. 1 DSA and publish the classification in the Official Journal of the EU. With a four-month deadline from publication, the obligations apply to the corresponding services, Art. 33(6) subpara. 2 DSA. If the services lose their classification as VLOPs or VLOSEs, the Commission cancels the designation pursuant to Art. 33(5) DSA. In this case, a transitional period of four months also applies until the obligations of Art. 34 et seq. DSA no longer apply to intermediary services, Art. 33(6) subpara. 2 sent. 2 DSA. 72

§ 3
Responsibility and liability of intermediaries

Literature: *Angelopoulos*, European Intermediary Liability in Copyright. A Tort-Based Analysis, Amsterdam 2016; *Angelopoulos*, 'Harmonizing Intermediary Copyright Liability in the EU: A Summary' in Frosio (ed), Oxford Handbook of Online Intermediary Liability, Oxford 2020, p. 315; *Arnold*, 'Intermediary Liabilty and Trade Mark Infringement: A Common Law Perspective' in Frosio (ed), Oxford Handbook of Online Intermediary Liability, Oxford 2020, p. 404; *Balkin*, 'Free Speech is a Triangle', Columbia Law Review 118, no. 7 (2018), 2011; *Balkin*, 'Old-school/new-school speech regulation', Harvard Law Review Vol. 127, no. 8 (2014), 2296; *Baumann*, Die Haftung von Domain-Registraren. Verantwortlichkeit eines neutralen Dienstanbieters für urheberrechtsverletzende Inhalte Dritter, Tübingen 2021; *Berberich/Seip*, 'Der Entwurf des Digital Services Act', GRUR-Prax 2021, 4; *Berberich/Conrad*, 'Plattformen und KI' in Ebers/Heinze/Krügel/Steinrötter (eds), Künstliche Intelligenz und Robotik, München 2020, p. 932; *Berger/Janal*, 'Eine Untersuchung zur Störerhaftung von Online Auktionshäusern', CR 2004, 917; *Bertermann*, 'LG Köln: Störerhaftung von Domain-Registraren für Inhalte von Webseiten', MMR 2015, 523; *Bornkamm*, 'E-Commerce Directive vs. IP Rights Enforcement. Legal Balance Achieved?', GRUR Int. 2007, 642; *Buiten*, 'From Intermediary Liability to Platform Regulation, JIPITEC 2021, 361; *Buiten/Streel/Peitz*, 'Rethinking Liability Rules for Online Hosting Platforms', International Journal of Law and Information Technology 2019, 139; *Busch/Mak*, 'Putting the Digital Services Act in Context: Bridging the Gap Between EU Consumer Law and Platform Regulation', EuCML 2021, 109; *Cauffman/Goanta*, 'A New Order: The Digital Services Act and Consumer Protection', European Journal of Risk Regulation 2021, 758; *Cogo/Ridolfi*, 'Administrative Enforcement in Europe' in Frosio (ed), Oxford Handbook of Online Intermediary Liability, Oxford 2020, p. 586; *Conrad*, 'Zum Modell der Rechteklärung und Rechteverwaltung auf Hosting-Plattformen', ZUM 2017, 289; *Conrad*, '§ 3 Verantwortlichkeit und Haftung von Intermediären', in Steinrötter (ed), Europäische Plattformregulierung – Rechtshandbuch, Baden-Baden 2023; *Conrad/Ampatziadis*, 'Und täglich grüßt das Murmeltier: Wird die Störerhaftung durch die Störerhaftung ersetzt?', GRUR 2023, 1504; *Czychowski/Nordemann*, 'Grenzenloses Internet – entgrenzte Haftung? Leitlinien für ein Haftungsmodell der Vermittler', GRUR 2013, 986; *Denga*, 'Die Technology Judgement Rule' in: Kuschel/Assmussen/Golla (eds), Intelligente Systeme – Intelligentes Recht, 2021, p. 63; *Douville/Netter*, Règlement sur les services numériques : de l'encadrement des plateformes communicationelles (1), RTD Com. 2023, 19; *Dreier/Leistner*, 'Urheberrecht im Internet: die Forschungsherausforderungen', GRUR 2013, 881; *Dreier/Schulze* (eds), Urheberrechtsgesetz: UrhG, 7th edition, Munich 2022; *Dubout*, 'Modérer la modération: le Digital Services Act ou la civilisation du numérique', RTD 2023, 7; *Farrand*, "Is This a Hate Speech?' The Difficulty in Combating Radicalisation in Coded Communications on Social media Platforms', European Journal on Criminal Policy and Research, 2023, 477; *Freytag*, 'Verantwortlichkeit für rechtswidrige Inhalte nach der E-Commerce-Richtlinie', CR 2000, 600; *Fromm/Nordemann* (eds), Urheberrecht, 12th edition, Munich 2018; *Frosio* (ed), The Oxford Handbook of Online Intermediary Liability, Oxford 2020; *Frosio*, 'Why Keep A Dog and Bark Yourself? From Intermediary Liability to Responsibility', Oxford International Journal of Law and Information Technology 2018, 1; *Frosio/Husovec*, 'Accountability and Responsibility of Online Intermediaries' in Frosio (ed), Oxford Handbook of Online Intermediary Liability, Oxford 2020, p. 613; *Frosio/Geiger*, 'Taking Fundamental Rights Seriously in the Digital Services Act's Platform Liability Regime', European Law Journal 2023, 1; *Frosio/Geiger*, 'Towards a Digital Constitution, How the Digital Services Act Shapes the Future of Online Governance' in João Pedro Quintais, et al. 'From the DMCA to the DSA: A Transatlantic Dialogue on Online Platform Regulation and Copyright' Verfassungsbooks, 1 Jan. 2024, p. 43; *Frosio/Mendis*, 'Monitoring and Filtering: European Reform or Global Trend?' in Frosio (ed), Oxford Handbook of Online Intermediary Liability, Oxford 2020, p. 544; *Gabriel*, Strafrechtliche Verantwortlichkeit für fremde Texte, Frankfurt/M. 2003; *Geiger/Frosio/Izyumenko*, 'Intermediary Liability and Fundemental Rights' in Frosio (ed), Oxford Handbook of Online Intermediary Liability, Oxford 2020, p. 138; *Geiger/Izyumenko*, 'Blocking Orders: Assessing Tensions with Human Rights' in Frosio (ed), Oxford Handbook of Online Intermediary Liability, Oxford 2020, p. 566; *Geiger/Jütte*, 'Platform Liability under Art. 17 of the Copyright in the Single Market Directive, Automated Filtering and Fundamental Rights: An Impossible Match', GRUR International 2021, 517; *Gerdemann/Spindler*, 'Das Gesetz über digitale Dienste (Digital Services Act) (part 1) – Grundlegende Strukturen und Regelungen für Vermittlungsdienste und Host-Provider', GRUR 2023, 3; *Gersdorf/Paal* (eds), Informations- und Medienrecht, 2nd edition, Munich 2021; *Goldman*, 'An Overview of the United States' Section 230 Internet Immunity', in Frosio (ed), Oxford Handbook of Online Intermediary Liability, Oxford 2020, p. 155; *Grabitz/Hilf/Nettesheim* (eds), Das Recht der Europäischen Union: EUV/AEUV, 77th edition, Munich 2022; *Grisse*, 'Was bleibt von der Störerhaftung? Bedeutung der 3. Änderung des TMG für die zivilrechtliche Systematik und Umsetzung der Vermittlung in Deutschland', GRUR 2017, 1073; *Grisse*, Internetangebotssperren – Zivilrechtliche Vermittlerhaftung von Internetzugangsanbietern, Tübingen 2018; *Grisse*, 'Haftung eines Domain-Registrars für Urheberrechtsverletzungen unter der Domain – Anmerkung zu BGH, Urteil vom 15.10.2020 – I ZR

13/19 – Störerhaftung des Registrars', ZUM 2021, 152; *Grünwald/Nüßing*, 'Vom NetzDG zum DSA: Wachablösung beim Kampf gegen Hate Speech? Diskussionsstand zu beiden Gesetzesvorhaben und deren Vereinbarkeit', MMR 2021, 283; *Gsell/Krüger/Lorenz/Reymann* (eds), beck-online Grosskommentar BGB, Munich 2022; *Paschke/Berlit/Meyer/Kröner* (eds), Hamburger Kommentar – Gesamtes Medienrecht, 4th edition, Baden-Baden 2021; *Grynbaum/Pailler/Le Goffic/Morlet*, Droit des activités numériques, 2nd edition, Paris 2023; *Hau/Poseck* (eds), Beck'sche Online Kommentare BGB, 64th Edition, Munich 2022; *Hennemann*, 'Die Inanspruchnahme von Zugangsvermittlern: Von der Störerhaftung zum Sperranspruch', ZUM 2018, 754; *Gersdorf/Paal* (eds), BeckOK Informations- und Medienrecht, 38th Edition, Munich 2022; *Hilty/Moscon*, 'Digital Markets, Rules of Conduct, and Liability of Online Intermediaries – Analysis of Two Case Studies: Unfair Commercial Practices and Trade Secrets Infringement', in Frosio (ed), Oxford Handbook of Online Intermediary Liability, Oxford 2020, p. 421; *Hoeren*, 'Anmerkung zur Entscheidung des BGH vom 23.9.2003 – VI ZR 335/02', MMR 2004, 166; *Hoeren*, 'Anmerkung zur Entscheidung des BGH vom 11.3.2004 – I ZR 304/01', MMR 2004, 672; *Hoeren*, 'Anmerkung zur Entscheidung des Europäischen Gerichtshofs vom 12.07.2011, C-324/09', MMR 2011, 596; *Sieber/Höfinger*, 'Teil 18 – Haftung', in Hoeren/Sieber/Holznagel (eds), Handbuch Multimedia-Recht, 60. Ergänzungslieferung, Munich 2023; *Hoeren/Yankova*, 'The Liability of Internet Intermediaries – The German Perspective', IIC 2012, 501; *Hofmann/Raue* (eds), Digital Services Act, Baden-Baden 2023; *Holznagel*, Notice and Take-Down-Verfahren als Teil der Providerhaftung, Tübingen 2013; *Holznagel*, 'Der neue § 7 Abs. 3 Satz 1 TMG: Richtervorbehalt für die zivilrechtliche Störerhaftung von Hostprovidern?', CR 2017, 738; *Holznagel*, 'Der Konflikt zwischen Art. 15 E-Commerce-RL und proaktiven Verhinderungspflichten von Host-Providern', ZUM 2018, 350; *Holznagel*, 'Versteckte Weichenstellungen und ausstehende Reparaturen bei den Regelungen zu Privilegierung, Haftung & Herkunftslandsprinzip für Provider und Online-Plattformen', CR 2021, 123; *Hofmann*, Der Unterlassungsanspruch als Rechtsbehelf, Tübingen 2017; *Hofmann*, 'Das Allgemeininteresse an der Verfügbarkeit von Internet im Spannungsverhältnis zum Schutz von Urheberrechten', GPR 2017, 176; *Hofmann*, 'Prozeduralisierung der Haftungsvoraussetzungen im Medienrecht – Vorbild für die Intermediärshaftung im Allgemeinen?', ZUM 2017, 102; *Hofmann*, 'Störerhaftung des Domain-Registrars im Urheberrecht', NJW 2021, 274; *Hofmann/Specht-Riemenschneider*, 'Verantwortung von Online-Plattformen', ZGE 2021, 49 (67); *Husovec*, Injunctions against Intermediaries in the European Union, Cambridge 2017; *Husovec*, 'Rising Above Liability: The Digital Services Act As a Blueprint for the Second Generation of Global Internet Rules', Berkeley Technology Law Journal 2023, 101; *Husovec/Urban*, 'Will the DSA have the Brussels Effect?' in João Pedro Quintais, et al. 'From the DMCA to the DSA: A Transatlantic Dialogue on Online Platform Regulation and Copyright' Verfassungsbooks, 1 Jan. 2024, p. 73; *Janal*, 'Der Entwurf eines Digital Services Acts: Neue Perspektiven der Verantwortung von Diensteanbietern der Informationsgesellschaft', K&R 2021, 6; *Janal*, 'Haftung und Verantwortung im Entwurf des Digital Services Act', ZeuP 2021, 227; *Janal*, 'Friendly Fire? Das Urheberrechts-Diensteanbieter-Gesetz und sein Verhältnis zum künftigen Digital Services Act', GRUR 2022, 211; *Jarass* (ed), Charta der Grundrechte der Europäischen Union, 4th edition, Munich 2021; *Jones*, Die urheberrechtliche Haftung von Intermediären im Rechtsvergleich, Tübingen 2020; *Kaesling*, 'Evolution statt Revolution der Plattformregulierung', ZUM 2021, 177; *Kavanagh/Fasshauer/White*, 'EU Data and Digital Drive: 10 Things to Know About the Digital Services Act', The Computer & Internet Lawyer 2023, 11; *Keber*, 'Netzsperren und die neue Clearingstelle Urheberrecht im Internet (CUII) – eine kritische Bestandsaufnahme aus Sicht der Internetnutzer:innen', CR 2021, 391; *Kitz*, 'Anmerkung zu LG Düsseldorf 23.05.2007 – 12 O 151/07', CR 2007, 603; *Kosseff*, The Twenty-Six Words that created the Internet, Ithaca 2019; *Kuczerawy*, From 'Notice and Takedown' to 'Notice and Stay Down': Risks and Safeguards for Freedom of Expression', in Frosio (ed), Oxford Handbook of Online Intermediary Liability, Oxford 2020, p. 525; *Kuczerawy/Ombelet*, 'Did the Romans get it Right?' in Taddeo/Floridi (eds), The Responsibility of Internet Service Providers, Cham 2017, 101; *Leistner*, 'Störerhaftung und mittelbare Schutzrechtsverletzung', GRUR-Beil. 2010, 1; *Leistner*, 'Grundlagen und Perspektiven der Haftung für Urheberrechtsverletzungen im Internet', ZUM 2012, 722; *Leistner*, 'The Commission's vision for Europe's Digital Future: Proposals for the Data Governance Act, the Digital Markets Act and the Digital Services Act – A critical primer', Journal of Intellectual Property Law & Practice 2021, 778; *Leistner*, 'Besprechung zu EuGH "Polen/Parlament und Rat"', GRUR 2022, 803; *Leistner/Grisse*, 'Sperrverfügungen gegen Access-Provider im Rahmen der Störerhaftung (Teil 1)', GRUR 2015, 19; *Leistner/Grisse*, 'Sperrverfügungen gegen Access-Provider im Rahmen der Störerhaftung (Teil 2)', GRUR 2015, 105; *Libertus*, 'Umfang und Reichweite von Löschungspflichten bei Rechtsverstößen im Internet', ZUM 2005, 627; *Loiseau*, 'Commerce électronique – Le Digital Services Act', Communication Commerce électronique n° 2, Février 2023; *Loiseau*, 'Commentaires - Contrats – Responsabilité', Communication Commerce électronique n° 5, Mai 2024, 1; *Lucas/Lucas-Schloetter/Bernault*, Traité de la propriété littéraire et artistique, 5th edition, Paris 2017; *Manara*, Droit du commerce électronique, Paris 2013; *Marsoof*, Internet Intermediaries and Trade Mark Rights, Milton Park 2019; *Meyerson*, 'Authors, editors and uncommon carriers: Identifying the "speaker" within the new media', Notre Dame Law Review 1995, 79; *Montagnani*, 'A new Liability Regime for Illegal Content in the Digital Single Market Strategy', in Frosio (ed), Oxford Handbook of Online Intermediary Liability, Oxford 2020, p. 295; *Mostert*, 'Intermediary Liability and Online

Trade Mark Infringement: Emerging International Common Approaches', in Frosio (ed), Oxford Handbook of Online Intermediary Liability, Oxford 2020, p. 369; *Säcker/Rixecker/Oetker/Limperg* (eds), Münchener Kommentar zum Bürgerlichen Gesetzbuch, 8th edition, Munich 2020; *Erb/Schäfer* (eds), Münchener Kommentar zum Strafgesetzbuch Nebenstrafrecht II Band 7, 3rd edition, München 2019; *Heermann/ Schlingloff* (eds), Münchener Kommentar zum Lauterkeitsrecht (UWG), Lauterkeitsrecht Band I, 3rd edition, Munich 2020; *Müller/Nordemann*, 'Die neue Clearingstelle im Urheberrecht im Internet (CUII) – Urheberrechtliche und verfassungsrechtliche Voraussetzungen der Selbstregulierung von Sperransprüchen in Deutschland', ZUM 2021, 507; *Müller-Terpitz/Köhler*, Digital Services Act, Munich 2024; *Nolte*, 'Hate-Speech, Fake-News, das »Netzwerkdurchsetzungsgesetz« und Vielfaltsicherung durch Suchmaschinen', ZUM 2017, 552; *Hamacher/Krings/Otto*, Nomos Kommentar Glücksspielrecht, Baden-Baden 2022; *Nordemann*, 'Neues zur Providerhaftung im Urheberrecht. Registrare, CDN- und DNS- Provider und ihre strukturell rechtsverletzenden Kunden', GRUR 2021, 18; *Nordemann/Steinbrecher*, 'Urheberrecht: Wirtschaftsübereinkunft gründet Clearingstelle', MMR 2021, 189; *Nunziato*, 'The Digital Services Act and the Brussels Effect on Platform Content Moderation', Chicago Journal of International Law 2023, 115; *Ohly*, Verhandlungen des 70. Deutschen Juristentages Hannover 2014 Bd. I: Gutachten Teil F: Urheberrecht in der digitalen Welt – Brauchen wir neue Regelungen zum Urheberrecht und dessen Durchsetzung?, 2014; *Ohly*, 'Die Verantwortlichkeit von Intermediären', ZUM 2015, 308; *Ohly*, 'Die Haftung von Internet-Dienstleistern für die Verletzung lauterkeitsrechtlicher Verkehrspflichten', GRUR 2017, 441; *Paal*, 'Anmerkung zu einer Entscheidung des EuGH, Urteil vom 03.10.2019 (C-18/18) – Zur Haftung von Intermediären für Rechtsverletzungen Dritter im Internet', JZ 2020, 92; *Pankoke*, 'Beweis- und Substanziierungslast im Haftungsrecht der Internetprovider', MMR 2004, 211; *Papaevangelou*, "The non-interference principle': Debating online platforms' treatment of editorial content in the European Union's Digital Services Act', European Journal of Communication, 2023, 466; *Pons/André/Borgat*, 'Contenus illicites en ligne, quelle est l'évolution du régime de responsabilité des hébergeurs ?', Pin Code 2021/3, 1; *Quintais/Appelman/ Fathaigh*, 'Using Terms and Conditions to apply Fundamental Rights to Content Moderation', German Law Journal, 2023, 881; *Raue*, 'Anmerkung zur Entscheidung des BGH vom 2.6.2022 – I ZR 140/15', GRUR 2022, 1308; *Reiffenstein/Blaschek* (eds), Konsumentenpolitisches Jahrbuch 2021, Vienna 2021; *Rössel*, 'Digital Services Act – Eingehende Analyse und Überprüfung der regulatorischen Neuerungen aus dem Trilog und potentielle Lücken', AfP 2023, 93; *Rosati*, 'Intermediary IP injunctions in the EU and UK experiences: when less (harmonization) is more?', GRUR Int. 2017, 206; *Roßnagel* (ed), Beck'scher Kommentar zum Recht der Telemediendienste, Munich 2013; *Rössel*, 'Vorschlag zur Harmonisierung der Verantwortlichkeit von Onlineplattformen', ITRB 2021, 35; *Schaefer*, 'Anmerkung zu BGH, Urteil vom 12. Mai 2010 – I ZR 121/08 – Sommer unseres Lebens', ZUM 2010, 699; *Schmid/Grewe*, 'Digital Services Act: Neues "Grundgesetz für Onlinedienste"?', MMR 2021, 279; *Loewenheim/Leistner/Ohly* (eds), Urheberrecht, 6th edition, Munich 2020; *Schulze/Staudenmayer* (eds), EU Digital Law, Baden-Baden 2020; *Schwemer*, 'Digital Services Act: A reform of the e-Commerce Directive and much more' in Savin/Trzaskowski (eds), Research Handbook on EU Internet Law, Cheltenham 2023; *Schwemer/Mahler/Styri*, 'Legal analysis of the intermediary service providers of non-hosting nature, Final re-port prepared for European Commission', University of Copenhagen Faculty of Law Legal Studies Research Paper Series, 2020; *Senftleben*, 'Breathing Space for CloudBased Business Models – Exploring the Matrix of Copyright Limitations, Safe Harbours and Injunctions', Journal of Intellectual Property, Information Technology and E-Commerce Law 2013, 87; *Senftleben*, 'Human Rights Outsourcing and Reliance on User Activism in the DSA' in João Pedro Quintais, et al. 'From the DMCA to the DSA: A Transatlantic Dialogue on Online Platform Regulation and Copyright' Verfassungsbooks, 1 Jan. 2024, p. 61; *Senftleben*, Intermediary Liability and Trade Mark Infringement: Proliferation of Filter Obligations in Civil Law Jurisdictions?, in Frosio (ed), Oxford Handbook of Online Intermediary Liability, Oxford 2020, p. 381; *Senftleben/Angelopoulos*, 'The Odyssey of the Prohibition on General Monitoring Obligations on the Way to the Digital Services Act: Between Article 15 of the E-Commerce Directive and Article 17 of the Directive on Copyright in the Digital Single Market' (22.10.2020), <https://ssrn.com/abstract=3717022> (last accessed: 26.01.2024); *Slot*, 'Case C-194/94, CIA Security International SA v. Signalson SA and Securitel SPRL, Judgment of the Full Court of Justice of 30 April 1996, not yet reported', Common Market Law Review 1996, 1035; *Sobola/Kohl*, 'Haftungsprivilegierung nach § 11 TDG – Grundsatzanalyse und Tendenzen der Rechtsprechung, CR 2005, 443; *Specht*, 'Ausgestaltung der Verantwortlichkeit von Plattformbetreibern zwischen Vollharmonisierung und nationalem Recht', ZUM 2017, 114; *Specht-Riemenschneider/Hoffmann*, 'Verantwortung von Online Plattformen – Ein Plädoyer für funktionszentrierte Verkehrspflichten' (2021) <https://www.vzbv.de/publikationen/nutzerrechte-auf-online-plattformen-absichern> (last accessed: 24.06.2024); *Spindler*, 'Dogmatische Strukturen der Verantwortlichkeit der Diensteanbieter nach TDG und MDStV', MMR 1998, 639; *Spindler*, 'Die Verantwortlichkeit der Provider für "Sich-zu-Eigen-gemachte" Inhalte und für beaufsichtigte Nutzer', MMR 2004, 440; *Spindler*, 'Europarechtliche Rahmenbedingungen der Störerhaftung im Internet – Rechtsfortbildung durch den EuGH in Sachen L'Oréal/eBay', MMR 2011, 703; *Spindler*, 'Weltweite Löschungspflichten bei Persönlichkeitsrechtsverletzungen im Internet', NJW 2019, 3274; *Spindler*, 'The Liability system of Art. 17 DSMD and national implementation – contravening prohibition of general monitoring duties?', JIPITEC 2020, 344; *Spindler*, 'Haftung von Infrastrukturbetreibern, insbesondere DNS-Resolver nach TMG und geplantem Digital Services Act', CR 2022, 318; *Spindler/Schmitz* (eds), Telemediengesetz: TMG, 2nd edition, Munich 2018; *Spindler/Schuster* (eds), Recht der elektronischen Medien, 4th edition, Munich 2019; *Tourkochoriti*, 'The Digital Services Act and the EU as the Global Regulator of the Internet', Chicago Journal of International Law, 2023, 129; *Wagner*, 'Haftung von Plattformen für Rechtsverletzungen (Teil 1)', GRUR 2020, 329; *Wagner*, 'Haftung von Plattformen für Rechtsverletzungen (Teil 2)', GRUR 2020, 447; *Wegmann/Kehl*, 'Mit Kanonen auf Spatzen? Die Auswirkungen von Digital Services Act und Digitale-Dienste-Gesetz auf digital aktive Unternehmen jenseits von TikTok, Facebook & Co.', BB 2024, 387; *Wiebe*, 'Providerhafung in Europa: Neue Denkanstöße durch den EuGH (Teil 1)', WRP 2012, 1182; *Wimmers/Nolte*, 'Wer stört? Gedanken zur Haftung von Intermediären im Internet – von praktischer Konkordanz, richtigen Anreizen und offenen Fragen', GRUR 2014, 16; *Zech*, 'The European Parliament proposal for a regulation on liability for the operation of artificial intelligence systems', ZGE 2022, 293.

I. General principles

1. Liability regimes as a pillar of the European fair balance on platforms

1 After years of discussion, preparatory works and studies, the legislator transferred the existing liability rules for internet service providers essentially unchanged from the E-Commerce Directive[1] to the DSA.[2] With few exceptions, the wording of the liability rules in Chapter II is identical to Art. 12 to 15 of the E-Commerce Directive. The legislator thus maintained the horizontal liability scheme introduced two decades ago in the pioneering age of the internet.

2 **Two US regulations served as the model** for this **special liability regime** for internet service providers: *First*, **Section 230 of the Communication Decency Act (CDA)** of 1996, a telecommunications regulation, which excludes to a wide extent liability of operators of interactive computer services for third-party content.[3] *Second*, the copyright safe harbour in the US **Digital Millennium Copyright Act (DMCA)** of 1998. Notably, the DMCA is the model for categorizing internet services into mere conduit (Art. 4 of the DSA), caching (Art. 5 of the DSA) and hosting (Art. 6 of the DSA).[4] Key concepts, such as the notice-and-take-down (NTD) and the Good Samaritan rule, now introduced to European law through Art. 7 of the DSA, also replicate models in the CDA and the DMCA.[5]

3 The **basic rule for the European liability regime** is that **internet service providers are not subject to a general obligation to monitor the information which they store for their users, nor to seek facts or circumstances indicating illegal activity. Instead,**

---

[1] Directive 2000/31/EC of the European Parliament and of the Council of 8 June 2000 on certain legal aspects of information society services, in particular electronic commerce, in the Internal Market ("Directive on electronic commerce"), OJ 2000 L 178, 1.

[2] Regulation (EU) 2022/2065 of the European Parliament and of the Council of 19 October 2022 on a single market for digital services and amending Directive 2000/31/EC (Digital Services Act), OJ 2022 L 277, 1. The legislative history and relevant draft documents are succinctly presented by Raue in Hofmann/Raue, Introduction para. 30 et seqq.

[3] Art. 230 CDA is described as a fundamental principle of the Internet era; see Kosseff, 2019; Nunziato Chi. J. Int. Law 2023, 115 (119).

[4] § 512(a)–(c) DMCA encompass the categories "*Transitory Digital Network Communications*", "*System Caching*", "*Information Residing on Systems*" and "*Networks At Direction of Users*". The stipulated liability provision for "Information *Location Tools*" (search engines) in § 512(d) DMCA was not incorporated; Relevant discussions on the DMCA, including Holznagel, 'Notice and Take-Down-Verfahren als Teil der Providerhaftung', 2013, p. 5 et seqq; Ohly, 'Verhandlungen des 70. Deutschen Juristentages Hannover 2014 Bd. I: Gutachten Teil F: Urheberrecht in der digitalen Welt – Brauchen wir neue Regelungen zum Urheberrecht und dessen Durchsetzung?', 2014, p. 95 et seq.; Hennemann in Gersdorf/Paal TMG § 7 mn. 4.

[5] Section 230 CDA; § 512(g)(1) DMCA; Holznagel, 'Notice and Take-Down-Verfahren als Teil der Providerhaftung', 2013, p. 23 et seqq., 54 et seqq. Nunziato Chi. J. Int. Law 2023, 115 (119) however, points out that "In contrast to the DSA, § 230(c) imposes no conditions on platforms to receive immunity from liability".

they must act expeditiously to disable access to or remove illegal information upon obtaining knowledge of the illegal character of the information and must otherwise comply with **orders of authorities and courts**. The liability regime thereby follows a **two-step approach** where the service provider's knowledge of specific illegal information or a court or administrative order are the pivotal points for enhanced obligations.

Unless service providers have knowledge of specific illegal activity, they are not liable under civil or criminal law or in any other way for third-party content. It is one of the essential decisions of the legislator that this liability privilege does not depend on whether, and in what way, service providers have taken precautions against infringements. With the exceptions of cases of abuse, **service providers are not subject to due diligence obligations or a duty to investigate content or information without cause**. Only upon obtaining **knowledge of an infringement** or when they have been **ordered to remove or take precautionary measures**, are service providers subject to obligations to disable access to or delete illegal content **(take-down)** and, if necessary, to prevent new uploads **(stay-down)**. 4

The liability provisions of the E-Commerce Directive were often described as *privileges* aimed at **guaranteeing legal certainty to the developing industry of internet service providers**. Those service providers were compared to "tender shoots" of the digital economy protected by the legislator from being "nipped in the bud" by imposing civil and criminal liability on them.[6] Conceiving of the liability regime in that way as a promotion for start-up activity would have suggested repealing Art. 12 to 15 of the E-Commerce Directive once the tender shoots evolved into flourishing companies.[7] Indeed, introducing enhanced obligations for platforms was the approach taken by the legislator in Art. 17 of the DSM Directive[8], which provides for a duty of care-based liability concept for copyright liability of service providers where content is shared. 5

In the legislative process for the DSA, the legislature examined a similar approach to that taken in copyright law for general liability rules but eventually opted against structural reform of the civil liability regime.[9] Instead, the legislature has **regulated various aspects of platform activity in Sections 3 to 4 of Chapter III and introduced enhanced obligations for very large online platforms**, albeit outside of the civil and criminal liability regime.[10] 6

This legislative choice confirms that the liability rules are not aimed at protecting service providers from regulatory burdens or liability. Rather, the liability rules of Chapter 7

[6] See Dreier/Leistner GRUR 2013, 881 (881) who refer to "extremely delicate shoots" that have since evolved into "dominating gatekeepers" (paraphrased from German); see also Ohly GRUR 2017, 441 (449); Loiseau Commerce électronique n° 2, 2023, 1.

[7] Leistner in Schricker/Loewenheim UrhG § 97 mn. 56; European Commission, Impact Assessment Report, SWD (2020) 348 final Part 2/2 p. 165 et seq. For a duty of care-based approach also Buiten/Streel/Peitz, 'Rethinking Liability Rules for Online Hosting Platforms' (11.03.2019), p. 15 et seq., <https://papers.ssrn.com/sol3/papers.cfm?abstract_id=3350693> (last accessed: 26.01.2024).

[8] Directive (EU) 2019/790 of the European Parliament and of the Council of 17 April 2019 on copyright and related rights in the digital single market and amending Directives 96/9/EC and 2001/29/EC, OJ 2019 L 130, 92.

[9] On the duty of care-based approach, see European Commission, Impact Assessment Report, SWD(2020) 348 final Part 2/2, p. 165; preceded by various studies, notably Sartor, 'Providers Liability: From the eCommerce Directive to the future' (2017) <https://www.europarl.europa.eu/RegData/etudes/IDAN/2017/614179/IPOL_IDA(2017)614179_EN.pdf> (last accessed: 26.01.2024); Nordemann, 'Liability of Online Service Providers for Copyrighted Content – Regulatory Action Needed?' (January 2018) <https://www.europarl.europa.eu/RegData/etudes/IDAN/2017/614207/IPOL_IDA(2017)614207_EN.pdf> (last accessed: 26.01.2024).

[10] Art. 92 DSA provides for early application of the DSA, including the liability regime, to very large online platforms and search engines four months after designation pursuant to Art. 33(4) DSA, and thus at the earliest 7 months after entry into force of the DSA.

II are justified by the goal of **balancing the multipolar interests which are inherent in the platform economy.**[11] Articles 4 to 10 of the DSA is a **response to the possible restrictions of (mainly) free speech, freedom of information of freedom of the arts** which would result from incentivizing services to avoid criminal responsibility and civil liability.[12]

8 The decision to shield internet service providers from liability responds to the fact that, in the absence of such a liability shield, service providers are prone to avoid any risk and tend to block too much content, rather than too little **(overblocking)**. The risk of overblocking is particularly acute where intellectual property right holders' area accorded strict remedies under civil and criminal law that are aimed at deterring and preventing infringements.[13] Carefully designing a system of nuanced duties of care to balance conflicting interests has not proven to avoid these dangers. Duties of care are developed in light of the circumstances. In practice, exactly which duties are determined to be reasonable in the particular case is subject to *ex post*-assessment in court and may be hard if not impossible to predict.[14] Litigating cases in grey areas is time-consuming and requires resources. Thus, it is likely that providers of vast amounts of information, content and offers will structure their business operations in a way that is aimed at avoiding disputes rather than test the boundaries of the law.

9 The CJEU recently highlighted these risks in the context of delisting requests from search engines. **In hard cases, it is cheaper for service providers to simply block content than to fight in court over the accessibility of information, opinions, content and offers from third parties.**[15] If overblocking occurs, third parties are the ones that bear the burden; their activities, often protected by fundamental rights, are impaired. The danger of externalising third party interests through the suppression of communication, which is also referred to as "collateral censorship",[16] has been clearly demonstrated by the discussion on Art. 17 of the DSM Directive.[17]

10 The liability regulations thus create the framework which enables **a balance of interest through the activities of digital intermediaries,** which are **considered desirable by society.**[18] The core of the model is to proceduralise the moderation of content in order to enable a case-by-case consideration of the interests affected and prescribe action by the intermediaries only to the extent that it serves to achieve the right balance of interests in the individual case.[19]

---

[11] On the balancing of interests on platforms Berberich/Conrad, 'Plattformen und KI' in Ebers/Heinze/Krügel/Steinrötter (eds), Künstliche Intelligenz und Robotik, p. 930, mn. 60 et seqq.

[12] F. Hofmann in Hofman/Raue, DSA intro to Art. 4 mn. 33 et seqq., sees three phases of legislative focus: The protection of a developing industry; followed by an effective protection for rightsholders; and finally a focus on user rights.

[13] Conrad ZUM 2017, 289 (293); Frosio/Geiger Eur. Law J. 2023, 1 (5).

[14] Aptly, para. 19 of the Dissenting Opinion in the case ECHR 16.6.2015 – App. no. 64569/09 – Delfi AS v Estonia: "Only divine legal counsel could have been sufficiently certain that a portal operator would be liable for a comment [...]".

[15] CJEU 8.12.2022 – case C-460/20, ECLI:EU:C:2022:962 para. 71 – TU, RE v Google LLC = GRUR 2023, 147 – TU.

[16] On the term Meyerson Notre Dame Law Review 1995, 79 (118) ("the silencing by a private party of the communication of others"); Balkin Harvard Law Review, 2014, 2296 (2309 et seq.). F. Hofmann in Hofmann/Raue, DSA intro to Art. 4 mn. 93, 100 also sees a growing danger of "collateral damage" for user rights when stricter liability regimes are applied.

[17] Regarding chilling effects and "de facto censorship" in this context, see Nolte ZUM 2017, 552 (560). Husovec BTLJ 2023, 101 (130) points out the similarity in the EU and the U.S., which also have a stricter rule for the online sharing of copyrighted works, Sec. 512 DMCA.

[18] Recital 1 DSA; see also AG Jääskinen 9.12.2010 – case C-324/09, ECLI:EU:C:2010:757 para. 53 = BeckRS 2010, 91402 – L'Oréal v eBay; Wimmers/Nolte GRUR 2014, 16 (17).

[19] Dubout RTD 2023, 7 (Introduction).

The CJEU has applied the same principles that evolved based on the E-Commerce Directive to analogue business models.[20] This clearly indicates that the interests involved, and the benefits and threats as well as the means of resolving them are not limited to the digital sphere. The underlying model of nuanced rights enforcement based on considerations of proportionality has been described as a **general concept of European law** serving as further justification of Art. 4 to 8 of the DSA.[21] **11**

In the DSA Impact Assessment, the Commission thus emphasis that the liability exemptions of the DSA represent a "**cornerstone for the fair balance**" in the internet economy: **12**

> "Any other model placing more legal risks on intermediaries would potentially lead to severe repercussions for citizens' freedom of expression online and traders' ability to conduct their businesses online and reach consumers. They would also be prohibitive for any new business, reinforcing the stronghold of very large players, able to sustain and, to a certain extent, externalize costs. Conversely, significantly decreasing the standard for hosting services to quality (sic!) for the liability exemption would severely affect the safety and trust in the online environment".[22]

The EU is not alone in pursuing this model. The European Court of Human Rights assumes that it is recognised in international law that internet service providers are not liable for third party content if they act immediately when they become aware of the illegality of the content.[23] **13**

2. Impact of fundamental rights on the liability rules

The high impact of the **fundamental rights dimension** of the liability rules, which are aimed at ensuring a fair balance of interests, has been one of the most important developments for this civil liability regime since it came into force. Questions of liability and responsibility have led to numerous judgements of the CJEU that have highlighted the importance of online platforms for the exercise of fundamental rights of its users and the CJEU has examined the incentives created by the liability rules from the perspective of possible interferences with fundamental rights which they cause. Issues of liability relating to the accessibility of content via online platforms have led to **landmark rulings in the fundamental rights jurisprudence of** the CJEU, the ECHR and the national courts.[24] **14**

---

[20] CJEU 7.7.2016 – case C-494/15, ECLI:EU:C:2016:528 para. 36 et seq. = GRUR 2016, 1062 – Tommy Hilfiger v Delta Center.

[21] F. Hofmann in Hofmann/Raue, intro to Art. 4 mn. 19.

[22] European Commission, Impact Assessment Report, SWD (2020) 348 final Part 1/2, mn. 170; also explicitly states: "The liability exemption of online intermediaries is a cornerstone for the fair balance of rights in the online world." referencing ECHR 12.10.2017 – App. No. 3877/14, BeckRS 2017, 161237 para. 84 – Tamiz v the United Kingdom.

[23] ECHR 12.10.2017 – 3877/14, BeckRS 2017, 161237 para. 84 – Tamiz v The United Kingdom.

[24] CJEU 26.4.2022 – case C-401/19, ECLI:EU:C:2022:297 para. 75 et seq. = GRUR 2022, 820 – Poland v Parliament and Council; AG Saugmandsgaard Øe 15.7.2021 – case C-401/19, ECLI:EU:C:2021:613 para. 129 et seq. = GRUR-RS 2021, 20614 – Poland v Parliament and Council; CJEU 22.6.2021 – joined cases C-682/18 and C-683/18, ECLI:EU:C:2021:503 para. 64 et seqq. = GRUR 2021, 1054 – YouTube and Cyando; CJEU 16.2.2012 – case C-360/10, ECLI:EU:C:2012:85 para. 41 et seq. = GRUR 2012, 382 – SABAM v Netlog; CJEU 24.11.2011 – case C-70/10, ECLI:EU:C:2011:771 para. 43 et seq. = GRUR 2012, 265 – Scarlet Extended SA v SABAM; CJEU 29.1.2008 – case C-275/06, ECLI:EU:C:2008:54 para. 61 et seq. = ZUM 2008, 288 – Promusicae v Telefónica de España SAU; ECHR 12.10.2017 – App. No. 3877/14, BeckRS 2017, 161237 para. 84 – Tamiz v The United Kingdom; BVerfG 06.11.2019 – 1 BvR 16/13, ZUM 2020, 58 – Recht auf Vergessen I; BVerfG 06.11.2019 – 1 BvR 276/17, ZUM-RD 2020, 1 – Recht auf Vergessen II; BVerfG 22.5.2019 – 1 BvQ 42/19, ZUM-RD 2019, 429 – Der III. Weg; Corte di Cassazione, 19.03.2019 – 9133/2015, GRUR Int. 2019, 952; Conseil constitutionnel, decision no. 2020–801

15 The scrutiny of liability rules under the aspects of fundamental rights has reached its peak in the CJEU's *Poland* decision, in which the court carefully scrutinized the effects of a liability concept based on duties of care. Only narrowly did Art. 17 of the DSM Directive pass the test of compatibility with primary Union law.[25] After this decision, the **importance of fundamental rights for the liability regime** cannot be overstated.[26]

16 Confronted with a web of conflicting interests on platform services, case law has developed the notion of "fair balance" as a **special manifestation of the principle of proportionality.**[27] *Firstly,* **users** cause the transmission and storage of information and offers and may be affected by service providers in their rights and freedoms, such as the freedom of expression, artistic and scientific freedom, property rights or the freedom to conduct their business (Art. 11, 13, 16, 17 of the CFR).[28] *Secondly,* **holders of intellectual property rights** may be affected by measures (or the absence of measures) of service providers in their property rights and their commercial activities (Art. 16, 17(2) of the CFR). *Thirdly,* **recipients** may be affected in their rights and freedoms, such as the freedom of information, their possible rights to data and commercial interests (Art. 7, 8, 11, 16 of the CFR).[29] *Fourthly,* the **rights and interests of the platform operators** must also be taken into account, mainly to pursue their commercial activities and make use of their property (Art. 16, 17 of the CFR).[30]

17 The premise of the fundamental rights scrutiny **is that effects of liability rules can be as serious as traditional regulatory interventions.**[31] If service providers are forced to use filtering measures to avoid liability, these may lead to restrictions on users' fundamental rights, such as their freedom of expression or entrepreneurial freedom. Unlike voluntary measures taken by service providers, these are **directly attributable to the legislature.**[32] If liability rules induce private individuals to control and restrict the

---

DC, 18.06.2020 (re the partial unconstitutionality of the French Loi Avia); öOGH 30.03.2020 – 4 Ob 36/20b MMR 2020, 685.

[25] CJEU 26.4.2022 – case C-401/19, ECLI:EU:C:2022:297 = GRUR 2022, 820 – Poland v Parliament and Council.

[26] Concerning the necessity for balancing fundamental rights Holznagel ZUM 2018, 350 (356 et seq.).

[27] Saugmandsgaard Øe characterizes the balancing test as the third limb of the proportionality test, see AG Saugmandsgaard Øe 15.7.2021 – case C-401/19, ECLI:EU:C:2021:613 para. 248 = GRUR-RS 2021, 20614 – Poland v Parliament and Council. For the balancing test see also Geiger/Jütte GRUR Int. 2021, 517 (522 et seq. and mn. 70); on the speech triangle on platforms Balkin Colum. L. Rev. 2018, 2011; see also the case law of the German Constitutional Court BVerfG 11.04.2018 – 1 BvR 3080/09, NJW 2018, 1667 – Stadionverbot; BVerfG 06.11.2019 – 1 BvR 16/13, ZUM 2020, 58 – Recht auf Vergessen I; BVerfG 06.11.2019 – 1 BvR 276/17, ZUM-RD 2020, 1 – Recht auf Vergessen II; BVerfG 22.05.2019 – 1 BvQ 42/19, ZUM-RD 2019, 429 – Der III. Weg; Frosio/Geiger Eur. Law J. 2023, 1.

[28] CJEU 26.4.2022 – case C-401/19, ECLI:EU:C:2022:297 para. 75 = GRUR 2022, 820 – Poland v Parliament and Council; Jarass in Jarass GrCh Art. 11, mn. 13, 15.

[29] CJEU 16.2.2012 – case C-360/10, ECLI:EU:C:2012:85 para. 43 = GRUR 2012, 382 – SABAM v Netlog.

[30] On the latter, CJEU 24.11.2011 – case C-70/10, ECLI:EU:C:2011:771 para. 46 = GRUR 2012, 265 – Scarlet Extended; CJEU 26.4.2022 – C-401/19, ECLI:EU:C:2022:297 para. 75 = GRUR 2022, 820 – Poland v Parliament and Council; this also applies in principle in data protection law, even if the CJEU did not consider the interests of the service providers to be decisive in the result here; see CJEU 13.5.2014 – case C-131/12, ECLI:EU:C:2014:317 para. 81 = NJW 2014, 2257 – Google Spain SL v AEPD and others; likewise BVerfG 6.11.2019 – 1 BvR 276/17 para. 120, ZUM-RD 2020, 1 – Recht auf Vergessen II; different opinion Wagner GRUR 2020, 329 (336).

[31] CJEU 26.4.2022 – case C-401/19, ECLI:EU:C:2022:297 para. 55 = GRUR 2022, 820 – Poland v Parliament and Council; Opinion of AG Saugmandsgaard Øe 15.7.2021 – case C-401/19, ECLI:EU:C:2021:613 para. 87 = GRUR-RS 2021, 20614 – Poland v Parliament and Council.

[32] CJEU 26.4.2022 – case C-401/19, ECLI:EU:C:2022:297 para. 55, 56 = GRUR 2022, 820 – Poland v Parliament and Council; on the obligation of private parties in the provision of public services BVerfG 22.2.2011 – 1 BvR 699/06, NJW 2011, 1201 – Freedom of assembly in an airport; BVerfG 18.7.2015 –

fundamental rights of others,[33] the European courts will scrutinize possible effects to avoid a disproportionate interference with fundamental rights.

The goal of creating a **suitable incentive system for a fair balance of interests** was thus the decisive reason for maintaining liability rules. For this goal to be realised, it is essential that the applicability of the liability regulations is not contingent upon the use of precautionary measures without cause.[34] Whilst the complex web of interests has not dissolved, it can be expected that the issues will resurface in areas where the legislature has introduced regulatory interventions and supervision. Art. 35(1) of the DSA demonstrates that these are subject to the same scrutiny as the fundamental rights in the context of the liability norms. **18**

3. European harmonisation of the liability regime

a) *Full harmonisation of the limitation of liability*

The main reason for transferring the liability rules of the E-Commerce Directive into a Regulation was to **overcome differences in national solutions and create uniform rules for service providers.**[35] Diverging national rules were the result not only of specialized regulatory interventions at Member State level (such as the German NetzDG[36]), but also national peculiarities in the implementation of the liability rules.[37] Faced with this patchwork of national solutions, the European legislature opted for a **directly binding Europe-wide solution.**[38] This must be considered in the interpretation and implementation of the provisions of Chapter II. **19**

b) *Art. 4 to 8 of the DSA as negative liability regulations and limitation of responsibility*

Although the liability limitation standards have a fully harmonising effect in their scope of application, they nevertheless only regulate one aspect of criminal and civil liability, namely a **negative condition for an offense or claim**. As with the E-Commerce Directive, Art. 4 to 8 of the DSA only regulate under which conditions service providers are *not* liable. They do not positively determine whether and under which conditions service providers can be held liable if Art. 4 to 6 of the DSA are not fulfilled. Under no circumstances, as was already stated in the explanatory memorandum to the proposal for the E-Commerce-Directive, should the provisions affect substantive rules governing any infringements that may be concerned.[39] **20**

Nevertheless, there have been **continuous discussions about the relationship between the liability provisions and substantive liability rules**. The legislator of the **21**

---

1 BvQ 25/15, NJW 2015, 2485 – "Bierdosen-Flashmob"; similarly BVerfG 11.4.2018 – 1 BvR 3080/09, NJW 2018, 1667 – Stadionverbot.

[33] The obligation of private parties to control third parties is also emphasised by Wagner GRUR 2020, 329.

[34] European Commission, Impact Assessment Report, SWD (2020) 348 final Part 1/2, p. 43, mn. 159.

[35] Recital 25 DSA. Kavanagh/Fasshauer/White The Computer & Internet Lawyer 2023, 11; for the E-Commerce Directive; Manara, p. 60.

[36] On the relationship of the DSA to the NetzDG Grünwald/Nüßing MMR 2021, 283 (285 et seqq.).

[37] The European Commission noted "[f]ragmented national laws", see Impact Assessment Report, SWD (2020) 348 final part 2/2, p. 94. On the "divergent national case law" already European Commission, Commission Staff Working Document SEC (2011) 1641 final, p. 26 et seq. For the case of German "Störerhaftung", see Conrad, '§ 3 Verantwortlichkeit und Haftung von Intermediären', in Steinrötter (ed), Europäische Plattformregulierung – Rechtshandbuch, § 3 mn. 21, 192 et seq.

[38] Critical that oversight is left to member state authorities, which could hinder harmonised enforcement, see Frosio/Geiger, Verfassungsbooks, 2024, 43 (52).

[39] Explanatory Memorandum to the Draft Directive 2000/31/EC (E-Commerce Directive), COM (1998) 586 final, p. 27.

DSA clarified the relationship once more: "Those rules should not be understood to provide a positive basis for establishing when a provider can be held liable, which is for the applicable rules of Union or national law to determine."[40] Discussions in recent years have shown, however, that this seemingly simple rule has repeatedly given rise to discussions in practice.

22 One of the rules limiting the responsibility of service providers is the **prohibition of imposing general monitoring measures and active fact-finding obligations on service providers** (Art. 8 of the DSA). The relevance of Art. 8 of the DSA is twofold: On the one hand, it prohibits that direct or indirect obligations are being imposed on service providers to monitor and investigate illegal content or information without reason. On the other hand, according to the case law of the CJEU, Art. 8 of the DSA (or its predecessor Art. 15 of the E-Commerce-Directive) has significance for stay-down measures that can be ordered against service providers (mn. 169 et seqq.).

23 The CJEU has thus recognised Art. 8 of the DSA (or Art. 15 of the E-Commerce Directive) as a **negative principle of responsibility** that limits measures at both European and national levels.[41] The DSA places the task to fine-tune obligations in individual cases in the hands of the Member States (cf. Art. 4(3), Art. 5(3) and Art. 6(4) of the DSA)[42], even though they may also be subject to special regulations at Union level (e.g., Art. 8(3) of the Directive 2001/29/EC). In applying their national laws, however, Member States are subject to European fundamental rights and must ensure that a fair balance between the different rights is achieved.

4. A horizontal liability regime in a multi-level system

a) Horizontal regulation for intermediaries

24 The main policy decision for Chapter II was to maintain the horizontal approach and the ground rules of the liability concept of the E-Commerce Directive.[43] In accordance with the purpose of the Digital Services Act as a regulatory instrument for digital services, Art. 4 to 9 of the DSA regulate the liability of service providers **comprehensively and conclusively**.

25 This means, on the one hand, that the liability rules set out in Chapter II **apply irrespective of the area of law** to which the otherwise applicable union or national legal matter belongs to (i.e. intellectual property rights, personality rights, protection of minors).[44] On the other hand, it means that **legal consequences and sanctions resulting from** violations are subject to the intermediary regulations irrespective of whether they

[40] Recital 17(1)(2) DSA.

[41] Husovec 2017, p. 118, refers to a "transplant" of provisions from the E-Commerce Directive into Directive 95/46/EC of the European Parliament and of the Council of 24 October 1995 on the protection of individuals with regard to the processing of personal data and on the free movement of such data (DP Directive), OJ 1995 L 281, 31, This is because the prohibition on monitoring and investigation limits measures under Article 11(1)(3) of the Enforcement Directive.

[42] Specht-Riemenschneider/Hoffmann, 'Verantwortung von Online Plattformen – Ein Plädoyer für funktionszentrierte Verkehrspflichten' (2021) <https://www.vzbv.de/publikationen/nutzerrechte-auf-online-plattformen-absichern> (last accessed: 24.06.2024), p. 45.

[43] European Commission, Impact Assessment Report, SWD (2020) 348 final Part 1/2, p. 48, para. 169; Berberich/Seip GRUR-Prax 2021, 4; Rössel AfP 2023, 93, 94; Farrand European Journal on Criminal Policy and Research 2023, 477 (486) ("path dependence"), critical of the approach Lucas/Lucas-Schloetter/Bernault 2017, mn. 1285, p. 1005.

[44] Explicitly rec. 17 DSA; for an application of the hosting rules under Art. 14 E-Commerce Directive to criminal liability, see BGH 12.09.2023 – 3 StR 306/22, BeckRS 2023, 32308 mn. 56 et seqq. – Cyberbunker. (liability exemption for hosting service denied because the enterprise deliberately contributed to illegal activities); See also rec. 20 DSA.

fall under civil law, criminal law or administrative law. Recital 17 of the DSA, which states that the liability exemptions "apply in respect of any type of liability as regards any type of illegal content, irrespective of the precise subject matter or nature of those laws", succinctly summarizes this principle.

26 The decision of the legislator to opt for a horizontal liability regime followed from the regulatory **aim of creating legal certainty for service providers throughout the Union**, without the need for special sector-specific regulations in the Member States on a case-by-case basis.[45] The DSA thereby avoids problems of classification as seen in sector-specific regulation, which are particularly burdensome where regulatory matters are classified differently across the member states. The difficulties in classifying injunctive relief, one of the key questions of the infamous German "Störerhaftung", confirm the merits of such an approach (→ mn. 143, 152 et seq.).

27 Due to the conscious decision of the legislature,[46] questions of classification remain in relation to the three service types "mere conduit", "caching" and "hosting". In practice, however, these questions have not shown to be critical as **the CJEU has interpreted the general prerequisites of the liability exemptions, particularly the central criterion of neutrality, in the same manner for all service categories.** Also, legal consequences often depend on general concepts such as the Good Samaritan-rule (Art. 7 of the DSA) or the prohibition of general monitoring (Art. 8 of the DSA) which apply to all service categories.[47]

b) Liability in a multi-level system: Separation of substantive and intermediary liability

28 The decision in favour of a horizontal cross-sector regime implies that the **conditions of the liability provisions of Art. 4 to 6 of the DSA are to be interpreted and applied regardless of whether the service provider is subject to liability under a sector-specific regulation of Union law or national law.** For instance, the question of whether liability would be assumed under provisions of trademark law or youth protection law plays no role in determining whether one of the liability exemptions of Art. 4, 5 or 6 of the DSA applies.

29 In relation to Member State law, this follows from the **primacy of European Union law.** The aim of harmonising the liability conditions for service providers across the Union[48] could not be reached if the applicability of European liability exemptions depend on whether liability exists under national law. It was one of the reasons why the liability rules were transferred from a directive to a regulation that Member States could not adopt individual approaches as to their interpretation. Even where the legislator has given Member States room to establish their own systems to order stay-down measures, national law must be applied in accordance with Union law (e.g., in Art. 9(1) of the DSA) and in particular, the fundamental rights and freedoms enshrined in the Charter.

30 In relation to other European Union law, Art. 4 to 9 of the DSA are ***leges speciales*** in their scope of application **and must therefore be observed with priority.**[49] Otherwise, the goal of creating legal certainty for service providers would not be achieved. However,

[45] Rec. 16 DSA.

[46] Rec. 19 DSA.

[47] Critical of the distinction Specht-Riemenschneider/Hoffmann, 'Verantwortung von Online Plattformen – Ein Plädoyer für funktionszentrierte Verkehrspflichten' (2021) <https://www.vzbv.de/publikationen/nutzerrechte-auf-online-plattformen-absichern> (last accessed: 24.06.2024), p. 13.

[48] Rec. 16 DSA.

[49] See Hilty/Moscon, 'Digital Markets, Rules of Conduct, and Liability of Online Intermediaries – Analysis of Two Case Studies: Unfair Commercial Practices and Trade Secrets Infringement', in Frosio (ed), Oxford Handbook of Online Intermediary Liability, p. 421 (431).

given the overlapping subject matter of the Regulation with other Union legislation, it cannot be ruled out that other regulations have an impact on the interpretation of the liability exemptions (e.g., on the "expeditious" action required upon notification, see mn. 131 et seqq.).

31 With this **principle of double priority,** the legislator took a clear stance in a discussion on the relationship between substantive laws and liability exemptions, a discussion that originated primarily in copyright law. While it was advocated that primary copyright liability should per se exclude the application of the hosting defence,[50] the CJEU rejected this approach: Primary liability under copyright law – and by extension: under other substantive areas of law – is not in itself decisive for the assessment of whether Art. 14(1) of the E-Commerce Directive (now Art. 6(1) of the DSA) applies.[51] Liability exemption and substantive liability are separate conditions.

32 The legislator of the DSA confirmed this principle. The liability exemptions of the DSA aim to establish a **legally secure liability framework**, that not only incentivizes socially desirable behaviour but also balances the interests of the parties involved.[52] **If the liability regime is applicable and results in a limitation of liability, this cannot be overridden by national or other Union legislation**. Such a clear separation is inherent in the nature of the liability rules as ***leges speciales*** **taking priority over national laws**. Hence, the fact that a service provider is primarily liable under a substantive liability rule does not mean that it cannot rely on the liability limitations outlined in Art. 4 to 6 of the DSA.

33 While the principle is clear, practice may be less so: **The conditions for substantive liability and the applicability of the DSA's liability rules may run parallel and overlap.** To the extent that substantive rules rely on identical or similar circumstances as the liability exemptions under the DSA, their application may be aligned. However, parallelism is possible but not always the case: The prerequisites for the infringement can differ from those for privileged liability and, consequently, from the liability exemption of the service provider who would otherwise be considered primarily liable. This is particularly evident when substantive liability provisions are based on the violation of duties of care, which the liability regime of the DSA excludes[53]. Additionally, the assessment may differ where a substantive liability provision only requires a degree of carelessness ("should have known"), while Art. 6 of the DSA requires actual knowledge.

34 It is an apparent contradiction with this principle that the German Bundesgerichtshof found that the hosting defence does not apply *per se* if the courts find primary liability in copyright law.[54] It is essential to recognize that the requirements **of both, the liability**

---

[50] In this regard, the clarification of AG Saumandsgaard Øe 16.7.2020 – joined cases C-682/18 and C-683/18, ECLI:EU:C:2020:586 para. 137 et seq. = GRUR-RS 2020, 18772 – YouTube and Cyando; the preliminary requests in the cases CJEU 15.9.2021 – case C-442/19, ECLI:EU:C:2021:769 = BeckRS 2021, 30065 – Stichting Brein and CJEU 24.8.2021 – case C-500/19, ECLI:EU:C:2021:692 = BeckRS 2021, 25128 – Puls 4 TV GmbH & Co. KG v YouTube LLC and Google Austria GmbH, in which the question was expressly raised, were no longer pursued by the national courts due to the decision CJEU 22.6.2021 – joined cases C-682/18 and C-683/18, ECLI:EU:C:2021:503 = GRUR 2021, 1054 – YouTube and Cyando.

[51] CJEU 22.06.2021 – joined cases C-682/18 and C-683/18, ECLI:EU:C:2021:503 para. 108 = GRUR 2021, 1054 – YouTube and Cyando; more clearly AG Saugmandsgaard Øe 16.07.2020 – joined cases C-682/18 and C-683/18, ECLI:EU:C:2020:586 para. 138–140 = GRUR-RS 2020, 18772 – YouTube and Cyando, to which the CJEU however refers.

[52] On legal certainty, rec. 16 DSA; on balancing conflicting interests, e.g. rec. 51 DSA.

[53] See Hilty/Moscon, 'Digital Markets, Rules of Conduct, and Liability of Online Intermediaries – Analysis of Two Case Studies: Unfair Commercial Practices and Trade Secrets Infringement', in Frosio (ed), Oxford Handbook of Online Intermediary Liability, p. 421 (431) for competition law.

[54] BGH 02.06.2022 – I ZR 140/15, GRUR 2022, 1308 para.122 – YouTube II; BGH 02.06.2022 – I ZR 135/18, GRUR 2022, 1328 para. 50 – uploaded III. Specifically, the issue was whether primary liability can

standard and the prerequisites outlined in Art. 4 to 6 of the DSA must be assessed independently and separately.[55]

5. Developing liability: the hybrid concept of the DSA

Although the liability exemptions have remained fundamentally unchanged as compared to the E-Commerce-Directive, there have been partial adjustments to their scope of application, and the legislator has provided clarification on certain issues. **The most significant change lies in the context of the liability exemptions**, which has been influenced by the introduction of new regulatory instruments. 35

a) *Copyright specific exception for online content-sharing service providers*

The most significant departure from the horizontal approach of the E-Commerce Directive has been the introduction of a **sector regime for copyright for online content-sharing service providers.** Online content-sharing services have been at the forefront of the discussions about a reform of the liability regime of intermediaries and the underlying discussions about a potential "value gap" resulting therefrom. These services are now subject to a distinct set of rules mandated by Art. 17 of the DSM Directive which have been transposed with notable differences in the Member States. These rules include the licensing of content, proactive stay-down measures and procedural rules to safeguard user rights. As Art. 17 of the DSM Directive is limited to copyright issues, and cases may involve other issues at the same time, the **liability regimes of Art. 17 of the DSM Directive and Chapter II of the DSA may apply simultaneously** (see for overlaps of DSA and DSM Directive → § 9 mn. 106 et seq.). 36

b) *Limited development of liability rules*

In the regulatory domain of Chapter II, the European legislator has identified the necessity for changes at various junctures. These changes are articulated in both recitals and new articles. Firstly, the relationship between the liability exemptions and substantive liability was clarified (→ mn. 42 et seqq.) and the case law on neutrality of service providers confirmed (→ mn. 60 et seqq.). *Secondly,* the recitals offer comprehensive clarifications on the covered services, leading to an expansion, particularly for ancillary services (→ mn. 69 et seqq., 102 et seqq.), while also establishing limits to prevent abuse (→ mn. 76). *Thirdly,* the legislator introduced a Good Samaritan provision in Art. 7 of the DSA, which clarifies the effects of pro-active investigations and filtering (→ mn. 77 et seqq.). *Lastly,* rules have been enacted for administrative orders following the identification of a legal violation (Art. 9 and 10 of the DSA; → mn. 181 et seqq.). 37

---

arise from the (alleged) non-fulfilment of stay-down obligations. This case was not decided by the CJEU 22.6.2021 – joined cases C-682/18 and C-683/18, ECLI:EU:C:2021:503 = GRUR 2021, 1054 – YouTube and Cyando, so that there are already doubts as to whether this complies with European law; CJEU, loc. cit., para. 89. In any case, an active role would have to be established separately for purposes of the DSA and does not follow from primary copyright liability. A general parallelism of the liability requirements cannot be inferred from the CJEU's YouTube and Cyando judgment, neither for copyright law nor for other areas of law; see CJEU 22.06.2021 – joined cases C-682/18 and C-683–18, ECLI:EU:C:2021:503 para. 107 = GRUR 2021, 1054 – YouTube and Cyando.

[55] Conrad/Ampatziadis GRUR 2023, 1504.

c) Limitation of liability in a regulatory context

38 The novelty of the DSA lies in the integration of the liability exemptions into **a broader framework of regulation.**[56] This new regulatory approach, which combined the existing liability framework with problem-oriented and graduated regulation of specific issues, was the guiding principle in the drafting of the DSA.[57] It constitutes a significant development, both in theory and practice and in view of the sometimes conflicting goals of the liability exemptions on the one side and regulatory instruments on the other, is likely to produce tensions between the sides of the regulation.

39 The new regulatory obligations include, on the *one hand,* the provisions in the DSA, particularly **due diligence obligations in Chapter III of the DSA** (→ § 4 mn. 4 et seq.; → § 5 mn. 18 et seq.), and most notably enhanced obligations of **very large online platforms in Section 5 of Chapter III** (e.g., Art. 34 and 35 of the DSA; → § 6 mn. 32 et seq., 48 et seq.). *On the other hand,* new **sector-specific regulations** have been introduced at both **European and national levels.** Notable examples include rules for providers of online audio-visual media services (Directive (EU) 2018/1808) or provisions to combat the dissemination of terrorist content online in Regulation (EU) 2021/784[58]. New instruments are continually being added,[59] reacting to trends in Member States that have introduced special regimes to combat criminal speech online (Germany, France)[60], or institutionalized intellectual property rights infringement by public authorities (e.g., Spain, Italy, Greece).[61] Given the coexistence of regulations and directives on the EU level and additional legislation on Member States-level, the complexity of the legal framework continues to increase. This jeopardizes the goal of European harmonisation, legal certainty; predictability, and, ultimately, the proper functioning of the internal market, one of the key goals of the DSA itself (Art. 1(1) of the DSA).

40 **The most significant evolution** from the E-Commerce Directive to the **DSA is the combination of an incentive structure** devised on the basis of criminal responsibility and civil law liability **with traditional regulatory instruments.** It results in a **hybrid regulatory scheme, which has been described as a graduated system of surveillance,**[62] where the same issues may be subject to criminal and civil law rules as well as regulatory oversight.

41 The fact that the particularly contentious issues relating to primary and secondary copyright liability have been addressed specifically in Art. 17 of the DSM Directive, and

[56] Buiten JIPITEC 2021, 361; Loiseau Commerce électronique n° 2 2023, 2.

[57] European Commission, Online platforms and the Digital Single Market – Opportunities and Challenges for Europe, COM(2016) 288/2, p. 9.

[58] Regulation (EU) 2021/784, Art. 3(3); crit. on the often lobby-driven selection of special sectoral regulatory instruments Janal ZEuP 2021, 227 (235).

[59] See for example the proposal for a regulation of liability for artificial intelligence systems, 2020/2014(INL) P9_TA(2020)0276; on this Zech ZGE 2022, 293.

[60] Such as the German NetzDG or the French LOI n° 2020–766 du 24 juin 2020; Rössel AfP 2023, 93, 94 holds NetzDG, Loi Avia and KoPl-G incompatible with the full harmonisation of the DSA. However, given the fragmented start of the DSA's application it remains unclear from when on the national laws are inapplicable. F. Hofmann/Raue in Hofmann/Raue, Introd. mn. 76 deem the further applicability of the NetzDG "highly dubious". ibid. mn. 80 for similar French and Austrian legislation; Wegmann/Kehl, BB 2024, 387, 388 notes that the German legislator intends to repeal core provisions of the NetzDG due to the DSA. Tourkochoriti Chi. J. Int. Law, 2023, 129 (132, 145) further addresses the conflicts of the DSA with U.S. (free speech) law; on this "Brussels Effect" of the DSA see also Nunziato Chi.J. Int. Law, 2023, 115 et passim; Quintais/Appelman/Fathaigh GLJ, 2023, 881 (889, 899 et seqq.) who deem (esp. Dutch and German) national court decisions to be of more relevance for securing fundamental rights than the aforementioned national laws; Husovec/Urban, Verfassungsbooks, 2024, 73 (76).

[61] See on the latter, Cogo/Ridolfi in Frosio, p. 586 (588 et seqq.).

[62] "Gradation de la surveillance ciblée", see Dubout RTD 2023, 7 (B.2.).

new regulatory instruments have been added, has provided some "**breathing space**" for the liability regime.[63] The legislature has used this to **cautiously expand the scope of application of the liability rules to ancillary services**[64] (→ mn. 69 et seqq.) and has encouraged **the use of voluntary measures to combat illegal content** (→ mn. 77 et seqq.). However, tensions may arise between the principles of limited liability and the absence of a duty of care, with the regulatory obligations imposed on very large online platforms and search services.[65]

6. The liability rules of the DSA as partial harmonisation in the European multi-level system

Chapter II of the DSA exempts intermediaries from liability under specifically regulated conditions but permits them to take corrective and preventive actions against infringements. The limitations of liability are **fully harmonising within their scope**, while the rules on orders against intermediaries allow **for national variations** within the boundaries set by European law. 42

The liability exemptions thus constitute a self-contained regulatory scheme that is separate and independent from substantive liability rules under European and national law (**principle of separation**). The European system operates **alongside substantive liability and sector-specific regulation of the responsibility of internet intermediaries.** Liability of intermediaries is thus regulated **in a hybrid form within the European multi-level system.** 43

In practice, this translates into a **two-limb assessment of liability**: *Firstly,* the conduct of the service provider must not fall under one of the liability exemptions (**negative condition**). *Secondly,* liability must exist under the relevant substantive rules (**positive condition**). As both conditions are a prerequisite for liability, the burden of proof for the elements of the liability exemptions and the existence of substantive liability lies with the claimant.[66] 44

Both conditions, negative and positive, must be fulfilled cumulatively, but are independent of each other. Consequently, the order in which the conditions are examined is irrelevant in practice. Discussions as to whether the European rules on intermediary liability constitute a pre- or post-filter have no practical relevance. If there is no liability due to the applicability of the liability exemptions or because the substantive law requirements are not met, further inquiry becomes unnecessary. The liability rules under the DSA also do not contain exceptions to liability so that the principle of narrow interpretation does not apply.[67] 45

[63] Concept by Senftleben JIPITEC 2013, 87: "Breathing Space for CloudBased Business Models".

[64] See Schwemer, 'Digital Services Act: A Reform of the e-Commerce Directive and Much More' (10.10.2022) <https://ssrn.com/abtract=4213014> (last accessed: 28.11.2023), p. 9 et seq.

[65] For a sceptical view see Montagnani, 'A new Liability Regime for Illegal Content in the Digital Single Market Strategy', in Frosio (ed), Oxford Handbook of Online Intermediary Liability, p. 295 (296).

[66] BGH 23.09.2003 – VI ZR 335/02, GRUR 2004, 74 (75) – Rassistische Hetze.

[67] AG Jääskinnen, 9.12.2010 – case C-324/09, ECLI:EU:C:2010:757 para. 136 = BeckRS 2010, 91402 – L'Oréal v eBay.

II. General application requirements and specifications

1. Subjective scope: The services concerned

a) Information society services

46 The liability exemption in Art. 4 to 6 of the DSA only apply to information society services. Art. 3(a) of the DSA provides that these services must be understood as defined in Art. 1(1)(b) of Directive (EU) 2015/1535 (Info-Directive). As per this definition, an information society service is "**any service normally provided for remuneration, at a distance, by electronic means and at the individual request of a recipient of services.**" This corresponds to the definition on which the E-Commerce Directive is based (cf. Art. 2(a) of the E-Commerce Directive in conjunction with Art. 1 no. 2 of Directive 98/34/EC).[68]

47 **The service must be provided electronically and at a distance**, meaning it is transmitted and received by any means from a starting point to an end point using equipment for the electronic processing and storage of data (Art. 1(1)(b) of the Info-Directive).

48 Neither the DSA nor the Info Directive provide clarification on the requirement that the service is usually provided **against remuneration.** However, it can be inferred that it is **not necessary for the user to pay a (separate) fee for the service provision.** It suffices if the activity is provided in connection with a service of an economic nature and is ultimately remunerated through a reimbursement or the price of the goods sold. Consequently, both advertising-financed business models and services provided without separate consideration as part of an economic offer fall within the scope of application of the liability rules. This is relevant, for instance, when services are provided by telecommunications providers as part of a "service package" and are ultimately remunerated by the customer through the internet connection fee. Similarly, when Wi-Fi connections are offered in hotels or other publicly accessible places, they form part of an economic activity and are thus provided against remuneration. Providers should also be eligible if the service is provided by the public sector and financed by levies or taxes (such as public libraries, schools or universities).

49 **In contrast, the rules of the DSA do not apply to private "services,"** particularly in the significant case of **private Wi-Fi networks.**

50 If a service provider offers more than one service, Chapter II only applies to the services that are considered information society services.[69]

51 Distinguishing information society services from other services offered by an operator can become more challenging when a service comprises various functionalities that, when considered individually, only partially fall within the scope of the liability rules. If these functionalities are inseparably linked as part of an overall offer, the determination hinges on the primary focus of the offer. **If the focus of the offer is on an information society service, the liability privilege applies to the entire service.**[70]

52 This should **also** apply also **when a service is offered on an optional basis, but as part of an information society service**. The most relevant example are **logistics**

---

[68] Directive 98/34/EC of the European Parliament and of the Council of 22 June 1998 laying down a procedure for the provision of information in the field of technical standards and regulations, OJ 1998 L 204, 37.

[69] Also rec. 15 DSA.

[70] See CJEU 3.12.2020 – case C-62/19, ECLI:EU:C:2020:980 para. 41–49 = MMR 2021, 309 – Star Taxi App SRL v Unitatea Administrativ Teritorială Municipiul Bucureşti prin Primar General and Consiliul General al Municipiului Bucureşti; CJEU 19.12.2019 – case C-390/18, ECLI:EU:C:2019:1112 para. 50 = MMR 2020, 171 – Airbnb Ireland; see also CJEU 20.12.2017 – C-434/15, ECLI:EU:C:2017:981 para. 40 = MMR 2018, 144 – Elite Taxi v Uber System Spain.

services on online marketplaces. Even if traders choose shipping services as an optional add-on, the service is usually a subordinate part of the overall offer.

b) Officers, employees and agents

The wording of Art. 4 to 6 of the DSA suggests that only the service providers are eligible under the liability exemptions. Pursuant to general principles this **excludes accessory liability** for officers, employees, or agents.[71] 53

The liability exemptions of the DSA do not seem to exclude, however, **original liability of officers, employees or agents of the service provider**. This creates tension with the purpose to facilitate the emergence and expansion of innovative digital services in the internal market (Recital 4 of the DSA). Considering this objective, it would be a contradictory if the liability privilege did not extend to the individuals who are carrying out the privileged activities.[72] The risk that liability rules create incentives that are contrary to the goal of an open and free internet, applies here as well. To ensure the effectiveness of the liability exemption, it should therefore **also apply to the individuals acting for the privileged service providers.**[73] 54

2. Information provided by users

a) Technical approach

Art. 4 to 6 of the DSA require that the **information is "provided by a recipient of the service."** This aligns with the concept of information "provided" by the user in Art. 12 to 14 of the E-Commerce Directive.[74] It is not necessary that the main purpose of the service consists in offering the possibility to provide information if this is one aspect of its activity.[75] 55

The fact that the wording hinges on the provision of information implies a **technical approach**, emphasising the person who uploads the information into the system and thus has control over its selection.[76] This interpretation is also confirmed by the recitals, which focus on the provision of information and cite, as negative examples, information provided under the editorial responsibility of the service providers. Recital 29 of the DSA also suggests an approach based on "technical functionalities" when classifying services for the purposes of Art. 4 to 6 of the DSA. 56

The entry criterion for the liability exemptions thus provides a relatively **broad filter**. The more important questions of application arise from the liability rules themselves 57

71 See on the relevant regulation in the German TMG Hennemann in Gersdorf/Paal TMG § 7 mn. 21; Sieber/Höfinger, 'Teil 18 – Haftung', in Hoeren/Sieber/Holznagel (eds), Handbuch Multimedia-Recht, Part 18.1 mn. 35.

72 Hennemann in Gersdorf/Paal TMG § 7 mn. 22; Sieber/Höfinger, 'Teil 18 – Haftung', in Hoeren/Sieber/Holznagel (eds), Handbuch Multimedia-Recht, Part 18.1 mn. 35; also Spindler MMR 1998, 639 (640).

73 Spindler in Spindler/Schmitz TMG intro to §§ 7–10 mn. 41; Hennemann in Gersdorf/Paal TMG § 7 mn. 22; Sieber/Höfinger, 'Teil 18 – Haftung', in Hoeren/Sieber/Holznagel (eds), Handbuch Multimedia-Recht, Part 18.1 mn. 35.

74 The German version of the DSA differs from the wording in the E-Commerce Directive whereas there is no difference between the E-Commerce Directive and the DSA in other language versions (the English language version reads "provided by a recipient"; the French version reads "informations fournies par un destinataire"; the Italian version reads "informazioni fornite da un destinatario" in both cases).

75 AG Saugmandsgaard Øe 16.07.2020 – joined cases C-682/18 and C-683/18, ECLI:EU:C:2020:586 para. 144 et seq = GRUR-RS 2020, 18772 – YouTube and Cyando.

76 Hennemann in Gersdorf/Paal TMG § 7 mn. 33; Altenhain in MüKoStGB TMG intro to § 7 mn. 24; Spindler MMR 2004, 440 (441).

and from the requirement that the service provider must behave neutrally and passively to benefit from the limitation of liability (→ mn. 60 et seqq.).

b) Provision of the information

58 Users are deemed to provide information **when they select the information and determine whether and for how long it will be accessible**. Service providers may organise the uploading process, e.g., by creating categories for the information, if it is the user who completes the relevant fields. Organizing the upload process and by extension, the information on the service may be helpful or necessary to ensure that the large amount of information is subsequently accessible in a useful manner. Input assistance tools also serve as auxiliary tools for users and do not change the character of the information as being provided by the user.

59 More difficult questions arise if the service provider checks uploaded information, arranges it, or offers certain functions for its retrievability. However, these questions regularly pertain to whether the service provider is acting neutrally (→ mn. 70).

3. Neutrality of the service provider

a) Active role and neutrality in the case law of the CJEU

60 According to CJEU case law, **the applicability of liability rules depends on whether the service provider acts neutrally or passively rather than actively.**[77] The normative foundation of the neutrality rules lies in Recital 42 of the E-Commerce Directive, which stipulates that the service provider's activity must be purely technical, automatic and passive, meaning it must not grant the service provider knowledge or control over the information that is transmitted or stored. While Recital 42 of the E-Commerce Directive only applied for access and cache providers, case law, even under the E-Commerce Directive, extended this criterion to all categories of service providers.

61 Over time, **neutrality has emerged as the central criterion for distinguishing between privileged and non-privileged activities**. Recognizing the pivotal role of this requirement, the DSA legislator has generalised and specified the neutrality requirement in Recital 18 of the DSA. In view of the significance of this central criterion, elevating the principle to a proper article in the DSA would have been natural.

62 The CJEU primarily developed the principle of neutrality for hosting services. In *L'Oréal/eBay*, the CJEU emphasised that the service provider must not only meet the requirements of Art. 14 of the E-Commerce Directive but must also act as **"an intermediary"**. This is not the case if the service provider operates beyond its passive and automatic role, engaging in activities that grant it knowledge or control over the data.[78]

63 Consequently, a service provider forfeits the liability exemption under two conditions: firstly, by becoming **active**, i.e., undertaking specific activities (**objective element**); secondly, these activities must result in the service provider gaining knowledge and control over specific content (**subjective element**).

[77] CJEU 23.3.2010 – joined cases C-236/08 to C-238/08, ECLI:EU:C:2010:159 para. 113 et seq. = GRUR 2010, 445 – Google and Google France; CJEU 12.7.2011 – case C-324/09, ECLI:EU:C:2011:474 para. 112 et seq. = GRUR 2011, 1025 – L'Oréal v eBay; crit. re this case law Janal GRUR 2022, 211 (215 et seq.); see on this criterion and its adoption in the DSA also Schwemer, 'Digital Services Act: A Reform of the e-Commerce Directive and Much More' (10.10.2022) <https://ssrn.com/abtract=4213014> (last accessed: 28.11.2023), p. 8 et seq.

[78] CJEU 12.7.2011 – case C-324/09, ECLI:EU:C:2011:474 para. 112 et seq. = GRUR 2011, 1025 – L'Oréal v eBay. A compilation of different relevant CJEU rulings regarding the scope of Art. 14 E-Commerce-Directive can be found in Quintais/Appelman/Fathaigh GLJ, 2023, 881 (886 et seq.).

Ultimately, this combines elements of Art. 4, 5 and 6 of the DSA. For Art. 4, it is crucial that the service provider refrains from certain activities concerning the transmitted information, i.e., remains passive (including no selection or modification of the content or its addressees). Conversely, for Art. 6 of the DSA, the knowledge of the service provider is decisive, rather than its active or passive role. Art. 5 of the DSA incorporates a combination of viewpoints. By **consolidating neutrality into a uniform rule,** the CJEU, now confirmed by the legislator, has levelled out the differences between the rules for different service providers. 64

The critical question is **what it means for a service provider to be neutral and what constitutes an active role**. While examples and criteria can be found in case law, a generalized formulation is lacking.[79] Specifically, the CJEU has ruled that an active role cannot be inferred from the fact that the service provider stores third-party offers on its servers,[80] charges for its service,[81] sets the payment terms,[82] makes general information available to its users,[83] determines the modalities of the service, or operates a social media platform[84]. This holds true even if the service provider is generally aware that users also utilise the service to store and make accessible infringing content.[85] 65

In contrast, the CJEU identified the selection of articles for the online presence of a daily newspaper in the *Papasavvas* case as an active behaviour. In this case, the service provider had specific knowledge of the content and exercised control over the distribution.[86] In such instances, one can characterize it as genuine **editorial control** over individual content.[87] 66

The CJEU has traditionally based its assessment on **objective circumstances** rather than the public's perception of the service. Therefore, a service provider does not forfeit its neutral role by checking content for compliance with the service guidelines or illegality and, if necessary, blocking information based on the results of such checks. This is now explicitly confirmed in Art. 7 of the DSA (→ mn. 77). The assessment is based on objective criteria. If the service provider curates its own offering, albeit from information and content provided by users, it if selects specific content based on content-related 67

---

79 Crit. Hoeren MMR 2011, 596 (605).

80 CJEU 12.7.2011 – case C-324/09, ECLI:EU:C:2011:474 para. 115 = GRUR 2011, 1025 – L'Oréal v eBay.

81 CJEU 12.7.2011 – case C-324/09, ECLI:EU:C:2011:474 para. 115 = GRUR 2011, 1025 – L'Oréal v eBay; CJEU 23.3.2010 – joined cases C-236/08 to C-238/08, ECLI:EU:C:2010:159 para. 116 = GRUR 2010, 445 – Google and Google France. French Courts also deemed an online marketplace (eBay) eligible for the hosting privilege, even if the hosting provider charges a fee, see Cour d'appel de Paris 04.04.2012, pôle 5 – ch. 1, decision no. 10/00878.

82 CJEU 23.3.2010 – joined cases C-236/08 to C-238/08, ECLI:EU:C:2010:159 para. 116 = GRUR 2010, 445 – Google and Google France.

83 CJEU 12.7.2011 – case C-324/09, ECLI:EU:C:2011:474 para. 115 = GRUR 2011, 1025 – L'Oréal v eBay; CJEU 23.3.2010 – joined cases C-236/08 to C-238/08, ECLI:EU:C:2010:159 = GRUR 2010, 445 para. 116 – Google and Google France.

84 CJEU 16.2.2012 – case C-360/10, ECLI:EU:C:2012:85 para. 27, 34 = GRUR 2012, 382 – SABAM/Netlog.

85 CJEU 22.6.2021 – joined cases C-682/18 and C-683/18, ECLI:EU:C:2021:503 para. 111 = GRUR 2021, 1054 – YouTube and Cyando. National Courts ruled in a similar fashion, e.g. in the Netherlands Leeuwarden Court of Appeal 22.05.2012, No.107.001.948/01, § 5.14.

86 CJEU 11.9.2014 – case C-291/13, ECLI:EU:C:2014:2209 para. 3, 46 = MMR 2016, 63 – Papasavvas.

87 On the development of French case law, Angelopoulos, 2016, p. 127 et seq.; Jones, 2020, p. 138 et seq.; Grynbaum/Pailler/Le Goffic/Morlet, 2023, pp. 1010 et seqq.; Lucas/Lucas-Schloetter/Bernault, 2017, mn. 1288 et seqq., p. 1007 et seq. See also Papaevangelou, Eur. J. Comm. 2023, 466 *passim* regarding a proposed, but ultimately rejected "non-interference principle" in favour of editorial content from media companies. Husovec BTLJ 2023, 101 (126 et seq.) points out the difference between platforms and "conventional publishers, such as newspapers": the former ones shall only be *accountable* while the latter ones shall be *liable*.

or aesthetic criteria, it assumes editorial responsibility and cannot rely on the liability limitations.[88]

68 **General advertising for the service** itself or its offerings does not lead to the service provider losing its neutral position. For internet marketplaces, however, the CJEU considers an active role if the service provider selects keywords for specific offers on the marketplace, indicating a link between the marketplace operator and the offer.[89] In contrast, advertising the online marketplace through keyword advertising is attributed to neutral general advertising. The key factor here is that the core service of the online marketplace lies in making specific offers accessible. If the specific offer is chosen based on general, automatically applied criteria, it is not actively promoted but forms part of the marketplace operator's overall offering.[90]

b) The characteristics of neutrality under the DSA

69 As a guiding principle, the legislator has, after extensive discussions and several preparatory studies, confirmed that established business models of platforms and social media services[91] should continue benefiting from liability privileges. The DSA explicitly clarifies that this principle extends to both existing and newly developed business models, provided they meet the requirements set out in Art. 4 to 6 of the DSA.[92] The determining factor is **not whether a business model is deemed "active" or "passive,"** but rather whether an activity of the service provider grants it **knowledge and control** over the specific content in question.[93]

70 Service functionalities that group or otherwise arrange content to facilitate retrieval, internal search functions or automated recommendations or advertisements continue to be considered neutral activities.[94] Common design and optimization mechanisms also do not establish an active role in the sense of the DSA, as long as they are of a **general nature and apply universally** to all information.[95] Importantly, the applicability of the

---

[88] See Rec. 18 DSA; see also BGH 4.4.2017 – VI ZR 123/16, GRUR 2017, 844 para. 19 et seq. – klinikbewertungen.de.

[89] CJEU 12.7.2011 – case C-324/09, ECLI:EU:C:2011:474 para. 115 = GRUR 2011, 1025 – L'Oréal v eBay; crit. Hoeren MMR 2011, 596 (605).

[90] See also Wiebe WRP 2012, 1182 (1188); Spindler MMR 2011, 703 (705); Spindler in Spindler/Schmitz TMG § 7 mn. 12, however not for Google Ads keyword advertising. National Courts also held that hosting provider remain eligible for the liability privilege as long as they do not promote particular offers, see Leeuwarden Court of Appeal, 22.05.2012, No.107.001.948/01; Tribunal judiciaire de Paris 28.06.2019, ch. 3, sec. 2, decision no. 18/00503.

[91] In this respect, very pronounced AG Saugmandsgaard Øe 16.7.2020 – joined cases C-682/18 and C-683/18, ECLI:EU:C:2020:586 para. 167 = GRUR-RS 2020, 18772 – YouTube and Cyando.

[92] Rec. 28 DSA with a number of examples.

[93] The Impact Assessment states: "From the [CJEU] rulings it can also be inferred, furthermore, that the relevant test is not whether a given platform is "active" or "passive", but whether the services provided play an active role which gives the platform knowledge or control over the illegal data stored." European Commission, Impact Assessment Report, SWD(2020) 348 final Part 2/2, p. 155.

[94] AG Saugmandsgaard Øe 16.7.2020 – joined cases C-682/18 and C-683/18, ECLI:EU:C:2020:586 para. 157 = GRUR-RS 2020, 18772 – YouTube and Cyando; Janal ZEuP 2021, 227 (240). In the same vein, French Courts decided that the (automatic) structuring of content does not deprive the hosting providers from the respective hosting privilege, Cour d'appel de Paris 04.04.2012, pôle 5 – ch. 1, decision no. 10/00878, Cour d'appel de Paris 15.06.2018, decision no. 17/09497 Tribunal judiciaire de Paris 10.01.2020, ch. 3, sec. 3, decision no. 17/10934.

[95] In the legislative process, these activities were sometimes misleadingly also referred to as active role or the business models as "active" host providers; see Sartor, 'Providers Liability: From the eCommerce Directive to the future (2017) p. 22 <https://www.europarl.europa.eu/RegData/etudes/IDAN/2017/614179/IPOL_IDA(2017)614179_EN.pdf>(last accessed: 28.11.2023).

liability provisions is not excluded merely because the service provider makes a causal contribution to the infringement.

Recital 18 of the DSA codified the criterion of **editorial control as the limit of neutral activity**, a standard utilized by the CJEU in *Papasavvas to* establish the boundary.[96] However, editorial activity should be understood in specific content-related terms, such as selecting content based on content-related criteria or modifying uploaded content. 71

Since the focus must always be on **specific information**, the applicability of liability limitations for a service does not require a uniform assessment. For instance, in the *L'Oréal/eBay* case, the CJEU excluded the application of hosting rules only to the extent that eBay advertised specific offers in a manner suggesting a link between eBay and the offer.[97] Even if a service makes available not only information provided by the user but also selects and posts information itself, the liability rules may apply to the former part while they would not apply to the latter.[98] 72

Given the explicit clarification that the limitation of liability also extends to **technical auxiliary functions**, auto-complete functionalities should be covered by the liability exemptions. German case law, which goes in a different direction[99] should be reconsidered in view of the more liberal approach of the DSA. The search function itself can be easily attributed to the auxiliary functions of the service and is thus covered by the privilege, in the same way as automatic suggestions. The autocomplete function is ultimately an element of the search function and is comparable to an input aid, to the extent it is algorithmically selected based on content neutral criteria. 73

The key consideration in each case is whether the activities of the service provider are of a general nature, applied in a consistent manner to all content or information, and can thus be classified as **service-related modalities,** or whether the service provider takes measures regarding specific content selected by it or the user. Only the latter activities provide the service provider with knowledge and control.[100] This aligns with the CJEU's assertion that the (lack of) knowledge of the illegality of specific content is crucial for applying the hosting rules. An action is considered active only if it is not applied "blindly" to all information stored on the service but is specific to one or more particular cases. 74

A specific provision on neutrality is found in the newly included Art. 6(3) of the DSA, which precludes the application of the limitation of liability for transaction platforms if the traffic cannot recognize the source of the information (→ mn. 134 et seqq; concerning obligations for transaction platforms under the DMA → § 12 mn. 26 et seq.). 75

c) *Abuse of rights*

Recital 20 of the DSA includes two clarifications that define the boundary of neutrality with cases that can be qualified as abusive. *Firstly,* the liability rules do not apply if the service provider **"collaborates"** with a user in engaging in unlawful activities. *Secondly,* the application is excluded if the service provider primarily conducts its activity **to** 76

[96] CJEU 11.9.2014 – case C-291/13, ECLI:EU:C:2014:2209 = MMR 2016, 63, para. 44 et seq. – Papasavvas.

[97] CJEU 12.7.2011 – case C-324/09, ECLI:EU:C:2011:474 para. 123 = GRUR 2011, 1025- L'Oréal v eBay.

[98] See e.g. OLG Hamburg 29.9.2010 – 5 U 9/09, MMR 2011, 49.

[99] BGH 14.5.2013 – VI ZR 269/12, GRUR 2013, 751 para. 20 – "Autocomplete".

[100] See also Manara, 2013, p. 76, for the distinction between an activity relating to the specific content (*contenu*) and one relating to the 'container' (*contenant*).

enable or facilitate the storage and dissemination of **unlawful** information.[101] This covers, for example sharehosters whose business model creates specific incentives for sharing illegal content.[102]

d) Good Samaritan Rule

77 Even though service providers are not obligated to take active precautions against infringement, and the liability privilege is not contingent on content checks for illegality, **voluntary measures against illegal content are widespread**. The E-Commerce Directive did not provide for cases in which a service provider becomes aware of illegal content through voluntary measures. Consequently, under the E-Commerce Directive, it was not explicitly excluded that precautionary measures against infringements could result in knowledge of illegal content and preclude the application of the liability shield.

78 Such an interpretation could rely on *L'Oréal/eBay*, which seemed to preclude the application of Art. 14(1)(a) of the E-Commerce Directive (now: Art. 6(1)(a) of the DSA) if the service provider had knowledge of illegal content through measures carried out on its own initiative.[103] Also, in *Glawischnig-Piesczek,* the Advocate General suggested that precautionary measures against repeated infringements could result in an active role and the loss of the liability privilege.[104] The tension between active precaution and the loss of privilege became further evident in the *Delfi* case of the European Court of Human Rights where a service provider was found liable for content that had not been identified in monitoring measures.[105]

79 As a result, it was widely held that negative consequences of voluntary measures created the wrong incentives.[106] Service providers found themselves in a **dilemma, being urged to implement general precautions against illegal content while simultaneously increasing their liability risk through the same measures.**[107] This not only led to inconsistencies, but also hindered the Commission's initiatives to motivate service providers to adopt voluntary measures. Examples of these initiatives include the "Code of Conduct on countering illegal hate speech online" (2016), the "Communication on tackling illegal content online" (2017), and the "Recommendation on measures to effectively tackle illegal content online" (2018).[108]

---

[101] Rec. 20 p. 2 DSA. Read in conjunction with rec. 21 DSA, Rössel AfP 2023, 93 (95) concludes that encryption and anonymisation do not exclude the application of the liability privilege; similar F. Hofmann in Hofmann/Raue, DSA intro to Art. 4 mn. 79.

[102] See CJEU 22.6.2021 – joined cases C-682/18 and C-683/18, ECLI:EU:C:2021:503 para. 101, 105 et seq. = GRUR 2021, 1054 – YouTube and Cyando.

[103] CJEU 12.7.2011 – case C-324/09, ECLI:EU:C:2011:474 para. 122 = GRUR 2011, 1025 – L'Oréal v eBay; confirmed in CJEU 22.6.2021 – joined cases C-682/18 and C-683/18, ECLI:EU:C:2021:503 para. 115 = GRUR 2021, 1054 – YouTube and Cyando.

[104] AG Szpunar 4.6.2019 – case C-18/18, ECLI:EU:C:2019:458 para. 73 = BeckRS 2019, 10236 – Glawischnig-Piesczek.

[105] ECHR 16.6.2015 – App. No. 64569/09, NJW 2015, 2863 para. 76, 162 – Delfi AS v. Estonia; on this, Kuczerawy/Ombelet Taddeo/Floridi 2017, 101 (104 et seq.).

[106] Leistner ZUM 2012, 722 (724); Leistner ' The Commission's vision for Europe's Digital Future: Proposals for the Data Governance Act, the Digital Markets Act and the Digital Services Act – A critical primer' (22.03.2021), p. 9 <https://papers.ssrn.com/sol3/papers.cfm?abstract_id=3789041≥; Schwemer 'Digital Services Act: A Reform of the e-Commerce Directive and Much More' (13.10.2022), p. 11 <https://ssrn.com/abtract=4213014> (both last accessed: 28.11.2023).

[107] This "moderator's dilemma" had already led to the introduction of the Samaritan rule in Art. 230 CDA; see on the term Goldman in Frosio, p. 155 (157 et seqq.).

[108] European Commission 'The EU code of conduct on countering illegal hate speech online' <https://commission.europa.eu/strategy-and-policy/policies/justice-and-fundamental-rights/combatting-discrimination-0/racism-and-xenophobia/eu-code-conduct-countering-illegal-hate-speech-online_endiscrimination-0/racism-and-xenophobia/eu-code-conduct-countering-illegal-hate-speech-online_en>

According to the newly introduced Art. 7 of the DSA, in line with its US model,[109] service providers remain eligible for the liability exemptions **if they conduct own-initiative investigations in good faith and in a diligent manner,** or take measures to detect, identify, and remove unlawful content or to block access.[110] This applies to measures undertaken voluntarily and on their own initiative, as well as those taken by service providers to comply with the requirements of Union and national law. Such information may emerge from cooperation with trusted flaggers (cf. Art. 22 of the DSA)[111] or from preventive mitigation measures implemented by the operators of very large online platforms under Art. 35 of the DSA, or precautionary measures against repeat infringements, whether voluntary or mandated by court order. **80**

4. No obligation to monitor; no pro-active investigation

Art. 8 of the DSA provides that operators of intermediary services may not be subjected to a general obligation to monitor the information they transmit or store, nor to actively seek facts or circumstances indicating illegal activity. The principle was already enshrined in Art. 15 of the E-Commerce Directive. It has been a crucial factor for the development of the European liability regime and is a central element in achieving a **fair balance between the interests involved**. **81**

The **general monitoring prohibition** is a general principle that is also applied in other regulatory instruments (e.g., Recital 16 of the InfoSoc Directive[112]; Art. 28(3)(2) of the AVMS Directive[113] or Art. 17(8) of the DSM Directive). The CJEU has interpreted the prohibition of general monitoring as a **manifestation of the principle of proportionality**[114]. The rule has been considered of fundamental importance to keep the internet a free and open domain.[115] **82**

(last accessed: 28.11.2023); European Commission, Communication from the Commission on tackling illegal content online, COM(2017) 555 final, p. 12 et seq.; Commission Recommendation (EU) 2018/334 on measures to effectively tackle illegal content online p. 7 et seq.; Rössel ITRB 2021, 35 (37) is critical of whether the chosen approach can actually resolve this contradiction. Schmid/Grewe MMR 2021, 279 (280), among others, approve of the innovation. For the development of the different instruments see Quintais/Appelman/Fathaigh, GLJ, 2023, 881 (887 et seqq.) and Farrand, Eur. J. Crim. Pol. Res., 2023, 477 (483 et seqq.).

[109] Section 230(c) CDA however, excludes liability for voluntary content moderation measures taken in good faith; Kaesling ZUM 2021, 177 (179); Rössel ITRB 2021, 35 (37).

[110] The French version is somewhat unclear but must be interpreted in line with the other language versions; see Douville/Netter RTD Com. 2023, p. 19, mn. 17; Rössel AfP 2023, 93 (96); on the draft, Kuczerawy ' The Good Samaritan that wasn't: voluntary monitoring under the (draft) Digital Services Act', (12.01.2021) <https://verfassungsblog.de/good-samaritan-dsa/> (last accessed: 28.11.2023); and F. Hofmann in Hofmann/Raue, DSA Art. 7 mn. 6; ibid. mn. 11, however, sees a continuation of the pre-DSA legal situation, see also rec. 26 "it should be clarified" that voluntary, good-faith activities do not forfeit Art. 4 et seq.

[111] See on such a case LG Hamburg 5.3.2010 – 324 O 565/08, MMR 2010, 433.

[112] Directive 2001/29/EC of the European Parliament and of the Council of 22 May 2001 on the harmonisation of certain aspects of copyright and related rights in the information society, OJ 2001 L 167, p. 10.

[113] Directive 2010/13/EU of the European Parliament and of the Council of 10 March 2010 on the coordination of certain provisions laid down by law, regulation or administrative action in Member States concerning the provision of audiovisual media services (Audiovisual Media Services Directive), OJ 2001 L 95, p. 1.

[114] CJEU 12.7.2011 – case C-324/09, ECLI:EU:C:2011:474 para. 139 = GRUR 2011, 1025 – L'Oréal v eBay; CJEU 24.11.2011 – case C-70/10, ECLI:EU:C:2011:771 para. 36 et seq. = GRUR 2012, 265 – Scarlet Extended; see Husovec, 2017, p. 118; Frosio/Geiger, Eur. Law J. 2023, 1 (8 et seq.).

[115] AG Saugmandsgaard Øe 15.7.2021 – case C-401/19, ECLI:EU:C:2021:613 para. 105 = GRUR-RS 2021, 20614 – Poland v Parliament and Council.

83 Art. 8 of the DSA serves as a **limitation on state or state-initiated monitoring and filtering measures**. Recital 30 of the DSA confirms: "Nothing in this Regulation should be construed as an imposition of a general monitoring obligation or a general active fact-finding obligation, or as a general obligation for providers to take proactive measures in relation to illegal content." This precludes obligations of fact finding as a prerequisite of the application of the liability exemptions, a principle that is not always respected by national case law.[116]

84 Recital 47 of the E-Commerce Directive already provided, however, that the general no monitoring-rule does not apply to monitoring obligations in specific cases and not to orders by public authorities in accordance with national law. This distinction is reiterated in Recital 30(1)(2) of the DSA. The issue when and to what extend service providers can be subject to obligations to prevent further infringements (stay-down) has been one of the most debated aspects of the European liability regime for intermediaries.

85 The CJEU consistently ruled that Art. 15 of the E-Commerce Directive (now: Art. 8 of the DSA) prohibits the imposition of general filtering systems requiring **general and continuous monitoring** to prevent any future infringement of rights.[117] This approach appears to exclude any obligation to search the entirety of the information stored by the service provider, even if the search is specific to a particular work or piece of information.[118]

86 In *Glawischnig-Piesczek*, the CJEU cautiously expanded its previously very restrictive case law in the area of defamation. Service providers can be obligated to block not only **specific information** but also **identical and equivalent information**, if it is sufficiently specific, and the service provider can **automatically** detect it **without the need to carry out an independent assessment**.[119]

87 In the **German discussion**, a distinction was made between general monitoring obligations and stay-down obligations triggered by, and limited to, specific illegal content. While general monitoring was prohibited, specific monitoring was not.[120] The distinction was also framed as *ex ante* versus *ex post* monitoring.[121] As a result, courts concluded that, in principle, service providers, once notified of illegal content, are obligated to take appropriate measures to prevent repeated cases of the same or an equivalent infringement.[122] While obligations are subject to a reasonableness-test, such a defence was left to enforcement proceedings.[123] As a premise of the distinction, it was

---

[116] The "shuttle process" developed by the BGH for service providers who must act upon notifications of content is not supported by rec. 30; see BGH 25 Oct. 2011 – VI ZR 93/10, NJW 2012, 148 para. 25 et seq. – Blog-Eintrag; Wagner GRUR 2020, 447 (453).

[117] CJEU 16.2.2012 – case C-360/10, ECLI:EU:C:2012:85 para. 34 et seqq. = GRUR 2012, 382- – SABAM/Netlog; CJEU 24.11.2011 – case C-70/10, ECLI:EU:C:2011:771 para. 36 et seqq. = GRUR 2012, 265 – Scarlet Extended; CJEU 22.6.2021 – joined cases C-682/18 and C-683/18, ECLI:EU:C:2021:503 para. 135 = GRUR 2021, 1054 – YouTube and Cyando.

[118] On the distinction between the object of the search (tracking down a specific file or work) and the body of information searched (all files stored with the host provider) Kuczerawy in Frosio, p. 525 (541); Senftleben/Angelopoulos, ' The Odyssey of the Prohibition on General Monitoring Obligations on the Way to the Digital Services Act: Between Article 15 of the E-Commerce Directive and Article 17 of the Directive on Copyright in the Digital Single Market' (04.01.2021), p. 8 et seq., <https://papers.ssrn.com/sol3/papers.cfm?abstract_id=3717022≥ (last accessed: 28.11.2023).

[119] CJEU, 3.10.2019 – case C-18/18, ECLI:EU:C:2019:821 para. 33 et seq – Glawischnig-Piesczek.

[120] See Leistner ZUM 2012, 722 (724); Spindler, JIPITEC 2020, 344 (para. 55); BGH 11.3.2004 – I ZR 304/01, GRUR 2004, 860 (862) – Internetversteigerung I.

[121] Bornkamm GRUR Int. 2007, 642.

[122] BGH 11.3.2004 – I ZR 304/01, GRUR 2004, 860 – Internetversteigerung I; BGH 12.7.2012 – I ZR 18/11, GRUR 2013, 370 para. 22 – Alone in the Dark.

[123] BGH 11.3.2004 – I ZR 304/01, GRUR 2004, 860 – Internetversteigerung I; Leistner/Grisse GRUR 2015, 105 (105 et seq.).

widely held that the liability exemptions did not apply to claims for cease-and-desist and injunctive relief (→ mn. 143).[124]

Early in the debate, *Hoeren* and *Yankova* have emphasised that fundamental rights are always at risk when the entirety of stored information is searched.[125] The weight of an interference **is only slightly reduced if the search is carried out after a piece of illegal information has been detected or in relation to a specific information or content.**[126] 88

For instance, if an access provider is ordered to search all private communications, the relevance to those whose emails are read would be little affected by whether the search relates to a specific object or occurs without cause or after an infringement has occurred. The relevance of such a limitation of the general monitoring obligation is highlighted by the position of the *Bundesgerichtshof*, which considers an infringement in **copyright law** to be of the same nature if it concerns the same work. The position is clearly problematic in light of the *Netlog* decision of the CJEU, where the prohibition of extensive monitoring and filtering duties was established for the first time.[127] 89

Nevertheless, it must be acknowledged that the CJEU in *Glawischnig-Piesczek* **abandoned the position that risks for the exercise of fundamental rights of the persons who stored the content do not per se exclude monitoring or stay-down obligations** which implicate the entirety of the stored information. At the same time, the CJEU did not conclude that monitoring obligations and a duty to filter are generally permissible if they concern a specific work or subject matter or are triggered by specific illegal information or content. 90

To resolve the apparent tension, the scheme of Art. 4 to 8 of the DSA must be taken into account: On the one hand, **Art. 8 of the DSA establishes the rule** that service providers are **not subject to a general duty to take precautions against infringements or to conduct investigations.** Art. 8 of the DSA is **not subject to any conditions** and applies **regardless of whether infringements have occurred or have been notified to the service provider**; this is reaffirmed by the last sentence of Recital 30 of the DSA. As a result, to rely on the liability exemptions in Art. 4 to 6 of the DSA, service providers are not required to monitor information, whether specific or general, whether *ex ante* or *ex post*. 91

On the other hand, the second sentence of Recital 30 of the DSA, in line with its predecessor in the E-Commerce Directive, contain a reference to obligations in specific cases. The reference to specific monitoring or stay-down obligations does not limit the general principle, however, which is supported by the rule that a Recital does not have the same legislative weight as an article of a regulation. Rather than limiting the general rules of Art. 8 of the DSAs, Recital 30 is a mere **reference** to **the possibility of member states to issue administrative or judicial take down or stay down-orders based on Art. 4 to 6 of the DSA.** While Art. 4 to 6 DSA contain only opening clauses for such orders, they are mandated by Art. 11(1)(3) of the Enforcement Directive and Art. 8(3) of the InfoSoc Directive. However, these orders under national law are subject to the general limits of EU law, in particular that they must be provided by law and respect the prin- 92

124 In this respect, Hoeren spoke of a "trick" to circumvent the TMG (then: TDG); see Hoeren MMR 2004, 672 (672).

125 Hoeren/Yankova IIC 2012, 501 (511); also Janal K&R 2021, 6 (8); Holznagel CR 2021, 123 (127 et seq.).

126 Critically also Angelopoulos, 2016, p. 161.

127 CJEU 16.2.2012 – case C-360/10, ECLI:EU:C:2012:85 = GRUR 2012, 382 – SABAM/Netlog. Also critical re the similar nature of an infringement in copyright law F. Hofmann in Hofmann/Raue, DSA Art. 8 mn. 24.

ciple of proportionality.[128] Importantly, only authorities and courts can issue these orders (→ mn. 150 et seqq.). Hence, Recital 30 merely underlines the two-step approach of the liability regime, namely the exemption of liability and duties to investigate before the provider has actual knowledge of illegal content and the possibility of administrative bodies or courts to issue orders which take into account proportionality in the individual case.

III. The prerequisites of the negative liability conditions

1. Mere conduit

93 Art. 4 of the DSA duplicates **Art. 12 of the E-Commerce Directive** without significant changes and supersedes **national implementing laws based thereon.** The Article includes a specific provision for services that transmit information via networks or offer access to such services. These services are not held liable for the information they transmit or provide access to[129], but they may be subject to official or judicial orders.

a) Principles

94 In Art. 3(g)(i), Art. 4(1) of the DSA, "**Mere conduit**" is defined as services that transmit information provided by a user in a communications network or provide access to a communications network.[130] In the first case, the service involves both the transmission and the information, while in the second case, providing access is sufficient.[131]

95 The term "**communication network**" is not explicitly defined in the DSA. However, it can be understood in the context of telecommunications law, where communication networks encompass transmission systems, switching and routing facilities, and other resources facilitating signal transmission through cable, radio, optical, or other electromagnetic devices. The technical design of the network or its predominant use for communication purposes is not the decisive factor; even electricity networks fall under Art. 4 of the DSA if they serve communication purposes.

96 Art. 4 of the DSA should be interpreted in a technical-functional manner, maintaining technology-neutrality. It encompasses both **wired and wireless communication services** and is open to accommodating new business models.[132] The provision is concerned with the technical communication process rather than specific information access or transmission. Contractual obligations or the presence of a contract are not determining factors[133].

97 Crucially, the service must involve enabling or facilitating access through a technical, automatic, and passive process ensuring information transmission. **Temporary storage** for technical reasons that exclusively serves the purpose of transmission, such as **buffering**, is included (Art. 4(2) of the DSA). In this context, the CJEU has emphasised

---

[128] Janal sees problems of delimitation GRUR 2022, 211 (216).

[129] In this respect, Art. 4 DSA contains a clarifying amendment compared to Art. 12 E-Commerce Directive.

[130] Leistner in Schricker/Loewenheim UrhG § 97 mn. 138.

[131] Spindler in Spindler/Schmitz/ TMG § 8 mn. 7.

[132] Rec. 28 DSA. The aim of Art. 4 DSA is to guarantee the functioning of the internet, F. Hofmann in Hofmann/Raue DSA Art. 4 mn. 4 et seq.

[133] CJEU 15.9.2016 – case C-484/14, ECLI:EU:C:2016:689 para. 44 et seq. = GRUR 2016, 1146 – McFadden/Sony Music; CJEU 27.3.2014 – case C-314/12, ECLI:EU:C:2014:192 para. 34 et seq. = GRUR 2014, 468 – UPC Telekabel.

whether proper or equally efficient transmission of information is feasible without storage, reflecting a rather lenient standard.[134]

To invoke the liability provisions of Art. 4 of the DSA, service providers must adhere to the **neutrality requirement** outlined in Art. 4(1)(a)–(c) of the DSA. They emphasise the principle that the liability regime of Art. 4 of the DSA only covers **automatic and technical transmission or access switching activities**. The characteristics outlined in these provisions should be interpreted with a focus on responsibility for the transmission of specific content, emphasising whether a content-related activity is being performed. The characteristics are exhaustive; whether a service provider has or should have knowledge in an individual case, is not relevant here.[135] **98**

For the requirement that the service provider must not have initiated the transmission himself (**Art. 4(1)(a) of the DSA**), the decisive factor is whether the information originates from the service provider or was selected by it for transmission. An example are messages from mobile network operators to customers or users in a specific cell (**cell broadcasting**). Messages are not attributed to the service provider, however, if it merely implements technical transmission processes initiated by the user (e.g., retrieval of internet pages).[136] **99**

Art. 4(1)(b) of the DSA covers situations where network operators or access intermediaries select or influence the recipients of the information. In this context, technical processes implemented by service providers that carry out the selection decisions of their users are not considered harmful. For example, **Spam filters** that merely affect the perception or filing of emails in a specific folder do not influence the recipients but are an additional service for users who have already received the emails.[137] **100**

According to **Art. 4(1)(c) of the DSA,** the service provider must not select or act on the information. **Technical interventions**, such as modifications to transmission protocols or the encryption of transmissions, are not considered harmful to the extent they do not **change content.**[138] **Push messages can be borderline cases, particularly** if the transmitted information is not defined by the user but selected by the provider.[139] **101**

b) Application

Due to the increasing technical complexity of **communication networks,** a variety of ancillary functionalities have emerged which are provided by network operators, content providers, and third parties. These services often comprise multiple components that may serve different purposes.[140] To address this complexity, the Commission conducted several investigations in the run up to the legislation, aiming to clarify the application **102**

---

134 CJEU 5.6.2014 – case C-360/13, ECLI:EU:C:2014:1195 para. 28 = ZUM 2014, 681 – Public Relations Consultants Association, on Art. 5(a) Directive 2001/29/EC (InfoSoc Directive); F. Hofmann in Hofmann/Raue DSA Art. 4 mn. 29 et seq. focuses on the (sole) purpose of the temporary storage ("carrying out the transmission") for determining, on a case-by-case basis, the permissible duration of the temporary storage.

135 VG Düsseldorf 08.11.2011 – 27 K 5887/10, ZUM-RD 2012, 362 (366 et seq.); VG Düsseldorf 29.11.2011 – 27 K 458/10, ZUM-RD 2012, 570 (575).

136 Jandt in Roßnagel TMG § 8 mn. 15; Spindler in Spindler/Schmitz TMG § 8 mn. 13; Hennemann in Gersdorf/Paal TMG § 8 mn. 21.

137 Spindler in Spindler/Schmitz TMG § 8 mn. 53; as far as emails are stored for a longer period of time, however, the activity is usually subject to Art. 6 DSA.

138 See already rec. 43 E-Commerce Directive; see now rec. 21(1)(3) DSA; Spindler in Spindler/Schmitz TMG § 8 mn. 15 et seq.; Hennemann in Gersdorf/Paal TMG § 8 mn. 23 et seqq.

139 Jandt in Roßnagel TMG § 8 mn. 17.

140 The facts of the case in OLG Köln GRUR 2021, 70 – HERZ KRAFT WERK are instructive.

of liability exemptions to **non-hosting intermediaries.**[141] The outcomes of these discussions are reflected in Recitals 28 and 29 of the DSA.

103 Overall, the tendency of the DSA is to adopt a more generous understanding of the liability exemptions, as long there is a **functional link to the communication process and subject to the principle of neutrality.** While the Recitals sometimes contain the (obvious) reservation that providers must meet the requirements of Art. 4 of the DSA, the explicit and sometimes multiple references to certain service types in connection with liability exemptions should be interpreted as a decision **in favour of eligibility for the liability exemptions.**[142]

104 The DSA covers ancillary services, even if they do not solely consist of providing **transmission or direct access services**. More restrictive case law under the E-Commerce Directive would need to be revised accordingly.[143] The key criterion is whether a service involves a **content-agnostic technical-administrative function** that holds considerable significance for **network access** or transmission, and where service providers typically lack knowledge of the specific transmitted information.

105 Typical cases falling under Art. 4 of the DSA include **operators of telecommunication networks** providing customers with internet access, known as access providers.[144] This also encompasses services like **voice telephony**[145] or **VPN networks. WLAN operators** are also included, particularly if they offer **wireless online access** as part of a commercial activity (→ mn. 49).

106 **DNS services**[146] have been explicitly mentioned in Recital 28 of the DSA as potential services eligible for liability privileges. These services play a crucial role in resolving user-entered URLs into numeric IPs, facilitating the transmission of information.[147] DNS services significantly contribute to providing access and enable effective internet communication possible. Here again, more restrictive case law under the E-Commerce Directive should be revisited in light of the more expansive approach under the DSA.[148][149]

107 The activities of **registrars,** whose service consists of registering domains for their customers with **registries** and forwarding necessary data to these registries, can also be regarded as auxiliary functions for transmission.[150] However, since registrars are not themselves involved in technical provision or **access provision**, it was argued that they are not privileged in terms of liability as access intermediaries.[151] With regard to the liability consequences, however, registrars were largely placed on an equal footing with access providers, even without privileged treatment.[152] Under the DSA, a direct application

---

[141] Schwemer/Mahler/Styri, 'Legal Analysis of the Intermediary Service Providers of Non-hosting Nature' (20.05.2021), mn. 108, <https://papers.ssrn.com/sol3/papers.cfm?abstract_id=3798494> (last accessed: 28.11.2023).

[142] Likewise Gerdemann/Spindler GRUR 2023, 3 (5).

[143] E.g., BGH 15.10.2020 – I ZR 13/19, GRUR 2021, 63 – Stoererhaftung des Registrars (Breach of Duty of Care).

[144] BGH 26.11.2015 – I ZR 3/14, BeckRS 2016, 1908 para. 23 – 3dl.am; on the exclusion of telecommunications services in the TMG above.

[145] Rec. 29 DSA.

[146] DNS stands for Domain Name System.

[147] Spindler in Spindler/Schmitz TMG § 8 mn. 45; Leistner/Grisse GRUR 2019, 19 (22).

[148] OLG Cologne 9.10.2020 – 6 U 32/20, GRUR 2021, 70 para. 98 – HERZ KRAFT WERKE; Spindler CR 2022, 318 mn. 21 et seqq.

[149] Spindler in Spindler/Schmitz TMG § 8 mn. 45; Leistner/Grisse GRUR 2019, 19 (22).

[150] In detail Baumann, 2021, p. 13; Bertermann MMR 2015, 523 (525).

[151] BGH 15.10.2020 – I ZR 13/19, GRUR 2021, 63 para. 14, 17, 25 et seq. – Stoererhaftung des Registrars; BGH 9.11.2011 – I ZR 150/09, GRUR 2012, 304 para. 53 – Basler Haar-Kosmetik; Nordemann GRUR 2021, 18 (19); on this in detail Baumann, 2021 p. 191 et seq.

[152] BGH 15.10.2020 – I ZR 13/19, GRUR 2021 para. 16 et seq.- Stoererhaftung des Registrars; Grisse ZUM 2021, 152 (153); Spindler CR 2022, 318 (mn. 31). 31); Hofmann NJW 2021, 274; left open by

of Art. 4 of the DSA also seems possible, referring to the rather generous tendency of the legislator.[153]

Content delivery networks (CDNs) consist of **caching and proxy servers** that enhance the efficiency of content delivery to end users. Functionally, CDNs play a role in the transmission process, but technically they also involve elements of caching or hosting. Recital 29 of the DSA leans towards categorizing this service more as caching, although this classification may depend on the specific design. Consequently, a general classification can be difficult.[154] **108**

The classification of **online search engines** under the categories of the E-Commerce Directive was previously unresolved.[155] Recital 28 of the DSA now explicitly includes search engines as services eligible for liability limitations. Additionally, Recital 29 of the DSA identifies paid **referencing services** as potential hosting services. Since these services fall under advertising-funded services in Chapter II, search engines fall under the same category, if their activity qualifies as "mere conduit", caching or hosting. The mention of search engines in the recitals indicates that the legislator assumes they are generally eligible for the exemption of liability.[156] **109**

In general, Recital 28 of the DSA reveals the legislator's intention to broadly define the privileged services. This extends beyond services that solely enable internet access from a technical standpoint to include those that enhance the usability of the internet, making it "socially adequate"[157] and providing technical support functions. To prevent an overly extensive exemption from liability, it is crucial for these services to confine themselves to **neutral, technical functions** without taking on an active role. **110**

Another supporting argument for assuming a broad exemption from liability is the explicit authority granted to national authorities to **order the cessation of an infringement** (Art. 4(3), Art. 5(2), Art. 6(4) of the DSA). This approach effectively balances the **111**

---

the CJEU 7.8.2018 – case C-521/17, ECLI:EU:C:2018:639 para. 40 et seqq. – Coöperatieve Vereniging SNB-REACT U.A./Deepak Mehta.

153 However, the BGH also based its exclusion of registrars on the definition of service provider – which is not changed by the DSA: BGH 15.10.2020 – I ZR 13/19, GRUR 2021, 63 para. 16 et seq. – Störerhaftung des Registrars.

154 OLG Köln 09.10.2020 – 6 U 32/20, GRUR 2021, 70 para. 69 – HERZ KRAFT WERK; on the question of whether this is a case of caching see below. Nordemann sees CDNs in a position between access provider and hosting provider, but does not consider an additional category of intermediaries necessary for this, J.-B. Nordemann 'The functioning of the Internal Market for Digital Services: responsibilities and duties of care of providers of Digital Services' (May 2020), p. 32 et seq., <https://www.europarl.europa.eu/RegData/etudes/STUD/2020/648802/IPOL_STU(2020)648802_EN.pdf> (last accessed: 28.11.2023). Against CDNs as mere conduit or caching service Köhler in Müller-Terpitz/Köhler DSA Art. 4 mn. 35 et seq.

155 National courts differed in their assessment of search engines: Crown Court, Gloucester, 06.02.2010 – ref. no. T20097013, summary available at: https://wilmap.stanford.edu/entries/r-v-rock-and-overton-2010-t20087573 ruled that a hyperlinking website was a mere conduit service; a Belgian Court, however, denied a liability privilege for a news search service since that service would actively edit content (see European Commission, Commission Staff Working Document SEC(2011) 1641 final, p. 27).

156 Although a formulation used by the Council, which emphasised the importance of search engines separately, did not prevail legislative process, the naming of search engines among the privileged services remained; see Council of the European Union, General Approach, No. Preliminary doc. 13203/21, p. 27, 116, available at <https://data.consilium.europa.eu/doc/document/ST-13203-2021-INIT/de/pdf> (last accessed: 28.11.2023). A clarification was called for, inter alia, by Janal ZEuP 2021, 227 (234, 254) and Ohly ZUM 2015, 308 (315); see also Rössel AfP 2023, 93 (94).

157 In this way re DNS services Spindler CR 2022, 318 mn. 13. Vice versa, inadequate behaviour, namely providing knowingly or actively supporting access to illegal activities, forfeits the privilege of Art. 4 DSA, not primarily because the access provider has actual knowledge of the illegal activity (which is irrelevant in the case of mere conduit services), but rather because he takes an active role, F. Hofmann in Hofmann/Raue DSA Art. 4 mn. 11, 19.

interests of service providers in conducting their economic activities with the need to prevent infringements, all without creating incentives for undesirable **overblocking**.

2. Caching

112 Art. 5 of the DSA mirrors Art. 13 of the E-Commerce Directive with slight adjustments and the Recitals introduce few new elements.[158] In general, this provision has proven to be less controversial, possibly because the relevant processes occur in the background.

a) *Caching service*

113 Compared to Art. 13 of the E-Commerce Directive, Art. 3(g)(ii), Art. 5 of the DSA provide a slightly broader definition of **caching**. A service is eligible if **temporary intermediate storage** enhances the efficiency or security of transmission to other users. Consequently, caching aimed solely at increasing security may also qualify for the caching exemption. Recital 29 of the DSA cites examples of caching services such as "the sole provision of content delivery networks, reverse proxies, or content adaptation proxies."

114 The temporary intermediate storage is to be **distinguished in two ways**: On the one side, if it lasts only as long as necessary for transmission, it falls under the category of mere conduit as outlined in an annex act (Art. 4(2) of the DSA; → mn. 97).[159] On the other side, if information is permanently mirrored, it constitutes a hosting service.[160]

115 The following services have been classified as caching: **Mirror servers**, which replicate content for the purpose of stockpiling, on the condition that the duration of the caching is reasonable, and the mirroring process is automatic;[161] **Usenet servers**, which decentralize networked servers operated by different providers by periodically synchronizing uploaded information.[162]

116 Caching services are not applicable to permanent storage, such as **archive and archiving servers** that store content permanently.[163] When providers of search engine services cache content for more efficient and faster service, this falls under the purview of Art. 5 of the DSA.[164] Other forms can fall under Art. 6 of the DSA.[165]

117 The characterization of **content delivery networks (CDN)** is inconsistent, primarily because these services comprise various components that differ in individual cases and

---

[158] J.-B. Nordemann 'The functioning of the Internal Market for Digital Services: responsibilities and duties of care of providers of Digital Services' (May 2020), p. 35 et seq., <https://www.europarl.europa.eu/RegData/etudes/STUD/2020/648802/IPOL_STU(2020)648802_EN.pdf> (last accessed: 28.11.2023). Köhler in Müller-Terpitz/Köhler DSA Art. 5 mn. 4 et seqq. points out that the CJEU never explicitly ruled on the caching privilege.

[159] Spindler in Spindler/Schmitz TMG § 9 mn. 3 with the example of intermediate email storage for Section 8 para. 2 TMG.

[160] Spindler in Spindler/Schmitz TMG § 9 mn. 3; F. Hofmann in Hofmann/Raue DSA Art. 5 mn. 36.

[161] OLG Düsseldorf 15.01.2008 – I-20 U 95/07, MMR 2008, 254 (256); Spindler in Spindler/Schmitz TMG § 9 mn. 8.

[162] They are partly assessed as a caching service (e.g. LG München 19.04.2007 – 7 O 3950/07, ZUM 2007, 496) and partly as a hosting service (e.g. Queen's Bench Division, 10.03.2006, [2006] EWHC 407 (QB); available at: http://www.bailii.org/ew/cases/EWHC/QB/2006/407.html); see Hoeren/Yankova IIC 2012, 501 (514); Kitz CR 2007, 603 (604); Spindler in Spindler/Schmitz TMG § 9 para. 10. It seems to be favourable to classify the initial server as a hosting service and the mirroring servers as a caching service.

[163] Libertus ZUM 2005, 627 (630); Spindler/Schmitz/Spindler TMG § 9 mn. 7.

[164] Hoffmann/Volkmann in Spindler/Schuster TMG § 9 mn. 8, 11; on the term "cache" also Ott in Gersdorf/Paal TMG § 9 mn. 2 et seqq.

[165] Gerdemann/Spindler GRUR 2023, 3 (5); Köhler in Müller-Terpitz/Köhler DSA Art. 5 mn. 45 et seqq.: case-by-case-analysis.

cannot be universally categorized. Consequently, the classification of a CDN depends on the specific activity of the service concerned.[166]

b) Additional requirements for the application

Caching service providers like access providers, are required to keep information unchanged (**Art. 5(1)(a) of the DSA**). However, technically induced alterations to the content are deemed acceptable, provided they serve the purpose of expediting transmission and ensuring the integrity of the original information.[167] Additionally, caching service providers must adhere to conditions related to accessing the information (**Art. 5(1)(b) of the DSA**). This is essential to prevent the undermining of access protections on the mirrored server. Thirdly, for the exemption from liability in caching (**Art. 5(1)(c) DSA**), it is necessary to observe industry-recognized and related rules for updating information.[168] If the lawful collection of usage data is collected on the mirrored server is "widely recognized and used by the industry", the caching service provider must not impede this collection (**Art. 5(1)(d) of the DSA**). The caching service provider is only required to leave lawful **data collection**, such as **counting statistics** or **cookies**, unaltered. In practice, this poses a challenge as the caching service provider, lacking insight into the processes of data collection on the mirrored server, cannot verify the legality of the data collection and typically allows or refrains from interfering with all data collections.[169] **118**

As a final requirement, the caching service provider must act "expeditiously", either through **deletion or blocking** of access, upon receiving "actual knowledge of the fact that the information at the initial source of the transmission has been removed from the network, or that access to it has been disabled, or that a judicial or an administrative authority has ordered such removal or disablement" (**Art. 5(1)(e) of the DSA**). **119**

3. Hosting

a) Services covered

Art. 6 of the DSA governs the liability of **services engaged in the storage of information provided by users of the service**. This provision is directly applicable to services that store information on behalf of users, with access restricted solely to the user. Notably, this encompasses cloud computing and web hosting.[170] **120**

[166] Mere conduit = Art. 12 Directive 2000/31/EC = Art. 4 DSA: OLG Hamburg 28.01.2009 – 5 U 255/07, ZUM-RD 2009, 439 (446) – Use Net II; LG Köln 30.01.2020 – 14 O 171/19, MMR 2020, 326 para. 73 et seq. – Cloudflare. Caching service = Art. 13 Directive 2000/31/EC = Art. 5 DSA: OLG Düsseldorf 15.01.2008 – I-20 U 95/07, ZUM 2008, 332 (334); OLG Cologne 09.10.2020 – 6 U 32/20, GRUR 2021, 70 para. 72 et seq. – HERZ KRAFT WERK, on this also Nordemann GRUR 2021, 18 (19); caching performance, at least for certain services of a CDN: J.-B. Nordemann 'The functioning of the Internal Market for Digital Services: responsibilities and duties of care of providers of Digital Services' (May 2020), p. 33 mn. 73 <https://www.europarl.europa.eu/RegData/etudes/STUD/2020/648802/IPOL_STU(2020)648802_EN.pdf> (last accessed: 28.11.2023), mn. 73: Rome Commercial Court – Cloudflare, summary available at <https://www.lexology.com/library/detail.aspx?g=22b049b3-bb0a-42c5-b785-e01b18820a1c> (both last accessed: 28.11.2023).

[167] Spindler in Spindler/Schmitz TMG § 9 mn. 17; Hoffmann/Volkmann in Spindler/Schuster TMG § 9 mn. 18; F. Hofmann in Hofmann/Raue DSA Art. 5 mn. 16 deems only deliberate changes as a forfeiture of the liability privilege, hence, changes based on technical malfunctions are still covered from the liability privilege.

[168] The language versions seem to be more aligned compared to the wording under the E-Commerce Directive. The French version referers to "*règles ... largement reconnue*", the Italian to "*norme... ampiamente riconosciuto*". In the German version of the E-Commerce Directive, reference was instead made to "Industriestandard".

[169] Hoffmann/Volkmann in Spindler/Schuster TMG § 9 mn. 29 et seqq.

[170] Rec. 29 DSA.

121 Additionally, Art. 6 of the DSA also covers business models where the stored content is not exclusively for the uploader´s use but is **also made accessible to third parties**. As per Recital 29 of the DSA, this includes "paid referencing services or services enabling sharing information and content online, including file storage and sharing," which can be categorized as hosting services. Storage of information on a permanent basis may also be exempt from liability.[171]

122 The following services, among others, can be eligible for the liability exemption under Art. 6 of the DSA: **File hosting services;[172], cloud computing (including indirect services to sub-cloud providers**[173], email services that retain emails as part of webmail services[174] (beyond mere forwarding), opinion forums[175], rating portals[176], and Usenet servers-assuming the originating server functions as a hosting provider and mirroring servers provide caching services.[177]

123 While it is said that the mere act of setting **hyperlinks** is not insufficient to warrant exemption from liability,[178] this does not exclude that services like search engines benefit from exemption of liability as their services are more complex and involve storage of information.

b) No knowledge of illegal activity

124 The most important condition for the liability exemption of Art. 6 of the DSA is that the service provider **does not have actual knowledge** of illegal activity or illegal content. As regards claims for damages, awareness **of facts or circumstances from which the illegal activity or the illegal content is apparent** is equivalent to actual knowledge.

125 As explicitly stated, knowledge refers to actual, **positive knowledge of individual illegal information.**[179] A general knowledge that illegal content is being distributed through the service, is not sufficient.[180] **Attribution of knowledge** of individual employees to the provider is held to follow general principles.[181]

126 Knowledge must concern not only the **content itself**, but also its illegal nature. This is clear from the wording of Art. 6(1)(a) of the DSA, which – in contrast to Art. 14(1)(a) of the E-Commerce Directive – refers to the illegality of both the activity and the content.[182] The focus is on whether the service provider has knowledge that it should block a certain content or information.[183]

---

[171] Hennemann in Gersdorf/Paal/ TMG § 10 mn. 17 et seqq.

[172] BGH 15.08.2013 – I ZR 80/12, GRUR 2013, 1030 (1032) – File Hosting Service; BGH 12.07.2012 – I ZR 18/11, GRUR 2013, 370 (para. 21 et seq.) – Alone in the Dark.

[173] Spindler in Spindler/Schmitz TMG § 10 mn. 12.

[174] Spindler in Spindler/Schmitz TMG § 10 mn. 82.

[175] BGH 27.03.2007 – VI ZR 101/06, GRUR 2007, 724 (725) – Meinungsforum.

[176] Spindler in Spindler/Schmitz TMG § 10 mn. 93.

[177] Spindler in Spindler/Schmitz TMG § 10 mn. 96.

[178] Spindler in Spindler/Schmitz TMG § 10 mn. 72; F. Hofmann in Hofmann/Raue Art. 6 mn. 35.

[179] BGH 23.9.2003 – VI ZR 335/02, GRUR 2004, 74 (75) – rassistische Hetze; OLG Brandenburg 16.12.2003 – 6 U 161/02, MMR 2004, 330 (331); Hennemann in Gersdorf/Paal TMG § 10 mn. 24.

[180] CJEU 22.6.2021 – joined cases C-682/18 and C-683/18, ECLI:EU:C:2021:503 para. 111 et seq. = GRUR 2021, 1054 – YouTube and Cyando; likewise already BGH 17.8.2011 – I ZR 57/09, BGHZ 191, 19 para. 19 = GRUR 2011, 1038 – Stiftparfüm; on the acquisition of such knowledge through automation see Schwemer, 2022, pp. 10 et seq., available at <https://ssrn.com/abtract=4213014> (last accessed: 28.11.2023).

[181] Hennemann in Gersdorf/Paal TMG § 10 mn. 25.

[182] By that, the corresponding question regarding Section 10 TMG has been answered by the legislator; see on TMG the references in Hennemann in Gersdorf/Paal TMG § 10 mn. 27 et seq.

[183] CJEU 22.6.2021 – joined cases C-682/18 and C-683/18, ECLI:EU:C:2021:503 para. 113 = GRUR 2021, 1054 – YouTube and Cyando; CJEU 23.3.2010 – joined cases C-236/08 to C-238/08, ECLI:EU:C:2010:169 para. 109 = GRUR 2010, 445 – Google and Google France.

In the case of **notification**, often in the form of a **cease-and-desist letter**, it is essential that there is adequate information to reasonably conclude, without conducting an own assessment, that the content or its dissemination is illegal[184]. Given that the service provider is not obligated to conduct an independent assessment, this implies that the illegality of the content must be manifest.[185] **127**

Art. 16 of the DSA now outlines specific requirements for the notice which confirms the principles outlined in the relevant case law (→ § 4 mn. 20 et seq.). **128**

c) No circumstantial knowledge in the case of claims for damages

In terms of damages, a hosting provider cannot invoke the liability exemption under Art. 6(1) of the DSA if it is aware of facts or circumstances from which the illegal activity or illegal content is apparent. **129**

The **criteria** for determining this **awareness** are not consistently assessed. Some argue that this limitation only applies to proven violations[186] while others contend that it narrows the exemption from liability, making it unavailable if service providers **negligently** fail to recognize the illegality of activities or content.[187] This latter perspective is supported by the need to avoid inconsistencies with general liability principles, wherein higher standards are required for criminal liability compared to a mere obligation to pay damages.[188] **130**

d) Expeditious action

If the hosting provider becomes **aware of the illegality or circumstances indicating illegality**, it can no longer invoke the liability exemption **unless it acts expeditiously to block access to or remove the illegal content** (Art. 6(1)(b) of the DSA).Therefore, a caching provider is obligated to swiftly remove or disable access to information stored at the original point of transmission or as directed by a judicial or administrative authority (Art. 5(1)(e) of the DSA; → mn. 119). **131**

The CJEU has clarified the interpretation of the **immediacy concept within the context of the E-Commerce Directive** and has ruled that there should be no delay in addressing a copyright infringement that causes disproportionate harm to the right **132**

184 CJEU – joined cases C-682/18 and C-683/18, ECLI:EU:C:2021:503 para. 116 = GRUR 2021, 1054 – YouTube and Cyando; CJEU 12.7.2011 – C-324/09, ECLI:EU:C:2011:474 para. 122 = GRUR 2011, 1025 – L'Oréal v eBay; BGH 2.6.2022 – I ZR 140/15, GRUR 2022, 1308 para. 115 – YouTube II; also already on "Stoererhaftung" (Breach of Duty of Care) BGH 19.3.2015 – I ZR 94/13, GRUR 2015, 1129 para. 42 – Hotelbewertungsportal.

185 CJEU 8.12.2022 – case C-460/20, ECLI:EU:C:2022:962 para. 72 – TU; on the requirement that the service provider must be able to take the blocking decision without conducting its own review CJEU 22.6.2021 – joined cases C-682/18 and C-683/18, ECLI:EU:C:2021:503 para. 122 – YouTube and Cyando; for France see Loiseau, Communication – Commerce électronique n° 2, Février 2023, p.2; for Germany BGH 13.09.2018 – I ZR 140/15, GRUR 2018, 1132 para. 49 – YouTube I; BGH 22.07.2010 – I ZR 139/08, GRUR 2011, 152 para. 45 – Kinderhochstühle im Internet I; BGH 30.04.2008 – I ZR 73/05, GRUR 2008, 702 para. 50 – Internetversteigerung III; F. Hofmann in Hofmann/Raue DSA Art. 6 mn. 41 et seq. elaborates on the requirements for a sufficient notice pursuant to Art. 16 para. 2 DSA, which leads to a presumption of knowledge, Art. 16 mn. 3 DSA; Köhler in Müller-Terpitz/Köhler DSA Art. 6 mn. 41 et seqq., 51 notes similarities between the notice prerequisites under European law with the requirements of a notice pursuant to Sec. 512c § 3 DMCA.

186 Hoeren MMR 2004, 166 (169).

187 Sieber/Höfinger, 'Teil 18 – Haftung', in Hoeren/Sieber/Holznagel (eds), Handbuch Multimedia-Recht, Part 18.1 mn. 90; Hoffmann/Volkmann in Spindler/Schuster TMG § 10 mn. 38.

188 Hoffmann/Volkmann in Spindler/Schuster TMG § 10 mn. 38; see on the state of the dispute also Hennemann in Gersdorf/Paal TMG § 10 mn. 32 et seqq. with corrigenda.

holder.[189] The CJEU's focus on disproportionate harm indicates that the timeframe for action depends on the specific circumstances of each case. For instance, if a service provider becomes aware of a substantial amount of illegal content[190], they may be given a longer period to take corrective measures compared to a situation involving a single infringement. Furthermore, content associated with severe impairments can generally be blocked or removed more swiftly than content where only financial concerns are at stake.

133 In this regard, legislative considerations also play a role. **Art. 3(3) of the Regulation (EU) 2021/784**[191] establishes an exceptionally short one-hour deadline for removing terrorist **online content**, particularly in cases involving official orders. While this timeframe may not directly apply to private notices, it is noticeably shorter than, for example, the timeframe for addressing copyright infringements, which typically do not pose a threat to life.

e) Special rule for liability under consumer protection law

134 Art. 6(3) of the DSA introduces a new rule which did not exist in the E-Commerce Directive. This provision excludes the limitation of liability under **consumer protection law for online platforms** that facilitate consumers in entering distance contracts. This exclusion applies when an average consumer can reasonably assume, based on the service's design, that the service or product originates either directly from the service provider or from a user controlled by it.

135 The purpose of this provision is to safeguard consumers engaging in online business transactions.[192] Instances triggering this provision include situations where the online platform fails to clearly display the trader's identity, withholds the trader's identity or contact details until after contract conclusion, or engages in marketing under its name instead of that of the third-party seller.[193] The determining factor is an objective assessment, considering all relevant circumstances.[194]

136 In several aspects, this provision stands out as an anomaly within **the liability framework and the general concept pursued in the DSA**. Generally, the legislator has based its intervention on the principle of leaving the liability exemptions untouched while introducing additional obligations through enhanced obligations. It remains unclear how the legislator justifies departing from that general approach, particularly in the context of the already extensively harmonised[195] transparency in consumer protection.

---

[189] CJEU 22.6.2021 – joined cases C-682/18 and C-683/18, ECLI:EU:2021:503 para. 141 = GRUR 2021, 1054 – YouTube and Cyando.

[190] For instance, in LG München I 30.6.2015 – 33 O 9639/14, MMR 2015, 831 (832) 1,000 works were at issue. The view of the BGH in BGH 15.8.2013 – I ZR 80/12, GRUR 2013, 1030 para. 59 according to which the review obligations of the interferer do not diminish even in the case of a notification of infringements in relation to more than 4,800 musical works and, if these cannot be fulfilled at the same time, only an exclusion of fault can be considered, is problematic.

[191] Regulation (EU) 2021/784 of the European Parliament and of the Council of 29 April 2021 on combating the dissemination of terrorist content online, OJ 2021 L 172, p. 79.

[192] See on the respective draft provision Art. 5 mn. 3 DSA Cauffman/Goanta EJRR, 2021, 758 (766); Specht-Riemenschneider/Bernzen in Reiffenstein/Blaschek p. 213 (223 et seq.).

[193] Rec. 24 DSA.

[194] Rec. 24 DSA; see Busch/Mak EuCML 2021, 109 (111) who proposed an exemplary list of circumstances to be considered. Art. 20 (2) ELI Model Rules on Online Platforms was proposed as an example for such a list.

[195] See only Article 6a of Directive 2011/83/EU introduced by the Omnibus Directive (Directive (EU) 2019/2161 of the European Parliament and of the Council of 27 November 2019 amending Council Directive 93/13/EEC and Directives 98/6/EC, 2005/29/EC and 2011/83/EU of the European Parliament

Furthermore, the applicability of limiting liability in this context relies on the user's perception, unlike the other liability conditions that are determined based on objective factors. Art. 6(3) of the DSA introduces a shift in perspective, differing significantly from liability aspects in other areas.[196] It is best understood as a **provision akin to preventing abuse,** allowing consumers who have entered a transaction based on trust in the service provider to hold them accountable. 137

IV. Legal consequences for the liability of service providers

1. Legal consequences if the liability exemptions apply

If the requirements of Art. 4 to 6 of the DSA are met, the service provider "shall not be liable" for the information transmitted or stored.[197] The **term "liability" must be interpreted broadly**, encompassing **all adverse consequences arising from the unlawfulness of transmitted, cached, or stored information**. This follows from the purpose of the liability exemptions to achieve a balance of different interests on platforms and the scheme of the DSA, which provides for regulatory oversight of the risks of illegal content rather than ordering through civil liability. 138

As to **criminal law sanctions**, a conduct may not be deemed unlawful if the provider complies with the requirements of the liability exemptions, and no adverse consequences can be attributed to it. Most importantly, no liability may attach to the service provider arising out of omissions to take certain precautionary measures. 139

The prohibition to attach liability to omissions extends to **duties of officers, employees and agents** to oversee and control the activity of a service provider. This is particularly relevant for the **criminal liability of officers and employees of service providers.** 140

Civil liability is also excluded, regardless of its classification in the legal system of the Member State. This includes **claims for damages,**[198] **unjust enrichment, actions performed without due authority,** and other legal grounds. It also extends to preparatory claims for information.[199] The legislator's decision not to impose proactive duties of care on exempted service providers implies that within the scope of the exemptions, there is no general tort liability for their conduct. The legislator assumed that the civil liability system might otherwise create incentives that hinder the exercise of fundamental rights of third parties. 141

The scope of the liability exemption may vary depending on the type of service and the content made available thereon. For example, service providers who exercise **editorial control** over the content on their websites, such as the online presence of press publications, generally do not benefit in that activity from the liability exemptions.[200] However, to the extent their websites also offer possibilities for **user interaction, they** 142

and of the Council on better enforcement and modernisation of Union consumer protection laws, OJ 2019 L 328, p. 7).

196 In trademark law, however, the CJEU recently anchored the elements of trademark use to similar criteria; see CJEU 22.12.2022 – case C-148/21, C-184/21, ECLI:EU:C:2022:1016 para. 43 et seq., 48 – Louboutin.

197 In the French and Spanish versions the term *'responsable' is* used, in the Italian *'responsabile'*. The German version changed from "haftet der Diensteanbieter nicht" ("the service provider is not accountable") in the E-Commerce Directive to "nicht verantwortlich" ("not liable") in the DSA.

198 CJEU 15.9.2016 – case C-484/14, ECLI:EU:C:2016:689 No. 5 and para. 74 = GRUR 2016, 1146 – McFadden/Sony Music.

199 J. B. Nordemann in Fromm/Nordemann UrhG § 97 mn. 185.

200 See CJEU 11.9.2014 – case C-291/13, ECLI:EU:C:2014:2209 = MMR 2016, 63 – Papasavvas.

are eligible for the liability exemptions. Conversely, if the service is fundamentally a **hosting service**, but the provider is notified about a specific illegal content and fails to act expediently, the liability exemption may not apply for the specific content of which the provider has been notified but will continue to apply for all other content.[201]

143 An intense debate existed, especially in Germany, as to whether the liability exemption also covers **cease-and-desists-claims and/or injunctive relief**.[202] In principle, the scope of application of the European liability rules does not depend on how claims or legal actions are classified within the national legal systems.[203] The crucial factor is not whether national law categorizes a claim as removal or injunctive relief, but rather the foundation and purpose of the claim. As the unequivocal wording of Art. 4 to 6 of the DSA make clear, any adverse consequences from the transmission or storage of unlawful information are excluded to the extent that the limitation exemption applies. This includes cease-and-desist claims.

144 The debate was in fact triggered by a misunderstanding of the scheme of the liability rules. Whereas the **liability exemptions also apply to cease-and-desist-claims**, this leaves unaffected the possibility for orders of national courts under national law in accordance with Art. 4(3), Art. 5(3) and Art. 6(4) of the DSA (→ mn. 150). Depending on the nature of the relevant national law instrument or remedy, these orders can be based on cease-and-desist claims. However, even then, orders must fulfil the requirements under Art. 4 to 6 of the DSA and respect the limitations on these orders mandated by European law, namely they must be issued by an administrative authority or court and must respect the principle of proportionality.

145 Furthermore, the imposition of liability for **costs of legal action** on the involved parties, including the reimbursement of warning and court costs, is also excluded during periods when the service provider's conduct falls under the limitation of liability standard.[204] This distinction should be made from the **costs associated with any blocking or precautionary measures** or legal costs arising from disputes over them.

2. Legal consequences if the liability exemptions do not apply

146 If the conditions for exemption from liability are not fulfilled or cease to exist, **the liability exemptions do not apply. Liability then depends on whether the requirements under the substantive provisions are fulfilled (positive condition).** The legislator has emphasized that these questions are independent, i.e., that ineligibility for the exemptions of liability does not automatically imply liability under the substantive provisions (→ mn. 32 et seq.).

147 This also addresses a question that the German *Bundesgerichtshof* has submitted to the CJEU in *YouTube/Cyando* but which has remained unanswered. Notably, the *Bundes-*

---

[201] The position of the *Bundesgerichtshof* which does not apply the liability exemptions for similar or equivalent repeat infringements, is not consistent with the CJEU case law; see BGH 2.6.2022 – I ZR 140/15, GRUR 2022, 1308 para. 118 et seqq. – YouTube II and Conrad/Ampatziadis GRUR 2023, 1504.

[202] From the German case law, see BGH 11.3.2004 – I ZR 304/01, GRUR 2004, 860 (862) – Internetversteigerung I; BGH 19.4.2007 – I ZR 35/04, GRUR 2007, 708 para. 41 et seq. – Internetversteigerung II; BGH 27.3.2012 – VI ZR 144/11, GRUR 2012, 751 para. 9 – RSS Feeds; BGH 27.7.2010 – I ZR 139/08, GRUR 2011, 152 para. 26 – Kinderhochstühle im Internet I; BGH 17.8.2011 – I ZR 57/09, GRUR 2011, 1038 para. 22, 26 – Stiftparfüm; BGH 12.7.2012 – I ZR 18/11, GRUR 2013, 370 para. 31 – Alone in the Dark; for the debate see e.g. Hoeren MMR 2004, 672 (672); Wimmers/Nolte GRUR 2014, 16 (20); Nordemann GRUR 2021, 18 (21); Specht ZUM 2017, 114 at mn. 15; Köhler in Müller-Terpitz/Köhler DSA Art. 4 mn. 8 et seqq.; for a French law perspective Lucas/Lucas-Schloetter/Bernault, 2017, mn. 1295, p. 1014.

[203] See for injunctive relief, Hofmann GPR 2017, 176 (180).

[204] CJEU 15.9.2016 – case C-484/14, ECLI:EU:C:2016:689 No. 5 and para. 75 = GRUR 2016, 1146 -McFadden/Sony Music.

gerichtshof had asked whether service providers that are not primarily liable under copyright law, may still be liable for damages as an infringer under Art. 11(1)(1) Enforcement Directive if they fail to meet the requirements for exemption from liability concerning reproduction (e.g., due to an *active role*).[205]

If the question is understood conditionally – whether the service provider is liable as an infringer *because* they play an **active role within the scope of liability limitation rules** – the answer is 'No'. The fact that not all of the conditions for the liability exemptions are fulfilled, has no bearing on the question of substantive liability.[206] On the one hand, primary liability under the substantive laws does not automatically result in ineligibility of the service provider for the liability exemptions. On the other hand, ineligibility for the liability exemptions does not per se result in substantive liability. The two regimes are separate. Were this not the case, the requirements of liability exemptions would *effectively* become positive elements for substantive liability rules. This is explicitly excluded by Recital 17 of the DSA. 148

This does not rule out a parallel **application of the law** where the criteria overlap. It is important to note, however, that Art. 11(1)(1) Enforcement Directive, frequently cited in this context,[207] is not a liability provision itself, but merely refers to the pertinent copyright, trademark or patent law liability requirements.[208] Playing an "active role" in connection with an offense may not be a criterion under the relevant substantive law, e.g., for the concept of 'communication to the public' in copyright law or for 'use' of a trademark in trademark law. In these cases, the assessment of the liability exemption and the substantive liability test may diverge. 149

V. Orders against intermediaries

Even if service providers benefit from the liability exemptions under Art. 4 to 6 of the DSA, they may, as is explicitly reserved in these provisions,[209] still be subject to **orders from a judicial or administrative authority** to terminate or prevent and infringements. Recital 25 of the DSA confirms that the orders include injunctive relief to remove or disable access to illegal content but must respect the limitations under European law. 150

In the hybrid multi-level construct of the European liability scheme, this opens the door to **national solutions and differences** under the umbrella of the overarching principles of the European system, namely the prohibition of general monitoring and pro-active investigation duties. 151

---

205 In this way the reasoning for the preliminary request referred in BGH 13.9.2018 – I ZR 140/15, GRUR 2018, 1132 para. 56 et seq. – YouTube: "Rather, in the view of the Senate, the infringer is also the service provider who does not limit himself to a neutral role in the communication to the public by users of his platform but plays an active role."

206 See also Conseil constitutionnel 10.06.2004, decision no. 2004–496 DC.

207 The CJEU had pointed out that in the absence of perpetrator liability (under trade mark law), liability based on other legal provisions "such as Article 14(1) of Directive 2000/31 or Article 11(1)(1) of Directive 2004/48" could be considered; CJEU 2.4.2020 – case C-567/18, ECLI:EU:C:267 para. 49 = GRUR 2020, 637 – Coty/Amazon.

208 GA Saugmandsgaard Øe 15.7.2021 – case C-401/19, ECLI:EU:C:2021:613 para. 105 = GRUR-RS 2021, 20614 – Poland v Parliament and Council.

209 Art. 4(3), Art. 5(3) and Art. 6(4) DSA.

1. Legal nature of orders

a) Mandatory involvement of state authorities or courts

152 Art. 4(3), Art. 5(3) and Art. 6(4) of the DSA provide that orders to terminate or prevent an infringement (**take down** and **stay down**) may be issued by a judicial or administrative authority in accordance with the laws of the Member States. The wording is taken form the relevant provisions in the E-Commerce-Directive but only refers to infringing content whereas the broader concept used in the DSA is illegal content. No difference should be made between these two concepts.

153 At the time of enactment of the E-Commerce Directive, due to the **differences between the laws of the Member States** often rooted in procedural laws and traditions, it seemed understandable to accept a lack of harmonization and build on national traditions. Since then, however, Member States have introduced powers to issue orders and the issues have been studied extensively in the legal literature.[210] A more unified approach would therefore seem possible and preferable. The legislature took an intermediate path introducing further transparency between Member States through information obligations (Art. 9 DSA), possibly hoping to achieve more standardization in practice. The topic is likely to remain relevant in the coming years. Further harmonisation seems inevitable.

154 The hesitancy of the legislator may still be rooted in **conceptual differences** as to the design of claims or remedies for removal and injunctions in Europe. These are partly substantive in nature and determined by the court, and partly procedural remedies, where the authority or the court determines legal consequences in case of illegal content.[211] Also, separating factual issues from procedural peculiarities of national law has not always been an easy task, even in the case law of the CJEU.[212]

155 While Art. 4(3), Art. 5(3) and Art. 6(4) of the DSA are framed in terms of a constitutive state order, they may allow for different forms of transposition.[213] Importantly, however, they prescribe that, in each case, a **balancing of interests** occurs by a state authority.

b) Injunctive orders

156 The request for blocking and prevention is issued **against the intermediary as a third party**, not as infringer.[214] Therefore, in accordance with the *L'Oréal* judgement of the CJEU, the situation is more complex and lends itself to other kinds of injunctions.[215] The authority or court must strike a **balance between the interests involved** which requires a **nuanced approach**; this is often disregarded in the court practice.

157 The orders call for **positive action**, not for cease-and-desist. This is evident not only in the removal through take-down, but even more so for preventive measures (stay-down). The notion, associated with injunctive relief, that the service provider is obligated to terminate the infringement, is often not feasible and at least, not proportionate. As the CJEU rightfully observed, measures against intermediaries "contribute to

---

[210] See, inter alia, Angelopoulos, 2016; Hofmann, 2017; Husovec, 2017; Jones, 2020; Ohly, 2014, p. 96 et seq.

[211] See Hofmann, 2017, p. 13 et seqq.; Husovec, 2017, p. 145 et seq.

[212] See AG Cruz-Villalón, 27.3.2014 – case C-314/12, ECLI:EU:C:2013:781 para. 61 = BeckRS 2013, 82229 – UPC Telekabel; CJEU 27.3.2014 – case C-314/12, ECLI:EU:C:2014:192 para. 61 = GRUR 2014, 468 – UPC Telekabel.

[213] In this sense also AG Saugmandsgaard Øe 15.7.2021 – case C-401/19, ECLI:EU:C:2021:613 para. 210 = GRUR-RS 2021, 20614 – Poland v Parliament and Council.

[214] CJEU 27.3.2014 – case C-314/12, ECLI:EU:C:2014:192 para. 53 = GRUR 2014, 468 – UPC Telekabel.

[215] CJEU 12.7.2011 – case C-324/09, ECLI:EU:C:2011:474 para. 129 – L'Oréal v eBay.

avoiding new infringements". Proportionality may require that the measures ordered are such that they may not necessarily completely terminate or prevent the infringement.[216]

The view of the CJEU that it may be less of an interference to allow the service provider to choose the means to achieve the desired result, is not without doubts.[217] If providers are ordered to achieve a certain result rather than take certain actions, they may resort to **excessive measures**. The countervailing principle, also expressed by the CJEU, namely that providers are obligated to protect the fundamental rights of third parties,[218] probably holds more aspirational value given that providers have a – likewise protected – interest to minimize the risk of liability. Hence, orders to achieve a certain result should be used with caution. 158

2. Prohibition of general monitoring and proportionality

Orders to address clear violations of the law are generally acceptable and, when appropriate, proportionate. Taking measures to prevent the reappearance of the same content, such as files, is considered a specific action, if these measures have a time limitation, they qualify as **specific measures according to Recital 30 of the DSA**.[219] The key issue from a proportionality point of view is which measures service providers must adopt to identify identical or equivalent content. 159

When service providers are mandated to remove not only the specific content, but also **similar or equivalent content**, and to prevent future uploads, it implies that providers must scrutinise all the information stored on their service, at the very least any future uploads. Typically, this requires the **implementation of automated filters** and create tension between the obligation to prevent further infringements and the prohibition of general monitoring (Art. 8 of the DSA). 160

The CJEU initially adopted a highly restrictive approach to preventive measures but cautiously expanded it in ***Glawischnig-Piesczeck*** (see mn. 90 et seqq.). Service providers may be compelled not only to prevent the re-upload of identical content, but also to block "equivalent information". However, this information must be clearly specified for the hosting provider to **automatically detect** it **without requiring an independent assessment**.[220] In the *Poland* judgment, the CJEU emphasised that service providers are never obligated to make an independent assessment of the illegality of the uploaded information.[221] In the *TU/Google case,* the CJEU once again highlights the potential threats that obligations to investigate can pose to the fundamental rights of third parties.[222] 161

Hence, the condition that the service provider must **be aware of the unlawful information** and is **not burdened with an obligation to independently assess whether content is unlawful** is crucial for determining the required measures. Therefore, it is 162

---

216 CJEU, 7.7.2016 – case C-494/15, ECLI:EU:C:2016:528 para. 34 = MMR 2016, 676 – Tommy Hilfiger.

217 CJEU 26.4.2022 – C-401/19, ECLI:EU:C:2022:297 para. 90–92 = GRUR 2022, 820 – Poland v. Parliament and Council; CJEU 27.3.2014 – case C-314/12, ECLI:EU:C:2014:192 para. 53 = GRUR 2014, 468 – UPC Telekabel; Grisse, 2018, p. 70 et seq.

218 CJEU 27.3.2014 – case C-314/12, ECLI:EU:C:2014:192 para. 55 = GRUR 2014, 468 – UPC Telekabel.

219 Hoeren/Yankova IIC 2012, 501 (529).

220 CJEU3.10.2019 – case C-18/18, ECLI:EU:C:2019:821, para.- 34 – 37 = GRUR 2019, 1208 – Glawischnig-Piesczek; Spindler NJW 2019, 3274; Paal JZ 2020, 92.

221 CJEU 26.4.2022 – case C-401/19, ECLI:EU:C:2022:297 para. 90 – 92 = GRUR 2022, 820 – Poland v Parliament and Council.

222 CJEU 8.12.22 – case C-460/20, ECLI:EU:C:2022:962 para.71 = GRUR-RS 2022, 34883 – TU.

vital that the criteria guiding the service provider's search for infringements **are specific and conducive to automated searches.**[223]

163 As a result, determining permissible measures involves **a case specific application of the principle of proportionality.**[224] Importantly, the proportionality test goes beyond the bilateral relationship between claimant and the service provider and includes the equitable balancing of multipolar interests.

3. Content of the orders

164 The CJEU has established that orders under Art. 11(1)(3) Enforcement Directive should be "equitable and proportionate". These orders should not be excessively costly, create barriers to legitimate trade, **or compel service providers to engage in constant monitoring of their users.**[225] The standard of review is based on European fundamental rights, if the measures are prescribed by European law.[226] However, there may be challenging questions regarding the delineation between national and European fundamental rights.[227]

165 Additionally, measures need to be **technically feasible.** Precautionary measures against renewed infringements should be capable of running automatically without requiring a separate assessment.[228] The crucial factor is whether the criteria leading to the infringement are specific enough. It's important to assess not only the effectiveness of the proposed measure in identifying new infringements, but also the potential impact of blocking lawful content (referred to as "*false positives*"). Filtering measures that cannot adequately distinguish between lawful and unlawful content are inadmissible.[229]

166 Orders must be **legally enforceable.** A frequent issue here are conflicts with telecommunications secrecy.[230] Enforceability becomes a particular issue for **orders that are global in scope,** a possibility not excluded by the CJEU. Assessing compatibility of an order on a worldwide scale is almost impossible and such orders are, in most cases disproportionate. In any event, **limitations for the geographical scope** of the orders may still arise from **international tort law and international jurisdiction.**[231]

---

[223] CJEU 3.10.2019 – case C-18/18-, ECLI:EU:C:2019:821 para. 34 = GRUR 2019, 1208 – Glawischnig-Piesczek; CJEU 8.12.22 – case C-460/20, ECLI:EU:C:2022:962 para. 71 = GRUR-RS 2022, 34883 – TU.

[224] BGH 17.5.2001 – I ZR 251/99, GRUR 2001, 1038 (1039 et seq.) – ambiente.de; BGH 22.7.2010 – I ZR 139/08, GRUR 2011, 152 para. 45 – Kinderhochstühle im Internet I; BGH 30.4.2008 – I ZR 73/05, GRUR 2008, 702 para. 50 – Internetversteigerung III; BGH 10.10.1996 – I ZR 129/94, GRUR 1997, 313 (315 et seq.) – Architektenwettbewerb; Cour de Cassation 27.03.2024, n°22-21.586, Loiseau, Commerce électronique n° 5 2024, 1.

[225] CJEU 7.7.2016 – case C-494/15, ECLI:EU:C:2016:528 para. 34 = MMR 2016, 676 – Tommy Hilfiger.

[226] CJEU 27.3.2014 – case C-314/12, ECLI:EU:C:2014:192 para. 44 et seq. = GRUR 2014, 468 – UPC Telekabel; CJEU 24.11.2011 – case C-70/10, ECLI:EU:C:2011:771 para. 41 = GRUR 2012, 265 – Scarlet Extended.

[227] See CJEU 29.7.2019 – case C-469/17, ECLI:EU:C:2019:623 = GRUR 2019, 934 – Funke Medien; BVerfG 06.11.2019 – 1 BvR 16/13, ZUM 2020, 58 – Recht auf Vergessen I; BVerfG 06.11.2019 – 1 BvR 276/17, ZUM-RD 2020, 1 – Recht auf Vergessen II; BVerfG 22.05.2019 – 1 BvQ 42/19, ZUM-RD 2019, 429 – Der III. Weg.

[228] CJEU 3.10.2019 – case C-18/18, ECLI:EU:C:2019:821 para. 34 = GRUR 2019, 1208 – Glawischnig-Piesczek; CJEU 8.12.22 – case C-460/20, ECLI:EU:C:2022:962 para. 71 = GRUR-RS 2022, 34883 – TU; also BGH 22.7.2010 – I ZR 139/08, GRUR 2011, 152 para. 39 – Kinderhochstühle im Internet I; BGH 19.4.2007 – I ZR 35/04 708, GRUR 2007, 708 para. 47 – Internetversteigerung II; see also OLG Stuttgart, 26.11.2020 – 2 U 147/18, GRUR-RS 2020, 45570 para. 126 – Alibaba.

[229] CJEU 26.4.2022 – C-401/19, ECLI:EU:C:2022:297 para. 86 = GRUR 2022, 820 – Poland v. Parliament and Council; Leistner GRUR 2022, 803 (805 et seq.).

[230] In this regard, Hennemann in Gersdorf/Paal TMG § 7 mn. 71; Leistner/Grisse GRUR 2015, 19 (22 et seq.).

[231] Spindler NJW 2019, 3274 (3276).

Measures must be **proportionate,** ensuring a **fair balance of interests**. This entails first that the measures should effectively put an end to the violation of rights.[232] Additionally, the ordered measures must be necessary, and if multiple options meet these criteria, the one imposing the least burden must be chosen.[233] Failure to do so would violate the service provider's rights under Art. 16 CFR and potentially infringe on the fundamental rights of other users, such as freedom of information.[234] 167

A specific aspect of proportionality involves the determination whether the operator should or must decide itself on the means to address the occurrence of certain illegal content (i.e., an obligation to achieve a certain result) or whether it is ordered to take certain measures (obligation to take certain actions). Here, a distinction seems appropriate: On the one hand, if multiple measures exist that are equally effective, the choice should **be left to the intermediary.**[235] In the same vein, the service provider should be granted a certain **margin of appreciation in designing and selecting technical systems.** This is even more important when systems work with artificial intelligence, where **duties of care relate to the system** rather than a specific result.[236] 168

On the other hand, in most cases, **general obligations to achieve a certain result,** ordering the blocking of specific content without restrictions and without defining the means are **disproportionate**. Since measures against infringements are typically not 100 % effective and can be circumvented, such an obligation would unreasonably burden the service provider and create the very incentives to overblocking that the liability exemptions are trying to avoid. If providers are uncertain about the required actions,[237] they will tend to choose the more extensive measure, even if it affects the rights of third parties.[238] 169

Finally, **obligations with no time limit are problematic.**[239] 170

It can be expected that the case law will continue to evolve and that more types of orders will be developed for different areas of application:[240] 171

---

232 CJEU 15.9.2016 – case C-484/14, ECLI:EU:C:2016:689 para. 95 = GRUR 2016, 1146 – McFadden/Sony Music.

233 See the decision of the French Conseil Constitutionell 10.06.2009, no. 2009–580-DC, Conseil constitutionnel 10.06.2009, no. 2009–580-DC, which limits the orders to what is strictly necessary ("les mesures strictement nécessaires à la préservation des droits en cause").

234 CJEU 15.9.2016 – case C-484/14, ECLI:EU:C:2016:689 para. 82 et seqq. = GRUR 2016, 1146 – McFadden/Sony Music; on the requirement of the least possible interference in Art. 16 CFR see CJEU 26.04.2012 – case C-510/10, ECLI:EU:C:2012:244 para. 57 = BeckRS 2012, 80766 – TV2.

235 On the aspect in general CJEU 27.3.2014 – case C-314/12, ECLI:EU:C:2014:192 para. 52 = GRUR 2014, 468 – UPC Telekabel; CJEU 26.4.2022 – case C-401/19, ECLI:EU:C:2022:297 para. 75 = GRUR 2022, 820 – Poland v Parliament and Council. On the combination of several possible measures Leistner/Grisse GRUR 2015, 19 (26 et seq.).

236 On system-related duties of care Berberich/Conrad, 'Plattformen und KI' in Ebers/Heinze/Krügel/Steinrötter (eds), Künstliche Intelligenz und Robotik, 2020, p. 930, para. 66; Denga, 'Die Technology Judgement Rule' in: Kuschel/Assmussen/Golla (eds), Intelligente Systeme – Intelligentes Recht, 2021, p. 63 ("technological judgement rule").

237 The matter is subject to scrutiny by AG Jääskinnen, 9.12.2010 – case C-324/09, ECLI:EU:C:2010:757 para. 181 = GRUR 2011, 1025 – L'Oréal v eBay.

238 CJEU 27.3.2014 – case C-314/12, ECLI:EU:C:2014:192 para. 44 et seq. = GRUR 2014, 468 – UPC Telekabel.

239 CJEU 12.7.2011 – case C-324/09, ECLI:EU:C:2011:474 para. 140 = GRUR 2011, 1025 – L'Oréal v eBay; Hoeren MMR 2004, 672 (673); Janal ZEuP 2021, 227 (252).

240 For nuanced duties in the case of libel, copyright and trademark infringements, Senftleben/Angelopoulos, 'The Odyssey of the Prohibition on General Monitoring Obligations on the Way to the Digital Services Act: Between Article 15 of the E-Commerce Directive and Article 17 of the Directive on Copyright in the Digital Single Market' (04.01.2021), p. 3 et seq., 14 et seq. <https://papers.ssrn.com/sol3/papers.cfm?abstract_id=3717022> (last accessed: 28.11.2023).

172 Blocking injunctions against internet service providers have been one of the first to prevent access to infringing content.[241] They are as effective as intrusive for third party rights and triggered intense debate. Differences have emerged in particular as regards subsidiarity, as some Member States require first that **reasonable measures are taken against the infringer or, if applicable, the host provider,**[242] where others do not.[243] In practice, network operators and rights holders have initiated cooperation and clearing mechanisms which are looked upon favourably by the DSA but may, as the discussions about Art. 17 of the DSM Directive have shown, be problematic for rights of third parties.[244]

173 As to **orders against host providers,** case law classifies potential measures based on the type of infringement. It is noteworthy that the precautionary measures ordered in the *Glawischnig-Piesczeck* case, which set the stage for CJEU case law, pertained to **manifest defamation.**[245] In the same vein, the *Delfi* case of the ECHR also involved manifest defamation.[246] While libel and defamation are challenging to detect by filters due to their contextual nature, and "equivalent" violations open up a broad field of argumentation[247], these violations tend to capture the attention of courts due to the personal involvement of individuals. Nevertheless, the CJEU has mandated a specification of the infringement and the possibility of automated examination in the case of extended stay-down obligations.[248] Similar developments can be seen in relation to the protections of minors where the importance of the protected interests call for increased efforts.[249]

174 In contrast, the CJEU highlighted in the Poland decision that **Art. 17 of the DSM Directive imposes an outcome-oriented obligation on service providers to ensure lawful content accessibility**. In contrast, the duty to prevent infringement only necessitates best efforts.[250] Consequently, **when in doubt,** copyright **property rights** should take a secondary position to **avoid excessive blocking**. The CJEU justifies this stance by asserting that the fundamental rights position of intellectual property owners is not unconditionally guaranteed.[251]

175 In **trademark law,** the risk of overly broad injunctions is generally held to be high.[252] Consequently, the CJEU has restricted measures to prevent trademark infringements **to**

---

241 See e.g., Marsoof, 2019, p. 178 et. seq; Geiger/Izyumenko, 'Blocking Orders: Assessing Tensions with Human Rights' in Frosio (ed), Oxford Handbook of Online Intermediary Liability, p. 566.

242 See BGH 26.7.2018 – I ZR 64/17, GRUR 2018, 1044 para. 42 et seq. – Dead Island; BGH, 13.10.2022 – I ZR 111/21, GRUR 2022, 1812 – DNS-Sperre; Rössel AfP 2023, 93 (95).

243 For France, see Lucas/Lucas-Schloetter/Bernault, Traité de la propriété littéraire et artistique, 2017, mn. 1301, p. 1019.

244 See Marsoof, 2019, p. 176 et seqq.; Arnold, 'Intermediary Liabilty and Trade Mark Infringement: A Common Law Perspective' in Frosio (ed), Oxford Handbook of Online Intermediary Liability, p. 404; on the fundamental rights issues Geiger/Izyumenko, 'Blocking Orders: Assessing Tensions with Human Rights' in Frosio (ed), Oxford Handbook of Online Intermediary Liability, p. 138.

245 CJEU 3.10.2019 – case C-18/18-, ECLI:EU:C:2019:821 = GRUR 2019, 1208 – Glawischnig-Piesczek.

246 ECHR 16.6.2015 – App. No. 64569/09, NJW 2015, 2863 – Delfi AS v. Estonia.

247 Hofmann/Specht-Riemenschneider ZGE 2021, 49 (67).

248 CJEU 3.10.2019 – C-18/18-, ECLI:EU:C:2019:821 para. 34 = GRUR 2019, 1208 – Glawischnig-Piesczek.

249 BGH 12.07.2007 – I ZR 18/04, GRUR 2007, 890 para. 40 – Jugendgefährdende Medien bei eBay.

250 CJEU 26.4.2022 – case C-401/19, ECLI:EU:C:2022:297 para. 78 = GRUR 2022, 820 – Poland v Parliament and Council.

251 CJEU 27.3.2014 – case C-314/12, ECLI:EU:C:2014:192 para. 61 = GRUR 2014, 468 – UPC Telekabel.

252 See for instance Mostert, 'Intermediary Liability and Online Trade Mark Infringement: Emerging International Common Approaches', in Frosio (ed), Oxford Handbook of Online Intermediary Liability, 368 (378); Senftleben/Angelopoulos, 'The Odyssey of the Prohibition on General Monitoring Obligations on the Way to the Digital Services Act: Between Article 15 of the E-Commerce Directive and Article 17 of the Directive on Copyright in the Digital Single Market' (04.01.2021), p. 3 et seq., 14 et seq. <https:/

"infringements of that kind by the same seller in respect of the same trademarks".[253] Otherwise, there is a concern about potential restrictions on legitimate trade such as the prohibition of parallel imports or the sale of exhausted goods. In any case, orders resulting in the withdrawal of goods bearing specific trademarks from the market are excluded.[254]

4. Costs of the measures

According to the case law of the CJEU, the provisions of the E-Commerce Directive do not prevent imposing the **costs of the respective measures on the service provider.**[255] The DSA does not explicitly regulate the question. The CJEU has stipulated that measures may not be excessively costly but did not further elaborate on the bearing of costs. 176

In any event, there is no European requirement that the service provider bears the costs of the measures. **European practices vary.**[256] Orders against intermediaries are based on the notion that the intermediaries have the means to stop the infringement. Their **obligation is thus one of assistance, not of liability in the strict sense.**[257] Therefore, it is widely acknowledged that in imposing measures on them, consideration must be given to the fact that the intermediary service provider is not the one committing the infringement itself.[258] 177

The argument that intermediaries must bear the costs because they benefit from the provision of their services, frequently encountered, is not conclusive, as right holders similarly benefit from the use of their rights or the measures to protect them.[259] The fact that service providers can be the ***"cheapest" cost avoider***[260] does not necessarily mean the measures ordered are "*cheap*", or that it is justified to impose them on service providers. 178

Therefore, **potential solutions** could involve imposing the incremental costs of requested measures on the applicants.[261] This approach might also create an incentive to ensure that measures are not applied excessively or for longer than necessary. 179

/papers.ssrn.com/sol3/papers.cfm?abstract_id=3717022> (last accessed: 28.11.2023); Marsoof, 2019, p. 155 et seqq.

253 CJEU 12.7.2011 – case C-324/09, ECLI:EU:C:2011:474 para. 141 = GRUR 2011, 1025 – L'Oréal v eBay; AG Jääskinen09.12.2010 – case C-324/09, ECLI:EU:C:2010:757 para. 181 et seq. – L'Oréal; CJEU 7.7.2016 – case C-494/15, ECLI:EU:C:2016:528 para. 34 et seqq. = MMR 2016, 676 – Tommy Hilfiger.

254 CJEU 12.7.2011 – case C-324/09, ECLI:EU:C:2011:474 para. 140 = GRUR 2011, 1025 – L'Oréal v eBay.

255 CJEU 15.9.2016 – case C-484/14, ECLI:EU:C:2016:689 para. 78 = GRUR 2016, 1146 -McFadden/Sony Music; also BGH 26.11.2015 – I ZR 174/14, GRUR 2016, 268 para. 37 – Stoererhaftung des Access-Providers.

256 See case law references in Husovec, 2017, p. 85 et seq.; 200 et seqq.; Rosati GRUR Int. 2017, 206 (210).

257 Jones, 2020, p. 198 uses the term auxiliary performance obligation; see Husovec 2017 with the subtitle "Accountable but not Liable?".

258 CJEU 27.3.2014 – case C-314/12, ECLI:EU:C:2014:192 para. 53 = GRUR 2014, 468 – UPC Telekabel.

259 Critical of the implicit assumption of responsibility also Lucas/Lucas-Schloetter/Bernault, Traité de la propriété littéraire et artistique, 2017, mn. 1305, p. 1021.

260 In this sense, for example, Leistner GRUR Beil. 2010, 1 (32); Frosio/Geiger, Eur. Law J. 2023, 1 (5) ("Calabresi-Coase paradigm of "least-cost avoiders").

261 See on the various cost items the English decision Cartier International AG v British Telecommunications plc [2014] WHC EWHC 3354 (Ch); [2015] Bus LR 298 (ChD); [2016] EWCA Civ 658, [2017] BusLR 1 [212] (UK); Arnold, inFrosio, 404; Leistner/Grisse GRUR 2015, 105 (112).

5. Transposition in Member States

180 As noted above, Member States have adopted or retained differing and sometimes diverging solutions to implement the possibility of ordering measures against intermediaries. France and Germany are contrasting examples. On the one hand, France has adopted, in its transposition of the E-Commerce-Directive, dedicated procedural rules to address orders against intermediaries which allow for judicial or administrative orders.[262] On the other hand, Germany has for a long time not introduced any dedicated rules for online intermediaries. The courts addressed this gap by applying the general concept of "**Störerhaftung**", essentially a doctrine of liability for duty of care which, despite some tentative legislative efforts, still dominates the practice of these orders.[263] While this doctrine of *Störerhaftung* has received wide attention in the literature, it remains at its core incompatible with the logic and structure of the European liability scheme for online intermediaries.[264]

6. Requirements for orders to take action against unlawful content

181 The **requirements** for administrative and court orders are outlined in Art. 9 of the DSA. Specially, Art. 9(2) of the DSA specifies the minimum information that the order must include (**Art. 9(2)(a) of the DSA**), necessary local restrictions (**Art. 9(2)(b) of the DSA**), as well as the language in which the order must be issued (**Art. 9(2)(c) of the DSA**). Additionally, Art. 9 of the DSA includes provisions on the procedure for issuing the orders and information obligations related to their execution. According to Art. 9(6) of the DSA, these provisions are without prejudice to national procedural law.

182 In practice, the **list of necessary components** of the order (Art. 9(2)(a) of the DSA) is likely to be particularly relevant. Accordingly, the legal basis for the order must be stated first (**no. i**). In the case of civil law orders, this would be the obligation of the intermediary to remove the possibility of access to the unlawful content. The same applies to the required justification of the unlawfulness (**no. ii**)).

183 To comply with the order, the service provider must be **informed as precisely as possible** about the content in question. **No. (iv)** specifies that the content can be identified by means of a URL address, and further information must be added if necessary.

184 Furthermore, the person subject to the order must be informed of which authority issued the order **(no. iii).** This enables the service provider to verify the authenticity of the order.[265] Finally, the orders must contain information on which authority, if any, is to be informed about the execution **(no. vi)** and which legal protection options exist **(no. v)**.[266]

7. Requirements for information orders

185 Art. 10 of the DSA governs the **criteria for information orders**. Subsection 2 of Art. 10 of the DSA outlines the essential details that must be included in the request

---

[262] See Loi n° 2004–575 du 21 juin 2004 pour la confiance dans l'économie numérique (LCEN); for an overview Pons/André/Borgat, Pin Code 2021/3 (N° 9), p. 1; Jones, 2020, p. 193 et seq.

[263] Explicit legislative bases for orders are now contained in § 7(4) TMG or Art. 109(3) of the MStV; BGH 26.7.2018 – I ZR 64/17, GRUR 2018, 1044 para. 42 et seq. – Dead Island; BGH, 13.10.2022 – I ZR 111/21, GRUR 2022, 1812 – DNS blocking; Hennemann ZUM 2018, 754.

[264] See for more detail Conrad, '§ 3 Verantwortlichkeit und Haftung von Intermediären', in Steinrötter (ed), Europäische Plattformregulierung – Rechtshandbuch, § 3 mn. 21, 192 et seq.

[265] Rec. 35 DSA.

[266] Details can be found in rec. 39 of the DSA; F. Hofmann in Hofmann/Raue DAS Art. 9 mn. 57 et seq. list further examples.

(**lit. a**), the specific content restrictions (**lit. b**), and stipulates the language and method for issuing and transmitting the order (lit. c). Additionally, Art. 10 of the DSA includes provisions addressing the order issuance process and information obligations. It is important to note that, as per Art. 10(6) of the DSA, these provisions do not override national procedural laws.

Regarding the information requirements under Art. 10(2)(a) of the DSA, distinctions **186** arise when compared to Art. 9(2)(a) of the DSA due to differences in the **content of the orders**. Instead of specifying content to be blocked via a URL, the requested information must be via identified using account names or other unique identifiers (**no. iii**).[267] Furthermore, rather than justifying unlawfulness, an explanation must be provided for why the information is necessary and why the information order is both essential and proportionate (**no. iv**).

8. Transmission of information on orders

If a national authority issues an order to address illegal content (Art. 9 of the DSA) or **187** an information order (Art. 10 of the DSA), it is required to transmit both the order and **information regarding its execution to the digital services coordinator of its respective Member State** (Art. 9(3) or Art. 10(3) of the DSA). Subsequently, the coordinator records this information in an information exchange system, facilitating communication with other authorities, the Commission, and the Panel (Art. 61 et seqq. of the DSA; Art. 9(4) or Art. 10(4) of the DSA, in each case in conjunction with Art. 85 of the DSA). The coordinator's obligation to disclose may be waived, especially if it conflicts with national criminal procedural law.[268]

This provision ensures that **competent authorities** in each Member State are in- **188** formed about orders issued in other Member States, facilitating a consistent exercise of discretion by these authorities.[269] Similar notification provisions are present in other legal acts of the European Union.[270] They serve as both procedural requirements and mechanisms to promote harmonisation, mitigating the emergence of trade barriers in harmonised legal domains.[271] Consequently, these provisions the harmonisation efforts of the EU legislator and represent a manifestation of loyal collaboration among Member States and between Member States and the Union.

267 Rec. 37 of the DSA clarifies that the information order can only relate to individual users.

268 Rec. 34 DSA.

269 Rec. 12 of the DSA provides guidance on the interpretation of the characteristic "illegal content" and thus demonstrates the importance of uniform application.

270 For example, Art. 5 Info Directive (EU) 2015/1535.

271 In this direction also Slot CML Rev. 1996, 1035; Rec. 2 DSA also sees the internal market affected by national legislation.

§ 4
Transparency obligations

Literature: *Achleitner*, Digital Markets Act beschlossen: Verhaltenspflichten und Rolle nationaler Wettbewerbsbehörden, NZKart 2022, 359; *Alexander*, Anwendungsbereich, Regelungstechnik und einzelne Transparenzvorgaben der P2B-Verordnung, WRP 2020, 945; *Alexander*, Transparenz in der Plattformwirtschaft, GRUR 2023, 14; *Busch/Dannemann/Schulte-Nölke*, Bausteine für ein europäisches Recht der Plattformökonomie, MMR 2020, 667; *Cornils*, Präzisierung, Vervollständigung und Erweiterung: Die Änderungen des Netzwerkdurchsetzungsgesetzes 2021, NJW 2021, 2465; *Ebner*, Weniger ist Mehr? Die Informationspflichten der DS-GVO – Eine kritische Analyse, 2022; *Ebner*, Information Overload 2.0?, ZD 2022, 364; *Flamme*, Schutz der Meinungsvielfalt im digitalen Raum, MMR 2021, 770; *Frank*, Inhaltemoderation, MMR 2022, 1026; *Gerpott*, Das Gesetz über digitale Dienste nach den Trilog-Verhandlungen, CR 2022, 516; *Gielen/Uphues*, Digital Markets Act und Digital Services Act, EuZW 2021, 627; *Hacker*, KI und DMA – Zugang, Transparenz und Fairness für KI-Modelle in der digitalen Wirtschaft, GRUR 2022, 1278; *Härting/Adamek*, Digital Services Act, IPRB 2021, 100; *Härting/Adamek*, Digital Services Act – ein Überblick, CR 2021, 165; *Janal*, Haftung und Verantwortung im Entwurf des Digital Services Acts, ZEuP 2021, 227; *Kalbhenn/Hemmert-Halswick*, EU-weite Vorgaben für die Content-Moderation in sozialen Netzwerken, ZUM 2021, 184; *Kerber*, Datenrechtliche Aspekte des Digital Markets Act, ZD 2021, 544; *Kocher*, Digitale Plattformarbeit – die Verantwortung von Marktorganisatoren, ZEuP 2021, 606; *Kuhlmann/Trute*, Die Regulierung von Desinformationen und rechtswidrigen Inhalten nach dem neuen Digital Services Act, GSZ 2022, 115; *Kumkar*, Plattform-Recht revisited: Umgang mit den Marktforderungen digitaler Plattformen de lege lata et ferenda, ZEuP 2022, 530; *Kuß/Lehmann*, Digital Services Act – Entwurf eines einheitlichen Rechtsrahmens für die EU-Digitalwirtschaft, DB 2021, 605; *Möllers/Kernchen*, Information Overload am Kapitalmarkt, ZGR 2011, 1; *Naumann/Rodenhausen*, Die P2B-Verordnung aus Unternehmenssicht: Herausforderungen für europäische Plattformen am Beispiel einer Hybrid-Online-Plattform, ZEuP 2020, 768; *Paal/Kieß*, Digitale Plattformen im DSA-E, DMA-E und § 19a GWB, ZfDR 2022, 1; *Paal/Kumkar*, Die digitale Zukunft Europas, ZfDR 2021, 97; *Peifer*, Die neuen Transparenzregeln im UWG (Bewertungen, Rankings und Influencer), GRUR 2021, 1453; *Podszun*, Empfiehlt sich eine stärkere Regulierung von Online-Plattformen und anderen Digitalunternehmen?, NJW-Beil. 2022, 56; *Podszun/Kersting*, Eine Wettbewerbsordnung für das digitale Zeitalter, ZRP 2019, 34; *Podszun/Offergeld*, Plattformregulierung im Zivilrecht zwischen Wissenschaft und Gesetzgebung: Die ELI Model Rules on Online Platforms, ZEuP 2022, 244; *Raue/Heesen*, Der Digital Services Act, NJW 2022, 3537; *Rohrßen*, Internetvertrieb 2019/20 – Vertriebsvorgaben, (Best-)Preis & Platform-to-Business-Verordnung, ZVertriebsR 2019, 341; *Rössel*, Digital Services Act: Haftungsprivilegierungen, Überwachung und Blockadeanordnungen, ITRB 2023, 12; *Savary*, Der Digital Services Act steht vor der Tür: ein Meilenstein in der Regulierung von Online-Plattformen?, BB 2022, Heft 10, I; *Spindler*, Der Vorschlag für ein neues Haftungsregime für Internetprovider – der EU-Digital Services Act (Teil 1), GRUR 2021, 545; *Spindler/Seidel*, Die Regulierung von Online-Plattformen, NJW 2022, 2730; *Voigt/Eschborn/Bastians*, Weitreichende neue Pflichten für Host-Provider, MMR 2022, 727; *Weiden*, Neue Informationspflichten im Namen des Verbraucherschutzes, NJW 2021, 2233.

A. Introduction

The need for "greater transparency" in the digital economy is currently a much-discussed topic. Additionally, corresponding transparency obligations are being sought not only by the Union legislator, but also increasingly by national legislators and represent a popular tool in the area of **self-regulation (see → § 6 mn. 7 et seqq.).** Particularly in the case of such regulations, which are at least also of a consumer protection or competition law nature, an increased degree of transparency represents the pivotal point.[1] Transparency is often both a **goal** and a **means to** achieve it.[2] One of the advantages of transparency obligations is that they allow the legislator to avoid abstract bans on certain types of behaviour; instead, they rely on an increased level of information that is intended to protect recipients from making heedless decisions.[3] As an overarching goal, transparency obligations thus serve to create an adequate **basis of information that** empowers recipients to make an informed decision. Consequently, transparency obligations should generally achieve their protective effect by providing "more" information.[4] Hence, there is an intertwining of information requirements and transparency requirements.[5] 1

The Union legislator has recently introduced a wide range of transparency obligations and has identified the creation of a **transparent online environment** as one of its main objectives. Thus, the DSA[6] also identifies as one of its objectives the creation of a safe and transparent online environment, which is to be achieved by means of clear, effective, predictable and balanced harmonised due diligence obligations for intermediary information society services.[7] In addition, the DSA aims to mitigate the **risks** traditionally associated with digital services, such as purely algorithmic decision-making, 2

[1] Peifer GRUR 2021, 1453 (1453) with reference to the German UWG.
[2] Alexander GRUR 2023, 14 (14).
[3] Peifer GRUR 2021, 1453 (1453); Gerpott CR 2022, 516 (526).
[4] Podszun/Offergeld ZEuP 2022, 244 (253); Alexander WRP 2020, 945 (950).
[5] Alexander GRUR 2023, 14 (14).
[6] Regulation (EU) 2022/2065 of the European Parliament and of the Council of 19 October 2022 on a Single Market For Digital Services and amending Directive 2000/31/EC (Digital Services Act), OJ L 277, 1.
[7] Rec. 40 DSA (supra n 6).

disinformation campaigns and the dissemination of illegal content.[8] For this purpose, a large number of regulations were introduced that regulate **extensive disclosure and information obligations** of the individual information society services and are intended to ensure an appropriate level of information as well as the awareness of the individual recipient.

3 However, transparency and information obligations have generally proven to be not entirely without flaws. With their ever-increasing implementation, it has become apparent that the sheer mass of information made available by them sometimes overwhelms the addressees (“**information overload**”). The result is rational apathy and simple disregard of the disclosed information.[9] Nonetheless, even from the perspective of those obliged to disclose information, the corresponding requirements sometimes affect critical areas. For example, the disclosure obligations often concern sensitive data and, if applicable, **business secrets**. Especially in those areas where the disclosure obligations also affect **algorithm-based business models**, a simultaneous encroachment on business and trade secrets of the companies is often unavoidable.[10] Here lies a risk of conflicts with the law on the protection of trade secrets, which in Germany (in implementation of the Know-How Directive[11]) has found expression in the Code for the Protection of Trade Secrets.

B. Transparency obligations under the DSA

4 Ensuring transparency in the area of the digital economy can be described as one of the supporting pillars of the DSA.[12] Transparency is essentially intended to prevent arbitrary and abusive decisions by information society services by making them (more) comprehensible. The DSA attempts to achieve these goals by means of various regulations. However, no uniform, generally applicable obligations have been created. As with the other provisions of the DSA, the transparency obligations are rather **asymmetrically** structured and depend on the nature of the services offered by the digital information society service as well as its size, whereby a moderate and problem-oriented regulation is to be offered.[13]

5 In terms of content, two major transparency categories can be differentiated. There are regulations on general **transparency reporting obligations** as well as special regulations to create **transparency in online advertising**. These regulatory complexes are supplemented by various other transparency and information obligations as well as the possibility of introducing **codes of conduct**.

I. Transparency reporting obligations

6 The first broad category imposes reporting obligations on information society services regarding the **content moderation** or content management they carry out. Accord-

---

[8] Kuß/Lehmann DB 2021, 605 (605).

[9] Cf. generally on the parallel problem on the capital market Möllers/Kernchen ZGR 2011, 1 (6 et seq., 11 et seq.) and on the data economy Ebner ZD 2022, 364 (365 et seq.).

[10] Peifer GRUR 2021, 1453 (1455).

[11] Directive (EU) 2016/943 of the European Parliament and of the Council of 8 June 2016 on the protection of undisclosed know-how and business information (trade secrets) against their unlawful acquisition, use and disclosure, OJ L 157, 1.

[12] Gielen/Uphues EuZW 2021, 627 (636).

[13] DSA P. 7.

ing to this, information society services must prepare transparency reports at regular intervals, whereby the scope of the obligations depends on the classification of the information society service. Especially in this field, it has often been shown in the past that decisions of the information society services were sometimes hardly – or **only with great difficulty – comprehensible for those** affected. The transparency reports now potentially enable public, parliamentary as well as judicial control and discussion of the appropriateness and effects of content moderation[14] and, thus, at the same time strengthen the **rights of recipients**.

The requirements for the depth of content and the extent of the reports are staggered and are largely based on the size of the information society service. The **intensity** and **number** of obligations to be fulfilled increase with the information society service's size. More specifically, the DSA lays out three size categories, for which it provides corresponding regulations. In terms of content, the respective regulations are structured consecutively,[15] so that larger information society services must also observe the requirements for smaller counterparts. This differentiated gradation of the individual size categories and the associated staggered requirements are intended to reflect the different technical and actual capabilities, but also the **specific risks** of the individual information society services and represent the result of an intensive balancing of interests on the part of the Union legislator.[16] 7

1. Provisions for all providers of intermediary services

First of all, Art. 15 DSA contains **basic provisions** on the annual transparency reporting obligations that apply to all providers of intermediary services. These relate quite generally to the deletion and blocking behaviour of information society services in the area of content moderation and in this respect show similarities to the German regulations of the **NetzDG**.[17] The NetzDG contains comparable obligations for social network providers. § 2 of the NetzDG also stipulates a reporting obligation, according to which, if the threshold of 100 complaints about illegal content is exceeded, a German-language report on the handling of complaints about illegal content on the respective platform must be prepared every six months.[18] However, the regulations of the DSA are more detailed compared to its German contemporary and the scope of application is much broader, as all providers per se are affected by this.[19] 8

In general, Art. 15 DSA requires the preparation of an annual report on the content moderation operated by the provider of switching services, including the measures it has taken as a result of the application and enforcement of their terms and conditions. The provisions of Art. 15 DSA are a **minimum requirement**. This means that information society services are free to publish transparency reports with greater frequency, i.e. more than once every six months. The requirements of Art. 15 DSA serve as a kind of basic requirement and therefore apply to all providers of intermediary services. Thus, the obligations of Art. 15 DSA are intended to ensure a basic and **appropriate level of** transparency and accountability. 9

Nevertheless, there are individual information society services that are exempted from the scope of application of the transparency reporting obligation. Thus, according to Art. 15(2) DSA, such providers of intermediary services that can be qualified as **micro** 10

---

14 Raue/Heesen NJW 2022, 3537 (3540).
15 Rössel ITRB 2023, 12 (13).
16 Savary BB 2022, Iss. 10, I.
17 Paal/Kieß ZfDR 2022, 1 (28).
18 Cf. also Cornils NJW 2021, 2465 (2467 et seq.).
19 Spindler GRUR 2021, 545 (551).

or small enterprises in the sense of the Annex of Recommendation 2003/361/EC[20] are exempt from these publication obligations. This is intended to avoid disproportionate burdens on such providers.[21] This decision is ultimately in line with a large number of European legal acts that aim to protect smaller market participants from additional bureaucratic burdens and to reduce the burden of their obligations.[22]

11 The requirements of Art. 15(1) DSA can be divided into two subtypes. There are regulations for the **content** as well as for the **formal design** of the transparency report.

a) Formal requirements

12 The formal requirements for the transparency report follow directly from the introductory of Art. 15(1)(1) DSA. These reports must be formulated in a **clear and easily comprehensible manner**. This requirement is straightforward, as the transparency reports are intended to reduce existing **information asymmetries** vis-à-vis the largest possible group of stakeholders. This requires that the reports are written in such a way that, for the most part, problems of comprehension are not to be expected. From a purely technical point of view, the reports must be written in a **machine-readable format** and be easily **available to the public**. The latter is the case if the reports are accessible to everyone. For the interpretation of the term "machine-readable format", reference can be made to Art. 2 no. 13 Directive (EU) 2019/1024[23]. According to this, a file format is machine-readable if it is structured in such a way that software applications can easily identify, recognise and extract specific data, including individual statements of fact, and their internal structure. The background to this requirement is probably that this should enable **automated analysis** with the help of AI tools[24] and thus also ensure the **comparability of** the respective reports over time and across different providers.

13 From a formal point of view, the Commission can also adopt **implementing acts** pursuant to Art. 15(3) DSA in which it sets out templates concerning the form, content and other details of reports, including harmonised reporting periods. Corresponding legal acts are again useful in order to achieve better comparability of the transparency reports among each other and also to be able to better compare the corresponding internal structures of the providers of intermediary services.

b) Content requirements

14 The DSA contains more detailed information on the content requirements for the transparency report. Specifically, Art. 15(1)(2) DSA stipulates five specific aspects the transparency report must address. However, the inclusion of one of these aspects can be waived if the information does not apply to the specific information society service. Still, the aspects named are not an exhaustive list. Instead, according to the wording of the standard ("in particular"), the transparency report only has to present and elaborate on these aspects. In addition, **other relevant aspects** can be included in the transparency report on a voluntary basis.

---

[20] OJ L 124, 36.

[21] Rec. 49 DSA (supra n 6).

[22] For the definition of micro-enterprises and SMEs cf. Commission Recommendation of 6 May 2003 concerning the definition of micro, small and medium-sized enterprises, OJ L 124, 36, available at <https://eur-lex.europa.eu/legal-content/EN/TXT/PDF/?uri=CELEX:32003H0361&from=EN> (last accessed: 11.07.2024).

[23] Directive (EU) 2019/1024 of the European Parliament and of the Council of 20 June 2019 on open data and the re-use of public sector information, OJ L 172, 56.

[24] Busch/Dannemann/Schulte-Nölke MMR 2020, 667 (670).

However, these five concrete content-related requirements can be subdivided again according to the **target group**. On the one hand, there are requirements that every provider of intermediary services must fulfil. On the other hand, there are also requirements that are solely applicable to a limited group of addressees by referring to more specific regulations. 15

aa) Content requirements for all providers of intermediary services

Some of the content requirements apply to all information society services. The first of these aspects requires a list of the number of orders received from Member State authorities and the median time taken by the information society service to actually take the action required by these orders. This requirement therefore concerns the **time taken to respond** to such orders. In other words, it is intended to provide information on the extent to which official deletion and information orders have been complied with.[25] This includes, among other things, orders to act against illegal content as defined in Art. 9 DSA as well as orders to provide information according to Art. 10 DSA. However, Art. 15(1)(2)(a) DSA does not limit these specific orders. Furthermore, the information is to be **broken down** further based on various parameters. These parameters include the type of illegal content concerned, the Member State issuing the order and the median time needed to inform the authority issuing the order or any other authority specified in the order, of its receipt, and to give effect to the order. This information offers outsiders the possibility to assess the **efficiency of the** existing internal structures for reacting to corresponding content of the information society service and especially to **compare them** with other providers of intermediary services. 16

A second content-related requirement, which is directed at all providers of intermediary services, concerns content moderation that was carried out without an official request. Art. 15(1)(2)(c) DSA requires the provision of meaningful and comprehensible information about content moderation engaged in at the **providers' own initiative.** This also includes information on the extent to which automated tools were used for this purpose. Furthermore, insight into the **internal structures of** the information society service is required, as measures taken to train and support the persons responsible for moderating content must also be disclosed. Again, the number and type of measures taken that affect the availability, visibility and accessibility of information provided by recipients must be disclosed. Finally, information on the ability of recipients to provide such information through the service and other relevant limitations of the service must be listed. For the sake of clarity, the information reported must be **broken down according to three criteria**: first, the type of illegal content or violation of the information society service's terms and conditions; second, the method used to detect it; and third, the type of restriction applied. 17

Art. 15(1)(2)(e) DSA regulates a further content-related requirement. According to this, information must be provided on the **use of automated means in** content moderation. However, this information is only to be included if corresponding means were actually employed. This case mainly concerns the use of automated procedures, especially in the form of **algorithms**. What is required here is a qualitative description, details of the precise purposes and the provision of indicators of the accuracy. In addition, the possible **rate of error** of the automated means used for this purpose as well as any safeguards applied in this context must be listed. Unlike the other requirements of Art. 15(1) DSA, this one explicitly does not name an addressee. However, solely due to its specific 18

---

[25] Raue/Heesen NJW 2022, 3537 (3540); generally, on administrative orders Kuhlmann/Trute GSZ 2022, 115 (118).

location in Chapter III Section 1 (Provisions for all providers of switching services), it can be assumed that the provision is also addressed to all providers of intermediary services.

19 A final content-related requirement results from Art. 15(1)(2)(d) DSA. According to this, the number of complaints received through the internal complaint-handling systems in accordance with the provider's **terms and conditions must be** included in the transparency report. The basis for each individual complaint as well as the relevant decision of the information society service must be stated. In addition, **efficiency aspects** in the form of the median time required until the final decision is taken and the number of cases in which these decisions were eventually reversed must also be noted here.

bb) Further requirements for special target groups

20 The other substantive requirements of Art. 15(1)(2) DSA are – in principle – addressed to all providers of intermediary services due to their location in Chapter III Section 1. Nevertheless, they will not be relevant for every information society service. For example, information must be disclosed on how the information society services have reacted to reports under the notification and redress procedure from Art. 16 DSA (so-called **notice and action mechanism**)[26] and to complaints via the **internal complaint-handling system** under Art. 20 DSA.[27] However, these procedures do not apply to all providers of intermediary services but are only addressed to certain information society services. Thus, despite its location in Chapter III Section 1 (Provisions applicable to all providers of intermediary services) of the DSA, Art. 15 DSA at least indirectly contains provisions that are not originally addressed to all providers of such services.

21 Thus, Art. 15(1)(2)(b) DSA regulates a further substantive requirement for **hosting service providers**. This results inevitably from the fact that the notice and action mechanism of Art. 16 DSA is only addressed to this particular group of addressees. The transparency report must state the number of notices submitted in accordance with Art. 16 DSA and break them down according to further criteria. First, the type of allegedly illegal content concerned as well as the number of notices submitted by trusted flaggers must be stated. Furthermore, any action taken pursuant to the notices must be listed. A differentiation must be made as to whether the respective measure was taken based on the law or the terms and conditions of the provider. Finally, the number of notices processed by solely using automatic means and the median time needed for taking the action must be indicated.

22 Another provision, which at least possibly has a reduced group of addressees, is Art. 15(1)(2)(d) DSA. According to this, the number of complaints received via the **internal complaint-handling system** must be disclosed. There are two types of internal complaint management systems. Only after an information society service has been classified as an online platform is it obliged to maintain a system that meets the requirements of Art. 20 DSA. Essentially, such a system must provide the recipient with the possibility to lodge **complaints electronically and free of charge** against decisions taken by the provider of the online platform. If, on the contrary, an information society service is not yet classified as an online platform, there are no specific requirements for such an internal complaint-handling system. Such a system is only mentioned in Art. 14(1) DSA. According to this, information society services must set out the procedural rules for their internal complaint-handling system in their terms and conditions. However, the DSA does not contain a direct obligation to set up such a system in these cases. In this

[26] Kuhlmann/Trute GSZ 2022, 115 (116 et seq.).
[27] Raue/Heesen NJW 2022, 3537 (3540).

respect, there is an actual obligation to maintain a corresponding system only for information society services who surpass the threshold to the online platform, but not for all other information society services.

Pursuant to Art. 15(1)(2)(d) DSA, the **number of complaints** received via the internal complaint management system must be disclosed. In addition to the mere number, information on the basis for those complaints, the decisions taken in respect of those complaints, the median time needed for taking those decisions and the number of instances where those decisions were reversed must also be disclosed. 23

c) *Summary*

Overall, it can be stated that the transparency reporting obligations directed at all providers of intermediary services are not only aimed at providing information on the removal and blocking of information that is considered illegal content or violates the provider's terms and conditions. Rather, it should give stakeholders additional **insights into the internal processes** of the information society service. For the first time, relevant factors such as the efficiency with which corresponding cases are reacted to, as well as the internal structures that are kept in place to deal with these issues, are to be effectively disclosed. In the long run, this will provide the basis for an **efficiency assessment** of the individual information society services as well as the possibility for a **direct comparison** of the individual actors. Furthermore, it will become clear whether the action of the information society service is primarily forced by outside complaints and to what percentage there is original action on the part of the information society services themselves. 24

2. Provisions for online platforms

In accordance with the staggered structure of the transparency reporting obligations, there are further requirements for providers of online platforms. These are set out in Art. 24 DSA. The obligations contained therein have different starting points and directions. 25

a) *Extensions of the transparency report according to Art. 15 DSA*

First of all, Art. 24(1) DSA extends the basic requirements of Art. 15 DSA on transparency reporting obligations for providers of online platforms. According to the wording, these are not optional but **disclosures of a mandatory nature**. These additional requirements are justified by the special responsibility and duties of online platforms.[28] The requirements contained herein are linked to the even more far-reaching special requirements imposed on online platforms by Section 3 of Chapter 3. 26

According to Art. 24(1)(a) DSA, the number of disputes submitted to the out-of-court dispute settlement bodies mentioned in Art. 21 DSA (see → § 5 mn. 6, 2 et seqq.) must be listed. Similar to Art. 15 DSA, the **outcomes of** the dispute resolution and **median duration** until the conclusion of the dispute resolution proceedings as well as the proportion of disputes in which the online platform providers implemented the decisions of the body must be stated. 27

Furthermore, according to Art. 24(1)(b) DSA, online platforms must publish reports on their activities to remove and block information that is considered **illegal content** or violates their terms and conditions. Specifically, this involves information on the number of suspensions as a measure to combat and protect against misuse according to Art. 23 28

[28] Rec. 65 DSA (supra n 6).

DSA. The information must be broken down based on the different alternatives contained in Art. 23 DSA. More specifically, a distinction must be made between suspensions enacted for the provision of manifestly illegal content, the submission of manifestly unfounded notices and the submission of manifestly unfounded complaints.

b) Obligation to publish the average number of monthly active recipients

29 Moreover, Art. 24(2) DSA contains further dissemination obligations that go beyond those of the transparency report. If this is primarily intended to provide an insight into the internal structures and the handling of illegal content as well as disputes, this obligation deals with the question of the **legal classification** of the online platform. Thus, Art. 24(2) DSA contains obligations to publish and communicate information on the average number of monthly active recipients of the service in the Union. This number is calculated as an average over the period of the past six months and in accordance with the methodology laid down in the delegated acts referred to in Art. 33(3) DSA. Both online platforms and online search engines are affected by this. The disclosure must be made for the first time by 17th of February 2023. Thereafter, the number of recipients must be updated on a rolling basis, **at least every six months**. This disclosure obligation was introduced primarily to enable the competent authorities to determine whether an online platform or an online search engine is to be considered a very large online platform or a very large online search engine and, thus, to impose the increased obligations of Art. 33 et seq. DSA.[29] Hence, the requirements have a **procedural character**.

30 In addition to these disclosure obligations, the Digital Services Coordinator at the place of establishment and the Commission have the possibility to **request** this information from online platforms or online search engines at any time pursuant to Art. 24(3)(1) DSA. In this case, this information must be updated without undue delay and at the moment of such request. In addition, it is possible to request additional information on the calculation as well as explanations and substantiation in respect of the data used pursuant to Art. 24(3)(3) DSA. However, these shall not contain any personal information. If the Digital Services Coordinator at the place of establishment has reason to believe, after reviewing the data, that a provider of an online platform or an online search engine meets the threshold of average monthly active recipients in the Union set out in Art. 33(1) DSA, it shall notify the Commission thereof pursuant to Art. 24(4) DSA. Thus, even in the **interim between two mandatory disclosures,** there is always the possibility to check whether the thresholds have been exceeded. However, since this is a separate procedure from the disclosure pursuant to Art. 24(2) DSA, this will probably have no influence on the publication periods.

c) Disclosure of the reasons for recipient restrictions following the provision of illegal content

31 Finally, pursuant to Art. 24(5)(1) DSA, providers of online platforms are obliged to provide the Commission with the decisions and the statements of reasons referred to in Art. 17(1) DSA, in a standard format and without undue delay after the decision. This concerns **restrictions imposed on the recipient** due to the provision of information with illegal content or due to a breach of the terms of use. This can range from mere restrictions on the visibility of individual information provided by the recipient to suspension or closure of the recipient's account. This information is fed into a publicly accessible machine-readable **database** managed by the Commission. In doing so, the

[29] Rec. 65 DSA (supra n 6).

providers of online platforms must ensure that the information transmitted does not contain any personal data. This is intended not only to increase the transparency of decisions by providers of online platforms, but also to enable monitoring. In order to promote efficient achievement of the objective, the narrow time criterion ("without undue delay") was included. This is to ensure that the database is **updated in real time.**[30]

3. Provisions for very large online platforms and very large online search engines

In addition to the listed transparency obligations, there is also a final level of stricter obligations for very large online platforms and very large online search engines. These are to be classified as "very large" if they exceed the **threshold of** an average monthly number of 45 million active recipients in the Union and have been **designated as such**, Art. 33(1) and (4) DSA. These additional obligations derive from Art. 42 DSA and are based on the specific **systemic risks associated** with the activities of such providers as well as the additional obligations imposed on them under this Regulation.[31] Again, a division can be made into three different types of supplementary transparency obligations. 32

a) *Supplementary information for the transparency report*

From a formal point of view, Art. 42(1) DSA initially provides for an **increased reporting frequency** of transparency reports for providers of very large online platforms or very large online search engines. Initially, the transparency report must be published at the latest by two months from the date of application specified in Art. 33(6) subpara. 2 DSA. Thereafter, the frequency increases to at least every six months. Thus, the reporting obligations for corresponding information society services are doubled. In addition to these technical aspects, Art. 42(2) DSA also imposes additional information requirements on providers of very large online search engines, which must be included on top of the information specified in Art. 15 and 24(1) DSA. According to the wording, these additions are again not optional, but **mandatory** information, which must also be published in at least one of the official languages of the Member States. This concerns three supplementary points, which, however, are again not always addressed to both online platforms and online search engines. 33

The additional requirements of Art. 42(2)(1)(a) DSA are directed exclusively at providers of very large online platforms. These must provide information on the **human resources** dedicated to content moderation in respect to the service offered in the Union. This information must also include the human resources used to comply with the obligations to maintain the reporting and redress mechanism under Art. 16 DSA and to deal with reports from trusted flaggers within the scope of Art. 22 DSA and within the framework of the internal complaints-handling system under Art. 20 DSA. The corresponding resources are to be **broken down** according to each applicable official language of the Member States. 34

In addition, Art. 42(2)(1)(b) DSA stipulates that the qualifications and linguistic expertise of the persons assigned to these tasks must be stated. Furthermore, information on the relevant training and the support available to the staff must be provided. 35

Finally, according to Art. 42(2)(1)(c) DSA, further information on the use of **automated means for moderating content** must be included. This supplements the basic 36

[30] Rec. 66 DSA (supra n 6).
[31] Rec. 100 DSA (supra n 6).

rule of Art. 15(1)(e) DSA and again concerns **algorithm-based decisions**. Specifically, additional indicators of accuracy and related information must be offered. These are in turn to be broken down by each official language of the Member States.

b) Additional information within the scope of publication pursuant to Art. 24(2) DSA

37 The recipient figures that must be published according to Art. 24(2) DSA must also be **supplemented** with additional information according to Art. 42(3) DSA. This regulation affects both providers of very large online platforms and those of very large online search engines. Furthermore, the average monthly recipients for each Member State must also be included in the general transparency report.

c) Additional transparency obligations

38 The last extended disclosures only apply to very large online platforms which, due to their reach, play a central, systemic role in promoting public debate and economic transactions. Smaller providers, on the other hand, are completely exempt from the obligations. These tie in with the **independent audit** obligations under Art. 37 DSA. This independent audit serves to ensure compliance with the due diligence obligations for a transparent and safe online environment contained in Chapter III of the DSA, as well as the commitments arising from the codes of conduct in Art. 45, 46 DSA and the crisis protocols referred to in Art. 48 DSA. For this purpose, at the latest three months after receipt of the audit report pursuant to Art. 37(4) DSA, various documents must be transmitted to the digital services coordinator at the place of establishment and the Commission without delay after completion.

39 Specifically, a report on the **results of the risk assessment** pursuant to Art. 34 DSA, the **audit report** pursuant to Art. 37(4) DSA itself as well as the **report on the implementation of the audit results** pursuant to Art. 37(6) DSA must be made available for this purpose. Furthermore, information on special remedial measures taken in accordance with Art. 35(1) DSA to adequately, proportionately and effectively mitigate the particular individual systemic risks must be included. Lastly, information on the consultations carried out by the provider to support the risk assessments and the design of the risk mitigation measures must be provided, where such consultations have been carried out.

40 Restrictions arise only from Art. 42(5) DSA. Thus, providers of a very large online platform or a very large online search engine are entitled to remove some individual cases from the publicly accessible information. However, this restriction is subject to additional conditions. For example, **removal is only permissible** in cases where the disclosure of the listed information would at the same time lead to the disclosure of confidential information of that provider or its recipients, cause significant vulnerabilities to the security of its service, undermines public safety or could pose harm to recipients. However, the possibility to remove such information only concerns the public part of the report. Nonetheless, the **full reports** shall continue to be sent to the Digital Services Coordinator at the place of establishment and to the Commission.

4. Summary

41 For the first time, the transparency reports will provide comprehensive **insights into content moderation** of the information society services. In this respect, it is to be expected that the currently existing information asymmetries will be at least partially reduced. As with many disclosure obligations, however, the question arises as to whether these will actually result in an improved information environment, especially for the

recipient. In order to effectively reduce the existing lack of transparency and to achieve the goals pursued with the DSA, the transparency reports must be **meaningful** and also at least somewhat **comparable.**[32] Whether this will actually be the case remains to be seen. In any case, the information society services will always have to weigh up between the protection of their business secrets and the transparency requirements incumbent on them.[33] It is yet to be seen, however, whether the reprisals to be feared in the case of a violation of the corresponding obligations are actually sufficiently serious so that the information society services, in case of doubt, see themselves obliged to disclose even sensitive information. In any case, it can be assumed that the transparency reporting obligations will lead to a considerable **additional effort** for the information society services concerned.[34]

II. Transparency of online advertising

The second large block of transparency obligations concerns online advertising. Until now, there were already corresponding **labelling obligations** according to Art. 7(2) of the Unfair Commercial Practices Directive[35], which, however, only affected the respective trader, i.e. the advertiser itself. This labelling obligation is now considerably expanded by the DSA and extended to online platforms, which is not least due to the fact that their main source of income is traditionally advertising revenue.[36] In addition, the Union legislator recognises **considerable risks**, especially in the area of advertising. For example, advertising itself could be illegal content, contribute to financial incentives for the publication or amplification of illegal or otherwise harmful content and activities online, or the discriminatory presentation of advertisements with an impact on the equal treatment and opportunities of citizens.[37] **42**

Where the DSA overlaps with the GDPR[38], it is noted that the transparency obligations only **complement** the specific requirements of the GDPR, but do **not amend** them. Such an overlap may occur in particular[39] regarding consents and the right to object to the processing of personal data (Art. 7 GDPR) concerning advertising on online platforms. It is precisely here that the transparency obligations of the DSA are intended to enable and facilitate recipients to make use of their rights as data subjects.[40] **43**

1. Provisions for online platforms

Regulations on transparency in online advertising do not exist for all providers of intermediary services, but **only** apply **above a certain size**. Thus, Art. 26 DSA, as the "low- **44**

[32] So also, Gielen/Uphues EuZW 2021, 627 (636) with reference to the transparency reports of the NetzDG, in which precisely these aspects were considerably criticised.

[33] Savary BB 2022, Iss. 10, I.

[34] Savary BB 2022, Iss. 10, I.

[35] Directive 2005/29/EC of the European Parliament and of the Council of 11 May 2005 concerning unfair business-to-consumer commercial practices in the internal market and amending Council Directive 84/450/EEC, Directives 97/7/EC, 98/27/EC and 2002/65/EC of the European Parliament and of the Council and Regulation (EC) No 2006/2004 of the European Parliament and of the Council (Unfair Commercial Practices Directive), OJ L 149, 22.

[36] Raue/Heese NJW 2022, 3537 (3542).

[37] Rec. 68 DSA (supra n 6).

[38] Regulation (EU) 2016/679 of the European Parliament and of the Council of 27 April 2016 on the protection of natural persons with regard to the processing of personal data and on the free movement of such data, and repealing Directive 95/46/EC (General Data Protection Regulation), OJ L 119, 1.

[39] In addition, note in particular Art. 5(1)(a), Art. 12–15 GDPR.

[40] Commission Explanatory Memorandum on the proposed Digital Services Act COM(2020), 825 final, 5.

est level" of transparency requirements in the area of advertising, is only addressed to online platforms. For information society services that are not to be classified as online platforms, however, there are **no special regulations** in this area. Thus, the DSA does not impose any additional transparency obligations on such information society services.

45 In terms of content, Art. 26 DSA only has a **protective character in favor of the recipients**, but not in favour of the advertisers. The latter are not considered at any point in the provisions of the DSA. Instead, Art. 26 DSA obliges the online platform to display to the recipient in a clear, concise, and unambiguous manner and in real time a conclusively regulated amount of information about the displayed advertising. This essentially includes that the information is an advertisement in the first place and by whom it was placed. Thus, Art. 26(1)(a) DSA provides for a **highlighted identification** of information as commercial advertising. For this purpose, recourse can be made to corresponding voluntary standards, which can be issued according to Art. 44(1)(h) DSA. However, the use of corresponding standards is at the discretion of the information society service. This regulation is intended to enable the recipient to recognise advertising beyond any doubt and not to be misled into clicking on corresponding banners under the false assumption of neutral information.

46 Furthermore, according to Art. 26(1)(b) DSA, the natural or legal person on whose behalf the advertisement is displayed must be recognisable. This is to make it clear to whom the corresponding advertising message is to be attributed and to increase **recognizability as an advertising message**. However, if the advertising is paid for by another natural or legal person, this person must also be recognisable according to Art. 26(1)(c) DSA.

47 Lastly, pursuant to Art. 26(1)(d) DSA, the online platform must provide meaningful information on the most important parameters for determining the recipients to whom the advertisement is presented. This includes, for example, information on whether the advertisement is **contextual** or **another type of** advertisement.[41] This creates special regulations that address so-called microtargeting, where advertising is not shown to everyone, but only to specific recipients.[42] Particularly in personalised advertisements using targeting techniques, which may match the interests of the recipient and possibly also appeal to the recipient's vulnerabilities, the Union legislator recognises a considerable **potential danger** and negative effects, which are in part also capable of increasing social damage. Specifically, disinformation campaigns or discriminating against certain groups are feared.[43] It is precisely in this area that the problems of algorithm-based decisions once again become clear. These are typically characterised by their **lack of transparency**, since the parameters that the algorithm uses for its decision-making usually remain largely unknown.[44] In order to address this problem, the Union legislator has recently introduced regulations that provide for more intensive regulation of such systems that are based exclusively on algorithm-based decisions.[45] The corresponding information in the context of transparency reports also falls into this category.

48 However, it seems problematic that it remains unclear which information is to be classified as "**significant**". General information such as recipient behaviour, access time or access location are unlikely to be included here, as this is generally known and, therefore, unlikely to be classified as "significant" or suitable for actually increasing the level

---

[41] Rec. 68 DSA (supra n 6).
[42] Kalbhenn/Hemmert-Halswick ZUM 2021, 184 (191).
[43] Rec. 69 DSA (supra n 6).
[44] Flamme MMR 2021, 770 (771).
[45] Kuß/Lehmann DB 2021, 605 (608); similarly Flamme MMR 2021, 770 (774).

of transparency.[46] It also remains unclear to what extent this information is available for the information society services at all. This is because the respective advertising spaces are often not marketed by themselves, but by **advertising networks**, so that the information society service may not have unhindered access to the necessary information.[47] In the long term, this problem may be addressed by introducing corresponding codes of conduct according to Art. 46 DSA (→ § 7 mn. 1, 9 et seqq.). In this respect, there are also fears of overlaps with the e-Privacy Regulation[48], which is currently still in the drafting stage and which, in addition to the GDPR, is also intended to regulate the problems of personalised advertising.[49]

Information must also be provided on how these parameters can be **changed under certain** circumstances. This information must be directly and easily accessible from the advertisement. How exactly this **easy access** can be designed in practice has not yet been conclusively clarified. It seems to make little sense to include this information with every advertisement banner or to list it in the immediate vicinity. It would be much more practicable to offer the online platforms the possibility to keep such parameters accessible by means of a corresponding **link** and a reference placed on it. Such a procedure seems sensible, not least to prevent information overload.[50] 49

As important as the clear recognisability of commercial information is, the question still arises as to whether the provisions of Art. 26 DSA offer actual added value. In terms of content, there is considerable **overlap with** Art. 6 E-Commerce Directive[51].[52] The latter already provides in its lit. a and lit. b that commercial communication, i.e. advertisement, must be clearly identifiable as such and that the natural or legal person on whose behalf the commercial communication is made shall also be clearly identifiable. Art. 26 DSA merely requests additional information regarding the parameters applied. It remains to be seen whether this is actually a significant gain in transparency in the eyes of the individual recipients. 50

An innovation compared to the first draft of the DSA is stipulated in Art. 26(2) DSA. This obliges online platforms to provide recipients with a **functionality to** declare whether the content they provide is or contains a commercial communication. This addresses the manifold problems that especially advertising messages on social media platforms such as Instagram entail. The labelling must be prominent and allow other recipients to clearly and unambiguously identify the advertisement recipient's information as commercial in real time. 51

2. Provisions for very large online platforms and very large online search engines.

The DSA provides further requirements for providers of very large online platforms or very large online search engines if they display advertisements. This further obliga- 52

---

[46] Kuß/Lehmann DB 2021, 605 (608).

[47] Härting/Adamek CR 2021, 165 (170 et seq.); Kuß/Lehmann DB 2021, 605 (608 et seq.).

[48] Proposal for a Regulation of the European Parliament and of the Council concerning the respect for private life and the protection of personal data in electronic communications and repealing Directive 2002/58/EC (Regulation on Privacy and Electronic Communications), of 10.1.2017, COM(2017), 10 final, available <https://eur-lex.europa.eu/legal-content/EN/TXT/PDF/?uri=CELEX:52017PC0010&from=EN≥ (last accessed: 11.07.2024).

[49] Cf. Härting/Adamek CR 2021, 165 (170 et seq.).

[50] Janal ZEuP 2021, 227 (268 et seq.).

[51] Directive 2000/31/EC of the European Parliament and of the Council of 8 June 2000 on certain legal aspects of information society services, in particular electronic commerce, in the Internal Market ('Directive on electronic commerce'), OJ L 178, 1.

[52] Janal ZEuP 2021, 227 (268).

tion is justified by the greater reach of such platforms and the special risks resulting from the behavioural analyses perfected by these platforms for targeted advertising.[53] Such providers are obliged to maintain a **repository** containing various information on the advertisements placed. Pursuant to Art. 39(1)(1) DSA, the information must be made publicly available in this repository for the entire period during which they present an advertisement and until one year after the advertisement was presented for the last time on their online interfaces. The repository must be designed in such a way that it is **reliable and searchable** according to several criteria. The information contained in the repository must be precise and complete. Only personal data of recipients of the service to whom the advertisement was or could have been presented shall be removed from the archive.

53 The information that providers of very large online platforms or very large online search engines must include is derived from Art. 39(2) DSA. However, according to the wording ("at least"), these are minimum requirements. The information society services concerned are permitted to include additional information in the archive. The **minimum information** includes the natural or legal person on whose behalf the advertisement is presented, the natural or legal person who paid for the advertisement, if there is a discrepancy with the advertiser in this respect, as well as, if applicable, the main parameters used to display the advertisement specifically to one or more certain groups of recipients or to exclude a certain group of recipients. In this respect, there are clear **overlaps with the** requirements of Art. 26(1) DSA, which contain the information that providers of online platforms must make available to their recipients. A further link to the rules for online platforms is provided by Art. 39(2)(f) in conjunction with Art. 26(2) DSA. According to this, information on commercial communications that recipients publish using the tool to be created by the platforms to identify advertising must also be included in the archive. In addition, the **content of the advertisement**, including the name of the product, service or brand and the subject matter of the advertisement, the period during which it was displayed, and the total number of recipients reached and, where applicable, aggregated figures broken down by Member State for the group or groups of recipients to whom the advertisement was targeted, must be included in the repository.

54 Only Art. 39(3) DSA contains an **exception** according to which certain information is not to be included in the repository. This is the case if a provider of a very large online platform or very large online search engine has removed or disabled access to a specific advertisement based on alleged illegality or incompatibility with its terms and conditions. Instead, in such cases, the legal basis on which the order to take action against illegal content or the justification on which the restriction of use is based must be provided pursuant to Art. 39(3) subpara. 1 sent. 2 DSA.

3. Appreciation

55 As sensible as increased transparency is, especially in the area of online advertisements, it remains more than questionable whether the DSA actually brings about significant progress. Because in terms of content, Art. 26 DSA is largely **redundant,** as corresponding regulations already exist in Art. 6 E-Commerce Directive. In addition, the DSA focuses exclusively on the interests of recipients and, thus, advertising addressees. However, the **interests of advertisers** are completely ignored. They too can suffer disadvantages from the opacity of advertisements via online platforms. For example, many advertisers have a considerable interest in knowing in which context the online platform

[53] Rec. 95 DSA (supra n 6); Kalbhenn/Hemmert-Halswick ZUM 2021, 184 (191 et seq.).

displays its advertisement and which content is (indirectly) financed by it.[54] After all, there is the likelihood that the advertisement addressees will associate the message with the other content in its direct vicinity. If this involves dubious content, e.g. of a radical nature, it is also in the interest of the advertiser to be informed about this in order to avoid damage to its image and, if necessary, to be given the opportunity to influence the advertisement context. This problem arises repeatedly and results from the fact that advertisement, especially via social media and search engines, is often automated and based on the intensity of recipient interaction, whereby the latter is often highest with attention-seeking content with possibly incorrect or radical information.[55] However, corresponding transparency obligations that address this well-known problem are missing entirely in the DSA.

III. General transparency and information obligations

In addition to these concrete transparency obligations for specific areas, there are other regulations that aim to **further inform** recipients and, thus, ultimately to create additional transparency. Some of these are more general regulations which indirectly lead to an increase in transparency, but some are also more far-reaching original transparency regulations in adjacent areas. Here, too, a subdivision based on the size of the information society service is possible. 56

1. Regulations for all providers of intermediary services

Corresponding indirect regulations for an additional gain in transparency result, among other things, from the more far-reaching specifications in the design of the **terms and conditions**. The Union legislator considers the associated encroachment on the contractual freedom of information society services to be appropriate in order to create the necessary transparency and to achieve an appropriate level of protection for recipients and to avoid unfair and arbitrary outcomes.[56] 57

This basic regulatory approach is not new. Rather, the Union legislator has already introduced additional provisions, particularly in the area of terms and conditions, in the **P2B-Reg.**[57], which also promise a gain in transparency (on this → § 17 mn. 27 et seqq.). The need for additional transparency arises especially in the field of **content moderation**. For example, the deletion of a large part of the content is not based on legal requirements, but on the **private autonomous decisions** of the information society services.[58] Thus, Art. 14 DSA is intended to prevent information society services from making **arbitrary** decisions about the removal or blocking of content that is not in accordance with their contractual terms.[59] For this reason, Art. 14 DSA establishes additional requirements for the wording of terms and conditions concerning manual or automated content moderation. This is intended to increase the **predictability of** corresponding decisions for recipients. In this respect, the algorithms used in this context become particularly relevant. As a consequence, the transparency obligation does not only concern the 58

54 Janal ZEuP 2021, 227 (269).

55 Cf. Janal ZEuP 2021, 227 (268) with the example of the British government, whose advertising messages were shown on YouTube in 2017 without their knowledge before the videos of Islamist hate preachers.

56 Rec. 45 DSA (supra n 6); also Härting/Adamek IPRB 2021, 100 (101).

57 Regulation (EU) 2019/1150 of the European Parliament and of the Council of 20 June 2019 on promoting fairness and transparency for business users of online intermediation services, OJ L 186, 57.

58 Raue/Heesen NJW 2022, 3537 (3540).

59 Spindler GRUR 2021, 545 (551).

terms and conditions per se, but also the procedures used in the area of content moderation.[60] Thus, according to Art. 14(1) DSA, all providers of intermediary services are obliged to provide **information in** their terms and conditions on any restrictions that they impose in relation to the use of their service in respect of information provided by the recipients of the service. These disclosures must also include information on any policies, procedures, measures and tools used for the purpose of content moderation, including algorithmic decision-making and human review, as well as the rules of procedure of their internal complaint handling system. In doing so, information society services are obliged under Art. 14(5) DSA to carry out a **comprehensive balancing of interests** and to act objectively and proportionately.

59 To ensure general comprehensibility, the relevant passages in the terms and conditions must be written in a **clear, plain, intelligible, user-friendly, and unambiguous language** and made publicly available in an easily accessible and machine-readable format. This regulation is reminiscent of the requirements for terms and conditions according to Art. 3(1) P2B-Reg., as its content is almost identical.

60 When drafting these passages, however, the addressees of the platform must also be taken into account. The **protection of minors**, which is already stipulated in Art. 28 DSA for providers of online platforms, is expanded upon. Such providers of intermediary services that are primarily directed at minors or that are predominantly used by minors shall, according to Art. 14(3) DSA, explain the relevant conditions for, and any restrictions on, the use of the service in such a way that (also) minors can understand. If the terms and conditions are subject to any significant **change**, the recipient shall be informed of this in accordance with Art. 14(2) DSA. This ought to increase transparency for the recipient which restrictions exist for the use of the services of the provider of intermediary services.

2. Regulations for online platforms

61 There are also more far-reaching transparency requirements for online platforms in the general regulations. For example, pursuant to Art. 23(4) DSA they are additionally obliged to set out in a diligent, objective and proportionate manner in their terms and conditions their rules for applying and enforcing the restrictions in the aforementioned **cases of abuse** (see → § 5 mn. 7, 9 et seq.). Furthermore, they need to disclose the facts and circumstances they use to classify conduct as abusive as well as the duration of a possible suspension. Here, too, the aim is not to interfere gratuitously with the individual contractual and creative freedom of information society services, but to achieve a sufficient **minimum level of clarity and precision of** the relevant rules and to ensure an **appropriate level of transparency.**[61]

62 A more specific supplementary transparency provision for providers of online platforms results from Art. 27 DSA. This applies exclusively to information society services who use **recommender systems.** They are obliged to increase transparency in this regard. Thus – again in the terms and conditions – the main **parameters that** they use in their recommender systems as well as all possibilities for recipients to modify or influence those main parameters must be set out. In doing so, the parameters must explain why certain information is suggested to the individual recipient. There are certain **minimum standards** for this information, which, according to Art. 27(2)(2) DSA, include the criteria that are most significant in determining the information suggested to the recipient as well as the reasons for the relative importance of those parameters. Finally, ac-

---

[60] Spindler GRUR 2021, 545 (551).

[61] Rec. 64 DSA (supra n 6).

cording to Art. 27(3) DSA, recipients must be provided with an easily accessible function by means of which the preferred option can be selected and changed at any time. That functionality shall be directly and easily accessible from the specific section of the online platform's online interface where the information is being prioritised.

Finally, there are transparency-related special regulations for providers of online plat- **63**
forms that enable consumers to conclude **distance contracts** with traders. According to Art. 29 DSA, micro or small enterprises are once more exempt from these regulations. These are linked to the creation of a safe, trustworthy and, in particular, transparent online environment for consumers as well as for other stakeholders, such as competing traders or holders of intellectual property rights. For example, online platforms that enable consumers to conclude distance contracts with traders are obliged under Art. 30 DSA to ensure that these traders provide the information designated therein and thus do not remain anonymous. This is to prevent traders from selling products and services in violation of the applicable rules.[62] To this end, relevant information society services must collect various information from traders using their online platform and make best efforts to assess whether this information is reliable and complete. This obligation is supplemented by a **right to information** on the part of consumers. If a relevant online platform provider becomes aware that an unlawful product or service has been offered by a trader to consumers in the Union through its services, it is obliged to inform the consumers who have acquired the unlawful product or service through its services about various aspects, including the identity of the trader and the relevant remedies.

3. Additional regulations for providers of very large online platforms and very large online search engines

Finally, and due to their special role and reach, further requirements apply to very **64**
large online platforms as well as very large online search engines.[63] According to Art. 14(6) DSA, such information society services shall publish their terms and conditions in the **official languages** of all the Member States in which they offer their services. Furthermore, in order to prevent "information overload", also an **easily accessible and machine-readable summary** of the terms and conditions, including the available remedies and redress mechanisms is to be made available to recipients, Art. 14(5) DSA. This includes the main elements of the information requirements, including the possibility of easily opting out from optional clauses.[64]

Additionally, Art. 38 DSA provides further requirements regarding the recommender **65**
systems used. Thus, the respective providers must consistently ensure that alternative options are available to the recipients of their service for the most important parameters of their recommender systems, which are not based on **profiling within the** meaning of the DSA (Art. 4 no. 4, Art. 22 DSA). This choice shall be directly accessible from the online interface where the recommendations are presented.[65]

IV. Granting access to data

Another aspect that can be subsumed under the term transparency obligation in the **66**
broadest sense is the obligation of very large online platforms to provide access to certain data to the Digital Services Coordinator at the place of establishment or to the

[62] Rec. 72 DSA (supra n 6).
[63] Rec. 48 DSA (supra n 6).
[64] Rec. 48 DSA (supra n 6).
[65] Rec. 94 DSA (supra n 6).

Commission upon their **reasoned request** pursuant to Art. 40(1) DSA (see → § 6 mn. 95 et seqq.). The use of this data is, however, **restricted to a specific purpose,** so that it may only be used to monitor and assess compliance with the DSA. Furthermore, according to Art. 40(2) DSA, various aspects such as the rights and interests of the concerned providers of very large online platforms or very large online search engines and recipients, including the protection of personal data, the protection of confidential information, in particular trade secrets, and the maintenance of the security of their service, must be considered. However, the provider has the possibility to **amend the request**. Thus, according to Art. 40(5) DSA, he can ask the requesting body to change the request if he either does not have access to the requested data (lit. a) or if granting access to the data will lead to significant vulnerabilities in the security of his service or in the protection of confidential information, in particular trade secrets (lit. b). In the latter case, the very large online platform is obliged under Art. 40(6) DSA to submit **proposals** for one or more alternative means through which access may be provided to the requested data or other data which are appropriate and sufficient for the purpose of the request.

67 Pursuant to Art. 40(4), (8–12) DSA, corresponding data access can also be granted to so-called **vetted researchers**. This possibility was generally welcomed, as it is hoped that it will provide additional insight into the opaque conditions within the platform economy. In particular, it aims to eliminate information asymmetries, ensure a resilient risk mitigation system and provide information to online platform providers, online search engine providers, digital service coordinators, other competent authorities, the Commission and the public.[66] However, access to data is also to be limited to this. For example, Art. 40(4) DSA explicitly ties access to the **exclusive purpose** of conducting research that contributes to the detection, identification and understanding of systemic risks in the Union pursuant to Art. 34(1) DSA, and to the assessment of the adequacy, efficiency and impacts of the risk mitigation measures pursuant to Art. 35 DSA. The procedure for obtaining the status of "vetted researcher" is essentially governed by Art. 40(8) and (9) DSA. This can only be granted for the specific research listed in the application. In addition, further conditions must be fulfilled, including in particular independence from commercial interests, research funding and compliance with data security and confidentiality requirements as well as the protection of personal data. This is primarily to ensure **proportionality** and adequate protection of rights and legitimate interests, including personal data, business secrets and other confidential information.[67]

68 However, the extent to which it will be possible in practice to actually gain access to such data is currently still very questionable and remains to be seen. This is because the wording of Art. 40(5) DSA does not oblige very large online platforms to elaborate on the reason for refusal or even to justify the existence of these circumstances. In the absence of the possibility to inspect the internal processes, it will be generally difficult for the requesting body to check the **justification for the refusal**. The same applies to the **alternative proposals** to be submitted under Art. 40(6) DSA. Here, too, it will hardly be possible to determine whether this represents a suitable alternative or not. This poses the acute danger that the much-welcomed possibility of data access will degenerate into a paper tiger. It is already feared that it will be largely at the discretion and favour of the providers of very large online platforms to pass on their data to authorities and researchers.[68]

---

[66] Rec. 96 DSA (supra n 6).

[67] Rec. 97 DSA (supra n 6).

[68] Kuß/Lehmann DB 2021, 605 (609); Gielen/Uphues EuZW 2021, 627 (636).

V. Codes of Conduct

In addition, the aforementioned transparency obligations are accompanied by the codes of conduct that the DSA provides for the elaboration in various areas (see → § 7 mn. 11 et seqq.). In general, these codes of conduct, which can be developed on a **voluntary basis**, are intended to contribute to the proper application of the DSA. For the question of transparency obligations, Art. 46 DSA is of particular interest, which concerns codes of conduct specifically for the area of online advertising and is intended to **promote the** achievement of the objectives and transparency obligations of the DSA overall. A wide rank of **stakeholders** should be **involved in the** development of the codes, so that they receive broad support. At the same time, this should also ensure that the codes are technically sound, effective and offer the highest levels of user-friendliness to ensure that the transparency obligations achieve their objectives.[69] According to Art. 46(2) DSA, the aim of such codes is to ensure the effective transmission of information that fully respects the rights and interests of all parties involved, as well as a competitive, transparent and fair environment in online advertising, in accordance with Union and national law, in particular on competition and the protection of privacy and personal data. 69

A code of conduct in the field of advertising is viewed as particularly useful because several players are generally involved in the provision of online advertising. For example, the advertiser and the provider who publishes the advertising do not usually convene themselves but are brought together by **intermediary services.**[70] In this complex process, the codes of conduct are intended to support and complement the transparency obligations of online platforms and very large online platforms laid down for advertising. The Union legislator hopes that this will provide **flexible and effective mechanisms** to facilitate and enhance the compliance with those obligations, notably as concerns the modalities of the transmission of the relevant information.[71] In addition, the Union legislator believes that such codes should also include measures to ensure that meaningful information about the **monetization of data** is appropriately shared throughout the value chain.[72] 70

VI. Appreciation

The various transparency obligations of the DSA address a large number of known problems of the digital economy and are basically suitable for reducing the existing lack of transparency, at least to some extent. Nevertheless, the existing regulations still have **weaknesses.** Ultimately, it remains unclear whether the chosen approach will actually lead to a noticeable increase in transparency in practice and thus achieve positive effects for recipients. Although the various disclosure obligations make countless additional pieces of information available, there is a risk of the classic danger of "information overload" with the consequence that the texts made available by the obligated parties are simply **not read by the respective recipients.**[73] The consequence would be that corresponding transparency regulations would ultimately prove to be **pointless** – possibly even counterproductive – and would merely represent an **additional expense** for 71

---

[69] Rec. 107 DSA (supra n 6).
[70] Rec. 107 DSA (supra n 6).
[71] Rec. 107 DSA (supra n 6).
[72] Rec. 107 DSA (supra n 6).
[73] Kuß/Lehmann DB 2021, 605 (609); Gielen/Uphues EuZW 2021, 627 (636).

the companies concerned.[74] Furthermore, the question arises whether the demands that the DSA places on the recipient are not ultimately too high. For example, the average recipient is expected to have an enormous **background understanding** for the mere comprehension of the information provided in order to actually be able to make an informed decision on the basis of that content.[75] However, this objection, which is generally directed against transparency and information obligations, can be countered by the fact that the information provided does not per se have to be read in full by every addressee. Rather, it will be sufficient to reduce the existing lack of transparency and problems in the digital sector if so-called "**professional readers**" such as consumer protection organisations, competition associations, but also competitors or public bodies in general, take note of the information provided, evaluate it and, if necessary, take the appropriate follow-up steps.[76] This control possibility in particular is often much more profitable than an individual evaluation by each recipient herself. In addition, increasing attention to an illustrative presentation of the information (by means of graphics, icons, etc.)[77] as well as a clear, simple and short wording of the information could be helpful,[78] which was also intended by the Union legislator.

72 Furthermore, the question arises as to whether the approach taken by the Union legislator of introducing mere transparency obligations does not fall **short** or, as the case may be, simply comes too late and is no longer sufficient. A closer look at individual provisions, such as the provisions on terms and conditions, illustrates the problem. The additional requirements of the DSA may make the individual passages in the terms and conditions of the platforms more comprehensible. However, it is questionable whether this is actually useful. In this respect, the very large online platforms that are significant in the market have extensive **power to shape the law**, since it is precisely with them that the so-called "tipping point" has been reached. A "tipping point" is typical in such markets, which show strong network effects and tend to cause a concentration on a few platforms, which subsequently act as central **gatekeepers**.[79] In these cases, the platforms have achieved such a strong market position that the market either threatens to tip or has already tipped. The recipients or providers are then left with little room for manoeuvre: in the absence of competition, they have to accept the conditions unilaterally dictated by the respective platform. In such a situation, however, the implementation of transparency obligations falls short or comes too late. These are supposed to guarantee protection through the provision of relevant information. In order for information to actually ensure an effective level of protection, however, it is imperative that the protected group of persons has or is given the opportunity to adapt their behavior or **change** their **decision-making behavior on the** basis of this information.[80] In the described scenario of a tilted market, however, such an adjustment is precisely not possible, as there are no longer any **alternative options for action** in the form of competing platforms. In this respect, the generalisation can be made that transparency obligations lose their

---

[74] Peifer GRUR 2021, 1453 (1454).

[75] Weiden NJW 2021, 2233 (2235).

[76] Peifer GRUR 2021, 1453 (1454).

[77] A monograph on the topic (in connection with the GDPR information obligations) was recently published in Ebner, Weniger ist Mehr? Die Informationspflichten der DSGVO – Eine kritische Analyse, 2022.

[78] Peifer GRUR 2021, 1453 (1454); also Weiden NJW 2021, 2233 (2235).

[79] Podszun/Kersting ZRP 2019, 34 (35).

[80] Spindler/Seidel NJW 2022, 2730 (2733) with reference to the example of Google; in Google's case, it is almost irrelevant how much information is provided in the GTCs about the ranking parameters, since already due to the market position on the search engine market there are de facto no more choices; Alexander WRP 2020, 945 (950).

efficiency with increasing platform size and strength of market position. Especially the problems surrounding the so-called GAFA (Google, Amazon, Facebook (Meta), Apple) can no longer be dealt with by this.[81] Insofar as the transparency regulations of the DSA concern tilted markets, it must be stated that these will probably no longer be able to contribute to improving the situation.

For the area of terms and conditions, it is also suggested that instead of merely 73
formal requirements, material regulations be implemented that address their fair design in terms of content and regulate them comprehensively and coherently.[82] However, it remains unclear what such a legal act could look like. On the one hand, the **contractual freedom** of the information society services must be considered, which would be significantly more restricted by these kinds of regulations than is the case with the current requirements laid out in the DSA. On the other hand, it will hardly be possible to establish legally secure regulations with verifiable quantitative criteria, if only because of the **different framework conditions** that prevail in the various digital sectors. Instead, it is to be expected that for a proportionate legal regulation, the information society services will have to be granted a broad scope for **design**, which would have to be taken into account, for example, through broad scope for interpretation in a corresponding legal act. However, in the case of standards that are broadly defined and in need of interpretation, the question arises as to whether these could actually still offer a noticeable added value. Instead, the implementation of an **effective procedure for** the review of terms and conditions of platforms with the corresponding power to shape law would be an important step. Here, for example, the instrument of the representative action, which has already been anchored in the P2B-Reg., could be generalised.[83] In addition, the question must be asked as to who specifically should fall within the scope of protection of corresponding provisions. In the case of online search engines, for example, the terms and conditions do not provide a suitable starting point for reducing a lack of transparency. This is because there is often too much rational apathy of the terms and conditions on the part of the addressees, i.e. the recipients. Finally, the recipient often does not enter into a close contractual relationship with the search engine operator, so that she is not significantly affected by the individual provisions.[84]

The basic approach of the DSA with its gradual catalogue of obligations oriented 74
to the size of the information society services is also criticised. This is because many transparency and due diligence obligations are only intended for information society services above a certain threshold, while many of the challenges mentioned are **already** applicable to **smaller platforms**, which are, however, subject to less control due to the less stringent requirements.[85] Overall, it will probably only become clear in the practical application of the size-based system whether the demarcations between the individual categories, some of which were disputed in advance, will actually lead to the intended appropriate differentiation.[86]

All in all, it remains to be said that transparency is only an effective means if it is 75
suitable for reducing information asymmetries and the corresponding requirements can also be effectively enforced and sanctioned in the event of non-compliance. Thus, the mere knowledge of the recipient about disadvantageous designs is of little use if she

---

[81] The problem of gatekeepers is primarily regulated in the DMA, cf. the remarks in rec. 77 et seq. In any case, the transparency obligations provided for there cannot adequately solve this problem either.

[82] Kumkar ZEuP 2022, 530 (562 et seq.).

[83] Similarly, Kumkar ZEuP 2022, 530 (563).

[84] Spindler/Seidel NJW 2022, 2730 (2733).

[85] Frank MMR 2022, 1026 (1028).

[86] Savary BB 2022, Iss. 10, I.

cannot choose any effective alternative **courses of action**.[87] Accordingly, the efficiency of transparency obligations is also related to the question of the effectiveness of the corresponding **sanction regulations**. However, at least regarding the existing information asymmetries concerning algorithm-based decisions, a certain gain in transparency can reasonably be expected.[88]

C. Transparency obligations under other EU legal acts

76 As already mentioned, the introduction of transparency rules is not specific to the DSA. On the contrary, there are already countless Union legal acts that make use of this instrument. These do not exclusively concern the digital economy. However, it is precisely in this area that there is an increasing focus on corresponding regulations. It follows, however, that ultimately there is **no uniform and coherent transparency approach** for the digital sector, but rather a **patchwork of** sector-specific transparency. Especially in the area of the platform economy, there are various important legal acts that contain transparency requirements somewhat similar to the DSA.

I. The Digital Markets Act

77 The DMA[89] can be described as a kind of **special law for gatekeepers** in which they are subjected to additional, more far-reaching obligations. The DMA also uses, at least in part, more far-reaching transparency obligations to break through the existing information asymmetries. However, it does not establish a comprehensive transparency approach, but merely introduces isolated regulations. In some respects, the DMA represents a continuation of the DSA with regard to transparency obligations, which in effect introduces a **fourth category of** information society services. However, these additional requirements do not only apply to information society services of a certain size. Rather, they must have an additional position of economic power as well as an overall economic significance in order to fall within the scope of application of the DMA (→ § 11 mn. 29 et seq.).

78 Further requirements, which also fall under the area of transparency obligations, are introduced for the area of **online advertising services**, among others. For example, there are obligations to provide additional information for online advertising (Art. 5(9) and (10) DMA) as well as obligations to disclose performance measuring tools used for advertising (Art. 6(8) DMA),[90] in order to reduce the lack of transparency and information asymmetry that exists especially in this sector.[91] The DMA thus further tightens the transparency obligations regarding online advertising for gatekeepers laid down in the DSA. The category "transparency obligation" can also include the **data access rights** according to Art. 6(10) and (11) DMA. According to these, the gatekeeper is obliged to grant commercial recipients and third parties, authorised by a commercial recipient, ac-

---

[87] Podszun NJW-Beil. 2022, 56 (59); Podszun/Offergeld ZEuP 2022, 244 (253 et seq.) on the comparable problem with the P2B-Reg. and the DMA.

[88] Gerpott CR 2022, 516 (523).

[89] Regulation (EU) 2022/1925 of the European Parliament and of the Council of 14 September 2022 on contestable and fair markets in the digital sector and amending Directives (EU) 2019/1937 and (EU) 2020/1828 (Digital Markets Act), OJ L 265, 1.

[90] See Hacker GRUR 2022, 1278 (1279).

[91] Kerber ZD 2021, 544 (547).

cess to certain data compiled by the gatekeeper.[92] One of the last connecting factors for further-reaching transparency obligations are the regulations on **rankings** according to Art. 6(5) DMA. In addition to a prohibition of self-preferential treatment, this provision contains a general transparency requirement for the conditions based on which the gatekeeper carries out the ranking process. In terms of content, it is assumed that the transparency obligations regarding rankings are comparable to those of the P2B-Reg. (→ mn. 79), so that the DMA does not result in any substantive changes in this respect.[93] Finally, there is also an **audit obligation under the DMA,** which results in an additional **disclosure obligation** for corresponding gatekeepers. According to Art. 15 DMA, gatekeepers must submit an independently audited description of any techniques for profiling of consumers that the gatekeeper applies to or across its core platform services to the Commission within six months of their designation.[94]

II. The P2B-Regulation

The so-called P2B-Reg. (→ § 16 mn. 1 et seqq.) serves to reduce information asymmetries by providing for various transparency and information obligations for online intermediary services and addressing the **particular risks of abuse** resulting from the enormous macroeconomic importance of corresponding platforms.[95] It essentially contains concrete transparency obligations at various levels, which are intended to flank cartel law, which has proven to be weak in this respect, with elements of contract and fairness law.[96] These requirements largely concern the relationship between online brokerage services and their commercial business partners, e.g. in the area of terms and conditions or the ranking parameters used. Thus, the P2B-Reg. clearly interferes with the platform operators' contractual freedom.[97] In addition, regarding the areas of regulation, there are also overlaps with the DSA in some cases, since the starting points are largely comparable. In these cases, the P2B-Reg., as a **lex specialis**, takes precedence over the DSA.[98] **79**

III. Regulation on combating the dissemination of terrorist content online (EU) 2021/784

The Regulation on addressing the dissemination of terrorist content online[99] also obliges hosting providers to a certain degree of transparency. These obligations are set out in particular in Art. 7 of the Regulation and also require the publication of a **transparency report**. This must essentially provide information on the measures taken by the hosting provider against the dissemination of terrorist content in a given calendar year. The terms of use must also set out their policy for combating the dissemination of terrorist content and, where appropriate, be supported by meaningful explanations of how **80**

---

92 Also Hacker GRUR 2022, 1278 (1280 et seq.).

93 Hacker GRUR 2022, 1278 (1282).

94 Achleitner NZKart 2022, 359 (361).

95 Spindler/Seidel NJW 2022, 2730 (2733); from a labour law perspective Kocher ZEuP 2021, 606 (628); Paal/Kumkar ZfDR 2021, 97 (109).

96 On this also Naumann/Rodenhausen ZEuP 2020, 768 (786 et seq.); Paal/Kumkar ZfDR 2021, 97 (109).

97 Rohrßen ZVertriebsR 2019, 341 (344).

98 Commission Explanatory Memorandum on the proposed Digital Services Act COM(2020), 825 final, 5.

99 Regulation (EU) 2021/784 of the European Parliament and of the Council of 29 April 2021 on addressing the dissemination of terrorist, OJ L 172, 79.

specific measures work. All in all, this is intended to achieve **transparent communication vis-à-vis the** recipients.[100] If there are overlaps with the DSA, the respective regulations complement each other, but the regulation on addressing the dissemination of terrorist online content also takes precedent as a **lex specialis.**[101]

D. Summary

81 Overall, the approach pursued with the DSA of additional requirements to increase the transparency of the digital economy is **neither new nor unique**. Various regulations already exist at the national level that have a similar goal. The EU legislator already has tried to break up opaque structures through transparency obligations, not only in the digital sector. However, the DSA will for the first time create a **uniform Union standard of transparency obligations** that will replace national regulations in the long run. The diverse transparency obligations of the DSA will probably at least lead to various problems in the digital sector becoming more **identifiable**. This is necessary for solving these issues in the long term – even if perhaps not necessarily with the existing instruments of the DSA. The current problem with regulating the digital economy is that the concrete business models, mechanisms of action and internal processes of large platforms, such as content moderation, are largely discretionary, which makes it difficult to take appropriate and targeted regulatory measures.[102] In this respect, there is hope that the DSA can provide a remedy.

82 Regarding the expected actual effects of the transparency obligations of the DSA, however, **no uniform judgement** is possible. Insofar as smaller platforms are affected, the requirements of the DSA may well fulfil the objectives pursued. With regard to such platforms, which are at the same time gatekeepers and operate on so-called tilted markets, these essentially come too late, however, as fair competition can no longer be established as a result.

83 In conclusion, it can be said that the transparency obligations of the DSA alone are, in any case, not suitable for ensuring effective platform regulation. In order for this goal, which is rather a task for society as a whole, to be achieved, a **coherent interaction of** civil law requirements as well as public law and criminal law control is required.[103] However, the DSA transparency requirements are a suitable instrument of civil law and, thus, a step in the right direction.

---

[100] Also, Voigt/Eschborn/Bastians MMR 2022, 727 (729).

[101] Commission Explanatory Memorandum on the proposed Digital Services Act COM(2020), 825 final, 5.

[102] Similarly, Gielen/Uphues EuZW 2021, 627 (636); Janal ZEuP 2021, 227 (273).

[103] Frank MMR 2022, 1026 (1028).

§ 5
Due diligence obligations, content moderation and procedural fairness

Literature: *Adelberg,* Hassrede in sozialen Netzwerken – Reichweite und Grenzen der Pflichten und Rechte der Netzwerkbetreiber, K&R 2022, 19; *Augsberg/Petras,* Deplatforming als Grundrechtsproblem, JuS 2022, 97; *Berberich/Seip,* Der Entwurf des Digital Services Act, GRUR-Prax 2021, 4; *Buiten,* The Digital Services Act From Intermediary Liability to Platform Regulation, JIPITEC 2021, 361; *Busch/Mak,* Putting the Digital Services Act in Context, EuCML 2021, 109; *Busch,* Der Digital Services Act: Ein neuer Rechtsrahmen für den Online-Handel?, ZdiW 2021, 88; *Denga,* Plattformregulierung durch europäische Werte: Zur Bindung von Meinungsplattformen an EU-Grundrechte, EuR 2021, 569; *Denga,* Das "Gesetz über Digitale Dienste" der Europäischen Union, in Ruffert (ed.), Die Regulierung digitaler Plattformen (2023), 9; *Dienstbühl,* Facebook muss gelöschten Beitrag mangels Grenzüberschreitung zur "Hassrede" wiederherstellen, GRUR-Prax 2019, 446; *Flamme,* Schutz der Meinungsvielfalt im digitalen Raum, MMR 2021, 770; *Friehe,* Löschen und Sperren in sozialen Netzwerken, NJW 2020, 1697; *Gerdemann,* Ein Stück Rechtsgeschichte zu den Grenzen der Meinungsfreiheit in sozialen Medien?, ZUM 2022, 364; *Gerpott,* Das Gesetz über digitale Dienste nach den Trilog-Verhandlungen, CR 2022, 516; *Gerpott,* Neue europäische Regeln für digitale Plattformen, CR 2021, 255; *Gielen/Uphues,* Digital Markets Act und Digital Services Act, EuZW 2021, 627; *Grünwald/Nüßing,* Vom NetzDG zum DSA: Wachablösung beim Kampf gegen Hate Speech?, MMR 2021, 283; *Härting/Adamek,* Digital Services Act – ein Überblick, CR 2021, 165; *Härting/Adamek,* Digital Services Act, IPRB 2021, 100; *Hennemann/Heldt,* Prozedurale Vermessung: Das Kuratieren kommunikativer Räume durch soziale Netzwerke, ZUM 2021, 981; *Hofmann/Specht-Riemenschneider,* Verantwortung von Online-Plattformen. Ein Plädoyer für ein funktionszentriertes Verkehrspflichtenkonzept, ZGE 2021, 48; *Hofmann/Sprenger,* Privatisierung der Rechtsdurchsetzung, UFITA 2021, 249; *Holznagel,* Zu starke Nutzerrechte in Art. 17 und 18 DSA, CR 2022, 594; *Holznagel,* Nutzerrechte bei Facebook: Klärung durch den BGH und bevorstehende Irrwege des EU-Gesetzgebers, CR 2021, 733; *Holznagel,* Chapter II des Vorschlags der EU-Kommission für einen Digital Services Act, CR 2021, 123; *Holznagel,* Put-back-Ansprüche gegen soziale Netzwerke: Quo Vadis?, CR 2019, 518; *Jäger,* Die unionsrechtskonforme Umsetzung der Sperrobliegenheiten nach Art. 17 DSM-RL: ein offenes Kapitel, ZUM 2021, 903; *Janal,* Friendly Fire? Das Urheberrechts-Diensteanbieter-Gesetz und sein Verhältnis zum künftigen Digital Services Act, GRUR 2022, 211; *Janal,* Haftung und Verantwortung im Entwurf des Digital Services Acts, ZEuP 2021, 227; *Janal,* Der Entwurf eines Digital Services Acts: Neue Perspektiven der Verantwortung von Diensteanbietern der Informationsgesellschaft, K&R 2021, 6; *Kaesling,* Evolution statt Revolution der Plattformregulierung, ZUM 2021, 177; *Kahl/Horn,* Sperrungen in sozialen Netzwerken: Verfahrensrechtliche Vorgaben des BGH, K&R 2021, 703; *Kalbhenn/Hemmert-Halswick,* EU-weite Vorgaben für die Content Moderation in sozialen Netzwerken, ZUM 2021, 184; *Kalbhenn/Hemmert-Halswick,* Der Regierungsentwurf zur Änderung des NetzDG. Vom Compliance-Ansatz zu Designvorgaben, MMR 2020, 518; *Kettemann/Schulz/Fertmann,* Anspruch und Wirklichkeit der Plattformregulierung, ZRP 2021, 138; *Krönke,* Privatverfahrensrecht in digitalen Grundrechtsnetzwerken, ZUM 2022, 13; *Kühling,* »Fake News« und »Hate Speech« – Die Verantwortung der Medienintermediäre zwischen neuen NetzDG, MStV und Digital Services Act, ZUM 2021, 461; *Kuhlmann/Trute,* Die Regulierung von Desinformationen und rechtswidrigen Inhalten nach dem neuen Digital Services Act, GSZ 2022, 115; *Kumkar,* Plattform-Recht revisited: Umgang mit den Marktordnungen digitaler Plattformen de lege lata et ferenda, ZEuP 2022, 530; *Kuß/Lehmann,* Digital Services Act – Entwurf eines einheitlichen Rechtsrahmens für die EU-Digitalwirtschaft, DB 2021, 605; *Laude,* DSA-Umsetzung abseits sehr großer Online-Plattformen, RDi 2024, 216; *Legner,* Der Digital Services Act – Ein neuer Grundstein der Digitalregulierung, ZUM 2024, 99; *v. Lewinski/Klink,* Compliance-Pflichten nach dem DSA – ein umfassender Überblick, RDi 2023, 183; *Lüdemann,* Digitalisierte Öffentlichkeiten und multipolare Grundrechtsverhältnisse, ZUM 2021, 640; *Lüdemann,* Grundrechtliche Vorgaben für die Löschung von Beiträgen in sozialen Netzwerken, MMR 2019, 279; *McColgan,* Das wird man ja wohl noch löschen dürfen? – Kontrollmaßstäbe für Meinungsregeln im Internet – Zugleich Besprechung von BGH 29.7.2021 – III ZR 192/20, RDi 2021, 605; *Mendelsohn,* Die "normative Macht" der Plattformen – Gegenstand der zukünftigen Digitalregulierung?, MMR 2021, 857; *Paal/Kieß,* Digitale Plattformen im DSA-E, DMA-E und § 19a GWB, ZfDR 2022, 1; *Peguera,* The Platform Neutrality Conundrum and the Digital Services Act, IIC 2022, 681; *Peukert,* Five Reasons to be Skeptical About the DSA, Verfassungsblog, 31.08.2021 <https://verfassungsblog.de/power-dsa-dma-04/> (last accessed: 23.06.2024); *Peukert,* Gewährleistung der Meinungs- und Informationsfreiheit in sozialen Netzwerken, MMR 2018, 572; *Peukert/Husovec/Kretschmer/Mezei/Quintais,* European Copyright Society – Comment on Copyright and the Digital Services Act Proposal, IIC 2022, 358; *Quintais/Schwemer,* The Interplay between the Digital Services Act and Sector Regulation: How Special is Copyright?, European Journal of Risk Regulation 2022, 191; *Raue,* Plattformnutzungsverträge im Lichte der gesteigerten Grundrechtsbindung marktstarker sozialer Netze, NJW 2022, 209; *Raue/Heesen,* Der Digital

Services Act, NJW 2022, 3537; *Raue,* Meinungsfreiheit in sozialen Netzwerken, JZ 2018, 961; *Rössel,* Digital Services Act, ITRB 2021, 35; *Rössel,* Digital Services Act, AfP 2021, 93; *Savova/Mikes/Cannon,* The Proposal for an EU Digital Services Act, CRi 2021, 38; *Schmid/Grewe,* Digital Services Act: Neues "Grundgesetz für Onlinedienste"?, MMR 2021, 279; *Schneiders,* Hate Speech auf Online-Plattformen, UFITA 2021, 269; *Schwartmann,* Muster-AGB für Meinungsneutralität – Ein Impuls zur Fortentwicklung von BGB und DSA, NJW 2022, 133; *Spieker gen. Döhmann/Westland/Campos* (eds.), Demokratie und Öffentlichkeit im 21. Jahrhundert – zur Macht des Digitalen, 2022 (cited Spiecker/Westland/Campos, Demokratie und Öffentlichkeit); *Spindler/Seidel,* Die Regulierung von Online-Plattformen, NJW 2022, 2730; *Spindler,* Der Vorschlag für ein neues Haftungsregime für Internetprovider – der EU-Digital Services Act (Teil 1), GRUR 2021, 545; *Spindler,* Der Vorschlag für ein neues Haftungsregime für Internetprovider – der EU-Digital Services Act (Teil 2), GRUR 2021, 653; *Spindler,* Die Zukunft des europäischen Haftungsrechts für Internet-Provider – der Digital Services Act, MMR 2023, 73; *Spoerri,* On Upload-Filters and other Competitive Advantages for Big Tech Companies under Article 17 of the Directive on Copyright in the Digital Single Market, JIPITEC 2019, 173; *Ukrow,* Rechtsdurchsetzung bei der Verbreitung von Hate Speech und terroristischen Inhalten, UFITA 2021, 223; *Voigt/Eschborn/Bastians,* Weitreichende neue Pflichten für Host-Provider – Kurzanalyse der Verordnung zur Bekämpfung der Verbreitung terroristischer Online-Inhalte, MMR 2022, 727; *Wagner,* Haftung von Plattformen für Rechtsverletzungen (Teil 1), GRUR 2020, 329; *Wagner,* Haftung von Plattformen für Rechtsverletzungen (Teil 2), GRUR 2020, 447; *Wimmers,* The Out-of-court dispute settlement mechanism in the Digital Services Act – A disservice to its own goals, JIPITEC 2021, 421; *Wölken/David,* Warum wir ein "digitales Grundgesetz" für Europa brauchen, PinG 2021, 169.

A. Overview

1 This chapter describes the legal framework of the DSA[1] for **notification, monitoring, moderation and dispute resolution in relation to user-generated content** that has been uploaded to hosting services and especially online platforms. Designed primarily as procedural rules, the provisions of the DSA are intended to balance the interests of all parties involved in content moderation in a fair and non-discriminatory manner. To this end, the DSA sets out notice and action mechanisms for illegal content, including mandatory information to affected users (Art. 16, 17), internal complaint-handling and external dispute settlement procedures (Art. 20, 21), the use of trusted flaggers (Art. 22) and protection measures against misuse (Art. 23). All such measures must also comply with general requirements for platform governance (Art. 14).

2 The DSA requirements for dealing with uploaded content, especially on online platforms, follow the general legislative **objectives** of the DSA: On one hand, the DSA seeks to establish **uniform EU-wide rules** for the cross-border use of online intermediary services. The EU Commission was concerned that increasingly diverging national EU member states' laws could impede the provision of cross-border intermediary services and negatively affect the internal market.[2] This applies in particular to national laws that tackle illegal content online (such as the German *Netzwerkdurchsetzungsgesetz*[3]), which are likely to be superseded by the DSA after its entry into force.[4] In this respect, the DSA aims at creating a 'level playing field' in all EU member states by means of **full harmonisation**[5]. The **horizontal** regulation of the DSA will establish cross-sectoral rules alongside other sector-specific regulations[6] such as Art. 17 DSM-Directive[7] (→ § 22

[1] Regulation (EU) 2022/2065 of the European Parliament and of the Council of 19.10.2022 on a Single Market For Digital Services and amending Directive 2000/31/EC (Digital Services Act), OJ L 277, 1. Unless stated otherwise, provisions referred to in this chapter are those of the DSA.

[2] Rec. 2 et seq., 40 DSA.

[3] Cf. for a discussion of the German *Netzwerkdurchsetzungsgesetz* (Network Enforcement Act, NetzDG) and a comparison of regulations, e.g. Grünwald/Nüßing MMR 2021, 283; for other EU member states' laws cf. Savova/Mikes/Cannon CRi 2021, 38 (43 et seqq.).

[4] Cf. Grünwald/Nüßing MMR 2021, 283 (287); Adelberg K&R 2022, 19 (21); Paal/Kieß ZfDR 2022, 1 (28); Gerpott CR 2022, 516 (522); Kuhlmann/Trute GSZ 2022, 115 (116); Hennemann/Heldt ZUM 2021, 981 (991); Peukert in Spiecker/Westland/Campos, Demokratie und Öffentlichkeit, p. 229 (246) for the example of the German *Netzwerkdurchsetzungsgesetz*.

[5] Rec. 9 DSA.

[6] Rössel ITRB 2921, 35 (36).

[7] Directive (EU) 2019/790 of the European Parliament and of the Council of 17.4.2019 on copyright and related rights in the Digital Single Market and amending Directives 96/9/EC and 2001/29/EC, OJ L 130, 92; cf. for further details on the DSM Directive Janal GRUR 2022, 211; Spindler MMR 2023, 73 (74).

mn. 2 et seq.), the AVM-Directive (EU) 2018/1808[8] or the Anti-Terrorism Regulation (EU) 2021/784.[9]

3 At the same time, the DSA aims at creating a **safe and transparent online environment**[10] with harmonised **due diligence obligations** for providers of intermediary services throughout the EU.[11] This is understood to serve mainly **non-economic objectives.**[12] The societal significance and political role of online platforms and especially communication platforms has been increasingly discussed in recent times. There is no doubt that online platforms are of paramount importance as **digital 'marketplaces for ideas and opinions'** that enable active societal participation in the process of forming public opinions and thus strengthen the democratic potential of civil societies.[13] However, platforms can also be used to host illegal content such as criminal, defamatory or otherwise illegal 'hate speech' or undesired content such as so-called 'fake news'. Whether these phenomena are caused by an attention economy that is immanent to platform business models[14] or whether the cause for such developments can also be found outside the platform economy[15] is debatable. In any case, online platforms will normally take **moderation measures** against unwanted content in their own interest (→ mn. 33), while their level of moderation 'harshness' may vary. The DSA now sets a benchmark for content moderation in two ways: At the 'lower' end of moderation standards measures **against illegal content** become mandatory and cannot leave illegal content unmoderated. However, at the 'upper' end, any moderation measures must at the same time **not** lead to **overblocking.** Overblocking is a term for misguided regulatory incentives due to which platforms would, in the event of doubt, rather remove contentious (but legal) content to avoid potential liability than keeping it online and defending it, because deleting is easier than a costly dispute.[16] These disincentives are correctly identified as a structural impairment to the freedoms of expression and communication[17], and they endanger in particular content in a legal 'grey area', which can-

[8] Directive (EU) 2018/1808 of the European Parliament and of the Council of 14.11.2018 amending Directive 2010/13/EU on the coordination of certain provisions laid down by law, regulation or administrative action in EU member states concerning the provision of audiovisual media services (Audiovisual Media Services Directive) in view of changing market realities, OJ L 303, 69.

[9] Regulation (EU) 2021/784 of the European Parliament and of the Council of 29.4.2021 on addressing the dissemination of terrorist content online, OJ L 172, 79; cf. on this topic Voigt/Eschborn/Bastians MMR 2022, 727.

[10] Rec. 40 DSA.

[11] Rec. 40 DSA.

[12] Paal/Kieß ZfDR 2022, 1 (11), (18).

[13] Denga EuR 2021, 569 (570).

[14] Gerpott CR 2022, 516 (517); Wölken/David PinG 2021, 169 (170); Kuhlmann/Trute GSZ 2022, 115 (120); Flamme MMR 2021, 770; Buchmann in Spiecker/Westland/Campos, Demokratie und Öffentlichkeit, p. 15 (25).

[15] Cf. Peukert in Spiecker/Westland/Campos, Demokratie und Öffentlichkeit, p. 229 (230 et seq.) who mentions uniform reporting in traditional media, which arguably supports a shift to online media that are more susceptible to fake news.

[16] Overblocking is therefore less a reproach against online platforms, who behave fully rational in this respect, but rather a structural incentive problem, cf. Wagner GRUR 2020, 447 (452); Kaesling ZUM 2021, 177 (179); Hofmann/Specht-Riemenschneider ZGE 2021, 48 (52); Gielen/Uphues EuZW 2021, 627 (635); Paal/Kieß ZfDR 2022, 1 (9); Denga EuR 2021, 569 (573 et seq.); McColgan RDi 2021, 605 (608).

[17] European Commission DSA Impact Assessment, 15.12.2020, SWD(2020) 348 final, mn. 57; Paal/Kieß ZfDR 2022, 1 (9); Raue JZ 2018, 961 (963); Wagner GRUR 2020, 447 (452); Hofmann/Sprenger UFITA 2021, 249 (260); Kalbhenn/Hemmert-Halswick MMR 2020, 518 (518 et seq.); cf. for the parallel discussion on the DSM-Directive (EU) 2019/790 also Opinion AG Saugmandsgaard Øe of 15.7.2021 in proceedings CJEU C-401/19, ECLI:EU:C:2021:613 = GRUR-RS 2021, 20614 mn. 140 seq, 198 – Republic of Poland/EP and Council; differentiating Holznagel CR 2022, 594 (603).

not be conclusively assessed to be legal or not in mass proceedings,[18] so that platforms have strong incentives to comply even with excessive and legally unfounded takedown requests.[19] In this respect, transparency measures for deleted content and complaint handling systems for uploading users are procedural safeguards for the freedoms of communication.[20] The DSA thus follows a dual objective to **curb illegal content** on one hand and likewise to **protect** users' **freedoms of communication** on the other.[21]

The DSA does **not** contain an obligation to remove '**harmful content**' as such, which was discussed in the legislative process,[22] except where such content is illegal at the same time (and without prejudice to the – rather vague – systemic obligations of very large online platforms, → § 6). The completely vague and hardly manageable term of 'harmful content' seems to include the controversial topics of hate speech, fake news and disinformation. As far as such content is illegal by law, there is no need for such a category. In other cases, a definition of what lawful statements would be 'harmful' and forbidden, which would trigger takedown or monitoring obligations, is highly problematic with regard to users' freedom of expression, freedom of information and platform operators' freedom to conduct their business. An impairment of fundamental rights through **legally uncertain** terms and, resulting from this, excessive compliance efforts can hardly be justified. Instead, the approach of the DSA to focus on illegal content in general due diligence obligations is more suitable to cater for the **freedom of expression and information**, which form the basis for an **open civic discourse, as required in democratically constituted societies**. Of course, the **voluntary** decision of platform operators to take action against certain forms of non-illegal content in accordance with their terms of service under their internal **platform governance** (→ mn. 33 et seq.) remains unaffected. Such contract-based restrictions and moderation policies are widely used and are even a competitive factor for platforms in a market for rules.[23] The DSA itself does not set out any provisions related to specific types of content or specific moderation standards, but instead offers a procedural framework (e.g. Art. 17, 20, 21) that seeks to ensure fair and non-discriminatory standards for handling content (also on the basis of a platform's general terms and conditions). In addition, the terms of service may themselves be subject to review under a fairness test according to the EU Unfair Terms Directive[24] and its implementing national laws, which may require to take into account the indirect effect of the affected parties' fundamental rights (→ mn. 38 et seqq.). 4

Within the DSA framework, one must always keep in mind that providers of online intermediary services usually act at the core of processes for forming and exchanging public opinions so that any regulation would not only affect their freedom to conduct 5

[18] This applies in particular to infringements of personality rights and decisions that require a complex balancing of interests, cf. Wagner GRUR 2020, 447 (452). Differentiating approaches, e.g. according to type of content or with use of pre-flagging, which is taken into account in pending complaint proceedings, were not implemented in the DSA; cf. on this topic Kaesling ZUM 2021, 177 (182).

[19] Raue JZ 2018, 961 (963) refers to 'phantom rights' that threaten the fundamental freedoms of third parties.

[20] Raue JZ 2018, 961 (969).

[21] Gerpott CR 2022, 516 (522); Schmid/Grewe MMR 2021, 279 (282); Kalbhenn/Hemmert-Halswick ZUM 2021, 184 (185); against overblocking cf. also Buiten JIPITEC 2021, 361 (378). This tension already became apparent in the legislative process, cf. for stricter platform requirements opinion of the Committee on the Internal Market and Consumer Protection of 28.5.2021, 2020/0361(COD), P9_A(2021)0356 – and for a stronger emphasis on user rights opinion of the Committee on Civil Liberties Justice and Home Affairs of 28.7.2021, 2020/0361(COD), LIBE_AD(2021)692898.

[22] Kuhlmann/Trute GSZ 2022, 115 (119); Kaesling ZUM 2021, 177 (182); Buiten JIPITEC 2021, 361 (366).

[23] Schmid/Grewe MMR 2021, 279 (280).

[24] Council Directive 93/13/EEC of 5.4.1993 on unfair terms in consumer contracts, OJ L 95, 29.

business, but also fundamental communication rights of their users.[25] This creates a **situation of multipolar interests** of platform operators and various user groups, which is acknowledged and emphasised in the recitals, as they repeatedly refer to the **EU Charter of Fundamental Rights** ('CFR') and in particular the right to freedom of expression and information of the users, to freedom of the service provider to conduct business, to non-discrimination and effective legal protection.[26] It is therefore foreseeable that the CFR will be a major benchmark for the interpretation of the DSA as EU secondary law (similar to moderation and filtering measures under Art. 17 DSM Directive[27]).[28] This also means that applying the complex DSA framework will often involve striking a **balance** between actions against (allegedly) illegal content on one hand, and appropriate safeguards on the other to protect fundamental communication rights, which constitute a democratic society,[29] as well as the entrepreneurial freedom of service providers and their economic and technical limits of action. Against that background, the framework of the DSA can ultimately be seen as an attempt to cut through the Gordian knot of conflicting interests by using a **protection of fundamental rights through procedure**[30] coupled with the requirement of **procedural fairness.** Whether this objective has been achieved in the DSA's final version remains to be seen (→ mn. 85 et seqq.).

6 In view of the **multitude** of **user-generated content**, which can potentially be illegal for a variety of reasons, an overarching 'horizontal' regulation with granular material requirements for all types of content is practically impossible to enact. For this reason, the DSA lays its focus primarily on **content-agnostic and technology-neutral**[31] **procedural requirements**[32] for platform operators to carry out content moderation and to implement specific processes for notifying, assessing and blocking content as well as handling possible complaints. Within this procedural framework, objectionable content will be examined at various levels, from a first review upon notice, over internal complaint-handling systems, adversarial out-of-court dispute settlement proceedings, to, ultimately, public state courts. Against that background, the DSA does not strictly require platform operators to find the 'right' results on the merits in the first assessment of individual cases (a task even state courts often struggle with), but rather imposes a **structural compliance obligation to establish processes and mechanisms** for procedural fairness, which are handled in a fair, diligent, non-arbitrary and non-discriminatory manner. The DSA thus sets out a **proceduralisation of content removal obligations and removal prohibitions**[33] by virtue of design specifications that aim at resolving

---

[25] Cf. on the significance of fundamental rights Adelberg K&R 2022, 19 (20); in the similar context of Art. 17 DSM Directive (EU) 2019/790 cf. CJEU 26.4.2022 – C-401/19, ECLI:EU:C:2021:613 = GRUR 2022, 820.

[26] Cf. rec. 3, 9, 22, 36, 40 et seq., 47, 51 et seq., 63 DSA. Uploading users affected by restricting measures can invoke their freedom of expression (Art. 11 (1) CFR). Users affected by insults or defamation can rely on Art. 7, 21 CFR. For platform operators, the freedom to conduct a business under Art. 16 CFR applies. For balancing these interests and rights cf. Kaesling ZUM 2021, 177 (182).

[27] Cf. CJEU 26.4.2022 – C-401/19, ECLI:EU:C:2021:613 = GRUR 2022, 820 mn. 45–47, 69 et seq., 75, 80 et seq. and Opinion AG Saugmandsgaard Øe of 15.7.2021, GRUR-RS 2021, 20614 mn. 4–6, 70 et seq., 140 et seq.

[28] Cf. Peukert/Husovec/Kretschmer/Mezei/Quintais IIC 2022, 358 (370); Gerpott CR 2021, 255 (260).

[29] Similar as here Gerpott CR 2022, 516 (523); Kuß/Lehmann DB 2021, 605.

[30] Cf. on the protection of fundamental rights through procedure from a German perspective BGH 29.7.2021 – III ZR 179/20, NJW 2021, 3179 mn. 84; Raue JZ 2018, 961; Hofmann/Sprenger UFITA 2021, 249 (264 et seqq.). See also Kraetzig/Lennartz NJW 2022, 2524 who are critical towards algorithmic decision-making in situations with balancing fundamental rights.

[31] Rec. 4 DSA.

[32] For this focus on procedural requirements, see Buchheim in Spiecker/Westland/Campos, Demokratie und Öffentlichkeit, p. 249 (258).

[33] Busch, ZdiW 2021, 88 (90); Gielen/Uphues EuZW 2021, 627 (636).

multipolar conflict situations of fundamental rights[34] and at achieving more moderation transparency.[35] Against this background, few individual 'wrong' decisions in this staged content evaluation process do not trigger any fines, but so would only systemic violations of compliance obligations to set up the respective processes (→ mn. 88).

B. Systematic structure and regulated types of service providers

The DSA follows in its structure a **gradual addressee-related approach**. This includes regulations that apply to all providers of intermediary services (Chapters I and II, Chapter III Section 1), or those that apply only to the sub-set of hosting service providers (Chapter III Section 2). Further obligations are even more narrowly focused on online platforms in general (Chapter III Section 3) or more specifically online platforms for concluding B2C distance contracts with traders (Chapter III Section 4). Finally, the DSA addresses very large online platforms that may create systemic risks and imposes certain obligations on them only (Chapter III Section 5). The latter rules are not discussed in this book chapter, but reference is made to this book's chapters → § 4 and → § 6. Accordingly, a platform's compliance obligations under the DSA may vary and gradually increase with the respective **type of service provider** concerned. 7

I. Hosting service providers

The obligations to set up a notice and action mechanism (Art. 16) together with the corresponding explanation requirements for restrictive measures (Art. 17) and the notification of suspected criminal offences (Art. 18) apply to all **hosting service providers, including online platforms**. Pursuant to Art. 3(g)(iii), hosting services, being a **subset of intermediary services,** are information society services (as defined in Directive (EU) 2015/1535[36]) that store information provided by a user on his request. For determining hosting services, the **principles developed** under the **E-Commerce Directive 2001/29/EC** and the existing CJEU case law can still be used (cf. for details → § 3 mn. 1 et seq.). Thus, this category generally includes e.g. webhosting, cloud storage, file storage and sharing services, and according to the recitals also advertising servers and paste bin services[37] regardless of their size.[38] In contrast, **other types** of **intermediary services** mentioned in Art. 3(g), i.e. mere conduit (access providers)[39] and caching, but also **content providers** who offer their own content and do not store any third-party content for users (such as video and music-on-demand services, online newspapers, company websites, blogs, etc.) are **not subject to the aforementioned obligations.** Content providers do not enjoy any liability privilege for their own content under Art. 6, but are not subject to the obligations of Art. 11 et seq. either. This is coherent and consistent. 8

[34] On this requirement cf. Raue JZ 2018, 961 (969); Wagner GRUR 2020, 447 (452 et seq.); Wagner ZUM 2022, 861 (867); Hofmann/Sprenger UFITA 2021, 249 (261 et seq.); Buchheim in Spiecker/Westland/Campos, Demokratie und Öffentlichkeit, p. 249 (255).

[35] Buchheim in Spiecker/Westland/Campos, Demokratie und Öffentlichkeit, p. 249 (258).

[36] Directive (EU) 2015/1535 of the European Parliament and of the Council of 9.9.2015 laying down a procedure for the provision of information in the field of technical regulations and of rules on information society services, OJ L 241, 1.

[37] Rec. 50 DSA.

[38] Rec. 50 DSA. For a narrower interpretation of hosting service providers in special cases see Laude RDi 2024, 216 (218).

[39] Cf. for a critique that access providers have no information obligations under the DSA when blocking content Janal K&R 2021, 6 (7).

Given that content providers are normally fully liable for their own content under general liability rules without a hosting privilege, there is no need to subject them to further procedural platform obligations. Special liability rules and due diligence obligations are therefore two sides of one coin.

9 Apart from online platforms, online B2C marketplaces and online search engines, the DSA does **not** set out any **further function-specific differentiation** of intermediary services.[40] This could foreseeably lead to **ambiguities** in the course of further technical development and will leave the details of fringe cases to be clarified by the courts. **Non-commercial** service providers are sometimes considered as not being affected by the DSA obligations, since the definition of intermediary services under the DSA is based on the definition of an information society service (Art. 3(g) and (a)), which requires a service that is normally provided for remuneration, at a distance, by electronic means and at the individual request of a recipient (Art. 1(b) Directive (EU) 2015/1535).[41] If one were to follow this argument, there would remain some room for regulation by EU member states.[42]

10 The implications of the DSA for **services without a central intermediary** (e.g. services based on distributed ledger technology) remain to be seen. While the DSA rules are tailored to centralised intermediary services,[43] there are good arguments that the liability privilege (Art. 6) should also apply to individual participants in a distributed network infrastructure (nodes)[44], since they have neither knowledge of, nor control over, the automatically processed content.[45] However, the procedures to be set up under the DSA as part of the due diligence obligations will often be difficult to implement in truly decentralised systems. This holds true in any case to **public permissionless distributed ledger** systems where it is hardly possible for individual participants to influence the processed data at all so that corresponding obligations (e.g. takedown) may be legally impossible to fulfil. Individual server instances of other **decentralised networks (e.g. Fediverse)** are also technical infrastructure operators and exempt from the obligations of Art. 20 et seq. DSA, if they fall under the threshold of Art. 19 for micro and small enterprises (→ mn. 17). However, the mere participation in decentralised networks will usually not constitute the operation of an intermediary service, even if data processing is for technical reasons partially carried out at users' devices.

II. Online platforms

11 The obligations to set up internal complaint-handling systems, to cooperate with external dispute settlement bodies as well as trusted flaggers, to implement misuse protec-

---

[40] Kaesling ZUM 2021, 177 (178); Kettemann/Schulz/Fertmann ZRP 2021, 138 (139).

[41] Cf. Spindler GRUR 2021, 545 (547); Gielen/Uphues EuZW 2021, 627 (634) arguing for a 'Wikipedia' regulation *de lege ferenda*. Since the type of service in question must *normally* be provided for remuneration, without having to consider its financing in each case, the DSA implications for non-profit services are unclear. In any case, it has to be noted in that context that the EU Commission has designated Wikipedia as a very large online platform on 25.4.2023.

[42] Spindler GRUR 2021, 545 (547). Ultimately, the CJEU will have to clarify this issue.

[43] Cf. for the comparable case of the GDPR that also hinges on one (or more contractually bound) entities as data controllers Berberich/Steiner EDPL 2016, 422 (424); Erbguth/Fasching ZD 2017, 560 (563).

[44] Cf. for distributed ledger technology under the E-Commerce Directive Saive CR 2018, 186 (190 et seq.); Ebers/Heinze/Krügel/Steinrötter KI/Berberich § 27 mn. 46.

[45] Cf. for application of these criteria as the basis of the liability privilege CJEU 23.3.2010 – C-236/08 to C-238/08, GRUR 2010, 445 mn. 114 et seq. – Google France; CJEU 12.7.2011 – C-324/09, GRUR 2011, 1025 mn. 111 et seq. – L'Oréal/eBay; see also Berberich GRUR-Prax 2017, 269.

tion measures and others (Art. 20–28) apply to all **online platforms**. As a **subset of hosting service providers,** online platforms must, by definition, fulfil the requirements of Art. 3(g)(iii) outlined above and in addition **store and disseminate information to the public at the request of a service recipient** (Art. 3(i)), unless this is a minor and ancillary feature (see → mn. 14 et seq. below for details on hybrid services). Dissemination to the public is defined by Art. 3(k) as making information available to a potentially unlimited number of third parties at the request service recipient who provided the information. **Examples** of online platforms include social networks or online marketplaces for goods and services (but not online shops with their own content); video sharing platforms or app stores for third-party apps.[46] Whether these services are offered to consumers (P2C), to traders (P2B) or to both sides of a market (P2B2C) is irrelevant,[47] unless specific DSA rules (such as those in section 4) only refer to activities vis-à-vis consumers or traders. Therefore, business-related B2B platform services and professional social networks also fall into the scope of Art. 19 et seq. The category of online platforms does **not include** mere hosting service providers with information storage only for certain users,[48] cloud computing and web hosting services as well as other technical infrastructure service providers (even if these are provided for online platforms),[49] or interpersonal communication services within the meaning of Directive (EU) 2018/1972,[50] such as e-mail or instant messaging services.[51] Online search engines also do not fall under the definition of online platforms with respect to their due diligence obligations, and the DSA addresses them separately.[52]

The main parameter to distinguish between hosting services and online platforms is 12
the **dissemination of information to the public** at the user's request. It is foreseeable that this concept will – similar to the discussion of communication to the public in copyright law under Art. 3 InfoSoc Directive 2001/29/EC[53] – raise serious questions of delimitation, at first on the role of platforms in dissemination, and secondly on the concept of public: According to the recitals, a **dissemination** of information should require making the information easily accessible to service recipients in general without further required actions by the uploading service recipient, irrespective of whether the information is actually accessed.[54] The dissemination must occur upon the **direct request of the uploader.**[55] Therefore, an online platform must directly perform the 'final act' in the user-driven dissemination of content; mere preparatory or technical infrastructure-related services are excluded here. In addition, information from one user must be disseminated, as intended by the service provider, to other users of the service who among them-

[46] Cf. for examples rec. 13 DSA; Schmid/Grewe MMR 2021, 279 (280), Kalbhenn/Hemmert-Halswick ZUM 2021, 184 (186); Grünwald/Nüßing MMR 2021, 283 (285).

[47] Spindler GRUR 2021, 653 (654).

[48] Rec. 13 DSA; Härting/Adamek CR 2021, 165 (166); Holznagel CR 2022, 594 (596).

[49] Rec.13 DSA.

[50] Directive (EU) 2018/1972 of the European Parliament and of the Council of 11.12.2018 on the European Electronic Communications Code, OJ L 321, 36. However, whether the CJEU case law on Art. 3 of the said directive can be directly applied to the DSA is questionable, cf. mn. 13.

[51] Rec. 14 DSA.

[52] Since online search engines are defined separately in Art. 3(j), and the DSA addresses them separately in Art. 14(6), 24(2)–(4) and Section 5, as well as in the rec. 41, 48, 57, 65, 75 et seq., these services must be systematically distinguished from online platforms within the meaning of Art. 3(i); cf. on this distinction also Gerpott CR 2022, 516 (519); differentiating Legner ZUM 2024, 99 (104); dissenting Raue/Heesen NJW 2022, 3537 (3538).

[53] Directive 2001/29/EC of the European Parliament and of the Council of 22.5.2001 on the harmonisation of certain aspects of copyright and related rights in the information society, OJ L 167, 10.

[54] Rec. 14 DSA.

[55] Rec. 14 DSA.

selves constitute a 'public'. The fact that users can publicly disseminate their content themselves or outside the service (such as when sending links to their content) does not, as such, re-qualify a host provider to be an online platform.

13 The concept of **public** is not defined in the DSA. Given that the recitals refer to an 'unlimited number of persons'[56], one may be inclined again to draw upon the concept of the public established in EU copyright law (Art. 3(1) Copyright Directive 2001/29/EC).[57] However, in the view taken here, it is not possible simply to rely on the CJEU case law on copyright for a more precise definition. Copyright use rights are usually interpreted broadly in accordance with their purpose to cover any commercial exploitation outside the private sphere to ensure an appropriate remuneration for authors. This is not the regulatory objective of the DSA, whose risk-based approach is rooted in balancing the interests of all parties involved and imposes considerable obligations on online platforms, which must not be maximised but remain proportionate.[58] According to the recitals, the decisive factor is how a potentially unlimited number of people gain access to the information: Information is public if there is a potentially unlimited number of recipients who are not determined by the uploader, such as generally publicly accessible content or groups to which everyone has access.[59] If, on the other hand, a **registration or admission** to a group is required (such as closed chat groups in instant messaging services), a differentiation must be made: This is made public if the admission occurs automatically without human decision or selection.[60] In contrast, if it is the uploader who determines the addressees, there is most likely no public dissemination of the uploaded information.

III. Hybrid or mixed services

14 The service classification under the DSA is also likely to raise questions for handling hybrid or mixed services with **several functionalities**. This concerns, for **example,** services that partially offer their own content, partially store user-generated content and partially disseminate it to the public. For example, a sales platform on the internet can act as a seller of its own products and at the same time operate a marketplace for third party traders. A video platform can offer its own editorially curated videos as well as user-generated content. An online newspaper or blog may operate a comment forum in addition to showing its own articles. Or the operator of a cloud computing service may also offer the publication of content. A content-oriented approach is not new here but has already been taken under the E-Commerce Directive[61]. Under the DSA, however, the classification and **delimitation** of services is no longer focused only on **liability issues**, but relevant also for the differentiated **due diligence obligations** and the calculation of applicable thresholds (e.g. user numbers).[62]

15 For such a differentiation, the DSA sets out a **functional service-related delimitation** in recital 15, according to which the provisions of the DSA only apply to those services, which fall within their respective scope of application. This delimitation applies to all relevant provisions of the DSA, not only to due diligence obligations but also to

---

[56] Rec. 14 DSA.

[57] Cf. Peukert/Husovec/Kretschmer/Mezei/Quintais IIC 2022, 358 (367).

[58] Cf. rec. 13 on the delimitation of online platforms in order to 'avoid imposing overly broad obligations'.

[59] Spindler GRUR 2021, 653; Gielen/Uphues EuZW 2021, 627 (634).

[60] Rec. 14 DSA.

[61] Cf. BGH 14.5.2013 – VI ZR 269/12 mn. 20.

[62] Gielen/Uphues EuZW 2021, 627 (635); on hybrid services see also Laude RDi 2024, 216 (217).

liability privileges. Accordingly, to take one hypothetical example, a media company that (i) provides its own content and also (ii) operates a social network and (iii) a messenger service would fall within the scope of Section III DSA only for (ii), but would enjoy the liability privilege as a host provider for (ii) and (iii).

Category	DSA Obligations	Liability privilege	Examples
Intermediary service	Art. 11–15	If applicable, liability privilege from Art. 4–6	Umbrella term (see below)
Hosting service provider (sub-case of intermediary service)	Art. 16–18 and all the above	Liability privilege from Art. 6	Cloud storage, web hosting, ancillary hosting features (e.g. comment areas)
Online platform (sub-case of hosting service provider)	Art. 19–28 and all the above	Liability privilege from Art. 6	Social networks, UGC video platforms
Online platform for B2C distance contracts (sub-case of online platform)	Art. 29–32 and all the above	Liability privilege from Art. 6	Online trading marketplaces
Very large online platforms (sub-case of online platform) and very large search engines	Art. 33 et seqq. (for online platforms also all of the above, if relevant)	Liability privilege from Art. 6	Very large online trading marketplaces, social networks and video sharing platforms (as far as VLOP criteria are fulfilled)
Content provider with own content	None under DSA	None under DSA	Online press, web shops, blogs, websites in general, audio and video streaming services (without user-generated content)
Interpersonal communication services	None under DSA	If applicable, liability privilege for infrastructure from Art. 6	E-mail; messenger (unless open user groups)

Specifically for the **differentiation between online platforms and host providers** the definition of Art. 3(i) draws a distinction in line with the **main focus** of such service: Service features do not re-qualify hosting service providers as online platforms if they are (i) a **minor and purely ancillary feature** of another service, or (ii) a **minor functionality** of the principal service that cannot be used for objective and technical reasons without the principal service, and in either case is no means to circumvent the DSA. In view of the various potential services and converging features in the market, this vaguely 16 formulated exception will foreseeably need to be clarified by the courts and ultimately by the CJEU.[63] As examples, the recitals do not classify as online platforms the comment sections of online media (unlike social networks),[64] or cloud computing and webhosting services, which could also disseminate content as a minor or ancillary feature.[65] Accordingly, it also seems conceivable that potentially open user groups, depending on their practical significance, may constitute a minor or ancillary feature within instant messaging services.[66] It is noteworthy that the recitals apply this distinction rule more generally to individual functionalities of another service (e.g. own content) so that the principal service in question appears not to strictly require a hosting service provider, but could be understood as a more general rule.[67] However, keeping in mind that this rule explicitly serves as a **privilege to avoid overly broad obligations triggered by less important functions,**[68] there are good reasons to argue that this general rule works only **in favour** but not to the detriment of service providers.

IV. Exemptions for small enterprises (Art. 19)

17 Art. 19 DSA mostly **exempts micro and small enterprises** (as defined in Recommendation 2003/361/EC[69]) from the application of the **online platform**-related Art. 20–28 to avoid a disproportionate burden[70], unless they are very large online platforms as defined in Art. 25.[71] For these companies, an introduction of mandatory content moderation and dispute settlement measures (see below) is voluntary. This also applies for a transitional period of 12 months after they lose this status.[72] The exemption in Art. 19 is relevant not only for **start-ups**, but also for smaller social networks that are independent from each other but enable data exchange via standardised interface protocols and thus allow users to communicate across services (so-called **Fediverse**). Here, each independent service operator of an instance must be assessed separately; the DSA does not provide a basis for a cross-provider assessment. However, the more general provisions for **hosting services** and **intermediary services** remain **applicable** under Art. 19, as well as

[63] Peukert/Husovec/Kretschmer/Mezei/Quintais IIC 2022, 358 (371); see also Laude RDi 2024, 216 (220) with a proposal of determining factors.

[64] Rec. 13 DSA.

[65] Rec. 13 DSA.

[66] Cf. for this discussion Kuhlmann/Trute GSZ 2022, 115 (115 et seq.).

[67] This is shown by the example in rec. 13 DSA for the comments section of online media: Online media are fully liable for their editorial content and therefore, unlike hosting service providers, not subject to the DSA. They only qualify as hosting service providers for user statements in their comments sections. The recital states that the comment section is ancillary to the main service of news publication under the editorial responsibility of the publisher, i.e. in its role as content provider, not as a host provider. With a focus on hosting the comment section, these very comments could hardly be seen as an ancillary but as a main feature.

[68] Rec. 13 DSA. This context supports the argument that such a delineation rule should, for reasons of proportionality, likewise apply to distinguish host providers from other intermediary services or content providers.

[69] Commission Recommendation 2003/361/EC of 6.5.2003 concerning the definition of micro, small and medium-sized enterprises (OJ 2003 L 124, 36). The applicable consolidation rules shall prevent circumvention attempts, cf. rec. 57 DSA.

[70] Rec. 57 DSA.

[71] Rec. 57 DSA.

[72] Critical Gerpott CR 2022, 516 (519) due to the short transitional period and the significant additional administrative burden. A possibility for non-profit or medium-sized enterprises as defined in Recommendation 2003/361/EC to apply for a general exemption, which was proposed by the European Parliament in the legislative process, was not included in the final version of the DSA.

the mandatory reporting of user numbers at request of the Digital Services Coordinator or the EU Commission (Art. 24(3)).

C. Notice and action mechanism for hosting service providers (Art. 16–18)

All hosting service providers (including online platforms), irrespective of their size, must establish procedures through which individual content on their services can be reported as allegedly illegal (**notice**) and through which the service provider then checks and decides whether to share this assessment and to take measures or not (**action**). Such notice and action mechanisms are mandatory for **illegal content** and must follow the procedural requirements set out in Art. 16 (→ mn. 19 et seqq.). Decisions to take **restrictive measures** must be explained to users by a sufficient **statement of reasons** (→ mn. 28 et seqq.). Providers must also report certain content that constitutes serious **criminal offenses** to law enforcement authorities (→ mn. 31). In that regard, the DSA further develops the previously existing notice-and-take-down procedure for hosting service providers. As before, such provider becomes liable for illegal third-party content only once he become aware of the illegality and does not immediately remove or block such content (→ § 3 mn. 120 et seqq.). 18

I. Notice procedure (Art. 16)

1. Scope of application: Illegal content

Establishing notice and action mechanisms is mandatory for **illegal content** only. Art. 16 does not require the implementation of such procedures for legal content that "only" violates contractual terms of use.[73] Thus, hosting service providers are free whether to use such procedures or not for merely "undesirable" content that is banned by their terms of service. However, it can be expected that notice-submitting users would regularly use existing mechanisms also for flagging content that violates the terms of service, as such content may be difficult for users to distinguish from illegal content before any professional assessment has been made. 19

Illegal content is any information that, in itself or in relation to an activity (including product sales and services), is not in compliance with EU law or the national law of any EU member state, irrespective of the precise subject matter or nature of that law (Art. 3(1)(h)). This definition is deliberately broad and based on the idea that anything that is **illegal offline** should also be **illegal online.**[74] It can refer to content that is **illegal in itself** (such as criminal forms of so-called hate speech[75] or terrorist content) or that is **related to illegal activities**. Examples in the recitals include sharing of sexual abuse images, the unlawful and unconsented sharing of private images, online stalking, the sale of 20

---

[73] This follows from the wording and definition in Art. 3(h), and also systematically from the *e contrario* argument that Art. 20(1) explicitly refers to both categories of (i) information that is incompatible with terms and conditions and (ii) illegal information. Similar Legner ZUM 2024, 99 (106).

[74] In this respect, the definition is broader than some EU member states' rules (like the German *Netzwerkdurchsetzungsgesetz* with an enumerative list of serious criminal offences, see Adelberg K&R 2022, 19 (21)).

[75] The specific laws for qualifying statements as a criminal offence are not fully harmonised and vary among EU member states. In German law, for instance, this could be defamation (*Beleidigung*, § 185 *Strafgesetzbuch*) or agitating defamation (*Verhetzende Beleidigung*, § 192a StGB; on the interpretation of this rather new law cf. Schwartmann NJW 2022, 133 (135)).

counterfeit products, illegal sales of live animals, illegal offers of accommodation services, offers that violate consumer protection law, or unlawful use of copyrighted material.[76] The broad criterion of merely relating to unlawful acts, however, will foreseeably raise **difficult questions of meaningful delimitation.** As a counter-example, eyewitness videos of a potential crime should not fall under this criterion.[77] One may doubt that the inductive, example-based approach of the recitals alone will suffice for legal certainty and a proportionate approach to limit the danger of overblocking in the latter case. Therefore, as a rough guidance proposal, an applicable test could be whether the upload of content is in itself an act of illegal **support** for or **execution** of the prohibited activity or not. Such a test could differentiate from cases where the uploaded content has no sufficient **inherent connection** to a generally illegal activity.[78] Anyway, cases where the illegality is not ascertainable in the uploaded content itself would hardly be recognisable by service providers, nor could they effectively verify the legality upon notice.

21 The DSA itself does not specify what is **illegal or not**, but rather presupposes this qualification. According to the recitals, illegality can result from **EU law** or from **national law** of EU member states in conformity with EU law, while it should be irrelevant what the precise nature or subject matter of the law in question is.[79] It is therefore conceivable that different EU member states may have **divergent substantive laws** in place for the assessment of illegality – and that the DSA may reach a limit on the intended harmonisation of laws here.[80] However, the extent of potential divergences will vary depending on the area of regulation. Divergences can be expected to be smaller in harmonised areas of law (e.g. copyright or consumer protection law) than in non-harmonised areas (e.g. substantive criminal law[81] or free speech laws[82]). This unfortunate **tension with the country of origin-principle**[83] is the price to be paid for the broad definition of illegality in the DSA. Ultimately, it is conceivable that even controversial provisions of a single EU member state (e.g. bans on certain opinions, political views or religious expressions) could suffice for illegality.[84] In that event, a safety net against

[76] Rec. 12 DSA.

[77] Rec. 12 DSA.

[78] For example, content as such should not be deemed illegal simply because uploading users do not have public law licences (e.g. business or media law licences) for their general activities. Otherwise, to take an example from German law on public broadcasters whose activities are tightly regulated, content created by public broadcasters outside the scope of their permitted activities (§ 32 MedienStV – *Medienstaatsvertrag*, Federal State Treaty on Media Broadcasts) would be illegal and could not be shared for that reason alone. The same could be true for companies with funding that violates EU state aid laws. Such an overreaching interpretation would conflict with the fact that the DSA adopts a content-centered view and is not an instrument to sanction other forms of general non-compliance with laws.

[79] Rec. 12 DSA; critical towards uniform rules for different types of illegal content also Härting/Adamek CR 2021, 165 (170).

[80] Kaesling ZUM 2021, 177; Kuhlmann/Trute GSZ 2022, 115 (119); Wimmers JIPITEC 2021, 421 mn. 21, 26. To make it even more complex, diverging laws of several EU member states may also be applicable on the merits under conflict of laws rules (cf. Dregelies MMR 2022, 1033 (1034)). This potential applicability of a multitude of legal systems for assessing illegal content may be a challenge posed on top of DSA compliance obligations. It remains to be seen how the practical application of the DSA will face this challenge. In any case, obligations must remain proportionate (cf. rec. 13 DSA on the avoidance of overly broad obligations).

[81] Kaesling ZUM 2021, 177.

[82] Denga EuR 2021, 569 (572) correctly points out the different standards of EU member states in the right of expression as a "cultural-relative phenomenon" within the EU, which even the Charter of Fundamental Rights does not completely assimilate.

[83] Kalbhenn/Hemmert-Halswick ZUM 2021, 184 (188).

[84] Critical especially on cross-border removal of content that is only illegal in individual EU member states: Opinion of the Committee on Civil Liberties Justice and Home Affairs of 28.7.2021, 2020/0361(COD), LIBE_AD(2021)692898, p. 3 mn. 7; Holznagel CR 2022, 594 (598).

prohibitions on specific content is at least created by the requirement that such national laws must still be in accordance with EU law[85] and, therefore, must also be tested against and interpreted in the light of the **Charter of Fundamental Rights.** Although this does not necessarily mean that the 'strictest' national regulation will prevail, it still creates significant legal uncertainties.

2. Procedural details

Notice submission requirements. The mandatory notice and action mechanisms must allow any individual or entity to notify specific items of information in a service as allegedly illegal. Not only recipients of a service are entitled to submit notices, but the notice procedure of Art. 16 must (unlike Art. 17 and 18) be accessible to **everyone.**[86] The submission of notices shall be possible exclusively **by electronic** means[87] in an **easily accessible** and **user-friendly manner.** This will usually require a contact address or input forms that are easy to find and understandable for average users, without hidden instructions or points of contact.[88] According to the recitals, the procedures should be clearly identifiable, located close to the information in question and at least as easy to find and use as notification mechanisms for content that violates the terms of service, if applicable.[89] The DSA does not prescribe a specific form of technical implementation, but Art. 16(2) contains some content-related design requirements to facilitate the submission of **sufficiently precise and adequately substantiated notices.** For instance, the submitting user must be able to give a substantiated **explanation** the alleged illegality, to indicate its exact electronic **location** (e.g. URL or other information required and appropriate according to the type of service), to provide his **name and email address**[90] (except in the case of serious offences), and a statement confirming his ***bona fide* belief in the accuracy and completeness** of the reported information and allegations. In addition, it should be possible to notify multiple specific items of allegedly illegal content through a single notice.[91] From a practical point of view, there is much leeway for the platform interface design, and it is also conceivable to set up different entry forms for different types of infringements along with upload options for evidence.[92] 22

Procedure and deadlines. After receipt of the notice and immediate **confirmation of receipt** to the notifying user (Art. 16(4)), hosting service providers must **process** all notices received and take a decision in a **timely, diligent, non-arbitrary and objective** manner (Art. 16(6)). This decision will then be communicated without undue delay to the notifying user, together with possibilities for legal redress (Art. 16(5)). These abstract procedural requirements are ultimately an attempt to bring an element of **procedural fairness** into the service provider's difficult task of balancing the conflicting interests and fundamental rights of users, notifiers and the service provider itself in its decision.[93] 23

[85] Rec. 12 DSA.

[86] Spindler GRUR 2021, 545 (552); Holznagel CR 2022, 594 (596); Raue/Heesen NJW 2022, 3537 (3540); Buchheim in Spiecker/Westland/Campos, Demokratie und Öffentlichkeit, p. 249 (267).

[87] The DSA does not specify further contact options, but does not exclude them either, cf. Spindler GRUR 2021, 545 (552).

[88] Spindler GRUR 2021, 545 (552).

[89] Rec. 50 DSA. However, this requirement will have to be qualified for such noticing individuals who are not themselves registered users with access to the service and therefore cannot perceive the content. The DSA does not contain any obligation for closed services to make content visible to non-users.

[90] Critical towards the requirement of an email address Härting/Adamek CR 2021, 165 (166).

[91] Rec. 50 DSA.

[92] Janal ZEuP 2021, 227 (252).

[93] Cf. rec. 52 for the balancing of fundamental rights, including, for the recipients of the service, the right to freedom of expression and of information, the right to respect for private and family life, the

This requires a diligent procedure according to standardised and non-discriminatory internal processes and rules, which are applied uniformly under the service provider's applicable review standards and which do not discriminate against any user groups or opinions as such (no political bias).[94] Article 16(6) therefore serves not only the interests of notifying users, but equally the interests of uploading users in diligent moderation decisions and, ultimately, of all users and the platform operator to avoid overblocking. In contrast to similar EU member states' laws[95], the DSA does not set out a specific and fixed **deadline** for decision-making. Rather, the hosting service provider has a **reasonable period of time for review and consideration,** because complex assessments of the facts and legal evaluations (especially in free speech cases) may be necessary,[96] depending on the type of content and infringement. In complex cases, sufficient evaluation time is necessary also to reduce the risk of overblocking, which would increase with rigid time limits.[97] Therefore, the deadlines for a timely decision may vary in individual cases. For normal notices, a service provider may have more time than for trusted flagger notifications.[98] At this stage of the content moderation procedure, the provider's decision can be drawn on the basis of information actually available (i.e. according to what is "on file" in the matter e.g. from the uploaded content or notices). Hosting service providers are **not obliged** to **find or clarify the relevant facts** in dispute proactively. Such an obligation would impose disproportionate efforts and a judge-like role in platform moderation mass proceedings. Nevertheless, providers are free under the DSA to hear the uploading users voluntarily. In such case, i.e. where the service provider does more than actually required for ascertaining the facts in the notice procedure, e.g. as the basis for balancing fundamental rights implications, it appears appropriate to grant an extended period of time.

24 **Automated decision-making**. Within the notice and action mechanism, hosting service providers may use automated means for processing or decision-making,[99] but must **inform** the notifying users and, in case of content-restricting measures, also the uploading users concerned (Art. 16(6) 2nd sent., Art. 17(3)(c)). This is different for internal complaint-handling systems or later escalation stages, which require some form of human review (→ mn. 49 et seq.). While manner and extent of using automatic filters are not specifically regulated[100], the general requirements of Art. 16(6) still apply for the entire procedure. This means in effect that the requirements to act diligently, non-arbitrar-

---

right to protection of personal data, the right to non-discrimination and the right to an effective remedy. For service providers, the freedom to conduct a business, including the freedom of contract, applies. For parties affected by illegal content, the right to human dignity, the rights of the child, the right to protection of property, including intellectual property, and the right to non-discrimination may apply, depending on the individual case.

94 Cf. also Kaesling ZUM 2021, 177 (182) against politically-driven decision-making in the context of platform governance.

95 Cf. for the German *Netzwerkdurchsetzungsgesetz* Grünwald/Nüßing MMR 2021, 283 (285); Härting/Adamek CR 2021 (165). Without a specified time limit, v. Lewinski/Klink RDi 2023, 183 (187) consider Art. 16(6) as addressing only clear violations.

96 Kaesling ZUM 2021, 177 (180); Gielen/Uphues EuZW 2021, 627 (635); Dregelies MMR 2022, 1033 (1035). However, voluntary industry agreements can provide for shorter times here, such as the EU Code of Conduct for Combating Illegal Hate Speech on the Internet, which various major online platforms have signed and which provides for 24 hours for various serious and criminal forms of hate speech.

97 Kuhlmann/Trute GSZ 2022, 115 (117); Raue/Heesen NJW 2022, 3537 (3540).

98 Spindler GRUR 2021, 653 (655).

99 Rec. 42 DSA; Spindler GRUR 2021, 545 (552); Kalbhenn/Hemmert-Halswick ZUM 2021, 184 (189); Raue/Heesen NJW 2022, 3537 (3540); Spindler MMR 2023, 73 (76); Legner ZUM 2024, 99 (106).

100 Rössel ITRB 2921, 35 (39). Currently, the vast majority of moderation decisions on large online platforms are automated, at least in the first stage, cf. empirically Peukert in Spiecker/Westland/Campos, Demokratie und Öffentlichkeit, p. 229 (239); Holznagel CR 2022, 594 (597).

ily and objectively in a manual case-by-case review will translate into similar obligations to generally set up and implement such automated systems with sufficient diligence in the creation, training (incl. data set selection) and monitoring of algorithms (also to avoid overblocking). According to the recitals, the used technology must be sufficiently reliable to limit the rate of errors to the maximum extent possible.[101] On the other hand, current technical limitations of algorithmic decision-making must also be taken into account.[102] If the DSA explicitly allows automated (first-level) decisions, the law cannot set out unrealistic requirements that automated decisions must always and in every single case be correct (whatever that would mean compared to a full legal review), because a certain inherent technically error rate must be accepted. In the systematic DSA framework an algorithmic response to notifications takes only the role of an automated first filter[103], whereas individual human balancing decisions occur at a later stage, because they are often difficult, time-consuming and more expensive.[104] Applying proportionate requirements here is therefore in line with the overall structure of content moderation, under which the DSA sets out a **cascade of successive procedures and escalation stages,** the costs of which per case will increase with escalation levels, but the overall case numbers may decrease at each stage after being solved.[105] Against this background, any structural obligation that aims at correctness of the first decisions should be limited here,[106] and the platform operator should have a certain discretion in choosing blocking and deletion measures.[107] In view of the DSA's objective to (also) avoid overblocking,[108] service providers have the right to (and should) apply restrictive measures with **reasonable restraint,** especially if the factual and legal situation is uncertain. Such an approach is still compliant with the DSA's systemic due diligence obligations.

3. Knowledge and liability

If a notice (i) contains all the **information** specified in Art. 16(2) and (ii) such information enables a diligent hosting service provider to ascertain that such content is **clearly[109] illegal without a detailed legal (and factual[110]) examination**, the provider is deemed to have knowledge of the illegality, and the liability privilege of Art. 6 ceases to 25

[101] Rec. 26 DSA; on the danger of false positives cf. Peukert VerfBlog, 31.8.2021 <https://verfassungsblog.de/power-dsa-dma-04> (last accessed: 23.06.2024); sceptical on this requirement Gerpott CR 2022, 516 (522).

[102] Cf. Opinion of the Committee on Civil Liberties Justice and Home Affairs of 28.7.2021, 2020/0361(COD), p. 4 mn. 13: 'Algorithms cannot reliably identify illegal content and routinely result in the suppression of legal content, including journalistic content.'

[103] Buchheim in Spiecker/Westland/Campos, Demokratie und Öffentlichkeit, p. 249 (256).

[104] Denga EuR 2021, 569 (574).

[105] Cf. on the aspect of procedural escalation under the DSA Buchheim in Spiecker/Westland/Campos, Demokratie und Öffentlichkeit, p. 249 (257); Holznagel CR 2022, 594 (596); Busch ZdiW 2021, 88 (90); on platform conflict resolution generally cf. Engert AcP 218 (2018), 304 (350). However, the user is always free to immediately approach state courts (→ mn. 84).

[106] Buchheim in Spiecker/Westland/Campos, Demokratie und Öffentlichkeit, p. 249 (256).

[107] Gerpott CR 2022, 516 (523).

[108] See → mn. 3 and rec. 51 and 53 DSA emphasising the freedom of expression and freedom of information.

[109] Cf. rec. 53 DSA for the requirement of clear illegality, which determines the standard in the (less specific) wording of Art. 16(3).

[110] Cf. on this criterion under the E-Commerce Directive CJEU 22.6.2021 – C-682/18, C-683/18, ECLI:EU:C:2021:503 = GRUR 2021, 1054 mn. 116 – Peterson; cf. on the application of this ruling also under the DSA Dregelies MMR 2022, 1033 (1036). Even if the DSA wording only refers to a legal examination, it nonetheless must imply a fact-finding, which is the basis for any legal assessment. In practice, such fact-finding by platforms can only occur on the basis of statements submitted by the individual users concerned.

apply in regard to this specific item of information. For such knowledge, it will not suffice that a notice only formally contains the elements set out in Art. 16(2). It is also necessary that the notice is **sufficiently precise and adequately substantiated** to allow a diligent economic operator to reasonably identify, assess and, where appropriate, act against the allegedly illegal content.[111] This knowledge includes awareness of the illegality, and it requires that the notified information is sufficiently specified[112] and correct, comprehensible as well as complete in its substance.[113] In contrast, the liability privilege persists if the underlying relevant facts are not sufficiently clear or if the legal assessment has uncertain results.[114] This will often be difficult in practice, especially in defamation cases where further contextual knowledge may be required for a viable assessment, which the service provider usually does not have, or in disputes between different rightholders.[115] The liability privilege will remain applicable at least until the expiry of a reasonable processing period, because otherwise service providers would *de facto* be forced, contrary to their obligations under Article 16(6), to block content immediately after a notice without time for a diligent examination.[116] But even after that examination, the service provider can still come to the conclusion that the content in question is not sufficiently identified as illegal and keep it available until illegality is established by means of an adversarial procedure with the parties involved (especially in free speech law cases after sufficient fact-finding).

II. Remedial decision and user notification

26 After having received and processed the notice, the hosting service provider must take a remedial decision. The DSA does not specify the content of such decision. Either, the decision can be to leave the allegedly illegal content on the platform in case of doubt, or to take one of various **measures** mentioned in Art. 17(1) to remove this content, to restrict its visibility, or other measures (for details on such restricting measures → mn. 52). The **legal benchmark for the remedial decision** is therefore the respective applicable **substantive law** under which content is considered illegal. In the event that the facts of the case cannot be sufficiently determined, or that the legal situation is not sufficiently clear from the available information, the service provider has the freedom to decide in its reasonable discretion, e.g. on the basis of applicable **rules of evidence.** Service providers are not obliged to delete content, which, to determine illegality, would require an independent assessment of the content by them in the light of the information provided[117]. Similarly, the choice of measures to be taken is a discretionary balancing decision of the service provider. For individual items of illegal content, the DSA itself does

---

[111] Rec. 22 DSA; Kaesling ZUM 2021, 177 (180); Janal ZEuP 2021, 227 (247); Adelberg K&R 2022, 19 (22); Holznagel CR 2021, 123 (126); Gielen/Uphues EuZW 2021, 627 (635); Schmid/Grewe MMR 2021, 279 (280).

[112] Janal ZEuP 2021, 227 (247).

[113] Holznagel CR 2021, 123 (126).

[114] Janal ZEuP 2021, 227 (247).

[115] For this reason, Janal K&R 2021, 6 (9) proposes a dispute resolution directly between the parties concerned.

[116] Kaesling ZUM 2021, 177 (180); cf. also rec. 22 DSA 2nd sent. for the requirement of taking into account the fundamental rights to freedom of expression and of information in such decision.

[117] Cf. by analogy for Art. 17 DSM-Directive (EU) 2019/790 CJEU 26.4.2022 – C-401/19, ECLI:EU:C:2021:613 = GRUR-RS 2021, 20614 mn. 89 et seq. – Republic of Poland v EP and Council. Given that this judgement is also based on balancing fundamental rights when handling illegal (copyright infringing) content in similar hosting situations, there are strong arguments to apply this test likewise under the DSA.

not set out subjective rights or claims for individuals to have such content deleted, but rather presupposes such claims in the applicable substantive law.[118] An individual **claim for deletion of content** will normally arise from the substantive law that declares such content to be illegal. However, for individual claims of users who submit notices the applicable substantive law may require that such users' own rights have been violated (→ mn. 48). The user who submits a notice must be **informed** of the remedial decision (Art. 16(5)). This same holds true if measures are not possible for technical or operational reasons.[119] In addition, the provider must inform about possibilities for redress against this decision, if the provider has not fulfilled the user's takedown request. In contrast to Art. 17, the DSA does **not** require any further specific **justification or statement of reason** to be given to notifying users.[120] Thus, the hosting service provider has no obligation to explain to them why objectionable content, which is kept available online, is considered lawful or not clearly illegal.

An ***ex ante*** **hearing for uploading users** prior to the decision to block or otherwise restrict their content is not expressly foreseen at this stage[121], and takes place later in the internal complaint handling procedure against this decision (Art. 20). However, this leads to a systematic friction in the DSA, because such a procedure has only to be set up by online platforms, but not by all hosting service providers.[122] Yet, service providers are free to consider voluntarily the legitimate interests of uploading users before taking such restriction measures. This plays a role mostly where service providers have already implemented corresponding "counter-notice" procedures, e.g. for DMCA procedures, or to handle alleged violations of their general terms and conditions.[123] Insofar as procedures mandated by EU member states' national laws go beyond the requirements of notice (Art. 16) and complaint handling (Art. 20) under the DSA[124], it is conceivable that these could no longer be mandatory at the level of the EU member states in view of full harmonisation,[125] but will nevertheless remain possible on a voluntary basis. 27

III. Statement of reasons for restrictions on uploading users (Art. 17)

Service providers must make all restriction measures sufficiently transparent for their users. According to Art. 17, restrictive measures imposed on user-provided content, which affect its visibility, its monetisation, the service as such or users' accounts ('restrictions'; on these measures in detail → mn. 52) must be **disclosed to the users concerned** at the latest when such measure is taken, together with a **clear and specific statement of reasons** (Art. 17(1) and (3)). This transparency requirement primarily aims at preventing the widespread practice of hidden restrictions on visibility (so called **shadow ban-** 28

[118] This is the flipside to the individual put-back claims, which the DSA also presupposes in existence, cf. Kaesling ZUM 2021, 177 (182).

[119] Rec. 51 DSA.

[120] Cf. Dregelies MMR 2022, 1033 (1036).

[121] Spindler GRUR 2021, 545 (553); Adelberg K&R 2022, 19 (22).

[122] Critical also Rössel ITRB 2921, 35 (40).

[123] Cf. rec. 50 DSA for equal treatment of the accessibility of reporting procedures for illegal content and content contrary to the general terms and conditions.

[124] In Germany, for instance, the Federal Supreme Court has developed by case law a procedure of proactive hearings for both sides, in particular for personality rights infringements, cf. BGH 25.10.2011 – VI ZR 93/10, GRUR 2012, 311. From a purely procedural point of view, large parts of the BGH proceedings for online platforms are likely to coincide with Articles 16, 17 and 20. Insofar as there are divergences in hearing obligations and investigative standards, the DSA is likely to take precedence here.

[125] Dissenting Holznagel CR 2022, 594 (598) for the aforementioned case law of the German Federal Supreme Court.

ning[126]). It applies to both a moderation decision as remedy after the notice procedure (Art. 16) and to other internally initiated moderation measures. This statement of reasons must be given in particular when restrictions are imposed (for the first time) after a notice has been submitted by another complaining user,[127] and where the DSA does not provide for a mandatory prior hearing of the uploading user.

29 The obligation to issue a statement of reasons applies in any case and regardless of the chosen manner or reason for the imposed restrictions. Such statement of reasons is particularly important and must be given also for fully automated blocking measures against uploading users with **content filter technology**, and in case of measures **against non-illegal content** on the basis of service provider's general terms and conditions.[128] **Exceptions** exist in the case of deceptive high-volume commercial content (e.g. online shops with a large number of counterfeit products) (Art. 17(2) subpara. 2) as well as for orders by public authorities (Art. 17(5)).

30 With its requirement to issue a statement of reasons, the DSA again does not determine a specific outcome or decision-making criteria;[129] as these will follow the standards of substantive law applicable to the respective restriction measure. Yet, the DSA sets out formal **minimum requirements** for a clear and specific statement of reasons in Art. 17(3) and (4): the statement must make clear which **specific restriction measure** has been taken as a result of the decision, as well as its territorial scope and duration (Art. 17(3)(a)). In addition, the reasons must state the **facts and circumstances relied on in taking the decision**, including whether it was taken after a notice pursuant to Art. 16 or based on voluntary own-initiative and, where strictly necessary, the identity of the notifier[130] (Art. 17(3)(b)) as well as the use of **automated means** for taking the decision or for content recognition (Art. 17(3)(c)). In case of allegedly illegal content, the **legal ground** relied on must be indicated together with explanations as to why the content is considered to be illegal on this basis (Art. 17(3)(d)); the same applies to content allegedly incompatible with the service provider's **terms and conditions** (Art. 17(3)(e)). Finally, users must receive clear and user-friendly information about **available legal redress** (Art. 17(3)(f)). Here again, the DSA sets out the general transparency requirement for the statement of reasons to be **clear and easily comprehensible** and as precise and specific as reasonably possible under the given circumstances for users to exercise their remedies (Art. 17(4)). This should usually require a brief, understandable subsumption of the facts under the stated legal basis, which may also include balancing the fundamental rights of the parties involved, if applicable. As far as decisions and statements of reasons under Art. 17 originate from online platforms (not only from host providers), these must be transmitted to the EU Commission for inclusion in a publicly accessible machine-readable database managed by the EU Commission (Art. 24(5)).

---

126 Cf. rec. 55 DSA.

127 Holznagel CR 2022, 594 (598).

128 Rec. 42 DSA. In that regard, the application scope of the mandatory statement of reasons under Art. 17 is broader than it is for the notice and action procedure under Art. 16.

129 Spindler GRUR 2021, 545 (552).

130 The identity is likely to be necessary especially in cases that involve individual rights (such as infringement of personality rights or defamation) in order to provide the uploading user and/or service provider with the information necessary for a legal defence under Art. 17(4), as well as in cases of intellectual property infringements, cf. rec. 54.

IV. Notification of criminal offences to public authorities (Art. 18)

The obligation to report suspicions of criminal offences was initially placed only on online platforms, but was later extended to all hosting service providers in the legislative process.[131] If the provider becomes aware of information that gives rise to the suspicion that a **criminal offence involving a threat to the life or safety of a person** has taken place, is taking place or is likely to take place, he shall promptly inform the law enforcement or judicial authorities of the relevant EU member state (alternatively, in cases of doubt, the state of establishment or Europol) and provide all available information (Art. 18). The DSA itself does not regulate in detail which criminal offences are meant here.[132] Recital 56 refers, by way of example, to such criminal offences as set out in Directive 2011/36/EU on preventing and combating trafficking in human beings,[133] in Directive 2011/93/EU on combating the sexual abuse of children[134] or in Directive (EU) 2017/541 on combating terrorism.[135] These grave criminal offences indicate at least that the criminal offences concerned by Art. 18 DSA must also be **quite serious and directly related to the life or safety of individuals** while minor offences will not suffice.[136] 31

D. Platform governance and content incompatible with service terms

Assessing the terms of service and handling content thereunder – especially for deleting content that is legal but undesirable for a target group-oriented business model – is only partially regulated in the DSA. Service providers are in principle free to set the rules for using their own offerings (→ mn. 33 et seq.). In doing so, however, they engage in private law enforcement that is regulated by the DSA with certain transparency requirements and with the obligation to apply and exercise restrictions in their terms of service in a diligent, objective and proportionate manner that takes into account fundamental rights (→ mn. 35 et seq.). In addition, terms of service will normally constitute general terms and conditions and are, at least vis-à-vis consumers, usually subject to a fairness test under the Unfair Terms Directive 93/13/EEC and their respective implementations in EU member states' national laws[137] (→ mn. 38 et seq.). 32

131 Cf. Art. 21 of the EU Commission's DSA draft, which was previously located in DSA Section 4.

132 Given that the possibly applicable criminal law of all EU member states may substantially diverge (cf. Tschorr MMR 2022, 1053 (1056)), this creates considerable legal uncertainty for platform operators. It remains to be seen how the practical application of the DSA will deal with this issue. In any case, the obligations must remain proportionate (cf. rec. 13 DSA on the avoidance of overly broad obligations).

133 Directive 2011/36/EU of the European Parliament and of the Council of 5.4.2011 on preventing and combating trafficking in human beings and protecting its victims, and replacing Council Framework Decision 2002/629/JHA, OJ L 101, 1.

134 Directive 2011/93/EU of the European Parliament and of the Council of 13.12.2011 on combating the sexual abuse and sexual exploitation of children and child pornography, and replacing Council Framework Decision 2004/68/JHA, OJ L 335, 1.

135 Directive (EU) 2017/541 of the European Parliament and of the Council of 15.3.2017 on combating terrorism and replacing Council Framework Decision 2002/475/JHA and amending Council Decision 2005/671/JHA, OJ L 88, 6.

136 For a similar approach to interpret the required seriousness from the stated examples cf. Tschorr MMR 2022, 1053 (1056). Kuhlmann/Trute GSZ 2022, 115 (118) refer to, for instance, calls for murder, calls for the destruction of (infrastructure) facilities or hijacking means of transport.

137 Council Directive 93/13/EEC of 5.4.1993 on unfair terms in consumer contracts, OJ L 95, 29. While details may vary, according to Janal GRUR 2022, 211 (217) this directive may be the basis of an EU-wide fairness test for platform terms.

I. Private platform governance as a regulatory principle

33 The power of service providers to control what types of content are uploaded to and made available through their platforms – often referred to as internal 'platform governance' – is usually formed and exercised by means of **contractual agreements** with users of their services. Regardless of whether they are named 'terms of service', 'community standards' or otherwise, these rules will normally, under the applicable contract law of EU member states, be part of numerous parallel contracts[138] that are concluded between the service provider on one hand and each (registered) user on the other and regulate the respective rights and obligations for using the provided services.[139] In this respect, platform governance rules are part of the **free business decision** of a service provider to determine the type content that can be uploaded, processed and made available by the platform and are therefore protected by the freedom to conduct business under Art. 16 CFR. Normally, these rules will also include the moderation of certain non-illegal, but undesired content. The fact that platforms act as **private rule-makers**[140] when they determine the conditions for the use of their offerings as '**internal platform law**'[141] is first and foremost rooted in their **private autonomy and freedom to contract,**[142] just as it is generally open to everyone who provides goods or services to do so under their own contractual rules for these offerings. The DSA recognizes this fundamental principle in Art. 14.[143] In the platform economy it is essential that service providers can create a binding framework for the collaboratively created platform content, which users must comply with and which allows the functioning of online platform services to all users.[144] Any such platform governance aims at **ensuring** the **suitability and quality** (in the broadest sense) of the goods traded and/or services delivered on the platform[145] and to protect users from opportunistic and harmful behaviour of a few other market participants.[146] Measures to this end may include, for example, the use of quality controls (e.g. to ensure minimum standards on marketplaces), the use of filters, the curation and/or moderation of content,[147] access controls or an effective reputation management for platform users.[148] In practice, the removal of illegal content will often be based also

---

[138] On the effect of the general terms of service as market rules beyond individual inter-partes contractual relationships cf. Kumkar ZEuP 2022, 530 (543 et seq.).

[139] Cf. for German contract law only BGH 29.7.2021 – III ZR 179/20, GRUR 2021, 1433 mn. 32; OLG Munich 7.1.2020 – 18 U 1491/19Pre, GRUR-RR 2020, 174 mn. 68; Adelberg K&R 2022, 19 (23); Hennemann/Heldt ZUM 2021, 981 (983); Kettemann/Schulz/Fertmann ZRP 2021, 138; critical towards such private rulemaking Mendelssohn MMR 2021, 857 (859).

[140] On this aspect in general, cf. Schweizer ZEuP 2019, 1; Heinz WuW 2019, 439 (442); Kumkar ZEuP 2022, 530 (532); Mendelssohn MMR 2021, 857 (858).

[141] On this concept in general, cf. Berberich, Virtuelles Eigentum, 2010, p. 245 et seqq.; Denga EuR 2021, 569 (571) refers in this respect to the 'constitution' of a platform model; see also Teubner ZaöRV 2003, 1; Glushko Berkeley Tech. L. J. 2007, 507 (511); Jankowich Tul. J. Tech. & Intell. Prop. 2006, 5 (10); generally on the scope of application of such internal rulemaking Mayer-Schönberger/Crowley NW. U. L. Rev. 2006, 1775 (1794).

[142] Kaesling ZUM 2021, 177 (182); on the design of transaction spaces by setting internal platform law as part of private autonomy and freedom to contract cf. Berberich, Virtuelles Eigentum, 2010, p. 250 et seq.

[143] Janal ZEuP 2021, 227 (231); Janal K&R 2021, 6 (8).

[144] Reidenberg, Governing Networks, p. 919 et seq.

[145] Engert AcP 218 (2018), 304 (351); Kumkar ZEuP 2022, 530 (534 et seq.).

[146] Engert AcP 218 (2018), 304 (352).

[147] Cf. on the moderation of content (also described as curation) Hennemann/Heldt ZUM 2021, 981; Denga EuR 2021, 569 (571); Buchmann in Spiecker/Westland/Campos, Demokratie und Öffentlichkeit, p. 15 (19); Djeffal in Spiecker/Westland/Campos, Demokratie und Öffentlichkeit, p. 177 (180 et seq.).

[148] Engert AcP 218 (2018), 304 (354 et seq., 370 et seq.); Jaekel, Die Macht der digitalen Plattformen, 2017, p. 49.

on (concurrent) breaches of the terms of service.[149] With regard to **communication platforms** and social networks in particular, whose business model is based on an exchange of opinions and information between users, the **moderation of user generated content** as such is nothing new, but has always been practised in online discussion forums (even in old dial-in mailbox systems before the existence of nowadays internet), for example by deleting inappropriate content ('off topic'), offensive content ('trolling') or illegal content. What is rather new, however, is the immense importance of online platforms as communication channels, the increasing societal polarisation of different opinions and more aggressive forms of expression, as well as the extent and impact of moderation efforts undertaken to deal with those general developments. Against this background, some platforms have spurred political discussions by adopting various measures in deleting, demonetarising and shadow banning non-illegal content for various reasons, which are sometimes perceived as intransparent, one-sided and politicising, while others have been criticised for acting too passively.

However, there are generally recognised **limits to private autonomy and freedom to contract**, which likewise apply to the 'internal law' of platforms that is formed by means of contract. To mention the most important ones from a practical perspective, at first, platform use agreements based on **general terms and conditions** must be comply with the EU Unfair Terms Directive and their respective implementations in EU member states laws.[150] (→ mn. 38 et seq.) Even if there is **no direct effect of fundamental rights obligation** for online platforms vis-à-vis their users,[151] questions of **indirect third-party effects** play an increasingly important role for the interpretation as well as for the non-discriminatory and proportionate enforcement of terms of use.[152] In addition, Art. 102 TFEU and/or national **competition laws** of EU member states on abuse of dominant market positions[153] may apply to market-dominant platforms. In a similar vein, to keep open contestable markets, the DMA regulates certain core platform services as an important gateway for business users to reach end users with significant impact on the internal market (so-called 'gatekeepers').[154] **34**

149 Adelberg K&R 2022, 19 (23).

150 As an example for the German implementation of the Unfair Terms Directive in Sec. 305 et seq. BGB (German Civil Code) this is standing case law and courts usually engage in scrutinizing the fairness of such online platforms terms of use, cf. only BGH 29.7.2021 – III ZR 179/20, GRUR 2021, 1433 mn. 30 et seq.; OLG Frankfurt a. M. 12.5.2016 – 22 U 205/14, NJW-RR 2016, 1070; KG 27.12.2018 – 23 U 196/13, GRUR-Prax 2019, 170; OLG Dresden 8.8.2018 – 4 W 577/18, NJW 2018, 3111 (3112); OLG Dresden 30.4.2021 – 4 W 118/21, MMR 2021, 566 mn. 14; OLG Dresden 8.3.2022 – 4 U 1050/21, MMR 2022, 479 mn. 8; OLG Karlsruhe 4.2.2022 – 10 U 17/20, GRUR-RS 2022, 1154 mn. 30 et seq.; LG München 11.10.2018 – 12 O 19277/17, ZD 2019, 174.

151 Rec. 38 DSA; Kaesling ZUM 2021, 177 (182).

152 Rec. 22 DSA; Spindler GRUR 2021, 545 (552).

153 The problematic cases discussed here are not so much cases of content moderation, but rather the preferential treatment of own offers of vertical integrated platforms on their own marketplaces (Heinz WuW 2019, 439 (442); Schweitzer ZEuP 2019, 1 (10); Engert AcP 218 (2018), 304 (367)), falsified ratings (Engert AcP 218 (2018), 304 (367)), falsified or misleading search results or changes to a ranking using extraneous criteria (cf. misleading search results or changes to a ranking using extraneous criteria (cf. in this regard BGH 27.4.2017 – I ZR 55/16, GRUR 2017, 1265 (1267 et seq.); LG München I 18.3.2015 – 37 O 19570/14, MMR 2016, 257 (258 et seq.); Büscher GRUR 2017, 433 (440 et seq.); Engert AcP 218 (2018), 304 (339)).

154 Regulation (EU) 2022/1925 of the European Parliament and of the Council of 14.9.2022 on contestable and fair markets in the digital sector and amending Directives (EU) 2019/1937 and (EU) 2020/1828 (Digital Markets Act), OJ L 265, 1.

II. Enforcement requirements for terms and conditions (Art. 14)

35 Contrary to what was has been discussed in the legislative process[155], the final version of the **DSA** does **not** contain a **fairness test on the substance of general terms** and conditions in platform service terms.[156] This approach appears right, since a substantive fairness test for terms in B2C contracts is already laid down in the Unfair Terms Directive and its respective implementations in EU member states. Apart from that, a general fairness test that scrutinizes the content of B2B contracts (beyond market abuse regulations or special sectoral provisions like in Art. 13 Data Act) is difficult to justify in view of private autonomy, freedom to contract, freedom of competition and freedom to conduct business. Thus, Art. 14 only sets out certain **transparency requirements and enforcement provisions** for general terms and conditions. These rules apply not only to providers of hosting services or to online platforms, but to **all providers of intermediary services** regardless of their size and market power.[157]

36 The concept of **general terms and conditions** under the DSA is understood in a broad sense and includes all clauses, irrespective of their name or form, which govern the contractual relationship between the provider of intermediary services and the recipients of the service (Art. 3(u)).[158] According to the transparency requirements of Art. 14(1)–(3), providers of intermediary services must include information on any **restrictions** on user-provided information in **clear, plain, intelligible,** user-friendly and unambiguous language in their general terms and conditions.[159] This includes information on all policies, procedures, measures and tools for **content moderation,** including algorithmic decision-making and human review, termination rights[160] as well as the **rules of procedure** for the internal complaint handling system as set out in Art. 20. Content moderation is broadly defined in Art. 3(t) as all automated or non-automated activities that are aimed, in particular, at detecting, identifying and addressing content provided by users that is illegal or incompatible with the terms and conditions, including all measures taken that affect the availability, visibility, and accessibility of that content, such as demotion, demonetisation, access blocking or removal, or that affect the ability of users to provide this content, such as termination or suspension of user accounts. This should practically amount to a transparency obligation for **all types of content-related measures** (on these measures in more detail → mn. 52). All terms must be made publicly available by the service provider in an easily accessible and machine-readable for-

[155] Cf. opinion of the Committee on the Internal Market and Consumer Protection, 28.5.2021, 2020/0361(COD), P9_A(2021)0356, p. 73 et seq. on one hand, and opinion of the Committee on Civil Liberties Justice and Home Affairs, 28.7.2021, 2020/0361(COD), LIBE_AD(2021)692898, p. 4, 62 as well as Art. 12(1) of the European Parliament's pre-trilogue DSA draft version on the other.

[156] According to rec. 45, the DSA sets out 'certain rules on the content, application and enforcement of the terms and conditions' of providers. Despite the reference to 'content' this statement cannot be interpreted as to introduce a substantive fairness test, but only refers to transparency requirements. Such a far-reaching encroachment on freedom to contract as a substantive fairness test for all providers of intermediary services is not reflected in the final wording of Art. 14 and could not only be based on ambiguous passages in the recitals after corresponding proposals of the European Parliament have been rejected in the trilogue. Dissenting Legner ZUM 2024, 99 (105).

[157] Spindler GRUR 2021, 545 (551); Denga in Ruffert, Die Regulierung digitaler Plattformen, p. 9 (19).

[158] The fact that the DSA – in contrast to Art. 3(2) Unfair Terms Directive – makes no reference to the requirement of pre-formulated contractual terms is unlikely to be significant in practice, as individually negotiated contract terms do not exist in the mass business between platforms and their users.

[159] From a transparency point of view, there is no objection to be made against the common practice of linking various corresponding policies in the general terms and conditions, provided that this is done in a sufficiently transparent manner and does not involve an excessive 'click-through effort'. Moreover, rec. 45 DSA allows the use of graphic elements for illustration.

[160] Rec. 45 DSA.

mat. Users must also be informed of significant **changes** to the terms,[161] and information to **minors** needs to be understandable for the target group. In addition, very large online platforms and very large search engines must provide a concise, easily accessible and machine-readable summary as well as a **translation** in the official languages of all EU member states where they offer their services (Art. 14(5) and (6)).

One provision in the DSA with probably high significance is the **enforcement control** for the aforementioned restrictions (and thus practically for all types of content moderation measures) enshrined in Art. 14(4). Although the DSA does not put a provider's general terms and conditions to the test for validity, it is their application and enforcement in individual cases, on which the DSA imposes certain limits under fundamental rights aspects: All providers of intermediary services shall act in a **diligent, objective and proportionate** manner in applying and enforcing the said restrictions, with due regard to the rights and legitimate interests of all parties involved, including the fundamental rights of service recipients, such as the freedom of expression, freedom and pluralism of the media, and other fundamental rights and freedoms as enshrined in the CFR. This also requires content moderation measures to be applied in a **non-discriminatory and non-arbitrary** manner[162], which in effect rules out politically motivated measures that favour or disadvantage individual opinions[163] (e.g. political bias, selective enforcement). For details on the general requirements for diligent, objective and non-arbitrary action see also → mn. 23. While the DSA does not impose a direct obligation on service providers to comply with a European set of values or fundamental rights,[164] it nonetheless reflects the indirect effect of fundamental rights as a benchmark for interpretation of (horizontal) civil law relationships in mass business transactions, which is also recognized in EU member state law.[165] Here, too, the fundamental rights of all parties involved (including service providers themselves[166]) must be appropriately balanced – and respective measures to take this into account are advisable, e.g. in applicable moderation policies. Without prejudice to the general discussion on the indirect effect of fundamental rights to the application of EU law in general (→ mn. 39), the DSA explicitly mandates to take such rights into account for its application as EU secondary law. 37

III. Substantive review of service terms under national laws

1. Application of the EU Unfair Terms Directive

The DSA itself does neither preclude a review of general terms and conditions on their substance and validity, nor does it supersede the **applicable substantive contract law** or specific provisions for such test. In particular, the DSA leaves the **Unfair Terms Directive** unaffected[167]. The Unfair Terms Directive ('UTD') regulates unfair terms in B2C consumer contracts (Art. 1(1) UTD). A contractual term (unless individually negotiated) shall be regarded as unfair if, contrary to the requirement of good faith, it causes a significant imbalance in the parties' rights and obligations arising under the contract to 38

---

[161] However, this duty to provide information does not affect the question of how unilateral amendments can change general terms and conditions under the respective applicable contract law of EU member states.

[162] Rec. 47 DSA; Janal ZEuP 2021, 227 (232).

[163] Kaesling ZUM 2021, 177 (183).

[164] Adelberg K&R 2022, 19 (23); critical Denga EuR 2021, 569 (581).

[165] Spindler GRUR 2021, 545 (551). See also → mn. 39 below.

[166] Cf. rec. 3 in general, and specifically for Art. 16 cf. rec. 52 DSA.

[167] Rec. 10 DSA; Kalbhenn/Hemmert-Halswick ZUM 2021, 184 (187); Mendelssohn MMR 2021, 857 (860).

the detriment of the consumer (Art. 3(1) UTD). The unfairness of such terms shall be assessed by taking into account the nature of the goods or services for which the contract was concluded, all circumstances at the time of its conclusion as well as all other applicable terms of the contract or of another dependent contract (Art. 4(1) UTD). However, the main subject matter of the contract and the adequacy of the price and remuneration are excluded from this fairness test (Art. 4(2) UTD). In any case, the notion of unfairness can also be derived from a lack of transparency, as the terms must be drafted in plain, intelligible language (Art. 5(1)(1)). **Unfair terms are not binding** on the consumer, but the remaining contract shall continue to be valid and binding upon the parties if it can continue in existence without the unfair terms (Art. 6(1) UTD). While EU member states have implemented these provisions into their national contract laws, they remain free to adopt or retain more stringent provisions (Art. 8 UTD)[168]. These consumer protection standards will also apply even if service providers choose another applicable law for their service contracts.[169] According to Art. 6(2)(2) Rome I Regulation[170] service providers are in general free to choose the applicable substantive law, but this choice must not deprive European consumers of their minimum legal protection at their place of habitual residence. This includes the consumer protection granted by the Unfair Terms Directive or its national implementations at the place of consumers' residence. Against this background, EU member states' **case law on the validity and interpretation of certain general terms and conditions** under the EU Unfair Terms Directive (or its national implementations) will most likely **continue to apply** also after the DSA has come comes into force. This also includes established EU member states' case law, according to which the general service terms of online platforms must be interpreted and applied in the light of the fundamental rights of all parties involved.[171] Such substantive law standards generally apply to the interpretation as well as to the case-by-case application of a service providers' general terms and conditions. The applicable contract law must therefore be taken into account not only by state courts, but also in internal complaint-handling systems and out-of-court dispute settlement proceedings pursuant to Art. 20 and 21.

2. Impact of fundamental rights in particular

39 Against the background that the Unfair Terms Directive has been implemented as part of **individual EU member states contract laws**, this chapter will not provide an exhaustive overview, but will exemplify the interpretation of service providers' terms with the approach taken by German courts for the implementation of the said fairness test in the German Civil Code. The following case law examples may therefore not strictly reflect the respective applicable law throughout the EU, but provide a rough guideline of what courts could consider as unfair terms under the aforementioned standards. The starting point for the review of content moderation measures under contract law is that any restrictive measure (in particular removal) must be justified and based on the respective contract (i.e. the terms of service) and may not be carried

[168] In Germany, for instance, the fairness test for general terms and conditions is not confined to B2C contracts but with some modifications also applies to general terms and conditions in B2B contracts, e.g. between platforms and professional users.

[169] Cf. BGH 29.7.2021 – III ZR 179/20, GRUR 2021, 1433 mn. 26.

[170] Regulation (EC) No 593/2008 of the European Parliament and of the Council of 17 June 2008 on the law applicable to contractual obligations (Rome I), OJ L 177, 6.

[171] Cf. for the example of Germany only BGH 29.7.2021 – III ZR 179/20, GRUR 2021, 1433 mn. 54 et seq.; highlighting the continuing importance of this case law under the DSA also Legner ZUM 2024, 99 (105).

out without reason.[172] The German Federal Supreme Court for instance allows a platform operator to impose regulations on content, such as a ban on certain types of undesirable (not illegal) statements, provided that this is **objectively justified** and is done by **weighing** the respective concerned fundamental rights in the individual case.[173] For the interpretation of the terms of service and the application of specific restriction measures, the **indirect effect of the fundamental rights of all parties** must be taken into account.[174] Comparable principles may apply at the level of EU law. While a general doctrine of interpretation of secondary EU law in the light of the fundamental rights enshrined in the CFR appears not yet generally acknowledged,[175] approaches to such methodology can nonetheless be found in CJEU practice, according to which the courts of EU member states must not only interpret their national law in a manner consistent with an implemented directive but also as not conflicting with fundamental rights or with the other general principles of EU law. Specifically for the fairness test in the Unfair Terms Directive, the CJEU case law has so far been focused on economic fairness of terms, e.g. in the context of loans, transparency requirements, or legal remedies so that questions of other fundamental rights have not yet found their way to be assessed here.[176] Yet, the methodology to interpret EU secondary law (also with implications for private law relationships) in the light of fundamental rights as such is supported by CJEU case law.[177] Therefore, it is argued that the CFR must be taken into account for

---

172 Cf. for the example of Germany BGH 29.7.2021 – III ZR 179/20, GRUR 2021, 1433 mn. 28; BGH 27.1.2022 – III ZR 12/21, NJW-RR 2022, 625 mn. 34, 49.

173 In this context, the conflicting multipolar interests of all parties involved must be resolved in such a way that their respective interests are balanced out as far as possible, cf. BGH 29.7.2021 – III ZR 179/20, GRUR 2021, 1433 mn. 59 et seq.; BGH 27.1.2022 – III ZR 12/21, NJW-RR 2022, 625 mn. 48; OLG Munich 12.4.2022 – 18 U 6473/20 PRE, GRUR-RS 2022, 11666 mn. 26; OLG Celle 20.1.2022 – 13 U 84/19, MMR 2022, 399 (400); OLG Dresden 8.8.2018 – 4 W 577/18, NJW 2018, 3111 (3114); OLG Düsseldorf 4.12.2020 – 7 U 131/19, GRUR-RS 2020, 41440 mn. 31.

174 Cf. for the example of Germany BGH 29.7.2021 – III ZR 179/20, GRUR 2021, 1433 mn. 54; BGH 27.1.2022 – III ZR 12/21, NJW-RR 2022, 625 mn. 43; OLG Munich 24.8.2018 – 18 W 1294/18, NJW 2018, 3115 mn. 27; OLG Dresden 8.8.2018 – 4 W 577/18, NJW 2018, 3111 (3113); OLG Düsseldorf 4.12.2020 – 7 U 131/19, GRUR-RS 2020, 41440 mn. 31; OLG Karlsruhe 25.6.2018 – 15 W 86/18, 25.6.2018 – 15 W 86/18, NJW 2018, 3110 mn. 18; KG 22.3.2019 – 10 W 172/18, NJW-RR 2019, 1260 mn. 17–19; OLG Nürnberg 4.8.2020 – 3 U 3641/19, GRUR-RR 2020, 543 mn. 53 et seq.; cf. also Raue JZ 2018, 961 (965).

175 Thus far, the case law of the CJEU only recognises a third-party effect of specific equality and social rights, but not of liberty rights, cf. Kingreen in Calliess/Ruffert, 6th ed. 2022, CFR Art. 51 mn. 27 with further references; cf. also Denga in Ruffert, Die Regulierung digitaler Plattformen, p. 9 (20).

176 Nonetheless, under the lens of economic and procedural fairness, the CJEU has already interpreted the UTD and their national implementations in the light of fundamental rights, namely Art. 47 CFR (cf. CJEU 17.07.2014 C-169/14, ECLI:EU:C:2014:2099, mn. 50 with interpretation of Art. 7 UTD in conjunction with Art. 47 CFR as basis for procedural equality rights, or CJEU 22.09.2022 C-335/21, ECLI:EU:C:2022:720, mn. 70 and CJEU 03.04.2019, C-266/18, ECLI:EU:C:2019:282, mn. 47, both emphasising that implementations of the UTD must i.a. provide for effective legal remedies under Art. 47 CFR).

177 Cf. for the interpretation of Art. 17 DSM-Directive (EU) 2019/790 CJEU 26.4.2022 – C-401/19, ECLI:EU:C:2021:613 = GRUR-RS 2021, 20614 mn. 89 et seq. – Republic of Poland v EP and Council, as well as Opinion AG Saugmandsgaard Øe of 15.7.2021 in proceedings CJEU C-401/19, ECLI:EU:C:2021:613 = GRUR-RS 2021, 20614 mn. 5, 87, 129. Cf. also for other EU directives that concern private law liability relationships CJEU 24.11.2011, C-70/10, ECLI:EU:C:2011:771 – Scarlet Extended, mn. 43 et seq. (balancing of fundamental rights); CJEU 27.03.2014, C-314/12, ECLI:EU:C:2014:192 – UPC Telekabel Wien, mn. 46; CJEU 29.01.2008, C-275/06, ECLI:EU:C:2008:54 – Promusicae = NJW 2008, 743 mn. 68; cf. more generally CJEU 26.06.2007, C-305/05, ECLI:EU:C:2007:383 – Ordre des barreaux francophones et germanophone, mn. 28 et seq.; CJEU 06.11.2003, C-101/01, ECLI:EU:C:2003:596 – Lindqvist = EuZW 2004, 245 mn. 87; cf. for balancing fundamental rights methodologically also CJEU 17.04.2018, C-414/16, ECLI:EU:C:2018:257 – Egenberger, mn. 81.

the interpretation of the general provisions of primary and secondary EU law, also in the context of private law relationships.[178]

40 Accordingly, for **(uploading) users** as addressees of restricting measures, their fundamental rights to freedom of expression (Art. 11(1) CFR), equality and non-discrimination (Art. 20, 21(1) CFR) must be taken into account.[179] **Platform operators** can invoke their freedom to conduct their business including the freedom of contract (Art. 16 CFR).[180] These rights do not only enshrine the freedom to participate in the competitive process by offering own services, but these rights also protect an appropriate scope for the design of a business model and economic development (e.g. with a target group of users who want to communicate on specific topics only or within a safe environment). Platform operators have a legitimate business interest in creating an attractive communication and advertising environment for both users and advertisers.[181] Likewise, they have a legitimate interest in (i) not being liable for potentially illegal content,[182] (ii) in creating communication rules that are as uniform as possible within the service, also in cross-border cases[183] and (iii) in competing with other platforms by setting certain quality and moderation standards for their users.[184] In that regard, the decision of what type of (non-illegal) content shall be moderated or not, and how strict the implemented moderation measures shall be, constitutes the very foundation of each platform's competitive freedom (but see → § 6 for the EU Commission's attempts to impose more control over content at least in case of very large online platforms). By adhering to certain communication quality standards, the interest of **other users** is also protected from violations of their right to private life, human dignity, and non-discrimination (Art. 1, 7, 21 CFR).[185] These (or similar) principles applicable for the interpretation and application of general terms and conditions under the respective applicable national contract law continue to apply after the DSA went into force.[186]

41 The impact of fundamental rights (in particular the freedom of expression) when applying such measures and enforcing restrictions may pose **difficult questions as to interpretation** of what has actually been said and drawing a line between what is permissible or not. This challenge, however, is not specific to platform regulation, but lies in the nature of all laws that regulate any forms of speech. The interpretation of

---

178 Pache in Pechstein/Nowak/Hände, Frankfurter Kommentar, 1st ed. 2017, CFR Art. 51 mn. 38; Hatje in Schwarze/Becker/Hatje/Schoo, EU-Kommentar, 4th ed. 2019, CFR Art. 51 mn. 22; cf. also Pötters in Preis/Sagan, Europäisches Arbeitsrecht, 2nd ed. 2019, Die Unionsgrundrechte, mn. 3.33.

179 For the indirect effect of such fundamental rights in the interpretation of terms of use under national contract law in the example of Germany cf. BGH 29.7.2021 – III ZR 179/20, GRUR 2021, 1433 mn. 61 et seqq.; BGH 27.1.2022 – III ZR 12/21, NJW-RR 2022, 625 mn. 45. For the significance of these fundamental rights under the DSA see rec. 3, 47, 51 et seq., 54, 63, 81, 86, 90, 150.

180 For the indirect effect of such fundamental rights in the interpretation of terms of use under national contract law in the example of Germany cf. BGH 29.7.2021 – III ZR 179/20, GRUR 2021, 1433 mn. 69; BGH 27.1.2022 – III ZR 12/21, NJW-RR 2022, 625 mn. 45 (according to which platform operators can also invoke their own freedom of expression). For the significance of platform operators' fundamental rights under the DSA see rec. 3 and 52.

181 Cf. BGH 29.7.2021 – III ZR 179/20, GRUR 2021, 1433 mn. 73; OLG Nürnberg 4.8.2020 – 3 U 3641/19, GRUR-RR 2020, 543 mn. 63.

182 BGH 29.7.2021 – III ZR 179/20, GRUR 2021, 1433 mn. 76 et seq.; OLG Nürnberg 4.8.2020 – 3 U 3641/19, GRUR-RR 2020, 543 mn. 68.

183 BGH 29.7.2021 – III ZR 179/20, GRUR 2021, 1433 mn. 50.

184 OLG Nürnberg 4.8.2020 – 3 U 3641/19, GRUR-RR 2020, 543 mn. 63.

185 For the indirect effect of such fundamental rights in the interpretation of terms of use under national contract law in the example of Germany cf. BGH 29.7.2021 – III ZR 179/20, GRUR 2021, 1433 mn. 75; BGH 27.1.2022 – III ZR 12/21, NJW-RR 2022, 625 mn. 46. For the significance of these fundamental rights under the DSA see rec. 52, 81.

186 Janal GRUR 2022, 211 (217).

statements (including their respective contexts), their assessment under applicable laws or terms, and the required consideration of fundamental rights create a considerable **risk of misjudgement**, which is even exacerbated with the use of automated systems.[187] This is all the more true in cases of justified critique, citations, irony, sarcasm, and missing context.[188] However, precisely these difficulties in handling content may be mitigated by the 'staged' moderation approach of the DSA: The risk of a certain and reasonable level of misjudgement through the use of automated systems in the notice mechanism is – at least under the current technological state of the art – inherent in this expressly permitted means of moderation. Any misjudgement at this automated first level moderation is to be corrected by human (internal) or even judicial (external) review at subsequent escalation levels. The DSA framework can therefore be seen as taking these problems into account from a procedural perspective, as it allows for mass decisions at the first level (with a certain error rate in a reasonable number of cases), which must then be corrected in mandatory appeal procedures (which also scrutinize fundamental rights implications in more detail that are difficult to tackle in a fully-automated review).

3. Exemplary case law guidelines from an EU member state's perspective

The following **summarized case law standards** present an **example** from a German perspective of how EU member states' courts could handle and **interpret general terms and conditions** in the context of online platforms when applying the EU Unfair Terms Directive and its implementation into national contract law, taking into account the **indirect effect of fundamental rights** in their interpretation on a case-by-case basis. Albeit the interpretation and validity of terms from a contract law perspective is not regulated by the DSA, it remains to be seen to what extent courts will also resort to these principles when applying the DSA and in particular Art. 14(4). This is not unlikely, given that the methodology (balancing of fundamental rights) and the subject matter of the legal test (scrutinizing moderation measures) are quite similar and may overlap under substantive contract law and under the regulatory framework for enforcement control by Art. 14(4) DSA. 42

As a starting point for the assessment under (in this example German) contract law implementing the EU Unfair Terms Directive, all **moderation measures** and especially the removal of content require an **objective reason**[189]. Platform operators' decisions in this regard must be comprehensible and their contractual basis must not hinge on subjective believes or fears, but on objective, verifiable facts.[190] As part of their private platform governance, service providers can set out in their terms general **thematic restrictions** as a general exclusion of certain types of content that do not correspond to the **purpose of the platform**[191] (e.g. a general ban on political discussions on a 43

[187] Cf. OLG Karlsruhe 4.2.2022 – 10 U 17/20, GRUR-RS 2022, 1154 mn. 43; on the challenges for laws that restrict free speech in general cf. Spindler in Spiecker/Westland/Campos, Demokratie und Öffentlichkeit, p. 75 (95); Denga EuR 2021, 569 (572); Schwartmann NJW 2022, 133 (137).

[188] Augsberg/Petras JuS 2022, 97 (105).

[189] BGH 29.7.2021 – III ZR 179/20, GRUR 2021, 1433 mn. 81; BGH 27.1.2022 – III ZR 12/21, NJW-RR 2022, 625 mn. 49; OLG Karlsruhe 4.2.2022 – 10 U 17/20, GRUR-RS 2022, 1154 mn. 38.

[190] BGH 29.7.2021 – III ZR 179/20, GRUR 2021, 1433 mn. 82; BGH 27.1.2022 – III ZR 12/21, NJW-RR 2022, 625 mn. 49; OLG Frankfurt a. M. 30.6.2022 – 16 U 229/20, GRUR-RS 2022, 15047 mn. 71; OLG Dresden 8.8.2018 – 4 W 577/18, NJW 2018, 3111 (3113); OLG Düsseldorf 4.12.2020 – 7 U 131/19, GRUR-RS 2020, 41440 mn. 35; OLG Karlsruhe 4.2.2022 – 10 U 17/20, GRUR-RS 2022, 1154 mn. 39.

[191] BGH 29.7.2021 – III ZR 179/20, GRUR 2021, 1433 mn. 81; OLG Dresden 8.8.2018 – 4 W 577/18, NJW 2018, 3111 (3113); Raue JZ 2018, 961 (968). See also Opinion of the Committee on Civil Liberties Justice and Home Affairs of 28.7.2021, 2020/0361(COD), p. 4, 62: "[T]erms and conditions shall respect fundamental rights and permit interferences with the free exchange of lawful information only where it is

specialised expert platform). It is also appropriate to set up a mandatory code of conduct in the terms of service that aims at **respectful interaction of users**, which prevents the risk of users and advertising partners turning away from a platform due to rude interaction manners. According to case law, however, a general communication platform that is not restricted to certain topics cannot prohibit its users to express (non-illegal) **individual opinions** or political views as such just for the sake of their stance.[192] Any bans on content or topics of speech must affect all users in a **non-discriminatory way.**[193] The content moderation and restriction practice must not create the structural danger of excluding parts of the public opinion spectrum in a one-sided, biased manner,[194] nor can a privatisation of communication spaces lead to a situation where societal conflicts can no longer be freely carried out.[195] Thus, a supposed protection against **being confronted with dissenting opinions** is not a legally recognisable interest, since taking note of and evaluating other people's opinions is inevitably entailed by the freedom of expression and desirable in a democratic society.[196] Users or user groups must not be treated differently only because of their opinions, and they cannot be excluded or sanctioned for that reason as such.[197] When interpreting and assessing contested user statements, this must be done from the perspective of a reasonable **average reader**[198] and in their **factual context,** without isolating them or taking them out of the context they were made in.[199] This applies in particular to links on content elsewhere or to quotations from third parties.[200] Posting mere links as such cannot be automatically interpreted as a statement of support or attribution.[201] **Ambiguous statements** cannot be equated with prohibited statements as long as a reasonable assessment gives no clear indication otherwise.[202]

44 Compared to opinions as such, the **way and manner of expression** can be moderated more strongly to ensure a **minimum level of decency** in debates.[203] In this context,

---

incompatible with the declared purpose of the service." This high hurdle did not ultimately become part of the DSA, but is likely to remain a recognised case of content moderation under contract law. However, the declared purpose itself cannot not be such as to contravene the aforementioned standards.

[192] BGH 29.7.2021 – III ZR 179/20, GRUR 2021, 1433 mn. 81; BGH 27.1.2022 – III ZR 12/21, NJW-RR 2022, 625 mn. 49; OLG Dresden 8.8.2018 – 4 W 577/18, NJW 2018, 3111 (3114); Schwartmann NJW 2022, 133 (135); Raue JZ 2018, 961 (967); cf. also Augsberg/Petras JuS 2022, 97 (106) on the responsibility of social media that opens up a general space of public discussion to maintain plurality in the discussion. If online platforms want to represent their own point of view, a less strict and more proportionate measure than deletion is always to distance themselves from user content, cf. Raue JZ 2018, 961 (968).

[193] OLG Frankfurt a. M. 30.6.2022 – 16 U 229/20, GRUR-RS 2022, 15047 mn. 71.

[194] Dienstbühl GRUR-Prax 2019, 446.

[195] Raue JZ 2018, 961 (966).

[196] OLG Nürnberg 4.8.2020 – 3 U 3641/19, GRUR-RR 2020, 543 mn. 67. No appropriate standard for general communication platforms is the creation of a feel-good atmosphere that prohibits critical statements (Raue JZ 961 (967); Augsberg/Petras JuS 2022, 97 (105) with reference to BVerfG 22.2.2011 – 1 BvR 699/06, NJW 2011, 1201). Thus, terms that prohibit content just due to users subjectively 'feeling hurt' or being 'triggered' would probably not pass these standards.

[197] OLG Nürnberg 4.8.2020 – 3 U 3641/19, GRUR-RR 2020, 543 mn. 80 et seq.

[198] OLG Munich 24.8.2018 – 18 W 1294/18, NJW 2018, 3115 mn. 31; OLG Düsseldorf 4.12.2020 – 7 U 131/19, GRUR-RS 2020, 41440 mn. 35; OLG Frankfurt a. M. 30.6.2022 – 16 U 229/20, GRUR-RS 2022, 15047 mn. 79; KG 22.3.2019 – 10 W 172/18, NJW-RR 2019, 1260 mn. 22.

[199] BGH 29.7.2021 – III ZR 179/20, GRUR 2021, 1433 mn. 86; OLG Munich 24.8.2018 – 18 W 1294/18, NJW 2018, 3115 mn. 31; OLG Düsseldorf 4.12.2020 – 7 U 131/19, GRUR-RS 2020, 41440 mn. 35; KG 22.3.2019 – 10 W 172/18, NJW-RR 2019, 1260 mn. 22.

[200] OLG Munich 7.1.2020 – 18 U 1491/19PRE, GRUR-RR 2020, 174 mn. 119.

[201] This was left open by OLG Dresden 8.3.2022 – 4 U 1050/21, MMR 2022, 479 mn. 13.

[202] Cf. OLG Düsseldorf 4.12.2020 – 7 U 131/19, GRUR-RS 2020, 41440 mn. 37 et seq., this may be different if a clear tendency can be derived from the context of a previous discussion, mn. 58.

[203] OLG Nürnberg 4.8.2020 – 3 U 3641/19, GRUR-RR 2020, 543 mn. 73; with this tendency also Schwartmann NJW 2022, 133 (136 et seq.).

even sharp, exaggerated or tasteless statements that may be perceived as inappropriate or politically incorrect by some users are covered by the freedom of expression. This applies in particular to controversial political or social issues, as long as the discussion is focused on the substance of these issues and do not disparage certain persons or groups of persons.[204] Here, the term '**hate speech**' is particularly difficult to handle. This term originates from US-American legal doctrines and appears – as such, unless it refers to illegal content[205] or is defined in more detail – conceptually too vague for content moderation.[206] Therefore, restrictions in general terms and conditions related to so called hate speech must be (and mostly are in practice) further **specified with subsumable objective criteria**. These approaches, speaking generally, normally amount to **prohibiting a blanket disparagement** or exclusion of people or groups of people.[207] Such prohibition of objectionable forms of expression must, however, leave unaffected the possibility of **expressing critical opinions**, including societal criticism, criticism of the media and censorship[208] or drastic criticism of political decisions.[209] To be distinguished from such a blanket disparagement of people is also the expression of accurate facts[210] or statistical statements,[211] the assessment of specific actions taken by persons[212] or criticism of persons or groups factually related to specific events[213] as well as ironic or sarcastic use of terms.[214] Under these free speech case law standards, it is fair to argue that appropriately worded and non-illegal statements for supporting or rejecting certain societal developments or political ideologies and criticism of persons (especially those in public life) cannot be prohibited – as opposed to inadmissible generalisations that disparage persons and are unrelated to specific facts or events.[215]

Dealing with so-called '**fake news**' or '**disinformation**' is not per se part of the 45
mandatory general due diligence obligations of the DSA for all online platforms and therefore primarily subject to individual private platform governance. However, a mechanism of **voluntary self-regulation** exists here with the Strengthened **Code of Practice on Disinformation**[216], which plays a role in particular for very large online platforms as

---

[204] OLG Düsseldorf 4.12.2020 – 7 U 131/19, GRUR-RS 2020, 41440 mn. 57.

[205] Hate speech in Council Framework Decision 2008/913/JHA of 28.11.2008 on combating certain forms and expressions of racism and xenophobia by means of criminal law refers i.a. to public incitement to violence or hatred against a group of persons or against a member of such a group on the basis of race, colour, religion, descent or national or ethnic origin, which EU member states shall make punishable. Insofar as this is already a criminal act, it is in any case illegal content as defined by the DSA. On criminal forms of hate speech, see Ukrow UFITA 2021, 223 (229 et seqq.).

[206] Cf. for the lack of a general legally binding definition and a variety of different approaches, cf. Ukrow UFITA 2021, 223 (227 et seq.); Schneiders UFITA 2021, 269 (274).

[207] Cf. for a differentiating and opinion-neutral approach Schwartmann NJW 2022, 133 (136 et seq.).

[208] OLG Karlsruhe 10.11.2021 – 14 U 46/19, GRUR-RS 2021, 51703 mn. 47 (irrespective of whether correct or whether majority or minority opinion).

[209] KG 22.3.2019 – 10 W 172/18, NJW-RR 2019, 1260 mn. 23; OLG Karlsruhe 10.11.2021 – 14 U 46/19, GRUR-RS 2021, 51703 mn. 47 (including criticism of immigration); OLG Nürnberg 4.8.2020 – 3 U 3641/19, GRUR-RR 2020, 543 mn. 116.

[210] OLG Oldenburg 1.7.2019 – 13 W 16/19, MMR 2020, 41 mn. 10.

[211] OLG Nürnberg 4.8.2020 – 3 U 3641/19, GRUR-RR 2020, 543 mn. 132.

[212] OLG Oldenburg 1.7.2019 – 13 W 16/19, MMR 2020, 41 mn. 11.

[213] Cf. OLG Frankfurt a. M. 30.6.2022 – 16 U 229/20, GRUR-RS 2022, 15047 mn. 71; OLG Nürnberg 4.8.2020 – 3 U 3641/19, GRUR-RR 2020, 543 mn. 111 (group of persons accused of lack of respect towards the legal system with reference to specific events), KG 22.3.2019 – 10 W 172/18, NJW-RR 2019, 1260 mn. 23 (polemical expression of fears).

[214] OLG Nürnberg 4.8.2020 – 3 U 3641/19, GRUR-RR 2020, 543 mn. 118.

[215] OLG Bamberg 16.6.2020 – 5 U 337/19, GRUR-RS 2020, 44668 mn. 36; OLG Nürnberg 4.8.2020 – 3 U 3641/19, GRUR-RR 2020, 543 mn. 125.

[216] The new 2022 Strengthened Code of Practice on Disinformation is currently signed by 44 companies and replaces the previous Code of Conduct from 2018, EU Commission, 16.06.2022 <https://digital-strate

a prospective risk mitigation measure under their specific obligations of Art. 35.[217] Adherence to this code, however, is not mandatory under the DSA, but may be just one factor among many for assessing the – rather vague – systemic obligations of very large online platforms (→ § 6).

46 Yet, **drawing a line** between what is considered harmful 'disinformation' – and thus would be excluded as the basis for individual opinion-forming at the outset – or what information is necessary for a public and democratic discourse and the process of individual opinion-forming in a pluralistic, open-minded society, is very difficult and extremely sensitive due to the direct **impact on citizens' fundamental rights.**[218] Various societal conflicts appear to be triggering an inflationary, sometimes politically motivated use of the 'fake news' label for discrediting content that is technically no false statement of fact. This problem of 'disinformation fight overreach' is exacerbated by some cases where moderation measures have allegedly been politically influenced or where fact-checking businesses themselves are accused of applying double standards. Any meaningful legal assessment of 'disinformation' must therefore rely on objective, general, non-biased, content-agnostic criteria: Disinformation requires per definition **false or misleading information.**[219] This does **not include** expressions of opinion, evaluations, forecasts, scientific studies (and references thereto), correct quotations marked as such, accurate statements of fact (unless the context necessary for their understanding is omitted), or such facts that are simply not clearly verifiable or falsifiable. To be distinguished from disinformation are also misleading advertising (which is regulated under consumer protection and/or fair trading laws), reporting errors, satire, parody or clearly identified partisan news and commentary.[220] There is in particular no general legal rule that, in case of doubt, unproven information equates with disinformation, as its suppression would massively curb the public discourse and fundamentally threaten free speech in an open democratic society. Findings of new facts may occur over time can lead to new assessments. This is even true for authoritative sources whose horizon of knowledge usually changes over time (also in the fields of science and health) and whose public information handling may sometimes be unduly influenced by politics. Therefore, a premature, interest-driven categorisation of unclear facts (or even of subjective assessments) as alleged disinformation, coupled with deleting such content or demonetising information sources, creates the risk of cutting off necessary discussions and discursive truth-finding.[221] Such a broad understanding and even suppression of alleged 'disinfor-

gy.ec.europa.eu/en/library/2022-strengthened-code-practice-disinformation> (last accessed: 23.06.2024). While some signatories have left since due to unclarities and differences what should be considered disinformation under free speech aspects, new signatories have joined including those whose business is fact-checking. The Code regulates various measures, including limiting the spread of disinformation through demonetisation and exclusion of advertising networks, transparency of political advertising, user empowerment and improving cooperation with fact-checkers and researchers.

[217] Cf. 2022 Code of Practice on Disinformation, preamble lit. j.

[218] Cf. on this conflict 2022 Code of Practice on Disinformation, preamble lit. b and c.

[219] Cf. 2022 Code of Practice on Disinformation, preamble lit. a. This can be further differentiated into disinformation in a narrower sense (i.e. spread with an intention to deceive or secure economic or political gain) or misinformation (shared without harmful intent) as well as various campaigns for the use thereof, cf. 2022 Code of Practice on Disinformation, preamble lit. a footnote 7–10.

[220] Cf. 2022 Code of Practice on Disinformation, preamble lit. a footnote 5.

[221] Critical in view of a changing information base also Peukert VerfBlog, 31.8.2021<https://verfassungsblog.de/power-dsa-dma-04> (ast accessed: 23.06.2024). The approach to rely on a proactive discourse to contain the effects of disinformation is not, in the view expressed here, a worrying protection gap, because severe cases are covered by criminal law, and the appropriate and adequate means of dealing with false information is not its removal, but rather, if necessary, references to reliable, neutral, corrective sources that enable users to review and assess the content themselves. It would be contradictory to apply on one hand in the commercial sphere the role model of the average, reasonably well-informed and reasonably

mation' would be at odds with EU fundamental rights standards. In addition, Article 14(4) DSA sets out the general requirement of non-discriminatory and non-arbitrary content moderation also in the realm of alleged disinformation (→ mn. 37). Therefore, service providers must act in an unbiased manner and use the same standards for such test regardless of the specific type of content in question.

IV. Put-back claim

In the event of an unlawful deletion or other restriction of user content, the **DSA** does regulate a **procedure**, but even in its final version it appears **not** to provide for an individual subjective claim of a user for restoration of such content (**put back**).[222] This can be understood by looking at the scope of the DSA, where the notion of illegality or compliance with the respective terms of service is a question to be answered by the **applicable substantive law**, which cannot be derived from the DSA itself. Thus, users of intermediary services and in particular online platforms may have such an individual claim under the respective applicable substantive contract law from their **user contract.** In Germany for instance, such claim is generally recognised in case law.[223] The existence of such claims is also implicitly presupposed by the DSA, as the internal complaint handling or reference to external dispute resolution would be of little use without a substantive claim for restitution, which decides under **standards outside the DSA** whether the user is successful or not.[224] Particularly in the B2B sector, a put back claim has considerable significance (for example between app stores and software developers in the case of deleted apps, between sales platforms and online shops in the case of blocking, or generally within a platform ecosystem involving as users professional third-party service providers).[225] 47

The same applies mutatis mutandis to the deletion of content. Again, the **DSA constitutes** a content-agnostic and first and foremost procedural regulation, and it does **not in itself** grant **any individual claims** for non-uploading users or even third parties to have deleted the content of other users, but rather presupposes such claims under applicable substantive law. Normally, notifying entities within the meaning of Article 16(1), who are not at the same time registered users, will most probably have no contractual claims 48

observant and circumspect consumer (settled case law of the CJEU, cf. only CJEU 16.7.1998 – C-210/96, GRUR Int 1998, 795 – Gut Springenheide; for an overview cf. Lettl GRUR 2004, 449 (453)), but to deny him this role model as a critical, self-standing citizen in the political process. Also, a scientific discourse cannot be silenced by content moderation just with reference to an alleged majority opinion at a given time.

222 Spindler GRUR 2021, 545 (553); Adelberg K&R 2022, 19 (22); v. Lewinski/Klink RDi 2023, 183 (188); probably also Buiten JIPITEC 2021, 361 (379); dissenting Kühling ZUM 2021, 461 (469). In particular, the duty of online platforms to correct unjustified decisions in the appeal procedure pursuant to Article 20(4) is a purely procedural duty and, according to the view expressed here, does not convey an individual claim, but must be measured against the standard of substantive law, which determines the existence and scope of such claim (→ mn. 59). This provision was already included in the EU Commission's DSA draft (as Art. 17(3)) and was not changed in the legislative process.

223 Such contractual claim would under German law be derived from a breach of contract (i.e. to publish the user's content unless illegal or forbidden by the terms of service), cf. BGH 29.7.2021 – III ZR 179/20, GRUR 2021, 1433 mn. 27; see also Spindler GRUR 2021, 545 (553); Janal ZEuP 2021, 227 (253); Wagner GRUR 2020, 447 (452). However, only users who have signed up to the terms of service will have such claim. Insofar as the users as defined in Art. 3 lit. b DSA should also include passive, only 'reading' users without registration (see → mn. 51), it is doubtful whether there is a contract in place.

224 Spindler GRUR 2021, 653 (654).

225 Janal ZEuP 2021, 227 (253).

against an online platform.[226] Claims under the applicable substantive law may exist first and foremost for a specific injured party under e.g. general tort law, criminal law or other sector specific laws (like intellectual property infringements).

E. Dispute resolution on online platforms

I. Internal complaint handling system (Art. 20)

1. General systematics and DSA framework

49 A new obligation for all online platforms is to establish for their users an electronic, easily accessible, free of charge internal complaint handling system. This obligation is an essential element in the DSA's **balancing act** between removing **illegal content** on the one hand and avoiding **overblocking** of lawful content on the other (→ mn. 3). In this respect, the aim of the internal complaint handling system is also to **protect uploading users** whose content has been deleted or otherwise restricted without sufficient basis. Art. 20 can therefore be seen as a mechanism for **fundamental rights protection through procedure**[227] by giving uploading users the right to be heard and to have their position assessed in a fair manner. Whether it is appropriate that the EU legislator in effect pushes online platforms into a judge-like role (at least in a first instance) and places the substantial burden of private law enforcement upon them (especially for 'horizontal' disputes between users) is debatable under different points of view.[228] However, if the legislator does so, then it is only consequent to demand the application of procedural principles based on the rule of law.[229] Similar mechanisms of internal dispute resolution can be found in other areas of platform regulation, such as Art. 17(9) DSM Directive or national laws[230].

50 The obligation to set up an internal complaint handling system primarily contains **procedural requirements** and does not pre-determine specific results in individual cases.[231] In view of the large conceivable spectrum of allegedly illegal content and disputes, this would neither be feasible nor is it the subject matter of the DSA. As set out before, the DSA as such does not specify the standard for determining illegality (in the case of allegedly illegal content) or contract violations (in the case of content allegedly being contrary to the terms of service). This assessment depends in every individual case on the **applicable substantive law** or the applicable terms of service, taking into account the fundamental rights of the parties involved. The DSA itself ensures that restricting decisions can be scrutinized under these standards. Moreover, the complaint handling procedure requires – unlike the preceding notice and action procedure – to have a **human review** for the first time. Even with numerous online platforms having implemented 'counter-notification' schemes as part of their notice-and-take-down procedure, an internal complaint handling mechanism in accordance with Art. 20 is now mandatory

---

[226] Cf. for German law also Spindler GRUR 2021, 545 (552 et seq.).

[227] Cf. on procedural safeguards for fundamental rights also BGH 29.7.2021 – III ZR 179/20, GRUR 2021, 1433 mn. 84; Raue JZ 2018, 961 (969); Augsberg/Petras JuS 2022, 97 (103).

[228] Cf. as critical towards this tendency Guggenberger NJW 2017, 2577; Mendelsohn MMR 2021, 857 (869); with correct differentiation as to the role of online platforms in multipolar legal relationships Raue JZ 2018, 961 (962); Hofmann/Sprenger UFITA 2021, 249. On such 'privatisation of enforcement' in general cf. also Kalbhenn/Hemmert-Halswick MMR 2020, 518 (521); Kaesling ZUM 2021, 177 (181).

[229] Hofmann/Sprenger UFITA 2021, 249 (261 et seqq.).

[230] In Germany for instance § 14 UrhDaG, § 3b NetzDG or § 10b 2nd sent. no. 6 TMG.

[231] Similarly Kalbhenn/Hemmert-Halswick ZUM 2021, 184 (188).

for **all online platforms except for micro or small enterprises** (→ mn. 17). The latter, however, have the option of setting up an internal complaint handling procedure on a voluntary basis[232] and, without the requirements of Art. 20, have bigger discretion in how doing so.

2. Eligibility to file and subject matter of complaints

51 In the EU Commission's draft, the complaint-handling procedure was designed as an appeal instance against restricting measures so that uploading users were entitled to file a complaint.[233] In the final version of the DSA, a complaint can also be filed against decisions to reject measures following the notice and action procedure (Art. 16). Therefore, **recipients of the service**, including individuals or entities that have submitted a notice, are **entitled to file a complaint**. This includes, on one hand, **uploading users** affected by moderation measures and, on the other hand, **users who gave notice** on allegedly illegal content in the notice procedure. In this respect, the subject matter of the complaint procedure differs depending on the applicant, but are mirror images of each other. According to the clear wording of the DSA, there is **no** obligation to make an internal complaint-handling system available to **external notifying parties** who are not at the same time recipients of the service.[234] What needs to be clarified in practice, however, is how broad the term 'recipient of the service' in Art. 3(b) can be interpreted. Such recipients are not only uploading users, but also passive (reading) users.[235] It is doubtful, however, whether this would include users without an account or registration.[236]

52 In the first (and practically more important) case, **subject matter** of the procedure are complaints lodged by uploading users against the service provider's decision on **restricting measures** mentioned in Art. 20(1) based on allegedly **illegal content** or content **incompatible with the terms and conditions**[237]. These can be decisions taken in individual cases after a notice and action procedure (Art. 16), but can also be any restrictive measures taken manually or automatically (e.g. by filters) in the context of proactive or reactive content moderation pursuant to Art. 17(1). Regardless of the slightly different wording, Art. 17(1)(a)–(d) and Art. 20(1)(a)–(d) both set out essentially the same moderation measures, which concern uploaded content (information), service provision, user accounts and/or monetisation and, in each case, their respective restriction or termination. These measures are:

- In relation to **content,** its **removal** (deletion), the temporary or permanent **disabling of access** (whether only for certain users or for all users), and any **restriction of visi-**

[232] Rec. 43 DSA.

[233] Cf. on the restriction to uploading users in the EU Commission draft Spindler GRUR 2021, 653 (654).

[234] Cf. also Holznagel CR 2022, 594 (596).

[235] Peukert/Husovec/Kretschmer/Mezei/Quintais IIC 2022, 358 (371). This also follows from Art. 3(p) at the end, according to which 'exposed' users are also counted as active users.

[236] Dissenting and for their inclusion Holznagel CR 2022, 594 (596). However, this question should only be practically relevant if users actually have the possibility of use. Uploading active users will practically be only those with registration, as upload possibilities normally do not exist without a registration and binding terms of service. For passive 'reading' users, registration requirements are still handled differently. In the view taken here, a complaint-handling procedure should be mandatory only for registered users, as it is designed as an enforcement mechanism for substantive user rights, not as a popular procedure open to everyone. Otherwise, the systematic distinction between the right of everyone to report (Art. 16) and the right of only users to initiate proceedings (Art. 20) would be undermined.

[237] Whether restricting measures are taken due to illegality or 'only' due to breach of contract is irrelevant. This relieves from the (sometimes difficult) distinction between these types of content for accessing the complaint-handling procedure.

bility compared to a normal display of content not affected by moderation measures. This also includes **demoting**[238] with the consequence that content only appears with lower priority or not at all in search functions (so-called shadow banning) or any other measures that limit the visibility, availability or accessibility of this information[239]. (Art. 20(1)(a), Art. 17(1)(a))
- Also, in relation to **content**, the permanent **termination**, temporary suspension or other **restriction** of generally offered opportunities for **monetisation** (e.g. advertising opportunities provided on online platforms or integration into advertising networks, or other types of payments to uploading users). (Art. 20(1)(d), Art. 17(1)(b))
- With regard to the **provision of services or access** to the online platform, their complete or partial (e.g. temporary or concerning only parts of the service or being limited to read-only status) **suspension** or **termination**. Compared to the next point, this concerns rather how the service is actually restricted rather than legal questions on how to handle the underlying service contract. A complete termination will, however, usually overlap with termination issues. This also covers threatening measures with an intimidating and preliminary effect in response to alleged violations, based on which a suspension may follow in the event of further violations ("strikes" or violation counters). (Art. 20(1)(b), Art. 17(1)(c))
- With regard to the **user account** or the service contract, its **suspension** or **termination**. (Art. 20(1)(c), Art. 17(1)(d))

53 The aforementioned list appears **enumerative**, but it includes all currently used common restriction measures, and the term "restriction" is formulated in a sufficiently open way to cover other impairments with negative effects that are not expressly mentioned.[240] Such a **broad interpretation** of the complaint handling system's **subject matter** takes into account the protection of the freedom of expression[241] and the pre-filtering function of Art. 20: The question whether restricting measures are objectively justified (or not) should be clarified (initially) in the internal complaint-handling system in order to speed up a decision and to avoid later court proceedings. Also, in order to avoid delimitation difficulties, in the event of doubt it seems advisable to make a decision on the merits.

54 In the second case, where **users file notices** within the meaning of Art. 16, the subject matter of the complaint mechanism is the online platform's **decision** not (or not sufficiently[242]) to take the aforementioned restricting **measures against illegal content** after a specific notice procedure initiated by the respective notifying user. In contrast to a complaint against taking restrictive measures, for a 'complaint of failure to act' it is not clear whether such procedure is mandatory for illegal content only, or also for content incompatible with the service providers' terms and conditions. This lack of clarity follows from the fact that the complaint-handling procedure in the case of notifying users, which was only included by the EU legislator in the trilogue, is systematically still based on the notice procedure under Art. 16 (and not Art. 17), which only applies to illegal

---

[238] Demoting is expressly mentioned in Art. 17(1)(a) as a sub-case of restrictions and is therefore also covered by the wording of Art. 20(1)(a). There are neither systematic nor teleological reasons to exclude demoting from the notion of restrictions here.

[239] Content-related 'fact checking' notes placed by service providers are also likely to be a restriction on the visibility of information, because they put into question its correctness (dissenting Holznagel CR 2022, 594 (596)). In view of their susceptibility to dispute and the pre-filtering function of Art. 20, systematic and teleologic arguments tend to include such measures in the internal complaint-handling system before further escalation steps apply (Art. 21 or state courts).

[240] Cf. rec. 58 DSA on the criterion of negatively affecting service recipients.

[241] Cf. rec. 54 DSA.

[242] Rec. 58 DSA.

content (→ mn. 19). The recitals, however, state that the complaint-handling mechanism should apply if platform operators have provided for voluntary notice procedures for content contrary to the terms and conditions.[243] It should be noted, however, that under applicable substantive law (at least under German law), notifying users may have no contractual claims against platform operators for the implementation of certain restrictive measures against other users, but only claims in the event of violations of their own rights (→ mn. 48). Thus, notifying users who are not infringed in their own rights may have no standing or claims to enforce platform governance rules against online platforms themselves, regardless of whether the DSA mandates access to a complaint procedure (without determining the outcome).

3. Procedural requirements

Access to the complaint handling system must be available **electronically** and **free of charge** for at least **six months** from the date on which restricted users are notified of the respective decision in accordance with Art. 17, or notifying parties in accordance with Art. 16(5) (Art. 20(2)). After that period requests in the complaint procedure no longer need to be processed. The **design requirements** in Art. 20(3) call for an **easy access, user-friendliness** as well as the possibility of submitting sufficiently precise and adequately substantiated complaints. In this respect, reference can be made to the similar requirements of the notice and action procedure (Art. 16).[244] Access should be provided in the context of typical user interaction areas; a link deep within help pages or the imprint alone is seen as insufficient.[245] In addition, free text fields and upload options for evidence may be useful.[246] Unnecessary formal requirements for users, such as a precise indication of legal provisions, or a detailed legal explanation, cannot be expected.[247] The fact that the complaint-handling must be an **internal** procedure means, in contrast to Art. 21, that applicants can turn directly to their respective service provider and do not have to engage with external third parties. A platform operator can of course make use of back-to-back **external third party services** for the processing of complaints, who act – as usual in customer care outsourcing – for him and in his name. 55

Submitted complaints must be handled **timely**, in a **non-discriminatory**, **diligent** and **non-arbitrary** manner (Art. 20(4)). These procedural requirements are intended to 56

243 This is not clear in the wording history of Art. 20 and is also systematically doubtful. It was only late in the legislative process that reporting users were included in Art. 20(1) (Art. 17(1) old draft version) on the initiative of the EU Council. The previously existing reference to content contrary to general terms and conditions in the case of user restrictions as defined in Art. 17 (Art. 15 old draft version) was based on the protection of uploading users' communication freedoms against overblocking. The subsequent inclusion of notifying users creates systemic frictions, as it is linked to the narrower subject matter of the notice and action procedure in Art. 16 (Art. 14 old draft version). If one takes the recitals at their word, a measure not mandated by the DSA (notice procedure for content contrary to the GTC) would lead to a considerable burden by expanding the complaint-handling procedure, but possibly without removal claims on the merits for users who are not themselves violated in their own (e.g. personality) rights. This may provide misaligned incentives to limit the notice and action procedure to its mandatory scope of application, i.e. illegal content only, in the first place.

244 Cf. Spindler GRUR 2021, 653 (654) who also supports a similar interpretation.

245 Holznagel CR 2022, 594 (598).

246 Contrary to Holznagel CR 2022, 594 (598), this appears not to be a mandatory requirement, but rather depends on design variants in individual cases. In this respect, the platform operator should have a large degree of discretion for interface design, as long as it fulfils the requirements of easy accessibility. This can also include a 'click-through' path or (appropriate and correct) warnings, e.g., on consequences of false notices.

247 Rec. 58 DSA.

ensure a **fair outcome.**[248] While these obligations are related to the processing of each individual case, they are in their nature general **systemic process-related obligations.** This means that their violation in an individual case (e.g. exceeding a deadline; careless processing) would not as such constitute a violation of the DSA punishable by fines,[249] but a systemic failure to implement appropriate processes could be. Therefore, platform operators must set up internal processes for appropriate processing and instruct their employees and, if applicable, their external service providers accordingly. As it is generally advisable from a compliance perspective, such internal processes, responsibilities and instructions should be adequately documented and their implementation regularly monitored. Sufficiently **diligent processing** normally requires an appropriate level of (personnel and material) **resources**, sufficient qualifications and, if necessary, training of the respective persons involved.[250] Decisions in the complaint-handling procedure must not be made solely on the basis of **automated means** (Art. 20(6)). Thus, and unlike in the notice and action procedure, it must be possible for users to approach an appropriately qualified human contact person. Yet, automated means may be used to **prepare and support** human decision-making, or, if used as primary means, with a subsequent manual review or supervision.[251] In general, a rule-based, standardised and structured internal decision-making practice also aims at avoiding **prohibited arbitrary and discriminating results.** Art. 20(4) requires strict **procedural equality**. This precludes, for example, giving preference to certain complaints[252] or handling the procedure differently for users with certain opinions or political views than for other users.

57 The service provider is **not obliged to actively investigate or clarify facts** in case of **unclear, complex or contradictory circumstances** brought forward by users on the merits of a dispute – e.g. in the case of alleged violations of personality rights or contradictory IP ownership claims between users. The DSA neither provides for such proactive obligations[253], nor would they be appropriate under CJEU case law[254] in view of the limited possibilities for fact-finding in mass proceedings and the preliminary filter function of the complaint-handling procedure. Thus, service providers are free to make **decisions 'according to the file'**[255] and only on the basis of the facts as currently presented to them by users. Unclear cases can be handled at the reasonable discretion of the service provider, e.g. according to general **principles of the burden of proof.** An online inter-

---

248 Rec. 58 DSA.

249 Contrary to Holznagel CR 2022, 594 (599), fines presuppose systemic failure of the due diligence obligations as such, and therefore are not triggered by individual decisions that eventually turn out to be 'wrong'.

250 The DSA's obligation for platform operators to provide internal complaint handling processes as a form of dispute resolution creates a certain tension between the quality of dispute resolution and the effort that can still be reasonably expected from platform operators. Against this background, it will not be possible to demand legal qualification, but the use of less qualified personnel should be compensated by the provision of guidelines for decisions and sufficient supervision. In the case of outsourcing to external service providers one can also expect – as it is market practice in the customer care sector – certain contractual minimum requirements for qualification and diligence as well as their verification through appropriate KPIs and reporting regulations.

251 Rec. 58 DSA; Spindler GRUR 2021, 653 (654); Dregelies MMR 2022, 1033 (1037).

252 Holznagel CR 2022, 594 (598).

253 Rössel ITRB 2921, 35 (39).

254 Cf. Opinion of AG Saugmandsgaard Øe of 15.7.2021 in case C-401/19, GRUR-RS 2021, 20614 mn. 198 and subsequently CJEU 26.4.2022 – C-401/19, ECLI:EU:C:2021:613 = GRUR-RS 2022, 8378 mn. 89 et seq. – Republic of Poland/EP and Council in the parallel context Art. 17 DSM Directive (EU) 2019/790 on the absence of an obligation to delete content that service providers would have to assess independently with regard to the lawfulness of the information provided; for the application of these rulings holdings in the context of the DSA cf. Wimmers JIPITEC 2021, 421 mn. 7 et seq.

255 Holznagel CR 2022, 594 (598).

mediary is hardly in the position to clarify the facts 'timely' in a court-like manner, nor would this be reasonable in adversarial disputes between users (e.g. in defamation cases or between users who both claim intellectual property ownership). This fact-finding is reserved for the decision-making bodies of later escalation levels such as the dispute resolution procedure (Art. 21) or state court proceedings. Therefore, a decision in the complaint-handling procedure may well deviate from a later court ruling (with a better factfinding) without suggesting a service provider's non-compliance with the DSA. In addition, an online platform is free to voluntarily undertake extra fact-finding measures to pacify disputes (e.g. several statement rounds in 'counter-notices', → mn. 27), provided it otherwise complies with the requirements of Art. 20.

The difficult question of what happens to **content that was blocked after a complaint** during this procedure (or ongoing disputes thereafter) was quite controversial in the legislative process. Where a final assessment is difficult and time-consuming, the risk of overblocking can also materialise in the course of time until blocked content is restored late thereafter.[256] The proposal of the European Parliament to clarify in Art. 14 that the DSA does not provide for an obligation to remove content under pending proceedings was not included in the final version of the DSA. On the other hand, the DSA is silent on any obligation how to handle this dilemma either. Ultimately, it will be left to the service provider how to handle legally unclear content to avoid overblocking, taking into account the liability risk. The DSA does not rule out a practice of keeping legally unclear content in principle available during pending proceedings until the matter has been clarified and the content been identified with sufficient certainty as illegal.[257] However, to avoid liability, online platforms must act expeditiously to remove such content as soon as they have a sufficient degree of knowledge of its illegality (Art. 6(1)). This decision by online platforms how to handle disputed content is of central importance insofar as it **allocates the burden of further initiative** on the notifier (for removal) or the uploading user (for reinstatement).[258] 58

4. Decision and remedial action

The platform operator's decision[259] on the merits of a complaint concerning illegality or incompatibility of content with the terms of service must follow the **standards of the respective applicable substantive law**. Against the background of limited factual knowledge, a decision 'according to the file' and the lack of proactive factfinding obligations (→ mn. 57), a platform operator may take such decision already on 'sufficient grounds', which may be below the standard of proof applicable in state courts. This lower threshold applies to both taking and reversing restrictive measures and therefore may open some discretion in practice where no conclusive assessment can be made. If it turns out that a restrictive measure taken (or inaction) was **unjustified**, it must be **reversed without undue delay** after a decision on the complaint (Art. 20(4) 2nd sent.). This case-by-case obligation to hand down a moderation decision and its implementation in 59

256 The German legislator, for example, recognised this problem when implementing Art. 17 of the DSM Directive (EU) 2019/790 in §§ 9 et seq. UrhDaG and created a rather complex system that differentiates according to the type of content, which content remains online during the clarification of its legality and which does not. The DSA does not provide for such a stay-up obligation; instead, the decision is left to the reasonable discretion of the service providers according to their legal assessment of the content.

257 Cf. on the parallel case of Art. 17 DSM Directive (EU) 2019/790 Opinion AG Saugmandsgaard Øe of 15.7.2021 in proceedings CJEU C-401/19, GRUR-RS 2021, 20614 mn. 198, 203 – Republic of Poland/EP and Council; CJEU 26.4.2022 – C-401/19, ECLI:EU:C:2021:613 = GRUR-RS 2022, 8378 mn. 89 et seq.

258 Cf. Hofmann/Sprenger UFITA 2021, 249 (266 et seq.).

259 Such decision must be taken; it is not sufficient to transmit the parties' communication, cf. Janal GRUR 2022, 211 (219).

Art. 20(4) are part of the general due diligence obligations and their **procedural implementation** for the platform operator. Hence, they do not confer any individual claim upon users that would go beyond claims under the applicable substantive law.[260] Even if one were to assume such individual claims, their scope would be reduced compared to claims under substantive law, because decisions may be made provisionally and only according to the 'state of the file', so that the DSA in no case grants individual claims to a 'correct' decision with factfinding on the merits in a way a court would do. Again, the DSA in itself does not alter the standards of applicable substantive law, under which any content or remedial action must be scrutinized.

60 The complainant shall be **informed** of the reasoned decision without undue delay (Art. 20(5)). If moderation measures are taken against uploading users for the first time, i.e. following a complaint against a previously rejected measure after a notice under Art. 16, the users concerned must also be informed in accordance with Art. 17.[261] Further information on available legal redress is mandatory (Art. 21 as well as, if applicable, actions before EU member state courts), but is meaningful only where the complaint has not been fully remedied.

61 It remains to be seen to what extent the internal complaint handling system will meet the intended objective of **pacifying disputes** and lead to **fair results.** On one hand, it is plausible that a larger number of cases can be settled if platform operators engage in a factual assessment of the case with individual feedback to users, which goes beyond automatically generated emails. On the other hand, the complaint procedure suffers from a structural flaw rooted in the triangular legal relationship between uploading user, platform operator and notifying infringed party[262]. This flaw stems from the fact that the complaint procedure is not designed as a 'horizontal' adversarial procedure between two affected users, but as a 'vertical' procedure between user and platform operator who would have to take the side of the other user. Apart from a platform's lack of incentives to defend lawful content (cf. → mn. 3 for the risk of overblocking), the complaint procedure appears little suitable for resolving direct disputes between users (e.g. infringements of personality rights, IP etc.). In particular, a **hearing of the 'other side'** as fundamental procedural right[263] is not mandatory.[264] If a complaint s lodged by an uploading user against a restrictive measure, the notifying user will already have had the opportunity to be heard in the preceding notice procedure.[265] But this is different in the reverse case of a notifier's complaint against the decision not to take restriction measures, in which the DSA sets out no mandatory hearing of the uploading user. This friction was caused by the (questionable, → mn. 54) inclusion of notifying parties as being entitled to lodge complaints, which was done only late in the legislative process. This could result in a first restriction measure being taken against an uploading user following a complaint brought by a notifying user against refusal to act (Art. 17), which then in turn would possibly open a (further) complaint procedure for the uploading user who faces this re-

---

260 Cf. Spindler GRUR 2021, 545 (553) and Adelberg K&R 2022, 19 (22) on restitution claims under the EU Commission draft, in which this provision was included as Art. 17(3), which was to that extent (i.e. except for including notifying entities in the wording) not changed in the legislative process.

261 Holznagel CR 2022, 594 (598).

262 For an analysis of this typical three-pole relationship in conflicts on online platforms, cf. Raue JZ 2018, 961 (962).

263 On this requirement as a procedural guarantee cf. Hofmann/Sprenger UFITA 2021, 249 (266).

264 Cf. Holznagel CR 2022, 594 (598); Spindler GRUR 2021, 653 (654).

265 Cf. Hofmann/Sprenger UFITA 2021, 249 (265) on similar procedures under German law (NetzDG and UrhDaG implementing the DSM Directive).

striction for the first time.[266] Against the background of that unclarity, it may make sense for platform operators in such cases to practically include uploading users in the first complaint procedure. The DSA does not prohibit such practice (→ mn. 57). The DSA only requires proceedings (and thus a legal hearing) to be conducted with the uploading user concerned, but not an unnecessary duplication of two proceedings with the same subject matter.

II. Out-of-court dispute settlement (Art. 21)

1. General

If the internal complaint handling system of online platforms does not lead to the resolution of the dispute, the **users entitled to lodge complaints** under Art. 20 can turn to **certified, independent out-of-court dispute settlement bodies** in accordance with Art. 21(1), which issue a non-binding vote. In this respect, the DSA follows the general trend towards out-of-court dispute resolution.[267] Service recipients must be **informed** of this possibility for redress in an easily accessible, clear and user-friendly manner (→ mn. 60). For platform operators, this creates **obligations** to implement the **procedural requirements** of Art. 21 and to **cooperate** with the respective chosen dispute settlement bodies. Legal recourse to **state courts** is always **open** for users (Art. 21(1) subpara. (3)), so that the jurisdiction of dispute settlement bodies is only supplementary.[268] Although not explicitly mentioned, the same applies to platform operators, who can seek recourse in state courts, too.[269] 62

2. Eligibility to file, subject matter, and principles of dispute settlement proceedings

The **subject matter** of out-of-court dispute settlement proceedings are the same decisions as in the internal complaint-handling procedure pursuant to Art. 20(1)[270] (→ mn. 51). Under the DSA's cascaded dispute resolving approach, these proceedings can be seen systematically as a continuation of a **preceding complaint procedure** on the same measures. However, according to the recitals, users should also be able to directly appeal to an external dispute settlement body alternatively to Art. 20.[271] This appears misguided and conflicting with the systemic escalation structure of Art. 16, 20 and then 63

---

[266] In line with Holznagel CR 2022, 594 (598), a statement of reasons pursuant to Art. 17 is also necessary in the case of a first-time moderation measure against an uploading user as a result of a complaint procedure by another notifying user. In the absence of a prior legal hearing for the uploading user or opportunity to take part in the procedure, the DSA systematics suggest there that they can initiate a complaint procedure within the meaning of Art. 20 against all moderation measures that affect themselves for the first time. Otherwise, the procedural rights of users provided by the DSA would be curtailed and users would be confronted with moderation decisions that they could only challenge for the first time under Article 21 or in court. This would also contravene the original purpose of Art. 20 to protect uploading users and to limit overblocking.

[267] Cf. only Directive 2013/11/EU on Alternative Dispute Resolution in Consumer Matters, OJ L 165, 63; Art. 17(9) DSM Directive.

[268] Cf. Rec. 44, 55 DSA.

[269] The DSA does not exclude this (in practice rather rare) possibility, and access to state courts is generally not restricted (cf. rec. 59 DSA) in order to maintain procedural equality in civil law proceedings.

[270] On the uniformity of the subject matter of the proceedings cf. also Holznagel CR 2022, 594 (596).

[271] Rec. 59 DSA; Holznagel CR 2022, 594 (599). This passage, inserted on the Council's initiative, is contrary to the systematic structure of the DSA as a cascaded escalation mechanism. Under the view taken here, immediate access to external dispute resolution under Art. 21 is required only if a procedure under Art. 20 could or was not carried out at all, or not in a timely manner.

Art. 21 DSA.[272] Even more, an interpretation of this recourse mechanism in the light of fundamental rights may require an attempt for a prior internal dispute resolution. This stems from the fact that the final version of the DSA poses a considerable burden on online platform operators especially by the unbalanced cost rules and the misguided, dispute-promoting incentive structures of Art. 21(5) (→ mn. 70) – which would at least be mitigated under the lens of proportionality if the number of disputes could be reduced in the preceding complaint procedure of Art. 20. If, on the other hand, one were to grant immediate access to Art. 21, at least the six-month preclusion period by way of reference to Art. 20(1) should be applied. It makes no sense in the procedural incentive structure why skipping meaningful (de-)escalation stages should even be rewarded with eliminating pacifying preclusion periods.

64 **Entitled** to file an application for out-of-court dispute settlement[273] are all **service recipients directly affected by decisions** pursuant to Art. 20(1). These are, on one hand, uploading users against whom restrictive measures have been taken and, on the other hand, notifying users whose respective requests were rejected in the internal complaint handling procedure (→ mn. 52, 54). Such users can be B2C end customers, but also B2B users (e.g. traders on a marketplace platform).[274] There is no provision for the platform operator itself to initiate the settlement procedure,[275] nor for third parties who are not at the same time service recipients. Also, the DSA does not set out any obligation to include notifying third parties in the procedure.[276]

65 **Parties and participants**. As it is the case with Art. 20, the dispute settlement is done in the **'vertical' relationship between user and online platform,** but not 'horizontally' between users themselves,[277] which might have been more appropriate in some adversarial cases such as defamation, infringement of subjective rights, or if clarification of the facts is required.[278] (→ mn. 61) Legal practice will also have to develop principles whether and to what extent – similar to court proceedings – other directly affected users or notifiers can be included here to foster procedural efficiency (e.g. with **dispute notices** to join on either side). On one hand, the DSA does not provide for the initiation of proceedings by the platform operator. On the other hand, this only means that users cannot be forced into a dispute settlement procedure by the service provider against their will. This does not rule out appropriate procedural frameworks of dispute settlement bodies, in particular for the clarification of the facts or for a direct dispute between two users who both turn against the service provider with contradicting claims, as long as a dispute as such is initiated by either user and not the platform operator. The DSA does not set out details in this regard, but only requires to have clear and fair rules of procedure in place (Art. 21(3)(f)). This leaves room for implementation and should allow some sort of 'horizontal' means of procedure between users, even more where similar rules in state court proceedings support the notion of their procedural fairness.

---

[272] Cf. for this cascaded structure Busch ZdiW 2021, 88 (90); Härting/Adamek IPRB 2021, 100 (103); Härting/Adamek CR 2021, 165 (168); Raue/Heesen NJW 2022, 3537 (3541); Buchheim in Spiecker/Westland/Campos, Demokratie und Öffentlichkeit, p. 249 (256); Buiten JIPITEC 2021, 361 (375); Wimmers JIPITEC 2021, 421 mn. 17. Generally critical of Art. 21 also Holznagel CR 2022, 594.

[273] Technically, the right to bring proceedings will be governed by the respective procedural rules of the concerned settlement-body. Yet, fulfillment of the DSA requirements decides whether platform operators are obliged to take part in these proceedings in the first place. If, for instance, proceedings are initiated by third parties, they will fall outside the scope of Art. 21 DSA.

[274] Spindler GRUR 2021, 653 (655); Busch ZdiW 2021, 88.

[275] Spindler GRUR 2021, 653 (654); Rössel ITRB 2921, 35 (40).

[276] Holznagel CR 2022, 594 (595).

[277] Janal GRUR 2022, 211 (219).

[278] Janal K&R 2021, 6 (9). On the enforcement of rights in platform-related multi-person relationships, see also Hofmann/Sprenger UFITA 2021, 249 (257 et seqq.).

Choice of dispute settlement body. Users are free to choose a certified dispute settlement body,[279] provided that the subject matter of the proceedings is within its scope of activity. Both parties shall **engage in good faith** with such settlement body with a view to resolving the dispute. Yet, platform operators may **refuse** to do so if a dispute has **already been resolved** concerning the same information and the same grounds of alleged illegality or incompatibility with its terms of service (Art. 21 (2) subpara. 2). This exception covers not only settled proceedings, but also other pending proceedings before state courts and other dispute settlement bodies.[280] However, assuming that the purpose of this exception is both procedural efficiency and similarity to the res judicata principle, it appears **unclear** whether it requires the **same parties** to be involved. On one hand, the protection of users as a central DSA objective tends to require so, as otherwise users could be cut off from access to Art. 21 proceedings only because another user has already carried out the procedure. On the other hand, arguments of procedural economy and proportionality can be invoked, and one may question whether the burden of online platforms with considerable procedural costs is appropriate in cases where another dispute settlement body has already decided a parallel issue. In any case, such a situation presupposes that the entire subject matter of the dispute is in effect the same and not related to individual circumstances or to the person of certain users (e.g. in the case of sharing of one and the same content by many users). Deviations in individual cases may already arise in view of a different context of users activities. Therefore, the scope of this exception will need to be clarified in practice. Furthermore, a cooperation may also be **dispensable under the good faith standard** of Art. 21(2) subpara. 1 under special circumstances in individual cases. Such cases, where good faith may be questioned, include **hasty applications** and obvious errors made by the platform operator without a prior internal complaint procedure[281] or if a decision has already been fully remedied in the internal complaint procedure, or if applicant has suffered no detriment. 66

Time limits. The proceedings must be concluded within a reasonable period of time, at the latest, however, within **90 calendar days**[282] and, in case of highly complex disputes, **180 calendar days** after receipt of the complaint, by making available the decision (Art. 21(4) subpara. 3). **Exceeding the time limit** has **no consequences** for the parties to the proceedings; legal recourse is open to them anyway and the duration of the proceedings is not their responsibility. However, a frequent and unjustified delay in processing beyond individual cases might cast doubt upon the dispute settlement body's certification requirements, in particular the sufficiency of necessary resources and/or expertise. 67

3. Decision and costs

The standards of the decision again follow the applicable **substantive law**, from which the alleged illegality of the content or incompatibility with the terms of service results.[283] In this respect, the dispute settlement body hands down a **quasi-judicial decision** based on enforceable subjective rights asserted in each case (if any, on substantive law claims → mn. 47 et seq.) and not a mediation proposal.[284] Therefore, the applicable 68

---

[279] Holznagel CR 2022, 594 (600).

[280] Rec. 59 DSA; Holznagel CR 2022, 594 (600).

[281] Holznagel CR 2022, 594 (600).

[282] The ninety day time limit is based on Art. 8(e) of Directive 2013/11/EU on Alternative Dispute Resolution in Consumer Matters, cf. opinion of the Committee on the Internal Market and Consumer Protection of 28.5.2021, 2020/0361(COD), P9_A(2021)0356, p. 87 et seq.

[283] Wimmers JIPITEC 2021, 421 mn. 35 correctly points out the potential applicability of different EU member state laws.

[284] Holznagel CR 2022, 594 (600 et seq.); Wimmers JIPITEC 2021, 421 mn. 44.

conflict of law rules must also be taken into account for determining the applicable substantive law.[285] The settlement body's decision is **not legally binding** (Art. 21(2) subpara. 3).

69 The **cost bearing rules** of the dispute settlement proceedings (Art. 21(5) subpara. 1) are **asymmetrical**. If the user initiating the proceedings **prevails,** the platform operator shall bear the fees of the proceedings and reasonable expenses incurred by the user in relation to the dispute (e.g. lawyers' fees in more complex cases[286]). In the opposite case of a user **losing the case**, the user is not required to reimburse any fees or other expenses of the platform operator.[287] Yet, the user may have to bear the full costs in cases where he manifestly acted in bad faith and this finding is part of the decision. From a procedural perspective, the platform operator must therefore have a right to apply for a corresponding declaratory judgment. It is, however, unclear in which cases this **misuse provision** applies. As a rough point of reference, one could draw upon the requirements of Art. 16(2) lit. d, which requires a confirmation of the *bona fide* belief for user notices that the notified information and allegations contained therein are accurate and complete. The **amount of procedural fees** for dispute settlement bodies or their calculation method must be announced in advance (Art. 21(5) subpara. 3). The fees charged to platform operators shall be reasonable and in no event exceed the costs incurred by such body, which **excludes** dispute settlement bodies working for **profit**. There is no obligation to cooperate with dispute settlement bodies who charge unreasonably high fees. For users, dispute resolution must be available free of charge or for a nominal fee (Art. 21(5) subpara. 2).

70 The asymmetric bearing of costs is **criticised,** because in the final DSA version uploading users and notifying users can both force online platforms into expensive dispute resolution without bearing any own cost risk, which leads to a complete decoupling from the substance of claims and success in proceedings, **even in the case of 'correct' moderation decisions.**[288] The original incentive structure of the asymmetric cost rules was to encourage 'correct' decisions[289] by 'pricing' overly heavy-handed moderation with a procedure initiated only by restricted uploading users in order to **prevent overblocking.**[290] This meaningful incentive structure has been **lost** in **the final version of the DSA,** where notifying and uploading users are both entitled to initiate proceedings. As a consequence, online platforms now may find themselves in a **conflict** between users' diverging ideas on what should be the right 'level' of moderation, which is difficult to resolve. Even more, in proceedings initiated by notifying users, the intended protection against overblocking (→ mn. 3) may even be reversed in terms of incentives. In addition, there are fears that some dispute settlement bodies may develop a user (group)-friendly bias. Since proceedings are initiated at the users' choice and almost always at the expense of

---

[285] Similarly Dregelies MMR 2022, 1033 (1034).

[286] Holznagel CR 2022, 594 (601).

[287] Janal ZEuP 2021, 227 (256); Spindler GRUR 2021, 653 (655); Schmid/Grewe MMR 2021, 279 (281); Gielen/Uphues EuZW 2021, 627 (635). The DSA does not clearly set out who will bear any nominal fees (Art. 21(5) subpara. 2) of the settlement body in such case. Art. 21(5) subpara. 1 only rules out reimbursements of the platform operator's costs, but does not go so far as to mandate covering the user's cost in the event he loses the case.

[288] Holznagel CR 2022, 594 (601 et seqq.) sees this as violating Art. 16 CFR, which protects the rights of platform operators. Critical in view of the platform's 'sandwich position' also Janal GRUR 2022, 211 (219 et seq.).

[289] The asymmetry under the Commission's draft, in which only uploading users were eligible to apply, was also understood as an incentive for better internal decisions, cf. Kaesling ZUM 2021, 177 (181).

[290] Holznagel CR 2022, 594 (595); Janal GRUR 2022, 211 (219); on substantive claims of publishing users (the enforcement of which is the purpose of Art. 21) as a 'counterweight' to overblocking cf. Raue JZ 2018, 961 (963 et seq.); Wagner GRUR 2020, 447 (452).

online platforms, a **forum shopping** to the most applicant-friendly dispute resolution bodies and a typical race to the bottom may be the consequence[291] -- also with respect to a biased handling of specific content like political or religious issues,[292] depending on who brings the proceedings first. All this may create **misguided incentives for content moderation** and a considerable burden for online platforms, while on the other hand the relief from any costs can hardly be justified, at least not for notifying institutions. The current cost structure is not only an encroachment on the entrepreneurial freedom of online platforms,[293] but it also undermines the structural guarantees of the DSA for the protection of the users' freedoms of communication (→ mn. 3). Against this background it is fair to argue that the freedom from costs for users should only apply to uploading users and, at most, to reporting users who also assert individual claims (e.g. for defamation), but not to those reporting users or reporting institutions who do not have an individual claim under substantive applicable law that could be enforced in court. Whether this interpretation can be done by teleological reduction of para. 5[294] or whether para. 5 is simply disproportionate in the final version of the DSA,[295] will have to be clarified by the courts. In any case, the misguided cost rules may support a **narrow interpretation of Art. 21** in all respects for proceedings initiated by notifying users.

4. Certification requirements for dispute settlement bodies

Dispute settlement bodies are organised under private law, but must be certified by public authorities.[296] This certification is granted upon **request** by the **Digital Services Coordinator** of the EU member state where the dispute settlement body is established and valid for a period of up to five years with the possibility of renewal. EU member states may also support the activities of or set up their own out-of-court dispute settlement bodies (Art. 21 (6)). The substantive **requirements for granting a certification** are (Art. 21 (3)): 71

- **Independence** from and **impartiality** vis-à-vis online platforms, their users and notifying persons or institutions (Art. 21(3) subpara. 1 (a): Since these requirements are set up as general *ex ante* certification requirements (and apply not only in specific proceedings), independence as a central requirement[297] must **generally be ensured vis-à-vis all** aforementioned groups, including potential participants in proceedings. Bodies controlled by or dependent on online platforms do not fulfil this requirement[298], nor do organisations that are directly or indirectly financially supported by them or that cannot clearly demonstrate their de facto independence, for instance due to economically important contracts, funding or committee representatives. For reasonable doubt, it will suffice that the body's members have close relationships with possible parties to the proceedings.[299] This applies to the influence of platform operators in the same way as to the influence of user associations or, more importantly, notifying institutions. State funding of dispute settlement bodies is pos-

[291] Holznagel CR 2022, 594 (599).

[292] Wimmers JIPITEC 2021, 421 mn. 35.

[293] Holznagel CR 2022, 594 (604).

[294] Holznagel CR 2022, 594 (604).

[295] See for the consequences of disproportionate interference with fundamental rights CJEU 22.11.2022 – C-37/20, C-601/20, ECLI:EU:C:2022:912 on the invalidity of provisions of the Money Laundering Directive (EU) 2018/843 on the grounds of Art. 7 and 8 CFR.

[296] Janal GRUR 2022, 211 (219).

[297] Kaesling ZUM 2021, 177 (181).

[298] Kaesling ZUM 2021, 177 (181); Janal K&R 2021, 6 (8).

[299] Holznagel CR 2022, 594 (599).

sible,[300] but must preserve their independence. It is argued that a user-friendly decision-making practice should not in itself question independence, as long as it is legally correct and plausible.[301] Independence must be secured by procedural rules and also apply on the level of natural persons in charge of resolving disputes, including rules on conflict of interest for the decision-making members.[302]

- **Necessary expertise** in one or more **specific areas** of the assessment of **illegal content** or the application and enforcement of **terms of service** (Art. 21(3) subpara. 1 (b)): Given the broad scope of potentially illegal content, this ability to effectively contribute to resolving a dispute can be assessed only on a sector-specific basis. An organisation specialised in the protection of minors will rarely have in-depth knowledge of consumer protection or copyright law – and vice versa. For the same reason, the **certification** is only **sector-specific** (Art. 21(3) subpara. 2(a)). In addition, the expertise must also relate to the respective **applicable substantive law,** because the merits of cases may potentially involve the laws of different EU member states (→ mn. 21).[303]
- **Remuneration** of members **independent from the outcome** of proceedings (Art. 21(3) subpara. 1 (c) as well as easy **accessibility** via **electronic** means of communication (including online upload of complaints and required documents) (Art. 21(3) subpara. 1 (d)).
- Ability to **resolve disputes swiftly, efficiently** and **cost-effectively** in at least one official EU language. For this purpose, a dispute settlement body must also have the necessary resources and expertise.[304] Since these efficiency requirements are related to the required expertise, they apply only in the respective certified area of activity (Art. 21 (3) subpara. 1 (e)).
- **Clear and fair rules of procedure** that are easily and publicly accessible: In practice, these rules should be similar to the procedural rules of organisations generally recognised in out-of-court dispute resolution, which normally reflect generally acknowledged principles of the rule of law as well as procedural details (such as the form of motions, procedural rights of the parties including the right to be heard and requirements to state reasons etc.) (Art. 21(3) subpara. 1 (f)).[305]

72 In the **certification**, the Digital Services Coordinator shall specify the areas of expertise, as well as the official language(s) of the proceedings (Art. 21(3) subpara. 2) and notify the certifications to the EU Commission for **publication** (Art. 21(8)). The certification is valid in all EU member states.[306] Dispute settlement bodies must prepare an annual **activity report** (including number of complaints received, decisions, duration of proceedings as well as any difficulties) for the Digital Services Coordinator; in addition, the Digital Services Coordinator prepares a **consolidated report** every two years (Art. 21(4)). If the Digital Services Coordinator learns through his own investigations or information from third parties that the necessary certification conditions are no longer

[300] Holznagel CR 2022, 594 (599).

[301] Holznagel CR 2022, 594 (599).

[302] Rec. 59 DSA.

[303] This should, at least in practice, somewhat reduce the danger of pan-European forum shopping between dispute resolution bodies in different EU member states (cf. Wimmers JIPITEC 2021, 421 mn. 27). It can be expected that a dispute settlement body certified, e.g., in Portugal will seldom have the expertise to judge on issues of German criminal law – and vice versa.

[304] Rec. 59 DSA.

[305] Holznagel CR 2022, 594 (600).

[306] Rec. 59 DSA. This is without prejudice to any limits that the scope of acknowledged expertise may pose, e.g., on the applicable substantive national law that determines the alleged illegality.

met, the certification must be **revoked** after consultation with the dispute settlement body (Art. 21(7)).[307]

III. Trusted Flaggers (Art. 22)

1. General

73 Online platforms must establish mechanisms and processes for the priority processing of notices originating from certain 'trusted flaggers'. Art. 22 regulates the status and approval of these trusted flaggers as well as the procedural rules applicable to their notices. This **fast-track approach for handling notices** is expected to tackle illegal content faster and more reliably,[308] especially since similar procedures are already in place at some online platforms on a voluntary basis.

2. Accelerated notice handling

74 Online platforms must take the necessary technical and organisational measures to ensure that notices submitted by trusted flaggers are given priority and are processed and decided without undue delay (Art. 22(1)). This **acceleration obligation** applies to notices that are submitted via the **regular notice procedure** according to Art. 16[309] and refer to subject matter within the trusted flagger's **designated area of expertise**. In line with the scope of the referenced Art. 16, Art. 22 only applies to **illegal content**, not to violations of the terms of service.[310] The final version of the DSA contains neither rules for a privileged processing of trusted correction notices against unjustified moderation of lawful content[311] nor for a trusted pre-flagging mechanism of lawful content.[312] Platform operators are therefore free to set up such mechanisms voluntarily. In addition, they may open other reporting channels with equal privilege and cooperate **voluntarily** with other notifying bodies. The same holds true for implementing other mechanisms to ensure the quality of uploaded content (e.g. a community flagging system for fake news).

75 The consequence of receiving a notice from a trusted flagger only entails its **priority processing.**[313] Such notices must be handled more quickly than normal notices, but the duration can vary, depending on the individual case, the type of illegal content and the quality of notices.[314] Art. 22 does not relate to the outcome and substance of decisions to take restricting measures or not. In particular, the DSA does **not** set out a presumption that notices from trusted flaggers would have a **higher degree of correctness** or would trigger liability-relevant knowledge within the meaning of Art. 14(3) more quickly than other sources of information. This will depend on the individual circumstances, e.g. the

---

[307] In the view expressed here, the certification requirements should be interpreted as also protecting the interests of third parties, namely platform operators who have to cooperate and bear the consequences and costs of decisions taken by e.g. unqualified settlement bodies, which means that they should also have subjective rights and standing to apply for a revocation.

[308] Rec. 61 DSA.

[309] On the other hand, according to rec. 42, trusted flaggers should also be able to contact the central contact point as defined in Art. 12. This contradiction can be resolved in such a way that, on one hand, accessibility must be ensured in any case, but prompt processing is only possible and can only be guaranteed if the notices are submitted via the channels provided for this purpose

[310] The use of trusted flaggers here is voluntary, Rec. 62 DSA.

[311] This was proposed by the European Parliament in the legislative process as Art. 19(1a).

[312] Kaesling ZUM 2021, 177 (182); Peukert/Husovec/Kretschmer/Mezei/Quintais IIC 2022, 358 (372).

[313] Rec. 61 et seq. DSA; Janal GRUR 2022, 211 (219); Kuß/Lehmann DB 2021, 605 (608); Kuhlmann/Trute GSZ 2022, 115 (117); Buiten JIPITEC 2021, 361 (375).

[314] Rec. 62 DSA.

content and quality of submitted notices. The treatment of notices that do not meet the requirements of Art. 16(2) or are submitted contrary to the admission requirements of Art. 22(2) is not explicitly spelled out (→ mn. 76). At least in the latter case, the revocation mechanism of Art. 22(7) is available, whereby a trusted flagger can lose his awarded status. However, it appears also inappropriate to subject online platforms to the obligations of Art. 22(1) in the case of **deficient notices**, which unnecessarily block content moderation resources that otherwise would be available for all users or other trusted flaggers. Therefore, it would be systematically sound to link the processing obligations of Art. 22(1) with the minimum notices requirements in Art. 16(2), which also apply to trusted flaggers.

3. Status requirements for Trusted Flaggers

76 An entity's status as trusted flagger is not granted by the platform operator,[315] but is **awarded upon application** by the Digital Services Coordinator of the EU member state where the applicant is established, provided that the applicant demonstrably fulfils the substantive **requirements** of Art. 22(2):

- Particular **expertise** and competence in detecting, identifying and notifying illegal content (Art. 22(2)(a)). The expertise must specifically relate to the handling of certain types of illegal content including the correct interpretation and use of applicable law, i.e. it requires at least certain **basic legal knowledge** (also in the respective applicable legal system). Purely journalistic competences, e.g. as 'fact checkers', are not sufficient.
- **Independence** from online platforms (Art. 22(2)(b)). Here, reference can be made to the requirements for dispute settlement bodies, provided that the DSA requires independence here only vis-à-vis online platforms, since trusted flaggers do not make decisions. The pursuit of collective interests, which has been discussed as an additional requirement in the legislative process, has not been included in the final version of the DSA, so that interest groups can now also act as trusted flaggers (if all other status requirements are met).
- Submission of notices in a **diligent, accurate and objective** manner (Art. 22(2)(c)). Similar as with dispute settlement bodies, such practice will de facto presuppose certain expertise and will be difficult to achieve without it. These requirements also include at least substantively correct and substantiated notices pursuant to Art. 16(2) without extraneous motives and according to non-discriminatory processing standards.

77 Only **institutions** (legal entities) can be awarded with a trusted flagger status, but **not individuals**.[316] **Examples** of trusted flaggers include – as far as they fulfil the aforementioned awarding requirements – public bodies, Europol,[317] NGOs, the INHOPE reporting network or organisations for reporting illegal racist depictions,[318] qualified entities from other EU legal acts,[319] industry and business associations, in the case of infringements of intellectual property rights also organisations of rightsholders,[320] but not indi-

---

315 Janal GRUR 2022, 211 (218). This is different, for example, in the case of voluntary authorisation of trusted flaggers under private law by the service provider.

316 Rec. 61 DSA; Kalbhenn/Hemmert-Halswick ZUM 2021, 184 (190).

317 Rössel ITRB 2921, 35 (41).

318 Rec. 61 DSA.

319 Schmid/Grewe MMR 2021, 279 (281).

320 Rec. 61 DSA; Rössel ITRB 2921, 35 (41).

vidual rightsholders[321] or individual companies. Government bodies must also apply for this status.[322] The lack of a strict **neutrality** requirement in comparison with Art. 21 can be compensated by taking into account in the approval process a wide diversity of trusted flaggers[323] (which can balance out the fact that e.g. industry associations and particular interests groups will usually be biased and/or focus only on certain content). All trusted flaggers must publish an annual **activity report** (Art. 22(3)) and submit it to the Digital Services Coordinator.

As soon as a trusted flagger no longer fulfils his status requirements, the Digital Services Coordinator that awarded the status shall **revoke** it after consultation (Art. 22(7)). 78
Reasons may be, for example, justified doubts about the expertise, methodological diligence, or objectivity of a trusted flagger, which the Digital Services Coordinator has obtained from his own investigations or from third party information. An **investigation** shall be carried out immediately upon information from platform operators about a significant number of insufficiently precise, inaccurate or inadequately substantiated notices, and the status as trusted flagger shall be suspended during this investigation period (Art. 22 par. 6). In this context, the Digital Services Coordinator must immediately investigate such information and can, within the scope of his investigative competence, e.g. submit requests for information to the trusted flagger. **Reporting unreliable trusted flaggers** is not only in the own interest of online platforms, but part of their obligations under the DSA to enable the Digital Services Coordinator to continuously check the status requirements.[324] Assuming that Art. 22(7) also protects the interest of online platforms to allocate moderation resources efficiently to fight illegal content without being impaired by unreliable trusted flaggers, they would, in the view expressed here, have a subjective right to apply for intervention by the Digital Services Coordinator.[325] Coordinators shall communicate status awards and revocations to the Commission (Art. 22(4)), which shall **publish** up-to-date information in a publicly accessible **database** (Art. 22(5)). For further details, the Commission may issue **guidelines** (Art. 22(8)). In the event of **misuse** of the notice mechanism by trusted flaggers, platform operators may take sanction measures set out in Art. 23(2) (e.g. suspension) also vis-à-vis trusted flaggers.[326]

IV. Measures and protection against misuse (Art. 23)

1. General

Art. 23 regulates measures of online platforms to **protect against misuse** of their services. This protection does not only serve the interests of online platforms themselves, but also those of all parties involved not to misuse resources necessary to curb illegal 79

[321] Janal GRUR 2022, 211 (218 et seq.).

[322] Raue/Heesen NJW 2022, 3537 (3541).

[323] It is unclear whether and according to which criteria the limitation of the total number of trusted flaggers mentioned in rec. 61 DSA is to be achieved. Particularly in view of particular interest groups that usually cover only certain areas of activity, a selection should ensure a broad range of trusted flaggers and will have to be made according to objective and non-discriminatory admission criteria and without political bias.

[324] Spindler GRUR 2021, 653 (655).

[325] Cf. for the parallel case of dispute resolution bodies and their certification requirements under Art. 21 (7) DSA above mn. 72.

[326] Similar as here Spindler GRUR 2021, 653 (655); Kaesling ZUM 2021, 177 (180). Although the status as a trusted flagger entitles to an accelerated handling of notices, it does not override the general mechanisms to protect platform operators and users from false notices and overblocking.

content.[327] Misuse may relate on one hand to the **upload** of illegal content **by users** (Art. 23(1)), and on the other hand to misuse of the **procedures for notifying content and complaints** pursuant to Art. 16 and 20 (Art. 23(2)). Both cases are mirror images of each other and considered as misuse in order to create an appropriate **balance** between containing illegal content on one hand and preventing overblocking through unfounded notices on the other.[328] Art. 23(1) and (2) set out not only the right but also the **obligation** for online platforms to **temporarily suspend** their services.[329] However, this obligation does not extend to other or more far-reaching measures (such as terminations or permanent restrictions) so that online platforms have considerable discretion to **implement** these sanctions in their general terms of service[330] as long as they comply with Art. 23(3) and with Art. 14(4), as applicable.

2. Suspension for uploading illegal content

80 Online platforms **suspend** their services for uploading users who **frequently** provide **manifestly illegal** content for an appropriate period of time and after prior warning. There is no exception for user accounts in the public interest, as it was discussed in the legislative process, e.g. for politicians.[331] Clarifying which content is manifestly illegal, recital 63 states that illegality must be **evident to laypersons without any substantive analysis** of the content. This perspective aims at uploading end users, not at a professional platform moderation team, and is correct in view of the sanction character of Art. 23. The threshold for being manifestly illegal is therefore high and will include obvious and serious cases (e.g. death threats, terrorism). It seems, however, less likely that this would cover more complex cases where the scope of the freedom of expression must be legally determined with a complex weighing of interests and context, or where alleged copyright infringements raise questions of interpretation of law, e.g. for limitations to copyright. Difficulties will also arise in the case of criminal laws that have to be interpreted in conformity with fundamental rights to achieve sufficient legal certainty. If these issues are subject to legal discussions, a layperson can hardly be expected to make such an assessment. Finally, Art. 23 does **not** cover content that only violates the **terms of service** without being illegal at the same time.[332] Yet, this only means that online platforms have no obligation to establish anti-misuse measures, but they are free to define objectionable content and take measures in their general terms of service, as long as these comply with the general requirements set out by law, most notably Art. 14(4) DSA and the Unfair Terms Directive (or their national implementations).[333]

3. Suspension for misuse of reporting and complaint procedures

81 Similar to the upload of illegal content, online platforms must also suspend the processing of notices and complaints (Art. 16 and 20) of those individuals or entities (including trusted flaggers[334]) who **frequently** submit **manifestly unfounded reports or complaints** (Art. 23(2)). In addition, as with Art. 23(2), further measures are possible

---

[327] Kuhlmann/Trute GSZ 2022, 115 (117); cf. also rec. 63 DSA.

[328] Cf. for Art. 23 as a necessary corrective against overblocking also Janal ZEuP 2021, 227 (264).

[329] Cf. Savova/Mikes/Cannon CRi 2021, 38 (41) on the Commission's DSA draft, which was adopted contrary to the European Parliament's proposal that online platforms are entitled to take such measures.

[330] Rec. 64 DSA.

[331] Opinion of the Internal Market and Consumer Protection Committee, 28.5.2021, 2020/0361(COD), P9_A(2021)0356, p. 91.

[332] Janal ZEuP 2021, 227 (264).

[333] Rec. 64 DSA.

[334] Spindler GRUR 2021, 653 (655); Kaesling ZUM 2021, 177 (180).

(e.g. account blocking for reporting users). Especially in the event that an internal complaint procedure (Art. 20) would not be seen as mandatory before conducting external dispute settlement proceedings (Art. 21) (→ mn. 63), it may be useful to include in the terms of service a provision for misuse of the **dispute settlement proceedings.** Art. 23 does not stipulate such an obligation, but neither rules it out. In view of the protection against misuse as a guiding principle recognised in the DSA, such a provision appears not inadequate in the general terms and conditions. In particular, the asymmetrical and misguided incentives of Art. 21(5) require stronger protection against abusive initiations of proceedings. Since the recitals do not differentiate between uploads and (later included) notices, the **standard** for manifestly unfounded notices appears to remain the **layperson's perspective.**[335] This is appropriate for reporting individuals for the same reasons as for uploading users, but less so for **professional reporting entities** including trusted flaggers. Here, determining what is unfounded should be in line with the professional standards and knowledge of these entities.

4. Requirements for anti-misuse decisions

Misuse remedy measures must generally be **appropriate, proportionate and effective**, and need to respect the rights and legitimate interests of all parties involved, including fundamental rights and in particular the freedom of expression.[336] As a general applicable principle, measures must not be taken arbitrarily.[337] According to Art. 23(4), online platforms themselves are responsible for **specifying** the requirements of Art. 23 transparently, and their **general terms of service** must set out in a clear and detailed manner their misuse policies together with examples. 82

In the event of misuse, uploading or notifying users may only be suspended for a **reasonable period of time** after **prior warning.** In that respect, the obligations under Art. 23 are two-sided: on the one hand, Art. 23 mandates a suspension (but not other measures) as minimum obligations for online platforms; on the other hand, it sets out minimum procedural requirements for any measure against misuse to protect also the interests of users.[338] All decisions on misuse must be made on a **case-by-case basis, timely, diligently** and in an **objective** manner (Art. 23(3)). These diligence requirements are similar to those in the notice procedure (→ mn. 24). The service provider must **take into account all relevant facts and circumstances apparent from the information available** to him when deciding on whether and which measures to take. This includes at least (i) the absolute **number** of illegal content or unfounded notices within a given timeframe as well as (ii) their relative **proportion** compared to all content or notices, (iii) the **gravity** and consequences of the misuse and (iv) the **intentions** pursued, if ascertainable. Further relevant circumstances have to be assessed to the extent available to the service provider, i.e. if they are **known from records** (e.g. in correspondence or ticket systems). As it is the case in the notice procedure, the DSA does not set out a proactive obligation for online platforms to engage in court-like fact-finding. The requirements for misuse to be assessed in each individual case will probably rule out a fully automated blocking without any human examination. For **abusively reporting trust-** 83

335 Rec. 63 DSA.

336 Cf. rec. 63 DSA.

337 Janal ZEuP 2021, 227 (264).

338 It may be discussed whether these minimum requirements even apply to the measures not covered by Art. 23. However, in view of the general obligation to take diligent, objective and proportionate moderation measures (cf. Art. 14(4), which will usually also cover the prohibition of uploading illegal content addressed general terms of service), there are good reasons to apply these standards of procedural fairness also to anti-misuse measures that go beyond Art. 23.

ed flaggers, who enjoy special privileges and can (mis-)use platform resources even with priority, these circumstances can be taken into account as an aggravating factor for assessing the gravity of misuse.

V. State court proceedings

84 The judicial procedure before state courts (e.g. for deletion of illegal content or for restoring unjustifiably deleted content or against user blocking) is not regulated in the DSA and is left to the EU member states,[339] and their respective general **laws of civil procedure.** National legal protection remains unaffected by the procedural requirements of the DSA.[340] This means that users have the right not only to go through the procedures provided for in the DSA, but also to immediately appeal to the national courts instead.[341] Whether this right could be effectively contracted out under applicable substantive law by platform terms of service is doubtful. However, it can be expected in practice that users will first and foremost use the dispute resolution mechanisms of the DSA, which are more easily accessible and more favourable for them, so that these procedures can fulfil their 'pre-filter' function.

F. Criticism

85 Criticism against the DSA can be raised under several points of view. First of all, the DSA should procedurally **balance** the **rights of all participants**. Whether this has been achieved in the final version of the DSA remains to be seen. A serious challenge for – especially smaller – online platforms are most likely the **significant efforts required** for the various mandatory stages of **content moderation**. Unlike in copyright law, for example, where infringements can meanwhile be ascertained quite effectively by automated content recognition systems,[342] assessing a potentially unlimited range of illegal types of content involves substantial efforts, which are even increased with manual case-by-case dispute resolution procedures.[343] The DSA therefore brings online platforms into a difficult **dilemma situation**, in which they are obliged to delete illegal content on one hand, while they are supposed to keep legally compliant content available on the other hand.[344] Against this background, concerns are raised that the

---

[339] Janal ZEuP 2021, 227 (256).

[340] Holznagel CR 2022, 594 (596).

[341] Gielen/Uphues EuZW 2021, 627 (635 et seq.); cf. also rec. 10 and 126 DSA regarding jurisdiction rules.

[342] Likewise Holznagel CR 2022, 594 (597).

[343] Cf. Janal GRUR 2022, 211 (219); Härting/Adamek CR 2021, 165 (169); Spindler GRUR 2021, 653 (654). Whether automated mass enforcement is possible and whether platforms are indeed always 'cheapest cost avoiders' for disputes (so argues Denga EuR 2021, 569 (577)) is doubtful and very dependent on the subject matter of the dispute. While this may well be the case for clear and technically recognisable copyright infringements, practice proves that this is not the case where difficult questions of fact need to be ascertained or a balancing of interests to be undertaken (especially in free speech cases). In addition, it will be decisive in practice to what extent the moderation procedures can actually and empirically fulfil a pacifying dispute filtering function.

[344] Cf. also for overblocking cases outside the DSA Holznagel CR 2022, 594 (604 et seq.); Peukert in Spiecker/Westland/Campos, Demokratie und Öffentlichkeit p. 229 (242); Wimmers JIPITEC 2021, 421 mn. 10; BGH 29.7.2021 – III ZR 179/20, GRUR 2021, 1433 mn. 77; OLG Nürnberg 4.8.2020 – 3 U 3641/19, GRUR-RR 2020, 543 mn. 68.

DSA could lead to significant **barriers to market entry** for new online platforms.[345] This potential consequence would directly undermine the aim of containing (the sometimes so perceived[346]) opinion power of big private platforms and would significantly impair natural competition against the generally strong positive network effects in the platform economy.[347]

With regard to the risk of **overblocking**, one can certainly fear **misguided incentives** in the final version of the DSA. Entangled by different detailed procedural provisions on how to keep online or take down content, platform operators will have to sail between Scylla and Charybdis in case of content that is not clearly illegal, and their decisions can foreseeably not satisfy both sides of uploading and notifying users at the same time. Even more, online platforms will often have to take on the role of a quasi-judge in the first instance, also for deciding disputes that actually should be carried out directly between users, e.g. about personality rights violations or intellectual property infringements. Such privatisation of law enforcement[348] is probably less the own wish of online platforms but rather a burdensome duty imposed upon them by the legislator. For this reason, the Commission's DSA draft originally provided only for complaints by uploading users as a 'counterweight' to unjustified moderation measures, which were intended to internalise the 'costs' of overblocking (→ mn. 70). In contrast, the final version of the DSA has jettisoned the EU Commission's carefully balanced incentive structure in favour of a two-sided complaint procedure also for notifying users, and above all combined with asymmetrical cost rules for the external dispute settlement procedure. Being approached from two opposing sides, online platforms are caught in the middle, structurally unable to take decisions that please both sides, and face the costs in any case. It is evident that this mechanism undermines the DSA objective to prevent overblocking, and this result should be corrected as far as possible through interpretation of the DSA in the light of fundamental rights and in particular the freedom of expression. 86

Finally, the DSA has left the issue of non-illegal but so called 'undesirable' or **'harmful' (but legal) content** to be handled by **individual platform governance** rules through their terms of service (→ mn. 33 et seq.). In that regard, the DSA only mandates their non-discriminatory, diligent, objective and proportionate enforcement (→ mn. 37). Thus, the policy discussion on the nature and definition of such 'harmful' (but legal) content and the inherent tension with the freedom of expression remains unsolved and appears to shift from mandatory general rules towards specific codes of conduct for VLOPs and to individual platform governance policies. In a pluralistic society, what is considered as harmful or not depends very much on the individual perspective and, if implemented as a general mandatory rule, would at least have to be specifically defined under the rule of law due to its direct impact upon fundamental rights. It 87

345 Cf. for technical filters Rössel ITRB 2921, 35 (39); Hofmann/Specht-Riemenschneider ZGE 2021, 48 (61); Dreier/Leistner GRUR 2013, 881 (895); cf. on the additional burden on small providers Gielen/Uphues EuZW 2021, 627 (634); Schmid/Grewe MMR 2021, 279 (282); Peukert VerfBlog, 31.8.2021 <https://verfassungsblog.de/power-dsa-dma-04> (last accessed: 23.06.2024); cf. on the parallel problem with Art. 17 DSM-Directive and the burden on small and medium-sized enterprises Janal ZEuP 2021, 227 (245); Spoerri JIPITEC 2019, 173.

346 In that vein cf. Kaesling ZUM 2021, 177; Gielen/Uphues EuZW 2021, 627; Amstutz AcP 218 (2018), 438 (443); Spindler/Seidel NJW 2022, 2730 (2733).

347 Cf. on concentration tendencies in the platform economy in general BKartA (German Federal Cartel Office), Background Paper Digital Economy dated 1.10.2015, 5; Paal/Kieß ZfDR 2022, 1 (4 et seq.); Kumkar ZEuP 2022, 530 (536).

348 Critical towards this tendency Guggenberger NJW 2017, 2577; correctly differentiating with regard to the position of online platforms themselves in multipolar legal relationships Raue JZ 2018, 961 (962); Hofmann/Sprenger UFITA 2021, 249.

is the legislator's task and should not be left to executing authorities to determine the boundaries of free speech. In principle, as long as content is not illegal, it seems preferable to give online platforms extensive freedom to design their offerings and allow them to enter into a regulatory competition of different platform governance models. It is fair to assume that too little content moderation with 'wild west' rules will have an equally deterring effect on users as excessive censorship and opinion-forming. Different platform governance models in that respect can create a free '**market for rules**'[349] that would optimally serve the interests of both platforms (in terms of freedom to conduct their business) and users (in terms of selecting an appropriate platform to match their preferences). However, this freedom to focus e.g. on fostering free speech or on creating a feel-good atmosphere presupposes that there are no overly high barriers to market entry and that there remains sufficient choice of different platform governance models.

G. Relationship to other provisions and miscellaneous

88 The enforcement of the DSA is primarily a public law matter[350] (see → § 8). The individual 'due diligence obligations' described in this chapter are **systemic service design obligations**, not duties to avert specific illegal content in individual cases.[351] In this respect, only a **systemic breach** of these obligations may give rise to the fines set out in the DSA,[352] not just single cases of failing to take down individual illegal content (without prejudice to losing the liability privilege for such specific content under Art. 6).

89 **Contractual claims** are not regulated in the DSA and remain unaffected (→ mn. 47 et seq.).[353] As a compensation provision for users, Art. 54 is seen as a liability standard with reference to the respective applicable law of EU member states.[354] With regard to contractual claims of users, such claims may often be limited or disclaimed in the terms of service, as far as permissible under applicable law. Contractual claims by third parties (e.g. notifying non-users) will usually not exist. Third parties whose rights have been violated by users (e.g. under defamation laws) may have the right to approach online platforms (or their infringing users) under other legal doctrines, e.g. applicable tort laws, but taking into account the liability rules of Art. 6 (→ § 3).

90 Finally, the DSA does not further clarify the **demarcation to other legal acts** and the interplay with their own procedural requirements (e.g. the complaint procedure according to **Art. 17 DSM-Directive** and its implementation in the EU member states[355] or the **Platform-to-Business Regulation**[356]). While these other rules remain in principle unaffected, it will have to be assessed whether these rules complement each other, or whether

[349] Major user movements away from as well as towards certain online platforms after a change in governance policies clearly show that the type and extent of moderation is significant for a large number of users and therefore represents an important competitive factor. Cf. on a market for rules here also Lüdemann ZUM 2021, 640 (643); Denga EuR 2021, 569 (574); Heinz WuW 2019, 439 (442).

[350] Buchheim in Spiecker/Westland/Campos, Demokratie und Öffentlichkeit, p. 249 (261).

[351] Janal ZEuP 2021, 227 (263).

[352] For the parallel legal situation in the German NetzDG cf. Peukert in Spiecker/Westland/Campos, Demokratie und Öffentlichkeit, p. 229 (245).

[353] Spindler GRUR 2021, 653 (661); Peukert/Husovec/Kretschmer/Mezei/Quintais IIC 2022, 358 (374 et seq.).

[354] Raue/Heesen NJW 2022, 3537 (3542 et seq.).

[355] Cf. Janal GRUR 2022, 211; Holznagel CR 2022, 594 (596); Peukert/Husovec/Kretschmer/Mezei/Quintais IIC 2022, 358; Quintais/Schwemer European Journal of Risk Regulation 2022, 191.

[356] Regulation (EU) 2019/1150 of the European Parliament and of the Council of 20.6.2019 on promoting fairness and transparency for business users of online intermediary services, OJ L 186, 57. In this regard, cf. Busch ZdiW 2021, 88 (90 et seq.).

one of them may take precedence as the more specific rule in some circumstances. Here, too, swift clarification in legal practice seems necessary, as the efforts to set up costly parallel structures for regulatory compliance would be unnecessary and disproportionate.

§ 6
Specifics for systemically important platforms

Literature: *Berberich/Seip*, Der Entwurf des Digital Services Act, GRUR-Prax 2021, 4; *Buck-Heeb/Dieckmann*, Selbstregulierung im Privatrecht, 2010; *Bradshag/Howard*, The Global Disinformation Order, 2019; *Buri/Hoboken, The* Digital Services Act (DSA) proposal: a critical overview, 2021; *Cappello* (ed.), Die Entschlüsselung des Gesetzespakets zu digitalen Diensten, IRIS Spezial, Europäische Audiovisuelle Informationsstelle, 2021; *Denga*, Plattformregulierung durch europäische Werte, EuR 2021, 569; *Denga* in: Ruffert (ed.), Die Regulierung digitaler Plattformen, 2023, 9; *Denga/Pohle/Hölzel*, Technikregulierung durch doppelte Delegation, RW 2020, 420; *Dewenter/Rösch*, Einführung in die Ökonomie der Medienmärkte, 2015; *Dürig/Herzog/Scholz* (eds.), Grundgesetz-Kommentar, Werkstand: 98. EL March 2022, Art. 20; *Eifert*, Rechenschaftspflichten für soziale Netzwerke und Suchmaschinen – Zur Veränderung des Umgangs von Recht und Politik mit dem Internet, NJW 2017, 1450; *Eifert/Metzger/Schweitzer/Wagner*, Taming the Giants: The DMA/DSA package (2021) 58 CML Rev 987; *European Data Protection Supervisor*, Opinion 1/2021 on the Proposal for a Digital Services Act; *Gerdemann/Spindler*, Das Gesetz über digitale Dienste (Digital Services Act) (Teil 1), GRUR 2023, 3; *Gerdemann/Spindler*, Das Gesetz über digitale Dienste (Digital Services Act) (Teil 2), GRUR 2023, 115; *Grimm*, Die Zukunft der Verfassung, 1991; *Hayek*, The Use of Knowledge in Society, The American Economic Review 1945, 519; *Hayek*, Die Anmaßung von Wissen, 1974; *Helberger/van Drunen/Vrijenhoek/Möller*, Regulation of news recommenders in the Digital Services Act: Empowering David against the Very Large Online Goliath, Internet Policy Review, Opinion, 26 February 2021; *Janal*, Haftung und Verantwortung im Entwurf des Digital Services Acts, ZEuP 2021, 227; *Künast*, Regeln für Wahlkämpfe im digitalen Zeitalter, ZRP 2019, 62; *Laux/Wachter/Mittelstadt*, Taming the few: platform regulation, independent audits, and the risks of caputre created by the DMA and DSA, Computer Law & Security Review 43 (2021) 105613; *v. Lewinski/Klink*, Compliance-Pflichten nach dem DSA – ein umfassender Überblick, RDi 2023, 183; *Loewenheim* (ed.), Handbuch des Urheberrechts, 3. Auflage 2021; *Müller*, Künftige Plattformregulierung und effektive Durchsetzung in Deutschland, MMR 2022, 1007; *Pariser*, The Filter Bubble, 2011; *Peukert*, Zu Risiken und Nebenwirkungen des Gesetzes über digitale Dienste (Digital Services Act), KritV 2022, 57; *Polański*, Some thoughts on data portability in the aftermath of the Cambridge Analytica scandal EuCML 2018, 141; *Raue/Heesen*, Der Digital Services Act, NJW 2022, 3537; *Volkmann*, Hate Speech durch Social Bots, MMR 2018, 58.

A. General overview

I. Scope of application

For providers of "very large online platforms" and "very large online search engines", far-reaching additional obligations are laid down in Chapter III, Section 5. Due to the specific reference to systemic risks, the term "systemically important platforms" will be 1 used in this chapter. Such platforms have at least 45 million active users in the European Union (Art. 33(1) DSA[1]) and thus reach more than 10 % of consumers within the Union.[2] The **tightening of the due diligence obligations for systemically important platforms** fits into the tiered structure of the DSA's due diligence obligations and is therefore ultimately an expression of the principle of proportionality. This is because the type and number of obligations are "directly linked to the scope of a service and its economic and social importance".[3]

2 A status comparable to "**critical infrastructure**" is imposed on system-relevant platforms within the framework of Section 5.[4] The background to this is the exposed position and the associated specific dangers that, in the opinion of the legislator, emanate from online platforms or search engines with an increased reach. Without doubt, they play a role that can no longer be neglected for public debates, economic transactions and the dissemination of information, opinions and ideas due to their large number of users.[5] The resulting great influence on online security, public opinion-forming, public discourse and the economy in general gives indeed rise to specific dangers,[6] which are to be countered by making particularly relevant providers liable.

II. Overview of the increased obligations for systemically important platforms

3

Article	Content
Art. 34	Risk assessment
Art. 35	Risk reduction
Art. 36	Crisis response mechanism
Art. 37	Independent audit
Art. 38	Recommendation systems
Art. 39	Additional transparency of online advertising
Art. 40	Data access and control
Art. 41	Compliance Department
Art. 42	Transparency reporting obligations
Art. 43	Supervisory fees

4 In view of their **exposed position for socio-political discourse,** providers of systemically relevant platforms are obliged to carry out a regular risk assessment (Art. 34). In

[1] Regulation (EU) 2022/2065 of the European Parliament and of the Council of 19.10.2022 on a single market for digital services and amending Directive 2000/31/EC (Digital Services Act), OJ L 277, 1. Unless another law is mentioned below, the provisions refer to the DSA.

[2] The "average monthly number of active users in the Union", which in future is to be calculated as an average over a period of six months, is used as a decisive factor, cf. Rec. 6; see also Müller MMR 2022, 1007 (1008).

[3] Müller MMR 2022, 1007 (1009); on this also Janal ZEuP 2021, 227 (232); Raue/Heese NJW 2022, 3537 (3542); on the risk-based tiered approach of the DSA see Gerdemann/Spindler GRUR 2023, 3 (3 et seq.); v. Lewinski/Klink RDi 2023, 183 (193 et seq.).

[4] Thus Berberich/Seip GRUR-Prax 2021, 4 (7).

[5] Rec. 75 DSA; see Eifert NJW 2017, 1450 (1454); specifically with regard to a market failure Eifert/Metzger/Schweitzer/Wagner (2021) 58 CML Rev 987.

[6] Rec. 79 DSA.

particular, "**systemic risks**", such as the dissemination of illegal content, the impact on elections or the mental health of users, which may arise from the design or operation of the services, are to be considered. Subsequently, identified risks are to be addressed by providers through appropriate and effective measures (Art. 35). The provision of Art. 36 on a **crisis response mechanism**, which was introduced late in the legislative process, stands out particularly from the section. Here, providers are obliged to take special measures in the event of a crisis, which even go beyond the increased obligations of the section.

Art. 37 obliges providers to undergo an annual **independent audit** to verify (among other things) compliance with the increased obligations of this section. Finally, Art. 38 and 39 focus on recommendation systems and online advertising and impose specific obligations on systemically relevant platforms in this regard. In addition, the actors concerned must grant both the Digital Services Coordinator and the Commission access to their internal data (Art. 40). This is to enable effective monitoring. Approved researchers are granted comparable access to research systemic risks and risk mitigation measures. 5

Art. 41 obliges the providers concerned to set up an adequately equipped **compliance department** to ensure an independent internal review of the providers' compliance with the regulation. In addition, increased transparency reporting obligations are imposed on providers (Art. 42). Finally, the late-introduced Art. 43 imposes an annual supervisory fee on providers. This is intended to cover the estimated costs incurred by the administration through the supervisory tasks under the Regulation. 6

III. Successful regulation through supervised self-regulation?

The obligation of systemically important platforms follows the concept of **supervised self-regulation.**[7] The providers concerned should first independently recognise and avert the dangers addressed by the DSA, at best without the need for intervention by the state. This represents a delegation of state regulatory tasks to the platform providers. Paradigmatic for this is the mechanism laid down in **Art. 34 and 35,** which obliges the providers to react independently in the course of appropriate risk mitigation measures after an independent assessment of their systemic risks. 7

The approach of self-regulation is not a special feature of the present section, but is also valid vis-à-vis the other providers addressed by the regulation, for example vis-à-vis providers of online platforms in Chapter III, Section 3. However, since systemically relevant platforms, as rightly recognised by the legislator, pose particular social and individual risks, the question of the **permissibility of the delegation of** state tasks is particularly grave here.[8] 8

In the starting point, the legitimacy and meaningfulness of a **decentralised approach to** legislation can be confirmed. This is because the companies to which the tasks have been delegated can, in principle, bear a **great deal of expertise about the dangers in their platform ecosystems**, without which effective prevention is difficult to imagine.[9] There is a certain similarity here with the concept of the ***obligation of private parties*** for 9

[7] On the structure also Cappello (ed.), Die Entschlüsselung des Gesetzespakets zu digitalen Diensten, 2021, p. 19 ff; on self-regulation by delegation: Denga/Pohle/Hölzel RW 2020, 420 et seqq.; comprehensively on this the volume by Buck-Heeb/Dieckmann, Selbstregulierung im Privatrecht, 2010.

[8] For more details, see also Denga in Ruffert (ed.), Die Regulierung digitaler Plattformen, 2023, p. 9, 23 ff.

[9] On the legitimacy of self-regulation Hayek already since the 1940s: The Use of Knowledge in Society, The American Economic Review 1945, 519; Hayek, The Presumption of Knowledge, 1974.

policing tasks.[10] In areas with increased sensitivity to fundamental rights, high demands must nevertheless be placed on the legitimacy of such delegation. For in situations in which there is a particular threat to the rights and interests of the subjects of fundamental rights, the state remains obliged to protect and thus to independently control and monitor the delegation – in any case, a delegation does not per se lead to the fulfilment of the state's duties to protect, but to their transformation. This follows from its duties to protect under fundamental rights and the theory of materiality.[11] A delegation of state duties can thus only take place if it is adequately compensated.

10 **Compensatory approaches** can be seen in the provisions of Art. 36, 37, 39, 40, 42, in which the DSA aims to **overcome the information asymmetries** between state agencies and private companies and also provides for **state powers of intervention.** For example, the independent audits to be carried out annually according to Art. 37 result in comprehensive audit reports, which provide an in-depth insight into whether the providers are complying with the obligations of the regulation. In addition, the providers concerned must themselves fulfil far-reaching reporting (Art. 42) and transparency obligations in dealing with online advertising (Art. 39). A central building block for eliminating the existing information asymmetries between companies and the administration is also Art. 40, which allows access to internal data by state authorities. In addition, the provision grants access for authorised researchers, which enables research into the systemic risks emanating from online platforms and search engines and thus counteracts the information deficit on the state side, especially in the medium and long term. Finally, the crisis response mechanism in Article 36 ensures the state's competence to oblige providers to take further measures in cases of crisis that are particularly sensitive to fundamental rights (for more details, see → mn. 53 et seqq.).

11 Art. 36, 37, 39, 40, 42 thus at least provide the basis for compensating for the delegation of state duties under Art. 34, 35, 38, 41, 43 to platform providers. In principle, the chosen regulatory technique seems worthy of approval despite the particular sensitivity to fundamental rights in dealing with systemically important platforms due to the considerable information deficit on the state side and the associated impossibility of effective danger prevention by the state. Powers of intervention without the necessary knowledge would be of no use. The DSA attempts to overcome the information asymmetry and provides for effective intervention measures for particularly sensitive situations. The state's duties to protect thus seem to be sufficiently safeguarded, especially since digital spaces of opinion and trade were not state-ordered at all for a long time.[12] Much will certainly depend on the **adequate equipment of the national authorities and the Commission,** because knowledge alone is not enough for effective administration; it must of course also be adequately processed. Only then can the state implement its monitoring duties at all.

IV. Overregulation and overblocking

12 Even a first glance at the obligations of Section 5 suggest that systemically relevant platforms will have to substantially adapt their business model and will need compre-

---

[10] More in detail Denga in Ruffert (ed.), The Regulation of Digital Platforms, 2023, p. 9, 23 ff.

[11] On the principle of materiality Dürig/Herzog/Scholz/Grzeszick GG Art. 20 mn. 105; on preventive regulation Grimm, Die Zukunft der Verfassung, 1991, p. 197 et seqq.

[12] With an overview of the history of platform regulation Denga EuR 2021, 569 (575 et seqq.) Today, "bad content" is still a major problem of the digital space, cf. European Commission, Open Public Consultation on the Digital Services Act Package, Ref. Ares(2020)7629347, p. 4.

hensive compliance management in the future. Whether the considerable bureaucratic effort to be expected on the part of the providers, and also the authorities, will ultimately lead to a more adequate handling of the increased risks in dealing with very large online platforms and search engines remains to be seen. In any case, it seems questionable whether **more bureaucracy** will actually lead to **more protection of fundamental rights.** The often **vague provisions,** especially on systemic risks under Article 34, are particularly problematic.

The comprehensive obligations under the regulation generally raise the problem of **13**
overblocking, in which a provider, in case of doubt about its compliance obligations to avoid liability, removes more rather than less content from the platform.[13] In Section 5, the risk prevention approach of Articles 34, 35, which is critical for communications regulation, could be increasingly reflected in overblocking in the form of preventive overregulation.[14] In order to counteract these concerns, Section 5 emphasises the preservation of the principle of proportionality with striking frequency, not least by referring to the consideration of the fundamental rights of the respective actors. Whether these references are enough to sufficiently counteract a potentially preventive blocking is doubtful, however.[15]

B. Specific obligations for providers of systemically important platforms

I. Definition of systemically important platforms

1. Basic concept

Art. 33 defines which online platforms or online search engines are to be understood **14**
as "very large online platforms" or "very large online search engines" (here in short: "systemically important platforms") and thus regulates the scope of application of Chapter III, Section 5. According to Art. 33(1), the section applies to such online platforms or search engines that have an average monthly number of **at least 45 million active users** in **the European Union and have** been **designated as very large online platforms or search engines.** The designation shall be made by decision of the Commission in accordance with the provisions of Art. 33(4).

The DSA identifies specific risks and disproportionate negative impacts once plat- **15**
forms demonstrate a user base that affects a "significant proportion" of the Union's population.[16] Such a significant reach is assumed from an operational threshold of 10 % of the population of the Union.[17] Art. 33(2) opens up the possibility of **adjusting** this operational threshold if the Union population increases or decreases by at least 5 %.[18] The possibility of adjustment ensures that the number of average monthly users continues to correspond to the operational threshold of 10 % of the population of the Union.

In its final version, Art. 33 includes not only "very large online platforms" but **also** **16**
"very large online search engines".[19] The Commission justifies the extension of the

---

[13] For a comprehensive discussion of the problem, see this handbook → § 5 mn. 3.
[14] Peukert KritV 2022, 57 (75 et seqq.).
[15] For more details, see Denga EuR 2021, 569 et seqq.
[16] Rec. 76 DSA.
[17] Rec. 76 DSA.
[18] Rec. 76 DSA.
[19] Originally, only "very large online platforms" were covered by the section, Art. 25 DSA-E. For example: Buri/Hoboken, The Digital Services Act (DSA) proposal: a critical overview, 2021, p. 31 et seqq.

scope of the regime with the crucial role of large online search engines when it comes to finding information and making it available on the internet.[20]

2. Calculation of the number of users

17 The relevant connecting factor of the definition is the "average monthly number of active users in the Union". The **number of users is recorded by the providers themselves**, which they must publish as part of their transparency reporting obligations under Art. 24(2) of the DSA; the Commission's decision is generally based on this data, Art. 33(4) subpara. 1 sent. 2 (→ mn. 22 et seq.). Recital 77 specifies how the number of users is to be determined. In addition, Art. 33(3) ensures[21] that the Commission is authorised, after consultation of the Body for the Adoption of Delegated Acts, to supplement the calculation method so that dynamic market and technological developments can also be reflected.[22]

18 According to Recital 77, the number of average monthly active users should reflect all those users who, in a given period of time, "actually use the service at least once by being exposed to information disseminated through the online interface of the online platform, such as by watching or listening to it or providing information".[23] The figure is calculated as an average over a period of six months.[24] On the one hand, the "use" of the service cannot be limited to an elaborate interaction with information (by clicking, commenting, linking, sharing etc), on the other hand, the number of active users cannot be equated with the number of merely registered, otherwise inactive users.[25] The middle ground mentioned in the recitals is convincing – in any case, **users who merely passively view information on the online interfaces of the respective platform** should **also** be included.[26]

19 **The one-time use of** the respective service **also** influences the number of active users. However, users who use different online interfaces of the same platform should only be counted once, even if they access a service via different URLs or domain names.[27] Possibilities for the technical implementation of these considerations are not specified in Art. 33 and Recital 77.

20 **Indirect uses are** explicitly **not to be taken into account**; this concerns cases in which, when using other services, the information of the provider to be rated is merely made accessible through linking or indexing. **Automated uses,** such as by *bots* or *scrapers,* should also **not** influence the number of active users. "Scraping" is the term used to describe technical procedures for reading text from computer screens and websites, thereby extracting relevant information in a targeted manner.[28] *Social bots in* particular, which generate machine interaction via "empty" accounts, have proven to be highly problematic in connection with the spread of *fake news.*[29] In principle, the DSA does not require providers to "track" their users; however, to the extent that they can record auto-

---

[20] Rec. 75 DSA.

[21] This is also reflected in rec. 77 DSA.

[22] Initial non-binding guidelines dated 1.2.2023 are available on the European Commission's website, <https://digital-strategy.ec.europa.eu/en/library/dsa-guidance-requirement-publish-user-numbers>, last accessed: 29.08.2024.

[23] Rec. 77 DSA.

[24] Rec. 76 DSA.

[25] Rec. 77 DSA.

[26] Rec. 77 DSA.

[27] Rec. 77 DSA.

[28] On scraping: Loewenheim UrhR-HdB/Leistner/Zurth § 49 mn. 137 et seqq.

[29] For example, Volkmann MMR 2018, 58 on hate speech by social bots.

mated uses, this is not prohibited.[30] Delegated acts pursuant to Art. 33(3) should also be considered for the implementation of these requirements.

3. Adjustment of the threshold value

Art. 33(2) requires the Commission to adopt delegated acts in accordance with Art. 87 to adjust the reference level for the systemic number of active monthly users in the Union if there is a future increase or decrease in population. Specifically, an **adjustment** shall be required if the **population of the Union increases or decreases by at least 5 %** compared to its population in 2020 or, after adjustment by a delegated act, compared to its population in the year in which the last delegated act was adopted. In such a case, the number shall be adjusted so that it again corresponds to the operational threshold of 10 % of the population of the Union in the year in which the delegated act was adopted. The figure shall be rounded up or down so that it can be expressed in millions. 21

4. Designation decision of the Commission and required information basis

The designation of a platform or search engine as a "very large online platform" or "very large online search engine" is made by **decision of the Commission** pursuant to Art. 33(4). Of central importance in the context of this decision is the question of the basis on which the number of "average monthly active users in the Union" is determined and thus the criteria set out in Recital 77 are applied. 22

Art. 33(4) subpara. 1 sent. 2 provides for three possible alternatives of information bases for the determination: 23

Standard	Content
Var. 1	on the basis of the data reported by the provider of the online platform or search engine pursuant to Art. 24(2)
Var. 2	on the basis of information requested pursuant to Art. 24(3)
Var. 3	on the basis of any other information available to the Commission

Art. 24 thus plays a decisive role within the framework of the information bases for determining user numbers. The transparency obligations for all online platforms are regulated here; they thus also apply to system-relevant platforms. 24

As a rule, the DSA obliges providers to **publish** information on the average monthly **number of their active users** in the Union every six months on "a **publicly accessible area of their online interface**", in accordance with Art. 24(2). 25

Pursuant to Art. 24(3), providers may furthermore be required, at the request of the Digital Services Coordinator of establishment and the Commission, to provide **information** within the meaning of Art. 24(2) (i.e. information on the average monthly number of their active users in the Union) **without delay**. In this context, additional information, explanations and justifications may also be requested; Art. 33(4) subpara. 1 sent. 2 var. 2 takes up this information. 26

Constellations in which providers do not comply with the requirements under Art. 24(2) and (3) are caught by Art. 33(4) subpara. 1 sent. 2 var. 3, where "**other information available to the Commission**" is mentioned. Thus, the application of section 5 27

[30] Rec. 77 DSA; this balancing act between freedom of surveillance and legitimisation of surveillance is also found in Art. 7 DSA, critically Denga in Ruffert (ed.), Die Regulierung digitaler Plattformen, 2023 (id.).

cannot be prevented by obstruction on the part of the platform providers. If a decision is taken on the basis of such "other information" within the meaning of Art. 33(4) subpara. 1 var. 3, or on the basis of additional information requested pursuant to Art. 24(3) (Art. 33(4) subpara. 1 sent. 2 var. 2), Art. 33(4) subpara. 3 grants the providers concerned a ten-day period to submit preliminary comments. The Commission then takes "due account" of these comments. This allows affected providers to catch up on their information obligations.

5. Rapid change in the number of users

28 Recital 78 takes into account the fact that the user base of an online platform or search engine can expand rapidly and thus achieve systemic relevance, with the associated effects on the internal market.[31] The economic background is the "**network effects**" typical of the platform economy, which can lead to exponential growth.[32] The Commission identifies evidence of such exponential growth in a high annual turnover or a high market capitalisation of an online platform or search engine.[33] In cases of exponential growth, Recital 78 assumes that the respective providers can be obliged to report more frequently on the number of active users. Thus, the requirement of reporting every six months according to Art. 24(2) can be adapted proportionately in order to determine the point in time at which the platform is to be considered a very large online platform or search engine.[34] Art. 24(3) empowers the Digital Services Coordinator of establishment as well as the Commission for this purpose.

6. Cancellation of the designation

29 According to Art. 33(5), the designation shall be revoked by the Commission if the systemically important platform does not have an average monthly number of active users equal to or below the number referred to in Art. 33(1) for an uninterrupted period of one year[35]. The online platform or search engine must therefore have an average monthly number of active users in the Union below 45 million during an uninterrupted period of one year. Thus, **falling below** the required number of users for a **short period of time** is **not sufficient for the designation to be revoked**.

7. Notification, publication and start of application

30 Finally, decisions within the meaning of Art. 33(4) and (5), i.e. decisions on the designation of an online platform or search engine or decisions on the withdrawal of such a designation, shall be notified by the Commission to the provider concerned without delay pursuant to Art. 33(6). The Commission shall also publish a **list of designated very large online platforms and search engines in** the **Official Journal of the European Union** and keep it up to date.

31 Finally, Art. 33(6) subpara. 3 regulates the temporal scope of the increased obligations of Chapter III, Section 5. Accordingly, the providers concerned are granted a period of

---

[31] Rec. 78 DSA.

[32] Rec. 78 DSA; in more detail on network effects Monopolkommission, Wettbewerbspolitik: Herausforderung digitale Märkte, 68th SG 2015, mn. 37; Dewenter/Rösch, Einführung in die Ökonomie der Medienmärkte, 2015, pp. 27; Clement/Schreiber, Internet Economics, 3rd ed. 2016, s. 273; BKartA, Working Paper: Market Power of Platforms and Networks, 2016, p. 97 et seq.; Mohr EuZW 2019, 265 (267); Denga ZGE 2020, 1 (13 et seq.).

[33] Rec. 78 DSA.

[34] Rec. 78DSA.

[35] The DSA – in all language versions – speaks of "above", which is an editorial oversight.

four months after notification of their designation pursuant to Art. 33(4) or the withdrawal of their designation pursuant to Art. 33(5), after the expiry of which the obligations of the Section shall apply or cease to apply.

II. Risk assessment

1. Basic concept

Art. 34 obliges very large online platforms to carry out an identification, evaluation and analysis of the systemic risks ("risk assessment") arising from the design, operation or use of the services […] (Art. 34(1)). The standard thus takes up the approach of **delegation or self-regulation of the platforms** by obliging them to independently assess the self-created risks (see → mn. 7 et seqq.). According to Art. 35, the assessments resulting from the risk assessment must then be implemented in the form of targeted risk reduction measures, which are also determined by the regulated actors themselves. 32

2. Systemic risks

Art. 34(1) lists four "systemic risks" to be identified, analysed and assessed in the risk assessment:[36] 33

Standard	Systemic risk
(a)	Dissemination of illegal content
(b)	Any actual or foreseeable adverse effects on the exercise of fundamental rights
(c)	Actual or foreseeable adverse effects on social debate, electoral processes and public security
(d)	Actual or foreseeable adverse effects in relation to gender-based violence, the protection of public health and minors, and serious adverse effects on the physical and mental well-being of a person

a) *Dissemination of illegal content*

The first systemic risk identified by the DSA is the **dissemination of illegal content** through the services of the very large online platforms and search engines. This includes, among other things, the "dissemination of depictions of sexual child abuse or unlawful hate speech or other types of misuse of the services for criminal offences, as well as unlawful activities such as a sale of goods or services […] prohibited by Union or national law".[37] Accordingly, the **unlawfulness of content is to be determined either by Union or applicable national law**. The providers are to carry out the assessment of illegality independently of the compatibility of the information with their general terms and conditions,[38] whereby the legislator clarifies that this is a legal assessment – and not an assessment by the providers themselves. The assessment does not affect the personal 34

[36] Rec. 80 DSA.
[37] Rec. 80 DSA.
[38] Rec. 80 DSA.

responsibility of the user of the online platforms or the owners of websites indexed by online search engines for a possible illegality of their conduct under other provisions.[39]

35 These considerations reveal the inherent **problems of the concept of "illegal content"**.[40] In particular, a large part of the content classified as "illegal" will be removed from the online platform or search engine by the providers concerned without having been subjected to a proper legal review beforehand.[41] Furthermore, against the background of the protection of freedom of expression, it seems misguided to make illegality dependent on the respective applicable national law, when in some Member States of the Union – especially in Poland and Hungary – there is a considerable risk that an unreasonable restriction of freedom of expression will occur.[42] From this it becomes clear that the concept of "illegal content" carries within itself the **risk of "overblocking"** – and thus of an unreasonable restriction of freedom of expression.[43] The concept of illegality requires clarifcation. In addition to the question of when content is to be classified as "illegal", it still seems questionable when such content is "disseminated" by online platforms or search engines. Recital 80 states that dissemination can occur (in particular) when access to illegal content "spreads rapidly and widely", for example through accounts with a particularly large reach,[44] and thus a large number of people come into contact with the content.

b) Any actual or foreseeable adverse effects on the exercise of fundamental rights

36 The second category of systemic risk is any actual or foreseeable **adverse effects on the exercise of fundamental rights**. Adverse effects on the exercise of the following fundamental rights are to be considered in particular:

Article	Fundamental right
Art. 1 CFR	Fundamental right to respect for human dignity
Art. 7 CFR	Fundamental right to respect for private and family life
Art. 8 CFR	Fundamental right to the protection of personal data
Art. 11 CFR	Fundamental right to freedom of expression and information (including media freedom and pluralism)
Art. 21 CFR	Fundamental right to non-discrimination
Art. 24 CFR	Rights of the child
Art. 38 CFR	Consumer protection

37 It is not clear when there is a "foreseeable adverse effect" on the exercise of fundamental rights. The **broad wording** again not only bears the risk of an overreaction

39 Rec. 80 DSA.

40 Denga EuR 2021, 569 et seqq.; Peukert KritV 2022 57 (69).

41 Buri/Hoboken, The Digital Services Act (DSA) proposal: a critical overview, p. 34.

42 Barata, The Digital Services Act and its impact on the right to freedom of expression: special focus on risk mitigation obligations, p. 18; Buri/Hoboken, The Digital Services Act (DSA) proposal: a critical overview, p. 34.

43 Barata, The Digital Services Act and its impact on the right to freedom of expression: special focus on risk mitigation obligations, p. 18; Buri/Hoboken, The Digital Services Act (DSA) proposal: a critical overview, p. 34.

44 Rec. 80 DSA.

on the part of the obligated platforms, but also lacks a balancing with any conflicting fundamental rights that may arise.[45]

Recital 81 gives examples of relevant risks, such as the **design of algorithmic systems** of systemically important platforms, the **misuse of a service for the transmission of abusive messages**, or other methods to **prevent freedom of expression** or to **hinder competition.**[46] The scattering of these examples illustrates the difficulties in dealing with the wording of the Regulation; there are almost innumerable situations that could be considered for adverse effects on the exercise of fundamental rights. In particular, it remains **unclear** what **level of adverse effect (or risk of such) is required** to constitute a systemic risk. **38**

Risks to the rights of the child are given particular importance. Here, for example, providers are to check "how easy it is for minors to understand the design and functioning of the service and in what way minors may be exposed through their service to content that may impair their health or their physical, mental or moral development".[47] With this, the legislator emphasises the **special need for protection of minors**, which of course continues in the digital space.[48] **39**

c) *Actual or foreseeable adverse effects on social debate, electoral processes and public safety*

The third category of systemic risk is actual or foreseeable adverse **effects on social debate, electoral processes and public security,** Article 34(1)(3)(c). A concretisation of this systemic risk is missing in the recitals.[49] Here, too, the enormous breadth of the term "adverse effects" must be criticised. With this risk-category, the European legislator is undoubtedly addressing fields in which the enormous effects and influences of very large online platforms and search engines have become clear in the past, such as in particular the presidential election in the United States in 2016 or the Brexit vote in the United Kingdom in 2016.[50] Against this backdrop, the explicit addressing of social debate and election processes seems to be a conclusive policy goal; it is another matter whether the assessment of such comprehensive processes should be imposed on private parties and whether it can be **delegated at all as an essential public question** (→ mn. 7 et seqq.). **40**

d) *Other risks*

As a final systemic risk, Art. 34(1) subpara. 2 (d) lists a **very broad catalogue** of issues, namely actual or foreseeable adverse effects in relation to gender-based violence, the protection of public health and of minors, as well as serious adverse effects on the physical and mental well-being of a person. Once again, the blatant vagueness of the norm should be pointed out; in particular, it is unclear how intensive the mental well-being of a (one?) person must be in order to be considered as a systemic risk. **41**

---

[45] Barata, The Digital Services Act and its impact on the right to freedom of expression: special focus on risk mitigation obligations, p. 18; Buri/Hoboken, The Digital Services Act (DSA) proposal: a critical overview, p. 34; Denga EuR 2021, 569 (591 et seqq.).

[46] Rec. 81 DSA.

[47] Rec. 81 DSA.

[48] For example: rec. 40, which mentions the particular vulnerability to discriminatory acts.

[49] Cf. rec. 82 DSA.

[50] On this, Künast, Regeln für Wahlkämpfe im digitalen Zeitalter ZRP 2019, 62 et seqq.; Przemysław Polański, Some thoughts on data portability in the aftermath of the Cambridge Analytica scandal EuCML 2018, 141 et seqq.

42 According to the considerations of the European legislator, the reasons for such risks can be "coordinated disinformation campaigns related to public health" or "the design of online interfaces that can stimulate behavioural addictions of users".[51] The first aspect is obviously linked to the experience of the Corona pandemic, during which online platforms and search engines were used to spread false news about the virus and vaccinations.

3. Platform-dependent factors for influencing systemic risks

43 Art. 34(2) specifies which **influencing factors** the providers must take into account in particular in their risk assessment. Art. 34(2) lists five factors, which are described in more detail in Recital 84.

Standard	Risk factor
(a)	Design of recommender systems and other relevant algorithmic systems
(b)	Content moderation systems
(c)	Applicable general terms and conditions and their enforcement
(d)	Systems for selecting and presenting advertisements
(e)	Data related practices of the provider

44 Furthermore, according to Art. 34(2) sent. 2, providers must analyse whether and how the systemic risks are influenced by intentional manipulation of the respective service by platform users or third parties. Such influence can be realised by an "inauthentic use or automated exploitation of the service, as well as by the amplification and the possibility of the rapid and wide dissemination of illegal content and of information incompatible with their general terms and conditions".

45 In addition, according to Art. 34(2) sent. 3, providers must take **regional and linguistic aspects** into account even if they are specific to a Member State. Consequently, aspects based on a regional limitation or on linguistic differences must also be taken into account in the context of the risk assessment.[52]

4. Obligation to transmit and retain data

46 According to Art. 34(3), providers are obliged to **keep the documents of the risk assessment for at least three years** after it has been carried out and to forward them to the Commission and the Digital Services Coordinator of establishment as required.

47 This is to ensure **continuity and interrelatedness of risk assessments** in order to track dynamic developments.[53] It can also facilitate investigations and enforcement actions.[54] Providers are therefore required to keep "all evidence" of a risk assessment carried out, including, for example, information on its preparation, underlying data and data on the testing of their algorithmic systems.[55]

[51] Rec. 83 DSA.
[52] Rec. 84 DSA.
[53] Rec. 85 DSA.
[54] Rec. 85 DSA.
[55] Rec. 85 DSA.

III. Risk mitigation

As a consequence of the risk assessment to be carried out under Art. 34, Art. 35 obliges the regulated providers of systemically important platforms to take **appropriate, proportionate and effective risk mitigation measures** tailored to the particular systemic risks identified. 48

Art. 35(1)(2)(a)–(k) lists examples of measures that may be considered. These are specified in recitals 87 and 88. The purpose of the measures is to contribute appropriately and effectively to reducing the identified risks.[56] The measures should also be **proportionate** against the background of the provider's **economic performance.** 49

Standard	Measure
(a)	Adaptation of the design, features or functioning of the services (including online interfaces)
(b)	Adaptation of the general terms and conditions and their enforcement
(c)	Adaptation of the content moderation procedures [...]
(d)	Testing and adaptation of algorithmic systems
(e)	Adaptation of the advertising systems [...]
(f)	Reinforcing internal processes, resources, auditing, documentation or supervision of activities
(g)	Start or adapt cooperation with trusted whistleblowers (Art. 22) and implementation of decisions of out-of-court dispute resolution bodies (Art. 21)
(h)	Start or adapt cooperation with other online platform providers or online search engines using the codes of conduct or crisis protocols referred to in Article 45 and Article 48
(i)	Awareness-raising measures and adaptation of online interfaces to give users more information
(j)	Targeted measures to protect the rights of the child
(k)	Ensuring that an item of information, whether it is a generated or manipulated image, sound or video content, which noticeably resembles existing persons, objects, places or other facilities or events and which falsely appears to a person to be genuine or truthful, is identifiable by a conspicuous marking when displayed on the online interfaces [...]

The effects of the measures on fundamental rights are to be explicitly taken into account in accordance with Art. 35(1) sent. 1. Provider of systemically relevant platforms need to **avoid unnecessary restrictions on the use of services**. In particular, any effects on freedom of expression are to be sufficiently and comprehensively taken into account.[57] In this way, the European legislator is attempting to address the problem of over-reaction in the form of "**overblocking**" (on this in detail → rec. 12 et seq.). Whether the simple emphasis on this goal can be sufficient despite the far reaching and vague obligations of the Regulation appears doubtful.[58] 50

[56] Rec. 86 DSA.
[57] Rec. 86 DSA.
[58] Critically also Peukert KritV 2022, 57 (61).

51 Art. 35(2) establishes an **annual reporting obligation of the Board**, which, in cooperation with the Commission, shall publish the most prominent recurring systemic risks as well as best practices to mitigate them, as reported or otherwise identified by the providers of systemically important platforms. The report is to be broken down by the member states in which the risks occurred. In cconformity with the approach of self-regulation, the affected providers are thus given significant assistance in implementing the examplary measures of Article 35(1) through the reports on typical risks and best practices for mitigation. The aim is to increase the effectiveness of self-regulation.

52 According to Art. 35(3), the Commission, in cooperation with the Digital Service Coordinators, may publish **guidelines** setting out best practices and possible measures in relation to risk mitigation measures. Again, due consideration shall be given to the possible impact of the measures on the fundamental rights of all stakeholders. The guidelines constitute further assistance for the benefit of the providers concerned and are thus, like the reports under Art. 35(2), elements in a system of effective self-regulation.

IV. Crisis response mechanism

1. Basic concept

53 Article 36 on a so-called "**crisis response mechanism**" was introduced late in the legislative process. The article empowers the Commission to adopt a decision in the event of a crisis that obliges providers of systemically important platforms to implement specific measures. According to the European legislator, in times of crisis it may become necessary for providers to take urgent specific measures in addition to the other measures provided for in the Regulation.[59] No doubt the legislator had the Corona pandemic in mind here, but also Russia's war of aggression against Ukraine. Other provisions of the Regulation remain unaffected by Art. 36.[60]

54 The European legislator also wants to **protect** the **fundamental rights of the citizens** in the event of a crisis. The principle of proportionality allows for more intensive measures in proportion to the increased danger. In each individual case, a comprehensive balancing of interests must be carried out, in which the platform's fundamental right to moderation and its freedom of enterprise are also appropriately taken into account.

55 Within the approach of self-regulation, which is comprehensively pursued in Chapter III Section 5, the provision can also be understood as a **necessary compensation for the delegation of protective state duties.** In the event of a crisis, the self-regulatory powers of platforms can thus be limited by at least partially reducing their discretion in exercising their guarantor position towards users and society.[61]

2. Special measures

56 Article 36(1) subpara. 1 (a)–(c) lists (exhaustively) specific measures that the Commission may oblige providers to take.

---

[59] Rec. 91 DSA.
[60] Rec. 91 DSA.
[61] On the providers' right of choice under Art. 36(5) see below → mn. 65 et seqq.

Standard	Measure
(a)	Assessment of whether, and if so to what extent and how, the operation and use of the services significantly contribute or are likely to contribute to a serious threat within the meaning of paragraph 2.
(b)	Identify and apply targeted, effective and proportionate measures, such as any of those provided for in Article 35(1) or Article 48(2), to prevent, eliminate or limit such contribution to the serious threat identified in accordance with point (a).
(c)	Reporting to the Commission, by a certain date or at regular intervals specified in the decision, on the evaluations referred to in point (a), on the precise content, implementation and qualitative and quantitative impact of the specific measures taken pursuant to point (b) and on any other issue related to those assessments or those measures, as specified in the decision.

Recital 91 lists **as examples of measures within the** meaning of Article 36(1)(b) 57 "adapting content moderation processes and increasing the resources dedicated to content moderation, adapting terms and conditions, relevant algorithmic systems and advertising systems, further intensifying cooperation with trusted flaggers, taking awareness-raising measures and promoting trusted information and adapting the design of their online interfaces".[62]

Finally, Art. 36(1) sent. 2 manifests that the principle of proportionality must also be 58 upheld in the context of these special measures, in a way that not only the seriousness of the threat, but also the urgency of the measure and "the actual or potential implications for the rights and legitimate interests of all parties concerned, including the possible failure of the measures to respect the fundamental rights enshrined in the Charter" must be taken into account. This emphasises that the **principle of proportionality** must be upheld even in the event of a crisis – the value of this rhetoric is, as already emphasised, questionable.

3. Definition of crisis

When a crisis occurs is defined by law in Art. 36(2). This is said to be the case when 59 "**extraordinary circumstances** lead to a serious **threat to public security or public health** in the Union or in **significant parts** of it".[63] By way of example, the Commission cites armed conflicts or acts of terrorism, natural disasters, pandemics and other serious cross-border threats to public health.[64] Since Art. 36 can oblige to take far-reaching measures, it must be emphasised against the background of the principle of proportionality when assessing whether a crisis has occurred that there must be a *serious* threat to the legal interests mentioned.

4. Requirements for the Commission decision

Art. 36(3) lays down requirements for the Commission's decision-making on the con- 60 crete crisis measures. Essentially, it must ensure that the measures taken can be taken within a short period of time, but at the same time that the mechanism is only used if and to the extent that this is **absolutely necessary** and that the measures taken under the

62 Rec. 91 DSA.
63 Rec. 91 DSA.
64 Rec. 91 DSA.

mechanism are effective and proportionate.[65] The requirements are thus intended to strike a balance between effectiveness and proportionality.

61 Thus, Art. 36(3)(a) states the necessity and proportionality of the measures taken, again calling for consideration of the "implications for the rights and legitimate interests of all parties concerned, including the possible failure of the measures to respect the **fundamental rights** enshrined in the Charter".

62 Art. 36(3)(b) then manifests the requirement to **set an appropriate deadline** for the providers within which the crisis measures according to para. 1 are to be taken. Within the framework of reasonableness, the urgency of the measure and the time required for its preparation and implementation must be taken into account. The appropriateness of a deadline shall be determined on the basis of the specific individual case.

63 Finally, Art. 36(3)(c) sets a **time limit** of a maximum of **three months** for the required measures.

5. Procedure for the adoption of resolutions

64 In the event of a decision being taken, the Commission shall immediately observe the procedural provisions set out in Art. 36(4). In doing so, it must notify the decision to the provider concerned (a), make it publicly accessible (b) and inform the Board with a request for comments and keep it informed (c). In particular, this takes into account the **transparency of the decision-making process.**

6. Right of choice of the provider

65 According to Art. 36(5), the right to choose the concrete measures to be taken remains with the respective provider, as long as they are "targeted, effective and proportionate". Despite the self-regulation compensated for in Art. 36 in the event of a crisis, the fundamental **decision-making leeway of the providers concerned thus remains.** This is consistent when one considers that especially in crisis situations, proximity and knowledge of the facts are decisive for the choice of concrete means of danger prevention; the regulation makes sense with regard to the comprehensive asymmetry of information between platform providers and the state.

7. Dialogue between supplier and Commission

66 Art. 36(6) manifests the possibility of a dialogue between the provider and the Commission, in which the effectiveness and proportionality of the measures are discussed. The **dialogue "may" take place at the request of the Commission or the respective provider** and must in particular shed light on whether the measures taken by the provider meet the requirements of Art. 36(3)(a) and (c), i.e. whether they are proportionate and comply with the maximum time limit of three months.

8. The Commission's right of supervision

67 The application of the targeted measures shall be monitored by the Commission in accordance with Art. 36(7), taking into account the development of the crisis. **The Commission shall report on** this to **the Board at least on a monthly basis**. If the Commission concludes in the course of the monitoring that the measures taken by the provider are ineffective or disproportionate, it may, after consulting the panel, request the provider to reconsider the measures by adopting a decision.

---

[65] Rec. 91 DSA.

In this way, the legislature compensates for the platforms' remaining discretion to choose according to Article 36(5) and can thus enable the administration to fulfil its monitoring duties, which remain especially in situations sensitive to fundamental rights. However, the compensation and framing of the delegation is clearly too weak at this point – **a "second chance" of the platform provider to avert danger does not seem appropriate in the event of a crisis.** 68

9. Right of amendment and extension of the Commission

Art. 36(8) empowers the Commission, on the recommendation of the Board, to amend the decision pursuant to Art. 36(1) or Art. 36(7) subpara. 2. According to Art. 36(8)(a), the Commission may revoke such a decision and request the provider to no longer apply the specific measures taken. If the reasons for the measures still exist, the Commission may also, according to Art. 36(8)(b), extend the decision by a **maximum of three months**; the extension is possible once ("no more than three months"). Finally, in the context of the amendment under Art. 36(8)(c), the Commission may take into account the experience gained, especially against the background of respect for fundamental rights – which seems self-evident. According to Art. 36(9), the requirements of paras. (1) to (6) apply to the amending decision. 69

10. Reporting obligation of the Commission

Finally, Art. 36(11) establishes a reporting obligation of the Commission towards the European Parliament and the European Council. The Commission must report annually, and in any case three months after the end of the crisis, on the application of the specific measures taken on the basis of these decisions. 70

V. Independent audit

1. Basic concept

Art. 37 obliges providers of systemically important platforms to undergo an independent audit at least once a year at their own expense. External audits are intended to ensure compliance with the obligations arising from the ordinance and, if applicable, additional commitments from codes of conduct and crisis protocols.[66] Against the background of the intended self-regulation, the independent audits according to Art. 37 **compensate for the delegation of state power through supervision**; the audit is a very essential sources of information available to the Commission. 71

2. Subject of the examination

Art. 37(1) regulates which obligations and commitments are covered by the independent audit. On the one hand, **all obligations set out in Chapter III are listed**, Art. 37(1)(a). On the other hand, commitments made in accordance with Art. 45 (codes of conduct) and 46 (codes of conduct for online advertising) and the crisis protocols mentioned in Art. 48 are included. 72

---

[66] Rec. 92 DSA; comprehensively on the dependency risks of the external auditors in an oligopolistic market Laux/Wachter/Mittelstadt Computer Law & Security Review 43 (2021) 105613, 7 et seqq.

3. Providers' duty of cooperation and handling of confidential information

73 Art. 37(2) subpara. 1 obliges the providers concerned to support and cooperate with the respective auditing organisations so that the examination can be carried out effectively, efficiently and in a timely manner. Providers are required to **provide access to relevant data and premises and to answer questions from the audit organisation**. In addition, auditors should also be able to use other objective sources of information.[67] In doing so, audits should be conducted "according to best industry practices and high professional ethics and objectivity, with due regard, as appropriate, to auditing standards and codes of practice".

74 Art. 37(2) subpara. 2 addresses the handling of sensitive information in the context of independent audits. This reveals the **conflict of interest** between the official interest in a **comprehensive, transparent and in-depth examination** and the interest of the providers concerned in being able to maintain the **confidentiality** of certain information relevant to the business model. On the one hand, Art. 37(2) subpara. 2 sent. 1 emphasises that the auditors shall ensure an appropriate level of confidentiality and compliance with confidentiality obligations with regard to information they receive in the course of the audits. On the other hand, Article 37(2) subparagraph 2 sent. 2 states that this must not have a detrimental effect on "the conduct of audits and other provisions of this Regulation, in particular the provisions on transparency, monitoring and enforcement". Finally, Article 37(2) subpara. 2 sent. 3 states that, where necessary for the purposes of the transparency obligations under Article 42(4), a version without confidential information shall be attached to the report. Within the framework of balancing confidentiality and transparency interests, the legislature has thus made a decision in favour of the public's transparency interests in the course of Art. 37(2) subpara. 2 sent. 2. At the same time, confidentiality is expressly recognised as a legitimate interest which is to be taken into account "according to reasonable discretion". This compromise seems plausible.

4. Requirements for the independent audit bodies

75 Art. 37(3) sets out the requirements that a body performing an independent audit within the meaning of Art. 37 should meet. Recital 92 concretises them to the effect that an engagement should be waived or, where appropriate, the audit mandate already accepted should be resigned if the auditors are not "**beyond doubt**" with regard to the strict requirements for independence and technical competence.

76 Art. 37(3)(a) sets out requirements for the independence of the review body. Thus, the audit organisation must be independent not only of the respective provider, but also of any legal entity associated with this provider, and must **not be in any conflict of interest** with them (cf. Art. 37(3)(a)). Art. 37(3)(a)(i)–(iii) specify these requirements: According to Art. 37(3)(a)(i), the audit organisation may not provide any non-audit services in connection with the audited matter for 12 months before and after the start of the audit. This exclusion of the provision of non-audit services between the provider and the audit organisation (or the obligation to do so) for a total of 24 months is intended to ensure comprehensive independence, although no cooling-off period is provided for as in the case of the audit of financial statements.[68] Furthermore, according to Art. 37(3)(a)(ii), the respective audit organisation may not have provided audit services within the meaning of this Article to the provider and related legal entities for a period of more

67 Rec. 92 DSA.

68 Gerdemann/Spindler GRUR 2023, 115 (124).

than ten consecutive years. Of course, the audit fees pursuant to Art. 37(3)(a)(iii) may not be made dependent on the outcome of the audit.

According to Art. 37(3)(b), the auditor must also have **proven expertise in** the field of risk management as well as technical competence and capacity. Recital 92 states that the body should in particular have the technical competence to test algorithms.[69] 77

Lastly, according to Art. 37(3)(c), the verifier must **demonstrably** operate **with objectivity** and in accordance with **professional ethics,** in particular on the basis of compliance with codes of conduct or other relevant standards. 78

5. Minimum content of the audit report

Pursuant to Art. 37(4), a written audit report must be prepared for each audit, which must contain the minimum content listed in Art. 37(4)(a)–(h). The legal requirements are specified in Recital 93. The background to this audit report is to enable a "**meaningful assessment**" of the activities carried out and the conclusions reached.[70] Therefore, the audit report should provide information on the measures taken by the respective provider to fulfil its obligations under the Regulation and, if necessary, make suggestions for improvement.[71] According to Recital 93, the audit report must then be sent to the Digital Services Coordinator of establishment, the Commission and the Board. However, this requirement is not clear from the wording of the egulation. 79

Standard	Minimum content
(a)	name, address and the point of contact of the provider of the very large online platform or of the very large online search engine subject to the audit and the period covered
(b)	name and address of the examining body(ies)
(c)	a declaration of interests
(d)	a description of the specific elements audited, and the methodology applied
(e)	a description and a summary of the main findings drawn from the audit
(f)	a list of consulted third parties
(g)	an audit opinion
(h)	operational recommendations in the event of a non-positive audit opinion

The audit opinion anchored in Art. 37(4)(g) is of central importance in the context of the audit report. This is based on the conclusions from the audit evidence and can be **"positive", "positive with comments"** or **"negative".**[72] Recital 93 specifies when which audit opinion is to be issued. Accordingly, a positive opinion is to be issued if all the evidence shows that the audited provider complies with the obligations of the Regulation and the commitments.[73] According to the strict wording of the recital, a single breach of duty is sufficient to prevent the issuance of a "positive" statement. A "positive report with observations" is to be issued if observations are added by the auditor which never- 80

[69] Rec. 92 DSA.
[70] Rec. 93 DSA.
[71] Rec. 93 DSA.
[72] Rec. 93 DSA.
[73] Rec. 93 DSA.

theless "do not have a material impact on the audit result".[74] A material impact on the audit result would be given if it becomes apparent at any point in the audit that the provider is not fulfilling obligations under the Regulation or commitments made. If there is no such case and the auditor nevertheless has to add a remark, this possibility therefore applies. If the audited provider does not fulfil the obligations of the Regulation or the commitments made, the auditor must issue a "negative audit opinion".[75]

6. Gaps in the report

81 **If it was not possible** for the auditor **to verify certain elements or to issue an opinion** on the basis of its investigations during the examination, the **circumstances and reasons** why the elements could not be examined must be **explained in** the examination report in accordance with Art. 37(5). This ensures that there are no arbitrary gaps in the scope of the audit report.

7. Consequences of a non-"positive" audit report

82 Finally, Art. 37(6) regulates how an affected provider must react in the event of a non-"positive" audit report. According to this, the provider must duly take into account all operational recommendations of the audit report and take the necessary measures to implement them. Within one month after receipt of the recommendations, the **implemented measures** must be **presented in a report** according to Art. 37(6) sent. 2. Any non-implementation of operational recommendations must be justified in the report and alternative measures to remedy the violations must be presented. In accordance with the narrow wording of Art. 37(6), which only exempts "positive" audit reports from these consequences, providers who receive a positive audit report "with comments" are also covered and have to report on the implementation of duties.

8. Possibility of supplementing the Commission

83 Finally, Art. 37(7) empowers the Commission to adopt delegated acts to supplement the above provisions where necessary. In particular, rules for the procedural steps, audit methods and report templates are listed here.

VI. Recommender systems

84 Art. 38 addresses providers of very large online platforms and search engines that use "recommender systems". According to Art. 3(s), a recommender **system** is "a **fully or partially automated system** used by an online platform **to suggest in its online interface specific information** to recipients of the service or **prioritise that information**, including as a result of a search initiated by the recipient of the service or otherwise determining the relative order or prominence of information displayed". The reason for this Regulation is the intention to encourage affected providers to evaluate and adapt the design of their recommender systems – and thus, for example, to initiate measures to avoid or minimise bias.[76] The legislator thus recognises the central role and the great influence of recommender systems in the use of system-relevant platforms, which can lead in par-

---

[74] Rec. 93 DSA.
[75] Rec. 93 DSA.
[76] Rec. 94 DSA.

ticular to the discourse-critical phenomenon of **filter bubbles.**[77] Amazon has filed a lawsuit against the Commission's order to i.a. publish its recommender systems under Art. 38 – the first case invoving the DSA and pointing towards the core dilemma of platform regulation, nameley the balance between transparency and confidentiality of business secrets.[78]

In addition and supplementary to the transparency obligations that apply to all online platforms with regard to their recommendation systems under Art. 27,[79] providers are required under Art. 38 to **offer at least one option for each of their recommender systems that is not** based on **"profiling".**[80] Profiling is defined by reference to the definition in Article 4(4) GDPR. Such an option should be made available to users as an alternative for the "most important parameters" of the recommendation systems.[81] The selection of alternatives should be directly accessible from the online interface on which the recommendations are presented. 85

However, it is **unclear which** parameters of recommendation systems are the "**most important**".[82] If a narrow interpretation of this term was applied, the providers concerned could already fulfil the obligations of Art. 38 with relatively restricted measures.[83] As a result, an extension of the obligations to all parameters of the recommender systems was partly demanded.[84] In addition, criticism was voiced to the effect that providers should be obliged to have a default setting without profiling instead of the opt-out option anchored in Art. 38.[85] 86

VII. Additional transparency of online advertising

1. Basic concept

Art. 39 establishes additional transparency obligations for providers of very large online platforms and search engines that display "online advertising" on their online interfaces. Since numerous **platform business models are** based significantly on the **placement of advertisements**, this regulation is inevitably of great importance.[86] According to Art. 3(r), advertising within the meaning of the norm is "information designed to promote the message of a legal or natural person, irrespective of whether to achieve commercial or non-commercial purposes, and presented by an online platform on its online interface against remuneration specifically for promoting that information". 87

The background to stricter transparency obligations for online advertising are the special risks associated with the use of advertising systems, which arise from the scope 88

---

[77] Bradshag/Howard, The Global Disinformation Order, 2019, s. 2 et seqq.; Pariser, The Filter Bubble, 2011.

[78] Until now only a summary ruling of the EGC was rendered, with partly success of Amazon in terms of Art. 39, T-367/23 R.

[79] Berberich/Seip GRUR-Prax 2021, 4 (5).

[80] Rec. 94 DSA.

[81] Rec. 94 DSA.

[82] Helberger/van Drunen/Vrijenhoek/Möller, Regulation of news recommenders in the Digital Services Act: empowering David against the Very Large Online Goliath, Internet Policy Review, Opinion, 26.2.2021, available at <https://policyreview.info/articles/news/regulation-news-recommenders-digital-services-act-empowering-david-against-very-large, last accessed: 29.08.2024.

[83] Helberger/van Drunen/Vrijenhoek/Möller, Regulation of news recommenders in the Digital Services Act: empowering David against the Very Large Online Goliath, Internet Policy Review, Opinion, 26.2.2021.

[84] EDPS, Opinion 1/2021 on the Proposal for a Digital Services Act, s. 26.

[85] EDPS, Opinion 1/2021 on the Proposal for a Digital Services Act, p. 16.

[86] Müller MMR 2022, 1007 (1009).

and the possibility of being able to reach users in a ***targeted*** manner on the basis of their behaviour (***targeted advertising***).[87] Through the additional transparency obligations, the European legislator is attempting in particular to balance out existing information asymmetries vis-à-vis the providers. This is because the area of online advertising stands out as a sphere where specific processes and modes of operation are hardly at all publicly available. Amazon has filed a lawsuit against the Commission's order to i.a. publish its advertising policy under Art. 39 – the first case invoving the DSA and pointing towards the core dilemma of platform regulation, nameley the balance between transparency and confidentiality of business secrets.[88]

2. Archiving obligation

89 Art. 39(1) obliges affected providers (i.e. those who display online advertising on their online interface) to compile the information listed in Art. 39(2) in a specific area of their online interface, i.e. a so-called **archive.** This archive must be made publicly available by the provider for the entire period during which the advertising is displayed and for one year after the last display of the advertising, "through a searchable and reliable tool that allows multicriteria queries".

90 In addition to **supervision**, the purpose of making information available to the public is also to enable **research** into new risks, such as manipulative techniques and disinformation or unlawful advertising as such.[89] In particular, "targeted advertising", i.e. advertising that is intended to specifically reach certain user groups, is to be targeted. The affectedness of minors, who are considered to be particularly worthy of protection, is also to be given special consideration.[90]

91 According to Art. 39(1) sent. 2, the provider shall ensure "that the **archive does not contain any personal data** of the users to whom the advertising was or could have been displayed". Nevertheless, the provider shall make "reasonable efforts" to present information as precisely and completely as possible.

3. Minimum content of the archive

92 Art. 39(2) lists the minimum content of the archive to be published by the provider.

Standard	Minimum content
(a)	the content of the advertisement, including the name of the product, service or brand and the subject matter of the advertisement
(b)	the natural or legal person on whose behalf the advertisement is presented
(c)	the natural or legal person who paid for the advertisement, if that person is different from the person referred to in point (b)
(d)	the period during which the advertisement was presented

87 Rec. 95 DSA.

88 Until now only a summary ruling of the EGC was rendered, with partly success of Amazon in terms of Art. 39, T-367/23 R.

89 Rec. 95 DSA.

90 Rec. 95 DSA.

Standard	Minimum content
(e)	whether the advertisement was intended to be presented specifically to one or more particular groups of recipients of the service and if so, the main parameters used for that purpose including where applicable the main parameters used to exclude one or more of such particular groups
(f)	the commercial communications published on the very large online platforms and identified pursuant to Article 26(2)
(g)	the total number of recipients of the service reached and, where applicable, aggregate numbers broken down by Member State for the group or groups of recipients that the advertisement specifically targeted

4. Exception for removed or blocked advertising

If a provider has removed or blocked access to a particular advertisement on the grounds of presumed illegality or incompatibility with its general terms and conditions, the information referred to in Art. 39(2)(a), (b) and (c) must not be included in the archive pursuant to Art. 39(3) subpara. 1 sent. 1. Thus, the content of the advertisement, the person in whose name the advertisement was displayed and, if applicable, the person who paid for the advertisement are not to be listed in the archive. Instead, according to Art. 39(3) sent. 2, the archive should contain **information on the legal basis** on which the advertising was blocked or removed (Art. 9(2)(a) and (i). In addition, the obligations to give reasons according to Art. 17(3) apply to the restriction of the reproduction of content. 93

5. Guidelines of the Commission

In order to provide guidance to providers, Art. 39(3) subpara. 2 empowers the Commission to publish guidelines, which it issues after consultation with the Board, qualified accredited researchers and the public. These are intended to provide information on the structure, organisation and functioning of the archives. 94

VIII. Data access and control

1. Basic concept

In order to enable monitoring of very large online platforms and search engines, Art. 40 requires the providers concerned to grant access to internal data to both the **Digital Services Coordinator of establishment and the Commission.** In addition, Art. 40 also allows **authorised researchers** comparable access to data for the purpose of conducting research on systemic risks and respective risk mitigation measures.[91] Art. 40 thus contributes significantly to the verifiability of security by platforms and serves to eliminate existing information asymmetries on the state side.[92] While the provision has innovative features,[93] it raises concerns about its strong impact on confidential information, especially in the form of business secrets.[94] 95

---

[91] Müller MMR 2022, 1007 (1009).
[92] To compensate for the legitimacy deficit: Denga/Pohle/Hölzel RW 2020, 420 et seqq.
[93] Buri/Hoboken, The Digital Services Act (DSA) proposal: a critical overview, p. 39.
[94] Peukert KritV 2022, 57 (81).

2. Data access for monitoring and evaluation of providers

96 The prerequisite for data access according to Art. 40(1) is a **justified request** by the Digital Services Coordinator of establishment or by the Commission. Subsequently, providers of systemically important platforms must disclose such information as is necessary for monitoring and assessing compliance with the Regulation.

97 Recital 96 specifies which information is to be covered by this. Explicitly covered are **algorithms** and thus a core area of the business activity of platforms. This may include all information necessary to assess risks and possible damages associated with the systems, as well as "data on the accuracy, functioning and testing of algorithmic systems for content moderation, recommender systems or advertising systems, including, where appropriate, training data and algorithms, or data on processes and outputs of content moderation or of internal complaint-handling systems within the meaning of this Regulation". Article 40(3) further specifies an obligation for providers to explain the design, logic, functioning and testing of their algorithmic systems.

98 Art. 40(2)2 stipulates a strict **purpose limitation of the use of data.** Requests for specific information on individual users or for compliance with other legislation cannot thus be based on Art. 40.[95] The Coordinator and the Commission are also explicitly obliged to take due account of the rights and interests of providers and users. Since access to provider data is a weighty intervention in their data-driven business model, a sensitive weighing of interests is required in any case.

99 Finally, providers must grant access within a **reasonable period of time.** When this is the case is to be determined according to the concrete circumstances of the individual case. According to Article 40(7), access must be provided via an "appropriate interface". This must be specified in the request for information and can also refer to online databases or application programming interfaces.

3. Research data access

100 Art. 40(4) entitles a specified group of researchers (in para. 8) to access data. The right of access is limited to research concerning the self-regulation of systemically important platforms under Art. 34, 35, i.e. the **detection, identification and understanding of systemic risks as well as the adequacy, effectiveness and impact of risk mitigation measures**. Thus, a strict purpose limitation corresponding to Art. 40(2) applies.

101 Research into the development and significance of systemic online risks is of particular importance to the European legislator. It is intended to **address** existing **information deficits** and thus ensure a resilient risk reduction system by making the research results available to providers, Coordinators, other competent authorities, the Commission and the public.[96] Recital 97 gives examples of possible research requests: these may concern, for example, the number of views or other types of access to content before it is removed.[97]

102 The detailed regulation of research data access in Art. 40(4)–(12) reveals an enormous sensitivity. Research data access is to be allowed only in narrowly defined cases and for narrowly defined purposes in order to do justice to the conflicting interests and rights of the providers concerned. According to Art. 40(13), the Commission may adopt delegated acts on technical conditions, purposes of use and compliance with the GDPR. Overall, the concept seems very **cumbersome,** so that its effectiveness in practice remains to be seen.

---

[95] Rec. 96 DSA.
[96] Rec. 96 DSA.
[97] Rec. 97 DSA.

4. Details of research data access

a) Qualification of the researchers

Researchers must fulfil all the conditions of Art. 40(8)(1)(a)–(g), whereupon the Digital Services Coordinator of establishment (of the provider) will grant[98] the **status of "approved researcher"**. The status is only valid in relation to the application for the research work specified in the respective application. 103

Standard	Requirement for the researcher
(a)	Affiliation to a research organisation as defined in Article 2 no. (1) of Directive (EU) 2019/790
(b)	Independence from commercial interests
(c)	Transparency of funding
(d)	Guarantee of data security, data protection and confidentiality
(e)	Demonstration of the necessity and proportionality of research data access
(f)	Conformity with purposes of Art. 40(4)
(g)	Publication of the results of the research within a reasonable period of time after the completion of the research and taking into account the rights and interests of the users of the service concerned, in accordance with Regulation (EU) 2016/679.

b) Communication of the research request

The research request is not to be addressed directly to the provider of systemically relevant platforms; rather, Art. 40(4) provides that the **request** must first be referred to the Digital Services Coordinator of establishment of the researcher or provider.[99] 104

The Coordinator involved shall carry out an **initial assessment in** accordance with Art. 40(8)(1)(a)–(g) and, if necessary, forward the research request after a positive finding to the Digital Services Coordinator of establishment, who shall take the final decision on the award, Art. 40(9) subpara. 2. 105

The Coordinator assessing a research request shall **inform the Commission** and the Board of its receipt, Art. 40(8) sent. 2. If the status of "approved researcher" is granted to a natural person or institution, the Coordinator shall inform the Board of the name, contact details as well as the purpose of the research submitted in the request, in accordance with Art. 40(11). 106

[98] This follows from Art. 40(9), but must be criticised – it would seem better for the coordinator to be responsible at the researcher's place of establishment, since the researcher's research requests can relate to different platforms with different establishments and only a central conferral of status offers efficiency advantages and a guarantee of neutrality; the approval decision of a coordinator must then be recognised throughout the EU.

[99] The researcher has a right of choice, cf. Art. 40(9) p. 1.

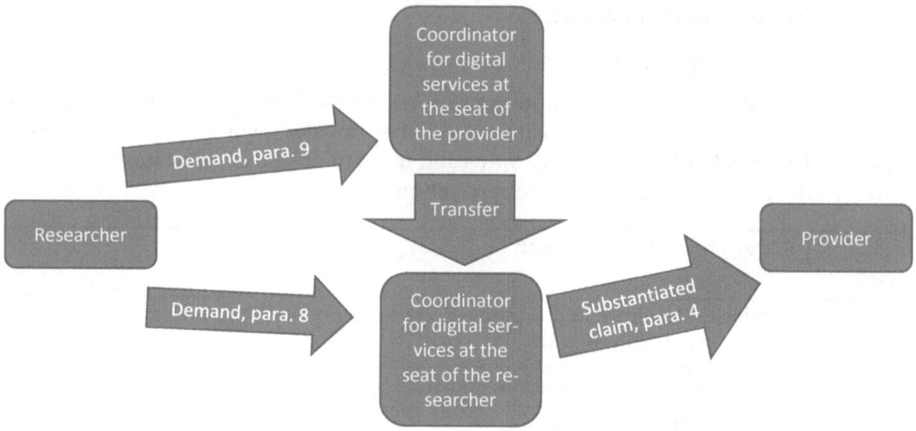

c) Admissibility and appropriateness of a research request

107 The **substantive requirements** for a research request itself are **not entirely clear**, as they are regrettably mixed up with the qualification of researchers themselves under Art. 40(8); here, concretisation through a delegated act would be desirable. In particular, it is not clear when an application becomes "sufficiently substantiated", which is a condition of the coordinator's request to a provider. Art. 40(8) concerns research applications to the effect that they "provide information on the funding of the research" ((c)) and demonstrate "that their access to the data and the time frames requested are necessary for, and proportionate to, the purposes of their research, and that the expected results of that research will contribute to the purposes laid down in paragraph 4" ((e)).

108 Recital 97 emphasises that any request should be "**proportionate**" and must adequately protect the respective rights and legitimate interests. This includes "personal data, trade secrets and other confidential information, of the very large online platform or of the very large online search engine and any other parties concerned, including the recipients of the service". In a possible balancing of interests, the legislator explicitly privileges the research interests in the context of its recitals. This is because consideration of the providers' commercial interests should not lead to a refusal of access, provided that the requested data are "necessary for the specific research objective pursuant to a request under this Regulation". Therefore, in such a constellation, providers have to ensure appropriate access for researchers, if necessary by implementing technical protection measures.[100]

d) Requests for amendments by suppliers

109 In contrast to official access requests, Art. 40(5) entitles providers affected by a research access **request** to submit an **amendment request** within 15 days. To justify this, the applicant can either claim that they are unable to grant access to the requested data because there is no access to it (a), or that granting access would lead to significant weaknesses in the security of the service or the protection of confidential information, such as trade secrets ((b)). Pursuant to Art. 40(6), the provider must at the same time submit proposals as to how access to the requested data can be granted otherwise or to other data that are appropriate and sufficient for the purposes of the request. The Digital

[100] Rec. 97 DSA.

Services Coordinator of establishment shall decide on the request within 15 days. In contrast to access requests for monitoring and evaluation under Art. 40(1), the providers concerned are thus given a certain possibility to react and defend themselves against research requests under Art. 40(4).

e) Immediate access to publicly available data

Pursuant to Art. 40(12), the providers concerned must grant authorised researchers access to data **without delay**, provided that it is **publicly available** via their online interface and that it contributes to the detection, identification and understanding of systemic risks in the Union. In doing so, the GDPR shall be complied with; where the purpose of the research allows, personal data shall only be transferred in anonymised or pseudonymised form.[101] Researchers who only fulfil the requirements listed in Article 40(8) subpara. 1 (b),(c),(d) and (e) should also benefit from immediate access to data, provided they are associated with non-profit institutions, organisations and associations and use the data exclusively for research purposes. The data to be analysed must contribute to the identification or understanding of systemic risks. As an example, access to "aggregated interactions with content from public pages, public groups, or public figures, including impression and engagement data [...]" is listed. Recital 98 declares voluntary cooperation between providers and researchers as the goal. 110

f) Termination of research data access

If the coordinator for digital services, who has granted the status of authorised researcher and submitted the reasoned request for data access to providers, determines that the authorised **researcher no longer fulfils the conditions** set out in Art. 40(8), he shall take a decision on the termination of access pursuant to Art. 40(10). An investigation to this effect may be carried out by the coordinator himself or on the basis of information provided by third parties. The coordinator shall subsequently inform the provider concerned of the decision. In addition, he shall give the authorised researcher the opportunity to comment before terminating the access. 111

IX. Compliance Department

1. Basic concept

Art. 41 obliges the providers of systemically important platforms to establish an independent and competent compliance function against the background of the particular complexity of the functioning of the systems used and the systemic risks for society associated with them.[102] Especially in the **context of self-regulation,** a well-organised compliance department forms the basis for complying with the complex requirements of the DSA in the first place; in addition, the DSA emphasises the compliance responsibility of the provider's management body. 112

2. Structure and tasks

According to Art. 41(1), providers of systemically important platforms must establish a compliance function that is independent of their operational departments and consists 113

[101] Rec. 98 DSA.

[102] This concept is borrowed from financial market regulation, cf. in particular Art. 22(2) and (3) of Regulation (EU) 2017/565.

of one or more compliance officers. In order to effectively ensure compliance with the DSA, it must have **sufficient authority, powers and resources** and have direct access to the provider's management body. In doing so, the department must be properly involved by the respective provider at an early stage in all matters related to this Regulation, "including in the risk assessment and mitigation strategy and specific measures".[103]

114 The tasks to be assumed by the department or the commissioners are set out in Art. 41(3)(a)–(f):

Standard	Task
(a)	Cooperation with the Digital Services Coordinator of establishment and with the Commission for the purposes of the DSA
(b)	Ensure that all risks referred to in Art. 34 are identified and properly reported and that reasonable, proportionate and effective risk-mitigation measures are taken in accordance with Art. 35
(c)	Organisation and supervision of the activities of the systemically important platform provider in connection with the independent audit pursuant to Art. 37
(d)	Informing and advising the management and employees of the systemically important platform provider about the relevant obligations under the DSA
(e)	Monitoring of the systemically important platform provider with regard to its obligations under the DSA
(f)	Where applicable, monitoring of compliance with the commitments made by the systemically important platform provider under the codes of conduct pursuant to Art. 45, 46 or the crisis protocols pursuant to Art. 48

3. Management of the compliance department

115 According to Art. 41(2), the head of the department must have **adequate professional qualifications, knowledge, experience and skills** to perform the duties provided for by law. Explicitly, the head must be an "independent manager" who is specifically responsible for the compliance function and is directly accountable to the provider's management body and communicates with it on the duties of the DSA, in particular on the realisation of systemic risks. The head may not be replaced without the prior consent of the provider's management body, Art. 41(2) subpara. 4. According to Art. 41(4), the name and contact details of the head must be communicated by the respective platform to the Digital Services Coordinator of establishment and the Commission.

4. Compliance obligations of the provider's management body

116 Art. 41 imposes specific obligations on the management body of the provider concerned. According to Art. 41(2) subpara. 1, it must carefully select the head of the compliance department on the basis of his or her "professional qualifications, knowledge, experience and skills". In addition, it has to "determine, supervise and assume liability" for the provider's corporate governance arrangements, which ensure **the independence of the compliance department**. This also includes determining the allocation of tasks

[103] Rec. 99 DSA.

within the organisation to avoid conflicts of interest and ensure responsible management of the systemic risks identified under Art. 34.

Pursuant to Article 41(6), the **provider's management body** shall review the strategies and measures for addressing, managing, monitoring and mitigating the identified systemic risks at least once a year. According to Art. 41(7), the management body shall devote **sufficient time to** the **review of measures related to risk management.** **117**

X. Transparency reporting obligations

1. Basic concept

Art. 42 imposes far-reaching transparency reporting obligations on the providers of systemically important platforms, which apply in **addition to the general transparency reporting obligation** for intermediary services under Art. 15 (→ § 4 mn. 25 et seq.). In the concept of self-regulation, transparency reporting obligations primarily serve to eliminate existing **information asymmetries** on the state side and enable state control and intervention. The background to the special obligations are the systemic risks arising from the business of the providers of systemically important platforms.[104] Consequently, the risk assessments carried out according to Article 34 and the measures taken according to Article 35 are at the centre of the special transparency reporting obligations.[105] **118**

2. Content of the special transparency reporting obligations

The providers of systemically important platforms must publish transparency reports **every six months** – instead of annually as provided for in Art. 15(1). The report must be published in at least one official language of the Member States of the European Union. In addition, the providers must include the average monthly number of users for each Member State in their reports in accordance with Article 42(3). **119**

The additional information compared to Art. 15 follow from Art. 42(2)(1)(a)–(c): **120**

Standard	Additional indication
(a)	human resources dedicated by the provider to the moderation of content related to the service offered in the Union, broken down by each relevant official language of the Member States, including for compliance with the obligations under Articles 16 (Reporting and redress procedures) and 22 (Trusted whistleblowers), as well as for compliance with the obligations under Article 20 (Internal complaints management system).
(b)	qualifications and language skills of the persons carrying out the activities referred to in Art. 42(2)(1)(a), as well as the training and support of such personnel
(c)	indicators of accuracy and related information according to Art. 15(1)(e) (use of automated means for moderating content), broken down by each official language of the Member States

[104] Rec. 100 DSA.
[105] Rec. 100 DSA.

3. Transmission and publication of the documents

121 Providers are obliged to submit the documents listed in Art. 41(4) to the Digital Services Coordinator of establishment and the Commission no later than three months after receipt of the audit report pursuant to Art. 37(4) without delay after completion and, in addition, to make them publicly available.

122 The following documents are included pursuant to Art. 42(4)(a)–(e):

Article	Underlay(s)
(a)	report on the results of the risk assessment according to Art. 34
(b)	specific remedial measures taken pursuant to Art. 35(1)
(c)	the audit report referred to in Art. 37(4)
(d)	the report on the implementation of the audit results referred to in Art. 37(6)
(e)	where applicable, information on the consultations carried out by the provider to support the risk assessments and the design of the risk mitigation measures

123 The provider is given the option in Art. 41(5) to **remove information from the publicly available reports** if it considers that the publication would lead to the disclosure of confidential information of the provider or users, cause significant vulnerabilities to the security of its service, compromise public safety or could harm users. However, in such a case, the provider shall submit the full report, including a justification for the removal of the information, to the Digital Services Coordinator of establishment and the Commission.

XI. Supervisory fees

1. Basic concept

124 The Commission levies an annual supervision fee on the providers of systemically important platforms, Art. 43(1). Each individual service for which the providers have been designated under Art. 33 is subject to the fee, Art. 43(3) subpara. 1. **Concrete supervisory measures vis-à-vis** the fee-paying provider are **not a prerequisite.** The purpose is to provide the Commission with the necessary resources in terms of staff, expertise and funding to enforce the DSA. The levying of the fee is done "in recognition of the fact that Member States should have the power to levy a supervisory fee on providers established in their territory for the supervisory and enforcement tasks carried out by their authorities".[106]

2. Cost recovery

125 According to Art. 43(2), the **total amount of the fees shall cover the estimated costs** incurred by the Commission in connection with its supervisory tasks under the DSA. In particular, the costs related to the designation under Art. 33, the establishment, maintenance and operation of the database under Art. 24(5) and the information exchange system under Art. 85, the referrals under Art. 59, the assistance to the Committee under

[106] Rec. 101 DSA.

Art. 62 and the supervisory tasks under Art. 56 and Chapter IV, Section 4 shall be taken into account.

The **annual supervision fee** is to be determined on the basis of the total costs incurred by the Commission in the performance of its supervisory tasks under the DSA; it is to be reasonably estimated in advance.[107] The providers of the very large online platforms and search engines thus bear the costs of the entire supervision regardless of concrete supervisory measures taken.[108] 126

3. Legal acts on fee setting and methodology

The amount of the annual supervisory fee shall be determined for each provider by the adoption of an **implementing act** of the Commission pursuant to Art. 43(3) subpara. 2. If several services of the provider have been designated as a very large online platform or search engine, several supervisory fees shall be charged to the provider in accordance with Art. 43(3) subpara. 1. 127

The Commission shall also adopt delegated acts concerning the methodology for calculating fees, in accordance with the principles laid down in Art. 43(5). In addition, the advisory procedure set out in Art. 88 shall be followed when adopting the implementing acts. The supervisory fees must also be proportionate. The requirements for the methodology refer to the points mentioned in Art. 43(4)(a)–(d): 128

Standard	Subject of the concretisation of the methods
(a)	determination of the costs incurred by the Commission in connection with its supervisory tasks under the DSA
(b)	determination of the individual annual supervisory fees pursuant to Art. 43(5)(b) and (c)
(c)	determination of the maximum overall limit pursuant to Art. 43(5)(c), i.e. the absolute maximum limit of 0.05 % of the provider's worldwide annual net revenue in the previous business year
(d)	payment details

Both when adopting the implementing acts pursuant to Art. 43(3) and when adopting the delegated acts pursuant to Art. 43(4), the principles set out in Art. 43(5)(a)–(c) shall be observed. Accordingly, the costs incurred in the previous year must be taken into account when estimating the total amount of the annual supervision fee (Art. 43(5)(a)). In addition, according to Art. 43(5)(b), the fee must be in proportion to the average monthly number of active users in the Union. Finally, Art. 43(5)(c) manifests an absolute cap on the supervisory fee of 0.05 % of the provider's worldwide annual net revenue in the previous financial year. 129

The principles are thus intended to ensure the **proportionality of the supervisory fees** vis-à-vis the providers concerned. Recital 101 states that the annual supervisory fee should be proportionate to the size of the service and that the individual annual supervisory fee should not exceed a ceiling to be determined for each provider of very large online platforms or search engines, taking into account its economic capacity. 130

[107] Rec. 101 DSA.
[108] Critically, Denga in Ruffert (ed.), The Regulation of Digital Platforms, 2023, 9.

4. Nature of the revenue

131 From the Commission's point of view, the supervisory fees charged pursuant to Art. 43(6) constitute external, earmarked revenue within the meaning of Art. 21(5) of Regulation (EU, Euratom) 2018/1046 of the European Parliament and of the Council.[109] According to Recital 101, these may be used to finance additional human resources or other expenditure incurred by the Commission in connection with the performance of the task entrusted to it by this Regulation.

5. Reporting obligation

132 According to Art. 43(7), the Commission is subject to an annual reporting obligation to the European Parliament and the Council, which includes the total amount of costs "for the performance of tasks under this Regulation" as well as the total amount of individual annual supervisory fees charged in the previous year.

XII. Temporal applicability

133 According to Art. 92, the DSA can apply to systemically important platforms four months after they have been designated as systemically important platforms under Art. 33(4). If the Commission designates a platform as systemically important before Okt. 17th 2023, it must comply with the requirements of the DSA and, in particular, of Chapter III, Section 5 – but conversely can also invoke the "good Samaritan clause" under Art. 7.[110]

[109] Regulation (EU, Euratom) 2018/1046 of the European Parliament and of the Council of 18.7.2018 on the Financial Regulation applicable to the general budget of the Union, amending Regulations (EU) No 1296/2013, (EU) No 1301/2013, (EU) No. 1303/2013, (EU) No 1304/2013, (EU) No 1309/2013, (EU) No 1316/2013, (EU) No 223/2014, (EU) No 283/2014 and Decision No 541/2014/EU and repealing Regulation (EU, Euratom) No 966/2012, OJ L 193, 1.7.2018, p. 1.

[110] More on this → § 3 mn. 82 et seqq.; as well as Cappello (ed.), The Decoding of the Digital Services Legislative Package, 2021, pp. 16 et seq., 40.

§ 7
Standards, codes of conduct and crisis protocols

Literature: *Berberich/Seip*, Der Entwurf des Digital Services Act, GRUR-Prax 2021, 4; *Buck-Heeb/Dieckmann*, Selbstregulierung im Privatrecht, 2010; *Buri/Hoboken*, The Digital Services Act (DSA) proposal: a critical overview, 2021; *Cappello* (ed.), Die Entschlüsselung des Gesetzespakets zu digitalen Diensten, IRIS Spezial, Europäische Audiovisuelle Informationsstelle, 2021; *Denga*, Plattformregulierung durch europäische Werte, EuR 2021, 569; *Denga/Pohle/Hölzel*, Technikregulierung durch doppelte Delegation, RW 2020, 420; *Dewenter/Rösch*, Introduction to the Economics of Media Markets, 2015; *Dürig/Herzog/Scholz* (eds.), Grundgesetz-Kommentar, Werkstand: 98th EL March 2022, Art. 20; *European Data Protection Supervisor*, Opinion 1/2021 on the Proposal for a Digital Services Act; *Grimm, Dieter*, Die Zukunft der Verfassung, 1991; *Hayek*, The Use of Knowledge in Society, The American Economic Review 1945, 519; *Hayek*, Die Anmaßung von Wissen, 1974; *Helberger/van Drunen/Vrijenhoek/Möller*, Regulation of news recommenders in the Digital Services Act: empowering David against the Very Large Online Goliath, Internet Policy Review, Opinion, 26 February 2021; *Janal*, Haftung und Verantwortung im Entwurf des Digital Services Acts, ZEuP 2021, 227; *Leupold/Wiebe/Glossner* (eds.), IT-Recht, 4th edition 2021; *Loewenheim* (ed.), Handbuch des Urheberrechts, 3rd edition 2021; *Müller*, Künftige Plattformregulierung und effektive Durchsetzung in Deutschland, MMR 2022, 1007; *Peukert*, Zu Risiken und Nebenwirkungen des Gesetzes über digitale Dienste (Digital Services Act), KritV 2022, 57 (75 et seq.); *Volkmann*, Hate Speech durch Social Bots, MMR 2018, 58.

A. Overview of Chapter III Section 6

I. Basic concept

1 Chapter III, Section 6 contains "other provisions on due diligence". In essence, Art. 44–48 contain **three instruments** that are intended to make it easier for providers of

intermediary services as defined in Art. 3(g) to **facilitate compliance with the due diligence obligations of the DSA**. The **voluntary standards** under Art. 44, **codes of conduct** under Art. 45–47 and **crisis protocols** under Art. 48 all address areas of life with a **special risk situation and sensitivity to fundamental rights,** where there is a special state interest in effective protection against perils. The purpose of the "other provisions" is to enable the actors regulated by the DSA to **independently comply with the** obligations imposed on them. Section 6 thus serves to enable **effective self-regulation** (in detail on this concept → § 6 mn. 7–11). However, if a provider implements the voluntary instruments, this is by no means equivalent to compliance with the obligations under the DSA; **no *safe harbour* is** created.[1] Neither do additional due diligence obligations emerge from the section.

II. Principle of voluntariness

2 The instruments anchored in Chapter III Section 6 are all characterised by the **principle of voluntariness**. Consequently, the providers concerned can in no way be obliged to implement the voluntary standards, codes of conduct or crisis protocols. Nor does any breach of the requirements themselves lead to sanctions.

3 The principle of voluntariness finds expression in the rights of the section manifested in favour of the Commission or the Board. In fact, instead of being mandatory, the **Commission can only "encourage and facilitate" the development and implementation of voluntary standards** (Art. 44(1), "encourage and facilitate" **the elaboration of voluntary codes of conduct** (Art. 45(1), 46(1), 47(1)) or **"encourage and facilitate" participation in the elaboration of crisis protocols** (Art. 48(2)). If the respective actors refuse to participate in the instruments of the section, the Commission cannot counteract this by means of coercive measures or sanctions. Its options are rather limited to the rights of request, such as the request for participation of the actors (Art. 45(2)), to take necessary measures (Art. 45(4) subpara. 3) or to revise a crisis protocol (Art. 48(5)).

4 In principle, providers themselves ensure that they comply with the due diligence obligations defined under Art. 44–48. Only within the framework of the Commission's right of request under Art. 45(2) can a provider's **refusal to participate** in a corresponding code of conduct "without adequate justification" lead to this being **taken into account when determining possible infringements** under the DSA.[2] In essence, however, this also does not represent a limitation of voluntariness, but is rather intended to counteract arbitrary behaviour by providers in the event of significant systemic risks pursuant to Art. 45(2).

III. Overview of the instruments of voluntary self-regulation

5 Chapter III, Section 6 establishes three different instruments of voluntary self-regulation – standards (Art. 44), codes of conduct (Art. 45–47) and crisis protocols (Art. 48):

[1] Rec. 102, 104 DSA.
[2] Exgr. 104 DSA.

	Standards Art. 44	Codes of Conduct Art. 45–47	Crisis protocols Art. 48
Character	The voluntary standards are intended to facilitate effective and consistent application of the obligations by providers. In particular, best technical practices are presented and sensitive areas such as online advertising, recommender systems and the protection of minors are addressed.	The codes of conduct shall contribute to the proper application of the DSA. Areas are to be identified in which codes will be implemented. In particular, the fight against illegal content and systemic risks will be targeted. In addition, codes for online advertising and in relation to accessibility will be targeted.	The crisis protocols are intended to contribute to a rapid, collective and cross-border response in the event of a crisis. The protocols add to the existing obligations under the Crisis Response Mechanism according to Art. 36.
Differences	Elaboration by standard-setting bodies.	Elaboration by the actors involved.	Elaboration by the actors involved.
	Deal primarily with technical standards.	Cover systemic risk, online advertising and accessibility.	Deal with crises.
	Time of drafting not determined.	Elaboration until Feb. 18th 2025.	Time of drafting not determined.
	Violations without consequences.	Systematic infringement leads to request by the Commission or the Panel, Art. 45(4) subpara. 3.	Consequences of infringement not specified, but right to request revision under Art. 48(5).

B. Standards

I. Basic concept

Art. 44 obliges the Commission to support and promote the development and implementation of "**voluntary standards**". These are to be established by European and international standard-setting bodies at least for the areas listed in Art. 44(1)(a)–(j).[3] In the context of self-regulation, voluntary standards serve to facilitate regulated providers' **compliance with the obligations under the DSA** by providing them with a set of due diligence requirements and technical best practices.[4] 6

The aim of voluntary standards is to facilitate **effective and consistent application of the obligations** under the DSA by providers. In addition to outlining best technical practices, standards can provide guidance for compliance in the areas of online advertising, recommendation systems and accessibility and protection of minors online.[5] 7

[3] CEN and ETSI in particular come into consideration here.
[4] Buri/Hoboken, The Digital Services Act (DSA) proposal: a critical overview, 2021, p. 42.
[5] Exgr. 102 DSA.

8 Standards can be considered in **particular** in areas where industry can develop **technical means to** assist service providers in complying with the DSA.[6] This can be considered, for example, for application interfaces, the design of general terms and conditions, external audits or the interoperability of advertising archives.[7]

9 In order to ensure that the voluntary standards not only reflect the state of the art, but also the behaviour of the respective users, Art. 44(2) provides for **support by the Commission in the** revision of the standards. Relevant information on the revision is to be kept publicly available and easily accessible according to Art. 44(2) sent. 2.

II. Areas of voluntary standard-setting

10 Art. 44(1)(a)–(j) specify areas in which voluntary standards are to be established.

Standard	Area	Explanation/Example
(a)	Electronic transmission of notifications pursuant to Art. 16	Art. 16-notifications are notifications of suspected illegal content on the services by persons or entities.
(b)	Templates, design and procedural standards for user-friendly communication with users about restrictions arising from the general terms and conditions and their amendments	The provider shall ensure user-friendly communication with its users about restrictions arising from the GTC or changes to the GTC. Such a restriction may occur when certain content is no longer displayed on online platforms.
(c)	Electronic transmission of reports by trusted whistleblowers according to Art. 22, also via application programming interfaces	According to Art. 22(1), providers of online platforms have to ensure a transmission of reports from trustworthy whistleblowers that guarantees priority treatment and prompt processing of these.
(d)	Special interfaces, including application programming interfaces, which facilitate the fulfilment of the obligations under Art. 39, 40	Art. 39 obliges the providers of very large online platforms and search engines to additional transparency obligations if they display online advertising. Art. 40 regulates data access and control by the Digital Services Coordinator, the Commission and authorised researchers vis-à-vis very large online platforms and search engines.
(e)	Auditing of very large online platforms and search engines pursuant to Art. 37	Art. 37 anchors an independent audit of very large online platforms and search engines to be carried out at least annually.

[6] Exgr. 102 DSA.
[7] Rec. 102 DSA and the list in Art. 44(a)–(j).

Standard	Area	Explanation/Example
(f)	Interoperability of the advertising archives referred to in Art. 39(2)	Art. 39 obliges the providers of very large online platforms and search engines to create an archive of the online advertising displayed. Interoperability is intended to enable smooth interaction between the archives.
(g)	Data transfer between advertising intermediaries within the framework of the transparency obligations according to Art. 26(1)(b), (c), (d)	According to Art. 26(1), providers of online platforms must ensure transparency vis-à-vis the user when displaying advertising. The following must be recognisable to the user: The information's character as advertising The person on whose behalf the advertisement is displayed The person who paid for the advertisement Information on the most important parameters for determining the users to whom the advertising is displayed.
(h)	Technical measures enabling compliance with the obligations on advertising contained in the Regulation, including the obligations relating to clearly visible labelling of advertising and commercial communications pursuant to Art. 26	The Regulation imposes specific obligations when it comes to the display of online advertising. Among other things, Art. 26 ensures that users are able to recognise advertising as such.
(i)	Selection interfaces and presentation of information on the main parameters of different types of recommender systems according to Art. 27, 38	Art. 27 obliges providers of online platforms to set out basic information on recommender systems used in their general terms and conditions. According to Art. 38, providers of very large online platforms and search engines shall furthermore submit at least one option for each of their recommendation systems that is not based on profiling pursuant to Art. 4(4) of Regulation (EU) 2016/679.
(j)	Standards for targeted measures to protect minors on the internet	Minors have a special need for protection, which is taken into account in the entire DSA.

C. Codes of conduct

I. Basic concept

11 According to Art. 45, the Commission and the Board shall encourage and facilitate the development of **voluntary codes of conduct** at Union level.[8] These shall also contribute to the proper application of the Regulation; special attention shall be paid to **combating illegal content and systemic risks.** Systemic risks are defined by the Regulation in Art. 34(1)(3)(a)–(d) in relation to very large online platforms and search engines (in detail → § 6 mn. 33–42). This includes:

- The dissemination of illegal content via the services, (a);
- Any actual or foreseeable adverse effects on the exercise of fundamental rights, (b);
- Actual and foreseeable adverse effects on social debate, electoral processes and public safety, (c);
- Actual and foreseeable adverse effects in relation to gender-based violence, the protection of public health, minors and serious adverse effects on physical and mental well-being, (d).

12 Recital 103 emphasises that the implementation of the codes should be measurable and subject to public supervision. At the same time, this should not conflict with the **voluntary nature of the codes,** i.e. it should not affect the freedom of choice of stakeholders.[9] Codes of conduct can be based on **existing self-regulatory measures** at Union level, such as the *Product Safety Pledge*, the Memorandum of Understanding on the Sale of Counterfeit Goods on the Internet, the Code of Conduct on Combating Unlawful Hate Speech on the Internet or the Code of Conduct on Combating Disinformation.[10]

II. Right of the Commission to request

13 Article 45(2) provides for the **Commission's right to request** providers of very large online platforms and search engines as well as competent authorities, civil society organisations and other relevant stakeholders **to participate in the development of voluntary codes of conduct**. The right to request applies if several very large online platforms or search engines are **affected by "significant" systemic** risks within the meaning of Art. 34(1). Since Art. 34(1)(3)(a)–(d) does not define when a "significant" systemic risk exists, it remains unclear when the Commission's right of request applies. On the other hand, "simple" systemic risks are hardly conceivable, so that the Commission may probably request the development of codes of conduct on a very large scale.

14 The request may also set out commitments to specific risk reduction measures as well as a framework for regular reporting on any measures taken and their results. At first glance, the right of request does not limit the fundamental voluntariness of the codes of conduct, since a **request** by the Commission **can be refused by** the provider concerned. Recital 104 nevertheless specifies that a provider's refusal to comply with a Commission request, if without adequate justification, may be taken into account for the purposes of establishing a possible infringement by the platform or search engine.

---

[8] They are already mentioned as a regulatory instrument under Art. 37 of the Services Directive (2006/123/EC).

[9] Exgr. 103 DSA.

[10] Exgr. 106 DSA.

III. Performance indicators and reports

According to Art. 45(3), in implementing the Codes of Conduct, the Commission and the Board shall work to ensure that the Codes of Conduct clearly set out their specific objectives and implement key **performance indicators** to measure the achievement of the objectives and to ensure that the Codes of Conduct take **into account the needs and interests of all stakeholders**. In doing so, the Commission and the Board shall also encourage **regular stakeholder reports** that cover all actions taken and their results. The reports shall be aligned with the key performance indicators of the codes. 15

Finally, Art. 45(3) emphasises that the performance indicators and reporting obligations should take into account the differences in size and capacity of the participants. This ties in with the principle of **proportionality** and ensures that smaller providers are not unduly burdened. 16

IV. Commission monitoring and evaluation law

Following on from Recital 103, which calls for measurable monitoring of the implementation of the codes subject to public oversight, Article 45(4) provides for regular **monitoring and evaluation by the Commission and the Board to ensure** that the codes of conduct meet the respective objectives and that the objectives pursued are achieved. The conclusions are then to be published. In addition, the Commission and the Body shall encourage and facilitate the regular review and adaptation of the Codes of Conduct in accordance with Article 45(4) subpara. 2. 17

If there is a systematic violation of the codes, the Commission and the Board may finally request the signatories of the codes of conduct to take the necessary measures pursuant to Art. 45(4) subpara. 3. This right to request does not prevent the voluntary nature of the codes; **systematic violations of the codes of conduct are not subject to sanctions.** 18

V. Article 46 Codes of conduct for online advertising

1. Basic concept

In order to contribute to more transparency along the value chain of online advertising, Art. 46 obliges the Commission to promote and facilitate **codes of conduct for online advertising**. According to Art. 46(1), the codes of conduct are to be linked to the existing transparency obligations for online advertising vis-à-vis providers of online platforms from Art. 26 and vis-à-vis providers of very large online platforms and search engines from Art. 36 and thus provide "flexible and effective mechanisms to support and improve compliance with these obligations".[11] Article 46 thus addresses not only the providers of very large online platforms and search engines within the meaning of Article 33, but all online platforms as defined in Chapter III, Section 3, on whose platforms advertising is displayed. In addition to the general codes of conduct in Article 45, which primarily address systemic risks, the Regulation provides for codes tailored to online advertising. This expresses the legislative recognition that online advertising poses a particular risk to fundamental rights and freedoms.[12] 19

---

[11] Exgr. 107 DSA.

[12] On the special risks of advertising systems: rec. 95 DSA.

2. Actors involved in the elaboration

20 As the provision of online advertising usually involves a variety of actors, the development of the codes of conduct should involve a wide range of stakeholders. This is to ensure broad support and work towards the goal of achieving the legal transparency obligations.[13] In addition, this broad participation should ensure that all legitimate interests of different stakeholders are taken into account in the development of the codes. **All stakeholders along the value chain** of online advertising can be considered for this: the advertisers, providers of the online platforms as well as intermediary services that bring the advertisers together with the provider who publishes the advertising,[14] organisations representing the users, civil society organisations or relevant authorities. Art. 46(4) allows the Commission to call on all actors along the value chain to promote and comply with the codes of conduct.

3. Minimum content of the codes of conduct

21 Through the codes of conduct for online advertising, the European legislator wants to promote a **competitive, transparent and fair environment for online advertising** in addition to an **effective transmission of information.** According to Art. 46(2) sent. 1, both objectives are subject to the constraints of "full respect for the rights and interests of all parties concerned" and conformity with Union and national law, in particular with regard to competition and the protection of privacy and personal data. In order to achieve these objectives, Art. 46(2)(2)(a)–(c) lists the **minimum content of codes of conduct** for online advertising "which the Commission shall promote".

22 According to Art. 46(2)(2)(a), the codes of conduct shall first cover "the transmission of information held by providers of online advertising intermediaries to recipients of the service concerning the requirements set in Article 26(1)(b), (c) and (d)". Among other things, the codes are thus intended to facilitate the transmission of **information about the advertiser** who pays for the advertising if he is different from the person on whose behalf the advertising is displayed (for more details → § 4 mn. 42–55).[15] The legislator thus addresses in particular constellations in which so-called "**influencers**" display advertising for third parties on the respective accounts of the online platforms or interfaces.

23 According to Art. 46(2)(2)(b), the codes shall also cover the "transmission of information held by providers of online advertising intermediaries to the repositories pursuant to Article 39". The **archive** includes, inter alia, the transmission of information on the **content of the advertisement** (Art. 39(2)(a)), **the person on whose behalf the advertisement is displayed** (Art. 39(2)(b)) or the **period** during which it was displayed (Art. 39(2)(d)) (for more details → § 6 mn. 89–92).

24 Finally, according to Art. 46(2)(2)(c), the codes for online advertising should include "**meaningful information on the monetisation of data**". Specified in Recital 107, the codes should thus contain measures that ensure an appropriate exchange of information on the monetisation of data throughout the value chain. Art. 46(2)(c) is thus intended to introduce a higher level of transparency into the field of data monetisation, which is characterised by a public information deficit, enabling clarification of the amount, procedure and design of monetisation.[16]

---

[13] Exgr. 107 DSA.
[14] Exgr. 107 DSA.
[15] Exgr. 107 DSA.
[16] On "external data monetisation", for example, Leupold/Wiebe/Glossner IT-R/Koehler mn. 5 et seqq.

4. Period of elaboration and date of entry into force

Art. 46(3) sets the time frame for the development and entry into force of the codes of conduct. The aim is to have the codes drawn up by one year after the date of application of the Regulation, i.e. **by Feb. 18th 2025.** The codes will finally be **applied** 18 months after the date of application, i.e. **from Aug. 18th 2025.** 25

VI. Accessibility Codes of Conduct

1. Basic concept

In order to promote full and effective participation in online services on an equal basis and to facilitate access to them for persons with disabilities, Art. 47 requires the Commission to promote and facilitate the development of appropriate codes of conduct on **accessibility**. According to Art. 47(2) sent. 1, this is to ensure the accessibility of the respective services in accordance with Union and national law in order to maximise the usability of the services by persons with disabilities. 26

In addition to the respective providers of online platforms and other relevant services, **user organisations, civil society organisations and public authorities** should also be involved. This broad participation is intended to ensure that all legitimate interests of different stakeholders are taken into account in the development of the codes. Unlike the relevant Recital 105, which only refers to the accessibility of very large online platforms and search engines, Article 47 addresses all providers of online platforms. It is therefore not necessary to exceed the threshold of active monthly users in the Union (cf. Art. 33). 27

The primary legal background of the norm is undoubtedly **Art. 26 CFR**, according to which the integration of persons with disabilities must be guaranteed. Following on from this, the specific codes of conduct as a voluntary option of self-regulation can sensitise the respective actors to issues of inclusion. 28

2. Minimum target

Art. 47(2)(2)(a)–(c) specifies the minimum objectives to which the codes of conduct must refer with regard to accessibility: 29

Standard	Destination	Explanation
(a)	Designing and adapting services to make them accessible to people with disabilities by making them perceptible, operable, understandable and robust	In order to ensure accessibility of services and thus maximum use by persons with disabilities, the aim is to design services in a perceptible, usable, understandable and robust manner, which is reflected in the design and adaptation of services. The design of the services or their adaptation shall therefore be carried out in a perceptible, operable, understandable and robust manner so that the services become accessible to persons with disabilities. The different needs arising from different forms of restrictions must be taken into account in the design and adaptation. For example, simple language and a clear design should be taken into account in the conception. In addition, a method of operation should be considered that can be carried out not only haptically by "click" but also auditorily.
(b)	Explain how services meet applicable accessibility requirements and make this information available to the public in a way that is accessible to people with disabilities	Services shall provide an explanation of how they comply with the applicable accessibility requirements. This explanation shall be made publicly available. Attention shall be paid to a presentation that makes the information accessible to persons with disabilities.[17]
(c)	Provide information, forms and measures under this Regulation in a way that is easy to find, easy to understand and accessible to persons with disabilities	Relevant information, forms and measures of the DSA shall be provided by the services in a way that is easy to find and understand. This shall make them accessible in particular to persons with disabilities.

3. Period of elaboration and period of entry into force

30 In parallel to the codes of conduct for online advertising from Art. 46(3), the codes of conduct relating to accessibility shall also be developed one year after the date of application of the Regulation, i.e. by **Feb. 18th 2025,** and subsequently applied from **Aug. 18th 2025**, i.e. 18 months after the date of application of the Regulation.

[17] The applicable accessibility requirements are mainly derived from Directive (EU) 2019/882 of 17 April 2019 on accessibility requirements for products and services, OJ 2019 L 151, 70.

D. Crisis protocols

I. Basic concept

In order to take into account the central role of very large online platforms and search engines in the dissemination of information, Art. 48 empowers the Commission to require the respective providers to establish voluntary crisis protocols. The aim is to coordinate a **rapid, collective and cross-border response in the event of a crisis.**[18] The voluntary crisis protocols from Art. 48 thus join the existing obligations of the providers of very large online platforms and search engines from the crisis response mechanism of Art. 36. 31

According to Art. 48(2) sent. 1, in order to implement the crisis protocols, the Commission shall encourage and facilitate the participation of the respective providers in their elaboration, testing and application. Even though this may primarily concern providers of very large online platforms and search engines, according to the clear wording of Art. 48(2) sent. 1, **smaller online platforms or search engines** that do not fall under the additional obligations of Chapter III Section 5 may also be included. 32

In addition to the respective providers, Art. 48(3) requires the Commission to involve, where appropriate, **Member State authorities, Union bodies and agencies and civil society organisations or other relevant organisations** in the development of the protocols. In the course of broad participation, parallel to the other instruments of voluntary self-regulation from Chapter III Section 6,[19] a consideration of all legitimate interests of the different circles is to be ensured. 33

II. Crisis situation

In order for the crisis protocols to be activated in accordance with Art. 48, a crisis within the meaning of this Article must occur. Art. 48(4)(c) provides that a clear procedure for determining a crisis must be laid down in the protocols. Since, in addition to the crisis protocols from Art. 48, Art. 36 in particular provides for a crisis response mechanism and Art. 36(2) contains the definition of a "crisis", the question arises to what extent this can be applied to Art. 48. Although Article 36(2), according to which a crisis exists if "**extraordinary circumstances lead to a serious threat to public security or public health in the Union or in significant parts of it**",[20] restricts its definition to "the purposes of this Article", i.e. to Article 36, the definitional approach from Article 48(1) sent. 2 is also based on the protected interests of public security and public health, so that a congruence of the concept of crisis can be assumed. By way of example, Recital 108 cites situations in which online platforms are misused for the rapid dissemination of illegal content or disinformation, or in which the rapid dissemination of reliable information is required. Here, the legislator obviously had the Corona pandemic in mind, in which the rapid dissemination of reliable information was necessary to protect the health of the population. 34

When determining the procedure for activating the protocol, the parties involved must take into account the concept of crisis within the meaning of Art. 48(4)(c). 35

---

[18] Rec. 108 DSA.

[19] Standards under Art. 44, Codes of Conduct under Art. 45–47.

[20] So also Rec. 91 DSA.

III. Elements of a crisis protocol

36 Article 48(4)(a)–(f) sets out the elements of a crisis protocol envisaged by the Commission.

Standard	Element	Explanation
(a)	specific parameters for determining the particular exceptional circumstances to be addressed by the crisis protocol and the objectives pursued thereby	The crisis protocol shall set out the specific parameters for determining the particular circumstances that the crisis protocol is intended to address. MaW shall outline which crises the crisis protocol is intended to address and its objectives.
(b)	the role of each stakeholder and the actions they have to take in preparation and after activation of the crisis protocol.	The roles of each person involved shall be outlined along with the actions that each person is required to take in preparation for and after activation of the protocol.
(c)	a clear procedure to determine when to activate the crisis protocol	In the course of a clearly defined procedure to determine when the Protocol is activated, it must be determined when a crisis exists within the meaning of the Protocol – and according to which this is to be determined (→ mn. 34).
(d)	a clear procedure for determining the period of time in which the measures to be taken after the activation of the crisis protocol are to be implemented and which is strictly limited to what is necessary to cope with the particular exceptional circumstances	In addition, a clear procedure must be established to determine the period of time in which the respective measures are to be carried out. In the course of the increased sensitivity to fundamental rights, this must be strictly limited to what is necessary.
(e)	safeguards to prevent adverse effects on the exercise of fundamental rights enshrined in the Charter, in particular freedom of expression and information and the right to non-discrimination	In the course of the increased sensitivity to fundamental rights, safeguards must be anchored that protect against adverse effects on the exercise of Charter fundamental rights. In particular, freedom of expression and information from Article 11 CFR and the right to non-discrimination from Article 21 CFR must be taken into account. For more details, see → mn. 37 et seq. below.

Standard	Element	Explanation
(f)	A procedure for public reporting of all measures taken, their duration and their results after the crisis situation has ended.	Finally, a procedure for public reporting on measures taken, their duration and their results must be established. Reporting must only take place after the crisis situation has ended.

IV. Protection of fundamental rights

In order to take into account the special **sensitivity to fundamental rights** of the far-reaching measures in the event of a crisis, the European legislator emphasises the **limitation of the crisis protocols to what is absolutely necessary.**[21] Thus, according to Art. 48(4)(d), it must be ensured that special measures are implemented that are "strictly limited to what is necessary for addressing the specific extraordinary circumstances concerned". In addition, according to Art. 48(4)(e), safeguards must be implemented within the framework of the Protocol to avoid negative effects on the fundamental rights enshrined in the Charter, in particular with regard to the freedoms of communication. 37

Recital 108 concretises this important limitation to the effect that the measure implies **no general obligation** of the participating providers **to monitor the transmitted or stored information or to actively search for facts or circumstances** indicating illegal content.[22] In order to ensure the protection of the fundamental rights referred to in Art. 48(4)(e) thus sought, the Commission may, according to Art. 48(5), request the parties to revise the Protocol. 38

V. Aimed measures

Art. 48(2)(2)(a)–(c) lists measures which the Commission intends to be covered by the crisis protocol. Of the three measures listed, the crisis protocols should include one or more. 39

Standard	Measure	Explanation
(a)	highlighting information on the crisis situation provided by Member States' authorities or at Union level or by other relevant reliable bodies, depending on the context of the crisis	In the context of pandemics, for example, platforms could highlight current information from the authorities, such as current case numbers or behavioural recommendations.
(b)	Ensure that the provider of mediation services designates a specific contact point for crisis management	This can be explicitly the electronic contact point mentioned in Art. 11 or, in the case of systemically relevant platforms, the compliance officer mentioned in Art. 41.

[21] Rec. 108 DSA.
[22] For more information on the freedom to monitor communications → § 3 mn. 23 et seqq.

Standard	Measure	Explanation
(c)	adapt the resources dedicated to compliance with the obligations set out in Articles 16, 20, 22, 23 and 35 to the needs arising from the crisis situation.	The adjustment of material and human resources must be realigned with the needs that have arisen as a result of the crisis situation. Explicitly emphasised here are resources for fulfilling the obligation to: – Establishment of a reporting and redress procedure (Art. 16) – Establishment of an internal complaints management system (Art. 20) – Establishment of measures for reporting by trusted whistleblowers (Art. 22) – Establishment of measures and protection against misuse (Art. 23) – Establishment of risk mitigation measures by very large online platforms and search engines (Art. 35).

VI. Consequences of a defective crisis protocol

40 If the Commission is of the opinion that a crisis protocol does not effectively deal with the crisis situation or does not protect the exercise of the fundamental rights referred to in Art. 48(4)(e), it may **request** the parties concerned to **revise the crisis protocol in** accordance with Art. 48(5). This can also be done by taking additional measures. This right to request does not prevent the crisis protocols from being voluntary.

§ 8
Enforcement: Powers of and cooperation with authorities

Literature: *Achleitner*, 'Das Durchsetzungsregime im Digital Markets Act: Private Enforcement unerwünscht?', ZöR 2023/2, 201; *Achleitner*, 'Governance im Digital Services Act: Zur erstarkenden Rolle der Europäischen Kommission und privater Akteure in der Plattformregulierung', in Hoffberger-Pippan/Ladeck/Ivankovics (Eds.), Jahrbuch 23 Digitalisierung und Recht, 2023, 107; *Achleitner*, Algorithmische Ausgestaltung des Publikums in sozialen Medien unter dem Digital Services Act im Lichte der Meinungsfreiheit, ÖZW 2023, 128; *Achleitner*, 'Der Digital Services Act als risikobasierte Regulierung. Zu den Auswirkungen des risikobasierten Ansatzes des DSA auf Desinformation und den Grundrechtsschutz', MR-Int 2022/4, 114; *Buri*, 'A Regulator Caught Between Conflicting Policy Objectives', 31.10.2022, Verfassungsblog, <https://verfassungsblog.de/dsa-conflicts-commission> (last accessed: 26.6.2024); *Cauffman/Goanta*, A New Order: The Digital Services Act and Consumer Protection, EJRR 2021, 758; *Husovec*, 'Injunctions against Intermediaries in the European Union', Cambridge 2017; *Husovec*, Principles of the Digital Services Act, 2024; *Monti/de Streel*, 'Improving EU Institutional design to better supervise digital platforms', Cerre Report, January 2022 <https://cerre.eu/publications/improving-eu-institutional-des ign> (last accessed: 26.6.2026); *Peukert/Husovec/Kretschmer/Mezei/Quintais*, 'European Copyright Society – Comment on Copyright and the Digital Services Act Proposal', IIC 2022, 358; *Polanski*, 'Revisiting country of origin principle: Challenges related to regulation e-commerce in the European Union', Computer Law & Security Review 2018, 562; *Reda/Selinger*, 'Digital Services Act: Europaparlament diskutiert Netzsperren', Verfassungsblog, 18.11.2022 <https://verfassungsblog.de/dsa-netzsperren/> (last accessed: 26.6.2024; *Thiel*, Zusammenarbeit der Datenschutzaufsicht auf europäischer Ebene, ZD 2021, 467.

A. Introduction

1 The enforcement and supervision of the DSA is shared between the authorities of the **Member States,** and the **European Commission (mixed enforcement system)**. They are additionally supported and advised by the European Board for Digital Services (EBDS → § 9 mn. 1 et seqq.).[1] The national authorities play a pivotal role in ensuring compliance with the DSA and collaborating with other regulatory bodies.[2] The enforcement of the DSA is, in principle, in the hands of the national authorities, except in specific instances where the European Commission is the enforcer. It depends on which intermediary services are involved.

2 The **European Commission**, assisted by the **Digital Services Committee**[3] (Art. 88), is the **central** (but not absolutely exclusive) **enforcement authority** for very large online platforms (VLOPs) and very large online search engines (VLOSEs). However, it has **exclusive competence** for both oversight and enforcement of **specific obligations** unique to the providers of VLOPs and VLOSEs, as set out in **Chapter III, Section 5** (→ § 6 mn. 1 et seqq.; → mn. 52 et seqq.). The purpose of this governance framework is to ensure that the DSA requirements specifically designed for VLOPs and VLOSEs are vigorously and effectively managed. For other obligations of VLOPs and VLOSEs providers, the Commission **shares competence** with national authorities (**concurrent competence**; → mn. 7 et seqq.; → mn. 43 et seqq.; → mn. 53 et seqq.).

3 Member States must designate a competent authority to act as the **Digital Services Coordinator (DSC)** (→ mn. 16). In addition to the DSC, other national authorities may be involved in the enforcement of the DSA. This arrangement establishes a **multi-layered enforcement** regime at the national level, operating across various administrative and political levels, such as both the state and federal levels in Germany. This setup poses challenges for effective enforcement at the Member State level due to varying organisational, human, and financial resources.

4 The DSA establishes a complex and multi-layered enforcement mechanism, based on **close collaboration** between all relevant bodies at both the Member State and EU levels. To facilitate this **collaborative approach** to regulation, an **information sharing system** (→ mn. 50) is being established. National authorities also face the challenge of reconciling different regulatory practices, policy objectives, procedural rules and institutional structures across Member States and, where necessary, departing from pre-existing national regulatory frameworks.[4]

5 The DSA, unlike the **DMA**,[5] explicitly allows for **private enforcement** through Art. 54. Users are expressly granted the right to seek compensation for any damage or loss from the intermediary service providers in accordance with national law.[6] Without prejudice to the provisions on the exemption from liability provided for in the DSA (→ § 3 mn. 1 et seqq.) as regards the information transmitted or stored at the request of a recipient of the service, a provider of intermediary services should be liable for the

[1] An EU-wide supervisory authority ('EU-Agency') for digital services was discussed, but the idea did not make it into the draft regulation, cf. European Parliament, A9–0177/2020, 5.10.2020, mn. 8.

[2] See rec. 111 DSA.

[3] This committee is a committee within the meaning of the Regulation (EU) No. 182/2011 (see Art. 88 DSA).

[4] Monti/de Streel, 'Improving EU Institutional design to better supervise digital platforms', Cerre Report, January 2022, p. 52.

[5] Achleitner ZöR 2023/2, 201.

[6] The proposal for the DSA did not yet contain such a provision; see also Peukert/Husovec/Kretschmer/Mezei/Quintais IIC 2022, 358 (374 et seqq.); Husovec, Principles of the Digital Services Act, 2024, 428 et seqq.

damages suffered by recipients of the service that are caused by an infringement of the obligations set out in the DSA.[7] While Art. 54 states that users have the right to seek damages when providers fail to comply with the DSA, the DSA does not address the conditions for liability, leaving them to be determined solely by the respective national laws of the Member States.

B. National enforcement and supervision

I. Competences

Member States (i.e. national authorities) are responsible for **monitoring** and **enforcing** the obligations set out in the DSA, except for those powers conferred on the European Commission in relation to very large online platforms (VLOPs) and very large online search engines (VLOSEs)) (Art. 56). 6

With regard to VLOPs and VLOSEs, the European Commission enjoys exclusive competence to supervise and enforce the additional and specific obligations set out in Chapter III, Section 5 (→ § 6 mn. 1 et seqq.) (Art. 56(2) and Art. 65(2)).[8] Although the DSA **centralises** the supervision of VLOPs and VLOSEs at the European Commission level (→ mn. 54 et seqq.), the supervision of these large 'big tech' intermediary services is not entirely removed from national authorities. For due diligence obligations that are not part of the additional and specific obligations set out in Chapter III, Section 5, the national authorities and the European Commission have **shared competence (concurrent competence**) (Art. 56 → mn. 52 et seqq.).[9] 7

If the **European Commission** has **not yet exercised** its powers in these cases, where competence is shared with national authorities (→ mn. 7), or has not initiated proceedings for the same infringement against providers of VLOPs and VLOSEs, the Member State where the provider is established is responsible. This means that the competent authority of that Member State is entitled to supervise and enforce the DSA, except for the obligations set out in Chapter III, Section 5 (Art. 56(4)). 8

Once the European Commission initiates proceedings against providers of VLOPs and VLOSEs, national authorities must refrain from taking independent action. The initiation of such proceedings by the Commission under Art. 66 effectively suspends the powers of the DSC and any other competent authority under Art. 56(4) to monitor and enforce obligations (Art. 66(2)(3)). In addition, the European Commission has the power to take over ongoing proceedings against providers of VLOPs and VLOSEs that were originally initiated by national authorities. In certain cases, the European Commission may also be called upon to enforce obligations on a subsidiary basis, irrespective of the intermediary service involved (→ mn. 34 et seqq.). 9

Member States are required to designate one or more authorities for the supervision of providers of intermediary services and the enforcement of the DSA's provisions (Art. 49). The DSA allows Member States to use **existing authorities** or, if necessary, to establish additional authorities for the DSA.[10] Given that the DSA intersects with various areas of law, including consumer, criminal, and data protection law, Member States 10

---

[7] See rec. 121 DSA.

[8] On these additional obligations, especially risk management, see Achleitner MR-Int 2022/4, 114 (116 et seqq.); Cauffman/Goanta, A New Order: The Digital Services Act and Consumer Protection, EJRR 2021, 758 (770 et seqq.).

[9] See rec. 125 DSA.

[10] See rec. 109 and 113 DSA.

are free to assign **specific authorities** based on their expertise in individual economic sectors or legal areas. Additionally, due to the multifaceted and cross-sectoral challenges that can result from unlawful actions by providers of intermediary services, **multidisciplinary** supervision will be essential, alongside robust **mechanisms for cooperation** between competent authorities. By **February 17 2024**, each Member State had to designate one of these competent authorities as a **Digital Services Coordinator (DSC)**. The requirements, powers, and responsibilities of Digital Services Coordinators, as articulated in Articles 50, 51, and 56, also extend to all other national competent authorities, as specified in Art. 49(4).

11 The DSA is based on the **country-of-origin principle.**[11] The Member State in which the main establishment of the provider of intermediary services is located has exclusive powers to supervise and enforce the DSA (Art. 56). The **main establishment** of the provider of intermediary services is presumed to be the Member State where the **head office** or **registered office,** within which the principal financial functions and operational control are exercised, is located.[12]

12 Regarding providers of intermediary services that **do not** have an establishment in the EU but that offer services within the EU and thus fall within the scope of the DSA, are required to designate in writing a **legal or natural person** as their **legal representative** in one of the Member States in which they offer their services (Art. 13). The enforcement and supervisory powers over these providers lie with the Member State where this legal representative is based (Art. 56(6)). If a provider of intermediary services does not designate a legal representative as outlined in Art. 13, all Member States (alongside the Commission for providers of VLOPs or VLOSEs) will have the authority to supervise and enforce the DSA (Art. 56(7)). In such circumstances, if a DSC intends to exercise its powers, it should inform all other DSCs and the European Commission. They must also ensure that the rights enshrined in the Charter of Fundamental Rights of the European Union are respected, in particular to avoid the same act being sanctioned more than once under the DSA (**ne bis in idem**). When the European Commission intends to act, it must notify all DSCs. After this notice, other Member States should avoid initiating proceedings for that specific infringement (Art. 56(7)).

13 The country-of-origin principle, which is also enshrined in the **E-Commerce Directive**[13], has been criticised for potentially creating a "**race to the bottom**" effect and encouraging **forum shopping.**[14] Indeed, there is a risk that certain national authorities will not intervene or will intervene insufficiently, leading to significant shortcomings in implementation. Under the **GDPR**[15] (which also upholds the country-of-origin principle), for example, Irish data protection authorities have been accused of being unduly cautious and inadequate in regulating large online platforms based in their territory.[16] Therefore, certain providers of intermediary services may strategically position them-

---

[11] For the country-of-origin principle cf. Polanski Computer Law & Security Review 2018, 562 (563 et seqq.).

[12] See rec. 123 DSA.

[13] Directive 2000/31/EC of the European Parliament and of the Council of 8 June 2000 on certain legal aspects of information society services, in particular electronic commerce, in the Internal Market ('Directive on electronic commerce') OJ 2000 L 178, 1.

[14] The anchoring of the country-of-origin principle in the DSA was criticised (e.g. by France), as it was feared that enforcement would be restricted, see Euractive DSA: Enforcement for very large online platforms moves towards EU commission, 3.11.2021.

[15] Regulation (EU) 2016/679 of the European Parliament and of the Council of 27 April 2016 on the protection of natural persons with regard to the processing of personal data and on the free movement of such data, and repealing Directive 95/46/EC (General Data Protection Regulation), OJ 2016 L 119, 1.

[16] Buri, A Regulator Caught Between Conflicting Policy Objectives, Verfassungsblog, 31.10.2022.

selves in Member States that are perceived to have a more 'lenient' approach to the enforcement of the DSA. Recognising this, the EU legislator, while retaining the essence of the country-of-origin principle, has granted the European Commission with a pivotal supervisory role, especially concerning VLOPs and VLOSEs (→ mn. 52 et seqq.).

14 However, the country-of-origin principle offers providers of intermediary services the crucial advantage of legal certainty. Under this principle, the Member State of their establishment acts as the sole authority, thus providing a **one-stop-shop mechanism**. This saves the providers from navigating through multiple authorities in different Member States, thereby reducing administrative burdens (→ see however mn. 13).

II. Digital Services Coordinators and national competent authorities

1. Introduction

15 Given the **cross-border** nature of intermediary services and the **horizontal scope** of the obligations laid down in the DSA,[17] a competent authority within a Member State had to be designated as a Digital Services Coordinator (DSC) by 17 February 2024 (Art. 49 et seq.).[18] The DSC is responsible for all matters relating to the application and enforcement of the DSA in the Member States and will act as a **single point of contact**[19], thereby reinforcing coherent enforcement and ensuring effective cooperation between the competent authorities across the Member States. The DSC serves as a **coordination hub** for cooperation among various competent authorities within the Member State and acts as the contact point for the European Commission, the European Board for Digital Services (EBDS), DSCs from other Member States, and users of intermediary services. Consequently, the DSA mandates close collaboration between DSCs and other national competent authorities, including the European Commission and the EBDS (Art. 49(2)). This implies, however, that compliance with the requirement for a strong cooperation mechanism will determine the effectiveness and efficiency of the DSA.

16 Where more than one competent authority is responsible for tasks under the DSA in a Member State, it is not intended to establish a **hierarchical** position of the DSC over other competent authorities in the performance of their tasks.[20] Although the DSC should not be considered as the 'first among equals' among national authorities, it should ensure the effective involvement of all relevant competent authorities. The designation of competent authorities and a DSC should take into account the division of powers for the regulation of digital services in the Member States (e.g. **competences at federal and state levels in Germany)**[21].

17 Where several authorities in a Member State are designated as responsible for the enforcement of the DSA, close cooperation between them is essential. This ensures a solid law enforcement in the Member States and equalises possible **knowledge asymmetries**. A clear delineation of the responsibilities of each authority is also crucial (Art. 49(2)(3)). Concerning the cooperation between the competent national authorities and the DSCs, Member States have the **discretion** to implement additional measures ('through appro-

[17] See rec. 110 DSA.

[18] See rec. 110 DSA.

[19] See rec. 110 DSA; rec. 110 refers to a 'single point of contact'.

[20] See rec. 110 DSA.

[21] In Germany, for example, both the federal state and the constituent states – the 'Länder' – have responsibilities in the area of digital services, so it would be problematic in terms of the prohibition on overlapping administrative responsibilities ('Mischverwaltung') to assign both federal and Länder responsibilities to one authority.

priate tools')[22] beyond the specific mechanisms outlined in the DSA. Examples include pooling of resources, the formation of joint task forces, joint investigations, and mutual assistance mechanisms to ensure efficient and resource-efficient enforcement of the DSA at the national level (Art. 49(2) and recital 110).

18 In addition to its coordinating role, the DSC has specific **enforcement tasks** under the DSA that cannot be delegated to other competent authorities. The DSC acts as a **central point of complaint** for the recipients of the service and any body, organisation or association mandated to exercise the rights conferred by the DSA. They have a **right to lodge a complaint** against providers of intermediary services in cases of alleged infringements of the DSA (Art. 53). The competent Member State for lodging complaints is the one where the recipient of the service is located or established. However, individuals or representative organisations should be able to lodge any complaint related to compliance with those obligations with the DSC in the territory where they **received the service**, without prejudice to the DSA's rules on allocation of competences.[23]

If a complaint doesn't fall within the competence of the DSC (either because it falls under the responsibility of another competent authority in its Member State or because it concerns a DSC in another Member State) – the DSC must **forward the complaint**. Throughout this process, both parties retain the **right to be heard** and must be kept properly informed of the status of the complaint (in accordance with national law). The DSA does not set a specific timeframe for the handling of complaints, leaving room for variations based on national procedural norms.

In addition, the DSC's responsibilities go beyond strict enforcement and supervision to include certain **administrative activities**. The DSC is solely responsible for accrediting a body as an **out-of-court dispute settlement** under Art. 21, granting **trusted flagger** status under Art. 22, facilitating **data access** for researchers under Art. 40 and drawing up **annual reports** on their activity under Art. 55. These powers are not transferable to other national authorities (Art. 49(4)).

2. Requirements for Digital Services Coordinators

19 Given the variety of providers of intermediary services and their use of advanced technology, the efficiency and effectiveness of enforcement depends to a large extent on the human and financial resources available to the competent national authorities and the DSC. To this end, the DSA explicitly mandates that all competent authorities be provided with 'all necessary resources' to carry out their tasks, including sufficient technical, financial, and human resources (Art. 50(1)).[24] Moreover, it is imperative that these authorities maintain absolute independence in their activities(Art. 50(2)). National authorities designated under the DSA must operate with full **independence** from both private and public entities. However, this independence does not exempt them from **appropriate accountability measures** aligned with national constitutions, such as financial oversight or reporting obligations to national parliaments. Moreover, the principle of independence does not impede **judicial scrutiny**, nor does it restrict collaboration and information exchange with other national entities like law enforcement or consumer protection authorities.

---

[22] Rec. 110 DSA.

[23] See rec. 118 DSA.

[24] The proposal for the DSA (in Art. 39) still only referred to 'adequate' resources. The requirements for DSCs set out in Art. 50 apply equally to all other competent national authorities in the Member States (Art. 49(4)).

Member States must ensure that their DSCs, along with other relevant national authorities, perform their DSA-related tasks in an '**impartial**, **transparent**, and **timely manner**' (Art. 50(1)). To facilitate this, Member States are empowered, in accordance with national law and EU law, to establish **funding mechanisms**, such as a **supervisory fee** applied directly to providers of intermediary services. However, this fee should only be imposed on providers whose main establishment is in the Member State in question. Moreover, the fee must be strictly limited to covering the necessary and proportionate costs associated with the tasks of the competent authorities, and its imposition must be transparent.[25] The stipulations delineated in Art. 50 pertain equally to the DSC and all other competent authorities (Art. 49(4)).

The activities of the DSC are subject to **transparency** and **accountability requirements**. Accordingly, the DSC must draw up an **annual report on their activities** under the DSA (Art. 55).[26] The DSC is responsible for ensuring that it consolidates all relevant information from other competent authorities within the Member State in this report (Art. 55(3)). The report should not only be made available to the public in a machine-readable format but should also be forwarded to both the European Commission and the EDBS. 20

The report should include:

- the total number of **complaints** received and an overview of their **follow-up**;
- the number and subject matter of **orders to act** against illegal content and orders to provide information issued by national judicial and/or administrative authorities of the DSC's Member State in accordance with Art. 9 and 10 (Art. 55(2)). It should also cover the **effects** given to those orders.

The DSC will obtain these data directly from the newly established information sharing system (see Art. 85, → mn. 50).

3. Powers of Digital Services Coordinators and national authorities

a) Introduction

The DSC and, where appropriate, other competent national authorities have the **investigative** and **enforcement powers** set out in Art. 51.[27] These powers must be **effective, dissuasive,** and **proportionate**, taking into account the **nature**, **gravity**, **recurrence** and **duration** of the (alleged) infringement. The economic, technical, and operational capacity of the provider of intermediary services concerned must also be taken into account (Art. 51(5)). It is for the Member States to lay down the specific conditions, rules, and procedures for the exercise of these powers (Art. 51(6)). In exercising these powers, the authorities must comply with national procedural and substantive rules, while ensuring respect for **fundamental rights.**[28] In particular, rights such as respect for private life, the rights of the defence, the right to be heard, access to the file and the right to an effective judicial remedy for all affected parties shall be safeguarded for all those affected (Art. 51(6)). 21

The provisions on the powers of the DSC set out in Art. 51 apply **equally** to any other competent authority designated by the Member States in accordance with Art. 49(1). 22

---

[25] See rec. 111 DSA.

[26] This obligation exclusively applies to the DSCs and is not applicable to other competent national authorities.

[27] The powers for DSCs set out in Art. 51 apply equally to all other competent national authorities (Art. 49(4)).

[28] See rec. 116 DSA.

Thus, the investigative and enforcement powers referred to in Art. 51 may be conferred either on the DSC itself or on another competent national authority.[29]

b) Powers of investigation

23 The powers of investigation include the right for national authorities to require the **immediate communication** ('without undue delay') of information from providers of intermediary services under their jurisdiction and from other persons acting for purposes relating to their trade, business, craft or profession and having knowledge of information relating to a suspected infringement of the DSA (including organisations performing the audits referred to in Art. 37 and 75) (Art. 51(1)(a)).

In addition, the national authorities are empowered to carry out **inspections** or to request a **judicial authority** to order the inspection of **any premises** that those providers of intermediary services or those persons use for purposes related to their trade, business, craft, or profession. They can also request **other public authorities** to conduct such inspections. During these inspections, they are authorised to examine, seize, take, or obtain **copies of information** relating to a suspected infringement in any form, irrespective of the storage medium (Art. 51(1)(b)). In addition, the competent authorities have the power to **ask** any member of staff or representative of providers of intermediary services or those persons to give explanations in respect of any information relating to a suspected infringement and to **record** the answers with their consent (Art. 51(1)(c)).

c) Enforcement powers

24 Enforcement powers include (Art. 51(2)):

- the power to **accept commitments** offered by intermediary services providers in relation to their compliance with the DSA and to make these commitments **binding** (Art. 51(2)(a));
- the power to **order the cessation of infringements** and, where appropriate, to impose **remedies** proportionate to the infringement and necessary to bring the infringement effectively to an end, or to request a judicial authority in their Member State to do so (Art. 51(2)(b));
- the power to impose **fines**, or to request a judicial authority in their Member State to do so, in accordance with Art. 52 (→ mn. 31) for failure to comply with the DSA, including with any of the investigative orders issued pursuant to Art. 51(1) (→ mn. 23) (Art. 51(2)(c);
- the power to impose a **periodic penalty**, or to request a judicial authority in their Member State to do so, in accordance with Art. 52 (→ mn. 31) to ensure that an infringement is terminated in compliance with an order issued pursuant to Art. 51(1)(b) or for failure to comply with any of the investigative orders issued to Art. 51(1)(a)–(c) (→ mn. 23) (Art. 51(2)(d));
- the power to adopt **interim measures** or to request a judicial authority in their Member State to do so, to avoid the risk of **serious harm** (Art. 51(2)(e)).

25 Art. 51(3) also provides for **repressive enforcement powers** as an **ultima ratio** in case of repeated non-cooperation and non-compliance with the DSA. These (tempora-

[29] According to Art. 49(4), the provisions for DSCs laid down in Art. 50, 51 and 56 also apply to all other competent national authorities. In the following, the term competent authority therefore refers equally to the DSC in relation to these provisions; the number of competent authorities and thus the concrete division of tasks may vary in the Member States. Conversely, this means that all other provisions except for Art. 50, 51 and 56 apply exclusively to DSCs and these cannot be transferred to other national authorities.

ry) **measures** may only be taken after all other powers under Art. 51 to bring about the cessation of an infringement have been **exhausted** and the infringement has **not been remedied** or is **continuing** and causing **serious harm**, which cannot be avoided through the exercise of other powers available under Union or national law. The competent national authority may apply these measures in the case of serious and persistent infringements only to providers of intermediary services falling within the competence of the Member State of that authority. The measures are based on a step-by-step approach. The **first measure** is to require the **management body** of the provider to take all **necessary measures.** This initial measure involves requiring the provider to examine the situation without 'undue delay', adopt and submit an **action plan** outlining the necessary measures to terminate the infringement, ensure that those measures are taken, and **report** on the actions implemented (Art. 51(3)(a)).

As a **secondary measure**, a **court order** may be issued **restricting recipients' access** (temporary) either to the service concerned by the infringement or, only where that is **not technically feasible**, to the **online interface**[30] of the provider of intermediary services on which the infringement takes place (Art. 51(3)) (so called **website blocking; internet shutdowns**) (→ for details mn. 26 et seqq.).

Given the serious consequences of temporarily restricting recipients' access to the service or to the online interface of the provider of the intermediary services, the DSA requires **preliminary** measures to act as an early warning system for the provider of the intermediary services. First, the competent authority must require the management body of the provider to make an **immediate assessment** of the situation. It is also required to request an **action plan** to remedy the infringement, followed by a **report** detailing the measures taken to remedy the infringement of the DSA (Art. 51(3)(a)). 26

If the initial measures prove insufficient, i.e., if the provisions of Art. 51(3)(a) are not adequately met, further action might be considered. If the competent authority considers that the infringement is continuing and has not been remedied, it may **temporarily** restrict recipients' access to the service affected by the infringement. Alternatively, if that's not technically feasible, **access to the online interface** of the intermediary service provider where the infringement occurs can be restricted. This is subject to two conditions: 27

- the infringement causes **serious harm** and,
- the infringement entails a **criminal offence** involving a threat to the **life or safety of persons.**

If these criteria are met, the competent authority may request that the competent **judicial authority** of its Member State to order the **temporary restriction** of access (Art. 51(3)(b)).[31] Thus, such a temporary restriction of access can only be imposed by a **court decision**. The Recitals list possible scenarios for these **last resort** measures, including websites containing or disseminating **child pornography**, actions detrimental to the **collective interests of consumers** and the misuse of intermediary services by third parties to infringe **intellectual property** rights.[32]

Such an order to restrict access should be addressed in principle at a provider of intermediary services, such as the relevant hosting service provider, internet service

---

[30] For the definition of the term 'online interface' see Art. 3(m) DSA.

[31] For a critical analysis see Reda/Selinger, Digital Services Act: European Parliament discusses net blocking, Verfassungsblog, 18.11.2022.

[32] See rec. 119 DSA; for a critical analysis in relation to copyright content see Peukert/Husovec/Kretschmer/Mezei/Quintais, European Copyright Society – Comment on Copyright and the Digital Services Act Proposal IIC 2022, p. 358 (374).

provider or domain registry or registrar, which is in a reasonable position to achieve that objective without unduly restricting access to lawful information.[33] The Union legislator leaves it to the Member States to lay down specific rules and procedures.

Any measures ordered must be **proportionate** to the nature, gravity, recurrence and duration of the infringement, without unduly restricting access to lawful information by recipients of the service concerned (Art. 51(3)(b)). Especially when such measures can affect the rights and interests of **third parties**, as might particularly be the case when access to online interfaces is restricted, it is necessary to implement special protective measures or **additional safeguards** alongside them (for details see → mn. 28).

28 Prior to submitting a request to the competent judicial authority for access restrictions, the competent national authority must invite all **interested parties** to provide **written observations**, detailing the measures it plans to request, and identifying the intended addressee or addressees thereof. A period of at least **two weeks** should be granted for this purpose (Art. 51(3)(b)).

Providers of intermediary services, the intended addressees and any other relevant third parties demonstrating a **legitimate interest**, also have the **right to participate** in the **proceedings** before the **judicial authority**. However, in instances where a national authority acts at the **request of the European Commission** pursuant to Art. 82, that national authority is **not obliged** to provide interested parties the opportunity to be heard. In such a cases, the European Commission must itself offer the opportunity to provide observations in advance (Art. 82(1) → mn. 96).

29 In accordance with Art. 51(3) the **blocking period** must initially be set at **four weeks**. However, the competent judicial authority may allow the competent authorities, which are still responsible for the supervision in this case, to **extend that period** for further periods of the same duration, up to a maximum number as determined by the judicial authority (Art. 51(3)(b)).

The national competent authority shall extend the period only under the following conditions (Art. 51(3)(b)):

- The provider of intermediary services has failed to take necessary measures to terminate the infringement.
- The temporary restriction does not unduly restrict access to lawful information for the recipients of the service, considering:
  - The number of recipients and
  - The existence of any adequate and readily accessible alternatives.

30 Restrictions on access to websites or online interfaces constitute a significant measure that must comply with fundamental rights, in particular the freedom of expression and information, as well as the freedom to conduct a business.[34] The ECJ clarified in the UPC Telekabel case that, in principle, court-ordered **website blocking** can be permissible, as long as a **fair balance** is achieved between the conflicting **fundamental rights** of the parties involved.[35] Additionally, any blocking measure must be '**strictly targeted**'[36] with respect to the freedom of information of users. In this sense the measures 'must serve to bring an end to a third party's infringement of copyright or of a related right but without thereby affecting internet users who are using the provider's services in order to

---

[33] See rec. 120 DSA.

[34] On this, see in particular with regard to copyright infringements and online gambling Husovec, p. 133 et seqq.

[35] ECJ 27.3.2014 – case C-314/12, ECLI:EU:C:2014:192 para. 46 et seq.; see also ECJ 29.1.2008 case – C275/06, ECLI:EU:C:2008:54 para. 68.

[36] ECJ 27.3.2014 – case C-314/12, ECLI:EU:C:2014:192 para. 56.

lawfully access information'[37]. This ensures that access to permissible content is not denied.[38] The ECtHR considers the blocking of an entire website to be an **'extreme measure'**, comparing it to the banning of a newspaper or television channel.[39] Both the ECJ and the ECtHR insist on procedural safeguards to ensure that affected parties have access to effective judicial remedies.[40] Consequently, Art. 51(3) (as well as Art. 82(1)(2)) lays down strict criteria for such blockings. While these measures are necessary, there is always a risk of abuse and they need to be carefully monitored by national authorities.[41]

4. Penalties

It is up to the Member States to decide on the sanctions to be applied in accordance with national law. Such sanctions must be **effective**, **proportionate**, and **dissuasive**, taking into account the nature, gravity, recurrence and duration of the infringement, in view of the public interest pursued, the scope and kind of activities carried out, as well as the **economic capacity** of the infringer.[42] In determining the penalties, consideration should be given to whether the provider of intermediary services concerned has systematically or recurrently failed to comply with its obligations. Additionally, factors such as the number of affected users and whether the provider is active in several Member States should be taken into account (Art. 52).[43] 31

The fines may not exceed **6 %** of the annual **worldwide turnover** of the provider of intermediary services concerned in the preceding financial year (Art. 52(3)). 32

A fine of up to **1 %** of the **annual income** or **worldwide turnover** of the provider of intermediary services or person concerned in the preceding financial year might be imposed for the supply of incorrect, incomplete or misleading information, failure to reply to or rectify incorrect, incomplete or misleading information and failure to submit to an inspection (Art. 52(3)). 33

The maximum amount of a **periodic penalty payment** shall be **5 %** of the average daily worldwide turnover or income of the provider of intermediary services concerned in the preceding financial year per day, calculated from the date specified in the decision concerned (Art. 52(4)). 34

C. Coordinated investigation and consistency mechanisms

I. Mutual assistance

The complex and **multi-layered enforcement system** of the DSA relies heavily on a **cooperation mechanism** among the concerned DSCs in the Member States, the European Commission, and the European Board for Digital Services. To achieve this, the DSA provides detailed and comprehensive provisions on mutual assistance and empha- 35

[37] ECJ 27.3.2014 – case C-314/12, ECLI:EU:C:2014:192 para. 56.

[38] ECJ 27.3.2014 – case C-314/12, ECLI:EU:C:2014:192 para. 56.

[39] ECtHR 23.6.2020 – App. No. 10795/14, para 38- Vladimir Kharitonov v Russia; ECtHR 23.6.2020 – App. no. 12468/15, 23489/15 and 19074/16, para. 37 – OOO Flavus and Others v Russia.

[40] See Reda/Selinger, Digital Services Act: European Parliament discusses netblocking, Verfassungsblog, 18.11.2022.

[41] See Reda/Selinger, Digital Services Act: European Parliament discusses netblocking, Verfassungsblog, 18.11.2022.

[42] See rec. 117 DSA.

[43] See rec. 117 DSA.

sises **a high level of cooperation** in this context (Art. 57)[44]. Mutual assistance primarily involves the **exchange of information** between the competent authorities in the Member States and the European Commission. It also mandates the DSC of establishment to inform all DSCs of destination, the European Commission, and the European Board for Digital Services about the opening of an investigation and the intention to take a final decision, including its assessment, in respect of a specific provider of intermediary services (Art. 57(1)).

36 Mutual assistance shall also include **mutual support** between the DSC of destination and the DSC of establishment for the purpose of an **investigation** (Art. 57(2)). The DSC of establishment can therefore request other DSCs to provide specific information regarding a specific provider of intermediary services or to exercise their investigative powers referred to a provider or to utilise their investigative powers (as per Art. 51(1)) with regard to specific information located in their Member State. In this context, Member States must lay down **national procedural rules** to ensure that the addressee of such investigative measures not only comply but are also **liable** for any non-compliance.[45]

37 The **request for mutual assistance** under Art. 57(1) mandates every DSC that receives such a request to take appropriate action (Art. 57(3)). The DSC concerned **must comply** with such request and inform the DSC of establishment about the action taken, without **undue delay** and no later than two months after its receipt, unless (Art. 53(3)(a)–(c)):

- the scope or the subject matter of the request is **not sufficiently specified**, justified, or proportionate in view of the investigative purposes; or
- neither the requested DSC nor other competent authority or other public authority of that Member State is **in possession of the requested information** nor can have access to it; or
- the request cannot be complied with **without infringing** Union or national law.

II. Cross-border cooperation among Digital Services Coordinators

38 The DSA provides for **cross-border cooperation** between the DSCs of destination and the DSC of establishment of the provider (Art. 58). If a **DSC of destination** has reasons to suspect that a provider of intermediary services has infringed provisions of the DSA negatively affecting users of the service in the Member State of that DSC, it may **request** the **DSC of establishment** to assess the matter and to initiate necessary investigatory and enforcement measures. However, this does not apply if the European Commission has **already initiated** an investigation for the same alleged infringement (Art. 58(1)). While the DSC of destination has the option to initiate cross-border cooperation in this instance, it is under **no obligation to do so** ('it may request') (Art. 58(1)).

39 Such requests for action should be based on **well-substantiated evidence** ('duly reasoned') showing the existence of an alleged infringement with negative impact on collective interests of the recipients of the service in its Member State or having a negative societal impact (Art. 58(3)).[46]

---

[44] See rec. 127 DSA.
[45] See rec. 127 DSA.
[46] See rec. 128 DSA.

Specifically, the request must be **duly reasoned** and should, at the very least, indicate (Art. 58(3)(a)–(b)):

- the **point of contact** of the provider of the intermediary services concerned as provided for in Art. 11;
- a **description of the relevant facts**, the provisions of the DSA concerned and the reasons why the DSC that sent the request, or the Board, suspects that the provider infringed this Regulation, including the description of the negative effects of the alleged infringement;
- **any other information** that the DSC that sent the request, or the Board, considers relevant, including, where appropriate, information gathered on its own initiative or suggestions for specific investigatory or enforcement measures to be taken, including interim measures.

At the **request** of at least **three DSCs of destination**, that have reason to suspect that a specific provider of intermediary services infringed the provisions of the DSA in a manner **negatively affecting recipients** of the service in their Member States, the **European Board for Digital Services** (EBDS) may request the **DSC of establishment** to investigate an alleged infringement, and take the necessary enforcement measures (Art. 58(2)). However, this only applies if the European Commission has not already taken action in the matter. 40

The EU legislator has made it clear that such a request for the involvement of the **DSC of establishment** is **only admissible** where the provider both infringes the DSA and affects users in the Member State concerned. This alternative route via the EBDS may increase the **(political) pressure** on the DSC concerned, highlighting the urgency of the matter and the potential delays in response. 41

While the DSC of destination is **not obligated to initiate** such a request (→ mn. 38), the DSC of establishment shall '**take utmost account**' of the request (Art. 58(1) and (2)). They are then required to, without **undue delay** and not later than **two months** following receipt of the request, communicate with both the DSC that sent the request and the EBDS, regarding their assessment of the alleged infringement and any enforcement measures taken or envisaged (Art. 58(5)). If **no notification** is received within this timeframe, the EBDS may **refer the matter** to the **European Commission**. The same applies if the EBDS disagrees with the assessment or the action taken or planned (Art. 59(1)). If the DSC of establishment considers that it does not have sufficient **information** to act on the request, it may either request further information (in accordance with Art. 57) or, alternatively, initiate a joint investigation in accordance with Art. 60(1) involving at least the requesting DSC (Art. 58(4)). 42

III. Referral to the European Commission

In certain cases, the DSA provides for referral to the European Commission ("**fall-back-option**"; Art. 59), i.e. matters initially dealt with by the national authorities are entrusted to the Commission. The referral to the Commission may be initiated in matters for which the national authorities have sole competence (pursuant to Art. 56) or where the national authorities exercise their competence because the Commission has not yet opened proceedings in this matter (pursuant to Art. 56(4)). The referral is a **discretionary** decision of the EBDS ("can"). This provision is intended to mitigate enforcement shortcomings due to delays on the part of national authorities, in this case the DSCs. 43

In particular, this **subsidiary oversight and enforcement mechanism** vested in the European Commission is authorised under the following circumstances (Art. 59(1)):

- **Failure to communicate in cross-border cooperation among DSCs**: In the context of cross-border cooperation between DSCs, if the notification required under Art. 58 is not received from the DSC of establishment within the timeframe set out in Art. 58(5).
- **Disagreement of the EBDS in cross-border cooperation**: In cases where the EBDS disagrees with the assessment or the measures taken or envisaged by the DSC of establishment in the context of a cross-border cooperation under Art. 58(5).
- **Deficiencies in the joint investigations of the DSC of establishment**: The EBDS may refer the matter to the Commission in case of identified deficiencies in the joint investigation process pursuant to Art. 60(3) involving the DSC of establishment (→ mn. 46 et seqq.)
  Specifically, the following **three scenarios** can trigger such a referral to the European Commission in the context of joint investigations (Art. 59(1) and Art. 60(3)(a)–(c)):
  - the DSC of establishment failed to communicate its preliminary position within the deadline set out in Art. 60(2);
  - the EBDS substantially disagrees with the preliminary position communicated by the DSC of establishment, or
  - the DSC of establishment failed to initiate the joint investigation promptly following the recommendation by the EBDS pursuant to Art. 60(1)(b).

44 Once the matter has been referred to the European Commission, and after its review, if the European Commission considers that the assessment or the investigatory or enforcement measures taken or envisaged under Art. 58(5) in the context of cross-border cooperation are **insufficient** ('to ensure effective enforcement') or **not in line with the DSA**, it will communicate its views to the DSC of establishment and the EBDS. Furthermore, the European Commission will request that the DSC of establishment re-evaluate the matter and take necessary measures (Art. 59(3)). The European Commission shall assess the matter within **two months** following the referral of the matter.

The DSC of establishment must then take the **necessary investigatory or enforcement measures** to ensure compliance with the DSA, taking '**utmost account**' to the views of the European Commission and the European Commission's request for review. The Commission shall set a deadline for the DSC to take the necessary measures.[47]

To ensure close cooperation, the DSC must **inform** the European Commission, the requesting DSC (→ mn. 38 et seqq.) or the EBDS about the measures taken within **two months** from that request for review (Art. 59(2) and (3)).

45 This '**fall-back option**' for the European Commission is particularly designed to mitigate the disadvantages of the **country-of-origin principle** enshrined in the DSA (→ mn. 13 et seq.). In the event of inadequate enforcement action by the DSC of the establishment failing to comply with the requirements of the DSA, it ensures the possibility of 'higher instance' oversight by the European Commission.[48]

---

[47] See rec. 129 DSA.

[48] See BEUC, The Digital Services Act, Position Paper, 2021, p. 32; see also Art. 11 of the Regulation (EC) No 1/2003.

IV. Joint investigations

In order to facilitate cross-border supervision and investigations of obligations laid down in the DSA in relation to providers of intermediary services operating in more than one Member State, a DSC of establishment may launch and lead joint investigations with the participation of one or more DSC concerned (Art. 60). This is carried out through the **information sharing system** (→ mn. 50).[49] 46

Furthermore, **other DSCs** that **prove a legitimate interest** in participating in a joint investigation, may equally request to do so (Art. 60(2)).

The recitals also indicate that other competent authorities may be involved where appropriate,[50] whereas this aspect is not as explicit in the text of the DSA in Art. 60. Art. 49(4), which is relevant in this context, extends the provisions applicable to the DSC under Articles 50, 51 and 56 to any other competent authority designated by Member States under Art. 49, but does not mention the Art. 60 at issue here (→ mn. 10). On that basis, it can be assumed that when Art. 60 mentions DSC, it **primarily** refers to the DSCs. The recitals do, nonetheless, recognise the possibility for other authorities to be involved where appropriate. However, additional DSCs may be involved unless the DSC of the establishment considers that an excessive number of authorities involved could jeopardise the effectiveness of the investigation, taking into account the characteristics of the alleged infringement and the lack of direct impact on the recipients of services in those Member States.[51]

The DSC of establishment may launch and lead joint investigations (Art. 60(1)(a)–(b)): 47

- at its **own initiative**, to investigate an alleged infringement of the DSA by a given provider of intermediary services in several Member States, or
- **upon recommendation of the EBDS**, acting on the request of at **least three DSCs** alleging, based on a reasonable suspicion, an infringement by a given provider of intermediary services affecting recipients of the service in their Member States.

The joint investigation is to be completed within a period of **three months**, unless the parties agree otherwise (Art. 60(2)) and will be led by the DSC of establishment. The joint investigation concludes with a **preliminary position** (with enforcement measures where applicable) of the DSC of establishment (**final report**)[52] which is then forwarded to the DSCs, the European Commission and the EBDS no later than one month after the end of the period for concluding the joint investigation (Art. 60(2)). The preliminary position shall take into account the views of all other DSCs participating in the joint investigations. Joint investigative activities may include various measures, such as coordinated data gathering exercises, pooling of resources, task forces, coordinated requests for information, or common inspections of premises.[53] 48

In order to ensure effective cooperation, the EBDS may in certain cases refer the matter to the European Commission pursuant to Art. 59 (Art. 6(3)) → mn. 43 et seqq.). Specifically, such a referral can be made in the following cases (Art. 60(3)(a)–(c)): 49

[49] See rec. 130 DSA.
[50] See rec. 130 DSA.
[51] See rec. 130 DSA.
[52] See rec. 130 DSA.
[53] See rec. 130 DSA.

- The DSC of establishment **failed to communicate** its preliminary position within the deadline set out in Art. 60(2).
- The EBDS substantially **disagrees** with the preliminary position communicated by the DSC of establishment.
- The DSC of establishment **failed to initiate** the joint investigation promptly following the recommendation by the EBDS pursuant to Art. 60(1)(b).

The participating DSCs shall cooperate in '**good faith**', taking into account – where applicable, the indications of the DSC of establishment and the EBDS's recommendation. The DSA does not, therefore, mandate that the DSC is obligated to implement the recommendations of the DSC of establishment or the EBDS.

D. Information sharing system

50 To allow a continuous and secure real-time exchange of information between the **DSCs, the EBDS and the European Commission**, Art. 85 mandates the establishment of a 'reliable and secure' information sharing system. All subsequent **communication** between DSCs, the European Commission and the EBDS is to take place via this system. It is expected that **other competent authorities** will be able to access this system if it proves essential for the fulfilment of their tasks (Art. 85(1)). The objective of this system is to facilitate communication between the relevant authorities in relation to the DSA.

51 The details and modalities for the functioning of the information sharing system and its interoperability with other relevant systems is laid down by the Commission in an **implementing act**, which was adopted in accordance with the **advisory procedure** referred to in Art. 88 (Art. 85(3)).[54]

E. Enforcement of obligations of providers of VLOPs and VLOSEs

I. Introduction

52 The European Commission plays a pivotal role in the supervision of very large online platforms (VLOPs) and very large online search engines (VLOSEs). They are subject to **enhanced supervision** due to their size and the potential impact they have on the digital landscape.[55] The European Commission's competence in this context is twofold: First, it has **exclusive competence** regarding specific and additional obligations to manage **systemic risks** imposed only on providers of VLOPs and VLOSEs under Chapter III, Section 5 (**centralised supervision**).[56] Second, it possesses shared competence (alongside DSCs or national authorities) concerning due diligence obligations that are not specifically only imposed on providers of VLOPs and VLOSEs, i.e. all other obligations of the DSA addressed to all providers of intermediary services (concurrent/shared competence).

53 The DSC and, where permitted by the DSA (see Art. 49(4) → mn. 10), other national authorities **share supervisory** responsibility over VLOPs and VLOSEs with the Euro-

[54] Commission Implementing Regulation (EU) 2024/607 of 15 February 2024 on the practical and operational arrangements for the functioning of the information sharing system pursuant to Regulation (EU) 2022/2065 of the European Parliament and of the Council (Digital Services Act), OJ L, 2024/607, 16.2.2024.

[55] See rec. 137 DSA.

[56] See rec. 125 DSA.

pean Commission with regard to compliance with obligations that are **not specifically only for VLOPs and VLOSEs** as outlined in Chapter III, Section 5 (**shared/concurrent competence** → mn. 6 et seqq.). This governance framework acknowledges the European Commission's capacity in addressing **systemic and cross-border infringements** by large online platforms. Furthermore, it provides Member States with the opportunity to apply their expertise on VLOPs and VLOSEs infringements that aren't systemic or cross-border in nature. It is for the European Commission to decide whether such a shared competence in regard of VLOPs and VLOSEs is appropriate. The European Commission retains the discretion to determine whether the supervision of VLOPs and VLOSEs (apart from the specific obligations under Chapter III, Section 5) is to be undertaken by the DSCs or by itself.[57] With regard to the European Commission's powers to supervise VLOPs and VLOS, the DSA generally mentions 'powers other than those laid down in Section 5 of Chapter III' (Art. 56(3)) and 'provisions of this Regulation' (Art. 66(1)), without making any specific limitations or exceptions to the supervision competence of the Commission in this context.[58] Recital 125 highlights that the European Commission may in many cases be better placed to deal with **systemic infringements** committed by providers of VLOPs and VLOSEs, whereas DSCs are more appropriate to deal with "**individual infringements** committed by these providers that do not raise systemic or cross-border issues". Recital 139 states and explicitly clarifies: 'In order to effectively perform its tasks, the Commission should maintain a **margin of discretion** as to the decision to initiate proceedings against providers of very large online platforms or of very large online search engines.'[59] According to these specifications, national authorities are to manage individual infringements committed by providers of VLOPs and VLOSEs that don't entail systemic or cross-border infringements, as indicated in recital 125 (see also Art. 65(2)). However, there is no explicit obligation to do so in the provisions of the DSA and the European Commission has a **margin of discretion** in this respect.

In order to avoid enforcement shortcomings and in the interests of efficiency, the **54**
European Commission has a prerogative of enforcement over the competent national authorities in those areas where the Commission and the authorities have shared competence: Once the European Commission has initiated proceedings against a provider of VLOPs or VLOSEs for the same infringement, the Member State (i.e. the DSC of establishment concerned and, where applicable, all competent national authorities) should **no longer be allowed to do so and be precluded from exercising their investigative and enforcement powers** in respect to the concerned provider of VLOPs and VLOSEs (Art. 56(4) and Art. 66(2)(3)).[60] This privilege of the European Commission to **take over proceedings** is designed to avoid duplication, inconsistencies, and risks associated with the **prohibition of double jeopardy (ne bis in idem)**.[61] In certain cases outlined in Art. 59, the EBDS can refer a particular matter to the European Commission (→ mn. 43 et seqq.).

The European Commission has supervisory powers similar to those under existing **55**
anti-trust rules, encompassing investigatory capabilities, access to data and the authori-

[57] See rec. 125 and 139 DSA.

[58] See rec. 139 DSA.

[59] Rec. 139 DSA.

[60] See also rec. 125 and 139 DSA. Art. 56(4): 'Where the Commission has not initiated proceedings for the same infringement, the Member State in which the main establishment of the provider of very large online platform or of very large online search engine is located shall have powers to supervise and enforce the obligations under this Regulation, other than those laid down in Section 5 of Chapter III, with respect to those providers.'

[61] See rec. 139 DSA; see Buri, A Regulator Caught Between Conflicting Policy Objectives, Verfassungsblog, 31.10.2022.

ty to impose fines. These powers are, in essence, analogous to those of the DSC or the competent national authorities (→ mn. 60 et seqq.). In order to finance the additional costs for the supervision of these large online platforms, the European Commission charges them an **annual supervisory fee** (Art. 43). The European Commission has adopted a **delegated Regulation** with the detailed **methodologies and procedures** regarding the supervisory fees, which specifies the criteria for the calculation of the supervisory fees. In particular it lays down the detailed methodology and procedure for the determination of the estimated costs and for the calculation of the individual fees.[62]

56 The European Commission has the **exclusive power** for supervision and public enforcement of the additional obligations to manage systemic risks imposed on providers of VLOPs and VLOSEs under Chapter III, Section 5 (→ § 6, mn. 1 et seqq.) (Art. 56(2)). In this context, the European Commission acts as the **sole and central enforcement and supervisory authority** and the **enhanced supervision** laid down in Art. 75 applies (→ mn. 82). Theses exclusive powers are without prejudice to certain administrative tasks to DSCs (or other national authorities), such as the vetting of researchers (Art. 40 → mn. 18).

57 By centralising the enforcement of the specific and additional obligations for VLOPs and VLOSEs providers with the European Commission, and granting the European Commission the right to take over any proceedings against VLOPs and VLOSEs providers under shared competences (→ mn. 53 et seqq.), the DSA provides for different enforcement provisions than the GDPR. The evaluation of the GDPR has shown that different legal traditions in law enforcement and different procedural rules in the Member States have led to the protracted enforcement of the GDPR (→ mn. 14).[63] However, the **centralisation of enforcement powers** at the level of the European Commission raises concerns about a potential **concentration of power** at EU level.[64] The European Commission must maintain a balance between its strong (political) role in the legislative process and its capacity as an independent supervisory and enforcement body for VLOPs and VLOSEs, together with its mandates under the DMA and competition law.[65] To what extent will the European Commission foster **synergies** between its mandates in relation to the DMA and the DSA? For example, how might information from a DSA-based investigation be used in **DMA proceedings**? The European Commission, in its emerging role as regulator of online platforms, wields extensive new powers, underlining the need for robust and clearly defined **control mechanisms** over its functions. The increasing influence of the European Commission, especially in the exercise of its executive powers, warrants critical scrutiny, particularly in the light of its **democratic legitimacy**. The European Commission now has the responsibility to demonstrate its independence, accountability, and transparency in its actions and to strengthen its position as an effective supervisory body.

---

[62] Commission Delegated Regulation (EU) 2023/1127 of 2 March 2023 supplementing Regulation (EU) 2022/2065 of the European Parliament and of the Council with the detailed methodologies and procedures regarding the supervisory fees charged by the Commission on providers of very large online platforms and very large online search engines, OJ L 2023 149, 16.

[63] See Thiel ZD 2021, 467 (468 et seqq.); Monti/de Streel, Improving EU Institutional design to better supervise digital platforms, Cerre Report, January 2022, p. 34 et seq.

[64] Achleitner, Governance im Digital Services Act: Zur erstarkenden Rolle der Europäischen Kommission und privater Akteure in der Plattformregulierung, in Hoffberger-Pippan/Ladeck/Ivankovics (Ed.), Jahrbuch 23 Digitalisierung und Recht, 2023, 107 (109 et seqq.); Buri, A Regulator Caught Between Conflicting Policy Objectives, Verfassungsblog, 31.10.2022; Monti/de Streel, Improving EU Institutional design to better supervise digital platforms, Cerre Report, January 2022, p. 55 et seqq.

[65] Monti/de Streel, Improving EU Institutional design to better supervise digital platforms, Cerre Report, January 2022, p. 55 et seq.

The European Commission is assisted in the enforcement of the DSA by the **European Board for Digital Services**, which enables it to benefit from the expertise of Member States. The requirement for the European Commission to develop expertise is explicitly mentioned in Art. 64, which mandates the European Commission to enhance its capacities and capabilities in cooperation with the DSCs and the EBDS and, if necessary, by providing personnel from the Member States. 58

The European Commission has established the **European Centre for Algorithmic Transparency (ECAT)** in Seville, Spain. This centre, officially inaugurated in April 2023, serves as a **hub of multidisciplinary expertise**. It combines the insights of data scientists, **AI specialists**, lawyers, and social scientists to scrutinise algorithms and pinpoint systemic risks. Algorithmic systems, which are central to shaping the visibility of online content, have sparked social and ethical debates. In response to these concerns, the DSA emphasises the need for **algorithmic accountability** and regular transparency assessments.[66] The aim of ECTAT is to aid the European Commission in ensuring that the providers of VLOPs and VLOSEs adhere to the obligations of the DSA. The centre not only delves deep into the workings of algorithms but also fosters collaborations with diverse stakeholders, industry, academia, and civil society, aiming to enhance algorithmic understanding and propose transparent methodologies. The centre's experts are tasked with analysing transparency paradigms, assessing systemic risks and promoting best practices in the field of **digital transparency**. Operating under the umbrella of the European Commission, ECAT's activities are steered by the **Joint Research Centre (JRC)** – the Commission's in-house scientific department – in close coordination with the Directorate-General for Communications Networks, Content and Technology (**DG CONNECT**).[67] 59

II. Initiation of proceedings by the European Commission and cooperation in investigation

1. Introduction

The responsibility for supervising the rules of the DSA primarily lies with the European Commission and the DSCs, or other competent national authorities, which share competence in most areas. However, the specific and additional obligations in Chapter III, Section 5, which relate exclusively to providers of VLOPs and VLOSEs, are supervised and enforced centrally and exclusively by the European Commission (Art. 56(3); Art. 66 → mn. 52 et seqq.). In general, the European Commission exercises its supervisory role by **initiating proceedings** under Art. 66 based on concrete **suspicions** against a particular provider. Nevertheless, the European Commission is entitled to exercise investigatory powers even before initiating proceedings under Art. 66(1). The initiation of proceedings by the European Commission pursuant to Art. 66(1) **relieves** the DSC, or any other competent authority of its supervisory and enforcement powers under the DSA pursuant to Art. 66(2) (Art. 56(4) → mn. 54). 60

Once the European Commission has decided to initiate proceedings under Art. 66, it must **notify** all DSCs and the EBDS (via the **information sharing system** → mn. 50) as well as the provider of the VLOPs or the VLOSEs concerned. Furthermore, in addition to the **mandatory notification** by the European Commission, the DSCs are obliged to

[66] Achleitner, Algorithmische Ausgestaltung des Publikums in sozialen Medien unter dem Digital Services Act im Lichte der Meinungsfreiheit, ÖZW 2023, 128.

[67] See <https://algorithmic-transparency.ec.europa.eu/index_en> (last accessed: 26.6.2024).

provide all relevant information on the alleged infringement without undue delay (Art. 66(2)). If, during the course of its proceedings, the European Commission identifies an infringement of the provisions of the DSA, it is empowered to issue a non-compliance decision (Art. 73, → mn. 76) and to impose fines (Art. 74, → mn. 84), in accordance with Art. 66(1).

61 In addition, the DSCs have the right to ask the European Commission to intervene in matters relating to VLOPs and VLOSEs. If a DSC considers that a provider of a VLOPs or VLOSEs has either infringed the specific and additional provisions of the DSA for VLOPs and VLOSEs (Chapter III, Section 5) or has systemically infringed any of the provisions of the DSA in a manner that **seriously affects** recipients of the services in its Member State, the DSC may request the European Commission to investigate the situation through the information sharing system (→ mn. 50). However, the DSA doesn't require the DSC to take any action. Any complaint to the European Commission must be properly reasoned (Art. 65(3)).

62 The European Commission and the DSC, in cooperation with other competent national authorities, have **shared** supervisory and enforcement powers with regard to due diligence obligations other than those specifically and additionally imposed on VLOP and VLOS providers by Chapter III, Section 5. This competence for VLOPs and VLOSEs will remain unless the European Commission decides to take over the procedure under Art. 66(2) (**shared competences** → mn. 7 et seqq. and mn. 53 et seqq.) The initiation of proceedings by the European Commission against a particular provider under the provisions of the DSA **relieves** the DSC and any other national authority concerned of its enforcement powers (→ mn. 8 and mn. 54 et seqq.).

63 The European Commission is entrusted with a number of powers that enable it to fulfil its designated responsibilities:

- Power to request for information (Art. 67);
- Power to take interviews and statements (Art. 68);
- Power to conduct inspections (Art. 69);
- Power to order interim measures (Art. 70);
- Power to declare commitments binding (Art. 71);
- Power to monitor the effective implementation and compliance (Art. 72).

These powers are analogous to those of national competent authorities (→ mn. 21 et seqq.) and reflect the European Commission's established powers under **antitrust** rules.

2. Requests for information and power to take interviews and statements

64 The European Commission can, either upon a **simple request** or by a **formal decision**, issue a request for information pursuant to Art. 67 during its proceedings against providers of VLOPs and VLOSEs. This request for information under Art. 67 may be directed not only at the providers of VLOPs or VLOSEs, but also at any other **natural** or **legal person** acting within the scope of their trade, business, craft, or profession who may possess information relevant to the suspected infringement of the provisions of the DSA. In addition, organisations that are required to conduct audits in accordance with Art. 37 and 75(2) may also be requested to provide information (Art. 67(1)).

65 The European Commission shall request the relevant information from the parties concerned in one of two ways: either by issuing a **simple request** or by issuing a **decision** that clearly states both the legal basis for the request and the purpose of the request. Moreover, the Commission must specify the information required, determine the period within which this information is to be provided, and outline the **fines** stipulated in

Art. 74 for providing insufficient information (Art. 67(2) and (3)). When the European Commission issues a request via decision, that decision must also highlight the right to have the decision reviewed by the Court of Justice of the European Union (Art. 67(3)).

The parties are obliged to respond to the request within a **reasonable time period** set by the European Commission. Furthermore, the DSC and other relevant authorities are obliged to provide the Commission with all necessary **information** upon request, in order to enable the Commission to exercise its powers (Art. 67(5)). The Commission is entitled to request access to data, information, databases and algorithms held by relevant individuals, as well as any clarifications that may be required in relation to them.[68] Furthermore, the Commission is empowered to conduct **interviews** and obtain statements from any natural or legal entity in order to gather the requisite information. However, this may only take place with the consent of the individual in question (Art. 68).

3. Power to conduct inspections

An inspection pursuant to Art. 69 may be conducted by **officials** of the European Commission and other **accompanying persons** authorised by the Commission. This inspection can occur at the premises of provider of the VLOPs and VLOSEs concerned, or at the premises of another person (Art. 67(1)). 66

The officials and other accompanying persons authorised by the European Commission are entitled to (Art. 69(2)(a)–(g): 67

- enter any premises, land and means of transport of the provider of the VLOP or VLOSE concerned or of the other person concerned;
- examine the books and other records related to the provision of the service concerned, irrespective of the medium on which they are stored and take or obtain copies of or extracts from such books or other records;
- require the provider of the VLOP or the VLOSE or the other person concerned to provide access to and explanations on its organisation, functioning, IT system, algorithms, data-handling and business practices and to record or document the explanations given;
- seal any premises used for purposes related to the trade, business, craft or profession of the provider of VLOP or VLOSE or of the other person concerned, as well as books or other records, for the period and to the extent necessary for the inspection;
- ask any representative or member of staff of the provider of the VLOP or VLOSE or the other person concerned for explanations on facts or documents relating to the subject-matter and purpose of the inspection and address questions to them.

If an inspection is ordered by the European Commission in a decision, the provider concerned is obliged to **comply** with the inspection (Art. 69(6)). The decision must specify the subject matter and purpose of the inspection, determine the date on which it is set to begin, and indicate the penalties (as pursuant in Art. 74 and 75). The Commission must also consult the DSC of the Member State on whose territory the inspection is to be carried out before taking its decision. 68

If the provider opposes the inspection, the Member State where the inspection is taking place should take the **necessary measures**, in line with its national law, upon the request of the Commission's officials or other accompanying persons. Necessary assistance, such as **coercive measures** should then be provided to support the Commission in its action (Art. 69(8)). If necessary, the DSC of the Member State concerned should

[68] See rec. 141 DSA.

seek authorisation from a national **judicial authority** at the request of the officials and other accompanying persons authorised by the Commission (Art. 69(9)).

69 In such cases, the national judicial authority before which a case has been brought must verify that the European Commission decision the decision is **authentic** and that the **coercive measures** envisaged are neither **arbitrary** nor **excessive** in relation to the subject matter of the inspection. The Commission, either directly or through the DSC of the concerned Member State, should, when necessary, provide the competent judicial authority with **detailed explanations.** However, the national judicial authority cannot challenge the need for the inspection and does not have access to information from the Commission's **case file.** The Court of Justice of the European Union has exclusive jurisdiction to review the legality of the Commission's decision (Art. 69(10)).

70 In accordance with the cooperation mechanism of the DSA, the DSCs, and other competent national authorities in the territory where the inspection is carried out shall assist the European Commission in its activities (Art. 69(3)). The Commission may also appoint auditors and experts to assist with the inspection. Officials of, and other persons authorised or appointed by, the DSCs of the Member State in which the inspection is to be conducted, shall actively assist the officials and other accompanying persons authorised by the Commission in relation to the inspection, at the request of that DSC or of the Commission (Art. 69(7)). For this purpose, they shall have the same powers as the officials of the Commission.[69]

71 Although Art. 69 already contains detailed and comprehensive provisions regarding the European Commission's power of inspection, there is a need to further delineate this **significant intervention power** of the Commission, which will be manifested as an **implementing act** that the Commission can adopt (Art. 83(a)).[70]

4. Interim measures

72 In proceedings that could lead to a decision of non-compliance according to Art. 73(1), the European Commission may, in situations of urgency due to the risk of serious damage to service recipients, order an **interim measure** against the provider of a VLOP or VLOSE based on a ***prima facie* finding** of an infringement (Art. 70).[71] Such an interim measure is **limited** to a specific time frame, but may be renewed when necessary and appropriate. All relevant decisions are subject to publication (Art. 80(1)). The Commission adopts a non-compliance decision, where it finds that the provider of the VLOP or VLOSE concerned does not comply with the interim measures (Art. 73(1)(b)) (→ mn. 76 et seqq.).

5. Commitments

73 During an ongoing monitoring or enforcement procedure, the provider of the VLOP or VLOSE can offer the Commission a **commitment** to ensure compliance with the relevant provisions of the Regulation (Art. 71). The provision in Art. 71 mirrors that of Art. 9 of Regulation (EC) No 1/2003[72], thereby drawing on well-established instruments in **antitrust law.** The European Commission may, at its discretion, make this commit-

---

[69] These are the powers enumerated in Art. 69(2).

[70] Commission Implementing Regulation (EU) 2023/1201 of 21 June 2023 on detailed arrangements for the conduct of certain proceedings by the Commission pursuant to Regulation (EU) 2022/2065 of the European Parliament and of the Council ('Digital Services Act'), OJ L 159, 22.6.2023, p. 51.

[71] See rec. 142 DSA.

[72] Council Regulation (EC) No 1/2003 of 16 December 2002 on the implementation of the rules on competition laid down in Articles 81 and 82 of the Treaty, OJ 2003 L 1, 1.

ment binding by means of a decision, which would at the same time (at least temporarily) close the procedure against the provider. This means that the Commission declares that there are **no further grounds for action**. The decision of the Commission must be published (Art. 80(1)). If the Commission determines that the commitment will not result in effective compliance, it has the right to reject the commitment in a reasoned decision at the conclusion of the proceedings (Art. 71(3)).

The Commission adopts a non-compliance decision, if it finds that the provider of the VLOP or VLOSE concerned does not comply with the commitment made binding (Art. 73(1)(c)) (→ mn. 76 et seqq.)

The European Commission may **reopen the** procedure at any time upon request or 74
on its own initiative (Art. 71(2)(a)–(c)):

- where there has been a **material change** in any of the facts on which the decision was based;
- where the provider of the VLOP or the VLOSE concerned acts **contrary** to its commitments; or
- where the decision was based on **incomplete**, **incorrect** or **misleading** information.

6. Monitoring actions

In order to monitor the effective implementation and compliance with the DSA, 75
Art. 72 empowers the European Commission to take the 'necessary actions'. These monitoring actions include directing the providers of VLOPs and VLOSEs to grant access to, and offer explanations relating to, their **databases** and **algorithms**. In addition, the European Commission may require these providers to retain all documents deemed necessary to assess both the enforcement of and compliance with the obligations under the DSA (Art. 72(1)).

To **enhance** its oversight capabilities, the European Commission may appoint **independent external auditors and experts**. Additionally, with the consent of the competent national authority concerned, the Commission can enlist experts and auditors from competent national authorities, such as **data protection** or **consumer protection** authorities,[73] to offer specialised expertise or knowledge in monitoring (Art. 72(2)).

III. Non-compliance and fines

1. Preliminary findings and non-compliance decision

a) Procedure

The European Commission adopts a **non-compliance decision**,[74] where it finds that 76
the provider of the VLOP or VLOSE concerned does not comply with one or more of the following (Art. 73(1)(a)–(c)):

- the relevant **provisions** of the DSA;
- **interim measures** ordered pursuant to Art. 70 (→ mn. 72);
- **commitments** made binding pursuant to Art. 71 (→ mn. 73 et seqq.).

Before adopting a non-compliance decision, the European Commission shall first 77
communicate its **preliminary findings** to the provider of the VLOP or VLOSE con-

[73] See also rec. 143 DSA.

[74] Providers of intermediary services (as legal persons) can bring an **action for annulment** against a Commission decision before the General Court of the EU pursuant to Art. 263 TFEU.

cerned. In these preliminary findings, the Commission will set out in detail the measures that it intends to take or that it considers that the provider should take in order to address effectively the problems identified (Art. 73(2)). This process ensures that the provider is afforded an opportunity to rectify any alleged infringements.

78 Following the initial phase, during which the European Commission presents its preliminary findings to the provider, the Commission is then able to adopt a non-compliance decision (Art. 73(3)). The non-compliance decision shall require the provider of the VLOP and the VLOSE concerned to take the **necessary measures** to ensure compliance with the decision within a **reasonable period** specified in the decision. Furthermore, the provider is required to provide the Commission with information on the measures which that provider intends to take in order to comply with the Commission's decision (Art. 73(3)). In addition, the provider must subsequently supply the Commission with a description of the measures it has taken to ensure compliance with the Commission's decision (Art. 73(4)).

79 If the European Commission determines that the provider **does not meet** the conditions enumerated in Art. 73(1) (→ mn. 76) for a non-compliance decision, it will close the investigation by a **decision**. This decision will be effective immediately (Art. 73(5)).

80 Before adopting a decision, the European Commission shall give the provider of the VLOP or the VLOSE concerned or other persons (referred to in Art. 67(1) → mn. 64) the opportunity of being heard on (Art. 79(1)(a)–(b)):[75]

- preliminary findings of the Commission and
- measures that the Commission may intend to take in view of the preliminary findings.

The parties concerned must submit their observations on the Commission's preliminary findings within a reasonable period fixed by the Commission itself, which may not be **less than 14 days** (Art. 79(2)). The recipients of the digital services in question are not included in the group of individuals entitled to submit comments and observations under Art. 79(1) and (2) (→ mn. 64), which means that they are not permitted to participate in the procedure.

81 The European Commission shall base its decision only on objections on which the parties concerned have been able to comment (Art. 79(3)). The **rights of defence** of the parties concerned shall be fully respected in the proceedings. The parties concerned have the right to access the Commission's file under the terms of a negotiated disclosure, subject to the legitimate interest of the provider concerned in the protection of its business secrets (Art. 79(4)).

b) Enhanced supervision of remedies

82 Where the European Commission adopts a **non-compliance decision** pursuant to Art. 73 as a result of a provider's infringement of a **specific obligation** under Chapter III, Section 5, which applies exclusively to providers of VLOPs and VLOSEs (→ mn. 56 et seqq.), the **system of enhanced supervision** under Art. 75 applies (i.e. the Commission shall make use of the enhanced supervision system). Art. 75 thus provides for intensified supervision of remedies for infringements of the obligations laid down in Chapter III, Section 5 for providers of VLOPs and VLOSEs. This is intended to address supervisory concerns arising from the '**potentially significant societal effects**'[76] of an

[75] See also rec. 146 DSA.
[76] See rec. 145 DSA.

infringement of the additional obligations to **manage systemic risk** that apply solely to VLOPs and VLOSEs.[77]

Providers must draw up an **action plan** setting out the measures they intend to take to terminate the infringement or to remedy it (Art. 75). The measures must include a commitment to perform an independent **audit** in accordance with Art. 37(3) and (4) (→ § 6 mn. 71) and shall specify the identity of the auditors and the methodology, timing, and follow-up of the audit (Art. 75(2)).[78] The provider shall communicate the action plan to the DSCs, the Commission and the EBDS within a reasonable period (Art. 75(2)). The measures may also include, where appropriate, a commitment to participate in a **relevant code of conduct** pursuant to Art. 45 (→ § 7 mn. 11). 83

Following the receipt of the action plan, the EBDS is required to communicate its opinion on the action plan to the European Commission within a period of **one month**. Subsequently, the Commission must determine within a one-month period whether the proposed measures outlined in the action plan are sufficient to rectify or terminate the infringement, and to establish a reasonable timeline for their implementation. The possible commitments to relevant **codes of conduct** shall be taken into account in its decision. The Commission will then **monitor** the implementation of the action plan. The provider of the VLOP or VLOSE concerned must provide the Commission with the audit report without undue delay after it becomes available. Furthermore, they are required to provide regular updates on the progress of the action plan. If necessary, the Commission may request additional information from provider of the VLOP or VLOSE within a given deadline ('reasonable period') (Art. 75(3)). The Commission informs the EBDS and the DSC of the implementation of the action plan.

The European Commission may implement necessary measures, including **periodic penalty payments** (Art. 76(1)) and **access restrictions** (Art. 82(1); see also Art. 51(3) → mn. 27) if the provider of the VLOP and the VLOSE (Art. 75(4)(a)–(c)):

- **fails** to provide any **action plan**, the audit report, the necessary updates, or any other additional information required within the given deadline; or
- the European Commission **rejects** the proposed action plan; or
- the European Commission considers, based on the audit report, any updates or additional information provided, that the implementation of the action plan is **insufficient** to terminate or remedy the infringement.

2. Fines and periodic penalty payments

The European Commission may adopt a decision, imposing **fines** (Art. 74) and periodic **penalty payments** (Art. 76). Such penalties target either the provider of the VLOP or VLOSE or, alternatively, other **natural or legal persons** as stipulated in Art. 67(1) (→ mn. 64) (Art. 74(2); Art. 76(1)). Before adoption a decision imposing fines (Art. 74(2)) the Commission shall communicate its preliminary findings (→ mn. 77 et seqq.) to the parties concerned (Art. 74(3)). When determining the amount of the fine, the Commission must consider the **gravity**, **duration**, and **recurrence** of the infringement (Art. 74(4)). 84

The European Commission may impose in a non-compliance decision (Art. 73 → mn. 76 et seqq.) on the provider of the VLOP or VLOSE concerned **fines not exceeding 6 %** of its total worldwide annual **turnover** in the preceding financial year (Art. 74). 85

[77] See rec. 145 DSA.
[78] See Achleitner MR-Int 2022/4, 114 (119).

Specifically, such fines may be imposed where the Commission finds that the provider, intentionally or negligently (Art. 74(1)(a)–(c)):

- **infringes** the relevant provisions of the DSA;
- fails to comply with a decision ordering **interim measures** under Art. 70; or
- fails to comply with a **commitment made binding** by a decision pursuant to Art. 71.

86 In certain cases, the European Commission may adopt a decision imposing **fines** not exceeding **1 %** of the total annual **income** or worldwide **turnover** in the preceding financial year. These fines shall be imposed either on the provider of the VLOP or VLOSE concerned or, alternatively, on other natural or legal persons as referred to in Art. 67(1) (→ mn. 64) (Art. 74(2)).

87 In particular, such fines may be imposed where the European Commission finds that the provider of VLOP or VLOSE intentionally or negligently (Art. 74(1)):

- supply incorrect, incomplete or misleading **information** in response to a simple request or request by a decision pursuant to Art. 67 (→ mn. 64 et seq.);
- fail to reply to the **request for information** by decision within the set period (→ mn. 64 et seq.);
- fail to **rectify** within the period set by the Commission, incorrect, incomplete or misleading **information** given by a member of staff, or fail or refuse to provide complete information;
- refuse to submit to an **inspection** pursuant to Art. 69 (→ mn. 66 et seqq.);
- fail to comply with the **measures** adopted by the Commission pursuant to Art. 72 (→ mn. 75); or
- fail to comply with the conditions for access to the **Commission's file** pursuant to Art. 79(4) (→ mn. 81).

88 The European Commission can adopt a **decision**, imposing **periodic penalty payments** on the provider of VLOP or VLOSE, or other persons specified in Art. 67(1) (→ mn. 64). These penalties can reach up to **5 %** of the average daily income or worldwide annual turnover in the preceding financial year per day, calculated from the date appointed by the decision (Art. 76).

89 The European Commission may adopt a decision, imposing **periodic penalty payments** in order to compel them to (Art. 76(1)(a)–(e)):

- supply correct and complete **information** in response to a decision requiring information pursuant to Art. 67;
- submit to an **inspection** which it has ordered by decision pursuant to Art. 69;
- comply with a decision ordering **interim measures** pursuant to Art. 70(1);
- comply with **commitments made legally binding** by a decision pursuant to Art. 71(1);
- comply with a **decision** pursuant to Art. 73(1), including where applicable the requirements it contains relating to the action plan referred to in Art. 75.

90 Fines and penalty payments for non-compliance with the DSA should be set at an **appropriate** level. This should be in line with the principles of **proportionality** and **ne bis in idem** (prohibition of double jeopardy). The European Commission, in collaboration with the relevant national authorities, is responsible for ensuring that these principles are adhered to. Specifically, the Commission should consider any fines and penalties previously imposed on the same legal person for identical facts, based on a final decision concerning an infringement of other Union or national rules. This ensures that the overall fines and penalties remain proportionate and reflect the **severity** of the infringements

committed. All decisions made by the Commission are subject to review by the Court of Justice of the European Union in accordance with the provisions of the TFEU.[79] The **Court of Justice of the European Union** has unlimited jurisdiction to review decisions by which the Commission has imposed fines and penalty payments (Art. 261 TFEU). The Commission may **annul**, **reduce**, or **increase** the imposed penalties (Art. 81).

3. Limitation period for the imposition and the enforcement of penalties

The powers of the European Commission to impose fines and periodic penalty payments and to enforce decisions concerning finds and periodic penalty payments (Art. 74 and 76) are subject to a limitation period of **five years** (Art. 77 and 78). 91

With regard to the powers conferred upon the Commission to impose fines and periodic penalty payments pursuant to Art. 74 and 76, the limitation period starts on the **day the infringement is committed**. In cases of continuous or repeated infringements, the time begins to run on the day the infringement **ceases** (Art. 77(2)). 92

Any action by the European Commission or the DSC, aimed at investigating or prosecuting the infringement, interrupts the limitation period (Art. 77(3)). Each interruption starts the time running afresh. Nevertheless, the limitation period shall conclude at the latest when a period of time equivalent to twice the limitation period has elapsed without the Commission imposing a fine or periodic penalty payment (Art. 77(4)). If proceedings concerning a decision of the Commission are subject of proceedings pending before the Court of Justice of the European Union, the limitation period is **suspended** (Art. 77(5)).

The powers conferred on the European Commission to enforce decisions concerning fines (Art. 74) and periodic penalty payments (Art. 76) are subject to a limitation period of **five years** (Art. 78). Time shall **begin to run** on the day on which the decision becomes final (Art. 78(2). 93

The limitation period for the enforcement of penalties is **interrupted** in the following cases (Art. 78(3)):

- by notification of a decision varying the original amount of the fine or periodic penalty payment or refusing an application for variation;
- by any action of the Commission, or of a Member State acting at the request of the Commission, designed to enforce payment of the fine or periodic penalty payment.

Each interruption **resets the time** (Art. 78(4)). The limitation period for enforcing penalties is **suspended** during a payment grace period or pursuant to a decision from the Court of Justice of the European Union or a national court (Art. 78(5)(a)–(b)).

4. Request for access restrictions and cooperation with national courts

As a **last resort**, where all powers to bring about the cessation of an infringement of the DSA have been exhausted, the European Commission may initiate **repressive enforcement powers** in the form of **restricting recipients' access** either to the service concerned by the infringement or, only where that is not technically feasible, to the **online interface** of the intermediary service provider on which the infringement takes place (Art. 82(1) and Art. 51(3)) (so called **website blocking**; **internet shutdowns** → mn. 25 et seqq.). 94

The DSA provision concerning the repressive powers of the Commission refers directly to Art. 51(3), which sets out the repressive measures relating to the DSC's powers

[79] Rec. 144.

over intermediary services. Therefore, Art. 51(3) also applies to providers of VLOPs and VLOSEs when it comes to the Commission's supervision. To this end, the European Commission requests the DSC of establishment to take action in this regard pursuant to Art. 51(3) (→ mn. 25 et seqq.).

In accordance with Art. 51, the DSC is obliged to request the provider to take the **necessary measures** at the **first instance** (Art. 51(3)(a)). Only after this is done – in a subsequent step – can the DSC apply to a **judicial authority** for a temporary restriction order. As a first step, the DSC must therefore ask the provider's management to draw up an action plan (Art. 51(3)(a) → mn. 25 et seqq.). When the DSC considers that the provider has **not** adequately met the requirements regarding the **action plan**, the DSC may request the competent **judicial authority** of its Member State to order a **temporary restriction of access** (Art. 51(3)(b)). A temporary restriction of access can only be imposed by a **court decision** (→ mn. 25 et seqq.).

95 In light of the significant consequences of such a measure, it is only an option once all other potential measures have been **exhausted**. Furthermore, it must be demonstrated that the infringement persists and causes substantial harm that cannot be avoided by the exercise of other powers under EU or national law (Art. 82(1)).

96 Prior to requesting that the DSC take action in accordance with Art. 51(3), the parties concerned must be granted the **right to be heard**. The European Commission shall invite interested parties to submit written comments within a period of at least **14 working days** (Art. 82(1)).

97 Access restrictions can only be imposed based on a **court decision** by a competent **national judicial authority**. Accordingly, the European Commission must initially seek the assistance of the DSC in requesting that the competent judicial authority of its Member State impose a temporary restriction on access (Art. 82(1) and Art. 51(3) → mn. 25 et seqq.) → mn. 94.

98 The European Commission is obliged to cooperate with national courts when such cooperation is required. It may submit **written observations** to the competent judicial authority, and, with the permission of that authority, can also **orally** present its views on the matter (Art. 82(2)). To prepare these opinions – and solely for this purpose – the Commission may request the competent judicial authority to provide the **necessary documents** for evaluating the case (Art. 82(2)).

99 When a national court rules on a matter that has already been addressed by a European Commission decision under the DSA, the court must not make any decisions that are **contrary** to those of the Commission. Furthermore, national courts **must avoid** making decisions that might **conflict** with a prospective Commission decision in **ongoing proceedings** under the DSA. In this context, the national court can evaluate if it's necessary to suspend its proceedings (Art. 82(3)). This provision is also relevant in the context of private enforcement (→ mn. 5). Art. 82 is in line with and doesn't prejudice Art. 267 TFEU (**Preliminary ruling**).

100 In order to guarantee a consistent implementation and enforcement of the DSA, and to ensure that national court decisions do not conflict with those adopted by the European Commission under the DSA, it is essential to maintain a good **exchange of information** between the involved authorities (→ mn. 4; mn. 50).[80]

[80] See rec. 147 DSA.

§ 9
Interplay and relationship with other legal acts

Literature: *Alexander,* Geschäftsgeheimnisse und Ranking-Transparenz – Spannungsfeld zwischen Schutz von Geschäftsgeheimnissen und neuen Informationspflichten für Anbieter von Online-Suchdiensten, MMR 2021, 690; *Busch,* Mehr Fairness und Transparenz in der Plattformökonomie? Die neue P2B-Verordnung im Überblick, GRUR 2019, 788; *Busch/Dannemann/Schulte-Nölke,* Bausteine für ein europäisches Recht der Plattformökonomie: Die ELI-Modellregeln für Onlineplattformen, MMR 2020, 667; *Busch/Mak,* Putting the Digital Services Act in Context: Bridging the Gap Between EU Consumer Law and Platform Regulation, EuCML 2021, 109; *Bydlinski,* Juristische Methodenlehre und Rechtsbegriff, 2nd edn, Stuttgart 2011; *Engeler,* Der Konflikt zwischen Datenmarkt und Datenschutz, NJW 2022, 3398; *Fenyves/Kerschner/Vonkilch* (Hrsg.), §§ 1 bis 43 ABGB, 3. Aufl. des von Dr. Heinrich Klang begründeten Kommentars zum Allgemeinen Bürgerlichen Gesetzbuch, Wien 2014; *Gerdemann/Spindler,* Das Gesetz über digitale Dienste (Digital Services Act) (Teil 1). Grundlegende Strukturen und Regelungen für Vermittlungsdienste und Host-Provider, GRUR 2023, 3; *Janal,* Friendly Fire? Das Urheberrechts-Diensteanbieter-Gesetz und sein Verhältnis zum künftigen Digital Services Act, GRUR 2022, 211; *Kreutz,* Der Webseitennutzungsvertrag – Fiktion oder unbekanntes Rechtsgeschäft?, ZUM 2018, 162; *Kühling/Sauerborn,* 'Dark patterns' unter der DS-GVO und dem DSA – Neue Herausforderung für die digitale Rechtsordnung, CR 2022, 226; *Leibold,* Schadensersatzansprüche sowie Inhalt und Streitwerte des Auskunftsanspruchs nach der DS-GVO – Eine Rechtsübersicht 2019–2021, ZD 2022, 18; *Leistner,* European Copyright Licensing and Infringement Liability Under Art. 17 DSM-Directive, ZGE, 2020, Vol. 2, p. 123; *Loy/Baumgartner,* Consent-Banner und Nudging – Tracking-Mechanismen: Wie viel 'Anstupsen' ist erlaubt?, ZD 2021, 404; *Martini/Drews/Seeliger/Weinzierl,* Dark Patterns – Phänomenologie und Antworten der Rechtsordnung, ZfDR 2021, 47; *Möller,* Dark Patterns in Consent-Bannern – Wie das Einwilligungserfordernis im Online-Tracking durch geschickte Designgestaltungen ausgehebelt wird: ein Drama in drei Akten, VuR 2022, 449; *Naumann/Rodenhausen,* Die P2B-Verordnung aus Unternehmenssicht: Herausforderungen für europäische Plattformen am Beispiel einer Hybrid-Online-Plattform, ZEuP 2020, 768; *Ohly,* UWG-Rechtsschutz bei Verstößen gegen die Datenschutz-Grundverordnung?, GRUR 2019, 686; Peukert/Husovec/Kretschmer/Mezei/Quintais, European Copyright Society – Comment on Copyright and the Digital Services Act Proposal, IIC 2022, 358; *Quintas/Schwemer,* The Interplay between the Digital Services Act and Sector Regulation: How Special Is Copyright?, European Journal of Risk Regulation 2022, 1; *Raue,* 'Unberührt' – das Verhältnis von DSA zur DSM-RL und zum UrhDaG, ZUM 2023, 160; Raue/Heesen, Der Digital Services Act, NJW 2022, 3537; *Riesenhuber,* § 10: Die Auslegung, in: Riesenhuber (Hrsg.), Europäische Methodenlehre, 4th edn, Berlin 2021; *Ruffert* (ed.), Die Regulierung digitaler Plattformen, 2023; *Schneider/Kremer,* Ein zweiter, kritischer Blick auf die P2B-Verordnung: Nachhaltige Veränderung des Plattformökosystems?, WRP 2020, 1128; *Schwamberger,* Anmerkung zu OGH 6 Ob 104/18h, GPR 2019, 57; *Schwamberger,* Die Folgen des datenschutzrechtlichen Widerrufs bei Verträgen über digitale Leistungen, ecolex 2021, 795; *Schweitzer,* Digitale Plattformen als private Gesetzgeber: Ein Perspektivwechsel für die europäische 'Plattform-Regulierung', ZEuP 2019, 1; *Sosnitza,* Bewertung und Rankings im Internet – Neue lauterkeitsrechtliche Anforderungen, CR 2021, 329; *Uebele,* Datenschutzrecht vor Zivilgerichten – Die Durchsetzung des Datenschutzrechts über UWG und UKlaG auf dem Prüfstand von Rechtsprechung und Gesetzgeber, GRUR 2019, 694; *Uitz,* Die EU-Platform-to-Business-VO – Europäische Regulierung der internetbasierten Plattformwirtschaft, 2022; *Wais,* B2B-Klauselkontrolle in der Plattform-Ökonomie: Der Kommissionsvorschlag für eine Verordnung über Online-Vermittlungsdienste, EuZW 2019, 221; *Weiß,* Öffnungsklauseln in der DS-GVO und nationale Verwirklichung im BDSG: Vollharmonisierung light, Baden-Baden 2022; *Wendehorst,* Rechtsdurchsetzung im Verbraucherrecht – materiellrechtliche Aspekte, 21. ÖJT Vol. II/1, Wien 2022.

A. Introduction

1 The Digital Services Act (DSA)[1] has **numerous points of contact with other European legal acts**. This has also been recognised by the European legislator. In contrast to the Commission's proposal,[2] which in part explicitly stated that the DSA is a *lex generalis* and that the legal acts take precedence as *leges speciales*,[3] the European legislator has now merely decreed in Art. 2(4) that the DSA is **'without prejudice'** to a number of explicitly cited legal acts.

2 The list in Art. 2(4) DSA is not exhaustive ('in particular'). In addition, the legislator uses **broad legal terms** ('Union law on copyright and related rights [...] consumer protection and product safety [...] on the protection of personal data'), which additionally lead to **legal uncertainty regarding the interaction with other legal acts.** This approach is elegant insofar as the legislator was not forced to reflect for each provision whether a more specific legal act, such as the P2B Regulation in case of ranking, takes precedence. In addition, however, the general approach poses major challenges for legal practitioners due to the uncertainty of the respective precedence. Finally, a speciality could even be to the advantage of the infringers in view of the strict sanctions of the DSA: Thus, assuming a speciality of the P2B Regulation, it could be argued that no administrative penalties can be imposed on the platform provider in case of a breach of the ranking requirements, because the P2B Regulation does not contain any administrative penalties.

3 In addition, the open formulations used by the European legislator in Art. 2(4) and the non-exhaustive list contained therein also mean that the interaction with other legal acts cannot, by its very nature, be dealt with conclusively. Therefore, the partial interaction with selected legal acts – the **Digital Markets Act** (DMA),[4] the **Platform-to-Business Regulation** (P2B Regulation),[5] the **Omnibus Directive**,[6] the **General Data Protection Regulation** (GDPR)[7] as well as the **DSM Directive**[8] – will be shown below.

B. Digital Markets Act (DMA)

4 The DMA proposal was presented by the European Commission on 15.12.2020 together with the DSA proposal. Together, the two legal acts are intended to ensure a **'fair and competitive economy'** and thus one of the three objectives of the European Commission's digital strategy. Both legal acts (DMA and DSA) form the regulatory package for a digital single market.

5 The question of the interplay of the two legal acts can thus be answered easily: While the DSA is intended to fundamentally reform the E-Commerce Directive[9] from 2000 by focusing on liability issues and illegal content of digital services, the DMA aims to supplement European antitrust law with ex ante regulations in order to close gaps or

[1] Regulation (EU) 2022/2065, OJ L 277, 1.
[2] COM(2020) 825 final.
[3] See rec. 9 COM(2020) 825 final: 'This Regulation is therefore without prejudice to those other acts which are lex specialis in relation to the generally applicable framework laid down in this Regulation'.
[4] Regulation (EU) 2022/1925, OJ L 265, 1.
[5] Regulation (EU) 2019/1150, OJ L 186, 57.
[6] Directive (EU) 2019/2161, OJ L 328, 7.
[7] Regulation (EU) 2016/679, OJ L 119, 1.
[8] Directive (EU) 2019/790, OJ L 130, 92.
[9] Directive 2000/31/EC, OJ L 178, 1.

weaknesses with regard to large, market-dominating and established online platforms (so-called digital gatekeepers). **Both legal acts complement each other**.

C. Platform-to-Business Regulation (P2B Regulation)

6 As simple as the interaction between the DSA and the DMA may have seemed, the interaction between the DSA and the P2B Regulation is just as difficult. As its name suggests, the P2B Regulation intends to promote 'fairness and transparency for business users of online intermediation services'. In doing so, the European legislator is breaking new ground, as the provisions in the P2B Regulation support antitrust law through specifications in fairness and contract law.[10] The European legislator is leaving the familiar path of ex post and case-by-case control of market-dominant companies and generally specifying **additional ex ante criteria** for the entire platform economy, irrespective of whether a relevant threshold has been exceeded.[11]

7 The P2B Regulation is limited in particular to regulating the **form and content of general terms and conditions** (GTC).[12] In this context, far-reaching initial considerations, such as the introduction of a general fairness test for P2B contracts modelled after Art. II-9:405 DCFR or the inclusion of a 'black list' similar to the Annex of the UCP Directive have been dropped.[13] The P2B Regulation establishes general transparency requirements for GTCs (Art. 3(1) P2B Regulation, → § 16 mn. 27 et seq.), provisions on the amendment of GTCs (Art. 3(2) P2B Regulation, → § 16 mn. 45 et seq.) on suspension and termination (Art. 4 P2B Regulation, → § 16 mn. 57 et seq.) and contains a 'rump version'[14] of the originally considered 'black list' in Art. 8. In addition, the regulation contains provisions on ranking (Art. 5 P2B Regulation, → § 16 mn. 88 et seqq.), ancillary goods and services (Art. 6 P2B Regulation, → § 16 mn. 62 et seqq.), differentiated treatment (Art. 7 P2B Regulation, → § 17 mn. 105 et seqq.), on access to data (Art. 9 P2B Regulation, → § 16 mn. 72 et seqq.), on best price clauses (Art. 10 P2B Regulation, → § 16 mn. 66 et seqq.), and on complaint management and mediation (Art. 11–13 P2B Regulation, → § 17 mn. 11 et seqq.).

8 The provision on **ranking** (Art. 5 P2B Regulation) is particularly relevant for the **interaction** with the DSA, which, in view of the provisions on recommender systems in the DSA (Art. 27, 38 DSA, → § 4 mn. 62 et seq.), raises the question of whether one of the two legal acts takes precedence in this respect. In the following, the overlaps and different provisions in the legal acts will first be shown. Subsequently, it will be explained that Art. 5 P2B Regulation supplements the provisions on recommender systems in the DSA and that, in principle, both legal acts are applicable.

I. Overlaps in the scope of application

9 The P2B Regulation distinguishes between provisions for 'online intermediation services' and those for 'providers of online search engines' (→ § 16, mn. 92, 110). It is ex-

[10] Cf. Busch GRUR 2019, 788 (789); see on the history and the need for legislative action: Uitz, Die EU-Platform-to-Business-VO, p. 30 et seqq.; Naumann/Rodenhausen ZEuP 2020, 768 (769); Schweitzer ZEuP 2019, 1 (1); see on the preliminary work of the European Law Institute (ELI) in the form of the elaborated 'ELI Model Rules for Online Platforms': Busch/Dannemann/Schulte-Nölke MMR 2020, 667.

[11] Cf. Busch GRUR 2019, 788 (789); Naumann/Rodenhausen ZEuP 2020, 768 (769).

[12] See on the differences to the Unfair Terms Directive: Wais EuZW 2019, 221 (224).

[13] Cf. Busch GRUR 2019, 788 (789).

[14] Cf. Busch GRUR 2019, 788 (791).

plained below that both providers fall under the scope of application of the P2B Regulation as well as that of the DSA.

1. Online intermediation services

10

Art. 3(i) DSA	Art. 2(2) P2B Regulation
'online platform' means a hosting service that, at the request of a recipient of the service, stores and disseminates information to the public, unless that activity is a minor and purely ancillary feature of another service or a minor functionality of the principal service and, for objective and technical reasons, cannot be used without that other service, and the integration of the feature or functionality into the other service is not a means to circumvent the applicability of this Regulation;	**'online intermediation services' means services which meet all of the following requirements: (a) they constitute information society services within the meaning of point (b) of Article 1(1) of Directive (EU) 2015/1535 of the European Parliament and of the Council; (b) they allow business users to offer goods or services to consumers, with a view to facilitating the initiating of direct transactions between those business users and consumers, irrespective of where those transactions are ultimately concluded; (c) they are provided to business users on the basis of contractual relationships between the provider of those services and business users which offer goods or services to consumers;**

In the case of online platforms – especially online intermediation services – there are basically **three legal relationships**. The first legal relationship is between the platform and the supplier on the platform (**'supplier-sided relationship'**), for example between the selling business and the online marketplace. 11

The second legal relationship is between the platform and the user (**'user-sided relationship'**), e.g. between the potential buyer and the online marketplace. 12

Finally, if a contract is concluded between a user and a supplier on an online intermediation service, the third legal relationship arises: the so-called **'user-supplier relationship'**. 13

The P2B Regulation is **personally applicable** only **between online intermediation services**, i.e. in particular online marketplaces, hotel booking portals, app stores, as well as **business users and corporate website users** (Art. 1(2) P2B Regulation). However, pure **B2B platforms** do not fall under the P2B Regulation (→ § 15 mn. 3).[15] In this respect, it can be assumed that the scope of application of the Regulation is essentially limited to the **'supplier-sided relationship'**. If both the user and the supplier are businesses, the Regulation is not applicable by virtue of this exception and only rare cases will be found in which non-commercial suppliers sell products to commercial users via a platform. In the case of hotel booking portals and app stores, this will usually be excluded by the very nature of the service. 14

Online intermediation services within the scope of the P2B Regulation also fall under the term 'online platform' in Art. 3(i) DSA.[16] The definition does not only include social networks, but in particular also platforms that enable consumers to conclude distance contracts with traders;[17] a separate section of the DSA is dedicated to such distance con- 15

[15] Cf. rec. 11 sent. 4 P2B Regulation: 'However, this Regulation should not apply to peer-to-peer online intermediation services without the presence of business users, pure business-to-business online intermediation services which are not offered to consumers, online advertising tools and online advertising exchanges which are not provided with the aim of facilitating the initiation of direct transactions and which do not involve a contractual relationship with consumers.'; critical on this exception: Busch GRUR 2019, 788 (790).

[16] Busch/Busch P2B Regulation Art. 5 mn. 5.

[17] Cf. rec. 13 DSA.

tracts (Art. 29 et seq. DSA), which in particular contains provisions on traceability of traders, compliance by design and a right to information (→ § 4 mn. 63).

2. Online search engines

16

Art. 3(j) DSA	Art. 2(5) P2B Regulation
'online search engine' means an intermediary service that allows users to input queries in order to perform searches of, in principle, all websites, or all websites in a particular language, on the basis of a query on any subject in the form of a keyword, voice request, phrase or other input, and returns results in any format in which information related to the requested content can be found;	**'online search engine' means a digital service that allows users to input queries in order to perform searches of, in principle, all websites, or all websites in a particular language, on the basis of a query on any subject in the form of a keyword, voice request, phrase or other input, and returns results in any format in which information related to the requested content can be found;**

17 The **definitions** of online search engines in the DSA and the P2B Regulation **differ.** On the one hand the DSA speaks of an 'intermediary service'. The P2B Regulation, on the other hand, of a 'digital service'. The **definitions of** the two legal acts **overlap**, if not coincide, with regard to online search engines. However, this only applies with regard to the definitions, **but not with regard to the scope of application** of the corresponding provisions. Chapter three, section five **DSA** (Art. 33 et seq. DSA, → § 6 mn. 1 et seq.), which also contains the definition of recommender systems, is **only applicable to very large online search engines** (Art. 33(1) DSA). These are search engines with more than **45 million** monthly active users.

II. Material overlaps in ranking and recommender systems

1. Definitions

18

Art. 3(s) DSA	Art. 2(8) P2B Regulation
'recommender system' means a fully or partially automated system used by an online platform to suggest in its online interface specific information to recipients of the service or prioritise that information, including as a result of a search initiated by the recipient of the service or otherwise determining the relative order or prominence of information displayed;	**'ranking' means the relative prominence given to the goods or services offered through online intermediation services, or the relevance given to search results by online search engines, as presented, organised or communicated by the providers of online intermediation services or by providers of online search engines, respectively, irrespective of the technological means used for such presentation, organisation or communication;**

a) Prominence of goods or services

19 A 'ranking' in the sense of the P2B Regulation exists in the case of a so-called **'prominence'.** In contrast, a 'recommender system' in the sense of the DSA does not only exist in the case of a 'prominence', but also in the case of a 'suggestion', a 'prioritisation' or another determination of the 'relative order'. It is not evident that the European legislator intended anything else to be understood by these terms in the DSA and the P2B Regulation. It is noteworthy, however, that one would understand 'ranking' to mean a certain prominence by determining the order of the search results listed. However, the words 'determining the relative order' are listed in the DSA next to 'prominence', which could mean, conversely, that **'prominence'** could **not be understood as 'determining**

the relative order'. A look at the other language versions shows that this is not a translation error.[18]

In addition, the definition in Art. 2(8) P2B Regulation only covers the prominence given to goods and services, whereas a recommender system under the DSA applies not only to goods and services, but to all information. Thus, the **scope of application of the DSA is broader** than that of the P2B Regulation. However, it can be assumed that the broad term of information, despite the lack of a definition in the DSA, also covers goods and services. 20

Thus, the words 'prominence given to the goods and services' as defined in Art. 2(8) P2B Regulation also fall under the wording 'suggest [...] specific information' or 'prioritise that information' of the recommender system of the DSA. However, the DSA goes beyond the P2B Regulation, which means that the concept of the recommender system is broader than that of the ranking in the P2B Regulation. 21

b) Relevance of search results

In addition to the prominence of goods and services, the term ranking also includes the 'relevance given to search results by online search engines'. This 'relevance' is likely to fall at least under the **broad provision of the DSA** ('or otherwise determining the relative order or prominence of information displayed'), because ultimately this 'relevance' is also only about specifying a certain order or prominence. 22

2. Transparency requirements for online intermediation services

23

Art. 27(1) DSA	Art. 5(1) P2B Regulation
Providers of online platforms that use recommender systems shall set out in their terms and conditions, in plain and intelligible language, the main parameters used in their recommender systems, as well as any options for the recipients of the service to modify or influence those main parameters.	**Providers of online intermediation services shall set out in their terms and conditions the main parameters determining ranking and the reasons for the relative importance of those main parameters as opposed to other parameters.**

The concept of ranking in the P2B Regulation also falls under the concept of recommender systems in the DSA. However, the latter contains a broader term, since it covers, for example, not only the prioritising of goods and services, but of all information. 24

Consequently, if the DSA and the P2B Regulation were applicable, the transparency requirements of both legal acts would have to be met with regard to the ranking. This raises **two central questions** for those subject to the law: (1) Does the P2B Regulation introduce additional requirements or can the transparency requirements of both legal acts be fulfilled by means of an information notice? (2) Does the violation of the transparency requirements lead to sanctions/liability under the DSA, the P2B Regulation or both legal acts? 25

a) Type and place of information for online intermediation services: 'plain and intelligible' in the GTCs

Both the P2B Regulation and the DSA oblige online intermediation services to include **information** on recommender system or ranking in the **general terms and** 26

[18] See, for example, the German version of Art. 2(8) P2B Regulation: '„Ranking" die relative Hervorhebung von Waren und Dienstleistungen [...]' and Art. 3(s) DSA: '[...] oder das auf andere Weise die relative Reihenfolge oder Hervorhebung der angezeigten Informationen bestimmt.'

conditions. In this respect, the European legislator seems to have abandoned the idea that the information has to be provided before the conclusion of the contract and that an additional provision stipulates that the information becomes part of a possibly concluded contract.[19] Instead, in both legal acts, the 'pragmatic way' was taken and the **information automatically becomes part of the contract as part of the GTC.** Ultimately, however, in order to become part of the contract, the GTC must be available before the contract is concluded.[20] The legislator disregards that the ranking parameters can also change from time to time, e.g. in the form of sales events such as 'Black Friday' or 'end of season sales'.[21] Unlike with online search engines in the P2B Regulation, however, there is **no obligation to keep** this ranking information **'always up-to-date'** for **online intermediation services.**[22]

27 There is concordance between the DSA and the P2B Regulation with regard to the way in which information is provided. Both stipulate that the general terms and conditions must be drafted in plain and intelligible language (Art. 3(1)(a) P2B Regulation; Art. 27(1) DSA). This criterion will not only fail those GTCs that are overbroad or formulated in a way that is incomprehensible to the average reader.[23] However, it should be noted that the P2B Regulation is only addressed to business users and thus the average business user is the criterion for determining the average reader and not the consumer.[24] The DSA, on the other hand, covers all natural and legal persons and thus also consumers. In this respect, it could well be assumed that although the same standard is to be understood with regard to the wording 'clear and comprehensible', a stricter standard is to be applied to the wording in the context of the DSA in view of the different addressees.

b) Content of the information: reasons for the relative weighting of the main parameters

aa) General

28 Both the information obligations under the DSA and those under the P2B Regulation[25] are aimed at **algorithm transparency.** This should enable users to **understand the** ranking and recommendations and to **optimise** the presentation of the **results.**[26] There is a general provision for transparency in both legal acts. According to Art. 5(1) P2B Regulation, the GTC must contain 'the main parameters determining ranking and the reasons for the relative importance of those main parameters as opposed to other parameters'. In contrast, according to Art. 27(1) DSA, the 'main parameters used in their recommender systems, as well as any options for the recipients of the service to modify or influence those main parameters [shall be set out]'.

---

[19] Cf. Art. 6(5) CRD: 'The information [...] shall form an integral part of the distance or off-premises contract and shall not be altered unless the parties expressly agree otherwise.'

[20] So now also explicitly Art. 3(1)(b) P2B Regulation: 'Providers of online intermediation services shall ensure that their general terms and conditions are easily available to business users at all stages of their commercial relationship with the provider of online intermediation services, including in the pre-contractual stage'.

[21] Cf. Naumann/Rodenhausen ZEuP 2020, 769 (790).

[22] However see Busch/Busch P2B Regulation Art. 5 mn. 38; European Commission, 'Guidelines on Transparency', 08.12.2020, OJ 2020 C 424, mn. 120, which assume an implicit obligation to provide up-to-date information. In my opinion, however, this is contradicted by the clearly different wording of Art. 5(1) and (2) P2B Regulation.

[23] Cf. Busch/Busch P2B Regulation Art. 5 mn. 34.

[24] Busch/Busch P2B Regulation Art. 5 mn. 34.

[25] Cf. Busch/Busch P2B Regulation Art. 5 mn. 1 et seqq.

[26] See rec. 24 P2B Regulation.

bb) General clause

When comparing the general clauses in the legal acts, it becomes apparent that these lead to the **same level of transparency.** Although the wording of Art. 5(1) P2B Regulation and Art. 27(1) DSA differ slightly. The 'relative weighting', however, is not to be understood differently from the 'options for the recipients of the service to modify or influence those main parameters'. There is a difference, however, that **only the general provision of the P2B Regulation** contains an obligation to state the **reasons for the relative weighting.** In the case of the DSA, this is found in the specifications (→ § 4 mn. 62 et seqq.). 29

cc) Specifications

30

Art. 27(2) DSA	Art. 5(5) P2B Regulation
The main parameters referred to in paragraph 1 shall explain why certain information is suggested to the recipient of the service. They shall include, at least: (a) the criteria which are most significant in determining the information suggested to the recipient of the service; (b) the reasons for the relative importance of those parameters.	**The descriptions referred to in paragraphs 1, 2 and 3 shall be sufficient to enable the business users or corporate website users to obtain an adequate understanding of whether, and if so how and to what extent, the ranking mechanism takes account of the following: (a) the characteristics of the goods and services offered to consumers through the online intermediation services or the online search engine; (b) the relevance of those characteristics for those consumers; (c) as regards online search engines, the design characteristics of the website used by corporate website users.**

There are also **different formulations** with regard to the **specifications** of the general provisions on transparency. These are due to the different regulatory objectives pursued by the two legal acts. The P2B Regulation only addresses the supplier-sided relationship, whereas the DSA addresses both the supplier-sided and the user-sided. In this respect, the transparency requirements in the supplier-sided relationship of the P2B Regulation are aimed at **tracking a ranking in the user-sided relationship**, namely vis-à-vis consumers. This is also logical insofar as there is no ranking as such vis-à-vis the supplier. The supplier usually does not see any search results or is offered possible products for purchase. However, this result can also be achieved with the specifications of the DSA. The DSA also wants to provide users with the greatest possible transparency with regard to the information suggested to them. Finally, the 'characteristics of the goods and services' according to Art. 5(5)(a) P2B Regulation are simply specific parameters or 'information' as defined in Art. 27(2)(a) DSA. The same applies to any influence on the parameters through the payment of remuneration. Finally, the obligation to provide information regarding the 'reasons for the relative importance of those parameters' (Art. 27(2)(b) DSA) is also consistent with that of Art. 5(1) P2B Regulation: 'Providers of online intermediation services shall set out in their terms and conditions the main parameters determining ranking and the reasons for the relative importance of those main parameters as opposed to other parameters'. 31

dd) Limits of the transparency obligations

32

DSA	Art. 5(6) P2B Regulation
–	**Providers of online intermediation services and providers of online search engines shall, when complying with the requirements of this Article, not be required to disclose algorithms or any information that, with reasonable certainty, would result in the enabling of deception of consumers or consumer harm through the manipulation of search results. This Article shall be without prejudice to Directive (EU) 2016/943.**

33 A key difference between the ranking-related transparency obligations of the P2B Regulation and the DSA is that Art. 5(6) P2B Regulation sets **limits to the transparency obligations.** The first sentence of the provision leads to a **balancing of interests** between those of business users in transparency and the fight against manipulative behavior.[27] This obligation intends to prevent diverse ranking manipulating practices.[28] Despite this legitimate interest, there is **no comparable provision** for transparency obligations for recommender systems **in the DSA**. The same applies to the second sentence of Art. 5(6) P2B Regulation, which addresses the **relationship with the Trade Secrets Directive.**[29] In the DSA, however, the Trade Secrets Directive is not listed in its Art. 2(4).

ee) Guideline competence

34

DSA	Art. 5(7) P2B Regulation
–	**To facilitate the compliance of providers of online intermediation services and providers of online search engines with and the enforcement of the requirements of this Article, the Commission shall accompany the transparency requirements set out in this Article with guidelines.**

35 Finally, Art. 5(7), the European Commission's competence to issue guidelines, is a **unique feature of the P2B Regulation**. A similar provision or competence is not to be found in the DSA. However, the guidelines do **not have the quality of a legal norm** and cannot have **any legal effect on** their own.[30] Rather, they will be a **'useful reference point'** for the ECJ for the interpretation[31] of the requirements for algorithm transparency in both the P2B Regulation and the DSA.

ff) Interim result

36 In summary, the European legislator has created largely the **same level of algorithm transparency for** online intermediation services in a **cumbersome manner in** Art. 5 P2B Regulation and Art. 27 DSA. Cumbersome because the legislator uses **different wording in the two provisions** and because the individual criteria are listed in a **differ-**

[27] Busch/Busch P2B Regulation Art. 5 mn. 73; Köhler/Bornkamm/Feddersen/Alexander P2B Regulation Art. 5 mn. 33; Alexander MMR 2021, 690 (695); Sosnitza CR 2021, 329 (333).

[28] Busch/Busch P2B Regulation Art. 5 mn. 72.

[29] Directive (EU) 2016/943, OJ L 157, 1.

[30] Cf. Busch/Busch P2B Regulation Art. 5 mn. 75; Köhler/Bornkamm/Feddersen/Alexander P2B Regulation Art. 5 mn. 35; European Commission, 'Guidelines on Transparency', 08.12.2020, OJ 2020 C 424 mn. 9.

[31] Cf. ECJ 7.3.2022 – C-310/99, ECLI:EU:C:2002:143 mn. 52 = BeckRS 2004, 76246 – Italy/Commission; ECJ 4.7.2000 – C-387/97, ECLI:EU:C:2000:356 mn. 89 = EuZW 2000, 531 – Commission/Greece.

ent place in the respective provisions: once in the general clause itself, once in the specification of this general clause.

The central differences between the provision in the P2B Regulation and in the DSA is, that the P2B Regulation provides for **limits to the transparency obligations** (Art. 5(6) P2B Regulation) and a **guideline competence of the European Commission** (Art. 5(7) P2B Regulation). However, the Guidelines under the P2B Regulation can also be used for the interpretation of Art. 27 DSA. 37

3. Transparency requirements for online search engines

38

Art. 38 DSA	Art. 5(2) P2B Regulation
In addition to the requirements set out in Article 27, providers of very large online platforms and of very large online search engines that use recommender systems shall provide at least one option for each of their recommender systems which is not based on profiling as defined in Article 4, point (4), of Regulation (EU) 2016/679.	**Providers of online search engines shall set out the main parameters, which individually or collectively are most significant in determining ranking and the relative importance of those main parameters, by providing an easily and publicly available description, drafted in plain and intelligible language, on the online search engines of those providers. They shall keep that description up to date.**

a) *Place of transparency requirements*

The DSA provides for **uniform transparency requirements for** online intermediary services and online search engines in the GTC.[32] In the P2B Regulation, in contrast, the European legislator has acknowledged that in the case of online search engines, the website is often visited but no contractual relationship is concluded with the provider of the website.[33] The visit or use of the website does not always necessarily lead to the conclusion of a so-called **website use contract**; this is rather a highly disputed question in the national legal systems.[34] Accordingly, Art. 5(2) P2B Regulation provides that the 'providers of online search engines shall set out the main parameters, which individually or collectively are most significant in determining ranking and the relative importance of those main parameters, by providing an easily and publicly available description, drafted in plain and intelligible language, on the online search engines of those providers.' Nevertheless, Art. 38 DSA only declares the requirements set out in Art. 27 DSA applicable on recommender systems in search engines (→ § 4 mn. 84 et seqq.). Thus, search engines also only have to provide information about recommender systems in their GTC. Nevertheless, the outcome of the two provisions may only vary in the wording, but not in practice. After all, according to Art. 14(1), the general terms and conditions must also be **'publicly available'** before the conclusion of a contract. Publicity is given, if the information can be retrieved without the business users having to register or log in beforehand.[35] Thus, both the requirements of the DSA and those of the P2B Regulation are fulfilled if the transparency requirements are included in the GTC of the search engine providers; *et vice versa*. 39

[32] Cf. Art. 38 DSA: 'In addition to the requirements set out in Art. 27, providers of very large online platforms and very large online search engines using recommender systems shall provide at least one option for each of their recommender systems that is not based on profiling in accordance with Art. 4(4) of Regulation (EU) 2016/679.'

[33] Cf. Köhler/Bornkamm/Feddersen/Alexander P2B Regulation Art. 5 mn. 14.

[34] Cf. in this regard Kreutz ZUM 2018, 162.

[35] Busch/Busch P2B Regulation Art. 5 mn. 49; cf. also rec. 26 P2B Regulation: Areas of websites where users have to log in or register should not be considered easily and publicly accessible in this respect.

40 Another central deviation appears with regard to the scope of application. The requirements of the DSA only apply to search engines that have an average monthly number of at least 45 million active users in the Union and that are designated as very large online search engines pursuant to Art. 33(4) DSA. In contrast, the P2B Regulation applies regardless of the monthly users.

b) Content of the transparency requirements

41 While the DSA merely declares the provisions on recommender systems to be applicable also to (very large) online search engines and additionally contains the requirement of an alternative without profiling under the GDPR (→ § 4 mn. 84 et seq.), the P2B Regulation provides for its own requirements for ranking in online search engines, the requirements of which **differ from** those for online intermediation services in at least **four essential aspects.**

aa) Reasons for the ranking

42 The first central difference between the **content of the transparency requirements with** regard to providers of online intermediation services and those of online search engines lies in the fact that in the case of the latter, according to the wording of Art. 5(2) P2B Regulation, information does not have to be provided on the reasons[36] for the relative weighting of the main parameters. The wording thus suggests that online search engines only have to indicate the relative weighting. This is treated by *Busch,* for example, as an editorial inaccuracy that has no effect on the content of the disclosure obligations.[37] However, the **clear wording of the provision** speaks against such an imprecision. It is true that the European Commission assumes in its guidelines for online search engines that the reasons for the relative weighting must be stated.[38] However, these guidelines are only to be seen as a **strong indication** for a certain interpretation; under no circumstances can these guidelines be used to interpret a law beyond the wording or – as in the present case – to supplement it.

bb) Duty to update

43 The second and central difference is that according to Art. 5(2) last sentence of the P2B Regulation, the information must be kept **'up-to-date'.** If there is a change in the relative weighting of the main parameters, the information must be updated.[39] A similar obligation is missing in the DSA. This could stem from the fact that in this case the transparency obligations are to be fulfilled in the GTC and these cannot be changed unilaterally without further ado after agreement. However, according to the opinion expressed here, it would still have been possible for the provider to undertake an obligation in the GTC to inform the user in the event of a change in the parameters.

---

[36] See Busch/Busch P2B Regulation Art. 5 mn. 32 et seqq.

[37] Busch/Busch P2B Regulation Art. 5 mn. 47.

[38] European Commission, Guidelines on Transparency, OJ 2020 C 424 mn. 22: 'Article 5(1) and (2) require providers to explain not only the main parameters but also the reasons for the relative weighting of these parameters compared to other parameters.'

[39] Busch/Busch P2B Regulation Art. 5 mn. 51; for an implicit corresponding obligation also for online intermediation services: Busch/Busch P2B Regulation Art. 5 mn. 38; European Commission, Guidelines on Transparency, OJ 2020 C 424 mn. 120.

cc) Consideration of the web design

The third deviation lies in the **specifications**. The P2B Regulation states that the providers of online search engines must also inform about the consideration of the design features of the website. The background to the provision is that search engines often prefer those websites that are characterised by a **high level of user-friendliness** or have a **responsive web design.**[40] 44

dd) Limits of the transparency obligation and guideline competence

Finally, with regard to online search engines – as with online platforms – the DSA does not contain any provisions on the **limits of transparency requirements** (Art. 5(6) P2B Regulation) and on possible **guidelines by the European Commission** (Art. 5(7) P2B Regulation). Here, reference can be made to the above statements (→ mn. 34). 45

4. Legal consequences of the violation of the transparency requirements

Before the possible priority application of the P2B Regulation or the DSA can be discussed, it is important to show what legal consequences the two legal acts prescribe in the event of a breach of the transparency requirements. 46

a) DSA

As is well known, the DSA relies on **a combination of self-regulation and the supervision by the Member State and the European Commission** to enforce breaches of the regulation. But there also exists a dispute resolution mechanism (→ § 5 mn. 49 et seqq.). 47

aa) Private enforcement

Private enforcement is strengthened by the claim for damages under Art. 54 DSA, which has been proposed by the European Parliament at a late stage of the legislation process. Users can claim for damages if intermediary services have violated user-related provisions of the DSA. Also in view of recital 121 sent. 2, this is an **imperfect liability standard,**[41] as it is to be applied 'in accordance with Union and national law' (Art. 54 DSA). In contrast to, for example, damages under the GDPR, the national requirements for fault, evidence, etc. must undoubtedly be applied in addition. In this respect, the European legislator decided not to model the private enforcement after the GDPR, but opted for a **legal fragmentation**. First of all, there is the anticipatory requirement to determine the applicable domestic law by means of conflict of laws. Finally, due to the national law that is then called upon to apply, there will always be situations that give rise to a claim for damages under the law of one country and not under the law of another. 48

bb) Public enforcement

The implementation of the DSA at national level has to be carried out by newly appointed **Member State authorities**, which are to be called **'Digital Services Coordinators'** (Art. 49 et seqq. DSA). The coordinator has to be an independent authority and be given investigative and enforcement powers by the member states (Art. 51 DSA), including the power to impose fines of up to 6 % of annual turnover (Art. 52(3) DSA). In addition, there is a **'European Board for Digital Services'** (Art. 61 et seqq. DSA), which advises the Commission and the Member States on the implementation of the DSA and 49

[40] Busch/Busch P2B Regulation Art. 5 mn. 69.
[41] Raue/Heesen NJW 2022, 3537 (3542).

contribute to its uniform application. The Commission has an important role in enforcing the obligations of very large online platforms and very large search engines (Art. 65 et seqq. DSA).

cc) Collective enforcement

50 The legal protection of the DSA can also be asserted **collectively** for consumers via the new **Directive on representative actions**[42] (Art. 90[43]) but there is also a **'representation option'** in Art. 86, which is already known in a similar form from the GDPR. Unlike Art. 80 GDPR, however, Art. 86 DSA is **not an opening clause**[44] and thus an **optional possibility for the Member States** to provide for a representation possibility in national law, but results autonomously from Art. 86 DSA. Like the possibility of representation under the GDPR, that of Art. 86 DSA will also be important outside of consumer transactions due to the Directive on representative actions.

dd) Possibility to sue under the Unfair Competition Act

51 For the GDPR there is an ongoing discussion whether violations of the Regulation can also be enforced by **competitors.**[45] This question has now been submitted (again) by the German Supreme Court (BGH).[46] The question can neither be answered with the wording, the systematic context nor the regulatory objectives of the GDPR. The same applies to the DSA, but with the central difference that the legal protection of the DSA is not 'without prejudice to any other administrative or judicial remedy', as under Art. 77 et seq. GDPR. The resulting legal fragmentation could speak **against a possibility of** legal action, if such a possibility is not necessarily due to the principle of effectiveness.

b) P2B Regulation

52 The P2B Regulation also **distinguishes** between **online intermediation services** and **online search engines in** terms of enforcement.

aa) Out-of-court dispute resolution for online mediation services

53 In the case of online intermediation services, there is a **multi-stage escalation process** (→ § 17 mn. 1 et seqq.).[47] The first measure of legal protection is dispute resolution within the framework of an internal complaint-handling system (Art. 11), which can generally be invoked in the event of alleged non-compliance by the platform with one of the obligations set out in the Regulation. The second option is mediation (Art. 2(12)) as an extrajudicial form of dispute resolution (Art. 12 and Art. 13).

---

[42] Directive (EU) 2020/1828, OJ L 409, 1.

[43] 'In Annex I to Directive (EU) 2020/1828, the following point is added: (68) Regulation (EU) 2022/2065 […]'.

[44] In other words, the optional possibility for member states to deviate from European regulations. See the comprehensive White Opening Clauses in the GDPR, especially p. 41 et seqq.

[45] See in particular BGH GRUR 2023, 264 mn. 12 et seq.; Ohly GRUR 2019, 868; Uebele GRUR 2019, 694, in each case with further references.

[46] BGH GRUR 2023, 264.

[47] Busch/Busch P2B Regulation Art. 11 mn. 4; see on this in particular Uitz Die EU-Platform-to-Business-VO p. 207 et seqq.

bb) Collective enforcement

Subsequently, the **possibility of judicial enforcement** is provided both against providers of online intermediation services and such of online search engines. In this context, Art. 14 P2B Regulation contains specific provisions for 'judicial proceedings by representative organisations or associations and by public bodies'. The provision contains rules on collective redress in its first paragraph: 'Organisations and associations that have a legitimate interest in representing business users or in representing corporate website users, as well as public bodies set up in Member States, shall have the right to take action before competent national courts in the Union, in accordance with the rules of the law of the Member State where the action is brought, to stop or prohibit any non-compliance by providers of online intermediation services or by providers of online search engines, with the relevant requirements laid down in this Regulation.' 54

cc) Enforcement of individual rights

Art. 14(9) P2B Regulation contains a provision on the enforcement of individual rights:[48] 'The right referred to in [Art. 14 I] shall be without prejudice to the rights of business users and corporate website users to start any action before competent national courts, in accordance with the rules of the law of the Member State where the action is brought, which is based on individual rights and aims to stop any non-compliance, by providers of online intermediation services or providers of online search engines, with the relevant requirements laid down in this Regulation.' 55

Finally, Art. 15 P2B Regulation contains a **general clause,** already known from many other legal acts, which imposes a general obligation on the Member States to **ensure adequate and effective enforcement** of the P2B Regulation by taking appropriate measures. 56

Art. 14 and 15 of the P2B Regulation raise three questions which cannot be clarified here: (1) Does individual legal protection exist only on the basis of Art. 14(9) P2B Regulation, or is such protection also possible under national contract law? (2) Does the P2B Regulation preclude competitors from taking legal action under the German Unfair Competition Act? (3) Do claims for damages also serve to 'prevent non-compliance [...]' within the meaning of Art. 14(9) P2B Regulation? 57

c) Differences between the legal acts

The central difference between the legal protection of the DSA and the P2B Regulation is obvious: While the DSA provides for extensive **administrative legal protection,** even with the establishment of a 'European Board for Digital Services', administrative legal protection is completely lacking in the P2B Regulation, at least at European level. Of course, the **Member States are free** to introduce administrative legal protection in accordance with Art. 15 of the P2B Regulation; however, they are not obliged to do so. 58

Furthermore, there are also **differences with regard to the private enforcement.** First of all, the mandatory establishment of an out-of-court dispute resolution mecha- 59

[48] Schneider/Krämer WRP 2020, 1128, mn. 65; LG München I BeckRS 2021, 10631: A right to bring an action also does not follow directly from Art. 14(3) and (4) (P2B Regulation), since § 8a UWG (German Act against Unfair Competition – Gesetz gegen den unlauteren Wettbewerb) is, according to its wording, a conclusive Member State regulation for infringements of the Regulation. The criticism here, however, is that Art. 14(9) is precisely not an opening clause, but the provision itself grants individual legal protection. In this respect, even if § 8a UWG is to be interpreted in the sense of the decision, the Regulation also takes precedence over Member State law. In conclusion, but on the effet utile, also Busch/Busch P2B Regulation Art. 5 mn. 77.

nism in the P2B Regulation should be mentioned; such a mechanism is missing in the DSA in the case of a violation of the provisions on recommender systems, since the DSA only obliges the providers to set out the rules of procedure of their internal complaint handling system in their GTC (Art. 14(1) DSA). Furthermore, depending on the interpretation of Art. 54 DSA and Art. 14(9) P2B Regulation, central differences may arise in the enforcement of individual rights. In particular, the possibility of competitors filing an action under unfair competition law on a violation of the transparency conditions, which is important in practice, does not seem to have been considered in either legal act. It could be argued that such a claim is affirmed under one legal act and denied under the other.

III. On the supplementary application of DSA and P2B Regulation

60 The scope of application of the P2B Regulation and the DSA overlaps with regard to both 'providers of online intermediation services' and 'providers of online search engines'. There are some key differences between the provisions of the P2B Regulation and the DSA with regard to transparency requirements and the legal consequences of violating them.

61 With regard to the relationship between the DSA and the P2B Regulation, it has been argued up to now that the more specific and detailed provisions of the P2B Regulation on ranking transparency are primarily applicable.[49] According to the view expressed here, however, when assessing the relationship in terms of transparency, not only the **transparency requirements** but also the consequences in the event of a **violation** must be taken into account. In the following, it will be argued that both the DSA and the P2B Regulation apply to ranking transparency.

1. No priority application of the DSA due to the lex posterior rule

62 In contrast to the proposal of the European Commission, which explicitly stated that the DSA is *lex generalis* and that many of the cited legal acts take precedence as *leges speciales*, the European legislator stipulated in Art. 2 that the DSA is 'without prejudice to other legal acts'. In fact, the later adoption of the DSA (publication in the Official Journal on 27.10.2022) compared to the P2B Regulation (publication in the Official Journal on 11.7.2019) could have resulted in the more recent act taking precedence over the older one.[50] *Lex posterior derogat legi priori.*[51] It is to be assumed that the legislator is well aware of its own laws and accordingly aligns more recent legal provisions with older legal provisions. However, it is decisive that the younger legislator, in case of doubt, wants to repeal all provisions opposing its new regulation.[52] The later law thereby repeals even more specific laws of a certain area of law if it is itself an intended **complete** and **final** regulation of an entire area of law[53] unless, of course, the legislature has ex-

[49] Busch/Busch P2B Regulation Art. 5 mn. 5; Hofmann/Raue/Grisse DSA Art. 27 mn. 39; see also Busch/Mak EuCML 2021, 109 (114).

[50] See Riesenhuber EurMethodenlehre-HdB/Riesenhuber mn. 30; see also Bydlinski Methodenlehre p. 572; Klang/Kerschner/Kehrer ABGB §§ 6, 7 mn. 30.

[51] Cf. on this rule of interpretation at European level: AG Stix-Hackl 03.05.2001 – C-145/99 – ECLI:EU:C:2001:240 mn. 49 – Commission v. Italy: 'common heritage of legal method'.

[52] Klang/Kerschner/Kehrer ABGB §§ 6, 7 mn. 30.

[53] See by way of example only RIS-Justiz RS0008900: In case of doubt, the later law repeals all, also the more specific laws of a certain field of law if it is itself a so-called codification, i.e. an intended complete and conclusive regulation of an entire field of law.

cluded this effect with a general clause.[54] Such an exclusion of the *lex posterior rule* is also present in Art. 2(4) DSA ('without prejudice'). The legislator obviously did not want to repeal any already existing (more specific) provisions with this legal act that would enter into force later. Thus, the DSA cannot claim precedence over the P2B Regulation on the basis of the *lex posterior rule.*

2. P2B Regulation is not a lex specialis in relation to the DSA

63 The DSA does not take precedence over the P2B Regulation. However, this applies *vice versa,* because the principle of speciality does not necessarily give precedence to the P2B Regulation. The principle of speciality, *lex specialis derogat legi generali,* intends to clarify the relationship between two regulations, one of which (special) contains all the constituent elements of the other (general) and at least one more.[55] If one legal act is 'without prejudice' to another, the ECJ has already assumed that one of the two legal acts prevails due to the principle of speciality.[56]

64 The question of whether a provision is 'special' within the meaning of this principle is regularly precisely the question to be clarified by **interpretation.**[57] Insofar as the legal consequences of the competing legal norms are compatible with each other, it depends on whether the legal consequences of the more specific norm for its area of application are, according to the regulatory intention of the law, only to supplement or modify the legal consequences of the more general norm or to take its place.[58] Thus, the principle of speciality regularly only describes the respective **result of interpretation.**[59]

65 Accordingly, it would have to be clarified whether the European legislator merely wants to **supplement** or **modify** the ranking provision of the DSA with that of the P2B Regulation or whether the provision in the P2B Regulation should completely **replace** the provisions of the DSA. The main argument against a speciality of the P2B Regulation is that this would completely **nullify the legal consequences** of the DSA. As explained above, both legal acts contain more or less unclear provisions on the collective or individual private enforcement, but only the DSA contains provisions for **legal protection under administrative law**. This legal protection of the DSA, similar to that of the GDPR, is extremely comprehensive. It concerns not only the possibility of imposing administrative fines of 6 % of annual turnover in the event of non-compliance, but also in particular the provisions on the interaction of national authorities and the establishment of a 'European Board for Digital Services'. Furthermore, a priority of the P2B Regulation would deprive the European Commission of its far-reaching enforcement rights with regard to ranking transparency obligations for very large online platforms and very large search engines due to the principle of speciality. Overall, the extensive enforcement provisions of the DSA speak against a priority of the P2B Regulation.

3. Consequences of the supplementary application of the P2B Regulation

66 According to the opinion expressed here, the P2B Regulation only provides for supplements to the DSA with regard to algorithm transparency. Consequently, both the transparency requirements of the DSA and those of the P2B Regulation must be com-

---

[54] Cf. RIS-Justiz RS0008900.

[55] Cf. Bydlinski Methodenlehre p. 465; Klang/Kerschner/Kehrer ABGB §§ 6, 7 mn. 27 et seqq.

[56] ECJ 3.7.2012 – C-128/11, ECLI:EU:C:2012:407 – GRUR 2012, 904 – UsedSoft mn. 56: It should further be recalled that Directive 2009/24, which specifically concerns the legal protection of computer programs, is lex specialis in relation to Directive 2001/29.

[57] Riesenhuber EurMethodenlehre-HdB/Riesenhuber mn. 31.

[58] Riesenhuber EurMethodenlehre-HdB/Riesenhuber mn. 31.

[59] Riesenhuber EurMethodenlehre-HdB/Riesenhuber mn. 31.

plied with. It should be noted in particular that only in the case of the P2B Regulation can the business user invoke the **limits of the transparency obligations** when deceiving or harming consumers through the manipulation of search results (Art. 5(6) P2B Regulation). In contrast, concerning online search engines, the P2B Regulation contains **more far-reaching obligations,** since these apply to all providers and the information must also **always be** kept **up to date.** However, the obligations under both legal acts are satisfied if information is provided in the general terms and conditions.

67 In the event of a breach of the transparency requirements, the legal consequences of the DSA and the P2B Regulation are opened if the breached provision can be found in **both legal acts.** If only one legal act applies, for example in the case of 'normal' search engines with a monthly number of users below 45 million, the provider is exposed to the consequences of this one legal act, in the example those of the P2B Regulation. If both legal acts are applicable, the supplier can decide whether a possible claim for damages is based on the violation of the DSA or the P2B Regulation.

68 Overall, it is important to note in legal protection that there is no system for **preventing contradictory decisions** either within legal acts or between legal acts. This problem is already known from other regulations, especially the GDPR, where the European Court of Justice recently ruled that the objective of creating a uniform level of data protection required the Member States to prevent contradictory decisions.[60] Similarly, the Member States should also be obliged, in particular with regard to the DSA, to create a uniform level of protection with regard to platforms and thus to prevent contradictory decisions on the basis of the DSA. Compared to other legal acts, however, no basis for preventing contradictory decisions is apparent.

D. Omnibus Directive

69

Art. 3(s) DSA	Art. 2(1)(m) UCP Directive
'recommender system' means a fully or partially automated system used by an online platform to suggest in its online interface specific information to recipients of the service or prioritise that information, including as a result of a search initiated by the recipient of the service or otherwise determining the relative order or prominence of information displayed;	'ranking' means the relative prominence given to products, as presented, organised or communicated by the trader, irrespective of the technological means used for such presentations, organization or communication;

70 The Omnibus Directive also introduced ranking transparency provisions in European consumer protection law, which are **based on the P2B Regulation.** However, since the P2B Regulation only applies to companies offering services on the platform and online intermediaries, and since appropriate transparency should also be ensured towards users (consumers), the Omnibus Directive introduces **similar transparency requirements towards consumers** in the Consumer Rights Directive[61] and the UCP Directive[62]. Accordingly, the UCP Directive now contains its **own definition** of ranking, which differs in part from that in the P2B Regulation. Accordingly, ranking is 'the relative prominence given to products, as presented, organised or communicated by the trader, irrespective of the technological means used for such presentations, organization or communication'. The Consumer Rights Directive uses the term ranking but does not

[60] ECJ 12.1.2023 – C-132/21, ECLI:EU:C:2023:2 = ZD 2023, 209 (with comment *Schwamberger*).
[61] Directive 2011/83/EU, OJ L 304, 64.
[62] Directive 2005/29/EC, OJ L 149, 21.

introduce its own definition. However, due to the joint adoption of the provisions with the Omnibus Directive, it can be assumed that under both legal acts the definition in the UCP Directive can be used.

According to Art. 2(4)(f), the DSA does **not affect** 'Union law on consumer protection'. This also includes the Omnibus Directive, the Consumer Rights Directive and the UCP Directive. In the following, it will be shown that the latter directives do not take precedence over the DSA, but that they provide supplementary provisions.[63] 71

I. Ranking in the UCP Directive

72

Art. 27(1) DSA	Art. 7(4a) UCP Directive
Providers of online platforms that use recommender systems shall set out in their terms and conditions, in plain and intelligible language, the main parameters used in their recommender systems, as well as any options for the recipients of the service to modify or influence those main parameters.	**When providing consumers with the possibility to search for products offered by different traders or by consumers on the basis of a query in the form of a keyword, phrase or other input, irrespective of where transactions are ultimately concluded, general information, made available in a specific section of the online interface that is directly and easily accessible from the page where the query results are presented, on the main parameters determining the ranking of products presented to the consumer as a result of the search query and the relative importance of those parameters, as opposed to other parameters, shall be regarded as material. This paragraph does not apply to providers of online search engines as defined in point (6) of Article 2 [P2B Regulation]**

In addition to the inclusion of the ranking definition in Art. 2, separate provisions on ranking were created. In the new Art. 7(4a) UCP Directive, the parameters already known from the P2B Regulation and the DSA are qualified as 'relevant information'. If a business offers consumers the possibility to search for goods or services of different providers, they must not be **withheld the** information according to which essential parameters the ranking of the offers in the results of the online search is determined and which weighting is given to these parameters in relation to other parameters. In addition, the new No. 11a of the Annex contains the prohibition of **surreptitious advertising** in search results. Accordingly, **paid advertising** or special payments to **influence the ranking** in search results must be **disclosed** to consumers. 73

The Directive applies regardless of where the conclusion of the legal transaction on the offered goods takes place. This transparency obligation includes not only **online marketplaces**, but also other **intermediation services** such as **comparison shopping engines,** whether or not they offer consumers the possibility to conclude a contract with the providers of the goods or services on their platform. It is disputed whether the search for goods and services of **different providers** must be made possible. For example, the German legislator assumes that online shops of businesses who only offer their own goods or services do not fall within the scope of application.[64] Whether the Omnibus Directive actually allows such a restriction is questionable as the wording opposes this *prima vista*. 74

In any case, operators of online search engines as defined in Art. 2(6) P2B Regulation are excluded from the scope of application of the provision. This is because Art. 5(2) 75

[63] See also Hofmann/Raue/Grisse DSA Art. 27 mn. 40 et seqq.

[64] BT-Drs. 19/27873, 36.

P2B Regulation already contains an obligation for operators of online search engines to inform the public about the essential parameters used to determine the ranking and their relative weighting.[65] Although **a duplication of transparency obligations is avoided**, the enforcement provisions of the UCP Directive – in particular the newly created Art. 11a UCP Directive – are not applicable when these obligations are broken. Consumers who have been harmed by unfair commercial practices have **access to adequate and effective remedies** under Art. 11a UCP Directive, including compensation for the **harm** suffered by the consumer and, where appropriate, **price reduction** or **termination of the contract**. In addition, sanctions are available under national law implementing Art. 13 UCP Directive, which obliges Member States 'either to impose fines through administrative procedures or to initiate legal proceedings for the imposition of fines, or both, the maximum amount of such fines being at least [sic!] 4 % of the trader's annual turnover in the Member State or Member States concerned.'

II. Ranking in the CRD

76

Art. 27(1) DSA	Art. 6a (1) CRD
Providers of online platforms that use recommender systems shall set out in their terms and conditions, in plain and intelligible language, the main parameters used in their recommender systems, as well as any options for the recipients of the service to modify or influence those main parameters.	**Before a consumer is bound by a distance contract, or any corresponding offer, on an online marketplace, the provider of the online marketplace shall, without prejudice to Directive 2005/29/EC, provide the consumer with the following information in a clear and comprehensible manner and in a way appropriate to the means of distance communication:** **(a) general information, made available in a specific section of the online interface that is directly and easily accessible from the page where the offers are presented, on the main parameters determining ranking, as defined in point (m) of Article 2(1) of Directive 2005/29/EC, of offers presented to the consumer as a result of the search query and the relative importance of those parameters as opposed to other parameters;**

77 The old CRD did not apply between platform and consumer, i.e. in the **user-sided relationship**, when the consumer did not conclude a contract with the platform or when the consumer does not pay a price for the use of the platform. The ranking is primarily carried out by the platforms; the supplier can only influence the ranking within the platform's ranking system. Thus, the European legislator decided to insert a new Art. 6a into the CRD, which additionally contains special obligations to inform for contracts concluded on online marketplaces, and also extended the scope of application to those cases in which the consumer provides personal data that is not necessary for the performance of the contract.

78 With the CRD, the European legislator attempts to include the provider of the online marketplace in this contractual relationship and to impose central information duties on him. However, these information duties cannot **have any effects on the user-sided relationship** between the consumer and the platform, when the user did not conclude a contract with the platform. If they concluded a contract, the breach of these obligation duties may lead to claims for damages against the platform, but cannot have any effect on the contract between the consumer and the trader, i.e. the user-supplier relationship.

[65] Rec. 21 Omnibus Directive.

The consequences of breaching the information obligations are again regulated in the CRD with a **general clause**: 'Member States shall ensure that adequate and effective means exist to ensure compliance with this Directive' (Art. 23 CRD). In addition, the Directive now contains strong administrative sanctions. According to Art. 24, the Member States must enact provisions on sanctions to be imposed in the event of violations of the Directive. According to a newly inserted paragraph, the Member States shall ensure that the penalties include the possibility 'either to impose fines through administrative procedures or to initiate legal proceedings for the imposition of fines, or both, the maximum amount of such fines being at least 4 % of the trader's annual turnover in the Member State or Member States concerned'. When read in conjunction with the DSA it is especially worthy to discuss whether sanctions of Art. 24 CRD can also be imposed on 'online marketplaces' when a contract has only been concluded with the trader.[66] It could be argued that such sanctions are mandatory due to the **principle of effectiveness**. In my view this would ultimately ignore the clear scope of the Directive. It only applies between traders and consumers and not between platforms and consumers. Consequently, the CRD is currently simply the **wrong place** to also regulate **sanctions against the platform**. 79

III. Interaction with the DSA

When the consumer did not conclude a contract with the platform, the scope of application of the DSA only **overlaps** with the UCP Directive, because in this case the CRD only sets out the contractual relationship between the trader and the consumer and not the 'user-sided relationship' between the platform and the consumer. In this respect, the newly introduced Art. 6a of the CRD can only have an effect on the contractual relationship and cannot have **any effect on the platform.** Thus, there is no overlap between the scope of application of Art. 27, 38 DSA and Art. 6a CRD, when a contract has not been concluded with the platform, but the requirements and legal consequences of the two legal acts exist side by side. 80

The situation is different with the UCP Directive and in situations where a contract is concluded between the consumer and the platform. The newly introduced provisions on ranking transparency in the UCP are also applicable to online intermediary services and overlap with Art. 27 DSA. However, it should first be noted that the transparency obligations of the UCP Directive fall short of those of the DSA in two respects. Firstly, the UCP Directive is decidedly **not applicable to search engines** and the corresponding legal protection, for example through the new Representative Actions Directive, is not available. Secondly, the transparency obligations also lag behind **those of the DSA in terms of content**. The UCP Directive does not contain any specifications of the transparency obligation corresponding to Art. 27(2) DSA. There is also no requirement to provide information on the 'reasons for the relative importance of those parameters'. Nor is it to be explained how consumers can 'modify or influence' the parameters. It cannot be assumed that the European legislator intended to exclude such central information obligations of the DSA through a speciality of the UCP Directive, in particular in the significant legal relationship between platforms and consumers. Therefore, it is more likely that the protection of the UCP Directive is additional to that of the DSA and thus 81

[66] Admittedly, in view of the implementation of Art. 24 CRD, especially in Austria and Germany, this should probably be the least of the problems regarding sanctions. Cf. Wendehorst Rechtsdurchsetzung im Verbraucherrecht – materiellrechtliche Aspekte, 21. ÖJT Vol. II/1, 20 et seq.

supplements the latter – like the P2B Regulation. The same applies to the CRD, when the platform and the consumer have entered into a contract.

E. GDPR

82 The DSA interacts with the requirements of the GDPR in **three ways.** On the one hand, as a **legal requirement,** the DSA can be the legal basis for the lawfulness of data processing (Art. 6(1)(c)). In addition, the DSA is the first European legal act to introduce **a separate provision on dark patterns.** However, this is only applicable if the provisions of the GDPR do not take effect, which is why the interaction of the GDPR and the DSA need to be explained. Finally, the DSA mentions the GDPR regarding its **ranking provisions.** In this context, it needs to be mentioned that those provisions are only additions to the GDPR, which do not lead to a GDPR violation, but to a DSA violation.

I. Data processing for compliance with a legal obligation

83 Under the GDPR, data processing is only lawful if it is based on a legal ground. These are listed in particular in Art. 6(1) GDPR. In addition to consent (Art. 6(1)(a)) and performance of a contract (Art. 6(1)(b)), on which numerous ECJ cases are pending,[67] processing in fulfilment of a legal obligation (Art. 6(1)(c)) or if it is necessary for the purposes of a legitimate interest (Art. 6(1)(f)) is particularly relevant.

84 Many of the obligations of the DSA for online intermediary services and online search engines can only be fulfilled if personal data is also processed for this purpose. This applies in particular to the obligations in the following provisions:[68]

- Orders to act against illegal content content (Art. 9 DSA)
- Orders to provide information (Art. 10 DSA)
- Notice and action mechanisms (Art. 16–18 DSA)
- Notification of suspicions of criminal offences (Art. 18 DSA)
- Internal complaint-handling system (Art. 20, 30 DSA)
- Out-of-court dispute settlement (Art. 21, 30 DSA)
- Trusted Flaggers (Art. 22 DSA)
- Measures and protection against misuse (Art. 23 DSA)
- Recommender system transparency (Art. 27 DSA)
- Traceability of traders (Art. 30 DSA)
- Crisis response mechanism (Art. 36 DSA)
- Additional online advertising transparency (Art. 39 DSA)
- Data access and scrutiny (Art. 40 DSA)

85 However, not every legal obligation to process personal data automatically leads to the lawfulness of the data processing. Rather, Art. 6(3) GDPR specifies the requirements and possibilities of the legal bases according to Art. 6(1)(c) and (e), in particular also for **orders** under **EU law** for data processing. The above-mentioned provisions must therefore also meet these requirements.

86 According to Art. 6(3) sent. 2 GDPR, the **purpose of the processing** must be determined initially in the legal basis or the purpose shall be 'necessary for the performance

[67] See the overview by Leibold ZD 2022, 18.

[68] This list corresponds to the list published by Veil on his Twitter channel: Veil, 14.11.2022, available at: <https://twitter.com/winfriedveil/status/1592214207013224448>, last accessed: 27.08.2024.

of a task'. The purpose does not have to be explicitly specified but can result from the context of the respective task.[69] In addition, the provision stipulates that the legal basis according to Art. 6(1)(c) may in principle also contain **further provisions** (Art. 6(3) sent. 3).[70] Finally, it is stated that the Union law authorising data processing must pursue a **public interest** and be proportionate to the legitimate purpose pursued. However, Art. 6(3) sent. 4 of the GDPR only has declaratory effect insofar as the principle of proportionality already results from other standards, in particular Art. 8 in conjunction with Art. 52 of the CFR.[71]

II. Dark patterns

One of the central novelties in the DSA is the is the provision to **combat** so-called **dark patterns.**[72] These practices intend or actually achieve to significantly **distort** or **impair** the ability of users to make **autonomous** and **informed choices** or **decisions.**[73] Such practices may be used to induce users to engage in undesirable behavior or make unintended choices that have negative consequences for them.[74] There is no 'one' dark pattern, but many different forms, which can be categorised as 'pressure', 'operational coercion', 'obstacles' and 'misleading'.[75] 87

A typical example of the first category ('pressure') is so-called *nagging*, i.e. the **repeated** request to perform a certain action, such as **accepting** the terms and conditions or **giving consent.** This also includes the display of a scarce number of available goods (*scarcity*), or that goods are only displayed as available for a certain time in the context of a countdown.[76] 88

Operational coercion includes typical **tying scenarios** in which certain services are only possible if a subscription or customer account is concluded, or if the (further) use of a service requires acceptance of the changed data protection settings or consent to data processing at all.[77] 89

Dark patterns can also occur in the form of **obstacles.** For example, in the context of *preselection,* choices have already been made, e.g. a tick has already been set. This also includes cases in which the various options have longer click paths and one option is preferred due to the natural click possibility (so-called *click fatigue*).[78] 90

Furthermore, dark patterns can also be used to make **surreptitious changes.** This is the case, for example, when additional costs are only displayed in the last step of an order, additional objects are added to the shopping basket, or services are automatically subscribed to.[79] 91

---

[69] Cf. Paal/Pauly/Frenzel DSGVO Art. 6 mn. 41.

[70] See Paal/Pauly/Frenzel DSGVO Art. 6 mn. 42 et seq.

[71] Cf. Paal/Pauly/Frenzel DSGVO Art. 6 mn. 45.

[72] On these, see in particular EDPB, Guidelines 3/2022 on Dark patterns, 2022, available at: <https://www.edpb.europa.eu/our-work-tools/our-documents/guidelines/guidelines-032022-deceptive-design-patterns-social-media_en> last accessed: 27.08.2024; Kühling/Sauerborn CR 2022, 226; Konsumentverket, Barriers to a well-functioning digital market, 2021, available at: <https://www.medvetenkonsumtion.se/wp-content/uploads/2021/05/Konsumentverket-underlagsrapport-barriers-digital-market.pdf> last accessed: 27.08.2024; Martini/Drews/Seeliger/Weinzierl ZfDR 2021, 47; from a data protection perspective: Loy/Baumgartner ZD 2021, 404; Möller VuR 2022, 449; Denga ZfDR 2022, 229.

[73] Cf. rec. 67 DSA.

[74] Cf. rec. 67 DSA.

[75] Martini/Drews/Seeliger/Weinzierl ZfDR 2021, 47 (52).

[76] Martini/Drews/Seeliger/Weinzierl ZfDR 2021, 47 (52).

[77] Martini/Drews/Seeliger/Weinzierl ZfDR 2021, 47 (52).

[78] Martini/Drews/Seeliger/Weinzierl ZfDR 2021, 47 (52).

[79] Martini/Drews/Seeliger/Weinzierl ZfDR 2021, 47 (52).

92 Finally, dark patterns often lead to **misdirection**. For example, when so-called *trick questions* are asked in which **confusing wording** is used, the design distracts from the content through conspicuous graphic elements (*misdirection*) or the click on a button leads to different results than usually expected. This also includes so-called *disguised ads*, i.e. advertising disguised as content or control elements.[80]

93 Art. 25 DSA intends to counter all dark patterns. Accordingly, online platform providers 'shall not design, organise or operate their online interfaces in a way that deceives or manipulates the recipients of their service or in a way that otherwise materially distorts or impairs the ability of the recipients of their service to make free and informed decisions."'.[81] In doing so, the European Commission may issue guidelines, in particular with regard to '(a) giving more prominence to certain choices when asking the recipient of the service for a decision; (b) repeatedly requesting that the recipient of the service make a choice where that choice has already been made, especially by presenting pop-ups that interfere with the user experience; (c) making the procedure for terminating a service more difficult than subscribing to it.' However, according to Art. 25(2) DSA, the 'dark patterns prohibition' in the DSA does not apply to practices covered by the GDPR. In the case of dark patterns, the DSA not only leaves the GDPR 'untouched', but is not applicable at all if the provisions of the GDPR apply. In the GDPR, dark patterns are opposed in particular by the provisions on the effectiveness and withdrawal of consent, as well as the general principles for the processing of personal data.[82] These will be briefly discussed below in order to show the interplay between the DSA and the GDPR in this respect as well.

1. Invalidity of consent

94 In particular, consent to the processing of personal data is only valid if it is given voluntarily and in an **informed manner.** With regard to dark patterns, **involuntariness** or a **lack of informed consent** could stem from the fact that the data subjects are **deceived** into believing that they have to give their consent to use a service, although this is **not actually necessary** and thus **involuntary consent** is given. In this respect, the ECJ also stated in **Orange Romania,**[83] that 'to ensure that the data subject enjoys genuine freedom of choice, the contractual terms must not mislead him or her as to the possibility of concluding the contract even if he or she refuses to consent to the processing of his or her data. Without information of that kind, the data subject's consent to the processing of his or her personal data cannot be regarded as having been given **freely** or, moreover, as having been given in an **informed manner**."'[84] Also, the withdrawal of consent could be made more difficult, for example, by *click fatigue*, which can also lead to the invalidity of consent.[85]

95 In addition, the requirement of **active consent** to data processing (Art. 4(11) GDPR, Recital 32 GDPR)[86] serves to prevent dark patterns in the form of *preselections*.[87] The controller is thereby deprived of the possibility to induce the data subject to consent through the technical design, namely by preselecting an option or the pre-ticked box.

[80] Martini/Drews/Seeliger/Weinzierl ZfDR 2021, 47 (52).
[81] See crit. on the EP proposal: Kühling/Sauerborn CR 2022, 226 (233).
[82] Kühling/Sauerborn CR 2022, 226; Loy/Baumgartner ZD 2021, 404; Möller VuR 2022, 449.
[83] ECJ 11.11.2020 – C-61/19, ECLI:EU:C:2020:901 = ZD 2021, 89 – Orange România.
[84] ECJ 11.11.2020 – C-61/19, ECLI:EU:C:2020:901 = ZD 2021, 89 – Orange România mn. 42, 51.
[85] See rec. 42 of the GDPR.
[86] See in this respect ECJ 1.10.2019 – C-673/17, ECLI:EU:C:2019:801 = MMR 2019, 732 (Moos/Rothkegel) – Planet49 mn. 55 et seqq.
[87] Cf. Kühling/Sauerborn CR 2022, 229 et seq.

Finally, dark patterns in the form of **operational coercion** are prevented by the **tying ban.**[88] As is well known, according to Art. 7(4) GDPR, 'when assessing whether consent is freely given, utmost account shall be taken of whether, inter alia, the performance of a contract, including the provision of a service, is conditional on consent to the processing of personal data that is not necessary for the performance of that contract.' The tying ban thus aims to prevent so-called 'take-it-or-leave-it' scenarios, in which the data subject is denied a service if consent is not given under data protection law. The scope of the tying ban is still **highly controversial.**[89] According to the Austrian Supreme Court, it does not prevent all tying in any case, but in the case of such tying, involuntary consent is to be assumed.[90] 96

2. Principles of data processing (Art. 5 GDPR)

However, the GDPR does not only specifically oppose dark patterns with the requirements for the effectiveness of consent, but also by means of the **general principles of data processing** laid down in Art. 5.[91] The principle of transparency (Art. 5(1)(a) alt. 3 GDPR) is addressed by the need to be informed when giving consent and framework of Art. 12 et seqq. GDPR. Only those who are aware of data processing can subsequently assert the **rights of data subjects** under the GDPR. The controller must provide the data subject with all information and notifications in a precise, comprehensible and easily accessible form in clear and simple language. More stringent requirements apply if the information is specifically addressed to children. The principle of transparency thus counteracts those dark patterns that prevent access to relevant information within the meaning of Art. 12 et seqq. GDPR (*hidden information*).[92] The same is likely to apply to obfuscating presentations and ambiguous information, changes of language or unnecessary and complex division of the information into several levels, as well as to misleading information in general.[93] 97

3. Data protection by design (Art. 25 GDPR)

Finally, dark patterns are also counteracted by the requirement of 'data protection by design' as set out in Art. 25 GDPR. This refers to the obligation to design products in such a way that they already take data protection concerns into account during their development, considering the associated effort and other disadvantages. Art. 25 GDPR also covers the design of the **application interfaces,** as it represents the **top level of the technical architecture** that guides the multi-layered process of data processing.[94] 98

However, this obligation requires contours and in this context the essential use case, namely *preselection*, is already sufficiently covered by the consent requirements. The same applies to very intensive *nagging patterns*, in which data subjects are required to give their consent to data processing at very short intervals.[95] However, further delineation will be necessary. The European Data Protection Board (EDPB) has already pub- 99

[88] Cf. Kühling/Sauerborn CR 2022, 226 (229).
[89] See in particular Schwamberger GPR 2019, 57; Schwamberger ecolex 2021, 795, both with further references.
[90] OGH GPR 2019, 57 (Schwamberger).
[91] Kühling/Sauerborn CR 2022, 226 (232 et seqq.).
[92] EDPB, Guidelines 3/2022, 19 et seqq.; Kühling/Sauerborn CR 2022, 226 (232).
[93] EDPB, Guidelines 3/2022, 24 et seqq., 34, 40; Kühling/Sauerborn CR 2022, 226 (232).
[94] Cf. Martini/Drews/Seeliger/Weinzierl ZfDR 2021, 47 (57).
[95] Cf. Martini/Drews/Seeliger/Weinzierl ZfDR 2021, 47 (58).

lished guidelines[96], with which Art. 25 GDPR becomes a powerful weapon to prevent dark patterns from a data protection perspective.

III. Profiling requirements

100 In addition to the provision on dark patterns in Art. 25, the DSA also refers to the GDPR in Art. 26, 28 and 38 regarding profiling. According to Art. 26(2), providers of online platforms may not display advertising to users that relies on profiling using special categories of personal data as defined in the GDPR. If the provider has sufficient certainty that the user in question is a **minor**, it may not display any advertising at all that is based on profiling using the user's personal data (Art. 28(2) DSA). Finally, the DSA sets forth in Art. 38 that providers of very large online platforms and very large online search engines that use recommender systems must provide at least one option for each of their recommender systems that is not based on profiling under the GDPR (→ § 4 mn. 84 et seqq.).

101 The Digital Services Act contains **two data processing prohibitions**: One for **minors in general** and one using **special categories of personal data**. Although processing is also generally prohibited under the GDPR and is only lawful if a permissive circumstance exists, consent is often used by data controllers as a panacea for any data processing and is sometimes also used for the highly problematic third-country transfer. In fact, **consent** can be used to allow almost **any data processing,** as long as it meets the strict requirements of the GDPR. However, it seems surprising, especially from a consumer law perspective, that the GDPR does **not set out any 'mandatory data protection law',**[97] i.e. certain facts and scenarios that cannot be justified by consent. Ultimately, it would also be possible for consumers to legitimise all actions and obligations contractually without any further ado, if this were not prevented by mandatory consumer protection law.

102 With Art. 26(3) and 28(2) DSA, **first parts of a 'mandatory data protection law'** appear; the processing activities ordered therein cannot be permitted by means of consent. However, violations of the provisions do not lead to a data protection offence and to the sanction and legal protection mechanisms of the GDPR. Rather, these cases are a violation of the DSA, which are an **addition and not an amendment to the GDPR**. The same applies to the obligation to offer an **alternative without profiling** under Art. 38 DSA for providers of very large online platforms and very large online search engines.

103 In this context, the GDPR could still be significant for the **interpretation of the term 'minor'** in Art. 28 DSA. Although the DSA wants to introduce a higher level of protection for 'minors' with this provision, nevertheless it lacks a definition or an age limit. This differs from the GDPR, which sets an age limit of 16 years and an opening clause for the Member States that can provide for a lower age limit up to the age of 13, with the provisions in Art. 8(2) GDPR.

104 The reference in Art. 28(2) DSA cannot also be used to refer to the age limit of the GDPR, but is limited to the profiling concept of the GDPR. Rather, the **interpretation** of the term minor must be made **according to the DSA,** whereby the guidelines of the European Commission (Art. 28(4) DSA), will (hopefully) also provide guidance. These guidelines are supposed to support the providers of online platforms in the application according to Art. 28(1) anyway.

---

[96] EDPB, Guidelines 3/2022.

[97] See on the criticism of consent in particular Engeler NJW 2022, 3398.

IV. Result

The DSA interacts with the provisions of the GDPR in **three ways.** On the one hand, the DSA as a legal requirement for data processing can lead to the **lawfulness of data processing** (Art. 6(1)(c) GDPR). However, the obligations set out in the DSA must be measured against the requirements of Art. 6(3) GDPR. In addition, the provisions on dark patterns in Art. 25 DSA are **only applicable** when the relevant provisions of the **GDPR no longer apply**. The GDPR tackles dark patterns in particular with the invalidity of consent as well as the principles of data processing and possibly also Art. 25 GDPR. In this respect, Art. 25 DSA is particularly important in the case of dark patterns independent from data processing, or if the data processing is not based on consent. Finally, Art. 26, Art. 28 and Art. 38 DSA **supplement** the **provisions of the GDPR** on profiling. Violations of these provisions are pure violations of the DSA and can therefore only be punished according to its sanctions and only the legal protection of the DSA can be claimed. This could be of particular importance with regard to legal actions based on national laws on unfair competition. 105

F. DSM Directive

The DSA and the DSM Directive overlap in particular with regard to liability privileges.[98] In the DSA, the restrictions on access, caching and hosting known from the E-Commerce Directive (Art. 4 et seqq. DSA) were adopted almost identically. However, these overlap with Art. 17 DSM Directive, which, due to the media discussion, became known primarily under the heading of **'upload filters'**. In the following, the **overlap in the scopes of application** and the **different conception** of the limitations of liability will first be explained and then it will be shown that Art. 17 DSM Directive must largely be classified as *lex specialis* to Art. 4 et seqq. DSA, but in addition, the DSA supplements the copyright liability regime in certain aspects.[99] 106

I. Scope of application

The European legislator adheres to the liability privileges of Art. 12–14 of the E-Commerce-Directive. Accordingly, the DSA contains privileges for mediating access to unlawful content (Art. 4: Access, → § 3 mn. 99 et seqq.), for short-term intermediate storage (Art. 5: Caching, → § 3 mn. 118 et seqq.) as well as for the storage of information provided by a recipient (Art. 6: Hosting, → § 3 mn. 126 et seqq.). However, the central difference to the directive is that these provisions – corresponding to the nature of a regulation – **no longer have to be implemented in national law**, but apply directly. The limitations of liability extend to any content that violates Union law or member state law; thus, it also covers copyright infringements in particular.[100] 107

[98] See also the comments by Raue ZUM 2023, 160 on the interaction of the two legal acts and the interplay of the DSA and Urheberrechts-Diensteanbieter-Gesetz (Act on the Copyright Liability of Online Content Sharing Service Providers – UrhDaG).

[99] See on this already Janal GRUR 2022, 211; Quintas/Schwemer European Journal of Risk Regulation 2022, 1; Raue/Hofmann/Hofmann Art. 2 mn. 57 et seq.; Peukert/Husovec/Kretschmer/Mezei/Quintais IIC 2022, 358; Raue ZUM 2023, 160.

[100] Cf. Janal GRUR 2022, 211 (212).

108 The focus of the following will be on the **hosting provider** (Art. 6 DSA).[101] According to the current wording[102] of the DSA, this provision could cover online search engines.[103] Not only the definition in Art. 3(j) DSA, but also the partial storage of content in connection with the forwarding to the content of third parties support this assumption.[104]

109 In contrast, Art. 17 DSM Directive applies to 'online content-sharing service providers' whose main purpose it is to store and provide public access to a large amount of copyright protected works or other subject matter uploaded by its users. It is also required that the provider organises and promotes this content for the purpose of making a profit. Crucial for the applicability of Art. 17 of the DSM Directive is the **main purpose of the activity**. Clear cases of application of the provision are video platforms such as *YouTube*.[105] Beyond that, however, the applicability of the provision is doubtful, especially with regard to **social networks.**[106] The main purpose of social networks is in particular to allow users to **present themselves** and **communicate** with each other and not to upload and forward **large amounts of copyright-protected material.**[107] It is conceivable, that the social networks, as they currently do in data protection law, for the applicability of Art. 6(1)(b) GDPR, try to define their main purpose via the general terms and conditions.[108] This could only be countered by an objective definition of the main purpose.[109] Furthermore, it is questionable whether 'live streaming' is also covered by the provision; ultimately, the videos in this case are only 'temporarily stored'.[110]

---

101 Janal GRUR 2022, 211 (215).

102 See Janal GRUR 2022, 211 (215) for criticism of the Commission's proposal in this regard.

103 Cf. Gerdemann/Spindler GRUR 2023, 3 (5).

104 Cf. Gerdemann/Spindler GRUR 2023, 3 (5).

105 Janal GRUR 2022, 211 (212).

106 Janal GRUR 2022, 211 (212).

107 Cf. Janal GRUR 2022, 211 (212); Leistner, European Copyright Licensing and Infringement Liability Under Art. 17 DSM-Directive, 2020, available at: <https://papers.ssrn.com/sol3/papers.cfm?abstract_id=3572040> last accessed: 28.08.2024, p. 19 et seqq.

108 See the submission of the OGH ZD 2021, 627.

109 On data protection law: EDPB, Guidelines 2/2019, mn. 22 et seqq.

110 See Leistner, European Copyright Licensing and Infringement Liability Under Art. 17 DSM-Directive, 2020, available at: <https://papers.ssrn.com/sol3/papers.cfm?abstract_id=3572040> last accessed: 28.08.2024, mn. 72.

II. Liability and privilege under the DSA and DSM Directive

110

Art. 6 DSA	Art. 17 DSM-RL
1. Where an information society service is provided that consists of the storage of information provided by a recipient of the service, the service provider shall not be liable for the information stored at the request of a recipient of the service, on condition that the provider: (a) does not have actual knowledge of illegal activity or illegal content and, as regards claims for damages, is not aware of facts or circumstances from which the illegal activity or illegal content is apparent; or (b) upon obtaining such knowledge or awareness, acts expeditiously to remove or to disable access to the illegal content.	**1. Member States shall provide that an online content-sharing service provider performs an act of communication to the public or an act of making available to the public for the purposes of this Directive when it gives the public access to copyright-protected works or other protected subject matter uploaded by its users. An online content-sharing service provider shall therefore obtain an authorisation from the rightholders [...] for instance by concluding a licensing agreement[...]. 4. If no authorisation is granted, online content-sharing service providers shall be liable for unauthorised acts of communication to the public [...] unless the service providers demonstrate that they have: (a) made best efforts to obtain an authorisation, and (b) made, in accordance with high industry standards of professional diligence, best efforts to ensure the unavailability of specific works and other subject matter for which the rightholders have provided the service providers with the relevant and necessary information; [...]**

111 In order to be able to invoke the liability privilege of Art. 6(1) DSA, a host provider must take **immediate** action as soon as it becomes **aware of the illegality** of content stored for its users or becomes aware of circumstances from which the illegality becomes obvious. In practice, this results in the obligation to **'notice and take down'**, i.e. to **block** infringing content upon notification of the rights holder. Furthermore, the DSA contains a 'Good-Samaritan-Rule', which clarifies the effects of pro-active investigations and filtering (Art. 7 DSA, → § 3 mn. 77 et seq) and stands in an ambivalent relationship with Art. 8, which provides that operators of intermediary services may not be subjected to a general obligation to monitor the information they transmit or store, nor to actively seek facts or circumstances indicating illegal activity.[111] Taking the previous case law of the ECJ into account, the general liability privilege for hosting providers does not apply if an intermediary service does not limit itself to the **neutral provision of its service** through purely technical and automatic processing of the data entered, but takes on an active role and gaining knowledge or control over this data.[112] For the determination of the 'active role', the current explanations in recital 20 of the DSA can be used. Accordingly, a **deliberate cooperation** between the intermediary service and the users for the purpose of **committing illegal acts** – and thus precisely not a neutral provision of services – cannot already be assumed if the provider provides encryption or other systems to prevent the identification of the users. Furthermore, the liability privilege should not apply if the provider offers its service **primarily for the purpose of facilitating illegal activities**. The mere fact that a service offers encrypted transmissions or another system that

[111] Denga, in Ruffert p. 14 et seq.
[112] ECJ 22.6.2021 – C-682, 683/18, ECLI:EU:C:2021:503 mn. 107 = GRUR 2021, 1054 – YouTube and Cyando.

makes it impossible to identify the user is not in itself considered to facilitate unlawful activities.[113]

112 Unlike Art. 6 DSA, Art. 17 DSM Directive does not **provide for a liability privilege** for the service provider, but sets out under which conditions the service provider must take responsibility for an act of communication to the public or an act of making available to the public for sharing online content (Art. 17(1) sent. 1 DSM Directive). This is a major conceptual difference between the two legal acts. Service providers who wish to avoid liability must obtain the authorisation of the right holders, for example by **concluding a licence agreement**, in order to reproduce works or other subject matter publicly or to make them publicly available (Art. 17(1) sent. 2 DSM Directive). If the authorisation is not granted, the service provider is not liable under Art. 17(4) if it has made **best efforts** to obtain permission and has immediately terminated the communication to the public of a work uploaded by users as soon as the rightholder requested so and gave a duly justified indication that the work was being communicated to the public without permission.

113 The interaction of Art. 6 DSA and Art. 17 DSM Directive is characterised by **numerous uncertainties** in the interpretation of the provisions. These uncertainties start with the scope of application, which may also overlap regarding social network providers. However, the younger legal act (DSA) leaves the older one (DSM Directive) **'unaffected'** in accordance with the general competition provision in Art. 2(4)(b) DSA. Due to the more specific scope of application of Art. 17 of the DSM Directive, it was previously assumed – as far as can be seen – that the copyright provisions were **partially special.**[114] In view of the more specific scope of application of the DSM Directive and the incompatibility of the two liability privileges, this is also to be agreed with. As far as copyrights are concerned, the exemption from liability of service providers when sharing online content for infringements by their users is therefore determined by the DSM Directive. This speciality is also explicitly stated in Art. 17(3) DSM-Directive: 'When an online content-sharing service provider performs an act of communication to the public or an act of making available to the public under the conditions laid down in this Directive, the limitation of liability established in Art. 14(1) of Directive 2000/31/EC [i.e. Art. 6 DSA] shall not apply to the situations covered by this Article.'

III. Prevention of future violations

114 According to the DSM Directive, a service provider does not only commit **its own act of communication** to the public or an act of making available to the public if the communication to the public of (potentially) infringing content is not **immediately terminated,** but also if it has made every effort, in accordance with high industry standards of professional diligence, to ensure that the future uploading of that work or other subject matter is prevented (Art. 17(4)(c)). For this prevention of future uploads, the **controversial upload filters** are necessary, at least for larger providers.

115 In contrast, the DSA explicitly provides for a **prohibition of general monitoring obligations** (→ § 3 mn. 86 et seqq.). However, this probably only refers to **follow-up checks** after an infringement,[115] because recital 30 in its final version explicitly refers to the relevant case law of the ECJ and thus in particular to its *Glawischnig* decision from

---

[113] Rec. 20 DSA.

[114] Janal GRUR 2022, 211; Quintas/Schwemer European Journal of Risk Regulation 2022, 1; Raue ZUM 2023, 164 et seqq.

[115] Cf. Gerdemann/Spindler GRUR 2023, 6.

2019.[116] Accordingly, it is reasonable to expect service providers to prevent the storage of corresponding content for the future, even if it is uploaded by other users or the content is merely **'similar in meaning'**, provided that ' automated search tools and technologies' are available.[117] It could be concluded that there is an obligation to use upload filters to prevent further violations of the same personality rights under the DSA.[118] However, the European legislator – probably also aware of the public controversy in the context of the legislative procedure for Art. 17 DSM Directive – has **refrained from** further specifying the technical requirements or differentiating between content with the same meaning and content with different meanings.[119]

It would have been desirable if the European legislator had also taken a **clear position** on a possible **'upload filter'** under the DSA. However, even in its current form, the existing regulation is clearly incompatible with the DSM Directive.[120] Indeed, it is not possible for the platform to comply with the requirements of one provision and the other at the same time; rather, they are designed as alternatives. In particular, it is not possible for a licensing option similar to the DSM Directive to be introduced under the DSA in the case of infringements.[121] Due to the incompatibility and the more specific scope of application of the DSM Directive, it must be assumed that the more specific DSM Directive also takes precedence over the DSA with regard to the prevention of future infringements. 116

IV. Reporting and redress system

117

Art. 16 DSA	Art. 17 DSM Directive
1. Providers of hosting services shall put mechanisms in place to allow any individual or entity to notify them of the presence on their service of specific items of information that the individual or entity considers to be illegal content. Those mechanisms shall be easy to access and user-friendly, and shall allow for the submission of notices exclusively by electronic means. 2. The mechanisms referred to in paragraph 1 shall be such as to facilitate the submission of sufficiently precise and adequately substantiated notices. To that end, the providers of hosting services shall take the necessary measures to enable and to facilitate the submission of notices containing all of the following elements:[...] 3. Notices referred to in this Article shall be considered to give rise to actual knowledge or awareness for the purposes of Article 6 in respect of the specific item of information concerned where they allow a diligent provider of hosting services to identify the illegality of the relevant activity or information without a detailed legal examination. [...]	**1. Member States shall provide that an online content-sharing service provider performs an act of communication to the public or an act of making available to the public for the purposes of this Directive when it gives the public access to copyright-protected works or other protected subject matter uploaded by its users. An online content-sharing service provider shall therefore obtain an authorisation from the rightholders [...] for instance by concluding a licensing agreement, [...]. 4. If no authorisation is granted, online content-sharing service providers shall be liable for unauthorised acts of communication to the public [...], unless the service providers demonstrate that they have: [...] (c) acted expeditiously, upon receiving a sufficiently substantiated notice from the rightholders, to disable access to, or to remove from their websites, the notified works or other subject matter, and made best efforts to prevent their future uploads in accordance with point (b).**

116 ECJ 3.10.2019 – C-18/18, ECLI:EU:C:2019:821 mn. 41 et seqq. – *Glawischnig.*
117 ECJ 3.10.2019 – C-18/18, ECLI:EU:C:2019:821 mn. 46 – *Glawischnig.*
118 Janal GRUR 2022, 216.
119 Cf. Janal GRUR 2022, 217; Gerdemann/Spindler GRUR 2023, 6.
120 Janal GRUR 2022, 217.
121 Janal GRUR 2022, 217.

118 In order to make use of the liability privilege in Art. 17 DSM Directive, the service provider must have **immediately** complied with a **'sufficiently substantiated notice'** by the right holder. However, the Directive does not contain any requirements for the notification and remedy procedure or their design.[122] It is unclear when the criterion 'receiving a sufficiently substantiated notice' is fulfilled, since service providers can 'receive' such a notice by phone, post, email or other means.

119 In contrast, Art. 16 DSA (→ § 5 mn. 18 et seqq.) obliges hosting service providers n to **establish procedures** for persons or entities to notify them of the presence on their services of individual items of information that the person or entity concerned considers to be unlawful content (Art. 16(1)). Also, they have to **facilitate** the submission of sufficiently accurate and appropriately reasoned **notifications** (Art. 16(2)). In addition, the hosting service provider must send a **confirmation of receipt** to the person making the notification (Art. 16(4) DSA) and notify that person without delay of its **decision** and of the **redress available** against that decision (Art. 16(5)). Finally, Art. 16(6) provides for the **modalities for processing** the notification: This must be done in a timely, diligent, non-arbitrary and objective manner.

120 The DSA clearly provides for **more detailed requirements for the reporting and redress system**, which nevertheless fall short of those of Art. 17(4)(c) DSM Directive in a crucial aspect: While the processing of reports under Art. 16(6) DSA only requires that reports be dealt with **'in a timely manner'**, the DSM Directive requires that reports be dealt with **'without undue delay'.**[123] In this respect, the legal acts not only provide for different, but also incompatible provisions on notifications. However, the DSM Directive does not take precedence due to its stricter regulatory content, but due to its more specific scope of application; the DSM Directive only applies to copyright infringements and not – like the DSA – to all infringements.[124] This speciality does **not completely supersede** Art. 16 DSA, but only concerns the modalities of processing the complaint and also in this case merely the time in which the platform must take action. Furthermore, the requirements of Art. 16 DSA remain in place and Art. 17(4)(c) DSM Directive does not conflict with them.[125] The lack of a notification and redress procedure does not lead to a violation of Art. 17(4)(c) DSA and thus to a communication to the public by the platform, but to a **violation of the DSA**. However, if such a procedure has been set up, notifications of potential copyright infringements can also be made via this procedure. It can be assumed that the notification of a potential infringement also means that the service provider has 'received' the notice within the meaning of Art. 17(4)(c) DSA – if the other requirements are met.[126]

[122] Raue ZUM 2023, 165 et seq.
[123] Raue ZUM 2023, 160 (166).
[124] Cf. however Raue ZUM 2023, 160 (163).
[125] Raue ZUM 2023, 160 (166).
[126] Cf. Raue/Hofmann/Hofmann Art. 2 mn. 57 et seq.; Peukert/Husovec/Kretschmer/Mezei/Quintais IIC 2022, 358 (363).

V. Internal complaint-handling system

Art. 20 DSA	Art. 17 DSM Directive
1. Providers of online platforms shall provide recipients of the service, including individuals or entities that have submitted a notice, for a period of at least six months following the decision referred to in this paragraph […]. **4. Providers of online platforms shall handle complaints submitted through their internal complaint-handling system in a timely, non-discriminatory, diligent and non-arbitrary manner. Where a complaint contains sufficient grounds for the provider of the online platform to consider that its decision not to act upon the notice is unfounded or that the information to which the complaint relates is not illegal and is not incompatible with its terms and conditions, or contains information indicating that the complainant's conduct does not warrant the measure taken, it shall reverse its decision referred to in paragraph 1 without undue delay. […]**	**9. Member States shall provide that online content-sharing service providers put in place an effective and expeditious complaint and redress mechanism that is available to users of their services in the event of disputes over the disabling of access to, or the removal of, works or other subject matter uploaded by them.** **Where rightholders request to have access to their specific works or other subject matter disabled or to have those works or other subject matter removed, they shall duly justify the reasons for their requests. Complaints submitted under the mechanism provided for in the first subparagraph shall be processed without undue delay, and decisions to disable access to or remove uploaded content shall be subject to human review. […]** 121

In addition, unlike the DSM Directive, the DSA contains **detailed requirements** for decisions on **deletion or blocking of content** (Art. 17 DSA, → § 5 mn. 49 et seq.) and on an effective internal complaints-handling system. According to Art. 20(1) DSA, online platforms shall provide their users for a period of at least **six months** after a decision with access to an effective internal complaint-handling system that enables them to lodge complaints, electronically and free of charge. The provider must process complaints in a **timely, non-discriminatory**, **diligent** and **non-arbitrary manner** (Art. 20(4) DSA). The provider of the online platform must also notify the complainant of the reasoned decision without delay and ensure that the decision was taken under the supervision of appropriately qualified staff (Art. 20(5) DSA) and not solely by automated means (Art. 20(6) DSA). 122

In the DSM Directive, on the other hand, there is only the requirement that the service provider 'put[s] in place an effective and expeditious complaint and redress mechanism'. The provision lacks more specifications for the design of this procedure. The key differences are that the DSA makes more detailed statements on the internal complaints management system, but the DSM Directive in turn requires a quicker decision; this must not only be made 'in a timely manner' but 'expeditiously'. As already explained with regard to the reporting and redress system, the DSM Directive is thus only *lex specialis* with regard to the temporal modalities compared to Art. 20 DSA. Furthermore, the notification and redress mechanisms of the DSA also apply to copyright infringements by online platforms and Art. 17 and 20 DSA constitute an 'effective complaint and redress procedure' within the meaning of Art. 17(9) DSM Directive.[127] 123

VI. Result

The DSA and the DSM Directive overlap with regard to their liability privileges. Here, 124
Art. 17 DSM Directive takes precedence due to the more specific scope of application

[127] Cf. Raue ZUM 2023, 166 et seqq.; Raue/Hofmann/Hofmann Art. 2 mn. 58 et seqq.; Peukert/Husovec/Kretschmer/Mezei/Quintais IIC 2022, 358 (363).

and the incompatibility of the two regulations, which is also explicitly stated in Art. 17(3) DSM Directive. Insofar as copyright is concerned, the exemption from liability of service providers when sharing online content for infringements of the rights of their users is therefore determined by the DSM Directive, which means that the provision on upload filters also applies. However, the speciality does not supersede all requirements of the DSA, but rather, with regard to the reporting and redress system, for example, only concerns the modalities of processing the complaint and in this case only the time in which the platform must take action. Furthermore, the requirements of Art. 16 DSA remain in place and do not conflict with Art. 17(4)(c). The same holds true for the internal complaint-handling system.

CHAPTER 2: DMA

§ 10
Introduction

Literature: *Akman*, 'Regulating competition in digital platform markets: a critical assessment of the framework and approach of the EU Digital Markets Act', European Law Review (ELR) 47 (2022), 85; *Alexiadis/de Streel*, Designing an EU Intervention Standard for Digital Platforms, 2020, https://t1p.de/em82j (cited as 'Digital Platforms'); *Argenton/Pruefer*, 'Search Engine Competition with Network Externalities', Journal of Competition Law & Economics (JCLE) 8 (2012), 73; *Ayres/Braithwaite*, Responsive Regulation, Oxford 1992; *Baldwin/Cave/Lodge*, Understanding Regulation: Theory, Strategy, and Practice, 2nd edn, Oxford 2011; *Basedow*, 'Das Rad neu erfunden: Zum Vorschlag für einen *Digital Markets Act*', Zeitschrift für Europäisches Privatrecht (ZEuP) 29 (2021), 217; *Baumol*, 'Contestable Markets: An Uprising in the Theory of Industry Structure', American Economic Review (AER) 72 (1982), 1; *Baumol*, Interview, Journal of Economic Perspectives (JEP) 15 (2002), 211; *Baumol/Lee*, Contestable Markets, Trade, and Development, World Bank Research Observer (WBRO) 6 (1991), 1; *Baumol/Panzar/Willig*, Contestable Markets and the Theory of Industry Structure, San Diego 1982; *Bongartz*, '§ 19a GWB – a keeper?', Wirtschaft und Wettbewerb (WuW) 2022, 72; *Botta*, 'Sector Regulation of Digital Platforms in Europe: Uno, Nessuno e Centomila', Journal of European Competition Law & Practice (JECLAP) 12 (2021), 500; *Braithwaite*, 'Types of responsiveness', in Drahos (ed), Regulatory Theory, Acton 2017; *Bundeskartellamt*, Marktmacht von Plattformen und Netzwerken, June 2016, https://t1p.de/664ua (cited as 'Marktmacht'); *Chirico*, 'Digital Markets Act: A Regulatory Perspective', Journal of European Competition Law & Practice (JECLAP) 12 (2021), 493; *Condorelli/Padilla*, 'Harnessing Platform Envelopment in the Digital World', Journal of Competition Law & Economics (JCLE) 16 (2020), 143; *Crémer/de Montjoye/Schweitzer*, Competition Policy for the Digital Era, 2019, https://op.europa.eu/s/y7j6 (cited as 'Competition Policy'); *de Streel/Feasey/Krämer/Monti*, Making the Digital Markets Act More Resilient and Effective, 2021, https://t1p.de/0l9te (cited as 'de Streel et al, Digital Markets Act'); *Ducci*, Natural Monopolies in Digital Platform Markets, Cambridge 2020; *Evans/Schmalensee*, 'The Industrial Organization of Markets with Two-Sided Platforms', Competition Policy International (CPI) 3 (2017), 151; *Franck/Peitz*, 'Digital Platforms and the New 19a Tool in the German Competition Act', Journal of European Competition Law & Practice (JECLAP) 12 (2021), 513; *France/Germany/Netherlands*, Strengthening the Digital Markets Act and Its Enforcement, 27.5.2021, https://t1p.de/c6ocx (cited as 'Digital Markets Act'; *Fritsch*, Marktversagen und Wettbewerbspolitik, 10th edn, Munich 2018; *Furman* et al, Unlocking Digital Competition, 2019, https://t1p.de/6ytpr (cited as: 'Furman Report'); *Gal/Petit*, 'Radical Restorative Remedies for Digital Markets', Berkeley Technology Law Journal (BTLJ) 36 (2021), 617; *Geradin*, What Is a Digital Gatekeeper? Which Platforms Should Be Captured by the EC Proposal for a Digital Market Act?, 2021, https://t1p.de/ecvj7 (cited as 'Gatekeeper'); *Gielen/Uphues*, 'Digital Markets Act und Digital Services Act', Europäische Zeitschrift für Wirtschaftsrecht (EuZW) 2021, 627; *Grünwald*, 'Gekommen, um zu bleiben? – § 19a GWB im Lichte des DMA-Entwurfs', Neue Zeitschrift für Kartellrecht (NZKart) 2021, 496; *Harrison/Zdzieborska/Wise*, Ne Bis in Idem: The Final Word?, Kluwer Competition Law Blog, 7.4.2022, https://t1p.de/uvujk; *Harta*, 'Der Digital Markets Act und das Doppelverfolgungsverbot', Neue Zeitschrift für Kartellrecht (NZKart) 2022, 102; *Haus/Weusthof*, 'The Digital Markets Act – a Gatekeeper's Nightmare?', Wirtschaft und Wettbewerb (WuW) 2021, 318; *Hillmer*, Daten als Rohstoffe und Entwicklungstreiber für selbstlernende Systeme, Baden-Baden 2021; *Hillmer*, 'Daten und Datennetzwerkeffekte als Innovationsfaktoren in selbstlernenden Systemen', Zeitschrift für Digitalisierung und Recht (ZfDR) 2021, 255; *Höppner*, Google's (Non-) Compliance with the EU Shopping Decision, 2020, https://t1p.de/olxzq (cited as 'Shopping Decision'); *Ibáñez Colomo*, 'The Draft Digital Markets Act: A Legal and Institutional Analysis', Journal of European Competition Law & Practice (JECLAP) 12 (2021), 561; *Kaplow*, 'On the Relevance of Market Power', Harvard Law Review (HLR) 130 (2017), 1303; *Kaplow*, 'Rules Versus Standards: An Economic Analysis', Duke Law Journal (DLJ) 42 (1992), 557; *Kerber*, 'Taming tech giants with a per-se rules approach? The Digital Markets Act from the "rules vs. standard" perspective', 2021, https://t1p.de/hmlyc (cited as 'Taming'); *König*, Actual competitive effects, hypothetical competitors, and the challenge of proving exclusionary conduct (Case T-604/18 Google Android), EU Law Live, 7.12.2022, https://t1p.de/6slvk; *König*, 'Big Data und Wettbewerbsrecht', in Borges/Keil (eds), Rechtshandbuch Big Data, Munich 2024; *König*, 'Form, Effects, or Both? The More Economic Approach and the European Commission's Decision in Google Search', European Law Review (ELR) 44 (2019), 680; *König*, 'The Role of German Authorities and Courts in the Implementation of the Digital Markets Act', European Competition and Regulatory Law Review (CoRe) 7 (2023) 112; *König*, 'Zum Verfassungsrang der Grundfreiheiten und des europäischen Wettbewerbsrechts', Europarecht (EuR) 2022, 48; *Kommission Wettbewerbsrecht 4.0*, Ein neuer Wettbewerbsrahmen für die Digitalwirtschaft, 2019, https://t1p.de/2u7e7 (cited as 'Wettbewerbsrahmen'); *Körber*, 'Lessons from the Hare and the Tortoise: Legally imposed self-regulation, proportionality and the right to defence under the DMA', Neue Zeitschrift für Kartellrecht (NZKart) 2021, 379 (Part 1), 436 (Part 2); *Krämer/Schnurr*, 'Big Data and Digital Markets Contestability: Theory of Harm and Data Access Remedies', Journal of Competition Law

& Economics (JCLE) 18 (2022), 255; *Kumkar*, 'Der Digital Markets Act nach dem Trilog-Verfahren – Neue Impulse für den Wettbewerb auf digitalen Märkten', Recht Digital (RDi) 2022, 347; *Lamadrid de Pablo/Bayón Fernández*, 'Why the Proposed DMA Might Be Illegal under Article 114 TFEU, and How to Fix It', Journal of European Competition Law & Practice (JECLAP) 12 (2021), 576; *Lancieri/Pereira Neto*, 'Designing Remedies for Digital Markets: The Interplay Between Antitrust and Regulation', Journal of Competition Law & Economics (JCLE) 18 (2022), 613; *Larouche/de Streel*, 'The European Digital Markets Act: A Revolution Grounded on Traditions', Journal of European Competition Law & Practice (JECLAP) 2021, 542; *Lomas*, Google antitrust complainants call for EU to shutter its Shopping Ads Units, TechCrunch, 18.10.2022, https://t1p.de/dpa7t; *Marsden*, 'Google Shopping for the Empress's New Clothes – When a Remedy Isn't a Remedy (and How to Fix it)', Journal of European Competition Law & Practice (JECLAP) 11 (2020), 553; *Marsden/Podszun*, Restoring Balance to Digital Competition – Sensible Rules, Effective Enforcement, 2020, https://t1p.de/1zv4k (cited as 'Digital Competition'); *Mestmäcker/Schweitzer*, Europäisches Wettbewerbsrecht, 3rd edn, Munich 2014; *Monti*, 'The Digital Markets Act: Improving Its Institutional Design', European Competition and Regulatory Law Review (CoRe) 5 (2021), 90; *OECD*, The Evolving Concept of Market Power in the Digital Economy, 2022, https://t1p.de/ra5b3; *Petit*, 'The Proposed Digital Markets Act (DMA): A Legal and Policy Review', Journal of European Competition Law & Practice (JECLAP) 12 (2021), 529; *Podszun*, 'The Digital Markets Act: What's in it for Consumers?', Journal of European Consumer and Market Law (EuCML) 11 (2022), 1; *Podszun/Bongartz/Langenstein*, 'The Digital Markets Act: Moving from Competition Law to Regulation for Large Gatekeepers', Journal of European Consumer and Market Law (EuCML) 10 (2021), 60; *Polley/Konrad*, 'Der Digital Markets Act – Brüssels neues Regulierungskonzept für Digitale Märkte', Wirtschaft und Wettbewerb (WuW) 2021, 198; *Prüfer/Schottmüller*, 'Competing with Big Data', Journal of Industrial Economics (JIE) 69 (2021), 967; *Schaefer/Sapi*, Learning from Data and Network Effects: The Example of Internet Search, 2020, https://t1p.de/30bs9 (cited as 'Learning'); *Schweitzer*, 'Digitale Plattformen als private Gesetzgeber: Ein Perspektivwechsel für die europäische "Plattform-Regulierung"', Zeitschrift für Europäisches Privatrecht (ZEuP) 27 (2019), 1; *Schweitzer*, 'The Art to Make Gatekeeper Positions Contestable and the Challenge to Know What Is Fair: A Discussion of the Digital Markets Act Proposal', Zeitschrift für Europäisches Privatrecht (ZEuP) 29 (2021), 503; *Scott Morton* et al, Market Structure and Antitrust Subcommittee Report, 2019, https://t1p.de/8yjzp (cited as 'Stigler Report'); *Stucke/Grunes*, Big Data and Competition Policy, Oxford 2016; *Vesterdorf/Fountoukakos*, 'An Appraisal of the Remedy in the Commission's Google Search (Shopping) Decision and a Guide to its Interpretation in Light of an Analytical Reading of the Case Law', Journal of European Competition Law & Practice (JECLAP) 9 (2018), 3; *Witt*, The More Economic Approach to EU Antitrust Law, Oxford 2016; *Zimmer/Göhsl*, 'Vom New Competition Tool zum Digital Markets Act: Die geplante EU-Regulierung für digitale Gatekeeper', Zeitschrift für Wettbewerbsrecht (ZWeR) 2021, 29.

A. Introduction

1 With the Digital Markets Act (DMA)[1], the European Union has created a **special set of obligations** for companies that act as ***gatekeepers*** in the digital economy. Gatekeepers provide ***core platform services*** such as online marketplaces, search engines, social networks or operating systems, and can therefore control the competitive conditions in markets that have developed around these services. The DMA aims to prevent the gatekeepers, which initially include **Alphabet/Google**, **Amazon**, **Apple**, **Booking, ByteDance/TikTok**, **Meta/Facebook** and **Microsoft** (→ mn. 30), from exploiting their **gatekeeping power** to the detriment of other companies and consumers. Markets in the digital economy should remain contestable and fair, i.e. open to competition and free from discrimination that is not objectively justified (for more details → mn. 17 et seqq.). The provision of core platform services by gatekeepers is therefore subject to strict rules of conduct. The EU Commission can enforce compliance with these rules, for example by imposing heavy fines for culpable infringements.

2 The history of the creation of the DMA and its regulatory concept leave no doubt that the DMA serves a **competition policy objective** (see → mn. 5 et seqq., mn. 17 et seqq.).[2] As a legal basis, the EU Commission used the **internal market competence** of Art. 114 TFEU (as in the case of the Digital Services Act – DSA[3]). As a result, the DMA was adopted in the ordinary legislative procedure pursuant to Art. 294 TFEU. However, the choice of Art. 114 TFEU as the legal basis for the DMA has been criticised in the literature.[4] Some authors consider Art. 103 TFEU in conjunction with Art. 352 TFEU to be more specific and therefore to take precedence over Art. 114 TFEU.[5] However, the wording of Art. 103 TFEU is very closely related to Art. 101, 102 TFEU and it therefore does not seem compelling to regard Art. 103 TFEU as the exclusive legal basis for all competition policy measures.[6] Instead, a narrow scope of application of Art. 103 TFEU is also suggested by the fact that the article provides for an abridged legislative procedure without the full participation of the European Parliament.[7] At the same time, it can hardly be denied that competition policy is an important part of internal market policy,[8] which speaks in favour of the applicability of Art. 114 TFEU. It does not even seem necessary to refer additionally to the flexibility clause of Art. 352 TFEU. From a practical point of view, it seems to be of little relevance whether the correct legal basis was chosen for the DMA. In particular, the choice of Art. 114 TFEU does not stand in the way of a **competition policy interpretation** of the DMA,[9] since the protection of undistorted competition is also part of the internal market policy.

3 The DMA was adopted on 14.9.2022 and entered into force on 1.11.2022. Its main provisions have been applicable since 2.5.2023 (cf. Art. 54 DMA). The first gatekeepers

---

[1] Regulation (EU) 2022/1925 of the European Parliament and of the Council of 14.9.2022 on contestable and fair markets in the digital sector, OJ 2022 L 265, 1.

[2] Convincingly Schweitzer ZEuP 29 (2021), 503 (517 et seq.).

[3] Regulation (EU) 2022/2065 of the European Parliament and of the Council of 19.10.2022 on a Single Market for Digital Services, OJ 2022 L 277, 1.

[4] Cf. Haus/Weusthof WuW 2021, 318 (319 et seq.); Basedow ZEuP 29 (2021), 217 (220 et seqq.); Zimmer/Göhsl ZWeR 2021, 29 (31 et seqq.); Lamadrid de Pablo/Bayón Fernández JECLAP 12 (2021), 576 et seqq.

[5] See e.g. Basedow ZEuP 29 (2021), 217 (221); Zimmer/Göhsl ZWeR 2021, 29 (31 et seqq.).

[6] But see Zimmer/Göhsl ZWeR 2021, 29 (33 et seq.), who consider Art. 103 TFEU to be applicable whenever there is a clear connection to competition.

[7] Cf. König EuR 2022, 48 (71) with further references.

[8] See also Protocol No. 27 to the Treaty of Lisbon, OJ 2008 C 115, 309.

[9] But see Zimmer/Göhsl ZWeR 2021, 29 (33 et seqq.).

were designated on 6.9.2023 (→ mn. 30).[10] Pursuant to Art. 3(10) DMA, the gatekeepers must fulfil their obligations under Art. 5, 6 and 7 DMA no later than six months after their designation. The gatekeepers designated on 6.9.2023 must therefore fulfil their obligations under Art. 5, 6 and 7 DMA since 7.3.2024.

4 The rest of the chapter is structured as follows: Section B describes the **policy background** of the DMA in more detail (→ mn. 5 et seqq.). Section C discusses and assesses the **objectives** of the DMA, i.e. the promotion of contestable markets and fairness in the digital economy (→ mn. 17 et seqq.). Section D explains the **regulatory concept** of the DMA in order to clarify the central ideas, instruments and mechanisms (→ mn. 25 et seqq.). In this context, the **institutional framework** of the DMA and the **enforcement regime** are also briefly presented. Finally, to round off the policy discussion, a number of **regulatory alternatives** are considered in Section E (→ mn. 54 et seqq.). In this context, a brief look is also taken at related legislative measures in EU Member States and outside the EU.

B. Policy background

5 The DMA is designed to address **competition concerns** that have arisen in a number of digital markets in recent years and that are widely considered to be difficult to address using traditional competition law instruments. The **EU Commission** has extensive expertise in this area, having addressed the specificities of digital markets in various **antitrust proceedings** and sector inquiries, as well as in the context of **merger control.** Notable examples include the *eBook cases*,[11] the various antitrust investigations against Alphabet/Google[12], Amazon,[13] Apple,[14] Meta/Facebook[15] and Microsoft,[16] the sector inquiries into e-commerce (2017)[17] and the Internet of Things (2022),[18] and numerous merger control decisions, such as in the *Microsoft/Skype* (2011),[19] *Facebook/WhatsApp* (2014)[20] and *Microsoft/LinkedIn* (2016)[21] cases. Further evidence of restrictions on competition in digital markets has come to light through investigations by **national competition authorities.** The German Federal Cartel Office (Bundeskartellamt), for example, has made important contributions through antitrust investigations, sector inquiries

[10] EU Commission, FAQ of 31.10.2022, QANDA/20/2349.

[11] EU Commission, Decision of 4.5.2017 – AT.40153 – Amazon (eBooks); Decision of 25.7.2013 – AT.39847 – eBooks (Penguin); Decision of 12.12.2012 – AT.39847 – eBooks (Hachette).

[12] EU Commission, Decision of 20.3.2019 – AT.40411 – Google AdSense; Decision of 18.7.2018 – AT.40099 – Google Android; Decision of 29.6.2017 – AT.39740 – Google Search (Shopping); see also EU Commission, Press release of 14.6.2023, IP/23/3207; Press release of 11.3.2022, IP/22/1703.

[13] Cf. EU Commission, Decision of 20.12.2022 – AT.40462 – Amazon Marketplace; Decision of 20.12.2022 – AT.40703 – Amazon Buy Box.

[14] EU Commission, Decision of 4.3.2024 – AT.40437 – Apple App Store Practices (music streaming); Press release of 16.6.2020, IP/20/1073.

[15] EU Commission, Press release of 19.12.2022, IP/22/7728; Press release of 11.3.2022, IP/22/1703.

[16] EU Commission, Decision of 16.12.2009 – AT.39530 – Microsoft (Tying); Decision of 24.3.2004 – AT.37792 – Microsoft.

[17] EU Commission, Final Report of 10.5.2017, COM(2017) 229.

[18] EU Commission, Final Report of 20.1.2022, COM(2022) 19.

[19] EU Commission, Decision of 7.10.2011 – M.6281.

[20] EU Commission, Decision of 3.10.2014 – M.7217.

[21] EU Commission, Decision of 6.12.2016 – M.8124.

and informal consultations.[22] Extensive **academic studies**[23] have also contributed to a relatively good understanding of the competition issues in the digital economy.

This section briefly outlines the specific features of digital markets that are relevant 6
to competition policy. The focus is on those circumstances which, from an economic point of view, may justify particularly intensive competition law enforcement or regulation. This is because the DMA is based on the premise that certain digital markets are characterised by **specific market failures** that cannot be adequately addressed by traditional competition law instruments. The limits of competition law enforcement in digital markets are also be briefly discussed below.

I. Special features of digital markets

The DMA is designed to address specific competition concerns in digital markets, 7
which can broadly be attributed to two causes: On the one hand, some digital markets, in particular platform markets, are characterised by a **tendency towards monopolisation**, which in extreme cases can take the form of a natural monopoly.[24] On the other hand, digital markets are often **multi-sided markets** where services are offered to at least two different groups of customers. If one of these groups consists of businesses (referred to in the DMA as "business users"), the service offered may be an important **gateway** for them to reach another group of customers ("end users"). The tendency towards monopolisation then has a double negative effect. Not only is there a risk of the typical negative welfare effects of high market concentration (e.g. higher prices, lower quality, less innovation), but there is also a risk of foreclosure of **secondary markets**. Such foreclosure may occur if the platform operator has ***gatekeeper power*** *(bottleneck power)*, i.e. if the platform operator can use its platform to control other companies' access to important customer groups. The platform operator can then influence the extent to which competition is possible on secondary markets.

The reasons why many platform markets tend to be monopolistic have been de- 8
scribed many times:[25] Strong ***economies of scale*** can mean that the average cost of a platform operator is lower the more customers it serves. The marginal cost of operating an online platform, i.e. the cost of processing an additional user request, is typically very low.[26] At the same time, overheads and fixed costs, such as the cost of research and (software) development and of the people working in these areas, are relatively high, as very sophisticated algorithms are usually required. Large groups of customers can make it easier to recoup these costs. On many online platforms, only one group of customers pays a monetary fee (e.g. advertisers in the case of a search engine), while others can use the service free of charge, but may have to provide data and attention in return (e.g. end users). Many online platforms are also characterised by **positive network effects**, i.e. the utility of the service increases as more users use the same

[22] Particularly noteworthy are the internationally discussed data abuse case against Facebook (see Bundeskartellamt, Decision of 6.2.2019 – B6–22/16), several sector inquiries under § 32e GWB and, more recently, the § 19a GWB proceedings, cf. Bundeskartellamt, Proceedings against large digital companies <https://t1p.de/torql> last accessed 25.8.2024.

[23] See e.g. Crémer/de Montjoye/Schweitzer, Competition Policy for the Digital Era, 2019; Furman et al, Furman Report, 2019; Scott Morton et al, Stigler Report, 2019.

[24] Cf. Ducci, Natural Monopolies, p. 10 et seqq. and passim.

[25] Cf. Rec. 2 DMA; Crémer/Montjoye/Schweitzer, Competition Policy, p. 19 et seqq.; Kommission Wettbewerbsrecht 4.0, Wettbewerbsrahmen, p. 15 et seqq.; Furman Report, para. 1.24 et seqq.; Bundeskartellamt, Marktmacht, p. 48 et seqq.

[26] These costs consist mainly of energy and server costs.

service. A further distinction can be made between direct and indirect network effects. A positive **direct network effect** occurs when users benefit from other users of the same customer group using the same service. This is the case with social networks, for example, because their communication functions become more attractive as more users can be reached through the network. A positive **indirect network effect** occurs when users benefit from other users of a different customer group using the same service. For example, an operating system becomes more attractive to end users the more software developers provide software for the operating system, and the utility of a search engine for advertisers increases the more end users use the search engine for their searches, thereby revealing their consumer preferences.

9 **Data-driven network effects** play a particularly important role in the monopolistic tendencies of many platform markets.[27] Such effects occur when users benefit indirectly from other users using the same service because the platform operator uses the user data to improve the service: the more users, the more data; the more data, the better the service; the better the service, the more users. Such self-reinforcing effects have been observed, for example, in search engines and navigation services,[28] where search results and suggestions become more refined as they are based on a larger set of data. The same applies to other platforms that use recommendation or ranking algorithms (e.g. social media, e-commerce). Controlling rich data sources can also be a good starting point for entering other markets where data-driven innovation can improve product or service quality. This strategy is referred to in the literature as **data-driven *envelopment*.**[29] Good access to data in one market is used as leverage to enter another market where the data is also relevant. By pushing forward, additional data sources may become available, which can then be used to secure existing market positions and to address even more markets, which can lead to a **domino effect**.[30]

10 Another problem in many digital markets is the existence of **significant barriers to market entry**. These can result from high overheads and fixed costs, as well as from the deterrent effect of economies of scale and network effects, which can make it seem hopeless to challenge the market position of incumbents.[31] A low propensity to switch on the part of end users, which may be due to **high switching costs** and the resulting **lock-in effects**, can also make market entry appear less attractive. An example of the latter is social networks, where users often invest a lot of time and effort in maintaining their profiles and networks, as well as in creating and sharing content. This may discourage them from switching to another platform, even if that platform actually offers a better service.[32] Similar barriers may also prevent switching between **digital ecosystems**, e.g. from services that were developed specifically for iOS devices and are integrated into Apple's ecosystem, e.g. through identification or payment services, to similar services based on Google Android.

---

[27] Krämer/Schnurr JCLE 18 (2022), 255 (259 et seqq.); Hillmer ZfDR 2021, 255 (263 et seqq.); Hillmer, Daten, p. 273 et seqq.; Prüfer/Schottmüller JIE 69 (2021), 967 (967 et seqq.); Schaefer/Sapi, Learning, p. 4; Stucke/Grunes, Big Data, mn. 14.01 et seqq.; for a more detailed discussion of the importance of data for competition in digital markets, see König in Borges/Keil, Big Data, Ch. 12.

[28] Prüfer/Schottmüller JIE 69 (2021), 967 (968); Ducci, Natural Monopolies, p. 57 et seqq.

[29] Krämer/Schnurr JCLE 18 (2022), 255 (261 et seq.); Condorelli/Padilla JCLE 16 (2020), 143 (182 and passim).

[30] Krämer/Schnurr JCLE 18 (2022), 255 (261); Prüfer/Schottmüller JIE 69 (2021), 967 (970).

[31] Cf. e.g. Stigler Report, p. 17 et seqq.; Furman Report, para. 1.65 et seqq.; Bundeskartellamt, Marktmacht, p. 56 et seq.

[32] Bundeskartellamt, Decision of 2.5.2022 – B6–27/21, para. 189 et seq.; Decision of 6.2.2019 – B6–22/16, para. 460 et seq. – Facebook.

These and other effects favour **high market concentration** and, in some cases, monopolisation. Economies of scale, network effects and lock-in effects can give market leaders an unassailable lead over their competitors, who are relegated to the fringes of the market. This is known as the ***"winner-takes-it-all"* effect** and ***tipping***.[33] Prominent examples are the entrenched positions of Google in the European markets for general search services and of Facebook in the markets for social networks for private users.[34] A key welfare problem of such "tipped" markets is that the **incentives to innovate** are reduced both for the market leader and for actual and potential competitors, because all relevant actors know that the position of the market leader can no longer be challenged by quality competition.[35] 11

Competition authorities have concluded that the following digital markets, among others, are each dominated by a single undertaking: **general search services** (Google),[36] online search advertising (Google),[37] online search advertising intermediation (Google),[38] licensing of smart mobile operating systems (Google),[39] Android app stores (Google),[40] provision of **online marketplace services** to third-party sellers (Amazon),[41] **social networking** for private users (Facebook),[42] online display advertising on social media (Facebook),[43] distribution of music streaming applications on Apple iOS devices (Apple)[44] and mobile wallets on Apple iOS devices (Apple).[45] 12

The fact that many platform operators have significant market power is particularly harmful from a competition policy perspective because platforms often serve as **infrastructure** for the development of business models and markets. Platform operators can then decide whether other companies have access to these secondary markets and, if so, on what terms. Entire **digital ecosystems** have developed around a number of particularly important platforms, which further strengthens the position of the platform operators. Through their terms of service, platform operators can shape the market environment and the conditions for competition in secondary markets.[46] An illustrative example is app stores as platforms and the downstream markets for the distribution of apps 13

---

33 Podszun/Bongartz/Langenstein EuCML 10 (2021), 60 (60 et seq.); Stigler Report, p. 11 et seqq.; Furman Report, p. 4; Bundeskartellamt, Marktmacht, p. 50 et seq.; Evans/Schmalensee CPI 3 (2017), 151 (164, 171 et seq.); Argenton/Pruefer JCLE 8 (2012), 73 (79 et seq.).

34 Cf. EU Commission, Decision of 18.7.2018 – AT.40099, para. 686 et seq. – Google Android; Decision of 27.6.2017 – AT 39740, para. 271 et seq. – Google Shopping; Bundeskartellamt, Decision of 2.5.2022 – B6–27/21, para. 176 et seq.; Decision of 30.12.2021 – B7–61/21, para. 275 et seq.; Decision of 6.2.2019 – B6–22/16, para. 423 et seq. – Facebook.

35 Krämer/Schnurr JCLE 18 (2022), 255 (259 et seq.); Prüfer/Schottmüller JIE 69 (2021), 967 (969).

36 Bundeskartellamt, Decision of 30.12.2021 – B7–61/21, para. 234 et seqq.; EU Commission, Decision of 18.7.2018 – AT.40099, para. 674 et seq. – Google Android; Decision of 27.6.2017 – AT.39740, para. 271 et seq. – Google Shopping.

37 EU Commission, Decision of 17.12.2020 – M.9660, para. 427 – Google/Fitbit; Decision of 20.3.2019 – AT.40411, para. 228 et seq. – Google AdSense.

38 EU Commission, Decision of 20.3.2019 – AT.40411, para. 274 et seq. – Google AdSense.

39 EU Commission, Decision of 18.7.2018 – AT.40099, para. 440, 446 – Google Android.

40 EU Commission, Decision of 18.7.2018 – AT.40099, para. 590, 598 – Google Android.

41 EU Commission, Press release of 20.12.2022, IP/22/7777; Bundeskartellamt, Decision of 5.7.2022 – B2–55/21, para. 87 et seqq.

42 Bundeskartellamt, Decision of 2.5.2022 – B6–27/21, para. 126 et seq.; Decision of 6.2.2019 – B6–22/16, para. 374 et seq.

43 EU Commission, Press release of 19.12.2022, IP/22/7728; cf. also Bundeskartellamt, Decision of 2.5.2022 – B6–27/21, para. 209 et seq.

44 EU Commission, Decision of 4.3.2024 – AT.40437 – Apple App Store Practices (music streaming); Press release of 30.4.2021, IP/21/2061.

45 EU Commission, Press release of 2.5.2022, IP/22/2764.

46 Crémer/de Montjoye/Schweitzer, Competition Policy, p. 60 et seqq.; Schweitzer ZEuP 27 (2019), 1 (4 et seqq. and passim).

(for further details see → § 12 mn. 32 et seq.). App store operators can use their terms of use to decide which apps are allowed, which minimum requirements must be met, e.g. with regard to data security and data protection, whether app developers have to pay a fee for using the app store, and how this fee is determined. As this example shows, control of a platform can create **gatekeeper power** because it may enable the platform operator to control and restrict other companies' access to important customer groups. This is particularly problematic if the platform operator is itself active in the relevant downstream markets or intends to enter these markets in the future, e.g. to gain access to additional data sources (cf. → mn. 9). In such situations, the platform operator may try to use its gatekeeper power to its own advantage and discriminate against other companies using the platform services. This may reduce the ability of actual and potential competitors to compete in secondary markets, which may result in consumers suffering from **higher prices, lower quality** and **less innovation**. In extreme cases, more and more secondary markets could tip in favour of the platform operator (see → mn. 11), which would further increase the negative welfare effects.

II. Limits of competition law

14 Theoretically, it would be conceivable to address the competition problems in digital markets solely through **competition law.** Platform operators often have considerable market power, which in critical cases can easily reach the level of a **dominant position** within the meaning of Art. 102 TFEU (cf. → mn. 12). The concept of **abuse** within the meaning of Art. 102 TFEU has also proved to be sufficiently open to cover new types of anticompetitive practices, as shown in particular by the ***Google Search (Shopping)*** decision and its confirmation by the General Court (GC).[47] The obligations under Art. 5–7 DMA have largely been formulated in response to ongoing or concluded competition law proceedings of the EU Commission and other competition authorities (for further details see → § 12 mn. 22 et seq.). This shows that, in formulating the DMA, the EU legislator was not primarily concerned with laying down obligations of conduct that go beyond competition law. Nor was the **enforcement regime** of competition law apparently seen as a central problem, as the enforcement regime of the DMA is strongly modelled on Regulation 1/2003,[48] the relevant framework of EU competition law. In some cases, the latter framework even provides for more far-reaching powers than the DMA. Pursuant to Art. 7(1) of Regulation 1/2003, for example, the EU Commission can sanction a single infringement of Art. 101, 102 TFEU with behavioural or structural **remedies**, whereas, under Art. 18(1) DMA, the Commission is only empowered to do so if a gatekeeper "systematically" fails to comply with its obligations under Art. 5–7 DMA. Moreover, under the DMA, the Commission cannot impose remedies by an ordinary decision, but must carry out a market investigation and adopt an implementing act (see → § 13 mn. 29 et seqq., mn. 83 et seqq.).

15 On the other hand, a real disadvantage of competition law is the **complexity** of the standards and tests to be applied.[49] In order to define the relevant markets, to determine the existence of a dominant position and to identify a restraint of competition, it is

[47] EU Commission, Decision of 27.6.2017 – AT.39740 – Google Search (Shopping); GC, Judgment of 10.11.2021 – T-612/17, ECLI:EU:T:2021:763 – Google Shopping. For further details, see König ELR 44 (2019), 680 et seq.

[48] Council Regulation (EC) No 1/2003 of 16.12.2002 on the Implementation of the Rules on Competition Laid Down in Articles 81 and 82 of the Treaty, OJ 2003 L 1, 1.

[49] Cf. Rec. 5, 11 DMA; Schweitzer ZEuP 29 (2021), 503 (507 et seq.); Crémer/Montjoye/Schweitzer, Competition Policy, p. 59 et seqq.; Stigler Report, p. 45 et seqq.; Furman Report, para. 3.7 et seqq.

usually necessary to evaluate and assess, from an economic and legal point of view, large amounts of evidence. Competition authorities can use their investigative powers to obtain the necessary information, but the process takes a long time. For example, the investigation in the ***Google Search (Shopping)*** case took almost seven years, those in the *Google Android* case just over three years and those in the German *Facebook case* just under three years. The so-called ***more economic approach*** – advocated by the EU Commission, among others – has also contributed to the complexity of competition law investigations by advocating a more precise economic analysis of alleged anti-competitive practices and their impact on consumers.[50] As a result, per se prohibitions and legal presumptions have largely been pushed back and replaced by empirical case-by-case analysis of the respective effects on competition and consumer welfare.[51] With the DMA, the wheel is now being turned back, at least for important parts of the digital economy: per se prohibitions are being reintroduced or, to a large extent, newly created, and effect-based assessments are being declared unnecessary. The aim is to make the law easier to apply and enforce. The fact that some decisions will be flawed from an economic point of view is deliberately accepted as the price to be paid for greater effectiveness (→ mn. 46 et seqq.).

Another weakness in the application of competition law in digital markets is not clearly addressed by the DMA: It has been very problematic in the past that public enforcement of competition law is essentially confrontational, based primarily on the threat of high fines, whereas **effective remedies** can usually only be designed in cooperation with the companies concerned.[52] The ***Google Search (Shopping)*** case is an illustrative example of this problem. In its decision, the EU Commission (as usual) did not demand any specific measures. Instead, it simply ordered Google to bring its infringement to an end and to inform the Commission in due course of the specific measures it would take.[53] This has led to ongoing disputes as to whether Google's measures, which have been modified several times, are sufficient to address the Commission's concerns.[54] Market participants continue to complain to the Commission because they believe that Google's search algorithm and website design do not comply with the requirements of the prohibition decision.[55] The Commission could have imposed more specific remedies under Art. 7(1) of Regulation 1/2003, for example by setting requirements for the presentation of search results and advertising on Google's websites, but it has shied away from doing so. In general, competition authorities tend to be reluctant to impose specific requirements on a company's business policy, preferring to rely on **voluntary remediation**. However, this strategy has only been partially successful against the major US tech companies, notably in the *eBook cases*[56] and in several investigations against Amazon.[57] 16

[50] Cf. Podszun EuCML 11 (2022), 1 (2); Schweitzer ZEuP 29 (2021), 503 (507 et seq.). For more detailed analysis of the more economic approach as a challenge for competition enforcement in digital markets, see König EU Law Live, 7.12.2022; König ELR 44 (2019), 680 et seqq.

[51] See EU Commission, Guidance paper on abusive exclusionary conduct, OJ 2009 C 45, 7; Mestmäcker/Schweitzer, Europäisches Wettbewerbsrecht, § 3 mn. 43 et seqq.; Witt, More Economic Approach, pp. 111 et seqq., 193 et seqq.; 231 et seqq.

[52] Cf. Lancieri/Pereira Neto JCLE 18 (2022), 613 (614 et seqq., 617 et seqq.); Monti CoRe 5 (2021), 90 (93 et seqq.); cf. also the far-reaching proposals of Gal/Petit BTLJ 36 (2021), 618 et seqq.

[53] Cf. EU Commission, Decision of 27.6.2017 – AT.39740, Art. 3 and 4 of the operative part.

[54] See, for example, Marsden JECLAP 11 (2020), 553 et seqq.; Höppner, Shopping Decision, pp. 79 et seqq., 171 et seqq.; Vesterdorf/Fountoukakos JECLAP 9 (2018), 3 et seqq.

[55] See for example Lomas, TechCruch, 18.10.2022.

[56] EU Commission, Decision of 4.5.2017 – AT.40153 – eBooks (Amazon); Decision of 12.12.2012 – AT.39847 – eBooks (Apple); Decision of 1.12.2011 – AT.39847 – eBooks (Hachette).

[57] Cf. EU Commission, Press release of 20.12.2022, IP/22/7777; also EU Commission, Decision of 4.5.2017 – AT.40153 – eBooks (Amazon); Bundeskartellamt, Case Report of 17.7.2019 – B2-88/18 –

Alphabet/Google, Apple, Meta/Facebook and Microsoft, on the other hand, have relied on confrontation, with the result that in many cases no effective remedy has been achieved for years. Although the DMA, like competition law, relies primarily on harsh sanctions, it at least contains some cautious approaches to facilitate **amicable solutions** between the Commission and the gatekeepers (for more details see → mn. 52).

C. Goals

17 The objectives of the DMA are controversial.[58] This is partly due to a not very successful attempt by the EU legislator to distance the **objectives of the DMA** from those of competition law.[59] The emphasis on the specificity of the DMA seems odd given the history of the DMA and the undeniable influence of competition law cases on the drafting of Art. 5–7 DMA.[60] The EU legislator has not explicitly addressed the reasons for insisting on the independence of the DMA from competition law, but it is likely that the main objective was to avoid conflicts with the ***ne bis in idem principle***.[61] According to the case law of the ECJ, this principle precludes further investigations (only) if a decision has already been taken in respect of (1) the same undertaking, (2) the same facts and (3) the same legal interests protected (so-called "triple identity" of offender, facts and legal interest).[62] The wording in the recitals of the DMA to the effect that the DMA protects a "different legal interest" from European competition law is probably aimed at the third condition.[63]

18 Art. 1(1) of the DMA states that the purpose of the DMA is "to contribute to the proper **functioning of the internal market**" and to ensure "**contestable** and **fair markets** in the digital sector […] to the benefit of business users and end users". The EU Commission's original draft was rightly criticised for being unclear about what exactly was meant by contestable and fair markets.[64] The final version of the DMA now includes clarifications in the recitals that should facilitate the interpretation and application of the DMA.

Amazon Business Solution Agreement; Case Report of 9.12.2013 – B6-46/14 – Amazon Price Parity Clause.

[58] See for example Akman ELR 47 (2022), 85 (106 et seqq.); Schweitzer ZEuP 29 (2021), 503 (509 et seqq.); Petit JECLAP 12 (2021), 529 (540); Körber NZKart 2021, 379 (380 et seq.); Podszun/Bongartz/Langenstein EuCML 10 (2021), 60 (61 et seqq.).

[59] Cf. rec. 11 sent. 2 and 3 DMA: "This Regulation pursues an objective that is complementary to, but different from that of protecting undistorted competition on any given market, as defined in competition-law terms, which is to ensure that markets where gatekeepers are present are and remain contestable and fair, independently from the actual, potential or presumed effects of the conduct of a given gatekeeper covered by this Regulation on competition on a given market. This Regulation therefore aims to protect a different legal interest from that protected by those rules and it should apply without prejudice to their application."

[60] Rightly criticised by Schweitzer ZEuP 29 (2021), 503 (509 et seqq.).

[61] Cf. Harta NZKart 2022, 102 et seqq.; Harrison/Zdzieborska/Wise, Kluwer Competition Law Blog, 7.4.2022.

[62] ECJ, Judgment of 14.2.2012 – C-17/10, ECLI:EU:C:2012:72, para. 97 – Toshiba. Cf. more recently also ECJ, Judgment of 22.3.2022 – C-117/20, ECLI:EU:C:2022:202, para. 44 et seq. – bpost.

[63] Rec. 11 sent. 3 DMA. The English version refers to the "legal interest […] protected", which is exactly the wording used in the Toshiba judgment of the ECJ (→ mn. 62).

[64] See, for example, de Streel et al., Digital Markets Act, p. 42 et seqq.; Schweitzer ZEuP 29 (2021), 503 (509 et seqq.); Körber NZKart 2021, 379 (380 et seq.); Podszun/Bongartz/Langenstein EuCML 10 (2021), 60 (62).

I. Internal market

The first objective of the DMA, to contribute to the proper functioning of the internal market, is largely clear.[65] It is obvious that the unity of the European market organisation for the digital sector would be jeopardised if the Member States were to pursue different regulatory approaches. Against this background, national go-it-alone measures such as the German § 19a GWB should be viewed critically. Moreover, the internal market objective of the DMA cannot simply be brushed aside, as the EU legislator has chosen Art. 114 TFEU as the legal basis for the DMA. Against this background, it is surprising and unconvincing that Art. 1(5) and (6) DMA leave the Member States a wide scope for their own regulatory activities.[66] This creates the risk that the DMA will not achieve its objective of preventing the fragmentation of the internal market. The companies concerned (not only the gatekeepers) would then suffer from less legal certainty and higher compliance costs. In view of these risks, it would have been more convincing if the EU legislator had clearly prohibited national regulations such as § 19a GWB, regardless of their specific design.[67] 19

II. Contestable markets

Less clear are the DMA's other two objectives, addressed in its title, of ensuring contestable and fair markets in the digital sector. Regarding *contestability*, the choice of this peculiar term seems to refer to the **theory of contestable markets** known from industrial economics.[68] This connection has been disputed in the literature,[69] but probably only in terms of the anti-interventionist bias that the theory has often been accused of having.[70] However, the main merit of the contestable markets theory is that it suggests that firms have little incentive to abuse their market power as long as they face ***potential* competition**. As a consequence, competition policy should respond to high market concentration with measures that lower barriers to market entry. The DMA certainly takes up this idea because, unlike, for example, the sector-specific frameworks for traditional network industries, it does not start from the premise that certain markets are lost to competition from the outset and *therefore* need to be regulated. Rather, the DMA makes it clear that it (also) aims to ensure the **contestability of core platform services** and of markets "where gatekeepers are present".[71] It is therefore evident that the EU legislator is not prepared to accept any (natural) monopolies in the digital economy and is not content to protect competition only in secondary markets. Instead, it assumes (perhaps somewhat naively) that the DMA obligations will strengthen the (potential) competitors of the gatekeepers to such an extent that the gatekeepers will become vulnerable in their main areas of business, i.e. in the core platform services, or that they will *feel* so vulnerable that they will refrain from exploiting their gatekeeper 20

---

[65] Cf. rec. 6–9 DMA.

[66] Rightly criticised by Lamadrid de Pablo/Bayón Fernández JECLAP 12 (2021), 576 (578 et seqq.).

[67] The prevailing view in the German literature is that § 19a GWB is not invalidated by the DMA, cf. → § 11 mn. 79; MüKoWettbR/Wolf GWB § 19a mn. 97; Bongartz WuW 2022, 72 et seq.; Zimmer/Göhsl ZWeR 2021, 29 (56 et seq.); more sceptically Grünwald NZKart 2021, 496 et seq.; Schweitzer ZEuP 29 (2021), 503 (517 et seq.).

[68] Baumol/Panzar/Willig, Contestable Markets and the Theory of Industry Structure, 1982; Baumol AER 72 (1982), 1 et seqq. For overviews see, e.g., Mestmäcker/Schweitzer, Europäisches Wettbewerbsrecht, § 26 mn. 76 et seqq.; Baumol/Lee WBRO 6 (1991), 1 et seqq.; Fritsch, Marktversagen, p. 184.

[69] See Schweitzer ZEuP 29 (2021), 503 (511); Monti CoRe 5 (2021), 90 (91 et seq.).

[70] Baumol JEP 15 (2002), 211 (220).

[71] Cf., for example, Art. 1(1), Art. 12(5), rec. 8, 11, 32, 97 DMA.

power to the detriment of other companies and consumers. In addition, however, the DMA is also intended to help keep secondary markets open to competition and to prevent exploitation or unfair treatment in these markets.

21 In light of these observations, the contestability objective is primarily relevant to those markets where core platform services are provided. The recitals of the DMA state that "contestability" should relate to "the ability of undertakings to effectively overcome barriers to entry and expansion and challenge the gatekeeper on the merits of their products and services".[72] Accordingly, Art. 12(5)(a) DMA expresses that the legislator considers contestability to be threatened by two types of practices of gatekeepers: on the one hand, conduct that prevents other companies from **entering the market** or **expanding** in the market and, on the other hand, conduct that impedes access to "**key inputs**", which could mean, for example, important data sources. Conversely, this also indicates how the contestability of core platform markets is to be ensured: by lowering barriers to market entry and expansion as well as legal rights to access key inputs. Examples of obligations under Art. 5–7 DMA which are intended to make core platform services contestable in this sense are the **prohibition of data bundling** under Art. 5(2)(b) DMA, the prohibition of **best price clauses** under Art. 5(3) DMA, the prohibition **of tying** under Art. 5(8) DMA, the obligation to provide **data portability** under Art. 6(9) DMA, the right of access to **search engine data** under Art. 6(11) DMA and the termination requirements under Art. 6(13) DMA (for further details, see → § 12 mn. 22 et seq.).

22 However, the DMA also recognises that in some cases the gatekeepers' positions may be so entrenched that their platforms no longer seriously compete with other platforms.[73] Examples include Google Search and Facebook, as well as certain operating systems (Android, iOS, Windows) and app stores (Apple App Store, Google Play). Amazon Marketplace can also be included in this group, although its position appears to be somewhat more contestable. In such cases, according to the EU legislator, the DMA should at least contribute to the protection and enhancement of competition on the platform, i.e. in downstream or **secondary markets.** Obligations that serve this purpose include, for example, the prohibition of obstructing customer communication under Art. 5(4) DMA, the obligation to **acknowledge external purchases** under Art. 5(5) DMA, the prohibition of **tying** under Art. 5(8) DMA, the prohibition on the **use of third party data** under Art. 6(2) DMA, the obligations to allow **uninstallations**, the free use of **third party software** and easy **switching** between services under Art. 6(3) sent. 1, Art. 6(4) and Art. 6(6) DMA, the prohibition of **self-preferencing** in rankings under Art. 6(5) DMA, the **interoperability obligation** under Art. 6(7) DMA and the **access rights** under Art. 6(10) and (12) DMA (for further details, see → § 12 mn. 22 et seqq.).

III. Fairness

23 The DMA also aims to ensure that the markets in the digital economy are fair. The recitals of the DMA explain that "unfairness" should relate to "an **imbalance** between the rights and obligations of business users where the gatekeeper obtains a **disproportionate advantage**".[74] Market participants should be able to "adequately capture the benefits resulting from their innovative or other efforts".[75] Interestingly, in some provisions of the DMA, the fairness objective refers only to **business users** and not to end

[72] Rec. 32 DMA.
[73] Rec. 32 sent. 6 DMA.
[74] Rec. 33 sent. 1 DMA.
[75] Rec. 33 sent. 2 DMA.

users, in particular consumers.[76] This suggests that the primary objective is not to prevent exploitation of consumers, but to create a fair market environment for companies other than gatekeepers. Art. 12(5)(b) of the DMA states that practices shall be considered unfair where "there is an *imbalance* between the rights and obligations of business users" and where "the gatekeeper obtains an advantage from business users that is *disproportionate* to the service provided by that gatekeeper to those business users". In essence, the goal is to prevent unequal treatment that is not objectively justified. Examples from the catalogues of Art. 5–7 DMA are the prohibition of obstructing **customer communications** under Art. 5(4) DMA, the obligation to recognise **external purchases** under Art. 5(5) DMA, the prohibition on the use of **third party data** under Art. 6(2) DMA, the obligation to allow the free use of **third party software** under Art. 6(4) DMA and the prohibition of **self-preferencing** in rankings under Art. 6(5) DMA. The fairness objective overlaps here and elsewhere with the objective of keeping secondary markets open to competition (→ mn. 22).

In some, albeit less central, provisions of the DMA, **end users** are also explicitly 24
included in the fairness objective.[77] Moreover, notwithstanding the subtleties of the fairness concept, there is no doubt that the DMA also serves to protect **consumers.** This can be seen, for example, in the fact that the DMA also aims to ensure low prices and high quality of products and services.[78]

D. Regulatory concept

In the following, the main cornerstones of the DMA's regulatory concept will be out- 25
lined in order to clarify the central **ideas, instruments** and **mechanisms** of the DMA. To this end, the basic idea of the status- and function-based regulation of the DMA and its scope of application will be explained in more detail. The central obligation regime, the institutional framework and the enforcement mechanisms of the DMA will also be presented and discussed in more detail.

I. Basic idea

The basic idea of the DMA's regulatory concept is quite simple: specific obligations, 26
which are easier to apply than the comparatively vague rules of competition law, are formulated for certain business activities (core platform services) of certain companies (gatekeepers) (for further details, see → mn. 15, 41 et seq.). In particular, the DMA dispenses with complex economic investigations. The obligations are to be enforced by means of a rather conventional **enforcement regime**, which, among other things, relies on the sole competence of the EU Commission and provides for broad investigative powers and strict sanctions (for further details, see → mn. 48 et seqq.).

The regulatory approach of the DMA is often referred to as **sector-specific regu-** 27
lation,[79] and the recitals of the DMA and materials from the legislative process also

[76] Cf. e.g. Art. 12(5)(b), rec. 2, 33 DMA. This is criticised by Podszun EuCML 11 (2022), 1 (3 et seqq.); Podszun/Bongartz/Langenstein EuCML 10 (2021), 60 (62); but see also de Streel et al., Digital Markets Act, p. 45.

[77] Cf. for example rec. 2, 4, 7 DMA.

[78] Rec. 4 DMA. See also the explicit reference to consumers in rec. 1, 8 DMA.

[79] See, for example, Akman ELR 47 (2022), 85 (86 et seq.); Botta JECLAP 12 (2021), 500 (500 et seq.); Chirico JECLAP 12 (2021), 493 (494); Larouche/de Streel JECLAP 2021, 542 (543); Polley/Konrad WuW 2021, 198 (198 et seq.).

point in this direction.[80] It is certainly true that the DMA contains rules that go beyond general competition law and are intended to take account of specific market failures and the resulting competition problems in the digital sector. The conduct requirements of Art. 5–7 DMA are also quite detailed and specific compared to competition law. This may justify speaking of regulation, even if the degree of concretisation is much lower than in the law of network industries or banking law, for example. It is also significant that the DMA complements the usual approach of competition law, which is based on individual, selective interventions, with permanent, detailed monitoring of a small subset of companies.

28 However, the classification of the DMA as ***ex ante* regulation** seems less convincing.[81] *Ex ante* regulation typically means that certain business decisions must be submitted to a **public authority** for prior review. It is characteristic that the authority's approval must be obtained before the respective decision can be implemented. The most important example is the *ex ante* control of network tariffs, for example in the energy sector.[82] However, the obligations of the DMA apply by operation of law (*ex lege*) and in principle do not require a prior decision or specification (→ mn. 39).[83] However, it is anything but unusual for legal provisions to apply *ex ante*. In the case of provisions that can be enforced by the imposition of fines, *ex ante* application is already required by the prohibition of retroactivity (*nulla poena sine lege praevia*), which is a fundamental right of justice (cf. Art. 49(1) sent. 1 CFR). In this respect, the DMA does not differ from competition law, the provisions of which also apply *ex ante*, and in particular, without prior specification by a competition authority.

II. Scope of application

29 The personal scope of application of the DMA is limited to gatekeepers within the meaning of Art. 2(1) DMA, and the material scope of application of the DMA is limited to core platform services as defined in Art. 2(2) DMA. Both concepts are considered in turn in this section.

1. Gatekeepers

30 The DMA applies only to gatekeepers, i.e. undertakings which provide core platform services and which are designated in accordance with Art. 3 DMA (cf. Art. 2(1) DMA). The details of the designation procedure and the relevant criteria are explained in Chapter 11 below. Only the **basic idea** is briefly presented here: Gatekeepers must always be designated as such by the EU Commission pursuant to Art. 3(4) or (8) DMA. This presupposes that the **criteria** of Art. 3(1) DMA are met, which is rebuttably presumed if the **thresholds** of Art. 3(2) DMA are exceeded. However, the thresholds are so high that only a very small group of undertakings is likely to exceed them. These include in particular **Alphabet/Google**, **Amazon**, **Apple**, **Booking**, **Bytedance/TikTok**, **Meta/Facebook**

---

[80] Rec. 7, 77 DMA; EU Commission FAQ of 31.10.2022, QANDA/20/2349; COM(2020) 842, 5.

[81] But see Akman ELR 47 (2022), 85 (86 et seq.); Ibáñez Colomo JECLAP 12 (2021), 561 (562); Polley/Konrad WuW 2021, 198 (198 et seq.); Zimmer/Göhsl ZWeR 2021, 29 (35); Kerber, Taming, p. 2. The characterisation as ex ante regulation seems appropriate (only) for the procedure under Art. 8(2) and (3) DMA, → § 12 mn. 11.

[82] Cf. Art. 6(1) of Directive (EU) 2019/994 of the European Parliament and of the Council of 5.6.2019 on Common Rules for the Internal Market for Electricity, OJ 2019 L 158/125, and Art. 18 of Regulation (EU) 2019/943 of the European Parliament and of the Council of 5.6.2019 on the Internal Market for Electricity, OJ 2019 L 158/54.

[83] Sceptical for the same reason Schweitzer ZEuP 29 (2021), 503 (mn. 112).

and **Microsoft**, which were designated as gatekeepers by the EU Commission on 6.9.2023 and 13.5.2024 (Booking).[84] At the time of writing, a market investigation into X (formerly Twitter) was still pending. Another candidate for gatekeeper status is Zalando, although this would depend on non-public data and their business development in recent months. Some other companies such as Airbnb, Alibaba, Ebay, Spotify, Tencent and Uber are likely to fall below the high turnover threshold of Art. 3(2)(a) DMA (EUR 7.5 billion in the EU in the last three financial years), while others such as SAP, Oracle, Paypal, Netflix and Tesla do not provide core platform services or are likely to fall below the equally high user thresholds of Art. 3(2)(b) DMA (45 million monthly active end users and 10,000 yearly active business users in the EU).

The **reasons** for the narrow definition of the personal scope of application are not openly discussed in the DMA or the accompanying materials. It is probably best justified by the need to make the most effective use of the EU Commission's limited resources and to respect the principle of proportionality. Both aspects suggest that the obligations of the DMA should only be imposed on the most powerful and influential companies in the digital economy. However, it is rightly criticised in the literature that the criteria of Art. 3(2)(a) DMA (turnover and market capitalisation/market value) are at best weak indicators of the existence of **gatekeeper power**.[85] Even companies whose services do not exceed these thresholds may control an "important gateway" to end users (cf. Art. 3(1)(b) DMA) and this is the crucial point from a competition policy perspective.[86] With the turnover and market capitalisation/market value related thresholds of Art. 3(2)(a) DMA, the EU has exposed itself to the criticism that it is trying to regulate certain companies and not certain business models.[87] From a competition economics perspective, however, a function-based rather than a status-based approach is called for: The decisive factor should be whether the economic activity in question is in need of regulation or not. The EU Commission should therefore proactively seek to identify gatekeeper positions below the thresholds of Art. 3(2) DMA and, if necessary, initiate proceedings under Art. 3(8) DMA. For this purpose, it would have been helpful if the **notification requirement** under Art. 3(3) DMA had already been triggered when the threshold of Art. 3(2)(b) DMA is exceeded (or even earlier if it is clear that a company provides at least one core platform service), and not only when all three quantitative thresholds of Art. 3(2) DMA are exceeded cumulatively. 31

Pursuant to Art. 3(8) in conjunction with Art. 17(4) DMA, the EU Commission may also designate as gatekeepers undertakings which do not yet enjoy an entrenched and durable position within the meaning of Art. 3(1)(c) DMA with regard to their core platform services, provided that it is foreseeable that they will enjoy such a position in the near future *(**"emerging gatekeepers"**)*. However, under Art. 17(4) DMA, such undertakings only have to fulfil those obligations from the catalogues of Art. 5–7 DMA which are expressly declared applicable by the Commission in the designation decision (→ § 12 mn. 7, 24). 32

2. Core platform services

The obligations of the DMA do not apply to all of the gatekeepers' business activities, but only to their core platform services. This follows directly from the wording of 33

[84] EU Commission, Press release of 13.5.2024, IP/24/2561; Press release of 6.9.2023, IP/23/4328.

[85] Geradin, Gatekeeper, p. 13 et seq.; Körber NZKart 2021, 379 (382 et seq.).

[86] For a more detailed assessment of gatekeeper power, see OECD, Market Power, p. 26; Crémer/Montjoye/Schweitzer, Competition Policy, p. 47 et seq.; Alexiadis/de Streel, Digital Platforms, p. 5 et seqq.; cf. also Basedow ZEuP 29 (2021), 217 (219).

[87] See, for example, Körber NZKart 2021, 379 (379 et seq., 382 et seq.).

Art. 5(1), Art. 6(1) and Art. 7(1) DMA, where the **obligation** to comply is limited to the core platform services listed in the designation decision pursuant to Art. 3(9) DMA. Pursuant to Art. 4(2) DMA, the EU Commission may subsequently add further core platform services to a an existing designation decision.

34 In view of these circumstances, the list of core platform services in Art. 2(2) DMA determines the **material scope of application** of the DMA. The DMA does not contain an abstract definition of a core platform service, but it follows from Art. 3(1)(b) DMA that such a service is "an important gateway for business users to reach end users". Art. 3(2)(b) DMA makes it clear that core platform services are typically used by both business users (cf. Art. 2(21) DMA) and end users (cf. Art. 2(20) DMA), i.e. they are offered on **multi-sided markets** in economic terms. The core platform services to which the DMA applies are listed in Art. 2(2) DMA. The **list** is initially exhaustive and can only be extended by means of an amendment to the DMA, which, like the DMA itself, would have to be adopted in accordance with the ordinary legislative procedure (cf. Art. 114(1), 294 TFEU). The EU Commission may prepare a legislative proposal by means of a market investigation pursuant to Art. 19 DMA.

35 Art. 2(2) DMA lists ten categories of core platform services: **online intermediation services** (in particular online marketplaces such as Amazon Marketplace, Facebook Marketplace and Zalando; app stores such as Google Play and Apple's App Store; and 'verticals' such as Booking, Google Shopping and Google Maps), **online search engines** (e.g. Google Search, Microsoft Bing), **online social networking services** (e.g. Facebook, Instagram, LinkedIn, TikTok, X), **video-sharing platform services** (e.g. YouTube), **number-independent interpersonal communication services** (NIICS; in particular email services such as Gmail, Outlook.com and Yahoo Mail; and instant messaging services such as WhatsApp, Facebook Messenger, iMessage and Skype), **operating systems** (e.g. Microsoft Windows, Android, iOS, iPadOS), **web browsers** (e.g. Google Chrome, Safari, Edge, Samsung Internet Browser), **virtual assistants** (e.g. Amazon Alexa, Google Assistant, Siri), **cloud computing services** (e.g. Amazon Web Services, Microsoft Azure, Google Cloud) and **online advertising services** when provided by an undertaking that also provides another core platform service (e.g. Amazon Advertising, Google Ads, Meta Ads, Microsoft Advertising, TikTok Ads, X Ads). In its initial designation decisions of 6.9.2023, the EU Commission identified a total of 22 core platform services.[88] Two more (Booking and iPadOS) were added by mid-2024. Ten other services were reviewed but were not categorised as core platform services or were still subject to a market investigation under Art. 17 DMA at the time of writing.

36 Taking into account that the obligations of Art. 5–7 DMA refer only to the core platform services of the gatekeepers and not to their other business activities, it becomes clear that the DMA is less concerned with the regulation of the gatekeepers than with the **regulation of the core platform services**. This is the right approach in terms of policy, as the specific competition problems of the digital economy arise only in individual markets or in relation to specific business models. They do not affect 'the' digital economy as a whole or all the activities of the seven gatekeepers designated so far.[89] However, the regulation of core platform services under the DMA is limited to core platform services that are provided by gatekeepers as defined in Art. 2(1) DMA.

37 It has been rightly pointed out in the literature that the existence of **gatekeeper power** depends primarily on whether and, if so, to what extent business users are **dependent** on

[88] EU Commission, Press release of 6.9.2023, IP/23/4328.
[89] Cf. rec. 2 of the DMA.

a particular platform service in order to be able to reach end users.[90] The DMA only indirectly refers to this aspect: Art. 3(1)(b) DMA presupposes that a core platform service is offered which is an "important" (not: indispensable) gateway to end users. Art. 3(2)(b) DMA is concerned with whether the service is used by a very large number of end users (45 million monthly active end users in the EU), but does not take into account, for example, the extent to which the user groups of different platform services overlap. For example, it seems possible that a large proportion of Amazon Marketplace users can be reached alternatively via Facebook Marketplace, Zalando or eBay, which could limit Amazon's gatekeeper power and prevent excessively anti-competitive behaviour.[91] On the other hand, the thresholds of Art. 3(2)(b) DMA are so high that business users may consider *any* core platform service exceeding these thresholds as an indispensable distribution channel. This is likely to be exacerbated by the fact that it is not easy for the business users concerned to determine whether and to what extent there is an overlap between the user groups of different platform services. As a result, business users may want to use all major gateway services in parallel (**supply-side multihoming**).

III. Duty regime

The core of the DMA are the three **catalogues of obligations** in Art. 5–7 DMA. The obligations formulated in these catalogues, which apply only to gatekeepers and only with regard to core platform services (→ mn. 29 et seqq.), have two main characteristics. Firstly, they are exhaustive. Unlike competition law, there is **no general clause** that could be used to justify obligations other than those set out in Art. 5–7 DMA. On the other hand, the obligations apply without any possibility of qualification or balancing, i.e. **no efficiency defence** or other justification is permitted. This is intended to avoid the problems that arise in the enforcement of competition law, where it is often necessary to carry out extensive economic analyses (→ mn. 15). 38

All obligations under Art. 5–7 DMA are ***self-executing***, i.e. they apply by operation of the law without the need for a prior decision by the EU Commission or any other authority. This is noteworthy because, when drafting the DMA, the EU Commission had originally considered providing for a 'black list' of self-executing prohibitions and a 'grey list' of authorisations, which could have been used by the Commission to prohibit further practices by means of an administrative decision.[92] Similarly, the German § 19a GWB is designed in such a way that undertakings of paramount significance for competition across markets (≈ gatekeepers) are not automatically subject to stricter prohibitions, but that the Bundeskartellamt has the power to order such prohibitions in individual cases. The DMA only provides for some leeway in Art. 6 and 7 DMA. Their obligations are also *self-executing*, but the Commission can specify them for individual gatekeepers by means of implementing acts pursuant to Art. 8(2) DMA. However, this is at the discretion of the Commission ("may"). 39

1. Specific obligations

The catalogues of obligations in Art. 5–7 DMA are characterised by a **high degree of specification**, at least compared to the broad standards of competition law. Each obligation stands on its own and is conclusively described with its requirements and legal con- 40

---

[90] Cf., for example, Geradin, Gatekeeper, p. 7 et seqq., with further references; de Streel et al., Digital Markets Act, p. 16 et seqq.

[91] Cf. Geradin, Gatekeeper, p. 13 et seq.

[92] Cf. Podszun/Bongartz/Langenstein EuCML 10 (2021), 60 (64).

sequences. There is no general prohibition clause, and analogies to Art. 5–7 DMA can only be permitted to a very limited extent due to the **exhaustive enumeration** and the procedures described in Art. 12 and Art. 19(3) DMA for updating or extending the catalogues. The decision of the EU legislator in favour of the enumeration technique has been criticised in the literature because, in view of the dynamic development of the digital economy, it bears the risk that the catalogues in Art. 5–7 DMA will soon become outdated.[93] However, the legislator deliberately chose this solution in order to increase **legal certainty** for the undertakings concerned and to facilitate the application and enforcement of the obligations and the DMA as a whole. This is in line with law and economics research, which emphasises that specific rules reduce **enforcement costs** and increase the likelihood of **compliant behaviour**.[94] Whether these objectives could not have been achieved with a general clause combined with examples (as in Art. 101, 102 TFEU, but with more narrowly tailored catalogues)[95] is now a moot question, as it must in any case be respected that the legislator deliberately rejected such an approach.

2. No effects analysis

41 Another characteristic of the obligations existing under Art. 5–7 DMA is that they must be complied with by the gatekeepers, regardless of the impact this may have on the markets and on consumers. In other words, while the DMA is intended to ensure contestable and fair markets and thus to protect competition in the digital economy for the benefit of consumers, it is irrelevant for the assessment of individual cases whether compliance with the obligations under Art. 5–7 DMA actually contributes to the achievement of these objectives. These articles establish **per se rules** that must be strictly complied with and do not provide for a case-by-case analysis of the effects of business practices. Nor do they allow for justifications or efficiency defences. Art. 8(1) sent. 2 DMA, which obliges the gatekeepers to achieve the objectives of the DMA, does not contradict this understanding. In view of the genesis and telos of the DMA, it must be assumed that the obligations of Art. 5–7 DMA are not intended to be qualified by this provision (→ § 12 mn. 9).

42 The per se approach means first of all that, unlike in competition law, there is no need to define markets or to establish market power. The DMA obligations are not linked to the existence of a dominant position, but to the status of a company as a gatekeeper. This is examined and established once in the procedure under Art. 3 DMA and is then irrevocably established for the application and enforcement of the obligations under Art. 5–7 DMA. A **market definition** is not to be carried out in this context, because according to the declared intention of the EU legislator, such an assessment "is not relevant to the designation as a gatekeeper".[96] The fact that the concrete determination of **market power** is not to be relevant is consistent with the overall concept of the DMA. This is because the determination of market power in the context of Art. 102 TFEU is primarily a rough filter for the likelihood of anti-competitive effects.[97] As such effects are not relevant for

[93] See, for example, Kumkar Rdi 2022, 347 (350 et seq.); Westermann ZHR 186 (2022), 325 (334 et seq.); Körber NZKart 2021, 436 (437); Basedow ZEuP 29 (2021), 217 (220); Podszun/Bongartz/Langenstein EuCML 10 (2021), 60 (65); Marsden/Podszun, Digital Competition, p. 54 et seq. Less critically Schweitzer ZEuP 29 (2021), 503 (532 et seq.), who refers to the adjustment mechanisms integrated into the DMA, such as the update procedure pursuant to Art. 12.

[94] Cf. Kaplow DLJ 42 (1992), 557 et seqq.; cf. also Kerber, Taming, p. 3 et seq.

[95] Gielen/Uphues EuZW 2021, 627 (630); Basedow ZEuP 29 (2021), 217 (220).

[96] Rec. 23(2) sent. 1 DMA.

[97] Cf. Kaplow HLR 130 (2017), 1303 (1328 et seq., 1332 et seq.).

the application of the obligations of the DMA, an analysis of market power is not necessary.

According to the basic concept and regulatory technique of the DMA, it is irrefutably assumed that the obligations regulated in Art. 5–7 DMA restrict the contestability of core platform services or are unfair. According to the declared intention of the EU legislator, a case-by-case examination of the **actual effects** of the respective practice should not take place.[98] This also means that the EU Commission does not have to prove that the gatekeeper's behaviour restricts competition or is detrimental to consumers in order to establish a breach of duty. It is sufficient to prove that the gatekeeper has failed to fulfil an obligation under Art. 5–7 DMA. The catalogues can be interpreted teleologically according to general principles. However, it is irrelevant for their application whether contestability and fairness are actually endangered in the concrete case. 43

There is also no possibility for the gatekeeper to prove that its conduct, although in breach of an obligation under Art. 5–7 DMA, does not limit the contestability of a core platform service or is not unfair in an individual case. It is the declared intention of the EU legislator that there should be no case-by-case examination of the actual affects, so that such balancing exercises or **defences** have no basis from the outset. The DMA does not provide for the possibility to justify a breach of duty. In particular, unlike competition law, it does not provide for an efficiency defence. 44

The fact that the DMA imposes the obligations under Art. 5–7 DMA independently of a case-by-case impact analysis and does not even allow for an efficiency defence or other factual justification is often criticised in the **literature.**[99] Indeed, at first sight it seems strange that the EU legislator, on the one hand, identifies contestability and fairness as the primary objectives of the DMA, but on the other hand prescribes certain conduct irrespective of whether it actually makes markets more contestable or fairer in the individual case. Whether the objectives are furthered in a particular case by compliance with the obligations is simply irrelevant to their validity and enforcement. Although the DMA pursues economic objectives, an economic analysis of the effects in a particular case is not relevant. The **disadvantages** of such an approach can be clearly identified.[100] Practices are prohibited even though they may not be harmful in the specific case. And practices are allowed even though they should actually be prohibited because they are capable of having harmful effects. The result may be that entrepreneurial activities are not undertaken when they would be economically beneficial, or that such activities are undertaken when there is a risk of welfare losses. In other words, it may be that the obligations of Art. 5–7 DMA are counterproductive in individual cases. 45

However, this is not an oversight, but has been deliberately accepted by the legislator in order to enable simple, quick and effective enforcement of the obligations under Art. 5–7 DMA. The basic concept of the DMA is based on the logic of **error costs,**[101] which is strongly influenced by experience with competition law. In the end, the legislator weighed up two alternatives: Of course, it would have been possible to continue with competition law, which, due to the economic methodology to be applied, on the one hand promises economically convincing results in each individual case, but on the other 46

---

[98] Rec. 11, 31 DMA.

[99] See e.g. Kumkar RDi 2022, 347 (351 et seq.); Westermann ZHR 186 (2022), 325 (333 et seq.); Schweitzer ZEuP 29 (2021), 503 (534 et seqq.); Zimmer/Göhsl ZWeR 2021, 29 (53 et seqq.); de Streel et al., Digital Markets Act, pp. 56 et seqq., 92.

[100] Cf. Zimmer/Göhsl ZWeR 2021, 29 (53 et seqq.); Kerber, Taming, p. 6 et seqq.

[101] See also Kerber, Taming, p. 3 et seqq., 11 et seq.; Crémer/Montjoye/Schweitzer, Competition Policy, p. 50 et seqq.; Kommission Wettbewerbsrecht 4.0, Wettbewerbsrahmen, p. 24 et seq.; Furman Report, para. 3.42 et seqq. (with respect to merger control).

hand is very costly to enforce. Given the limited resources of the competition authorities, there would be a risk of error costs in the form of permanent ***under-enforcement,*** which means that not all harmful behaviour is stopped in time. An alternative would be a regime that is economically less precise than competition law, but easier to enforce. Error costs then arise primarily in the form of ***over-enforcement,*** because the lack of fine-grained economic assessments leads to the prohibition and sanctioning of behaviour that is actually not harmful in individual cases. The legislator has deliberately chosen the second path because, in view of the special competition problems of the digital economy, it has apparently come to the conclusion that it promises lower error costs overall and is more sensible from an economic point of view.[102]

47 The EU legislator's decision to dispense with an effects analysis was based primarily on the conviction that it was precisely such economic assessments that had paralysed competition law enforcement in the digital sector in recent years (→ mn. 14 et seq.).[103] The resulting economic damage is apparently estimated to be high. At the same time, it would be naive to believe that optimal results can be achieved with the DMA. In contrast to the few per se prohibitions of competition law (e.g. regarding horizontal price agreements), the per se rules of the DMA are empirically on shaky ground.[104] The positive and negative **effects** of their enforcement on the markets remain to be seen. Since the economic effects of a certain practice are ordinarily not taken into account in individual investigation procedures pursuant to Art. 20 et seqq. DMA, it would be good if these effects were at least examined in **market investigations**, e.g. under Art. 19 of the DMA, in order to prevent possible undesirable developments. They should also be examined in the context of the evaluation pursuant to Art. 53 DMA, which is due for the first time by 3.5.2026.

IV. Enforcement

48 The enforcement regime of the DMA, which is primarily based on official investigations and strict sanctions, is modelled on the **Regulation 1/2003,**[105] but is also characterised by an effort to **speed up** proceedings as much as possible. This can be seen, for example, in the material presumption of Art. 3(2) DMA, which is intended to make costly investigations unnecessary, at least as a rule, and in the fact that in some cases quite short processing periods are provided for (cf. e.g. Art. 3(4), Art. 8(2) subpara. 2 sent. 2, Art. 9(1) sent. 4, Art. 10(1) sent. 2 DMA). In addition, gatekeepers are subject to numerous cooperation and information obligations (cf. Art. 3(3), Art. 8(1) sent. 1, Art. 11, 14, 15 DMA), which considerably facilitate investigations by the Commission.

49 The obligations of the DMA are enforced exclusively by the **EU Commission.** In particular, it is the Commission that designates companies as gatekeepers under Art. 3(4) and (8) DMA, conducts market investigations under Art. 16 et seq. DMA and, pursuant to Art. 20 et seqq. DMA, may initiate investigation proceedings to enforce the obliga-

---

[102] Cf. also the recommendation of Crémer/Montjoye/Schweitzer, Competition Policy, p. 50 et seqq., who, however, argued for presumptions which the gatekeeper could have rebutted.

[103] Cf. rec. 5, 10 and 11 DMA.

[104] The obligations under Art. 5–7 DMA are mainly based on individual competition law decisions, which are controversial in terms of competition policy and of which only very few have been confirmed by court decisions, cf. for example Kumkar RDi 2022, 347 (350); Ibáñez Colomo JECLAP 12 (2021), 561 (568); Zimmer/Göhsl ZWeR 2021, 29 (54 et seq.); Podszun/Bongartz/Langenstein EuCML 10 (2021), 60 (65).

[105] Council Regulation (EC) No 1/2003 of 16.12.2002 on the Implementation of the Rules on Competition Laid Down in Articles 81 and 82 of the Treaty, OJ 2003 L 1, 1.

tions under Art. 5–7 DMA. Thus, the legislator did not follow the demands made during the legislative process[106] for the involvement of the national competition authorities. An argument in favour of the exclusive competence of the EU Commission is that the number of gatekeepers will remain very small and that **procedural efficiency** as well as the chances for a constructive '**regulatory dialogue**' (→ mn. 52) should be significantly increased if all supervisory powers are bundled in a single authority with corresponding scope for action.[107] The disadvantage is that the resources of the Member State authorities remain unused.[108] This makes it all the more urgent to give the relevant units of the Commission the necessary clout as soon as possible.

If a gatekeeper fails to fulfil its obligations under Art. 5–7 DMA, the Commission 50 may issue a **non-compliance decision** pursuant to Art. 29 DMA. This decision must be taken in accordance with the advisory procedure under Art. 50(2) DMA, i.e. after obtaining the opinion of the Digital Markets Advisory Committee, to which the Commission must pay "utmost account" pursuant to Art. 4 of the Comitology Regulation.[109] The Committee is composed of representatives of the Member States, cf. Art. 3(2) of the Comitology Regulation. According to Art. 29(5) DMA, the decision of non-compliance must in any event state that the infringement is to be brought to an end. If the gatekeeper has intentionally or negligently breached its obligations, a **fine** may be imposed in the non-compliance decision under Art. 29 DMA, cf. Art. 30(1) DMA. The fine may amount to up to 10 % of the total worldwide turnover of the gatekeeper in the last business year preceding the decision. The broad definition of an undertaking in Art. 2(27) DMA applies, i.e. the turnover of an entire group of companies may be taken into account.

If the Commission finds that a gatekeeper has systematically failed to comply with its 51 obligations under Art. 5–7 DMA and has maintained, strengthened or expanded its gatekeeping position, it may impose **behavioural and structural remedies** on the gatekeeper in accordance with Art. 18(1) sent. 3 DMA in order to ensure effective compliance with the requirements of the DMA. Pursuant to Art. 18(3) DMA, systematic non-compliance is to be presumed if the Commission has taken at least three non-compliance decisions against a gatekeeper within a period of eight years. The measures imposed must be proportionate and necessary. Structural measures may include the obligation to divest a certain business area or parts thereof or to refrain from certain corporate acquisitions or mergers (cf. Art. 18(2) DMA).[110]

The enforcement regime of the DMA is rather **confrontational**, as evidenced by the 52 Commission's far-reaching investigative powers and the strict sanctions. This carries the risk that the gatekeepers will not be very cooperative, similar to their behaviour in several competition law proceedings (→ mn. 16). The **regulatory dialogue** originally envisaged by the Commission remains fragmentary in the final version of the DMA. There is some room for the **specification** of the obligations under Art. 6 and 7 DMA, especially

[106] Cf. France/Germany/Netherlands, Digital Markets Act, p. 2; Schweitzer ZEuP 29 (2021), 503 (539 et seqq.); Podszun/Bongartz/Langenstein EuCML 10 (2021), 60 (66); Zimmer/Göhsl ZWeR 2021, 29 (51 et seq.).

[107] For more details, also on other aspects, see Monti CoRe 5 (2021), 90 (92 et seq.); Petit JECLAP 12 (2021), 529 (539); Larouche/de Streel JECLAP 2021, 542 (558); de Streel et al., Digital Markets Act, p. 72 et seq.

[108] Monti CoRe 5 (2021), 90 (93); Zimmer/Göhsl ZWeR 2021, 29 (51 et seq.); Podszun/Bongartz/Langenstein EuCML 10 (2021), 60 (67); Schweitzer ZEuP 29 (2021), 503 (539 et seq.); Haus/Weusthof WuW 2021, 318 (323).

[109] Regulation (EU) No 182/2011 of the European Parliament and of the Council of 16.2.2011 Laying Down the Rules and General Principles Concerning Mechanisms for Control by Member States of the Commission's Exercise of Implementing Powers, OJ 2011 L 55, 13.

[110] EU Commission FAQ of 31.10.2022, QANDA/20/2349.

in the procedure under Art. 8(2) and (3) DMA. In addition, the DMA in Art. 25 provides for the instrument of **commitments**, which is known from competition law, but only for proceedings for systematic non-compliance under Art. 18 DMA. It is also worth mentioning that the Commission may issue **guidelines** under Art. 47 DMA in order to facilitate the compliance of gatekeepers with their obligations under Art. 5–7 DMA. Beyond these facilitating mechanisms, however, there is a lack of formalised instruments with which the Commission could provide assistance and advice to the gatekeepers and reward cooperative behaviour as part of a ***'responsive regulation'***.[111] For example, Art. 30(4) DMA does not provide for positive behaviour after the infringement to be taken into account in the imposition of fines. It remains to be seen whether the Commission will at least use the discretion granted to it in many places of the DMA[112] for a constructive dialogue with the gatekeepers.

53 Nowhere in the DMA is there any mention of **private enforcement,** e.g. through actions for injunctions and damages, although the Commission emphasises that the DMA is directly applicable in all Member States as a regulation under Art. 288(2) TFEU and must also be enforced by national courts.[113] The German Federal Ministry of Economic Affairs and Climate Action has taken a similar view and ensured with the 11th Amendment to the **German Competition Act** (*Gesetz gegen Wettbewerbsbeschränkungen*, "GWB")[114] that actions based on the DMA are subject to similar rules as actions for breach of competition law.

E. Alternatives

54 The DMA can be seen in the context of similar legislation that has been enacted or is currently under discussion in EU Member States and outside the EU. These legislative proposals have been preceded by thorough competition policy studies and have been the subject of extensive expert debate. Despite considerable overlap and similarities between the individual initiatives, **regulatory approaches** have emerged that differ from the DMA, some of which are briefly outlined below. The main purpose is to illustrate which choices were central to the design of the DMA and where the main differences with other legislation lie. It remains to be seen whether the DMA's regulatory approach will prove superior to alternative approaches.

55 An early predecessor of the DMA is the German **§ 19a GWB**, which was introduced by the 10th Amendment to the GWB ("GWB Digitisation Act") of 18.1.2021[115] and entered into force one day later. A similarity to the DMA is that § 19a GWB also aims to impose special obligations on certain undertakings, which are referred to as "**undertakings of paramount significance for competition across markets**". Whether an undertaking has this status is to be examined in a special administrative procedure, just as under Art. 3 DMA. So far, the Bundeskartellamt has designated Alphabet/Google, Amazon, Apple and Meta/Facebook as undertakings with paramount significance for compe-

[111] Cf. Ayres/Braithwaite, Responsive Regulation. For overviews see Braithwaite in Drahos, Regulatory Theory, p. 117 et seqq.; Baldwin/Cave/Lodge, Understanding Regulation, p. 259 et seqq.

[112] Cf. e.g. Art. 3(5) sent. 2 and 3, Art. 4(1), Art. 8(2), Art. 9(1) and (2), Art. 10(1), Art. 17(1), Art. 18(1), Art. 19(1), Art. 21 et seqq., Art. 24(1), Art. 25(1), Art. 30(1) DMA.

[113] EU Commission FAQ of 31.10.2022, QANDA/20/2349.

[114] See König CoRe 7 (2023), 112 et seqq.

[115] German Federal Law Gazette, 2021 I 2.

tition across markets pursuant to § 19a(1) GWB.[116] There is also an ongoing case against Microsoft.[117] An important difference is that – in contrast to Art. 3(2) DMA – no presumptions are made, so that the determination under § 19a(1) GWB is comparatively burdensome. More importantly, § 19a(2) GWB – in contrast to Art. 5–7 DMA – does not formulate any directly applicable obligations, but merely empowers the Bundeskartellamt to issue **prohibition decisions.** The prohibitions of § 19a(2) GWB are therefore not *self-executing*, but only apply to a specific company if it is ordered to do so by a corresponding decision. This means that an additional step is necessary, which, however, has the great advantage that the requirements of § 19a(2) GWB can be tailored to the specific addressee and the market situation in each individual case.[118] Another difference to the DMA is that § 19a GWB is designed as a competition law provision, so that, for example, the procedural law and the sanctions of the GWB are applicable. The DMA, on the other hand, was deliberately placed outside the competition law framework by the EU legislator (→ mn. 17 et seqq.), so that procedural issues etc. had to be regulated independently.

Other EU Member States have also amended their national competition laws to **56** better address anti-competitive behaviour in digital markets. In **Italy,** for example, an amendment to the national competition law entered into force in the autumn of 2022, introducing, among other things, a **presumption of dependence** to the detriment of digital platforms, which play a central role as providers of intermediary services.[119] It also codified new examples of abusive behaviour, including the prevention of multihoming.

In the **UK**, the **Digital Markets, Competition and Consumer Bill** (DMCC Bill) aims **57** to extend the powers of the Competition and Markets Authority (CMA), which, in anticipation, had already established the **Digital Markets Unit** (DMU) in April 2021.[120] The plans for a special pro-competitive regime for digital markets largely stem from the **Furman Report,** which was published back in spring 2019.[121] However, the DMCC Bill was not passed until May 2024 after lengthy deliberations in the UK Parliament and with the government.[122] Among other things, the authors of the Furman Report recommended that the DMU be established and that special rules of conduct be drawn up for companies with a ***"strategic market status"*** (SMS).[123] In addition, the DMU should promote greater data mobility and open data standards in order to actively encourage competition and innovation in the area of data-driven business models. Again, a similarity to the DMA lies in the fact that specific obligations are to be formulated for certain, particularly powerful companies, over and above the existing competition law. In all likelihood, the number of SMS companies will be as small as the number of gatekeepers under Art. 3 DMA. However, a more flexible approach will be taken with regard to the obligations, based on codes of conduct, which can be more easily tailored to individual SMS companies and amended than the broadly formulated obligations of Art. 5–7 DMA, which are directly applicable by operation of law.[124] There are also indications

116 Bundeskartellamt, Decision of 3.4.2023 – B9-67/21 – Apple; Decision of 5.7.2022 – B2–55/21 – Amazon; Decision of 2.5.2022 – B6–27/21 – Meta/Facebook; Decision of 30.12.2021 – B7–61/21 – Alphabet/Google.

117 Bundeskartellamt, Press release of 28.3.2023.

118 Cf. Schweitzer ZEuP 29 (2021), 503 (535 et seq.); Franck/Peitz JECLAP 12 (2021), 513 (520 et seqq.).

119 DLA Piper Blog, 28.9.2022, <https://t1p.de/tny47> last accessed 26.8.2024.

120 Cf. CMA, Digital Markets Unit, 7.4.2021, <https://t1p.de/lgm6f> last accessed 26.8.2024.

121 Furman et al, Furman Report, 2019.

122 UK Parliament, Digital Markets, Competition and Consumers Act 2024, <https://bills.parliament.uk/bills/3453> last accessed 26.8.2024; UK Government, Autumn Statement 2022, para. 3.32.

123 On this and the following Furman Report, p. 9.

124 Furman Report, p. 9.

that the DMU intends to rely more on **negotiated solutions** and 'soft' regulatory instruments than provided for in the DMA, which is largely designed as a traditional ***command-and-control regulation*** with strict obligations and dissuasive sanctions.

58 Complementary regulatory tools to protect competition are also being discussed in the **U.S.,** although they have not yet made it beyond the draft stage. An interesting proposal is the **Open App Markets Act** (OAMA),[125] which was introduced by Democrats in the Senate and the House of Representatives in August 2021. It would impose certain behavioural obligations on app store providers with more than 50 million users in the U.S. (i.e. Apple and Google in particular) in order to protect competition in app markets for the benefit of consumers. Many of the OAMA's obligations are strikingly similar to the corresponding provisions of the DMA. For example, Sec. 3(a) OAMA, similar to Art. 5(7) DMA, would prohibit making the distribution of an app dependent on the use of a particular system for **in-app purchases** (→ § 12 mn. 36).[126] It also provides for a **prohibition of most-favoured-nation treatment,** which is reminiscent of Art. 5(3) DMA. Sec. 3(b) OAMA is intended to prohibit restrictions on **customer communications** similar to Art. 5(4) DMA. Sec. 3(c) OAMA, similar to Art. 6(2) DMA, regulates that **data** from apps of third party companies may not be used to compete with these companies. Sec. 3(d) OAMA prescribes **options** reminiscent of Art. 6(3), (4) and (6) DMA. Sec. 3(e) OAMA formulates a **prohibition of self-preferencing** similar to Art. 6(5) DMA. Finally, Sec. 3(f) OAMA contains a far-reaching **interoperability obligation** similar to Art. 6(7) DMA. An important difference to the DMA is, of course, that the OAMA is intended to apply only to certain app store providers and not to other platform services. However, another piece of legislation, the **American Innovation and Choice Online Act** (AICOA),[127] has been introduced in Congress to fill this gap. However, as the OAMA, the AICOA did not yet make it beyond the draft stage. If adopted, the AICOA would apply to certain, particularly large online platforms such as Google Search, Amazon Marketplace and Facebook. The primary purpose of the AICOA is to prohibit **self-preferencing** in rankings and other discriminatory conduct by platform operators.[128] An important difference with the DMA is that the AICOA would allow for certain justifications.[129] However, both bills, the OAMA and the AICOA, died at the end of the 117th Congress, and given the change in the majority in the House of Representatives, it remains to be seen whether they will be reintroduced in the current Congress and, if so, with what outcome.

59 Despite the clear international trend towards a regulation of certain digital markets that goes beyond competition law, it should not be concealed that the authors of the numerous **studies on competition policy** that have been prepared in recent years, among others on behalf of governments and competition authorities, have mostly advocated less far-reaching approaches than those that have now been implemented with the DMA.[130] The legislator has preferred to be bold, but has entered unchartered territory, especially

---

125 S. 2710/H.R.7030, available at <https://t1p.de/ykbj4> last accessed 26.8.2024.

126 Sec. 3(a) OAMA, like its European counterpart, is likely to have been inspired by complaints from market participants and in particular the *Epic Games v Apple* case, which is based on antitrust law, see U.S. District Court Northern District of California, Order of 10.9.2021 – Case No. 4:20-cv-05640-YGR, available with further information at <https://t1p.de/x59o5> last accessed 26.8.2024. See also U.S. Court of Appeals (9th Cir.), 67 F.4th 946 (2023).

127 S. 2992/H.R.3816, available at <https://t1p.de/hc5hq> last accessed 26.8.2024.

128 Cf. Sec. 3(a) AICOA.

129 Cf. Sec. 3(b) AICOA.

130 Cf. for example Crémer/de Montjoye/Schweitzer, Competition Policy, p. 125 et seqq.; Kommission Wettbewerbsrecht 4.0, Wettbewerbsrahmen, p. 6 et seq., Furman Report, p. 138 et seqq.; Stigler Report, p. 59 et seqq.

with some last-minute changes during the legislative process. The impact of the DMA on competition in the digital economy cannot be exactly predicted at this stage. It will therefore be crucial to keep a close eye on developments in the relevant markets and to readjust if necessary.

§ 11
Scope of application and relationship to other instruments

Literature: *Achleitner*, Digital Markets Act beschlossen: Verhaltenspflichten und Rolle nationaler Wettbewerbsbehörden, NZKart 2022, 359; *Akman*, Regulating competition in digital platform markets: a critical assessment of the framework and approach of the EU Digital Markets Act, ELR 2022, 85; *Alexander*, Anwendungsbereich, Regelungstechnik und einzelne Transparenzvorgaben der P2B-Verordnung, WRP 2020, 945; *Alexiadis/De Streel*, The EU's Digital Markets Act: Opportunities and Challenges Ahead, BLI 2022, 163; *Bania*, Fitting the Digital Markets Act in the existing legal framework: the myth of the "without prejudice", Eur. Compet. J. 2023, 116; *Basedow*, Das Rad neu erfunden: Zum Vorschlag für einen Digital Markets Act, ZEuP 2021, 217; *Beems*, The DMA in the broader regulatory landscape of the EU: an institutional perspective, Eur. Compet. J. 2023, 1; *Bongartz*, § 19a GWB – a keeper?, WuW 2022, 72; *Botta*, Sector Regulation of Digital Platforms in Europe, JECLAP 2021, 500; *Brauneck*, Der Digital Markets Act (DMA) – das neue, bessere digitale EU-Wettbewerbsrecht?, RDi 2023, 27; *Bulowski*, Regulierung von Internetkommunikationsdiensten: Zur Anwendbarkeit des Telekommunikationsrechts auf Voice over IP, Instant Messaging und E-Mail-Dienste, 2019 (cit.: Internetkommunikationsdienste); *Burchardi*, Die Selbstbegünstigung von Plattformunternehmen im Fokus des Kartell- und Regulierungsrechts, NZKart 2022, 610; *Busch*, Mehr Fairness und Transparenz in der Plattformökonomie? – Die neue P2B-Verordnung im Überblick, GRUR 2019, 788; *Cabral/Haucap/Parker/Petropoulos/Valetti/Van Alstyne*, The EU Digital Markets Act – A Report from a Panel of Economic Experts, 2021 (cit.: Report from a Panel of Economic Experts); *Christodoulou/Holzwarth*, Die neue Vertikal-GVO: Das moderne Vertriebskartellrecht 3.0, NZKart 2022, 540; *Colomo*, The Draft Digital Markets Act: a legal and institutional analysis, JECLAP 2021, 561; *Crémer/Crawford/Dinielli/Fletcher/Heidhues/Schnitzer/Scott Morton*, Fairness and Contestability in the Digital Markets Act, JREG, 2023, 973 (cit.: Crémer et al.); *Crémer/De Montjoye/Schweitzer*, Competition policy for the digital era: Report for the European Commission (2019); *De Pablo/Fernández*, Why the Proposed DMA Might Be Illegal under Article 114 TFEU, and How to Fix It, JECLAP 2021, 576; *Deselaers*, Die ersten Verfahren des Bundeskartellamts nach § 19a GWB – gelöste und ungelöste Fragen, NZKart 2024, 366; *De Streel/Cave/Feasey/Krämer/Monti*, Digital Markets Act: Making economic regulation of platforms fit for the digital age, CERRE Recommendation Paper 11–2020; *Dietrich/Vinje*, The European Commission's proposal for a Digital Markets Act; *Drewes/Meyer/Moss*, Update: Europäische Plattformregulierung, RDi 2024, 310; *Drexl et al.*, Postition Statement of the Max Planck Institute for Innovation and Competition of 2 May 2023 on the implementation of the Digital Markets Act (DMA), GRUR Int. 2023, 864; *Furman et al.*, Unlocking digital competition, Report of the Digital Competition Expert Panel of the HM Treasury, 2019 (cit.: Digital Competition Expert Panel); *Galle/Dressel*, Private Rechtsdurchsetzung des DMA – Stand und Perspektiven, EuZW 2024, 107; *Gerpott*, Report und Technik: Das Gesetz über digitale Märkte nach den Trilog-Verhandlungen, CR 2022, 409; *Gersdorf*, Regulierung der OTT-Dienste, in: Körber/Kühling, Regulierung – Wettbewerb – Innovation, 2017, 185; *Gielen/Uphues*, Digital Markets Act und Digital Services Act – Regulierung von Markt- und Meinungsmacht durch die Europäische Union, EuZW 2021, 627; *Grünwald*, Gekommen, um zu bleiben? – § 19a GWB im Lichte des DMA-Entwurfs, NZKart 2021, 496; *Grünwald*, "Big Tech"-Regulierung zwischen GWB-Novelle und Digital Markets Act – Missbrauchsaufsicht über (Digital-)Unternehmen im europäischen Kontext, MMR 2020, 822; *Grünwald/Döpkens*, Cloud Control? – Regulierung von Cloud Computing-Angeboten, MMR 2011, 287; *Harta*, Der Digital Markets Act und das Doppelverfolgungsverbot, NZKart 2022, 102; *Hartmann*, Die europäische Regulierung audiovisueller Mediendienste: Kohärenz des materiellen Anwendungsbereichs der AVMD-Richtlinie für hybride Onlineangebote vor dem Hintergrund der Medienkonvergenz, 2019 (cit.: Mediendienste); *Haucap/Schweitzer*, Die Begrenzung überragender Marktmacht digitaler Plattformen im deutschen und europäischen Wettbewerbsrecht, PWP 2021, 17; *Heinze*, Der kartelldeliktische Schadensersatzanspruch nach der Richtlinie 2014/104/EU – Baustein oder Fremdkörper im europäischen Haftungsrecht?, ZEuP 2020, 281; *Heinze*, Der internationale Anwendungsbereich des digitalen Binnenmarkts. Eine Skizze, in: Ius Vivum: Kunst – Internationales – Persönlichkeit. Festschrift für Haimo Schack zum 70. Geburtstag, 440; *Heinze/Warmuth*, Das Sonderprozessrecht der Datenschutz-Grundverordnung, ZZPInt 2016, 175; *Herbers*, Der Digital Markets Act (DMA) kommt – neue Dos and Don'ts für Gatekeeper in der Digitalwirtschaft, RDi 2022, 252; *Higer/Patt*, „Kampf gegen Windmühlen" – ist eine Abwendung der Gatekeeper-Benennung nach dem DMA tatsächlich überhaupt möglich?, NZKart 2024, 78; *Hon*, Cloud / Hosting Providers Beware? An Unintended Consequence of the P2B Regulation, SCL 2020; *Horstkotte/Jannausch*, Ne bis in idem im Europäischen Wettbewerbsrecht, IWRZ 2022, 147; *Jenny*, Competition Law Enforcement and Regulation for Digital Ecosystems: Understanding the issues, facing the Challenges and moving forward, Concurrences No. 3–2021, 38; *Kalbhenn*, Medien- und wettbewerbsrechtliche Regulierung von Messenger-Diensten, ZUM 2022, 266; *Kerber*, Datenrechtliche Aspekte des Digital Markets Act, ZD 2021, 544; *Klump*, "Think twice" – Die private Rechtsdurchsetzung des DMA nach dem Referentenentwurf zum Wettbewerbsdurchsetzungsgesetz, in: Kirk/Offergeld/Rohner, Kartellrecht in der Zeitenwende, 2023, 131; *Klusmann/Schley*, Einmal ist keinmal? Der EuGH und der Grundsatz ne bis in idem, NZKart 2022, 264; *Koenig/Mezey*, Schießt die Regulierung digitaler Märkte über das Ziel hinaus?, N&R 2022, 192; *Kohser/Jahn*, Die P2B-Verordnung – Neue Pflichten für Plattformbetreiber und Suchmaschinenanbieter, GRUR-Prax 2020, 273; *Körber*, Legally imposed self-regulation, proportionality ant the right to defence under the DMA – Part 1, NZKart 2021, 379; *Kruse/Maturana*, Unionsrechtliche Grenzen einer missbrauchsunabhängigen Entflechtung, EuZW 2022, 798; *Kühling/Hildebrandt/Bulowski*, Die Zukunft der Interoperabilitätsregulierung für OTT-Kommunikationsdienste, K&R 2022, 670; *Kumkar*, Der Digital Markets Act nach dem Trilog-Verfahren – Neue Impulse für den Wettbewerb auf digitalen Märkten, RDi 2022, 347; *Lettl*, Der neue § 19a GWB, WRP 2021, 413; *Lodoabă*, An overview on the Scope of the Digital Markets Act: Fair Practices Versus Ex-Ante Competition Law, Bologna Law Review 2023, 43; *Maturana*, Verteidigungsrechte im Digital Markets Act, GRUR 2023, 1158; *Mell/Grance*, The NIST Definition of Cloud Computing, NIST Special Publication 800–145; *Monti*, The Digital Markets Act – Institutional Design and Suggestions for Improvement, TILEC Discussion Paper No. 4–2021; *Morozovaite*, The future of anticompetitive self-preferencing: analysis of hypernudging by voice assistants under article 102 TFEU, Eur. Compet. J. 2023, 410; *Müller*, Die "pflichtenbezogene" Regulierung digitaler Märkte in der EU – der neue Digital Markets Act, InTeR 2022, 93; *Noskova*, Virtual assistants as gatekeepers for consumption? – how information intermediaries shape competition, Eur. Compet. J. 2023, 30; *Paal/Kumkar*, Wettbewerbsschutz in der Digitalwirtschaft, NJW 2021, 809; *Petit*, The Proposed Digital Markets Act (DMA): A Legal and Policy Review, JECLAP 2021, 529; *Podszun*, Private Enforcement and Gatekeeper Regulation: Strengthening the Rights of Private Parties in the Digital Markets Act, JECLAP 2022, 254; *Podszun/Bongartz/Langenstein*, The Digital Markets Act: moving from Competition Law to Regulation for Large Gatekeepers, EuCML 2021, 60; *Polley/Konrad*, Der Digital Markets Act – Brüssels neues Regulierungskonzept für Digitale Märkte, WuW 2021, 198; *Ribera Martínez*, An inverse analysis of the digital markets act: applying the Ne bis in idem principle to enforcement, Eur. Compet. J. 2023, 86; *Richter/Gömann*, Private Enforcement des DMA – Ein Ausblick am Beispiel Amazons, NZKart 2023, 208; *Schallbruch*, Die EU-Richtlinie über Netz- und Informationssicherheit: Anforderungen an digitale Dienste, CR 2016, 663; *Schweitzer*, The Art to Make Gatekeeper Positions Contestable and the Challenge to Know What Is Fair: A Discussion of the Digital Markets Act Proposal, ZEuP 2021, 503; *Scott Morton/Caffarra*, The European Commission Digital Markets Act: A translation, Vox EU CEPR, 5 January 2021; *Spindler/Seidel*, Die Regulierung von Online-Plattformen, NJW 2022, 2730; *Tribess*, P2B-Verordnung zur Förderung von Fairness und Transparenz von Online-Diensten, GWR 2020, 233; *Uitz*, Die EU-Platform-to-Business-VO (P2B-VO), 2023 (cit.: P2B-VO); *Van den Boom*, What does the Digital Markets Act harmonize? – exploring interactions between the DMA and national competition laws, Eur. Compet. J. 2023, 57; *Voigt/Reuter*, Platform-to-Business-Verordnung – Neue Anforderungen für Anbieter von Online-Vermittlungsdiensten und Online-Suchmaschinen ab Juli 2020, MMR 2019, 783; *Wiedemann*, Data Protection and Competition Law Enforcement in the Digital Economy: Why a Coherent and Consistent Approach is Necessary, IIC 2021, 915; *Witt*, The Digital Markets Act – Regulating the Wild West, CMLR 2023, 625; *Wolf/Brüggemann*, Der Digital Markets Act und § 19a GWB, in: Kirk/Offergeld/Rohner, Kartellrecht in der Zeitenwende, 2023, 365; *Zimmer*, Der Digital Markets Act – Neue Regeln für marktmächtige Plattformen, NZG 2022, 145; *Zimmer/Göhsl*, Vom New Competition Tool zum Digital Markets Act: Die geplante EU-Regulierung für digitale Gatekeeper, ZWeR 2021, 29; *Zimmer/Nittenwilm*, For whose sake, and by which means? Fairness Concepts in European Law. A reflection on the occasion of recent European legislation, especially the passage of the Digital Markets Act, ZEuP 2022, 820; *Zober*, Durchsetzung des DMA-E und dessen Verhältnis zum Kartellrecht, NZKart 2021, 611; *Zurth/Pless*, #transparenz: Die Kennzeichnung nutzergenerierter Werbung in sozialen Netzwerken unter der neuen AVMD-Richtlinie – Teil 1, ZUM 2019, 414.

A. Scope of application

1 According to Art. 1(2), the DMA applies to "core platform services provided or offered by gatekeepers to business users established in the Union or end users established or located in the Union, irrespective of the place of establishment or residence of the gatekeepers and irrespective of the law otherwise applicable to the provision of service". The scope of application is thus determined by a **functional element** (provision or offering of **core platform services** within the meaning of Art. 2 no. 2 DMA, → mn. 6 et seqq.) and a **territorial element** (for business users established in the Union or end users established or located in the Union, → mn. 64 et seqq.). The territorial element is limited by **personal requirements** for the users (business users and end users) and, most importantly, for the service provider, who must be designated by the Commission as a gatekeeper within the meaning of Art. 2 no. 1 DMA in conjunction with Art. 3 DMA based on specific thresholds (→ mn. 43 et seqq.).

The **purpose** of the DMA is to ensure "for all businesses,[1] contestable[2] and fair[3] markets in the digital sector[4] [...] to the benefit of business users and end users" (Art. 1(1) DMA). This establishes the further requirement that the core platform service must be offered in the **digital sector**, i.e. in the sector of products and services provided through or by means of information society services (→ mn. 9) (Art. 2 no. 4 DMA). The core platform service must therefore be a service provided **at a distance, by electronic means** and **at the individual request of a recipient** (Art. 2 no. 3 DMA in conjunction with Art. 1(1)(b) Single Market Transparency Directive[5], → mn. 9). 2

While the definition of the substantive scope on the basis of specific activities (in the case of the DMA, provision or offering of core platform services) and the territorial scope on the basis of the focus on users established or residing in the Union is similar to previous regulations,[6] the DMA breaks new ground with the restriction to gatekeepers to be designated by the Commission. The Union's digital market regulations have so far objectively defined their addressees primarily on the basis of their activities (cf. for example, Art. 1(2) in conjunction with Art. 2 no. 2, 3 P2B Regulation[7], Art. 2(1) DSA[8]), sometimes combined with exceptions for small and medium-sized enterprises.[9] The new regulatory approach is justified by the particular dangers for the negotiating balance and fairness on markets for certain core platform services[10] which arise from the characteristics of core platform services[11] and from the emergence of particularly powerful companies favoured by them, the so-called gatekeepers (→ mn. 6 et seqq.).[12] As a result of pronounced scale economies, strong network effects, lock-in effects caused by the multi- 3

[1] The objective of the DMA is not achieved when the contestability is upheld solely for other gatekeepers, GC 17.07.2024 – T-1077/23, ECLI:EU:T:2024:478 paras. 307 et seqq. = BeckRS 2024, 16880 – ByteDance v Commission; cf. rec. 32 DMA.

[2] On the term rec. 32 DMA; see also ECJ 21.2.1973 – 6/72, ECLI:EU:C:1973:22 para. 29 = NJW 1973, 966 – Continental Can; Communication from the Commission – Guidance on the Commission's Enforcement Priorities in Applying Article 82 EC Treaty to Abusive Exclusionary Conduct by Dominant Undertakings, COM(2008) 832 final, OJ 2009 C 45/7 para. 30.

[3] On the term rec. 33 DMA and recital 3 P2B Regulation; generally Zimmer/Nittenwilm ZEuP 2022, 820.

[4] Van den Boom Eur. Compet. J. 2023, 57 (61) argues that the term "sector" is not accurate and views the DMA as "thematic regulation".

[5] Directive (EU) 2015/1535 of the European Parliament and of the Council of 9 September 2015 laying down a procedure for the provision of information in the field of technical regulations and of rules on Information Society services (2015) OJ L 241/1.

[6] For a comparison of the rules of territorial scope in the legal acts of the Union on the Digital Single Market Heinze, in: FS Schack, 2022, 440.

[7] Regulation (EU) 2019/1150 of the European Parliament and of the Council of 20 June 2019 on promoting fairness and transparency for business users of online intermediation services (2019) OJ L 186/57.

[8] Regulation (EU) 2022/2065 of the European Parliament and of the Council of 19 October 2022 on a Single Market For Digital Services and amending Directive 2000/31/EC (2022) OJ L 277/1.

[9] Small and medium-sized enterprises can in principle also be gatekeepers, but their ability to impair contestability must be examined particularly carefully, because the DMA "primarily targets large undertakings with considerable economic power rather than medium-sized, small or micro enterprises" (recital 24 DMA). However, an orientation towards the size of companies can be found, for example, in IT security law, where it can be explained in terms of the security function, because in addition to the area of activity, the size of a company is also decisive for its security relevance, cf. Art. 2(1) Directive (EU) 2022/2555 of the European Parliament and of the Council of 14 December 2022 on measures for a high common level of cyber security across the Union, amending Regulation (EU) No 910/2014 and Directive (EU) 2018/1972, and repealing Directive (EU) 2016/1148 (NIS 2 Directive) (2002) OJ L 333/80.

[10] See rec. 4–5, 7, 11 DMA.

[11] See rec. 2–3 DMA.

[12] See rec. 13–14 of the DMA.

sidedness and data driven advantages[13], core platform services tend to concentrate and create particularly powerful companies that can sometimes control entire platform ecosystems and with which new market operators can only compete under difficult conditions.[14] In the view of the Union legislator, general EU competition law does not counter these particular dangers sufficiently effective, inter alia because of its ex-post control. In addition, a dominant position[15] may not always be ascertainable, especially since Art. 101 and 102 TFEU are "based on an individual assessment of market positions and behaviour, including its actual or potential effects and the precise scope of the prohibited behaviour, and [...] provide for the possibility of undertakings to make efficiency and objective justification arguments for the behaviour in question".[16]

4 Therefore, the DMA pursues an **objective** that complements the objective of general competition law (protection of undistorted competition), but is to be distinguished from it:[17] The DMA wants to "ensure that markets where gatekeepers are present are and remain contestable and fair".[18] Since the particular threats to contestability[19] and fairness[20] are, according to the understanding of the Union legislator, not per se linked to the offer of core platform services,[21] but only if the service is operated by an undertaking that meets the three criteria for gatekeepers set out in Art. 3(1) DMA,[22] the DMA regulates – with few exceptions (cf. Art. 14 DMA) – only the core platform services offered by gatekeepers, which is reflected at the level of the scope of application in a corresponding personal application requirement. The DMA is thus not – unlike, for example, the GDPR (cf. Art. 1(1) GDPR[23]: protection of personal data) – concerned with the regulation or prohibition of specific conduct (such as the handling of personal data) of all actors. The DMA is also not – unlike, for example, the P2B Regulation (cf. Art. 1(1) P2B Regulation) – about fairness and transparency on digital platforms in general. Rather, it only regulates those actors who can jeopardise the goal of "contestable markets in the digital sector" (Art. 1(1) DMA). In this way, the Union legislator creates, in addition to the rules of Union law on unfair competition, EU competition (antitrust) law[24] and the sectoral rules on the regulation of market access and market conduct (regulatory law, e.g. in the areas of energy or telecommunications) a further group of norms which, due to its fun-

---

[13] Rec. 2 DMA.

[14] Rec. 3 DMA.

[15] Rec. 5 DMA.

[16] Rec. 10 DMA; on the approach of the DMA rec. 11 and rec. 23 subpara. 2 DMA.

[17] On the inclusion of equal opportunities for economic operators in the objective of ensuring a system of undistorted competition, however, ECJ 1.7.2008 – C-49/07, ECLI:EU:C:2008:376 para. 51 = EuZW 2008, 605 – MOTOE; ECJ 13.12.1991 – 18/88, ECLI:EU:C:1991:474 para. 25 = EuZW 1992, 250 – RTT/GB-Inno-BM; ECJ 19.3.1991 – 202/88, ECLI: ECLI:C:1991:120 para. 51 = EuZW 1991, 345 – Terminal Equipment.

[18] Rec. 11 and Art. 1(1) DMA.

[19] On the term rec. 32 and Art. 12(5)(a) DMA. See also already ECJ 21.2.1973 – 6/72, ECLI:EU:C1973:22 para. 29 = NJW 1973, 966 – Continental Can; Communication from the Commission – Guidance on the Commission's Enforcement Priorities in Applying Article 82 EC Treaty to Abusive Exclusionary Conduct by Dominant Undertakings, COM(2008) 832 final (2009) OJ C 45/7 para. 30.

[20] On the term, see rec. 33 and Art. 12(5)(b) DMA and rec. 3 P2B Regulation; Colomo JECLAP 2021, 561; Alexiadis/de Streel BLI 2022, 163, 171 et seq.; also on the interplay between contestability and fairness van den Boom Eur. Compet. J. 2023, 57, 62 et seq.; generally Zimmer/Nittenwilm ZEuP 2022, 820; Crémer et al. JREG 2023, 973; Beems Eur. Compet. J. 2023, 1 (4 et seqq.); Akman ELR 2022, 85 (106 et seqq.).

[21] Rec. 15(1) DMA.

[22] Rec. 15(2) DMA.

[23] Regulation (EU) 2016/679 of the European Parliament and of the Council of 27 April 2016 on the protection of natural persons with regard to the processing of personal data and on the free movement of such data, and repealing Directive 95/46/EC (2016) OJ L 119/1.

[24] On the demarcation between fair trading law and antitrust law in Union law Peifer/Heinze Einl. C. mn. 50 et seqq.

damental detachment from the case-by-case assessment of the effects of specific conduct[25], is close to regulatory law[26]. However, unlike classical regulatory law, the DMA only or at least predominantly serves to compensate for market failures[27]. The realisation of public interest objectives such as the provision of services of general interest or the security of supply, which are important in traditional regulatory law, are not the focus of the DMA. In EU digital law, public interest objectives are rather pursued by other legal acts such as the DSA.[28]

Due to its focus on compensating for market failures, the DMA overlaps significantly with competition law. Thus, questions of **demarcation to the general competition** rules of the Union and the Member States inevitably arise, which are addressed in Art. 1(5)–(7) DMA (→ mn. 76 et seqq.). Moreover, Art. 1(3) DMA excludes the markets for electronic communications networks as defined in Art. 2 no. 1 and no. 4 of the EECC Directive[29], which are already regulated under telecommunications law. With regard to interpersonal communications services as defined in Art. 2 no. 5 of the EECC Directive, Art. 1(4) DMA clarifies that the DMA is without prejudice to the powers and responsibilities granted to the national regulatory and other competent authorities by virtue of Art. 61 of that Directive (→ mn. 73 et seqq.). As the structure of the scope of application provision in Art. 1 DMA is similar to the parallel provision in Art. 1 P2B Regulation, a **parallel interpretation** seems appropriate.[30] 5

I. Substantive scope

Concerning its substantive scope, the DMA – pursuant to its Art. 1(2) – requires the provision or offering of one of the **core platform services** listed exhaustively in Art. 2 no. 2 DMA. In the opinion of the legislator, low contestability and unfair practices are more frequent and more pronounced for these services than for other services, especially if they are widespread and commonly used services that directly mediate between business users and end users.[31] This is due to extreme scale economies and low marginal costs, very strong network effects, the multisidedness of the services and the associated ability to connect many business users with many end users, lock-in effects, the lack of multi-homing, vertical integration and data driven advantages.[32] The underlying assumption is that these effects create particularly high barriers to entry with regard to the core platform services covered by the DMA, which create or consolidate monopolistic or oligopolistic market structures, giving some companies a central role with various dependency relationships which offer the possibility of abusive behaviour.[33] Accordingly, with the list in Art. 2 no. 2, the DMA includes in its scope only those digital services "that are most broadly used by business users and end users and where concerns about 6

[25] Rec. 11 DMA: "independently from the actual, potential or presumed effects of the conduct of a given gatekeeper covered by this Regulation on competition on a given market".

[26] Cf. Burchardi NZKart 2022, 610 (615), who classifies the duties of the DMA in essence not as competition law duties but as regulatory law duties of conduct.

[27] Cf. rec. 5, 11 DMA.

[28] Scott Morton/Caffarra Vox EU CEPR, 5 January 2021.

[29] Directive (EU) 2018/1972 of the European Parliament and of the Council of 11 December 2018 establishing the European Electronic Communications Code (2018) OJ L 321/36.

[30] On the admissibility of interpretation across legal acts Heinze ZEuP 2020, 281 (283).

[31] Rec. 13 DMA.

[32] Rec. 2 and 13 DMA. On the consideration of these factors in the procedure of rebutting the presumptions (→ mn. 52 et seq.) of Art. 3(2) DMA, GC 17.07.2024 – T-1077/23, ECLI:EU:T:2024:478 paras. 171 et seqq. = BeckRS 2024, 16880 – ByteDance v Commission.

[33] Kumkar RDi 2022, 347 (348); Zimmer NZG 2022, 145.

weak contestability and unfair practices by gatekeepers are more apparent".[34] In general, for the purposes of the DMA, the term "core platform services" is to be understood in a **technology neutral** way, so that it covers services that are "provided on or through various means or devices" up to and including connected televisions or embedded digital services in vehicles.[35] The list of core platform services can be expanded in the ordinary legislative procedure (Art. 19(3)(a) DMA). Non-profit services such as collaborative projects (e.g. Wikipedia) are not considered as core platform services.[36]

7 Contrary to the proposals of the European Parliament in the trilogue, streaming services[37], payment services and connected TVs have not been included in the DMA. Nor does the DMA refer to a **digital ecosystem** of at least two interrelated platform services or an activity in a dual role, for example as marketplace operator and trader on a marketplace. This contrasts with proposals before the DMA was adopted[38] which suggested to limit the application of the DMA by a criterion of "digital ecosystem".[39] The reference to the control of entire "platform ecosystems" can still be found in the general description of the threats to competition in recital 3 of the DMA, in the definition of contestability in recital 32 of the DMA and in recital 64 of the DMA on number-independent interpersonal communications services.

1. Online intermediation services (Art. 2 no. 2(a))

8 Pursuant to Art. 2 no. 5 DMA, online intermediation services are those as defined in Art. 2 no. 2 P2B Regulation[40], with Amazon Marketplace or App Stores (Art. 2 no. 14 DMA) mentioned as examples in the literature.[41] The legal definition in Art. 2 no. 2 P2B Regulation is deliberately designed by the legislator to be technology neutral.[42] Accordingly, an online intermediary service has three prerequisites: First, it must be an **information society service** within the meaning of Art. 1(1)(b) Single Market Transparency Directive (EU) 2015/1535[43] (Art. 2 no. 2(a) P2B Regulation). Secondly, it must allow

---

[34] Rec. 13(6) DMA.

[35] Rec. 14 DMA.

[36] Rec. 2(6) DMA.

[37] Cf. Impact Assessment Report SWD(2020) 363 final, para. 128; critically Podszun/Bongartz/Langenstein EuCML 2021, 60, 64.

[38] French Government/Ministry for Economic Affairs (Germany)/Ministry of Economic Affairs (Netherlands) ("friends of an effective Digital Markets Act"), Strengthening the Digital Markets Act and Its Enforcement, 1; De Streel/Cave/Feasey/Krämer/Monti CERRE Recommendation Paper 11–2020, 10, 12; likewise Monopolkommission Sondergutachten 82: Empfehlungen für einen effektiven und effizienten Digital Markets Act (2021) mn. 38 et seq. with suggested wording; Arbeitskreis Kartellrecht, Digital Markets Act: Perspektiven des (inter)nationalen Wettbewerbsrechts (2021) 12 et seq.; rejecting Zimmer/Göhsl ZWeR 2021, 29 (37).

[39] Gerpott CR 2022, 409 (412), however, probably sees this as a supplementary criterion in Art. 3(8)(g) DMA.

[40] Regulation (EU) 2019/1150 of the European Parliament and of the Council of 20 June 2019 on promoting fairness and transparency for business users of online intermediation services (2019) OJ L 186/57.

[41] Achleitner NZKart 2022, 359 (360); in the legislative process, it was suggested that the "very broad (collective) category" of online intermediary services should be explicitly named in the interest of legal certainty, just like the other core platform services, for example by explicitly listing "online marketplaces for electronic commerce" and "voice assistance services", Monopolkommission Sondergutachten 82: Empfehlungen für einen effektiven und effizienten Digital Markets Act (2021) mn. 41. The proposal was not taken up, perhaps also because of the already existing parallel regulation in Art. 2 No. 2 P2B Regulation.

[42] Rec. 10 P2B Regulation, in general on technology neutrality also rec. 14 DMA.

[43] Directive (EU) 2015/1535 of the European Parliament and of the Council of 9 September 2015 laying down a procedure for the provision of information in the field of technical regulations and of rules on Information Society services (2015) OJ L 241/1.

business users to offer goods or services to consumers with a view to facilitating the **initiating of direct transactions** between those business users and consumers (Art. 2 no. 2(b) P2B Regulation). It is neither necessary that these transactions take place nor that they take place on the operator's platform (Art. 2 no. 2(b) in conjunction with recital 10 P2B Regulation). Thirdly, classification as an online intermediary service requires that the service is provided based on a **contractual relationship** between the provider of those services and business users which offer goods or services to consumers (Art. 2 no. 2(c) P2B Regulation).

An **information society service** within the meaning of Art. 1(1)(b) of the Single Market Transparency Directive (EU) 2015/1535 is any service normally provided for remuneration, at a distance, by electronic means and at the individual request of a recipient of services.[44] First of all, the intermediation must be a service within the meaning of Art. 56, 57 TFEU,[45] which is hardly problematic. The requirement of a service "normally provided for remuneration" also includes services that are not remunerated by those who receive them,[46] as long as it is an economic activity at all.[47] The requirement of remuneration only excludes the actions of persons outside their trade, business or profession.[48] The term "**information society service**" is to be understood **broadly** and covers all economic activities that can take place online, in particular also the "services contributing to facilitating relations between persons engaged in online sales activities and their customers",[49] and intermediation services which bring together suppliers and demands for services without at the same time making an offer for the services sought.[50] The fact that the transactions mediated between the commercial users of the online intermediary service and the consumers are concluded "in part offline" does not prevent the intermediary service from being classified as an online intermediary service.[51] However, an information society service does not exist if the intermediary service is an **integral part of an overall service** that cannot legally be classified as an information society service (e.g. Uber is therefore not an information society service, but a transport service,[52] Airbnb, on the other hand, is an information society service, not an accommodation service;[53] the difference is seen, among other things, in the lower degree of control 9

44 See also the reproduction of the definition in recital 17(2) eCommerce Directive 2000/31/EC; ECJ 6.10.2020 – C-511/18, C-512/18, ECLI:EU:C:2020:791 para. 198 = NJW 2021, 531 – La Quadrature du Net; ECJ 7.8.2018 – C-521/17, ECLI:EU:C:2018:639 para. 42 = GRUR 2018, 921 – SNB-REACT; ECJ 23.3.2010 – C-236/08 to C-238/08, ECLI:EU:C:2010:159 para. 110 = GRUR 2010, 445 – Google France and Google: "services which are provided at a distance, by means of electronic equipment for the processing and storage of data, at the individual request of a recipient of services, and normally in return for remuneration".

45 Cf. ECJ 3.12.2020 – C-62/19, ECLI:EU:C:2020:980 para. 43 = MMR 2021, 309 – Star Taxi.

46 BT-Drs. 14/6098, 21 et seq.; see also ECJ 19.12.2019 – C-390/18, ECLI:EU:C:2019:1112 para. 46 = MMR 2020, 171 – Airbnb Ireland: irrelevant whether the fee for the intermediary service is charged to the tenant or the landlord; ECJ 4.5.2017 – C-339/15, ECLI:EU:C:2016:689 para. 36 = GRUR 2017, 627; ECJ 15.9.2016 – C-484/14, ECLI:EU:C:2016:689 para. 41 = NJW 2016, 3503 – Mc Fadden.

47 ECJ 11.9.2014 – C-291/13, ECLI:EU:C:2014:2209 para. 28 et seq. = MMR 2016, 63 – Sotiris Papasavvas.

48 Rec. 18(8) eCommerce Directive 2000/31/EC.

49 ECJ 7.8.2018 – C-521/17, ECLI:EU:C:2018:639 para. 42 = GRUR 2018, 921 – SNB-REACT.

50 ECJ 20.12.2017 – C-434/15, ECLI:EU:C:2017:981 paras. 35, 37 et seq., 40 = GRUR 2018, 308 – Uber Systems Spain: if an offer of another (e.g. transport) service is made at the same time as the intermediary service, the intermediary service is only an integral part of the overall service, so that there is no longer an "information society service".

51 Rec. 11(3) P2B Regulation.

52 ECJ 20.12.2017 – C-434/15, ECLI:EU:C:2017:981 para. 40 = GRUR 2018, 308 – Uber Systems Spain; ECJ 19.12.2019 – C-390/18, ECLI:EU:C:2019:1112 para. 50 = MMR 2020, 171 – Airbnb Ireland; ECJ 3.12.2020 – C-62/19, ECLI:EU:C:2020:980 para. 49 = MMR 2021, 309 – Star Taxi.

53 ECJ 19.12.2019 – C-390/18, ECLI:EU:C:2019:1112 paras. 52 et seqq. = MMR 2020, 171 – Airbnb Ireland: intermediary service separable from the actual real estate business (rental), as not aimed at the

over the direct service providers – landlord or driver – with Airbnb compared to Uber[54]). **"Service provided at a distance"** describes a service "provided without the parties being simultaneously present" (Art. 1(1)(b)(i) Single Market Transparency Directive (EU) 2015/1535). This is not the case if the supplier and the recipient are physically present at the same time, even if electronic devices are used.[55] A **"service provided by electronic means"** is a service which "is sent initially and received at its destination by means of electronic equipment for the processing (including digital compression) and storage of data, and entirely transmitted, conveyed and received by wire, by radio, by optical means or by other electromagnetic means" (Art. 1(1)(b)(ii) Single Market Transparency Directive (EU) 2015/1535, cf. also Art. 2(h)(ii) third indent eCommerce Directive 2000/31/EC). This also covers access to a communications network and the mere transmission or storage of information.[56] It is not sufficient that the service is provided with electronic means but in material form[57] or by telephone/fax[58]. A "service provided at the **individual request of a recipient**" is a service "provided through the transmission of data on individual request" (Art. 1(1)(b)(iii) Single Market Transparency Directive (EU) 2015/1535).[59] This excludes services "provided by transmitting data without individual demand for simultaneous reception by an unlimited number of individual receivers (point to multipoint transmission)" such as television broadcast as defined in Art. 1(1)(e) AVMSD 2010/13/EU,[60] radio services and teletext (via television signal).[61]

10 Allowing users to **offer goods or services** is to be understood broadly. Thus, in addition to actual sales offers, all forms of advertising and product presentation fall under this,[62] but not the offer of online dating. Online payment services (cf. also Art. 2 no. 16 DMA) are also not online intermediary services within the meaning of Art. 2 no. 2(b) P2B Regulation (Art. 1(3) and recital 11 P2B Regulation), as they do not mediate the offer of goods or services. However, online intermediary services can also be active in the

---

direct realisation of an accommodation service, but at providing a tool to facilitate the conclusion of accommodation contracts on the basis of a structured list of accommodations.

[54] ECJ 19.12.2019 – C-390/18, ECLI:EU:C:2019:1112 paras. 66 et seqq. = MMR 2020, 171 – Airbnb Ireland.

[55] On examples of services not covered Recital 18(10) eCommerce Directive 2000/31/EC and Annex I No. 1 Single Market Transparency Directive (EU) 2015/1535: medical examinations or treatment in a doctor's surgery using electronic equipment where the patient is physically present; consultation of an electronic catalogue in a shop with the customer on site; plane ticket reservation at a travel agency in the physical presence of the customer by means of a network of computers; electronic games made available in a video arcade where the customer is physically present. However, only those services which are inseparably linked to a physically supplied service are excluded ECJ 2.12.2010 – C-108/09, ECLI:EU:C:2010:725 paras. 37, 39 = GRUR 2011, 243 – Ker-Optika.

[56] Rec. 18(5) eCommerce Directive 2000/31/EC.

[57] For examples, Annex I of Single Market Transparency Directive (EU) 2015/1535: automatic cash or ticket dispensing machines; access to road networks, car parks etc., charging for use, even if there are electronic devices at the entrance/exit controlling access and/or ensuring correct payment is made.

[58] For examples, Annex I Single Market Transparency Directive (EU) 2015/1535: voice telephony services, telefax/telex services, services provided via voice telephony or fax, telephone/telefax consultation of a doctor, telephone/telefax consultation of a lawyer, telephone/telefax direct marketing.

[59] Rec. 18(7) eCommerce Directive 2000/31/EC; ECJ 19.12.2019 – C-390/18, ECLI:EU:C:2019:1112 para. 48 = MMR 2020, 171 – Airbnb Ireland.

[60] Accordingly, "'television broadcasting' or 'television broadcast' (i.e. a linear audiovisual media service) means an audiovisual media service provided by a media service provider for simultaneous viewing of programmes on the basis of a programme schedule".

[61] Annex I Single Market Transparency Directive (EU) 2015/1535; recital 18(6) eCommerce-RL 2000/31/EC, which still refers to the definition of television broadcasting according to Art. 1(a) of the now repealed Directive 89/552/EEC.

[62] Köhler/Bornkamm/Feddersen/Alexander, 41st edition 2023, P2B-VO Art. 2 mn. 10; differing Uitz P2B-VO 50.

area of financial services and mediate the services listed in Annex II Single Market Transparency Directive (EU) 2015/1535, which are not exhaustive (investment services, insurance and reinsurance operations, banking services, operations relating to pension funds or services relating to dealings in futures or options).[63] The reference to Art. 2 no. 2 P2B Regulation proves difficult with regard to the requirement that the service must enable business users to offer goods or services to **consumers** (Art. 2 no. 2(b) P2B Regulation). This is because, in contrast to the P2B Regulation, the DMA is in principle not limited to B2C platforms due to the shift from consumer to end user (→ mn. 38 et seqq.).[64] However, the explicit and unqualified reference to Art. 2 no. 2 P2B Regulation is likely to be understood as a restriction to B2C platforms (including mixed platforms on which both B2C and B2B and C2C contracts are brokered) in the area of online intermediary servives, even if this neither corresponds to the structure of the other platform services, which also cover the B2B relationship, nor does it do justice to the design of the end user concept[65] (→ mn. 38 et seqq.).[66] The consumer as a connecting factor is alien to the DMA, because it is based in principle on a situational consideration of the economic function of individual market participants. Thus, end users in general should be treated in the same way as consumers. Even if it would therefore make sense to extend the reference to Art. 2 no. 2 P2B Regulation to cases in which an online intermediary service enables commercial users to offer goods or services to **end users** (and not only consumers), the explicit and unrestricted reference to Art. 2 no. 2 P2B Regulation with recital 11(4) P2B do not permit such an interpretation as the DMA currently stands (different for online search engines → mn. 13).

Furthermore, an online intermediary service requires that **direct transactions** are mediated between the business users of the service and consumers, i.e. the intermediary service must not itself become the contractual partner of the consumer. If (as may be the case with Amazon, for example) both transactions between end users and consumers are mediated and contracts are concluded between the platform operator and the consumers, this does not prevent the service from being classified as an online intermediary service (cf. Art. 6 P2B Regulation). But the online intermediation service must "aim to facilitate the initiating of direct transactions between business users and consumers, irrespective of whether the transactions are ultimately concluded online, on the online portal of the provider of online intermediation services in question or that of the business user, offline or in fact not at all".[67] The intermediation of transactions must therefore not only be of a marginal character.[68] Finally, the online intermediation service must be provided on the basis of a **contractual relationship** between the provider of those services and the business users which offer goods or services to consumers, although it has not been conclusively clarified according to which law the existence of a contract is to be determined.[69] It is supposed to be sufficient for this that the business user and the platform operator express their intention to be bound in an unequivocal 11

[63] Rec. 14 DMA.

[64] Cf. rec. 15 DMA: Mediation not only between business users and end users, but also between end users and end users does not prevent the service from being classified as a gateway for business users to reach end users.

[65] In this respect also rec. 14 DMA.

[66] This is also the conclusion of Podszun/Bongartz/Langenstein EuCML 2021, 60 (63); see also Impact Assessment Report SWD(2020) 363 final, para. 128.

[67] Rec. 10(3) P2B Regulation.

[68] Rec. 10(4) P2B Regulation.

[69] For a determination based on national law BeckOK UWG/Tribess, 20th edition 2023, P2B-VO Art. 2 mn. 11a; Busch/Schulte-Nölke P2B-VO Art. 2 mn. 39; for an autonomous determination Uitz P2B-VO 55.

manner on a durable medium (Art. 2 no. 13 P2B Regulation) without an express written agreement necessarily being required.[70]

12 Apart from exclusive B2B or C2C marketplaces, the usual **online marketplaces** as defined in Art. 2(n) UTP Directive[71] and Art. 2 no. 17 Consumer Rights Directive[72] fall under the term online intermediary service.[73] **Price comparison platforms** are also covered, provided they operate on the basis of a contractual relationship with the business user and not merely on the basis of scraping (in the latter case, however, Art. 2 no. 6 DMA may apply, → mn. 14), as well as platforms for arranging service appointments.[74] Art. 2 no. 14 DMA specifies that **App stores** are online intermediation services focused on software applications (Art. 2 no. 15 DMA). According to recital 11 of the P2B Regulation, the intermediation can be conducted based on product advertising on social media or with the aid of voice assistance technology. An online intermediation service can therefore also be an online social networking service (→ mn. 15) and, under certain circumstances, a virtual assistant (→ mn. 28).[75] The same applies to video-sharing platform services (→ mn. 16 et seq.). Whether cloud computing services also fall under Art. 2 no. 2 P2B Regulation is disputed.[76] In the case of the DMA, this is probably not the case due to the independent provision covering these services in Art. 2 no. 2(i).

Concerning online intermediation services, the Commission designated Amazon[77] regarding its Marketplace, Meta[78] regarding its Marketplace, Apple[79] regarding its App Store, Booking[80] regarding Booking.com and Alphabet[81] regarding Google Shopping, Google Play and Google Maps as gatekeepers.

2. Online search engines (Art. 2 no. 2(b))

13 According to Art. 2 no. 6 DMA, online search engines are services within the meaning of Art. 2 no. 5 P2B Regulation. They are digital services that allow users to perform searches of all websites or all websites in a particular language based on a query and to receive results in which the users can find information related to the requested content. The search engines Google, Yahoo or Bing can be named as examples. The requirement derived from the definition of "provider of online search engines" in Art. 2 no. 6 P2B

---

[70] Rec. 10(6) P2B Regulation.

[71] Directive 2005/29/EC of the European Parliament and of the Council of 11 May 2005 concerning unfair business-to-consumer commercial practices in the internal market and amending Council Directive 84/450/EEC, Directives 97/7/EC, 98/27/EC and 2002/65/EC of the European Parliament and of the Council and Regulation (EC) No 2006/2004 of the European Parliament and of the Council (2005) OJ L 149/22.

[72] Directive 2011/83/EU of the European Parliament and of the Council of 25 October 2011 on consumer rights, amending Council Directive 93/13/EEC and Directive 1999/44/EC of the European Parliament and of the Council and repealing Council Directive 85/577/EEC and Directive 97/7/EC of the European Parliament and of the Council (2011) OJ L 304/64.

[73] Rec. 11 P2B Regulation; Alexander WRP 2020, 945 (947).

[74] Busch GRUR 2019, 788 (789); Kohser/Jahn GRUR-Prax 2020, 273; Voigt/Reuter MMR 2019, 783 (784).

[75] Critically Bania Eur. Compet. J. 2023, 116 (120 et seq.).

[76] Busch/Schulte-Nölke P2B-VO Art. 2 mn. 36; Hon SCL 2020.

[77] Commission Decision of 5 September 2023 C(2023) 6104 final, summary OJ C 2023/905.

[78] Commission Decision of 5 September 2023 C(2023) 6105 final, summary OJ C 2023/1029. Meta challenges the decision by action for annulment, T-1078/23, OJ C 2024/561.

[79] Commission Decision of 5 September 2023 C(2023) 6100 final, summary OJ C 2023/548. Apple challenges the decision by action for annulment, T-1080/23, OJ C 2024/563. Apple argues that there are in fact multiple separate App Stores depending on the type of device. On Apple's argument in the context of circumvention → mn. 47.

[80] Commission Decision of 13 May 2024 C(2024) 3176 final, summary OJ C 2024/4360.

[81] Commission Decision of 5 September 2023 C(2023) 6101 final, summary OJ C 2023/549.

Regulation that the users must also include consumers[82] does not apply to the DMA in the absence of a reference to Art. 2 no. 6 P2B Regulation. Since every search engine inevitably has end users, there is no need to identify them separately besides in the context of the thresholds (→ mn. 51) laid down in Art. 3(2) DMA. The search engine must search "in principle all websites". Search functions on individual databases or websites – even if these themselves constitute a core platform service – do not fall within the scope of the DMA.[83]

Price comparison platforms can be online search engines if they obtain their data by scraping websites. However, this only applies if the websites to be evaluated have not already been determined in advance, as the search must be possible in principle on all or all websites of a language according to Art. 2 no. 5 P2B Regulation.[84] (on price comparison platforms as online intermediation services → mn. 12) **14**

Concerning online search engines the Commission designated Alphabet[85] regarding Google Search as a gatekeeper.

Concerning Microsoft's search engine Bing the commission initiated the procedure according to Art. 17(3) DMA (→ mn. 53),[86] which led to the acceptance of the rebuttal.[87]

3. Online social networking services (Art. 2 no. 2(c))

According to Art. 2 no. 7 DMA, online social networking services are platforms (on the concept of platform see Art. 3(i) DSA) on which end users can **connect and communicate** with each other, **share content** and **discover other users and content** across multiple devices. Primarily covered are the classic and well-known social networks that connect people as a core function (e.g. Facebook by Meta, but also Instagram, LinkedIn, TikTok and Snapchat). If applied literally, video-sharing platform services (→ mn. 16 et seq.) and online intermediation services (→ mn. 8 et seqq.) would also be covered, for which, however, there are independent rules in the DMA (Art. 2 no. 2(a), (d) and no. 5, 8 DMA). The term social network therefore requires an interpretation based on the three characteristics mentioned in Art. 2 no. 7 DMA. Due to the intention to regulate classic social networks, it should be decisive that, from the perspective of end users, the contacting, communicating and sharing of content is the focus of the use and not merely accessory. For example, although comment functions are regularly available on video-sharing platforms, these usually only play a subordinate role alongside the accessing of the videos offered. Such comment sections therefore do not make a video sharing platform a social network within the meaning of Art. 2 no. 2(c) DMA. **15**

In order to distinguish between services which allow networking of end users or communication between them (cf. Art. 2 no. 9 DMA on communication services) and genuine social networks, it must therefore be determined – on the basis of market perception – what is to be regarded as the **main purpose of the core function** of the service. Thus, in the case of social networks, the contact and communication function, content sharing function and discovery function has to be of significant extent and not only of

---

[82] Busch/Schulte-Nölke P2B VO Art. 2 mn. 59.

[83] BeckOK UWG/Tribess, 20th edition 2023, P2B-VO Art. 2 mn. 22; Busch/Schulte-Nölke P2B-VO Art. 2 mn. 64; Köhler/Bornkamm/Feddersen/Alexander, 41st edition 2023, P2B-VO Art. 2 mn. 34; Tribess GWR 2020, 233 (234); Uitz P2B-VO 60.

[84] This will probably only be the case when using so-called web crawlers.

[85] Commission Decision of 5 September 2023 C(2023) 6101 final, summary OJ C 2023/549.

[86] Commission Decision of 5 September 2023 C(2023) 6078 final.

[87] Commission Decision of 12 February 2024 C(2024) 806 final, summary OJ C 2024/2709.

secondary importance.[88] The technical specifics of the algorithms utilized to determine the displayed content (e.g. social graph or content/interest graph) are without relevance for the classification of the service as a social networking service.[89] Still, this does not exclude that in individual cases a service can be both a video-sharing platform service (→ mn. 16 et seq.) and an online social networking service. To determine the number of business users (→ mn. 38 et seqq., 51), it is essential to consider that there are several ways for utilising social networks for business purposes, extending beyond mere advertising (→ mn. 31 et seqq.).[90]

Concerning online social networking services the Commission designated Meta[91] regarding Facebook and Instagram, ByteDance[92] regarding TikTok and Microsoft[93] regarding LinkedIn as gatekeepers.

Concerning X (formerly Twitter) the commission initiated the procedure according to Art. 17(3) DMA (→ mn. 53),[94] which led to the acceptance of the rebuttal.[95]

4. Video-sharing platform services (Art. 2 no. 2(d))

16 According to the reference to Art. 1(1)(aa) of the AVMSD[96], video-sharing platform services are services as defined by Art. 56, 57 TFEU where the principal purpose of at least one essential functionality is devoted to providing **programmes or user-generated videos**, for which the provider has no editorial responsibility, to the general public by means of electronic communications networks (within the meaning of Art. 2(a) of the Framework Directive 2002/21/EC[97]) for information, education or entertainment. Furthermore, the organisation of the videos must be determined by the provider, which may also be done by automatic means or algorithms in particular by displaying, tagging and sequencing. According to the broad definitions in Art. 1(1)(b), (ba) AVMSD, the terms programme and user-generated video cover all sequences of moving images with or

---

[88] Bongartz/Kirk, in: HK-DMA Art. 2 mn. 46.

[89] Commission Decision of 5 September 2023 C(2023) 6102 final, para. 57.

[90] Cf. GC 17.07.2024 – T-1077/23, ECLI:EU:T:2024:478 paras. 273 et seqq. = BeckRS 2024, 16880 – ByteDance v Commission.

[91] Commission Decision of 5 September 2023 C(2023) 6105 final, summary OJ C 2023/1029. Meta challenges the decision regarding Facebook by action for annulment, T-1078/23, OJ C 2024/561.

[92] Commission Decision of 5 September 2023 C(2023) 6102 final, summary OJ C 2023/552. Although TikTok also meets the definition of a video-sharing platform the Commission refrained from a double designation. ByteDance challenged the decision by action for annulment. However, ByteDance has not challenged the classification as online social networking service, GC 17.07.2024 – T-1077/23, ECLI:EU:T:2024:478 para. 158 = BeckRS 2024, 16880 – ByteDance v Commission.

[93] Commission Decision of 5 September 2023 C(2023) 6106 final, summary OJ C 2023/551.

[94] Commission Decision of 13 May 2024 C(2024) 3117 final.

[95] DG COMP <https://digital-markets-act.ec.europa.eu/commission-concludes-online-social-networking-service-x-should-not-be-designated-under-digital-2024-10-16_en> (last accessed: 19.10.2024).

[96] Directive 2010/13/EU of the European Parliament and of the Council of 10 March 2010 on the coordination of certain provisions laid down by law, regulation or administrative action in Member States concerning the provision of audiovisual media services (2010) OJ L 95/1, as amended by Directive (EU) 2018/1808 of the European Parliament and of the Council of 14 November 2018 amending Directive 2010/13/EU on the coordination of certain provisions laid down by law, regulation or administrative action in Member States concerning the provision of audiovisual media services (Audiovisual Media Services Directive) in view of changing market realities (2020), OJ L 303/69. On the concept of video-sharing platform, see also the Guidelines on the practical application of the essential functionality criterion of the definition of a 'video-sharing platform service' under the Audiovisual Media Services Directive (2020) OJ C 223/3.

[97] Directive 2002/21/EC of the European Parliament and of the Council of 7 March 2002 on a common regulatory framework for electronic communications networks and services (2002) OJ L 108/33. Repealed by Art. 125 of the EECC Directive (EU) 2018/1972.

without sound and differ only in the way they have been created.[98] The duration of the videos is irrelevant according to Art. 1(1)(b), (ba) AVMSD.[99] According to these criteria, YouTube in particular falls under Art. 2 no. 2(d) DMA. TikTok, in view of the importance of making user-generated videos available and the availability of corresponding tools, could (also) be regarded as a video-sharing platform service, even if it qualifies also as an online social networking service (→ mn. 15) within the meaning of Art. 2 no. 2(c) DMA. Not a video sharing service, but an on-demand audiovisual media service[100] are the services of **video streaming services** such as Netflix, Amazon Prime Video or Apple TV.

Since the purposes covered are very broadly defined as information, education and entertainment, it is questionable whether they are actually significant.[101] However, it is decisive that the services are directed at the **general public**, so that **closed user groups** are excluded.[102] Since closed user groups can be assumed to have their focus on the communicative networking element, corresponding services will generally be classified as online social networking services (→ mn. 15) or interpersonal communications services (→ mn. 18 et seqq.). 17

Concerning video-sharing platform services the Commission designated Alphabet[103] regarding Youtube as a gatekeeper.

Although TikTok also meets the definition of a video-sharing platform, the Commission refrained from a double designation.[104]

5. Number-independent interpersonal communications services (Art. 2 no. 2(e))

Number-independent interpersonal communications services are, according to Art. 2 no. 7 of the EECC Directive[105], services which neither establish a connection to publicly assigned numbering resources nor enable communication with corresponding numbers. An interpersonal communications service is a service normally provided for remuneration[106] that enables a direct interpersonal and interactive exchange of information via electronic communications networks between a finite number of persons, Art. 2 no. 5 EECC Directive. Thus – in contrast to the number-based services of Art. 2 no. 6 EECC Directive – these are communication services which **cannot establish a connection to the public telephone network.**[107] This primarily, but not exclusively, covers the classic mail and messenger services (so-called OTT communication services) (e.g. WhatsApp, Gmail, Skype, Microsoft Teams).[108] 18

[98] Zurth/Pless ZUM 2019, 414 (416 et seq.).

[99] Before the express clarification in the text of the Directive already: ECJ 21.10.2015 – C-347/14, ECLI:EU:C:2015:709 para. 20 = GRUR 2016, 101 – New Media Online.

[100] On the definition Art. 1(1)(g) AVMSD 2010/13/EU; in detail Hartmann Mediendienste 58 et seqq.; recital 27 AVMSD explicitly mentions video-on-demand as an example of an on-demand audiovisual media service. Critical of the non-inclusion of those under the DMA Podszun/Bongartz/Langenstein EuCML 2021, 60 (64).

[101] Affirmative Hoeren/Sieber/Holznagel MMR-HdB/Holznagel/Hartmann, 58th update, ch. 3 mn. 45.

[102] Hoeren/Sieber/Holznagel MMR-HdB/Holznagel/Hartmann, 58th update, ch. 3 mn. 50.

[103] Commission Decision of 5 September 2023 C(2023) 6101 final, summary OJ C 2023/549.

[104] Commission Decision of 5 September 2023 C(2023) 6102 final, summary OJ C 2023/552.

[105] Directive (EU) 2018/1972 of the European Parliament and of the Council of 11 December 2018 establishing the European Electronic Communications Code (2018) OJ L 321/36.

[106] Remuneration is also to be affirmed if the user is exposed to advertising for access to the service, recital 16 of the EECC Directive (EU) 2018/1972.

[107] Bulowski Internetkommunikationsdienste 83.

[108] Herbers RDi 2022, 252 (254); Kühling/Hildebrandt/Bulowski K&R 2022, 670.

19 In principle, the term therefore does not cover services which exclusively enable the user to make classic telephone calls via an Internet connection. However, it should not be concluded from this that such services automatically fall outside the scope of the DMA. This is because most of these communication services **also offer** the possibility of **direct communication** between users without a publicly assigned number. As soon as this is the case, it can no longer be assumed for the purposes of the DMA that the communication is number-based and the **entire service** is to be assessed as a number-independent interpersonal communication service within the meaning of Art. 2 no. 2(e) DMA. The reason for this are the different purposes of the EECC Directive and the DMA: While the EECC Directive as technology regulation provides for a clear technical separation of number-bound and number-independent interpersonal communication services,[109] the DMA aims to regulate the entire platform from an economic perspective. It must therefore be examined whether, according to the **common usage**, the **main purpose** of the service is communication between users without a publicly assigned number. A splitting of the service into its individual functions is not to be carried out due to the holistic view of the platform. However, a service that enables interpersonal communication only as a **secondary function** associated with another service, such as the communication channel in online games, is not an interpersonal communications service within the meaning of Art. 2 no. 6 of the EECC Directive.[110]

20 A compensation for this broad interpretation of the term "number-independent interpersonal communications services" is found in the exception of Art. 1(3)(b) DMA (→ mn. 73 et seqq.). Since OTT communication services do not fall under the strict regulation of the EECC Directive, unequal conditions of competition were feared by telecommunications providers.[111] Only a broad interpretation of the term "number-independent interpersonal communications services" can ensure that providers of OTT communications services do not escape regulation under the DMA by also offering a connection to the public network. If such a mixed service exists, it must be decided based on the exception in Art. 1(3)(b) DMA whether the transposition laws for the EECC Directive or the DMA apply with regard to individual types of conduct.

21 In contrast, against the background of the objectives and the regulatory structure, the argument that the DMA constitutes the counterpart to strict telecommunications regulation and should thus counteract the substitution of conventional telephone services by OTT communication services appears not convincing.[112] The DMA is intended to ensure the contestability and fairness of the market *in* which the gatekeeper is active, and not to protect neighbouring markets from crowding out – possibly due to innovation.

22 To **determine the number of users** pursuant to Art. 3(2)(b) DMA, only those users of the service are to be considered who (at least also) use the service for communication without a numbering resource on both sides.

Concerning number-independent interpersonal communications services, the Commission designated Meta[113] regarding WhatsApp and Messenger as gatekeeper.

Alphabet's Gmail and Microsoft's Outlook.com are number-independent interpersonal communications services within the meaning of Art. 2 no. 2(e) DMA but regard-

---

109 Gersdorf, in: Körber/Kühling Regulierung – Wettbewerb – Innovation 201.

110 Rec. 17 EECC Directive.

111 Kühling/Hildebrandt/Bulowski K&R 2022, 670 (670 set seq.).

112 In this direction probably Kühling/Hildebrandt/Bulowski K&R 2022, 670 (670 et seq.).

113 Commission Decision of 5 September 2023 C(2023) 6105 final, summary OJ C 2023/1029. Meta challenges the decision by action for annulment, T-1078/23, OJ C 2024/561.

less of exceeding the thresholds in Art. 3(2) DMA not considered as important gateways within the meaning of Art. 3(1)(b) DMA.[114] (→ mn. 52 et seq.)

Concerning Apple's iMessage, the commission initiated the procedure according to Art. 17(3) DMA (→ mn. 53),[115] leading to the acceptance of the rebuttal.[116]

6. Operating systems (Art. 2 no. 2(f))

No uniform definition of an operating system has been established in computer science. Apart from exceptional cases, it can be said that an operating system is software that runs in kernel mode.[117] This rather general definition is made more specific by referring to the two main tasks of an operating system, firstly the managing of hardware resources and secondly the provision of a clean abstract set of operating resources for applications.[118] Art. 2 no. 10 DMA defines an operating system as a system software that controls the **basic functions** of hardware or software and enables **software applications to run** on it. The DMA thus also seems to define an operating system by referring to its technical tasks. Thus, the control of the basic functions of hardware and software corresponds to the management of hardware resources, while the ability to run software applications can be roughly aligned with the clean abstraction of operating resources. That the possibility of executing software applications is not a prerequisite in the technical sense already follows from the nature of the operating system itself. If the operating system itself is software, the execution of software must already be possible without the operating system. If the DMA now requires that an operating system enables the execution of software applications, this is to be understood in the sense that the operating system enables software applications to access the hardware **by means of the abstraction it provides.** The control of basic functions is already achieved by the fact that the operating system controls the hardware components necessary for the operation of the actual computing operations without the need for a further software application. 23

Whether device drivers also fall under the term operating system seems questionable. Although these offer an abstraction of the operating resources present in the device, they must take the diversion via another operating system to enable the execution of software applications. In the absence of software applications, it must be assumed that drivers are not operating systems within the meaning of Art. 2 no. 10 DMA. 24

It remains unclear under which conditions software constitutes an operating system if it does not control the basic functions of hardware. Art. 2 no. 10 DMA explicitly provides for the possibility that an operating system can control the basic functions of software ("or software"). However, the possibility of also executing other software applications is given in many software applications via so-called plug-ins and add-ons. If the focus of these "software operating systems" were to be on enabling the execution of other applications, the concept of an operating system would in fact be a comprehensive catch-all for the inclusion of numerous computer programs in the DMA. At the very 25

---

[114] Commission Decision of 5 September 2023 C(2023) 6101 final, summary OJ C 2023/549; Commission Decision of 5 September 2023 C(2023) 6106 final, summary OJ C 2023/551.

[115] Commission Decision of 5 September 2023 C(2023) 6077 final. Apple challenges the decision by action for annulment insofar as it is predicated on a finding that iMessage is a number-independent interpersonal communications service, T-1079/23, OJ C 2024/562, T-1080/23, OJ C 2024/563. On the independent contestability of the Commission's decision to open a market investigation → mn. 62.

[116] Commission Decision of 12 February 2024 C(2024) 785 final, summary OJ C 2024/2710. Apple however challenges the decision by action for annulment insofar as it is predicated on a finding that iMessage is a number independent interpersonal communications service, T-214/24, OJ C 2024/3623. On the independent contestability of the implementing act concluding the market investigation → mn. 62.

[117] Tanenbaum/Bos, Modern Operating Systems, 4th edition 2015, 3.

[118] Tanenbaum/Bos, Modern Operating Systems, 4th edition 2015, 3 (3 et seq.).

least, therefore, it must be required that the **basic functions of the software** are controlled. The DMA does not provide answers to the questions of what *software* is, when its basic functions are controlled and how the operating system is then to be distinguished from the application.[119] In general usage and in the context of information technology, an operating system is usually only understood as software that controls the basic functions of the *hardware.* The inclusion of the control of software therefore leads to considerable difficulties of demarcation. If no restrictive interpretation has been established, in principle any software application that allows plug-ins or add-ins can be considered an operating system according to the wording of Art. 2 no. 10 DMA. The number of potential gatekeepers is thus likely to expand considerably – probably unintentionally – although this is limited by the fact that the provider of the corresponding control software must fulfil the criteria of a gatekeeper as defined in Art. 3(1) DMA.

Concerning operating systems, the Commission designated Microsoft[120] regarding Windows, Alphabet[121] concerning Android (incl. middleware such as Play Services) and Apple regarding iOS[122] and iPadOS[123] (after conducting a market investigation,[124] Art. 3(8), 17 DMA; → mn. 55 et seqq.) as gatekeepers.

7. Web browsers (Art. 2 no. 2(g))

26 According to Art. 2 no. 11 DMA, web browsers are software applications (Art. 2 no. 15 DMA) that enable end users (→ mn. 38 et seqq.) to access and interact with web content. This web content must be hosted on web servers connected by networks *such as the Internet.* This explicitly includes stand-alone web browsers as well as web browsers integrated or embedded in software or similar. In addition to the well-known web browsers for general use (e.g. Chrome, Safari or Internet Explorer), this also includes browser libraries provided for app development and applications for accessing pages via (peer-to-peer) overlay networks. The requirement of hosting on web servers does not stand in the way of including peer-to-peer networks, because a PC technically differs from a web server only in its function. If a PC is used as a host, it is (functionally) also to be regarded as a web server. However, the required interaction with the web content must be carried out by the user himself and not merely by the computer, so that applications for file sharing by means of protocols for decentralised distribution, such as BitTorrent clients, in principle do not fall under this provision. It may be different only if the accessing of torrent index sites is made possible.

27 In the Commission proposal, web browsers were not yet mentioned as core platform services. They were only included in the trilogue procedure.[125] In view of the existing oligopoly in web browsers, the inclusion is to be welcomed. Due to the technical specifications for website operators set by the operators of the major browsers, they offer a considerable potential for abusive practices.[126] As an example of the influence of the browser operators, Google's announced and (partly) reversed phase-out of support

---

119 Welcoming this due to flexibility reasons Report from a Panel of Economic Experts, 2021, 9.

120 Commission Decision of 5 September 2023 C(2023) 6106 final, summary OJ C 2023/551.

121 Commission Decision of 5 September 2023 C(2023) 6101 final, summary OJ C 2023/549.

122 Commission Decision of 5 September 2023 C(2023) 6100 final, summary OJ C 2023/548. Apple challenges the decision regarding the interoperability obligations (Art. 6(7) DMA; → § 12 mn. 64) by action for annulment based on a violation of the European Charter of Fundamental Rights (CFR), T-1080/23, OJ C 2024/563.

123 Commission Decision of 29 April 2024 C(2024) 2500 final, summary OJ C 2024/4374.

124 Commission Decision of 5 September 2023 C(2023) 6076 final.

125 Achleitner NZKart 2022, 359 (360).

126 Rec. 43 DMA.

for so-called third-party cookies in its browser Chrome can be mentioned, which has caused considerable unrest in the advertising industry.[127]

Concerning web browsers, the Commission designated Apple[128] regarding Safari and Alphabet[129] regarding Google Chrome as gatekeepers.

Samsung's Internet Browser is a web browser within the meaning of Art. 2 no. 2(h) DMA but regardless of exceeding the thresholds in Art. 3(2) DMA not an important gateway within the meaning of Art. 3(1)(b) DMA.[130] (→ mn. 52 et seq.)

Concerning Microsoft's browser Edge, the commission initiated the procedure according to Art. 17(3) DMA (→ mn. 53),[131] leading to the acceptance of the rebuttal.[132]

8. Virtual assistants (Art. 2 no. 2(h))

According to Art. 2 no. 12 DMA, virtual assistants are any form of software which **28** can process demands, tasks or questions and which provides access to other services or controls connected physical devices. Examples include Amazon Alexa or Apple Siri. The input can also be in audio, visual or written form. Virtual assistants were not yet included in the original Commission proposal. Their inclusion is justified by the danger virtual assistants may cause for competition as described in the sector enquiry "Consumer Internet of Things"[133].[134] The report is not binding for the interpretation of the term "virtual assistant", as it at best reflects the views of the Commission, but not of Council and Parliament.[135] For practical purposes, however, the final report can provide information on the Commission's view of how the term is to be understood and consequently also whether a service offered falls within the scope of the DMA in the Commission's view. The report can thus be informative in assessing whether the Commission expects a notification.

9. Cloud computing services (Art. 2 no. 2(i))

According to Art. 2 no. 13 DMA, cloud computing services are those as defined in **29** Art. 4 no. 19 NIS Directive[136]. These are digital services that enable access to a scalable[137]

[127] Critical on the inclusion of web browsers Alexiadis/de Streel BLI 2022, 163, 174; on the current developments on so-called tracking Wiedemann IIC 2021, 915.

[128] Commission Decision of 5 September 2023 C(2023) 6100 final, summary OJ C 2023/548.

[129] Commission Decision of 5 September 2023 C(2023) 6101 final, summary OJ C 2023/549.

[130] Commission Decision of 5 September 2023 C(2023) 6103 final, summary OJ C 2023/550.

[131] Commission Decision of 5 September 2023 C(2023) 6078 final.

[132] Commission Decision of 12 February 2024 C(2024) 806 final, summary OJ C 2024/2709.

[133] European Commission, Final Report – sector inquiry into consumer Internet of Things, COM(2022) 19 final.

[134] Achleitner NZKart 2022, 359 (360); Herbers RDi 2022, 252 (254); Bongartz/Kirk, in: HK-DMA Art. 2 mn. 66; in detail on the inclusion of virtual assistants Noskova Eur. Compet. J. 2023, 30; on virtual assistants under Art. 102 TFEU Morozovaite Eur. Compet. J. 2023, 410.

[135] For a stronger consideration Herbers RDi 2022, 252 (254).

[136] Directive (EU) 2016/1148 of the European Parliament and of the Council of 6 July 2016 concerning measures for a high common level of security of network and information systems across the Union (2016) OJ L 194/1; for the recast as NIS-2 Directive, see Directive (EU) 2022/2555 of the European Parliament and of the Council of 14 December 2022 on measures for a high common level of cyber security across the Union, amending Regulation (EU) No 910/2014 and Directive (EU) 2018/1972 and repealing Directive (EU) 2016/1148 (NIS-2 Directive) (2022) OJ L 333/80.

[137] On the term "scalable" rec. 33(2) NIS-2 Directive (EU) 2022/2555: "computing resources that are flexibly allocated by the cloud service provider, irrespective of the geographical location of the resources, in order to handle fluctuations in demand".

and elastic pool[138] of shareable[139] computing resources[140]. Accordingly, they must be computing resources that are flexibly allocated according to current demand and that are made available to several independent users when processed separately.[141] **Software as a Service** (SaaS), **Platform as a Service** (PaaS), **Network as a Service** (NaaS) and **Infrastructure as a Service** (IaaS) fall under this broad definition.[142] However, it is uncertain whether cloud computing services in this sense also include **application service providing** and private clouds in which dedicated hardware (so-called single tenancy) is made available to customers.[143]

30 In principle, the wording would also cover social networks and messenger services that enable shared file storage, as this requires the use of computing power, which, from a strictly technical point of view, would also include the sending and sharing of files.[144] This extension, caused by the (too) broad wording, misses the regulatory objective, because social networks are regulated separately by Art. 2 no. 7 DMA and messenger services by Art. 2 no. 9 DMA. A cloud computing service should therefore only be assumed (following the distinction of technical-functional main and secondary functions of audiovisual media services in the AVMS Directive) if the provision of SaaS, PaaS, NaaS or IaaS is the **main purpose** of a not merely secondary function of the service according to the **common usage**. The merely incidental provision of storage space, for example with webmail providers, does not make the service a cloud computing service.

10. Online advertising services (Art. 2 no. 2(j))

31 Different from the other platform services, the DMA does not contain a legal definition of the term online advertising service.[145] Instead, Art. 2 no. 2(j) DMA gives examples and thus merely describes the term. On the basis of these examples, online advertising services can be understood as **advertising brokerage services** that broker digital advertising space in the broadest sense.[146] However, the display of ads in other services of the gatekeeper is still part of the advertising service.[147] The term is not limited to "pro-

[138] The term "elastic pool" describes computing resources that are "provided and released according to demand in order to rapidly increase or decrease resources available depending on workload", rec. 33(2) NIS-2 Directive (EU) 2022/2555.

[139] The term "shareable" describes computing resources "provided to multiple users who share a common access to the service, but where the processing is carried out separately for each user, although the service is provided from the same electronic equipment", rec. 33(2) NIS-2 Directive (EU) 2022/2555.

[140] Computing resources "include resources such as networks, servers or other infrastructure, operating systems, software, storage, applications and services", rec. 33(1) NIS-2 Directive (EU) 2022/2555.

[141] Beucher/Ehlen, in: Kipker Cybersecurity-HdB, 2nd edition 2023, ch. 14 mn. 220; Buchberger, in: Schenke/Graulich/Ruthig BSIG § 2 mn. 16, which, however, require a large number of users with reference to rec. 17 NIS Directive 2016/1148. Correctly, however, in the case of flexible allocation by the provider, two independent users are sufficient. However, with such a small number of users, the criteria for gatekeeper status under Art. 3(1) DMA will hardly be met, so that the DMA will not be applicable for this reason.

[142] Rec. 33(1) NIS-2 Directive 2022/2555; on categorisation Mell/Grance NIST Special Publication 800–145.

[143] Grünwald/Döpkens MMR 2011, 287; Beucher/Ehlen, in: Kipker Cybersecurity-HdB, 2nd edition 2023, ch. 14 mn. 221; on the general understanding of the term James, in: Leupold/Wiebe/Glossner IT-Recht Part 11.2 mn. 3 et seq.; Meents, in: FA-InfoTechnologieR ch. 7 mn. 257. However, Schallbruch CR 2016, 663 (666) for the inclusion of virtual instances of standard software such as Microsoft Office 365 and shared project management systems such as Slack; likewise Bongartz/Kirk, in: HK-DMA Art. 2 mn. 73.

[144] Schallbruch CR 2016, 663 (666).

[145] See also rec. 45 DMA.

[146] Art. 5(10), 6(8), rec. 45 subpara. 2 DMA describe this simply as "inventory".

[147] Commission Decision of 5 September 2023 C(2023) 6101 final, summary OJ C 2023/549.

grammatic advertising"[148] so that it includes advertising space on websites and video and audio content as well as product placements and other forms of "influencer marketing".[149] It is sufficient that end users are usually shown a product or service in return for payment.[150] If the advertising is not placed on the platform operator's own website, the website operators are to be considered business users alongside the advertisers (on the concept of "corporate website users" → mn. 42).

An advertising service is only a core platform service if its operator operates another core platform service in one of the other forms of Art. 2 no. 2 DMA. However, it is sufficient if the thresholds regarding the number of users according to Art. 3(2)(b) DMA are fulfilled by the advertising service, but not by the other platform service. This is intended to cover situations in which a gatekeeper operates several services (including at least one core platform service pursuant to Art. 2 no. 1(a)–(i) DMA), which do not individually reach 45 million active end users and 10 000 business users per year (cf. Art. 3(2)(b) DMA). The advertising service linked to them may nevertheless reach these thresholds because it is used across different platforms. In this case, the platform service as defined in Art. 2 no. 2(a)–(i) DMA would not be an important gateway to end users as defined in Art. 3(1)(b) DMA, but the advertising service would be, so that a designation as gatekeeper is possible. A **link between** the advertising service and the other core platform service is **not required**. In particular, the advertising service does not have to be offered or operated within the other platform service, but can also be operated (exclusively) on third-party websites. 32

The fact that advertising services themselves also fall under the concept of core platform services is to be welcomed in view of the importance of online advertising for initiating contractual relationships with consumers. However, the **link to the operation of another platform service,** which may have remained in the DMA as an echo of the discussion on the requirement of a digital ecosystem (→ mn. 7, 46), is questionable and can only be justified with the unconvincing assumption of the legislator that the operation of an advertising network can only take place on its own platform. However, the operation of the advertising network can be detached from that of the actual platform. For example, Google Ads takes care of the advertising business for many smaller website operators in return for a share of the revenues. The (potential) market power of such external advertising networks is not diminished by this, but on the contrary strengthened by the greater coverage.[151] Tying to another platform service also leads to arbitrary results. For example, there is no reason why an operating system provider with less than 45 million end users can be designated as a gatekeeper when operating an online advertising network, while video streaming providers[152] can operate a corresponding advertising network even with several hundred million of end users without falling in the scope of the DMA. 33

148 Although rec. 45 DMA refers to the complexity of online advertising due to programmatic advertising.

149 Differing probably Bongartz/Kirk, in: HK-DMA Art. 2 mn. 12, referring to the mention of "programmatic advertising" in rec. 45 DMA.

150 Similar with recourse to Directive 2006/114/EC Bongartz/Kirk, in: HK-DMA Art. 2 mn.12.

151 Rec. 44 DMA recognises this possibility in principle.

152 Critical of the non-inclusion Podszun/Bongartz/Langenstein EuCML 2021, 60 (64).

Concerning online advertising services the Commission designated Meta[153] regarding MetaAds, Amazon[154] regarding Amazon Advertising and Alphabet[155] regarding its advertising services as gatekeepers.

The Commission accepted the rebuttals (→ mn. 52 et seq.) submitted by X[156] (formerly Twitter) and ByteDance[157] (TikTok) regarding their advertising services. Concerning Microsoft Ads the Commission initiated the procedure according to Art. 17(3) DMA (→ mn. 53),[158] which led to the acceptance of the rebuttal.[159]

11. New platform services

34 It is also possible for new platform services to be included in the DMA, e.g. future platform services based on artificial intelligence. For this purpose, the Commission conducts a market investigation pursuant to Art. 19 DMA (→ § 13, mn. 42 et seqq., 97 et seqq.) regarding the platform service to be included and submits a legislative proposal to the Council and the European Parliament for the **inclusion of further services** in Art. 2 no. 2 DMA. The effectiveness of this (supposedly long) procedure has been questioned in view of the dynamics of the digital sector.[160] However, the problem is smaller as it may seem. Apart from the fact that an extension of the strict regulatory requirements of the DMA should be democratically decided and on the facts be convincingly justified, in view of the very high threshold values, it can hardly be assumed that a market "tips" so quickly or unpredictably that this could not be recognised by the Commission in time and addressed by initiating the procedure according to Art. 19 DMA. The developments of the last decades show that the services covered today by the DMA rose in importance for several years. During this time, the growth of oligopolistic and monopolistic structures did not come over night, but developed over several years. With this experience, it is obvious that the Commission would and should carry out a market investigation precisely in this growth phase. Moreover, the time for the market investigation was reduced from 24 months to 18 months (Art. 19(3) DMA). The argument that the legislative procedure itself takes too long is also not convincing. The adoption of the DMA itself is proof enough that European legislative procedures can also proceed quickly. In the case of the mere inclusion of a single service, this process is likely to be much shorter. If an undesirable market development is resolved within this period, regulation by the DMA is not necessary, which ideally should already be established as a result of the market investigation.

A market investigation pursuant to Art. 19 DMA can be requested by three or more Member States (Art. 41(3)(b) DMA). The request is not binding (Art. 41(5) DMA). The decision to open a market investigation remains at the discretion of the Commission.[161]

---

[153] Commission Decision of 5 September 2023 C(2023) 6105 final, summary OJ C 2023/1029.

[154] Commission Decision of 5 September 2023 C(2023) 6104 final, summary OJ C 2023/905.

[155] Commission Decision of 5 September 2023 C(2023) 6101 final, summary OJ C 2023/549. In contrast to Alphabets delineation, the Commission views all Alphabet services concerning advertising as one single platform service, including Google Analytics, AdSense and the display of the ads.

[156] Commission Decision of 13 May 2024 C(2024) 3156 final.

[157] Commission Decision of 13 May 2024 C(2024) 3153 final.

[158] Commission Decision of 5 September 2023 C(2023) 6078 final.

[159] Commission Decision of 12 February 2024 C(2024) 806 final, summary OJ C 2024/2709.

[160] Kumkar RDi 2022, 347 (349); Monti TILEC Discussion Paper No. 4–2021, 10 (10 et seq.); Schweitzer ZEuP 2021, 503 (521); Zimmer/Göhsl ZWeR 2021, 29 (39 et seq.).

[161] Gappa/Käseberg, in: HK-DMA Art. 41 mn. 3.

The Member States may bring an action for annulment (Art. 263(2) TFEU) against the Commission's decision not to open a market investigation.[162]

When it has been argued that the Council and the Parliament could also amend the regulation without the procedure of Art. 19 DMA,[163] this is true from a legal point of view but misjudges the political effects of the procedurally anchored market investigation. By carrying out the market investigation according to the DMA, the Commission creates the basis for negotiations with the Council and the Parliament, which would subsequently have to give good reasons for a refusal to include the service concerned. 35

Also, the existing (very comprehensive) powers of the Commission under the DMA are not unduly expanded by Art. 19 DMA.[164] The fact that the Commission was not directly given the competence to add further services is primarily due to political reasons. The Member States may have an interest in excluding domestic – or for tax reasons domestically established – platform services from the application of the DMA. The current compromise text of the DMA has only been made possible by the fact that primarily the large US tech companies are covered. The political decision as to which other services and thus companies should be covered by the DMA, which has far-reaching regulatory implications, should not be made by the Commission alone, if only for reasons of democratic legitimacy.[165] 36

II. Personal scope

In defining its personal scope of application, the DMA refers to, on the one hand, a provider of core platform services within the meaning of Art. 2 no. 2 DMA, who has been designated as **gatekeeper** pursuant to Art. 3 DMA, and, on the other hand, to business users or end users. 37

1. Business users and end users

The terms business user (Art. 2 no. 21 DMA) and end user (Art. 2 no. 20 DMA) are **mutually exclusive**. Together with the provider of the platform service, they form the totality of all persons coming into contact with the platform service. A demarcation of business users and end users may seem dispensable due to their mutually exclusive but collectively exhaustive nature. However, the thresholds in Art. 3(2) DMA (→ mn. 47 et seqq.) and the different requirements for the territorial scope of application (→ mn. 64 et seqq.), which is determined according to the establishment of business users and the establishment or location of end users (Art. 1(2) DMA), make a clear definition necessary. 38

Business users are natural or legal persons who use core platform services acting in commercial or professional capacity for the purpose of or in the course of providing goods or services to end users (Art. 2 no. 21 DMA). This definition is very similar to the definition in Art. 2 no. 1 P2B Regulation and the definition of trader in Art. 2 no. 2 Consumer Rights Directive (CRD)[166], so that a parallel interpretation may seem obvious. 39

---

162 Only if the Commission does not react at all to such a request an action for failure to act pursuant to Art. 265 TFEU exceptionally is admissible.

163 Schweitzer ZEuP 2021, 503 (521); Zimmer/Göhsl ZWeR 2021, 29 (39 et seq.).

164 According to Art. 49 in conjunction with Art. 12 DMA, the Commission can independently determine further obligations for gatekeepers.

165 Differing Schweitzer ZEuP 2021, 503 (521); Zimmer/Göhsl ZWeR 2021, 29 (40).

166 Directive 2011/83/EU of the European Parliament and of the Council of 25 October 2011 on consumer rights, amending Council Directive 93/13/EEC and Directive 1999/44/EC of the European

However, the view that case law and literature on the definition of consumer in Art. 2 no. 2 CRD can be used, as it has been argued correspondingly for the P2B Regulation,[167] is rejected in recital 14(5) for the DMA. The ECJ has consistently ruled that the term "trader" – and consequently the term "business user" – is to be defined negatively by distinguishing it from the counter term "consumer".[168] In the DMA, by contrast, the counter concept to "business user" is not that of consumer, but that of "end user", which is not congruent with the concept of consumer (cf. recital 14(5) DMA).

40 The decisive criterion for distinguishing between "business user" and "end user" is therefore not the connection of the use with business or professional activities, but the **provision of goods and services** or the **demand** for them. Thus, recital 14(5) DMA clarifies that the term "end user" is intended to include, in certain circumstances, users "that are traditionally considered business users, but in a given situation do not use the core platform services to provide goods or services to other end users", such as companies using cloud computing services for their own purposes. This is only consistent if one regards that the definition of "business" in the DMA is establishing a new criterion – different from Art. 2 no. 2 CRD – by focusing on the provision of goods or services on the platform.[169] A buyer on a B2B platform is thus explicitly not subject to the term "business user" in Art. 2 no. 21 DMA, but is obviously not a consumer either. The fact that Art. 2 no. 21 DMA nevertheless requires a connection to commercial or professional activities is only intended to make consumers on the "supplier side" part of the group of end users. In comparison to the distinction between traders/consumers, the group of **business** users is thus limited to all **traders** that act as **providers** of goods and services, while end users are all other (also traders) users who act as (potential) **demanders**, as well as consumers on the supply side.[170]

41 The consequences of Art. 2 no. 20 and no. 21 DMA for the inclusion of **exchange platforms** in the DMA are not entirely clear. As a starting point, it can be stated that all consumers as users of exchange platforms fall under the term end user, since their exchange offer is not made in the course of a business or professional activity. Difficulties only arise when commercial users mutually provide goods and services to each other via a platform. If Art. 2 no. 21 DMA is applied literally, one could assume that there is no provision of goods or services to end users in this case and thus no commercial users, because according to Art. 2 no. 20 DMA end users are only persons who do not act as commercial users. If the alleged "end users" use the platform in the course of their commercial or professional activities to provide goods or services, one could therefore be inclined to deny them end user status. However, this would run counter to the objective of the DMA to ensure "for *all*[171] businesses, contestable and fair markets in the digital sector […] to the benefit of business users and end users" (Art. 1(1), on the concept of the digital sector Art. 2 no. 4 DMA). The wording in Art. 2 no. 21 DMA that the provision of the goods or services must be to *end users* should therefore be understood on exchange platforms in such a way that the dual role both as a provider (also acting commercially) and as a buyer of goods or services does not prevent the qualification as an end user in

---

Parliament and of the Council and repealing Council Directive 85/577/EEC and Directive 97/7/EC of the European Parliament and of the Council (2011) OJ L 304/64.

[167] Busch/Schulte-Nölke P2B-VO Art. 2 mn. 5; Köhler/Bornkamm/Feddersen/Alexander, 41st ed. 2023, P2B-VO Art. 2 mn. 4; Uitz P2B-VO 65.

[168] ECJ 3.10.2013 – C-59/12, ECLI:EU:C:2013:634 para. 33 = NJW 2014, 288 – BKK/Wettbewerbszentrale; ECJ 4.10.2018 – C-105/17, ECLI:EU:C:2018:808 para. 33 = GRUR 2018, 1154 – Kamenova.

[169] For this reason, the application of the principles developed in regard of Art. 2 no. 2 Consumer Rights Directive on Art. 2 No. 1 P2B Regulation also appears questionable.

[170] Cf. Bongartz/Kirk, in: HK-DMA Art. 2 mn. 107 but also mn. 103.

[171] Emphasis added.

the role of a buyer. Recital 14 DMA also states that the notion of end user should, in *certain circumstances*, include users who are normally considered to be business users *if* they do not use core platform services to provide goods and services to end users in a particular situation, such as companies using cloud computing services for their own purposes. Accordingly, undertakings that demand goods or services on core platform services for their own purposes should be considered end users in that role as demanders, even if at the same time they also use the platform in the course of a commercial or professional activity for providing goods or services to end users.

The concept of **corporate website users**, familiar from the P2B Regulation (Art. 2 no. 7 P2B Regulation), is not to be found in the DMA. If they use a core platform service to provide goods or services, they are to be characterised as business users.[172] **42**

2. Gatekeeper

Only an operator of core platform services (→ mn. 6 et seqq.) that has been designated in the procedure pursuant to Art. 3 DMA is subject to regulation by the DMA as a gatekeeper within the meaning of Art. 2 no. 1 DMA. The Commission shall publish an updated list of all gatekeepers and core platform services designated by decisions pursuant to Art. 3(9) DMA (Art. 4(3) DMA). **43**

a) *Undertaking*

Prior to the new version of Art. 3 DMA in the trilogue procedure, there was extensive discussion about which (legal) person should be designated as gatekeeper. It was proposed that the operator of a core platform service should be designated as gatekeeper, but the turnover and other figures of the undertaking "to which it [the gatekeeper] belongs" should be decisive for the characterisation as gatekeeper.[173] This discussion has now been resolved: It is always the undertaking which is considered as the gatekeeper. According to Art. 2 no. 27 of the DMA, an **undertaking** is an **entity engaged in economic activity**, regardless of its legal status and the way in which it is financed, including all linked enterprises or connected undertakings that form a group through the direct or indirect control of an enterprise or undertaking by another. The DMA thus adopts the functional concept of undertaking developed by the ECJ[174] in European competition law. This explicit clarification was necessary because the DMA is based on the competence of Art. 114 TFEU. The concept of undertaking under competition law is therefore not necessarily transferable to the DMA,[175] especially since the application of the concept of undertaking even in private competition tort law was controversial for a long time until clarification by the ECJ[176] and is still uncertain in other legal contexts, for example, in the GDPR.[177] In the DMA, the criteria developed by the ECJ on the concept of undertaking are to be applied, since terms that are used in the same way in different **44**

---

172 See also the definitions for active business users of online search engines and web browsers in Annex E.

173 Critically, Zimmer/Göhsl ZWeR 2021, 29 (40 et seq.), (48).

174 ECJ 23.4.1991 – C-41/90, ECLI:EU:C:1991:161 para. 21 = NJW 1991, 2891 – Höfner and Elser; ECJ 17.2.1993 – C-159/91 and C-160/91, ECLI:EU:C:1993:63 para. 17 = NJW 1993, 2597 – Poucet and Pistre; ECJ 10.1.2006 – C-222/04, ECLI:EU:C:2006:8 para. 107 = EuZW 2006, 306 – Cassa di Risparmio di Firenze; ECJ 11.7.2006 – C-205/03, ECLI:EU:C:2006:453 para. 25 = EuZW 2006, 600 – FENIN; ECJ 12.7.2012 – C-138/11, ECLI:EU:C:2012:449 para. 35 = EuZW 2012, 835 – Compass-Datenbank; ECJ 10.9.2009 – C-97/08 P, ECLI:EU:C:2009:536 para. 54 = EuZW 2009, 816 – Akzo Nobel.

175 Zimmer/Göhsl ZWeR 2021, 29 (35).

176 ECJ 14.3.2019 – C-724/17, ECLI:EU:C:2019:204 paras. 28 et seqq. = NJW 2019, 1197 – Skanska; on the discussion Heinze ZEuP 2020, 281 (293).

177 On the extension of corporate liability beyond competition law Heinze ZEuP 2020, 281 (293). For the Brussels Ia Regulation, see also ECJ 4.7.2024 – C-425/22, ECLI:EU:C:2024:578 para. 44 – MOL.

European legal acts generally have the same meaning in the interest of unity and coherence of the Union legal order, at least if the Union legislator has not expressed a different intention and the legal act in question is based on the principles and provisions of the subject matter in question.[178] Since the definition from competition law was deliberately adopted in the DMA and the DMA is deliberately designed as a supplement to the general competition rules,[179] it is "based on the principles and provisions of the relevant subject area", so that the concept of undertaking is to be interpreted consistently. One might only consider a diverging interpretation if the case law on the concept of undertaking under competition law were to change substantially. Then the question would arise whether the European legislator intended to adopt the understanding of the term at the time of the DMA, so that only the *status quo* at the time of the enactment of the DMA can be referred to and an own interpretation oriented towards the DMA would become necessary. However, such a change in the highly differentiated case law is not to be expected, so that the principles developed by the ECJ on the concept of an undertaking under competition law[180] can be reverted to.

b) General requirements

45 The requirements for designation as a gatekeeper are set out in Art. 3(1) DMA. According to this, an operator of core platform services (→ mn. 6 et seqq.) must have a **significant impact** on the internal market (a), the platform service provided must serve business users as an important **gateway** to reach end users (b) and the company must enjoy an **entrenched and durable position** in its operations or such a position must at least be foreseeable in the near future[181] (c). The DMA thus essentially establishes a functional criterion (gateway function) and a relevance criterion (impact on the internal market). The further requirement of an entrenched and durable position primarily serves the purpose of not having to initiate proceedings where the (presumed) risks for competition do not materialise or materialise only for a very short time. The designation as gatekeeper is made **in relation to a core platform service** that serves as an important gateway for business users to reach end users (Art. 3(1)(b) DMA), i.e. only for "those of their core platform services that individually constitute an important gateway for business users to reach end users".[182] Accordingly, in the designation decision pursuant to Art. 3(4) or (8) DMA, the Commission lists the core platform services of the undertaking in question which are to be regarded as an important gateway within the meaning of Art. 3(1)(b) DMA (Art. 3(9) DMA). In this context, the "fact that it is possible that an undertaking providing core platform services not only intermediates between business users and end users, but also between end users and end users should not preclude the conclusion that such an undertaking is or could be an important gateway for business users to reach end users".[183]

46 It is not necessary for the designation that the undertaking has a **dominant position** in the sense of competition law.[184] Since neither a determination of the relevant market

[178] ECJ 4.10.2011 – C-403/08 and C-429/08, ECLI:EU:C:2011:631 para. 188 = GRUR 2012, 156 – Football Association Premier League/Murphy; ECJ 3.7.2012 – C-128/11, ECLI:EU:C:2012:407 para. 60 = NJW 2012, 2565 – UsedSoft; Peifer/Heinze Einl. C mn. 25.

[179] Rec. 11 DMA.

[180] Calliess/Ruffert/Weiß TFEU Art. 101 mn. 25 et seqq. with further references.

[181] The term "near future" is not defined by the DMA. Following Käseberg/Gappa, in: HK-DMA Art. 3 mn. 5, however, it seams reasonable to refer to the three-year review period in Art. 4(2) DMA.

[182] Rec. 15 DMA.

[183] Rec. 15 DMA.

[184] Cf. rec. 5 DMA.

nor a qualitative analysis of market dominance is required, the gatekeeper designation has the advantage of greater speed compared to classic instruments of competition law.[185] In contrast to general competition law, it is also not necessary to determine the actual, possible or presumed **effects** of a gatekeeper's conduct on the market in order to determine gatekeeper status.[186] Nor was a general **efficiency defence**, i.e. the reference to overriding efficiency gains through a certain conduct of the gatekeeper, for instance in the form of a possible exemption from some of the obligations under Art. 5 et seqq. DMA,[187] included in the DMA. An efficiency defence should therefore not be taken into account to determine the scope of application of the DMA, at least not as a general defence.[188] The requirement of a "**digital ecosystem**" proposed as a fourth criterion for gatekeeper status, i.e. that the gatekeeper operates at least two interrelated platform services or is active in a dual role, for example as a marketplace operator and trader on a marketplace, as proposed before the adoption of the DMA,[189] was not included in the DMA either.[190] Nevertheless, the benefits and disadvantages associated with the existence or absence of an ecosystem may be taken into account in the assessment of the gateway criterion in the procedure of rebutting (→ mn. 52 et seq.) the presumption in Art. 3(2) DMA.[191] The determination of the requirements of Art. 3(1) DMA for the gatekeeper status can be based on the **fulfilment of quantitative thresholds** (Art. 3(2) DMA) in the procedure according to Art. 3(3) and (4) DMA or, if the thresholds of Art. 3(2) DMA are not met, based on the **qualitative aspects of Art. 3(8) DMA** in the procedure according to Art. 17 DMA.

c) Gatekeeper status due to fulfilment of thresholds (quantitative criteria, Art. 3(2) DMA)

According to Art. 3(2) DMA, it "shall be presumed [in the sense of a rebuttable presumption, → mn. 52 et seq.]" that an undertaking fulfils the conditions for gatekeeper status set out in Art. 3(1) DMA as soon as certain **thresholds** are reached. The Commission is empowered to adopt delegated acts in the procedure under Art. 49 DMA, in compliance with Art. 37 DMA, to determine the methods for deciding whether the quantitative thresholds in Art. 3(2) DMA are met (Art. 3(6) DMA), without, however, changing **47**

---

185 Report from a Panel of Economic Experts, 2021, 28; Zimmer/Göhsl ZWeR 2021, 29 (38 et seq.); on the underlying difficulties in competition law Crémer/de Montjoye/Schweitzer Competition policy for the digital era (2019) and European Commission, Impact Assessment Report SWD(2020) 363 final, para. 119; for the UK: Digital Competition Expert Panel (2019); for a comparison to the proposed New pro-competition regime (December 2020 CMA135) see Jenny Concurrences No. 3–2021, 38 paras. 170 et seqq.

186 Rec. 11 DMA.

187 Monopolkommission Sondergutachten 82: Empfehlungen für einen effektiven und effizienten Digital Markets Act (2021) mn. 167 with suggested wording.

188 Rec. 23 subpara. 2 DMA; critically Kumkar, in: FK-KartellR DMA Art. 3 mn. 54.

189 French Government/Ministry for Economic Affairs (Germany)/Ministry of Economic Affairs (Netherlands) ("friends of an effective Digital Markets Act"), Strengthening the Digital Markets Act and Its Enforcement, 1; De Streel/Cave/Feasey/Krämer/Monti CERRE Recommendation Paper 11–2020, 10, 12; likewise Monopolkommission Sondergutachten 82: Empfehlungen für einen effektiven und effizienten Digital Markets Act (2021) mn. 38 et seq. with suggested wording; rejecting Zimmer/Göhsl ZWeR 2021, 29 (37); Alexiadis/de Streel BLI 2022, 163, 176.

190 Gerpott CR 2022, 409 (412), however, sees this as a supplementary criterion in Art. 3(8)(g). The reference to the control of entire "platform ecosystems" can still be found in the general explanation of the dangers to competition in rec. 3 DMA, in the definition of contestability in rec. 32 DMA and in rec. 64 DMA on number-independent interpersonal communication services. Cf. Commission Decision of 5 September 2023 C(2023) 6102 final, mn. 130.

191 GC 17.07.2024 – T-1077/23, ECLI:EU:T:2024:478 paras. 131 et seqq. = BeckRS 2024, 16880 – ByteDance v Commission.

the quantitative thresholds themselves.[192] Under the **anti-circumvention rule** of Art. 13(1) DMA, the designation of an undertaking as a gatekeeper is not prevented by the fact that the company segments, divides, fragments or splits the core platform services by contractual, commercial, technical or other means in order to avoid exceeding the quantitative thresholds of Art. 3(2) DMA. Apple argued that its App Store (→ mn. 8 et seqq.) and its web browser (→ mn. 26 et seq.) Safari are in fact multiple services depending on the type of device (e.g. PC, smartphone, tablet computer) they are running on. The Commission did not follow this argument and designated Apple as a provider of *one* software application store and *one* web browser.[193]

48 A **significant impact on the internal market** within the meaning of Art. 3(1)(a) DMA is assumed if the company (1) provides the same core platform service in **at least three Member States** of the Union (cf. Art. 1(3)(b), (c) Merger Regulation[194]) and (2) either has an **annual turnover** in the Union of at least EUR 7.5 billion in each of the last three financial years *or* if its **average market capitalisation** or – in the case of unlisted companies – its equivalent fair market value in the previous financial year amounted to at least EUR 75 billion (Art. 3(2)(a) DMA).[195] In contrast to the turnover criterion, it is not relevant for the market capitalisation criterion whether it is mainly based on business activities outside the EU.[196] The market capitalisation value should be "based on a level that reflects the average market capitalisation of the largest publicly listed undertakings in the Union over an appropriate period".[197] In this context, "a market capitalisation at or above the threshold in the **last financial year** should give rise to a **presumption** that an undertaking providing core platform services has a significant impact on the internal market"; a market capitalisation which is at least equal to the threshold for **at least three years** can be "considered as further **strengthening that presumption**".[198] In individual cases, a detailed examination of the factors affecting market capitalisation may be necessary, for example "where the market capitalisation of the undertaking providing core platform services in preceding financial years was significantly lower than the threshold and the volatility of its market capitalisation over the observed period was disproportionate to overall equity market volatility or its market capitalisation trajectory relative to market trends was inconsistent with a rapid and unidirectional growth".[199] It is therefore possible to rebut the indicative effect of the market capitalisation criterion for the existence of a "significant impact on the internal market" within the meaning of Art. 3(1)(a) DMA even if the threshold value is reached.

49 The DMA assumes that an undertaking with a high group turnover in the Union that also meets the threshold for the number of users of core platform services in the Union has "a relatively strong ability to monetise those users".[200] Where there is not a high group turnover but a high market capitalisation in relation to the same threshold for the number of users in the Union, the DMA considers that the undertaking has "a

[192] Rec. 22 DMA.

[193] Commission Decision C(2023) 6100 final, summary OJ C 2023/548 paras. 12 et seq. Apple challenges the decision regarding its App Store by action for annulment, T-1080/23, OJ C 2024/563.

[194] Council Regulation (EC) No 139/2004 of 20 January 2004 on the control of concentrations between undertakings (2004) OJ L 24/1.

[195] Rec. 17 subpara. 1 DMA.

[196] GC 17.07.2024 – T-1077/23, ECLI:EU:T:2024:478 paras. 104 et seqq. = BeckRS 2024, 16880 – ByteDance v Commission; cf. Commission Decision of 5 September 2023 C(2023) 6102 final, mn. 124; critically Higer/Patt NZKart 2024, 78 (83 et seq.).

[197] Rec. 17 subpara. 2 DMA.

[198] Rec. 18 DMA.

[199] Rec. 19 DMA.

[200] Rec. 17 subpara. 2 DMA.

relatively significant potential to monetise those users in the near future".[201] The monetisation potential "in turn reflects, in principle, the gateway position of the undertakings concerned".[202] Apart from their relevance in determining monetisation potential, the indicators of high group turnover and high market capitalisation "reflect the financial capacity of the undertakings concerned, including their ability to leverage their access to financial markets to reinforce their position",[203] for example to acquire other (possibly currently or potentially competing) companies.[204] In addition, market capitalisation reflects expectations of the company's future position and impact in the domestic market, even if its current turnover is (still) relatively low.[205] The two criteria thus describe two similar but distinct situations of impact on the internal market. The fact that one of them is not fulfilled can be considered in the rebuttal of the presumption. However, due to the alternative nature of the criteria this alone cannot be considered as sufficient grounds for rebutting the presumption.[206]

Regarding the threshold values it is worth noting that the original Commission proposal already set the threshold at EUR 6.5 billion turnover and a market value of EUR 65 billion. The raising of the thresholds in the trilogue procedure can therefore also be understood as a "compensation" for the inclusion of web browsers (→ mn. 26 et seq.) and virtual assistants (→ mn. 28) as core platform services.[207] The threshold criterion is not a concretisation of market dominance under Art. 103(2)(c) TFEU, but a mere notability criterion for determining a **potential threat** to the contestability of the market and thus goes beyond general competition law.[208] **50**

According to Art. 3(2)(b) of the DMA, an **important gateway to end users** within the meaning of Art. 3(1)(b) of the DMA can be assumed if the core platform service had an average of at least **45 million end users established or located in the Union** (Art. 2 no. 20 DMA, → mn. 38 et seqq.) and **10 000 business users established in the Union** (Art. 2 no. 21 DMA, → mn. 38 et seqq.) in the previous financial year. The characteristic of being a gateway thus depends on the fact that a "very high number of business users [...] depend[209] on a core platform service to reach a very high number of monthly active end users". In this case, the undertaking providing the service can "influence the operations of a substantial part of business users to its advantage".[210] The fact that the provider of the core platform services not only intermediates between business users and end users, but also between end users and end users, does not preclude the finding that such an undertaking is or could be an important gateway for business users to reach end users.[211] In setting the thresholds, the Union legislator requires a significant percentage **51**

---

201 Rec. 17 subpara. 2 DMA.

202 Rec. 17 subpara. 2 DMA.

203 Rec. 17 subpara. 2 DMA.

204 Rec. 17 subpara. 2 DMA.

205 Rec. 17 subpara. 2 DMA.

206 GC 17.07.2024 – T-1077/23, ECLI:EU:T:2024:478 paras. 85 et seqq. = BeckRS 2024, 16880 – ByteDance v Commission.

207 Parliament had even demanded EUR 8 billion in annual turnover or EUR 80 billion in market capitalisation, see Gerpott CR 2022, 409 (412).

208 Zimmer/Göhsl ZWeR 2021, 29 (31); differing Basedow ZEuP 2021, 217 (222); Borges, in: Borges/Keil Big Data § 1 mn. 45; cf. GC 17.07.2024 – T-1077/23, ECLI:EU:T:2024:478 para. 198 = BeckRS 2024, 16880 – ByteDance v Commission; Kumkar, in: FK-KartellR DMA Art. 3 mn. 18; König, in: Borges/Keil Big Data § 12 mn. 17.

209 It is not implausible that a business user depends on the service in question, solely due to the prevalence of multi-homing on the market for the specific core platform service, GC 17.07.2024 – T-1077/23, ECLI:EU:T:2024:478 para. 210 = BeckRS 2024, 16880 – ByteDance v Commission.

210 Rec. 20 DMA.

211 Rec. 15 DMA.

of the total Union population for the number of end users, while the threshold for commercial users is based on a significant percentage of undertakings using core platform services.[212] In the interest of legal certainty for gatekeepers, the factors for determining and calculating the number of users per core platform service are set out in the Annex to the DMA.[213] The Annex also contains a table with definitions for the users of each platform service. The Commission is empowered to change the calculation method and indicators of the user numbers in the Annex (Art. 3(7) DMA) but not the quantitative thresholds themselves.[214] The specification of the exact calculation method for the user numbers is necessary, as the gatekeepers are obliged to notify the Commission when the thresholds are reached (Art. 3(3) DMA) on their own initiative. The benefits or disadvantages (not the existence/absence per se) associated with the existence or absence of a digital ecosystem can be used in an overall assessment to rebut (→ mn. 52 et seq.) the presumption of the core platform service being an important gateway.[215] The same applies to the factors laid out in recitals 2, 13 DMA.[216]

An **entrenched and durable position** is presumed according to Art. 3(2)(c) DMA if the **numbers of users** mentioned in Art. 3(2)b DMA have been reached in **each of the last three financial years,** because in this case the contestability of its position is considered limited[217].[218] This excludes from the DMA services with short-term fluctuations in user numbers, which are not uncommon in the digital economy due to short-lived trends. In light of the DMA's objective (→ mn. 2) to ensure fair and contestable markets "for all businesses"[219] it is insufficient for a rebuttal (→ mn. 52 et seq.) of this presumption if other gatekeepers compete with the undertaking in question.[220]

52 The thresholds of Art. 3(2) DMA are designed as **rebuttable presumptions**: Pursuant to Art. 3(5) subpara. 1 DMA, the undertaking providing core platform services may, as part of its notification pursuant to Art. 3(3) DMA (→ mn. 54), submit by means of "sufficiently substantiated arguments" that "exceptionally, although it meets all the thresholds in paragraph 2, due to the circumstances in which the relevant core platform service operates, it does not satisfy the requirements listed in paragraph 1". The arguments must be submitted in an annex to the notification and must clearly identify to which of the criteria in Art. 3(1) DMA they relate (Art. 3(3) Implementing Regulation 2023/814[221]). The **burden of proof** for rebuttal lies with the company concerned.[222] Even though it is thus possible to rebut the presumptions in paragraph 2, the wording of

[212] Rec. 20 DMA.

[213] Rec. 20 DMA. For determining the number of business users it is not sufficient to recourse on the number of users who (voluntarily) registered or declared themselves as such, GC 17.07.2024 – T-1077/23, ECLI:EU:T:2024:478 paras. 273 et seqq. = BeckRS 2024, 16880 – ByteDance v Commission.

[214] Rec. 20, 22 DMA.

[215] GC 17.07.2024 – T-1077/23, ECLI:EU:T:2024:478 paras. 131 et seqq. = BeckRS 2024, 16880 – ByteDance v Commission.

[216] GC 17.07.2024 – T-1077/23, ECLI:EU:T:2024:478 paras. 174 et seqq. = BeckRS 2024, 16880 – ByteDance v Commission.

[217] A certain degree of contestability can still exist, GC 17.07.2024 – T-1077/23, ECLI:EU:T:2024:478 para. 300 = BeckRS 2024, 16880 – ByteDance v Commission.

[218] Rec. 21 DMA; GC 17.07.2024 – T-1077/23, ECLI:EU:T:2024:478 paras. 296 et seq. = BeckRS 2024, 16880 – ByteDance v Commission.

[219] Art. 1(1) DMA.

[220] GC 17.07.2024 – T-1077/23, ECLI:EU:T:2024:478 paras. 303 et seqq. = BeckRS 2024, 16880 – ByteDance v Commission.

[221] Commission Implementing Regulation (EU) 2023/814 of 14 April 2023 on detailed arrangements for the conduct of certain proceedings by the Commission pursuant to Regulation 2022/1925 of the European Parliament and of the Council (2023) OJ L 102/6.

[222] Rec. 23 subpara. 1 DMA; cf. GC 17.07.2024 – T-1077/23, ECLI:EU:T:2024:478 paras. 59, 138 = BeckRS 2024, 16880 – ByteDance v Commission.

Art. 3(5) subpara. 1 DMA ("exceptionally [...] does not satisfy the requirements"), Art. 3(5) subpara. 3 DMA ("manifestly calling into question the presumptions") and Recital 23 DMA ("in exceptional circumstances, to rebut the presumption") suggests that rebuttal is only possible in special cases.[223] This results in a high standard of proof "in the sense that the arguments [...] must be capable of showing, with a high degree of plausibility, that the presumptions [...] are called into question".[224] It has to be noted that the high standard of proof cannot require the undertaking to take excessive or unrealistic steps.[225] It is not necessary to adduce evidence which rebuts the presumption once and for all.[226] In considering a possible rebuttal of the threshold presumption, the Commission will only take into account arguments that "directly relate to the quantitative criteria, namely the impact of the undertaking providing core platform services on the internal market beyond revenue or market cap,[227] such as its size in absolute terms, and the number of Member States in which it is present; by how much the actual business user and end user numbers exceed the thresholds and the importance of the undertaking's core platform service considering the overall scale of activities of the respective core platform service; and the number of years for which the thresholds have been met".[228] However, this does not mean that every argument must be expressed in figures.[229] In contrast, rebuttal or justification "on economic grounds seeking to enter into market definition or to demonstrate efficiencies deriving from a specific type of behaviour by the undertaking" is not taken into account, as this is not relevant for the designation as gatekeeper (on the irrelevance of both an effects test and a market definition and efficiency defence → mn. 46).[230] Also a rebuttal based on the objectives (→ mn. 2) of the DMA is not permissible.[231] In view of the difficult proof of rebuttal and the otherwise quite rigid catalogue of obligations, it was proposed that the Commission issues guidelines on rebutting the presumption rules,[232] which, however, cannot be conclusive because of the case-by-case examination of the respective service. Supposedly, the Commission is not bound by previous decisions concerning other undertakings or core platform services.[233] Whether or not this is convincing in view of the primary law principle of equal treatment may be questioned.

---

[223] Podszun/Bongartz/Langenstein EuCML 2021, 60 (63); critically Kumkar, in: FK KartellR DMA Art. 3 mn. 47. In view of the rebuttals accepted (→ mn. 53), fears that rebuttals would be virtually impossible proved unfounded, cf. Drewes/Meyer/Moss RDi 2024, 310 (312).

[224] GC 17.07.2024 – T-1077/23, ECLI:EU:T:2024:478 para. 71 = BeckRS 2024, 16880 – ByteDance v Commission.

[225] GC 17.07.2024 – T-1077/23, ECLI:EU:T:2024:478 para. 142 = BeckRS 2024, 16880 – ByteDance v Commission; cf. ECJ 21.1.2016 – C-74/14, ECLI:EU:C:2016:42 para. 41 = NZKart 2016, 133 (134) – Eturas.

[226] GC 17.07.2024 – T-1077/23, ECLI:EU:T:2024:478 para. 66 = BeckRS 2024, 16880 – ByteDance v Commission.

[227] As turnover and market capitalisation are mentioned in Art. 3(2) and rec. 17 DMA, recital 23 cannot be interpreted in a way that precludes the utilisation of these criteria as arguments for a rebuttal, GC 17.07.2024 – T-1077/23, ECLI:EU:T:2024:478 para. 91 = BeckRS 2024, 16880 – ByteDance v Commission.

[228] Rec. 23 subpara. 1 DMA. The list of elements in rec. 23 subpara. 1 DMA is not exhaustive, GC 17.7.2024 – T-1077/23, ECLI:EU:T:2024:478 paray. 49 et seq. = BeckRS 2024, 16880 – ByteDance v Commission.

[229] GC 17.7.2024 – T-1077/23, ECLI:EU:T:2024:478 paras. 47 et seq., 51 = BeckRS 2024, 16880 – ByteDance v Commission.

[230] Rec. 23 subpara. 2 DMA.

[231] GC 17.07.2024 – T-1077/23, ECLI:EU:T:2024:478 paras. 323 et seqq. = BeckRS 2024, 16880 – ByteDance v Commission.

[232] Higer/Patt NZKart 2024, 78 (84); Kumkar RDi 2022, 347; Zimmer/Göhsl ZWeR 2021, 29 (38 et seq.); Kumkar, in: FK-KartellR DMA Art. 3 mn. 48.

[233] GC 17.7.2024 – T-1077/23, ECLI:EU:T:2024:478 para. 68 = BeckRS 2024, 16880 – ByteDance v Commission; cf. GC 14.9.2022 – T-575/20, ECLI:EU:T:2022:551 para. 95 = BeckRS 2022, 23233 – SŽ

53 The **procedure for rebutting the threshold presumption** depends on whether the objections raised by the company are to be considered "sufficiently substantiated" so that they "manifestly call into question" the presumption. If this is not the case, the Commission may reject the objections within the time limit of Art. 3(4) DMA (45 working days after receipt) without proceeding to the procedure under Art. 17 DMA, which is otherwise applicable to designation below the thresholds under Art. 3(8) DMA (Art. 3(5) subpara. 2 DMA). If, on the other hand, the company's objections clearly rebut the presumptions pursuant to Art. 3(2) DMA, the Commission may, within the period of 45 working days after receipt of the objections and notwithstanding the rebuttal of the presumption of threshold value, open the procedure pursuant to Art. 17(3) DMA for the designation of the undertaking as gatekeeper below the threshold values (Art. 3(5) subpara. 3 DMA). If, finally, the company could not prove that the core platform service in question does not meet the requirements of Art. 3(1) DMA despite the sufficiently substantiated objections, the Commission shall designate the company as gatekeeper in the procedure under Art. 17(3) DMA (Art. 3(5) subpara. 4 DMA). It is debatable whether the Commission can assume that the presumption has been rebutted even if the company has not provided any evidence to this effect. Ultimately, this decision is also likely to be within the Commission's discretion.[234]

So far, the Commission has accepted the rebuttals concerning Microsoft's[235] communication service Outlook.com, Samsung's[236] web browser, Google's[237] communication service Gmail and the online advertising services of X[238] (formerly Twitter) and ByteDance[239] without conducting a market investigation. After conducting market investigations (Art. 3(5), 17(3) DMA) concerning Apple's[240] iMessage, the social network X[241] (formerly Twitter) and Microsoft's[242] Bing, Edge and Microsoft Advertising the Commission accepted the respective rebuttals.

d) *Obligation to notify (Art. 3(3) DMA) and designation based on thresholds (Art. 3(4) DMA)*

54 As soon as an operator reaches the threshold values of Art. 3(2) DMA, it must inform the Commission of this within two months and transmit the corresponding data

– Tovorni promet v Commission; GC 23.5.2019 – T-370/17, ECLI:EU:T:2019:354 para. 79 = BeckRS 2019, 9350 – KPN v Commission; GC 25.3.2015 – T-556/08, ECLI:EU:T:2015:189 para. 197 = BeckRS 2016, 80523 – Slovenská pošta v Commission; GC 9.9.2009 – T-301/04, ECLI:EU:T:2009:317 para. 55 = EWS 2009, 438 = BeckRS 2009, 70991 – Clearstream v Commission; GC 14.12.2005 – T-210/01, ECLI:EU:T:2005:456 paras. 118 et seqq. = WuW 2006, 77 = BeckRS 2007, 70282 – General Electric v Commission.

234 Differing Drewes/Meyer/Moss RDi 2024, 310 (312).

235 Commission Decision of 5 September 2023 C(2023) 6106 final, summary OJ C 2023/551.

236 Commission Decision of 5 September 2023 C(2023) 6103 final, summary OJ C 2023/550.

237 Commission Decision of 5 September 2023 C(2023) 6101 final, summary OJ C 2023/549.

238 Commission Decision of 13 May 2024 C(2024) 3156 final.

239 Commission Decision of 13 May 2024 C(2024) 3153 final.

240 Opening decision: Commission Decision of 5 September 2023 C(2023) 6077 final. Apple challenges the decision by action for annulment insofar as it is predicated on a finding that iMessage is a number-independent interpersonal communications service, T-1079/23, OJ C 2024/562. Decision accepting rebuttal: Commission Decision of 12 February 2024 C(2024) 785 final, summary OJ C 2024/2710. Apple however challenges the decision by action for annulment insofar as it is predicated on a finding that iMessage is a number-independent interpersonal communications service, T-214/24, OJ C 2024/3623. On the independent contestability of the decision to open a market investigation and the implementing act concluding the market investigation → mn. 62.

241 Opening decision: Commission Decision of 13 May 2024 C(2024) 3117 final.

242 Opening decision: Commission Decision of 5 September 2023 C(2023) 6078 final; decision accepting rebuttal: Commission Decision of 12 February 2024 C(2024) 806 final, summary OJ C 2024/2709.

(Art. 3(3) subpara. 1 DMA; so-called notification solution). Originally, a period of three months was envisaged for this notification, but this was shortened in the trilogue procedure. After (possibly delayed) submission of the information, the Commission designates the undertaking as gatekeeper within 45 working days after receipt of the complete information (Art. 3(3) subpara. 3 DMA in conjunction with para. 4).[243] A market definition and a finding of a dominant position are not required.[244] If the undertaking fails to notify or only complies with the obligation incompletely or incorrectly, the Commission may designate the company as a gatekeeper based on the information available to it (Art. 3(3) subpara. 2 DMA). In addition, a fine pursuant to Art. 30 DMA (→ § 14 mn. 39 et seqq.) may be imposed. The modalities of the notification are delineated in Art. 2, 4, 11 in conjunction with Annexes I, II of the Commission Implementing Regulation 2023/814[245]. While the notification is under review the undertaking is required to inform the Commission about any relevant changes (Art. 3(3) Implementing Regulation 2023/814).

e) *Gatekeeper designation below the thresholds based on qualitative criteria (Art. 3(8) DMA)*

Pursuant to Art. 3(8) DMA, the Commission may also designate an operator as a gatekeeper if the thresholds of Art. 3(2) DMA have not been reached, but the general objective requirements of Art. 3(1) DMA – significant impact on the internal market, function as an important gateway for business users to reach end users and current or foreseeable entrenched and durable position (→ mn. 45) – are nevertheless met (for designation as a gatekeeper in the event of rebuttal of the threshold presumption, see → mn. 53). To determine these conditions, the Commission must carry out the procedure pursuant to Art. 17 DMA, i.e. in particular a market investigation (→ § 13 mn. 12 et seqq.), in which the following criteria (Art. 3(8) subpara. 1 DMA) must be taken into account: (a) the size of the undertaking (including its turnover, market capitalisation, operations and position), (b) the number of business users and end users, (c) data driven advantages (in particular access to and collection of data and analytics capabilities) and network effects,[246] (d) scale and scope effects (including with regard to data and activities outside the Union), (e) lock-in effects[247] on business users and end users, including switching costs and behavioural bias reducing the ability to switch or multi-home,[248] (f) a conglomerate corporate structure or vertical integration of the undertaking that allows it to combine data, cross subsidise or otherwise leverage its position to its 55

[243] Late designation does not affect the legality of the decision, Drewes/Meyer/Moss RDi 2024, 310 (311).

[244] Rec. 5 DMA. Rather, the DMA assumes an abstract threat due to potential market power, so that such a threat need not exist in fact; cf. GC 17.07.2024 – T-1077/23, ECLI:EU:T:2024:478 para. 298 = BeckRS 2024, 16880 – ByteDance v Commission; Müller InTeR 2022, 93; Petit JECLAP 2021, 529 et seq.; Zimmer NZG 2022, 145; Zimmer/Göhsl ZWeR 2021, 29 n. 22; differing Basedow ZEuP 2021, 217 (222).

[245] Commission Implementing Regulation (EU) 2023/814 of 14 April 2023 on detailed arrangements for the conduct of certain proceedings by the Commission pursuant to Regulation 2022/1925 of the European Parliament and of the Council (2023) OJ L 102/6.

[246] On the interplay between ecosystems and network effects GC 17.7.2024 – T-1077/23, ECLI:EU:T:2024:478 paras. 152 et seqq., 160 = BeckRS 2024, 16880 – ByteDance v Commission.

[247] On the interplay between ecosystems and lock-in effects GC 17.07.2024 – T-1077/23, ECLI:EU:T:2024:478 para. 160 = BeckRS 2024, 16880 – ByteDance v Commission.

[248] The criterion of multi-homing was added in the Draft Report on the proposal for a regulation of the European Parliament and of the Council Contestable and fair markets in the digital sector, Amendment 45 (so-called "Schwab Report"); cf. Report on the proposal for a regulation of the European Parliament and of the Council on contestable and fair markets in the digital sector (Digital Markets Act), Amendments 79, 88, 94, 30.11.2021, A9-0332/2021.

advantage, and (g) the catch-all of "other structural business or service characteristics".[249] In addition, "a very high market capitalisation, a very high ratio of equity value over profit or a very high turnover derived from end users of a single core platform service can be used as indicators of the leveraging potential of such undertakings and of the tipping of the market in their favour".[250] Apart from market capitalisation, "high relative growth rates are examples of dynamic parameters that are particularly relevant to identifying such undertakings providing core platform services for which it is foreseeable that they will become entrenched and durable".[251] The objective of the test, which takes into account **both qualitative and quantitative thresholds**, is "preserving and fostering innovation and the quality of digital products and services, the degree to which prices are fair and competitive, and the degree to which quality or choice for business users and for end users is or remains high".[252] In contrast, it militates against a classification as a gatekeeper if the company providing the core platform service is a **medium-sized, small or micro enterprise**. In that case, careful consideration must be given to whether such an undertaking would indeed be "able to substantially undermine the contestability of the core platform services, since this Regulation primarily targets large undertakings with considerable economic power rather than medium-sized, small or micro enterprises".[253] In its decision, the Commission also takes into account the **foreseeable development** regarding the criteria, such as pending mergers (Art. 3(8) subpara. 3 DMA). If the undertaking does not comply with the Commission's investigative measures, the Commission may take a decision based on available information on the quantitative thresholds (Art. 3(8) subpara. 4 DMA).[254] The undertaking has the right to be heard and access to files (Art. 34 DMA in conjunction with Art. 8 Implementing Regulation 2023/814[255]) and can inform the Commission of its views (Art. 6 Implementing Regulation 2023/814).[256] Three or more Member States may request the Commission to conduct a market investigation pursuant to Art. 17 DMA (Art. 41(1) DMA). The request is not binding; the decision to open a market investigation remains at the discretion of the Commission.[257] The Member States may bring an action for annulment (Art. 263(2) TFEU) against the Commission's decision not to open a market investigation.[258]

So far, the Commission has initiated the proceeding according to Art. 3(8), 17 DMA regarding Apple's operating system iPadOS,[259] which led to its designation as gatekeeper.[260]

56 The designation under Art. 3(8) DMA, even if the threshold values are not reached, does not aim to prevent an entrenched market position of the undertaking, but is intended to ensure the contestability of the market from the earliest possible point in time

[249] On the criticism of these criteria Körber NZKart 2021, 379, 383.

[250] Rec. 25 DMA.

[251] Rec. 25 DMA.

[252] Rec. 25 DMA.

[253] Rec. 24 DMA.

[254] Rec. 23 subpara. 2 DMA.

[255] Commission Implementing Regulation (EU) 2023/814 of 14 April 2023 on detailed arrangements for the conduct of certain proceedings by the Commission pursuant to Regulation 2022/1925 of the European Parliament and of the Council (2023) OJ L 102/6.

[256] In detail Maturana GRUR 2023, 1128 (1161 et seqq.).

[257] Cf. Art. 41(5) DMA; Gappa/Käseberg, in: HK-DMA Art. 41 mn. 3.

[258] Only if the Commission does not react at all to such a request an action for failure to act pursuant to Art. 265 TFEU exceptionally is admissible.

[259] Commission Decision of 5 September 2023 C(2023) 6076 final.

[260] Commission Decision of 29 April 2024 C(2024) 2500 final, summary OJ C 2024/4374.

– "before the market tips irreversibly"[261].[262] If an undertaking without an entrenched market position is designated as a gatekeeper pursuant to Art. 3(8) DMA because such a position is foreseeable, the Commission can and may – for reasons of proportionality – only declare one or more of the obligations pursuant to Art. 5(3)–(6) DMA and Art. 6(4), (7), (9), (10), (13) DMA applicable, Art. 17(4) DMA.[263] In doing so, it must declare applicable only those obligations "that are necessary and appropriate to ensure that the services in question remain contestable and enable the qualified risk of unfair conditions and practices to be avoided"[264]. The aim is (only) to prevent the gatekeeper from obtaining an established and lasting position by **unfair means** (Art. 17(4) DMA).[265] In this respect, obligations that prevent the transfer of market power and obligations that facilitate provider switching and parallel use of several services come into consideration.[266]

The designation of a gatekeeper based on a market investigation ensures the timely applicability of the DMA. Thus, the Commission does not have to wait until a lasting and consolidated market position exists to start the designation procedure but can already take action if there is a foreseeable threat to the contestability of a platform market.[267] The fear that a market could tip during the market investigation is unfounded. Despite the rapidly changing circumstances in digital markets, it cannot be assumed that a market will tip so quickly. Scenarios in which the Commission considers a tipping to be possible and this occurs within 12 months appear rather unlikely. 57

f) Consequences of the designation as gatekeeper

The consequence of the designation as gatekeeper is that the undertaking concerned must comply with the obligations (→ § 12) resulting from the gatekeeper status (i.e. either Art. 5–7 DMA or – in the case of designation pursuant to Art. 3(8) in conjunction with Art. 17(4) DMA – the obligations listed in the designation decision pursuant to Art. 17(4)(1) DMA) no later than six months after one of its core platform services has been listed in the designation decision (Art. 3(10) DMA). In doing so, the obligations must be complied with in relation to each of the platform services listed in the designation decision, whereby a conglomerate position of the gatekeeper is to be taken into account when applying the obligations.[268] The time limit starts with the publication of the decision according to Art. 44(1) DMA and is calculated according to the general rules of Regulation (EEC) No. 1182/71. The Commission may impose implementing measures on the gatekeeper by decision, which on the one hand "should be designed in an effective manner" and take into account the characteristics of core platform services and any risks of circumvention, but on the other hand must be in line with the principle of proportionality and the fundamental rights of both the companies concerned and third parties.[269] In addition to the obligations under Art. 5–7 DMA, a gatekeeper must also comply with the obligation to provide information on concentrations (Art. 14 DMA) and 58

[261] Rec. 26(4) DMA; also Rec. 28 DMA: possibility to "intervene in time and effectively".
[262] Cf. in this respect Art. 17(4)(2); also Kerber ZD 2021, 544 (544 et seq.); differing Zimmer/Göhsl ZWeR 2021, 29 (45).
[263] Rec. 26 DMA.
[264] Rec. 27 DMA.
[265] Rec. 27 DMA.
[266] Rec. 27 DMA.
[267] Rec. 28 DMA.
[268] Rec. 29 DMA.
[269] Rec. 29 DMA.

provide an independently verified description of its consumer profiling techniques used for its core platform services mentioned in the designation decision (Art. 15(1) DMA).

g) Review of gatekeeper status by Commission

59 In view of the rapidly changing and complex technological circumstances and business practices, the DMA provides for a regular review – limited in time in the interest of legal certainty – of the gatekeeper status.[270] Thus, the Commission shall review **at least every three years** whether the designated undertakings still fulfil the requirements of Art. 3(1) DMA and whether, if necessary, the list of core platform services classified as gateways must be supplemented, Art. 4(2) subpara. 1 DMA. However, not every change in the factual situation requires a change in the designation decision, but only if, based on a case-by-case assessment, the "change in the facts also leads to a change in the assessment".[271] The Commission is also authorised outside the three-year period to review, amend or revoke a designation decision pursuant to Art. 3 DMA at any time, either ex officio or upon request, if the facts have changed substantially (Art. 4(1)(a) DMA) or if the decision was based on incomplete, incorrect or misleading information (Art. 4(1)(b) DMA, on possible fines in this case Art. 30(3)(a) DMA). The review procedure does not suspend the gatekeeper's duties (Art. 4(2)(1)(3) DMA). The Commission shall examine at least on an annual basis whether new undertakings ought to be designated, Art. 4(2) subpara. 2 DMA.

h) Review of gatekeeper designation by the courts

60 Due to the self-executing nature of the DMA, in general no direct legal action can be brought against the applicability of individual provisions of Art. 5–7 of the DMA to the gatekeeper – except under Art. 8(2), 9, 10 and in the case of Art. 17(4) DMA (→ mn. 56). It is however conceivable to argue that one or more specific obligations of Art. 5–7 DMA violate primary law in an action against a fine or another administrative measure addressed to the gatekeeper. The most important defence is therefore to take action against the designation as gatekeeper. The designation decision is a directly binding legal act vis-à-vis the designated undertaking (Art. 288(4) TFEU). Since this is an act of an EU institution with external legal effect,[272] an **action for annulment** can be brought against the designation decision pursuant to Art. 263(4) TFEU.[273] The competent court is the General Court (Art. 256 (1) TFEU). In principle, the action for annulment does **not** have **suspensive effect** (Art. 278(1) TFEU), but an application for a preliminary injunction (Art. 278(2) TFEU) can be filed in parallel.[274] ByteDance did so, but the General Court dismissed the application for interim measures.[275] If the requirements of Art. 3(1) DMA (→ mn. 45 et seq.) are not met, the General Court shall declare the designation decision null and void *ex tunc* (Art. 264(1) TFEU). This also applies if the thresholds of Art. 3(2) DMA have not been reached and the requirements of Art. 3(1) DMA cannot be established by other means. According to the General Court, beyond the arguments and evidence provided with the notification (Art. 3(5) DMA in conjunc-

[270] Rec. 30 DMA.
[271] Rec. 30 DMA.
[272] For more details on the subject matter of the action, see Thiele, in: EnzEuR III § 9 mn. 35 et seqq.
[273] Witt CMLR 2023, 625 (644); Käseberg/Gappa, in: HK-DMA Art. 3 mn. 28; Kumkar, in: FK-KartellR DMA Art. 3 mn. 76; differing Dietrich/Vinje CRi 2021, 33 (37).
[274] Wägenbaur, in: EnzEuR III § 7 mn. 34.
[275] GC 9.2.2024 – T-1077/23 R, ECLI:EU:T:2024:94 = WuW 2024, 266 = BeckEuRS 2024, 765698.

tion with Art. 2(3) Implementing Regulation 2023/814[276]), the undertaking may submit new arguments and evidence in the court procedure only to challenge a matter of law or matters of the decision it was unable to comment on during the administrative procedure.[277] Whether this is in accordance with the right to be heard appears questionable. An error in the reasoning of the Commission's decision will only result in annulment of the decision if the error could have had a decisive influence on the outcome.[278]

Pursuant to Art. 256(1) subpara. 2 TFEU in conjunction with Art. 58 of the Statute of the ECJ, an **appeal** against the decision of the General Court may be lodged with the ECJ within two months. The appeal is limited to legal review, thus there is no review of the facts. The appeal does **not have suspensive effect** (Art. 60 Statute ECJ). 61

In the case of a designation in the procedure pursuant to Art. 17 DMA (→ mn. 53, 55 et seqq.), the designation decision pursuant to Art. 3(8) DMA can also be challenged. However, the decision to initiate the market investigation pursuant to Art. 16(1) DMA as well as the implementing act to conclude the market investigation pursuant to Art. 17(1) DMA are – similar to the market investigation pursuant to Art. 17 Regulation (EC) No. 1/2003 – **merely preparatory measures** without any external legal effect, so that they cannot be the subject of an action for annulment.[279] An independent contestability would only be possible if these measures not only prepared a final decision, but decided conclusively on a separable aspect, which, however, in the concept of the DMA only takes place with the designation decision according to Art. 3(8) DMA. Any errors in the market investigation can therefore be asserted with an action for annulment against the designation decision. If an undertaking without an entrenched market position has been designated as a gatekeeper pursuant to Art. 17(4) DMA, the declaration of applicability of the **individual obligations** is also fully reviewable by the General Court in an action for annulment. If only the application of one or more obligations under Art. 5(3)–(6) or Art. 6(4), (7), (9), (10) or (13) DMA is not necessary or appropriate, partial nullity is declared with regard to these obligations. 62

Likewise, in the context of the procedure of review of the status of gatekeeper pursuant to Art. 4 DMA (→ mn. 59), the action for annulment is in principle admissible, because the rejection of an application to amend or repeal a legal act is also an act within the meaning of Art. 263 TFEU.[280] The decisive factor is therefore that an application for review is filed at all. Only if the Commission does not react at all to such a request an action for failure to act pursuant to Art. 265 TFEU is exceptionally admissible. 63

[276] Commission Implementing Regulation (EU) 2023/814 of 14 April 2023 on detailed arrangements for the conduct of certain proceedings by the Commission pursuant to Regulation 2022/1925 of the European Parliament and of the Council (2023) OJ L 102/6.

[277] GC 17.07.2024 – T-1077/23, ECLI:EU:T:2024:478 paras. 234 et seqq. = BeckRS 2024, 16880 – ByteDance v Commission.

[278] GC 17.07.2024 – T-1077/23, ECLI:EU:T:2024:478 para. 112 = BeckRS 2024, 16880 – ByteDance v Commission; GC 10.4.2024 – T-445/22, ECLI:EU:T:2024:228 para. 104 = BeckRS 2024, 6579 – Columbus Stainless v Commission; GC 20.9.2019 – T-650/17, ECLI:EU:T:2019:644 paras. 97, 348 = BeckRS 2019, 22477 – Jinan Meide Casting v Commission; GC 15.12.2010 – T-427/08, ECLI:EU:T:2010:517 para. 161 = GRUR Int 2011, 527 (536) – CEAHR v Commission; GC 9.7.2008 – T-301/01, ECLI:EU:T:2008:262 para. 307 = BeckRS 2009, 70101 – Alitalia v Commission; GC 12.9.2007 – T-60/05, ECLI:EU:T:2007:269 para. 77 = BeckRS 2008, 70212 – Ufex and Others v Commission; 14.5.2002 – T-126/99, ECLI:EU:T:2002:116 para. 49 = BeckRS 2002, 168810 – Graphischer Maschinenbau v Commission.

[279] Differing Akman ELR 2022, 85 (92). Nevertheless, Apple brought an action for annulment against the classification of iMessage as a number-independent interpersonal communications service, T-1080/23, OJ C 2024/563.

[280] ECJ 24.11.1992 – C-15/91 and C-108/91, ECLI:EU:C:1992:454 para. 22 = EuZW 1993, 415 – Buckl; GC 1.2.2023 – T-708/21, ECLI:EU:T:2023:49 para. 58 = BeckRS 2023, 1867.

ByteDance filed an action for annulment against the designation as gatekeeper regarding its online social networking service (→ mn. 15) TikTok. The General Court has dismissed the action.[281] Apple brought an action against the designation based on its online intermediation service (→ mn. 8 et seqq.) App Store and its operating system (→ mn. 23 et seqq.) iOS.[282] Meta seeks the annulment of the designation regarding its communications service (→ mn. 18 et seqq.) Messenger, its social networking service Facebook and its intermediation service Marketplace.[283]

III. Territorial scope

64 According to Art. 1(2) of the DMA, which is modelled on Art. 1(2) P2B Regulation, the DMA applies to core platform services provided or offered by gatekeepers to business users established in the Union or to end users established or located in the Union, irrespective of the place of establishment or residence of the gatekeepers and irrespective of the law otherwise applicable to the provision of services. The rules of the DMA are thus designed as **overriding mandatory provisions** (Art. 9 Rome I Regulation[284], Art. 16 Rome II Regulation[285]), because they apply independently of the otherwise (e.g. via the Rome Regulations) applicable law.[286] Insofar as other laws are applicable in addition to the DMA, e.g. in the context of private enforcement (e.g. for contractual relationships or tortious liability claims), the supplementary application of these other norms is determined according to the general rules of European private international law.[287] Accordingly, the law applicable to contracts is determined by Art. 3 et seqq. Rome I Regulation, the law applicable to non-contractual obligations by Art. 6(3) Rome II Regulation.[288] However, in the case of a supplementary application of primary law competition rules (Art. 101, 102 TFEU), their application is not determined according to Art. 6(3) Rome II, but based on the criterion of the qualified effects of a restriction of competition on the Union market.[289] In practice, there should rarely be any differences between the application of the DMA on the basis of the provision and offer criterion of Art. 1(2) DMA, the application of the general EU competition rules on the basis of the criterion of qualified effects (Art. 101, 102 TFEU) and the application of competition tort law on the basis of the market affected by the restriction of competition (Art. 6(3)(a) Rome II Regulation).

---

[281] GC 17.7.2024 – T-1077/23, ECLI:EU:T:2024:478 para. 68 = BeckRS 2024, 16880 – ByteDance v Commission.

[282] T-1080/23, OJ C 2024/563.

[283] T-1078/23, OJ C 2024/561.

[284] Regulation (EC) No 593/2008 of the European Parliament and of the Council of 17 June 2008 on the law applicable to contractual obligations (2008) OJ L 177/6.

[285] Regulation (EC) No 864/2007 of the European Parliament and of the Council of 11 July 2007 on the law applicable to non-contractual obligations (2007) OJ L 199/40.

[286] The same result is reached if one regards Art. 1(2) DMA as a conflict rule "in relation to particular matters" within the meaning of Art. 23 Rome I Regulation and Art. 27 Rome II Regulation. However, the qualification of the DMA as an overriding mandatory rule fits better than the classification as a "conflict rule".

[287] Cf. Bauermeister, in: BeckOGK Rom II-VO Art. 6 mn. 228.

[288] The fact that the DMA pursues an objective that is to be distinguished from general competition law (cf. rec. 11 DMA) should not prevent a qualification as competition law under conflict of laws, because the concepts of substantive law and conflict of laws are not necessarily congruent.

[289] In this regard, ECJ 17.9.2017 – C-413/14 P, ECLI:EU:C:2017:632 paras. 40 et seqq. = NZKart 2016, 541 – Intel; previously ECJ 27.9.1988 – 89/85, ECLI:EU:C:1988:447 para. 16 = NJW 1988, 3086 – Wood Pulp; see also Art. 6(3)(a) Rome II Regulation; fundamentally United States v. Aluminium Co of America, 148 F.2d 416 (2d Cir. 1945).

1. Establishment and residence of the gatekeeper irrelevant

The **international applicability** of the DMA is determined solely on the basis of the provision or offering of the platform service to business users or end users established or located in the Union. According to Art. 1(2) DMA, it is irrelevant where the provider of the core platform service has its establishment or residence. As in other legal acts of the Digital Single Market, this is a shift from the link to the establishment of the service provider to the location of the service recipient in the Union. However, a certain connection of the service to the Union in the form of an offer or provision of the service to business users or end users established in the Union is required (→ mn. 66 et seqq.).[290] This approach (connection to the offer or provision of the service in the Union) is compatible with public international law (→ mn. 90), just as the connection to the qualifying effects on the Union market in general competition law is compatible with public international law.[291] Similar to the traditional conflict-of-laws connection points for the protection of consumers and employees, the criterion of offer or provision of services to users in the Union serves to protect the users of the service, but also to ensure a certain – fair and contestable – regulation of the markets in the digital sector across the Union. At first glance, one may doubt the effectiveness of this approach, as it is not – like Art. 79(2) GDPR – flanked by a binding jurisdiction in the Union or the obligation to designate an agent for service of process or a single point of contact (cf. Art. 11, 12 DSA). However, in view of the extensive activity of the gatekeepers in the Union, the international jurisdiction of the European authorities (which is not explicitly regulated in the DMA) can be justified with the criterion of qualified effect.[292] In the context of enforcement under private law, no problems should arise either because, as a rule, the prerequisites for jurisdiction under national law (such as §§ 29, 32 ZPO in Germany) against third-state domiciled gatekeepers will usually be fulfilled by the offer or provision of their service in the Union. 65

2. Establishment and location of users in the Union

The business users for whom the platform service is offered must be established in the Union. The term **"establishment"** is to be interpreted autonomously under Union law. Despite different objectives (in the GDPR, the concept of establishment defines the establishment of the data controller bound by the GDPR, in the DMA, the concept of establishment defines the users protected by the DMA), it is possible to make use of the definition of establishment developed for the purposes of data protection law by the ECJ[293], 66

[290] Similarly, Art. 3(2) GDPR, Art. 2(1) DSA, Art. 1(2) P2B Regulation, Art. 2(1)(a) Draft AI Regulation, whereby the use of an AI system in the Union is also sufficient, Art. 2(1)(b) Draft AI Regulation; for a comparison of the rules of territorial scope in the legal acts of the Union on the Digital Single Market Heinze, in: FS Schack, 2022, 440.

[291] In this regard, ECJ 17.9.2017 – C-413/14 P, ECLI:EU:C:2017:632 paras. 40 et seqq. = NZKart 2016, 541 – Intel; previously ECJ 27.9.1988 – 89/85, ECLI:EU:C:1988:447 para. 16 = NJW 1988, 3086 – Wood Pulp; see also Art. 6(3)(a) Rome II Regulation; fundamentally United States v. Aluminium Co of America, 148 F.2d 416 (2d Cir. 1945).

[292] In this regard, ECJ 17.9.2017 – C-413/14 P, ECLI:EU:C:2017:632 paras. 40 et seqq. = NZKart 2016, 541 – Intel.

[293] ECJ 1.10.2015 – C-230/14, ECLI:EU:C:2015:639 paras. 28, 35 = NJW 2015, 3636 – Weltimmo. See also ECJ 13.4.2014 – C-131/12, ECLI:EU:C:2014:317 paras. 52, 55 et seqq. = NJW 2014, 2257 – Google Spain: data processing need not be carried out "by" but only "in the context of the activities" of the establishment (para. 53 on the broad interpretation); ECJ 5.6.2018 – C-210/16, ECLI:EU:C:2018:388 paras. 54 et seqq. = NJW 2018, 2537 – Wirtschaftsakademie Schleswig-Holstein.

which can also be found in recital 22 GDPR[294]. This is possible because the concept of establishment under data protection law is based on the general concept in Art. 49 TFEU[295]. A similar understanding as in data protection law is also found in Art. 125 EU Trade Mark Regulation[296]. The narrower term in Art. 7 no. 5 Brussels Ibis Regulation[297] is less appropriate, as the understanding in Art. 7 no. 5 Brussels Ibis Regulation is influenced by the aim of tailored rules on special jurisdiction and procedural purposes.[298]

67 Accordingly, an establishment presupposes the **effective and real exercise of activity through stable arrangements**. This can be a branch or a subsidiary, the specific legal form or personality (independent company, part of another company etc.) is irrelevant. In the case law of the ECJ, the notion of establishment is interpreted broadly.[299] The ECJ allows even minor activities to suffice for this,[300] so that even small offices or the setting up of bank accounts or post office boxes can count as an establishment.[301] Mere mailboxes or the operation of servers do not fall under the concept of establishment.[302]

68 **End users** are deemed to be located in the Union if they are established in the Union or physically present in the territory of the Union within the meaning of Art. 52 TEU, Art. 355 TFEU. The understanding of Art. 3(2) GDPR ("subjects who are in the Union") can also provide guidance in this respect. The concept is based purely on physical presence in the territory of the Union, without – in principle – any integration requirement, minimum duration of stay or intention to stay.[303] As a result, the DMA does not apply if platform services are offered or provided to business users without an establishment in the Union, through which they offer goods or services to end users outside the Union which are not established in the Union.

3. Offering or provision of platform services to users

69 Crucial to the applicability of the DMA is the final requirement that the platform service is offered **to users** falling within the territorial scope of the DMA. In view of the global accessibility and usability of platform services, it is not sufficient that business users or end users use or can use the service. The service must also be specifically offered or provided *to* users. When interpreting this term, it makes sense to refer back to the understanding of the "direction to"-criterion as developed for Art. 17(1)(c) of the Brussels I-bis Regulation[304] of

---

[294] Previously, rec. 19 of Directive 95/46/EC of the European Parliament and of the Council of 24 October 1995 on the protection of individuals with regard to the processing of personal data and on the free movement of such data (1995) OJ L 281/31.

[295] ECJ 1.10.2015 – C-230/14, ECLI:EU:C:2015:639 paras. 28 et seq. = NJW 2015, 3636 – Weltimmo.

[296] Regulation (EU) 2017/1001 of the European Parliament and of the Council of 14 June 2017 on the European Union trade mark (2017) OJ L 154/1.

[297] Regulation (EU) No 1215/2012 of the European Parliament and of the Council of 12 December 2012 on jurisdiction and the recognition and enforcement of judgments in civil and commercial matters (2012) OJ L 351/1.

[298] On the differences between the concept of establishment under data protection law and Art. 7 no. 5 Brussels I-bis Regulation and the approximation to Art. 125 EU Trade Mark Regulation Heinze/Warmuth ZZPInt 2016, 175, 185 et seqq. (on Art. 79(2)(1) GDPR).

[299] ECJ 13.5.2014 – C-131/12, ECLI:EU:C:2014:317 para. 53 = NJW 2014, 2257 – Google Spain; ECJ 1.10.2015 – C-230/14, ECLI:EU:C:2015:639 para. 25 = NJW 2015, 3636 – Weltimmo.

[300] ECJ 1.10.2015 – C-230/14, ECLI:EU:C:2015:639 para. 31 = NJW 2015, 3636 – Weltimmo.

[301] Zerdick, in: Ehmann/Selmayr DSGVO Art. 3 mn. 9; Ernst, in: Paal/Pauly DSGVO Art. 3 mn. 8.

[302] Zerdick, in: Ehmann/Selmayr DSGVO Art. 3 mn. 9; Ernst, in: Paal/Pauly DSGVO Art. 3 mn. 8.

[303] Hanloser, in: BeckOK DatenschutzR, 43rd edition 2021, DSGVO Art. 3 mn. 27.

[304] Regulation (EU) No 1215/2012 of the European Parliament and of the Council of 12 December 2012 on jurisdiction and the recognition and enforcement of judgments in civil and commercial matters (2012) OJ L 351/1.

2012 and Art. 6(1)(b) of the Rome I Regulation[305]. This is justified because recital 9 of the P2B Regulation on Art. 1(2) P2B Regulation – which was the model for the provision in Art. 1(2) DMA – explicitly refers to the direction criterion of the Brussels Ibis Regulation and the Rome I Regulation. Moreover, the concept of direction in Art. 17(1)(c) of the Brussels Ibis Regulation and Art. 6(1)(b) of the Rome I Regulation is the basis of the concept of direction in Art. 3(2)(a) and recital 23 of the GDPR as well,[306] which also argues in favour of a reception of this concept in Art. 1(2) of the DMA. According to Art. 17(1)(c) of the Brussels Ibis Regulation and Art. 6(1)(b) of the Rome I Regulation, an activity is directed to the Union if there are objective indications that customers in the Union are to be addressed.[307] This is the case if, on the basis of an overall assessment of the circumstances, the trader was prepared to conclude a contract with consumers in the state in question – transferred to the DMA: in the Union.[308] The mere accessibility of the website in the Union is not a sufficient indication in this respect, but other factors are needed, such as the use of a language or currency commonly used in one or more Member States, combined with the possibility of ordering goods and services in that language, or the mention of customers or users located in the Union, which indicate that the responsible person intends to offer goods or services to persons in the Union.[309] When applying the direction criterion, it is important to bear in mind that the DMA has different objectives and a different regulatory approach than the rules on consumer choice of laws: While consumer conflict of law rules deal with the protection of consumers in contractual relationships, the DMA aims at the protection (also) of business users who rely on a gatekeeper's core platform service as a gateway to reach end users (Art. 3(1)(b) DMA) and more generally at ensuring fair and contestable digital markets (Art. 1(1) DMA).[310] In addition, the end users do not necessarily have to be in a contractual relationship with the gatekeeper. The understanding of direction in Art. 17(1)(c) Brussels Ibis Regulation and Art. 6(1)(b) Rome I Regulation, which is geared towards consumer protection in contractual obligations, may therefore not sufficiently cover certain threats to the protective goals of the DMA, especially since the DMA – unlike the P2B Regulation[311] – does not contain a reference to the case law of the ECJ on Art. 6 Rome I Regulation and Art. 17(1)(c) Brussels Ibis Regulation.[312] It therefore seems appropriate to assume an offering to users in the Union for the purposes of the DMA already if there are either objective indications that the platform operator **intends to use its service or promotes the use of its service** in the Union, in which case the consumer law criteria can be applied (intended conclusion of a contract with users in the Union), or if it **takes any economic advantage of the use in the Union** in the knowledge of the existence of use in the Union.[313] Thus, the platform operator is free to escape the scope of the DMA without having to ensure effective blocking of any use in the Union. At the same time, however, it can no

[305] Regulation (EC) No 593/2008 of the European Parliament and of the Council of 17 June 2008 on the law applicable to contractual obligations (2008) OJ L 177/6.

[306] Hanloser, in: BeckOK DatenschutzR, 43rd edition 2021, DSGVO Art. 3 mn. 33.

[307] Leible, in: NK-BGB, 3rd edition 2019, Rome I Art. 6 mn. 54; Staudinger, in: Rauscher Brussels Ia-VO Art. 17 mn. 13a.

[308] ECJ 7.10.2010 – C-585/08, C-144/09, ECLI:EU:C:2010:740 para. 76 = NJW 2011, 505 – Pammer; rec. 23 GDPR: "In order to determine whether such a controller or processor is offering goods or services to data subjects who are in the Union, it should be ascertained whether it is apparent that the controller or processor envisages offering services to data subjects in one or more Member States in the Union".

[309] Rec. 23 GDPR.

[310] The GDPR also does not focus exclusively on the direction of an offer to the Union (Art. 3(2)(a) GDPR), but additionally on the monitoring of data subjects' behaviour in the Union (Art. 3(2)(b) GDPR).

[311] Rec. 9 P2B Regulation.

[312] Differing Käseberg/Gappa, in: HK-DMA Art. 1 mn. 9.

[313] In particular, the use of personal data and/or the placement of advertisements may be considered.

longer take any economic advantage of the use in the Union which will normally mean that it can no longer use its platform service as a gateway (→ mn. 45, 51) in the Union.

IV. Entry into force and application

70 The entry into force (subpara. 1) and the date of application (subpara. 2) of the DMA are set out in Art. 54 DMA. The Regulation entered into force on the twentieth day following its publication in the Official Journal (Art. 297(1)(3)(2) TFEU); Art. 54(1) DMA is merely of declaratory nature. The DMA was published in the Official Journal on 12 October 2022 and thus entered into force on 1 November 2022.

71 Pursuant to Art. 54(2) DMA, the Regulation applies in principle six months after its entry into force, i.e. as of 2 May 2023. According to subpara. 3, Art. 3(6) and (7) as well as Art. 40, 46–50 DMA are exempt from this, as they already apply as of the entry into force on 1 November 2022. The earlier application of these provisions enabled the Commission to make the necessary preparations for effective enforcement of the DMA already during the six-month transitional period.[314] Articles 42 and 43 DMA apply from 25 June 2023.

72 The notifications of the companies pursuant to Art. 3(3) DMA had therefore to be received by the Commission eight months after the entry into force on 1 November 2022 and thus by 3 July 2023. The designations had then to be made within 45 working days, i.e. by 6 September 2023 at the latest. The obligations of the gatekeepers took effect six months later (Art. 3(10) DMA), i.e. as of 7 March 2024 at the latest.

B. Sectoral exemption for telecommunications services

73 Pursuant to Art. 1(3) DMA, the Digital Markets Act does not apply to "markets related to" electronic communications networks within the meaning of Art. 2 no. 1 EECC Directive (EU) 2018/1972[315] and electronic communications services within the meaning of Art. 2 no. 4 EECC Directive (EU) 2018/1972[316]. According to the last half-sentence of Art. 1(3)(b) DMA, this exclusion does not apply to number-independent interpersonal communication services (Art. 2 no. 9 DMA in conjunction with Art. 2 no. 7 EECC Directive (EU) 2018/1972[317], → mn. 18 et seqq., e.g. messenger services such as

---

[314] Käseberg/Gappa, in: HK-DMA Art 54 mn. 2.

[315] According to Art. 2 No. 1 EECC Directive (EU) 2018/1972, electronic communications networks are "transmission systems, whether or not based on a permanent infrastructure or centralised administration capacity, and, where applicable, switching or routing equipment and other resources, including network elements which are not active, which permit the conveyance of signals by wire, radio, optical or other electromagnetic means, including satellite networks, fixed (circuit- and packet-switched, including internet) and mobile networks, electricity cable systems, to the extent that they are used for the purpose of transmitting signals, networks used for radio and television broadcasting, and cable television networks, irrespective of the type of information conveyed".

[316] According to Art. 2 No. 4 of the EECC (EU) 2018/1972, electronic communications services are services "normally provided for remuneration via electronic communications networks, which encompasses, with the exception of services providing, or exercising editorial control over, content transmitted using electronic communications networks and services, the following types of services:

(a) 'internet access service' as defined in point (2) of the second paragraph of Article 2 of Regulation (EU) 2015/2120;

(b) interpersonal communications service; and

(c) services consisting wholly or mainly in the conveyance of signals such as transmission services used for the provision of machine-to-machine services and for broadcasting".

[317] According to Art. 2 no. 7 of the ECCU Directive (EU) 2018/1972, a number-independent interpersonal communications service is "an interpersonal communications service which does not connect with

WhatsApp). Thus, gatekeepers have to ensure the interoperability of number-independent interpersonal communication services (Art. 7 DMA; → § 12 mn. 54 et seqq.). The exemption of Art. 1(3) DMA is motivated by the fact that telecommunication providers are already comprehensively regulated by the European Electronic Communications Code in the EECC Directive (EU) 2018/1972.

In the Commission's proposal, all interpersonal communications services were excluded from the exception in Art. 1(3) DMA. The final version of the DMA aims at convergence between the sectoral exemption of Art. 1(3) DMA and the application of the DMA to number-independent interpersonal communications services pursuant to Art. 2 no. 2(e) DMA. Still, this does not automatically mean that operators are only subject to regulation for number-based interpersonal communications services under the EECC Directive or to regulation under the DMA for number-independent communications services. For example, a platform service can offer both number-based and number-independent communications services. While according to the EECC Directive a number-based communications service as defined in Art. 2 no. 6 EECC Directive exists if communication with users with publicly assigned numbers is enabled, the DMA takes a more comprehensive approach. The regulation of number-based interpersonal communications services under the EECC Directive may place high demands on their operation, but it only covers a small part of the business activities of platform operators. The DMA, on the other hand, looks at the entire platform service. Therefore, if a platform service combines number-based and number-independent interpersonal communications services, the exclusion under Art. 1(3) DMA only covers the part of the service that enables communication with networks with publicly assigned numbering resources. The general obligations of the gatekeeper as well as the obligations regarding number-independent communication remain unaffected. 74

Pursuant to Art. 1(4) of the DMA, for interpersonal communications services as defined in Art. 2 no. 5 of the EECC Directive (EU) 2018/1972, the supervisory powers and responsibilities concerning telecommunications undertakings (e.g. regarding access and interconnection) granted to national regulatory authorities by Art. 61 of the EECC Directive (EU) 2018/1972 and to other competent authorities by Art. 61(2)(1)(b), (c) of the EECC Directive (EU) 2018/1972 remain unaffected. However, the rules and powers of the DMA only apply to number-independent interpersonal communications services anyway, due to the re-exemption in Art. 1(3)(b) DMA, so that Art. 1(4) DMA is also only relevant for such services.[318] Therefore, if an undertaking offers number-independent interpersonal communications services and is thus subject to telecommunications regulation and is also a gatekeeper within the meaning of Art. 3 DMA and is thus subject to the DMA, the obligations and powers under the EECC Directive and the DMA (cf. Art. 7 DMA) coexist. The competent authorities pursuant to Art. 61 of the EECC Directive can therefore take the measures listed therein independently of the requirements of the DMA, including the imposition of an obligation to make the services interoperable (Art. 61(2)(c) of the EECC Directive (EU) 2018/1972), because Art. 61(2)(c) of the EECC Directive (EU) 2018/1972 pursues different objectives (of telecommunications law) than the DMA in ensuring "end-to-end connectivity". 75

publicly assigned numbering resources, namely, a number or numbers in national or international numbering plans, or which does not enable communication with a number or numbers in national or international numbering plans".

[318] Käseberg/Gappa, in: HK-DMA Art. 1 mn. 14.

C. Relationship to other legal acts

I. Union and national competition law (Art. 1(6) DMA) and private enforcement

76 Pursuant to Art. 1(6)(1) and recital 10, the DMA does **not affect the application of Art. 101, 102 TFEU**. This is consistent considering that the DMA is only based on the internal market competence pursuant to Art. 114 TFEU and, according to recital 11, pursues objectives that are complementary to, but nevertheless distinct from competition law. The DMA defines its objective as ensuring fair and contestable markets in the digital sector (Art. 1(1) DMA).[319] It is therefore regulatory law that is motivated by competition objectives (→ mn. 4).[320] Consistent with this approach, the DMA was not based on Art. 103 TFEU.[321] The DMA and Art. 101, 102 TFEU remain applicable in parallel also if a national competition authority acts on the basis of Art. 101, 102 TFEU[322] while the Commission conducts proceedings on the basis of the DMA. As a consequence of parallel applicability of the DMA and Art. 101, 102 TFEU, the **Vertical Block Exemption Regulation** (VBER)[323] and the DMA coexist without affecting each other. This is demonstrated by the fact that the exempted narrow parity obligations pursuant to Art. 5(3) DMA are prohibited for gatekeepers.[324] The parallelism of the DMA and Union competition law also has consequences for **private enforcement**. On the one hand, the obligations under the DMA can in principle be enforced by private parties insofar as rights and obligations of individual affected parties derive from the DMA (cf. Art. 39 DMA).[325] In so far as this is the case, the principle of effectiveness establishes minimum requirements for private enforcement as a matter of Union law.[326] In addition, Art. 42 DMA declares the Representative Actions Directive[327] applicable. On the other hand, the **Competition Damages Directive**[328] only applies to "an infringement of Articles 101 or 102 TFEU or of national competition law" to the extent that the latter "predominantly

[319] In the Inception Impact Assessment, there was still talk of "fair" and "undistorted", Ref. Ares(2020)2877634, 2. This change only serves to differentiate from competition law, cf. Käseberg/Gappa, in: HK-DMA Art. 1 mn. 5.

[320] Schweitzer ZEuP 2021, 503 (509 et seq.); Spindler/Seidel NJW 2022, 2730 (2731); Wolf/Brüggemann, in: Kirk/Offergeld/Rohner 365 (366): regulatory law close to competition; differing Petit JECLAP 2021, 529.

[321] This was advocated by Basedow ZEuP 2021, 217 (225); Grünwald MMR 2020, 822 (826); it was still envisaged in the Inception Impact Assessment "New Competition Tool", Ref. Ares(2020)2877634, 2; in detail de Pablo/Fernández JECLAP 2021, 576.

[322] In addition, Art. 5(1) and Art. 11(6) in conjunction with Art. 3 of Council Regulation (EC) No 1/2003 of 16 December 2002 on the implementation of the rules on competition laid down in Articles 81 and 82 of the Treaty (2003) OJ L 1/1, as well as § 50(1) of the german GWB.

[323] Commission Regulation (EU) 2022/720 of 10 May 2022 on the application of Article 101(3) of the Treaty on the Functioning of the European Union to categories of vertical agreements and concerted practices (2022) OJ L 134/4.

[324] Christodoulou/Holzwarth NZKart 2022, 540 (543).

[325] Cf. BR-Drs. 168/23, 17; in detail Galle/Dressel EuZW 2024, 107; Podszun JECLAP 2022, 254; Richter/Gömann NZKart 2023, 208.

[326] On the principle of effectiveness in general and the requirements in the area of the claim for damages Heinze, Schadensersatz im Unionsprivatrecht (2017) 54 et seqq., 497 et seqq.; see also ECJ 20.9.2001 – C-453/99, ECLI:EU:C:2001:465 = GRUR 2002, 367 – Courage; ECJ 13.7.2006 – C-295/04 to C-298/04, ECLI:EU:C:2006:461 = EuZW 2006, 529 – Manfredi.

[327] Directive (EU) 2020/1828 of the European Parliament and of the Council of 25 November 2020 on representative actions for the protection of the collective interests of consumers (2020) OJ L 409/1.

[328] Cf. Art. 2 No. 1 Directive 2014/104/EU of the European Parliament and of the Council of 26 November 2014 on certain rules governing actions for damages under national law for infringements of the com-

pursues the same objective" as Art. 101, 102 TFEU. The Damages Directive therefore does not apply to the DMA – which pursues objectives distinct from competition law – by virtue of Union law.[329] In Germany, this gap has been closed by the legislator of the 11th GWB (German law against restraints of competition) amendment. It extended the rules of the GWB on civil law claims and remedies to violations of obligations under Art. 5–7 DMA by supplementing, inter alia, § 33(1) and § 89b(5)(1) GWB,[330] so that there is a parallelisation of remedies in German national law.[331]

For the application of provisions other than Art. 101, 102 TFEU, Art. 1(6)(2) DMA adds that the application of the DMA under certain conditions does not affect the application of **national competition law** ((a) and (b)) and of the European (**Merger Regulation**[332]) and national merger control provisions (c). The obligation to inform about mergers in Art. 14 DMA and the possibility of an acquisition prohibition (Art. 18(2) DMA) thus apply in addition to the Merger Regulation and national merger control law.[333] 77

Regarding the **parallel applicability of national competition law** and the DMA in accordance with Art. 1(6)(a) and (b) DMA, a distinction must be made: National competition laws "prohibiting anti-competitive agreements, decisions by associations of undertakings, concerted practices and abuses of dominant positions" (Art. 1(6)(a) DMA), i.e. **"corresponding national competition rules"**[334] like **§§ 1 and 19 GWB**, which according to recital 11 DMA (like Art. 101, 102 TFEU) pursue other objectives than those of the DMA, remain unaffected by the DMA.[335] National competition laws "**prohibiting other forms of unilateral conduct**"[336] remain unaffected by the DMA[337] according to Art. 1(6)(b) DMA **only** "insofar as they are applied to undertakings other than gatekeepers or amount to the imposition of further obligations on gatekeepers".[338] The national competition rules "**prohibiting other forms of unilateral conduct**", as is clarified in the explanatory recital 10 of the DMA, refer to national competition rules "that are based on an **individualised assessment** of market positions and behaviour, including its actual or potential **effects** and the precise scope of the prohibited behaviour, and which provide for the possibility of undertakings to make **efficiency and objective justification** arguments for the behaviour in question".[339] Article 1(6)(b) DMA is thus likely to be limited 78

petition law provisions of the Member States and of the European Union (2014) OJ L 349/1; Heinze ZEuP 2020, 281 (284).

329 Basedow ZEuP 2021, 217 (223).

330 BGBl. 2023 I 294; cf. BR-Drs. 168/23, 39, 46.

331 Critically Klumpe, in: Kirk/Offergeld/Rohner 131; on the cooperation of national courts and the Commission Art. 39 DMA.

332 Council Regulation (EC) No 139/2004 of 20 January 2004 on the control of concentrations between undertakings (2004) OJ L 24/1.

333 Zimmer/Göhsl ZWeR 2021, 29 (34).

334 Rec. 10 DMA.

335 The applicability of these national provisions in addition to Art. 101, 102 TFEU is regulated in Art. 3(2) of Regulation (EC) No 1/2003.

336 On their admissibility also Art. 3(2)(2) of Regulation (EC) No. 1/2003.

337 On the applicability of national provisions which "predominantly pursue an objective different from that pursued by Articles 81 and 82 of the Treaty [Articles 101 and 102 TFEU]", in addition to Union competition law (i.e. from the point of view of competition law) also Article 3(3) of Regulation (EC) No. 1/2003, on this Peifer/Heinze Einl. C mn. 55 et seqq.

338 The adjustment goes back to the Schwab Report EP 2020/0374(COD), Amendment No. 31 and the efforts to leave a certain scope of application to § 19a GWB in addition to the DMA, see Grünwald NZKart 2021, 496 (498).

339 Rec. 10 DMA.

to national competition rules which – in contrast to the DMA itself[340] – require a case-by-case examination of market position and practices, including their effects, and allow justification on the basis of efficiencies or other objective justifications. By contrast, if national provisions establish obligations that are independent of effects and justification (such as the DMA), they are not unaffected by the DMA on the basis of Art. 1(6)(b) DMA, but are subject to Art. 1(5) DMA and can only be permissible under Art. 1(5)(2) DMA.[341] If, again, the national rules are impact-related and establish behavioural obligations under national competition law, they remain permissible alongside the DMA according to Art 1(6)(b) DMA "insofar as they are applied to undertakings other than gatekeepers" (i.e. to undertakings which either do not offer core platform services as defined in Art. 2 no. 2 DMA and therefore cannot be designated as gatekeepers within the meaning of the DMA or offer core platform services but have not been designated as gatekeepers within the meaning of Art. 2 no. 1 DMA[342]) or "amount to the imposition of further obligations on gatekeepers" (i.e. obligations going beyond those in Art. 5–7 DMA).

79 An example of national law permissible under Art. 1(6)(b) DMA is the German **§ 19a GWB,**[343] which adheres to the requirement of a position of market power[344] in the form of paramount significance for competition across markets[345] and provides for both an impact-related individual case assessment and a possibility of justification (§ 19a(2) GWB). This is why it remains applicable alongside the DMA in the cases mentioned in Art. 1(6)(b) DMA (application to non-gatekeepers[346] or imposition of obligations going beyond Art. 5–7 DMA, e.g. concering other services than the core platform service).[347]

---

340 Rec. 23 subpara. 2 DMA. The DMA also assumes an abstract threat due to potential market power, so that such a threat need not actually exist, Müller InTeR 2022, 93; Petit JECLAP 2021, 529 et seq.; Zimmer NZG 2022, 145; Zimmer/Göhsl ZWeR 2021, 29 n. 22; differing Basedow ZEuP 2021, 217 (222).

341 Käseberg/Gappa, in: HK-DMA Art. 1 mn. 24.

342 The wording of Art. 2 No. 1 DMA suggests that for the gatekeeper status for the purposes of Art. 1(6)(2)(b) DMA (a parallel question arises with regard to the "status of a gatekeeper" in Art. 1(5)(2) DMA) only the designation by the Commission should be taken into account, according to Käseberg/Gappa, in: HK-DMA Art. 1 para. 19, 27; Bongartz WuW 2022, 72 (73); Grünwald NZKart 2021, 496 (497 et seq.): Act of designation by the Commission required. However, this has the remarkable consequence that the act of designation leads to a change in the regulatory regime and, in the case of stricter national regulations, even to a relaxation of the obligations for the gatekeeper, because with the designation as gatekeeper the blocking effect under Art. 1(5)(1) DMA is triggered. Nevertheless, the wording "gatekeeper" combined with the legal definition in Art. 2 No. 1 DMA should preclude abstractly referring to the requirements of Art. 3(1) DMA and consequently also the thresholds of Art. 3(2) DMA.

343 An overview of the proceedings is available on the BKartA's website, BKartA, 02.07.2024 <https://www.bundeskartellamt.de/SharedDocs/Publikation/DE/Downloads/Liste_Verfahren_Digitalkonzerne.pdf> (last accessed: 19.10.2024).

344 Which, in addition to overwhelming cross-market importance, also includes market dominance as well as relative and superior market power, cf. Lettl WRP 2021, 413 (415); differing König, in: Borges/Keil Big Data § 12 mn. 17, 48.

345 Lettl WRP 2021, 413 (415); Zimmer/Göhsl ZWeR 2021, 29 (59); Kumkar, in: FK-KartellR DMA Art. 1 mn. 53; doubtful in relation to the Commission proposal Podszun/Bongartz/Langenstein EuCML 2021, 60 (66 et seq.); BT-Drs. 19/23492, 73 et seq. clarifies that § 19a GWB is a form of control of abusive practices.

346 See also Botta JECLAP 2021, 500 (503 et seq.).

347 Wolf/Brüggemann, in: Kirk/Offergeld/Rohner 365 (368) and Haucap/Schweitzer PWP 2021, 17, 22 et seqq., both with a detailed comparison of § 19a GWB and the DMA; Zimmer/Göhsl ZWeR 2021, 29 (58 et seq.) also in favour of the application of Art. 1(6)(b) DMA with reference to the broad interpretation of the unilateral act as defined in Regulation (EC) No. 1/2003; Käseberg/Gappa, in: HK-DMA Art. 1 mn. 28; Kumkar, in: FK-KartellR DMA Art. 1 mn. 49; Lodoabă Bologna Law Review 2023, 43 (73); differing Polley/Konrad WuW 2021, 198 (199); Paal/Kumkar NJW 2021, 809 (815); Gielen/Uphues EuZW 2021, 627 (631); Witt CMLR 2023, 625 (663); Deselaers NZKart 2024, 366 (369); cf. Wissenschaftliche Dienste des Deutschen Bundestags, WD 7-3000-114/21 with further references.

§ 20(3a) GWB is also linked to the criterion of market power and therefore remains unaffected by the DMA.[348]

Against the special requirements for the application of national competition rules in Art. 1(6)(2) DMA it has been objected that the DMA is explicitly based on the internal market competence of Art. 114 TFEU and – in contrast to, for example, the Competition Damages Directive[349] – a deliberate decision was made not to make use of the competence of Art. 103(1) TFEU because it was foreseeable that the regulatory content of the DMA would exceed the limits of competition competence and unanimity in the Council required for an extension of competence according to Art. 352 TFEU would not have been achieved.[350] From this question of competence, an argument for the interpretation of Art. 1(6)(2) DMA has been derived: The starting point is the statement that the internal market competence does not create a general competence of the Union for all areas concerning the internal market.[351] Rather, Art. 114 TFEU is concerned with impediments to the internal market by diverging laws in the Member States, not by the conduct of private individuals.[352] Since the correct legal basis is determined by the main object of the legal act,[353] an interpretation of the DMA that focuses on competition law would lead to its nullity. If one wants to avoid nullity of the DMA because of the choice of an incorrect legal basis,[354] one should interpret the DMA in such a way that the regulatory areas covered by Art. 103(1) TFEU are excluded from the DMA. According to this view, national competition law must therefore only be measured against European competition law, not the DMA. If Member State competition law was compliant with EU competition law or was covered by an opening clause, the DMA could no longer take precedence. In this understanding, Art. 1(6)(a) and (b) of the DMA only have a declaratory effect, since apart from the autonomous classification of Member State rules as competition law, no further requirements for compatibility with the DMA must be met. Competition law provisions are all those that concern measures within the meaning of Art. 3(2)(2) of Regulation (EC) No. 1/2003[355].[356] 80

However, these competence-motivated objections can already be taken into account by the interpretation of Art. 1(6)(a) and (b) DMA as proposed here: National competition provisions within the meaning of Art. 3(2)(2) of Regulation (EC) No. 1/2003 are subject to Art. 1(6)(a) or (b) DMA and thus remain unaffected by the DMA even without a corrective interpretation. Only national competition provisions which, like the DMA, establish obligations of conduct that are independent of effects and justification do not fall under Art. 1(6)(b) DMA and are thus (in principle) covered by the blocking effect of the DMA according to Art. 1(5)(1) DMA (subject to sentence 2). But as, accord- 81

---

[348] Zimmer/Göhsl ZWeR 2021, 29 (59); Kumkar, in: FK-KartellR DMA Art. 1 mn. 49.

[349] Directive 2014/104/EU of the European Parliament and of the Council of 26 November 2014 on certain rules governing actions for damages under national law for infringements of the competition law provisions of the Member States and of the European Union (2014) OJ L 349/1.

[350] Zimmer/Göhsl ZWeR 2021, 29 (33).

[351] ECJ 17.3.1993 – C-155/91, ECLI:EU:C:1993:98 para. 19 = NVwZ 1993, 872 – Directive on Waste; ECJ 5.10.2000 – C-376/98, ECLI:EU:C:2000:544 para. 83 = NJW 2000, 3701 – Tobacco Advertising I; Khan, in: Geiger/Khan/Kotzur, 6th edition 2017, AEUV Art. 114 mn. 16.

[352] Basedow ZEuP 2021, 217 (221).

[353] ECJ 17.3.1993 – C-155/91, ECLI:EU:C:1993:98 paras. 19 et seq. = NVwZ 1993, 872 – Directive on waste; ECJ 29.4.2004 – C-338/01, ECLI:EU:C:2004:254 para. 55 – Commission v Council; ECJ 8.9.2009 – C-411/06, ECLI:EU:C:2009:518 para. 46 = NVwZ 2009, 1481 – Shipments of waste.

[354] In conclusion assuming the nullity: Basedow ZEuP 2021, 217 (221 et seq.); de Pablo/Fernández JECLAP 2021, 576; Zimmer/Göhsl ZWeR 2021, 29 (35).

[355] Council Regulation (EC) No. 1/2003 of 16 December 2002 on the implementation of the rules on competition laid down in Articles 81 and 82 of the Treaty (2003) OJ L 1/1.

[356] Zimmer/Göhsl ZWeR 2021, 29 (58); cf. Bongartz WuW 2022, 72 (74).

ing to the understanding of the legislator of the DMA, such provisions pursue an objective that is only complementary to the general competition provisions, but not identical to them,[357] they also do not fall under Art. 103 TFEU, so that no argument can be based on a blocking effect of that provision (Art. 103 TFEU) either.[358]

82 Finally, the potentially cumulative application of the DMA alongside European and national competition law raises the question of the scope of the **prohibition of double jeopardy** (Art. 50 CFR, non bis in idem). According to the criteria of the (recent) case law of the ECJ[359], however, double punishment of conduct under Art. 102 TFEU and Art. 30 DMA in conjunction with Art. 5, 6 DMA may be possible.[360] In these cases, however, the fine already imposed must be offset in the second proceeding for reasons of equity.[361]

II. Other Union law

83 For the relationship with Union law other than competition law, recital 12 DMA clarifies that the DMA applies "without prejudice to the rules resulting from other acts of Union law regulating certain aspects of the provision of services", in particular the GDPR and the ePrivacy Directive 2002/58/EC, the P2B Regulation, the Unfair Commercial Practices Directive 2005/29/EC, the AVMS Directive 2010/13/EU, the Payment Services Directive (EU) 2015/2366, Directive (EU) 2019/790 on copyright in the digital single market, as well as Directive (EU) 2019/882 on accessibility requirements for products and services and Directive 93/13/EEC on unfair terms in consumer contracts.

84 In relation to the **P2B Regulation,** the parallel application of the DMA can be explained by the asymmetrical approach of the DMA: Its rules are not imposed on all market participants, but only on a certain (small) group which, in the opinion of the legislator, pose a particular threat to the fairness on the market due to their size and position.[362] In relation to the **Unfair Terms in Consumer Contracts Directive**[363] the demarcation can be explained by the fact that the Unfair Terms in Consumer Contracts Directive is not aimed at the contestability and fairness of markets, but at consumer protection, so that the transposition laws pursuant to Art. 1(5)(2) DMA remain unaffected by the DMA.[364] The same applies to the **Consumer Rights Directive**[365] and the **Digital**

---

357 Rec. 11 DMA.

358 It is true that the legislator with its understanding in rec. 11 of the DMA cannot prescribe the interpretation of the primary law competence title of Art. 103 TFEU, which ultimately has to be clarified by the ECJ. However, it seems entirely justifiable that the Union legislator develops its own understanding of the scope of the competence norms, which would ultimately have to be tested before the ECJ.

359 ECJ 22.3.2022 – C-117/20, ECLI:EU:C:2022:202 = NZKart 2022, 203 – bpost; ECJ 22.3.2022 – C-151/20, ECLI:EU:C:2022:203 = NZKart 2022, 200 – Nordzucker.

360 Brauneck RDi 2023, 27 (32); Horstkotte/Jannausch IWRZ 2022, 147, 152; Klusmann/Schley NZKart 2022, 264 (266); Käseberg/Gappa, in: HK-DMA Art. 1 mn. 33; Kumkar, in: FK-KartellR DMA Art. 1 mn. 61; Witt CMLR 2023, 625 (649 et seqq.); critically Achleitner NZKart 2022, 359 (365); Harta NZKart 2022, 102 (106 et seq.); Ribera Martínez Eur. Compet. J. 2023, 86; Zober NZKart 2021, 611 (615).

361 Kumkar, in: FK-KartellR DMA Art. 1 mn. 61; Harta NZKart 2022, 102 (104); cf. rec. 86 DMA; ECJ 14.12.1972 – 7/72, ECLI:EU:C:1972:125 = BeckRS 2004, 73557 – Boehringer Mannheim; ECJ 13.2.1969 – 14/68, ECLI:EU:C:1969:4 = GRUR Int 1969, 264 – Walt Wilhelm.

362 In detail Bania Eur. Compet. J. 2023, 116 (119); cf. Busch/Busch P2B-VO Einl. mn. 17.

363 Council Directive 93/13/EEC of 5 April 1993 on unfair terms in consumer contracts (1993) OJ L 95/29.

364 Basedow ZEuP 2021, 217 (224 et seq.).

365 Directive 2011/83/EU of the European Parliament and of the Council of 25 October 2011 on consumer rights, amending Council Directive 93/13/EEC and Directive 1999/44/EC of the European Parliament and of the Council and repealing Council Directive 85/577/EEC and Directive 97/7/EC of the European Parliament and of the Council (2011) OJ L 304/64.

Content and Services Directive[366]. The UCPD[367] also remains unaffected by the DMA due to the different nature of the legal consequences in case of a violation.[368] The DMA and the **Data Act** also leave each other unaffected. However, the designation as gatekeeper leads to an exclusion from the right of access to data.[369]

III. Other national law (Art. 1(5) DMA)

The DMA contains two provisions on the relationship to national law: Art. 1(5) and Art. 1(6) DMA. While Art. 1(5) DMA deals with the general relationship to Member State provisions, Art. 1(6)(a) and (b) DMA offer two special opening clauses for national competition provisions ((c) concerns national merger control provisions) (on Art. 1(6) DMA → mn. 76 et seqq.). Despite being the more specific provision for competition law, para. 6 does not have a blocking effect on para. 5.[370] Since the DMA explicitly pursues a purpose that is distinct from competition law[371] and Art. 1(6) DMA only covers certain national competition rules (→ mn. 78 et seqq.), national competition provisions may also fall under Art. 1(5)(1) DMA (e.g. if they are prohibitions similar to the DMA and independent of individual cases) or may exceptionally be permissible under Art. 1(5)(2) DMA.[372] **85**

The starting point to determine the blocking effect of the DMA for national law is the prohibition in Art. 1(5)(1) of the DMA for Member States to impose no "further obligations" on gatekeepers "for the purpose of ensuring contestable and fair markets" in order to avoid fragmentation of the internal market. Member states are thus prohibited from introducing and/or applying national provisions "which are within the **scope** of and pursue the **same objectives** as this Regulation",[373] i.e. to ensure contestable and fair markets in the digital sector (Art. 1(1) DMA). This blocking effect is obvious in view of the chosen internal market competence (Art. 114 TFEU). It also makes it clear that the DMA does not merely aim at minimum harmonisation. **86**

On the other hand, in order to ensure that the DMA does not block any conceivable regulation of gatekeepers by national legislators, Art. 1(5)(1) DMA, according to Art. 1(5)(2) DMA, does not "preclude Member States from imposing obligations on undertakings, including undertakings providing core platform services, for matters falling outside the scope of this Regulation, provided that those obligations are compatible with **87**

---

366 Directive (EU) 2019/770 of the European Parliament and of the Council of 20 May 2019 on certain aspects concerning contracts for the supply of digital content and digital services (2019) OJ L 136/1.

367 Directive 2005/29/EC of the European Parliament and of the Council of 11 May 2005 concerning unfair business-to-consumer commercial practices in the internal market and amending Council Directive 84/450/EEC, Directives 97/7/EC, 98/27/EC and 2002/65/EC of the European Parliament and of the Council and Regulation (EC) No 2006/2004 of the European Parliament and of the Council ('Unfair Commercial Practices Directive') (2005) OJ L 149/22.

368 Cf. esp. Art. 11a UCPD; differing Bania Eur. Compet. J. 2023, 116 (126 et seqq.) who considers several prohibitions in the DMA to be "rules regulating specific aspects of unfair commercial practices" within the meaning of Art. 3(4) UCPD.

369 Art. 5(3), 6(2)(d), rec. 40 Regulation (EU) 2023/2854 of the European Parliament and of the Council of 13 December 2023 on harmonised rules on fair access to and use of data and amending Regulation (EU) 2017/2394 and Directive (EU) 2020/1828 (2023) OJ L 2854/1; critically, Koenig/Mezey N&R 2022, 192.

370 Differing Kumkar, in: FK-KartellR DMA Art. 1 mn. 34, 39; probably differing Käseberg/Gappa, in: HK-DMA Art. 1 mn. 21; Drexl et al GRUR Int. 2023, 864 (866).

371 Rec. 11 DMA.

372 Differing Basedow ZEuP 2021, 217 (224), who sees all national competition rules covered by Art. 1(6) DMA.

373 Rec. 9 DMA.

Union law and do not result from the fact that the relevant undertakings have the status of gatekeepers within the meaning of this Regulation". Member States are thus permitted to enact national rules also for gatekeepers and also in the digital sector, as long as they pursue **other objectives than the DMA**. According to the explanation in recital 9 of the DMA, Art. 1(5)(2) DMA is intended to allow Member States to apply "to gatekeepers within the meaning of this Regulation other national rules which pursue **other legitimate public interest objectives** as set out in the TFEU [Art. 36, 52] or which pursue **overriding reasons of public interest** as recognised by the case law of the [ECJ]", such as the protection of consumers or the prevention of unfair competition.[374] However, due to the express provision of Art. 1(5)(2) DMA, it should not be sufficient to open national regulatory sovereignty that the national legal act merely pursues a different objective than the DMA. It should also be necessary that it is a matter "falling outside the scope of this Regulation [i.e. the DMA]" and that the obligations "do not result from the fact that the relevant undertakings have the status of a gatekeeper within the meaning of this Regulation" (and – of course – that the obligations comply with Union law). Since the substantive scope of the DMA is defined by the gatekeeper status (Art. 1(2) DMA) and since Art. 1(5)(2) DMA precisely intends to open up regulation of core platform services for reasons other than the objectives of the DMA, the reference to the scope of application of the DMA in Art. 1(5)(2) DMA should not be understood as referring to the provision of core platform services in general, but solely to the regulation of gatekeepers to ensure contestable and fair markets in the digital sector.[375]

D. International aspects

I. Private international law

88 Since gatekeepers generally pursue global business models,[376] conflict of laws problems inevitably arise with regard to the application of the DMA. However, according to Art. 1(2) of the DMA, which provides for a very broad territorial scope (→ mn. 64 et seqq.), the application of the DMA does not depend on the classic conflict-of-law rules (such as the Rome I Regulation or the Rome II Regulation). Rather, the DMA is applicable "irrespective of the law otherwise applicable to the provision of service" (Art. 1(2) DMA).[377] The DMA thus creates **overriding mandatory provisions** within the meaning of Art. 9 Rome I Regulation and Art. 16 Rome II Regulation, which define their own territorial scope of application (specifically: by Art. 1(2) DMA) and are to be applied independently of the law otherwise applicable.

89 As a rule, the character of the DMA as an overriding mandatory provision does not have any effect on the Member State's law that applies under general conflict-of-law rules because the DMA has **precedence** over the Member States' laws. This is different if the application of the general conflict of law rules lead to the law of a third country be-

[374] A similar question about the objective of national rules in relation to the objectives of general European competition law already arises today in the context of the blocking effect of European competition law according to Art. 3(1) and (2) of Regulation (EC) No. 1/2003. According to Art. 3(3) of Regulation (EC) No. 1/2003, the blocking effect of European competition law according to Art. 3(1) and (2) of Regulation (EC) No. 1/2003 shall not "preclude the application of provisions of national law that predominantly pursue an objective different from that pursued by Articles 81 and 82 of the Treaty [Art. 101 and 102 TFEU]". This refers primarily to the law on fair competition, Peifer/Heinze Einl. C mn. 55 et seqq.

[375] Cf. Käseberg/Gappa, in: HK-DMA Art. 1 mn. 17 et seq.

[376] Rec. 7 DMA.

[377] With the same reasons for the P2B Regulation Busch/Schulte-Nölke P2B-VO Art. 1 mn. 46.

ing applicable; in this respect, application of the DMA is only possible via Art. 9(1) Rome I Regulation or Art. 16 Rome II Regulation[378]. Problems may arise, however, if the proceedings in which the question of the applicability of the DMA arises are conducted before the courts of a third country. In this case, the conflict-of-law rules of the third state, specifically the rules on mandatory rules there, decide on the applicability of the DMA. Whether, in the case of a threatened non-application of the DMA in the third state, a choice of court agreement in favour of the third state court covers claims arising from the DMA at all[379] and, if applicable, can be regarded as ineffective from the perspective of courts in the EU[380] and whether the lis pendens of the third state proceedings would be disregarded in the context of § 261 ZPO by analogy or whether the decision rendered by courts in a third state would not be recognised in the EU is an open question. The latter two aspects are likely to depend primarily on whether one counts the DMA among the rules of public policy within the meaning of § 328(1) no. 4 ZPO and which requirements determine a violation of public policy in the case of non-application of the DMA.[381]

II. Public international law

The Union must exercise its powers in compliance with international law.[382] Accord- 90
ing to the "Lotus principle", the Member States and, derived from this, the Union, enjoy unrestricted sovereignty and thus legislative competence.[383] All that is required is a link between the facts of the case and the territory (genuine link).[384] In view of the fact that the DMA may apply to gatekeepers from all over the world, a violation of the public international law prohibition of extraterritorial application may be considered. However, the DMA is linked to the residence and establishment (→ mn. 66 et seqq.) of the user and thus has a sufficient connection to the territory of the Union. Thus, the Lotus criteria seem to be fulfilled. In legal practice, however, it must be taken into account that the Union depends on the cooperation of third countries for extraterritorial law enforcement.[385]

---

378 Regulation (EC) No. 864/2007 of the European Parliament and of the Council of 11 July 2007 on the law applicable to non-contractual obligations.

379 Against the inclusion of claims for damages for violations of Article 101 TFEU in a choice of court agreement under the Brussels I-bis Regulation ECJ 21.5.2015 – C-352/13, ECLI:EU:C:2015:335 para. 69 – NZKart 2015, 307 – CDC Hydrogen Peroxide; on the extension of this interpretation to § 40 ZPO LG München I 7.2.2020 – 37 O 18934/17, NZKart 2020, 145 mn. 115 et seqq. (juris) – LKW-Kartell; for the inclusion of claims under Article 102 TFEU in a choice of court agreement under the Brussels I-bis Regulation, by contrast, ECJ 24.10.2018 – C-595/17, ECLI:EU:C:2018:854 paras. 28 et seq. = NJW 2019, 349 – Apple Sales/eBizcuss.com; on the criticism Ahrens/Heinze Wettbewerbsprozess ch. 15 mn. 24.

380 Cf. correspondingly on the non-application of European law on sales agents by an agreed US court BGH 5.9.2012 – VII ZR 25/12, ZVertriebsR 2013, 89.

381 Recently on the setting aside of an arbitral award for breach of public policy (§ 1049 (2)(2)(b) ZPO), which also includes §§ 19, 20, 21 GWB, BGH 27.9.2022 – KZB 75/21, NZKart 2023, 30 mn. 12 et seqq. – Steinbruch-Schiedsspruch.

382 ECJ 27.2.2018 – C-266/16, ECLI:EU:C:2011:864 para. 47 = BeckRS 2018, 1880 – Western Sahara Campaign UK; ECJ 21.12.2011 – C-366/10, ECLI:EU:C:2011:864 para. 123 = NVwZ 2012, 226 – Air Transport Association of America; ECJ 24.11.1992 – C-286/90, ECLI:EU:C:1992:453 para. 9 = BeckRS 2004, 76004 – Poulsen and Diva Navigation.

383 PCIJ 1927 P.C.I.J. (ser. A) No. 10 (Sept. 7), 18 et seq. – S.S. Lotus (Fr. v. Turk.).

384 ICJ Rep. 1955, 4, 24 et seqq. – Nottebohm Case.

385 On corresponding problems with the enforcement of the NetzDG Kalbhenn ZUM 2022, 266.

§ 12
Obligations for gatekeepers

Literature: *Achleitner*, 'Digital Markets Act beschlossen: Verhaltenspflichten und Rolle nationaler Wettbewerbsbehörden', Neue Zeitschrift für Kartellrecht (NZKart) 2022, 359; *Akman*, 'Regulating competition in digital platform markets: a critical assessment of the framework and approach of the EU Digital Markets Act', European Law Review (ELR) 47 (2022), 85; *Ann*, Patentrecht, 8th edn, Munich 2022; *Burchardi*, 'Die Selbstbegünstigung von Plattformunternehmen im Fokus des Kartell- und Regulierungsrechts', Neue Zeitschrift für Kartellrecht (NZKart) 2022, 610; *Cabral* et al., The EU Digital Markets Act – A Report from a Panel of Economic Experts, 2021, https://t1p.de/glbo9 (cited as 'Report'); *de Streel/Feasey/Krämer/Monti*, Making the Digital Markets Act More Resilient and Effective, 2021, https://t1p.de/0l9te (cited as 'de Streel et al., Digital Markets Act'); *Ellger*, 'Konditionenmissbrauch nach § 19 GWB durch Datenschutzverstoß – Der Facebook-Fall des Bundeskartellamts', Wirtschaft und Wettbewerb (WuW) 2019, 446; *Galle/Burdinski*, 'Neuste Entwicklungen bei vertikalen Beschränkungen', Europäische Zeitschrift für Wirtschaftsrecht (EuZW) 2021, 439; *Gerpott*, 'Das Gesetz über digitale Märkte nach den Trilog-Verhandlungen', Computer und Recht (CR) 2022, 409; *Haus/Weusthof*, 'The Digital Markets Act – a Gatekeeper's Nightmare?', Wirtschaft und Wettbewerb (WuW) 2021, 318; *Herbers*, 'Der Digital Markets Act (DMA) kommt – Neue Dos and Don'ts für Gatekeeper in der Digitalwirtschaft', Recht Digital (RDi) 2022, 252; *Höppner*, 'Duty to Treat Downstream Rivals Equally: (Merely) a Natural Remedy to Google's Monopoly Leveraging Abuse', European Competition and Regulatory Law Review (CoRe) 1 (2017), 208; *Höppner*, Google's (Non-) Compliance with the EU Shopping Decision, 2020, https://t1p.de/olxzq (cited as 'Shopping Decision'); *Hoffer/Lehr*, 'Onlineplattformen und Big Data auf dem Prüfstand – Gemeinsame Betrachtung der Fälle Amazon, Google und Facebook', Neue Zeitschrift für Kartellrecht (NZKart) 2019, 10; *Ibáñez Colomo*, 'The Draft Digital Markets Act: A Legal and Institutional Analysis', Journal of European Competition Law & Practice (JECLAP) 12 (2021), 561; *Karbaum/Schulz*, '"Antitrust Litigation 2.0" – Private Enforcement beim DMA?', Neue Zeitschrift für Kartellrecht (NZKart) 2022, 107; *Kerber*, 'Datenrechtliche Aspekte des Digital Markets Act', Zeitschrift für Datenschutz (ZD) 2021, 544; *Khan*, 'Amazon's Antitrust Paradox', Yale Law Journal (YLJ) 126 (2017), 710; *König*, Actual competitive effects, hypothetical competitors, and the challenge of proving exclusionary conduct (Case T-604/18 Google Android), EU Law Live, 7.12.2022, https://t1p.de/6slvk; *König*, Big Data und Wettbewerbsrecht, in Borges/Keil (eds), Rechtshandbuch Big Data, Munich 2024; *Körber*, 'Die Facebook-Entscheidung des Bundeskartellamtes – Machtmissbrauch durch Verletzung des Datenschutzrechts?', Neue Zeitschrift für Kartellrecht (NZKart) 2019, 187; *Körber*, 'Lessons from the Hare and the Tortoise: Legally imposed self-regulation, proportionality and the right to defence under the DMA', Neue Zeitschrift für Kartellrecht (NZKart) 2021, 379 (Part 1), 436 (Part 2); *Krämer/Schnurr*, 'Big Data and Digital Markets Contestability: Theory of Harm and Data Access Remedies', Journal of Competition Law & Economics (JCLE) 18 (2022), 255; *Krämer/Shekhar*, Regulating Algorithmic Learning in Digital Platform Ecosystems through Data Sharing and Data Siloing: Consequences for Innovation and Welfare, 2022, https://t1p.de/mrrld (cited as 'Algorithmic Learning'); *Kühling/Ceni-Hulek/Engelbracht*, 'Alles wieder auf Anfang – Zur kartellrechtlichen Bewertung enger Bestpreisklauseln auf Hotelportalen', Neue Zeitschrift für Kartellrecht (NZKart) 2021, 76; *Kumkar*, 'Der Digital Markets Act nach dem Trilog-Verfahren', Recht Digital (RDi) 2022, 347; *Larouche/de Streel*, 'The European Digital Markets Act: A Revolution Grounded on Traditions', Journal of European Competition Law & Practice (JECLAP) 12 (2021), 542; *Lichtenberg*, 'Die Bedingungen des App Stores auf dem Prüfstand', Neue Zeitschrift für Kartellrecht (NZKart) 2021, 551; *Lohse*, 'Facebook und die Verarbeitung der off-Facebook-Daten nach der DS-GVO: Ein Fall für die kartellrechtliche Missbrauchsaufsicht?', Neue Zeitschrift für Kartellrecht (NZKart) 2020, 292; *Lomas*, Google antitrust complainants call for EU to shutter its Shopping Ads Units, TechCrunch, 18.10.2022, https://t1p.de/dpa7t; *Mackenrodt/Wiedemann*, 'Zur kartellrechtlichen Bewertung der Datenverarbeitung durch Facebook und ihrer normativen Kohärenz mit dem Datenschutzrecht und dem Datenschuldrecht', Zeitschrift für Urheber- und Medienrecht (ZUM) 2021, 89; *Marsden*, 'Google Shopping for the Empress's New Clothes – When a Remedy Isn't a Remedy (and How to Fix it)', Journal of European Competition Law & Practice (JECLAP) 11 (2020), 553; *Mohr*, 'Kartellrechtlicher Konditionenmissbrauch durch datenschutzwidrige Allgemeine Geschäftsbedingungen', Europäische Zeitschrift für Wirtschaftsrecht (EuZW) 2019, 265; *Monti*, 'The Digital Markets Act: Improving Its Institutional Design', European Journal of Competition & Regulatoy Law (CoRe) 5 (2021), 90; *Petit*, 'The Proposed Digital Markets Act (DMA): A Legal and Policy Review', Journal of European Competition Law & Practice (JECLAP) 12 (2021), 529; *Perez*, Epic and Match's antitrust case against Google heads to jury trial on November 6, TechCrunch, 19.1.2023, https://t1p.de/6izak; *Podszun*, 'Should Gatekeepers Be Allowed to Combine Data? Ideas for Art. 5(a) of the Draft Digital Markets Act', Gewerblicher Rechtschutz und Urheberrecht International (GRUR-Int) 2022, 197; *Podszun/Bongartz/Kirk*, 'Digital Markets Act – Neue Regeln für Fairness in der Plattformökonomie', Neue Juristische Wochenschrift (NJW) 2022, 3249; *Podszun/Bongartz/Langenstein*, 'The Digital Markets Act: Moving from Competition Law to Regulation for Large Gatekeepers', Journal of European Consumer and Market Law (EuCML) 10 (2021), 60; *Polley/Konrad*, 'Der Digital Markets Act – Brüssels neues Regulierungskonzept für digitale Märkte', Wirtschaft und Wettbewerb (WuW) 2021, 198; *Reumann/Weber*, 'Selbstbegünstigung im Kartellrecht – Marktmachtmissbrauch superdominanter Plattformen?', Neue Zeitschrift für Kartellrecht (NZKart) 2022, 314; *Schweitzer*, 'The Art to Make Gatekeeper Positions Contestable and the Challenge to Know What Is Fair: A Discussion of the Digital Markets Act Proposal', Zeitschrift für Europäisches Privatrecht (ZEuP) 29 (2021), 503; *Scott Morton/Caffara*, The European Commission Digital Markets Act: A translation, VoxEU, 5.1.2021, https://t1p.de/6sp9z; *Vesterdorf/Fountoukakos*, 'An Appraisal of the Remedy in the Commission's Google Search (Shopping) Decision and a Guide to its Interpretation in Light of an Analytical Reading of the Case Law', Journal of European Competition Law & Practice (JECLAP) 9 (2018), 3; *Zimmer/Göhsl*, 'Vom New Competition Tool zum Digital Markets Act: Die geplante EU-Regulierung für digitale Gatekeeper', Zeitschrift für Wettbewerbsrecht (ZWeR) 2021, 29.

A. Introduction

The catalogues of obligations in Art. 5–7 DMA are the heart of the DMA, as they determine how the gatekeepers must behave on European markets in the future. The catalogues contain both **prohibitions**, such as the data processing prohibitions of Art. 5(2) DMA, the tying prohibition of Art. 5(8) DMA and the prohibition of self-preferencing in rankings under Art. 6(5) DMA, as well as **obligations**, such as the transparency obligations under Art. 5(9) and (10) DMA, the data portability obligation of Art. 6(9) DMA or the data access obligations under Art. 6(10) and (11) DMA. Since prohibitions can be reformulated as obligations to refrain, both types of behavioural requirements can simply be referred to as obligations. All obligations under Art. 5–7 DMA are aimed at preventing gatekeeper practices that would limit the contestability of core platform services (or downstream markets, cf. → § 10 mn. 22) or would be unfair (cf. Art. 12(1) and (5) DMA).[1] In particular, the purpose is to lower **barriers to market entry** and to prevent gatekeepers from extending their power to related markets (so-called *monopoly leveraging*).[2] In addition, the obligations should help to ensure that users of core platform ser- 1

[1] For more details on contestability and fairness see → § 10 mn. 20 et seqq., 23 et seq.

[2] Cf. on this and the following EU Commission, Impact Assessment Report of 15.12.2020, SWD(2020) 363, Part 2, 49 et seqq. On monopoly leveraging cf. Höppner CoRe 1 (2017), 208 (210 et seqq.).

vices can more easily switch to other services and have stronger incentives to do so, and that business users are not discriminated against.

2 The obligations under Art. 5–7 DMA apply only to **gatekeepers**[3] and only with regard to their **core platform services,**[4] as defined by the EU Commission in the designation decision pursuant to Art. 3(9) DMA. This follows directly from the wording of Art. 5(1), 6(1) and 7(1) DMA, as they each refer to the designation decision and Art. 3(9) DMA. As the first designation decisions were issued at the beginning of September 2023 and the obligations under Art. 5–7 DMA must be fulfilled no later than six months after the designation decision pursuant to Art. 3(10) DMA, the users of core platform services should be able to benefit from the new framework since March 2024 (→ § 10 mn. 3).

3 Understanding the content of Art. 5–7 DMA is made difficult by the fact that there is **no internal order** to the catalogues of obligations.[5] No prioritisation can be derived from the structure of the catalogues, nor has the legislator attempted to sort the obligations thematically, e.g. according to their respective objectives or the core platform services for which they are particularly relevant in individual cases (cf. also → mn. 4, 22 et seq.).[6] However, there is an important difference between the obligations under Art. 5 DMA on the one hand and those under Art. 6 and 7 DMA on the other, as only the latter can always be specified in the procedure under Art. 8(2) DMA. For the obligations under Art. 5 DMA, a specification by the Commission is only possible under Art. 8(2) sent. 3 DMA if the Commission initiates proceedings for circumvention under Art. 13 DMA.

4 The remainder of this chapter is structured as follows: First, the **basic principles** of the DMA obligations regime are presented in more detail (B) than in the introduction (→ § 10 mn. 38 et seqq.). Secondly, the **individual obligations** from the catalogues of Art. 5–7 DMA are discussed and analysed, together with their prerequisites and legal consequences (C). For this purpose, a structure has been chosen that does not follow the (not very helpful) structure of Art. 5–7 DMA, but focuses on the **core platform services** according to Art. 2(2) DMA. This is intended to show which obligations are particularly relevant in which context. In addition, the approach takes into account that very different **competition problems** can be identified in relation to the different core platform services. Therefore, it seems necessary to consider which platform services are involved in each context and which challenges arise in this context when interpreting and applying Art. 5–7 DMA.

B. Key elements of the obligations regime

5 The main features of the DMA obligations regime have already been outlined in the introduction (→ § 10 mn. 38 et seqq.). The basic principles are therefore only briefly recalled below. In addition, the provisions of Art. 8–13 DMA, which concern, among other things, the specification and updating of obligations and exceptions to their general applicability, are also discussed.

---

[3] Art. 2(1) DMA; → § 10 mn. 30 et seqq.; → § 11 mn. 43 et seqq.

[4] Art. 2(2) DMA; → § 10 mn. 33 et seqq.; → § 11 mn. 6 et seqq.

[5] Critically Akman ELR 47 (2022), 85 (112 et seq.); Gerpott CR 2022, 409 para. 21; Haus/Weusthof WuW 2021, 318 (321); Podszun/Bongartz/Langenstein EuCML 10 (2021), 60 (65); Körber NZKart 2021, 436 (437 et seq.); Petit JECLAP 12 (2021), 529 (535); Kerber ZD 2021, 544 (547).

[6] The latter was suggested, for example, by Akman ELR 47 (2022), 85 (112 et seq.) and Körber NZKart 2021, 436 (438).

I. General principles

The obligations under Art. 5–7 DMA apply only to **gatekeepers** and only in relation to their **core platform services** (→ mn. 2). Compared to the competition law prohibitions in Art. 101, 102 TFEU, the DMA obligations are very **specific**, which should allow for their effective enforcement (→ § 10 mn. 40). Nevertheless, it is often criticised in the literature that the requirements of the obligations are not sufficiently clear. This is said to make them difficult to apply and to create considerable legal uncertainty.[7] All obligations under Art. 5–7 DMA apply automatically by operation of law, i.e. they are ***self-executing*** and do not need to be activated by a prior administrative decision, as is the case, for example, with the prohibitions under the German § 19a(2) GWB. The obligations must be fulfilled no later than six months after the decision pursuant to Art. 3(4) or (8) DMA, designating the respective undertaking as a gatekeeper (cf. Art. 3(10) DMA). 6

Pursuant to Art. 3(8) in conjunction with Art. 3(1)(c) DMA, the EU Commission may also designate an undertaking as a gatekeeper if it does not yet enjoy an **entrenched and durable position** with regard to its core platform services, but it is "foreseeable that it will enjoy such a position in the near future". For such cases, Art. 17(4) DMA provides that the Commission may only declare the obligations under Art. 5(3)–(6) and Art. 6(4), (7), (9), (10) and (13) DMA applicable and that it shall only declare those obligations applicable which are appropriate and necessary to prevent the gatekeeper concerned from achieving, by unfair means, an entrenched and durable position in its operations. For this particular group of gatekeepers (*"emerging gatekeepers"*), the obligations under Art. 5–7 DMA are therefore not *self-executing*, but must be activated by a prior decision.[8] 7

The gatekeepers themselves must ensure **compliance** with the obligations (cf. also Art. 13(3) DMA) and demonstrate compliance to the EU Commission, Art. 8(1) sent. 1 DMA. They must also submit a **report** to the Commission as early as six months after their designation as gatekeepers pursuant to Art. 11(1) DMA, describing in a detailed and transparent manner the measures taken to ensure compliance with the obligations under Art. 5–7 DMA. The Commission may monitor and investigate the compliance of the gatekeepers pursuant to Art. 20 et seq. DMA and, if necessary, take measures against non-compliance, such as prohibition decisions or fines. 8

The obligations under Art. 5–7 DMA apply irrespective of the **actual effects** of compliance on competition and consumers in individual cases (→ § 10 mn. 41 et seqq.). The rationale is that it should be possible to verify compliance with the obligations without complex economic analyses. This is intended to ensure **effective enforcement** of the obligations, free from the difficulties that the legislator believes have become ubiquitous in the enforcement of competition law (→ § 10 mn. 15, 42 et seq.). Against this background, it may prove to be problematic that Art. 8(1) sent. 2 DMA states that the gatekeepers' measures "shall be effective in achieving the objectives of this Regulation and of the relevant obligation".[9] Presumably, this is only intended to prevent gatekeepers from resorting to an overly formalistic fulfilment of their obligations that does not correspond to the "spirit" of the DMA. Conversely, however, gatekeepers could also argue that they 9

[7] Akman ELR 47 (2022), 85 (110 et seq.); Körber NZKart 2021, 436 (437); Petit JECLAP 12 (2021), 529 (535); Schweitzer ZEuP 29 (2021), 503 (534 et seqq.); Cabral et al., Report, p. 10; de Streel et al., Digital Markets Act, p. 59 et seqq.

[8] Cf. Körber NZKart 2021, 436.

[9] A similar problem may be posed by Art. 8(1) sent. 3 DMA, which provides that the gatekeepers' measures must comply with the GDPR (Regulation (EU) 2016/679), the ePrivacy Directive (Directive 2002/58/EC) and legislation on cyber security, consumer protection and product safety. This may also invite efforts to undermine the strict enforcement of obligations under Art. 5–7 DMA, as gatekeepers may invoke conflicting objectives to justify their behaviour.

do not have to comply with certain obligations under Art. 5–7 DMA, if and to the extent that they can demonstrate that such compliance would not further the objectives of the DMA in the specific situation. If the effective enforcement of the DMA is not to be jeopardised, such justifications can only be accepted in very exceptional cases, if at all (→ § 10 mn. 41). As a general rule, it must be irrebuttably presumed that compliance with the obligations under Art. 5–7 DMA serves the purposes of the DMA.

II. Specification, Art. 8 DMA

10 According to Art. 8(2) and (3) DMA, the EU Commission may, on its own initiative or at the request of a gatekeeper, adopt an **implementing act** specifying the **measures** to be taken by the gatekeeper in order to fulfil its obligations under Art. 6 and 7 DMA. For this purpose, the Commission must initiate an **investigation procedure** pursuant to Art. 20 in conjunction with Art. 50(2) DMA, which must be completed within six months, Art. 8(2) subpara. 2 sent. 2 DMA. Third parties may submit comments pursuant to Art. 8(6) DMA. In determining the measures to be implemented, the Commission must ensure that the measures are **effective** in achieving the objectives of the DMA and the relevant obligation under Art. 6 and 7 DMA, and that they are **proportionate** in the specific circumstances, Art. 8(7) DMA. As a general rule, the possibility of specification is limited to obligations under Art. 6 and 7 DMA. Obligations listed in the catalogue of Art. 5 DMA can only be specified if the Commission initiates proceedings for circumvention under Art. 13 DMA (→ mn. 21).

11 As the procedure under Art. 8(2) and (3) DMA is not linked to a prior infringement of the law, the specification of obligations by the Commission is a paradigmatic case of ***ex ante* regulation** (→ § 10 mn. 28). According to the legislator, this is intended to facilitate a **regulatory dialogue** in which the Commission and the gatekeepers work together constructively to devise effective and proportionate measures.[10] The initiation of proceedings pursuant to Art. 8(2) and (3) DMA is at the **discretion** of the Commission. However, taking into account the principles of equal treatment, proportionality and good administration (cf. Art. 8(3) subpara. 1 sent. 2 DMA), it will hardly be possible for the Commission to refuse to examine a specific proposal by a gatekeeper. It is also to be expected that the Commission will seek **amicable solutions** in order to avoid lengthy litigation on the interpretation of Art. 6 and 7 DMA and to be able to achieve quick results. However, it remains to be seen how willing the gatekeepers will be to reach negotiated solutions.[11]

III. Exceptions

12 In order to ensure proportionality, Art. 9 and 10 DMA provide that the Commission may allow for exceptions from the obligations under Art. 5–7 DMA under certain conditions. However, the requirements are very high. Art. 9 DMA concerns cases in which the economic viability of the gatekeeper would be endangered by compliance with the obligations under Art. 5–7 DMA. Art. 10 DMA allows exemptions for reasons of public health and public security. The DMA does not provide for a general possibility of justification or efficiency defence (→ § 10 mn. 44).

[10] Cf. rec. 65(2) DMA.

[11] For more information on the gatekeepers' conduct in competition law proceedings, see → § 10 mn. 16.

1. Suspension, Art. 9 DMA

Art. 9(1) DMA empowers the Commission to suspend a specific obligation under Art. 5–7 DMA in whole or in part by means of an implementing act if the **economic viability** of the gatekeeper's operation in the European Union would otherwise be endangered. It is not entirely clear what is meant by 'economic viability', especially since Art. 2 DMA does not contain a definition. The term is also used in the competition law rules on **inability to pay**, where it refers to situations where high fines could drive undertakings into bankruptcy.[12] Moreover, since Art. 9(1) DMA refers not only to the economic viability of the specific platform service for which the suspension is requested but to that of the gatekeeper's entire **business operation** in the European Union, it seems virtually impossible, at least for Alphabet, Amazon, Apple, Meta and Microsoft, that Art. 9 DMA will be applied in the near future. The fact that the threat to economic viability under Art. 9(1) DMA must also be due to **exceptional circumstances** beyond the gatekeeper's control does not make it any easier. The recitals give the example of an unforeseen external shock that has temporarily eliminated a significant part of end user demand for the relevant core platform service.[13] 13

2. Exemption, Art. 10 DMA

The power of the EU Commission to grant exemptions under Art. 10(1) DMA is unlikely to be of much greater practical relevance, as such exemptions can only be granted for reasons of **public health** or **public security**, Art. 10(3) DMA. A possible application could be exemptions from the data processing prohibitions under Art. 5(2) and Art. 6(2) DMA, e.g. for disease control and prevention, or the prevention of acts of violence including self-harm. However, Art. 5(2) sent. 3 DMA already refers to the justifications of Art. 6(1)(c), (d) and (e) GDPR, which allow data processing in the public interest even without the consent of the data subject, and should be able to cover situations such as those mentioned above. The scope of Art. 6(2) DMA is limited to data that is used in competition with other undertakings. An application of Art. 10 DMA therefore seems unlikely. 14

IV. Updating, Art. 12 DMA

Art. 12(1) DMA empowers the Commission to **supplement** the obligations of Art. 5 and 6 DMA by means of delegated acts in accordance with Art. 49 DMA. With this authorisation, the legislator has made use of the power of delegation in Art. 290 TFEU. The scope and limits of the authorisation in Art. 12(1) DMA are determined by Art. 12(2) DMA, which specifies in detail which updates may be made in the **simplified procedure** of Art. 12 DMA. Adjustments going beyond this narrow scope can only be made by amending the DMA itself, which can only be done through the **ordinary legislative procedure** under Art. 294 TFEU. As a rule of thumb, it can be said that the simplified procedure under Art. 12 DMA can only be used to extend or specify existing obligations under Art. 5 and 6 DMA. Substantial amendments, on the other hand, such as the creation of new obligations or the deletion of existing ones, must be made in accordance with the ordinary legislative procedure. 15

In order to prepare a delegated act within the meaning of Art. 12(1) DMA, the Commission must conduct a **market investigation** pursuant to Art. 19 DMA (see → § 13 16

[12] Cf. EU Commission, Guidelines on Fines 2006, OJ 2006 C 210, 2, para. 35.
[13] Rec. 66 DMA.

mn. 42 et seqq., 97 et seqq.). According to Art. 19(3) sent. 1 DMA, the investigation must be completed within 18 months. The final report it to be submitted to the European Parliament and the Council and, where appropriate, shall be accompanied by a draft delegated act supplementing the DMA or a legislative proposal to amend the DMA in the ordinary legislative procedure, Art. 19(3) sent. 2 DMA. However, the Commission always has the right to initiate an ordinary legislative procedure even without a market investigation, as its right of initiative derives directly from Art. 294(2) TFEU and is not limited by Art. 19 DMA.

17 Within the framework of Art. 12(2) DMA, delegated acts according to Art. 12(1) DMA may provide for supplements to the obligations under Art. 5 and 6 DMA which are necessary to address practices that limit the **contestability** of core platform services or that are **unfair** in the same way as the practices addressed by the obligations laid down in Art. 5 and 6 DMA, cf. Art. 12(1) sent. 2 DMA. Art. 12(5) DMA explains in more detail when this is the case. In addition, the **requirements** of Art. 12(2) DMA must also be observed, but these provide the Commission considerable leeway. To mention just two examples, it would be possible to extend the prohibition of tying in Art. 5(8) DMA to services which are not core platform services (cf. Art. 12(2)(g) DMA) or to create additional data access rights along the lines of the right of access to search engine data under Art. 6(11) DMA (cf. Art. 12(2)(e) DMA). In the first years of application of the DMA, however, the Commission should be more than busy enforcing the existing obligations. Later, supplements according to Art. 12 DMA may become more important, especially in view of the very dynamic development of business models in the digital sector.[14] However, amending the DMA through the ordinary legislative procedure of Art. 294 TFEU is not too difficult, either, and has the advantage of greater legitimacy.

18 Art. 12(3) and (4) DMA empowers the Commission to amend or supplement certain aspects of the **obligations under Art. 7** DMA by means of delegated acts. The procedure is similar to that for the adoption of delegated acts according to Art. 12(1) DMA. The requirements are not listed in Art. 12(2) DMA, but directly in Art. 12(3) and (4) in conjunction with Art. 12(5) DMA.

V. Anti-circumvention, Art. 13 DMA

19 Art. 13 DMA makes it clear that gatekeepers must not circumvent their obligations under the DMA. Two different objects of regulation can be distinguished: Art. 13(1) and (2) DMA concern circumvention in the context of the gatekeeper designation procedure under Art. 3 DMA, the other paragraphs of Art. 13 DMA relate to circumvention of the obligations under Art. 5–7 DMA. With regard to the **designation procedure** under Art. 3 DMA, Art. 13(1) sent. 1 DMA stipulates that undertakings providing core platform services must not segment their services in order to circumvent the quantitative thresholds of Art. 3(2) DMA. If there is a suspicion of an effort to engage in such behaviour, the Commission may investigate the facts pursuant to Art. 13(2) DMA. If the thresholds would have been exceeded without the segmentation, the Commission may designate the undertaking as a gatekeeper according to Art. 3(4) DMA, Art. 13(1) sent. 2 DMA.

20 According to Art. 13(3) DMA, gatekeepers must ensure that the obligations under Art. 5–7 DMA are "fully and effectively" complied with.[15] This requirement is further specified in Art. 13(4)–(6) DMA. Art. 13(4) DMA, the most general of the three provi-

[14] Cf. Schweitzer ZEuP 29 (2021), 503 (532 et seqq.).
[15] Cf. also Art. 5(1), Art. 6(1), Art. 7(1) and (2), Art. 8(1) sent. 1 DMA.

sions, is quite comprehensive. It states that gatekeepers shall not engage in any behaviour that undermines **effective compliance** with the obligations in Art. 5–7 DMA, regardless of whether that behaviour is "of a contractual, commercial or technical nature, or of any other nature" or consists in the use of "*behavioural techniques*" or "*interface design*". Art. 13(5) DMA contains additional specifications with regard to **consent requirements** under data protection law (cf. e.g. Art. 5(2) DMA). Art. 13(6) DMA specifies that gatekeepers must not discriminate against users for exercising their rights and choices under Art. 5–7 DMA and that they must not make the exercise of these rights and choices unduly difficult. The drafting of the requirements of Art. 13(4)–(6) DMA, some of which are formulated in a very detailed and specific manner, appears to have been motivated by the concern that users of core platform services might be induced by the gatekeepers not to make use of the possibilities offered by Art. 5–7 DMA. One could imagine that end users might be influenced by certain **design decisions** to inadvertently grant **consent** under Art. 5(2) DMA or not to use the possibility of **switching** under Art. 6(6) DMA or the right to **data portability** under Art. 6(9) DMA. Indeed, a conceptual problem of the DMA is that its success depends largely on the extent to which business users and end users will actually make use of the possibilities offered by Art. 5–7 DMA. This cannot be enforced by any public authority, but depends largely on user preferences and behaviour. Nevertheless, Art. 13(4)–(6) DMA should at least prevent gatekeepers from deliberately undermining the effectiveness of Art. 5–7 DMA.

If a gatekeeper circumvents or attempts to circumvent an obligation under Art. 5–7 **21** DMA in a manner described in Art. 13(4)–(6) DMA, the EU Commission may initiate an investigation procedure under Art. 20 DMA and issue an **implementing act** pursuant to Art. 8(2) DMA to specify the measures to be taken by the gatekeeper. It is particularly noteworthy that in the context of anti-circumvention, a **specification** under Art. 8(2) DMA is also possible in relation to obligations under Art. 5 DMA, which is not otherwise provided for in Art. 8(2) DMA. A broad interpretation and application of Art. 13 DMA would therefore give the Commission more room for manoeuvre under Art. 8(2) DMA. Paradoxically, it may even be in the **interest of a gatekeeper** to raise suspicions of a circumvention or attempted circumvention under Art. 13 DMA. This is because it is the only way to ensure that the Commission may also specify obligations under Art. 5 DMA, which may well be welcomed by the gatekeeper due to the increased legal certainty. Art. 13(8) DMA makes it clear that Art. 13 DMA does not affect the Commission's powers under Art. 29–31 DMA. Thus, even in cases of circumvention, non-compliance decisions can be issued and, where appropriate, fines and periodic penalty payments can be imposed if the relevant conditions are met.

C. Individual obligations

The remainder of this chapter focuses on the presentation and analysis of the obliga- **22** tions arising from the catalogues of Art. 5–7 DMA. The structure of the discussion does not follow the unsystematic structure of Art. 5–7 DMA, but the list of **core platform services** in Art. 2(2) DMA. This is intended to show which obligations are particularly relevant in which context. Furthermore, from a competition policy point of view, it is appropriate to focus on the core platform services as these are the "important gateways" (cf. Art. 3(1)(b) DMA), which are of central importance for competition and the business opportunities of other companies. Most core platform services have already been the focus of **competition law investigations**, which have helped to identify the competition problems that arise in the relevant context. In view of the history of the creation of the DMA and its competition policy objectives (→ § 10 mn. 5 et seq., 17 et seq.), it seems appropriate to take due account of these findings in the interpretation and application of Art. 5–7 DMA.

23 Some of the obligations in Art. 5–7 DMA are not specifically related to individual core platform services, but are broadly designed to apply in all gatekeeping contexts. These include Art. 5(6) DMA, which prohibits gatekeepers from preventing or restricting business users or end users from **raising issues of non-compliance** by the gatekeeper with a competent authority or court. Another example is Art. 6(13) DMA, which prohibits gatekeepers from making it unduly difficult to **terminate** the provision of core platform services. The **supplementary obligations** of cooperation and transparency in Art. 8 et seq. DMA are also relevant for all gatekeepers and all core platform services. These include the obligation to demonstrate compliance pursuant to Art. 8(1) sent. 1 DMA, the reporting obligation under Art. 11 DMA, the obligation to inform about concentrations under Art. 14 DMA and the obligation to audit consumer profiling techniques under Art. 15 DMA. The obligation to establish a **compliance function** and to appoint at least one compliance officer under Art. 28 DMA should also be mentioned in this context. These obligations in particular make it clear that the DMA aims to subject gatekeepers to permanent and relatively close **regulatory monitoring**.

24 With regard to ***emerging gatekeepers*** designated by the Commission pursuant to Art. 3(8) in conjunction with Art. 17(4) DMA, it should be noted that they only have to comply with those obligations from the catalogues of Art. 5–7 DMA that the Commission declares applicable in the designation decision (→ mn. 7). When selecting the obligations, the Commission must take into account the restrictions of Art. 17(4) sent. 1 and 2 DMA.

I. Intermediation services

25 Online intermediation services within the meaning of Art. 2(2)(a), (5) DMA are primarily online marketplaces, app stores and vertical search engines ('verticals') such as price comparison websites or mapping services. Gatekeeper positions are particularly likely to exist in **online marketplaces** (Amazon Marketplace, Facebook Marketplace) and **app stores** (Apple App Store, Google Play). This is also where the biggest competition problems have arisen so far, as several recent competition law cases have shown. In the following, the focus will therefore be on the obligations in Art. 5–7 DMA that are particularly relevant for gatekeepers' online marketplaces and app stores.

1. Online marketplaces

26 According to Art. 2(17) of the Consumer Rights Directive 2011,[16] online marketplaces are services using software, including websites and applications, operated by or on behalf of a trader, which allow consumers to conclude distance contracts with other traders or consumers. By far the most important **online marketplace** that is clearly operated by a gatekeeper is Amazon Marketplace.[17] The EU Commission has also designated Facebook Marketplace as a core platform service operated by a gatekeeper.[18] The same applies to Booking, which is, however, described as a 'vertical' rather than a marketplace. For other major online marketplaces such as HRS, Zalando, Otto Market,

[16] Directive 2011/83/EU, OJ 2011 L 304/64, as amended by Directive (EU) 2019/2161, OJ 2019 L 328/7.
[17] Cf. EU Commission, Decision of 5.9.2023 – DMA.100018.
[18] EU Commission, Decision of 5.9.2023 – DMA.100044.

Airbnb and eBay, the Commission has not yet determined that their operators are gatekeepers under Art. 3(1) and (2) DMA. Therefore, these marketplaces do not qualify as core platform services. The markets for **online marketplace services** are often highly concentrated, which is due to network effects and high barriers to market entry.[19] From a competition policy perspective, it is therefore important to keep at least the downstream retail markets open to competition.

With respect to **Amazon Marktplace** in particular, both the EU Commission and national competition authorities, including the Bundeskartellamt, the German competition authority, have found that Amazon holds a **dominant position** in various geographic markets for the provision of online marketplace services to third party sellers.[20] There have also been repeated allegations that Amazon is abusing its market power in violation of Art. 102 TFEU and §§ 19, 20 GWB. The EU Commission recently concluded two investigations by accepting commitments.[21] The Bundeskartellamt has also already concluded several proceedings and is currently investigating whether Amazon is illegally using price control mechanisms to the detriment of third party sellers and whether Amazon is making it unduly difficult for third party sellers to trade in certain branded products (so-called *"brandgating"*).[22] 27

Art. 5–7 DMA contain a number of obligations which have been influenced by competition law investigations into online marketplaces or which are of particular importance to operators of such marketplaces if they are gatekeepers. An explicit reference to online intermediation services is made in Art. 5(3) DMA concerning the **prohibition of most-favoured customer clauses** (also referred to as 'most-favoured nation' (MFN) clauses due to the widespread use of such clauses in bilateral investment treaties).[23] Under this provision, a gatekeeper shall not prevent business users from offering the same products or services to end users through third-party online intermediation services or through their own direct online sales channel at prices or conditions that are different from those offered through the online intermediation services of the gatekeeper. This prohibits, for example, **bestprice clauses**, which have been addressed by competition authorities in relation to, inter alia, hotel booking platforms and the distribution of e-books.[24] These are clauses in distribution agreements between marketplace operators and business users which state that the business users may not offer lower prices outside the marketplace than on the marketplace itself. Best price clauses may apply to all distribution channels ("**wide best price clauses**") or only to certain, more precisely defined distribution channels ("**narrow best price clauses**"). Best price clauses are usually defended on the grounds that the marketplace operator cannot recoup its investment in the marketplace if end users use the services offered (e.g. search and comparison functions) but then switch to cheaper distribution channels to conclude the contract (**free-rider problem**).[25] However, best price clauses can restrict the competition between marketplace operators and also on downstream markets where business users of the market- 28

[19] Cf. e.g. Bundeskartellamt, Decision of 5.7.2022 – B2–55/21, para. 174 et seqq.

[20] EU Commission, Press release of 20.12.2022, IP/22/7777; Bundeskartellamt, Decision of 5.7.2022 – B2–55/21, para. 87 et seq.

[21] EU Commission, Press release of 20.12.2022, IP/22/7777.

[22] Bundeskartellamt, Press release of 14.11.2022.

[23] Critically on this restriction de Streel et al., Digital Markets Act, pp. 53, 88.

[24] Cf. EU Commission, Decision of 4.5.2017 – AT.40153 – Amazon (eBooks); Bundeskartellamt, Decision of 22.12.2015 – B9–121/13 – Booking; Decision of 20.12.2013 – B9–66/10 – HRS; Decision of 26.11.2013 – B6–46/12 – Amazon.

[25] Bundesgerichtshof, Decision of 18.5.2021, BGHZ 230, 88 = NZKart 2021, 499 = GRUR 2021, 1213 (mn. 69 et seq.); OLG Düsseldorf, Decision of 4.6.2019 – VI-Kart 2/16 (V), NZKart 2019, 379 (382); Kühling/Ceni-Hulek/Engelbracht NZKart 2021, 76 (76 et seq.); Galle/Burdinski EuZW 2021, 439 (443).

place offer their services.[26] The Bundeskartellamt has therefore prohibited the use of wide and narrow best price clauses by the operators of hotel booking platforms[27] and this has been confirmed by the Bundesgerichtshof (BGH), the German Federal Court of Justice.[28] The DMA also prohibits the use of both types of best price clauses if the operator of the respective marketplace is a gatekeeper. Already at the end of 2013, **Amazon** committed to the German Bundeskartellamt not to use best price clauses in its general distribution agreements for Amazon Marketplace.[29] With regard to distribution agreements for e-books, in particular, the company later made a similar commitment to the EU Commission.[30]

29 Another obligation of particular relevance to online marketplaces is the **prohibition on processing third-party data** under Art. 6(2) DMA. According to this provision, a gatekeeper shall not use, in competition with business users, any data that is not publicly available that is generated or provided by those business users in the context of their use of the relevant core platform service.[31] The precise scope of the processing prohibition, which applies also to data generated or provided by customers of the business users, is further clarified by Art. 6(2) sent. 2 DMA. The prohibition is apparently inspired by two **competition law investigations** by the EU Commission against Amazon and Meta/Facebook.[32] In the first case, the Commission's preliminary assessment was that **Amazon** had abused its dominant position in the market for online marketplace services by systematically using non-public business data of third party sellers for its own retail business in competition with these sellers.[33] In particular, it was found that Amazon Retail's algorithms and employees used data from third party sellers to identify products that Amazon itself should sell, to find suppliers, to negotiate wholesale prices and conditions, and to set prices for Amazon's own retail offerings.[34] The case was recently concluded with the Commission accepting **commitments** in which Amazon promised to stop using third party sellers' data for its own retail business.[35] In the second case, the Commission's preliminary assessment was that **Meta/Facebook** abused its dominant position in the markets for social networks and for online display advertising on social media by, among other things, imposing unfair trading conditions on online classified ad services competing with **Facebook Marketplace.**[36] In particular, the Commission was concerned by the fact that Facebook's terms and conditions allowed Meta/Facebook to use advertising-related data from competitors for the benefit of Facebook Marketplace. Art. 6(2) DMA now generally prohibits gatekeepers from such practices, irrespective of the actual effects on competition, provided that the data is generated or provided in connection with the use of a core platform service. As a consequence, gatekeepers will have to ensure a certain degree of **data unbundling** *("data siloing")*[37] for their online marketplaces in order to comply with the prohibition on processing third-party data.

---

[26] Cf. Kühling/Ceni-Hulek/Engelbracht NZKart 2021, 76 (77 et seq.).

[27] Bundeskartellamt, Case report of 9.3.2016 – B9–121/13; Case report of 5.3.2014 – B9–66/10.

[28] Bundesgerichtshof, Decision of 18.5.2021, BGHZ 230, 88 = NZKart 2021, 499.

[29] Bundeskartellamt, Case report of 9.12.2013 – B6–46/12.

[30] EU Commission, Decision of 4.5.2017 – AT.40153.

[31] For further details, including a discussion of the economic background of the data processing prohibitions, see König in Borges/Keil, Big Data, Ch. 12.

[32] See also the analysis by Khan YLJ 126 (2017), 710 (780 et seqq.).

[33] EU Commission, Press release of 20.12.2022, IP/22/7777; Press release of 10.11.2020, IP/20/2077.

[34] EU Commission, Communication Amazon Marketplace, OJ 2022 C 278, 8 para. 4.

[35] EU Commission, Press release of 20.12.2022, IP/22/7777.

[36] EU Commission, Press release of 19.12.2022, IP/22/7728.

[37] Cf. Krämer/Schnurr JCLE 18 (2022), 255 (275 et seqq.); Krämer/Shekhar, Algorithmic Learning, p. 2 et seq.

The **prohibition of self-preferencing** in Art. 6(5) DMA is also of great importance for online marketplaces. According to this provision, a gatekeeper may not treat its own services and products more favourably than similar services or products offered by a third party in **ranking** and related activities such as indexing and crawling.[38] Instead, the gatekeeper must apply transparent, fair and non-discriminatory conditions to such ranking. It follows from Art. 2(22) DMA that the prohibition of self-preferencing only applies to online intermediation services, social networks, video sharing platforms, virtual assistants and search engines. In the area of competition law, since the ***Google Search (Shopping)*** decision of 2017, the EU Commission has taken the view that self-preferencing may constitute an abuse of a dominant position within the meaning of Art. 102 TFEU.[39] It is particularly noteworthy in the context of Art. 6(5) DMA that online marketplaces have been a focus of such investigations: In the ***Amazon Buy Box case***, the EU Commission's preliminary assessment was that Amazon had abused its dominant position as a provider of marketplace services by unduly favouring its own retail offers and those of marketplace sellers using Amazon's logistics and delivery services to the detriment of other marketplace sellers and consumers.[40] In particular, the case concerned the criteria used to select the winner of the "*Buy Box*", i.e. the seller with whom the purchase contract is automatically concluded if the customer does not actively select another seller from a list on the product website. The Commission also concluded that the criteria used to select sellers and offers for Amazon's Prime programme also unduly favoured Amazon itself and the marketplace sellers using Amazon's logistics and delivery services. The investigation was recently concluded by the Commission accepting **commitments**.[41] In these commitments, Amazon undertook to treat all marketplace sellers equally when selecting them for the Buy Box, to prominently display a second competing offer alongside the Buy Box, and to establish non-discriminatory terms and criteria for qualifying marketplace sellers and offers for Amazon Prime. 30

A final provision worth highlighting in the context of online marketplaces is Art. 6(10) DMA on **data access rights**, as this provision is likely to benefit business users of gatekeeper marketplaces such as Amazon Marketplace. According to Art. 6(10) DMA, a gatekeeper shall provide business users with "effective, high-quality, continuous and real time access" to data provided or generated in the context of the use of a core platform service by those business users or their customers. Access to the data must be provided free of charge. Evidence from competition law investigations suggests that Art. 6(10) DMA is aimed primarily at anticompetitive "privacy policies" of app store operators and web browser providers (→ mn. 37). However, the provision is also relevant to **online marketplaces**, as illustrated in particular by the cases concerning the processing of third-party data discussed above (→ mn. 29). These cases have clearly shown that the data provided or generated on online marketplaces can be of significant importance for competition in downstream retail markets. While Art. 6(2) DMA limits the possibilities of the marketplace operator to use this data for its own benefit, Art. 6(10) DMA clarifies who is actually entitled to use the data and reap the associated benefits: the business users who generate or provide the data, either themselves or indirectly with the help of their customers. 31

38 The restriction of the prohibition of self-preferencing to rankings is criticized by Haus/Weusthof WuW 2021, 318 (322 et seq.).

39 EU Commission, Decision of 27.6.2017 – AT.39740.

40 EU Commission, Communication Amazon Marketplace, OJ 2022 C 278, 8 para. 7 et seqq.

41 EU Commission, Press release of 20.12.2022, IP/22/7777.

2. App stores

32 Art. 2(14) DMA defines "software application stores" (app stores) as a type of online intermediation service that focuses on software applications (cf. Art. 2(15) DMA) as the intermediated product or service. The most prominent examples are Apple's **App Store** for iPhones and other mobile devices running on Apple operating systems (especially iOS) and Google's **Play Store**, which is used on devices with Android as the operating system. The EU Commission designated both as core platform services in September 2023.[42] Both app stores have also been the focus of competition law investigations. The EU Commission has concluded that app stores for different operating systems must be distinguished for the purposes of product market definition and that Apple and Alphabet/Google each dominate the markets for the distribution of apps in their respective ecosystems with their app stores.[43] As app stores are important **gateways to downstream markets** for the sale of apps, the main competition concern is to ensure that app stores can be used by app developers under transparent, fair and non-discriminatory conditions.

33 The DMA is intended to contribute to this objective through a number of obligations. One example is the **prohibition of most-favoured customer clauses** under Art. 5(3) DMA, which applies to all online intermediation services, including app stores (cf. → mn. 28). Best-price clauses have not been a major concern in the context of app stores so far, but this may be due to the fact that there has been no competition between app stores on Apple devices and only little competition on Android devices. However, the DMA aims to change this, in particular through the obligation to allow the free installation of third party app stores under Art. 6(4) (→ mn. 62). The prohibition of most-favoured customer clauses could therefore become more important in the future.

34 Some of the provisions of Art. 5 and 6 DMA are clearly aimed at behaviour that has been observed in the past, particularly in connection with app stores. This includes, for example, the **prohibition of obstructing customer communication** in Art. 5(4) DMA. According to this provision, gatekeepers must allow business users of their core platform services to communicate and promote offers to end users and to conclude contracts with end users. These options must be available to the business users free of charge. The obligation not to interfere with customer communications is clearly influenced by the competition law investigations against **Apple**.[44] The most prominent case concerns the App Store and the markets for **music streaming apps** and was triggered by a complaint from Spotify.[45] In a preliminary assessment, the Commission found that Apple had abused its dominant position in the distribution of music streaming apps on Apple devices and had restricted competition between music streaming apps (including Spotify and Apple Music). In particular, the Commission was concerned with the fact that Apple requires app developers who want to distribute their apps through the App Store to process transactions within their apps (so-called **in-app purchases**, e.g. purchases of subscriptions or additional services) through Apple's own system for in-app purchases. However, since Apple then charges a **commission** of typically 30 %,[46] it may be more attractive for app developers to process transactions outside the app (e.g. through their own websites,

---

[42] EU Commission, Decision of 5.9.2023 – DMA.100013; Decision of 5.9.2023 – DMA.100002.

[43] EU Commission, Decision of 18.7.2018 – AT.40099, para. 306 et seq., 590 et seq. – Google Android; Press release of 30.4.2021, IP/21/2061; cf. also Bundeskartellamt, Decision of 30.12.2021 – B7–61/21, para. 317 et seq.

[44] Cf. EU Commission, Press release of 16.6.2020, IP/20/1073.

[45] On the following EU Commission, Press release of 30.4.2021, IP/21/2061; Press release of 16.6.2020, IP/20/1073.

[46] For an assessment under competition law, see Lichtenberg NZKart 2021, 551 (552 et seqq.).

which are not controlled by Apple). The Commission found that Apple's contractual terms made it difficult for app developers to communicate to their app users within their apps that purchases should be made outside the apps. This was clearly intended to prevent app developers from circumventing Apple's system for in-app purchases and the payment of the 30 % commission. In its preliminary assessment, the Commission found that Apple's restrictive contractual clauses violated Art. 102 TFEU. This was confirmed by the final decision of 4 March 2024, in which the Commission imposed a fine of 1.84 billion euros on Apple.[47] The final decision is no longer focused on exclusionary effects on music streaming markets or the appropriateness of the 30% commission. Instead, the Commission has focused entirely on the anti-steering provisions with which Apple prohibits app developers from advertising within the app for the conclusion of transactions outside the app. The Commission considers this to be an exploitative abuse through unfair trading conditions (cf. Article 102(a) TFEU) because the freedom of choice of app developers and their customers is restricted, which ultimately leads to higher prices. In any case, Art. 5(4) DMA now makes such practices by gatekeepers even more difficult, regardless of their actual effects on competition.

In the same context, two other requirements of Art. 5 DMA are also relevant. Firstly, 35 Art. 5(5) DMA obliges gatekeepers to allow end users, who use a business user's software application, to access and use content, subscriptions, features and other items through the gatekeeper's core platform service even if these items were acquired without using that service.[48] Like Art. 5(4) DMA, this obligation to recognise **external transactions** is clearly inspired by the EU Commission's ***Apple App Store/music streaming*** investigation. To be clear, the Commission did not find that Apple refused to recognise external transactions in apps on Apple devices.[49] On the contrary, the Commission explicitly found that Apple allows users of music streaming apps on Apple devices to use **music subscriptions** in their app, even if they were purchased outside the app. For example, users of the Spotify app on Apple devices can use the paid-for Spotify Premium service in the app if they have purchased the subscription on Spotify's own website and paid for it using a payment service of their choice. Apple "only" prevents subscriptions from being made within the app without using Apple's own system for **in-app purchases** and also makes it difficult for app developers to direct their app users to subscription options outside the app (→ mn. 34). It is clear, however, that competition would be all the more restricted if external transactions in apps were not recognised at all on Apple devices. Anyone wishing to use Spotify Premium on an iPhone would then have to pay for the subscription through Apple's system for in-app purchases and Spotify would have no way of avoiding paying the 30 % commission to Apple. Against this background, Art. 5(5) DMA, as well as the corresponding provision of Art. 5(4) DMA, which prohibits interference with customer communications, are intended to help ensure that the markets for the distribution and payment of digital content are not monopolised by gatekeepers, but remain as open as possible to competition.

Secondly, Art. 5(7) DMA clarifies that a gatekeeper shall not require end users or 36 business users to use an identification service, a web browser engine or a payment service of the gatekeeper in the context of services provided by a business user using a core platform service of the gatekeeper. The same applies, inter alia, to technical services supporting the provision of payment services, and **payment systems for in-app purchases** are specifically mentioned as an example. Once again, the influence of the ***Apple App***

---

[47] EU Commission, Decision of 4.3.2024 – AT.40437 – Apple App Store Practices (music streaming).

[48] This obligation is criticized by Zimmer/Göhsl ZWeR 2021, 29 (42) because of possible free rider problems.

[49] Cf. EU Commission, Press release of 30.4.2021, IP/21/2061.

Store/music streaming investigation is evident, as payment services are at the centre of Spotify's allegations regarding Apple's App Store rules. Specifically, Spotify has complained to the EU Commission and in an accompanying PR campaign not least about the fact that Apple requires the use of its own payment system to process in-app purchases and then charges a 30 % commission on many transactions.[50] Spotify argues that this distorts competition in the market for music streaming apps, as Spotify and other independent providers of music streaming apps either suffer significant cost disadvantages compared to Apple's own service Apple Music or have to forego in-app purchases, thus losing an important distribution channel. The Commission came to a similar conclusion in its preliminary assessment of the case and later in the final decision. In particular, it found that most streaming providers pass on the cost of the 30 % commission to their users.[51] According to the Commission, this distorts competition in the market for music streaming applications and consumers have to pay higher prices for their in-app subscriptions. Art. 5(7) DMA is intended to make such behaviour by gatekeepers more difficult. In addition, the provision seems to aim at maintaining the competition between **payment service providers**, which has been quite active so far. Despite the somewhat cautious wording ("shall […] not require"), it seems fair to assume, given the background and purpose of Art. 5(7) DMA, that the legislator wants business users of core platform services to be completely free to decide whether and, if so, which identification services, web browser engines and payment services they use in their apps. For app store operators, this is likely to mean that their payment services and systems for in-app purchases will soon face greater competition.

37 In view of the great importance that the providers of apps and app stores attach to data, the **data processing prohibitions** of Art. 5(2) and Art. 6(2) DMA (see → mn. 29, 40, 45 et seq., 67) as well as the **data access rights** under Art. 6(10) DMA also play an important role in the context of app stores. The provision on data access rights is particularly worth highlighting, as ongoing investigations by national competition authorities already indicate how important it could soon become (see also → mn. 31). Art. 6(10) DMA obliges gatekeepers to provide business users with "effective, high-quality, continuous and real-time access" to data provided or generated in the context of the use of a core platform service by those business users and their customers. Access to the data must be provided free of charge. The provision is likely to target, among other things, anti-competitive **"privacy frameworks"** of app store providers.[52] Such frameworks have already been examined by competition authorities under competition law. For example, the German Bundeskartellamt opened an investigation into Apple's tracking rules in June 2022.[53] This is one of the first proceedings based on the new § 19a(2) GWB (→ § 10 mn. 55). In addition, the Bundeskartellamt is investigating a violation of Art. 102 TFEU. Specifically, the issue is whether Apple's **App Tracking Transparency Framework** makes it more difficult for other companies to access user data, thereby giving Apple a competitive advantage. The App Tracking Transparency Framework must be used by app developers if they want to collect and analyse user data in an app that runs on an Apple device and is offered through Apple's App Store.[54] If the app developer does not comply with the tracking rules, Apple will not include the app in its App Store. The processing of

[50] Cf. Spotify, Time to Play Fair <https://www.timetoplayfair.com/> last accessed 26.8.2024.

[51] EU Commission, Decision of 4.3.2024 – AT.40437 – Apple App Store Practices (music streaming), paras 607 et seqq.; Press release of 30.4.2021, IP/21/2061.

[52] For further details, including a discussion of the economic background, see König in Borges/Keil, Big Data, Ch. 12.

[53] Bundeskartellamt, Press release of 14.6.2022.

[54] Cf. Apple, App Tracking Transparency <https://t1p.de/l84w7> last accessed 26.8.2024.

user data within an app may be necessary, for example, to serve personalised advertisements to end users in order to recoup the investment in developing the app. The App Tracking Transparency Framework provides that, with regard to tracking, app developers must obtain a specific consent from their users, which goes beyond the consent as it is required under data protection law (i.e., the GDPR). However, according to the Bundeskartellamt's preliminary assessment, Apple itself does not obtain such specific consent for its own apps.[55] This could give Apple unjustified advantages in app and advertising markets. Art. 6(10) DMA strengthens the position of business users vis-à-vis gatekeepers in such situations because it grants them a right to effective, high-quality, continuous and real-time access to the data generated by their services. This makes it clear that, for example, app store providers may not block app developers' efforts to collect and process data, but on the contrary must support them by providing access to data. With regard to personal data, Art. 6(10) subpara. 2 DMA requires that the end users concerned opt in to the sharing of their data. In addition, app developers must of course comply with the GDPR. However, gatekeeper app store operators are no longer allowed to demand data protection beyond what is required by data protection law.

Finally, another important obligation in the context of app stores is the obligation to **38**
provide **FRAND access** under Art. 6(12) DMA.[56] According to Art. 6(12) subpara. 2 DMA, gatekeepers shall apply general conditions of access to app stores, online search engines and online social networking services that are *"fair"*, *"reasonable"*, and *"non-discriminatory"*). The DMA thus adopts the FRAND concept, which is known from intellectual property law and in particular from the licensing of standard-essential patents.[57] Moreover, Art. 6(12) subpara. 2 DMA requires the relevant gatekeepers to publish general conditions of access, including an alternative dispute settlement mechanism. With respect to app stores, in particular, the right to FRAND access, which can also be enforced in **civil proceedings** due to the direct applicability of the DMA (→ § 10 mn. 53),[58] protects app developers from having their apps arbitrarily not included in or removed from gatekeeper app stores, such as the Apple App Store or the Google Play Store. In general, app store operators should have an interest in offering as many apps as possible through their app stores. However, especially when a dispute arises between an app store operator and an app developer, removing an app from the app store can be used as a sanction. This danger is illustrated, for example, by the US case ***Epic Games v Apple***. One of the causes of this dispute was that Apple removed the video game Fortnite from its App Store after the developer, Epic Games, deliberately violated Apple's app development guidelines, which Epic claimed were unlawful because of the aforementioned obligation to use Apple's payment system for in-app purchases and the resulting obligation to pay a 30 % commission (see also → mn. 34, 36).[59] It should be noted that Art. 6(12) DMA does not prevent app store operators from setting **minimum standards** for the apps they distribute (e.g. for the purpose of protecting children), but the requirements must be fair, reasonable and non-discriminatory, and they must be applied in such a way.[60] The EU

55 Bundeskartellamt, Press release of 14.6.2022.

56 See also Ibáñez Colomo JECLAP 12 (2021), 561 (565).

57 Cf. on the related competition problems ECJ, Judgment of 16.7.2016 – C-170/13, ECLI:EU:C:2015:477 – Huawei.

58 Cf. Podszun/Bongartz/Kirk NJW 2022, 3249 (mn. 48); Kumkar RDi 2022, 347 (mn. 21); Karbaum/Schulz NZKart 2022, 107 (109); less optimistic with regard to private enforcement of DMA rights Haus/Weusthof WuW 2021, 318 (324).

59 U.S. District Court Northern District of California, Judgment of 10.9.2021 – Case No. 4:20-cv-05640-YGR, available with further information at <https://t1p.de/x59o5> last accessed 26.8.2024.

60 The FRAND concept can also be used for price control, e.g. with regard to the usual commission fees of 30 %, see e.g. Lichtenberg NZKart 2021, 551 (555); Polley/Konrad WuW 2021, 198 (204). However,

Commission may specify details for individual gatekeepers in the procedure under Art. 8(2) DMA. In addition, it is likely that the civil courts will quickly help to bring the FRAND concept to life in the context of app stores through their decisions in private lawsuits, as Art. 6(12) DMA seems well-suited for private actions.

II. Search engines

39 Online search engines within the meaning of Art. 2(2)(b), (6) DMA are primarily web search engines that are designed to search for information on all websites in the World Wide Web. The most important example is **Google Search**, offered by Alphabet/ Google, which is very significant from a competition policy point of view. The EU Commission has designated Google Search as a core platform service in September 2023.[61] It is also considered designating Microsoft's Bing, but decided not to do so after conducting a market investigation under to Art. 17(3) DMA.[62] The EU Commission has found that Google has held a dominant position on the markets for the provision of general search services in the EEA since 2008.[63] Google's dominance is based, inter alia, on stable **market shares** above 90 %, significant **economies of scale** and **scope**, the absence of **multi-homing**, strong **brand effects** and extremely strong **data-driven network effects**. Taken together, these factors make Google's dominant position appear almost unassailable. Nevertheless, the DMA aims to promote competition between different search engine operators, inter alia by means of Art. 6(11) DMA (→ mn. 42). In addition, the DMA contains a number of provisions aimed at preventing Google from using its power in the search engine market to restrict competition in downstream and other related markets (in particular through so-called ***monopoly leveraging*** and **data-driven *"envelopment"***) (cf. → § 10 mn. 9).

40 Due to the great importance of data collection and analysis in the operation of a search engine, the **data processing prohibitions** of Art. 5(2) DMA are particularly relevant in the context of gatekeeper search engines. Although they are generally considered to be primarily inspired by the German ***Facebook* case** and the situation with social networks (→ mn. 45),[64] these prohibitions are likely to be equally relevant to Google's business model. Art. 5(2) DMA specifically contains four different prohibitions: Gatekeepers may not, for the purpose of providing online advertising services, process personal data of end users who use third-party services that make use of a core platform service (lit. a); they may not combine personal data from a core platform service with personal data from another service (lit. b) or cross-use it in another service (lit. c); and they may not sign in end users to other services in order to combine personal data (lit. d). However, these prohibitions do not apply if the end user concerned has been given the "specific choice" and has **consented** to the data processing in accordance with Art. 4(11) and Art. 7 GDPR. As a result of these prohibitions and the consent requirement, end users

concrete standards would still have to be developed. The criteria for determining FRAND-compliant royalties for standard essential patents will hardly be applicable, as they are very patent- and product-specific, cf. only Ann, Patentrecht, Ch. 43 mn. 39 et seq.

[61] EU Commission, Decision of 5.9.2023 – DMA.100004.

[62] EU Commission, Decision of 12.2.2024 – DMA.100015.

[63] EU Commission, Decision of 18.7.2018 – AT.40099, para. 674 et seq. – Google Android; Decision of 27.6.2017 – AT.39740, para. 271 et seq. – Google Search (Shopping); cf. also Bundeskartellamt, Decision of 30.12.2021 – B7-61/21, para. 234 et seq. In the Czech Republic, according to the Commission's findings, Google's dominant position has existed since 2011.

[64] Podszun/Bongartz/Kirk NJW 2022, 3249 (mn. 20); Kumkar RDi 2022, 347 (mn. 44); Akman ELR 47 (2022), 85 (94); Polley/Konrad WuW 2021, 198 (201 et seq.); Kerber ZD 2021, 544 (545).

should be able to choose whether to allow the processing of data across services (e.g. in order to receive a better, more personalised user experience or to avoid paying a monetary fee) or to opt for a service-specific separation of data collections *("**data siloing**")* (cf. → mn. 29), in which they do not receive such advantages but benefit from better data protection. The data processing prohibitions and the consent requirement are clearly intended to strengthen the **data sovereignty** of end users and to prevent a data-driven "***envelopment***" by gatekeepers (→ § 10 mn. 9).[65] However, the required data separation could have far-reaching consequences for Google and its business model, which is based on vertical and horizontal integration. This is illustrated by a competition law case brought by the German **Bundeskartellamt**. According to a commitments decision issued in October 2023, the Bundeskartellamt found that Google's data processing terms and practices violated German competition law.[66] Specifically, the proceedings were based on § 19a(2) sent. 1 no. 4a GWB, which is directed against conduct similar to that described in Art. 5(2) DMA. Among other things, the Bundeskartellamt found, that Google's terms allowed it to combine data from important services such as Google Search, YouTube, Google Play, Google Maps and the Google Assistant. In addition, Google was accused of collecting data from third party websites and apps and processing it together with data from Google services. The Bundeskartellamt argued that Google did not inform end users about these data processing practices in a sufficiently transparent manner and did not offer sufficient choice. In particular, the Bundeskartellamt argued that users should be able to limit data processing to individual Google services. The case was closed with a commitments decision after Google offered to change its data processing conditions and give users more choice, which the Bundeskartellamt considered sufficient to alleviate its competition concerns. Whether the Commission will adopt an equally restrictive interpretation of Art. 5(2) DMA depends, inter alia, on how the requirement of a "**specific choice**" in Art. 5(2) DMA is to be understood (cf. → mn. 45). The recitals emphasise that gatekeepers must offer a "less personalised but equivalent alternative" in order to ensure freedom of choice.[67]

Another obligation with considerable relevance for search engines is the **prohibition of self-preferencing** in Art. 6(5) DMA. According to this provision, gatekeepers may not treat more favourably, in ranking (cf. Art. 2(22) DMA) and related activities, services and products offered by themselves over similar services or products offered by third parties. Rather, rankings must be based on transparent, fair and non-discriminatory conditions. While the prohibition of self-preferencing also applies, pursuant to Art. 2(22) DMA, to online intermediation services, social networks, video-sharing platforms and virtual assistants, its genesis is closely linked to search engines and the EU Commission's ***Google Search (Shopping)* decision**.[68] In this decision, the Commission concluded that Google had favoured its own price comparison service Google Shopping over competing price comparison services in Google Search results, thereby infringing Art. 102 TFEU.[69] The Commission found that Google's self-preferencing had deprived its competitors in the markets for price comparison services of potential traffic and users, leading to higher fees for merchants/advertisers and ultimately to higher prices for 41

[65] On the latter, see Monti CoRe 5 (2021), 90 (91).

[66] On the following, see Bundeskartellamt, Decision of 5.10.2023 – B7-70/21 – Google data processing conditions; Press release of 11.1.2023; Press release of 25.5.2021.

[67] Rec. 36 DMA.

[68] For further details, see Burchardi NZKart 2022, 610; Reumann/Weber NZKart 2022, 314; Hoffer/Lehr NZKart 2019, 10 (16 et seqq.).

[69] EU Commission, Decision of 27.6.2017 – AT.39740, para. 341 et seq.

consumers.[70] A central part of the argument was that Google had used the search engine as leverage to monopolise the downstream market for price comparison services (so-called ***monopoly leveraging***).[71] While the decision remains controversial from a competition policy perspective, the legal reasoning was upheld by the GC.[72] With Art. 6(5) DMA, the EU legislator recognised the prohibition of self-preferencing, at least for gatekeepers and in relation to rankings, and exempted the Commission from the requirement to prove competitive harm.[73] However, the main challenge in the *Google Search (Shopping)* case, which has not yet been satisfactorily resolved, was to reach an agreement with Google on the **concrete measures** to be taken to end the self-preferencing (→ § 10 mn. 16).[74] Since the Commission's initial prohibition decision in 2017, Google has repeatedly implemented new designs for the display of search results, price comparison offers and other advertising on Google Search. The Commission has reviewed these changes and has occasionally requested improvements. However, the Commission continues to receive complaints from market participants who are not satisfied with what has been achieved so far.[75] This shows how difficult it can be for competition authorities to monitor and ensure compliance with their decisions in a rapidly changing market environment. In this respect, the DMA has the advantage that it is designed for permanent, much closer supervision of gatekeepers and that the possibility of specification under Art. 8(2) DMA creates a certain scope for **regulatory dialogue** (→ § 10 mn. 49, 52). It remains to be seen, however, whether the new instruments can effectively prevent self-preferencing by search engine operators.

42 Another obligation of particular importance for gatekeepers operating search engines is the obligation to provide **access to search engine data** under Art. 6(11) DMA. According to this provision, gatekeepers shall provide other search engine operators, at their request, with access to ranking, query, click and view data generated by end users on the gatekeepers' search engines. Such access shall be provided on *"fair"*, *"reasonable"*, and *"non-discriminatory"* terms.[76] Where personal data is concerned, it may only be made available in **anonymised form**. In addition to Art. 6(3) sent. 2 (→ mn. 66) and Art. 6(6) DMA (→ mn. 63), Art. 6(11) DMA is one of the provisions intended to improve the contestability of search engine markets. The legislator is not content with Google's quasi-monopoly, but has the ambitious goal of strengthening other search engine operators such as DuckDuckGo and Startpage in order to promote competition on search engine markets. This is a big step towards an **interventionist competition policy**, the success of which remains to be seen. The practical application of Art. 6(11) DMA raises a number of questions, many of which will probably have to be clarified by the EU Commission through specifications under Art. 8(2) DMA. For example, Art. 6(11) DMA is not very specific as to how the data access should be structured, especially in comparison with Art. 6(10) DMA. While the latter speaks of free, effective, high-quality, continuous and real-time access to aggregated and non-aggregated data, Art. 6(11) DMA only specifies certain types of search engine data and refers to the **FRAND concept** (see → mn. 38). The contrast with Art. 6(10) DMA suggests that access to search engine data

[70] EU Commission, Decision of 27.6.2017 – AT.39740, para. 452 et seqq., 589 et seqq.

[71] For further details, see Höppner CoRe 1 (2017), 208 (210 et seqq.).

[72] GC, Judgment of 10.11.2021 – T-612/17, ECLI:EU:T:2021:763. Google appealed against the GC's judgment on 20.1.2022. The case is being considered by the ECJ under case number C-48/22 P.

[73] The per se approach with respect to self-preferencing is criticised by Polley/Konrad WuW 2021, 198 (201). On the background of the limitation to rankings, see Achleitner NZKart 2022, 359 (361).

[74] See, for example, Marsden JECLAP 11 (2020), 553 et seqq.; Höppner, Shopping Decision, p. 79 et seqq., 171 ff.; Vesterdorf/Fountoukakos JECLAP 9 (2018), 3 et seqq.

[75] See, for example, Lomas, TechCruch of 18.10.2022.

[76] On the economic background, see König in Borges/Keil, Big Data, Ch. 12.

need **not** be provided **free of charge**, which may be justified by the fact that Art. 6(10) DMA concerns data that was generated with a service of the respective data access petitioner, whereas Art. 6(11) DMA concerns data that was generated by the gatekeeper and its customers. While in the first case it can be argued that the value creation is brought about by the access petitioner and therefore the data should be economically attributed to the petitioner, this cannot be claimed in the second case. It is also questionable whether access claims under Art. 6(11) DMA can be satisfied with **aggregated data sets** or whether the applicant can also request access to certain non-aggregated data. The recitals emphasising the importance of aggregated data sets suggest the former.[77] Finally, it is unclear whether Art. 6(11) DMA requires gatekeepers to provide for **continuous access** to data in **real time**. While such access is explicitly mentioned in Art. 6(10) DMA, Art. 6(11) DMA contains no such wording. However, the purpose of Art. 6(11) DMA, which is to strengthen competing search engines in competition with Google, argues in favour of continuous real-time access. This is because the timeliness of the data is very important for the quality of the search results. If the idea is really to make Google's position contestable,[78] this will hardly be possible without real-time access to Google's search engine data.

Finally, the obligation to provide **FRAND access** under Art. 6(12) DMA is also of **43** particular importance in the context of search engines. This provision requires gatekeepers to apply *fair*, *reasonable* and *non-discriminatory* general conditions of access for business users to their app stores, search engines and social networks. Details have already been discussed in the section on app stores (→ mn. 38). For search engines, the FRAND requirement means that websites cannot be arbitrarily removed from the search index or demoted in the ranking. Thus, any unequal treatment that is not objectively justified is prohibited, even beyond the prohibition of self-preferencing under Art. 6(5) DMA.

III. Social networks

Social networks within the meaning of Art. 2(2)(c), (7) DMA are platforms that en- **44** able end users to connect and communicate with each other, in particular through chats, posts, videos and recommendations. From a competition law perspective, a further distinction is made between **social networks for private users** (e.g. Facebook) and **professional or business networks** (e.g. LinkedIn).[79] Both the EU Commission and the German Bundeskartellamt have found that **Meta/Facebook** dominates the (national) markets for social networks for private users in the EEA.[80] In the case of professional networks, **LinkedIn** is the clear market leader. This was already established in the Commission's *Microsoft/LinkedIn decision* of 2016, when LinkedIn still faced stronger competition from local competitors, at least in some national markets (e.g. Xing in Germany).[81] The EU Commission has designated Facebook, Instagram and LinkedIn as core platform services in September 2023.[82] Somewhat more surprising was the designation of

---

[77] Rec. 61 sent. 2 DMA.

[78] Cf. rec. 61 sent. 5 DMA.

[79] EU Commission, Decision of 6.12.2016 – M.8124, para. 86 et seq. – Microsoft/LinkedIn; Bundeskartellamt, Decision of 2.5.2022 – B6–27/21, para. 127 et seq.; Decision of 6.2.2019 – B6–22/16, para. 277 et seq. – Facebook.

[80] EU Commission, Press release of 19.12.2022, IP/22/7728; Bundeskartellamt, Decision of 2.5.2022 – B6–27/21, para. 163 et seq.; Decision of 6.2.2019 – B6–22/16, para. 374 et seq. – Facebook.

[81] EU Commission, Decision of 6.12.2016 – M.8124, para. 282 et seq. – Microsoft/LinkedIn.

[82] EU Commission, Decision of 5.9.2023 – DMA.100020; Decision of 5.9.2023 – DMA.100017.

TikTok,[83] which also led to the designation of ByteDance as a sixth gatekeeper in addition to the obvious 'Big Five'. A market investigation into X (formerly Twitter) was still pending in the summer of 2024. Social networks are strongly characterised by **direct network effects**, as users benefit directly from others using the same platform. This can lead to strong **lock-in effects**, which in turn can lead to a low willingness to switch or multi-home. **Data-driven network effects** and **economies of scale and scope** also contribute to the fact that social network markets tend to be highly concentrated.

45 As social networks are typically based on a business model built around (personalised) **advertising**, gatekeepers operating a social network will have to take into account the data-related obligations under Art. 5(2), 6(2) and (10) DMA. Of particular importance are the **data processing prohibitions** of Art. 5(2) DMA, which are clearly inspired by the German ***Facebook case*** concerning anti-competitive data bundling.[84] In this case, the Bundeskartellamt prohibited Facebook, on the basis of § 19(1) GWB, from combining and analysing data across different services such as Facebook, WhatsApp and Instagram without the specific consent of the users.[85] In addition, the decision prohibits Facebook from combining data collected through the use of other companies' websites and apps (e.g. through the Facebook login or the "Like" button) with data collected on Facebook without the specific consent of the user. The decision has attracted a lot of attention, particularly because of the Bundeskartellamt's reasoning regarding the relationship between competition law and data protection laws, such as the GDPR.[86] The Bundesgerichtshof (BGH), Germany's highest civil court, refused to grant Facebook temporary legal protection and confirmed the Bundeskartellamt's decision in a lengthy and detailed judgment.[87] However, the BGH's reasoning was very different, relying more on consumer sovereignty and contractual freedoms than on data protection law. In the main proceedings, the Düsseldorf Higher Regional Court referred a number of questions on the relationship between competition law and data protection to the ECJ for a preliminary ruling.[88] In its judgment, the ECJ confirmed that national competition authorities may rely on breaches of the GDPR in order to establish an infringement of competition law.[89] Art. 5(2) DMA takes up some aspects of the *Facebook case*, but goes beyond the prohibitions imposed by the Bundeskartellamt and generalises them to all gatekeepers and all core platform services. Specifically, Art. 5(2) DMA contains four different prohibitions: Gatekeepers shall not process, for the purpose of providing online advertising services, personal data of end users who use third party services (lit. a); they shall not combine personal data from a core platform service with personal data from another service (lit. b) or cross-use such data in another service (lit. c); and they shall not sign in end users to other services in order to combine personal data (lit. d). The prohibitions do not apply if the end user concerned has been given the "specific choice" and has subsequently **consented** to the data processing in accordance with Art. 4(11) and Art. 7 of the GDPR (see → mn. 40).[90] Thus, regardless of the outcome of the German competition law proceedings, Meta/Facebook will continue to be prevented from combining data from different services unless it offers a specific choice and users consent to the data

---

[83] EU Commission, Decision of 5.9.2023 – DMA.100040.

[84] For further details, see Kerber ZD 2021, 544 (545 et seqq.); Hoffer/Lehr NZKart 2019, 10 (18 et seq.).

[85] Bundeskartellamt, Decision of 6.2.2019 – B6–22/16, para. 1 of the operative part and para. 522 et seq. – Facebook.

[86] See for example Mackenrodt/Wiedemann ZUM 2021, 89; Lohse NZKart 2020, 292; Mohr EuZW 2019, 265; Körber NZKart 2019, 187; Ellger WuW 2019, 446.

[87] Bundesgerichtshof, Decision of 23.6.2020, BGHZ 226, 67 = NZKart 2020, 473 = GRUR 2020, 1318.

[88] See also AG Rantos, Opinion of 20.9.2022 – C-252/21, ECLI:EU:C:2022:704.

[89] ECJ, Judgment of 4.7.2023 – C-252/21, ECLI:EU:C:2023:537 – Meta Platforms and Others.

[90] The link with the GDPR is criticised by Polley/Konrad WuW 2021, 198 (201 et seq.).

bundling.[91] Much will depend on how the Commission and the courts interpret the "specific choice" requirement.[92] The recitals state that gatekeepers should offer a "less personalised but equivalent alternative" without making the use of the core platform service or certain functionalities conditional on the end user's consent.[93] The **less personalised alternative** should not be different from the service provided to end users who consent to the data processing under Art. 5(2) DMA and it should not be of a lower quality, unless the reduction in quality is a direct consequence of the gatekeeper's inability to process certain personal data.[94] As a result, users should effectively be able to choose between a personalised user experience with a low level of data protection and a non-personalised variant with a high level of data protection. For Meta/Facebook, the new rules mean that it will have to adapt the services it offers in the EEA and in particular add the second, less personalised alternative. It is noteworthy that the legislator is making it more difficult for potential competitors to differentiate themselves in the market with privacy-friendly business models. Art. 5(2) DMA will therefore only have a pro-competitive effect if gatekeepers refrain from certain data processing practices altogether, because this would reduce data-driven network effects and lower barriers to market entry (cf. → § 10 mn. 9 et seq.). On the other hand, to the extent that gatekeepers do indeed offer less personalised alternatives (which some users may prefer), Art. 5(2) DMA primarily promotes **data protection** and not competition.

To the extent that social networks, such as Facebook and LinkedIn, are also used by **46** business users as a kind of 'infrastructure' through which they offer their services to end users, the **prohibition on the processing of third-party data** under Art. 6(2) DMA and the **right of data access** under Art. 6(10) DMA may also become relevant. While Art. 5(2)(a) DMA 'only' prohibits the processing of third party data for advertising purposes, Art. 6(2) DMA also prohibits the use of third party data in competition with business users whose services or customers generated or provided the data. Art. 6(10) DMA assigns the right to use such data to the relevant business user. Specifically, the provision requires gatekeepers to provide business users, upon request, with "effective, high-quality, continuous and real-time access" to data provided or generated in the context of the use of a core platform service of the gatekeeper by the business user or its customers (→ mn. 31, 37).

With regard to Meta/Facebook in particular, competition authorities have recently **47** criticised the fact that some of the undertaking's services can only be used with a **Facebook account.** For example, the German Bundeskartellamt initiated proceedings against Meta in December 2020 for, among other things, requiring a Facebook account in order to use Meta's **virtual reality products** (Meta Quest/Oculus).[95] Meta has now abandoned this requirement and offers the independent Meta Account as an alternative. The Bundeskartellamt has welcomed this step, but is continuing the proceedings in order to monitor further developments.[96] In another case, the EU Commission objected to Facebook linking its online classifieds service **Facebook Marketplace** to the social network.[97] The DMA does not prohibit such practices *per se*. The **prohibition of signing in users** to other services according to Art. 5(2)(d) DMA is narrowly drafted and appears to be

[91] See also § 19a(2) sent. 1 no. 4 GWB, which, however, is not self-executing.

[92] For a sceptical assessment from a consumer policy perspective, see Podszun GRUR-Int 2022, 197 (199).

[93] Rec. 36(1) sent. 6 DMA.

[94] Rec. 37 sent. 1 DMA.

[95] Bundeskartellamt, Press release of 10.12.2020.

[96] Bundeskartellamt, Press release of 23.11.2022.

[97] EU Commission, Press release of 19.12.2022, IP/22/7728.

primarily intended to prevent circumvention of the data bundling prohibition under Art. 5(2)(b) DMA. The **prohibition of tying** under Art. 5(8) DMA is also relevant in this context, but it is quite limited. The fact that the provision explicitly prohibits subscription and registration requirements makes it clear that it is directed against the integration of user accounts across services (→ mn. 59). However, Art. 5(8) DMA only prohibits the tying of two core platform services, not the tying of a core platform service and another service. This has been rightly criticised in the literature, as such a narrow tying prohibition cannot prevent core platform services from being used as leverage to monopolise related services that do not (yet) qualify as core platform services.[98] Art. 12(2)(g) DMA shows that the legislator was aware of this problem, but decided against a broader tying prohibition in Art. 5(8) DMA. In its present form, Art. 5(8) DMA prohibits, inter alia, the tying of two social networks (e.g. Facebook – Instagram) or of a social network and a number-independent interpersonal communication service (e.g. Facebook – WhatsApp), provided that the services meet the requirements of Art. 3(1)(b), (2)(b) DMA (cf. Art. 3(9) DMA). However, a tie between a core platform service and another service (e.g. Facebook – Meta Quest) remains permissible under the provision.

48 Another important requirement in the context of social networks is the obligation to provide **FRAND access** under Art. 6(12) DMA. This provision requires gatekeepers to apply *fair*, *reasonable*, and *non-discriminatory* conditions to business users' access to their app stores, search engines and social networks. Details have already been described in the section on app stores (→ mn. 38).

IV. Video-sharing platforms

49 **Video-sharing platforms** within the meaning of Art. 2(2)(d), (8) DMA are services whose principal purpose is to make available to the general public programmes or user-generated videos for which the provider of the video-sharing platform does not have editorial responsibility, in order to inform, entertain or educate, and whose organisation is determined by the provider of the video-sharing platform (see also Art. 1(1)(aa) AVMSD). **Non-curated video portals** such as YouTube or Twitch are covered by this definition, although for the latter it is unclear whether it meets the requirements of Art. 3(1)(b), (2)(b) DMA (the EU Commission seems to have come to the opposite conclusion, as it has not designated the platform as a core platform service). YouTube was designated by the Commission as a core platform service in September 2023.[99] Video-on-demand platforms such as Netflix, Amazon Prime Video and Disney+ are not covered by the definition of video-sharing platforms. It is noteworthy that video-sharing platforms have not been the focus of competition law investigations so far. In its investigation of Alphabet/Google's gatekeeper position under § 19a(1) GWB, the German Bundeskartellamt found that the undertaking has a strong position of economic power ("starke wirtschaftliche Machtposition") in video sharing (with YouTube).[100]

50 Obligations of particular importance for video-sharing platforms include the **data processing prohibitions** of Art. 5(2) DMA and the **tying prohibition** of Art. 5(8) DMA. Thus, Alphabet/Google may not integrate YouTube too closely with its other services and, in particular, may only combine the data obtained through YouTube with data from other services under the conditions of Art. 5(2) DMA (see → mn. 40, 45). Pursuant to

[98] Krämer/Schnurr JCLE 18 (2022), 255 (314 et seq.).
[99] EU Commission, Decision of 5.9.2023 – DMA.100005.
[100] Bundeskartellamt, Decision of 30.12.2021 – B7-61/21, para. 323.

Art. 2(22) DMA, the **prohibition of self-preferencing** under Art. 6(5) DMA also explicitly applies to video-sharing platforms, although there are no known cases of self-preferencing in the context of such platforms. The **data portability obligation** under Art. 6(9) DMA is also likely to have some relevance for video-sharing platforms.

V. Number-independent interpersonal communication services

Number-independent interpersonal communications services (NIICS) within the meaning of Art. 2(2)(e), (9) DMA are services which, without the use of telephone numbers, enable direct interpersonal and interactive exchange of information between a finite number of persons, whereby the persons initiating or participating in the communication determine its recipients (see also Art. 2(5) and (7) EECC). Art. 2(5) EECC also assumes that such services are normally provided for remuneration, but in practice this seems to be the exception rather than the rule. Services which enable interpersonal and interactive communication only as a minor ancillary feature that is intrinsically linked to another service are not covered by the definition of interpersonal communication services (cf. Art. 2(5) EECC). Important subtypes of number-independent interpersonal communication services are **email services** such as Gmail and Yahoo Mail and **instant messaging services** such as WhatsApp, Facebook Messenger and Skype. The EU Commission has designated WhatsApp and Facebook Messenger as core platform services in September 2023.[101] Gmail and Outlook.com have not been designated.[102] The same applies to Apple's iMessage, but only after a market investigation according to Art. 17(3) DMA.[103] 51

Since number-independent interpersonal communication services are often based on a business model built around (personalised) advertising, the **data processing prohibitions** of Art. 5(2) DMA (cf. → mn. 40, 45) are relevant for gatekeepers operating such services. In particular, these prohibitions make it more difficult to analyse data from communication services in order to display personalised advertising in other services, a practice that has been quite common up to now. However, Art. 5(2) DMA enables the end users concerned to give their specific consent to the aggregation of data across services, after being offered a specific choice by the relevant gatekeeper. The prohibition on the processing of third-party data under Art. 6(2) DMA and the right of access to data under Art. 6(10) DMA, on the other hand, are likely to be less relevant for communication services. This is because business users conduct far less business with end users through such services than, for example, through online intermediation services or social networks. 52

The **tying prohibition** of Art. 5(8) DMA is also likely to be of some importance for number-independent interpersonal communication services. Communication services are often a central element of gatekeeper ecosystems, as shown by Gmail and WhatsApp. However, according to Art. 5(8) DMA, gatekeepers shall not require business users or end users to subscribe to or register with another core platform service as a condition for using a core platform service. This prohibition also makes it more difficult to use cross-service user accounts (such as the Google Account, the Facebook Account, or Apple ID). However, Art. 5(8) DMA only prohibits the tying of two or more core platform services, not the tying of a core platform service with another service. 53

[101] EU Commission, Decision of 5.9.2023 – DMA.100024.
[102] EU Commission, Decision of 5.9.2023 – DMA.100023; Decision of 5.9.2023 – DMA.100006.
[103] EU Commission, Decision of 12.2.2024 – DMA.100022.

54 The central provision for number-independent communications services operated by gatekeepers is Art. 7 DMA. According to this provision, which was not yet part of the Commission's original draft for the DMA and which does not apply to other core platform services, gatekeepers shall ensure the **interoperability** of their number-independent interpersonal communication services designated under Art. 3(9) DMA with such communication services of other providers. Interoperability is to be achieved in several stages (→ mn. 55). While interoperability is already taken for granted with respect to e-mail services through the use of internet protocols such as SMTP, POP and IMAP, the interoperability requirement for **instant messaging services** will lead to far-reaching changes. For example, Meta/Facebook will need to ensure that WhatsApp can also receive messages from messaging apps such as Threema and Signal, and that WhatsApp users can send messages to these apps. However, interoperability is only required if the provider of the other interpersonal communications service requests it, which is far from guaranteed, especially for services with high security and privacy standards.[104] In addition, companies that are not gatekeepers are not obliged to provide interoperability, so end users may continue to face difficulties when trying to communicate with each other using different services. With the interoperability requirement, the legislator aims to mitigate the strong direct **network effects**[105] that have so far hampered competition between number-independent interpersonal communication services because they play into the hands of the gatekeepers with their extensive services. The reduction of network effects is intended to improve the contestability of the relevant markets, which seems to be particularly important to the legislator as number-independent communication services are often a central cornerstone of integrated ecosystems.[106]

55 The interoperability requirement must be met in three stages, depending on the design and functionality of the communications service. Details may be specified by the Commission for each gatekeeper in the procedure under Art. 8(2) DMA (→ mn. 10 et seq.). As a first step, interoperability must be ensured with regard to **end-to-end text messages** and the exchange of **files** between **individual end users**. According to Art. 7(2)(a) DMA, this obligation becomes effective immediately with the designation decision under Art. 3(9) DMA, i.e. for the first gatekeepers already in September 2023 (cf. → § 10 mn. 3). This is remarkable because, according to Art. 3(10) DMA, the other obligations of the DMA do not have to be fulfilled until six months after the designation decision (i.e. in March 2024, at the earliest). However, the requirement of Art. 7(2)(a) DMA is qualified by the fact that applications for interoperability under Art. 7(5) DMA can only be submitted after the publication of the reference offer within the meaning of Art. 7(4) DMA. However, this reference offer need not be published until six months after the designation decision pursuant to Art. 7(4) sent. 2 DMA (→ mn. 56). Notwithstanding the different and somewhat complicated regulatory technique, a synchronisation with Art. 3(10) DMA has thus been achieved. As a second step, interoperability must also be ensured for text messages and files exchanged via **group chats**. This requirement is to be met within two years of the designation decision pursuant to Art. 7(2)(b) DMA. The third step is to ensure interoperability for **voice and video calls**, whether between individual end users or in the form of group chats. For the implementation of this last step, the gatekeepers have four years after the designation decision pursuant to Art. 7(2)(c) DMA. The time limits set out in Art. 7(2) DMA may be extended by the Commission pursuant to Art. 7(6) DMA.

---

[104] Cf. Reuter, Netzpolitik.org, 8.7.2022, <https://t1p.de/v768c> last accessed 26.8.2024.
[105] Rec. 64 sent. 1 DMA.
[106] Cf. rec. 64 sent. 2 DMA.

As emphasised above (→ mn. 54), interoperability is only to be implemented if requested by the provider of another number-independent interpersonal communications service. The interoperability obligation then only applies in relation to the other service in question; gatekeepers are not generally obliged to develop their interpersonal communication services with open interfaces. If interoperability is requested, it must be provided **free of charge** in accordance with Art. 7(1) DMA, in particular by providing the necessary technical interfaces. Art. 7(3) DMA emphasises that the **level of security** offered by the gatekeeper to its own end users must be maintained for all interoperable services. If end-to-end encryption is used, as in the case of WhatsApp, this must therefore also be maintained for communication between services. It remains to be seen how independent providers of communication services will deal with this requirement. Conversely, it is also an open question how gatekeepers will react to the fact that some competing providers of communication services follow stricter security standards. According to Art. 7(4) DMA, gatekeepers must publish a **reference offer** containing the technical details and general conditions for interoperability. The reference offer must be published within the time limit laid down in Art. 3(10) DMA, i.e. no later than six months after the designation decision pursuant to Art. 3(9) DMA. Requests for interoperability may then be made, which the gatekeeper concerned must meet within **three months** by achieving interoperability for all relevant communication functions concerned (cf. Art. 7(2) DMA). 56

Art. 7(7) DMA clarifies that end users of number-independent interpersonal communications services shall remain free to decide whether they wish to use the interoperable functions. Furthermore, Art. 7(8) DMA emphasises that personal data should only be exchanged between providers of communications services to the extent strictly necessary to achieve effective interoperability. The interoperability requirement is primarily intended to improve the end user's **choice**,[107] but the increased interconnection of previously independent communications services should neither reduce **consumer sovereignty** nor jeopardise existing levels of **data protection** and **security**. Whether this can be achieved in practice remains to be seen. 57

VI. Operating systems

An operating system within the meaning of Art. 2(2)(f), (10) DMA is a **system software** that controls the basic functions of the hardware or software and enables software applications to run on it. According to this definition, the type of hardware is irrelevant. It thus covers operating systems for **PCs** (e.g. Microsoft Windows) as well as those for **smartphones** and other mobile or home entertainment devices (e.g. Google Android, iOS, iPadOS, tvOS, watchOS). Operating systems are important from a competition policy perspective because they form the basis of entire ecosystems that develop around the devices concerned. In particular, they are important gateways to the downstream markets for **software applications**, which are themselves very diverse, ranging from web browsers to productivity software (word processing, spreadsheets, etc.) to computer games. In the *Google Android* decision, the EU Commission found that **Android** and **iOS** belong to different product markets from a competition law perspective because Android can be licensed by device manufacturers, while iOS is only used by Apple itself.[108] The Commission has also found that Google has been dominant in the market 58

[107] Cf. rec. 64(3) DMA.
[108] EU Commission, Decision of 18.7.2018 – AT.40099, para. 238 et seq.

for licensable operating systems for mobile devices since 2011.[109] In the case of Apple's proprietary operating systems, Apple's dominance seems even more evident. Microsoft also clearly continues to dominate 'its' market (licensable operating systems for PCs) with **Windows.**[110] The EU Commission has designated Android, iOS and Windows as core platform services in September 2023.[111] Apple's iPadOS was designated a few months later after a market investigation under Art. 17(3) DMA.[112]

59 Of particular importance for gatekeepers offering operating systems seems to be the **prohibition of tying** according to Art. 5(8) DMA. According to this provision, gatekeepers may not require business users or end users to subscribe to or register with another core platform service as a condition for using a core platform service of the gatekeeper. At first glance, the provision appears to be inspired by competition law tying cases such as *Microsoft* and *Google Android*.[113] The ***Microsoft* decision** concerned, inter alia, the tying of the Windows operating system with the Windows Media Player.[114] In hindsight, it seems to have been the precursor of a whole series of decisions on platform markets. In the ***Google Android*** decision, the Commission found that Google had abused its dominant position in the market for Android app stores by tying the Google Search and Google Chrome apps to the Play Store.[115] The tying product was not the Android operating system, but the Play Store, which is closely related to Android. Comparing Art. 5(8) DMA in the light of these two decisions, however, it is striking that the provision is surprisingly narrow in two respects: First, it only prohibits the tying of two core platform services, not the tying of a core platform service with another service.[116] The tying of an operating system with a search engine or a web browser would therefore be covered, but not the tying with a media player as in the *Microsoft* case. Second, according to its wording, Art. 5(8) DMA only prevents gatekeepers from requiring business users or end users to "subscribe to or register with" another core platform service. The provision thus seems to refer only to those core platform services that require the creation of a **user account**. This is typically not the case for search engines and web browsers. Taking the wording seriously, Art. 5(8) DMA seems to be primarily directed against tying to platform services that require **registration**, such as social networks and interpersonal communication services. Interpreted in this way, the tying prohibition makes it more difficult for gatekeepers to use integrated user accounts across platform services.[117] For example, it would be contrary to Art. 5(8) DMA if Meta required users to have a Facebook account in order to use WhatsApp. However, tying can also pose risks to contestability and fairness in other contexts, as the *Microsoft* and *Google Android* cases have shown. Whether the Commission will seek to extend the tying prohibition in Art. 5(8) DMA beyond its narrow wording to other cases of application is not yet foreseeable.

60 There is, however, another provision that is intended to make the integration of services more difficult, and it is directly relevant to operating systems. This provision is Art. 6(3) DMA, which obliges gatekeepers to allow and technically enable end users to

---

[109] EU Commission, Decision of 18.7.2018 – AT.40099, para. 440 et seq.

[110] Cf. EU Commission, Decision of 24.3.2004 – COMP/37.792, para. 429 et seqq.

[111] EU Commission, Decision of 5.9.2023 – DMA.100009; Decision of 5.9.2023 – DMA.100025; Decision of 5.9.2023 – DMA.100026.

[112] EU Commission, Decision of 29.4.2024 – DMA.100047.

[113] See, for example, Akman ELR 47 (2022), 85 (94 et seq.). But see also Scott Morton/Caffarra, Digital Markets Act, mn. 9.

[114] EU Commission, Decision of 24.3.2004 – COMP/37.792, para. 792 et seqq.

[115] EU Commission, Decision of 18.7.2018 – AT.40099, para. 754, 877 et seq.

[116] This limitation is rightly criticized by Krämer/Schnurr JCLE 18 (2022), 255 (314 et seq.).

[117] See, for example, Polley/Konrad WuW 2021, 198 (204).

easily un-install software applications and to easily change default settings. The **obligation to enable uninstallations** under Art. 6(3) subpara. 1 DMA is, by its very wording, directed exclusively at gatekeepers offering operating systems. It is clearly inspired by the EU Commission's competition law investigations in the *Microsoft* and *Google Android* cases. The ***Microsoft* decision** concerned, among other things, the tying of the Windows operating system with the Windows Media Player. At the time, the Windows Media Player was an integral part of Windows and could not be uninstalled.[118] The Commission concluded that Microsoft had caused significant competitive harm in the media player market. It required Microsoft to offer Windows without the Media Player in the future.[119] The ***Google Android* decision** concerned, among other things, the tying of the Google Search and Google Chrome apps with the Play Store, which is itself tightly integrated with the Android operating system.[120] The tying was based on Google's *Mobile Application Distribution Agreements* (MADAs) with manufacturers of smartphones and other mobile devices. Under these agreements, manufacturers had to promise to pre-install the Google Search and Google Chrome apps on their devices if they wanted a licence to use the Play Store. Neither application can be uninstalled on Android devices.[121] The Commission found that the tying gave Google significant competitive advantages in the markets for general search services and web browsers on mobile devices, thereby reinforcing its dominant position in the markets for general search services. Both cases concerned so-called ***monopoly leveraging***, i.e. the extension of a dominant position to a downstream market.[122] In the context of these competition law investigations, it is particularly noteworthy that Art. 6(3) subpara. 1 DMA does not prohibit gatekeepers from pre-installing software applications on their operating systems. It only requires that the applications can be easily uninstalled. Whether end users will make use of this option is questionable, especially because of the so-called **default effect** *(status quo bias)*. This refers to the tendency of many consumers to prefer the option that does not require an active decision or leaves the current situation unchanged. In the *Android* decision, the default effect and the behavioural economics insights on which it is based rightly played an important role in the Commission's reasoning.[123] The wording of Art. 6(3) subpara. 1 DMA seems rather cautious and leaves the gatekeepers considerable room for manoeuvre, which is however limited by Art. 6(3) subpara. 2 DMA (→ mn. 61). On the other hand, it should be noted that according to Art. 6(3) subpara. 1 DMA it must also be possible to easily uninstall **software applications** that are not part of the provision of core platform services. This is important in order to make *monopoly leveraging* more difficult and to protect competition in secondary markets that have not (yet) tipped towards a gatekeeper. This relatively broad scope should be particularly emphasised in comparison with Art. 5(8) DMA, which is limited to the tying of core platform services.

Pursuant to Art. 6(3) subpara. 2 sent. 1 DMA, gatekeepers shall allow and technically enable end users to easily change the **default settings** of their operating systems, virtual assistants and web browsers that direct or steer end users to the gatekeepers' products or services. Pursuant to Art. 6(3) subpara. 2 sent. 2 DMA, this obligation includes in partic- **61**

[118] EU Commission, Decision of 24.3.2004 – COMP/37792, para. 310.

[119] EU Commission, Decision of 24.3.2004 – COMP/37792, Art. 6 of the operative part.

[120] EU Commission, Decision of 18.7.2018 – AT.40099. The decision was confirmed by GC, Judgment of 14.9.2022 – T-604/18, ECLI:EU:T:2022:541. For more details on this judgment, see König, EU Law Live, 7.12.2022. Google appealed against the GC's judgment. The case is now being heard by the ECJ under case number C-738/22 P.

[121] Cf. EU Commission, Decision of 18.7.2018 – AT.40099, para. 801 et seqq., 913 et seqq.

[122] Cf. Höppner CoRe 1 (2017), 208 (210 et seqq.).

[123] EU Commission, Decision of 18.7.2018 – AT.40099, para. 778 et seq.

ular, in the case of operating systems, that end users must be prompted to select the **online search engine, virtual assistant** or **web browser** to which the gatekeeper's operating system should direct or steer the user by default. The choice is to be made from a list of the main available service providers. The gatekeeper must display this list when the end user uses for the first time an online search engine, virtual assistant or web browser of the gatekeeper listed in the designation decision pursuant to Art. 3(9) DMA. The legislator thus relies on so-called ***choice screens***, which are already known from the ***Microsoft (tying)*** case.[124] The Commission closed this case by accepting commitments in which Microsoft promised to actively offer Windows users a choice between different web browsers. The aim was to reduce the dominance of Internet Explorer, which came pre-installed on Windows systems and was the most widely used web browser at the time. Today, in response to the Commission's decision in the *Google Android* case, Google also offers a choice screen for selecting between different search engines on Android devices.[125] Art. 6(3) subpara. 2 DMA requires gatekeepers offering operating systems to provide such a choice screen to allow users to select a search engine, a virtual assistant and a web browser, provided that the gatekeeper itself offers such services and that they are listed in the designation decision under Art. 3(9) DMA. This is particularly relevant for Google with respect to **Chrome, Google Search** and the **Google Assistant** on Android systems, and for Apple with respect to **Siri** and the **Safari** web browser on Apple operating systems. On the other hand, it was initially not clear whether the Commission would also consider Microsoft's Edge browser and Bing search engine as important gateways within the meaning of Art. 3(1)(b) DMA. It finally decided not to designate them as core platform services in February 2024.[126] This was probably the right decision, as in these two cases the choice screen requirement could have harmed competition on the relevant markets. This is because users could have been induced to choose Chrome, Safari and Google Search, which are more widely used across devices and systems than Edge and Bing.[127] The Commission could have sought to remedy such counterproductive effects through specifications under Art. 8(2) DMA. However, the Commission is not entitled – except within the narrow framework of Art. 9 and 10 DMA – to grant exemptions from the obligation under Art. 6(3) subpara. 2 DMA.

62 Another requirement, which is particularly relevant for gatekeepers offering operating systems, is the obligation to **enable the use of third party software** pursuant to Art. 6(4) DMA. Specifically, gatekeepers must enable software applications and app stores offered by other companies to be installed and effectively used on their operating systems. In addition, gatekeepers must not prevent software applications and app stores from other companies from being set as the default and must enable end users to carry out this change easily. According to Art. 6(4) subpara. 2 and 3 DMA, exceptions are only allowed if they are "strictly necessary and proportionate" to protect the integrity of the hardware or the operating system or to avert security risks. Art. 6(4) DMA is intended in particular to allow so-called **sideloading**, i.e. downloading and installing software applications and app stores without using the respective 'official' app store, i.e. the Play Store on Android systems and Apple's App Store on Apple operating systems. The provision is clearly inspired by competition law investigations into app stores and in particular the EU Commission's ***Apple App Store/music streaming*** case (see → mn. 34 et seq.). In contrast to Google, Apple has so far not allowed third party app stores on its operating sys-

---

[124] EU Commission, Decision of 16.12.2009 – COMP/39530.

[125] Cf. Google, About the choice screen, 12.6.2023 <https://www.android.com/choicescreen/> last accessed 26.8.2024.

[126] EU Commission, Decision of 12.2.2024 – DMA.100028; Decision of 12.2.2024 – DMA.100015.

[127] Cf. Bundeskartellamt, Decision of 30.12.2021 – B7-61/21, para. 234 et seqq., 322.

tems.[128] As a result, Apple controls the distribution of software applications for Apple devices and can impose restrictive contractual terms on software developers, e.g. with regard to data processing and tracking. The counter-example of Google, however, shows that a dominant position in app stores can be achieved even if alternative app stores are allowed, and that sideloading is not a panacea.[129] Google does not appear to have any less bargaining power vis-à-vis software developers than Apple. This is particularly evident in the highly controversial commission fees, which are hardly lower for Google's Play Store than for Apple's App Store and have also been criticised and complained about by software developers.[130] Even the largely unrestricted admission of software applications and app stores from other companies is therefore no guarantee of effective competition in software markets and between app stores. Here, too, the **default effect** is likely to play a fatal role (see → mn. 60). Nevertheless, it seems plausible that the opening of app store and software application markets pursuant to Art. 6(4) DMA will have at least some positive effects on the stimulation of competition in these markets. The practical effects, for example whether there will be a significant reduction in the level of commissions, remain to be seen.

Also of particular relevance to operating system providers is the **prohibition on restricting switching options** under Art. 6(6) DMA. According to this provision, gatekeepers may not impose technical or other restrictions on the ability of end users to switch between or subscribe to different software applications and services accessed through the gatekeeper's core platform service. In the Commission's original draft of the DMA, the provision was intended to apply only to operating system providers,[131] which underlines its importance in this context. It is clear from the recitals that the main objective is to ensure the contestability of **upstream and downstream markets** that develop around core platform services (e.g. markets for software applications, digital products and services, internet access services) and to let competition, rather than gatekeepers, decide who will prevail in these markets.[132] 63

Another requirement with particular relevance for gatekeepers offering operating systems is the **interoperability obligation** in Art. 6(7) DMA. According to the first sentence of subparagraph 1, gatekeepers must enable service providers and hardware providers, free of charge, to effectively interoperate with **hardware and software features** accessed or controlled via an operating system or virtual assistant of the gatekeeper as they are available to services or hardware provided by the gatekeeper. Art. 6(7) subpara. 1 sent. 2 DMA also obliges gatekeepers to allow business users and alternative providers of services provided together with or in support of core platform services (so-called ***ancillary services***) to interoperate effectively and free of charge with the **operating system, hardware or software features** as they are available to or used by the gatekeeper in providing such services, regardless of whether the features are part of an operating system. Exceptions are allowed under Art. 6(7) subpara. 2 DMA only if they are strictly necessary and proportionate to ensure that the integrity of the operating system, virtual assistant or hardware and software features provided by the gatekeeper is not compromised. These rules are clearly inspired by the EU Commission's competition law 64

128 Gurman, Bloomberg, 13.12.2022, <https://t1p.de/4ltpv> last accessed 26.8.2024.
129 Cf. EU Commission, Decision of 18.7.2018 – AT.40099, para. 590 et seq.
130 See, for example, the U.S. case *Epic Games* v. *Google*; Perez, TechCrunch, 19.1.2023.
131 Cf. Art. 6(1)(e) of the draft DMA, COM(2020) 842.
132 Rec. 52 and 53 DMA.

investigation in the ***Apple Pay* case.**[133] In this case, the Commission's preliminary view was that Apple abused its dominant position in the markets for mobile wallets on iOS devices by preventing other mobile wallet providers from using iOS devices' *Near Field Communication (NFC)*. This is wireless technology, communication protocols and software that allow users make payments with their device in a similar way to a debit or credit card, by simply holding the device up to a reader in a shop *("tap and go")*. Apple uses the NFC technology for its own Apple Pay app, but had so far excluded other mobile wallet providers from using it. The Commission was concerned that Apple was thereby restricting competition in the markets for mobile wallets for iOS devices, stifling innovation and reducing consumer choice. The case was later closed with a commitments decision after Apple had promised to open access to the *tap and go* technology on iPhones.[134] Art. 6(7) DMA aims to prevent gatekeeper behaviour similar to Apple's restrictive practices in the future by requiring that competing service or hardware providers have the same access to the hardware and software features of the operating system as the gatekeeper itself. The interoperability obligation vis-à-vis hardware providers is primarily intended to benefit providers of so-called wearables, i.e. smartwatches and other devices worn on the body, which are often only fully functional when connected to a main device (e.g. a smartphone).[135]

VII. Web browsers

65 According to the definition in Art. 2(11) DMA, web browsers are software applications that enable end users to access and interact with web content hosted on servers connected to networks such as the Internet. It is emphasised that the definition covers not only standalone web browsers, but also web browsers that are integrated or embedded in other software. Important examples include **Google Chrome**, **Microsoft Edge** and Apple's **Safari** browser. The EU Commission has designated Chrome and Safari as core platform services in September 2023.[136] Samsung's Internet Browser has not been designated, resulting in Samsung not being considered a gatekeeper.[137] Microsoft's Edge was subjected to a market investigation under Art. 17(3) DMA, but then got a pass.[138] In the Commission's original draft of the DMA, web browsers were not yet included in the core platform services as defined in Art. 2(2) DMA. They were added during the legislative process to take into account "recent enforcement experience" and "broader developments".[139] So far, browsers have not played a very significant role in competition law investigations. The EU Commission has found that browsers for PCs and browsers for mobile devices need to be distinguished in **product market definition**,[140] but not browsers for different operating systems.[141] However, the Commission makes an exception for browsers such as Apple's Safari, which are designed from the outset to run only

[133] EU Commission, Press release of 2.5.2022, IP/22/2764. Interoperability also played an important role in the first Microsoft case, see EU Commission, Decision of 24.3.2004 – COMP/37.792, para. 144 et seqq.
[134] EU Commission, Decision of 11.7.2024 – AT.40452 – Apple Mobile Payments.
[135] Rec. 55 DMA.
[136] EU Commission, Decision of 5.9.2023 – DMA.100008; Decision of 5.9.2023 – DMA.100027.
[137] EU Commission, Decision of 5.9.2023 – DMA.100038.
[138] EU Commission, Decision of 12.2.2024 – DMA.100028.
[139] EU Commission FAQ of 31.10.2022, QANDA/20/2349.
[140] EU Commission, Decision of 18.7.2018 – AT.40099, para. 369 et seq. – Google Android; Decision of 16.12.2009 – AT.39530, para. 17 et seq. – Microsoft (Tying).
[141] EU Commission, Decision of 18.7.2018 – AT.40099, para. 381 et seq. – Google Android.

on certain operating systems.[142] In the markets for non-OS-specific web browsers for mobile devices, Google Chrome is by far the leading browser.[143] Chrome is also the clear market leader for browsers for PCs. From a competition policy perspective, browsers are particularly important because of their close links with **search engines**. For example, in the ***Google Android* decision**, the EU Commission found that the linking of the Google Chrome app with the Play Store and the Google Search app was primarily aimed at strengthening Google's dominant position in the national markets for general search services.[144]

An important requirement for gatekeepers offering web browsers is the obligation under Art. 6(3) subpara. 2 DMA to enable end users to easily change the **default settings** of the gatekeepers' operating systems, virtual assistants and web browsers, provided that these settings direct or steer end users to the gatekeeper's products or services. Pursuant to Art. 6(3) subpara. 2 sent. 2 DMA, this means in particular that end users, when using a gatekeeper's web browser listed in the designation decision pursuant to Art. 3(9) DMA for the first time, must be asked to select from a list of the main available service providers the **online search engine** to which the browser should direct or steer the user by default. This obligation reflects the fact that web browsers typically direct users to a search engine website when the user simply types one or more search terms into the browser's address bar, rather than a specific internet address (Uniform Resource Locator – URL). Google Chrome uses Google Search by default, so the widespread use of the browser secures and strengthens Google's dominant position in the markets for general search services. On Android devices, in response to the EU Commission's *Google Android* decision, a **choice screen** is now used to allow users to actively choose between different search engines when configuring the device.[145] In the future, Google will have to offer such a choice directly in Chrome according to Art. 6(3) DMA, for all versions of the browser and independent of the operating system. The same applies to Apple and Safari, as the latter was found to be a core platform service in September 2023.[146] On the other hand, the obligation under Art. 6(3) DMA does not apply to Microsoft and Edge as the Commission does not consider Edge as an important access gateway within the meaning of Art. 3(1)(b) DMA after having conducted a market investigation under Art. 17(3) DMA.[147] 66

In the context of web browsers, the **data processing prohibitions** of Art. 5(2) and Art. 6(2) DMA as well as the **right of access to data** under Art. 6(10) DMA may also be relevant. This is illustrated, for example, by a competition law investigation of the UK Competition and Markets Authority (CMA) into Google's **Privacy Sandbox**.[148] This is an initiative to replace existing **tracking technologies** such as third-party cookies, advertising IDs and fingerprinting with more privacy-friendly technologies. However, there are concerns that Google could use data protection as an excuse to restrict other companies' ability to collect personal data and use it for personalised advertising. This could further strengthen Google's position in the markets for online advertising. Against this background, the CMA opened an investigation in January 2021 to examine the Privacy Sandbox from a competition law perspective.[149] The scope of the investigation was 67

142 EU Commission, Decision of 18.7.2018 – AT.40099, para. 387 et seq.
143 EU Commission, Decision of 18.7.2018 – AT.40099, para. 947 et seq.
144 EU Commission, Decision of 18.7.2018 – AT.40099, para. 969 et seq.
145 Cf. Google, About the choice screen, 12.6.2023 <https://www.android.com/choicescreen/> last accessed, 26.8.2024.
146 EU Commission, Decision of 5.9.2023 – DMA.100027.
147 EU Commission, Decision of 12.2.2024 – DMA.100028.
148 Cf. CMA, Case overview, available at <https://t1p.de/s29it> last accessed 26.8.2024.
149 CMA, Press release of 8.1.2021, <https://t1p.de/gumc7> last accessed 26.8.2024.

similar to that of the German Bundeskartellamt's investigation into Apple's **App Tracking Transparency Network**, which has already been discussed above in the context of app stores (→ mn. 37). While the German investigation is still ongoing in the summer of 2024, the CMA accepted commitments from Google in February 2022 and closed its investigation.[150] The authority was primarily concerned about Google's intention to remove the ability to use third-party cookies and other features from Google Chrome as part of the Privacy Sandbox project. In response, Google agreed to allow third-party cookies for the time being and to involve the CMA and the Information Commissioner's Office (ICO) in the development of the Privacy Sandbox. Google has also promised not to favour its own advertising services and to better inform other companies and the public about its plans to develop tracking technologies. The DMA prohibits the **bundling of data across services** without specific consent in Art. 5(2) and certain types of **third-party data processing** in Art. 6(2) (→ mn. 29, 46). Furthermore, Art. 6(10) DMA clarifies that gatekeepers must provide business users with free, effective, high-quality, continuous and real-time access to data provided or generated by the business users or their customers (→ mn. 31, 37). Gatekeepers must therefore not only refrain from impeding **access to data** by other companies, but must actively guarantee it. For personal data, however, the right of access under Art. 6(10) DMA only applies to the extent that there is a direct connection with the products or services offered by the relevant business user and the end users concerned have consented to the data sharing.

VIII. Virtual assistants

68 A virtual assistant within the meaning of Art. 2(2)(h), (12) DMA is a software that can process demands, tasks or questions, including those based on audio, visual, written input, gestures or motions, and that provides access to other services or controls connected physical devices. Well-known examples include **Amazon Alexa**, **Siri**, **Google Assistant** and Microsoft's **Cortana**. However, none of these services were designated as core platform services in the EU Commission's first decisions in September 2023 or later until summer 2024.[151] As a result, the DMA does not yet apply to virtual assistants. In the Commission's original draft of the DMA, virtual assistants were not yet part of the core platform services. Their inclusion during the legislative process is partly due to the Commission's sector inquiry into the Internet of Things for consumers.[152] The Commission found that the markets for voice assistants are characterised by high **barriers to market entry**, mainly due to high investment costs and the deterrent presence of vertically integrated companies with large ecosystems (in particular Google, Amazon, Apple).[153] Market participants had indicated, inter alia, that there were **exclusivity and tying practices** related to voice assistants and that it was often not possible to use multiple voice assistants on one device.[154] They also complained about the de facto **gatekeeping position** of virtual assistant providers, which allowed them to control the relationship between service providers and their users, in particular by restricting access to data.[155] It was also seen as problematic that virtual assistant providers themselves have better **access to data** and can favour their own services in downstream markets. In this context,

[150] CMA, Decision of 11.2.2022 – Case No. 50972; Press release of 11.2.2022, <https://t1p.de/165ez> last accessed 26.8.2024.
[151] EU Commission, Press release of 6.9.2023, IP/23/4328.
[152] EU Commission FAQ of 31.10.2022, QANDA/20/2349.
[153] COM(2022) 19, para. 13 et seqq.
[154] COM(2022) 19, para. 46.
[155] COM(2022) 19, paras 42 et seqq., 47.

some market participants also expressed concerns that virtual assistant providers could limit the **interoperability** of these applications with other providers' services or hardware, thereby putting them at a competitive disadvantage.[156]

An important requirement for gatekeepers offering virtual assistants is the obligation under Art. 6(3) subpara. 2 DMA to enable end users to easily change the **default settings** of a gatekeeper's virtual assistant if those settings direct or steer end users to the gatekeeper's products or services. In addition, Art. 6(3) DMA requires that end users, when using a gatekeeper virtual assistant for the first time, must be asked to select the **online search engine** to which the virtual assistant should direct or steer them by default from a list of the main available service providers. This requirement reflects the fact that virtual assistants are often closely integrated with search engines. As with operating systems (→ mn. 61) and web browsers (→ mn. 66), the aim is to ensure that a gatekeeper's control over a virtual assistant cannot easily be used as leverage to dictate a particular search engine to users, thus giving the gatekeeper an unjustified advantage in competition with other search engine operators. However, it could be problematic that virtual assistants are defined in Art. 2(12) DMA as processing, among other things, "tasks or questions". As a result, gatekeepers may try to integrate complex **search algorithms** directly into their virtual assistants in order to avoid the use of a separate search engine and thus the application of Art. 6(3) subpara. 2 DMA. The user's right of choice according to Art. 6(3) subpara. 2 sent. 2 DMA would then be largely undermined. 69

Also important in the context of virtual assistants is the **interoperability obligation** under Art. 6(7) DMA (cf. → mn. 64). According to this provision, gatekeepers must allow service providers and hardware providers to effectively interoperate, free of charge, with **hardware and software features** that are accessed or controlled via an operating system or a virtual assistant as they are available to services or hardware provided by the gatekeeper. The inclusion of virtual assistants appears to be influenced by, among other things, the EU Commission's ***Apple App Store/music streaming* investigation**, which has already been discussed above in connection with app stores (→ mn. 35 et seq., 62). The investigation is largely driven by recurring complaints from Spotify and other market participants, who are concerned not only about the 30 % commission and restrictions on their customer communication on iOS devices, but also about discrimination in access to hardware and software features. For example, it has long been impossible to control competing music streaming apps such as Spotify on iOS devices using the voice assistant Siri.[157] Instead, voice commands to play music were always directed to Apple's own streaming app, Apple Music. Later, it became possible to control competing music streaming apps with Siri voice commands, but if no such app was explicitly named by the user, Apple Music was still the default for playing music. In the future, gatekeepers will be prohibited from such practices, as Art. 6(7) DMA requires that competing providers of services (e.g. apps) or hardware (e.g. smartwatches, fitness trackers) have the same access to hardware and software features as the gatekeeper providing the virtual assistant. 70

IX. Cloud computing

Cloud computing services within the meaning of Art. 2(2)(i), (13) DMA are digital services that "enable access to a scalable and elastic pool of shareable computing re 71

[156] COM(2022) 19, para. 17 et seqq., 41.

[157] See on this and the following Spotify, How we got here, <https://t1p.de/mw3y3> last accessed 26.8.2024.

sources" (cf. Art. 2(19) NIS Directive). The definition covers remote access to computing capacity, data storage, software applications and other **computing resources** that are not available or operated on local IT systems, but are accessed via the Internet through a website or software application. Cloud computing can be used to provide a wide variety of services, so that the scope of application of Art. 2(2)(i), (13) DMA is theoretically very broad. The DMA does not specify which cloud services the legislator had in mind. From a technical point of view, a distinction can be made between remote access to software and/or data storage (***Software as a Service,*** *SaaS*; e.g. Google Workspace, Microsoft 365, Google Drive), to a platform for the development of web applications (***Platform as a Service,*** *PaaS*; e.g. Microsoft Azure, Amazon Web Services, Google App Engine) or to physical infrastructure such as computing capacity and storage (***Infrastructure as a Service,*** *IaaS*; e.g. Amazon Web Services, Microsoft Azure). The EU Commission did not identify any cloud computing services as core platform services in its first decisions in September 2023. As a result, the DMA does not yet apply to cloud services.

72 Cloud computing services are not specifically mentioned in any of the provisions of Art. 5–7 DMA, are only briefly mentioned in the recitals and have so far not played an important role in competition law enforcement. It is therefore largely unclear where the legislator sees the main competition policy challenges with regard to this type of core platform service. On the other hand, it is not difficult to predict a certain practical significance of the **data processing prohibitions** of Art. 5(2) and Art. 6(2) DMA as well as the **data access right** according to Art. 6(10) DMA. Art. 5(2) DMA prohibits the bundling of data across services without the specific consent of the user and has already been described in more detail above in connection with social networks (→ mn. 45). The prohibition on processing third-party data under Art. 6(2) DMA is also likely to be particularly relevant for providers of cloud computing services (cf. already → mn. 29, 46). According to this provision, a gatekeeper shall not use, in competition with business users, any non-publicly accessible data generated or provided by these business users in the context of their use of the relevant core platform service. The data covered is further specified in Art. 6(2) subpara. 2 DMA. The restrictions resulting from Art. 5(2) and Art. 6(2) DMA seem to be particularly relevant for gatekeepers offering cloud computing services. In particular, they do not allow such gatekeepers to process data stored in their clouds by business users or their customers for advertising purposes without specific consent (cf. Art. 5(2)(a) DMA). Gatekeepers are also prohibited from using the data in their clouds in competition with business users (cf. Art. 6(2) DMA). The recitals emphasise that, in the context of cloud computing services, this prohibition applies to "data provided or generated by business users of the gatekeeper in the context of their use of the cloud computing service […] or through its software application store that allows end users of cloud computing services access to software applications".[158]

73 Art. 6(10) DMA clarifies that gatekeepers must provide business users, upon their request and free of charge, with effective, high quality, continuous and **real-time access to data** provided or generated in the context of the use of a core platform service by the business users or their customers (cf. → mn. 31, 37). This requirement may also be relevant for providers of cloud computing services. This is obvious, for example, when a software developer uses a **cloud-based software development** and **hosting platform** of a gatekeeper *(platform as a service)* to make a web application available to its customers. In such a situation, the gatekeeper has access to the data because it controls the platform and all related data streams. Legally, however, the software developer is at least granted a right of access to the data under Art. 6(10) DMA, albeit not to the exclusion of the gate-

[158] Cf. rec. 48 DMA.

keeper. This allocation of access rights can be justified above all by the fact that the creation of the data in such cases is (also) based on the creation of value by the software developer. Whoever initiates the generation of data should also be allowed to use the data.

X. Online advertising services

Finally, according to Art. 2(2)(j) DMA, core platform services also include **online advertising services** such as "any advertising networks, advertising exchanges and any other advertising intermediation services" provided by an undertaking which provides at least one other core platform service referred to in Art. 2(2) DMA. Thus, pure advertising service providers are not subject to the DMA, but only advertising services provided by undertakings that are already considered to be gatekeepers due to other services they provide. These are mainly the advertising services of the **'Big Five'**, namely Google Ads (formerly Google AdWords), Amazon Ads, Meta Ads, Apple Search Ads and Microsoft Advertising. The EU Commission has designated Google Ads, Amazons Ad and Meta Ads as core platform services in September 2023.[159] Microsoft Advertising has not been designated after a market investigation under Art. 17(3) DMA.[160] Apple's advertising business has not yet been investigated, which suggests that it does not meet the thresholds of Art. 3(2) DMA. The advertising services of X (formerly Twitter) and TikTok also got a pass. Online advertising services are important from a competition policy perspective because the core platform services of the DMA are often based on business models that rely on (personalised) advertising. Alphabet/Google, for example, generated more than 80 % of its global group revenues from online advertising in 2020.[161] Competition authorities have frequently addressed online advertising markets in competition law investigations. Examples include the EU Commission's ***Google AdSense* decision**[162] and the recently concluded or ongoing investigations into the 'Jedi Blue' agreement between Google and Meta/Facebook,[163] Google's advertising technology services[164] and Apple and Google's tracking restrictions (→ mn. 37, 67).[165] 74

In the context of online advertising services, the **prohibitions on data processing** under Art. 5(2) and Art. 6(2) DMA are of particular importance. Art. 5(2) DMA prohibits the bundling of data across services without the specific consent of the user and has already been described in more detail above (→ mn. 40, 45). Particularly noteworthy is Art. 5(2)(a) DMA, which prohibits gatekeepers from processing, for the purpose of providing **online advertising services**, the personal data of end users who use third party services, unless the gatekeeper obtains the specific consent of the user. For example, the control over a core platform service such as a social network or an app store may not be used as leverage to analyse the communications between a business user and its customers on the platform for advertising purposes. Art. 6(2) DMA also prohibits gatekeep- 75

159 EU Commission, Decision of 5.9.2023 – DMA.100010; Decision of 5.9.2023 – DMA.100016; Decision of 5.9.2023 – DMA.100035.

160 EU Commission, Decision of 5.9.2023 – DMA.100034.

161 Bundeskartellamt, Decision of 30.12.2021 – B7-61/21, para. 3.

162 EU Commission, Decision of 20.3.2019 – AT.40411.

163 EU Commission, Press release of 11.3.2022, IP/22/1703, CMA, Press release of 11.3.2022, <https://t1p.de/ltmv3> last accessed 26.8.2024.

164 EU Commission, Press release of 22.6.2021, IP/21/3143; CMA, Press release of 26.5.2022, <https://t1p.de/pzjpt> last accessed 26.8.2024.

165 Bundeskartellamt, Press release of 14.6.2022; CMA, Press release of 11.2.2022, <https://t1p.de/s29it> last accessed 26.8.2024.

ers from using, in **competition** with business users, any non-publicly available data generated or provided by the business users or their customers in the context of their use of a core platform service. The recitals clarify that the prohibition also applies with respect to data obtained by a gatekeeper from business users through a core platform service for the purpose of providing online advertising services.[166] In such a situation, the gatekeeper may only use the data for the provision of the advertising services and not in competition with the business user, e.g. on upstream or downstream product or service markets. This is to take account of the **dual role** and consequent lack of neutrality of gatekeepers, who often provide not only core platform services and related online advertising services, but are also active in upstream or downstream markets where they compete with the business users of their platform services.

76 Of central importance for gatekeepers providing advertising services are also the **transparency obligations** under Art. 5(9) and (10) and Art. 6(8) DMA. According to Art. 5(9) DMA, gatekeepers shall provide each advertiser to whom they supply advertising services, at the request of the advertiser and free of charge, with information on a daily basis about each advertisement placed by the advertiser. The information must relate in particular to the aspects referred to in Art. 5(9)(a)–(c) DMA, including the prices and fees paid by the advertiser and the remuneration received by the publisher.[167] However, the remuneration may only be disclosed on an ad specific basis if the publisher agrees. Otherwise, the gatekeeper must only inform the advertiser of the daily average remuneration received by the relevant publisher. Art. 5(10) DMA contains a parallel provision according to which, conversely, publishers must be provided, on a daily basis and free of charge, with information about the advertisements displayed in their inventory (i.e. advertising space on their websites or in their applications). The background to both provisions is that the conditions under which gatekeepers provide advertising services have often been "non-transparent" and "opaque".[168] According to the legislator, transparency has even decreased following the introduction of "new privacy legislation" (apparently a reference to the GDPR).[169] As a result, advertisers and publishers often lack sufficient information and knowledge about the advertising services they use, which affects their ability to compare offers and switch to other advertising providers.[170] The transparency obligations in Art. 5(9) and (10) DMA are intended to improve the **comparability** of offers, increase the **ability and willingness to switch** and stimulate competition. This should have a positive impact on advertising costs and the prices of the advertised products and services,[171] which, given the importance of advertising markets, promises significant benefits for consumers. In order to achieve sufficient transparency and comparability, the price and cost information should be broken down to the level of individual advertisements. The information must also be provided on a daily basis and free of charge. Gatekeepers will also have to disclose the criteria they use to calculate their prices. These are ambitious requirements that should actually increase the transparency of the online advertising markets. It will be interesting to see how this will affect competition.

---

166 Rec. 47 sent. 4 DMA.

167 The term "publisher" refers to the provider of the website, application or other channel through which the advertisement is displayed.

168 Rec. 45 sent. 1 DMA; cf. also CMA, Online Platforms and Digital Advertising, Final Report, 2020, para. 5.334 et seqq.; Bundeskartellamt, Sector Inquiry Online Advertising, Discussion Report (in German), August 2022, para. 202. The executive summary is available in English.

169 Rec. 45 sent. 3 DMA.

170 Rec. 45 sent. 4 DMA.

171 Rec. 45 sent. 5 and 6 DMA.

Also relevant for providers of online advertising services is the right of access under Art. 6(8) DMA. This provision requires gatekeepers to provide advertisers and publishers, upon their request and free of charge, with access to the **performance measuring tools** and **data** they need to conduct their own independent verification of the advertisements inventory. The data must be provided by the gatekeepers in such a way that advertisers and publishers can use their own verification and measurement tools to assess the performance of the core platform services provided by the gatekeepers. The wording of Art. 6(8) DMA appears to be very broad, in particular as it is not limited to any specific core platform service. However, the reference to advertisers and publishers as well as the "verification of the advertisements inventory" suggest a close connection with Art. 5(9) and (10) DMA. The recitals also confirm that Art. 6(8) DMA is intended to apply exclusively to advertising services.[172] The separation from Art. 5(9) and (10) DMA is apparently due to the fact that the legislator has defined the right of access under Art. 6(8) DMA in a rather unspecific manner and therefore probably wanted to allow a specification under Art. 8(2) DMA. In any event, Art. 6(8) DMA also aims to increase the transparency of online advertising markets and to stimulate competition by improving the comparability of competing offers.[173] While Art. 5(9) and (10) DMA focus on price and cost information, Art. 6(8) DMA also aims to improve the ability of advertisers and publishers to evaluate and compare the **effectiveness** of advertising services. Overall, this should enable them to make informed decisions about which advertising services to use. 77

172 Cf. rec. 58 DMA.
173 Cf. rec. 58 DMA.

§ 13
Market investigation

Literature: *Achleitner*, 'Digital Markets Act beschlossen: Verhaltenspflichten und Rolle nationaler Wettbewerbsbehörden', NZKart 2022, 359; *Basedow*, 'Reinventing the Wheel: On the Proposal for a Digital Markets Act', ZEuP 2021, 217; *Budsizinki/Mendelsohn*, 'Regulating Big Tech: From Competition Policy to Sector Regulation?', Ilmenau Economics Discussion Papers, Vol. 27, No. 168; *Cabral/Haucap/Parker/Petropolous/Valetti/Van Alstyne*, 'The EU Digital Markets Act: A Report from a Panel of Economic Experts', Luxembourg 2021; *Colomo*, 'The Draft Digital Markets Act: A Legal and Institutional Analysis', Discussion Paper, 2021; de *Streel/Feasey/Kreamer/Monti*, 'Making the Digital Markets Act More Resilient and Effective', Recommendation Paper, Centre on Regulation in Europe, 2021; *Dietrich/Vinje*, 'The European Commission's proposal for a Digital Markets Act – In search of a 'golden standard' for appropriate ex ante regulation of large digital players', CRi 2021, 33; Friends of an effective Digital Markets Act, 'Strengthening the Digital Markets Act and its Enforcement', First Position Paper, 27.5.2021; *Geradin*, 'What is a digital gatekeeper? Which platforms should be captured by the EC proposal for a Digital Market Act?', Discussion Paper, 2021; *Gerpott*, 'Neue Pflichten für große Betreiber digitaler Plattformen – Vergleich von § 19a GWB und DMA-Kommissionsvorschlag', NZKart 2021, 273; *Gielen/Uphues*, 'Digital Markets Act und Digital Services Act. Regulierung von Markt- und Meinungsmacht durch die Europäische Union', EuZW 2021, 627; *Haus/Weusthof*, 'The Digital Markets Act – a Gatekeeper's Nightmare?', WuW 2021, 318; *Herbers*, 'Der Digital Markets Act (DMA) kommt – neue Dos and Don'ts für Gatekeeper in der Digitalwirtschaft', RDi 2022, 252; *Jovanovic/Greiner*, 'DMA: Überblick über den geplanten EU-Regulierungsrahmen für digitale Gatekeeper. Paradigmenwechsel im Umgang mit digitalen Plattformen?', MMR 2021, 678; *Kettemann/Schulz/Fertmann*, 'Anspruch und Wirklichkeit der Plattformregulierung. Kommissionsentwürfe der Rechtsakte zu digitalen Diensten und Märkten', ZRP 2021, 138; *Körber*, 'Lessons from the Hare and the Tortoise: Legally imposed self-regulation, proportionality and the right to defence under the DMA – Part 1', NZKart 2021, 379; *Künstner*, 'Risks of legal and factual bypassing of the objectives and regulatory content of the Digital Markets Act. A proposal to strengthen the Digital Markets Act in the current legislative process', 2022; *Kumkar*, 'Der Digital Markets Act nach dem Trilog-Verfahren', RDi 2022, 347; *Larouche/de Streel*, 'The European Digital Markets Act: A Revolution Grounded on Traditions', JECLP 12(7) (2021), 542; *Lettl*, 'Das Gesetz über digitale Märkte (Digital Markets Act – DMA)', WRP 2022, 1453; *Monti*, 'The digital markets act: improving its institutional design', European Competition and Regulatory Law Review 5(2) (2021), 90; *Motta/Peitz/Schweitzer* (eds), Market Investigations. A New Competition Tool for Europe?, 2022; *Paal/Kieß*, 'Digitale Plattformen im DSA-E, DMA-E und § 19a GWB', ZfDR 2022, 1; *Paal/Kumkar*, 'Die digitale Zukunft Europas. Europäische Strategien für den digitalen Binnenmarkt', ZfDR 2021, 97; *Petit*, 'The proposed digital markets act (DMA): a legal and policy review', JECLP 12(7) (2021), 529; *Podszun/Bongartz/Langenstein*, 'The Digital Markets Act: Moving from Competition Law to Regulation for Large Gatekeepers', EuCML 2021, 60; *Podszun/Schwalbe*, 'Digitale Plattformen und GWB-Novelle: Überzeugende Regeln für die Internetökonomie?', NZKart 2017, 98; *Savary*, 'Regulierung von Gatekeeper-Plattformen', RDi 2021, 117; *Schweitzer*, 'The Art to Make Gatekeeper Positions Contestable and the Challenge to Know What Is Fair: A Discussion of the Digital Markets Act Proposal', ZEuP 2021, 503; *Schweitzer*, 'The New Competition Tool: Its institutional set up and procedural design', Expert Report for the EU Commission, 2020; *Schweitzer/Gutman*, 'Unilateral Practices in the digital market: An overview of EU and national case law', e-competition 2021, Art. N° 101045; *Verbraucherzentrale Bundesverband*, 'Wahlfreiheit von Verbrauchern und effektiven Wettbewerb in digitalen Märkten sicherstellen', Positionspapier, 2021; *Zimmer/Göhls*, 'Vom New Competition Tool zum Digital Markets Act: Die geplante EU-Regulierung für digitale Gatekeeper', ZWeR 2021, 29; *Zober*, 'Durchsetzung des DMA-E und dessen Verhältnis zum Kartellrecht', NZKart 2021, 611.

A. Introduction

1 With market investigations, the DMA provides for a **special procedure** to ensure contestability and fairness in the digital sector. The Commission's broad investigative powers allow it to gather information on market structures, digital business models and entrepreneurial behaviour.[1] This will reduce possible information gaps between the enforcement authority and digital companies.[2] Market investigations serve both effective enforcement and regulatory updating.

2 There is only a partial similarity with the **sector inquiry** procedure, which the Commission is authorised to conduct under European competition law pursuant to Art. 17

[1] Kettemann/Schulz/Fertmann ZRP 2021, 138 (139).

[2] Achleitner NZKart 2022, 359 (366); Cabral/Haucap/Parker/Petropolous/Valetti/Van Alstyne, The EU Digital Markets Act: A Report from a Panel of Economic Experts, 2021, p. 28; Paal/Kumukar ZfDR 2021, 97 (113); Schweitzer ZEuP 2021, 503 (532).

Regulation (EC) No. 1/2003.[3] The German competition authority has corresponding powers under § 32e German Act against Restraints of Competition (ARC). Sector inquiries serve to uncover restrictions and distortions of competition within an economic sector.[4] In contrast, market investigations can be initiated for three different purposes. Market investigations are designed to enforce the DMA in two ways. Firstly, they can be initiated with the objective of **designating gatekeepers** (Art. 17). Secondly, the Commission is obliged to conduct a market investigation if it intends to remedy **systematic non-compliance** (Art. 18). Market investigations for these purposes are directed against a specific undertaking. Since the DMA does not affect the application of European and German competition law, cf. Art. 1(6), the power of the Commission and the national competition authorities to conduct sector inquiries remains intact.

3 Thirdly, market investigations take into account the fast pace of digital economy. They highlight the **need for timely updates** to the DMA that may arise in light of new core platform services and new practices. A market investigation will enable the Commission to carry out a swift analysis of the need for adaptation (Art. 19). This takes into account the fact that the chosen **rule-based approach** of the DMA is generally not very flexible compared to the broad general clauses of European competition law. However, in order to effectively regulate dynamic and rapidly evolving digital business models, flexibility is crucial.[5] During the legislative process, consideration was also given to introducing a market investigation in the event that antitrust enforcement powers do not allow for a sufficiently rapid response to identified threats to contestability and fairness.[6] However, the Union legislator did not take up this proposal.

4 Market investigations are similar to the **New Competition Tool** discussed before the DMA came into force. Among other things, expanded powers of intervention by the Commission were proposed as a new instrument for better enforcement of competition law.[7] In this context,–similar to the regulatory approach now implemented in the DMA the focus was on the early identification of market structures that pose a threat to competition.[8] It was considered to allow an intervention already before the realisation of market dominance or abuse within the meaning of Art. 102 TFEU.[9] The DMA's market investigations also show certain parallels with the market investigations carried out by the Competition and Market Authority of the United Kingdom.[10]

5 Market investigations are **lengthy** procedures.[11] The prescribed maximum durations and possible extensions vary depending on the reason for the investigation. Market

---

[3] Krauskopf/Brösamle in Schmidt/Hübener Der neue DMA § 8 mn. 3 et seqq.

[4] The German competition authority can also initiate a sector inquiry if there is a well-founded suspicion of qualified infringements of consumer law provisions, cf. Klose in Wiedemann KartellR-HdB § 52 mn. 56a.

[5] Podszun/Bongartz/Langenstein EuCML 2021, 60 (61).

[6] Friends of an effective Digital Markets Act, Strengthening the Digital Markets Act and its Enforcement, 9.9.2021, p. 1, 3 <https://www.bmwi.de/Redaktion/DE/Downloads/XYZ/zweites-gemeinsames-positionspapier-der-friends-of-an-effective-digital-markets-act.pdf?__blob=publicationFile&v=4> (last accessed: 10.9.2023).

[7] Schweitzer, The New Competition Tool: Its institutional set up and procedural design, Expert Report for the EU Commission, 2020, p. 5 et seqq. <https://ec.europa.eu/competition/consultations/2020_new_comp_tool/kd0420574enn.pdf> (last accessed: 10.9.2023).

[8] Motta/Peitz/Schweitzer Market Investigations p. 1 (8).

[9] Schweitzer, The New Competition Tool: Its institutional set up and procedural design, Expert Report for the EU Commission, 2020, p. 5 et seqq. <https://ec.europa.eu/competition/consultations/2020_new_comp_tool/kd0420574enn.pdf> (last accessed: 10.9.2023).

[10] Competition and Market Authority, Guidelines for market investigations, 2013 <https://assets.publishing.service.gov.uk/government/uploads/system/uploads/attachment_data/file/284390/cc3_revised.pdf> (last accessed: 10.9.2023).

[11] Krauskopf/Brösamle in Schmidt/Hübener Der neue DMA § 8 mn. 41.

investigations that serve the proper implementation of the DMA in the form of the designation of a gatekeeper or the adoption of remedies in the event of systematic non-compliance should generally be terminated after 12 months by the adoption of implementing acts (for deviations from this deadline → mn. 67 et seq.). In order to complement a market investigation aimed at identifying updating needs of the DMA, the Commission shall publish a report after 18 months at the latest. This report shall be accompanied, if appropriate, by a legislative proposal or a draft delegated act.

The provisions on market investigation are laid down in Chapter IV of the DMA, 6
Art. 16–19. Art. 16 regulates the conditions for initiating and resuming market investigations. Art. 17 governs market investigations for the designation of gatekeepers. Art. 18 contains provisions on market investigations in case of systematic non-compliance with the obligations under Art. 5–7. Art. 19 addresses market investigations in relation to new services and new practices.

In the Commission draft, the provisions on market investigation were set out in 7
Art. 14–17 DMA draft.[12]

B. Reasons

I. Designating gatekeepers (Art. 17)

1. Gatekeeper position and presumption

Pursuant to Art. 17, the Commission may initiate a market investigation to examine 8
whether an undertaking holds a **gatekeeper position**. According to recital 3, gatekeepers are characterised by considerable economic power, which may enable them to control entire platform systems in the digital economy. According to the Union legislator, this concerns a few large companies that provide core platform services (→ § 11 mn. 1). When an undertaking is designated as gatekeeper, it has to comply with the obligations laid down in Art. 5, 6, 7 within 6 months after a core platform service has been listed in the designation decision.

The requirements for a gatekeeper position are laid down in **Art. 3(1)** (→ § 12 9
mn. 45 et seqq.). Accordingly, a gatekeeper is an undertaking that has a significant impact on the internal market (lit. a), provides a core platform service which is an important gateway for business users to reach end users (lit. b), and enjoys an entrenched and durable position, in its operations, or it is foreseeable that it will enjoy such a position in the near future (lit. c). The gatekeeper position is determined with regard to core platform services as defined in Art. 2(2) (→ § 12 mn. 6 et seq.). An undertaking will be designated as a gatekeeper if it holds such a position regarding at least one core platform service. It is also possible to classify an undertaking as a gatekeeper with regard to several core platform services.[13]

In general, it is the Commission's responsibility to set forth and prove the require- 10
ments of the gatekeeper position. In order to accelerate the procedure, **Art. 3(2)** provides for a **rebuttable presumption** (→ § 12 mn. 47 et seqq.). It is linked to quantitative thresholds regarding turnover and user numbers.[14] When the thresholds are reached, the undertaking concerned is obliged to report on it. It must notify the Commission within

---

[12] COM(2020) 842 final, 51–53.

[13] Achleitner NZKart 2022, 359 (360).

[14] Basedow ZEuP 2021, 217 (219); Gielen/Uphues EuZW 2021, 627 (629). Crit. on the connecting factors of the presumption Körber NZKart 2021, 379 (379).

two months. The presumption requires, in particular, that the undertaking has generated an annual turnover of at least EUR 7.5 billion in the Union in each of the last three financial years and that it had at least 45 million monthly active end users established or staying in the Union and at least 10.000 annually active commercial users established in the Union in the previous financial year. If the thresholds are met, the gatekeeper is designated in a simple notification procedure pursuant to Art. 3(3)–(5) (→ § 12 mn. 54).[15]

11 If the **presumption does not apply**, the determination of the gatekeeper position is significantly more complex for the Commission. A detailed case-by-case examination is required. Art. 17 provides for a market investigation procedure for this purpose.[16] There are two situations in which the presumption does not apply: Firstly, it is not applicable if an undertaking **does not meet the thresholds** set out in Art. 3(2), cf. Art. 17(1). Secondly, a market investigation is required for the gatekeeper designation if the undertaking reaches the thresholds but submits **sufficiently substantiated arguments** against its gatekeeper position, cf. Art. 17(3). In both cases, the Commission must initiate a market investigation if it intends to clarify whether and with respect to which core platform services the undertaking holds a gatekeeper position.

2. Non-achievement of the thresholds (Art. 17(1))

12 Designation as a gatekeeper requires the conduct of a market investigation, cf. Art. 17(1), if the undertaking does not satisfy the requirements of the presumption under Art. 3(2). The conditions are not met if the undertaking does not reach either the turnover threshold or the user threshold or both thresholds. This also includes the case of the '*emerging gatekeeper*', who currently does not have an entrenched and durable position but will attain one in the near future.[17]

13 The Commission conducts its investigation based on the general **objective requirements** stated in Art. 3(1). This is made clear by rec. 24(1)(1). In addition, according to rec. 25(1)(1), the quantitative threshold values, cf. Art. 3(2), shall be taken into account. Recital 25(1)(2) sets out the goals of a market investigation for designating a gatekeeper. The Commission must pursue the objectives of preserving and fostering innovation and the quality of digital products and services, the degree to which prices are fair and competitive, and the degree to which quality or choice for business users and for end users is or remains high.

14 A gatekeeper position is not the same as a dominant position within the meaning of Art. 102 TFEU (→ § 12 mn. 45). An undertaking does not have to be dominant in order to be designated as a gatekeeper.[18] In addition, the designation process **does not require the delineation of markets.**[19] **Art. 3(8)** lists numerous **aspects** and thereby specifies what must be taken into account (→ § 12 nm. 55 et seqq.). These aspects are partly similar to the criteria of § 19a(1) of the German Act against Restraints of Competition (ARC) for determining paramount significance for competition across markets ('überragende marktübergreifende Bedeutung für den Wettbewerb'), but ultimately go beyond the catalogue of § 19a ARC.[20]

---

[15] Jovanovic/Greiner MMR 2021, 678 (680).
[16] Basedow ZEuP 2021, 217 (219).
[17] Krauskopf/Brösamle in Schmidt/Hübener Der neue DMA § 8 mn. 10.
[18] Gerpott NZKart 2021, 273 (275); Paal/Kieß ZfDR 2022, 1 (12).
[19] Kumkar RDi 2022, 347 (349); Petit Journal of European Competition Law & Practice 12(7) (2021), 529 (534).
[20] Gerpott NZKart 2021, 273 (275).

15 The elements of Art. 3(8) are not subject to any order or weighting. They open up a **wide scope** for the Commission. It must conduct a case-by-case assessment.[21] At the same time, the elements offer possible points of attack for the judicial review of designation decisions.[22] In order to strengthen legal certainty, they should be further specified. The Commission does not have the power to issue delegated acts in this regard, cf. Art. 49. However, a concretisation would be possible, e.g. in the form of guidelines.

16 Art. 3(8)(2)(a) mentions the **size of undertaking** including turnover, market capitalisation, operations and position. According to recital 25(1)(4), these elements can be used as indicators of the leveraging potential of undertakings and of the tipping of markets in their favour. As an undertaking grows in size, it tends to be easier for it to exploit **cost advantages.**[23] The variable costs for platform services are usually low.[24] If the undertaking concerned is a medium-sized, small or micro enterprise, it should be carefully examined, in accordance with recital 24(1)(2), whether such an undertaking, despite its small size, would be able to significantly undermine the contestability of core platform services.

17 Pursuant to Art. 3(8)(2)(b), the **number of business users using the core platform service to reach end users and the number of end users** shall be taken into account. Large numbers of users can make the undertaking an important gateway, cf. rec. 20(1). With the size of the undertaking and the number of users, the elements on which the presumption of Art. 3(2) is based are also taken into account in the qualitative assessment. Therefore, the extent to which the turnover and user figures of the undertaking concerned are below the presumption thresholds is also relevant.

18 Art. 3(8)(2)(c) adds **network effects and data driven advantages** to the list of criteria, in particular in relation to that undertaking's access to, and collection of, personal data and non-personal data or analytics capabilities. Both direct and indirect network effects can strengthen the economic power of platform operators. Direct network effects occur between users of the same group. One example is social networks. Their attractiveness to end users increases with the total number of end users on the platform.[25] Indirect network effects occur when the value of the platform to one group of users increases because the number of users from another group increases.[26] In the data-driven digital economy, competitive advantages also arise from the analysis and evaluation of large amounts of data.[27] They can make it possible to offer precisely tailored services or to develop them further. Possible economies of scale and scope from which the undertaking benefits – also in relation to data and, where relevant, to its activities outside the Union – must also be taken into account pursuant to Art. 3(8)(2)(d).

19 Furthermore, the **lock-in of business users and end users,** including switching costs and behavioural bias reducing the ability of business users and end users to switch or multi-home, may be relevant when determining a gatekeeper position under Art. 3(8)(2)(e). Lock-in effects increase with the costs of switching. They tie users to the platform.[28]

---

[21] Lettl WRP 2022, 1453 (1457).
[22] Herbers RDi 2022, 252 (255).
[23] Savary RDi 2021, 117 (118).
[24] Kühnen in Loewenheim/Meessen/Riesenkampff/Kersting/Meyer-Lindemann GWB § 18 mn. 109.
[25] Savary RDi 2021, 117 (118).
[26] Paal in BeckOK InfoMedienR GWB § 18 mn. 10.
[27] Podszun/Schwalbe NZKart 2017, 98 (100).
[28] Savary RDi 2021, 117 (118).

If multi-homing is not common, for example, because the platform operators offer similar services,[29] this may also increase market power.[30]

20 A **conglomerate corporate structure** or **vertical integration** may enable an undertaking to cross subsidise, to combine data from different sources or to leverage its position. These circumstances should also be addressed according to Art. 3(8)(2)(f). Finally, Art. 3(8)(2)(g) contains a catch-all clause according to which other structural business or service characteristics may be taken into account.

21 Pursuant to Art. 3(8)(3), the Commission shall discontinue **foreseeable developments** with a view to the above elements. This also includes planned mergers involving another undertaking providing core platform services or providing any other services in the digital sector or enabling the collection of data. The forward-looking nature of gatekeeper designation takes into account the dynamic nature of the platform economy (on the content of the designation decision → mn. 80 et seq.). In April 2024, the Commission closed a market investigation into Apple's iPadOS.[31] The core platform service had not met the presumption requirements set out in Art. 3(2). However, on the basis of a qualitative assessment under Art. 3(8), the Commission found that the operating system was an important gateway for business users to reach end users. It argued that although the number of end users did not reach the threshold of Art. 3(2), they were close to it and were expected to increase.[32] The Commission also constituted lock-in effects regarding both end users and business users, Art. 3(8)(e).[33]

3. Rebuttal of the presumption (Art. 17(3))

22 A market investigation for the purpose of designating a gatekeeper is also required if the undertaking rebuts the presumption of its gatekeeper position under Art. 3(2). In September 2023, the Commission had launched four market investigations for designating gatekeepers. In these investigations, the Commission intended to examine whether the platform services of Microsoft named Bing, Edge and Microsoft Advertising and the platform service iMessage of Apple qualify as gateways although they submitted a rebuttal according to Art. 3(5).[34] In February 2024, the Commission closed these market investigations by accepting Microsoft's rebuttals. It decided not to designate the undertaking as gatekeepers in relation to the core platform services under investigation.[35] The Commission also concluded that Apple should not be designated as a gatekeeper in relation to its number independent interpersonal communication core platform service iMessage.[36] It found that the 'results of the market investigation indicate that business users who use Messages for Business generally consider this service to be of limited im-

---

[29] Cf. Podszun/Schwalbe NZKart 2017, 98 (100).

[30] Geradin, What is a digital gatekeeper? Which platforms should be captured by the EC proposal for a Digital Market Act?, working paper, 2.4.2021, p. 17 <https://papers.ssrn.com/sol3/papers.cfm?abstract_id=3788152> (last accessed: 10.9.2023).

[31] Commission 29.4.2024 – DMA.100047 – Apple –iPadOS.

[32] Commission 29.4.2024 – DMA.100047 mn. 32 et seqq. – Apple –iPadOS.

[33] Commission 29.4.2024 – DMA.100047 mn. 37 et seqq. – Apple –iPadOS.

[34] Commission 5.9.2023 – DMA.100028 – Microsoft – web browers; Commission 5.9.2023 – DMA.100034 – Microsoft – online adversting services; Commission 5.9.2023 – DMA.100015 – Microsoft – online search engines; Commission 5.9.2023 – DMA.100022 – Apple – number-independent interpersonal communications services.

[35] Commission 12.2.2024 – DMA.100028 – Microsoft – web browsers; Commission 12.2.2024 – DMA.100034 – Microsoft – online advertising services; Commission 12.2.2024 – DMA.100015 – Microsoft – online search engines.

[36] Commission 12.2.2024 – DMA.100022 – Apple – number-independent interpersonal communications services.

portance to reach end-users.'[37] In May 2024, the Commission has opened a market investigation into the online social networking service X.[38] Although the undertaking met the thresholds for designation, it submitted a rebuttal arguing that the social networking service does not qualify as an important gateway.[39]

In order to rebut the presumption, the undertaking must present **substantiated arguments** that it is not a gatekeeper despite reaching the thresholds, cf. Art. 3(5)(1) (→ § 12 mn. 52 et seq.). The arguments must be suitable to **manifestly call into question** the presumption. According to recital 23(1)(1), rebutting the presumption is to be limited to '**exceptional circumstances**'. On the one hand, these strict requirements prevent undertakings from blocking or delaying the notification procedure without reasonable grounds.[40] On the other hand, undertakings should remain able to raise serious objections to their presumed gatekeeper position.[41] 23

If an undertaking submits arguments to rebut the presumption, the Commission proceeds as follows: It first checks whether the arguments are **sufficiently substantiated.** If they are not, the Commission rejects them within 45 working days. In this case, the **notification procedure** within the meaning of Art. 3(3),(4) remains in force (→ § 12 mn. 53). No market investigation is initiated, cf. Art. 3(5)(2). If, however, the Commission is of the opinion that the undertaking has been able to manifestly call into question the presumption, it initiates a market investigation pursuant to Art. 17(3), Art. 3(5)(3) within **45 working days** after receiving the undertaking's information. 24

The arguments considered as substantiated are specified in recital 23(1)(3). Elements which directly relate to the quantitative criteria of Art. 3(2) are taken into account. These include the impact of the undertaking providing core platform services on the internal market beyond revenue or market cap, such as **its size in absolute terms**, and the number of Member States in which it is present. In addition, it shall be examined the extent to which the number of actual business users and end-users **exceeds the thresholds** and the importance of the undertaking's core platform service considering the **overall scale of activities**. The number of years over which the thresholds have been met is also factored in. Accordingly, the more the turnover and user figures of the undertaking concerned exceed the thresholds, the more difficult it will be to rebut the presumption. Justifications on **purely economic grounds** are not taken into account, as this is irrelevant for the gatekeeper position.[42] As an example, rec. 23(1)(2) mentions efficiency gains.[43] It would be beneficial for legal certainty if the Commission were to specify the criteria that can be taken into account for the purpose of rebutting the presumption by issuing guidelines.[44] In 2023, the Commission has taken up several aspects in Art. 2 of its Implementing Regulation (EU) 2023/814 of 14 April 2023 on detailed arrangements for the conduct of certain proceedings. However, room for specification remains. 25

---

37 Commission 12.2.2024 – DMA.100022, mn. 32 – Apple – number-independent interpersonal communications services.

38 Commission 13.5.2024 – DMA.100041 – X – online social networking services.

39 Commission, Commission designates Booking as a gatekeeper and opens a market investigation into X, press release, IP/24/2561, 13.5.2024 <https://ec.europa.eu/commission/presscorner/detail/en/IP_24_2561> (last accessed: 5.7.2024).

40 Hebers RDi 2022, 252 (255).

41 Geradin, What is a digital gatekeeper? Which platforms should be captured by the EC proposal for a Digital Market Act?, working paper, 2.4.2021, p. 15 <https://papers.ssrn.com/sol3/papers.cfm?abstract_id=3788152> (last accessed: 10.9.2023).

42 Käseberg/Gappa in Podszun DMA Art. 3 mn. 19.

43 Crit. on this Körber NZKart 2021, 379 (384).

44 Likewise Kumkar RDi 2022, 347 (350); Zimmer/Göhls ZWeR 2021, 29 (38 et seq.).

26 The required direct reference to the quantitative criteria clearly limits the possibility of rebutting the presumption.[45] Behind this is the goal of a quick and simple enforcement of the DMA.[46] In particular, the aspects that can be taken into account in the context of rebutting the presumption are **significantly narrower** than those included in the catalogue of qualitative criteria of Art. 3(8).[47] The latter is only the yardstick for designating a gatekeeper if either the thresholds are not reached or the arguments presented in relation to the quantitative criteria clearly invalidate the presumption.[48]

27 To what extent the high rebuttal requirements of Art. 3(5) are convincing depends largely on whether the presumption criteria chosen in Art. 3(2) for the gatekeeper position are persuasive.[49] While some in the legislative process called for further restrictions on rebuttal[50] or supported the current provision,[51] others see the current provision as a misguided simplification of enforcement that comes at the expense of a substantive review of the gatekeeper position and could lead to overenforcement.[52] In favour of the latter view is the fact that contestability could be ensured regardless of the quantitative criteria due to other market structures, e.g. if multi-homing is common and switching between platforms is possible for users without significant effort.[53] This could create competitive pressure and make it easier for (potential) competitors to enter the market.

28 If the Commission initiates a market investigation as a result of the rebuttal of the presumption, it examines whether a gatekeeper position exists on the basis of the **objective requirements** of Art. 3(1),(8). In this respect, the examination programme is similar to that of a market investigation initiated as a result of the thresholds not being reached (→ mn. 12 et seq.).[54] If the market investigation shows that the undertaking could not prove that the core platform services it provides do not constitute a gatekeeper position within the meaning of Art. 3(1), the Commission shall designate the undertaking as a gatekeeper in an implementing act (on the content of the designation decision → mn. 80 et seq.).

II. Systematic non-compliance (Art. 18)

1. Principles

29 The Commission may carry out a market investigation pursuant to Art. 18 in order to examine whether a gatekeeper **systematically fails to comply with its obligations** under

[45] Some even consider them to be factually unrebuttable, cf. Colomo, The Draft Digital Markets Act, p. 29 et seq.

[46] Haus/Weusthof WuW 2021, 318 (321); Petit Journal of European Competition Law & Practice 12(7) (2021), 529 (534).

[47] Dissenting Dietrich/Vinje CiR 2021, 33 (37).

[48] Zimmer/Göhls ZWeR 2021, 29 (38).

[49] Critically on this Colomo, The Draft Digital Markets Act, p. 30; Schweitzer ZEuP 2021, 503 (525).

[50] Schwab, Draft Report on the proposal for a regulation of the European Parliament and of the Council Contestable and fair markets in the digital sector, 2020/0374(COD), p. 34, who had called for '*compelling substantiated arguments*' in place of the wording now in force.

[51] Zimmer/Göhls ZWeR 2021, 29 (39); de Streel/Feasy/Kreamer/Monti, Making the Digital Markets Act More Resilient and Effective, 2021, p. 26.

[52] Geradin, What is a digital gatekeeper? Which platforms should be captured by the EC proposal for a Digital Market Act?, working paper, 2.4.2021, p. 15 <https://papers.ssrn.com/sol3/papers.cfm?abstract_id=3788152> (last accessed: 10.9.2023); Haus/Weusthof WuW 2021, 318 (321); Körber NZKart 2021, 379 (384).

[53] Haus/Weusthof WuW 2021, 318 (321); Körber NZKart 2021, 379 (384).

[54] De Streel/Feasy/Kreamer/Monti, Making the Digital Markets Act More Resilient and Effective, 2021, p. 24.

Art. 5–7 (→ § 13 mn. 22 et seq.). If the Commission comes to this conclusion and also discovers that the gatekeeper has maintained, strengthened or expanded its position, it can adopt **behavioural and structural remedies** in an implementing act (→ mn. 84 et seqq.). This is an important difference to the procedure according to Art. 20, with which the Commission prosecutes 'simple' infringements, i.e. those below the threshold of systematic non-compliance. In this procedure, the Commission cannot impose any remedies. It can only issue a decision of non-compliance (cf. Art. 29) and impose a fine (cf. Art. 30). The Union legislature considers fairness and contestability in the digital sector to be **particularly impaired** in the case of systematic infringements. Having repeatedly violated the obligations, the gatekeeper has shown some reluctance to comply with the rules.[55] In this respect, the enforcement mechanism of the DMA is more restrained than that of European competition law. According to Art. 7 of Regulation (EC) No. 1/2003, remedies can already be imposed in the event of a single competition law infringement.[56] The DMA, however, considers them **ultima ratio**.

2. Systematic non-compliance with the obligations under Art. 5, 6, 7

a) *Presumption of Art. 18(3)*

If the Commission has issued at least **three non-compliance decisions** within the meaning of Art. 29 (→ § 15 mn. 74 et seq.) against the gatekeeper within a period of **eight years** prior to the opening of the market investigation, the gatekeeper shall be deemed to have engaged in systematic non-compliance with the obligations pursuant to Art. 18(3). In the draft DMA, this period was still five years.[57] 30

Art. 18(3) contains an **irrebuttable presumption** of systematic non-compliance.[58] The wording of Art. 18(3), according to which systematic non-compliance 'shall be deemed to have engaged in systematic non-compliance' if the above-mentioned requirements are met, is similar to that of Art. 3(2), which establishes a presumption for the gatekeeper position. However, in contrast to Art. 3(2), the presumption laid down in Art. 18(3) does not allow undertakings to rebut it. This is consistent with rec. 75(1)(2), which states that 'this [systematic non-compliance] is the case' where the Commission has issued three non-compliance decisions within a period of eight years. 31

The wording of Art. 18(3) clarifies that systematic non-compliance does not require the gatekeeper to repeatedly violate the same obligation. Three violations of **different obligations** are sufficient. This is made clear in rec. 75(1)(2), according to which the non-compliance decisions 'can concern different obligations'. 32

Furthermore, it is not required that the non-compliance decisions concern the same core platform service. While it could be argued against this that the non-compliance must contribute to the maintenance, strengthening or expansion of the gatekeeper position (→ mn. 40 et seq.),[59] the wording of Art. 18(3) supports a broad understanding. It 33

---

[55] De Streel/Feasy/Kreamer/Monti, Making the Digital Markets Act More Resilient and Effective, 2021, p. 71.

[56] Gerpott NZKart, 2021, 273 (278). Crit. on this Monti European Competition and Regulatory Law Review 5(2) (2021), 90 (95).

[57] COM(2020) 842 final, 52.

[58] Bundeskartellamt [German Competition Authority], Digital Markets Act: Perspektiven des (inter)nationalen Wettbewerbsrechts, p. 33; Gerpott NZKart 2021, 273 (278). Dissenting Huerkamp/Nuys in Podszun DMA Art. 18 mn. 4.

[59] Coates, The EU's draft Digital Markets Act (DMA): enforcement powers, and the curious treatment of Article 25, 21st Century Competition: Reflections on Modern Antitrust, 3.2.2021 <https://www.twentyfirstcenturycompetition.com/2021/02/the-eus-draft-dma-enforcement-powers-and-the-curious-treatment-of-article-25/> (last accessed: 10.9.2023).

refers to non-compliance decisions that were issued against a gatekeeper in relation to 'any of its core platform services' (i.e. not necessarily 'the same core platform service'). This is in line with rec. 75(1)(2), which explicitly states that non-compliance decisions may concern '**different core platform services**'.

34 In contrast, there are stricter requirements regarding **repeated infringements** when it comes to determining the height of fines. The possibility of imposing a higher fine under Art. 30(2) (fine of up to 20 % (instead of 10 % under Art. 30(1)) of the total worldwide turnover achieved in the preceding financial year) only applies if the repeated non-compliance constitutes of 'the same or a similar infringement of an obligation laid down in Art. 5, 6 or 7 in relation to the same core platform service' (→ § 15 mn. 55).

35 Moreover, the three infringements need **not** be committed and fined **consecutively.** It is also possible that three Art. 20 proceedings are conducted against the gatekeeper at the same time and brought to a closure at the same time.[60]

36 It is questionable how to deal with **further infringements** that take place shortly after the first three infringements that constitute systematic non-compliance. If the Commission has already adopted remedies with regard to the first three infringements, which are not suitable to deal with the fourth and possibly fifth infringement, the question arises whether one further infringement is sufficient to reactivate the power to investigate the market or whether three further infringements (i.e. six infringements in total) are required instead. Notwithstanding the possibility of determining systematic non-compliance even beyond the requirements of Art. 18(3) (below → mn. 37 et seq.), the latter is likely to be the case. An infringement **cannot be used several times** to initiate a market investigation. In this case, the objectives of the DMA are not impaired with the intensity that Art. 18 requires for a market investigation. The risks posed by violations for which a market investigation has been carried out are mitigated by the remedies already imposed.

b) Systematics beyond Art. 18(3)?

37 Systematic non-compliance can also occur if the requirements of Art. 18(3) are not met.[61] Otherwise, there would have been no need for a separate introduction of a concept of systematic non-compliance in addition to Art. 18(3). The DMA does not contain any further indications to specify the term. However, Art. 18(3) suggests that the Union legislature understands the term 'systematic' in the sense of **repeated** or regular.[62] Grammatically, the term can also be understood as a subjective component of **intention** or

[60] Portuese, The Digital Markets Act: The Path to Overregulation, CPI Columns Europe, 13.6.2022 <https://www.competitionpolicyinternational.com/the-digital-markets-act-the-path-to-overregulation/> (last accessed: 10.9.2023).

[61] Similarly Coates, The EU's draft Digital Markets Act (DMA): enforcement powers, and the curious treatment of Article 25, 21st Century Competition: Reflections on Modern Antitrust, 3.2.2021 <https://www.twentyfirstcenturycompetition.com/2021/02/the-eus-draft-dma-enforcement-powers-and-the-curious-treatment-of-article-25/> (last accessed: 10.9.2023); Louven, Vorschlag für einen Digital Markets Act – Marktuntersuchungen, CR-online.de Blog, 13.3.2021 <https://www.cr-online.de/blog/2021/03/13/vorschlag-fuer-einen-digital-markets-act-marktuntersuchungen/> (last accessed: 10.9.2023): '*Der EU-Kommission bleibt der Spielraum zur eigenständigen Feststellung systematischer Verstöße.*'; Podszun HK-DMA/Huerkamp/Nuys DMA Art. 18 mn. 6.

[62] Budsizinki/Mendelsohn, Regulating Big Tech: From Competition Policy to Sector Regulation?, Ilmenau Economics Discussion Papers, 27(154), 10; Commission, DMA Impact Assessment Report, SWD(2020) 363 final, 16.12.2020, mn. 170 <https://ec.europa.eu/digital-single-market/en/news/impact-assessment-digital-markets-act> (last accessed: 10.9.2023); Schweitzer/Gutman, Unilateral Practices in the digital market: An overview of EU and national case law, e-competition 2021, Art. no. 101045.

orderliness.[63] However, proof of fault is not a constitutive condition for affirming systematic non-compliance.[64] The interpretation of the term should take into account which additional powers the Commission receives in the case of systematic non-compliance: It can adopt behavioural and structural remedies. Thus, systematic non-compliance are to be affirmed if remedies are necessary to restore contestable and fair markets in the digital sector.

Against this background, it should not only be considered the **number and frequency** of violations, but also their **severity and duration** as well as any intentional action when determining the systematic nature of non-compliance.[65] For example, it has been suggested that systematic non-compliance should already be affirmed in the case of two infringements, provided that the same obligation is affected, because this suggests that remedies are necessary to restore contestability and fairness.[66] 38

In the absence of sufficient evidence of systematic non-compliance, the Commission cannot initiate a market investigation. Instead, the procedure under Art. 20 is available, which can be terminated by a non-compliance decision (→ § 15 mn. 74 et seqq.). In case of urgency due to the risk of serious and irreparable damage for business users or end users of gatekeepers, it may adopt an implementing act ordering interim measures against a gatekeeper pursuant to Art. 24 (→ § 15 mn. 84 et seqq.). 39

3. Maintaining, strengthening or expanding the gatekeeper position

The Commission can only impose remedies if, in addition to the systematic non-compliance, a further condition is met: the gatekeeper acting in breach of obligation must have maintained, strengthened or extended its position. This is to be examined on the basis of the **objective requirements** of Art. 3(1). According to rec. 75(1)(3), maintenance, strengthening or expansion can be presumed if, despite the enforcement actions taken by the Commission, the gatekeeper still holds or has further consolidated or entrenched its importance as a gateway for business users to reach end users. 40

The wording of Art. 18(1) does not make it clear whether systematic non-compliance must be the **cause** for maintaining, strengthening or extending the gatekeeper position. The problem is defused in comparison to the regulation proposed in the draft version,[67] as it is now sufficient that the gatekeeper maintains its position. The draft version had called for a strengthening or expansion. Nevertheless, the question arises whether the systematic nature of non-compliance must have helped the gatekeeper to prevent a weakening of its position. The need for a causal link is supported by the fact that systematic non-compliance poses **particular risks** to the goals of the DMA, insofar as the gatekeeper was at least able to maintain or even strengthen its position as a result.[68] The very fact that the gatekeeper was able to maintain its position shows that non-compliance decisions and the imposition of fines were not sufficient to ward off the threats to contestability and fairness in digital markets. Accordingly, a causal link between systematic non- 41

[63] Coates, The EU's draft Digital Markets Act (DMA): enforcement powers, and the curious treatment of Article 25, 21st Century Competition: Reflections on Modern Antitrust, 3.2.2021 <https://www.twentyfirstcenturycompetition.com/2021/02/the-eus-draft-dma-enforcement-powers-and-the-curious-treatment-of-article-25/> (last accessed: 10.9.2023).

[64] Huerkamp/Nuys in Podszun DMA Art. 18 mn. 10.

[65] Huerkamp/Nuys in Podszun DMA Art. 18 mn. 7.

[66] Orange, Committed to Europe: Orange's position on the European Commission's proposal for a Digital Markets Act Regulation, 1.4.2021 <https://www.orange.com/sites/orangecom/files/documents/2021-05/Orange%20views%20on%20the%20Digital%20Markets%20Act_April%202021.pdf> (last accessed: 10.9.2023).

[67] Cf. COM(2020) 842 final, 52.

[68] Monti European Competition and Regulatory Law Review 5(2) (2021), 90 (95).

compliance and maintenance, strengthening or expanding the gatekeeper position is required.[69]

III. New services and new practices (Art. 19)

1. Proposals to amend the DMA

42 The Commission may conduct a market investigation under Art. 19 to examine whether **new platform services** should be included in Art. 2 no. 2 and to identify **new practices** that limit the contestability of digital markets or are unfair, but which the DMA has so far not effectively addressed. The aim of such a market investigation is to identify the **need for updating** the rules of the DMA. Therefore, the Commission concludes it with the publication of a report, to which it may attach a proposal to amend the regulation or a draft delegated act (→ mn. 98 et seqq.).

43 With this type of market investigation, the Union legislator has partially taken up the ideas originally discussed under the **New Competition Tool**. It had been considered to enable a market investigation to identify structural risks for competition without already requiring indications of entrepreneurial conduct in breach of obligation.[70] The reason for this is the dynamic nature of the digital economy. As a result, the services in the digital sector and the types of practices relating to these services can change quickly and to a significant extent, cf. rec. 77(1)(1). Without a swift amendment of the provisions of the DMA, the regulation would run counter to the purpose of effectively regulating the risks to **contestability and fairness** in digital markets (cf. rec. 77(1)(2)). When conducting a market investigation pursuant to Art. 19, the Commission must, according to rec. 77(1)(6), develop a **solid evidentiary basis** enabling it to make proposals for adjustment. Pursuant to Art. 19(1)(2), it must also take into account all relevant results from proceedings pursuant to Art. 101, 102 TFEU concerning digital markets as well as any other relevant developments. In the recent past, it has been mainly antitrust abuse proceedings in which abusive practices in the digital sector have been assessed.

44 Pursuant to rec. 78(1)(2) and (3) the possibility of the Commission to examine an infringement of Art. 101, 102 TFEU in connection with new services and new practices remains unaffected. Any antitrust proceedings are governed by the provisions of Regulation (EC) No. 1/2003. Rec. 78 (1)(4) emphasises that in urgent cases where there is a risk of serious and irreparable damage to competition, the Commission may consider taking **interim measures pursuant to Art. 8 of Regulation (EC) No. 1/2003**. When identifying new services and practices under Art. 19, it must be taken into account that the objectives of the DMA are **not identical** to those of European competition law.[71] According to Art. 1(6), rec. 11(1)(2), the objectives complement each other. Nevertheless, the purpose of preserving contestability and fairness in digital markets differs from the protection of undistorted competition.

---

[69] Jovanovic/Greiner MMR 2021, 678 (681); Louven, Vorschlag für einen Digital Markets Act – Marktuntersuchungen, CR-online.de Blog, 13.3.2021 <https://www.cr-online.de/blog/2021/03/13/vorschlag-fuer-einen-digital-markets-act-marktuntersuchungen/> (last accessed: 10.9.2023); Verbraucherzentrale Bundesverband, Wahlfreiheit von Verbrauchern und effektiven Wettbewerb in digitalen Märkten sicherstellen, p. 19; dissenting Podszun HK-DMA/Huerkamp/Nuys DMA Art. 18 mn. 15.

[70] Motta/Peitz/Schweitzer Market Investigations p. 1 (12). Originally, however, it was further considered to combine market investigation with powers of intervention.

[71] On the controversial relationship between the DMA and competition law, see Budzinski/Mendelsohn, Regulating Big Tech: From Competition Policy to Sector Regulation?, Ilmenau Economics Discussion Papers, Vol. 27, No. 154, 15 ff; Harta NZKart 2022, 102 (105).

2. New services

In a market investigation pursuant to Art. 19, the Commission may examine whether new services should be included in the list of core platform services in **Art. 2 no. 2** (→ § 12 mn. 6 et seq.). According to rec. 77(1)(5), it may propose to amend or further detail the list. The market investigation should provide a solid evidentiary basis for this. The aim of any proposed amendment is to keep Art. 2 up to date and thus provide an effective and holistic regulatory solution, cf. rec. 77(1)(2). If the Commission comes to the conclusion that it wishes to propose an amendment, it may append a **legislative proposal** to its report (→ mn. 98 et seq.). 45

3. New practices

The Commission may launch a market investigation to identify practices that limit the contestability of core platform services or are unfair but are not addressed by the current version of the DMA. 46

According to rec. 69(1)(1), the obligations of the DMA should only be updated if a thorough investigation into the nature and impact of specific practices show that they are unfair or limiting contestability in the same manner as the unfair practices laid down in the DMA. With regard to the scope of the current set of obligations, the **anti-circumvention provision of Art. 13** must be taken into account (→ § 13 mn. 19 et seq.). According to this, a gatekeeper is also prohibited from circumventing the obligations in any of the ways standardised in Art. 13(5)–(7). In particular, a gatekeeper may not engage in any conduct that undermines effective compliance with the obligations, regardless of whether the conduct is of a contractual, commercial, technical or of any other nature, or consists in the use of behavioural techniques or interface design, cf. Art. 13(4), rec. 79(1)(3). 47

In order to update the set of obligations, the Commission cannot only submit a **legislative proposal**. According to Art. 49 in conjunction with Art. 12, it also has the power to adopt **delegated acts** (→ mn. 100 et seqq.; → § 13 mn. 15 et seqq.). Art. 12(5) specifies when the objectives of contestability and fairness give rise to adopting delegated acts.[72] A practice limits the contestability of core platform services if it is engaged in by gatekeepers and is capable of impeding innovation and limiting choice for business users and end user, cf. Art. 12(5)(a). A practice is unfair if there is an imbalance between the rights and obligations of business users and the gatekeeper obtains an advantage from business users that is disproportionate to the service provided by that gatekeeper to those business users, cf. Art. 12(5)(b). 48

C. Opening

I. Competence

Market investigations are carried out by the **Commission,** cf. Art. 17(1), Art. 18(1), Art. 19(1). According to Art. 16(5), it may ask one or more national competent authorities to assist it in its market investigation. Art. 38(6) concretises this by stating that the Commission may request the assistance of **national competition authorities.**[73] For market investigations into new services and new practices, Art. 40(7) emphasises that 49

[72] Seeliger in Podszun DMA Art. 12 mn. 25 et seqq.
[73] Huerkamp/Nuys in Podszun DMA Art. 16 mn. 27.

the **high-level group** may provide the Commission with expertise on the need to amend, add or remove rules in the DMA.

50 The consultation of further bodies is not mandatory for the Commission.[74] This also applies to the Digital Markets Advisory Committee pursuant to Art. 50(1) as well as the high-level group for the Digital Markets Act to be established pursuant to Art. 40.

51 For the practical arrangements of the proceedings concerning the market investigations, the Commission may adopt **implementing acts** pursuant to Art. 46(1)(i) to provide for detailed rules.

II. Initial suspicion

52 Market investigations are **administrative procedures**. Art. 16 merely sets out formal requirements for the opening of a market investigation. Art. 17 of Regulation (EC) No. 1/2003 states that where the trend of trade between Member States, the rigidity of prices or other circumstances 'suggest' that competition may be restricted or distorted within the common market the Commission may conduct its inquiry. In contrast to that, the wording of Art. 17–19 is vague regarding the requirement of an **initial suspicion.** There should at least be sufficient indications for the existence of a specific reason to investigate the market.[75] This means that there must either be indications of a gatekeeper position, systematic non-compliance or the existence of new services or new practices.

III. Initiation ex officio

53 The Commission generally initiates a market investigation **ex officio**. In doing so, it usually has the **discretion to take action.**[76] Accordingly, it does not have to initiate a market investigation even if there is an initial suspicion. Criteria for the decision to open an investigation are, among other things, the importance of the investigation for realising the objectives of the DMA, the Union interest or the private interests of affected users.[77] The principles set out in recital 69 on the procedure of Art. 20 apply mutatis mutandis to market investigations. Accordingly, the Commission decides at its own discretion on the initiation of proceedings.

IV. Initiation due to a request

54 Member States may request the Commission to open a market investigation pursuant to **Art. 41**. The requirements for an **initiation request** depend on the reason for the market investigation. Both a market investigation for designating a gatekeeper, cf. Art. 17, and a market investigation due to new services and new practices, cf. Art. 19, can only be requested by **at least three Member States**, cf. Art. 41(1),(3). In the case of systematic non-compliance already **one Member State** may request to open a market investigation, cf. Art. 41(2).

55 In all cases, the requesting Member States shall provide reasonable grounds supported by evidence in accordance with Art. 41(4). For a request regarding a market investiga-

---

[74] Krauskopf/Brösamle in Schmidt/Hübener Der neue DMA § 8 mn. 28.

[75] Krauskopf/Brösmle in Schmidt/Hübener Der neue DMA § 8 mn. 7; Zober NZKart 2021, 611 (613); dissenting Huerkamp/Nuys in Podszun DMA Art. 16 mn. 18.

[76] Huerkamp/Nuys in Podszun DMA Art. 16 mn. 8.

[77] Cf. on competition law Ritter/Wirtz in Immenga/Mestmäcker VO 1/2003 Art. 7 mn. 10.

tion in relation to new services and new practices, the evidence shall include information on newly introduced offers of products, services, software or features which raise concerns of contestability or fairness, whether implemented in the context of existing core platform services or otherwise. Within **four months** of receiving a request, the Commission shall assess whether there are reasonable grounds to open a market investigation pursuant to Art. 41(5). The Commission is obliged to examine the initiation request. However, it still has **discretion** in deciding whether to initiate an investigation.[78] The Commission shall publish its results of the **assessment** of the request.

In the course of the legislative process, it was proposed to allow for a request for initiation from private parties who are significantly affected by breaches of obligations under Art. 5, 6 and 7.[79] The Union legislator did not take up this proposal. According to Art. 27(1), private parties only have the possibility to inform the Commission or the national competition authorities about practices or behaviour of gatekeepers that may that falls within the scope of the DMA. National competition authorities have to transfer the information to the Commission under Art. 27(3) if they consider that a violation of Art. 5–7 has occurred. 56

V. Opening decision

The market investigation shall be opened by a **formal decision** pursuant to Art. 16(1). The decision shall state the date of opening of the market investigation, the subject matter, and purpose of the market investigation, cf. Art. 16(3). Since the Commission keeps its decisions to initiate sector enquiries brief, cf. Art. 17 of Regulation (EC) No 1/2003, it can be assumed that this will also be the case for decisions to open market investigations.[80] 57

In contrast to what was still envisaged in the draft proposal of the DMA,[81] the opening decision shall be **published**, cf. Art. 44(1)(1). In the publication, the Commission must state the names of the parties involved and the main content of the decision, taking into account legitimate interests of gatekeepers or third parties in the **protection of their confidential information**, cf. Art. 44(1)(2), (2). 58

D. Implementation

I. Powers of the Commission

The Commission's powers in a market investigation are similar to those in a sector inquiry as defined in Art. 17 of Regulation (EC) No 1/2003, but in some cases go beyond them. They are intended to enable the Commission to make a well-founded decision on a thorough factual basis.[82] 59

[78] Gappa/Käseberg in Podszun DMA Art. 41 mn. 3; Krauskopf/Brösamle in Schmidt/Hübener Der neue DMA § 8 mn. 29.

[79] Künstner, Dangers of Legal and Factual Circumvention of the Digital Markets Act's Objectives and Regulatory Content: A Proposal to Strengthen the Digital Markets Act in the Current Legislative Process, LobbyControl – Initiative for Transparency and Democracy, 22.2.2022, p. 6 <https://www.lobbycontrol.de/wp-content/uploads/LobbyControl-Gutachten-Digital-Markets-Act.pdf> (last accessed: 10.9.2023).

[80] Zober NZKart 2021, 611 (613).

[81] COM(2020) 842 final, 61.

[82] Zimmer/Göhls ZWeR 2021, 29 (45).

60 Pursuant to Art. 21, the Commission may request **information** by simple request or by decision (→ § 15 mn. 16). The power to request information is more far-reaching than that provided for in Art. 18 of Regulation (EC) No. 1/2003 for antitrust proceedings, since according to Art. 21, rec. 80(1)(2), the Commission may request access to any data and algorithms of undertakings and information about testing, and explanations of them.[83] According to recital 80(1)(2), this power is to be granted to the Commission regardless of who possesses this information. It is also independent of the form of the information, its format, the storage medium or the place of storage. The undertaking concerned may have to provide additional explanations. Its obligations to cooperate tend to be more far-reaching than in cartel proceedings.[84] The Union legislator considered this necessary given the information asymmetry which characterises the digital sector.

61 The Commission may also interview any natural or legal person who has consented thereto, cf. Art. 22 (→ § 15 mn. 21). The **interviews** may be recorded by any technical means. Pursuant to Art. 23, the Commission is also authorised to conduct **inspections.** This power, known as 'dawn raids', is modelled on the corresponding power in antitrust proceedings, cf. Art. 20 of Regulation (EC) No. 1/2003 (→ § 15, mn. 24).

62 For market investigations due to new services and new practices, Art. 19(2) adds that the Commission may **consult third parties.** These include, inter alia, business users and end users of services under investigation, as well as business users and end users who are subject to practices under investigation.

63 If the information consulted by the Commission contains **professional secrecy**, it is not authorised to disclose them under Art. 36(4). In its preliminary findings in a market investigation, the Commission must ensure that interested third parties can only inspect a non-confidential summary, Art. 18(5)(1).

II. Rights and obligations of undertakings

64 In the context of the market investigation, the **fundamental rights** of the parties, in particular their right to be heard, must be protected.[85] In market investigations for designating gatekeepers (Art. 17) and in market investigations into systematic non-compliance (Art. 18), undertakings have the opportunity to **comment** on the Commission's preliminary findings and the intended measures pursuant to Art. 34(1). For this purpose, the Commission may set a time limit of **at least 14 days**, cf. Art. 34(2). According to Art. 34(3), the Commission is only allowed to base its decisions on such preliminary findings on which the undertakings have had the opportunity to comment.

65 According to Art. 34(4)(2), the rights of defence of the undertakings concerned include the **right to access** the Commission's **file** in accordance with the disclosure requirements. Confidential information and internal documents of the Commission and the competent authorities of the Member States are excluded from inspection. In particular, correspondence between the Commission and the competent authorities of the Member States is excluded.

66 When the Commission initiates a market investigation with a view to designating a gatekeeper, the undertaking concerned also has another responsibility: If it fails to comply with the investigative measures ordered by the Commission even after the expiry of a reasonable period of time, the Commission may designate the undertaking as gatekeeper on the basis of the facts available to it, cf. Art. 3(8)(4).

---

[83] Krauskopf/Brösamle in Schmidt/Hübener Der neue DMA § 8 mn. 33.
[84] Zober NZKart 2021, 611 (613).
[85] COM(2020) 842 final, 5; Zober NZKart 2021, 611 (613).

III. Duration

1. General remarks

Different maximum durations of investigation are provided for each type of market investigation. In the case of market investigations regarding the designation of a gatekeeper or systematic non-compliance, additional deadlines apply within which the Commission must notify the undertakings concerned of its preliminary findings. With clear deadlines, the Union legislator wants to promote legal certainty according to rec. 73(1)(2). **Possibilities for extension** are only provided for in the case of market investigations to examine systematic non-compliance. This is intended to **accelerate** the enforcement of the DMA.[86] In its impact assessment report, the Commission had even advocated mandatory deadlines.[87] **67**

During the legislative process, the time limits in the draft version have been repeatedly criticised. They were considered too long, given the objective of the investigations.[88] The time limits now in force range from five months for market investigations in cases where an undertaking rebuts the gatekeeper presumptino (Art. 17) to 18 months for market investigations with reagrd to new services and practices (Art. 19). They represent a compromise between the procedural objective of examining the relevant subject matter in detail and reducing information asymmetries on the one hand, and the concern for speedy enforcement or updating of the DMA on the other hand.[89] **68**

2. Market investigation for designating gatekeepers

According to Art. 17(1)(2), a market investigation for designating gatekeepers shall be terminated within **12 months** if the undertaking does not meet the thresholds of Art. 3(2). Pursuant to Art. 17(2)(1), the Commission shall notify the undertaking concerned of its **preliminary findings** after only **six months.** It must explain whether, in its preliminary view, it is appropriate to designate the undertaking as a gatekeeper. It also names the core platform services which it considers to be affected according to its preliminary findings. **69**

If the market investigation is initiated as a result of a clear rebuttal of the gaterkeeper presumption under Art. 3(2), the Commission shall conclude the investigation within **five months,** cf. Art. 17(3)(1). According to Art. 17(3)(2), it shall communicate its preliminary findings after three months. In this case, the undertaking itself has already provided some facts and arguments for the assessment. **70**

The time limit is calculated on the basis of the date indicated as the date of initiation in the opening decision (→ mn. 57). The wording only requires the Commission to '**endeavour**' to meet the deadline. This contrasts with the mandatory nature of the time limit, which was emphasised in the legislative process. A systematic consideration also speaks in favour of this: Only for market investigations as defined in Art. 18 does the DMA explicitly provide for a possibility to extend the deadline. Art. 17, 19 do not contain any corresponding provisions. Therefore, the time limit of 12 months should nor- **71**

---

[86] Podszun/Bongartz/Langenstein EuCML 2021, 60 (66).

[87] Commission, DMA Impact Assessment Report, SWD(2020) 363 final, 16.12.2020, mn. 194 <https://ec.europa.eu/digital-single-market/en/news/impact-assessment-digital-markets-act> (last accessed: 10.9.2023).

[88] Podszun/Bongartz/Langenstein EuCML 2021, 60 (66); Zimmer/Göhsl ZWeR 2021, 29 (45).

[89] Schweitzer/Gutman, Unilateral Practices in the digital market: An overview of EU and national case law, e-competition 2021, Art. no. 101045.

mally be observed and may only be exceeded in exceptional cases if the Commission provides reasons for this.[90]

3. Market investigation into systematic non-compliance

72 A market investigation into systematic non-compliance must be completed within **12 months** from the date specified in the opening decision pursuant to Art. 18(1)(2). The Commission must issue **preliminary findings** within **six months.** In it, it shall explain whether it takes the preliminary view that the gatekeeper has systematically failed to comply with the obligations of the DMA and what remedies it considers necessary and appropriate, cf. Art. 18(4).

73 Interested **third parties** may also comment on the preliminary findings. Art. 18(5) provides that the Commission shall publish a non-confidential summary of the case and the remedies that it is considering imposing. Third parties may comment on this within a reasonable period of time. In addition to allowing interested parties to participate, this is intended to provide a means of reviewing the remedies before they are applied, cf. rec. 75(1)(6). The market investigation into systematic non-compliance is the only type of market investigation for which the participation of third parties is mandatory.[91]

74 As the only one of the three types of market investigation, procedures within the meaning of Art. 18 **can be extended at any time**. According to Art. 18(7), this applies both to the time limit for publishing the preliminary findings and to the time limit for adopting the final implementing act. The extension must be **objectively justified** and proportionate. Generally, the focus will be on the **investigative burden** associated with reviewing the maintenance, strengthening or expansion of the gatekeeper position as a result of systematic non-compliance. In addition, the examination of which remedial measures (→ mn. 84 et seq.) are appropriate and proportionate can be time-consuming. The same holds true if the gatekeeper offers commitments (→ mn. 91 et seq.).

75 The deadlines cannot be extended arbitrarily. Extensions may not exceed a total of six months. Consequently, the Commission must issue its preliminary findings after 12 months at the latest and its final decision **after 18 months at the latest**. In contrast, no statutory deadlines are provided for the gatekeeper to make commitments. Nor are there any for the implementation of remedial measures.

4. Market investigation into new services and new practices

76 The longest (initial) period is provided for in Art. 19 for the market investigation in relation to new services and new practices. It is **18 months**. There is no extension option. In the draft DMA, a period of 24 months was proposed,[92] which was criticised as too long.[93] Rec. 77(1)(4) now states that the Commission should review whether the DMA need to be amended within an appropriate time frame in order to ensure legal certainty. Even if the market investigation within the meaning of Art. 19 is not directed against a specific undertaking, it can still hang like a 'sword of Damocles' over already designated gatekeepers who expect to have to quickly adapt their business models to a modified DMA obligations catalogue.

---

[90] Huerkamp/Nuys in Podszun DMA Art. 17 mn. 7.

[91] Huerkamp/Nuys in Podszun DMA Art. 18 mn. 56; Krauskopf/Brösamle in Schmidt/Hübener Der neue DMA § 8 mn. 16.

[92] COM(2020) 842 final, 53.

[93] Haus/Weusthof WuW 2021, 318 (321); Monti, The Digital Markets Act – Institutional Design and Suggestions for Improvement, TILEC Discussion Paper No. 2021-04, 11; Podszun/Bongartz/Langenstein EuCML 2021, 60 (66).

E. Termination

I. Designation decision (Art. 17)

1. Form and procedure

77 The Commission concludes a market investigation on the designation of a gatekeeper, cf. Art. 17, with an **implementing act** in which it sets out its decision. According to Art. 290 TFEU, an implementing act is a legal act without legislative character.[94] In principle, the implementation of Union legal acts falls within the competence of the Member States. However, if there is a need to ensure uniform implementation, the Commission (and in exceptional cases the Council) may be empowered to adopt implementing acts.[95] In market investigations for the purpose of designating a gatekeeper, the Commission adopts an individual implementing decision. It will designate a gatekeeper if it comes to this conclusion in its investigation.

78 The individual implementing decision shall be adopted in accordance with the **committee procedure** referred to in Art. 50(2), rec. 100(1)(2) (→ § 11 mn. 50). Art. 4 of Regulation (EU) No. 182/2011 specifies the procedure: First, the Digital Markets Advisory Committee, Art. 50(1), shall give its opinion. In the event of a vote, this shall take place on the basis of a simple majority of its members. The Commission then decides on the draft implementing act to be adopted. In doing so, it shall take as far as possible into account the outcome of the Committee's deliberations and the opinion delivered.

79 Pursuant to Art. 50(4), the Commission shall communicate the opinion of the Committee together with the decision to the addressee of the individual decision. It shall also publish the opinion together with the individual decision, subject to professional secrecy.

2. Content

a) Principles

80 In the designation decision, the Commission shall list the relevant **core platform services** which are provided by the undertaking, and which are an important gateway for business users to reach end users pursuant to Art. 3(1)(b), cf. Art. 3(9). The gatekeeper shall fulfil the obligations set out in Art. 5, 6, 7 no later than six months after one of its core platform services has been listed in the designation decision, cf. Art. 3(10).

b) Designation of gatekeepers without an entrenched and durable position

81 The Commission may also designate an undertaking as a gatekeeper if it does not yet have an entrenched and durable position in its operations, but will foreseeably enjoy such a position in the **near future** (emerging gatekeepers). In this case, the decision is based on a **prediction**. A timely intervention of the obligations shall prevent a tilting of the market.[96] In the designation decision, only those obligations are to be declared applicable that are necessary and appropriate to prevent that the gatekeeper concerned achieves an entrenched and durable position in its operations., cf. rec. 74(1)(3) (→ § 12 mn. 56). Art. 17(4) lists the obligations that can be declared applicable to emerging gatekeepers. These are Art. 5(3)–(6) and Art. 6(4),(7),(9),(10),(13) (→ § 13 mn. 25 et seqq.).

---

[94] Krauskopf/Brösamle in Schmidt/Hübener Der neue DMA § 8 mn. 11.
[95] Nettesheim in Grabitz/Hilf/Nettesheim TFEU Art. 291 mn. 2.
[96] Körber NZKart 2021, 379 (383).

82 The criteria of 'an entrenched and durable position in the near future' and 'foreseeability' are accompanied by legal uncertainty. The advance intervention option is criticized in part to the effect that a prediction regarding a future tipping of the market is hardly reliable.[97] Some are of the opinion that in view of the duration of the market investigation of up to 12 months, the designation decision may be issued too late, even with regard to an emerging gatekeeper. The market could already collapse while the investigation is in progress.[98]

II. Remedies (Art. 18)

1. Form and procedure

83 If the Commission concludes in its market investigation that the gatekeeper has systematically failed to comply with its obligations under Art. 5–7 and as a result has maintained, strengthened or extended its position, it may lay down **remedies** in an implementing act. The **implementing act** is adopted under the **advisory procedure** of Art. 50(2) (→ mn. 77 et seq.). The reason for the adoption distinguishes the implementing act from those adopted under the regulatory dialogue pursuant to Art. 8. In the latter case, implementing acts serve to establish measures to ensure compliance with the gatekeeper obligations under Art. 6, 7. The gatekeeper can request the initiation of a regulatory dialogue. However, the opening of the dialogue is at the discretion of the Commission (→ § 13 mn. 11). In this respect, it is a matter of coordinating the implementation of its duties with the Commission.[99] The imposition of remedies after conducting a market investigation, in contrast, serves to restore contestability and fairness after systematic non-compliance.

2. Content

a) Behavioural remedies

84 The Commission may impose both behavioural and structural remedies. The choice of remedies must respect the **principle of proportionality**. Remedies must be proportionate and necessary to ensure effective compliance with the obligations, cf. Art. 18(1)(2).

85 **Behavioural** remedies include an order to bring an infringement to an end, and to refrain from taking any action having the same effect.[100] The order may, for example, consist of ordering the gatekeeper concerned to refrain from signing in end users to other services of the gatekeeper in order to combine personal data, cf. Art. 5(2)(d), or from preventing or restricting users from raising any issue of non-compliance by the gatekeeper with any relevant public authority, cf. Art. 5(6). Remedies can also require the undertaking to act positively.[101] What these measures will look like is still unclear. This

[97] Dietrich/Vinje Cri 2021, 33 (37); Petit Journal of European Competition Law & Practice 12(7) (2021), 529 (534).

[98] Zimmer/Göhsl ZWeR 2021, 29 (44).

[99] Herbers RDi 2022, 252 (258).

[100] Anweiler in Loewenheim/Meessen/Riesenkampff/Kersting/Meyer-Lindemann VO 1/2003 Art. 7 mn. 49.

[101] Huerkamp/Nuys in Podszun DMA Art. 18 mn. 21; Breit in Von der Groeben/Schwarze/Hatje VO 1/2003 Art. 7 mn. 13.

applies in particular to those measures with which the Commission intends to remedy systemic or structural deficiencies beyond individual breaches of obligations.[102]

Art. 18(2) clarifies that the remedies may also include the temporary prohibition of the gatekeeper concerned from entering into concentrations (cf. Art. 3 of Regulation (EC) No. 139/2004). The prohibition may be ordered with regard to core platform services or other services provided in the digital sector or enabling the collection of data, which are affected by the systematic non-compliance. If the Commission orders a prohibition of concentration, it supplements the notification requirements about intended concentrations, cf. Art. 14. The question whether the Commission can issue a temporary prohibition of concentration does not depend on whether the prohibited concentrations fall under the regime of European merger control pursuant to Art. 1 of Regulation (EC) No. 139/2004. The assessment of mergers under the SIEC test is equally irrelevant. The Commission may also temporarily prohibit concentrations that would not have led to a significant impediment to effective competition. Instead, the relevant question is whether the prohibition of concentration is suitable to remedy the systematic infringement in a proportionate manner.[103] 86

b) Structural remedies

Structural remedies typically interfere with property rights of the gatekeeper concerned.[104] They affect the corporate structure.[105] These include, for example, the sale or division of parts of the undertaking.[106] As a last resort, unbundling may be considered. 87

Unlike Art. 16(2) of the draft DMA,[107] Art. 18 **does not contain a provision on the subsidiarity of structural remedies**. In this respect, the legal consequences of the DMA go beyond those under Art. 7 of Regulation (EC) No. 1/2003. In antitrust proceedings, structural remedies can only be imposed if there are no equally effective behavioural remedies or if these would impose a greater burden on the undertaking concerned. In this respect, the Union legislator has taken up the criticism of the subsidiarity clause expressed in the legislative procedure. It was argued that structural remedies are not subsidiary in every case, even if the principle of proportionality is upheld.[108] Moreover, in view of the diverging goals, it was not appropriate to model Art. 18 on the rules of the antitrust procedure.[109] 88

Despite the lack of a subsidiarity clause, the **principle of proportionality** must be observed in the choice of remedies to be imposed.[110] Regarding structural remedies, it is pointed out that their restrained use in the context of platform regulation is in line with the approach to electronic communications regulation that has been pursued by European policymakers for years.[111] Moreover, the potentially disruptive nature of innovations in the digital environment should be taken into account when identifying 89

---

[102] Budzinski/Mendelsohn, Regulating Big Tech: From Competition Policy to Sector Regulation?, Ilmenau Economics Discussion Papers, Vol. 27, No. 154, 10.

[103] With further details Huerkamp/Nuys in Podszun DMA Art. 18 mn. 38–50.

[104] Cf. Breit in von der Groeben/Schwarze/Hatje VO 1/2003 Art. 7 mn. 14.

[105] Huerkamp/Nuys in Podszun DMA Art. 18 mn. 22.

[106] Gerpott NZKart 2021, 273 (278).

[107] COM(2020) 842 final, 52. Art. 16(2) of the draft version read: 'The Commission may impose structural remedies under paragraph 1 only if either no equally effective behavioural remedy can be considered or if such a remedy would be more burdensome for the gatekeeper concerned than a structural remedy.'

[108] Podszun/Bongartz/Langenstein EuCML 2021, 60 (66).

[109] Larouche/de Streel Journal of European Competition Law & Practice 12(7) (2021), 542 (553).

[110] Podszun/Bongartz/Langenstein EuCML 2021, 60 (66).

[111] Larouche/de Streel Journal of European Competition Law & Practice 12(7) (2021), 542 (553).

appropriate remedies.[112] Such innovations could be initiated, inter alia, by platform operators restructuring or expanding their business model to compete with other providers. In view of this, structural remedies could possibly have an inhibiting effect on innovation.[113]

90 When it comes to competition law enforcement, structural remedies for repeated infringements have, as far as can be seen, not yet acquired any practical significance.[114] Whether they are suitable to preserve contestability and fairness of digital markets in cases of systematic non-compliance is also assessed differently. With reference to the generally difficult assessment of the suitability of structural measures, it is argued that they will also prove largely fruitless within the context of the DMA.[115]

c) Commitments

91 A gatekeeper may offer **commitments** pursuant to Art. 25 in order to remedy the identified systematic non-compliance and to ensure compliance (→ § 15 mn. 34). If the Commission considers the commitments offered to be suitable, it can **declare** them **binding** in an implementing act. Some are of the opinion that the competitive settlement procedure would have offered a more suitable option for consensual dispute resolution with gatekeepers.[116] In the case of systematic non-compliance, the gatekeeper has already behaved unlawfully to such an extent that it must be denied the 'offer' of commitments.[117]

92 The DMA only provides for the possibility of commitments in the context of market investigations. In proceedings under Art. 20, which may be initiated for a single breach of obligations, gatekeepers cannot offer commitments. This has been criticised.[118] Some believe that commitments could expedite the process, helping to eliminate violations in a timely manner.[119] Others point out that commitments can increase investigation efforts.[120] The DMA aims to create an enforcement mechanism that responds to the dynamics of digital business models. It is therefore understandable that the Union legislator wanted to reserve the possibility of commitments for market investigations. These are designed as a lengthy, investigation-intensive procedure. Commitments allow gatekeepers to bring in expertise and thus contribute to reliably reducing the risks to contestability and fairness posed by systematic non-compliance.

93 If a gatekeeper offers commitments, it is up to the Commission to examine whether they are suitable to ensure effective compliance with the obligations under Art. 5–7. In doing so, it may, in accordance with rec. 76(1)(3), take into account the tests carried out by the gatekeeper to demonstrate the effectiveness of the commitments offered in practice. If the Commission finds that the commitments are suitable and therefore intends to make them binding, it will first publish a non-confidential summary of the case and the main content of the commitments, cf. Art. 18(6). This is to give interested third parties

---

[112] Larouche/de Streel Journal of European Competition Law & Practice 12(7) (2021), 542 (553).

[113] Larouche/de Streel Journal of European Competition Law & Practice 12(7) (2021), 542 (553).

[114] Commission, Impact Assessment Report, SWD(2020) 363 final, 16.12.2020, mn. 172.

[115] Budsizinki/Mendelsohn, Regulating Big Tech: From Competition Policy to Sector Regulation?, Ilmenau Economics Discussion Papers, 27(154), 10.

[116] De Streel/Feasy/Kreamer/Monti, Making the Digital Markets Act More Resilient and Effective, 2021, p. 71.

[117] De Streel/Feasy/Kreamer/Monti, Making the Digital Markets Act More Resilient and Effective, 2021, p. 71.

[118] Monti European Competition and Regulatory Law Review 5(2) (2021), 90 (95).

[119] Monti European Competition and Regulatory Law Review 5(2) (2021), 90 (95); Zober NZKart 2021, 611 (616).

[120] Ritter/Wirtz in Immenga/Mestmäcker VO 1/2003 Art. 9 mn. 1.

the opportunity to comment within a reasonable period. If the Commission refuses to make the commitments binding because they cannot ensure effective compliance, it must explain the reasons in the decision concluding the proceedings pursuant to Art. 25(3).

3. Enforcement

The Commission must regularly **review** remedies to ensure that the gatekeeper is effectively complying with its obligations, cf. Art. 18(8)(1). 94

According to Art. 26(1), the Commission shall take the necessary actions to monitor the effective implementation and compliance with its decisions pursuant to Art. 18. In particular, it may require the gatekeeper to **retain** any **documents** it deems relevant to assessing compliance., cf. Art. 26(1)(2). In addition, according to Art. 26(2), **independent external experts** and auditors as well as officials from competent national authorities of the Member States may be appointed to assist the Commission in monitoring the obligations and measures and to assist it with specific expertise or knowledge. 95

If a gatekeeper fails to comply with the remedies or with commitments made legally binding, the Commission may initiate proceedings pursuant to Art. 20 and issue a **decision of non-compliance**, cf. Art. 29(1)(c). **Penalty payments** may be imposed up to a maximum of 5 % of the average daily worldwide turnover in the preceding financial year, cf. Art. 31(1)(b), (g). In addition, the Commission may impose a **fine** of up to 10 % of the total worldwide turnover in the preceding financial year pursuant to Art. 30(1)(c), (e). A fine can only be imposed if the undertaking has intentionally or negligently violated remedies or commitments made legally binding. 96

III. Proposing amendments (Art. 19)

1. Report

The Commission shall conclude a market investigation into new services or new practices by submitting a **report**, cf. Art. 19(3), setting out its assessment of the need to amend the DMA or to adopt delegated acts. If the Commission considers legislative action necessary, it may accompany its report with a **proposal for the amendment of the regulation** or a **draft delegated act.** The report shall be submitted to the European Parliament and the Council, where appropriate, in accordance with Art. 19(3)(2). 97

2. Legislative proposal

Together with the report, the Commission may submit a legislative proposal to include additional **services** in the list of core platform services laid down in Art. 2 no. 2 or **new obligations in Chapter III.** Art. 19(3)(3) adds that the Commission may also propose to delete services from the list of core platform services or obligations in Art. 5–7. 98

An amendment of the DMA then requires action by the European legislator through the **ordinary legislative procedure**, cf. Art. 294 TFEU. Legislative proposals by the Commission must be endorsed by both the European Parliament and the Council.[121] 99

3. Draft delegated act

The Commission may attach to its report a draft delegated act **supplementing the obligations laid down in Art. 5, 6, 7.** The Commission may also propose amendments 100

[121] On the procedure Kluth in Calliess/Ruffert TFEU Art. 294 mn. 5–11.

to the obligations set out in **Art. 7.** If, however, the Commission comes to the conclusion that it wishes to delete any of the obligations, this is only possible by amending the DMA, cf. Art. 19(3)(3).[122]

Further details on the authority and procedure for updating or amending the catalogue of obligations by means of delegated acts are set out in Art. 12 in conjunction with Art. 49. Accordingly, contrary to what was discussed during the drafting of the DMA with the New Competition Instrument, the Commission cannot take concrete action after the end of an investigation. It can, however, adopt abstract general regulations.[123]

101 According to Art. 290(1) TFEU, delegated acts are **non-legislative acts of general application**. They serve to supplement or amend non-essential elements of a legislative act.[124] By delegating such powers to the Commission, the Union legislator is working to ensure that the DMA is swiftly adapted to new developments in the digital economy.[125] The procedure for adopting delegated acts is much faster than the ordinary legislative procedure for proposals to amend the regulation.[126]

102 **Art. 12** delegates to the Commission the power to adopt delegated acts in respect of various matters. According to Art. 12(1),(2), the Commission is empowered to supplement the obligations in Art. 5, 6 by delegated acts. Art. 12(3),(4) provides for powers to amend Art. 7: By means of delegated acts, the list of basic functionalities identified in Art. 7(2) can be amended by adding or removing functionalities of number-independent interpersonal communications services. In addition, the obligations in Art. 7 may be supplemented by the Commission specifying the manner in which they are to be fulfilled in order to ensure their effective compliance. Additions and amendments must be aligned with the objectives of the DMA. Supplemented or amended provisions must serve to counter practices that limit the contestability of core platform services or are unfair, cf. Art. 12(5).

103 Since the powers to adopt delegated acts pursuant to Art. 12 are based on the central obligations of the gatekeepers in Art. 5–7, there is a certain **tension with the requirements of Art. 290(1) (2)(2) TFEU.**[127] According to this, the 'essential elements of an area' are reserved for the legislative act. A delegation of power is excluded in this respect. It can only be used to supplement or amend non-essential elements. Against this background, some Member States criticised the scope of the delegation of power in Art. 12 during the drafting process of the DMA.[128] In fact, it seems questionable whether it is limited to non-essential areas of the DMA. Nevertheless, Art. 12 is in conformity with European primary law. Case law interprets the concept of essentiality in a sector-specific manner. In the agricultural sector, the ECJ has taken into account that the fast-moving market conditions require swift legislative action.[129] With this consideration, a comparably narrow interpretation of the concept of essentiality is required in the digital sector.[130]

104 Pursuant to Art. 49(2), the aforementioned powers shall be conferred for an initial period of **five years** from the entry into force of the DMA. The delegation shall be tacitly extended if neither the European Parliament nor the Council objects in due time. In ad-

[122] Huerkamp/Nuys in Podszun DMA Art. 19 mn. 9.

[123] Zimmer/Göhls ZWeR 2021, 29 (49).

[124] ECJ 17.3.2016 – case C-286/14, ECLI:EU:C:2016:183 mn. 42 – Parliament v Commission.

[125] Seeliger in Podszun DMA Art. 12 mn. 1.

[126] Jovanovic/Greiner MMR 2021, 678 (682).

[127] Achleitner NZKart 2022, 359 (361); Podszun/Bongartz/Langenstein EuCML 2021, 60 (65); Krauskopf/Brösamle in Schmidt/Hübener Der neue DMA § 8 mn. 23.

[128] Council, Progress Report, 2020/0374/COD, mn. 17.

[129] ECJ 13.7.1975 – case C-23/75, ECLI:EU:C:1975:142 mn. 10 et seq. – Rey Soda v Cassa Conguaglio Zucchero.

[130] Seeliger in Podszun DMA Art. 12 mn. 11; Zimmer/Göhsl ZWeR 2021, 29 (50).

dition, the European Parliament and the Council may revoke the delegation of power at any time in accordance with Art. 12(1),(3),(4), cf. Art. 49(3)(1).

Art. 49(4)–(6) provide for **procedural rules** for the adoption of delegated acts in the aforementioned cases. The Commission is obliged to consult the experts appointed by each Member State. The delegated act shall enter into force only if no objection has been expressed either by the European Parliament or the Council within a period of two months of notification of that act. 105

F. Resumption and review

The Commission may exceptionally **reopen** a market investigation that it has closed. This requires a specific reason in order not to break the validity of the implementing acts adopted at the time of termination.[131] The reasons are laid down in Art. 16(4). A **reason for reopening** exists if the facts on which a decision adopted under Art. 17, 18 or 19 was based have changed in a material respect, cf. Art. 16(4)(a). According to Art. 16(4)(b), the Commission may also reopen a market investigation if the decision was based on incomplete, incorrect or misleading information. 106

In addition, further **review mechanisms** are tailored to the specific occasions for market investigations. They partly overlap with the grounds for reopening applicable to all market investigations, but in some cases go further. For example, the Commission must review designations of a gatekeeper – irrespective of the procedure in which they were made – at least **every three years** pursuant to Art. 4(2)(1). The designation of a gatekeeper is thus designed from the outset for a limited period of time.[132] If the Commission finds that the facts on which it once based its designation decision have changed, it issues a decision confirming, amending or revoking the original decision. In contrast to the reopening under Art. 16(4), the review of the gatekeeper position may be requested. The grounds for application correspond to those of Art. 16(4). According to rec. 30(1)(5), an amendment of the decision due to a change of facts is only required if it leads to a change in the assessment. This is to be determined on the basis of a case-by-case assessment of the facts and circumstances, cf. rec. 30(1)(6). 107

Following a market investigation into **systematic non-compliance**, the Commission is entitled to amend the remedies imposed if, **following a new market investigation**, it finds that they are not effective, cf. Art. 18(8)(2).[133] To this end, according to rec. 75(1)(7), the Commission should be able to reopen proceedings in the event that the remedies prove to be ineffective. Any amendment of remedies should be done **prospectively**. 108

If a market investigation into systematic non-compliance has been determined by commitments that have been declared binding, the Commission may, upon request or on its own initiative, reopen the procedure if one of the reasons set out in **Art. 25(2)** applies. These include a material change in the facts on which the decision was based (lit. a), non-compliance with the commitments (lit. b), the fact that the decision was based on incomplete, incorrect or misleading information provided by the partied (lit. c) and the finding that the commitments do not prove to be effective (lit. d). 109

---

131 Huerkamp/Nuys in Podszun DMA Art. 16 mn. 22.
132 Huerkamp/Nuys in Podszun DMA Art. 18 mn. 36.
133 Krauskopf/Brösamle in Schmidt/Hübener Der neue DMA § 8 mn. 19.

G. Legal protection

I. Opening decision

110 The decision to initiate an investigation is **not a contestable act**. This also applies to market investigations within the meaning of Art. 17 and Art. 18, which are directed against a specific undertaking or a specific gatekeeper. This is because the initiation of a market investigation does not change the legal situation of the party concerned.[134]

111 There is also **no legal protection** against a decision to initiate a market investigation under Art. 19. No undertaking is affected by the decision. However, it seems possible that companies may object to specific investigative measures. Consequently, the legality of the decision to open an investigation may have to be clarified as an incidental matter.[135]

II. Legal acts terminating the investigation

112 The undertaking concerned may bring an **action for annulment** before the GC against a designation decision and against remedies, Art. 263(4) TFEU.[136] In principle, it has **no suspensive effect,** cf. Art. 278 TFEU. Pursuant to Art. 104 of the Rules of Procedure of the General Court[137], the undertaking concerned may file an application for suspension of the execution of the challenged decision.[138]

113 There is no legal remedy against proposals to amend the DMA and draft delegated acts published by the Commission as a result of a market investigation into new services and new practices. Should the proposal for a regulation or the draft delegated act be adopted in the ordinary legislative or advisory procedure, privileged plaintiffs within the meaning of Art. 263(2) TFEU may bring an action for annulment at any time. Undertakings do not have standing to bring an action because they are not directly affected. These are abstract-general regulations.

---

134 Huerkamp/Nuys in Podszun DMA Art. 16 mn. 13; Schütte/Thomas in Wiedemann KartellR-HdB § 49 mn. 189 et seq.

135 Cf. Hennig in Immenga/Mestmäcker VO 1/2003 Art. 17 mn. 49.

136 Huerkamp/Nuys in Podszun DMA Art. 16 mn. 14.

137 OJ 2015 L 105, 1.

138 Cf. Anweiler in Loewenheim/Meessen/Riesenkampff/Kersting/Meyer-Lindemann VO 1/2003 Art. 7 mn. 66.

§ 14
Powers of and cooperation with authorities/enforcement

Literature: *Bien/Käseberg/Klumpe/Körber/Ost,* Die 10. GWB-Novelle, 2021; *Friends of an effective Digital Markets Act,* Strengthening the Digital Markets Act and its Enforcement, First Position Paper of 27 May 2021; *Bechtold/Bosch/Brinker,* EU-Kartellrecht, 4th ed. 2023.

The enforcement of the Digital Markets Act (DMA)[1] takes up its overall objective of achieving an "*approximating* [of] *diverging national laws*" (cf. recital 8). The objective of averting a (potential) fragmentation of the internal market is explicitly to be achieved through the centralised enforcement of the DMA by the European Commission (cf. recital 9, 91).[2] 1

[1] Regulation (EU) 2022/1925 of the European Parliament and of the Council of 14 September 2022 on contestable and fair markets in the digital sector and amending Directives (EU) 2019/1937 and (EU) 2020/1828 (Digital Markets Act); OJ L 265, 1.

[2] In the European Commission's internal organization, the Directorate General Connect and the Directorate General for Competition are responsible for the application and enforcement of the DMA.

2 The exclusive responsibility of the European Commission envisaged in the original draft of the DMA has been watered down, at least in parts, in response to much criticism – among other things with reference to the limited resources available at the European Commission – and a German-French-Dutch alternative proposal[3]. Instead, the final text of the DMA provides for "close cooperation" or "coordinated enforcement measures" within the European Competition Network (ECN) and at least some responsibilities for the national competition authorities to initiate proceedings (→ mn. 95).

A. Overview

3 The DMA creates a **largely centralised** and **prime responsibility of the European Commission** to enforce it.[4] The various powers of the European Commission are essentially related to the (potential) status of the undertaking as a gatekeeper or central platform service as well as the compliance with the DMA provisions. These provisions are linked to the (self-executing) obligations for gatekeepers and, in case of non-compliance, empower the European Commission to initiate proceedings to designate an undertaking as a gatekeeper and enforce compliance with the gatekeeper obligations. At a glance:

Behaviour of the company	Power of the European Commission
Gatekeeper status	
Failure to notify by undertaking pursuant to Art. 3(3) subpara. 1 DMA and failure to comply with deadline in the request for information, Art. 3(3) subpara. 2 DMA	**Designation** by the European Commission, Art. 3(3) subpara. 2 DMA
Notification by undertaking or delayed information in the event of a request for information pursuant to Art. 3(3) subpara. 2 DMA	**Designation** by the European Commission without undue delay and at the latest within 45 working days after receiving the complete information, Art. 3(3) subpara. 3, (4) DMA

[3] Friends of an effective Digital Markets Act, Strengthening the Digital Markets Act and its Enforcement, First Position Paper, Federal Ministry of Economic Affairs and Climate Action, 27.05.2021, <https://www.bmwi.de/Redaktion/DE/Downloads/M-O/non-paper-friends-of-an-effective-digital-markets-act.html> (only available in German language) (last accessed: 16.08.2024).

[4] Regarding the relationship between the DMA and national legislations such as Section 19a Act against Restraints of Competition (ARC) → § 12 mn. 76 et seqq.

Behaviour of the company	Power of the European Commission
In case of sufficiently substantiated arguments provided by undertaking to exceptionally rebut the presumed gatekeeper status	If the European Commission takes the view that the rebuttal of the presumptions in Art. 3(2) DMA is unsubstantiated: **Rejection** of the submitted arguments by the European Commission without further (market) investigation, Art. 3(5) subpara. 2 DMA; If the European Commission takes the view that the rebuttal of the presumptions in Art. 3(2) DMA is substantiated: the European Commission can initiate a **market investigation** within 45 days, Art. 3(5) subpara. 3, (4), Art. 17(3) DMA
If the qualitative requirements of Art. 3(1) DMA are met, but not all the quantitative thresholds specified in Art. 3(2) DMA are satisfied	Conduct a **market investigation** to designate gatekeepers, Art. 3(8), Art. 17 DMA; In case of a persistent failure to cooperate with the European Commission after a corresponding request for cooperation by the European Commission: Designation as gatekeeper, Art. 3(8) subpara. 3 DMA
Request to reconsider, amend, and/or repeal of gatekeeper status due to substantial change in facts or designation decision based on incomplete, incorrect or misleading information	Upon request or after initiative of the European Commission, Commission may reconsider, amend or repeal designation decision, Art. 4(1) DMA; Ongoing fulfilment of the qualitative requirements mentioned in Art. 3(1) DMA: **review** by the European Commission at least every three years, Art. 4(2) subpara. 1 DMA; Potential **first-time qualification** of new undertakings offering core platform services: examination by the European Commission at least once a year, Art. 4(2) subpara. 2 DMA
Obligations of gatekeepers	
Infringement of anti-circumvention clause, Art. 13 DMA	Opening of **proceedings** against the gatekeeper by the European Commission, Art. 8(2) subpara. 1, 2 DMA
Exceptional adjustment of the self-executing obligations	Opening of **proceedings** by the European Commission at the request of the gatekeeper, Art. 8(2) subpara. 1, (3) DMA
Exceptional suspension of the obligations pursuant to Art. 5, 6, 7 DMA due to exceptional circumstances at the reasoned request of the gatekeeper	Adoption of an **implementing act** by the European Commission at the latest three months following receipt of the gatekeeper's complete reasoned request, Art. 9(1) DMA

Behaviour of the company	Power of the European Commission
Specific obligation pursuant to Art. 5, 6 or 7 DMA	**Implementing act exempting the gatekeeper** for grounds of public safety and public health by the European Commission, Art. 10 DMA
Merger control, Art. 14 DMA	Gatekeepers are obliged to **inform** the European Commission of intended **concentrations** not satisfying the thresholds of Regulation (EC) No. 139/2004[5] if they meet the criteria for change of control pursuant to Regulation (EC) No. 139/2004. However, according to the wording of the provision, this is not a notification of a concentration pursuant to Regulation (EC) No. 139/2004, but a mere obligation to inform the European Commission. Accordingly, such an information or the failure to inform does not enable the European Commission to examine or even prohibit the respective merger. Only Art. 14(5) DMA and a referral by the national competition authority to the European Commission pursuant to Art. 22 Regulation (EC) No. 139/2004 provide for such powers.

4 To fulfil the responsibilities under the DMA and to enforce the duties of conduct and cooperation imposed on the gatekeeper and on other companies, in addition to the market investigation (→ § 14 mn. 14 et seqq.) the European Commission has various powers to **investigate, enforce** and **monitor** as well as to **sanction** certain conducts. These powers are provided in Chapter V of the DMA. They range from specific investigative measures such as requests for information and inspections to sanctions such as fines and periodic penalty payments as well as remedies.

B. Investigative, enforcement and monitoring powers

5 The European Commission's powers to investigate, enforce and monitor are **partly identical to the powers provided in Regulation (EC) No. 1/2003**[6]. Against that background, many **disputes arising** in connection with the powers provided in Regulation (EC) No. 1/2003 will likely also become an issue when applying Art. 21 et seqq. DMA.[7] In particular, the **necessity** of certain measures, disputes around "**legal privilege**", dealing with **private documents and devices** and **electronic inspections** will most likely also play a role in the application of the DMA. These problems were well known to the European legislator due to the public consultation on the effectiveness of Regulation

[5] Council Regulation (EC) No. 139/2004 of 20 January 2004 on the control of concentrations between companies ("EC Merger Regulation"); OJ L 24, 1.

[6] Council Regulation (EC) No. 1/2003 of 16 December 2002 on the implementation of the rules on competition laid down in Articles 81 and 82 of the Treaty; OJ L 1, 1.

[7] Schmidt/Hübener/Reims, Das neue Recht der digitalen Märkte, 2023, Sec. 10 para. 33.

(EC) No. 1/2003 and the Implementing Regulation (EC) No. 773/2004[8], which was conducted in parallel to the DMA. Considering this, it is almost anachronistic to apply powers originating from Regulation (EC) No. 1/2003, which are **twenty years old** and are currently under revision, to the DMA. It remains to be seen whether, at least as regards Chapter V of the DMA, in the course of the revisions of Regulation (EC) No. 1/2003 and Regulation (EC) No. 773/2004, a **first revision** of the DMA will already take place soon.

I. General information

1. Initial suspicion

The European Commission can initiate investigations already **prior to the opening of a formal proceeding** regarding the possible adoption of decisions pursuant to Art. 8 (compliance with obligations for gatekeepers), Art. 29 (non-compliance decision) or Art. 30 (imposition of a fine), Art. 20(2) DMA. 6

Still, "fishing expeditions", i.e. investigations without any initial suspicion, would be unlawful. Since using the investigatory powers provided under Regulation (EC) No. 1/2003 requires at least an **initial suspicion** of a potential infringement of Art. 101, 102 TFEU[9], there are good reasons to apply the same standard in the context of Art. 21 et seqq. DMA for opening an investigation into a potential infringement of substantive or procedural law.[10] 7

2. Information by third parties, Art. 27 DMA

Like in general antitrust law, grounds for an initial suspicion can arise from **the European Commissions' own market observations**, but also be based on **information provided by third parties.** The third party can either inform the **national authority responsible for enforcing the provisions listed in Art. 1(6) DMA** or **directly the European Commission**, Art. 27(1) DMA. With the antitrust ***whistle-blower tool,*** the European Commission has already created the respective technical requirements for that.[11] 8

However, neither the national authority nor the European Commission are obliged to take actions based on the information provided by third parties, Art. 27(2) DMA. 9

In case the national authority has been informed and subsequently concludes, based on the information received, that there may be an infringement of the DMA, it shall refer that information to the European Commission, Art. 27(3) DMA. Even in this scenario, there are good arguments that the **European Commission has full discretion to decide** whether to take follow-up measures based on the information referred to them by the national authority or not. This is because the information the European Commission obtains via the detour of the national authority remains "information received" pursuant to Art. 27(1) DMA, even if they are initially received by the national authority. The European Commission therefore has a **broad discretion** as regards the appropriate measures according to Art. 27(2) DMA. Otherwise, the arbitrary decision of the third party 10

---

[8] Commission Regulation (EC) No. 773/2004 of 07 April 2004 relating to the conduct of proceedings by the Commission pursuant to Articles 81 and 82 of the EC Treaty; OJ L 123, 18.

[9] Bechtold/Bosch/Brinker Regulation (EG) Nr. 1/2003 Art. 18 mn. 4; Immenga/Mestmäcker/Hennig Regulation (EG) Nr. 1/2003 Art. 18 mn. 9.

[10] Podszun HK-DMA/Podszun DMA Art. 21 mn. 5.

[11] European Commission, Reporting system <https://comp-eu.whistleblowernetwork.net/setup> (last accessed 16.08.2024).

to which authority it submits the information would limit the discretion of the European Commission regarding its action.[12]

11 However, in case the European Commission **does not take any action** based on the information referred to it by the national authority, this does not lead to a subsidiary competence of the national authority. Rather, the primary competence remains with the European Commission. However, the national authority has full discretion to initiate an investigation pursuant to Art. 38(7) DMA (for more details → mn. 101 et seqq.).

3. No hierarchy

12 The use of the investigatory powers by the European Commission does not only require that there is an initial suspicion (→ mn. 6 et seqq.). Furthermore, the respective investigative measure needs to serve the fulfilment of the tasks assigned to the European Commission by the DMA. In that regard, the DMA, as well as Regulation (EC) No. 1/2003, do **not provide for any hierarchy between specific investigative measures.**

II. Requests for information, Art. 21 DMA

13 As part of its investigations, Art. 21 DMA confers on the European Commission the power to **request information** from undertakings and associations of undertakings to provide all necessary information.

14 Art. 21(1) DMA requires that the information is deemed "**necessary**". Whether and when this is the case is disputed under Regulation (EC) No. 1/2003, especially regarding the **far-reaching requests for information by the European Commission,** which require undertakings to search for documents and information based on predefined and generic search terms set by the European Commission. Even though in the antitrust context the European Court of Justice grants the European Commission **broad discretion** to assess the necessity of requested documents and information for an investigation, this discretion is not unlimited.[13] In particular, **the purpose of the request for information limits the scope of "necessity".**[14] Given that Art. 21 DMA and Art. 18 Regulation (EC) No. 1/2003 are largely identical, the principles developed for the interpretation of "necessity" under Art. 18 Regulation (EC) No. 1/2003 can also be applied to Art. 21 DMA. Accordingly, requests are only allowed if, **at that stage in the procedure, the request may legitimately be regarded as having a connection with the presumed infringement.**[15] Since the judicial control of the "necessity" is linked to the purpose of the request for information, this purpose must be **specified sufficiently precise** by the European Commission.[16]

15 Information to be provided under a request for information may be supplied both **by the representatives of undertakings as well as by duly authorised lawyers**, Art. 21(4) sentences 1, 2 DMA. However, if the information is supplied by a duly authorised lawyer, the undertaking is not exempted from its duty of care regarding the information. The undertaking remains fully responsible if the information supplied is incomplete, incorrect, or misleading, Art. 21(4)(3) DMA.

---

[12] Similarly, Podszun HK-DMA/Lahme/Ruster DMA Art. 27 mn. 3 et seqq.

[13] Podszun HK-DMA/Podszun DMA Art. 21 mn. 10 et seq.

[14] ECJ 18.10.1989 – 374/87, ECLI:EU:C:1989:387 para. 16 = BeckRS 2004, 71022.

[15] ECJ 29.10.2020 – T-451/20 R, ECLI:EU:C:2020:515 para. 38 = BeckRS 2020, 28669.

[16] ECJ 10.3.2016 – C- 248/14 P, ECLI:EU:C:2016:150 para. 28 = BeckRS 2016, 80466.

Like in general European antitrust procedural law, the European Commission can choose between a **simple request for information** (Art. 21(1) DMA) and a **formal decision to supply information** (Art. 21(3) DMA): 16

- In both cases, the **legal basis,** the **purpose of the request for information** as well as the **possibilities for legal protection** must be stated, and it must be specified which information is required as well as the deadline for the provision of the information, Art. 21(2), (3) DMA. Given the imminent sanctions for supplying incomplete, incorrect or late information (see below), the European Commission must set **adequate deadlines** and, if deemed necessary, grant extensions.[17]
- The **simple request for information** (RFI) does **not** constitute a **formal duty to cooperate** for the undertaking. This follows from Art. 30(3)(e), (f) DMA e contrario which only regulates the setting of fines in the event of failure to provide information in the case of a formal decision to supply information (see below). Based on that wording, the European Commission can, however, impose sanctions in the case of **incomplete, incorrect, or misleading information.** These sanctions are limited to **fines** (Art. 21(2), Art. 30(3)(f) DMA). However, imposing sanctions for providing incomplete information on a simple request for information (RFI) is **incompatible with the fact that there is no duty to cooperate in case of a simple request for information.** If the undertaking is under no obligation to cooperate, it cannot be held liable if it provides incomplete information. Moreover, in the case of a voluntary provision of information, information can only be "incorrect" if it is "misleading" at the same time. Therefore, the reference in **Art. 30(3)(f) half sent. 2 DMA** is to be **interpreted narrowly** so that it only sanctions incorrect or misleading information provided in response to a formal decision to supply information pursuant to Art. 21(3) DMA.
  The simple request for information is not subject to judicial review.
- In contrast to that, the **formal decision to supply information** establishes a **formal duty to cooperate**. Accordingly, the European Commission can impose **fines** (Art. 30(3)(e), (f) DMA) or **periodic penalty payments** (Art. 31(1)(c) DMA) not only in the case of incomplete, incorrect, or misleading information, but also in case of a **failure to provide** information or if the information is **not provided in time.**

The main difference to the parallel provision of Art. 20 Regulation (EC) No. 1/2003 is that the simple request for information as well as the formal decision to supply information also explicitly refers to ***"data and algorithms of undertakings and information about testing"*** (Art. 21(1)(2), (3)(2) DMA) and the European Commission can request **explanations** in that regard (Art. 21(1)(2) DMA).[18] 17

In contrast to the investigative powers granted to the European Commission pursuant to Regulation (EC) No. 1/2003, the investigative measures by the European Commission to enforce the DMA are not subject to the judicial review by the **Hearing Officer.** This is particularly the case for the simple request for information (Art. 18(2) Regulation (EC) No. 1/2003 in conjunction with Art. 4(2)(b) of the Decision of the President of the European Commission of 13 October 2011 on the function and terms of reference of the Hearing Officer in certain competition proceedings[19]) as well as the deadlines set by the European Commission for responding to the formal decision to supply informa- 18

[17] Art. 10 Commission implementing regulation (EU) 2023/814 of 14 April 2023 on detailed arrangements for the conduct of certain proceedings by the Commission pursuant to Regulation (EU) 2022/1925 of the European Parliament and of the Council ("**Implementing Regulation**"); OJ L 102, 6.

[18] Podszun HK-DMA/Podszun DMA Art. 21 mn. 12.

[19] OJ L 275, 29.

tion. In the case of Art. 18(3) Regulation (EC) No. 1/2003, the addressee of the decision can refer the matter to the Hearing Officer to decide on whether an extension of the time limit should be granted (Art. 4(2)(c) of the Decision of the President of the European Commission of 13 October 2011 on the function and terms of reference of the Hearing Officer in certain competition proceedings). In contrast to that, as regards deadlines under to Art. 21(3) DMA, only the **European Commission decides on the length of the time limit** regarding decisions to supply information (cf. Art. 10 Implementing Regulation to the DMA).

III. Interviews and taking statements, Art. 22 DMA

19 Art. 22 DMA stipulates the power of the European Commission to interview and take statements from natural or legal persons. Recital 82, with its reference to obtaining information from "*any*" natural or legal person, clarifies that the power to interview – in parallel to Regulation (EC) No. 1/2003 – aims at **natural or legal persons that are not already the subject of requests for information** (Art. 21 DMA) **and inspections** (Art. 23 DMA).

20 If a legal person is interviewed, the relevant natural persons must be made available by the legal person for the interview. In contrast to Art. 21 DMA, the provision only allows to conduct an **oral interview rather than putting any requests in writing**. It may also be carried out on the premises of "*an undertaking*", cf. Art. 22(2) DMA. As an argumentum e contrario to Art. 22(2) DMA and in the absence of an explicit authorisation, these interviews may **not take place on the private premise of a natural person.**[20]

21 The interview is subject to the **consent** from the person who is being interviewed. There are good reasons to assume that the consent – like the consent pursuant to Art. 19(1) Regulation (EC) No. 1/2003 – does not have any **formal requirements** and is **revocable at any time.**[21] This should also apply to cases of an interview of **a legal entity,** where the legal entity and its representatives have consented to the interview, but the person to be interviewed on behalf of the legal entity refuses to consent. The same should apply to the reverse case, where the natural person who is being interviewed makes a statement despite a prohibition from the undertaking to make any such statements. Regardless of any means in civil or labour law between the undertaking and a natural person to enforce a duty to make a statement, obtaining **consent cannot be coerced. It is neither possible to coerce any consent in case of an interview of a natural or legal person nor does the consent become invalid because of a diverging instruction given in the internal relationship between the undertaking and the natural person.** At the same time, **incorrect** or **incomplete statements** cannot be sanctioned. Art. 30 and 31 DMA do not contain a reference to Art. 22 DMA in this regard.

22 If the interview is conducted on the premises of an undertaking, the European Commission shall inform the national competent authority of the Member State that is enforcing the DMA and in whose territory the interview takes place, Art. 22(2) DMA. In this context, it can be assumed that the provision is likely to refer only to undertakings that are themselves or whose employees are related to the subject matter of the investigation. It remains to be seen whether the European Commission will also conduct interviews in hotels, like the enforcement of Regulation (EC) No. 1/2003. In this case, like Art. 19(2) Regulation (EC) No. 1/2003, there should probably be no obligation to inform

---

[20] In contrast to the powers of the European Commission in antitrust procedural law (cf. Art. 21 Regulation (EC) No. 1/2003), an inspection of private premises is not possible, → mn. 20.

[21] Podszun HK-DMA/Podszun DMA Art. 22 mn. 1.

the national authority since the interview does not take place on the premises of an undertaking.

23 In contrast to European antitrust procedural law, where the European Commission's power to record interviews is only indirectly[22] regulated, Art. 22(1)(2) DMA expressly provides for such a measure. Since the wording of Art. 22(1)(2) DMA is similar to that of Art. 3(3) Regulation (EC) No. 773/2004 and since both, the wording of Art. 22(1)(2) DMA and that of Art. 3(3) Regulation (EC) No. 773/2004 suggest that the European Commission's power to record is facultative, it can be assumed that the case law of the ECJ on Art. 3(3) Regulation (EC) No. 773/2004 is also applicable to Art. 22(1)(2) DMA. It follows from that that recording the statement as such is obligatory for the European Commission. The European Commission is only free to choose the technical means used for the recording.[23] Although the Implementing Regulation to the DMA does not contain an explicit obligation of the European Commission to **provide the interviewed person with the recording for approval,**[24] if follows from the prerequisite that a consent for the interview is required and the voluntary character of the statement that any recording must be provided to the person giving evidence and that it must be approved by him or her.[25]

IV. Inspections, Art. 23 DMA

24 In addition, the European Commission may conduct **inspections** pursuant to Art. 23 DMA to carry out its duties under the DMA, as far as these are **necessary.**[26] The competences of the European Commission largely correspond to those in Art. 20 Regulation (EC) No. 1/2003.

25 In particular, Art. 23(2) DMA grants European Commission staff the power to enter the premises, land and means of transport of undertakings and associations of undertakings (lit. (a)), to examine books and business records (lit. (b)), to take copies of and extracts from such books and records (lit. (c)), to seal the business premises and books or records of any kind for the duration of the inspection (lit. (e)), and to ask any representative or employee of the undertaking or association of undertakings for explanations of facts or documents relating to the subject matter and purpose of the inspection and to record their answers with any technical means (lit. (f)).

26 Like in European antitrust procedural law, there is only an **obligation to submit to an inspection** if this was ordered by a corresponding **decision** by the European Commission (Art. 23(6) DMA, Art. 20(4) Regulation (EC) No. 1/2003).[27] In contrast to European antitrust procedural law, cf. Art. 20(4)(3) Regulation (EC) No. 1/2003, and following the general approach of the DMA of being enforced centrally by the European Commission, the **member states** in whose territory the inspection is to be conducted are **not to be heard** before **the decision is adopted.** The national authorities referred to in Art. 1(6) DMA **only have an assisting role** in case of inspections conducted by the European Commission.

22 Art. 3 mn. 3 Regulation (EC) No. 773/2004 in conjunction with recital 25 Regulation (EC) No. 1/2003.

23 ECJ 06.09.2017 – C- 413/14 P, ECLI:EU:C:2017:632 para. 90 et seq. = NZKart 2017, 525.

24 The situation is different in antitrust procedural law, Art. 3(3)(2) Regulation (EC) No. 773/2004.

25 Podszun HK-DMA/Podszun DMA Art. 22 mn. 3.

26 On the interpretation of the criterion of necessity and the associated difficulties of delimitation → mn. 14.

27 Podszun HK-DMA/Podszun DMA Art. 23 mn. 17.

27 Pursuant to Art. 23(8) DMA, the Member States are obliged to provide any **assistance required** to carry out the inspection, including, **if deemed necessary, assistance by police forces or of an equivalent enforcement authority**, if the undertaking opposes an inspection.[28] If the assistance requires **authorisation from a judicial authority** under national law, the officials must apply for such authorisation from the competent court (Art. 23(9) DMA). In this case, the competent **court** only has **limited room for a judicial review**. In particular, it may not review the legality of the inspection as such. This is the exclusive right of the European Court of Justice. The power of the national court is therefore limited to assessing whether the **decision from the European Commission is authentic,** as well as (not) arbitrary and **proportionate**. As regards the latter, the court may hear either the European Commission or the competent national authority responsible for the enforcement of the provisions referred to in Art. 1(6) DMA regarding the background that led to the presumption of an infringement of the DMA, as well as regarding the gravity of the alleged breach and the nature of the undertaking's involvement.

28 In addition – and in contrast to Regulation (EC) No. 1/2003 – the European Commission may also **request the assistance of independent external experts and auditors** pursuant to Art. 26(2) DMA for the purpose of carrying out inspections, Art. 23(3) DMA.

29 Another important difference to the European Commission's powers of inspection pursuant to Regulation (EC) No. 1/2003 is that the European Commission has **no power to inspect other premises, in particular private residences.** The DMA does not provide for a provision comparable to Art. 21 Regulation (EC) No. 1/2003. This is proportionate since the DMA contains duties directly affecting the gatekeeper and its specific business activities. Unlike for potential infringements of Art. 101, 102 TFEU, the information relevant for an investigation can usually be found only at the premises of the undertaking and not on private premises.

30 Insofar as private documents are located on premises, land and means of transport of undertakings and associations of undertakings, the inspection may not cover these. However, the **rebuttable presumption** which has been recognised in the antitrust context that **documents kept on the undertaking's premises are business documents** likely will also apply in this case. Private devices used by employees for business purposes (***bring your own device***) are not considered as private devices in this context.[29]

31 Pursuant to Art. 23(2)(d) DMA, the European Commission may, beyond an inspection, **require the undertaking to provide access to and explanations on its organisation, functioning, IT system, algorithms, data-handling and business practices** and record the explanations given by any technical means.

32 In addition to the physical inspections of premises and documents, Art. 23 DMA – similar to Art. 20 Regulation (EC) No. 1/2003 – also allows for **electronic inspections**. The European Commission can freeze the entire computer system to prevent the deletion of data, temporarily block e-mail traffic within the undertaking and access all electronic data, including data stored outside the EU or on external servers or in a cloud, and electronic data stored on local devices (desktop PCs) as well as mobile devices (laptops, smartphones, external storage media).[30] In that regard, in antitrust practice large amounts of data are initially searched and copied on the basis of specific predefined

---

[28] Podszun HK-DMA/Podszun DMA Art. 23 mn. 24 et seq.

[29] Cf. for antitrust law Explanatory note on Commission inspections pursuant to Art. 20(4) Council Regulation No. 1/2003, para. 10, European Commission, revised 03.2024, < https://competition-policy.ec.europa.eu/system/files/2021-03/inspections_explanatory_note_en.pdf> (last accessed, 16.08.2024).

[30] Podszun HK-DMA/Podszun DMA Art. 23 mn. 12.

search terms. The manual review and marking of the data as relevant, irrelevant or privileged is then continued in the facilities of the European Commission.

To the extent that documents or data are subject to **legal privilege**[31], the rules set by courts and in practice with regard to Art. 20 Regulation (EC) No. 1/2003 should also be applied to Art. 23 DMA. Hence, there is no obligation to disclose correspondence exchanged between the undertaking and an (EU/EFTA) attorney as long as it relates to the subject matter of the proceeding.[32] **Correspondence between in-house lawyers is not protected.**[33] In the event of disagreement between the European Commission and the undertaking as to whether the documents in question are subject to legal privilege, the **"sealed envelope" procedure** applied in antitrust practice and by the European courts should also be used. In this case, the European Commission puts documents, for which there is a dispute on whether these are legally privileged, and no ad-hoc decision can be made, in a sealed envelope without further examination and continues the examination in the facilities of the European Commission in the presence of the undertaking concerned. 33

V. Commitments, Art. 25 DMA

If a gatekeeper offers **commitments** for the relevant core platform services in the context of a market investigation pursuant to Art. 18 DMA in order to comply with the obligations set out in Art. 5, 6 and 7 DMA and if the European Commission considers these to be **appropriate**, the European Commission may declare them binding and **declare that there are no further grounds for action**, Art. 25(1), (3) DMA (see in detail → § 14 mn. 83 et seq.). 34

VI. Monitoring, Art. 26 DMA

Pursuant to Art. 26(1) DMA, the European Commission shall monitor whether the gatekeeper effectively implements and complies with the obligations laid down in Art. 5, Art. 6 and Art. 7 DMA or in decisions by the European Commission adopted pursuant to Art. 8, 18, 24, 25 and 29 DMA by taking the **necessary actions**. For this purpose, pursuant to Art. 26(1)(2) DMA the gatekeeper may be obliged to **retain** all **documents** deemed to be relevant to assess the implementation of and compliance with these obligations and decisions. Even though Art. 26(1)(2) DMA does not specify the retention period in more detail, the obligation to retain will in **any case** apply for **the period of the existence of the designation** (three years, cf. Art. 4(2) DMA), unless **national laws on retention** already provide for longer retention periods for business documents.[34] 35

Similar to the monitoring of commitments in the context of merger control decisions by the "Monitoring Trustee" (Art. 20a(1) Implementing Regulation (EC) No 802/2004[35]), Art. 26(2) DMA allows the appointment of **external experts, auditors** 36

---

[31] ECJ 14.9.2010 – C-550/07 P, ECLI:EU:C:2010:512 para. 41 = DStR 2010, 2270; Bien/Käseberg/Klumpe/Körber/Ost/Klumpp/Seitz, Die 10. GWB-Novelle, 2021, para. 370 et seq.

[32] ECJ 14.9.2010 – C-550/07 P, ECLI:EU:C:2010:512 para. 41 = DStR 2010, 2270.

[33] ECJ 14.9.2010 – C-550/07 P, ECLI:EU:C:2010:512 para. 44 = DStR 2010, 2270; critically LMRKM/Barthelmeß/Rudolf VerfVO Art. 18 mn. 49.

[34] According to Sec. 257(4) German Commercial Code after six or ten years.

[35] Commission Regulation (EC) No. 802/2004 of 7. April 2004 implementing Council Regulation (EC) No. 139/2004 on the control of concentrations between undertakings; OJ L 133, 1.

and officials of the national competent authorities to assist the European Commission.[36]

C. Behavioural or structural remedies, Art. 18 DMA

37 In the event of **systematic non-compliance** with the obligations imposed on the gatekeeper, the European Commission may conduct a **market investigation**, Art. 18(1) DMA. To ensure compliance with the relevant behavioural obligations, the European Commission may in these cases not only impose fines but moreover impose behavioural or structural remedies on the gatekeeper, Art. 18(1) DMA, see in detail → § 14 mn. 14 et seqq.

D. Possible sanctions

38 In addition to imposing fines, to enforce the numerous duties imposed on the gatekeeper, the European Commission can also impose periodic penalty payments to compel the undertaking to comply with a certain behaviour. These powers are similar to the powers laid down in Art. 23 and Art. 24 Regulation (EC) No. 1/2003.[37]

I. Fines, Art. 30 DMA

39 Art. 30 DMA distinguishes between infringements of **substantive or procedural provisions** of the DMA. This differentiation is important for the consideration of the **amount of the fine** and the **potential addressee for such sanction**: In case of substantive infringements the fine can amount up to 10 % and in case of repeated infringements even up to 20 % of the total worldwide turnover in the preceding financial year. In this case, the fine can be imposed only on gatekeepers (Art. 30(1), (2) DMA). In contrast to that, breaches of procedural provisions can be fined with up to 1 % of the total worldwide turnover of the preceding financial year and can be imposed also other undertakings or associations of undertakings rather than only gatekeepers (Art. 30(3) DMA).

1. Formal opening of proceedings

40 Imposing a fine requires the **formal opening** of the proceedings against the undertaking concerned by a **decision**, Art. 20(1) DMA.

2. Infringement

a) Infringements of substantive law, Art. 30(1), (2) DMA

41 Imposing of a fine on the gatekeeper for a breach of substantive law requires that the European Commission adopts an implementing act setting out the findings of non-compliance, i.e. a **non-compliance decision** pursuant to Art. 29 DMA. In the non-compliance decision the European Commission finds that the gatekeeper intentionally or negligently

[36] Podszun HK-DMA/Podszun DMA Art. 26 mn. 4 et seq.
[37] Podszun HK-DMA/Huerkamp/Nuys DMA Art. 30 mn. 2.

- **does not comply with** any of the **obligations laid down in Art. 5, 6 or 7 DMA,** Art. 29(1)(a), Art. 30(1)(a) DMA;
- **does not comply with the decision** adopted by the European Commission pursuant to Art. 8(2) DMA obliging gatekeepers to **take measures pursuant to Art. 6, 7 DMA,** Art. 29(1)(b), Art. 30(1)(b) DMA;
- **does not comply with remedies** imposed pursuant to Art. 18(1) DMA, Art. 29(1)(c), Art. 30(1)(c) DMA;
- **does not comply with interim measures** imposed pursuant to Art. 24, Art. 29(1)(d), Art. 30(1)(d) DMA; or
- **does not comply with commitments made legally binding pursuant to Art. 25 DMA,** Art. 29(1)(e), Art. 30(1)(e) DMA.

b) Infringements of procedural law

The European Commission can impose fines on undertakings – both gatekeepers and other undertakings or associations of companies that are not gatekeepers – that intentionally or negligently **42**

- fail to provide the **information** required for assessing their designation as gatekeepers pursuant to Art. 3 DMA within the set deadline, or supply incorrect, incomplete or misleading information (Art. 30(3)(a) DMA);
- fail to comply with the **obligation to notify** the European Commission of **meeting the thresholds** pursuant to Art. 3(3) DMA (Art. 30(3)(b) DMA);
- fail to notify or supply incorrect, incomplete or misleading information regarding a **proposed concentration** pursuant to Art. 14 DMA (Art. 30(3)(c) DMA);
- fail to supply the **description of any techniques for profiling of consumers** required pursuant to Art. 15 DMA or supply incorrect, incomplete or misleading information (Art. 30(3)(d) DMA);
- fail to provide **access to data, algorithms or information about testing** in response to a **request for information made pursuant to Art. 21(3) DMA** (Art. 30(3)(e) DMA);
- fail to provide the information required in a **formal decision to supply information pursuant to Art. 21(3) DMA within the set deadline** or supply **incorrect, incomplete or misleading information or explanations** requested pursuant to Art. 21 DMA or given in an interview pursuant to Art. 22 DMA (Art. 30(3)(f) DMA). For the **restrictive interpretation** of Art. 30(3)(f) **half sent. 2 DMA** in case of incorrect or misleading information regarding a simple request for information pursuant to Art. 21(1) DMA → mn. 16;
- fail to **rectify, within the deadline set by the European Commission, incorrect, incomplete or misleading information** given by a representative or a member of staff relating to an **inspection pursuant to Art. 23 DMA** (Art. 30(3)(g), half sent. 1 DMA) or **fail or refuse to provide complete** information on facts relating to the subject matter and purpose of an inspection pursuant to Art. 23 DMA (Art. 30(3)(g), half sent. 2 DMA);
- **refuse to submit to an inspection pursuant to Art. 23 DMA** (Art. 30(3)(h) DMA);
- **fail to comply with the obligations** imposed by the European Commission pursuant to Art. 26 (Art. 30(3)(i) DMA);
- fail to introduce a **compliance function** in accordance with Art. 28 DMA (Art. 30(3)(j) DMA); or
- fail to **comply with** the **conditions for access to the files of the European Commission pursuant to Art. 34(4) DMA** (Art. 30(3)(k) DMA).

3. Fault

43 The imposition of a fine requires **intent or negligence** in the case of both an infringement of substantive and (merely) of procedural law.

44 As in European antitrust law, **the accusation of fault directly refers to the undertaking respectively the gatekeeper**, even if the accusation of fault is derived from the conduct of the natural person acting on behalf of the undertaking respectively the gatekeeper.

45 Following the principles developed in antitrust law, the conduct of the natural person can already be attributed to the undertaking if the **conduct happens under the official duties of the person acting**[38] **or in connection with a corresponding official instruction**.[39] This does not require a formal power of representation.

46 Based on the principles developed for European antitrust procedural law, it can be assumed that a conduct happened **intentionally** if the undertaking or the gatekeeper have been **aware of the infringement of the obligation or if it could not have been unaware that the respective conduct was unlawful. Negligence** can be assumed if the natural person acting **should have been aware of the infringement.**[40] For both, intent and negligence, similar to European antitrust procedural law, any **lack of knowledge regarding the legal situation** does not exempt the undertaking from its liability.[41] However, it remains to be seen how the European Commission will deal with the requirements of the DMA, which are still partially unclear, as well as the lack of specification through explanatory guidelines or FAQs, like these which have been established for European antitrust procedural law, as well as with the **lack of corresponding case law**. Even if such lack of knowledge might in general not lead to the exemption from intent or negligence, the European Commission can (and should) consider the still existing legal uncertainty when setting the amount of a fine.[42]

47 Regarding the **amount of the fine**, the DMA does not differentiate between intent and negligence. However, a differentiation between the two forms of fault should be applied in practice, as it is difficult to exercise the rights of defence fully and properly without knowing whether the European Commission is pursuing a case based on intent or negligence. In addition, the severity of the infringement must be considered when fixing the amount of a fine (Art. 30(4) DMA), as an infringement committed negligently constitutes a less severe infringement (see below → mn. 52).

---

[38] LMRKM/Nowak VerfVO Art. 23 mn. 17; Bechtold/Bosch/Brinker Regulation (EG) No. 1/2003 Art. 23 mn. 36; MüKoEuWettbR/Engelsing/Schneider Regulation (EG) No. 1/2003 Art. 23 mn. 36.

[39] ECJ 7.2.2013 – C-68/12, ECLI:EU:C:2013:71 para. 25 = EuZW 2013, 438: The only relevant criterion is whether the person acting is entitled to act for the undertaking; LMRKM/Nowak VerfVO Art. 23 para. 17; Immenga/Mestäcker/Biermann Regulation (EG) No. 1/2003 Art. 30 para. 16; Podszun HK-DMA/Huerkamp/Nuys DMA Art. 30 mn. 66; Immenga/Mestmäcker/Biermann Regulation (EG) No. 1/2003 Art. 23 para. 16; Podszun HK-DMA/Huerkamp/Nuys DMA Art. 30 para. 66; Schmidt/Hübener/Reims, Das neue Recht der digitalen Märkte, 2023, Sec. 10 para. 9.

[40] Podszun HK-DMA/Huerkamp/Nuys DMA Art. 30 para. 62 et seqq.; Schmidt/Hübener/Reims, Das neue Recht der digitalen Märkte, 2023, Sec. 10 para. 9.

[41] ECJ 9.11.83 – 322/81, ECLI:EU:C:1983:313 para. 107 = BeckRS 2004, 70794; LMRKM/Nowak Regulation (EG) Nr. 1/2003 Art. 23 para. 20; NK-EuWettbR/Kienapfel Regulation (EG) No. 1/2003 Art. 23 para. 40.

[42] For example, the European Commission reduced a fine for an infringement of Art. 101 TFEU by 20 % because "on the one hand, the Commission has not yet applied a practice of sanctioning cartels solely on the basis of an infringement of Article 101(1)(b) of the Treaty but on the other hand, restrictions of technical development are expressly mentioned in the Treaty as an example of a restriction of competition. The Commission therefore considers it as appropriate to exceptionally reduce the fines to be imposed on all parties by 20 %." European Commission Decision 8 July 2021 – AT.40178 para. 235.

4. Calculation of fines

a) Assessment criteria

The European Commission has a **broad discretion** in setting the amount of the fine. In any case, the **gravity,** the **duration,** and a **repetition of non-compliance** must be taken into account (Art. 30(4) half sent. 1 DMA).[43] In case of an infringement of procedural law, the **delay caused to the proceedings** by the infringement is also to be considered (Art. 30(4), half sent. 2 DMA). 48

In contrast to European antitrust (procedural) law, the European Commission has not yet released any explanatory guidelines or notices for infringements of the DMA.[44] However, **the methodology** applied by the European Commission for the **setting of fines** regarding an infringement of Art. 101, 102 TFEU appears to be applicable to infringements of the core compliance obligations of gatekeepers under Art. 5, 6, 7 and 8(2) DMA.[45] 49

When it comes to setting the fine, like in the practice for antitrust law, the **first step** is to **determine a basic amount** that reflects the **gravity of the infringement.** This is determined by reference to the **turnover to which the infringement directly or indirectly is related**, the **duration** of the breach and the **impact** it had. The turnover relating to the infringement also appears to be an appropriate starting point in the context of the DMA as the caps on the amount of the fine provided for in Art. 30 DMA are also turnover-related. Based on that, the relevant turnover related to the infringement would be the **turnover generated** in the EEA **in the last full business year of the infringement with the core platform service to which the compliance obligation relates to.**[46] In light of the diversity of the compliance obligations and the associated potential infringements, it is sensible to differentiate not only **between infringements of procedural and substantive law**, but also within these two groups of infringements **according to the type compliance obligation**, and, thus, to differentiate according to the severity of the infringement. The reason for that is that a varying number of users are likely to be affected depending on the type of compliance obligation. As regards the duration (Art. 30(4) DMA) and the severity of the respective infringement, these should be **determined on a case-by-case basis, considering the respective compliance obligation that has been infringed.**[47] 50

As a **second step,** this basic amount would be **adjusted** considering all **factors that increase or reduce the fine.**[48] Although according to Art. 30(4) DMA and the general principles of antitrust law, the fact that the infringement is **repeatedly** committed generally increases the fine, in the context of the DMA it is doubtful whether the repetition of an infringement as such can be considered an aggravating factor when setting the fine. This is because the fact that the infringement has been repeatedly committed already triggers an increase of the cap from 10 % to 20 % (cf. Art. 30(2) DMA) for infringements pursuant to Art. 30(1) DMA. Thus, the repetition itself is already part of the infringement in the context Art. 30(2) DMA. Considering this twice and also as an aggravating factor when adjusting a fine would breach the prohibition of double jeopardy. 51

---

[43] Regarding recurrence Podszun HK-DMA/Huerkamp/Nuys DMA Art. 30 mn. 38 et seq.

[44] Commission Notice on Immunity from fines and reduction of fines in cartel cases, 8 December 2006; OJ C 298, 17.

[45] Similarly, Schmidt/Hübener/Reims, Das neue Recht der digitalen Märkte, 2023, Sec. 10 para. 14. Similarly Podszun HK-DMA/Huerkamp/Nuys DMA Art. 30 mn. 96 et seqq.

[46] Podszun HK-DMA/Huerkamp/Nuys DMA Art. 30 mn. 71.

[47] Podszun HK-DMA/Huerkamp/Nuys DMA Art. 30 mn. 74.

[48] Podszun HK-DMA/Huerkamp/Nuys DMA Art. 30 mn. 83 et seqq.

52 The fact that an infringement was only committed **negligently** should be considered as a mitigating factor.

53 **It is doubtful**, whether an increase of the fine **is permissible** solely to **ensure deterrence.**[49] In contrast to antitrust law, which prevents negative effects *ex post*, the DMA aims for a proactive, positive shaping of the competitive order.

54 On the relationship between the DMA and general antitrust law and the question of whether parallel proceedings under the DMA and general (European or national) antitrust law can be conducted in parallel → mn. 12, mn. 76 et seqq.[50]

b) Cap of fines

55 Art. 30(1), (2) DMA provide for a cap regarding the fines to be imposed for infringements of **substantive law. It caps the fine at 10 %**, in the case of a **repeated infringement of 20 %**, of the gatekeeper's total worldwide turnover in the preceding business year. For **infringements of procedural law**, Art. 30(3) DMA caps the fine at **1 %** of the total worldwide turnover of the preceding financial year of the undertaking committing the infringement.

56 In the case of gatekeepers as well as undertakings or associations of undertakings, the turnover of the entire group of undertakings including all **directly and indirectly affiliated undertakings** within the meaning of Art. 3(2) Regulation (EC) No. 139/2004 must be **considered** (Art. 2 no. 1, no. 27, no. 28 DMA).

c) Judicial review of fines imposed

57 The European Court of Justice has unlimited jurisdiction to review decisions and the related discretion of the European Commission when imposing fines, Art. 45 DMA.

II. Periodic penalty payments, Art. 31 DMA

58 To enforce the **obligations listed** in Art. 31(1) DMA, which can be imposed on undertakings by way of a decision, the European Commission may impose **daily** periodic penalty payments on undertakings amounting up to 5 % of the average daily worldwide turnover in the preceding financial year. The periodic penalty payment differs from the fine not only in terms of its calculation and its absolute amount, but, contrary to the fining decision, it **does not require any fault.** The **only** decisive factor for imposing a periodic penalty payment is the **fact of (non-)compliance with the obligations imposed by the European Commission.**

59 Periodic penalty payments can be adopted in order to compel undertakings to

- comply with the **behavioural remedies** specified by the European Commission in a decision adopted pursuant to **Art. 8(2) DMA** (Art. 31(1)(a) DMA);
- compliance with the **behavioural remedies** imposed in course of a **market investigation** pursuant to Art. 18(1) DMA (Art. 31(1)(b) DMA);
- the correct and complete **response** to a **formal decision to supply information pursuant to Art. 21 DMA** (Art. 31(1)(c) DMA);
- to ensure **access to data, algorithms and information about testing** in the context of a **formal decision to supply information pursuant to Art. 21 DMA** in response to a request made pursuant to Art. 21(3) DMA (Art. 31(1)(d) DMA);

---

[49] In contrast to Podszun HK-DMA/Huerkamp/Nuys DMA Art. 30 mn. 11.
[50] See also Podszun HK-DMA/Huerkamp/Nuys DMA Art. 30 mn. 14 et seq.

- to submit to an **inspection** which was ordered by a decision taken pursuant to Art. 23 DMA (Art. 31(1)(e) DMA);
- to comply with **decision ordering interim measures** taken pursuant to Art. 24 DMA (Art. 31(1)(f) DMA);
- to comply with **commitments** pursuant to Art. 25(1) DMA (Art. 31(1)(g) DMA);
- to comply with the **measures imposed in a non-compliance decision** pursuant to Art. 29(1) DMA (Art. 31(1)(h) DMA).

The amount of the total penalty payment to be imposed may be **subsequently reduced** in case of **compliance with the respective obligation,** Art. 31(2) DMA. **60**

The European Court of Justice has unlimited jurisdiction to review and the related discretion of the European Commission when imposing a periodic penalty payment, Art. 45 DMA. **61**

III. Limitation period

Regarding the limitation period and the calculation of the respective deadline, a **distinction** must be drawn between the **limitation period for the imposition of sanctions and the limitation period for the enforcement of sanctions.** **62**

1. Limitation period for the imposition of penalties, Art. 32 DMA

The limitation period for the imposing fines (Art. 30 DMA) and periodic penalty payments (Art. 31 DMA) is **five years,** Art. 32(1) DMA. In contrast to Art. 25(1) Regulation (EC) No. 1/2003, Art. 32 DMA does **not** differentiate **between infringements of procedural and substantive law** regarding the duration of the limitation period.[51] **63**

The limitation period **starts running** on the day on which the infringement is committed. However, in the case of continued or repeated infringements, it only starts running on the day on which the infringement ceases, Art. 32(2) DMA.[52] **64**

According to Art. 32(3)(1) DMA, generally all acts of the European Commission for the purpose of a market investigation or proceedings in respect of an infringement interrupt **the limitation period**, provided that the **interrupting action** is **notified to at least one undertaking which has participated in the infringement**, Art. 32(3)(2) DMA. **65**

In particular, Art. 32(3)(3) DMA lists as **events which interrupt the limitation period** **66**

- **requests for information** by the European Commission (lit. (a)) – the limitation period shall be interrupted with effect from the date on which the action is notified to the undertaking (Art. 32(3)(2) DMA);
- **written authorisations to conduct inspections** issued to its officials by the European Commission (lit. (b)) – according to Art. 32(3)(2) DMA, the interruption of the limitation period only comes into effect upon notification to at least one undertaking which has participated in the infringement; as well as
- the **opening of a proceeding pursuant to Art. 20 DMA** by the European Commission.

Based on the wording of Art. 32(3)(1), (3) DMA, it does **not** provide for **an exhaustive list** of events interrupting the limitation period. Yet, in any case the event must be committed by the European Commission. Unlike Art. 25(3) Regulation (EC) No. 1/2003, which expressly extends the interruption of the limitation period to actions by national

[51] Critically Podszun HK-DMA/Huerkamp/Nuys DMA Art. 32 mn. 5.
[52] Podszun HK-DMA/Huerkamp/Nuys DMA Art. 32 mn. 6 et seqq.

competition authorities, there is no corresponding reference in Art. 32(3) DMA. Hence, for example, requests by the member states pursuant to Art. 41 DMA cannot interrupt the limitation period.

67 **All undertakings involved in a potential infringement benefit** from the **interruption of limitation.** Otherwise, in case of several undertakings participating in an infringement, there remains uncertainty for these undertakings as to whether and when there might have been event by the European Commission which interrupted the limitation period, particularly since in practice undertakings might have been notified about the event at different points in time.[53]

68 Each interruption starts time running of the limitation period afresh, Art. 32(4) DMA. The European Commission can therefore **take investigative actions several times and in a row**, each of which leads to a fresh start of the limitation period. Imposing a fine or periodic penalty payment is in general only permissible until the maximum limitation period of ten years has elapsed, Art. 32(4)(2) DMA. However, the maximum limitation period is extended by the time during which the limitation period is suspended pursuant to Art. 32(5) DMA, Art. 32(4)(3) DMA.

69 Pursuant to Art. 32(5) DMA, **the limitation period** is **suspended** as long as **the decision imposing a fine or periodic penalty payment of the European Commission is under appeal before the European Court of Justice.** In contrast to an interruption, the suspension **only** applies **to the respective undertaking which filed the appeal** as in this case, and contrary to the actions interrupting the limitation period – once the appeal has been published in the Official Journal, there is transparency for all undertakings when the appeal has been filed. Hence, there is no remaining uncertainty like with actions interrupting the limitation period as to when the interruption might kick in.

2. Limitation period for the enforcement of penalties, Art. 33 DMA

70 The limitation period for the enforcement of fines (Art. 30 DMA) and penalty payments (Art. 31 DMA) is **five years**, Art. 33(1) DMA and **begins to run** from the **day on which the decision** imposing the fine or periodic penalty payment becomes **final,** Art. 33(2) DMA.

71 Art. 33(3) DMA **provides for an exhaustive list of events interrupting the limitation period**:

- the **notification of a decision adapting** the original amount of the fine or periodic penalty payment or **refusal of** an application for adapting the amount, Art. 33(3)(a) DMA;
- any action of the European Commission or a Member State, acting at the request of the European Commission, designed to **enforce payment** of the fine or periodic penalty payment, Art. 33(3)(b) DMA.

72 Each interruption shall start time **running afresh,** Art. 33(4) DMA.

73 The limitation period for enforcement of penalties is **suspended**

- for so long as **time to pay is allowed**, Art. 33(5)(a) DMA; or
- for so long as enforcement of payment is **suspended** pursuant to a decision of the European Court of Justice or to a decision by the national court, Art. 33(5)(b) DMA.

[53] For antitrust law see Art. 25(4) Regulation (EC) No. 1/2003; Immenga/Mestmäcker/Biermann Regulation (EC) No. 1/2003 Art. 25 mn. 22.

E. Course and closure of proceedings

I. Non-compliance decision, Art. 29 DMA

74 The European Commission can set out its findings regarding the **non-compliance of the gatekeeper with specific obligations and measures to remedy an infringement** in a non-compliance decision.

75 The adoption of a non-compliance decision **requires** the **formal opening of proceedings** and is the **prerequisite for the imposing sanctions.**[54]

76 The **opening of proceedings** by means of a decision (Art. 20(1) DMA)

is **condition for**

↓

Decisions pursuant to Art. 8, 29, 30 DMA. The non-compliance decision sets out that a gatekeeper

- **does not comply with obligations** laid down in Art. 5, 6 or 7, Art. 30(1)(a) DMA;
- **does not comply with measures laid down** by the European Commission in a resolution adopted pursuant to Art. 8(2), Art. 30(1)(b) DMA;
- **does not comply with remedies imposed** in course of a market investigation pursuant to Art. 18(1), Art. 30(1)(c) DMA;
- **does not comply with interim measures** imposed pursuant to Art. 24 DMA, Art. 30(1)(d) DMA, or
- **does not comply with commitments** made legally binding pursuant to Art. 25 DMA, Art. 30(1)(e) DMA.

77 The **non-compliance resolution** (Art. 29 DMA)

is a **condition for**

↓

the **imposing of a fine** on a gatekeeper in **the case of an infringement of substantive law**, Art. 30(1), (2) DMA. However, in the case of mere infringement of procedural law, the non-compliance resolution is not a formal condition for imposing a fine on an undertaking, including gatekeepers, Art. 30(3) DMA.

78 Before adopting a non-compliance resolution, the European Commission shall communicate to the gatekeeper its **preliminary findings** regarding, *inter alia*, the **infringement** as well as the **measures** the European Commission considers taking or that it considers that the gatekeeper should take to **effectively address** the preliminary findings, Art. 29(3) DMA. In this context, the European Commission may also consult third parties, Art. 29(4) DMA.

79 The European Commission "shall endeavour" to adopt the non-compliance resolution within **twelve months from the opening of the proceedings** pursuant to Art. 20(1) DMA, Art. 29(2) DMA. According to the wording of the provision, this is **not a fixed time limit**, but rather a **voluntary commitment** by the European Commission. It should be noted that the twelve-month period does not refer to the entire investigation proceeding. It **only starts with the adoption of an opening decision pursuant to Art. 20(1) DMA**. However, the European Commission is already entitled to the various investigative powers before opening proceedings according to Art. 20(1) DMA,

---

[54] Podszun HK-DMA/Podszun DMA Art. 29 mn. 4.

Art. 20(2) DMA, so that the **total duration of a proceeding from the first investigative measures to the adoption of a non-compliance decision can also be significantly longer** and, in view of the limited resources of the European Commission, probably will be so.

80 The final step of proceedings is the adoption of a non-compliance decision or if such a **non-compliance resolution** is not to be adopted, a decision closing the proceedings, Art. 29(5), (7) DMA.

81 The non-compliance decision is **structured into three main parts** (Art. 29(5) DMA):[55] It contains

- an **order to cease and desist** with the non-compliance directed at the gatekeeper,
- the stipulation of a **specific deadline** to cease and desist and
- obliges the gatekeeper to **provide an explanation as to how it intends to comply with the decision.**

82 In accordance with the non-compliance decision, the gatekeeper must then **provide** the European Commission with the **description of the measures that it has taken to ensure compliance with the non-compliance resolution** (Art. 29(6) DMA).

83 The European Commission can enforce compliance with the measures imposed in a non-compliance decision by imposing (daily) **periodic penalty payments** on the gatekeeper, Art. 31(1)(h) DMA.

II. Interim measures, Art. 24 DMA

84 The procedure for issuing a non-compliance resolution is accompanied by the European Commission's power to adopt interim measures against the gatekeeper in case of **urgency due to the risk of serious and irreparable damages for business users and end users of gatekeepers.**

85 Similar to antitrust law (Art. 8 Regulation (EC) No. 1/2003), the requirements for imposing such interim measures are high. The **exceptional nature** of this measure is also reflected in the fact that the European Commission **cannot adopt** the decision on its own, but **only with the involvement of the Digital Markets Advisory Committee,** Art. 24(1)(3), Art. 50 DMA.

86 The European Commission must already have **opened a proceeding for the adoption of a non-compliance decision**, Art. 24(1)(2), Art. 20(1), Art. 29(1) DMA.[56] In addition, **there must be a *prima facie* finding of an infringement of obligations pursuant to Art. 5, 6, 7 DMA.** Hence, the standard of proof for the existence of an infringement is lowered compared to the standard of proof regarding a non-compliance resolution. Following the practice in antitrust law, **a summary assessment of the facts must at first sight show good reasons for the existence of an infringement of the obligations pursuant to Art. 5, 6, 7 DMA.** This does not require (absolute) certainty as to whether there is actually an infringement.[57] To effectively exercise the rights of defence against the threatened adoption of interim measures and comparable to the decision opening the proceeding pursuant to Art. 20(1), (29) DMA, the European Commission shall **inform** the gatekeeper about the **preliminary findings.**[58]

---

[55] Podszun HK-DMA/Podszun DMA Art. 29 mn. 5 et seqq.

[56] Cf. also rec. 84.

[57] ECJ 22.12.2004 – T-201/04 R, ECLI:EU:T:2004:372 para. 404 = BeckRS 2004, 15619.

[58] Cf. for antitrust law Immenga/Mestmäcker/Ritter/Wirtz Regulation (EG) Nr. 1/2003 Art. 8 mn. 8.

Interim measures can only be adopted in case of **urgency**. Urgency within the meaning of Art. 24(1)(1) DMA requires the risk of a **serious and irreparable damage to business users or end users of the gatekeeper**. The intervention by interim measures together with the non-compliance decision thus serves the purpose of preventing **developments that are difficult to be reversed.**[59] 87

Accordingly – and in consideration of the lowered standard of proof with regard to the existence of a potential infringement – interim measures may only preserve the *status quo* and have a provisional nature. 88

Moreover, they may only be imposed for **a specified period of time**, which may be **renewed**, in case and to the extent this is necessary and appropriate, Art. 24(1)(3) DMA. Once interim measures have been imposed, but the gatekeeper changes its conduct in a way that the corresponding risk either disappears or the imminent damage is neither serious nor irreparable, the **urgency ceases to exist retroactively**. As a consequence, the European Commission has to **annul** the measures **with *ex nunc* effect.**[60] 89

According to the wording – and as recognised for the identical wording of Art. 8(1) Regulation (EC) No. 1/2003 – it is within the **discretion** of the European Commission to adopt interim measures. In principle, potential business users or end users of the gatekeeper are **not entitled to claim** to the imposition of interim measures by the European Commission. 90

F. Professional secrecy, Art. 36 DMA

The information collected pursuant to the DMA may, in principle, only be used **for the purposes of the DMA**, Art. 36(1) DMA. 91

This does not apply to information that gatekeepers submit to the European Commission as part of the **reporting obligations for mergers**. These can be used under Regulation (EC) No. 139/2004 as well as under the national merger rules, Art. 14, Art. 36(2) DMA. 92

Similarly, Art. 36(3) DMA provides for an exception for information collected in the context of the **assessment of compliance with the obligations for profiling of consumers**, which, according to Art. 36(3), Art. 15(1) DMA, may be used for the purposes of both, the DMA and the **General Data Protection Regulation.**[61] 93

Any use of the information outside these exceptions is not **permitted**. This applies particularly to any **antitrust proceedings** conducted against gatekeepers, namely pursuant to Art. 102 TFEU. 94

G. Cooperation with national authorities

The role of the **national authorities** for the enforcement of the DMA is basically **limited to cooperation obligations and supporting the European Commission**. The information exchanged between the European Commission and national authorities mainly goes to the European Commission. Unlike in the enforcement of Art. 101, 102 TFEU, there is no reciprocal information flow. 95

---

[59] Rec. 84 DMA.

[60] For cartel procedure law, ECJ 10.3.2005 – T-184/01, ECLI:EU:T:2005:95 para. 35 et seqq. = BeckRS 2005, 156101.

[61] Regulation (EU) 2016/679 of the European Parliament and of the Council of 27 April 2016 on the protection of natural persons with regard to the processing of personal data and on the free movement of such data, and repealing Directive 95/46/EC (General Data Protection Regulation); OJ L 119, 1.

96 Moreover, the national authorities do **not** have **the power to impose sanctions.**

97 The far-reaching primary competence of the European Commission is safeguarded on the one hand by the enforcement competences expressly assigned to the national authorities in Art. 1(6) DMA, which are meant to be outside the scope of the DMA,[62] and on the other hand by the ***effet utile* and principle of loyalty** (Art. 4(3) subpara. 3 TEU) codified in Art. 1(7) DMA.[63] According to this principle, the Member States may **not adopt decisions which run counter to decisions of the European Commission under the DMA**.

I. General duty of cooperation and consultation of national authorities, Art. 1(7)(2), Art. 37 DMA

98 According to Art. 37(1) DMA, the European Commission and the Member States shall work in close **cooperation** and **coordinate** their enforcement actions regarding gatekeepers. In doing so, the national authorities shall **provide** the European Commission with **information** they have received.[64]

99 The European Commission may also **consult** national authorities, where appropriate, on all matters relating to the application of the DMA, Art. 37(2) DMA.

II. Support of the European Commission

100 The national authorities shall, upon request, support the European Commission to exercise its powers so that the latter is better able to carry out its duties under the DMA.[65] Accordingly, the European Commission may ask one or more national competent authorities to **assist** in its **market investigations** (Art. 16(5), Art. 38(6) DMA) and in **inspections** (Art. 23(3), (7) DMA). According to the DMA, these are in principle "core activities" of the European Commission. Whether and to what extent the European Commission will ask for such support remains to be seen in practice and will depend on the resources available at the Directorate General Connect and the Directorate General for Competition.

III. Investigations by the national competition authorities

101 Art. 38 DMA provides for rules on the **cooperation with national competition authorities**. The provision was only included in the draft at a late stage, after disputes on due process and conflicts of competence between the European Commission and national competition authorities became apparent. From an antitrust law perspective, technology companies from the USA have already been a priority in the enforcement agenda of the national competition authorities before the DMA has been created.[66] Furthermore, as part of the 10th amendment to the Act against Restraints of Competition (ARC) and before the DMA came into force, the German legislator created a national competence (Sec. 19a ARC) which also allows a targeted approach against Big Tech.

---

[62] On the difficulties of qualifying and classifying Sec. 19a ARC → mn. 12, mn. 76 et seqq.

[63] Rec. 90.

[64] Rec. 90.

[65] Rec. 90.

[66] FCO 6.2.2019 – B6-22/16; FCO 5.7.2022 – B2-55/21.

The DMA recognises the **risk of a duplication of work and overlapping investigations resulting from this conflict of competences.**[67] In light of this, Art. 38(2), (3) DMA stipulate **reporting obligations** of the national competition authorities regarding the opening and the closure of proceedings initiated against gatekeepers by national competition authorities within their remaining competences pursuant to Art. 1(6) DMA, Art. 38(2) DMA. The latter relates to any investigations by the national competition authorities dealing with **infringements of antitrust law**. According to Art. 38(2) DMA, the European Commission shall be **informed in writing of the first formal investigative measure, before or immediately after the beginning of that.** A similar reporting obligation does also exist where a national competition authority intends to impose obligations on gatekeepers, Art. 38(3) DMA. This applies especially to **imposing fines on gatekeepers.**[68] The reporting obligation does not apply to **national merger proceedings involving gatekeepers**, Art. 38(4) DMA. 102

In addition to the "residual competences" of the national competition authorities to enforce infringements outside the scope of the DMA, Art. 38(7) DMA creates **a derivative competence of the national competition authorities.**[69] National competition authorities may, in the context of an exclusive competence of the European Commission, by their own initiative conduct **investigations** against gatekeepers regarding possible infringements of Art. 5, 6 and 7 DMA. This is in particular relevant for cases where it **cannot be determined before the start of the investigations whether a gatekeeper's behaviour is capable of infringing the DMA, antitrust rules or even both.**[70] However, before taking the first formal investigative measure the national authority must **inform** the European Commission **in writing** in order to preserve the European Commission's primary competence, Art. 38(7) DMA. Subsequently, the **European Commission is then free to decide whether to open its own proceedings.** 103

If the European Commission decides to (formally) open its own proceedings pursuant to Art. 20 DMA, **the competence of the national competition authority ends.** As a result, the European Commission becomes the sole enforcer of the DMA, Art. 38(8)(1) DMA. Also, an already ongoing investigation of the national competition authority ends, Art. 38(8)(2) DMA. 104

Although Art. 38(8) DMA **transfers the competence from the national competition authority to the European Commission** only after opening of proceedings pursuant to Art. 20 DMA, the European Commission's **discretion** should be **reduced to zero** regarding the various investigative powers it has before opening proceedings according to Art. 20(2) DMA (→ mn. 6). Accordingly, the European Commission shall not use its investigatory powers in parallel to investigations conducted by national competition authorities. This is in line with the meaning and purpose of the provision, which aims to avoid a duplication of work (cf. recital 91). Moreover, the national competition authority must report to the European Commission on the findings of its investigation in any event, Art. 38(8)(2) DMA. Hence, there is **no reason for a parallel investigation** by the European Commission. In any case, taking investigate measures in parallel would not be "necessary" within the meaning of Art. 21, 23 DMA (on necessity → mn. 14). 105

Furthermore, in practice, the national (competition) authorities will probably also conduct **their own investigations** pursuant to Art. 27(1), (3) DMA. According to Art. 27(3) DMA, they are entitled to receive information on potential infringements by gatekeepers provided by third parties (→ mn. 8 et seqq.). However, the national authori- 106

[67] Rec. 91.
[68] Rec. 91.
[69] Podszun HK-DMA/Käseberg/Gappa DMA Art. 38 mn. 25 et seqq.
[70] Rec. 91.

ties are **only obliged to submit the information to the European Commission – and thus to transfer the proceeding – if the national authorities conclude that there *"may be an issue of non-compliance"* with the DMA** (Art. 27(3) DMA). The DMA does not specify the **degree of certainty** that the national authority must have gained in this regard. In light of the European Commission being the primary enforcer of the DMA, this threshold will likely be fulfilled at least in case of an **initial suspicion of an infringement** as at this point the European Commission could initiate investigations on its own by virtue of its own competences (in this regard → mn. 6).

CHAPTER 3:
P2B REGULATION

§ 15
Scope of application

Literature: *Alexander*, 'Anwendungsbereich, Regelungstechnik und einzelne Transparenzvorgaben der P2B-Verordnung', WRP 2020, 945; *Busch* (ed), Verordnung (EU) 2019/1150 zur Förderung von Fairness und Transparenz für gewerbliche Nutzer von Online-Vermittlungsdiensten (P2B-VO), Munich 2022; Callies/Ruffert (eds), EUV/AEUV Das Verfassungsrecht der Europäischen Union mit Europäischer Grundrechtecharta, 6th edn, Munich 2022; Dauses/Ludwig (eds), Handbuch des EU-Wirtschaftsrechts, Munich 2023; *Fritzsche/Münker/Stollwerck* (eds), Beck'scher Onlinekommentar UWG, 22nd edn, Munich 2023; *Köhler/Bornkamm/Feddersen* (eds), Gesetz gegen den unlauteren Wettbewerb, 42nd edn, Munich 2024; *Kühling/Buchner* (eds), Datenschutz-Grundverordnung/BDSG, 4th edn, Munich 2024; *Naumann/Rodenhausen*, 'Die P2B-Verordnung aus Unternehmenssicht: Herausforderungen für europäische Plattformen am Beispiel einer Hybrid-Online-Plattform', ZEuP 2020, 768; Paal/Pauly (eds), Datenschutzgrundverordnung. Bundesdatenschutzgesetz, 3rd edn, Munich 2021; *Riesenhuber*, Europäische Methodenlehre, 4th edn, Berlin 2021; *Wais*, 'B2B-Klauselkontrolle in der Plattform-Ökonomie: Der Kommissionsvorschlag für eine Verordnung über Online-Vermittlungsdienste', EuZW 2019, 221.

A. Introduction

The **origins of** the Regulation on Promoting Fairness and Transparency for Business Users of Online Intermediation Services[1], better known as the Platform-to-Business Regulation (P2B Regulation) lie in the European Commission's 2015 Digital Single Market Strategy.[2] The e-commerce sector inquiry quickly drew attention to the platform economy.[3] Platforms are intermediaries between traders and consumers (B2C) or between traders themselves (B2B). However, the platform economy exhibits problematic 1

[1] Regulation (EU) 2019/1150 of the European Parliament and of the Council of 20 June 2019 on promoting fairness and transparency for business users of online intermediation services, OJ 2019 L 186, 57.

[2] European Commission, 'A Digital Single Market Strategy for Europe', 6.5.2015, COM(2015) 192 final.

[3] European Commission, 'Initiating an inquiry into the e-commerce sector pursuant to Article 17 of Council Regulation (EC) No 1/2003', 6.5.2015, COM(2015) 3026 final.

tendencies: 46 % of business users surveyed reported they had encountered problems with platforms.[4] Key concerns included the market power of platforms, their lack of transparency, and potential self-preferencing.[5]

2 In response, the **Commission's proposal of** 2018[6] focused on transparency obligations regarding general terms and conditions, rankings, data access and exclusive arrangements, procedural regulations, such as the introduction of a mediation and complaints procedure, and representative actions.[7] Moreover, the European Parliament wanted to include substantive fairness obligations, such as controls on the content of general terms and conditions, a ban on wide most favoured nation clauses, a restriction on narrow most favoured nation clauses, and a right of access to data.[8] However, the Council of the European Union rejected these amendments and preferred a 'formal concept of fairness', instead of substantive requirements.[9]

3 In its **final form,** the P2B Regulation aims to establish a fair, predictable, sustainable, and trusted online business environment within the internal market[10] and a competitive, fair, and transparent online ecosystem where companies act responsibly.[11] Indirectly, the regulation also aims to protect consumers. Not only do the recitals frequently refer to consumer protection, consumer welfare, and the interests of consumers, but platforms that exclusively mediate between commercial users (B2B) are excluded from the scope of application.[12] As with the Consumer Rights Directive[13], the regulation's legal basis is Art. 114 TFEU. As a regulation, it is directly applicable in the EU Member States. Hence, its transposition into national law serves only as a clarification. Its content comprises a blend of contract law, unfair trade law, and antitrust law.[14]

4 The **relationship of the P2B Regulation to other legal provisions** is of great practical significance. Art. 1(4) explicitly states that national competition and unfair trade law remain applicable alongside the P2B Regulation, as does national contract law (including laws on general terms and conditions). According to Art. 1(5), the same applies to relevant EU provisions, e.g. competition or consumer protection law.

5 **The Digital Markets Act** (DMA)[15] can be seen as an extension of the P2B Regulation. It focuses on market power and regulates substantive issue such as self-preferencing, data access, most favoured nation clauses, that the Council rejected for the P2B Regulation (cf. Art. 5(3),(9),(10) and Art. 6(5),(8) and (11) DMA).

6 In order to define the **scope** of the regulation, the term 'platform' includes online intermediation services and online search engines. Additionally, the term 'business' encompasses both business users and corporate website users. These two groups constitute

---

[4] European Commission, 'Impact Assesment', 26.4.2018, SWD(2018) 138 final, with further reference.

[5] Tribess in Fritzsche/Münker/Stollwerck P2B Reg Art. 1 mn. 2.

[6] European Commission, 'Proposal for a regulation of the European Parliament and of the Council on promoting fairness and transparency for business users of online intermediation services, 26.4.2018, COM(2018) 238 final.

[7] Busch in Busch P2B Reg Introduction mn. 4.

[8] Busch in Busch P2B Reg Introduction mn. 5.

[9] Busch in Busch P2B Reg Introduction mn. 6.

[10] Rec. 7 P2B Regulation.

[11] Rec. 3 P2B Regulation.

[12] Rec. 9 P2B Regulation.

[13] Directive 2011/83/EU of the European Parliament and of the Council of 25 October 2011 on consumer rights, amending Council Directive 93/13/EEC and Directive 1999/44/EC of the European Parliament and of the Council and repealing Council Directive 85/577/EEC and Directive 97/7/EC of the European Parliament and of the Council, OJ 2011 L 304, 64.

[14] Alexander in Köhler/Bornkamm/Feddersen P2B Reg Art. 1 mn. 5.

[15] OJ 2022 L 265, 1.

the 'P' and 'B' in the P2B Regulation. The next three sections each cover one of the three dimensions of the scope of application: personal, substantive, and geographical.

B. Personal scope

While the regulation indirectly protects consumers, it directly protects only **two specific groups of businesses**: business users and corporate website users. In summary, both terms meet the criteria of undertaking under EU law,[16] and their definitions are almost identical.[17] Businesses of all sizes are protected, even though the initial focus was on small and medium-sized enterprises.[18] 7

I. Business users

Business users are defined in Art. 2(1) as legal persons or private individuals who offer goods or services to consumers through online intermediation services in connection with their 'trade, business, craft or profession'. The terminology used in this definition is unusual. The regulation prefers the term 'private individual' over 'natural person'.[19] This raises the question whether the term 'business user' in the P2B Regulation corresponds to the term 'trader' in EU consumer law.[20] The same sequence of adjectives qualifies the activity, indicating at least a close relationship between the two terms. The only justification for the regulation not using the term trader – apart from a drafting error[21] – is that 'business user' denotes a different perspective and goal of protection.[22] From a linguistic-structural point of view, business 'users' are likely closer to consumers than traders. 8

Essentially, the question is whether the online intermediation service is used in connection with a permanent, self-employed **activity** offered on the market for remuneration.[23] The partial redundancy of 'trade, business, craft or profession' likely aims to cover varying definitions in the Member States, such as in Germany, where certain 'liberal professions' of a scientific, artistic, or pedagogic nature are not considered trades or businesses.[24] The activity does not have to be carried out full time or with the intention of making a profit.[25] But the use of the online intermediation service must form part of this activity. While the wording only requires that the use is connected to this activity, the activity must not merely serve as the occasion. The following activities do not qualify the acting party as a business user: an employee selling used work clothes on eBay,[26] a travelling salesman offering a ride on a carpooling or ridesharing app (e.g. BlaBlaCar), an employee renting out their company flat on Airbnb while on holiday. 9

This raises further questions about distinguishing between business users and consumers. The most important case concerns the so-called **'gig economy'**. Examples include individuals who offer rides with their own vehicle via Uber or those who bring 10

---

[16] Schulte-Nölke in Busch P2B Reg Art. 1 mn. 13.
[17] Schulte-Nölke in Busch P2B Reg Art. 2 mn. 2.
[18] Naumann/Rodenhausen ZEuP 2020, 768 (777).
[19] Schulte-Nölke in Busch P2B Reg Art. 2 mn. 4.
[20] Schulte-Nölke in Busch P2B Reg Art. 2 mn. 3, with reference e.g. to Art. 2 No. 2 Consumer Rights Directive.
[21] Schulte-Nölke in Busch P2B Reg Art. 2 mn. 4.
[22] Schulte-Nölke in Busch P2B Reg Art. 2 mn. 5.
[23] Schulte-Nölke in Busch P2B Reg Art. 2 mn. 6.
[24] Schulte-Nölke in Busch P2B Reg Art. 2 mn. 6.
[25] Schulte-Nölke in Busch P2B Reg Art. 2 mn. 6.
[26] Schulte-Nölke in Busch P2B Reg Art. 2 mn. 6.

food from restaurants to customers via a delivery service (e.g. Uber Eats and Delivery Hero). The legislator might have used the term 'private individual' for these cases, since Art. 2(7) uses 'natural persons' for corporate website users. These activities were traditionally carried out by employees for an employer, so the question of a P2B relationship between the parties did not arise.

11 However, businesses are increasingly acting as intermediary platforms between users and service providers who are classified as self-employed. On 9.12.2021, the European Commission presented a proposal for a directive[27] that establishes a presumption that such a relationship counts as employment if a digital labour platform controls certain elements of the performance of work.[28] Regardless of this proposal, labour law protection will often be stronger than the protection offered by the P2B Regulation. These (**'false self-employed'**) service providers could be excluded from the scope of the regulation, as the relationship in question is regulated by more specific labour law. However, 'gig workers' could be classified as both employees under national law and as business users for the purposes of the P2B Regulation.[29] It remains to be seen whether there will be a need for this after the aforementioned proposal is adopted. At the very least, the argument that the P2B regulation needs to address the gaps caused by varying legal frameworks in different Member States will become obsolete.[30]

12 On the other hand, one could imagine the unwritten sub-category of **'false business users'**. Users who do not meet the objective criteria to be classified as business[31] could still invoke the P2B Regulation if the platform provider created the impression that they are business users.[32] These service providers would have the option to either invoke the provisions of the P2B Regulation or the potentially more advantageous national labour law. A German court found that the P2B Regulation does not necessarily supersede regulations in other areas of law (in this case competition law), even if it is applicable.[33]

13 Another case concerns private individuals who could cross the line to business users due to their **extensive use** of the online intermediation service. This includes 'powersellers' on eBay, permanent hosts on Airbnb, and drivers who generate positive income by continuously offering ride-shares. This requires a case-by-case analysis. Consumer protection laws often categorise this group as business users to ensure that consumers are afforded the highest level of protection when engaging with them. Under the P2B Regulation, the status of business users serves this very group. However, the regulation does not state that the protection of business users must be as strong as the protection afforded to consumers under consumer protection law. Thus, the threshold for private individuals who extensively use platforms could be higher than that under consumer protection law.

II. Corporate website users

14 The second group of businesses is **corporate website users**. Art. 2(7) defines these as natural or legal persons who offer goods or services to consumers through an online interface (mainly a website or application) for purposes related to their trade, business,

[27] European Commission, 'Proposal for a directive of the European Parliament and of the Council on improving working conditions in platform work', 9.12.2021, COM(2021) 762 final.
[28] Art. 4(1) alt. 1 COM(2021) 762 final.
[29] Schulte-Nölke in Busch P2B Reg Art. 2 mn. 10.
[30] See Schulte-Nölke in Busch P2B Reg Art. 2 mn. 10.
[31] Schulte-Nölke in Busch P2B Reg Art. 2 mn. 6.
[32] This is at least the result of Schulte-Nölke in Busch P2B Reg Art. 2 mn. 11.
[33] LG München 15.5.2021 – 37 O 21/21, MMR 2021, 995 mn. 75.

craft, or profession. This definition largely coincides with that of business users. Hence, only the additional characteristics are described below.

15 A corporate website first requires an **online interface**. This is defined as any software, including (parts of) web pages and (mobile) applications. This concept is understood broadly.[34] It includes traditional websites (e.g. web shops), applications and software for computers and mobile devices, as well as corporate profiles on other platforms (e.g. a Facebook Page or Google Maps Page). The latter is only included if the profile was **actively created**, commissioned, or at least approved by the business owner.[35] Profiles and pages created automatically (e.g. through 'scraping' or with metadata) or by customers do not make the respective business owner a corporate website 'user'. This means that a business owner with a profile or page created by customers on Google Maps must first claim this page in order to enjoy the rights of the regulation. However, corporate website users can terminate their relationship with the online search engine, e.g., by preventing indexing through conventions (e.g. through a robots.txt file) or technical means (e.g. through 'captchas').

C. Substantive scope

16 The substantive scope complements the personal scope by defining the addressees of the regulation.[36] However, the substantive scope itself has a strong personal element because it defines in Art. 2(2) and (5) the providers of **two specific types of platforms**: online intermediation services and online search engines. Most of the regulation addresses online intermediation services.[37] Only isolated provisions apply to online search engines, (e.g. parts of Art. 5 and 7). But the substantive scope for online search engines is broader, as the regulation requires no contractual relationship between the provider and the business user.

17 The **size of the platform** does not play a role for the application of the P2B Regulation, unlike in the case of the DMA. It also applies to small platforms. Instead of determining market power based on economic size, the regulation focuses on the structural bargaining power of platforms. This power results in particular from the indirect network effects of the data economy, which leads to the dependence of small business users on platforms.[38] Similarly, contract law rules on general terms and conditions assume structural power of those who set these conditions, without considering the specific economic circumstances.[39]

I. Online intermediation services

18 Art. 2(2) defines **online intermediation services** as information society services that, on a contractual basis, enable business users to offer goods or services to consumers. The Commission explicitly mentions examples such as e-commerce marketplaces, short-

[34] Schulte-Nölke in Busch P2B Reg Art. 2 mn. 72.
[35] Schulte-Nölke in Busch P2B Reg Art. 2 mn. 72.
[36] Alexander in Köhler/Bornkamm/Feddersen P2B Reg Art. 1 mn. 23.
[37] This is already supported by the title of the regulation; see also: Alexander WRP 2020, 945 (947).
[38] Rec. 2 P2B Regulation.
[39] Busch in Busch P2B Reg Introduction mn. 9.

term accommodation rental platforms, application stores, and social media platforms for businesses.[40]

1. Information society services

19 Art. 2(2)(a) requires an **information society service** as defined in Art. 1(1)(b) of the Information Society Services Directive[41]. This consists of three main elements, with the restriction that the activity must generally be provided for remuneration. The service must be provided: a) upon individual request, b) at a distance, and c) by electronic means (→ § 2 mn. 5).

a) Provision at the individual request of the recipient

20 Art. 1(1)(b)(iii) of the Information Society Services Directive defines a service as provided at the **individual request of the recipient** if it is provided 'through by the transmission of data on individual request'. The recipient of the service must first make a request to the service provider. The latter receives this request and transmits data compiled for the recipient. In contrast, the directive does not cover services where the provider transmits data concurrently to an unlimited number of recipients (so-called 'point-to-multipoint transmission'[42]). Annex I No. 3 of the Information Society Services Directive lists as examples of this live television programmes based on a broadcasting schedule (Art. 1(1)(e) AMS Directive[43]) and their time-shifted reception (e.g. near-video-on-demand, in which in television programmes are broadcasted in a staggered manner to enable 'connection' at a later date[44]), radio services and teletext received through the television signal. Additionally, analogue and digital radio, as well as online radio services and live streams (e.g. on Twitch or Youtube) are not transmitted upon individual request.

b) Provision at a distance

21 Art. 1(1)(b)(i) of the Information Society Services Directive defines a service as **provided at a distance** if it is provided 'without the parties being simultaneously present'. This includes traditional distance selling via the internet or telephone, where the recipient is not at the premises or in the presence of an employee of the provider. Examples include orders placed via the Internet, phone, or applications. However, the use of electronic or internet-based tools does not automatically fulfil the definition. Annex I of the directive clarifies that if a travel agent books an airline ticket over the internet for a customer who is physically present in the agency, this booking is not provided at a distance. The same applies to electronic games in an amusement arcade and electronic catalogues in a shop. The latter case likely includes 'digital kiosks' (e.g. in fast food restaurants), where customers select and pay for their goods to then pick them up at the counter without the help of a salesperson. The same should apply if a customer present in the

---

[40] European Commission, 'Q&A EN Communication 2020' (9.7.2020) <https://ec.europa.eu/newsroom/dae/document.cfm?doc_id=68300> (last accessed: 02.07.2024), p. 12.

[41] Directive (EU) 2015/1535 of the European Parliament and of the Council of 9 September 2015 laying down a procedure for the provision of information in the field of technical regulations and of rules on Information Society services (Information Society Services Directive), OJ 2015 L 241, 1.

[42] Ernst in Paal/Pauly GDPR Art. 4 mn. 147.

[43] Directive (EU) 2018/1808 of the European Parliament and of the Council of 14 November 2018 amending Directive 2010/13/EU on the coordination of certain provisions laid down by law, regulation or administrative action in Member States concerning the provision of audiovisual media services (Audiovisual Media Services Directive), OJ 2018 L 303, 69.

[44] Oster/Wagner in Dauses/Ludwigs E. V. mn. 89.

shop uses their mobile phone instead of a digital kiosk. However, it is difficult to precisely delineate the boundaries, as customers can move between the shop and public spaces during the process. Another example of Annex I is the patient who is physically present in a doctor's surgery being examined or treated using electronic equipment.

c) *Electronic delivery*

22 Art. 1(1)(b)(i) of the Information Society Services Directive defines a service as **electronically provided** if it is 'sent initially and received at its destination by means of electronic equipment for the processing […] and storage of data' and the transport of the data is transmitted entirely 'by wire, by radio, by optical means or by other electromagnetic means'. On the one hand, this excludes analogue distance selling services (e.g. mail ordering catalogues), including distance selling of CD-ROMs or software on other physical storage media. But it also excludes electronic services that are not provided through an electronic processing or inventory system. This includes voice telephony services (e.g. access codes for making cheaper international calls via override providers), fax/telex services, services provided through voice or fax (e.g. directory enquiry and hotline services), medical or legal advice, and direct marketing by telephone/fax. Finally, Annex 1 No. 1 excludes electronic services that have a material content, such as ATMs and ticket machines, as well as machines granting access to toll roads and car parks. The decisive element seems to be that the material service is provided directly at the machine. Thus, this should not apply to gambling machines that enable users to place bets (e.g. on sporting events) with remote providers via the internet.

d) *Service normally provided for remuneration*

23 Art. 1(1)(b) of the Information Society Services Directive requires that the service must normally be **provided in exchange for payment**. Payment often takes the form of a brokering fee (e.g. for taxi or hotel services). However, the term information society service is also used in the e-commerce Directive[45] and the GDPR[46]. In addition, electronic communications services are defined similarly in the e-communications Code as 'normally provided for remuneration'.[47] We can assume a consistent understanding of the concept of remuneration in these closely related provisions. For these areas, it is recognised that the services are provided for remuneration if they are offered on a commercial basis.[48] This goes beyond financial considerations from the users and includes advertisement-based financing from third parties, consideration in the form of user data, and when the service is offered as self-promotion for the provider (e.g. a 'free trial period').[49] Art. 1(1)(b) does not even require that the specific service in question be provided on a commercial basis. The wording 'normally for remuneration' only means that the type of service must usually be offered commercially (e.g. by other providers), not

---

[45] See Art. 2(a) Directive 2000/31/EC of the European Parliament and of the Council of 8 June 2000 on certain legal aspects of information society services, in particular electronic commerce, in the Internal Market ('Directive on electronic commerce'), OJ 2000 L 178, 1, which refers for this definition to Directive 98/34/EC of the European Parliament and of the Council of 22 June 1998 laying down a procedure for the provision of information in the field of technical standards and regulations, OJ 1998 L 204, 37.

[46] See Art. 4 no. 25 GDPR, which refers directly to the Information Society Services Directive.

[47] Art. 2 no. 5 Directive (EU) 2018/1972 of the European Parliament and of the Council of 11 December 2018 establishing the European Electronic Communications Code.

[48] Buchner/Kühling in Kühling/Buchner GDPR Art. 4 no. 25 mn. 6.

[49] Buchner/Kühling in Kühling/Buchner GDPR Art. 4 no. 25 mn. 6 et seq., with reference to ECJ 15.9.2016 – case C-484/14, ECLI:EU:C:2016:689 = GRUR 2016, 1146 mn. 41 et seq. – Tobias Mc Fadden v Sony Music Entertainment Germany GmbH.

necessary by the provider in question. Also, the term 'service' does not necessarily entail a financial consideration.[50]

2. Intermediation service

24 Art. 2(2)(b) further requires that the information society service be an **intermediation service**. It does so if it enables business users to 'offer goods or services to consumers' by brokering direct transactions between these groups. Since the platform must mediate between consumers and business users, three different relationships arise: A contractual relationship must exist between the platform and the business user (→ mn. 28 et seq.), a transaction between the consumer and the business user must be foreseeable (although not certain), and the consumer must, at the very least, use the platform *de facto*. The concept of 'business user' is the same as for the personal scope of application (→ mn. 8 et seqq.). The term 'consumer' is also used in the same way as for determining the geographical scope of application (→ mn. 52). The concept of goods or services does not require any new interpretation either, as it aligns the broad interpretation of primary EU law.

a) Transactions

25 Direct **transactions between consumers and business users must be initiated** on the platform, but it is irrelevant whether the transactions are *actually concluded*. The term transaction is closely related to the exchange of goods and services. The initiation comprises all actions that help to make a subsequent contract possible. This includes pre-contractual aspects such as creating a user account, starting a trial subscription, or providing free credit that the user can use later. In contrast, actions do not facilitate initiating a transaction if their aim is to change or terminate the contract or assert secondary rights arising from the contract. Thus, services that assist users in terminating their contracts (e.g. Aboalarm, Resilier.com, Kündigen.com) and certain 'legal tech' offers (e.g. Reclamador, RightNow, Wenigermiete.de, Flightright, Lagere-huur.nl) are not governed by the P2B Regulation. For the P2B regulation, it is irrelevant whether this transaction could be legally concluded or would be null and void for violating legal prohibitions (e.g. brokering illegal gambling).[51]

26 The transaction does not have to be completed on the platform. The rider of 'irrespective of where those transactions are ultimately concluded' only clarifies this aspect. It is irrelevant whether a transaction is completed on the platform of the intermediation service, on the website of the business user, offline, or not at all.[52] Thus, even comparison portals (e.g. Check24, Go.Compare, Verivox) and specialised product search engines (e.g. Google Shopping, Idealo, PriceRunner, Beslist.nl, Kelkoo) initiate transactions, despite (usually) referring consumers to business websites after displaying the results. Likewise, the parties can conclude a contract offline.[53] Someone who uses a platform (such as Quandoo, TheFork, Tablebooker) to reserve a table at a restaurant only completes the actual transaction (ordering a meal) when they arrive at the restaurant. The same applies to classified ads or second-hand shops (e.g. Facebook Marketplace,

---

[50] Thus, the ECJ also does not limit the concept of service in Art. 56 TFEU to services with direct financial consideration, but includes services financed by advertising: ECJ 26.4.1988 – case C-352/85, ECLI:EU:C:1988:196 = NJW 1989, 2189 mn. 16 – Bond van Adverteerders and others v The Netherlands State.

[51] Schulte-Nölke in Busch P2B Reg Art. 2 mn. 29.

[52] This is also the list in rec. 10 P2B Regulation.

[53] Rec. 11 P2B Regulation states that the transactions can be concluded at least 'partially offline'.

Kleinanzeigen.de, Marktplaats.nl, LeBonCoin, Segundamano.es, Gumtree) where buyers and sellers are connected, but the actual sale takes place offline (e.g. after inspecting the goods). However, this only applies if the seller is a business user.

b) Facilitation

The platform must facilitate the initiation of this transaction. While the wording implies an active role of the platform (e.g. directly approaching consumers), facilitation could be as simple as enabling business users to offer their goods and services. The element of facilitation specifies how the platform must allow business users to offer their goods and services. Facilitation narrows the scope from general enabling to ***purposeful enabling***. Short message services (e.g. X, formerly Twitter) or messenger services (e.g. WhatsApp, Signal, Telegram, Snapchat) also enable users to initiate a transaction (in a broader sense), because users can communicate on these platforms. However, these platforms do not enable such transactions *purposefully*. For example, they do not offer categories and classifications for goods and services, geographical restrictions (search radius), separate variables for prices, or the ability for users to search for specific shopping criteria. 27

3. Contractual relationship as a basis

This intermediation activity must be based on a **contractual relationship** between the online intermediation service provider and the business user. As is appropriate for a digital services regulation, this contract can be concluded in any form. Nor does it matter which legal system governs the contract.[54] 28

Whether this contract must be **effective and legally binding** (under the applicable law) is more complicated. Such a requirement could lead to significant difficulties in court because the regulation's scope would depend on the interpretation of national contract law. Moreover, platform service providers could avoid the regulation's applicability by terminating the contract with the business user. Nevertheless, some consider this requirement necessary, at least if a business user invokes the regulation to bring claims against the platform provider in court.[55] However, the wording of Art. 2(2)(c) only requires that the activity is provided '*on the basis* of a contractual relationship' (and not on the basis of a valid contract). 29

Rec. 10 clearly states that a contractual relationship should be deemed to exist if both parties have **expressed their intention** to be bound on a durable medium. This expression of intention is distinct from a legally binding contract. The (only explanatory) Commission Q&A document merely repeats that a contractual relationship exists if the parties 'express their intention to be bound in an unequivocal and verifiable manner'.[56] An unequivocal and verifiable 'declaration' of the intention to be bound is not equivalent to an enforceable contract. Instead, the legal effect of a contract can be influenced by formal requirements, provisions on the permissible content of the contract, errors made during the contract's conclusion, and subsequent legal actions. 30

A final decision must consider the **spirit and purpose** of the requirement of a contractual basis. This method of interpretation is particularly important in EU law.[57] Art. 2(2)(c) uses the contractual basis to distinguish the relationship between the busi- 31

---

54 Schulte-Nölke in Busch P2B Reg Art. 2 mn. 39.

55 Schulte-Nölke in Busch P2B Reg Art. 2 mn. 41–43.

56 European Commission, 'Q&A EN Communication 2020' (9.7.2020) <https://ec.europa.eu/newsroom/dae/document.cfm?doc_id=68300> (last accessed: 02.07.2024), p. 11.

57 Riesenhuber, p. 307.

ness user and the platform provider from *de facto* usage (e.g. between the platform provider and the consumer) and the pre-contractual initiation of a transaction (between the business user and the consumer). Unlike in these relationships, the parties must be willing to commit themselves. The regulation imposes obligations on the parties before the P2B contract is concluded (e.g. Art. 3(1)(b)) and upon termination of the contract (e.g. Art. 4(2)). Even after the termination of the contractual relationship, a business user must be able to rely on the regulation to claim that the platform provider did not provide them with a statement of reasons 30 days before termination. Hence, the requirement of a contractual basis is met when the platform provider concludes or intends to conclude contracts with business users.[58]

32 Only the recitals require that the intention to be bound must be expressed on a **durable medium.** Art. 2(13) defines a durable medium as any medium that allows business users to retrieve and view information unchanged for an adequate period of time. This includes, for example, confirmation emails, downloadable confirmations, or permanently retrievable messages within an app.

33 Some argue that the **lack** of a declaration on a durable medium should be without consequences.[59] The regulation purportedly aims to unilaterally protect business users from platform providers, and the former cannot influence compliance with the formal requirement.[60] Moreover, Art. 2(2)(c) does not even require a durable medium. One could also interpret rec. 10 to imply that a contractual relationship should exist at *least* when the intention to be bound is expressed on a durable medium. While this provision prevents higher formal requirements than 'expression on a durable medium', it does not aim to establish minimum requirements. Nevertheless, in the absence of a durable medium, the business user relying on the regulation must prove that they have entered into a contract with the online mediation service provider. The aim of protecting business users cannot render the question entirely irrelevant, as this formal aspect determines the scope of application in the first place (instead of just imposing rights and obligations).

II. Online search engines

34 The second type of platform, besides online intermediation services, is **online search engines**. Only a few of the obligations of the regulation also apply to them. The main difference compared to online intermediation services is that the regulation applies even without a contractual basis between the platform provider and business users of online search engines (referred to as 'corporate website users').[61] This leaves two relationships between the three relevant actors: Firstly, there is at least a de facto use of the online search engine by consumers. Secondly, there is at least a pre-contractual offering of goods and services to consumers by corporate website users.

1. Digital service

35 The online search engine must be a 'digital service'. The regulation notably does not use the term information society service (as it does for online intermediation services). There are few clues to interpret the concept of a 'digital' service, as it is not used anywhere else in the regulation. Obviously, the service must be based on digital information, i.e. information expressed as digits. It must also be an 'online' search engine.

[58] At least in the case of public enforcement: Schulte-Nölke in Busch P2B Reg Art. 2 mn. 40.
[59] Schulte-Nölke in Busch P2B Reg Art. 2 mn. 47.
[60] Schulte-Nölke in Busch P2B Reg Art. 2 mn. 47.
[61] Alexander in Köhler/Bornkamm/Feddersen P2B Reg Art. 1 mn. 21.

Hence, it must be provided electronically at a distance via the Internet. This excludes information hotlines where human operators answer inquiries over the phone. However, if the same service is provided automatically through a voice assistant application, it would likely qualify as a digital service. A digital service does not require that it is normally provided for a fee.[62] However, this makes no difference for most search engine providers (e.g. Google, Baidu, Bing, Duckduckgo), as they are financed by advertising, which would be sufficient (→ mn. 23).

2. Search engine

The primary function of an online **search engine** is to receive search queries from users and provide them with results. The term must be understood in a technologically neutral way.[63] A search query can consist of words or a group of words, voice input, music (e.g. Shazam, SoundHound, provided these services do not only search a limited database), photographs of objects or labels (e.g. Google Lens), or uploading images (e.g. Google Reverse Image Search, TinEye) or videos (e.g. Shutterstock, Berify, Bing Visual Search). Theoretically, a search could be initiated by selecting various criteria (without using keywords) to determine the desired information. An AI chat website can also constitute a search engine if the artificial intelligence searches the internet for its answers (e.g. Bing with ChatGPT-4, Google Gemini, Perplexity AI). 36

After processing the search query, the search engine displays **results** to users. The format for this is irrelevant, but these results must enable users to access additional information about this content. This could take the form of displaying just one result (e.g. in the case of the Google's 'I'm feeling lucky' search) or a list of results.[64] Results also include voice output containing the desired information (e.g. with Apple's Siri or Amazon's Alexa) and other forms of possible output. For example, the search engine could highlight a specific location in a virtual or augmented reality application or provide navigation instructions within a map or navigation application.[65] These results also allow users to learn more about the requested information. Results can also be found behind a payment barrier, commonly known as a paywall.[66] Information behind a paywall allows users to access more details about their search topic, provided they are willing to pay. 37

3. General-purpose search

The search engine must be capable of searching for the topic across **all websites** (or at least all websites in a specific language). This differentiates general-purpose search engines (also called 'horizontal' search engines[67]) from topic-specific ('vertical') search engines and a website's search function. The latter two are limited either thematically (e.g. Google News) or in terms of the sources searched (e.g. Wolfram Alpha or the catalogue search of a university library). Often, both forms are mixed. Google offers a general-purpose search engine on its homepage, as well as topic-specific search engines like Google Books, Scholar, and News. Again, the search mechanism should be viewed with a technologically neutral approach.[68] It does not matter whether the search engine 38

[62] Schulte-Nölke in Busch P2B Reg Art. 2 mn. 60.
[63] Rec. 13 P2B Regulation.
[64] Schulte-Nölke in Busch P2B Reg Art. 2 mn. 65.
[65] Schulte-Nölke in Busch P2B Reg Art. 2 mn. 66.
[66] For a different opinion see: Schulte-Nölke in Busch P2B Reg Art. 2 mn. 67.
[67] Haucap/Kehder, 'Suchmaschinen zwischen Wettbewerb und Monopol: Der Fall Google' 28.10.2013 <https://www.econstor.eu/bitstream/10419/76802/1/751556580.pdf> (last accessed: 02.07.2024), p. 5.
[68] Rec. 13 P2B Regulation.

only works with crawlers and indexes, combines the search results of several other search engines (meta-search), or incorporates elements of 'social bookmarking' (i.e. user ratings to curate the results).

III. Services explicitly excluded

39 The regulation explicitly excludes certain services from its substantive scope of application. Art. 1(3) excludes online payment services, online advertising tools, and online advertising exchanges. Rec. 11 excludes B2B and C2C platforms, software for search engine optimisation (SEO), ad blockers, and certain hardware interfaces. The examples are partially declaratory (e.g. B2B platforms), but some serves as the basis for excluding such services (e.g. online advertising exchanges). All services mentioned in Art. 1(3) are excluded, as the second part ('which are not provided with the aim of the facilitating the initiation of direct transactions and which do not involve a contractual relationship with consumers') is a non-restrictive relative clause providing additional information. It does not limit the exception to services that do not aim to facilitate transactions. The grammatical interpretation shows that the second part is introduced by the relative pronoun 'which', while a restrictive relative clause would likely be introduced by 'that' (for clarification).

40 **Online payment services** (e.g. Paypal, iDEAL, Klarna, Bancomat Pay, Google Pay, Apple Pay) do not qualify as online intermediation services since they do not initiate transactions. Instead, they are 'inherently auxiliary' to a transaction, as they allow fulfilling a contract that was already concluded.[69] These services do not fulfil the role of an intermediary that brings two parties together. Rather, a different party (e.g. the merchant as a business user) connects the consumer with the online payment service. This means that the online payment service provider does not have a 'gatekeeper role',[70] which it could abuse in connection with its inherent platform market power.

41 **Online advertising tools and online advertising exchanges,** on the other hand, could be considered as online intermediation services. They are information society services that are provided, at least indirectly, upon the individual request of a consumer. They enable business users to initiate transactions by displaying advertisements. When consumers click on advertisements and are redirected to a business user's website, the latter can initiate a transaction. Art. 1(3) constitutes an explicit exception and excludes these services. The rationale behind this policy decision may be that most provisions of the P2B regulation cannot be effectively applied to advertisements.[71] Another argument might be that advertising networks do not have as strong network effects as intermediation platforms. Unlike online marketplaces, advertising networks do not become more attractive for users with more advertising partners.

42 Platforms for transactions between consumers only (**C2C**) or between business users only (**B2B**) do not constitute online intermediation services, as the definition explicitly requires that both consumers and business users must use the service.

43 **Search engine optimisation** software offers business users the possibility to enhance their chances of being discovered by consumers (or other businesses) through a search engine. However, this function is not an intermediary activity. A lot of support activities, such as selling computer hardware or offering cloud computing or hosting services to

---

[69] Rec. 11 P2B Regulation.

[70] In this sense: Naumann/Rodenhausen ZEuP 2020, 768 (776), although this term is now more commonly associated with the DMA.

[71] Schulte-Nölke in Busch P2B Reg Art. 1 mn. 39.

a business user, lay the foundation for business users to contact consumers. However, putting business users in a position where they can make independent efforts to reach consumers is different from connecting business users with consumers.

The main purpose of **ad blockers** is to prevent the possibility of initiating transactions (through advertising). This raises the question of why this example was explicitly included. The answer could be the business model of some ad blockers, which do not block advertising from paying businesses.[72] 44

Hardware interfaces are technical means that connect hardware and software applications.[73] This includes any kind of operating systems (e.g. Windows or iOS).[74] These do not qualify as online intermediation services because they do not facilitate the initiation of transactions. Rec. 11 states that they require increased transparency if they integrate online intermediation services. This provision covers operating systems that include voice assistants (e.g. Siri, Cortana, Google Assistant and Google Gemini) or search functions (e.g. Google Search on Android). 45

D. Geographical scope

Art. 1(2) requires two cumulative conditions under the **modified marketplace principle** to determine the geographical scope.[75] First, the business user must be established in the EU. Second, their goods or services must be directed at consumers who are in the EU for at least part of the transaction. This creates a sufficient link to the EU to legitimise the regulation.[76] But the regulation also applies to purely domestic situations without any cross-border elements.[77] 46

The element of **platform operators** has no geographical limitation of the scope of application, as these 'typically have a global dimension'.[78] One may question this premise, especially since the P2B Regulation does not (like the DMA) apply only when certain thresholds are met. Additionally, this can lead to challenges when the regulation grants business users a legal claim against a platform operator outside the EU, but no jurisdiction to enforce it.[79] 47

The geographical scope as part of the applicability of the regulation is assessed in **two steps:** (1.) Are the business users domiciled or established in the EU? And (2.) do they direct their offers to consumers in the EU?[80] 48

I. Business users established in the EU

In the **first step,** a business user must demonstrate that they are domiciled or established within the EU. If public authorities enforce the regulation, it is sufficient 49

[72] See on this so-called 'whitelisting': OLG Hamburg 15.3.2018 – 5 U 152/15, GRUR-Prax 2018, 268.

[73] Rec. 11 P2B Regulation.

[74] Schulte-Nölke in Busch P2B Reg Art. 1 mn. 41.

[75] Tribess in Fritzsche/Münker/Stollwerck P2B Reg Art. 1 mn. 12; Schulte-Nölke, on the other hand, describes the geographical scope of application as a combination of the seat principle and the marketplace principle: Schulte-Nölke in Busch P2B Reg Art. 1 mn. 16.

[76] Schulte-Nölke in Busch P2B Reg Art. 1 mn. 16.

[77] Wais EuZW 2019, 221 (222).

[78] Rec. 9 P2B Regulation.

[79] Schulte-Nölke in Busch P2B Reg Art. 1 mn. 18.

[80] This test pattern is also proposed by the European Commission: European Commission, 'Q&A EN Communication 2020' (9.7.2020) <https://ec.europa.eu/newsroom/dae/document.cfm?doc_id=68300> (last accessed: 02.07.2024), p. 13.

that some business users meet this criterion. The Digital Services Act[81] (DSA) defines the geographical scope (for platform operators) through either an establishment in *or* a significant orientation towards a Member State.[82] However, such orientation is not enough to meet the first step of the geographical scope for the P2B regulation.

50 The criterion of '**established**' must be clarified. This term must be interpreted solely under EU law, meaning that definitions from the jurisdictions of the EU Member States cannot be utilised.[83] The regulation, however, provides no explanation for the term. In EU law, the concept of establishment can be interpreted broadly (as seen in the GDPR). This means that any permanent establishment that supports effective and actual activities is considered sufficient.[84] The term can also be interpreted more narrowly in the sense of Art. 49 TEU. This means that even an office in the EU is insufficient if it only represents the infrastructure necessary for operations.[85] Using a broad interpretation could incentivise business users to establish a branch office in the EU to benefit from the P2B provisions.[86] One may question the effectiveness of this incentive, considering that rights granted by the regulation are limited. One must also question the benefit to the EU from such a *minimum presence*. A comparison with the alternative for natural persons, which is residence, supports a narrow interpretation. If the alternative requirements 'establishment' and 'residence' are not somewhat comparable, natural and legal persons would be treated substantially differently.

II. Directed at consumers in the EU

51 The **second step** is to assess whether these business users from the EU offer their goods or services to consumers 'located in the Union for part of the transaction'.[87]

52 Art. 2(4) defines a **consumer** as a natural person who acts for a purpose that is not included in the definition of a business user (→ mn. 8 et seqq.). This corresponds to the definition of Art. 2 Consumer Rights Directive[88]. However, since individual consumers do not derive any rights from the regulation, there will not be many delineation problems. This is because it suffices for the platform to *also* target consumers.[89] Most open platforms, i.e. those that do not require proof of being a business user, will fulfil this requirement.[90] Is it justified to limit the regulation to B2C platforms only?[91] Business users may find themselves in a disadvantaged bargaining position vis-à-vis platforms that have a strong market position. However, the regulation focuses on structural market power (→ mn. 17). It appears to assume that business users are more willing to search for suppliers for a longer period of time, especially if this creates a lasting business relationship.

53 For the geographical assessment, only the **physical presence** during (part of) the transaction is relevant.[92] Consumers do not need to be domiciled or permanent resi-

[81] OJ 2022 L 277, 1.
[82] Rec. 7 et seq. DSA.
[83] Schulte-Nölke in Busch P2B Reg Art. 1 mn. 19.
[84] Schulte-Nölke in Busch P2B Reg Art. 1 mn. 19 et seq.
[85] Korte in Calliess/Ruffert TFEU Art. 49 mn. 29 et seq.
[86] Schulte-Nölke in Busch P2B Reg Art. 1 mn. 20.
[87] Rec. 9 P2B Regulation.
[88] OJ 2011 L 304, 64.
[89] Schulte-Nölke in Busch P2B Reg Art. 2 mn. 56.
[90] Schulte-Nölke in Busch P2B Reg Art. 2 mn. 57.
[91] Podszun in Busch P2B Reg Art. 7 mn. 168.
[92] Schulte-Nölke in Busch P2B Reg Art. 1 mn. 22.

dents in the EU, or nationals of a Member State.[93] If several steps of the transaction occur in different countries, it is enough for a single element to be carried out while the consumer is in the EU.[94] This criterion will be negligible in practice. Again, the regulation does not grant rights to individual consumers. Hence, it will be rare for all consumers of a business to perform only part of the transaction in the EU. One such rarity would be travel service providers who cater to consumers initiating transactions outside the EU, but only completing them when visiting the EU. One may question the legitimacy of limiting the regulation to only consumers within the EU.[95] After all, the same relationship between the platform and EU business can also exist in relation to non-EU customers.

The business users must **offer** their goods and services to these EU consumers. They do so if it is apparent that they direct their activities towards consumers in the EU.[96] While this initially depends on the format of the business user's offer,[97] the actions of third parties can be attributed to them if they willingly and knowingly use the service of said party.[98] Even the platform itself can be considered such a third party, meaning that its orientation towards EU consumers can meet this criterion. 54

The offer's content is aimed at EU consumers when business users express their willingness to enter into a contract with consumers in the EU.[99] But the mere accessibility of the website in the EU is not enough.[100] Instead, indicators are that the business user offers delivery to the EU, navigation directions from the EU, or accepts payment in an EU currency.[101] Another indicator might be that the website is available in an official EU language. However, some official EU languages are also spoken outside the EU, and there are population groups within the EU who speak non-EU languages.[102] 55

There are certain ways for the platform to **prevent** this. It is insufficient for the platform to not be directed at consumers in the EU. The platform could prohibit business users from offering goods or services to consumers in the EU through contractual terms. However, this could circumvent the P2B Regulation, e.g. if a platform technically enables and simultaneously legally prohibits users from addressing EU consumers. The P2B regulation recognises the greater bargaining power of platforms and their ability to unilaterally set terms and conditions.[103] The goal of the regulation is more effectively achieved if such a contradiction means that the regulation applies. The platform must take all realistic measures to effectively prevent business users from targeting consumers in the EU. Otherwise, the platform falls within the geographical scope of the regulation. On the other hand, the platform is not within the scope of the regulation if business users deliberately bypass otherwise effective restrictions. Under such circumstances, 56

---

[93] Rec. 9 P2B Regulation.

[94] Schulte-Nölke in Busch P2B Reg Art. 1 mn. 22.

[95] Wais EuZW 2019, 221 (222 et seq.).

[96] Rec. 9 P2B Regulation.

[97] A different approach takes Schulte-Nölke in Busch P2B Reg Art. 1 mn. 26.

[98] Schulte-Nölke in Busch P2B Reg Art. 1 mn. 24.

[99] Tribess in Fritzsche/Münker/Stollwerck P2B Reg Art. 1 mn. 19.

[100] ECJ 7.12.2010 – case C-585/08, ECLI:EU:C:2010:740 = NJW 2011, 505 mn. 69 – Peter Pammer v Reederei Karl Schlüter GmbH & Co. KG (C-585/08) and Hotel Alpenhof GesmbH v Oliver Heller (C-144/09); as a decision on Council Regulation (EC) No 44/2001 of 22 December 2000 on jurisdiction and the recognition and enforcement of judgments in civil and commercial matters, OJ 2001 L 12, 1 this must be considered per rec. 9.

[101] Partially based on ECJ 7.12.2010 – case C-585/08, ECLI:EU:C:2010:740 = NJW 2011, 505 mn. 83 et seq. – Peter Pammer v Reederei Karl Schlüter GmbH & Co. KG (C-585/08) and Hotel Alpenhof GesmbH v Oliver Heller (C-144/09).

[102] In this sense also: Schulte-Nölke in Busch P2B Reg Art. 1 mn. 28.

[103] Rec. 2 P2B Regulation.

it is no longer apparent that business users are offering their goods and services to EU consumers. If an online marketplace excludes delivery to the EU, payment in EU currencies, and registration for consumers with an EU address, the platform is not subject to the regulation solely because business users provide a contact option via email for delivery to the EU in the description of the goods.

§ 16
Requirements for terms and conditions and market conduct

Literature: *Alexander*, Kollektive und individuelle Rechtsdurchsetzung bei Zuwiderhandlungen gegen die VO (EU) 2019/1150, WRP 2021, 1375; *Alexander*, Anwendungsbereich, Regelungstechnik und einzelne Transparenzvorgaben der P2B-Verordnung, WRP 2020, 945; *Assion* (Hrsg.), TTDSG, Telekommunikation-Telemedien-Datenschutz-Gesetz, Handkommentar, 2022 (zit. Assion/*Bearbeiter*); *Busch*, Mehr Fairness und Transparenz in der Plattformökonomie?, GRUR 2019, 788; *Eickemeier/Brodersen*, Die neue P2B-Verordnung für die Stärkung der Rechte gewerblicher Nutzer von Online-Vermittlungsdiensten und Suchmaschinen, K&R 2020, 397; *von Westphalen*, b2b-Plattform-Verordnung: Das AGB-Recht vor weitreichenden Veränderungen, BB 2020, 579; *Höppner/Schulz*, Die EU-Verordnung 2019/1150 für Fairness und Transparenz von Online-Vermittlungsdiensten ("P2B-Verordnung"), ZIP 2019, 2329; *Höppner/Schulz*, EU-Verordnung für Online-Intermediäre: Begrenzung digitaler Marktmacht oder Bürokratie(papier)tiger?, K&R-Beilage 2019, 44; *Höppner*, Google Search (Shopping): Etablierte Missbrauchskriterien für digitalen Präzedenzfall, WuW 2017, 421; *Kohser/Jahn*, Die P2B-Verordnung – Neue Pflichten für Plattformbetreiber und Suchmaschinenanbieter, GRUR-Prax 2020, 273; *Louven*, Kartellrechtlicher Rechtsschutz gegen unberechtigte Verkäuferkonto-Sperren durch Amazon, K&R 2021, 685; *Rochet/Tirole*, Two-Sided Markets: A Progress Report, RJE 2006, 645; *Rochet/Tirole*, Platform Competition in Two-Sided Markets, JEEA 2003, 990; *Rohrßen*, Internetvertrieb 2019/20 – Vertriebsvorgaben, (Best-)Preise & Platform-to-BusinessVerordnung, ZVertriebsR 2019, 341; *Schneider/Kremer*, Ein zweiter, kritischer Blick auf die P2B-Verordnung: Nachhaltige Veränderung des Plattformökosystems?, WRP 2020, 1128; *Spindler/Seidel*, Die Regulierung von Online-Plattformen, NJW 2022, 2730; *Tribess*, Datenzugangsrechte in der Plattformökonomie, ZD 2020, 440; *Tribess*, P2B-Verordnung zur Förderung von Fairness und Transparenz von Online-Diensten, GWR 2020, 233; *Voigt/Reuter*, Platform-to-Business-Verordnung, MMR 2019, 783; *Wais*, B2B-Klauselkontrolle in der Plattform-Ökonomie: Der Kommissionsvorschlag für eine Verordnung über Online-Vermittlungsdienste, EuZW 2019, 221.

A. Introduction

1 In Art. 3 to 10 P2B Regulation[1], the legislator has created the **information obligations** that providers of online intermediation services and online search engines must observe. As will be shown structurally in the following, on the one hand these can be viewed from a perspective concerning the law of terms and conditions of the companies covered vis-à-vis business users. On the other hand, such actions are also covered that cannot be described as terms and conditions, such as explanations or actual actions. This concerns in particular de facto activities of online search engines with meaning for corporate website user.[2]

2 In both constellations, the platforms covered are active in competition in a way that can affect the economic success of other companies. These are **dependent** on the platform services in a special way. The P2B Regulation takes up the user relationship between the platforms and business users or corporate website user and establishes special requirements.[3]

[1] Regulation (EU) 2019/1150 of the European Parliament and of the Council of 20 June 2019 on promoting fairness and transparency for business users of online intermediation services, OJ 2019 L 186, 57.

[2] Alexander WRP 2020, 945 (948).

[3] Alexander WRP 2020, 945 (950), on the concept of AGB see further below.

B. Purposes and interpretation rules of the Regulation

Two different definitions form the interface on the applicable legal obligations. The first designates online intermediation services offered to business users. The second designates online search engines that enable any user to conduct searches via keyword entries and thus potentially also find users with a company website. Both tie in with general observations on **platforms** and can therefore be described as their varieties. In each case, the **typical triangular relationship of** interest mediation between different user groups occurs in connection with their use by users with corporate websites or the contractual use of services by business users and their appearance vis-à-vis consumers.[4] 3

In general, the legal regulations are directed at the providers of online intermediation services and the relationship with their business users. However, there are various additional regulations that are directed at providers of online search engines. This concerns the provisions in Art. 5(2), (5)(c) P2B Regulation on ranking and in Art. 7(2) P2B Regulation on differentiated treatment. It is clear from these provisions that the requirements relate to the **de facto explanatory behaviour.** This follows from the fact that the activity of an online search engine is regularly not based on a contractual basis, but the services are de facto used by the users. 4

The narrow concept of consumer from Art. 2 no. 4 P2B Regulation is important here, which is based on the general concept from consumer protection law and is not based on the concept of consumer under competition law. It is only decisive in the sense of a negative definition that consumers act for purposes that are outside their commercial, business, craft or professional activity. Based on the definitions of the provider of online intermediation services and the provider of online search engines presented below, a so-called "infection" of the services used is not relevant, i.e. if individual natural persons nevertheless use the offers for the aforementioned purposes of a commercial, business, craft or professional activity. Rather, the actual offer of the obligated companies to a group of consumers on one platform site is decisive. If individuals are no longer consumers, a classification into the user group of business users or corporate website user is also open for discussion. 5

I. Regulatory purposes as standards of interpretation

According to Art. 1(1) P2B Regulation, the purpose of the legal provisions is to contribute to the smooth functioning of the internal market by ensuring that adequate transparency, fairness and effective remedies are created for business users of online intermediation services and corporate website user with regard to search engines. A competition-theoretical classification of the smoothly functioning internal market can be left aside, because the purpose only covers a "contribution". However, this "contribution" is to be ensured by laying down appropriate transparency, fairness and effective remedies. In contrast, the title of the regulation reads "promoting fairness and transparency". 6

The three purposes mentioned above must be used as a **guide for the interpretation** of all legal provisions. In doing so, the regulations are not always to be considered in isolation according to one of the three purposes. Depending on the regulation, one or more of them may be programmatic for the application. The above remarks mean that the respective legal provisions must be interpreted autonomously according to the regulatory purpose of the P2B Regulation. 7

---

[4] Rochet/Tirole JEEA 2003, 990 (1029 et seq.); Rochet/Tirole RJE 2006, 645 (666 et seq.).

II. Applicable law

8 Due to Art. 1(4) P2B Regulation, general civil law remains unaffected and thus also contract law and law of unfair competition.[5] On the one hand, this means that, for example, in the area of applicable German law, the general control of terms and conditions according to §§ 305 et seqq. BGB remain applicable in principle, insofar as the relevant aspects are not regulated by the Regulation. On the other hand, the Regulation is **lex specialis** to general civil law. It is therefore to be interpreted according to its own rules, independent of the previous practice in the law on terms and conditions. However, a practical effect of the P2B Regulation in the sense of prima facie conclusions on the law on terms and conditions cannot be ruled out. For example, the provisions of the Regulation could serve as a guideline for the review of the control of terms and conditions under § 307(2) no. 1 BGB.[6]

9 According to Art. 1(5) P2B Regulation, the Regulation applies **without prejudice to** general Union legislation, in particular that relating to judicial cooperation in civil matters, competition, data protection, protection of business secrets, consumer protection, electronic commerce and financial services. These instruments shall be applicable in parallel. Likewise, according to Art. 1(4) P2B Regulation, the applicability of the Member States' provisions on unfair competition and unilateral acts remain unaffected. The applicable national civil law is also not affected.

10 These regulations serve to clarify that the P2B Regulation is by no means a comprehensive or even conclusive set of regulations, but rather a condensed representation of some areas that have been identified as to be regulated. Substantive regulatory references are largely **fragmentary**. In practice, it is supplemented by the aforementioned regulations of substantive law.[7] Whether and which regulation has priority of application can be delimited solely according to the respective scope of application and regulatory purpose.[8] Therefore, cases with a scope of application of the P2B Regulation cannot be considered solely on the basis of this regulation, but regularly require the inclusion of the complementary applicable substantive law provisions outside the regulation.[9]

11 This relationship between the P2B Regulation and general law has a significant impact on the general scope of interpretation of this regulation. This is because, particularly in the case of transparency obligations, it presupposes underlying conduct on the part of the platform in the form of a design decision. Accordingly, the question may arise as to whether this underlying conduct is conclusively regulated under substantive law by the P2B Regulation.[10] An example of this is the provision in Art. 4(5)(2) P2B Regulation on the exclusion of the need for a statement of reasons for the termination of services. According to this provision, a statement of reasons is not necessary if the provider of online intermediation services can prove repeated violations of his applicable terms and conditions and this has led to the complete termination of the online intermediation services in question before. The regulation does not regulate which specific violations could be decisive. This is consequently subject to the respective substantive law.[11]

---

[5] Busch/v. Westphalen P2B-VO Art. 2 mn. 84.

[6] Busch/v. Westphalen P2B-VO Art. 2 mn. 85.

[7] For example, Art. 10 of the P2B Regulation only provides for regulations explaining the reasons why the possibilities of business users are restricted to offer their goods and services at other conditions by other means. Whether these reasons are legally permissible in each case is a question of general law, such as antitrust law in the case of most favoured nation clauses.

[8] Busch/Schulte-Nölke P2B-VO Art. 1 mn. 42.

[9] Kohser/Jahn GRUR-Prax 2020, 273 (275).

[10] V. Westphalen/Thüsing/Hoeren IT-Verträge mn. 125.

[11] See Rec. 36 S. 3 P2B Regulation.

On the other hand, in connection with the consequence of voidness from Art. 3(3) P2B Regulation, it is discussed to what extent general regulations of civil law could still be applicable.

12 As a European regulation, the P2B Regulation is to be **interpreted autonomously.**[12] It is sector-specific regulatory law with effects on market behaviour and in particular the contracts used in this context.[13] Even if parallels to contract law, in particular the law on terms and conditions, may frequently arise, cross-references from literature and case law have rather anecdotal added value, but cannot replace this autonomous interpretation. This applies even more so, as the cases covered by the P2B Regulation can be those from the entire area of the European Union, i.e. also with references to Member States other than the Federal Republic of Germany. Within the scope of application of the Regulation, it takes precedence over Member State law.[14] If legal questions have to be answered outside the scope of the P2B Regulation,[15] this is governed by the applicable law, which in turn is determined within the framework of international private law.[16]

13 The fact that German law, and thus the law on terms and conditions, is applicable in the described examination procedure is within the scope of what is practically relevant, as is the **applicability of other jurisdictions**. It is therefore not helpful and in many cases even misleading to always make questions on the interpretation of the P2B Regulation dependent on conclusions from German law of terms and conditions. Due to the different regulatory purposes and the autonomous interpretation, the abbreviation "AGB" is not used here for clarification purposes.

III. Terms and conditions covered

14 For the further legal classification of the provisions of the P2B Regulation, the terms used are important. Central to this are the **terms and conditions,** which are flanked by the actual market behaviour of the addressed platforms. The provisions in Art. 3 et seqq. P2B Regulation mainly refer to terms and conditions between providers of online intermediation services and their business users. Only few specific provisions address the relationship between providers of online search engines and their users as well as corporate website users.[17]

15 The definition of terms and conditions in Art. 2 no. 10 P2B Regulation is quite close to that according to the general term terms and conditions as known in consumer law[18], but is **not congruent.**[19] First of all, it is decisive that these are terms or provisions which regulate the contractual relationship between the provider of online intermediation services and their business users, irrespective of their designation or form. It is not decisive that they are contractual terms themselves. A regulation can also already be made by the de facto circumstances. A further criterion is the unilateral determination by the provider of the online intermediation services, which is made by way of an overall assessment.[20] Not decisive in this overall assessment should be isolated considerations of

[12] Alexander WRP 2020, 945 (950).
[13] Höppner/Schulz K&R-Beilage 2019, 44 (45).
[14] Busch/Schulte-Nölke P2B-VO Art. 1 mn. 47.
[15] For example, the admissibility of reasons for a restriction of platform services to be provided in accordance with Art. 3 para. 1 lit. d P2B Regulation.
[16] Busch/Schulte-Nölke P2B-VO Art. 1 mn. 45 et seqq.
[17] Wais EuZW 2019, 221 (222).
[18] Council Directive 93/13/EEC of 5 April 1993 on unfair terms in consumer contracts OJ 1993 L 95, 29.
[19] Alexander WRP 2020, 945 (950); Wais EuZW 2019, 221 (228).
[20] Köhler/Bornkamm/Feddersen/Alexander P2B-VO Art. 2 mn. 47.

the relative size of the parties concerned, the fact that negotiations have taken place or the fact that individual provisions in these terms and conditions may have been the subject of negotiations and jointly determined by the respective provider and the respective business user.

16 **The geographical scope of application of** the regulation follows from Art. 1(2) P2B Regulation due to a combination of the principle of the country of establishment and the principle of the place of market.[21] This is also due to the specific circumstances of a platform's activities vis-à-vis several user groups, in this case the business users and corporate website users on the one hand and the consumers as their market counterpart on the other. The first criterion of the **country of establishment principle is based** on whether the business users and corporate website user have their place of business or residence in the European Union. The second criterion of the **place of market principle is based on** the offer of goods or services by the business users and corporate website users to consumers located in the European Union through the online intermediation services or online search engines. The Regulation thus applies extraterritorially irrespective of where the providers of the online intermediation services or online search engines are located and thus constitutes a so-called priority conflict rule.[22] This means that it has priority over the other conflict-of-law rules of international private law. In addition, due to its specific significance for the protection of the public interest, it constitutes a so-called overriding norm.[23] That means, it must be applied regardless of the choice of law clauses in a contract or the applicable laws of a state.

1. Online intermediation services and business users

17 According to the definition in Art. 2 no. 2 P2B Regulation, three requirements must be met for classification as an online intermediation service. First, it must be an **information society service within the** meaning of Art. 1(1)(b) Directive (EU) 2015/1535 of the European Parliament and of the Council of 9.9.2015 laying down a procedure for the provision of information in the field of technical regulations and of rules on information society services[24]. It must be a service normally provided for **remuneration** electronically at a distance and at the individual request of a recipient. The wording " normally provided for remuneration " means, as in similar constellations, that the opportunity of a monetary remuneration is sufficient.[25] However, a direct, positively determined remuneration > 0 is not required. Typically, a platform will not demand a monetary remuneration from one user group, but from another user group it will. The price to the first user group can be considered as zero discount.[26] This occurs within the framework of a business model covered by the P2B Regulation, which creates sufficient network effects on the basis of this incentivisation to offer the other user group the opportunity for brokered transactions.

18 Furthermore, these services must enable business users to offer goods or services to consumers by **facilitating** the initiation of direct transactions between these business users and consumers.[27] It is not decisive whether these transactions are ultimately concluded. This criterion describes the classic intermediary function of platforms. The

---

[21] Rec. 9 P2B Regulation.

[22] Busch/Schulte-Nölke P2B-VO Art. 1 mn. 46.

[23] Busch/Schulte-Nölke P2B-VO Art. 1 mn. 47.

[24] ABl. 2015 L 241, 1.

[25] Klarstellend im deutschen Recht hierzu § 18 Abs. 2a GWB, vgl. dazu BeckOK InfoMedienR/Paal GWB § 18 mn. 3.

[26] For more details, see Immenga/Mestmäcker/Fuchs TFEU Art. 102 mn. 63d.

[27] Rohrßen ZVertriebsR 2019, 341 (344).

preceding link to the information society service makes it clear that the platforms must be digital. The decisive factor here is that the intermediary service alone must be classified as an electronically provided service. The mediated goods or services are not important for this assessment.

Finally, these information society services with their intermediation services must be provided to business users offering goods or services to consumers on the basis of a **contractual relationship.** This criterion also focuses on the typical platform services. What is important here, however, is the contractual relationship as the basis for the provision of services. Whether and how these conditions were included, on the other hand, is not relevant for this assessment. 19

According to Art. 2 no. 3 P2B Regulation, a provider is any natural or legal person who provides or offers to provide the service to business users. According to Art. 2 no. 1 P2B Regulation, a business user is any private person or legal entity that acts in the course of a business or professional activity and offers goods or services to consumers via online intermediation services. This must be done for purposes related to a commercial, business, craft or professional activity. The scope of application is likely to be very broad and, in case of doubt, also include micro-entrepreneurs or intentional business users. 20

2. Differences to the German law on terms and conditions

In this context, it is not a matter of indications of negotiation as in general terms and conditions law.[28] On the one hand, the standard should be based on the purpose of the regulation to ensure the smooth functioning of the internal market in connection with the appearance of the platforms mentioned. This goes beyond the purpose of terms and conditions law to resolve certain contractual imparities between the user and his direct counterparty. Rather, the purpose of protection is extended to the mediated relationship between business users and their consumer customers. The provider of online intermediation services should have to take into account certain **minimum standards for** the relationship between its commercial customers and their consumer customers, unencumbered by the otherwise applicable general rules.[29] This corresponds to the specific need for protection of the business user if he is not in a position to influence the terms and conditions of the contract due to the specific competitive circumstances.[30] 21

Secondly, this specific definition of purpose results in a relationship of lex specialis. As a rule, the existence of terms and conditions will therefore always be assumed for providers of online intermediation services, even if negotiations have taken place.[31] This should apply even if the provider unconditionally accepts the terms and conditions of its business users. In this case, the provisions of Art. 3 et seq. P2B Regulation could not be waived and would also apply. Insofar as these would then constitute restrictions on the services, the providers would again be obliged to provide information. 22

3. Explanations as de facto market conduct

The term "terms and conditions" does not include behavior which is to be taken on the basis of the specific obligations in Art. 3 et seq. P2B Regulation by providers of online search engines. Some provisions require the obligated parties to behave in a manner that is detached from a contractual relationship. This applies, for example, to the obliga- 23

---

28 Wais EuZW 2019, 221 (222).

29 Busch/v. Westphalen P2B-VO Art. 2 mn. 83; Wais EuZW 2019, 221 (228).

30 Busch/v. Westphalen P2B-VO Art. 2 mn. 114.

31 For more details, see Wais EuZW 2019, 221 (228).

tion under Art. 5(2) P2B Regulation to provide clear and comprehensibly formulated **explanations** of main ranking parameters. The same applies to the obligation to explain differentiated treatments according to Art. 7(2) P2B Regulation. Both obligations require de facto explanatory behaviour that is independent of the existence of or inclusion in terms and conditions and instead takes into account only the de facto use of the services. Nevertheless, it is not excluded that such necessary explanations are included in regulations that are close to terms and conditions. In addition, some providers of online intermediation services will have a dual role and at the same time be providers of an online search engine. In these cases, they must additionally comply with the requirements for providers of online search engines.

24 Art. 2 no. 5 P2B Regulation defines the term online search engine. Unlike online intermediation services, it does not depend on a classification as an information society service within the meaning of Directive (EU) 2015/1535, but it must be a **digital service** alone. This service must allow users to enter queries in order to receive results in any format after a search on any topic. The provision lists as possible queries, by way of example, keyword, voice input, group of words or other input. The search on any topic is carried out in principle on all websites or limited to all websites of a certain language. As a result, the user receives information related to the content requested by the query.

25 According to Art. 2 no. 6 P2B Regulation, any natural or legal person who provides or offers to provide the service to consumers is classified as a provider of online search engines. The difference to the provider of online intermediation services is that the latter definition is primarily based on the offer to business users, who in turn provide services to consumers. However, the providers of online search engines also operate in the triangular relationship typical to platforms. The decisive third role is played by corporate website users, which are defined in Art. 2 no. 7 P2B Regulation. According to this, they must offer goods or services via an online interface for purposes related to their commercial, business, craft or professional activity. Consequently, these are businesses.[32] As a further difference to providers of online intermediation services, it is not necessary that the service offer is made on the basis of a contractual relationship.

26 Similar actual obligations arise from Art. 3(5) P2B Regulation. According to this, the provider of online intermediation services must ensure that the business users are clearly **recognisable** as providers of goods or services. This provision precludes, for example, a design in which the provider of the relevant goods or services is not directly recognisable as such on an intermediary service. Accordingly, it is inadmissible in particular that the platform operators improve their own competitive positions by preventing or worsening the disclosure of the identity of the business users.[33]

C. Transparency requirements in detail

27 Although the P2B Regulation is intended to serve the purposes of ensuring adequate transparency, fairness and effective remedies, the majority of regulations relate to **transparency**. Remedies are to be ensured primarily formally through an internal complaint management system and mediation. Transparency should serve the purpose of ensuring that business users are informed about necessary remedies in the first place. The objective of ensuring fairness is related to this in that it is strengthened by adequate and effective transparency.[34] Transparency rules can mitigate imbalances between platform

[32] Busch/Schulte-Nölke P2B-VO Art. 2 mn. 70.
[33] Köhler/Bornkamm/Feddersen/Alexander P2B-VO Art. 3 mn. 52; Tribess GWR 2020, 233 (235).
[34] Cf. for example rec. 8 p. 1 and 51 P2B Regulation.

and business users by balancing information and creating predictability for the business user.[35] The fact that fairness is not completely lost alongside transparency is also shown by the provision in Art. 18(2)(b) P2B Regulation, according to which the Commission should also take into account the effectiveness of any codes of conduct drawn up in improving fairness in its triennial review. However, independent regulations related to fairness are generally not found in the P2B Regulation.

Art. 3 P2B Regulation contains the general regulations with regard to ensuring transparency. They are partly supplemented by regulations on special contractual provisions in Art. 8 P2B Regulation. The regulations apply irrespective of the specific content and regulatory purpose of the respective terms and conditions. The subsequent provisions of Art. 4–7 as well as 9 and 10 P2B Regulation, on the other hand, represent **typified measures** by providers of online intermediation services and operators of online search engines who are subject to additional specific obligations. The general regulations on terms and conditions are only directed at the contractual relationship between providers of online intermediation services and their business users. They are divided into the basic transparency obligations according to Art. 3(1) P2B Regulation, which apply to all terms and conditions of providers of online intermediation services. They correspond to the requirements of the German transparency requirement, although the regulatory consequences differ.[36] Insofar as these providers intend to make changes, Art. 3(2) P2B Regulation makes further provisions in this regard. In the event of any violations of these paragraphs, Art. 3(3) P2B Regulation provides for the voidness of the terms and conditions. 28

I. Clear and understandable wording

Art. 3(1)(a) P2B Regulation stipulates that the terms and conditions of providers of online intermediation services must be formulated in a clear and comprehensible manner. Rec. 15 explains that business users should be able to see from the terms and conditions applicable to a contractual relationship which commercial terms and conditions for the use, termination and suspension of online intermediation services the provider of online intermediation services considers to provide. This serves the purpose of **predictability** in the business relationship. Conversely, the aforementioned recital does not consider terms and conditions to be drafted in a clear and comprehensible manner if they are vague or imprecise or do not regulate information on important commercial issues in sufficient detail and thus do not provide the business user with a reasonable degree of foreseeability in the most important aspects of the contractual relationship. Especially in the case of misleading formulations, the legislator already considers this to be the case. It will depend on the view of the average business user.[37] 29

II. Easily available

Art. 3(1)(b) P2B Regulation stipulates that the terms and conditions must be easily available to business users at all times in their business relationship with the provider of online intermediation services, including during the pre-contractual phase. There are no explicit form requirements or statements in the recitals in this regard. Only in the case of 30

---

[35] See rec. 15 P2B Regulation.
[36] V. Westphalen/Thüsing/Hoeren IT-Verträge mn. 125.
[37] Busch GRUR 2019, 788 (790).

changes is there a provision in Art. 3(2)(1) P2B Regulation that the information must be provided on a durable medium.[38] Similar to the requirements for clear and comprehensible regulations, however, the average business user must be taken as the yardstick.[39] It depends on the user's **accessibility** and the **predictability** of the business relationship.[40] Whether the terms and conditions are readily available is determined by the circumstances of the individual case and the standard of the average business user.[41] The continuous and open provision on the respective website of the online mediation service as well as its provider should be sufficient in any case.[42] It requires a clear indication by the provider of the place and circumstances of availability.[43]

31 Easy availability is not given in case access to the terms and conditions is granted first only after a prior registration or on the basis of a formal **request.**[44] This would reverse the burden of proof regarding the fact of easy availability and burden the business user with the initiative regarding the extent of foreseeability. However, prior registration cannot be required precisely because this also potentially creates a contractual relationship about which the business user would have to obtain foreseeability. The easy availability would then not refer to the phase before the conclusion of the contract, which includes any contract negotiations.[45] A request would mean that the provider of online intermediation services would continue to have the informational lead. However, there is no legitimate interest under the P2B Regulation in the terms and conditions not being available for everyone to see. Nor can it be argued from a systematic point of view with Art. 5(2) P2B Regulation, since this provision regulates the additional obligations for providers of online search engines that are not presented in terms and conditions. Moreover, Art. 10(1)(1) P2B Regulation further requires that the reasons for restrictions on the possibilities to offer other terms and conditions by other means must be stated and made "readily available to the public".[46] However, public availability is already no longer given in the case of access only after registration or request.[47] Sending by mail can therefore only be an alternative to maintain easy availability, for example in cases of temporary website outages.[48]

III. Basic information contained

32 Art. 3(1)(c)–(e) P2B Regulation imposes **content requirements** on the terms and conditions of providers of online intermediation services that go beyond the general requirements on the foreseeability of the business relationship.[49]

[38] Schneider/Kremer WRP 2020, 1128 (1131).
[39] Köhler/Bornkamm/Feddersen/Alexander P2B-VO Art. 3 mn. 12.
[40] BeckOK UWG/Wais P2B-VO Art. 3 mn. 6.
[41] Köhler/Bornkamm/Feddersen/Alexander P2B-VO Art. 3 mn. 12.
[42] BeckOK UWG/Wais P2B-VO Art. 3 mn. 7; Busch GRUR 2019, 788 (790).
[43] Wais EuZW 2019, 221 (225); but leaving open BeckOK UWG/Wais P2B-VO Art. 3 mn. 11.
[44] However, BeckOK UWG/Wais P2B-VO Art. 3 mn. 7, justifies this with a legitimate interest in the fact that not everyone can see it.
[45] Köhler/Bornkamm/Feddersen/Alexander P2B-VO Art. 3 mn. 13.
[46] Cf. Busch/Höppner/Wick P2B-VO Art. 10 mn. 22, who see only an "editorial difference"; in contrast, Köhler/Bornkamm/Feddersen/Alexander P2B-VO Art. 10 mn. 10 for an independent meaning of the public duty to inform consumers.
[47] BeckOK UWG/Fritzsche P2B-VO Art. 10 mn. 22.
[48] With reference to a teleological reduction in the case of merely temporary lack of technical accessibility Höppner/Schulz ZIP 2019, 2329 (2336).
[49] Köhler/Bornkamm/Feddersen/Alexander P2B-VO Art. 3 mn. 7.

1. Stating reasons for restricting the provision of the platform

According to Art. 3(1)(c) P2B Regulation, providers of online intermediation services must ensure that their terms and conditions specify the grounds on which a decision may be taken to suspend or terminate the provision of their online intermediation services to business users, in whole or in part, or to restrict them in any other way. These regulations are closely related to general antitrust law, which is not superseded by the P2B Regulation. Within the scope of application of the prohibition of abuse of market power, it may be impermissible for an obligated platform to restrict or discontinue its services if this is done **without objective reason.**[50] In the context of the P2B Regulation, a restriction is understood to be any quantitative or qualitative reduction of the services owed.[51] The obligation to provide concrete reasons for a block, on the other hand, is regulated in Art. 4(1) P2B Regulation. 33

a) Abstract duty to implement contractual clauses

The regulation provides for an abstract obligation to **state the** reasons.[52] According to recital 22 subpara. 2 P2B Regulation, the business users should be able to review the decision regarding the restriction to see whether he can successfully challenge it. It goes on to say that the justification for the restriction should state the reasons for the decision, with reference to the reasons that the provider had already set out in advance in the terms and conditions. The prior designation of the reasons in the terms and conditions is thus constitutive for the permissible implementation of blocking. 34

b) Legitimate reasons

Recital 22 subpara. 1 P2B Regulation addresses "legitimate reasons" on the basis of which a provider of online intermediation services may decide to restrict. What is legitimate is not discussed below in the regulation. Rather, legitimate reasons are **considered as to be constitutive.**[53] The obligation to designate from Art. 3(1)(c) P2B Regulation only regulates that any reasons are designated at all.[54] From a systematic point of view, this also results from the exception to the specific justification requirement in Art. 4(5) subpara. 2 P2B Regulation, as these require repeated breaches of pre-existing terms and conditions. If, on the other hand, a reason stated in the terms and conditions is not legitimate, a restriction subsequently made or decided upon may already be inadmissible according to respectively applicable general substantive law. 35

Synonyms for a legitimate interest such as "important" or "considerable" are not sufficient, as these do not make the exact and foreseeable criteria and requirements clear and thus the reasons are not **verifiable for** the business users.[55] Examples of rules describing inadmissible conduct may be permissible. If there are no legitimate reasons, any blocking on the basis of the terms and conditions is already excluded for this reason. 36

The provisions of Art. 4(4)(1)(a) and (b) P2B Regulation presuppose that there may be other reasons for the termination of intermediary services in addition to the reasons provided by the provider of online intermediation services in the terms and conditions. 37

---

[50] Introductory Louven K&R 2021, 685.

[51] Köhler/Bornkamm/Feddersen/Alexander P2B-VO Art. 3 mn. 15.

[52] Köhler/Bornkamm/Feddersen/Alexander P2B-VO Art. 4 mn. 5.

[53] Agreeing also BeckOK UWG/Wais P2B-VO Art. 3 mn. 19.

[54] BeckOK UWG/Wais P2B-VO Art. 3 mn. 20; for a substantive requirement of a legitimate reason Eickemeier/Brodersen K&R 2020, 397 (399); Voigt/Reuter MMR 2019, 783 (785).

[55] Cf. rec. 15 p. 1 P2B-VO; Köhler/Bornkamm/Feddersen/Alexander P2B-VO Art. 3 mn. 17; BeckOK UWG/Wais P2B-VO Art. 3 mn. 18.

These are reasons provided for by law, over which the provider has no influence, but which he must follow.

c) Implementation of a block due to the terms and conditions

38 If terms and conditions contain permissible reasons, a provider of online intermediation services may apply them to **individual cases** pursuant to Art. 4(1) P2B Regulation and, if the conditions are met, restrict or suspend the provision of its intermediary services or terminate them pursuant to Art. 4(2) P2B Regulation. If it does so, it must provide the business user concerned with the reasons for the decision on a durable medium at the latest at the same time as the restriction takes effect. Pursuant to Art. 4(5) subpara. 1 P2B Regulation, the reasons for the decision must explain the specific case and its circumstances and state why the restriction is being imposed. This also includes any notifications from third parties.

39 In the case of a complete termination, the provider must also observe a **30-day period** pursuant to Art. 4(2) P2B Regulation. Pursuant to Art. 4(4) subpara. 1 P2B Regulation, the provider of online intermediation services does not have to observe a time limit in the cases listed therein of a statutory or officially ordered obligation, mandatory national law or proof that the business user concerned has repeatedly violated the applicable terms and conditions and that this has led to the complete termination of the online intermediation services concerned.

40 Exceptionally, the provider of online intermediation services does not have to give reasons if he is either not allowed to disclose them due to legal or officially ordered obligations or if he can prove that the business user concerned has **repeatedly violated** the applicable terms and conditions and this has led to the complete termination of the online intermediation services concerned. However, the obligation to state reasons is replaced here by a burden of proof, which in the end also amounts to the fact that the restriction must be justified case by case.

2. Information on additional distribution opportunities

41 Another obligation according to Art. 3(1)(d) P2B Regulation concerns information on additional distribution channels or possible partner programmes through which the provider of online intermediation services could market the goods and services offered by the business user. Recital 16 P2B Regulation explains that business users should be clear about where and to whom their goods or services are marketed. The terms additional distribution channels or possible partner programmes are to be understood in a technology-neutral way. Other websites, software applications or other intermediary services are not exhaustively listed. These means could influence the intermediation services of the platform in an indirect way that might not be foreseeable for business users.[56] It could possibly even contradict their interests by targeting a clientele that is not intended to be targeted according to the marketing strategy of the business user or by displaying the goods and services on another platform.[57] In order to re-establish predictability here, the business users should be informed about the instruments used.[58]

42 Not all possible additional distribution options are to be presented, but only those that the provider of online intermediation services currently uses or would use.[59] The

[56] BeckOK UWG/Wais P2B-VO Art. 3 mn. 22.
[57] Köhler/Bornkamm/Feddersen/Alexander P2B-VO Art. 3 mn. 22.
[58] Busch GRUR 2019, 788 (791).
[59] BeckOK UWG/Wais P2B-VO Art. 3 mn. 23.

use of further distribution options not yet presented would then have to be carried out in the context of changes pursuant to Art. 3(2) P2B Regulation.

3. Information on intellectual property rights

Finally, the general transparency obligations under Art. 3(1)(e) P2B Regulation include the obligation to provide general information on the effects of the terms and conditions on the ownership and control of intellectual property rights of business users. This provision also has the purpose of making the business relationship predictable for business users.[60] Business users should be able to **foresee the legal situation.**[61] By way of example and not exhaustively, Recital 17 of the P2B Regulation lists logos, trade marks and business names, whereby the scope of application can extend to all intellectual property rights.[62] 43

According to recital 17 P2B Regulation, providers of online intermediation services should keep general information or, "if they wish so ", more detailed information. This does not mean that the amount of information is always at the discretion of the platform. Rather, the information must meet the criterion of foreseeability, which is equally likely to be determined by the circumstances of the individual case and the standard of a reasonable business user. Further information is required in particular if the terms and conditions are intended to regulate the ownership and control of intellectual property rights differently from the legal situation or if special rights are to be granted.[63] Thus, the higher the interests of the business users are affected or their predictability of the business relationship with regard to intellectual property rights would be limited without the information, the higher the standard of justification. 44

IV. Amendment of the terms and conditions

Art. 3(2) and (4) P2B Regulation provide for regulations on the amendment of terms and conditions by providers of online intermediation services. Not regulated is the amendment by business users, which, however, also has little practical relevance. Art. 3(4) P2B Regulation provides for an easing of the transposition deadline in certain cases. 45

1. Retroactive amendments

In connection with the amendment of terms and conditions, Art. 8(a) P2B Regulation prohibits **retroactive** amendments. In these cases, there is a lack of foreseeability for business users.[64] The provision is considered the only one with a substantive content, whereby the voidness according to Art. 3(3) P2B Regulation is probably left out.[65] In any case, in addition to the transparency requirements of Art. 3(2) P2B Regulation, which must be observed, it contains substantive requirements in the form that it protects business users from material burdens that could occur as a result of retroactive application.[66] 46

---

[60] Rec. 17 P2B Regulation.

[61] BeckOK UWG/Wais P2B-VO Art. 3 mn. 26.

[62] Köhler/Bornkamm/Feddersen/Alexander P2B-VO Art. 3 mn. 25; Busch/v. Westphalen P2B-VO Art. 3 mn. 326.

[63] Eickemeier/Brodersen K&R 2020, 397 (399); Busch GRUR 2019, 788 (791); Busch/v. Westphalen P2B-VO Art. 3 mn. 327.

[64] Rec. 32 P2B Regulation.

[65] v. Westphalen/Thüsing/Hoeren IT contracts mn. 125; Höppner/Schulz ZIP 2019, 2329 (2335).

[66] BeckOK UWG/Wais P2B-VO Art. 8 mn. 4.

Corresponding retroactive effects are prohibited regardless of whether they have been effectively implemented in accordance with Art. 3(2), (4) P2B Regulation.

47 **Two exceptions** apply, firstly compliance with a legal or regulatory obligation and secondly beneficial changes for the business user. In both cases, the business user is not considered to be in need of protection.[67] The retroactive amendment of the terms and conditions in cases of statutory obligation must be distinguished from retroactivity by law.[68] This is because retroactive corrections of the terms and conditions to the permanently applicable state of the law are also covered. Whether a retroactive effect by law is permissible depends on the respective applicable general law. Obligations imposed by authorities are conceivable in particular in cartel law.

48 Whether a regulation is advantageous for the business user depends on the circumstances of the individual case. The regulation does not specify whether the advantage is legal or economic. However, the purpose of the regulation and the protection of the business user suggest that an advantage must be **comprehensive**, i.e. it must not contain any disadvantages that are not reflected in the balance sheet.

2. Duty to inform

49 The provider of online intermediation services must inform the users concerned of any proposed change to their terms and conditions in accordance with Art. 3(2) subpara. 1 P2B Regulation. This must be done on a **durable medium in** accordance with Art. 2 no. 13 P2B Regulation.[69] Since terms and conditions according to Art. 2 no. 10 P2B Regulation broadly encompass all conditions or provisions that govern the contractual relationship, changes that may relate to the content of the service are also covered by the obligation to inform.[70]

3. Implementation period

50 Art. 3(2) P2B Regulation prescribes a lead time of at least 15 days. Only after this period may the proposed changes be implemented. If the change results in necessary technical or business adjustments for the business users, the providers of online intermediation services must also allow **longer periods** in accordance with Art. 3(2) subpara. 1 sent. 3 P2B Regulation. According to Art. 3(4) P2B Regulation, no time limit, not even a longer one, must be granted in the case of extraordinary circumstances. If the changes are made due to legal or officially ordered obligations, compliance with these obligations must prevent the time limit being set. This will often be the case for the same reasons with which an urgency of the implementation of the obligation is ordered. In addition, the provider of online intermediation services should be able to act immediately to avert unforeseen and immediate dangers from cyber security risks.

51 Pursuant to Art. 3(2) subpara. 4 of the P2B Regulation, business users may **waive** the time limit by a written declaration or a clearly confirming act, with the consequence that the changes take effect immediately. Unless an extended period of more than 15 days applies, the posting of new goods or services in the online intermediation services before the expiry of the deadline can be considered as such a waiver.

---

[67] Köhler/Bornkamm/Feddersen/Alexander P2B-VO Art. 8 mn. 9 et seq.
[68] On the latter, see in detail Busch/v. Westphalen P2B-VO Art. 8 mn. 10 et seqq.
[69] Köhler/Bornkamm/Feddersen/Alexander P2B-VO Art. 2 mn. 61.
[70] Köhler/Bornkamm/Feddersen/Alexander P2B-VO Art. 3 mn. 28.

4. Right of termination of the business user

Pursuant to Art. 3(2) subpara. 3 P2B Regulation, the business user affected by a proposed change has a specific right of termination before the expiry of the period. Unless a shorter period is provided for in the contract, the termination takes effect within 15 days of receipt of the notification of the change. Thus, in the event of termination, the business user does not have to tolerate the amended terms and conditions for a single day. The provision does not prescribe a specific form, so that the respective applicable Member State regulations apply.[71] 52

V. Consequence of voidness in case of violations of Art. 3(1) and (2) P2B Regulation

Art. 3(3) P2B Regulation orders the voidness of terms and conditions if they do not meet the requirements of Art. 3(1) P2B Regulation or contravene the provisions of Art. 3(2) P2B Regulation. In principle, this corresponds to the regulation under § 306(1) BGB. However, open questions arise regarding the consequences of voidness. 53

1. Absolute voidness

According to recital 20, the invalidity of the regulation should apply **erga omnes** and **ex tunc.**[72] Erga omnes means that the invalidity applies equally and directly to every user without the need for a further declaratory act.[73] 54

2. Substantive scope of the voidness

According to recital 20, the voidness should only apply to those provisions of the terms and conditions that do not comply.[74] Provided that the remaining provisions can be considered **separately** from these void provisions, they should continue to be valid and enforceable. In practice, this means a prohibition on the reduction of the respective clause in order to preserve its validity while at the same time applying the respective applicable law.[75] 55

Whether the provisions do not meet the requirements of Art. 3(1) and (2) P2B Regulation and to what extent separate consideration is possible depends on the **extent of the respective infringement.**[76] It is therefore already conceivable that there is an overall voidness due to a violation of the principle of easy availability.[77] On the other hand, the infringements under Art. 3(1)(a), (c) and (e) of the P2B Regulation could be presented in formally isolated regulatory texts and then allow for separate consideration, so that the invalidity does not extend to the remaining conditions.[78] This, however, only makes sense if the terms and conditions provide for regulations on the respective areas at all. From this interpretation follows the obligation of the provider of online intermediation services to clarify provisions or negative representations with regard to Art. 3 (1)(c)–(e) 56

[71] Köhler/Bornkamm/Feddersen/Alexander P2B-VO Art. 3 mn. 41.

[72] Busch/v. Westphalen P2B-VO Art. 3 mn. 364.

[73] BeckOK UWG/Wais P2B-VO Art. 3 mn. 55.

[74] BeckOK UWG/Wais P2B-VO Art. 3 mn. 43.

[75] Schneider/Kremer WRP 2020, 1128 (1133); Köhler/Bornkamm/Feddersen/Alexander P2B-VO Art. 3 mn. 49.

[76] AA: Köhler/Bornkamm/Feddersen/Alexander P2B-VO Art. 3 mn. 45: "evaluative consideration taking into account the interests of the parties".

[77] BeckOK UWG/Wais P2B-VO Art. 3 mn. 46.

[78] Alexander WRP 2020, 945 (951).

P2B Regulation.[79] If, for example, a provider of online intermediation services does not specify, in accordance with Art. 3(1)(c) P2B Regulation, the reasons for which he may restrict the provision of services to business users in whole or in part in any way, the invalidity sanction could come to nothing.[80] The failure to provide a regulation would anticipate the consequence of voidness. If, on the other hand, the terms and conditions contain provisions which are, however, insufficient, the application of the voidness would lead to an isolated voidness if considered separately. Accordingly, a comprehensive voidness of the entire set of terms and conditions makes more sense, since otherwise the provider without any implementation of the provisions would be in a better position than the one with a deficient implementation.[81] This is also supported by the voidness effect intended by the legislator for all users.

57 A restriction of this interpretation can result from the criterion of **foreseeability.** If, for example, provisions are not made which, according to the reasonable assessment of business users, are not to be expected, for example because they would be superfluous, their absence would not affect foreseeability. To include regulations here at all would possibly have the opposite effect and be perceived as unclear and incomprehensible. But even this restriction should only apply to those general contents that are not covered by Art. 3(1)(c)–(e) P2B Regulation. For with regard to these, the business users should at least expect clarifying regulations.

58 In the case of amendments to the terms and conditions made in breach of the duty to grant a fixed period of notice and therefore deemed void, the terms and conditions should be considered as if they had never existed. If only the amendments to the terms and conditions violate the transparency obligations and if they can be considered separately, the previous terms and conditions remain applicable.[82] The application of general law is only relevant if the invalidity affects the entire regulation or all terms and conditions.

3. Legal consequences of voidness

59 However, there is no general provision on content control similar to § 307(1)(1), (2) BGB. The P2B Regulation only provides for transparency control. Due to the absolute voidness of the terms and conditions, there seems to be no room for recourse to general contract law.[83] Thus, in the scope of application of German law, **no supplementary interpretation of the contract** according to §§ 133, 157 BGB would be possible.[84]

60 This result already seems questionable according to the clear wording of Art. 1(4)(1) P2B Regulation and the purpose of the regulation. This is because the principle that **general law** continues to apply alongside the P2B Regulation would be broken at this point. This could further lead to the assumption that the business user would lose his contractual basis solely due to a legal violation by the provider of the online mediation service.[85] A resolution of this conflict arises directly from the provision of Art. 3(3) P2B Regulation, which only orders the absolute voidness of the terms and conditions, but nothing more. Absolute voidness therefore only means that the terms and conditions de-

[79] This also follows from rec. 15 P2B Regulation.
[80] Cf. BeckOK UWG/Wais P2B-VO Art. 3 mn. 52.
[81] BeckOK UWG/Wais P2B-VO Art. 3 mn. 48; Busch/v. Westphalen P2B-VO Art. 3 mn. 373.
[82] v. Westphalen BB 2020, 579 (585); Köhler/Bornkamm/Feddersen/Alexander P2B-VO Art. 3 mn. 48.
[83] v. Westphalen/Thüsing/Hoeren IT contracts mn. 125; v. Westphalen BB 2020, 579 (585).
[84] v. Westphalen BB 2020, 579 (585) with further examples.
[85] Alexander WRP 2020, 945 (951) already doubts this.

sired by the provider do not apply. He cannot therefore make the desired arrangements, but reverts to the status of the applicable general law.[86]

61 It is still open whether invalidity will mean that business users will no longer be able to rely on **regulations that are favourable to** them. On the one hand, it is argued that the protective purpose no longer justifies the consequence of voidness if the regulations concerned represent an advantage for the business user.[87] However, in view of the clear wording and the unambiguous explanations in recital 20, there is no room for a teleological reduction. The business user could also raise the objection of bad faith if the provider does not provide the services as could be expected. If necessary, this could also be related to "cherry-picking" if he nevertheless invokes invalidity at another point. However, whether and to what extent this plea is possible is likely to be a question of the applicable substantive law outside the Regulation to be determined for the case.[88]

VI. Information on ancillary goods and services

62 Art. 6 P2B Regulation allows transparency for business users in the case of additional offers that may **compete** with them.[89] These can be offered either by the online intermediation service provider itself or by third parties. The provider must then include information in its terms and conditions about the nature of the ancillary goods and services offered and whether and under what conditions the business user is also entitled to offer its own ancillary goods and services through the online intermediation services.

63 According to the legal definition in Art. 2 no. 11 P2B Regulation, ancillary goods or services are those goods and services that are offered to the consumer prior to the conclusion of the transaction initiated by means of the online intermediation services, in addition and supplementary to the main goods or services offered by the business user through the online intermediation services. In this context, additional and complementary means that the goods or services are **functionally related to** the main goods or services by being dependent on them and directly related to them.[90] They must therefore be complementary offers by means of which a provider of online intermediation services or a third party can exert competitive pressure on business users. This does not include direct competing offers to the brokered goods or services of the business users or so-called third party offers without such a functional connection, for example if the online intermediation services are also offered for other types of goods or services.[91]

64 The transparency obligation in Art. 6 P2B Regulation first requires the inclusion of a description of the type of ancillary goods and services offered. If the offers are not made by the provider of online intermediation services himself, but by third parties, he must **describe** these offers by **category**.[92] However, this can only be done analogously if and to the extent that there is a temporal and functional connection between these offers and the main offers of the business user.[93] On the other hand, the business user must again

[86] Cf. clearly Köhler/Bornkamm/Feddersen/Alexander P2B-VO Art. 3 mn. 46.

[87] BeckOK UWG/Wais P2B-VO Art. 3 mn. 57; Köhler/Bornkamm/Feddersen/Alexander P2B-VO Art. 3 mn. 43.

[88] Köhler/Bornkamm/Feddersen/Alexander P2B-VO Art. 3 mn. 46; Schneider/Kremer WRP 2020, 1128 (1132).

[89] Busch/Busch P2B-VO Art. 6 mn. 2; Köhler/Bornkamm/Feddersen/Alexander P2B-VO Art. 6 mn. 1.

[90] Rec. 29 P2B Regulation.

[91] Busch/Busch P2B-VO Art. 6 mn. 16; BeckOK UWG/Fritzsche P2B-VO Art. 6 mn. 9.

[92] BeckOK UWG/Fritzsche P2B-VO Art. 6 mn. 16; Köhler/Bornkamm/Feddersen/Alexander P2BVO Art. 6 mn. 5; Busch/Busch P2B-VO Art. 6 mn. 19.

[93] Busch/Busch P2B-VO Art. 6 mn. 16.

be able to assess, in the sense of predictability, whether and how a competitive situation may arise for him as a result of the complementary offers.[94]

65 In addition to the competitive effects of the offer of ancillary goods and services, the business user must also be able to assess whether and under what conditions it is possible for him to **enter the market with** regard to the complementary offers. This requires first of all an explicit provision as to whether this possibility exists at all or not. If it does not exist, it is a non-competition clause that must be regulated in the terms and conditions.[95] However, Art. 6 P2B Regulation does not impose an equal treatment or opening obligation with regard to the offer of ancillary goods or services.[96] Such representations must be made according to Art. 7 P2B Regulation.

VII. Information on most favoured nation treatment

66 Art. 10(1) P2B Regulation prescribes information obligations regarding restrictions on the possibility of offering other terms by other means. This regulation also covers the so-called most favoured nation clauses, but also parity clauses or best price clauses.[97] If such clauses exist, the provider must state the most important economic, commercial or legal reasons. Art. 10(2) P2B Regulation clarifies the character of the provision as an obligation to provide information in order to maintain transparency. The substantive admissibility of MFNs is also governed here by the general provisions, in particular antitrust law.[98] The provision does not have its own **substantive effects.**[99]

1. Restrictions on the possibilities for offers on other terms by other means

67 The regulation covers all conduct in connection with the provision of online intermediation services which aims at such an effect.[100] Thus, **mere de facto conduct** is also subject to the duty to inform.[101] Thus, the provider does not have to have had the restrictive conditions granted to him beforehand in his terms and conditions in order to inform about them.[102] However, only restrictions of the providers of online intermediation services themselves are covered, not restrictions outside their sphere of influence. The provision explicitly refers only to offers to consumers under Art. 2 no. 4 P2B Regulation, not to other businesses.[103] However, it is comprehensively applicable if a contractual provision or practice does not differentiate between offers to consumers and businesses.[104] Therefore, corresponding clarifications are recommended.

68 The wording of Art. 10(1)(1) P2B Regulation does not provide for any restrictions as to how the restrictions take place.[105] In accordance with the purpose of the provision, it

---

[94] BeckOK UWG/Fritzsche P2B-VO Art. 6 mn. 17; Köhler/Bornkamm/Feddersen/Alexander P2B-VO Art. 6 mn. 6.

[95] BeckOK UWG/Fritzsche P2B-VO Art. 6 mn. 18; for a merely clarifying presentation Köhler/Bornkamm/Feddersen/Alexander P2B-VO Art. 6 mn. 7.

[96] Busch/Busch P2B-VO Art. 6 mn. 21 et seq.

[97] Busch/Höppner/Wick P2B-VO Art. 10 mn. 1.

[98] See in particular Köhler/Bornkamm/Feddersen/Alexander P2B-VO Art. 10 mn. 13, who points out a lack of legalisation effect of the P2BVO under substantive law; further Rohrßen ZVertriebsR 2019, 341 (343).

[99] Busch/Höppner/Wick P2B-VO Art. 10 mn. 17.

[100] Busch/Höppner/Wick P2B-VO Art. 10 mn. 10.

[101] Busch/Höppner/Wick P2B-VO Art. 10 mn. 1; aA BeckOK UWG/Fritzsche P2B-VO Art. 10 mn. 10.

[102] Busch/Höppner/Wick P2B-VO Art. 10 mn. 19.

[103] BeckOK UWG/Fritzsche P2B-VO Art. 10 mn. 9.

[104] BeckOK UWG/Fritzsche P2B-VO Art. 10 mn. 13; Busch/Höppner/Wick P2B-VO Art. 10 mn. 9.

[105] Busch/Höppner/Wick P2B-VO Art. 10 mn. 14.

is to be interpreted broadly and covers **all alternative distribution channels** to the platform. Typical restrictions are parity clauses with which providers contractually prohibit their commercial customers from posting better offers via other distribution channels than on the platform. Narrow parity clauses usually refer to sales via the business user's own channels, whereas broad parity clauses also refer to additional intermediation services of other providers. The business users then have fewer opportunities to compete with the offers on the platform. Furthermore, broad parity clauses have a negative effect on the competitive conditions of alternative intermediation services if no better offers can be posted on them. These effects can be further intensified in the case of best price clauses. Due to these negative effects on competition, such most-favoured-nation practices are to be assessed very cautiously under antitrust law.[106]

The wording refers to "the same goods and services". Given the purpose of creating transparency on MFN practices, it should be interpreted broadly to cover all rules that make it difficult for business users to offer competitive alternatives.[107] It is sufficient that, from the consumer's point of view, the goods or services are comparable to those covered by the intermediary services. This also applies to requirements regarding menus, for example,[108] as they represent a qualitative difference.[109] Not covered by the information obligation, however, are restrictions on the distribution of merely similar or complementary offers.[110] Complementary offers would merely supplement the goods or services offered on the online intermediation service. In the case of similar offers, other models, other equipment or other brands may also be covered.[111] If these are specifically described but covered by a generic scope of intermediation services, the restriction nevertheless applies to the same services.[112] This is not the case for specialised intermediation services which only refer to certain models, equipment or brands. Restrictions on other models, equipment or brands that go hand in hand with this are not covered by Art. 10(1)(1) P2B Regulation. 69

2. Statement of reasons

Art. 10(1)(1) prescribes a basic duty to provide information in the terms and conditions on the existing restrictions. These must be made easily available to the **public,** i.e. they must be viewable and easy to find by anyone without prior registration.[113] If the most-favoured-nation treatment does not result from the contractual terms themselves, but from the actual actions of the provider of online intermediation services, the terms and conditions contain purely informal statements on this without any regulatory character of their own.[114] 70

Providers of online mediation services do not have to state every reason, but only the **most important** ones. This serves to indicate factual justification reasons and thus simplifies reviewability.[115] If the reasons are less important, the substantive admissibility of MFN treatment alone is questionable. A typical reason for MFN practices is often seen 71

106 Busch/Höppner/Wick P2B-VO Art. 10 mn. 3 with further references.
107 More restrictive, however, Köhler/Bornkamm/Feddersen/Alexander P2B-VO Art. 10 mn. 6.
108 Citing this example, Busch/Höppner/Wick P2B-VO Art. 10 mn. 10.
109 Köhler/Bornkamm/Feddersen/Alexander P2B-VO Art. 10 mn. 7.
110 BeckOK UWG/Fritzsche P2B-VO Art. 10 mn. 13.
111 BeckOK UWG/Fritzsche P2B-VO Art. 10 mn. 13.
112 For example, the distribution conditions for a car brand outside a platform for the intermediation of cars without restriction of a brand.
113 BeckOK UWG/Fritzsche P2B-VO Art. 10 mn. 22.
114 Cf. however BeckOK UWG/Fritzsche P2B-VO Art. 10 mn. 19.
115 Köhler/Bornkamm/Feddersen/Alexander P2B-VO Art. 10 mn. 12.

in the avoidance of the free-rider problem.[116] Since the information obligation of Art. 10(1)(2) P2B Regulation only serves the presentation of transparency, the actual indication of reasons that exist at all is sufficient.[117] Whether it is a suitable reason for MFN treatment, on the other hand, depends on the respective applicable substantive law, which might lead to different results.[118] If no reason is given, a breach of the applicable substantive law provision is likely in addition to the breach of the duty to inform. Thus, the provider of online intermediation services is forced to explain the factual reasons via the regulation.[119]

VIII. Data access during the ongoing contractual relationship

72 Art. 9 P2B Regulation prescribes specific information obligations regarding data access during the existing contractual relationship. Art. 8(c) P2B Regulation, on the other hand, regulates information on data access after the end of the contractual relationship. Specific features regarding the differentiated presentation with regard to access to data result from Art. 7(3)(a) P2B Regulation.

1. Information provided

73 The wording of Art. 9 P2B Regulation refers to data. However, this term is to be **interpreted broadly** in this context according to the protective purpose of the regulation and independently of any data protection classifications.[120] It refers to all information that is made available or generated.[121]

74 An exception applies to data generated by the online intermediation service provider itself or data that the provider feeds in from **third-party sources.**[122] These are not provided or generated by business users or consumers.[123] Thus, the provider does not have to inform about their access, nor the lack of such access. In this respect, the provision excludes proprietary data as privileged. Difficulties may arise in differentiating between proprietary data and aggregated third-party data according to Art. 9(2)(c) P2B Regulation. This conflict can be resolved, at least in the context of transparency obligations, by a negative explanation supplementing the regulation on access to third-party data, namely that there is no further access to data. Whether the accompanying denial of access to data, on the other hand, is permissible depends on general law.[124] In particular for competition law or sector-specific access claims, the question of whether the data is proprietary data is regularly irrelevant.[125]

75 The above remarks in turn gain considerable significance with regard to the question of when data is made available. According to the purpose of the provisions, it cannot be a question of knowing while acting, but only of **de facto competitive behavior.**[126] This

[116] In summary, Busch/Höppner/Wick P2B-VO Art. 10 mn. 2.
[117] BeckOK UWG/Fritzsche P2B-VO Art. 10 mn. 19.
[118] This is also supported by Köhler/Bornkamm/Feddersen/Alexander P2B-VO Art. 10 mn. 12.
[119] BeckOK UWG/Fritzsche P2B-VO Art. 10 mn. 21.
[120] Tribess ZD 2020, 440 (441).
[121] Busch/Podszun P2B-VO Art. 9 mn. 40; Köhler/Bornkamm/Feddersen/Alexander P2B-VO Art. 9 mn. 7.
[122] Busch/Podszun P2B-VO Art. 9 mn. 72.
[123] Busch/Podszun P2B-VO Art. 9 mn. 65.
[124] Höppner/Schulz ZIP 2019, 2329 (2335).
[125] Cf. for German law in particular Section 20 (1a) sentence 3 GWB, according to which it is not decisive for the assessment of the inequity of the denied data access whether a market for the data in question has been opened so far.
[126] Busch/Podszun P2B-VO Art. 9 mn. 66.

will be very easy to determine in the case of registration data or information entered in fields, masks or search engines. However, there will be overlaps with the concept of generation in the course of provision, which is to be understood as a further catch-all term. This is data that is also automatically generated in the course of the provider's provision of the intermediary service.[127] These will regularly arise without knowledge from business users or consumers. The data collected is independent of whether or not intermediation services have actually been provided.

2. Obligation to explain

Providers of online intermediation services must inform business users "adequately" by means of the explanation referred to in paragraph 1, according to Art. 9(2) P2B Regulation. This is also a mere transparency obligation.[128] The business users should thereby be enabled to understand the possibility of using the data to increase their added value.[129] The **appropriateness of the explanation is** based on the purpose of the provision, which serves the information interests of the business users. This is contrasted with the possible legitimate interests of the provider of online intermediation services, which regularly take a back seat to the obligation to provide information.[130] 76

This is supplemented by the requirement that information must be provided about both the existing and the **non-existing access.** The subject of the explanation must therefore be the existence or absence of technical or contractual access to personal or other data or both. In contrast to Art. 8(c) P2B Regulation, this covers further categories of data that are not limited to those that the business user has provided or that have arisen during his use.[131] 77

If the provider grants access to data in accordance with its terms and conditions, these terms and conditions shall be subject to the requirements and limitations of the applicable **general law**. Insofar as the provider organises access to data in accordance with this, it shall clearly set out to business users the scope, nature and conditions of their access to certain categories of data as well as their use.[132] 78

The provider must also explain if **access does not exist**. Whether and how this is to be assessed under substantive law depends on general law. In particular, it may be questionable whether sector-specific and competition law provisions require mandatory access to be granted or whether non-existent access is inadmissible.[133] If such access is to be granted, but is not or insufficiently presented in the terms and conditions, two consequences result: Firstly, it is a violation of the transparency obligation from Art. 9 P2B Regulation, which is enforced within the framework of the sanction regime resulting from this.[134] Secondly, and without prejudice to this, the business user can enforce the substantive existing data access according to the rules of the respective applicable law. However, the enforcement of mandatory data access will regularly not be reasonable for individual data subjects. However, the transparency obligation and its independent enforceability re-establish collective legal protection, which leads to clarification of the ex- 79

---

[127] Busch/Podszun P2B-VO Art. 9 mn. 70.

[128] Busch/Podszun P2B-VO Art. 9 mn. 128.

[129] Rec. 33 P2B Regulation.

[130] On the balancing of interests Köhler/Bornkamm/Feddersen/Alexander P2B-VO Art. 9 mn. 10; Tribess ZD 2020, 440 (442).

[131] Köhler/Bornkamm/Feddersen/Alexander P2B-VO Art. 9 mn. 6.

[132] Rec. 33 P2B-VO.

[133] BeckOK UWG/Tribess P2B-VO Art. 9 mn. 8.

[134] Tribess ZD 2020, 440 (442); critical on the limits, however, Alexander WRP 2021, 1375 (1380 et seq.).

isting possibilities. In addition, the transparency obligation for differentiated treatment applies according to Art. 7(3)(a) P2B Regulation.

80 Art. 9(2) P2B Regulation prescribes **minimum requirements**[135] for circumstances that the provider of online intermediation services must explain. This means that the terms and conditions must contain differentiated presentations of the individual regulatory points. These are:

- Access to data by the provider of online intermediation services (Art. 9(2)(a) P2B Regulation)
- Access by business users to their own data (Art. 9(2)(b) P2B Regulation)
- Access to generally available data (Art. 9(2)(c) P2B Regulation)
- Provision of data to third parties (Art. 9(2)(d) P2B Regulation)

a) Access to data by the provider of online intermediation services

81 The regulation in Art. 9(2)(a) P2B Regulation concerns the online intermediation service provider's **own access to** data. For technical reasons, the provider will already have access to all data for the purpose of operation, which must be pointed out. If the provider uses additional service providers, it must be pointed out that access may not be available as a result, and at the same time, pursuant to Art. 9 (2)(d) P2B Regulation, the provision of data to third parties. Affiliated companies count as belonging to the provider.[136] Since the obligation to explain thus refers to the provider with all its economically active units, it must also be shown which affiliated companies receive access and under what conditions. This has particular implications for any group companies that compete with the business users on a horizontal level. For if these receive privileged access to data due to their connection with the provider, they simultaneously have a competitive advantage. Whether this is justified and can be permissibly exploited depends on general law, in particular cartel law. The transparency obligation can also serve the purpose of pointing out general competition law problems at an early stage.

82 Furthermore, reference must be made to access that **goes beyond mere operation**. This means that the provider must also point out any privileged access to data. This provision thus enables greater transparency, for example by disclosing competitive advantages of the platform or self-beneficiaries.[137] Whether this conduct would be permissible again depends on general substantive law, in particular antitrust provisions.

83 The term "other data" is very broad. It also includes **communication content** that is generated, for example, when the provider accesses the platform's own messenger.[138] Accordingly, the provider of online mediation services must also explain whether and under what conditions it accesses the communication of such services. Whether this access is permissible depends on the respective applicable law, in particular the national telecommunications data protection implemented on the basis of Directive 2002/58/EC (ePrivacy) as well as the secrecy of telecommunications. It should be noted that due to the specific relationship of this Directive to the GDPR, its provisions do not apply in parts and thus, in particular, no access pursuant to Art. 6(1)(1)(f) of the GDPR comes into consideration. If data is accessed beyond what is necessary to provide the service, consent must be obtained.[139] Since the legal requirements are also conditions of the provider for access, he must also explain these in his terms and conditions.

---

[135] Tribess ZD 2020, 440 (442).
[136] Busch/Podszun P2B-VO Art. 9 mn. 31.
[137] Rec. 33 P2B Regulation.
[138] Busch/Podszun P2B-VO Art. 9 mn. 68.
[139] Cf. on the need for and requirements of consent Assion/Assion TTDSG § 3 mn. 138 et seqq.

b) Access by business users to their provided data

Art. 9(2)(b) P2B Regulation concerns the access of business users to data **resulting from their use** of the online intermediation service.[140] This covers data provided by the business user as well as data generated in the course of providing these services to this business user and the consumers of the business user's goods and services. Further data access must be explained according to Art. 9(2)(c) P2B Regulation. Therefore, a clear or even conclusive definition of the data covered is irrelevant. Since the provision only serves transparency purposes, it does not make any statement on the controversial question of the allocation of data or even a so-called "ownership of data". It is therefore all the more decisive that the provider himself explicitly clarifies which data the business user can access and under which conditions. 84

c) Access by business users to generally available data

In addition, according to Art. 9(2)(c) P2B Regulation, it must be explained whether and how a business user can obtain access to **data of third parties** that are based on the use of the online intermediation service. This covers data made available or generated in the course of the services provided to all business users and consumers, i.e. not solely based on the use of the one business user himself who could obtain access. This provision is intended to force transparency about the extent to which pooling of data can be accessed. At the same time, this may lead to an increased exchange of data.[141] Furthermore, the explanations can create transparency about the risk of an exchange of information that may be inadmissible under cartel law.[142] 85

d) Provision of data to third parties

Art. 9(2)(d) P2B Regulation is related to the **commercialisation of data** by third parties.[143] These are regularly service providers who exploit data as part of their business models. A restriction to commercial third parties is not envisaged, so that NGOs, parties, authorities or other consumers are also covered.[144] In particular, business users should be informed whether they can refuse the transfer of data. Because of Art. 9(3) P2B Regulation, the transfer of data to third parties is subject to the permissibility of data protection and telecommunications secrecy law. 86

3. Checklist

The following checklist is recommended for the presentation of the explanatory obligations arising in particular from Art. 9(2) P2B Regulation:[145] 87

- Access to data by the provider of online intermediation services
  - Present or not present
  - Categories of data[146] (personal data, other data, in particular communication content)

---

140 In summary, Köhler/Bornkamm/Feddersen/Alexander P2B-VO Art. 9 mn. 12.
141 Rec. 35 P2B Regulation.
142 Busch/Podszun P2B-VO Art. 9 mn. 125 et seqq.
143 Rec. 34 P2B Regulation.
144 Busch/Podszun P2B-VO Art. 9 mn. 92.
145 Cf. also Busch/Podszun P2B-VO Art. 9 mn. 105.
146 But see rec. 33, p. 3 P2B Regulation: "The explanation should be proportionate and could refer to general access conditions rather than a comprehensive list of actual data or categories of data".

  - Conditions (affiliates, view, access, timeliness, scope and availability, processing, use, usability, self-restrictions)
- Access of business users to their own data
  - Present or not present
  - Categories of data (type of data, timeliness)
  - Technical access (technical requirements, viewing, access, timeliness, scope and availability, format, editing, use)
  - Contractual access (conditions, obligations, usability, restrictions)
- Access by business users to generally available data
  - Present or not present
  - Categories of data (type of data, differentiation from own data, topicality, aggregation, anonymisation, pseudonymisation)
  - Technical access (technical requirements, viewing, access, timeliness, scope and availability, format, editing, use)
  - Contractual access (conditions, obligations, usability, restrictions)
- Provision of data to third parties
  - Present or not present
  - Designation of data (type of data, timeliness, aggregation, anonymisation, pseudonymisation)
  - Purpose, scope and format of disclosure
  - Third party designation
  - Possibilities for refusing the transfer of data

IX. Ranking

88 Art. 5 of the P2B Regulation provides for information obligations on the process and the establishment of a ranking. The provision is in addition to the other obligations. In particular, it does not provide for rules on differentiated treatment on the basis of the ranking.[147] Nor does it make any statement as to whether a particular ranking result or procedure is permissible under substantive law. This depends on the respective applicable general law.[148] From an antitrust law perspective in particular, several cases of application have recently arisen in connection with platforms.[149] Whether an increased duty of transparency and thus the hoped-for informedness actually leads to the desired competitive successes appears questionable if competitors have no possibilities of evasion, especially if additional tipping effects can be ascertained.[150] However, the provision also aims at **improving the choice of** consumers, who can influence the market power relations with their selection decisions.[151] The results of a ranking can also be tantamount to a delisting or restriction of intermediation services, so that in these cases information obligations could be activated according to Art. 4 P2B Regulation.

89 The requirements are more detailed with regard to rankings on online search engines. This also results from the fact that corporate website user regularly have **no contractual relationship** with the provider of online search engines. On the basis of Art. 5(7) P2B Regulation, the Commission has issued guidelines in which it specifies the transparency

---

[147] Busch/Busch P2B-VO Art. 5 mn. 23.

[148] Cf. in particular Busch/Busch P2B-VO Art. 5 mn. 5 et seqq.

[149] See for example Commission 27.6.2017 – AT.39740 – Google Search (Shopping); CFI 10.11.2021 – T-612/17 – Google Shopping; Höppner WuW 2017, 421.

[150] Spindler/Seidel NJW 2022, 2730 (2733).

[151] See rec. 24 P2B Regulation; point 41 of the Ranking Transparency Guidelines refers to this.

requirements in rankings.[152] The guidelines are not binding, but they are highly indicative.[153]

1. Concept of ranking

The term ranking is legally defined in Art. 2 no. 8 P2B Regulation. According to this, it is supposed to be a **relative highlighting of** goods and services offered via online intermediation services. Relative highlighting means an evaluative sorting of comparable goods and services.[154] Ranking is the result of a search that is presented to consumers. It should not depend on the means used.[155] The term is technology-neutral and should be interpreted broadly.[156] Equally decisive for a ranking is the relevance attributed to search results by online search engines. The definition makes it clear that a ranking can be organised, presented and communicated by providers of online mediation services as well as by online search engines. A typical example is the integration of an online search engine into the offer of an online intermediation service. 90

The representation is not limited to a mere text list, but can include all perceptible highlights, such as cartographic ones.[157] A relative presentation of the goods and services directly next to each other is not mandatory. A highlighted presentation of only one mediated offer – such as that of a hybrid platform itself – is also the subject of a ranking.[158] 91

2. Specific features for providers of online search engines

Since providers of online search engines regularly lack a contractual relationship, Art. 5(2) P2B Regulation contains specific provisions. They must provide clear and comprehensible **explanations** in their online search engines, which are public and easily available. They must keep these up-to-date at all times.[159] The wording "in" adds to the obligation to make them easily available and public. The explanation must therefore be presented in such a way that it can be directly understood in connection with the provision of the online search engine. 92

3. Representational obligations

The provision of Art. 5 P2B Regulation also serves to establish **predictability**.[160] According to this provision, providers should not arbitrarily determine the main parameters for the ranking. Whether the determination is arbitrary is determined by the respective applicable substantive law. However, this verifiability can be facilitated by the fact that the criteria for the presentation of the ranking are available at all. However, the purpose of the provision is not exhausted in this. Business users and users with corporate 93

[152] Leitlinien zur Transparenz des Rankings gemäß der VO (EU) 2019/1150 des Europäischen Parlaments und des Rates vom 8.12.2020; im Folgenden: Leitlinien 2020 ABl. 2020 C 424/01, 3 (Rankingtransparenz-Leitlinien); on the concretisation effect BeckOK UWG/Wais P2B-VO Art. 5 mn. 24.

[153] BeckOK UWG/Wais P2B-VO Art. 5 mn. 24.

[154] Busch/Busch P2B-VO Art. 5 mn. 22; Köhler/Bornkamm/Feddersen/Alexander P2B-VO Art. 2 mn. 43.

[155] BeckOK UWG/Wais P2B-VO Art. 5 mn. 2.

[156] Busch/Busch P2B-VO Art. 5 mn. 23.

[157] Cf. Busch/Busch P2B-VO Art. 5 mn. 23; in principle, an auditory presentation is also conceivable, although additional circumstances must be added here, as a lecture takes place one after the other.

[158] Busch/Busch P2B-VO Art. 5 mn. 24.

[159] BeckOK UWG/Wais P2B-VO Art. 5 mn. 12.

[160] Rec. 24 P2B-VO; Schneider/Kremer WRP 2020, 1128 (1134).

websites should also be able to improve the presentation or goods and services or some of the inherent characteristics of the goods and services.[161]

a) Main parameters

94 Art. 5(1) P2B Regulation provides for the presentation of the parameters that *determine* the ranking of a provider of online intermediation services. According to Art. 5(2) P2B Regulation, the parameters that are *most important* for determining the ranking are to be presented. This wording does not result in a different consideration, since in both cases there can be a variety of possible selection criteria.[162] What is decisive is that the providers capture the inherent **dynamic character of the ranking in a static explanation** and present foreseeable influences.[163]

95 The main parameters do not include the underlying **logic** of a ranking.[164] This follows on the one hand from Art. 5(6)(1) P2B Regulation, according to which it is not necessary to disclose algorithms or information that would with sufficient certainty lead to the possibility of consumers being deceived or harmed by the manipulation of search results. In addition to preventing manipulation by third parties, this is also intended to prevent the platform from having to disclose the core area of its business performance.[165] Accordingly, the regulations based on the Directive on the protection of business secrets remain unaffected pursuant to Art. 5(6)(2) P2B Regulation. On the other hand, Art. 5(5) P2B Regulation concretises the explanations according to how the criteria listed there are taken into account by the ranking mechanism.

96 The regulation itself lists as main parameters all general criteria, processes and specific signals involved in the algorithms, or other adjustment or downgrading mechanisms used in the context of ranking. Numerous other examples are given in the **Ranking Transparency Guidelines in** their Appendix I. Whether these need to be explained depends on their respective influence on the ranking in question.[166] The greater the influence of a parameter, therefore, the more likely it is to be explained.[167] Parameters with only a minor influence do not need to be explained. Since the presentation of rankings has a decisive influence on the selection decisions of users, their point of view must be taken into account.[168]

97 If, on the other hand, parameters move from a relative weighting to the background as main parameters, this may necessitate a **change in the main parameters.** In the case of terms and conditions of providers of online intermediation services, this requires an amendment in accordance with Art. 3 P2B Regulation.[169] In the case of online search engines, there is an obligation to update in accordance with Art. 5(2)(2) P2B Regulation.[170]

---

[161] Rec. 24 P2B Regulation.

[162] For an explanation regarding online search engines Köhler/Bornkamm/Feddersen/Alexander P2B-VO Art. 5 mn. 13.

[163] Point 46 Ranking Transparency Guidelines.

[164] BeckOK UWG/Wais P2B-VO Art. 5 mn. 21.

[165] Busch/Busch P2B-VO Art. 5 mn. 2.

[166] Busch/Busch P2B-VO Art. 5 mn. 26; BeckOK UWG/Wais P2B-VO Art. 5 mn. 3.

[167] No. 42 Ranking Transparency Guidelines.

[168] No. 17 Ranking Transparency Guidelines; Köhler/Bornkamm/Feddersen/Alexander P2B-VO Art. 5 mn. 28.

[169] Cf. No. 46 at the end of the Ranking Transparency Guidelines, with more references in footnote 11.

[170] BeckOK UWG/Wais P2B-VO Art. 5 mn. 12.

b) Reasons for relative prominence

Art. 5(5) P2B Regulation prescribes a catalogue for the presentation of the main parameters, by means of which the information obligations are specified.[171] According to this, business users or corporate website users must be able to form an appropriate understanding with regard to the main parameters[172] as to whether, how and to what extent the ranking mechanism takes into account the criteria listed there. The provision describes the **minimum content** of the terms and conditions or explanations at this point.[173] It differentiates between providers of online mediation services and providers of online search engines. The provision under Art. 5(5)(c) P2B Regulation only applies to the latter. 98

aa) Offer characteristics

Business users and users with business websites should be able to improve the **presentation** of their goods and services or some of the inherent characteristics of the goods or services.[174] Therefore, Art. 5(5)(a) P2B Regulation requires that the explanations take into account the characteristics of the goods and services offered to consumers via the respective platform. The provision thus ties in with the qualitative characteristics by means of which business users or corporate website user can distinguish themselves from one another in competition with their offers.[175] These form the most important basis for an arbitrary ranking representation. Inherent characteristics of goods and services refer to their immediate features. However, the provision is not limited to this and also covers indirect characteristics.[176] This also includes customer reviews, as these relate to the evaluation by the addressed consumer group and have an impact on rankings.[177] Insofar as these do not have to be presented first due to their relevance for consumers according to Art. 5(5)(b) P2B Regulation, they can already represent an indirect characteristic and thus a characteristic requiring explanation. This may be the case, for example, with particularly high customer ratings. 99

bb) Relevance of the offer for consumers

The above-mentioned characteristics can also have an impact on consumers' decisions. These are made on the basis of the relative relevance of the characteristics, i.e. depending on whether a match has taken place with an individual consumer that can lead to a successful mediation.[178] Accordingly, Art. 5(5)(b) P2B Regulation prescribes an independent duty of consideration. This is linked to the platforms' mediation services with regard to commercial offers to consumers.[179] 100

cc) Design of the corporate website

Art. 5(5)(c) P2B Regulation only applies to providers of online search engines. In the case of these, the goods and services are not displayed on the provider's own website, but on the user's corporate website. These are recorded in the online search engines and dis- 101

[171] In detail, Busch/Busch P2B-VO Art. 5 mn. 62 et seqq.; BeckOK UWG/Wais P2B-VO Art. 5 mn. 17.
[172] Busch/Busch P2B-VO Art. 5 mn. 63.
[173] Busch/Busch P2B-VO Art. 5 mn. 62.
[174] Rec. 24 P2B Regulation.
[175] Busch/Busch P2B-VO Art. 5 mn. 66.
[176] Köhler/Bornkamm/Feddersen/Alexander P2B-VO Art. 5 mn. 27.
[177] Busch/Busch P2B-VO Art. 5 mn. 66.
[178] Busch/Busch P2B-VO Art. 5 mn. 68.
[179] Busch/Busch P2B-VO Art. 5 mn. 68.

played in the ranking. The **design of** the corporate website[180] can have an impact on its ranking in the search engine.[181] The provision requires the provider to explain whether and how it takes such criteria into account in its ranking.

c) Influencing the ranking in return for payment

102 Just as rankings can represent relative selection decisions of the provider, these could be **influenced in return for a fee.** Art. 5(3) P2B Regulation stipulates that the respective providers must explain these possibilities and, in particular, how fees affect the ranking. Direct and indirect fees are covered.[182] In the case of hybrid platforms, the obligation to provide information on differentiating treatments also applies.

103 Firstly, information must be provided on whether the ranking is influenced at all by the payment of a fee. Secondly, the provider must inform about the effects of the fee on the ranking. This explains the wording of the provision that the influence of payment is one of the **main parameters**. It must always be reflected, even if it may only have a minor influence on the ranking from the provider's point of view.

d) Inspection of third-party notices in the event of changes or delistings

104 Art. 5(4) P2B Regulation concerns specific delistings of corporate website user on online search engines on the basis of a **notification from a third party**, i.e. not the ranking parameters.[183] Since these regularly have no direct contractual relationship with the provider of an online search engine, they would find it difficult to enforce their rights in the event of a delisting. At the same time, there is a potential for abuse by third parties who submit false reports and thus contribute to the delisting.[184] The provider of a search engine has a subsequent duty to inform in the form that he must make the content of the notification available to the corporate website user for inspection. The user must be enabled to examine the content in order to be able to prevent improper use.[185] This provision does not apply to providers of online intermediation services, for which a corresponding duty of notification may, however, be imposed by contract.

X. Differentiated treatment of goods and services

105 According to Art. 7(1) P2B Regulation, providers of online intermediation services must explain any differentiated treatment of goods and services if they are offered by the provider itself or by business users controlled by it. The provision mainly covers information on **self-favouring practices** by hybrid platforms.[186] These are platforms which, in addition to their intermediary activities, also compete directly with their business users on the horizontal level in the form of self-distribution.[187] Due to their position as providers of online intermediation services, they have a competitive edge and privileged access to resources and information. In addition, the commercial conditions of the inter-

---

[180] Rec. 26 P2B Regulation gives the example of optimisation for display on mobile devices.

[181] Busch/Busch P2B-VO Art. 5 mn. 69 et seq.

[182] For explanation see Appendix II Ranking Transparency Guidelines.

[183] BeckOK UWG/Wais P2B-VO Art. 5 mn. 16; Köhler/Bornkamm/Feddersen/Alexander P2B-VO Art. 5 mn. 23.

[184] BeckOK UWG/Wais P2B-VO Art. 5 mn. 16.

[185] Köhler/Bornkamm/Feddersen/Alexander P2B-VO Art. 5 mn. 25; cf. rec. 26 UAbs. 2 P2BVO, according to which the content of this notification could also be made accessible via a publicly accessible online database.

[186] Busch GRUR 2019, 788 (793).

[187] Rec. 30 P2B-VO.

mediary service lead to an economic better position of the self-distribution compared to the business users. Whether these practices are permissible depends on general law.

1. Controlled business users

The wording covers the provider of online intermediation services itself as well as business users who are controlled by this provider. The **concept of control** is based on Art. 2 no. 9 P2B Regulation according to Art. 3(2) Regulation (EC) No. 139/2004 (Merger Control Regulation)[188]. Prima facie, the concept seems to cover a relationship only with an affiliated group subsidiary.[189] According to this, the presence of a parent company as a business user of online intermediation services would not be covered. This does not correspond to the meaning and purpose of the provision, as the obligation to provide explanations under Art. 7 P2B Regulation could be circumvented by simple corporate law arrangements. Accordingly, a link to the general definition of an undertaking under cartel law would be more appropriate.[190] 106

However, the wording of control can also be made fruitful in this context. For Art. 3(2) of the Merger Control Regulation sees control as being based on rights, contracts or other means which individually or jointly, taking into account all the factual or legal circumstances, confer the possibility of exercising a decisive influence on the activity of an undertaking. The only decisive factor is therefore a **determining influence**. In principle, this can be exercised independently of the subordination in a group structure. The wording is correspondingly open. The provision mentions two standard examples, firstly the share of assets in the enterprise, secondly the determining influence on the composition, deliberations or decisions of the organs of the enterprise through rights or contracts. The decisive factor is already the possibility to participate in strategically important decisions of the enterprise, which can also result de facto from the circumstances.[191] This results from an autonomous interpretation of the concept of control.[192] The concept of control chosen in Art. 7 P2B Regulation thus presupposes the determining economic influence of the provider of online intermediation services.[193] However, such an influence already exists due to the operator status with regard to the intermediary service and the associated at least factual possibility to exclude every business user and thus also every group company from using the services. In addition, in this case, there are sufficient personnel interrelationships.[194] The provider thus has the possibility to exert a negative influence on the business activity of the respective company.[195] 107

2. Duty to explain

Providers of online intermediation services must explain any differential treatment in their terms and conditions. This explanation must refer to the most important **economic, commercial or legal considerations underlying such differentiated treatment,** 108

---

188 VO (EG) Nr. 139/2004 des Rates vom 20.1.2004 über die Kontrolle von Unternehmenszusammenschlüssen ("EG-Fusionskontrollverordnung") (ABl. 2004 L 24, 1).

189 Busch/Podszun P2B-VO Art. 7 mn. 157; Köhler/Bornkamm/Feddersen/Alexander P2B-VO Art. 7 mn. 6.

190 Busch/Podszun P2B-VO Art. 7 mn. 158.

191 Immenga/Mestmäcker/Körber FKVO Art. 3 mn. 28; BeckOK InfoMedienR/Rinne VO 139/2004 Art. 3 mn. 3.

192 Immenga/Mestmäcker/Körber FKVO Art. 3 mn. 27.

193 LMRKM/Riesenkampff/Steinbarth FKVO Art. 3 mn. 17.

194 Immenga/Mestmäcker/Körber FKVO Art. 3 mn. 57.

195 Immenga/Mestmäcker/Körber FKVO Art. 3 mn. 33; LMRKM/Riesenkampff/Steinbarth FKVO Art. 3 mn. 23.

according to Art. 7(1)(2) P2B Regulation. In practice, the question of when a consideration is not among the most important and therefore does not need to be explained is not relevant. For in this case, either another consideration will constitute a sufficient objective reason or there will be a lack of sufficient justification with the consequence that the differentiated treatment may be inadmissible under the rules of general law and in particular antitrust law.

109 As regards the scope of the obligation to provide explanations, recital 30 of the P2B Regulation states that the obligation should apply to the level of online intermediation services as a whole, but not to the level of the individual goods and services offered via these services. This serves the purpose of maintaining **proportionality**. In view of the main reasons to be presented and the purpose of ensuring transparency, it would therefore be sufficient to clarify the fact that a differentiated treatment of self-distribution takes place.[196]

3. Specific features for providers of online search engines

110 Art. 7(2) P2B Regulation contains one of the specific provisions directed at providers of online search engines. These regularly do not provide their services to consumers on the basis of documented contracts, but the services are **actually** used. The provision also prescribes a duty of explanation here. Unlike Art. 7(1) P2B Regulation, this provision does not provide for any requirements regarding the manner of explanation. There is also no obligation to present the most important reasons in accordance with Art. 7(1)(2) P2B Regulation. The explanations must therefore correspond to the purpose of transparency and must be openly accessible.[197]

4. Individual measures of the obligor to be explained

111 Art. 7(3) P2B Regulation prescribes non-exhaustive[198] standard examples in which providers of online intermediation services as well as providers of online search engines have to provide special explanations.[199] The wording "where appropriate" means that these explanations must be provided insofar as differentiated treatments are carried out.[200] Conversely, there does not have to be a **negative description of** non-existent differentiated treatment. The requirements all refer to the presentation of the existence of and the provider's reasons for the differentiated treatments. The first half-sentence is of particular importance, as it already provides explanations for the case that differentiated treatment exists at all.

a) Differentiated access to data

112 Pursuant to Art. 7(3)(a) P2B Regulation, the explanations must include information on any access by the provider or the business users or users with a business website controlled by the provider to the data provided by business users, users with a business website or consumers for the use of the online intermediation services or online search engines in question or generated in the course of providing these services. The only infor-

---

[196] Busch/Podszun P2B-VO Art. 7 mn. 148.

[197] Busch/Podszun P2B-VO Art. 7 mn. 142.

[198] Busch/Podszun P2B-VO Art. 7 mn. 138 with further examples. One could also mention the question of the extent to which providers of online intermediary services or providers of online search engines exclude business users controlled by them or corporate website users from using their services.

[199] BeckOK UWG/Wais P2B-VO Art. 7 mn. 13.

[200] Köhler/Bornkamm/Feddersen/Alexander P2B-VO Art. 7 mn. 15; BeckOK UWG/Wais P2B-VO Art. 7 mn. 15.

mation to be provided is the extent to which differential treatment is applied and the considerations on which it is based.[201] This provision uses the same **broad concept of data** as Art. 9(2)(a) P2B Regulation, which focuses on the creation of the data when using the platform.[202] Both personal data and other data are covered. Whether and how this access is permissible is not relevant, as only the actual possibility is decisive.[203] It is also not relevant whether granting access to business users or users with a corporate website could be permissible in order to avoid differentiated treatment. The decisive factor here is the fact that privileged access is granted at all. Thus, even if reference were made to the lack of access to data pursuant to Art. 9(2)(a) P2B Regulation, the circumstance of a different treatment of the provider and the business users or users with a corporate website controlled by him would also have to be referred to.[204]

b) Differentiated ranking measures

Art. 7(3)(b) P2B Regulation supplements the requirements on ranking according to **113**
Art. 5 P2B Regulation. According to this, providers of online intermediation services or providers of online search engines must explain differentiated treatment if this relates to ranking or other settings applied by the provider that influence consumers' access to goods or services. Any restriction on free access between certain businesses and consumers must be explained.[205]

This may cover the following examples: Goods or services of the provider's platform **114**
operator or companies controlled by it are always mentioned in the first places of the ranking. Consumers are specifically directed to goods or services of the provider's platform operator or the companies controlled by it, for example through a prominent link in the user account. This can also be done by a separate display of one's own goods or services in the ranking, for example by a **marking**, the prominent display of one's own logo if the offers of the other companies are made without a logo, or any other highlighting. Indirect differentiations in the type of presentation or perceptibility are also covered.[206]

c) Differentiated charges

According to Art. 7(3)(c) P2B Regulation, any direct or indirect fees for the use of the **115**
online intermediation services or online search engines in question and the differentiated treatment that takes place must be presented. This provision is in addition to the provision in Art. 5(3) P2B Regulation, according to which information must be provided on the possibility of the ranking being influenced by a fee. Differentiated fees are always present in cases of **hybrid platforms,** insofar as these demand a fee at all from business users or corporate website users. This is because the providers regularly exempt themselves from a fee. Remuneration is not limited to monetary consideration, but can include all direct or indirect counter-values, as long as they are provided for use.[207]

Due to the hybrid position, business users or users with a corporate website thus pay **116**
a fee which at the same time benefits their own competitor.[208] At the same time, the

---

[201] BeckOK UWG/Wais P2B-VO Art. 7 mn. 14.
[202] Busch/Podszun P2B-VO Art. 7 mn. 81.
[203] Cf. → mn. 81; Busch/Podszun P2B-VO Art. 7 mn. 83 et seqq.
[204] Busch/Podszun P2B-VO Art. 7 mn. 74.
[205] Busch/Podszun P2B-VO Art. 7 mn. 97.
[206] Cf. Busch/Podszun P2B-VO Art. 7 mn. 99 with further references.
[207] Busch/Podszun P2B-VO Art. 7 mn. 114.
[208] For detailed information on the competitive background, see Busch/Podszun P2B-VO Art. 7 mn. 104.

costs of the independent companies are increased compared to self-distribution. The transparency regulation from Art. 7(3)(c) P2B Regulation is intended to compensate for these competitive problems with an information obligation. Since it is aimed precisely at companies with vertical integration, any internal settlements should be irrelevant.[209] In this case, there would already be no remuneration that companies pay each other.

d) Differentiated access to pre-placement services

117 Finally, according to Art. 7(3)(d) P2B Regulation, access to services, functions or technical interfaces must be explained which are relevant to the business user or the corporate website user and which are **directly related to** or complementary to the use of the online intermediation services or online search engines in question. The conditions and any remuneration charged for the use of these services, functions or technical interfaces must also be explained. Here, too, the provider must explain his differentiated treatments. This applies especially to cases where platforms control additional services that are relevant to the economic activity of business users or users with corporate websites.[210] The latter should thus be able to assess their general economic dependence on the intermediary services and the platform as a whole. The provision has a certain catch-all effect compared to the other regulatory examples, as it covers all other privileged accesses of the platform and its controlled company. With its overarching information obligations, it also fulfils a support function for the preparation of private legal enforcement.

XI. Information about termination by business users

118 According to Art. 8(b) P2B Regulation, providers of online intermediation services must include information in their terms and conditions about the conditions under which business users can terminate the contractual relationship with the provider. This constellation thus describes reverse circumstances to the termination by the provider according to Art. 4 P2B Regulation, whereby violations do not lead to voidness.[211] It does not cover the statutory termination conditions, but only those that the provider allows himself to be granted.[212] Accordingly, it does **not impose an obligation to regulate** grounds for termination.[213] The situation is different in the case of contractual restrictions of statutory termination options.[214] This provision also serves to create more transparency and predictability.[215]

119 According to the recitals, it should be possible to fulfil the conditions for the termination of online intermediation services in a proportionate manner and without undue difficulties.[216] A material requirement for the termination options does not result from the provision, but from the respective applicable law.[217]However, the provision of Art. 8(b) P2B Regulation is intended to ensure that information must also be provided about those conditions that are disproportionate and cause unreasonable difficulties in termi-

---

209 Busch/Podszun P2B-VO Art. 7 mn. 107.
210 Busch/Podszun P2B-VO Art. 7 mn. 118.
211 BeckOK UWG/Wais P2B-VO Art. 8 mn. 7.
212 Köhler/Bornkamm/Feddersen/Alexander P2B-VO Art. 8 mn. 13; BeckOK UWG/Wais P2B-VO Art. 8 mn. 12.
213 BeckOK UWG/Wais P2B-VO Art. 8 mn. 11.
214 Köhler/Bornkamm/Feddersen/Alexander P2B-VO Art. 8 mn. 13.
215 Rec. 32 P2B Regulation.
216 Rec. 32 P2B Regulation.
217 BeckOK UWG/Wais P2B-VO Art. 8 mn. 12.

nation. This is again related to **foreseeability**, here with less favourable termination options. Included are therefore all forms and modalities of contract termination, such as unilateral or consensual termination options, special formal requirements, time limits or grounds for exclusion.

XII. Remaining data access after expiration of the contract

Art. 8(c) P2B Regulation contains a further regulation for the post-contractual relationship[218] between business users and providers of online intermediation services. If the contract is terminated, difficulties may arise for business users during the **transition.** For example, due to the previous use of online intermediation services, a considerable amount of provided or generated data may have accrued. In this context, business users should be made aware of the fact that access to this data may no longer exist or of the conditions under which such access may exist after the end of the contractual relationship. Since the wording does not provide for a restriction to a specific manner of termination, this provision applies to all contract terminations.[219] **120**

The information requirements differ in parts from those under Art. 9 P2B Regulation. In particular, only information provided or generated by the business user is covered. This means that information only has to be provided on whether and how the business users can access the data relating to **their use.** Accordingly, no more information is required regarding the additional data covered by Art. 9 P2B Regulation. **121**

Technical and contractual access shall be described, both in terms of existence and non-existence. Legal data access or transfer claims are not covered. Contractual access means **data licences that extend beyond the** end of the contractual relationship.[220] Since this provision also only serves the purpose of foreseeability, it is not to be interpreted in such a way that data access rights are substantively established. This remains at the entrepreneurial discretion of the provider, which may be limited according to the applicable law, including antitrust law. A failure to provide information about non-existent technical or contractual access to data therefore does not establish a positive data access claim in favour of business users.[221] Since the scope and content of the contractually granted data access depends on the respective applicable law, licensing of data that is not subject to intellectual property law is also possible in principle. In addition, because of the intellectual property rights that may be granted, Art. 3(1)(e) P2B Regulation applies. **122**

---

[218] This is different from Art. 9 P2B Regulation, which applies during the existing contractual relationship.

[219] BeckOK UWG/Wais P2B-VO Art. 8 mn. 14.

[220] Busch/v. Westphalen P2B-VO Art. 8 mn. 44.

[221] Critical of this is also Busch/v. Westphalen P2B-VO Art. 8 mn. 45 et seq.

§ 17
Complaint-handling, mediation, enforcement and monitoring

Literature: *Busch*, Mehr Fairness und Transparenz in der Plattformökonomie?, GRUR 2019, 788; *Kohser/Jahn*, Die P2B-Verordnung – Neue Pflichten für Plattformbetreiber und Suchmaschinenanbieter, GRUR-Prax 2020, 273; *Potacs*, Effet utile als Auslegungsgrundsatz, EuR 2009, 465; *Russlies*, Die Abmahnung im gewerblichen Rechtsschutz, 2021; *Schneider/Kremer*, Ein zweiter, kritischer Blick auf die P2B-Verordnung: Nachhaltige Veränderung des Plattformökosystems?, WRP 2020, 1128; *Tribess*, Datenzugangsrechte in der Plattformökonomie, ZD 2020, 440; *Tribess*, P2B-Verordnung zur Förderung von Fairness und Transparenz von Online-Diensten, GWR 2020, 233; *Voigt/Reuter*, Platform-to-Business-Verordnung, MMR 2019, 783.

A. Introduction

Art. 11–17 P2B Regulation[1] create a **comprehensive and multi-layered set of instruments** to help achieve the objectives of the Regulation.[2] However, the system of alternative dispute resolution mechanisms, such as the mandatory internal complaint management systems (Art. 11 P2B Regulation) or mediation procedures (Art. 12, 13 P2B Regulation), individual and collective rights of action (Art. 14 P2B Regulation), the monitoring functions of the Commission (Art. 16 P2B Regulation) and the call for the establishment of codes of conduct (Art. 17 P2B Regulation), is not exhaustive. The P2B Regulation does not provide for any real enforcement instruments of its own in the sense of enforceable claims.[3] 1

Rather, Art. 15 P2B Regulation assigns the Member States the task of **ensuring adequate and effective enforcement of the P2B Regulation** (Art. 15(1) P2B Regulation) and of creating and enforcing effective, proportionate and dissuasive provisions in the event of infringements (Art. 15(2) P2B Regulation). However, Member States are not obliged to create new enforcement mechanisms. In particular, there is no obligation to provide for ex officio enforcement or to set fines (Recital 46). By the end of June 2023, 21 Member States had adopted national laws to enforce the P2B Regulation, while future legislation preparing the ground for enforcement of the P2B Regulation is envisaged in a further four Member States. More than 15 Member States currently enforce the P2B Regulation through a public authority responsible for its effective enforcement. This includes Germany that has enacted respective legislation in May 2024.[4] 2

The provisions of Art. 11–17 P2B Regulation do, however, take into account the declared **objective of the legislator** to create effective remedies in the event that providers of online intermediation services or providers of online search engines violate the provi- 3

[1] Regulation (EU) 2019/1150 of the European Parliament and oft the Council of 20 June 2019 on promoting fairness and transparency for business users of online intermediation services, OJ L 186, 57.

[2] Köhler/Bornkamm/Feddersen/Alexander P2B-VO Art. 11 mn. 1.

[3] Busch/Höppner/Wick P2B-VO Art. 15 mn. 9; Tribess GWR 2020, 233 (237).

[4] COM(2023) 525 final, 11; Art. 1 of the 'Gesetz zur Durchführung der Verordnung (EU) 2022/2065 des Europäischen Parlaments und des Rates vom 19. Oktober 2022 über einen Binnenmarkt für digitale Dienste und zur Änderung der Richtlinie 2000/31/EG sowie zur Durchführung der Verordnung (EU) 2019/1150 des Europäischen Parlaments und des Rates vom 20. Juni 2019 zur Förderung von Fairness und Transparenz für gewerbliche Nutzer von Online-Vermittlungsdiensten und zur Änderung weiterer Gesetze' of 6 May 2024 <https://www.recht.bund.de/bgbl/1/2024/149/VO.html> (last accessed: 28 August 2024); Busch/Höppner/Wick P2B-VO Art. 15 mn. 7.

sions of the P2B Regulation to the detriment of their business users (cf. Art. 1(1) P2B Regulation).[5]

4 Complaint management systems set up on a voluntary basis by the platform economy prior to the entry into force of the P2B Regulation have **not proved sufficiently effective** in this respect, in particular due to the dependency of business users on the platforms and their fear of 'retaliation' by the operators (Recital 5).[6] In a survey of business users of online platforms carried out by the Commission in the run-up to the legislative procedure for the P2B Regulation, almost half (46 %) of the business users participating in the survey stated that online platform operators exploit their strong market position, for example by sudden and unexplained unilateral changes to general terms and conditions or by delisting of products, services or businesses or suspension of accounts without clear statement of reasons, which in some cases significantly limits the ability of business users to develop their business.[7]

5 The mechanisms for **enforcing rights are different** for providers of online intermediation services and providers of online search engines. For example, only providers of online intermediation services are obliged to set up internal complaint management systems and to appoint mediators in accordance with Articles 11 and 12 of the P2B Regulation. Exceptions apply to providers of online intermediation services that qualify as small enterprises as defined in the Annex to Commission Recommendation 2003/361/EC (→ mn. 17).

B. Individual enforcement of rights

6 Even if, in view of the dependence of business users on online intermediation services or of corporate website users on online search engines, there is a justified concern that **users will shy away from disputes with providers** (→ mn. 13), the legislator has attached central importance to individual enforcement under the P2B Regulation. Particularly in the relationship between providers of online intermediation services and business users of such online intermediation services, the alternative dispute resolution mechanisms provided for in Articles 11 and 12 P2B Regulation are an attempt to remove existing obstacles to the individual enforcement of the rights of business users and the prosecution of infringements by providers of online intermediation services.[8]

7 This is to be ensured by **a fair internal complaint-handling system based on the principles of equal treatment** (Art. 11 P2B Regulation). Providers of online intermediation services must enable business users of their platform to clarify, free of charge, violations of the provisions of the P2B Regulation as well as technical problems and other conduct of the provider of online intermediation services that affects business users. The internal complaint-handling system must be easily accessible and enable disputes to be resolved within a reasonable time (→ mn. 32). Business users have the right to have their complaint duly considered and to receive a case-by-case decision with clear and understandable reasons (→ mn. 40). The general terms and conditions (→ mn. 20) of online intermediation services must provide all relevant information on access to the internal complaint-handling system and how it operates (→ mn. 40).

---

[5] Busch/Busch P2B-VO Art. 11 mn. 1.

[6] BeckOK UWG/Tribess P2B-VO Art. 1 mn. 10 et seq.

[7] SWD(2018) 138 final, Part 1/2, 11; BeckOK UWG/Tribess P2B-VO Art. 1 mn. 3 et seq.

[8] Köhler/Bornkamm/Feddersen/Alexander P2B-VO Art. 11 mn. 1 et seq.; Busch/Busch P2B-VO Art. 11 mn. 4.

If a business user's complaint cannot be resolved through the internal complaint-handling system, mediation should be attempted. Alternative dispute resolution procedures should also be used for other disputes relating to the provision of online intermediation services. Providers of online intermediation services are therefore obliged under Art. 12(1) to designate in their general terms and conditions at least two **impartial and independent mediators** with which they are willing to engage (→ mn. 45). The designated mediators must be able to act without undue delay and provide mediation services in the language of the general terms and conditions of the online intermediation services on terms that are affordable for business users (→ mn. 55). 8

The possibility for business users of online intermediation services to use internal complaint management systems or mediation procedures within the meaning of Art. 11, 12 P2B Regulation to settle disputes with the providers of online intermediation services does not affect the right of these business users or the right of the providers of online intermediation services to **take legal action**. For the mediation procedure, Art. 12(5) P2B Regulation expressly states that a court action may be brought at any time before, during or after the mediation procedure. Recital 37 also clarifies for the area of internal complaint management systems that efforts to reach an agreement through the internal complaint management procedure shall not affect the right of providers of online intermediation services or business users to bring an action before a court at any time during or after the internal complaint-handling procedure. In particular, business users of online intermediation services have access to the legal remedies established (or existing) by Member States in accordance with Art. 15 P2B Regulation (→ mn. 74). 9

As there is **no obligation to provide alternative dispute resolution mechanisms for disputes between corporate website users and online search engine providers** in accordance with Articles 11 and 12 of the P2B Regulation, corporate website users will in any event be dependent on the ordinary courts to enforce their rights in the event of violations of the P2B Regulation, unless the online search engine providers voluntarily set up or provide internal complaint systems, mediation centres or similar instruments. 10

I. Internal complaint-handling systems

Providers of online intermediation services are **obliged to set up internal complaint-handling systems** (Art. 11 P2B Regulation). This internal complaint-handling system must be easily accessible to business users, free of charge, and must ensure that complaints are dealt with within a reasonable time frame. It must be based on the principles of transparency and equal treatment applied to equivalent situations, and treating complaints in a manner which is proportionate to their importance and complexity (Art. 11(1)(2) P2B Regulation). The offer or use of an internal complaint-handling system does not restrict the possibility for business users or providers of online intermediation services to seek legal redress (→ mn. 74). 11

1. Purpose of internal complaint-handling systems

The purpose of internal complaint-handling systems is to provide **access to immediate, suitable and effective possibilities of redress**, in particular for business users whose use of the relevant online intermediation services has been restricted, suspended or terminated (Recital 37). Business users should not have exclusive recourse to the ordinary courts for the resolution of disputes with providers of online intermediation- 12 tion services.[9] According to the legislator, the internal complaint-handling systems of providers of online intermediation services should be designed in such a way that a significant proportion of complaints can be solved bilaterally by the provider of online intermediation services and the relevant business user in a reasonable period of time (Recital 37).

13 It is not clear whether the introduction of internal complaint-handling systems can actually reduce the number of disputes or whether it has already done so. To do so, it would be necessary to overcome the obstacle identified by business users prior to the entry into force of the P2B Regulation, namely the lack of communication on the part of the providers of online intermediation services. Given the **imbalance of power and the dependency of business users** on the relevant online intermediation services, it remains to be feared that the relevance of internal complaint-handling systems will essentially be limited to disputes where a business user would seek an amicable solution with the provider of online intermediation services even without a formalised complaint-handling procedure.[10]

2. Obligation to set up internal complaint-handling systems

14 The obligation to set up internal complaint-handling systems applies only to providers of online intermediation services in accordance with Art. 11 P2B Regulation (→ § 16 mn. 18). There is no corresponding obligation under the P2B Regulation for online search engines. The internal complaint-handling system must be set up by providers of online intermediary services **irrespective of the existence of specific complaints.** It is a compliance structure, the practical necessity of which is not at the discretion of the providers of online intermediation services.[11]

a) Relationship to the DSA

15 The relationship between the obligation under Art. 11 P2B Regulation and the obligation for online platform providers to set up internal complaint-handling systems pursuant to Art. 20 of the Digital Services Act (Regulation (EU) 2022/2065; DSA)[12] has not yet been clarified.12 Online intermediation services within the meaning of Art. 2 no. 2 P2B Regulation (→ § 16 mn. 18) may also be online platforms within the meaning of Art. 3(i) DSA, so that providers are obliged to set up internal complaint-handling systems in accordance with both Art. 11 P2B Regulation as well as Art. 20 DSA. Art. 2(4)(e) DSA clarifies that the P2B Regulation remains unaffected by the provisions of the DSA. The legislator's wording that the P2B Regulation (and other legal instruments referred to in Art. 2(4) DSA) 'supplement and specify' the DSA, suggests that the provisions of Art. 11 P2B Regulation should be regarded **as lex specialis vis-à-vis the DSA** with regard to the relationship between business users and providers of online intermediation services within the meaning of the P2B Regulation.[13]

16 As far as procedural matters within the meaning of Art. 11 P2B Regulation, business users are therefore referred to the internal complaint-handling systems set up in accordance with Art. 11 P2B Regulation. Business users do not have **the right to choose**

[9] BeckOK UWG/Tribess P2B-VO Art. 11 mn. 5.

[10] BeckOK UWG/Tribess P2B-VO Art. 11 mn. 7; Köhler/Bornkamm/Feddersen/Alexander P2B-VO Art. 11 mn. 23; Busch GRUR 2019, 788 (791), Voigt/Reuter MMR 2019, 783 (784 et seq.).

[11] BeckOK UWG/Tribess P2B-VO Art. 11 mn. 8.

[12] Regulation (EU) 2022/2065 of the European Parliament and of the Council of 19 October 2022 on a Single Market for Digital Services and amending Directive 2000/31/EC (Digital Services Act), OJ L 277, 1.

[13] Busch/Busch P2B-VO Art. 11 mn. 2.

whether they wish to pursue such infringements also or exclusively via an internal complaint-handling system set up by the provider for the purposes and procedural objects in accordance with Art. 20 DSA, which functions differently in detail and which is therefore recognised as advantageous.[14]

b) *Obligated parties according to Art. 11 P2B Regulation*

Providers of online intermediation services that are **small enterprises** within the meaning of the Annex to Commission Recommendation 2003/361/EC[15] are exempted from the obligations of Art. 11 P2B Regulation with regard to the costs of setting up and operating internal complaint management systems (Recital 38). Small enterprises are defined as those which employ fewer than 50 persons and whose annual turnover or annual balance sheet total does not exceed EUR 10 million. The consolidation rules contained in Commission Recommendation 2003/361/EC, in particular on the allocation of employee and turnover figures within groups of companies, are intended to ensure that any circumvention is prevented (Recital 38).[16] 17

Irrespective of this, small enterprises may set up internal complaint-handling systems **on a voluntary basis.**[17] Internal complaint-handling systems set up by small enterprises in this way do not have to comply with the requirements of Art. 11 P2B Regulation. Therefore, it would be permissible for a small enterprise to set up an internal complaint-handling system for the cases listed in Art. 11(1) P2B Regulation, to provide transparent information about it in accordance with Art. 11(3) P2B Regulation, and to process incoming complaints in accordance with the requirements of Art. 11(1) P2B Regulation, but not to submit or publish the reports required by Art. 11(4) P2B Regulation.[18] 18

The same applies if providers of online intermediation services that do not fall within the scope of the exception under Art. 11(5) P2B Regulation, disclose the internal complaint-handling system they have set up for breaches of other **obligations of the provider of online intermediation services under other laws or contractual agreements**. The provisions of Art. 11 P2B Regulation do not apply in this respect either, i.e. in particular there are no reporting obligations for providers of online intermediation services.[19] 19

c) *Information and reporting obligations of the providers*

Providers of online intermediation services are obliged to be **transparent** about the functioning of their internal complaint-handling systems. All relevant information concerning access and functioning must already be included in the general terms and conditions in accordance with Art. 11(3) P2B Regulation (→ mn. 21). In addition, the effectiveness and practical functioning of the internal complaint-handling systems must be reported on regularly in the form of public evaluation reports pursuant to Art. 11(4) P2B Regulation (→ mn. 22).[20] 20

---

14 Busch/Busch P2B-VO Art. 11 mn. 2.
15 OJ 2003 L 124, 36.
16 BeckOK UWG/Tribess P2B-VO Art. 11 mn. 2 et seq.
17 Köhler/Bornkamm/Feddersen/Alexander P2B-VO Art. 11 mn. 5; Busch/Busch P2B-VO Art. 11 mn. 39.
18 BeckOK UWG/Tribess P2B-VO Art. 11 mn. 4.
19 BeckOK UWG/Tribess P2B-VO Art. 11 mn. 24.
20 BeckOK UWG/Tribess P2B-VO Art. 11 mn. 37.

aa) Terms and conditions

21 In their general terms and conditions, providers of online intermediation services must provide their business users with all relevant information on **access to and the functioning of their internal complaint-handling system**. In particular, procedural issues relating to the accessibility of the internal complaint-handling system must be set out (→ mn. 32). From the perspective of the providers of online intermediation services, it is also advisable to explain, by way of example, which complaints can be dealt with through the internal complaint-handling system (→ mn. 24) and, conversely, for which constellations the internal complaint-handling system is not available.[21]

bb) Evaluation and publication of reports

22 Information on the functioning and effectiveness of the internal complaint-handling system must be made **easily available to the public** by providers of online intermediation services and must be reviewed at least annually. In the event of significant changes in the functioning of the internal complaint-handling system or significant changes regarding the effectiveness of the internal complaint-handling system, the information shall be updated by the provider of online intermediation services.[22]

23 The **purpose of the publication requirement** is to make it easier for business users to understand the main types of problems that may arise in connection with the provision of different online intermediation services and the possibilities for resolving these problems quickly and effectively on a bilateral basis (Recital 37). According to Art. 11(4) subpara. 2 P2B Regulation, the published reports on the functioning and effectiveness of the internal complaint-handling system must therefore include, in particular, the total number of complaints lodged, the main types of complaints, the average time period needed to process the complaints and aggregated information regarding the outcome of the complaints.[23]

3. Possible subjects of the proceedings

24 In order to use the internal complaint-handling system, the **business user must be the complainant**. The behaviour or problems complained about must have an 'impact' on the complainant. A business user can already initiate the internal complaint-handling procedure if even a suspected non-compliance with one of the obligations of the provider of online intermediation services under the P2B Regulation has an impact on the business user concerned (Art. 11(1)(2)(a) P2B Regulation). The requirement that the specific business user be affected prevents complaints from the general public and thus an overload or misuse of the internal complaint-handling systems. Complaints that do not indicate that the complaining business user is directly affected would be inadmissible and would not trigger the obligation to conduct a thorough investigation pursuant to Art. 11(2) P2B Regulation on the part of the provider of online intermediation services.[24]

25 Notwithstanding the decision to provide for the possibility of an internal complaint-handling procedure in certain situations (e.g. pursuant to Art. 4(3) P2B Regulation in

[21] BeckOK UWG/Tribess P2B-VO Art. 11 mn. 38 et seq.; Köhler/Bornkamm/Feddersen/Alexander P2B-VO Art. 11 mn. 32; Busch/Busch P2B-VO Art. 11 mn. 33 et seqq.

[22] BeckOK UWG/Tribess P2B-VO Art. 11 mn. 40 et seq.; Busch/Busch P2B-VO Art. 11 mn. 38.

[23] BeckOK UWG/Tribess P2B-VO Art. 11 mn. 42; Köhler/Bornkamm/Feddersen/Alexander P2B-VO Art. 11 mn. 33 et seqq.

[24] BeckOK UWG/Tribess P2B-VO Art. 11 mn. 22 et seq.; Busch/Busch P2B-VO Art. 11 mn. 14.

cases of restriction, suspension or termination; → § 17 mn. 33), an **internal complaint-handling procedure must be made available to business users in three key areas.**[25]

Pursuant to Art. 11(1) subpara. 2(a) P2B Regulation, the internal complaint-handling system is open to business users in all cases in which **the alleged non-compliance of the provider of online intermediation services** with its obligations under the P2B Regulation has an impact on the business user making the complaint. This applies in particular to infringements of the requirements for terms and conditions as set out in Art. 3, 8 P2B Regulation or in the procedure for the restriction, suspension and termination of the provision of services under Art. 4 P2B Regulation as well as in the ranking (Art. 5 P2B Regulation), in the offer of ancillary goods and services (Art. 6 P2B Regulation), in the differentiated treatment (Art. 7 P2B Regulation), in data access (Art. 9 P2B Regulation) or in the restriction of the possibility for business users to offer other conditions by other means (Art. 10 P2B Regulation). However, alleged breaches by the provider of online intermediation services of the obligations relating to the provision of the internal complaint-handling system itself (Art. 11 P2B Regulation) would also be admissible subjects of complaint, as would alleged breaches in the area of mediation (Art. 12 P2B Regulation).[26] 26

Business users may also initiate an internal complaint-handling procedure on the grounds that **technical problems** arise in direct connection with the provision of an online intermediation service that affect the business user making the complaint (Art. 11(1)(2)(b) P2B Regulation). This includes, for example, cases in which the offers of a business user cannot be displayed or retrieved or cannot be displayed or retrieved correctly due to errors within the technical platform of the online intermediation service, as well as connection problems and crashes of the online intermediation service.[27] The fact that a link between the technical problem and the provision of the online intermediation service is a precondition for the business user to use the internal complaint-handling system in turn excludes general complaints. This is because the internal complaint-handling system is not available to business users in respect of technical problems that are outside the control of the provider of online intermediation services in the first place (e.g. problems with the business user's Internet connection).[28] 27

Art. 11(1)(2)(c) P2B Regulation is ultimately a **catch-all provision** which also gives business users the opportunity to attempt to clarify other measures via the internal complaint-handling system. The provision is to be interpreted broadly.[29] The prerequisite is that the challenged other measure of the provider of online intermediation services is directly related to the provision of online intermediation services. Possible objects of complaint would be, for example, measures that force a business user to change the presentation of his goods or services offered via the relevant online intermediation service several times within a short period of time (e.g. due to changes in database structures).[30] The non-disclosure of the business user's data after termination of the contract would also fall under Art. 11(1)(2)(c) P2B Regulation.[31] 28

25 BeckOK UWG/Tribess P2B-VO Art. 11 mn. 21.
26 BeckOK UWG/Tribess P2B-VO Art. 11 mn. 25; Busch/Busch P2B-VO Art. 11 mn. 14.
27 BeckOK UWG/Tribess P2B-VO Art. 11 mn. 26 et seqq.; Busch/Busch P2B-VO Art. 11 mn. 15.
28 BeckOK UWG/Tribess P2B-VO Art. 11 mn. 27; Busch/Busch P2B-VO Art. 11 mn. 15.
29 BeckOK UWG/Tribess P2B-VO Art. 11 mn. 29 et seqq.; Busch/Busch P2B-VO Art. 11 mn. 17.
30 BeckOK UWG/Tribess P2B-VO Art. 11 mn. 30.
31 Busch/Busch P2B-VO Art. 11 mn. 19.

4. Design of internal complaint-handling systems in accordance with Art. 11 P2B Regulation

29 The legislator has essentially left the specific design of the internal complaint-handling systems to the providers of online intermediation services. Art. 11(1) and (2) P2B Regulation are limited to a few 'clichéd formulations'[32] that leave providers of online intermediation services a relatively **wide margin of manoeuvre** in the design of the internal complaint-handling system with regard to the requirements of the specific online intermediation service.[33] The background to this is the consideration that providers of online intermediation services must be granted an appropriate degree of flexibility in the design of the internal complaint-handling systems to be set up and in the handling of individual complaints (Recital 38).[34]

30 Providers of online intermediation services may also outsource the specific design of their internal complaint-handling systems and the handling of incoming complaints from business users to **external service providers** or another type of company (Recital 33). However, in the case of outsourcing the tasks pursuant to Art. 11 P2B Regulation, it must be ensured that such an external service provider or other corporate structure has the full authority and ability to ensure that the internal complaint-handling system complies with the requirements of the P2B Regulation (Recital 33).[35]

31 Overall, the **administrative burden** for providers of online intermediation services in setting up and operating internal complaint management systems should be minimised (Recital 38). In addition, providers of online intermediation services should be able to respond appropriately, where necessary, to any misuse of such systems that may be targeted by some users (Recital 38).[36]

a) Requirements and procedural principles

32 Internal complaint-handling systems must comply with the requirements of Art. 11(1) subpara. 2 P2B Regulation. The submission of a complaint by a business user via the internal complaint-handling system of an online intermediation service has **no suspensive effect** with regard to the alleged infringement of the P2B Regulation or the contested measure. Providers of online intermediation services should be able to maintain their decision during the complaint procedure (Recital 37).[37]

aa) Easy accessibility

33 The internal complaint-handling system must be easily accessible to business users of an online intermediation service (Art. 11(1) subpara. 2 sent. 1 P2B Regulation). It is not clear from the recitals of the P2B Regulation which criteria the legislator intends to use to assess easy accessibility.[38]

34 **Language barriers** should be avoided to meet the requirement of accessibility. However, business users are not entitled to have the internal complaint-handling procedure conducted in their own language, e.g. in German. Particularly in the case of international online intermediation services, where communication between business users and the relevant provider of online intermediation services takes place exclusively in English, an

---

[32] Busch GRUR 2019, 788 (795).

[33] Busch/Busch P2B-VO Art. 11 mn. 20; BeckOK UWG/Tribess P2B-VO Art. 11 mn. 12.

[34] Busch/Busch P2B-VO Art. 11 mn. 20; BeckOK UWG/Tribess P2B-VO Art. 11 mn. 11.

[35] BeckOK UWG/Tribess P2B-VO Art. 11 mn. 9.

[36] BeckOK UWG/Tribess P2B-VO Art. 11 mn. 13.

[37] BeckOK UWG/Tribess P2B-VO Art. 11 mn. 10; Busch/Busch P2B-VO Art. 11 mn. 4.

[38] BeckOK UWG/Tribess P2B-VO Art. 11 mn. 14.

internal complaint-handling system in accordance with Art. 11 P2B Regulation may also be offered exclusively in English without jeopardising easy accessibility. It is sufficient to offer the internal complaint-handling system in the language that is otherwise available for the use of the relevant online intermediation services.[39]

Complex **additional registration procedures** for the internal complaint-handling system, on top of the existing registration as a business user of the online intermediation services, appear questionable with regard to the requirement of easy accessibility. This would create barriers to the use of the internal complaint-handling system by business users, the dissuasive effect of which would be contrary to the objectives of effective dispute resolution. However, it would be permissible to require business users to agree to additional terms of use (e.g. special procedural rules) before using the internal complaint-handling system in order to prevent misuse of the internal complaint-handling system or to obtain a contractual remedy against such misuse.[40] 35

It would also be contrary to the requirement of accessibility to conduct internal complaint-handling procedures in the form of face-to-face meetings that require business users to be present at a specific location. Instead, internal complaints systems should be accessible electronically or by other means of remote communication.[41] However, fully **automated internal complaint-handling systems** (e.g. using artificial intelligence) are likely to violate business users' right to an individual response to their complaint.[42] 36

bb) Free of charge

Access to the internal complaint-handling system must be **free of charge for business users** (Art. 11(1) subpara. 2 sent. 1 P2B Regulation). Therefore, the use of the internal complaint-handling system may not be made dependent on the payment of a fee.[43] Indirect costs, such as the obligation to download fee-based software products for the purpose of using the internal complaint-handling system or the obligation to submit notarised documents, would also be inadmissible. And 'indirect costs', such as economic disadvantages during or after a complaint, cannot be imposed on business users.[44] 37

cc) Handling within a reasonable time frame

Pursuant to Art. 11(1) no. 2 sent. 1 P2B Regulation, providers of online intermediation services must organise their internal complaint-handling systems in such a way that a significant proportion of complaints can be solved bilaterally by the provider of online intermediation services and the relevant business user **in a reasonable period of time** (Recital 37).[45] The P2B Regulation does not provide any concrete guidance as to what period of time can be considered reasonable for the handling and resolution of a complaint. Taking into account the fact that the consequences of a breach of the P2B Regulation, technical problems or other unauthorised actions can have a significant impact on the ability of business users to develop their business, and conversely that, despite the need to assess individual cases, providers of online intermediation services will develop certain routines for dealing with particular complaints based on a large number of simi- 38

[39] BeckOK UWG/Tribess P2B-VO Art. 11 mn. 18; Busch/Busch P2B-VO Art. 11 mn. 22.
[40] BeckOK UWG/Tribess P2B-VO Art. 11 mn. 15.
[41] BeckOK UWG/Tribess P2B-VO Art. 11 mn. 17.
[42] Busch/Busch P2B-VO Art. 11 mn. 10; BeckOK UWG/Tribess P2B-VO Art. 11 mn. 17a.
[43] BeckOK UWG/Tribess P2B-VO Art. 11 mn. 16.
[44] Köhler/Bornkamm/Feddersen/Alexander P2B-VO Art. 11 mn. 17.
[45] BeckOK UWG/Tribess P2B-VO Art. 11 mn. 20.

lar cases, time limits should not be set too generously. It should therefore be ensured that the complaint is dealt with within a few weeks.[46]

dd) Transparency, equal treatment and appropriateness

39 The internal complaint-handling system set up for an online intermediation service must be based on the **principles of transparency and equal treatment** applied to equivalent situations. Complaints must be handled in a manner which is proportionate to their importance and complexity (Art. 11(1) subpara. 2 sent. 2 P2B Regulation).[47]

b) Procedure

40 Art. 11(2) P2B Regulation describes the procedure for internal complaint-handling after receipt of the business user's complaint with a few rather general requirements. This is to ensure that providers of online intermediation services retain **sufficient and appropriate flexibility** with regard to the specific design of their internal complaint-handling systems (Recital 37).[48]

41 Providers of online intermediation services must ensure that any complaint lodged is **duly considered** (Art. 11(2)(a) P2B Regulation). Internal complaint-handling systems must be designed to find an appropriate solution to the problem raised. To the extent that this is necessary in order to deal adequately with the problem raised, the provider of online intermediation services must also ensure that due consideration is given to any follow-up action that may be required in view of the complaint.[49]

42 Complaints from business users must be dealt with **swiftly and effectively**, taking into account the importance and complexity of the issue raised (Art. 11(2)(b) P2B Regulation). Complex legal problems may justify a longer processing time on the part of the provider of online intermediation services than the resolution of complaints which are less intrusive for business users but which, in their assessment, are easier to resolve as part of the internal complaint management procedure because they can be clearly resolved in favour of one side or the other, regardless of the potentially significant impact on the business user making the complaint (e.g. in the case of a disputed restriction, suspension or termination pursuant to Art. 4 P2B Regulation). Prioritisation is required, which should be based in particular on the impact of the subject matter of the complaint on the complaining business user.[50] In order to mitigate the negative consequences for the business user concerned and to avoid claims for damages, providers of online intermediation services are free to suspend the enforcement of a disputed measure on a voluntary and provisional basis (→ mn. 32).

43 Upon completion of the review by the provider of online intermediation services, the complainant must be informed of the outcome of the internal complaint-handling procedure (Art. 11(2)(c) P2B Regulation). The information must be drafted in plain and intelligible language with regard to the outcome. The business user making the complaint should be able to understand the outcome of the internal complaint-handling procedure and, in particular, the consequences of the outcome for its further use of the relevant online intermediation services. The **obligation to provide information** is in turn part of

---

[46] Busch/Busch P2B-VO Art. 11 mn. 29.

[47] BeckOK UWG/Tribess P2B-VO Art. 11 mn. 19, Köhler/Bornkamm/Feddersen/Alexander P2B-VO Art. 11 mn. 19 et seqq.

[48] BeckOK UWG/Tribess P2B-VO Art. 11 mn. 31.

[49] BeckOK UWG/Tribess P2B-VO Art. 11 mn. 32; Köhler/Bornkamm/Feddersen/Alexander P2B-VO Art. 11 mn. 28; Busch/Busch P2B-VO Art. 11 mn. 24.

[50] BeckOK UWG/Tribess P2B-VO Art. 11 mn. 33 et seq.; Busch/Busch P2B-VO Art. 11 mn. 28.

the internal complaint-handling procedure, so that the obligation to process and communicate the result swiftly in accordance with Art. 11(2)(b) P2B Regulation must also be observed in this respect.[51]

44 Business users have the right to an **individualised statement of reasons** for the decision taken within the framework of the internal complaint-handling system (Art. 11(2)(c) P2B Regulation). Accordingly, it would be inadmissible to provide business users only with pre-formulated text modules as justification without reference to the individual case. However, the use of standardised texts is compatible with Art. 11(2)(c) P2B Regulation if they are combined with a description of the facts of the individual case and the grounds of appeal. What is important is that it is clear to the business user making the complaint that the provider of online intermediation services has dealt with the individual case in question.[52]

II. Mediation in accordance with Art. 12 P2B Regulation

45 Providers of online intermediation services are required to specify in their terms and conditions **two or more mediators** with whom they are willing to engage (→ mn. 50). The purpose of appointing mediators is to reach an out-of-court settlement with business users of any disputes that may arise in the relationship between a business user and the provider of online intermediation services in relation to the provision of the online intermediation service in question. In particular, mediation is intended to contribute to the resolution of complaints from business users that could not be resolved by using the internal complaint-handling system (Art. 11 P2B Regulation; → mn. 11) (Art. 12(1) subpara. 1 P2B Regulation).

46 Participation in mediation is **voluntary for both parties** (Art. 12(3) P2B Regulation; → mn. 68) and does not prevent the business user or the provider of online intermediation services from taking legal action (Art. 12(5) P2B Regulation; → mn. 74). The parties themselves remain responsible for the procedure and may initiate and terminate it at any time (Recital 40).[53] The mediation procedure is subject to the principle of good faith (→ mn. 63). A reasonable proportion of the total costs of mediation will also be borne by the provider of online intermediation services in each individual case (→ mn. 53).

47 With regard to mediation procedures, providers of online intermediation services are also subject to **further information obligations**: at the request of a business user, providers of online intermediation services must provide information on the functioning and effectiveness of mediation in connection with their activities (Art. 12(6) P2B Regulation; → mn. 72).

1. Purpose of mediation

48 The purpose of mediation is to avoid lengthy and costly court proceedings between business users and providers of online intermediation services (Recital 40). Art. 12 P2B Regulation serves to provide business users with **efficient, rapid and thus effective redress possibilities** in the event of disputes with the provider of online intermediation services (Art. 1(1) P2B Regulation; → § 16 mn. 3).[54]

[51] BeckOK UWG/Tribess P2B-VO Art. 11 mn. 35; Köhler/Bornkamm/Feddersen/Alexander P2B-VO Art. 11 mn. 30 et seq.

[52] BeckOK UWG/Tribess P2B-VO Art. 11 mn. 36.

[53] BeckOK UWG/Tribess P2B-VO Art. 12 mn. 23 et seq.; Köhler/Bornkamm/Feddersen/Alexander P2B-VO Art. 12 mn. 2.

[54] BeckOK UWG/Tribess P2B-VO Art. 12 mn. 5; Busch/Höppner/Wick P2B-VO Art. 12 mn. 2.

49 As a rule, mediation will represent the second stage of dispute resolution and will concern cases that could not already be resolved within the framework of an internal complaint management procedure.[55] Nevertheless, Art. 12 P2B Regulation is not limited to these cases and provides business users with a comprehensive opportunity to bring forward behaviour of providers of online intermediation services which they consider unfair in an orderly procedure and, if necessary, to settle the dispute in this way.[56] Mediation is therefore **not limited to the subjects of the procedure under Art. 11(1) subpara. 2 P2B Regulation**.

2. Obligation to appoint mediators

50 Except in the case of small enterprises (→ mn 53), the terms and conditions of providers of online intermediation services must designate at least two mediators with whom the provider of online intermediation services is willing to engage. However, the obligation to appoint certain mediators does not bind either the business users of the online intermediation service in question or the provider of online intermediation services in the sense that the mediation would only be possible with the participation of these previously appointed mediators. The parties may also jointly appoint another mediator of their choice to resolve a dispute between them (Recital 40).[57]

51 The obligation to designate a minimum number of mediators is intended to ensure their neutrality (Recital 40). It is necessary to name **personally appointed mediators**; a reference to mediation organisations would not fulfil the obligation under Art. 12(1) P2B Regulation. This necessity can be seen by comparing Art. 12(1) P2B Regulation with Art. 13 P2B Regulation. While Art. 13 P2B Regulation refers to 'mediation organisations', the obligation of providers of online mediation services under Art. 12(1) P2B Regulation always refers to 'mediators'.[58]

a) Obligated parties according to Art. 12 P2B Regulation

52 The obligation to appoint mediators pursuant to Art. 12 P2B Regulation in order to promote the out-of-court settlement of disputes, as well as the obligation to set up internal complaint-handling systems under Art. 11 P2B Regulation (→ mn. 14), **only apply to providers of online intermediation services**. Providers of online search engines are not subject to such obligations.[59]

53 By analogy with Art. 11 P2B Regulation, Art. 12 P2B Regulation also exempts providers of online intermediation services from the obligation to appoint mediators if they qualify as **small enterprises** within the meaning of the Annex to Commission Recommendation 2003/361/EC (Art. 12(7) P2B Regulation). The background to this is again that these small enterprises should not be burdened with the costs and administrative effort associated with the necessary appointment of mediators in the general terms and conditions (Recital 41). Small enterprises are defined as those employing fewer than 50 persons and whose annual turnover or annual balance sheet total does not exceed EUR 10 million.[60]

---

[55] Busch GRUR 2019, 788 (791).

[56] BeckOK UWG/Tribess P2B-VO Art. 12 mn. 6; Köhler/Bornkamm/Feddersen/Alexander P2B-VO Art. 11 mn. 11; Voigt/Reuter MMR 2019, 783 (785).

[57] BeckOK UWG/Tribess P2B-VO Art. 12 mn. 7 et seqq.; Köhler/Bornkamm/Feddersen/Alexander P2B-VO Art. 12 mn. 12.

[58] BeckOK UWG/Tribess P2B-VO Art. 12 mn. 7 et seq.; Busch/Höppner/Wick P2B-VO Art. 12 mn. 10.

[59] BeckOK UWG/Tribess P2B-VO Art. 12 mn. 1.

[60] BeckOK UWG/Tribess P2B-VO Art. 12 mn. 2; Busch/Höppner/Wick P2B-VO Art. 12 mn. 48.

Nevertheless, small enterprises can make use of the possibilities offered by mediation or even actively promote it by designating mediators or mediation organisations in their general terms and conditions (Recital 41). For these small enterprises in particular, it may also be attractive to make use of specialised out-of-court dispute resolution mechanisms (Art. 13 P2B Regulation), which may have been set up by platform economy associations (→ mn. 65). If small enterprises make use of the option to appoint mediators voluntarily in their general terms and conditions, they do not have to comply with the requirements of Art. 12(2) P2B Regulation. Art. 12 P2B Regulation does not apply to these voluntary offers as a whole. Small businesses would therefore not be subject to the obligations to bear a reasonable share of the costs (→ mn. 53) or to disclose information on the functioning and effectiveness of mediation (→ mn. 72) with regard to the **voluntary provision of mediation services.**[61] 54

b) Requirements for mediators

Art. 12(2) P2B Regulation defines a number of **requirements** which the mediators appointed pursuant to Art. 12(1) P2B Regulation. These conditions are intended to ensure that the mediation process is accessible, fair and as swift, efficient and effective as possible (Recital 40).[62] Mediators must therefore be impartial and independent, offer their mediation services on terms that are affordable for the business users of the online intermediation services concerned, provide their mediation services in the language of the terms and conditions governing the contractual relationship between the provider of online intermediation services and the business user concerned, be easily accessible either physically in the place of establishment or residence of the business user, or remotely using communication technologies, be able to provide their mediation services without undue delay and have a sufficient understanding of general business-to-business commercial relations, allowing them to contribute effectively to the attempt to settle the disputes. 55

These criteria are partly identical in content to the **general requirements of the Directive 2008/52/EC** (Mediation Directive), e.g. with regard to the impartiality and independence of the mediator, but in some cases go beyond them.[63] 56

aa) Impartiality and independence

Mediators must be **impartial and independent** (Art. 12(2)(a) P2B Regulation). Mediators may therefore not represent their own interests, the individual interests of the parties or the interests of third parties in their work as mediators. Rather, the mediator is obliged to be impartial and must therefore protect the interests of all parties equally (cf. Art. 3(b) Mediation Directive).[64] The mediator must not have any legal (e.g. right of appointment of a third party), economic or other factual ties which, due to their intensity, influence his or her mediation activity. The mediator shall be free from any dependence, including on third parties, and shall not be subject to any special relationship with the parties. Only in this way can the core of the mediator's activity, namely his independence, be preserved (cf. Art. 3(a) Mediation Directive).[65] 57

---

[61] BeckOK UWG/Tribess P2B-VO Art. 12 mn. 3 et seq.; different opinion Busch/Höppner/Wick P2B-VO Art. 12 mn. 48.

[62] BeckOK UWG/Tribess P2B-VO Art. 12 mn. 10; Köhler/Bornkamm/Feddersen/Alexander P2B-VO Art. 12 mn. 14.

[63] BeckOK UWG/Tribess P2B-VO Art. 12 mn. 10.

[64] BeckOK UWG/Tribess P2B-VO Art. 12 mn. 11; MüKoZPO/Ulrici MediationsG §§ 1–9 mn. 25.

[65] BeckOK UWG/Tribess P2B-VO Art. 12 mn. 12; MüKoZPO/Ulrici MediationsG §§ 1–9 mn. 26.

bb) Affordable conditions

58 Mediation must remain affordable for business users. Accordingly, designated mediators are obliged to offer their services at **reasonable conditions for business users** (Art. 12(2)(b) P2B Regulation), i.e. at market rates, including hourly rates.[66]

59 This criterion is also taken into account in Article 12(4) P2B Regulation, which stipulates that providers of online intermediation services must always bear **a reasonable share of the total costs of mediation**, taking into account all relevant aspects of the case (Recital 41). This will further reduce costs for business users. This makes it easier for them to use mediation, which is in line with the aim of the P2B Regulation to create effective remedies for breaches of the P2B Regulation by providers of online intermediation services. The mediator is requested to make a suggestion on the issue of the bearing of costs, taking into account Art. 12(4) P2B Regulation. The proportion of the costs of the mediation procedure to be borne by the provider of online intermediation services in each individual case should be determined in particular by taking into account all relevant elements of the case at hand, in particular the relative merits of the claims of the parties to the dispute, the conduct of the parties, as well as the size and financial strength of the parties relative to one another.[67]

cc) Language of mediation

60 Designated mediators must be able to conduct the mediation procedure in the **language of the terms and conditions** governing the contractual relationship between the provider of online intermediation services and the business user (Art. 12(2)(c) P2B Regulation). Therefore, if the terms and conditions of the online intermediation services were written in English, a business user would also have to accept mediation in English. A claim that a German-language mediation service must also be provided cannot be derived from Art. 12(2) P2B Regulation. This provision corresponds to the provision in the area of internal complaint-handling systems (→ mn. 34).[68]

dd) Seat of the mediator

61 Mediators need to be **easily accessible** to business users. This does not necessarily require physical proximity in the sense that the mediators must be located in the same place as the business users, or at least in their vicinity. Art. 12(2)(d) P2B Regulation explicitly states that easy accessibility by means of remote communication technology (e.g. videoconferencing systems) is sufficient.[69]

62 However, mediators providing their services from a location **outside the Union** may only be appointed by providers of online mediation services under certain conditions. Article 12(1) subpara. 2 P2B Regulation allows this only if recourse to the services of these mediators does not effectively provide the business users concerned with legal protection under Union law or the law of a Member State. In addition to the provisions

[66] BeckOK UWG/Tribess P2B-VO Art. 12 mn. 13; Köhler/Bornkamm/Feddersen/Alexander P2B-VO Art. 12 mn. 20.

[67] BeckOK UWG/Tribess P2B-VO Art. 12 mn. 29 et seq.; Köhler/Bornkamm/Feddersen/Alexander P2B-VO Art. 12 mn. 21 et seq.

[68] BeckOK UWG/Tribess P2B-VO Art. 12 mn. 14; Busch/Höppner/Wick P2B-VO Art. 12 mn. 40 et seqq.

[69] BeckOK UWG/Tribess P2B-VO Art. 12 mn. 15; Busch/Höppner/Wick P2B-VO Art. 12 mn. 42.

of the P2B Regulation itself, particular mention should be made here of the applicable laws regarding protection of personal data and trade secrets (Recital 40).[70]

ee) Availability without undue delay

63 In view of the potentially existential consequences of a conflict with the provider of online intermediation services for business users (as well as for internal complaint-handling systems; → mn. 38), the implementation of a mediation procedure is also subject to a requirement to expedite. The mediators named in the terms and conditions must therefore be able to provide their services **without undue delay** (Art. 12(2)(e) P2B Regulation), i.e. within days.[71]

ff) Knowledge of the mediator

64 Art. 12(2)(f) P2B Regulation requires mediators to have a **sufficient understanding of business-to-business terms and conditions** to be able to contribute effectively to an attempt at dispute resolution. However, special or even basic knowledge of online intermediation services is not a prerequisite for appointment as a mediator. However, an adequate understanding of the functioning of online intermediaries and the reliance of business users on online intermediation services is likely to be as important for the chances of success of a mediation as a basic knowledge of terms and conditions.[72]

c) Special mediation organisations

65 Art. 13 P2B Regulation contains the **Commission's call** for the establishment of specialised mediation organisations, which are still lacking (Recital 43). Art. 13 P2B Regulation does not oblige providers of online intermediation services or associations in the platform economy to actually set up their own specialised mediation services. Failure to do so is therefore not sanctioned.[73]

66 The **establishment of specialised organisations providing mediation services** is intended to facilitate the resolution of disputes relating to the provision of online intermediation services through mediation (Recital 43). The involvement of mediators with expertise in the field of online intermediation services and in the different economic sectors in which these services are offered is intended to add to the confidence both parties have in the mediation process. In this way, the legislator hopes to increase the likelihood of that process leading to a swift, just and satisfactory outcome (Recital 43).[74]

67 Even if the requirements for designated mediators under Art. 12(2) P2B Regulation apply to mediation organisations established under Art. 13 P2B Regulation, it is doubtful whether the establishment of mediation organisations by providers of online mediation services or the associations representing them can actually contribute to strengthening the confidence of business users in the mediation process. Rather, it is to be feared that such mediation organisations – notwithstanding the obligation to be impartial and inde-

---

70 BeckOK UWG/Tribess P2B-VO Art. 12 mn. 16; Köhler/Bornkamm/Feddersen/Alexander P2B-VO Art. 12 mn. 13; Busch/Höppner/Wick P2B-VO Art. 12 mn. 46.

71 BeckOK UWG/Tribess P2B-VO Art. 12 mn. 17; Busch/Höppner/Wick P2B-VO Art. 12 mn. 43.

72 Busch/Höppner/Wick P2B-VO Art. 12 mn. 44 et seq.; BeckOK UWG/Tribess P2B-VO Art. 12 mn. 18 et seq.

73 BeckOK UWG/Tribess P2B-VO Art. 13 mn. 1.

74 Köhler/Bornkamm/Feddersen/Alexander P2B-VO Art. 12 mn. 16; BeckOK UWG/Tribess P2B-VO Art. 13 mn. 3 et seq.

pendent in this respect (→ mn. 57) – would be exposed to the **criticism of being too close to the platform economy.**[75]

3. The mediation process

68 The mediation process is subject to **general rules** and is not defined in detail in the P2B Regulation. The P2B Regulation merely stipulates that providers of online intermediation services and business users must participate in good faith in all mediation attempts pursuant to Art. 12 P2B Regulation, irrespective of the voluntary nature of the mediation (Art. 12(3) P2B Regulation; → mn. 48). Providers of online intermediation services are also obliged to disclose information before and during mediation (Art. 12(6) P2B Regulation; → mn. 72).

a) Principle of good faith

69 In accordance with the **principle of good faith**, providers of online intermediation services should consider any request from a business user to initiate a mediation procedure (Recital 40).[76]

70 Business users are also bound and obliged by the principle of good faith once a mediation procedure has been initiated (Recital 42). In particular, **misuse of the mediation system by business users** would violate the principle of good faith (Recital 42). In particular, bad faith by business users is presumed where a business user brings proceedings on a subject in relation to which that business user has previously brought proceedings seeking mediation and the mediator has determined in that case that the business user has not acted in good faith (Recital 42). Repeated unsuccessful mediation attempts in relation to the same business user may also entitle providers of online intermediation services to refuse a further mediation attempt on the basis of the principle of good faith (Recital 42).[77]

71 It also follows from the principle of good faith that providers of online intermediation services must **justify their refusal to mediate on a case-by-case basis.** In particular, the above-mentioned conduct of a business user should not restrict its ability to initiate mediation proceedings in a case where the mediator has determined that the subject matter of the mediation is not related to previous cases (Recital 42).[78] A business user does not act in bad faith if it refuses mediation because the mediator does not meet the requirements of Art. 12(2) P2B Regulation (→ mn. 55).[79]

b) Information obligations

72 Business users have the **right to obtain from the provider of online intermediation services information** on the functioning and effectiveness of mediation in the area of the specific online intermediation service before mediation starts and also during the mediation process (but not after it has ended[80]). In this respect, there is no obligation

[75] BeckOK UWG/Tribess P2B-VO Art. 13 mn. 5 et seq.; Busch/Höppner/Wick P2B-VO Art. 13 mn. 3.
[76] BeckOK UWG/Tribess P2B-VO Art. 13 mn. 25; Busch/Höppner/Wick P2B-VO Art. 12 mn. 16.
[77] BeckOK UWG/Tribess P2B-VO Art. 13 mn. 26 et seq.; Busch/Höppner/Wick P2B-VO Art. 12 mn. 16.
[78] BeckOK UWG/Tribess P2B-VO Art. 13 mn. 28; Köhler/Bornkamm/Feddersen/Alexander P2B-VO Art. 12 mn. 18.
[79] Köhler/Bornkamm/Feddersen/Alexander P2B-VO Art. 12 mn. 19.
[80] Köhler/Bornkamm/Feddersen/Alexander P2B-VO Art. 12 mn. 28.

to make this information publicly available, unlike the reports to be made on the functioning and effectiveness of internal complaint-handling systems (→ mn. 20).[81]

Furthermore, the information to be provided to business users under Art. 12(6) P2B Regulation is **not specified in a manner comparable to Art. 11(4) P2B Regulation** (→ mn. 22). However, the content and the way in which the information is presented should enable business users to gain an overview of the prospects of success of an amicable resolution of a dispute prior to a mediation attempt. Reports on the functioning and effectiveness of mediation should therefore in any event include information on the number of mediations conducted in relation to the specific online intermediation service, the main subjects of mediation, the time taken for mediation and the outcome of the mediations in an aggregated form.[82] 73

III. Individual legal action

The alternative dispute resolution mechanisms provided for in Art. 11, 12 P2B Regulation do not affect the right of business users and providers of online intermediation services to **take legal action** before, during or after the internal complaint management procedure or mediation (→ mn. 9). Since the P2B Regulation does not provide for alternative dispute resolution mechanisms for the relationship between providers of online search engines and corporate website users (→ mn. 10), providers of online search engines and corporate website users will in any case be referred to the ordinary courts to resolve disputes relating to the obligations under the P2B Regulation.[83] 74

The claims of providers of online intermediation services against their business users or of providers of online search engines against corporate website users are not subject to any special requirements in connection with the P2B Regulation. In the following, therefore, only the individual claims of business users of online intermediation services or corporate website users against providers of online search engines will be examined in more detail, insofar as they relate to breaches of obligations under the P2B Regulation. Since the P2B Regulation does not contain its own basis for claims, but instead calls on the Member States to create appropriate enforcement instruments (Art. 15 P2B Regulation; → mn. 33), the **basis for claims must be sought exclusively in national law**. Its applicability is determined by the general rules of private international law. German law is discussed below. 75

1. Claims under unfair competition law

In particular, in the relationship between business users and providers of online intermediation services, claims for individual enforcement of the obligations under the P2B Regulation may arise under **unfair competition law**. However, claims under unfair competition law are also conceivable in the relationship between corporate website users and providers of online search engines. The provisions of the P2B Regulation are rules of market conduct within the meaning of Sec. 3a of the German Act against Unfair Competition (Gesetz gegen den unlauteren Wettbewerb, UWG),[84] so that a violation of 76

---

[81] BeckOK UWG/Tribess P2B-VO Art. 13 mn. 21 et seq.

[82] BeckOK UWG/Tribess P2B-VO Art. 13 mn. 22; Köhler/Bornkamm/Feddersen/Alexander P2B-VO Art. 12 mn. 28.

[83] Köhler/Bornkamm/Feddersen/Alexander P2B-VO Art. 14 mn. 47.

[84] Busch/Höppner/Wick P2B-VO Art. 15 mn. 9; Köhler/Bornkamm/Feddersen/Köhler UWG § 3a mn. 1.293a; Tribess GWR 2020, 233 (238); Tribess ZD 2020, 440 (444); Kohser/Jahn GRUR-Prax 2020, 273 (275).

Sec. 8 et seq. UWG may give rise to claims for removal and injunctive relief as well as other consequential claims, in particular claims for damages.

a) *Competitive relationship between business users and providers of online intermediation services*

77 There is potentially a **concrete competitive relationship** between the providers of online intermediation services and the business users of the online intermediation service; the same applies to the relationship between corporate website users and the providers of online search engines. According to the case law of the German Federal Court of Justice (Bundesgerichtshof, BGH), such a relationship exists 'if both parties attempt to sell similar goods or services to the same group of end consumers and the competitive behaviour of one party is therefore likely to hinder or disrupt the other party. Since, in the interest of effective individual protection under unfair competition law, there are generally no high requirements for the existence of a concrete competitive relationship, it is sufficient that the infringer is in some way in competition with the affected party in the individual case. Therefore, a concrete competitive relationship is to be assumed if there is an interaction between the advantages that one party seeks to achieve for its business or that of third parties by a measure and the disadvantages that the other party suffers as a result, in the sense that its own competition may be promoted and the competition of third parties may be impaired and the goods or services offered by the parties are in competition with each other'.[85]

78 The substitution relationship between the offers of business users or corporate website users and those of providers of online intermediation services or providers of online search engines, and even more so the possibility of impeded competition in favour of providers of online intermediation services or providers of online search engines, were the main **motives of the legislator** in creating the regulatory framework of the P2B Regulation. Where a provider of online intermediation services offers certain goods or services to consumers through its own online intermediation services or through a business user over which it exercises control, it may be in direct competition with other business users of its online intermediation services over which it does not exercise control (Recital 30). The same competitive relationship may exist between the provider of an online search engine and corporate website users where both (directly or, in the case of the provider of an online search engine, through its affiliates) offer certain goods and services to consumers through the same online search engine (Recital 31).

79 These considerations are **directly reflected** in the P2B Regulation. Art. 7(1) P2B Regulation requires providers of online intermediation services to inform business users of 'any differentiated treatment which they give, or might give, in relation to goods or services offered to consumers through those online intermediation services by, on the one hand, either that provider itself or any business users which that provider controls and, on the other hand, other business users. That description shall refer to the main economic, commercial or legal considerations for such differentiated treatment.' (→ § 17 mn. 108) According to Art. 7(2) P2B-Regulation, providers of online search engines are obliged to provide a corresponding explanation with regard to the different treatment of their own and third-party offers in the context of the use of an online search engine (→ § 17 mn. 109). Art. 7(3) P2B Regulation lists specific content for which information must be provided. The references to data access rights or ranking mechanisms refer to

[85] BGH 5.11.2020 – I ZR 234/19, GRUR 2021, 497 mn. 15 – Zweitmarkt für Lebensversicherungen (Secondary market for life insurance policies); discussion and further resources at Köhler/Bornkamm/Feddersen/Köhler UWG § 2 mn. 107 et seqq.

Art. 5, 9 P2B Regulation and prove that the P2B Regulation as a whole is based on the idea that a concrete competitive relationship may exist between providers of online intermediation services and business users or providers of online search engines and corporate website users in accordance with fair trading standards.

b) No exclusion of competitors' claims by Sec. 8a UWG

The position of Sec. 8a, which was added to the UWG as part of the Act to Amend the Telemedia Act and Other Laws of November 13, 2000,[86] and its **effects on the sanctioning of violations of the P2B Regulation under unfair competition law** have not yet been clarified. Sec. 8a UWG provides that 'notwithstanding Sec. 8(3)', the associations, organizations and public bodies referred to in Art. 14(3) and (4) P2B Regulation are entitled to assert claims pursuant to Sec. 8(1) UWG. 80

aa) Blocking effect of Sec. 8a UWG

The prevailing view is that **Sec. 8a UWG is a lex specialis to Sec. 8(3) UWG**, with the consequence that, according to this view, only the associations, organizations and public bodies mentioned in Art. 14(3) and (4) P2B Regulation should be entitled to assert claims and bring actions under Sec. 8(1) UWG in conjunction with Sec. 3a UWG in the event of a violation of the P2B Regulation.[87] According to this view, competitors (including business users or corporate website users) are referred to other national legal bases, such as antitrust law, competition law, civil law, or trade secret law, for the assertion of claims based on a violation of the P2B Regulation.[88] 81

bb) Extension effect of Sec. 8a UWG

According to other authors, Sec. 8a UWG should not have a blocking function. Sec. 8a UWG is therefore **not to be understood as a restriction but, on the contrary, as an extension of the right to file an action**.[89] According to this view, in addition to the associations, organizations and public bodies entitled to bring an action under Art. 14(3), (4) P2B Regulation, competitors entitled to file a claim under Sec. 8(3) no. 1 UWG and, in particular, associations (Sec. 8(3) no. 2 UWG) and qualified organizations for the protection of consumer interests (Sec. 8(3) no. 3 UWG) would also be able to bring an action against infringements of the P2B Regulation. Whether this should also apply to Chambers of Industry and Commerce, Chambers of Crafts, other professional associations under public law or trade unions (Sec. 8(3) no. 4 UWG) remains unclear. 82

This view is based on the **meaning and purpose of Art. 14, 15 P2B Regulation**. The legislator did not intend Art. 14 P2B Regulation to be understood as the only enforcement mechanism, but rather clearly expressed through Art. 15 P2B Regulation that the Member States must provide for further effective and dissuasive enforcement possibilities. It would be inconsistent with this if the UWG were to restrict the possibilities of enforcing the P2B Regulation under unfair competition law via Sec. 8a UWG.[90] 83

Unlike associations under Art. 14(3) P2B Regulation, which only represent the interests of business users in a vertical relationship with the providers of online intermedia- 84

[86] BGBl. 2020 I 2456.

[87] LG Stuttgart 22.4.2021 – 11 O 10/21, MMR 2021, 1000 mn. 89; Köhler/Bornkamm/Feddersen/Köhler UWG § 8a mn. 4; MüKoUWG/Fritzsche UWG § 8a mn. 3; Russlies Abmahnung GewRS § 5 mn. 189.

[88] LG Stuttgart 22.4.2021 – 11 O 10/21, MMR 2021, 1000 mn. 89; Schneider/Kremer WRP 2020, 1128 mn. 65.

[89] Busch/Höppner/Wick P2B-VO Art. 15 mn. 13.

[90] Busch/Höppner/Wick P2B-VO Art. 15 mn. 12.

tion services, associations within the meaning of Sec. 8(3) no. 2 UWG represent the interests in a horizontal relationship. Consumer associations within the meaning of Sec. 8(3) no. 3 UWG should therefore also be entitled to sue for violations of the P2B Regulation, as the Regulation also serves to protect consumers. Transparency obligations in the area of rankings or best price clauses are **also important from a consumer perspective.**[91]

cc) Mediating concept

85 According to the **mediating concept** advocated here, Sec. 8a UWG has a blocking effect with regard to the bodies named in Sec. 8(3) nos. 2–4 UWG but does not affect the possibility for competitors to bring an action within the meaning of Sec. 8(3) no. 1 UWG.[92] Individual legal protection under unfair competition law remains possible. However, collective redress by way of representative action is only available to associations, organisations and public bodies which are entitled to do so under Art. 14(3) and (4) P2B Regulation (→ mn. 101).

(1) Wording of Sec. 8a UWG

86 The wording of Sec. 8a UWG is **unclear** and can only be described as a failure. The provision was included in the bill at short notice in order to ensure that the Unfair Competition Act complies with European Union law.[93] It remains unclear to what extent Sec. 8a UWG is intended to deviate from Sec. 8(3) UWG. A narrow interpretation in the sense that 'exclusively' the associations, organisations and public bodies mentioned in Art. 14(3) and (4) of the P2B Regulation are entitled to enforce the P2B Regulation under fair trading law is just as conceivable as an interpretation according to which Sec. 8a UWG was intended to enable 'also' the bodies mentioned therein to enforce it. Since Sec. 8a UWG expressly lists the associations, organisations and public bodies mentioned in Art. 14(3) and (4) P2B Regulation, but does not mention competitors, it is also possible to interpret Sec. 8a UWG as referring only to collective enforcement, while leaving individual claims under unfair competition law completely unaffected.

(2) Systematic approach and materials

87 According to the explanatory memorandum to the new law, the legislator's intention with Section 8a UWG was merely to provide **'clarification'**[94]. However, there was no need for clarification with regard to individual enforcement in the event of infringements of the P2B Regulation. According to Art. 14(9) P2B Regulation, the right of representative action should not affect the possibilities of individual enforcement provided for by the laws of the Member States. A clarification in this sense therefore already takes place at the level of Union law itself and would be superfluous in the context of the UWG. The fact that, according to the declared will of the legislator, the enforcement of rights in the event of infringements of the P2B Regulation is to take place via the Unfair Competition Act[95] indicates that the legislator did not see any need to include a clarification in this respect in the UWG.

---

[91] Busch/Höppner/Wick P2B-VO Art. 15 mn. 13.

[92] Like here Harte-Bavendamm/Henning-Bodewig/Goldmann UWG § 8a mn. 9; BeckOK UWG/Tribess P2B-VO Art. 1 mn. 26.

[93] BT-Drs. 19/20664, 8.

[94] BT-Drs. 19/20664, 8.

[95] BT-Drs. 19/20664, 8.

Systematically, it must also be taken into account that according to Art. 1(4) P2B Regulation, provisions of the Member States which, in accordance with Union law, prohibit or penalise unilateral acts or unfair commercial practices are **expressly not to be affected** by the P2B Regulation, unless the P2B Regulation itself regulates the relevant aspects differently.[96] On the other hand, Art. 14(3) P2B Regulation does not allow the conclusion that the legislator has restricted the rights of competitors in deviation from the general provisions or that it has restricted the prosecution of violations of the P2B Regulation under unfair competition law to the bodies mentioned in Art. 14(3) and (4) P2B Regulation. On the contrary: As a closer look at Art. 15 P2B Regulation shows, the legislator was aware that enforcement of the law by the bodies named in Art. 14(1) P2B Regulation would not be suitable to ensure an effective and dissuasive enforcement of the P2B Regulation. 88

In view of this, a need for clarification on the part of the German legislator **could only arise with regard to the relationship between Art. 14(3) and (4) P2B Regulation and Sec. 8(3) no. 2–4 UWG**. In this respect, a clarifying delimitation of the legal standing of associations and public bodies is understandable and also sensible in order to exclude any uncertainty as to the legal standing of associations and public bodies from the outset, which would otherwise only be resolved by the courts and the ECJ. 89

(3) Effet utile

The view advocated here is the most effective way of enforcing the P2B Regulation and thus fulfils the **requirement of 'effet utile'**[97]. This is because, on the one hand, the special conditions provided for in the P2B Regulation with regard to representative actions (Art. 14(3) and (4) P2B Regulation; → mn. 101) are duly enforced without restricting the rights of individual prosecution. 90

In order for the P2B Regulation to be fully effective, it is not necessary to further extend the group of parties entitled to bring claims. If public bodies within the meaning of Sec. 8(3) no. 4 UWG were allowed to bring actions in addition to the bodies established under Art. 14(4) P2B Regulation (→ mn. 113), the provision of Art. 14(4) P2B Regulation would ultimately be completely empty. The same applies to associations within the meaning of Sec. 8(3) no. 2 UWG in relation to organisations and associations established in accordance with the special provisions of Art. 14(3) P2B Regulation (→ mn. 104). The opposing view overlooks the fact that the organisations and associations established in accordance with Art. 14(3) P2B Regulation represent the collective interests of commercial users as a whole, irrespective of whether these relate to the vertical or horizontal relationship. There is **no need for an additional right of action for consumer organisations**. This is because the consumer protection character of some of the provisions of the P2B Regulation is merely mediated by the strengthening of the legal position of commercial users and corporate website users. This is a side effect of the enforcement of the P2B Regulation, but not its actual regulatory purpose. 91

(4) Result

Insofar as the infringements complained of by business users of online intermediation services or corporate website users against providers of online search engines relate to the horizontal relationship between user and provider, there is a **direct right of action and standing under Sec. 8(1), (3) no. 1 UWG in conjunction with Sec. 3a UWG**. In 92

[96] BeckOK UWG/Tribess P2B-VO Art. 1 mn. 25.

[97] EuGH 17.9.2002 – C-253/00, DVBl 2002, 1620 mn. 30 et seq. – Muñoz und Superior Fruiticola; cf. Potacs EuR 2009, 465.

view of the dualism between a vertical and a horizontal relationship between providers and users expressly laid down in the P2B Regulation, there is no need for a 'connecting provision' comparable to Sec. 8a UWG.[98] The wording limit of Sec. 8a UWG is not violated. Other competitors of providers of online intermediation services or providers of online search engines are also entitled to make claims and bring actions. Under the conditions of Sec. 8(1), (3) no. 1 UWG in conjunction with Sec. 3a UWG, they can also take action against violations of the P2B Regulation.

2. Contractual claims

93 Breaches of the transparency obligations of the P2B Regulation by providers of online intermediation services are likely to give rise to claims for damages under Sec. 280(1), 282, 241(2) of the German Civil Code (Bürgerliches Gesetzbuch, BGB) as a **breach of ancillary contractual obligations**.[99] A claim for damages may also arise under Sec. 280(1), 282, 241(2), 311(2) BGB in the context of a pre-contractual obligation between a business user and a provider of online intermediation services.[100] In practice, it is likely that there will be no causal damage resulting from a breach of transparency obligations, so that claims by business users of online intermediation services based on this would remain without effect.[101]

94 The fulfilment of individual transparency obligations of the P2B Regulation for providers of online intermediation services, e.g. those relating to ranking (Art. 5 P2B Regulation; → § 17 mn. 93) or the justification of a restriction, suspension or termination (Art. 4(1), (2) P2B Regulation; → § 17 mn. 33), can be enforced by the business users concerned as **independent contractual ancillary obligations**. However, if only (also) pre-contractual transparency obligations are affected, e.g. with regard to the internal complaint handling system (Art. 11 P2B Regulation; → mn. 11) or mediation (Art. 12 P2B Regulation; → mn. 45), independent actionability must be rejected.[102]

95 As there is no contractual relationship between the providers of online search engines and their corporate website users,[103] contractual claims cannot be considered.

3. Tort claims

96 For corporate website users in particular, an individual claim against a provider of online search engines for breach of obligations under the P2B Regulation may also be **based on tort law**. The infringed provision of the P2B Regulation would then have to be understood as a protective right within the meaning of Sec. 823(2) BGB, so that claims for injunctive relief in conjunction with Sec. 1004(1) BGB are also conceivable by analogy. Claims under Sec. 826 BGBfor wilful damage to morals are also possible. With regard to claims for damages, it will again be difficult to prove causal damage.[104]

---

[98] Advocating this need: Köhler/Bornkamm/Feddersen/Alexander P2B-VO Art. 14 mn. 48.

[99] Busch/Höppner/Wick P2B-VO Art. 15 mn. 22; Köhler/Bornkamm/Feddersen/Alexander P2B-VO Art. 14 mn. 49; Busch GRUR 2019, 788 (792); Tribess GWR 2020, 233 (238); Tribess ZD 2020, 440 (443); Voigt/Reuter MMR 2019, 783 (787).

[100] Busch/Höppner/Wick P2B-VO Art. 15 mn. 22; Köhler/Bornkamm/Feddersen/Alexander P2B-VO Art. 14 mn. 49.

[101] Busch/Höppner/Wick P2B-VO Art. 15 mn. 22.

[102] Busch/Höppner/Wick P2B-VO Art. 15 mn. 23.

[103] Busch/Höppner/Wick P2B-VO Art. 15 mn. 22.

[104] Busch/Höppner/Wick P2B-VO Art. 15 mn. 22; Köhler/Bornkamm/Feddersen/Alexander P2B-VO Art. 14 mn. 53.

C. Collective legal action

97 Art. 14 P2B Regulation gives certain organisations and associations as well as qualified public bodies the possibility of bringing an action for infringement of the P2B Regulation by providers of online intermediation services or providers of online search engines. In particular, this is intended to prevent future damage that could affect the viability of business relationships in the online platform economy (Recital 44).[105]

98 The creation of the representative action under the P2B Regulation is due in particular to the legislator's analysis in the run-up to the legislative process, according to which various factors, such as lack of financial resources, fear of "retaliation" and exclusive provisions on the choice of applicable law and place of jurisdiction in the general terms and conditions of the providers of online intermediation services or online search engines, may **limit the effectiveness of the existing possibilities for individual judicial redress** (Recital 44; → § 16 mn. 1).[106]

99 The P2B Regulation does not provide for separate sanction mechanisms for the enforcement of the P2B Regulation by organisations, associations or public bodies (→ mn. 2). According to Art. 15 P2B Regulation, Member States are obliged to ensure **appropriate and effective enforcement of the P2B Regulation**. The details of possible claims and the procedural organisation therefore depend on the applicable national law (Recital 46).[107]

100 In Germany, **Sec. 8a UWG** gives the organisations, associations and public bodies entitled under Art. 14(3) and (4) P2B Regulation to take legal action against infringements of the P2B Regulation (→ mn. 101).[108] Notwithstanding individual legal action (Art. 14(9) P2B Regulation; → mn. 87), their right to take legal action is exclusive; the bodies mentioned in Art. 8(3) no. 2–4 UWG do not have the right to take legal action with regard to the P2B Regulation (→ mn. 92).

I. Parties entitled to sue

101 In order to ensure that the organisations and associations entitled to bring collective actions under Art. 14(1) P2B Regulation effectively and appropriately exercise the right granted to them, they must **fulfil certain criteria**. These requirements are intended, in particular, to prevent abusive conduct through the ad hoc establishment of organisations or associations for the purpose of filing a particular action or actions, as well as the filing of actions for profit (Recital 44). Art. 14(3) P2B Regulation therefore provides that organisations or associations must be properly constituted in accordance with the law of a Member State, must not be profit-making and must pursue their objectives on a permanent basis (→ mn. 104).[109]

102 In addition, undue influence by third parties on the decision-making of the relevant organisations and associations must be excluded (→ mn. 111). In order to **avoid conflicts of interest**, this should in particular prevent organisations or associations representing business users or corporate website users from being unduly influenced by providers of online intermediation services or providers of online search engines

[105] Busch/Höppner/Wick P2B-VO Art. 14 mn. 1.
[106] Busch/Höppner/Wick P2B-VO Art. 14 mn. 1; BeckOK UWG/Dämmer P2B-VO Art. 14 mn. 2.
[107] Busch/Höppner/Wick P2B-VO Art. 15 mn. 1; BeckOK UWG/Dämmer P2B-VO Art. 14 mn. 3.
[108] Busch/Höppner/Wick P2B-VO Art. 14 mn. 3.
[109] Busch/Höppner/Wick P2B-VO Art. 14 mn. 26 et seqq.; BeckOK UWG/Dämmer P2B-VO Art. 14 mn. 5.

(Recital 44). This is to be achieved by requiring full disclosure of information on membership and sources of funding (Art. 14(3)(2) P2B Regulation).[110]

103 Art. 14(4) P2B Regulation contains **requirements for the establishment of public bodies** for the purpose of prosecuting infringements of the P2B Regulation (→ mn. 113). These bodies must be established in accordance with the relevant national law and be expressly empowered to bring such proceedings either in the collective interest of the parties concerned or in the general interest (Recital 44).[111]

1. Organisations and associations

104 Art. 14(3) P2B Regulation contains a catalogue of requirements that qualified entities must fulfil in order to be entitled to bring an action under Art. 14(1) P2B Regulation. Art. 14(3)(2) P2B Regulation obliges organisations and associations to **publish all information** on who their members are and on their sources of funding. Publication is not only required vis-à-vis the parties involved in legal proceedings, but the information must also be made available to the general public (e.g. by publication on the association's website).[112]

a) Proper establishment

105 Pursuant to Art. 14(3)(1)(a) P2B Regulation, qualified entities must be **properly established under the law of a Member State**. This does not necessarily have to be the law of the Member State in which an action is brought, or another associational activity is carried out. It is sufficient that the organisations and associations have partial legal capacity enabling them to bring representative actions in their own name.[113]

106 The group of eligible organisations and associations is therefore **very broad**. This is in line with the use of the term 'organisations and associations' in other European legal acts. Neither the P2B Regulation nor Art. 80 of the General Data Protection Regulation (Regulation (EU) 2016/673)[114] or other legal acts make a systematic distinction between organisations and associations. The pair of terms is therefore generally understood as an expression of the legislator's intention to draw the circle of authorised entities as wide as possible.[115] Only natural persons are excluded.[116]

b) Permanent representation of collective interests

107 Art. 14(3)(1)(b) P2B Regulation requires that organisations and associations pursue objectives that are **in the collective interest** of the group of business users or corporate website users that they represent on a permanent basis. A certain number of members or homogeneity within the membership is not required,[117] e.g. with regard to the branch of

---

[110] Busch/Höppner/Wick P2B-VO Art. 14 mn. 36; BeckOK UWG/Dämmer P2B-VO Art. 14 mn. 5 et seqq.

[111] Busch/Höppner/Wick P2B-VO Art. 14 mn. 42 et seqq.; BeckOK UWG/Dämmer P2B-VO Art. 14 mn. 8.

[112] Busch/Höppner/Wick P2B-VO Art. 14 mn. 36 et seq.; Köhler/Bornkamm/Feddersen/Alexander P2B-VO Art. 14 mn. 33.

[113] Busch/Höppner/Wick P2B-VO Art. 14 mn. 29; Köhler/Bornkamm/Feddersen/Alexander P2B-VO Art. 14 mn. 9.

[114] Regulation (EU) 2016/679 of the European Parliament and of the Council of 27 April 2016 on the protection of natural persons with regard to the processing of personal data and on the free movement of such data, and repealing Directive 95/46/EC (General Data Protection Regulation), OJ L 119, 1.

[115] Busch/Höppner/Wick P2B-VO Art. 14 mn. 28; Sydow/Marsch/Kreße DS-GVO Art. 80 mn. 4.

[116] Busch/Höppner/Wick P2B-VO Art. 14 mn. 28; Sydow/Marsch/Kreße DS-GVO Art. 80 mn. 5.

[117] Busch/Höppner/Wick P2B-VO Art. 14 mn. 30.

industry, the range of goods and services or the online intermediation services or online search engine used.

Proof that the collective interests of the members are represented is generally provided by the objects of the activities set out in the statutes. However, the existence of articles of association is not a mandatory requirement under Art. 14(3) P2B Regulation. Whether a statute is required for a particular organisation or association depends solely on the legal provisions of the Member State in which the organisation or association is duly established (→ mn. 105). In the absence of a statute required by association law, the general rules of presentation and proof apply to prove the representation of collective interests.[118] 108

In order to exclude ad hoc foundations for individual proceedings (→ mn. 101), the organisation or association must be **permanently** active in the context of collective representation of interests. The P2B Regulation does not specify the period required for this. The one-year period laid down in Sec. 8b(2) no. 2 UWG for associations within the meaning of Sec. 8 UWG also appears to be a suitable, albeit non-binding, standard for the purposes of the P2B Regulation.[119] 109

c) Activity with non-profit making character

Organisations and associations entitled to take legal action in accordance with Art. 14(1) P2B Regulation **may not pursue a profit-making objective** (Art. 14(3)(1)(c) P2B Regulation). This term is to be interpreted independently under European Union law and is not to be equated with non-profit status under tax law. Organisations and associations may cover their costs but may not focus their activities on generating profits from legal proceedings. It is not the individual legal proceedings that are decisive, but the overall view of the activities of the organisations or associations.[120] 110

d) No undue influence by any third party providers of financing

Qualified entities should represent the collective interests of their members **independently of undue influence from third-party donors**; this applies in particular to undue influence from contributions from providers of online intermediation services or providers of online search engines (Art. 14(3)(1)(d) P2B Regulation). Third-party donors are all persons outside the association itself; contributions from its members are therefore not covered.[121] 111

It is irrelevant for the question of undue influence whether the contribution is made once, several times or regularly, as long as it constitutes a conflict of interest on the part of the organisation or association by virtue of its amount or the **overall circumstances**. If an association is improperly influenced by third-party donors, it will lose its status as a qualified organisation altogether. Therefore, the right to bring an action does not expire only for a specific procedure for which or in which undue influence could be established.[122] Art. 14(3)(1)(d) P2B Regulation is to be interpreted broadly in the sense of an effective enforcement of the P2B Regulation through association actions: Funding by 112

118 Busch/Höppner/Wick P2B-VO Art. 14 mn. 30.

119 Busch/Höppner/Wick P2B-VO Art. 14 mn. 31.

120 BGH 4.7.2019 – I ZR 149/18, NJW 2019, 3377 mn. 45 – Umwelthilfe; Busch/Höppner/Wick P2B-VO Art. 14 mn. 32; Köhler/Bornkamm/Feddersen/Alexander P2B-VO Art. 14 mn. 25 et seq.

121 Busch/Höppner/Wick P2B-VO Art. 14 mn. 33 et seq.; Köhler/Bornkamm/Feddersen/Alexander P2B-VO Art. 14 mn. 27.

122 Busch/Höppner/Wick P2B-VO Art. 14 mn. 35.

third parties, in particular from the platform economy, should remain the exception and be limited to 'unsuspicious' individual cases.[123]

2. Public bodies

113 Art. 14(4) P2B Regulation sets out the conditions under which public bodies are authorised to enforce the P2B Regulation under civil law. Apart from being established, the only condition is that the public body is **'authorised'** under the law of the Member State concerned. The P2B Regulation does not impose any further conditions; in particular, the requirements of Art. 14(3) P2B Regulation do not apply.[124] Just as organisations or associations under private law are not limited to bringing an action in the Member State in which they are established, public bodies authorised under Art. 14(4) P2B Regulation may also bring actions throughout the entire territory of the Union.[125]

114 In Germany, public bodies **have not yet been authorised** to do so. In particular, the public bodies entitled to assert claims under unfair competition law (Chambers of Industry and Commerce, Chambers of Crafts and other professional associations) pursuant to Sec. 8(3) no. 4 UWG could be considered. This would be an obvious assignment, as these organisations are already legally mandated to represent the interests of their members; the representation of interests, also in the context of the platform economy, would usefully complement the mandate of the chambers in view of the new economic circumstances.[126] There are also calls for the Federal Antitrust Office to be given a mandate.[127] This also seems appropriate, as the Federal Antitrust Office has already been given further regulatory powers in the platform economy as a result of the latest amendments to antitrust regulations.[128]

3. List of entities entitled to bring an action

115 The legislator considered that a **list of organisations, associations and public bodies entitled to bring an action**, to be maintained by the Commission, could further simplify the judicial process. Art. 14(5) to (8) P2B Regulation therefore contains provisions by means of which the organisations, associations and public bodies which, in the opinion of the Member States, should be entitled to bring a representative action can be notified to the Commission (Art. 14(5) P2B Regulation). In the course of this notification, Member States should refer in particular to the relevant national provisions under which the organisation, association or public body has been established and, where applicable, to the relevant public register in which the organisation or association is entered (Recital 45).[129]

116 This possibility of designation by Member States is intended to provide a**dditional legal certainty and predictability** on which business users and corporate website users can rely. At the same time, it is intended to make court proceedings more efficient and faster (Recital 45).[130]

117 The Commission is therefore obliged under Art. 14(6) P2B Regulation to publish a list of these organisations, associations and public bodies in the Official Journal of the

---

[123] Busch/Höppner/Wick P2B-VO Art. 14 mn. 35.

[124] Busch/Höppner/Wick P2B-VO Art. 14 mn. 43; Köhler/Bornkamm/Feddersen/Alexander P2B-VO Art. 14 mn. 20.

[125] Busch/Höppner/Wick P2B-VO Art. 14 mn. 44.

[126] Busch/Höppner/Wick P2B-VO Art. 14 mn. 46.

[127] Busch GRUR 2019, 788 (796).

[128] Busch/Höppner/Wick P2B-VO Art. 14 mn. 46; crit. Köhler/Bornkamm/Feddersen/Alexander P2B-VO Art. 14 mn. 38.

[129] Busch/Höppner/Wick P2B-VO Art. 14 mn. 50; BeckOK UWG/Dämmer P2B-VO Art. 14 mn. 9.

[130] Busch/Höppner/Wick P2B-VO Art. 14 mn. 49.

European Union.[131] In accordance with Art. 14(7) P2B Regulation, inclusion in this list serves as **rebuttable evidence** that the organisation, association or public body is entitled to bring an action.[132]

So far, only a **few Member States have made use of the possibility** of designation. Austria has notified the Commission of three public bodies, Ireland of one and Spain is the only Member State to have designated an association under private law as an authorised body under Art. 14(3) P2B Regulation.[133] 118

Due to the considerable simplifications that the presumption effect of Art. 14(7) P2B Regulation for organisations and associations in the context of proving their eligibility, they have a **legal claim** against the competent public body to actually be named and notified to the Commission for the purpose of publication upon request and if the conditions of Art. 14(3) P2B Regulation are met. Even if the wording of Art. 14(5) P2B Regulation ('may') could indicate that only a decision free of discretionary errors must be made by the competent public authority, the claim is unconditional.[134] 119

If a Member State or the Commission has **concerns about a designation**, the Member State that has designated an organisation, association or public body is obliged to investigate these concerns and, if necessary, revoke the designation (Art. 14(8) P2B Regulation).[135] 120

II. Filing a collective action

Organisations, associations. and public bodies that meet the requirements of Art. 14(3) and (4) of the P2B Regulation are **entitled to bring an action**, with the court having to assess the entitlement to bring an action on a case-by-case basis in accordance with the criteria set out in Art. 14(3) P2B Regulation and Art. 14(4) P2B Regulation (Recital 45). There is a rebuttable presumption that the requirements of Art. 14(3) and (4) P2B Regulation for organisations or associations and public bodies which have been designated by a Member State in accordance with Art. 14(5) P2B Regulation (Art. 14(7) P2B Regulation; → mn. 115).[136] 121

Organisations or associations within the meaning of Art. 14(3) P2B Regulation (but not public bodies within the meaning of Art. 14(4) P2B Regulation) must also establish and prove a **'legitimate interest'** in the concrete legal action (Art. 14(1) P2B Regulation). This requirement corresponds to the need for legal protection under German civil procedural law. The court before which the matter is brought must examine whether the association's action, if successful, would benefit the business users or corporate website users it represents and thus fall within the purpose of the association's formation (→ mn. 107). For example, a legitimate interest could be lacking if an association explicitly represented the interests of holiday home landlords on online booking portals but took action against the practices of an online marketplace for fitness instructors. Similarly, the explicit representation of the interests of members from one Member State may not constitute a legitimate interest to bring an action against a platform that does not operate in that Member State and has no intention of doing so. However, in the 122

131 Busch/Höppner/Wick P2B-VO Art. 14 mn. 47; BeckOK UWG/Dämmer P2B-VO Art. 14 mn. 10.
132 Busch/Höppner/Wick P2B-VO Art. 14 mn. 49; BeckOK UWG/Dämmer P2B-VO Art. 14 mn. 11.
133 OJ 2021 C 402, 5; BeckOK UWG/Dämmer P2B-VO Art. 14 mn. 10.1.
134 Busch/Höppner/Wick P2B-VO Art. 14 mn. 50.
135 Busch/Höppner/Wick P2B-VO Art. 14 mn. 51.
136 Busch/Höppner/Wick P2B-VO Art. 14 mn. 5 et seqq.; Köhler/Bornkamm/Feddersen/Alexander P2B-VO Art. 14 mn. 21.

interest of effective enforcement of the P2B Regulation, the requirements for a legitimate interest should not be too high.[137]

123 The right to bring a representative action is **governed by the law of the Member State** in which the action is brought against a provider of online intermediation services or a provider of online search engines (Art. 14(1) P2B Regulation). According to the view of the Federal Court of Justice in its established case law, according to which, in the context of collective actions, procedural standing also follows from substantive standing[138], it is ultimately irrelevant, especially from the perspective of EU law, whether the requirements of Art. 14(1) P2B Regulation already refer to the admissibility of the action or only to its merits.[139]

124 The object of the collective action pursuant to Art. 14(1) of the P2B Regulation may be **the 'stop' or 'prohibition' of the pursued non-compliance with the P2B Regulation** by a provider of online intermediation services or a provider of online search engines. In essence, therefore, these are claims for the removal of an infringement that has already occurred or, with a view to the future, for the cessation of future infringements of the obligations under Art. 3–12 P2B Regulation.[140] As violations of the P2B Regulation are violations of market conduct rules (→ mn. 76), claims for injunctive relief arise in particular under the Unfair Competition Act. Sec. 8a UWG stipulates that organisations, associations and public bodies established in accordance with Art. 14(3), (4) P2B Regulation may assert claims for injunctive relief pursuant to Sec. 8(1) UWG in conjunction with Sec. 3a UWG by way of class action (→ mn. 92) instead of the bodies mentioned in Sec. 8(3) no. 2–4 UWG (→ mn. 85).

125 **Agreements on jurisdiction or applicable law** included in the general terms and conditions of online intermediation services or online search engines are irrelevant in the context of a collective action. This is because the association bringing the action is acting on its own behalf and is not asserting the rights of its members. However, the association itself has no contractual relationship with the providers of online intermediation services or online search engines which could bind it to the provisions of their general terms and conditions. The question of the (international) jurisdiction of the courts and the applicable law is therefore governed by general rules which, according to Art. 1(4) and (5) P2B Regulation, expressly remain unaffected by the Regulation.[141]

126 Accordingly, the courts of the **relevant marketplace** have jurisdiction as the place where the unlawful act took place, namely the contested infringement of the P2B Regulation (Art. 7 no. 2 Brussels Ia Regulation[142]; Art. 5 no. 3 Lugano Convention; sec. 32 German Civil Procedure Act (Zivilprozessordnung, ZPO)). In the case of online intermediation services, the marketplace is the place where the online intermediation service in question is provided, i.e. the market or markets to which the platform is directed according to the criteria of Art. 17(1)(c) alt. 3 Brussels Ia Regulation. For online search engines, it is obvious to consider the market or markets on which the corporate website users are primarily active as the marketplace.[143]

---

[137] Busch/Höppner/Wick P2B-VO Art. 14 mn. 40 et seq.

[138] BGH 13.9.2018 – I ZR 26/17, NJW 2018, 3581 mn. 12 – Prozessfinanzierer (litigation funder).

[139] Busch/Höppner/Wick P2B-VO Art. 14 mn. 6 et seq.; Köhler/Bornkamm/Feddersen/Alexander P2B-VO Art. 14 mn. 8.

[140] Busch/Höppner/Wick P2B-VO Art. 14 mn. 9 et seq.; Köhler/Bornkamm/Feddersen/Alexander P2B-VO Art. 14 mn. 13.

[141] Busch/Höppner/Wick P2B-VO Art. 14 mn. 13.

[142] Regulation (EU) No 1215/2012 of the European Parliament and of the Council of 12 December 2012 on jurisdiction and the recognition and enforcement of judgments in civil and commercial matters, OJ L 351, 1.

[143] Busch/Höppner/Wick P2B-VO Art. 14 mn. 17.

III. Registries of unlawful acts

Art. 14(2) P2B Regulation provides that Member States may exchange relevant judicial decisions on unlawful acts committed by providers of online intermediation services or providers of online search engines. However, Art. 14(2) P2B Regulation does not impose any obligation. For the **exchange of information**, appropriate registries may be used or established. Such registries could contribute to the uniformity of jurisprudence in the Member States, without, of course, the inclusion of a court decision being binding on other courts in the same or another Member State.[144] 127

D. Monitoring by the European Commission

According to Art. 16 P2B Regulation, the Commission is obliged to monitor the application of the Regulation on an ongoing basis. This **monitoring task** is closely linked to the Commission's obligation to evaluate the P2B Regulation (Art. 18(1) P2B Regulation).[145] For the first time on 13 January 2022 and every three years thereafter, the Commission should have determined or the Commission should determine whether additional rules, e.g. for the enforcement of the P2B Regulation, are necessary to ensure a fair, predictable, sustainable and trusted online business environment in the internal market (Art. 18(2) no. 2 P2B Regulation). 128

On 12 September 2023, the Commission presented a first report on the implementation and impact of the P2B Regulation. While noting the initial positive effects of the P2B Regulation, the Commission recognises that its full potential has not yet been realised. In particular, providers of online intermediation services often do not comply with the Regulation, while at the same time there is a lack of awareness among business users of the rights granted to them by the P2B Regulation. The P2B Regulation will only be fully effective in conjunction with complementary legislation, in particular the Digital Markets Act (DMA; Regulation (EU) 2022/1828) and the Digital Services Act (DSA; Regulation (EU) 2022/2065). The Commission's report is based on an external study analysing the effectiveness of the P2B Regulation in the first two years after its application in July 2020. To this end, the study team used various tools such as interviews, surveys, focus groups with business users and a review of the terms and conditions of platforms of different sizes and content orientations. The Commission notes that the P2B Regulation has so far been insufficiently implemented, in particular with regard to transparency requirements, e.g. with regard to the restriction, suspension and termination of the use of online intermediation services. With regard to complaint-handling mechanisms, there were significant differences in the number of complaints processed. Only a few online intermediation service providers offered compulsory mediation services. There were no specialised mediation organisations. In response to the sobering results of the review, the Commission intends to take measures to help enforce the P2B Regulation, but for the time being remains vague in describing its plans. Information campaigns will be launched to raise awareness among both providers and users. Other planned activities concern mediation services in the area of SME platforms and the establishment of codes of conduct. Finally, the Commission calls on the Member 129

---

[144] Busch/Höppner/Wick P2B-VO Art. 14 mn. 52; Köhler/Bornkamm/Feddersen/Alexander P2B-VO Art. 14 mn. 44.

[145] Busch/Busch P2B-VO Art. 16 mn. 5.

States to create instruments in national law for the effective enforcement of the P2B Regulation.[146]

130 **Close cooperation between the Commission and the Member States** is provided for in the monitoring and evaluation of the P2B Regulation (Art. 16(1)(1) P2B Regulation; see also Art. 18(3) P2B Regulation). The Member States shall assist the Commission by providing it, upon request, with any relevant information gathered including about specific cases (Art. 16(1)(3) P2B Regulation).[147]

131 The Commission is also required to fulfil its monitoring role by carrying out relevant studies (Art. 16(2) P2B Regulation). In this context, the Commission should work towards the establishment of a broad network for the exchange of information, making use of relevant expert bodies, centres of excellence and the **Observatory on the Online Platform Economy** (Recital 47). The prominent role of the Observatory on the Online Platform Economy is also underlined in the evaluation of the P2B Regulation. Its opinions and reports must be taken into account by the Commission (Art. 18(4) P2B Regulation). In connection with the P2B Regulation, the Observatory on the Online Platform Economy is primarily concerned with strategies and methods to ensure, expand and improve the general awareness of professional users with regard to their rights in the platform economy. Another focus of the work of the Observatory on the Online Platform Economy is to analyse the interactions between the P2B Regulation and other legal acts of the Union and to ensure coherence (e.g. with the Unfair Commercial Practices Directive; Directive 2005/23/EC[148]) or the Digital Services Act). Finally, the Observatory on the Online Platform Economy shall examine the relevance and appropriateness of codes of conduct (→ mn. 133) in the context of the P2B Regulation.[149]

132 Providers of online intermediation services are also obliged to cooperate with the Commission in the context of the monitoring of the P2B Regulation. The Commission may obtain information from them (but surprisingly not from the providers of online search engines[150]), also for the purpose of the evaluation pursuant to Art. 18 P2B Regulation (Art. 16(1)(4) P2B Regulation). **Providers of online intermediation services should cooperate in good faith with the Commission** by facilitating the collection of the relevant data where necessary (Recital 47). However, breaches of this obligation to cooperate cannot be sanctioned under the P2B Regulation.[151] According to the legislator's intention, monitoring should also be facilitated by the fact that the P2B Regulation improves the overall transparency of business relations between business users and providers of online intermediation services as well as between corporate website users and providers of online search engines (Recital 47).

---

[146] COM(2023) 525 final; SWD(2023) 300 final; Busch/Busch P2B-VO Art. 16 mn. 5.

[147] BeckOK UWG/Fritzsche P2B-VO Art. 16 mn. 4.

[148] Directive 2005/29/EC of the European Parliament and of the Council of 11 May 2005 concerning unfair business-to-consumer commercial practices in the internal market and amending Council Directive 84/450/EEC, Directives 97/7/EC, 98/27/EC and 2002/65/EC of the European Parliament and of the Council and Regulation (EC) No 2006/2004 of the European Parliament and of the Council ('Unfair Commercial Practices Directive'), OJ L 159, 22.

[149] Study on evaluation of the Regulation (EU) 2019/1150 on promoting fairness and transparency for business users of online intermediation services (the P2B Regulation) < https://op.europa.eu/en/publication-detail/-/publication/d6a287b5-5116-11ee-9220-01aa75ed71a1/language-en/ > (last accessed: 28 August 2024).

[150] Busch/Busch P2B-VO Art. 16 mn. 9.

[151] Busch/Busch P2B-VO Art. 16 mn. 11.

E. Voluntary commitments through codes of conduct

133 According to the legislator, codes of conduct drawn up either by the service providers concerned or by the organisations or associations representing them may **contribute to the proper application of the P2B Regulation** (Recital 48). Art. 17 P2B Regulation takes account of this conviction with a multi-layered request from the Commission. However, due to the Commission's lack of enforcement powers, the provision is more of an 'appellative programme requirement'.[152]

134 Providers of online intermediation services and organisations or associations representing them, together with business users, including SMEs, and their representative organisations, should **develop codes of conduct** to support the proper application of the P2B Regulation, taking account of the specific features of the various sectors in which online intermediation services are provided, as well as of the specific characteristics of SMEs (Art. 17(1) P2B Regulation). Similar requirements can be found in a number of other Union legal acts, in particular and including certain enforcement powers of the Commission in Art. 45–47 of the Digital Services Act (DSA, Regulation (EU) 2022/2065). However, the instrument of voluntary self-commitment of the online economy has already existed at Union level for more than 20 years. Already Art. 16 of the eCommerce Directive (Directive 2000/31/EC)[153] encourages associations to self-regulate in order to promote the objectives of the Directive.[154]

135 In addition, providers of online intermediation services are required to adopt and implement **industry-specific codes of conduct** if such codes exist and are widely applied (Art. 17(3) P2B Regulation). In contrast to Art. 17(1) P2B Regulation, which requires the creation of new codes of conduct, the request under Art. 17(3) P2B Regulation refers to codes of conduct that already exist and are widely used.

136 In the context of online search engines, their providers and the organisations and associations representing them should draw up codes of conduct that are specifically designed to ensure the proper application of the requirements for ranking under Art. 5 P2B Regulation (Art. 17(2) P2B Regulation). An example of an existing code of conduct in the area of online search engines is the '**Code of Conduct for Search Engine Providers**' ('Verhaltenskodex für Suchmaschinenanbieter') adopted on 21 December 2004 by the German association 'Freiwillige Selbstkontrolle Multimedia-Diensteanbieter e.V. (FSM)'.[155] Section 2 of this code of conduct also contains rules of conduct for the transparent preparation and presentation of search results, which are reminiscent of the transparency obligations for providers of online search engines (in particular from Art. 5 and 7 P2B Regulation), but fall far short of the level of transparency required by the P2B Regulation.[156]

---

[152] Busch/Busch P2B-VO Art. 17 mn. 2.

[153] Directive 2000/31/EC of the European Parliament and of the Council of 8 June 2000 on certain legal aspects of information society services, in particular electronic commerce, in the Internal Market ('Directive on electronic commerce'), OJ L 178, 1.

[154] For examples of codes of conduct established on the basis of this Directive, see Busch/Busch P2B-VO Art. 17 mn. 5.

[155] Verhaltenssubkodex für Suchmaschinenanbieter der FSM (VK-S) <https://www.fsm.de/files/2022/03/2004-12-21_fsm_verhaltenssubkodex_suchmaschinenanbieter.pdf> (last accessed: 28 August 2024).

[156] Busch/Busch P2B-VO Art. 17 mn. 10.

CHAPTER 4: EU MEDIA FREEDOM ACT

§ 18
The European Media Freedom Act

Literature: *Bakke/Sitter*, 'The EU's Enfants Terribles: Democratic Backsliding in Central Europe since 2010', Perspectives on Politics 2020, 22; *Bátorfy/Urbán*, 'State advertising as an instrument of transformation of the media market in Hungary', East European Politics 2020, 44; *Beaujean/Oelke/Wierny*, 'Immer mehr Verordnungen aus Brüssel und ihre Auswirkungen auf die Medienregulierung – Wie viel Handlungsspielraum verbleibt für die Mitgliedstaaten?', MMR 2023, 11; *Bleyer-Simon/Brogi/Carlini/Da Costa Leite Borges/Nenadić/Palmer/Parcu/Trevisan/Verza/Žuffová*, 'Monitoring Media Pluralism In The Digital Era' (EU Media Pluralism Monitor), San Domenico di Fiesole 2023; *Bleyer-Simon/Brogi/Carlini/Nenadic/Palmer/Parcu/Verza/Viola de Azevedo Cunha/Žuffová*, 'Monitoring Media Pluarlism In The Digital Era' (EU Media Pluralism Monitor), San Domenico di Fiesole, 2021; *Brühann*, 'Pluralismus und Medienkonzentration im Binnenmarkt – Beitrag zum Expertengespräch des Europäischen Medieninstituts am 12. Mai 1993 in Saarbrücken', ZUM 1993, 600; *Calliess/Ruffert* (eds), EUV/AEUV – Das Verfassungsrecht der Europäischen Union mit Europäischer Grundrechtecharta, 6th edn, Munich 2022; *Citino*, 'Verso l'European Media Freedom Act – la strategia europea contro le minacce al pluralismo e all'indipendenza dei media da una prospettivade iure condendo', MediaLaws – Rivista di diritto dei media, 2022, 232; *Cole/Etteldorf*, Future Regulation of Cross-Border Audiovisual Content Dissemination – A Critical Analysis of the Current Regulatory Framework for Law Enforcement under the EU Audiovisual Media Services Directive and the Proposal for a European Media Freedom Act, Baden-Baden 2023; *Cremer*, 'Grundrechtsverpflichtete und Grundrechtsdimensionen nach der Charta der Grundrechte der Europäischen Union', EuGRZ 2011, 545; *D. Dörr*, 'Die Entwicklung des Medienrechts', NJW 1997, 1341; *R. Dörr*, 'Mehr Medienfreiheit wagen! Aktuelle EU-Initiativen zur Regulierung der Medien', AfP 2023, 206; *R. Dörr/Weber*, 'Der European Media Freedom Act (EMFA) und seine Bedeutung für die nationale Medienregulierung', AfP 2023, 383; *Dregelies*, 'Digital Services Act – Ein Überblick über den neuen Rechtsrahmen für das Internet', MMR 2022, 1033; *Dregelies*, 'Europäische Persönlichkeitsrecht(e)? – Das Spannungsfeld von Persönlichkeitsschutz sowie Meinungs- und Pressefreiheit auf Ebene der EU' in Kubis/Peifer/Raue/Stieper (eds), Ius Vivum: Kunst – Internationales – Persönlichkeit, Festschrift für Haimo Schack zum 70. Geburtstag, Baden-Baden 2022, p. 951; *Dregelies*, 'Verbraucherschutz im Digital Services Act', VuR 2023, 175; *van Drunen/Papaevangelou/Buijs/Fathaigh*, What can a media privilege look like? Unpacking three versions in the EMFA, Journal of Media Law 15 (2023), 152; *Eberle*, 'Das europäische Recht und die Medien am Beispiel des Rundfunkrechts', AfP 1993, 422; *Eberle*, 'Das Fernsehen im Zugriff des europäischen Rechts' in Becker/Bull/Seewald (eds), Festschrift für Werner Thieme, Köln/Berlin/Bonn/München 1993, p. 939; *Gamito*, Consistent regulatory and self-regulatory mechanisms for media freedom in the Digital Single Market. The European Media Freedom Act (EMFA) as meta-regulation, Computer Law & Security Law 48 (2023) 105799, 1; *Gersdorf/Paal* (eds), BeckOK Informations- und Medienrecht, 41th edn, Munich 2023; *Glocke*, Publizistischer Quellenschutz im deutschen und europäischen Recht, Baden Baden 2017; *Gounalakis/Zagouras*, 'Publizistische Vielfaltsicherung – Eine Aufgabe für Europa?', JZ 2008, 652; *Grabitz/Hilf/Nettesheim* (eds), Das Recht der Europäischen Union, 80th supplement, Munich 2023; *von der Groeben/Schwarze/Hatje* (eds), Europäisches Unionsrecht – Vertrag über die Europäische Union – Vertrag über die Arbeitsweise der Europäischen Union – Charta der Grundrechte der Europäischen Union, 7th edn, Baden-Baden 2015; *Gundel*, 'Die zweite Fassung der Tabakwerberichtlinie vor dem EuGH: Weitere Klärungen zur Binnenmarkt-Harmonisierungskompetenz der Gemeinschaft', EuR 2007, 251; *Hain*, 'Sicherung des publizistischen Pluralismus auf europäischer Ebene?', AfP 2007, 527; *Henke*, 'Kulturelle Integration in der Europäischen Union unter dem europäischen Urheberrecht' in Kubis/Peifer/Raue/Stieper (eds), Ius Vivum: Kunst – Internationales – Persönlichkeit, Festschrift für Haimo Schack zum 70. Geburtstag, Baden-Baden 2022, p. 159; *Hillgruber*, 'Die Verwirklichung des Binnenmarktes durch Rechtsangleichung – Gemeinschaftsziel und -kompetenz ohne Grenzen?', in Krause/Veelken/Vieweg (eds), Recht der Wirtschaft und der Arbeit in Europa – Gedächtnisschrift für Wolfgang Blomeyer, Berlin 2004, p. 597; *Hofmann/Raue* (eds), Digital Services Act: DSA, Article-by-Article Commentary, Baden-Baden 2024; *Holtz-Bacha*, 'Freedom of the media, pluralism, and transparency. European media policy on new paths?', European Journal of Communication 2023, 1; *Jahn*, 'Europarichter überziehen ihre Kompetenzen', NJW 2008, 1788; *Jarass*, Charta der Grundrechte der Europäischen Union: GRCh unter Einbeziehung der sonstigen Grundrechtsregelungen des Primärrechts und der EMRK, 4th edn, Munich 2021; *Jotzo*, 'Der EuGH als Interimsnormgeber im digitalen Urheberrecht', ZGE 9 (2017), 447; *Karpenstein/Mayer* (eds), Konvention zum Schutz der Menschenrechte und Grundfreiheiten – EMRK, 3rd edn, Munich 2022; *Keller/Eggert*, Zur wirtschaftlichen Lage der deutschen Zeitungen 2023, BDZV-Branchenbeitrag 2023; *Klumpp/Witte Paz*, Weniger Zusammenschlüsse – mehr Medienfreiheit?, AfP 2024, 101; *Knodel*, Medien und Europa, Baden-Baden 2018; *Knothe*, 'Der EMFA – Lackmustest für das EUZBLG – Verhandlungsführung bzgl. des European Media Freedom Acts auf Grundlage des Gesetzes über die Zusammenarbeit von Bund und Ländern in Angelegenheiten der Europäischen Union', AfP 2023, 377; *Kraetzig*, 'Europäische Medienregulierung –

Freiheit durch Aufsicht?', NJW 2023, 1485; *Leible*, 'Viel Rauch um Nichts?', GPR 2007, 1; *Maierhöfer*, 'EuGH, 12. 12. 2006 — Rs. C-380/03 Bundesrepublik Deutschland./.Europäisches Parlament und Rat der EU. Gemeinschaftsrechtliches Verbot der Tabakwerbung', JZ 2007, 463; *Malferrari*, 'Der European Media Freedom Act als intra-vires-Rechtsakt', EuZW 2023, 49; *Marauhn*, '§ 4 Freedom of Expression, Freedom of Assembly and Association' in Ehlers /Becker (eds), European fundamental rights and freedoms, Berlin 2007, 97; *Meyer/Hölscheidt* (eds), Charta der Grundrechte der Europäischen Union, 5th edn, Baden-Baden 2019; *Meyer-Ladewig/Nettesheim/von Raumer*, EMRK Europäische Menschenrechtskonvention, 5th edn, Baden-Baden 2023; *Möstl*, 'Grenzen der Rechtsangleichung im europäischen Binnenmarkt – Kompetenzielle, grundfreiheitliche und grundrechtliche Schranken des Gemeinschaftsgesetzgebers', EuR 2002; *Muto*, 'European Media Freedom Act: la tutela europea della libertà dei media', MediaLaws – Rivista di diritto dei media 2022, 209; *J. Nguyen/Valadkhani/A. Nguyen/Wake*, 'Press Freedom and the Global Economy: The Cost of Slipping Backwards', Journalism Studies 2021, 339; *Nielsen*, Die Medienvielfalt als Aspekt der Wertesicherung der EU, Berlin 2019; *Ory*, 'Medienfreiheit – Der Entwurf eines European Media Freedom Act', ZRP 2023, 26; *Pampel*, Rechtsnatur und Rechtswirkungen horizontaler und vertikaler Leitlinien im reformierten europäischen Wettbewerbsrecht, Baden-Baden 2005; *Pechstein/Nowak/Häde* (eds), Frankfurter Kommentar zu EUV, GRC und AEUV, 2nd edn, Tübingen 2023; *Sata/Karolweski*, 'Caesarean politics in Hungary and Poland', East European Politics 2020, 206; *Schack*, Urheber- und Urhebervertragsrecht, 10th edn, Baden-Baden 2021; *Schwarze*, 'Die Kompetenzen der Europäischen Gemeinschaft auf dem Gebiet der Kultur', in Schwarze/Becker (eds), Geistiges Eigentum und Kultur im Spannungsfeld von nationaler Regelungskompetenz und europäischem Wirtschafts- und Wettbewerbsrecht, Baden-Baden 1998, p. 125; *Schwarze*, 'Grenzen der Harmonisierungskompetenz der EG im Presserecht – Zugleich eine Anmerkung zum zweiten Vorschlag der Kommission über eine Tabakwerbe-Richtlinie vom 30. Mai 2001', ZUM 2002, 89; *Schwarze/Becker/Hatje/Schoo* (eds), EU-Kommentar, 4th edn, Baden-Baden 2019; *Skouris*, 'Medienrechtliche Fragen in der Rechtsprechung des EuGH – Grundrechtliche Aspekte des Medienrechts und Charta der Grundrechte der EU', MMR 2011, 423; *Spindler/Schuster* (eds), Recht der elektronischen Medien, 4th edn, Munich 2019; *Stein*, 'Keine Europäische 'Verbots'-Gemeinschaft – das Urteil des EuGH über die Tabakwerbeverbot-Richtlinie', EWS 2001, 12; *Stock*, 'Medienfreiheit in der EU nur 'geachtet' (Art. 11 Grundrechtscharta) – Ein Plädoyer für Nachbesserungen im Verfassungskonvent', EuR 2002, 566; *Streinz* (ed), EUV/AEUV – Vertrag über die Europäische Union, Vertrag über die Arbeitsweise der Europäischen Union, Charta der Grundrechte der Europäischen Union, 3th edn, Munich 2018; *Sznajder*, European Media Freedom Act and its implications for both merger control and media pluralism: the Polish perspective, E.L. Rev. 49 (2024), 66; *Tettenborn*, 'Europäische Union: Rechtsrahmen für die Informationsgesellschaft', MMR 1998, 18; *Thomas*, 'Die Bindungswirkung von Mitteilungen, Bekanntmachungen und Leitlinien der EG-Kommission', EuR 2009, 423; *Ukrow*, 'Core problems of public international law regarding the regulation of the 'media sector' with respect to possible tensions with EU law' in Cole/Ukrow/Etteldorf (eds), On the allocation of competences between the European Union (EU) and its member states in the media sector – An analysis with particular consideration of measures concerning media pluralism, Baden-Baden 2021, p. 26; *Ukrow*, 'Framework for the allocation of competences under EU primary law' in Cole/Ukrow/Etteldorf (eds), On the allocation of competences between the European Union and its member states in the media sector – An analysis with particular consideration of measures concerning media pluralism, Baden-Baden 2021, p. 57; *Zeno-Zencovich*, The EU's Regulation of Speech: A Critical View, U.Pac.L.Rev. 55 (2024), 175.

On 16.9.2022, the Commission presented a proposal for the European Media Freedom Act (EMFA Proposal).[1] With this regulation the Commission wants to **reorganise the internal media market** (recital 2). This followed a decade-long debate on whether and how the Union should be allowed to take action in media law. After the Council adopted its negotiating mandates for the trilogue on 21.6.2023 (EMFA-EC)[2] and the European Parliament on 3.10.2023 (EMFA-EP)[3], an agreement was already reached in the trilogue procedure in December 2023. On 13 March 2024, the Parliament gave its final approval to the EMFA,[4] meaning that the final version is now available.[5] This chapter will provide an overview of the EMFA and the history of its origins. 1

A. Introduction and problem description

The European Union is not only growing together economically, but also politically. More and more decisions that affect our everyday lives are no longer made exclusively in the national capitals, but also in Brussels, Strasbourg, and Luxembourg. The Union's legislative procedure, which gives Member States an important role through the European Council, means that what happens in Germany or Spain is also relevant to the Danish or Polish population. And although there are still national parties in the European Parliament, they are grouped together in European political groups. 2

Nevertheless, political debates are still largely conducted on a national level,[6] which is certainly also due to the different languages of the European Union. Some media 3

[1] Proposal for a regulation establishing a common framework for media services in the internal market (European Media Freedom Act) and amending Directive 2010/13/EU, COM(2022), 457.

[2] EC 10954/23.

[3] EP P9_TA(2023)0336. A total of 448 MPs voted in favour, 102 against (with votes coming in particular from the ECR, ID and non-attached MEPs) and 75 abstained (in particular ECR, ID and The Left).

[4] There was an even larger majority than before. A total of 464 MPs voted in favour, 92 against (with votes coming in particular from the ECR, ID and non-attached MEPs) and 65 abstained.

[5] P9_TA(2024)0137.

[6] Dregelies in Kubis/Peifer/Raue/Stieper Europäische Persönlichkeitsrecht(e)? – Das Spannungsfeld von Persönlichkeitsschutz sowie Meinungs- und Pressefreiheit auf Ebene der EU, p. 951 (952). It is deduced from this that no Union regulation is required due to this lack of a Union-wide market for opinions; Schwarze ZUM 2002, 89 (95); Hain AfP 2007, 527 (531). In contrast, the ECJ already stated in 2006 that the cross-border distribution of newspapers is not an exception and that distribution via the internet extends cross-border perception even further, ECJ 12.12.2006 – case C-380/03, ECLI:EU:C:2006:772 para. 54 – Germany v Parliament and Council; agreeing Gundel EuR 2007, 251 (255); Leible GPR (2007), 1 (with reference to railway station kiosks). The fact that foreign media content is actually perceived is shown by the problems of personality rights that arise in the international civil procedure law, see

are trying to close the gap by targeting the EU as a whole rather than the people of a particular Member State.[7] In addition, media products have always been and continue to be **consumed across borders.**[8] Improved foreign language skills, AI-based translation tools, internal EU migration and the internet are likely to lead to media being consumed more frequently not only in their country of origin. However, such developments can be hindered by different media law regulations, but also by the different levels of rights relating to personality in the Member States.[9] It is desirable for the European project that a **framework** is created **to enable a European debate.**[10]

4 Irrespective of this, some media groups are also present in other Member States with their own offerings, such as Axel Springer Verlag with its Polish subsidiary company Ringier Axel Springer Polska and the newspapers Fakt, Newsweek Polska and numerous other publications. This is probably also due to the media antitrust laws of the Member States, which in some cases prevent further takeovers in their own Member State, with the result that companies move to other Member States.[11] This can result in media concentrations not only at national level, but throughout the EU.

5 It should therefore be noted that media are already consumed across borders and that media companies are economically operating in other Member States.

B. Danger for the media

I. The special significance of media

6 Media are not economic goods like any other.[12] They enjoy special protection under fundamental rights (Art. 11(2) CFR, Art. 10 ECHR), which goes beyond the freedom to conduct a business (Art. 16 CFR), as well as special (economic)[13] privileges.[14] This spe-

Dregelies in Kubis/Peifer/Raue/Stieper Europäische Persönlichkeitsrecht(e)? – Das Spannungsfeld von Persönlichkeitsschutz sowie Meinungs- und Pressefreiheit auf Ebene der EU, p. 951 (955 et seqq.).

[7] For example, eureporter.co, politico.eu, euractive.com or Euronews, which is subsidised by the EU Commission. In addition, there are Member States with the same official languages such as Germany and Austria (see for example ECJ 26.6.1997 – case C-368/95, ECLI:EU:C:1997:325 para. 2 – Vereinigte Familiapress Zeitungsverlags- und vertriebs GmbH v Bauer Verlag) or Ireland and Malta as well as closely connected Member States such as the Scandinavian countries.

[8] See for example the facts of ECJ 7.3.1995 – case C-68/93, ECLI:EU:C:1995:61 – Shevill and Others v Presse Alliance; ECJ 25.10.2011 – joined cases C-509/09 and C-161/10, ECLI:EU:C:2011:685 – eDate Advertising and Others; ECJ 17.6.2021 – case C-800/19, ECLI:EU:C:2021:489 – Mittelbayerischer Verlag. See also Dregelies in Kubis/Peifer/Raue/Stieper Europäische Persönlichkeitsrecht(e)? – Das Spannungsfeld von Persönlichkeitsschutz sowie Meinungs- und Pressefreiheit auf Ebene der EU, p. 951 (955 et seqq.).

[9] Dregelies in Kubis/Peifer/Raue/Stieper Europäische Persönlichkeitsrecht(e)? – Das Spannungsfeld von Persönlichkeitsschutz sowie Meinungs- und Pressefreiheit auf Ebene der EU, p. 951 (952).

[10] Dregelies in Kubis/Peifer/Raue/Stieper Europäische Persönlichkeitsrecht(e)? – Das Spannungsfeld von Persönlichkeitsschutz sowie Meinungs- und Pressefreiheit auf Ebene der EU, p. 951 et seqq.

[11] Knodel Medien und Europa, p. 213. MediaForEurope (formerly Mediaset S.p.A.) is not only the market leader in Italy and Spain, but has also increased its stake in the German ProSiebenSat.1 Media to over 25 per cent (cf. https://www.spiegel.de/wirtschaft/silvio-berlusconi-medienaufsicht-prueft-beteiligung-an-prosieben-a-d40189b5-53cd-4a30-9bdc-bcf5d12c656d (last accessed: 25.06.2024)). AxelSpringer AG, on the other hand, became increasingly active in foreign markets after the takeover of ProSiebenSat. 1 Media was prohibited, see for example Gounalakis/Zagouras JZ 2008, 652 (654 fn. 31).

[12] Also Sznajder E.L. Rev. 49 (2024), 66 (67); dissenting view Kraetzig NJW 2013, 1485 mn. 8.

[13] This enables the EU to charge reduced VAT rates for books, newspapers, and magazines. Extended to electronic publications by Directive (EU) 2018/1713.

[14] Thus, the protection of journalistic sources is subject to Art. 10 ECHR, ECtHR 27.3.1996 – App. No. 17488/90 para. 46 – Goodwin v the United Kingdom; Glocke, p. 162 et seq. and thus also Art. 11 CFR

cial treatment is based on the **political**[15] **and cultural**[16] **importance** of the media. Without functioning media, no democracy can work and it is difficult to disseminate cultural content.[17] The major internet platforms have created media distribution services that can have an impact on political debates which should not be underestimated. Declining circulations and the associated lower advertising revenues as well as rising paper prices are putting newspapers under pressure[18] and can lead to their insolvency or takeovers.

7 The **influence** that the media can have **on the economy** should also not be underestimated: A negative article about a company can limit its economic opportunities; reporting on corruption can end the company's market influence. Restrictions on press freedom have a proven negative impact on economic growth.[19]

II. Concrete threat to media freedom and pluralism

8 Media diversity and freedom can be jeopardised by various means. The most obvious are **direct attacks** to undermine the control function. The media have always been exposed to attacks on their freedom due to their function as a 'watchdog'[20] and as a democratic space for debate. Direct attacks on journalists are particularly alarming: in recent years, journalists have repeatedly paid for their work with their lives, particularly in connection with corruption.[21]

9 Less obvious, but also a direct attack, are attempts to reduce media plurality **by taking over media companies** or supporting them with state funding. However, media plurality can also be undermined by the fact that a changing market environment – fewer subscriptions and therefore a drop in advertising revenue – has led to many companies no longer being viable and therefore disappearing completely from the market or being bought up. Within the EU, **insufficient market plurality** is currently seen as the greatest threat.[22] This finding is not new, as the danger of (cross-border) media concentration has been discussed for some time.[23] However, the attempt to regulate media concentration throughout the EU by means of a directive failed in 1997.[24]

(Glocke, p. 194). Art. 85 GDPR also opens up the possibility for Member States to provide for exceptions to data protection for journalistic work (media privilege).

15 When a national media market is EU, Bayer, 'Missing Freedom Act' (Verfassungsblog, 15.9.2022) <https://verfassungsblog.de/missing-freedom-act/> (last accessed: 25.06.2024).

16 Thus, mass media fall under the concept of culture in Art. 167 TFEU, Ferreau in Spindler/Schuster Art. 167 TFEU mn. 4. Media transport culture and thus make it accessible to society in the first place and they create identity by disseminating certain content, Knodel Medien und Europa, p. 32 et seq.

17 See rec. 1a EMFA-EP (P9_TA(2023)0336, Amendment 2).

18 For the German market, Keller/Eggert Zur wirtschaftlichen Lage der deutschen Zeitungen 2023, p. 3. Even the increase in sales on the digital market is not enough to compensate for the losses, Keller/Eggert, Zur wirtschaftlichen Lage der deutschen Zeitungen 2023, p. 5.

19 J. Nguyen/Valadkhani/A. Nguyen/Wake Journalism Studies 2021, 399 (410 et seq.).

20 The role of the 'public watchdog' in the interpretation of Art. 10 ECHR is repeatedly emphasised by the ECtHR, for example ECtHR 20.5.1999 – App. No. 21980/93 para. 59, 68 – Bladet Tromsø and Stensaas v Norway; 28.06.2018 – App. No. 60798/10 and 65599/10 para. 89 – M.L. and W.W. v Germany.

21 One example is the murder of Jan Kuciak, Hajdari, 'Slovak tycoon Marián Kočner acquitted again over killing of journalist Ján Kuciak' (Euronews, 19.5.2023) <https://www.euronews.com/2023/05/19/slovak-tycoon-marian-kocner-acquitted-for-the-killing-of-journalist-jan-kuciak> (last accessed: 25.06.2024).

22 Bleyer-Simon/Brogi/Carlini/Da Costa Leite Borges/Nenadić/Palmer/Parcu/Trevisan/Verza/Žuffová Monitoring Media Pluarlism In The Digital Era, p. 156.

23 See for example the various resolutions of the EP, e.g. of 15.02.1990, OJ 1990 C 68/137 et seq., of 16.09.1992, OJ 1992 C 284/44 et seq.; of 27.10.1994, OJ 1994 C 323, 157 (see Brühann ZUM 1993, 600 et seq.); of 15.06.1995, OJ 1995 C 166, 133; of 20.11.2002, OJ 2004 C 25E, 205 et seq.; of 25.09.2008, OJ 2010 C 8E, 85 et seq. From academia, for example Gounalakis/Zagouras JZ 2008, 652 (654).

24 Gounalakis/Zagouras JZ 2008, 652 (655).

III. Social media platforms and the media

10 **Platforms** such as Instagram, X and Facebook are of great importance for media companies to disseminate their information, but also for journalists to obtain information. Due to their reach and the algorithms used, certain content is perceived more strongly, and the platforms thus have an influence on the political debate.[25] Therefore, it is often not a conscious decision of the individual which media content they consume – it is rather what social media presents to them.[26] The platforms also benefit from the content of the media services, as these attract users and thus generate additional advertising revenue. Advertising revenue that the media lack. The market power and therefore the ability of platforms to set their own rules has been analysed in many ways.[27] Elon Musk in particular blocked journalists he did not like on X[28] as well as documentaries[29]. All of this has an influence on media plurality that should not be underestimated.

IV. The special case of Hungary and Poland

11 The development in **Hungary** is particularly **drastic**.[30] Media freedom has been gradually eroded by Orbán's second government since 2010: while Hungary was still ranked 23rd in 'Reporters Without Borders' global press freedom rankings in 2010, it was only 72nd in 2023.[31] The Freedom House Study classifies Hungary as only 'partly free' and ranks the country as one of the worst decliners of the last ten years.[32] This is because Orbán's allies have taken over important regional and national newspapers,[33] and a new media law has given the government de facto power over the media.[34] However, dependencies can also arise from the fact that state advertising contracts are only awarded to pro-government media.[35] Even in the first Orbán government, the official and publicly declared aim was to end the alleged 'discrimination against the right-wing press' with state money.[36] State advertising funds (especially from the state lottery company) have since been redirected to the Fidez press.[37] This has made fair competition impossible and has distorted the media market.[38] As a result, the **Hungarian media** now **serve**

[25] Gamito Computer Law & Security Review 48 (2023) 105799, 1 (1 et seq.).

[26] Sznajder E.L. Rev. 49 (2024), 66 (75).

[27] Gamito Computer Law & Security Review 48 (2023) 105799, 1 (1 et seqq.) (with further references).

[28] Taylor, 'Elon Musk reinstates Twitter accounts of suspended journalists' (The Guardian, 17.12.2022) <https://www.theguardian.com/technology/2022/dec/17/elon-musk-reinstates-twitter-accounts-of-suspended-journalist> (last accessed: 25.06.2024).

[29] Reuters, 'Musk says unaware why Twitter India pulled posts on BBC documentary critical of Modi' (Reuters, 12.04.2023) <https://www.reuters.com/world/india/musk-says-unaware-why-twitter-india-pulled-posts-bbc-documentary-critical-modi-2023-04-12/> (last accessed: 25.06.2024).

[30] For more details, see Holtz-Bacha, European Journal of Communication 2023, 1 (2 et seqq.); European Commission, 'Rule of Law Report 2023, Hungary', SWD/2023/817, p. 27 et seqq.

[31] <https://rsf.org/en/index?year=2010> and < https://rsf.org/en/index?year=2023> (last accessed: 25.06.2024).

[32] Freedom House, Freedom In The World 2023, p. 12.

[33] Bakke/Sitter Perspectives on Politics 2020, 22 (26).

[34] Sata/Karolewski East European Politics 2020, 206 (212); Holtz-Bacha European Journal of Communication 2023, 1 (2).

[35] Bakke/Sitter Perspectives on Politics 2020, 22 (25).

[36] Bátorfy/Urbán East European Politics 2020, 44 (49).

[37] Bátorfy/Urbán East European Politics 2020, 44 (49).

[38] Bátorfy/Urbán East European Politics 2020, 44 (60 et seq.).

Orbán and his Fidez.[39] Even pressure from the Commission has not yet achieved any improvements in the area of media freedom.[40]

Something similar was[41] observed in **Poland**. The PiS government in Poland also tried to reduce the press landscape's plurality[42] but failed because the media are partly in foreign hands.[43] Pressure is also exerted by the fact that broadcasting licences are only renewed after a considerable delay.[44] This unfair – politically motivated – unequal treatment of individual media companies causes economic advantages for some companies. Nevertheless, at least small improvements can be recognised in Poland,[45] even if the situation remains highly problematic overall. After the last parliamentary elections in October 2023, however, the motto 'Jeszcze Polska nie zginęła'[46] ('Poland is not yet lost') will probably apply again. 12

V. Fundamental rights and the state's duty to protect

Media and media professionals are protected by fundamental rights, in particular by **Art. 10 ECHR** and **Art. 11 CFR**. Art. 10 ECHR not only constitutes to a right of defence against state interference, but also a **state duty to protect.**[47] Thus, there is a positive obligation to protect the media and media professionals from violence[48] and to set a framework so that 'a range of opinion and comment' is accessible[49]. This is because freedom of opinion is jeopardised if private or state actors obtain a dominant position over the media and are thus able to influence editorial work.[50] Despite Art. 6(2)(1) TFEU, the EU has not yet acceded to the ECHR. Art. 6(1)(2) TFEU also stipulates that accession does not extend the competences of the Union.[51] The positive obligations therefore do not 13

39 Sata/Karolewski East European Politics 2020, 206 (212).

40 European Commission, 'Rule of Law Report 2023, Hungary', SWD/2023/817, p. 1, 27 et seqq.

41 By voting out the PiS government in October 2023, there is hope that Poland will once again make progress in the area of press freedom.

42 Sata/Karolewski East European Politics 36 (2020), 206 (212), see also Sznajder E.L. Rev. 49 (2024), 66 (66).

43 Bakke/Sitter Perspectives on Politics 20 (2020), 22 (26).

44 Wójcik, 'EMFA and its Uphill Battle for Media Freedom and Democracy in the EU' (Verfassungsblog, 14.06.2023) <https://verfassungsblog.de/emfa-and-its-uphill-battle-for-media-freedom-and-democracy-in-the-eu/> (last accessed: 25.06.2024); Sznajder E.L. Rev. 49 (2024), 66 (76). See also European Commission, 'Rule of Law report, 2023, Poland', SWD/2023/821, p. 2, which does not yet see any improvements here.

45 For example, on the transparency of ownership structures, European Commission, 'Rule of Law report, 2023, Poland', SWD/2023/821, p. 25.

46 First sentence of the Polish national anthem.

47 Cornils in BeckOK InfoMedienR Art. 10 EMRK mn. 11; Daiber in Meyer-Ladewig/Nettesheim/von Raumer Art. 10 EMRK mn. 69; Mensching in Karpenstein/Mayer Art. 10 EMRK mn. 12; Ukrow, Core problems, p. 265, 314; Marauhn, § 4 Freedom of Expression, Freedom of Assembly and Association, p. 97 mn. 26.

48 ECtHR 16.03.2000 – App. No. 23144/93 para. 42 et seq. – Özgür Gündem v Turkey; ECtHR 14.09.2010 – App. No. 2668/07 para. 137 et seq. – Dink v Turkey; ECtHR 30.01.2023 – App. No. 24738/19 para. 78 ('establishing an effective system for the protection of journalists') – Gaši and others v Serbia.

49 ECtHR 17.9.2009 – App. No. 13936/02 para. 100 – Manole and others v Moldova; ECtHR 7.6.2012 – App. No. 38433/09 para. 134 ('put in place an appropriate legislative and administrative framework to guarantee effective pluralism') – Centro Europa 7 S.R.L. and Di Stefano v Italy.

50 ECtHR 17.9.2009 – App. No. 13936/02 para. 98 – Manole and others v Moldova.

51 So-called 'Kompetenzklausel' [engl. competence clause] (Pache in Frankfurter Kommentar Art. 6 TFEU mn. 36) or 'Begrenzungsklausel' [engl. limitation clause] (Hatje in Schwarze/Becker/Hatje/Schoo Art. 6 TFEU mn. 7), which is also referred to as a 'Angstklausel' [engl. fear clause] of the Member States before an active fundamental rights policy; Kingreen in Calliess/Ruffert Art. 6 TFEU mn. 13.

bind the EU if it lacks the competence.[52] This is the case in media law, meaning that the protection rights derived by the ECtHR from the ECHR do not apply to the Union itself.[53] When legislating, however, the Union legislator must take the ECHR into account.

14 Art. 11 CFR is intended by the legislator to correspond to Art. 10 ECHR.[54] As an independent fundamental right, Art. 11(2) CFR includes respect for media freedom and its plurality. The legislator refers to the ECJ case Stichting Collectieve Antennevoorziening Gouda v Commissariaat voor de Media[55] and the Television without Frontiers Directive 89/552/EWG.[56] This suggests an economically liberal understanding of Art. 11(2) CFR, as the aim of the Television without Frontiers Directive 89/552/EWG was to enable the free movement of services in the Member States.[57] However, the ECJ ruled in the aforementioned judgement that the protection of media pluralism could, in principle, be a reason to restrict the freedom of services.[58] Even if independent protection rights can be derived from Art. 11 CFR, these do not bind the Union because of a lack of competence.[59]

C. Union competence to enact the EMFA

15 The Commission bases the EMFA on **Art. 114 TFEU**. Poland, Germany, Austria, and Hungary criticised the chosen legal basis in the Council.[60] In the EP, the ID[61] and ECR[62] groups in particular expressed loud doubts. In addition, some German academics[63] and

52 Schwerdtfeger in Meyer/Hölscheidt Art. 51 CFR mn. 72 et seqq.; Cremer EuGRZ 2011, 545 (547).

53 Cornils in BeckOK InfoMedienR Art. 11 CFR mn. 28 et seq.; Kingreen in Calliess/Ruffert Art. 51 CFR mn. 35 points out that due to the lack of competence of the EU, no positive duty to protect has yet been established by the ECJ for any fundamental right.

54 Explanations relating to the Charter of Fundamental Rights from 14.12.2007 (2007/C 302/02), C303/21.

55 ECJ 25.7.1991 – case C-288/89, ECLI:EU:C:1991:157 – Stichting Collectieve Antennevoorziening Gouda/Commissariaat voor de Media.

56 Explanations relating to the Charter of Fundamental Rights from 14.12.2007 (2007/C 302/02), C303/21.

57 In this sense Bernsdorff in Meyer/Hölscheidt Art. 11 CFR mn. 17, who also considers this to be 'nicht zwingend' [engl. 'not mandatory'].

58 ECJ 25.7.1991 – case C-288/89, ECLI:EU:C:1991:157 para. 23 – Stichting Collectieve Antennevoorziening Gouda/Commissariaat voor de Media.

59 Cornils in BeckOK InfoMedienR Art. 11 CFR mn. 29; Bernsdorff in Meyer/Hölscheidt Art. 11 CFR mn. 20 (on para. 2).

60 Deutsche Ständige Vertretung EU, Diplomatische Korrespondenz from 19.4.2023 (BRUEEU_2023-04-19_74444), p. 2.

61 See the speech by Catherine Griset (France, Rassemblement National) on behalf of the ID ('D'abord, parce que la Commission prend appui sur l'argument faux qu'il existe un marché européen des médias.'), <https://www.europarl.europa.eu/doceo/document/CRE-9-2023-10-03-ITM-005_DE.html> (last accessed: 25.06.2024).

62 See the speech by Elżbieta Kruk (Poland PIS, member of the Rada Mediów Narodowych, the National Media Council) on behalf of the ECR ('Narusza tym samym postanowienia Traktatu o funkcjonowaniu Unii Europejskiej wskazanego jako podstawa prawna.'), <https://www.europarl.europa.eu/doceo/document/CRE-9-2023-10-03-ITM-005_DE.html> (last accessed: 25.06.2024).

63 Kraetzig NJW 2023, 1485 mn. 7 et seq.; Etteldorf, Why the Words 'But' and 'However' Determine the EMFA's Legal Basis (Verfassungsblog, 13.6.2023) (last accessed 25.06.24); and for the media industry Beaujean/Oelke/Wierny MMR 2023, 11 et seq.; also doubting Ory ZRP 2023, 26 (28 et seq.); Klumpp/Witte Paz, AfP 2024, 101 mn. 9. Dissenting view, Malferrari EuZW 2023, 49 (49 et seq.); R. Dörr/Weber AfP 2023, 383 mn. 14 et seqq. (for the public service media providers). Previously doubting that a competence for harmonisation in 'the area of media diversity protection' can be derived from Art. 114 TFEU, Ukrow, Framework, p. 57 (100).

the German Bundesrat (Federal Council)[64] doubted that Art. 114 TFEU could be used as a legal basis.

I. Criticising the legal basis – a German tradition

Criticism, particularly from Germany, is not new.[65] The German federal states had particularly opposed the Television without Frontiers Directive 89/552/EWG,[66] but also the attempts to issue a Directive on Media Concentration[67]. The Germans were also critical of legal acts that pursued purposes other than the harmonisation of the internal market and had an impact on the media sector, such as the Tobacco Advertising Directive 2003/33/EC. Back in 1993, Eberle stated the following about the German position on European media law: 'While the EC's competence under broadcasting law was constantly disputed from a German perspective, the EC Commission made use of it'.[68] 16

II. The reference to Art. 167 TFEU

The fact that Art. 114 TFEU is a sufficient legal basis is disputed, in particular with reference to Art. 167 TFEU.[69] It is claimed that in order to base the EMFA on Art. 114 TFEU, the '**main focus**' ('*Schwerpunkt*') of the regulation must be on the economic aspect of the media,[70] which is not the case with the EMFA.[71] Thus, some standards of the EMFA 'do not exclusively serve to promote the internal market'[72], rather, most of the standards are 'media policy'[73] and thus fall within the competence of the Member States.[74] The German Bundesrat (Federal Council) is also of the opinion that the press and radio concern primarily local and regional, but not cross-border issues, and therefore do not require uniform EU regulation.[75] At the beginning of the legislative process, the Regulatory Scrutiny Board also called on the Commission to clarify why Art. 114 TFEU grants a competence and for greater respect for the **principle of subsidiarity**.[76] 17

---

64 BR-Drs. 514/22 (B).

65 The Hungarian and Polish criticism is not surprising either, as the EMFA is directed precisely against their methods of undermining media freedom.

66 BR-Drs. 127/88. See Knothe AfP 2023, 377.

67 BR-Drs. 77/93 on the Green Paper Pluralism and media concentration in the internal market – an assessment of the need for Community action, COM (92) 480 final from 23.12.1992. On the other hand, Brühann ZUM 1993, 600 (604), considers a media concentration rule at Union level to be permissible.

68 Eberle in FS Thieme, p. 939 = AfP 1993, 422 ('Während aus deutscher Sicht die rundfunkrechtliche Kompetenz der EG beständig bestritten wurde, hat die EG-Kommission von ihr Gebrauch gemacht').

69 Kraetzig NJW 2023, 1485 mn. 7 et seq.; Etteldorf, Why the Words 'But' and 'However' Determine the EMFA's Legal Basis (Verfassungsblog, 13.6.2023) <https://verfassungsblog.de/why-the-words-but-and-however-determine-the-emfas-legal-basis/> (last accessed: 25.06.2024); and for the media industry Beaujean/Oelke/Wierny MMR 2023, 11 (11 et seq.). Also doubting Ory ZRP 2023, 26 (28 et seq.).

70 Kraetzig NJW 2023, 1485 mn. 8. It is also sometimes claimed that media regulation must not be 'the focus', for example Ukrow, Framework, p. 57 (106) with reference to ECJ 17.3.1993 – case C-155/91, ECLI:EU:C:1993:98 para. 20 – Commission v Council, whereby this decision concerns the delimitation of various possible competence norms.

71 Beaujean/Oelke/Wierny MMR 2023, 11 (15). Previously, Knodel Medien und Europa, p. 219 et seq., with the same arguments against a directive on media concentration in general.

72 'nicht ausschließlich der Förderung des Binnenmarkts'.

73 'medienpolitisch'.

74 Beaujean/Oelke/Wierny MMR 2023, 11 (15).

75 BR-Drs. 514/22 (B), p. 2.

76 Regulatory Scrutiny Board, SEC/2022/322 final, 27.7.2022, p. 8.

Following adjustments by the Commission, however, the Board gave the green light.[77] There also seems to be less doubt in many Member States that Art. 114 TFEU can serve as a basis for the Union`s competences.[78] The Legal Service of the Council of the European Union also came to the conclusion that the Commission could rely on Art. 114 TFEU.[79]

III. No main focus necessary

1. Decisive factor

18 Art. 114 TFEU does **not require** – as it is sometimes claimed[80] – that internal market harmonisation must be the **main focus** (‘*Schwerpunkt*’) of the regulation,[81] nor does the case law of the ECJ provide any indications of this:[82] rather, the ECJ has established that Art. 114 TFEU can be applied as an authorising basis, even if another regulatory purpose is the ‘decisive factor’.[83] It is only inadmissible to rely on Art. 114 TFEU in order to circumvent the explicit prohibitions on harmonisation.[84]

---

[77] Regulatory Scrutiny Board, SEC/2022/322 final, 27.7.2022, p. 1.

[78] This is for example the case in Italy: Italian Chamber of Deputies Opinion of 20 July 2023 on the EMFA-E, p. 5 <https://connectfolx.europarl.europa.eu/connefof/app/exp/COM(2022)0457> (last accessed: 25.06.2024); Muto MediaLaws – Rivista di diritto dei media 2022, 209 (225 et seq.); Gamito Computer Law & Security Review 48 (2023) 105799, 1 (7 et seqq.); probably also Citino MediaLaws – Rivista di diritto dei media 2022, 232 (250 et seq.); dissenting opinion Zeno-Zencovich, U.Pac.L.Rev. 55 (2024), 175 (180). Also Rucz/Irion/Senftleben: Contribution to the public consultation on the European Media Freedom Act (IViR 2022), <https://www.ivir.nl/publicaties/download/Position-paper-European-Media-Freedom-Act-consultation-1.pdf>, p. 7 (Netherlands) (last accessed: 25.06.2024). Critically, however, Sznajder E.L. Rev. 49 (2024), 66 (70) (Poland); Netherlands Senate, Opinion of 20 December 2022 on the EMFA-E, p. 1. Czech Senate, Irish House of the Oireachtas and the Portuguese Parliament do not problematise the basis of competence. In the EP, the ID and ECR groups in particular doubted the Union's competence, see above → fn. 61 et seq. In addition to Germany, Poland, Hungary and Austria questioned the competence in the Council (→ fn. 60).

[79] Opinion of the Legal Service of the Council of the European Union from 4.4.2023, 8089/23.

[80] For example, Kraetzig NJW 2023, 1485 mn. 8. It is also sometimes claimed that media regulation must not be ‘the focus’, for example Ukrow, Framework, p. 57 (106) with reference to ECJ 17 March 1993 – case C-155/91, ECLI:EU:C:1993:98 para. 20 – Commission v Council, whereby this decision concerns the delimitation of various possible competence norms.

[81] AG Fennelly 15.6.2000 – C-376/98 para. 66 – Germany v European Parliament and Council; Möstl EuR 2002, 318 (327 et seq.); Leible GPR 2007, 1.

[82] Tietje in Grabitz/Hilf/Nettesheim Art. 114 TFEU mn. 125 et seqq.; Hillgruber Die Verwirklichung des Binnenmarktes durch Rechtsangleichung – Gemeinschaftsziel und -kompetenz ohne Grenzen, p. 597 (608); Gundel EuR 2007, 251 (253). Criticising the case law of the ECJ: Stein EWS 2001, 12 (15) (sympathising with the 'main focus' criterion); Maierhöfer JZ 2007, 463 (465) (claiming that case law contradicts the wording of the EC Treaty); Hain AfP 2007, 527 (533).

[83] ECJ 5.10.2000 – case C-376/98, ECLI:EU:C:2000:544 para. 88 – Germany v Parliament and Council; ECJ 12.12.2006 – case C-380/03 para. 92 – Germany v Parliament and Council; ECJ 10.2.2002 – case C-491/01, ECLI:EU:C:2002:741 para. 62 – The Queen v ex parte British American Tobacco (Investments) Ltd and Imperial Tobacco Ltd; ECJ 14.12.2004 – case C-434/02, ECLI:EU:C:2004:800 para. 32 – Arnold André GmbH & Co. KG v. Landrat des Kreises Herford; ECJ 12.7.2005 – case C-154/04, ECLI:EU:C:2005:449 para. 30 – Alliance for Natural Health and Others; ECJ 4.5.2016 – case C-547/14, ECLI:EU:C:2016:325 para. 60 – Philip Morris Brands SARL and Others (all decisions on health protection); ECJ 3.12.2019 – case C-482/17, ECLI:EU:C:2019:1035 para. 36 – Czech Republic v Parliament and Council. If, on the other hand, several bases of competence are available, recourse to Art. 114 TFEU is inadmissible if the legal act only has a ‘incidental effect’ on harmonisation and the ‘main object’ is another; ECJ 17.3.1993 – case C-155/91, ECLI:EU:C:1993:98 para. 19 et seq. – Commission of the European Communities v Council of the European Communities; Tietje in Grabitz/Hilf/Nettesheim Art. 114 TFEU mn. 125 on this ‘main focus’ criterion and against a transfer to vertical competence disputes.

[84] ECJ 5.10.2000 – case C-376/98, ECLI:EU:C:2000:544 para. 79 – Germany v Parliament and Council; ECJ 10.2.2002 – case C-491/01, ECLI:EU:C:2002:741 para. 190 – British American Tobacco (Investments)

2. Prohibition of harmonisation

19 As the ECJ rulings cited relate to health protection, there are doubts as to whether the considerations can also be applied to media law[85] and reference is made to the 'prohibition of harmonisation' in Art. 167(5) TFEU[86]. However, the ECJ has since clarified its case law to the effect that the legislator can also rely on Art. 114 TFEU if one of the interests mentioned in Art. 114(3) TFEU is a **decisive factor.**[87] It is true that only health, safety, environmental and consumer protection are mentioned there, but not the protection of the media. However, the ECJ emphasises elsewhere that the pluralism of the media 'undoubtedly constitutes a legitimate aim in the general interest [...] the importance of which in a democratic and pluralistic society must be stressed in particular'.[88]

20 The '**prohibition of harmonisation**' in Art. 167(5) TFEU should also not be overrated. This only means that the EU has no original competence to harmonise the cultural area and refers to the permissible support measures of Art. 167.[89] If cultural areas are also harmonised, Art. 167(5) TFEU does not prevent this.[90] The aim of the Article is to **prevent cultural standardisation** and to **support the cultures** of the Member States.[91] However, the EMFA is not aimed at cultural harmonisation – on the contrary: by attempting to maintain plurality in the media market and to protect the work of journalists and other media professionals, the culture of the Member States is protected and supported. Nevertheless, it follows from Art. 167(4) and (5) TFEU that the Union legislator must take particular care to respect the cultural autonomy of the Member States when adopting harmonisation measures.[92]

3. Considerations of fundamental rights

21 According to Art. 11(2) CFR, the freedom of the media and its plurality must be respected. However, the legislative history and Art. 51(2) CFR cast doubt on whether Art. 11(2) CFR can be cited as an argument. The Fundamental Rights Convention decided – at Germany's insistence – against the wording 'ensure' and in favour of 'respected' in order to prevent the EU from gaining additional powers.[93] Even then, it was warned – particularly in view of the situation in Italy and Berlusconi's media group – that quality

Ltd. and Imperial Tobacco Ltd.; Hillgruber Die Verwirklichung des Binnenmarktes durch Rechtsangleichung – Gemeinschaftsziel und -kompetenz ohne Grenzen, p. 597 (608); Gundel EuR 2007, 251 (253).

85 Hain AfP 2007, 527 (533). Expressly against this is Nielsen, p. 83.

86 Hain AfP 2007, 527 (533). In general on the prohibition of harmonisation in the cultural area, Niedobitek in Streinz Art. 167 TFEU mn. 55; Fechner in von der Groeben/Schwarze/Hatje Art. 167 TFEU mn. 42; Ukrow/Ress in Grabitz/Hilf/Nettesheim Art. 167 TFEU mn. 179.

87 ECJ 3.12.2019 – case C-482/17, ECLI:EU:C:2019:1035 para. 36 – Czech Republic v Parliament and Council.

88 ECJ 22.1.2013 – case C-283/11, ECLI:EU:C:2013:28 para. 52 – Sky Österreich v Österreichischer Rundfunk; ECJ 3.9.2020 – case C-719/18, ECLI:EU:C:2020:627 para. 57 – Vivendi v Autorità per le Garanzie nelle Comunicazioni. Previously referred to as 'one of the fundamental pillars of a democratic society', ECJ 13 December 2001 – case C-340/00 P, ECLI:EU:C:2001:701 para. 18 – Commission v Cwik.

89 Schwarze, Kompetenz der EG, p. 125 (152).

90 Fechner in von der Groeben/Schwarze/Hatje Art. 167 TFEU mn. 43; Nielsen Die Medienvielfalt als Aspekt der Wertesicherung der EU, p. 77 et seq.; Henke Kulturelle Integration in der Europäischen Union unter dem europäischen Urheberrecht, p. 159 (162).

91 Ukrow/Ress in Grabitz/Hilf/Nettesheim Art. 167 TFEU mn. 180a; Ukrow, Framework, p. 57 (105 et seq.); Hain AfP 2007, 527 (533).

92 Schwarze, Kompetenz der EG, p. 125 (152) ('Gebot der kulturellen Rücksichtnahme' [engl. imperative of cultural consideration). Cf. Ukrow, Framework, p. 57 (106). Dissenting view probably Henke Kulturelle Integration in der Europäischen Union unter dem europäischen Urheberrecht, p. 159 (162) ('keine inhaltliche Begrenzung' [engl. no substantive limitation]).

93 Stock EuR 2002, 566 (575); Skouris MMR 2011, 423 (426); Streinz in Streinz Art. 11 CFR mn. 17.

assurance measures and measures to protect the media market might be needed.[94] As Art. 51(2) CFR clarifies that the CFR should not result in an extension of competences, the exact wording of Art. 11(2) CFR is irrelevant.[95] Nor does it follow from the wording of Art. 11(2) CFR that the EU may not intervene in the media law of the Member States.[96]

22 Thus, Art. 11(2) CFR does not justify an extension of competences but supports the assumption that the protection of the freedom of the media and its plurality is a decisive factor that may be pursued in the harmonisation of the internal market.

4. The role of the ECJ

23 Finally, a practical argument should not be underestimated: so far, the ECJ has not attracted attention by stopping the harmonisation of the EU.[97] This may be criticized, however, it is highly doubtful that the ECJ will exercise restraint at present, particularly in light of the significant risks that media freedom and the European democracy face. Especially as it has increasingly emphasised the particular importance of media plurality.[98]

5. Conclusion

24 As the protection of the media's freedom and its plurality is a particular value in the Union, the **Union can pursue this protection** as a decisive factor alongside internal market harmonisation. Politically, the Member States have cleared the way. After initial criticism, Germany also agreed to the EMFA and thus accepted that it can be based on Art. 114 TFEU. However, it follows from Art. 167 TFEU that the Union must proceed with restraint and take particular account of the Member States' specific characteristics.

D. Regulatory objective of the EMFA

25 According to Art. 1(1) EMFA, common rules are to be created for the proper functioning of the internal media market while '**safeguarding the independence and pluralism of media services**' (French: *tout en préservant l'indépendance et le pluralisme des services de médias*; German: *unter Wahrung der Unabhängigkeit und des Pluralismus von Mediendiensten*). The European legislator emphasises the particular significance of the media 'unique role in the internal market' (French: *unique dans le marché intérieur*; German: *einzigartige Rolle im Binnenmarkt*), which are an important source of information and means to disseminate opinions, recital 1 EMFA. In the trilogue procedure, the reference to the significance of the media within the process of the formation of public opin-

[94] Stock EuR 2002, 566 (575).

[95] Calliess in Calliess/Ruffert Art. 11 CFR mn. 26; Glocke Publizistischer Quellenschutz im deutschen und europäischen Recht, p. 183. See also Bernsdorff in Meyer/Hölscheidt Art. 11 CFR mn. 20.

[96] Knecht in Schwarze Art. 11 CFR mn. 10.

[97] For example, Hillgruber Die Verwirklichung des Binnenmarktes durch Rechtsangleichung – Gemeinschaftsziel und -kompetenz ohne Grenzen, p. 597 (607), recalling earlier objections that the ECJ sees itself as a motor of integration; critical of this development Jahn NJW 2008, 1788 (1788 et seq.) 'Europarichter überziehen ihre Kompetenzen' [engl. European judges exceed their competences]). Exemplary is the action of the ECJ in copyright law: Jotzo ZGE 2017, 447 (447 et seq.) 'Der EuGH als Interimsnormgeber im digitalen Urheberrecht' [engl. The ECJ as interim legislator in digital copyright law]). Critical Schack, mn. 160 (criticising 'Kompetenzüberschreitung' [engl. 'exceeding competences']).

[98] ECJ 22.1.2013 – case C-283/11, ECLI:EU:C:2013:28 para. 52 – Sky Österreich v Österreichischer Rundfunk; 3.9.2020 – case C-719/18, ECLI:EU:C:2020:627 para. 57 – Vivendi v Autorità per le Garanzie nelle Comunicazioni.

ion was added to recital 1 EMFA. The protection of media freedom and media pluralism is of particular importance for the internal market, recital 2 EMFA.[99]

26 New **economic opportunities** have arisen as a result of internationalisation and digitalisation, rec. 2(1)(2) et seq. EMFA. The legal fragmentation caused by the different legal systems of the Member States is an obstacle to the free movement of media in the internal market, rec. 4(1)(6) EMFA. The Proposal still lacked the specific highlighting of various market failures that are said to be due to digitalisation, rec. 4(1)(1) EMFA. As **online platforms** play a particularly important role in the distribution of media content, they are able to generate a significant proportion of advertising revenue, rec. 4(1)(2) et seq. EMFA. Another new addition is that national legal differences have a negative impact on the economic activity of media services, recital 5 EMFA.[100] The reason for this was certainly also to counter criticism of the lack of Union competence. The regulations also contain provisions that concern less media industry aspects. They explicitly emphasise, for instance, the protection of editorial independence (recital 17), the free flow of trustworthy information (recital 16) and the protection of sources (recital 19 et seq.).

E. Contents

I. Overview and scope

27 The EMFA has four chapters, with Chapter I (Art. 1–2) containing the general provisions and Chapter 4 (Art. 25–28) the final provisions. Chapter II regulates the rights and duties of media service providers and recipients (Art. 3–6). Chapter 3 (Art. 7–25), which is intended to set a framework for regulatory cooperation, is the most extensive.

28 Although Art. 1 EMFA contains the term 'scope' (French: *champ d'application*; German: *Geltungsbereich*) in its title, it only states that the Regulation is intended to regulate the proper functioning of the internal market for media services. According to Art. 2 EMFA, media services are services whose 'principal purpose (…) consists in providing programmes or press publications, under the editorial responsibility of a media service provider, to the general public, by any means, in order to inform, entertain or educate'. This definition is considered by some to be too narrow.[101] Recital 8 EMFA Proposal (now recital 11) was surprising, according to which video sharing or very large platforms can also be media service providers.[102] This would mean that they would be subject to the obligations of Art. 18 EMFA, but at the same time benefit from the privileges. This is justified by the fact that these platforms have begun to take editorial control over some content.[103] Parliament has prevailed with the demand that to concretise rec. 11(1)(4) EMFA to the effect that providers of platforms are only media service providers if they exercise editorial control.[104]

29 The EMFA is not intended to be exhaustive, but rather allows the Member States to issue '**more detailed or stricter rules**' (French: *règles plus détaillées ou plus strictes*; Ger-

99 Parliament was unable to assert itself with a reference to the special cultural meaning of the media, P9_TA(2023)0336 (Amendement 2).

100 This proposal came from the Council, rec. 4a EMFA-EC.

101 Barata, Protecting Media Content on Social Media Platforms (Verfassungsblog, 25.11.2022) <https://verfassungsblog.de/emfa-dsa/> (arbitrary and discriminatory) (last accessed: 25.06.2024).

102 Dissenting view probably Sznajder E.L. Rev. 49 (2024), 66 (71).

103 Critical of this is Barata, Protecting Media Content on Social Media Platforms (Verfassungsblog, 25.11.2022) <https://verfassungsblog.de/emfa-dsa/> (last accessed: 25.06.2024).

104 P9_TA(2023)0336 (Amendment 12).

man: *ausführlichere oder strengere Vorschriften*) for Chapter II and Chapter III Section 5 ('Requirements for well-functioning media market measures and procedures') and Article 25 ('Allocation of public funds for state advertising and supply or service contracts'), Art. 1(3) EMFA. The EMFA Proposal only spoke of 'more detailed' rules, while both the Parliament and the Council called for the addition of 'or stricter'. Both also wanted the member states to be able to deviate from Art. 25. Such an **opening clause** ('more detailed or stricter rules') is also contained in Art. 4(1) AVMS Directive 2010/13/EU. Although, this is concretised by recitals 41 and 83 AVMS Directive 2010/13/EU such concretisation is (still) lacking in the EMFA.[105]

30 Such **opening clauses** serve the idea of subsidiarity but hinder legal harmonisation and thus increase the effort for media service providers who want to operate across borders.[106] The reason that Parliament and Council both wanted to allow stricter rules is probably due to the opinion of the Council Legal Service. It had proposed such an addition in order to remain within the legal basis of Art. 114 TFEU.[107]

II. Rights and duties of media service providers and recipients (Chapter II)

1. Rights of recipients of media services, Art. 3 EMFA

31 Art. 3 EMFA claims that the member states have to respect the **right of recipients** of media services 'to have access to a plurality of editorially independent media content and ensure that framework conditions are in place in line with this Regulation to safeguard that right, to the benefit of free and democratic discourse'. The right to receive news and content is reminiscent of Art. 11(1)(2) CFR,[108] according to which every person has the right 'to receive and impart information and ideas without interference by public authority and regardless of frontiers' and Art. 10(1)(2) ECHR.

32 Art. 3 EMFA was intended to establish a 'right of recipients of media services' (French: *Droit des destinataires de services de médias*; German: *Recht der Empfänger von Mediendiensten*) – which is now only formulated as such in the title of Art. 3 EMFA. Some saw Art. 3 EMFA Proposal as an individual right of access to news.[109] Rather, Art. 3 EMFA could only be understood as a **prohibition for the Member States** to un-

---

105 The ECJ 3.2.2021 – case C-555/19, ECLI:EU:C:2021:89 para. 41 – Fussl Modestraße Mayr v SevenOne Media GmbH, ProSiebenSat.1, TV Deutschland GmbH, ProSiebenSat.1 Media SE concludes from Art. 4(1) and recitals 41 and 83 AVMS Directive 2010/13/EU that a national rule that is more detailed or stricter must nevertheless serve the objective of the directive or the respective article (in this case, the protection of viewers). The fact that the contested national provision regulates a situation that is not regulated by the Directive is irrelevant (Against this, Ukrow, 'Sicherung regionaler Vielfalt – Außer Mode? Anmerkungen aus Anlass des Urteils des Europäischen Gerichtshofs vom 3. Februar 2021, Rs. C-555/19, Fussl Modestraße Mayr GmbH v SevenOne Media GmbH, ProSiebenSat.1 TV Deutschland GmbH, ProSiebenSat.1 Media SE', p. 7 (EMR 10.2.2021) <https://emr-sb.de/wp-content/uploads/2021/02/EMR_Aktuelles-Stichwort-zum-EuGH-Urteil-in-Sachen-Fussl-Modestrasse-Mayr.pdf> (last accessed: 25.06.2024).

106 With a view to ECJ 3.2.2021 – case C-555/19, ECLI:EU:C:2021:89 para. 41 – Fussl Modestraße Mayr v SevenOne Media GmbH, ProSiebenSat.1, TV Deutschland GmbH, ProSiebenSat.1 Media SE it can also be assumed in the context of the EMFA that the ECJ will interpret the opening clause rather narrowly.

107 Opinion of the Legal Service of the Council of the European Union from 4.4.2023, 8089/23 mn. 18 and 21.

108 See Cole/Etteldorf Future Regulation of Cross-Border Audiovisual Content Dissemination, p. 102. The wording of Art. 3 EMFA Proposal was based even more clearly on the CFR.

109 R. Dörr AfP 2023, 206 mn. 19.

lawfully restrict editorial freedom and access to the media.[110] This comprehension serves as the basis of the final version: Member States must respect the right of recipients. In addition, they have to ensure (French: *veillent*, German: *gewährleisten*) framework conditions to guarantee access to 'a plurality of editorially independent media content' (French: *une pluralité de contenus médiatiques indépendants sur le plan editorial*, German: *einer Vielzahl von redaktionell unabhängigen Medieninhalten*). This final wording is a link between the proposals of the Council and the Parliament: while the Council only wanted the first half-sentence, the Parliament also demanded an obligation for the Member States ('shall ensure')[111]. It remains to be seen how strong the ECJ will make this obligation.

2. Rights of media service providers, Art. 4 EMFA

Art. 4(1) EMFA is intended to guarantee the **freedom of business** of media companies and para. 2 to guarantee editorial work. While media companies' freedom of business is generally protected by Art. 16 CFR, Art. 11(2) CFR and Art. 10 ECHR also apply to the necessary activities of the media. Restrictions on this freedom are possible, but they must be 'necessary in a democratic society', Art. 10(2) ECHR.[112] This limitation of the possibility of restriction also applies within the framework of Art. 11(2) CFR.[113] The EMFA incorporates this protection into secondary EU law and enables the Commission to take action against Member States in the event of violations. 33

According to Art. 4(1) EMFA, media service providers may only be restricted in their economic activities by restrictions 'allowed pursuant to Union Law'. However, Art. 4(1) EMFA is in Chapter II, to which the Member States may adopt 'more detailed or stricter provisions' in accordance with Art. 1(3) EMFA. Accordingly, the member states can adopt rules that further strengthen the 'editorial freedom and independence' (Art. 4(1)(1) EMFA, French: *la liberté éditoriale et l'indépendance*, German: *redaktionelle Freiheit und Unabhängigkeit*) of media service providers. 34

The member states have 'to ensure that journalistic sources and confidential communications are effectively protected', Art. 4(3)(1) EMFA. This is concretised by Art. 4(3)(2) EMFA. Member states are not allowed to 'oblige' (French: *obliger*, German: *Verpflichtung*) media service providers, the editorial staff or third persons, who have a relationship to the aforementioned, to disclose 'information related to or capable of identifying journalistic sources', Art. 4(3)(a) EMFA. This provision was a proposal of the Council, Art. 4(2a)(a) EMFA-EC. 35

Also Art. 4(3)(b) EMFA **protects journalist sources**. Hereafter it is prohibited to 'detain, sanction, intercept or inspect' (French: *placer en détention, sanctionner, intercepter ou soumettre à une inspection*; German: *Inhaftierung, Sanktionierung, Abfangen oder Untersuchung*) media service providers, the editorial staff or third persons, who have a relationship to the aforementioned for the purpose of obtaining information about journalistic sources. It's also prohibited to 'surveillance or search and seizure' (German: *Überwachung, Durchsuchung oder Beschlagnahme*, French: *une surveillance, ou à une perquisition et à une saisie*) for the purposes of obtaining this information. 36

---

[110] Art. 3 should be taken into account in particular if the Member States wish to adopt 'more detailed or stricter' rules within the meaning of Art. 1(3) EMFA.

[111] P9_TA(2023)0336 (Amendment 103).

[112] Jarass in Jarass Art. 11 CFR mn. 18; Glocke Publizistischer Quellenschutz im deutschen und europäischen Recht, p. 185.

[113] Streinz in Streinz Art. 11 CFR mn. 14; cf. ECJ 28.10.1992 – case C-219/91, ECLI:EU:C:1992:414 para. 38 – Ter Voort, which adopted the principle of Art. 10(2) ECHR even before the CFR came into force.

37 Under certain conditions, Member States may make **exceptions** to para. 3(a) and (b), Art. 4(4) EMFA. The prerequisite is that there is a legal basis (a), it is compatible with Art. 52(1) of the Charter of Fundamental Rights and with other Union law (b), it is justified by an 'overriding reason of public interest' (French: *une raison impérieuse d'intérêt général*; German: *überwiegender Grund des Allgemeininteresses*) and the measure is proportionate (c) and there is a decision by a judicial authority (d), Art. 4(4) EMFA.

38 It is forbidden to use '**intrusive surveillance software**' (French: *un logiciel de surveillance intrusif*; German: *intrusive Überwachungssoftware*) to obtain data from journalistic sources, Art. 4(3)(c) EMFA. Use may be permitted in exceptional cases, Art. 4(5) EMFA. The prerequisite is that the conditions of Art. 4(4) EMFA are met, Art. 4(5)(a) EMFA, and that it is a particularly serious offence within the meaning of Art. 4(5)(b) EMFA. Furthermore, the use of surveillance software is only permitted if the measures pursuant to para. 3(a) and (b) are not likely to succeed.

39 All measures under Art. 4(4) EMFA and Art. 4(5) EFMA must be reviewed 'regularly' (French: *régulièrement*, German: *regelmäßig*) by a judicial authority or an independent decision-making body. The right to effective legal protection must be guaranteed, Art. 4(8) EMFA.

40 With all these restrictions on the measures, the legislator is responding to the numerous criticisms. For example, it was criticised that Art. 4(2) EMFA Proposal falls short of the requirements of Art. 10 ECHR developed by case law.[114] However, these concerns were likely to be unfounded. This was because Art. 4(2) EMFA Proposal would not be understood as an exhaustive regulation, but rather interpreted within the framework of the general principles of EU law and fundamental rights.[115] Nevertheless, the **clarification** in the EMFA is welcome, as it facilitates the application of the law.

3. Public service media provider, Art. 5 EMFA

41 Art. 5 EMFA contains regulations on **public service media providers**. A public service media provider is 'a media service provider which is entrusted with a public service remit under national law and receives national public funding for the fulfilment of such a mission', Art. 2(3) EMFA. In the draft, the conditions were still separated by an 'or' and not connected by an 'and'. This was criticised by German public media.[116]

42 Art. 5(1) EMFA obliges the Member States to ensure that public service media providers provide '**in an impartial manner a plurality of information and opinions**'.[117] At the suggestion of the Council and the Parliament, it was added that public service media providers are 'editorially functionally independent' (French: *indépendance éditoriale et fonctionnelle*; German: *redaktionell und funktional unabhängig*).[118] The *management structures* shall be appointed through a transparent, open and non-discriminatory procedure, Art. 5(2)(2).[119]

43 According to Art. 5(3)(2) EMFA, the Member States must ensure that public service media providers have 'adequate, sustainable and predictable' (French: *suffisantes,*

---

[114] Voorhoof, European Media Freedom Act and the protection of journalistic sources: still some way to go (Inforrm's Blog 18.11.2022) <https://inforrm.org/2022/11/18/european-media-freedom-act-and-the-protection-of-journalistic-sources-still-some-way-to-go-dirk-voorhoof/> (last accessed: 25.06.2024).

[115] Cole/Etteldorf Future Regulation of Cross-Border Audiovisual Content Dissemination, p. 103.

[116] R. Dörr/Weber AfP 2023, 383 mn. 27 et seq.

[117] In the draft, this was not formulated as an obligation of the member states but as an obligation of the public service media. Critical, as this would be a disregard of the Amsterdam Protocol's limits of competence, R. Dörr/Weber AfP 2023, 383 mn. 35 et seq. with further references.

[118] R. Dörr/Weber AfP 2023, 383 mn. 34 see no difference to the current German legal situation.

[119] P9_TA(2023)0336 Amendment 119.

durables et prévisibles, German: *angemessen, nachhaltig und vorhersehbar*) **financial resources**. The Council has thus established that the financing procedures should also be based on 'transparent and objective criteria laid down in advance', Art. 5(3)(1) EMFA. The Member States should appoint 'independent authorities' to monitor compliance of Art. 5(1)–(3) EMFA, Art. 5(4) EMFA.

4. Transparency duties of media service providers, Art. 6 EMFA

Art. 6 EMFA contains special **transparency obligations** for media service providers. **44** In the draft, these should only apply to media service providers 'providing news and current affairs content'. This was rightly criticised by Academics.[120] After all, reports on non-current information also have an influence on social discussion and, for example, the cultural self-image of a society (especially in the case of information on historical events). Consequently, Parliament proposed that the obligation should apply to all media service providers.[121]

They must provide their recipients with information about their **legal name** and **con- 45** **tact details** (Art. 6(1)(a) EMFA), the names of their direct or indirect **owners** who are able to 'influence on the operation and strategic decision making' (Art. 6(1)(b) EMFA) and the names of their 'beneficial owners'[122] (Art. 6(1)(c) EMFA). The draft did not yet include the requirement to state the 'total annual amount of public funds for state advertising' and 'from third-country public authorities or entities', Art. 6(1)(d) EMFA. All information must be 'easily and directly accessible' (French: *aisément et directement accessibles*; German: *leicht und direkt zugänglich*).[123] The reason for this transparency rule is that it is necessary for the assessment of information to recognise whether conflicts of interest exist, recital 32(1). The national regulatory authorities must create databases on media ownership, Art. 6(2) EMFA.

The 'Monitoring Media Pluralism' report called for greater transparency of **owner- 46** **ship structures**.[124] Directive (EU) 2018/1808 had already introduced a provision into the AVMS Directive 2010/13/EU in Art. 5(2) which allows Member States to oblige media service providers to disclose their ownership structure to recipients.[125]

In addition, Art. 6(3) EMFA contains the duty of media service providers providing **47** news and current affairs content to 'take measures that they deem appropriate with a view to ensure the independence of individual editorial decisions'. It is not clear why this only applies to media service providers that provide news and current affairs.

That these rules do not apply to micro enterprises, as envisaged in the draft (Art. 6(3) **48** EMFA Proposal), has been dropped in the final version.

---

[120] Cole/Etteldorf Future Regulation of Cross-Border Audiovisual Content Dissemination, p. 29.

[121] P9_TA(2023)0336 Amendment 125.

[122] The EMFA refers to Art. 3 no. 6 Anti-money laundering Directive (EU) 2015/849 for the definition of the term 'beneficial owner'.

[123] Obligations to make information 'easily and directly accessible' can be found in various places in EU legislation and in sometimes slightly different formulations, see for example Art. 30(7)(1) DSA ('clear, easily accessible and comprehensible manner'), Dregelies in Hofmann/Raue Art. 30 DSA mn. 51.

[124] Bleyer-Simon/Brogi/Carlini/Da Costa Leite Borges/Nenadić/Palmer/Parcu/Trevisan/Verza/Žuffová Monitoring Media Pluralism In The Digital Era, p. 156 et seq. The danger of a lack of transparency has already been pointed out in previous years, e.g. Bleyer-Simon/Brogi/Carlini/Nenadic/Palmer/Parcu/Verza/Viola de Azevdo Cunha/Žuffová Monitoring Media Pluralism In The Digital Era, p. 150.

[125] This did not result in an obligation. Germany, for example, has not made use of the new option.

III. National regulatory authorities or bodies, Art. 7 EMFA

49 The **national regulatory authorities** named in Art. 30 AVMS Directive 2010/13/EU are responsible for the application of Chapter III (Art. 7–24 EMFA), Art. 7(1) EMFA. When applying the EMFA, they must fulfil the requirements of Art. 30 Directive 2010/13/EU, Art. 7(2) EMFA. The Parliament wanted to include that the regulatory authority must be *'legally distinct from the government and functionally independent from their respective governments and from any other public or private body'*, Art. 7(2a) EMFA-EP,[126] whereby this is already required under Art. 30(1) AVMS Directive 2010/13/EU. Consequently, the proposal was not adopted. The regulatory authorities must have sufficient financial, human and technical resources, Art. 7(3) EMFA. They must be granted appropriate investigative powers, Art. 7(4)(1) EMFA.

IV. European Board for Media Services, Art. 8–12 EMFA

50 The newly established '**European Board for Media Services**' (Art. 8(1) EMFA) is to replace the ERGA, para. 2. The Board is to be **independent** and is not bound by any instructions, Art. 9 EMFA. It is composed of representatives of the national regulatory authorities, Art. 10(1) EMFA, who each have one vote (para. 2) and decide by a two-thirds majority (para. 3). In addition, a non-voting member of the Commission is represented on the Board, Art. 10(6) EMFA. The task of the Board is to advise and **support the Commission** on the application of the EMFA (Art. 13(2)(1) EMFA). It makes its expertise available for this purpose (Art. 13(2)(a) EMFA), promotes the exchange of information between the regulatory authorities (Art. 13(2)(b) EMFA), draws up opinions to different questions (Art. 13(2)(d) EMFA), draws up opinions on the outcome of a dialogue between a very large online platform and a media service provider (Art. 13(2)(e) EMFA), draws up opinions with respect to regulatory or administrative measures in accordance with Art. 21(4) EMFA, draws up opinions on draft assessments or draft opinions of national regulatory authorities or bodies (Art. 13(2)(g) EMFA), draws up opinions with respect to media market concentrations which are likely to affect the functioning of the internal market for media services (Art. 13(2)(h) EMFA), supports the Commission in drawing up guidelines (Art. 13(2)(i) EMFA), mediates in the event of disagreements between national regulatory authorities (Art. 13(2)(j) EMFA), fosters the cooperation on harmonised standards (Art. 13(2)(k) EMFA), coordinates relevant measures by national regulatory bodies related to the dissemination of or access to content of media services from outside of the Union that target or reach audiences in the Union (Art. 13(2)(l) EMFA), organises the structured dialogue in accordance with Art. 19 EMFA (Art. 13(2)(m) EMFA), fosters the exchange of best practices related to the deployment of audience measurement systems (Art. 13(2)(n) EMFA), exchanges experience and best practices on media literacy (Art. 13(2)(o) EMFA) and draws up a detailed annual report on its activities and tasks (Art. 13(2)(p) EMFA).

51 The organisation and structure of the Board is **reminiscent of the European Data Protection Board**, Art. 68 et seq. GDPR Regulation (EU) 2016/679.[127] **Doubts** have been expressed **regarding independence**, as in many areas the Board can only act at the request of the Commission and the secretariat of the Board is provided by the Commis-

[126] P9_TA(2023)0336 Amendment 144.

[127] Cf. Cole/Etteldorf Future Regulation of Cross-Border Audiovisual Content Dissemination, p. 46 (expressly only on Art. 69 GDPR Regulation (EU) 2016/679).

sion, Art. 11 EMFA.[128] The Parliament rightly proposed that the Board should have a separate and independent secretariat, which only takes instructions from the Board.[129] However, as the Board's **competences are limited**,[130] the risk is likely to be low, even if the Commission's influence is considered high.

52 The Parliament did not succeed with its proposal to establish an 'Expert Group to the Board', which should be made up of representatives from the media sector, Art. 11a(1) EMFA-EP.[131] But a special consultation mechanism was introduced, Art. 12 EMFA. If the Board deals with issues that go beyond the audiovisual sector, representatives from the relevant media sector of the member states are to be invited, Art. 12(1) EMFA.

V. Regulatory cooperation and convergence, Art. 14–17 EMFA

53 The EMFA is also intended to **strengthen cooperation** between national regulatory authorities. From the legislator's point of view, 'structured cooperation' is missing in the previous system of the AVMS Directive 2010/13/EU, rec. 43(1)(2) EMFA. A national regulatory authority or body should now be able to **request assistance or cooperation** in order to exchange information or take measures for the uniform application of the Chapter III EMFA or AVMS Directive 2010/13/EU, Art. 14(1) EMFA. The requested authority can only refuse a request, if it is not competent (Art. 14(3)(a) EMFA), if the answer would violate the law (Art. 14(3)(b) EMFA) or if the scope of the request is unjustified or disproportionate (Art. 14(3)(c) EMFA). The requested authority shall do 'its utmost' (French: *faite met tout en oeuvre*, German: *unternimmt ihr Möglichstes*) to answer 'with undue delay' (French: *sans retard injustifié*, German: *unverzüglich*). The requesting authority may refer the matter to the Board if it is of the opinion that the requested authority has not acted sufficiently. In case of a 'serious and grave risk of limitation of the freedom to provide or receive media services' (French: *un risque sérieux et grave de limitation de la liberté de fournir ou de recevoir des services de médias*, German: *ernsthafte und schwerwiegende Gefahr der Beeinträchtigung der Freiheit, Mediendienste bereitzustellen oder zu empfangen*) or in case of 'serious and grave risk of prejudice to public security' (French: *un risque sérieux et grave d'atteinte à la sécurité publique*, German: *ernsthafte und schwerwiegende Gefahr einer Beeinträchtigung der öffentlichen Sicherheit*) the requesting authority may request to receive a response within 14 days, Art. 14(6) EMFA.

54 Art. 15 EMFA is intended to enforce Art. 28b AVMS Directive 2010/13/EU more effectively. For example, one national regulatory authority can request another to enforce the obligations for video-sharing platform providers under Art. 28b(1)–(3) AVMS Directive 2010/13/EU, Art. 15(1) EMFA. These duties include, for example, the protection of minors (Art. 28b(1)(a) AVMS Directive 2010/13/EU), protection against videos containing incitement to group-related hatred and violence (Art. 28b(1)(b) AVMS Directive 2010/13/EU) and protection against videos containing terrorist, child pornography and racist and xenophobic offences (Art. 28b(1)(c) AVMS Directive 2010/13/EU). In addition, Art. 28b(2) in conjunction with Art. 9 AVMS Directive 2010/13/EU requires that numerous conditions are met in order to regulate commercial communications.

128 Cole/Etteldorf Future Regulation of Cross-Border Audiovisual Content Dissemination, p. 9; and for the private media industry Beaujean/Oelke/Wierny MMR 2023, 11 (15 et seq.). See also Zeno-Zencovich, U.Pac.L.Rev. 55 (2024), 175 (180).

129 P9_TA(2023)0336 Amendment 160.

130 Bayer, Missing Freedom Act (Verfassungsblog, 15.9.2022) <https://verfassungsblog.de/missing-freedom-act/> (last accessed: 25.06.2024) who correctly points out, however, that due to the competence of the panel, the opinion can certainly exercise informal power.

131 P9_TA(2023)0336 Amendment 162.

55 According to Art. 28a AVMS Directive 2010/13 in conjunction with Art. 3(1) InfoSoc Directive 2000/31, the authority in whose jurisdiction the video-sharing platform is established is responsible for enforcing Art. 28b (country of origin principle). The resulting problems (in particular inactive national authorities) are well known. Art. 15(1) EMFA can help to increase the **pressure on national authorities**. However, there is no sanction mechanism. If there are differences of opinion between the authorities, the Body shall conduct mediation, Art. 15(3) EMFA. Art. 15 EMFA is therefore a step in the right direction. However, the willingness of the competent national authority to co-operate is still required. Nevertheless, Art. 15 EMFA could increase the pressure exerted by the Commission and the ECJ.

VI. Provision of media services in a digital environment, Art. 18–20 EMFA

56 Online platforms have become particularly important in the **distribution of media content**. Providers of very large online platforms are obliged by Art. 18(1) EMFA to enable media service providers to post certain information about themselves. The **DSA** has a comparable standard for online shops, Art. 31 DSA.[132] However, the media providers have the right to refuse the self-declaration, recital 53(1) EMFA.

57 Media service providers are to be given the opportunity to declare that they are media service providers (Art. 18(1)(a) EMFA) and that they comply with Art. 6(1), Art. 18(1)(b) EMFA. Furthermore they must have the possibility to declare 'that they are editorially independent from Member States, political parties, third countries and entities controlled or financed by third countries', Art. 18(1)(c) EMFA, and 'that they are subject to regulatory requirements for the exercise of editorial responsibility […] and to oversight by a competent national regulatory authority', Art. 18(1)(d) EMFA. Also, they must be able to 'declare that they do not provide content generated by artificial intelligence systems without subjecting it to human review or editorial control', Art. 18(1)(e) EMFA, 'provide their legal name and contact details', Art. 18(1)(f) EMFA and 'provide the contact details of the relevant national regulatory authorities', Art. 18(1)(g) EMFA. At the Council's proposal,[133] it was included that the **VLOPs shall obtain confirmation** from the relevant national authority in the event of 'reasonable doubt' (French: *doute raisonnable*; German: *begründeter Zweifel*) that the requirements of Art. 18(1)(d) are actually fulfilled, Art. 18(1)(2) EMFA. The EMFA does not explain when reasonable doubt exists. This is particularly interesting because, according to Art. 18(7) EMFA, it is generally possible to reject the self-declaration of the media service provider or to declare it invalid. The recitals are also silent on this. However, 'recognised civil society organisations, fact-checking organisations' (French: *organisations de la société civile reconnues, y compris les organisations de vérification des faits*; German: *anerkannte Organisationen der Zivilgesellschaft, einschließlich Faktenüberprüfungsorganisationen*) and other relevant professional organisations should have the opportunity to point out non-compliance with the requirements for self-declaration, recital 53(5). Overall, the VLOPs have a **duty to scrutiny**, which, although it falls short of Art. 30(2)(1)[134] and Art. 31(3) DSA[135], is certainly comparable to them. If a VLOP rejects the self-declaration or declares it in-

---

[132] See also Dregelies in Hofmann/Raue Art. 31 DSA mn. 1 et seqq.; Dregelies VUR 2023, 175 (180 et seq.).

[133] Parliament also made a similar proposal, P9_TA(2023)0336 Amendment 217.

[134] See also Dregelies in Hofmann/Raue Art. 30 DSA mn. 24 et seqq.

[135] See also Dregelies in Hofmann/Raue Art. 31 DSA mn. 25 et seqq.

valid, the media service provider can resort to the mediation procedure pursuant to Art. 12 P2B-Regulation (EU) 2019/115 or out-of-court dispute resolution pursuant to Art. 21 DSA,[136] Art. 18(7) EMFA. The Parliament was unable to assert itself with the demand that the VLOPs shall 'ensure that decisions concerning content moderation and any other actions they undertake do not negatively impact media freedom and pluralism', Art. 17(1)(1) EMFA-EP.[137]

As online platforms are so important for the dissemination of content, any **blocking of content** is subject to special rules, Art. 18(4) EMFA. Providers of VLOP that intend to suspend the provision of its online intermediation services in relation to content provided by a media service provider or to restrict the visibility of such content because it violates the platform's T&Cs, should inform the media service provider prior to the suspension in accordance with Art. 4(1) P2B Regulation (EU) 2019/1150 and Art. 17(4) DSA, Art. 18(4)(a) EMFA. The media service provider has the **'opportunity to reply'** (French: *la possibilité de répondre*, German: *Gelegenheit zu antworten*) within 24 hours. This timeframe can be shorter in a case of a crisis as in Art. 36(2) DSA, Art. 18(4)(b) EMFA. The provider of the VLOP may only decide to suspend or restrict visibility once the reply from the media service provider has been received or the deadline has expired, Art. 18(4)(b) EMFA. This **privileges media service providers** over other users of the platform. At first glance, this seems convincing, as media service providers have a special significance in the dissemination of information. However, if one look at who can be considered a media service provider, the privileged status appears less convincing. For this reason, there were calls in the legislative process to delete Art. 18 EMFA altogether.[138] This media privilege shall not apply if the VLOP is obligated to Art. 28, 34 and 35 DSA and Article 28b Directive 2010/13/EU or to other rules of the Union law relating to illegal content, Art. 18(4)(3) EMFA. 58

Art. 18(4) EMFA does not specify the legal consequences of how the VLOPs must respond to the media service provider's reply.[139] The added value of Art. 18(4) EMFA is likely to unfold in conjunction with the DSA. According to Art. 16(3) DSA, the notification by a user that content is illegal has the consequence that the VLOP has knowledge or awareness within the meaning of Art. 6 DSA. However, this only applies if it is possible to establish the unlawfulness 'without a detailed legal examination', Art. 16(3) DSA.[140] However, if the media service provider makes a statement as to why the content is not unlawful and should therefore not be deleted, this should regularly lead to a 'detailed legal examination' being necessary. The legal consequence of Art. 16(3) DSA should therefore not occur if the media service provider has submitted a detailed reply. 59

Providers of online intermediation services (P2B Regulation (EU) 2019/1150) respectively providers of online platforms (DSA) must provide an **internal complaint-handling system**. This system can also be used by media service providers. According to Art. 18(5)(1) EMFA a complaint of a media service provider must 'processed and decid- 60

---

136 On Art. 21 DSA in detail Dregelies in Hofmann/Raue Art. 21 DSA et seqq.

137 P9_TA(2023)0336 Amendment 207.

138 EU DisinfoLab, Policy Statement of Article 17 of the Proposed European Media Freedom Act, (Eu DisinfoLab, 24.1.2023) <https://www.disinfo.eu/advocacy/policy-statement-on-article-17-of-the-proposed-european-media-freedom-act/> (last accessed: 25.06.2024): Art. 18 EMFA also jeopardises the effectiveness of the DSA.

139 Bujis, Article 17 Media Freedom Act & the Digital Services Act: aligned or alienated? (DSA Observatory) <https://dsa-observatory.eu/2022/11/25/article-17-media-freedom-act-the-digital-services-act-aligned-or-alienated/> (last accessed: 25.06.2024) (on the draft); v. Drunen/Papaevangelou/Buijs/Fathaigh, Journal of Media Law 15 (2023), 152 (156 et seq.) on the draft and the proposals of the Council and Parliament.

140 In detail Raue in Hofmann/Raue Art. 16 DSA mn 47 et seqq.

ed upon with priority and without undue delay' (French: *soient traitées et résolues en priorité et sans retard injustifié*; German: *vorrangig und unverzüglich bearbeitet und entschieden warden*). The media service provider may be 'represented by a body' (French: *être représenté par un organisme*; German: *durch eine Stelle vertreten lassen*).

61 The Body regularly organises a structured dialogue between the providers of VLOPs as well as media service providers and civil society, Art. 19(1) EMFA.

62 Art. 20 EMFA contains a special **right for users**. According to this, users shall have the **right to customise the configuration of devices or interfaces** according to their interests and wishes, Art. 20(1) EMFA. Manufacturers and developers must ensure that the devices and interfaces allow the default setting to be changed 'freely and easily', Art. 20(2) EMFA. At Parliament's proposal, it has been included that also manufacturers and developers are obliged to ensure that the identity of the media service provider is clearly visible, Art. 20(3) EMFA.[141]

VII. Media market measures and procedures, Art. 21–24 EMFA

63 Art. 21 EMFA sets the framework for national media law. All measures that affect the operation of media service providers in the internal market must be 'duly justified and proportionate' (French: *dûment justifiées et proportionnées*, German: *hinreichend gerechtfertigt und verhältnismäßig*) as well as 'reasoned, transparent, objective and non-discriminatory' (French: *motivées, transparentes, objectives et non discriminatoires*, German: *begründet, transparent, objektiv und nichtdiskriminierend*), Art. 21(1) EMFA.[142] This currently appears to be lacking in some Member States. Every media service provider has the **right to effective legal protection** and access to an independent appellate body in order to defend themselves against measures pursuant to para. 1, Art. 21(3) EMFA. This body can but does not have to be a court, Art. 21(3)(2) EMFA. The Commission or a media service provider which is affected can request the Body to issue an opinion on a national measure, Art. 21(4) EMFA. The Board may also issue a statement on its own initiative, Art. 21(4) EMFA. Even if no explicit sanction mechanism is mentioned, this opens up the possibility for media service providers to take legal action against certain measures – and gives the ECJ the opportunity to intervene if the referral procedure is used. It also opens up the possibility for the Commission to take action against Member States using the infringement procedure. The Council and the Parliament[143] have ensured that para. 1 applies only if 'media pluralism or editorial independence' are liable to be affected.

64 The legislator considers different national rules not only justified, but even 'conducive' (French: *propices*, German: *zuträglich*) for media pluralism, rec. 60(1)(1) EMFA. Member States can thus take account of the specific local circumstances. However, different national rules hinder the freedom of establishment and the freedom to provide services, cf. rec. 60(1)(2) EMFA. In the media sector, there is a risk that national law will be used to restrict media freedom, as it is the case in Hungary, for example.[144] Art. 21 EMFA can now be an effective **door opener for the Commission and the ECJ** to repeal discriminatory regulations in individual member states. At the same time, there is enough flexibility for the Member States to react to national peculiarities.

[141] P9_TA(2023)0336 Amendment 237.

[142] Sznajder E.L. Rev. 49 (2024), 66 (70) sees this as a violation of Art. 167 TFEU.

[143] P9_TA(2023)0336 Amendment 238.

[144] It therefore seems questionable whether a directive is sufficient to prevent measures in states that attempt to restrict media freedom, Sznajder E.L. Rev. 49 (2024), 66 (68) (with a special polish perspective).

According to Art. 22(1) EMFA, Member States must adopt rules if the **media concentration** has a significant impact on media pluralism and editorial independence. This means that what was fought against intensively for many years and what Germany in particular wanted to prevent[145] now seems to have been achieved. The Italian Commissioner Mateo Monti had already tried to get a Directive against media concentration off the ground in 1997 but was defeated by his colleagues.[146] As media concentrations on the national markets of the Member States were also to be regulated by the Monti draft, the competence of the EC was disputed.[147] A new attempt was made in 2007,[148] which also failed. The prevention of media concentration had so far been seen as the responsibility of the Member States, which enacted different regulations to this end.[149] However, different media concentration rules lead to an impairment of the internal market.[150] In addition, a purely national approach leads to **transnational media concentration** being overlooked. In addition, some member states – such as Poland – do not take the influence of a merger on media plurality into account at all.[151] 65

Art. 22 EMFA only applies if there is a '**significant impact**' (French: *effet important*, German: *erheblich [...] auswirken*) **on media pluralism and editorial independence**. It is not specified when an impact is 'significant', so it will be up to national legislators to draft practicable regulations.[152] It can be assumed that the ECJ will ensure that Art. 22 EMFA is not rendered meaningless by a too narrow national implementation. It seems that the merger must have an impact on both media plurality and editorial independence.[153] This is suggested by the wording ('and') and the legislative history[154] of Art. 22(1) EMFA. If editorial independence is maintained in a merger, the negative impact on media plurality is also likely to be less. Nevertheless, there is a risk that the cumulative requirement will restrict Art. 22(1) EMFA too much.[155] 66

The rules for assessments of media market concentrations must be transparent, objective, proportionate and non-discriminatory, Art. 22(1)(a) EMFA. For the term 'concentration' (French: *concentration*, German: *Zusammenschluss*), reference is made to the definition in Art. 3 Regulation (EC) No 139/2004 (Merger Regulation), Art. 2(15) EMFA. It is positive that it is therefore possible to refer to the case law on Art. 3 Regulation (EC) No 139/2004 (Merger Regulation)[156], which simplifies the application of Art. 22 EMFA. The companies involved must be obliged to notify the merger in advance and to co-operate with the authorities, Art. 22(1)(b) EMFA. The assessment of the merger should be carried out by the national regulatory authorities, or they must be involved, 67

---

145 See → mn. 11.

146 Gounalakis/Zagouras JZ 2008, 652 (655). The proposal never made it past the internal draft stage of a 'non-paper'. The focus was on television, radio and daily newspapers. The ownership share of an entrepreneur in the media market was to be limited to 30 per cent of the total audience or customer quotas, Tettenborn MMR 1998, 18 (20 fn. 31). See also D. Dörr NJW 1997, 1341 (1342).

147 Tettenborn MMR 1998, 18 (20).

148 SEC/2007/32, on this for example Gounalakis/Zagouras JZ 2008, 652 (655 et seqq.).

149 For example, Brühann ZUM 1993, 600 (601).

150 Brühann ZUM 1993, 600 (601 et seq.).

151 Sznajder E.L. Rev. 49 (2024), 66 (74).

152 Klump/Witte Raz, AfP 2024, 101 mn. 20.

153 Sznajder E.L. Rev. 49 (2024), 66 (71 et seq.).

154 The CULT Committee (A9-0264/2023 Amendment 92) had proposed deleting 'and editorial independence', but apparently already had no majority in favour of this demand in Parliament (see P9_TA(2023)0336 Amendment 243).

155 Sznajder E.L. Rev. 49 (2024), 66 (71 et seq.).

156 Klump/Witte Raz, AfP 2024, 101 mn. 18.

Art. 22(1)(c) EMFA.[157] The notification of mergers should be objective, non-discriminatory and proportionate, Art. 22(1)(d) EMFA. The timeframes for the assessments must be regulated, Art. 22(1)(e) EMFA.

68 According to Art. 22(2) EMFA, the impact of the concentration on media pluralism 'including its effects on the formation of public opinion and on the diversity of media services and the media offering on the market' (Art. 22(2)(a) EMFA), the safeguards for the editorial independence (Art. 22(2)(b) EMFA) and whether the acquiring and acquired entities are economically sustainable without the merger (Art. 22(2)(c) EMFA) must be taken into account when assessing a merger. In the trialogue negotiations, it was added that the Commission's annual rule of law report concerning media pluralism and media freedom (Art. 22(2)(d) EMFA) and the commitments made by the parties to ensure media pluralism and editorial independence (Art. 22(2)(e) EMFA) must be taken into account.

69 The Commission can issue **guidelines** on the elements of Art. 22(2)(a)–(c) EMFA with the support of the Board, Art. 21(3) EMFA. If a concentration 'may affect the functioning of the internal market', the Board must be invited to comment in advance, Art. 22(4) EMFA. In the absence of such an invitation, the Commission can invite the Board to comment, Art. 22(1) EMFA.

70 According to Art. 22(2) EMFA, it is the **impact on the national media market** that matters. This follows from recitals 64(1)(4) ('a given media market in one or more Member States', French: *un marché des médias donné dans un ou plusieurs États members*, German: *einem bestimmten Medienmarkt in einem oder mehreren Mitgliedstaaten*) and 68(1)(1) ('pluralistic media markets' [plural]) EMFA and from the fact that the Board is only to be consulted if the internal market is impaired, Art. 22(4) EMFA. Art. 22(2) EMFA does not provide a rigid specification of when media pluralism is jeopardised – for instance, whether the market or audience share is decisive. It is questionable whether such a stipulation follows from the guidelines that can be issued in accordance with Art. 22(3) EMFA. Although **Union guidelines** do not bind the courts,[158] they should not be underestimated as an aid to interpretation. As Art. 24 EMFA lays down rules for audience measurement, the results of such measurements could certainly be used for merger control purposes.

VIII. Audience measurement, Art. 24 EMFA

71 The **measurement of readers, listeners or viewers** has an influence on the acquisition of advertising and the prices to be achieved, recital 69(1)(1) EMFA. Transparency duties are intended to ensure that the data is comprehensible, recital 70. The systems and methods used to measure audience figures must therefore comply 'with principles of transparency, impartiality, inclusiveness, proportionality, non-discrimination and verifiability', Art. 24(1) EMFA. Advertisers and media service providers must have the possibility to receive information on the methodology by companies that measure audience, Art. 24(2) EMFA.

[157] Whether these bodies are actually 'independent' (Art. 7(2) in conjunction with Art. 30 AVMS Directive 2010/13/EU) is likely to be a problem in some Member States, Sznajder E.L. Rev. 49 (2024), 66 (75) (with reference to Poland).

[158] Pampel Rechtsnatur und Rechtswirkungen horizontaler und vertikaler Leitlinien im reformierten europäischen Wettbewerbsrecht, pp. 88, 104; Thomas EuR 2009, 423 (426); Dregelies MMR 2023, 243 (247).

IX. Allocation of state advertising, Art. 25 EMFA

The allocation of **state advertising** can be an effective means of covertly promoting certain media that are loyal to the government, thereby placing other media providers at a competitive disadvantage. According to Art. 25(1) EMFA, public funds or any other consideration or advantage to media services providers or to providers of online platforms must be allocated in accordance with 'transparent, objective, proportionate and non-discriminatory criteria' (French: *des critères transparents, objectifs, proportionnés et non discriminatoires*, German: *transparenten, objektiven, verhältnismäßigen und nicht-diskriminierenden Kriterien*). Online platforms were not yet included in the draft of Art. 25(1) EMFA (Art. 24(1) EMFA Proposal). This was added to the law at the suggestion of the EP, which also wanted search engines to be included.[159] 72

Member States 'shall seek' (French: *s'efforcent*, German: *sind bestrebt*) to ensure that the advertising material is distributed to as many different service providers as possible. The wording 'shall seek' is surprisingly restrained and does not impose any real obligation on the Member States. 73

Online platforms were not yet included in the draft of Art. 25(1) EMFA (Art. 24(1) EMFA Proposal). This was added to the law at the suggestion of the EP, which also wanted search engines to be included. 74

F. Conclusion

The European Media Freedom Act's ambitious name has given rise **to much hope and criticism**. Hope, because media freedom is under serious threat in some Member States and the extremely large online platforms are endangering rather than improving media diversity and quality. Criticism because it was seen as undermining the Member States' competences in the media sector. 75

The EMFA is **unlikely to be a major success** for media freedom. Numerous measures prove to be too toothless for this and are dependent on the co-operation of the Member States' authorities. It is questionable whether this will have any effect, especially in Hungary. However, the EMFA could provide the Commission with a lever to enforce the fundamental rights protection of media freedom under Art. 11 CFR and Art. 10 ECHR in the Member States. It is therefore an important step that must be followed by others. 76

However, concerns that the Member States' competences could be undermined or that the Commission could abuse its power in relation to the media are probably unfounded. The provisions of the EMFA only grant the minimum protection that is already applicable law under Art. 11 CFR and Art. 10 ECHR – although there is a lack of effective enforcement mechanisms. In addition, there are numerous rules that attempt to provide a framework for media regulation. This should help to reduce discrimination against foreign media companies. 77

[159] P9_TA(2023)0336 Amendment 270.

CHAPTER 5: PLATFORM SPECIFICS OF OTHER EU LEGAL ACTS

§ 19
Platform-specific requirements of the Data Governance Act

Literature: *Fanderl/Niclas/von Blumenthal*, 'EU Data Governance Act', ITRB 2022, 145; *Hinrichs*, 'The Data Act: A Missed Opportunity for Consumers', PinG 2022, 217; *Hornung/Schomberg*, 'Datensouveränität im Spannungsfeld zwischen Datenschutz und Datennutzung: das Beispiel des Data Governance Acts', CR 2022, 508; *Miadzvetskaya*, 'Data Governance Act: On International Transfers of Non-Personal Data and GDPR Mimesis', European Data Protection Law Review 2023, 13; *Richter*, 'Looking at the Data Governance Act and Beyond: How to Better Integrate Data Intermediaries in the Market Order for Data Sharing', GRUR International 2023, 458; *Roßnagel*, 'Grundrechtsschutz in der Datenwirtschaft – Vorsorgepflichten in der Data-Governance', ZRP 2021, 173; *Schildbach*, 'Zugang zu Daten der öffentlichen Hand und Datenaltruismus nach dem Entwurf des Daten-Governance-Gesetzes', ZD 2022, 148; *Schütrumpf/Person*, 'Gaia-X: Vernetzte Infrastrukturen für eine europäisch geprägte Datenwirtschaft', RDi 2022, 281; *Schwartmann/Mühlenbeck*, 'Datenschutz durch Ermöglichungstechnik – Anonymität und Pseudonymität nach der DSGVO im Kontext von Data Act-Entwurf und Data Governance Act', RDV 2022, 264; *Specht-Riemenschneider/Blankertz/Sierek/Schneider/Knapp/Henne*, 'Die Datentreuhand – Ein Beitrag zur Modellbildung und rechtlichen Strukturierung zwecks Identifizierung der Regulierungserfordernisse für Datentreuhandmodelle', MMR-Beil. 2021, 25; *Spindler*, 'Schritte zur europaweiten Datenwirtschaft – der Vorschlag einer Verordnung zur europäischen Data Governance', CR 2021, 98; *Steinrötter*, 'Das Konzept einer datenaltruistischen Organisation', DuD 2021, 794; *Steinrötter*, 'Datenaltruismus', ZD 2021, 61; *Veil*, 'Der Data Governance Act und sein Verhältnis zum Datenschutzrecht', PinG 2023, 1.

A. DGA – part of the European data strategy

1 The **Data Governance Act**[1] entered into force on 23.6.2022 – 20 days after publication in the Official Journal of the European Union[2]. The new rules will apply 15 months after their entry into force on 24.9.2023 (Art. 38 DGA). With this regulation, the EU aims to promote the sharing and the use of idle data and create an alternative to the concentrated data power of large technology corporations, especially from the USA and China. The DGA is intended to establish structures in compliance with the existing legal framework that enable and promote data-driven innovation. The DGA's goal is to reconcile the use of data with the protection of personal data as well as trade secrets, copyrights, and industrial property rights. Similarly, these protection rights should not slow down or even prevent innovation, but rather strengthen confidence in the secure and lawful use of data. The DGA includes rules on the re-use of data held by public sector bodies (Chapter II DGA), the provision of data sharing services (Chapter III DGA), data altruism organisations (Chapter IV DGA) and the establishment of a European Data Innovation Board (Chapter VI DGA).

I. Objective

2 The Commission has recognised that data is at the heart of profound economic and social change and that **data-driven innovation** has enormous potential.[3] However, companies have so far only shared data with each other on a voluntary basis to a very limited extent.[4] In the Commission's view, data intermediation services, therefore, have a

[1] Regulation (EU) 2022/868 of 30.5.2022 on European data governance and amending Regulation (EU) 2018/1724 (Data Governance Act), OJ 2022 L 152, 1.

[2] OJ 2022 L 152, 1 (44).

[3] Rec. 2 DGA; European Commission, 'A European strategy for data', 19.2.2020, COM(2020) 66 final, 2 et seq.

[4] Röhl/Bolwin/Hüttl, 'Datenwirtschaft in Deutschland. Wo stehen die Unternehmen in der Datennutzung und was sind ihre größten Hemnisse?' (Studie des Instituts der deutschen Wirtschaft im Auftrag des Bundesverbands der Deutschen Industrie eV, 24.2.2021) <https://bdi.eu/publikation/news/datenwirtschaft-in-deutschland> (last accessed: 18.9.2024), p. 40.

key role to play in this data economy.[5] Accordingly, they could become actors facilitating the exchange of significant amounts of data,[6] in particular by supporting voluntary data sharing practices between companies.[7]

Today's **data economy** is characterised by a few, large players with considerable market power, so that, in particular, SMEs and start-ups with limited financial, legal and operational resources rarely succeed in gaining a foothold.[8] The European data economy is in danger of being increasingly left behind by competition from the USA and China,[9] which also benefit from strong concentration effects and comparatively few restrictions based on data protection regulations.[10] This development is to be countered with a '**European way**' by promoting data exchange and use while, at the same time, maintaining high data protection, security and ethical standards.[11] A competition between different data economies is emerging.[12] 3

The Commission envisages the creation of common **European data spaces** in which **independent data intermediaries** enable non-discriminatory access to the data economy.[13] The data economy should also be open to smaller companies through the neutrality of data access and the guarantee of data transferability (portability) and interoperability, and lock-in effects should thus be avoided.[14] The DGA is intended to create a harmonised framework for the exchange of data and facilitate the cooperation of different actors within the data ecosystems.[15] This regulation ultimately aims 'to develop further the borderless digital internal market and a human-centric, trustworthy and secure data society and economy'[16]. However, much data is stored somewhere untapped and underutilised, especially when it comes to pursuing research and innovation purposes in the public interest.[17] This is where the DGA comes in, establishing a Union-wide framework for data governance to increase trust among individuals and businesses in data sharing and re-use of data.[18] To **strengthen trust in data intermediaries,** the DGA provides for harmonised requirements for the provision of data intermediation services so that data subjects and data holders, but also data users, have better control over access to and lawful use of their data.[19] The labels 'data intermediation services provider recognised in the Union' and 'data altruism organisation recognised in the EU' are intended to strengthen trust in these data intermediaries by linking these designations to compliance with the DGA's requirements.[20] Such data intermediaries 4

[5] Rec. 27 DGA; Spindler CR 2021, 98 (99) mn. 2.

[6] Cf. Steinrötter DuD 2021, 794 (797).

[7] Rec. 27 DGA.

[8] European Commission, 'A European strategy for data', 19.2.2020, COM(2020) 66 final, 3 et seq., 9; Roßnagel ZRP 2021, 173 (176); Schütrumpf/Person RDi 2022, 281 (288).

[9] Cf. Roßnagel ZRP 2021, 173 (173).

[10] European Commission, 'A European strategy for data', 19.2.2020, COM(2020) 66 final, 4, 17; Schütrumpf/Person RDi 2022, 281 (281).

[11] European Commission, 'A European strategy for data', 19.2.2020, COM(2020) 66 final, 4, 27 et seqq.; see also Schütrumpf/Person RDi 2022, 281 (282, 288) on the private sector Gaia-X initiative, which is to be regarded as complementary.

[12] Roßnagel ZRP 2021, 173 (176).

[13] Rec. 27 DGA; European Commission, 'A European strategy for data', 19.2.2020, COM(2020) 66 final, 5 et seqq.

[14] Rec. 2 DGA; European Commission, 'A European strategy for data', 19.2.2020, COM(2020) 66 final, 12, 23 et seq.

[15] Rec. 3 DGA.

[16] Rec. 3 DGA.

[17] Rec. 6 DGA.

[18] Rec. 5 et seq. DGA; Spindler CR 2021, 98 (99) mn. 2.

[19] Rec. 32 DGA.

[20] Rec. 3 DGA.

should be independent: there should be a strict separation between the intermediation of data by neutral data intermediaries on the one hand, and the provision and use of the data on the other, in order to avoid conflicts of interest.[21]

II. Subject matter and scope of application

5 With the DGA, the EU creates a notification and supervisory framework for the provision of data intermediation services (Art. 1(1)(b) DGA) and lays down conditions for the re-use of certain data held by public sector bodies (Art. 1(1)(a) DGA). In order to promote the provision and use of data for certain purposes in the general interest, it also creates a set of rules that allows entities collecting and processing data provided for such purposes to register on a voluntary basis (Art. 1(1)(c) DGA). Furthermore, the DGA lays the foundation for the establishment of a European Data Innovation Council (Art. 1(1)(d) DGA).

6 The DGA thus lays down rules for the *how* of data intermediation rather than the *if*.[22]

1. Which services fall within the scope of application?

7 The DGA applies to **data intermediation services**. These are services which aim to establish commercial relationships for the purpose of data sharing between an undetermined number of data subjects and data holders on the one hand, and data users on the other.[23] Such services may also serve to exercise data subjects' rights in relation to personal data. Examples of data intermediation services include data marketplaces on which businesses make data available to others, data sharing ecosystems, and data pools established jointly by several natural or legal persons with the intention to license the use of such data pools to interested parties.[24]

8 If an undertaking offers a variety of data-related services, only those activities that relate directly to the provision of data intermediation services fall within the scope of the DGA.[25] Cloud storage, analytics services, data sharing software, internet browsers or browser plug-ins, and email services are not considered data intermediation services under the DGA.[26] Also excluded from the scope of the DGA are services that collect and aggregate, enrich or transform data from data holders and license the use of the resulting data to data users, without establishing a commercial relationship between data holders and data users.[27] Services that function as a 'closed system' are also excluded. This includes services that are used exclusively by one data holder to use their own data or are used by multiple legal persons in a closed group (e.g., in the context of supplier or customer relationships or of collaborations established by contract), in particular to ensure the functionalities of objects and devices connected to the Internet of Things.[28]

9 These examples clearly show that the focus of the DGA is the *intermediation* of data – personal and non-personal – between data holders and data users. It is about services that aim to establish business relationships between potential data users on the one hand, and data subjects as well as data holders on the other hand.[29] This Regulation

[21] Rec. 33 DGA.
[22] Cf. Schildbach ZD 2022, 148 (149).
[23] Rec. 28 DGA; cf. also the legal definition in Art. 2 no. 11 DGA.
[24] Rec. 28 DGA.
[25] Rec. 28 DGA.
[26] Rec. 28 DGA.
[27] Rec. 28 DGA.
[28] Rec. 28 DGA.
[29] Rec. 29 DGA.

does not set out any stipulations for the collection of data or their use per se, nor does it create a legal basis for these activities.

2. No establishment of new access or re-use rights

Public access to official documents provides for transparency and plays an important role in a democratic society.[30] However, the DGA does **not directly extend such access rights**. National and EU law on granting access to official documents remains unaffected by the DGA.[31] Article 1(2) DGA clarifies that this regulation does not create an obligation for public sector bodies to allow the re-use of data, nor does it release them from their confidentiality obligations under existing law. Each Member State should, in principle, be able to decide – subject to Union law on transparency requirements for public sector bodies – whether data held by public sector bodies is made available for re-use, and also to what extent such access is restricted in terms of purpose and scope.[32] Consequently, the DGA does not establish a new legal basis for access or re-use rights with respect to data held by public sector bodies.[33] Moreover, the DGA does not create an additional legal basis for the processing of personal data (Art. 1(3) DGA). 10

III. Interplay with other legal acts

The DGA is a horizontal, i.e., cross-sectoral regulation[34], interlaced with numerous other European and national legal acts, e.g., regulations on data held by public bodies, on the protection of personal data as well as on existing and planned sector-specific Union law, such as on the European Health Data Space[35] and on access to vehicle data. The Data Governance Act also forms **part of the** Commission's **European strategy for data**[36] of 19.2.2020. Although the DGA is intended to promote cooperation in the area of data use, competition law continues to apply within the scope of this regulation (Art. 1(4) DGA). As a result, there is an inherent risk for the respective data intermediaries that a joint data sharing platform is deemed to restrict competition.[37] 11

1. Embedded in the European data strategy

The European strategy for data aims to realise a **single European data space**, a **single market for data.**[38] By creating attractive economic policy conditions, the EU is to achieve a share of the data economy[39] at least equal to its economic weight by 2030 – this forms the EU's ambitious goal.[40] As part of the implementation of the European strategy for data, the DGA is to create cross-sectoral organisational concepts and structures for data access and use that enable data-driven innovation while complying with the 12

---

30 Rec. 11 DGA.

31 Rec. 11 DGA.

32 Rec. 11 DGA.

33 Cf. Spindler CR 2021, 98 (101) mn. 8.

34 Cf. European Commission, 'A European strategy for data', 19.2.2020, COM(2020) 66 final, 14; rec. 3 DGA.

35 European Commission, 'Proposal for a Regulation of the European Parliament and of the Council on the European Health Data Space', 3.5.2022, COM(2022) 197 final.

36 European Commission, 'A European strategy for data', 19.2.2020, COM(2020) 66 final.

37 Spindler CR 2021, 98 (108) mn. 46; Richter GRUR International 2023, 458 (468).

38 European Commission, 'A European strategy for data', 19.2.2020, COM(2020) 66 final, 5.

39 This refers to the data stored, processed and put to valuable use in Europe.

40 European Commission, 'A European strategy for data', 19.2.2020, COM(2020) 66 final, 5.

requirements of the existing legal framework.[41] The aim is to create suitable framework conditions by means of Union-wide, harmonised governance regulations that favour dynamic and flourishing data ecosystems.[42] Neutral data intermediaries are to increase the willingness to share data.[43] Both cross-sectoral data use and data use in shared sector-specific data spaces[44] should be strengthened. The interoperability of data is to be promoted through the creation of standards. In addition, new frameworks for data altruism are to make it easier for individuals to 'donate' their data for charitable purposes.[45]

13 As the first legislative initiative within the framework of the European data strategy, the DGA must be considered in **conjunction with the complementary Data Act**[46] (→ § 20 mn. 1 et seqq.).[47] The Data Act represents a comprehensive set of rules for access to and use of personal and non-personal data alike, namely to promote the use of industrial data.[48] Other laws and legislative projects that have originated from the European data strategy are the DMA (→ §§ 10 et seqq.), the DSA (→ §§ 1 et seqq.) and the the AI Act[49] (→ § 21 mn. 1 et seqq.).

2. No change to sector-specific Union law for access to and re-use of data

14 Existing legal provisions on **access to or re-use of certain categories of data**, in particular with regard to the granting of access to and disclosure of official documents, are not affected by the DGA (Art. 1(2)(a) DGA). The same applies to existing obligations of public bodies to allow the re-use of data or the requirements relating to the processing of non-personal data (Art. 1(2)(b) DGA). Insofar as **sector-specific regulations** already require compliance with certain additional technical, administrative, or organisational requirements, including through authorisation and certification procedures, these shall continue to apply. However, such sector-specific additional requirements must be non-discriminatory, proportionate and objectively justified (Art. 1(2) DGA).

---

[41] European Commission, 'A European strategy for data', 19.2.2020, COM(2020) 66 final, 10, 14; Spindler CR 2021, 98 (99) mn. 1.

[42] European Commission, 'A European strategy for data', 19.2.2020, COM(2020) 66 final, 14.

[43] Specht-Riemenschneider et al. MMR-Beil. 2021, 25 (25).

[44] European Commission, 'A European strategy for data', 19.2.2020, COM(2020) 66 final, 30 et seqq. contains the annex 'Common European data spaces in strategic sectors and domains of public interest'. It outlines the creation of various sector- and domain-specific European data spaces, namely an Industrial Data Space, a European Green Deal Data Space, a Mobility Data Space, a Health Data Space, a Financial Data Space and an Energy Data Space.

[45] European Commission, 'A European strategy for data', 19.2.2020, COM(2020) 66 final, 15.

[46] Regulation (EU) 2023/2854 of 13.12.2023 on harmonised rules on fair access to and use of data and amending Regulation (EU) 2017/2394 and Directive (EU) 2020/1828 (Data Act), OJ 2023 L 2854, 1.

[47] European Commission, 'A European strategy for data', 19.2.2020, COM(2020) 66 final, 14 et seqq.; European Commission, 'Proposal for a Regulation of the European Parliament and of the Council on harmonised rules on fair access to and use of data (Data Act)', 23.2.2022, COM(2022) 68 final, 5; Hinrichs PinG 2022, 217 (218); Richter GRUR International 2023, 458 (469).

[48] European Commission, 'Proposal for a Regulation of the European Parliament and of the Council on harmonised rules on fair access to and use of data (Data Act)', 23.2.2022, COM(2022) 68 final, 3.

[49] Regulation (EU) 2024/1689 of 13.6.2024 laying down harmonised rules on artificial intelligence and amending Regulations (EC) No 300/2008, (EU) No 167/2013, (EU) No 168/2013, (EU) 2018/858, (EU) 2018/1139 and (EU) 2019/2144 and Directives 2014/90/EU, (EU) 2016/797 and (EU) 2020/1828 (Artificial Intelligence Act), OJ 2024 L 1689, 1.

3. Interplay between DGA and GDPR

The objectives of the DGA to promote the sharing and re-use of data inevitably bring it into some **tension with the GDPR**[50],[51] for example with the principle of purpose limitation[52] pursuant to Art. 5 (1)(b) GDPR. According to this data protection principle, personal data[53] must be collected for specified, explicit and legitimate purposes and may not be further processed in a way incompatible with that initial purpose. Blanket consent by data subjects to data intermediaries for all possible purposes is not permitted.[54] Art. 5(1)(b) GDPR and Sec. 27(1) Bundesdatenschutzgesetz (German Federal Data Protection Act – BDSG) provide for certain exceptions to the principle of purpose limitation (for example, in the case of re-use for archiving purposes in the public interest, for scientific or historical research purposes or for statistical purposes). Nevertheless, the tension between DGA and data protection requirements is so great that the legislator felt compelled to include a clarification in the DGA. As a general rule, the GDPR requirements for lawful processing of personal data are to some extent to be seen as a prerequisite for processing such data under the DGA.[55] The DGA is considered by some to be an attempt to reconcile data use and data protection.[56] 15

The relationship between the DGA and the GDPR as well as other regulations[57] on the protection of personal data is explicitly set out in Art. 1(3) DGA. According to this provision, the GDPR fully applies to the processing[58] of personal data in connection with the DGA. This is also true with regard to the powers of the supervisory authorities. In case of conflict with the DGA, the relevant **law on the protection of personal data** takes **precedence** over the provisions of the DGA (as explicitly stipulated by Art. 1(3) DGA).[59] The existing law on the protection of personal data shall also prevail over the DGA in those cases where personal and non-personal data are inextricably connected in a single data set.[60] However, the concepts of personal data and identifiability within the meaning of the GDPR should not be deemed absolute, so as to leave sufficient room for identity protection by means of pseudonymisation and anonymisation, on which the DGA relies as technical measures to ensure data protection while, at the same time, enabling data use.[61] 16

---

50 Regulation (EU) 2016/679 of 27.4.2016 on the protection of natural persons with regard to the processing of personal data and on the free movement of such data and repealing Directive 95/46/EC (General Data Protection Regulation), OJ 2016 L 119, 1.

51 Steinrötter ZD 2021, 61 (61).

52 Cf. Roßnagel ZRP 2021, 173 (175).

53 For the definition of 'personal data', see Art. 4 no. 1 GDPR.

54 Specht-Riemenschneider et al. MMR-Beil. 2021, 25 (40).

55 Schwartmann/Mühlenbeck RDV 2022, 264 (267).

56 Roßnagel ZRP 2021, 173 (175).

57 Namely Regulation (EU) 2018/1725 of 23 October 2018 on the protection of natural persons with regard to the processing of personal data by the Union institutions, bodies, offices and agencies and on the free movement of such data, and repealing Regulation (EC) No 45/2001 and Decision No 1247/2002/EC, OJ 2018 L 295, 39; Directive (EC) 2002/58 of 12 July 2002 concerning the processing of personal data and the protection of privacy in the electronic communications sector (Directive on privacy and electronic communications), OJ 2002 L 201, 37 and Directive (EU) 2016/680 of 27 April 2016 on the protection of natural persons with regard to the processing of personal data by competent authorities for the purposes of the prevention, investigation, detection or prosecution of criminal offences or the execution of criminal penalties, and on the free movement of such data, and repealing Council Framework Decision 2008/977/JHA, OJ 2016 L 119, 89.

58 For the definition of 'processing', see Art. 4 no. 2 GDPR.

59 Veil PinG 2023, 1 (2).

60 Rec. 4 DGA.

61 Schwartmann/Mühlenbeck RDV 2022, 264 (267); Spindler CR 2021, 98 (104 et seq.) mn. 30; cf. Roßnagel ZRP 2021, 173 (176).

17 Moreover, the DGA does not expand the catalogue of possible legal basis for the processing of personal data pursuant to Art. 6 GDPR.[62] Consequently, data intermediaries cannot rely on the DGA as a legal basis for the lawfulness of the processing of personal data. Some are voicing criticism over this, as a new legal basis could have created incentives for businesses to act as data intermediaries in the first place.[63] The DGA is also not intended to change anything with respect to the information requirements laid down in the GDPR.[64] Insofar as their activities concern personal data, data intermediation services providers are therefore obliged to comply with the GDPR requirements – regardless of whether they act as controllers or processors within the meaning of the GDPR.[65] Thus, **central obstacles** to data sharing such as legal grey areas under data protection law and a lack of legal certainty regarding anonymisation remain unresolved.[66]

B. Requirements for data intermediation services

18 Chapter III DGA (**'Requirements applicable to data intermediation services'**) regulates the provision of data intermediation services. First, it specifies which data intermediation services fall within the relevant scope of application (Art. 10 DGA). Art. 11 DGA then explains the requirements and framework conditions for the registration of data intermediaries with the competent authorities. Art. 12 DGA contains as its core the requirements for the provision of data intermediation services. Finally, the competent authorities for data intermediaries (Art. 13 DGA) and their activities to monitor and enforce compliance with the DGA requirements are outlined, including possibilities to issue penalties in case of violations (Art. 14 DGA).

I. Definitions

1. Data intermediation services

19 A **'data intermediation service'** is defined in Art. 2 no. 11 DGA as 'a service which aims to establish commercial relationships for the purposes of data sharing between an undetermined number of data subjects and data holders on the one hand and data users on the other, through technical, legal or other means, including for the purpose of exercising the rights of data subjects in relation to personal data […]'. In addition, the following four types of services listed in Art. 2 no. 11(a)–(d) DGA are excluded from this legal definition in the sense of a negative definition:

- Lit. a: 'services that obtain data from data holders and aggregate, enrich or transform the data for the purpose of adding substantial value to it and license the use of the resulting data to data users, without establishing a commercial relationship between data holders and data users' (**data preparation and data licensing**).
- Lit. b: 'services that focus on the intermediation of copyright-protected content[67]' (**content intermediaries**).

---

[62] Art. 1(3) DGA; rec. 4 DGA.

[63] Specht-Riemenschneider et al. MMR-Beil. 2021, 25 (32); Steinrötter DuD 2021, 794 (798).

[64] Rec. 4 DGA.

[65] Rec. 35 DGA.

[66] Schildbach ZD 2022, 148 (152); Specht-Riemenschneider et al. MMR-Beil. 2021, 25 (26); cf. Schütrumpf/Person RDi 2022, 281 (281).

[67] The distinction between 'content' and 'data' is likely to lead to some difficulties in applying these provisions; cf. Spindler CR 2021, 98 (101) mn. 21.

- Lit. c: 'services that are exclusively used by one data holder in order to enable the use of the data held by that data holder, or that are used by multiple legal persons in a closed group, including supplier or customer relationships or collaborations established by contract, in particular those that have as a main objective to ensure the functionalities of objects and devices connected to the Internet of Things' (**closed data systems**).
- Lit. d: 'data sharing services offered by public sector bodies that do not aim to establish commercial relationships'. This refers to services provided by public sector bodies which allow the re-use of either protected data in their possession in accordance with the DGA or the use of any other data, but which are not aimed at establishing commercial relationships.[68]

Possible data intermediation services within the meaning of the regulation may also include bi- or multilateral data sharing and the creation of data sharing platforms or databases.[69] Data intermediation services also include the establishment of a specific infrastructure to connect data subjects and data holders, respectively, with data users.[70] 20

2. 'Data intermediation services provider recognised in the Union'

If a data intermediary meets the requirements and conditions regarding notification (Art. 11 DGA) and the provision of data intermediation services (Art. 12 DGA), it can obtain a compliance confirmation by the competent authority upon request and thus voluntarily undergo an ex-ante assessment (Art. 11(9) DGA). Receipt of such confirmation then entitles the data intermediary to use the label 'data intermediation services provider recognised in the Union' and a corresponding logo in accordance with Art. 11(9) DGA. This logo is intended to facilitate the recognition of trustworthy data intermediaries. Data subjects and data holders should be able to easily identify data intermediation services providers recognised in the Union through this logo and thus gain more trust in them.[71] To this end, the Commission has determined the design of a common logo by means of an implementing act (Art. 11(9) DGA).[72] To protect the logos from improper use, they will be registered as trademarks.[73] According to Art. 11(9) DGA, the data intermediation services providers recognised in the Union are to use this logo in a clearly visible manner on every publication associated with their data intermediation services in order to contribute to the distribution and awareness of the logo. It will be interesting to see how many data intermediaries actually submit themselves to a **voluntary compliance assessment** under Art. 11(9) DGA because they expect to gain a competitive advantage by using the label and logo.[74] 21

[68] Rec. 29 DGA.

[69] Rec. 27 DGA.

[70] Rec. 27 DGA.

[71] Rec. 43 DGA.

[72] European Commission, 'Commission Implementing Regulation (EU) 2023/1622 of 9.8.2023 on the design of common logos to identify data intermediation services providers and data altruism organisations recognized in the Union', OJ 2023 L 200, 1.

[73] European Commission, 'Logos for data intermediaries and data altruism organisations recognised in the Union' (9.8.2023) <https://digital-strategy.ec.europa.eu/en/library/logos-data-intermediaries-and-data-altruism-organisations-recognised-union> (last accessed: 18.9.2024). Under this link, the logos are also available for download.

[74] Hornung/Schomberg CR 2022, 508 (514) mn. 32.

3. Additional definitions

22 For some terms such as 'personal data', 'data subject', 'consent' or 'processing', the DGA refers to the corresponding legal definitions in Art. 4 GDPR. However, especially with regard to non-personal data, the Regulation introduces some new definitions. According to Art. 2 no. 8 DGA, **'data holders'** are legal persons (including public bodies and international organisations) or natural persons (who are not at the same time 'data subjects' with respect to the data in question), which have the right under applicable law to grant access to or to share certain personal data or non-personal data. Data subjects and data holders as potential data providers on the one side are interacting with **'data users'** on the other side. According to the legal definition in Art. 2 no. 9 DGA, these are natural or legal persons who have lawful access to certain personal or non-personal data and have the right, including under the GDPR in case of personal data, to use that data for commercial or non-commercial purposes.

II. Scope of application and conditions for data intermediation services

23 The provision of certain data intermediation services listed in Art. 10 DGA requires a **notification** pursuant to Art. 11 DGA and is subject to certain **conditions** set out in Art. 12 DGA. The scope of application of these requirements, thus, includes (i) intermediation services between data holders and potential data users (Art. 10(a) DGA), (ii) intermediation services between data subjects or natural persons which wish to make their personal or non-personal data, respectively, available, and potential data users (Art. 10(b) DGA) as well as (iii) services of data cooperatives (Art. 10(c) DGA). In addition to the provision of the technical or other means as a prerequisite of such services, the intermediation services according to Art. 10(a) DGA also include the bilateral or multilateral exchange of data or the establishment of platforms or databases that enable the exchange or joint use of data. Finally, the establishment of specific infrastructure for the interconnection of data holders with data users also belongs to this category of data intermediation services.

24 By contrast, according to Art. 15 DGA, recognised data altruism organisations and other not-for-profit entities expressly do **not fall within the scope** of Chapter III DGA, insofar as they collect data provided by natural or legal persons in the context of data altruism for objectives of general interest, unless those organisations and entities aim to establish commercial relationships between an undetermined number of data subjects and data holders on the one hand and data users on the other.

1. Notification obligation (Art. 11 DGA)

25 Anyone intending to offer one of the data intermediation services listed in Art. 10 DGA must **submit a notification to the competent authority** (Art. 11(1) DGA). The notification procedure must be designed in a non-discriminatory manner by the competent authority, which has to ensure that the procedure does not distort competition (Art. 11(7) DGA). The competent authorities may charge fees for the notification, which shall be proportionate and objective (Art. 11(11) DGA). Pursuant to Art. 11(6) DGA, the notification must contain the following information: the name of the data intermediary (lit. a), legal status, form, ownership structure, relevant subsidiaries and, where applicable, commercial register number (lit. b), address of the main establishment in the EU, and, where applicable, of any branches in another Member State or of the legal rep-

resentative (lit. c), a public website with complete and up-to-date information on the data intermediary and its activities (lit. d), contact persons and contact details of the data intermediary (lit. e), description of the data intermediation service and its categorisation pursuant to Art. 10 DGA (lit. f) as well as the estimated date for starting the activity, if different from the date of the notification (lit. g). If these details change or if a data intermediation service is discontinued, the data intermediary must inform the competent authority in due time (Art. 11(12) and (13) DGA).

After the submission of a notification, data intermediaries can start their activities in all Member States according to Art. 11(4) and (5) DGA, in compliance with the requirements of Chapter III DGA and – as is well worth noting – **without an ex-ante assessment** by the authorities of compliance with the DGA requirements.[75] Such an assessment is only carried out upon request (Art. 11(9) DGA); the possibility of such an ex ante assessment upon request was added in the trilogue.[76] A data intermediary may request the competent authority to confirm in a declaration within one week after a duly and fully completed notification that the respective data intermediary has submitted the notification in accordance with Art. 11(1) DGA and that it contains the information required under Art. 11(6) DGA (Art. 11(8) DGA). 26

The Commission maintains a central, regularly updated **public register of all data intermediaries** providing their services in the EU (Art. 11(10) DGA). 27

2. Conditions for providing data intermediation services (Art. 12 DGA)

Art. 12 DGA defines the **conditions** under which the data intermediation services named in Art. 10 DGA may be provided. Particularly important and impactful for the business model are the obligation to provide **access on fair, transparent and non-discriminatory terms** (Art. 12(f) DGA) and the **purpose limitation** stipulated by Art. 12(a) DGA. In the sense of a 'one size fits all' approach[77], the DGA lays down the following requirements for all types of data intermediaries. 28

a) No use of data for own purposes (Art. 12(a) DGA)

One of the core requirements for the provision of data intermediation services lies in the purpose limitation: data intermediaries may not use the data for which they provide data intermediation services for any other purposes (Art. 12(a) DGA). The only permitted purpose is to make this data available to data users. Furthermore, the data intermediation services must be provided through a separate legal entity. Accordingly, the data intermediaries are to act as **neutral third parties**.[78] 29

b) Prohibition of tying (Art. 12(b) DGA)

According to Art. 12(b) DGA, the pricing and other commercial terms for the provision of data intermediation services may not be made dependent on whether and to what extent the data holder or the data user uses other services of the same provider or an affiliated company. 30

[75] Roßnagel ZRP 2021, 173 (174 et seq.); Spindler CR 2021, 98 (101) mn. 19.
[76] Hornung/Schomberg CR 2022, 508 (512) mn. 22.
[77] Specht-Riemenschneider et al. MMR-Beil. 2021, 25 (32).
[78] Hornung/Schomberg CR 2022, 508 (512) mn. 21.

c) *Use of metadata (Art. 12(c) DGA)*

31 If **metadata** (e.g., date, time, geodata) relating to the activities of a natural or legal person is collected in the course of the provision of data intermediation services, it may only be used for the development of the respective data intermediation service according to Art. 12(c) DGA. Such data may be used by data intermediaries, for example, to detect fraud or to strengthen cyber security and must be made available to data holders upon request.

d) *Format conversions and interoperability (Art. 12(d) DGA)*

32 In principle, data intermediaries should enable the exchange of data in the format in which they receive it. However, Art. 12(d) DGA provides for some important exceptions, which are primarily intended to promote **interoperability.** Thus, a conversion into another format is indicated (i) if this improves interoperability within and between sectors, (ii) if the data user requests this, (iii) if Union law requires this, or, (iv) if this serves harmonisation with international and European data standards.

e) *Additional tools and services (Art. 12(e) DGA)*

33 In addition to data intermediation, data intermediaries are also allowed to offer a number of additional specific tools and services, which are aimed at data subjects or data holders and are primarily intended to facilitate data exchange (Art. 12(e) DGA). These tools and services may serve, for example, to temporarily store, maintain, convert, anonymise or pseudonymise the data. However, these complementary tools and services may only be used upon request by or with the consent of the data holder or the data subject. Furthermore, the third-party tools offered in this context may not be used for any other purpose.

f) *Fair, transparent, and non-discriminatory access (Art. 12(f) DGA)*

34 A key condition for the provision of data intermediation services is set out in Art. 12(f) DGA. According to this provision, data intermediaries must ensure that the procedure for access to the respective data intermediation service is fair, transparent, and non-discriminatory for all stakeholders. This includes prices as well as terms and conditions. With these **'FAND' terms**[79], the legislator opted for a less restrictive standard in the design of the access regulation than in, for example, Art. 6(11) and (12) DMA, which require gatekeepers to grant access on 'FRAND'[80] terms.

g) *Fraud and abuse prevention (Art. 12(g) DGA)*

35 According to Art. 12(g) DGA, data intermediaries must have procedures in place to prevent fraudulent or abusive practices by parties seeking to gain access through their services.

h) *Business continuity (Art. 12(h) DGA)*

36 In the **event of its insolvency,** a data intermediary must, according to Art. 12(h) DGA, enable an **adequate continuation of the provision of its services.** If the data intermediation service also includes the storage of data, a data intermediary must establish mechanisms that allow data holders and data users to access, transfer or retrieve their

[79] Short for 'fair and non-discriminatory'.
[80] Short for 'fair, reasonable and non-discriminatory'.

data. Where the data intermediary acts as a broker between data subjects and data users, mechanisms shall also be put in place to enable the exercise of data subjects' rights.

i) Interoperability (Art. 12(i) DGA)

According to Art. 12(i) DGA, each data intermediary must take appropriate measures, for example by using open standards used in the respective sector, in order to ensure **interoperability** with other data intermediaries. 37

j) Prevention of unlawful data access/unlawful data transfer (Art. 12(j) DGA)

According to Art. 12(j) DGA, data intermediaries must take **appropriate technical, legal and organisational measures to** prevent the unlawful transfer of or access to non-personal data. In addition to Union law, the national law of the respective Member State also serves as a guideline for lawfulness. 38

k) Obligation to report infringements (Art. 12(k) DGA)

Art. 12(k) DGA stipulates that data intermediaries must **inform** data holders without delay in the event of an unauthorised transfer, access or use of the non-personal data shared by them. The notification obligations in the event of personal data breaches are based on Art. 33 and 34 GDPR, which provide for the notification of the supervisory authority and the data subjects under certain conditions. 39

l) Security level (Art. 12(l) DGA)

In order to ensure an **appropriate level of security** for the storage, processing and transmission of non-personal data, data intermediaries must take the necessary measures according to Art. 12(l) DGA. If competitively sensitive information is involved, data intermediation services providers must even ensure 'the highest level of security'. 40

m) Services for data subjects (Art. 12(m) DGA)

Art. 12(m) DGA sets out special requirements for data intermediaries offering **services to data subjects.** They must act in the data subjects' best interest when facilitating the exercise of data subjects' rights. This includes informing and advising data subjects, before they give their consent, in a concise, transparent, intelligible, and easily accessible manner about intended data uses by data users and the standard terms and conditions pertaining to such uses. However, data subjects cannot instruct data intermediaries to enforce their data subject rights, unless the data intermediaries fulfil the requirements of Art. 80 GDPR, i.e., in particular, act without the intention of making a profit.[81] 41

n) Tools for obtaining consent or permissions (Art. 12(n) DGA)

If a data intermediary provides **tools** by means of which data subjects can give their **consent** or data holders their **permission** for processing, Art. 12(n) DGA requires that, where relevant, it must specify the third-country jurisdiction in which the data use is intended to take place. Furthermore, such data intermediation services providers must simultaneously provide data subjects and data holders with tools to also withdraw their consent or permission for data processing. 42

---

[81] Specht-Riemenschneider et al. MMR-Beil. 2021, 25 (42 et seq.).

o) *Obligation to maintain a log record (Art. 12(o) DGA)*

43 Finally, Art. 12(o) DGA stipulates that data intermediaries must keep a **record** of their data intermediation activities.

3. Designation of a legal representative in the EU

44 A data intermediary established in several EU Member States is subject to the legal jurisdiction of the Member State in which its primary place of business is located (Art. 11(2) DGA). If a data intermediary does not have an establishment in the EU but offers the data intermediation services mentioned in Art. 10 DGA, it must designate a **legal representative** in one of the Member States in which those services are offered (Art. 11(3) DGA). The data intermediary is then subject to the legal jurisdiction of that Member State (Art. 11(3) DGA). The legal representative serves as a single point of contact for questions in connection with the provided data intermediation services, namely for the competent authorities, but also for data subjects and data holders (Art. 11(3) DGA). Furthermore, the representative shall cooperate with the competent authorities and, upon their request, comprehensively demonstrate which measures the data intermediary has taken to comply with the DGA requirements (Art. 11(3) DGA).

45 Without full harmonisation of supervisory and enforcement practices across the authorities in the EU Member States, some differences in enforcement between the competent authorities are to be expected. This may lead to a certain amount of **forum shopping** by data intermediaries for the most advantageous competent authority[82] – similar to the forum shopping regarding the designation of a legal representative for non-EU controllers or processors in accordance with Art. 27 GDPR.

III. Competent authorities and monitoring of compliance

46 For the enforcement of the regulation, Art. 13 DGA provides for the designation of authorities responsible for data intermediation services for each Member State. According to Art. 14 DGA, these authorities are to monitor the compliance of data intermediaries with the requirements of the DGA.

1. Designation and cooperation with other authorities

47 Art. 13(1) DGA provides that each Member State shall designate one or more competent authorities responsible for carrying out the tasks related to the notification procedure for data intermediation services. However, the powers of the competent authorities for data intermediation services do not affect the powers of other authorities with which they have some overlap (e.g., data protection authorities, national competition authorities, cyber security authorities). Instead, in order to ensure a consistent application of the DGA, the DGA provides for a **close cooperation** and **exchange of information** between these authorities. In addition, Art. 26 DGA contains specific requirements for the competent authorities. Accordingly, they must be independent and perform their duties impartially, transparently, consistently, reliably and in a timely manner, while ensuring fair competition and non-discrimination (Art. 26(1) and (2) DGA).

[82] Cf. Schildbach ZD 2022, 148 (150); Spindler CR 2021, 98 (104) mn. 30.

2. Monitoring of compliance with the DGA requirements and penalty options

According to Art. 14 DGA, the **competent authorities** for data intermediaries **monitor and supervise** the compliance of data intermediation services providers with the requirements of Chapter III DGA 'Requirements applicable to data intermediation services'. They may also exercise their control on the basis of a request by a natural or legal person (Art. 14(1) DGA). In order to fulfil its monitoring task, the competent authority may, according to Art. 14(2) DGA, request from data intermediaries any information necessary to verify compliance with the requirements of Chapter III DGA. However, such a request must be proportionate and substantiated. If a data intermediary has its main establishment or legal representative in one Member State, but provides services in other Member States, the competent authorities of the different Member States shall cooperate and assist each other (Art. 14(7) DGA). According to Art. 14(7) DGA, this cooperation between authorities can include both an exchange of information for the purposes of their tasks and a substantiated request that another authority take the measures referred to in Art. 14 DGA. 48

If the competent authority identifies one or more violations of the DGA requirements, it shall notify the provider in question. The provider shall be given the opportunity to state its views within 30 days of the receipt of the notification (Art. 14(3) DGA). Pursuant to Art. 14(4) DGA, the authority may require a data intermediary to cease such an infringement within a reasonable period of time, or, in case of serious breaches, without delay. In addition, the authority shall take **appropriate and proportionate measures** to ensure compliance with the DGA requirements, including various sanctioning options listed in Art. 14(4)(a)–(c) DGA. To ensure that the competent authorities have effective sanctioning mechanisms at their disposal, they are empowered to (i) impose dissuasive fines through administrative proceedings (including periodic penalties and penalties with retroactive effect), initiate legal proceedings to impose fines, or both (Art. 14(4)(a) DGA), (ii) require a postponement of the start or a suspension of the provisions of the data intermediation service until the implementation of the changes requested by the authority (Art. 14(4)(b) DGA) or (iii) in case of serious or repeated infringements which have not been remedied by the respective data intermediary despite notification by the authority, require the cessation of the provision of the data intermediation service altogether (Art. 14(4)(c) DGA). If such a cessation of the data intermediation service has been ordered, the authority shall notify the Commission, whereupon the Commission shall remove the provider from the register of data intermediaries (Art. 14(4) DGA). Once a breach of the DGA requirements has been remedied, the respective data intermediary shall again notify the authority, which in turn informs the Commission (Art. 14(4) DGA). 49

A **provider not established in the EU** may be ordered by the authority to postpone the commencement of its activities as a data intermediary or to suspend such activities until a legal representative has been designated or the necessary information has been provided, demonstrating compliance with the DGA requirements, in accordance with Art. 14(5) DGA. 50

If the authority imposes **measures** on a data intermediary pursuant to Art. 14(4) or Art. 14(5) DGA, it shall notify the provider thereof without delay, including the reasons as well as the steps necessary to remedy the respective deficiencies (Art. 14(6) DGA). Furthermore, according to Art. 14(6) DGA, the authority shall provide the respective data intermediary with a reasonable grace period of no more than 30 days to comply with these measures. 51

C. Requirements for data altruism organisations

52 With the Data Governance Act, the EU also aims to promote **data altruism,** which is defined as the provision and use of data for purposes that serve objectives of general interest. To this end, Chapter IV of the DGA establishes a legal framework for recognised data altruism organisations in order to increase trust in such organisations and, thus, promote the exchange and use of data for such purposes. The requirements for data altruism organisations are more stringent compared to the requirements for (other) data intermediation services.[83] The reasoning behind this is that a voluntary donation of data requires all the more trust that the data will actually be used for the envisioned charitable purposes.

I. Concept of 'data altruism' and 'data altruism organisation recognised in the Union'

53 The legislature has recognised the great potential that the use of data holds not only for the private sector, but also for the **common good.**[84] Accordingly, the 'donation' of such data by data subjects and data holders is to be encouraged. The legal definition of 'data altruism' in Art. 2 no. 16 DGA understands this to mean the voluntary sharing of data on the basis of the consent of data subjects or the permission of data holders, respectively, to allow the use of their data without seeking or receiving a reward (excluding compensation for the costs caused by the provision of the data). The pursued objectives of general interest include, in addition to supporting scientific research, healthcare, combating climate change, improving mobility, improving the provision of public services and public policy making, and facilitating the development, production and dissemination of official statistics.[85] In this context, one of the objectives of the DGA is to contribute to the emergence of sufficiently large data pools through data altruism to enable **data analytics** and **machine learning** in the EU.[86] The Member States are also to play an active role in achieving this goal. Art. 16 DGA provides that Member States may establish organisational and/or technical arrangements and national policies to facilitate and promote data altruism.

54 Paramount for the success of this endeavour is to ensure, through the DGA's high standards for data altruism organisations, the necessary **trust** that the data provided in the context of data altruism will actually be used for charitable purposes.[87] In order to establish this trust, data altruism organisations that meet the requirements of the DGA may register in a public register and then use the designation 'data altruism organisation recognised in the Union' and a common logo for such recognised organisations (cf. Art. 17(2) DGA).[88] In addition, the Commission shall adopt implementing acts establishing and developing a **European** data altruism **consent form** to enable the collection of consents and permissions in all Member States in a uniform format, thereby facilitating the collection of data (Art. 25(1) DGA).

[83] Hornung/Schomberg CR 2022, 508 (512) mn. 24.
[84] Rec. 45 DGA.
[85] Rec. 45 DGA.
[86] Rec. 45 DGA.
[87] Rec. 46 DGA.
[88] Steinrötter DuD 2021, 794 (795).

II. Requirements for data altruism organisations

1. General requirements for registration

In a similar manner to the procedure for (other) data intermediation services providers, Art. 17 et seqq. DGA provide for recognised data altruism organisations to be registered – albeit voluntarily – in a corresponding public register. For registration in a public national register of recognised data altruism organisations, an entity must, according to Art. 18(a)–(e) DGA, (i) carry out data altruism activities (lit. a), (ii) be a legal person established pursuant to national law to meet objectives of general interest as provided for in national law, where applicable (lit. b), (iii) operate on a **not-for-profit basis** and act legally independent from any entity that operates on a for-profit basis (lit. c), (iv) carry out the data altruism activities through a structure that is functionally separate from other activities (lit. d), and (v) comply with the rulebook referenced in Art. 22(1) DGA no later than 18 months after its entry into force (lit. e). 55

2. Registration procedure

If an entity fulfils the requirements set out in Art. 18 DGA, it may **apply for registration in the national public register of data altruism organisations recognised in the Union** in the Member State where it is established or – if it is established in more than one Member State – in which it has its main establishment (Art. 19(1) and (2) DGA). If the entity does not have an establishment in the EU, it shall designate a legal representative in one of the Member States in which it provides data altruism services (Art. 19(3) DGA). This legal representative shall cooperate with the competent authorities, provide them with comprehensive information and also serve as a point of contact for the data subjects or data holders (Art. 19(3) DGA). 56

The **requirements for the application for registration** outlined in Art. 19(4) DGA go beyond those for the application for data intermediation services under Art. 11(6) DGA (→ mn. 25). Thus, in addition to the requirements also set out in Art. 11(6) DGA, an altruism organisation must provide information on the statutes of the entity (Art. 19(4)(c) DGA), its sources of income (Art. 19(4)(d) DGA), the objectives of general interest it intends to promote by collecting data (Art. 19(4)(h) DGA), as well as the type of data it intends to control or process and – in the case of personal data – the categories of such data (Art. 19(4)(i) DGA). 57

In contrast to the registration of recognised providers of data intermediation services, Art. 19(5) DGA provides for a standard **assessment of compliance with the requirements** for data altruism organisations **prior to registration**.[89] If the result of the competent authority's evaluation of the application is positive, it will register the organisation in the national register within 12 weeks of its receipt. This registration is valid in all Member States (Art. 19(5) DGA). The registration and any changes to the information are (further) notified by the authorities to the Commission, which updates the public Union register of recognised data altruism organisations accordingly (Art. 19(7) DGA). 58

3. Transparency requirements

In addition to the conditions for registration in the register, recognised data altruism organisations must fulfil various **transparency requirements.** Thus, according to Art. 20(1)(a)–(d) DGA, they must keep full and accurate records of (i) all natural or legal persons who have been given the possibility to process the data in their possession 59

[89] Hornung/Schomberg CR 2022, 508 (513) mn. 26.

(including contact details) (lit. a), (ii) the date or duration of the processing of data (lit. b), (iii) the purpose of the processing (lit. c), and (iv) any fees paid (lit. d). Furthermore, according to Art. 20(2) DGA, recognised data altruism organisations must prepare a comprehensive **annual activity report** and submit it to the competent authority; its minimum content is set out in Art. 20(2)(a)–(e) DGA.

4. Specific requirements to safeguard the rights and interests of data subjects and data holders

60 Beyond the registration and transparency requirements, recognised data altruism organisations must observe further requirements when providing their activities as specified in Art. 21 DGA:

- **Information obligation** (Art. 21(1) DGA): Organisations must inform data subjects or data holders prior to the processing of their data in a clear and comprehensible manner about the objectives of general interest and – in the case of personal data – about the specified, explicit, and legitimate purpose for which they allow data processing by data users. In the case of processing in a third country, the location shall also be named.
- **Purpose limitation** (Art. 21(2) DGA): The organisations may not use the data for **purposes** other than those of general interest for which the data subject or the data controller have authorised the processing. Misleading marketing practices to obtain data are prohibited.
- **Tools for obtaining consent and permissions** (Art. 21(3) DGA): The data altruism organisation shall provide appropriate tools for obtaining consent or permissions, respectively, for data processing. These tools should also make it easy to withdraw such consent or permission.
- **Appropriate level of security** (Art. 21(4) DGA): For the storage and processing of non-personal data collected on the basis of data altruism, organisations must ensure an appropriate level of security.
- **Obligation to notify breaches** (Art. 21(5) DGA): In the event of an unauthorised transfer, access or use, a data altruism organisation must, without delay, notify the relevant data holder which had shared the non-personal data.
- **Data use in a third country** (Art. 21(6) DGA): If the organisation enables data processing by third parties outside the EU, it must specify the respective third-country jurisdiction in which the data use is intended to take place.

5. Rulebook

61 In order to specify and supplement the requirements of the DGA, the Commission shall adopt delegated acts for the establishment of a **rulebook** (Art. 22(1) DGA). The rulebook shall be prepared in close cooperation with data altruism organisations and relevant stakeholders (Art. 22(2) DGA). According to Art. 22(1)(a)–(d) DGA, this rulebook shall include appropriate information requirements to enable an informed granting of consent or permission for data processing, appropriate technical requirements and security requirements for an adequate level of security, so-called communication roadmaps as well as recommendations on interoperability standards.

III. Competent authorities and monitoring of compliance

Each Member State shall designate one or more **authorities** responsible for the public national register of data altruism organisation recognised in the Union (Art. 23(1) DGA). Insofar as its tasks relate to the processing of personal data, it shall cooperate with the relevant data protection authority and other relevant sectoral authorities (Art. 23(3) DGA). If a data altruism organisation is active in several Member States, the respective competent authorities shall cooperate and exchange the necessary information (Art. 24(6) DGA). Further requirements for the competent authorities, such as their independence, are outlined in Art. 26 DGA. **62**

Pursuant to Art. 24(1) DGA, the competent authorities shall **monitor and supervise** compliance of recognised data altruism organisations with the requirements laid down in Chapter IV DGA, including at the request of a natural or legal person. For this purpose, the authorities may request from the data altruism organisations any information necessary to verify compliance with the DGA requirements (Art. 24(2) DGA). If violations are found, the authority notifies the respective organisation and provides it with 30 days to state its views (Art. 24(3) DGA). In order to enforce the DGA requirements, the authority may, according to Art. 24(4) DGA, require the cessation of an infringement and shall take **appropriate and proportionate measures** to ensure compliance. **63**

If a data altruism organisation fails to remedy a breach of the requirements set out in the DGA after having been notified by the competent authority, it may no longer refer to itself as a 'data altruism organisation recognised in the Union' and will be removed from the relevant registers. **64**

D. Re-use of data held by public sector bodies

For the **re-use of certain categories of data held by public sector bodies,** the DGA lays down some framework conditions. These apply to data that are protected on grounds of (Art. 3(1)(a)–(d) DGA): **65**

- commercial confidentiality (lit. a);
- statistical confidentiality (lit. b);
- protection of intellectual property rights of third parties (lit. c); and
- protection of personal data not falling within the scope of Directive (EU) 2019/1024[90] (lit. d).

According to Art. 3(2) DGA, data held by public undertakings (lit. a), cultural and educational establishments (lit. c) and data protected for reasons of public security (lit. d) are **excluded from the scope of application** of these provisions. **66**

I. Conditions for the re-use of protected data

Art. 5 DGA sets out the conditions for the re-use of the categories of data referred to in Art. 3(1) DGA. Both the conditions for allowing such re-use and the procedure for requesting it must be publicly available for transparency purposes (Art. 5(1) DGA). With regard to the categories of data, the purposes of re-use and the nature of the data, the conditions for re-use must be **non-discriminatory, transparent, proportionate and** **67**

[90] Directive (EU) 2019/1024 of the European Parliament and of the Council of 20.6.2019 on open data and the re-use of public sector information, OJ 2019 L 172, 56.

objectively justified and must not restrict competition (Art. 5(2) DGA). The same applies to any fees: public sector bodies may charge fees for allowing the re-use of such data, but these must be transparent, non-discriminatory, proportionate and objectively justified and must not restrict competition (Art. 6(1) and (2) DGA). In particular, these conditions are intended to promote access to such data for SMEs and start-ups, as well as to facilitate scientific research – accordingly, preferential treatment of such research is considered non-discriminatory.[91] However, the DGA leaves it up to the authorities to decide how the conditions are to be designed in detail and presents them with the challenge of mastering the balancing act between protecting the data and intellectual property on the one hand and promoting the re-use of the data on the other hand.[92]

68 In order to ensure the protection of these data,[93] public sector bodies are ***allowed to*** impose **additional requirements** for **re-use** according to Art. 5(3) DGA. These include the anonymisation of personal data (lit. a (i)), the aggregation or preparation of confidential commercial information or content protected by intellectual property rights (lit. a (ii)), the provision of a secure virtual or physical processing environment in which the re-use takes place and data is made available for remote access or physical access, respectively (lit. b and c). These requirements, thus, rely primarily on technical and organisational data protection measures such as anonymisation and pseudonymisation.[94] If national law does not provide for special safeguards with regard to applicable confidentiality obligations, the public sector body may only allow the use of data provided under additional requirements according to Art. 5(3) DGA if the re-user complies with a confidentiality obligation (Art. 5(5) DGA). Accordingly, disclosure of information that may have been accessible despite the protective measures is prohibited if this could affect the rights and interests of third parties. Therefore, according to Art. 5(5) DGA, re-users are specifically prohibited from re-identifying data subjects (**prohibition of re-identification**). Accordingly, they must take technical and operational measures to prevent re-identification and notify the public sector body – in addition to informing the respective supervisory authority and the data subjects in accordance with the GDPR[95] – of any data breaches that could lead to the re-identification of the data subjects. The same applies under Art. 5(5) DGA for non-personal data: If there is an unauthorised re-use of such data, the re-user must immediately inform the legal persons whose rights and interests could be affected, if necessary, with the help of the public sector body.

69 In order to safeguard the integrity of data protection, the public sector body has the right to verify the process, the means and any results of the data processing carried out by the re-user (Art. 5(4) DGA). If it concludes that the results contain information jeopardising the rights and interests of third parties, the public sector body may prohibit the use of such results (Art. 5(4) DGA).

70 Art. 5(7) DGA stipulates that it is mandatory to respect **intellectual property rights** when re-using data.

71 In cases where re-use is not allowed under Art. 5(3) and (4) DGA, Art. 5(6) DGA provides that the public sector body shall support potential re-users in obtaining the necessary consent or permissions from data subjects and data holders whose rights and interests may be affected by the re-use. For example, the public sector body could pro-

[91] Rec. 15 DGA.
[92] Roßnagel ZRP 2021, 173 (174); Spindler CR 2021, 98 (100) mn. 9; Veil PinG 2023, 1 (7).
[93] This is merely an option, cf. Roßnagel ZRP 2021, 173 (174); Spindler CR 2021, 98 (100) mn. 10.
[94] Schwartmann/Mühlenbeck RDV 2022, 264 (267); Spindler CR 2021, 98 (100) mn. 6.
[95] Cf. rec. 15 DGA.

vide **assistance** by offering technical means to forward consent or permission requests from re-users.[96]

II. Specific requirements for the transfer of non-personal data to third countries

72 Not least to protect against intellectual property theft or industrial espionage, **additional requirements** apply to **the transfer of non-personal data to third countries.**[97] There is no need for a regulation regarding personal data in the DGA, as the prevailing GDPR already contains comprehensive provisions in this regard.[98] Indeed, the DGA 'echo[s] concepts that are already in use in the GDPR'[99], in particular regarding international data transfers. According to Art. 5(14) DGA, a data transfer to third countries is only permitted if the respective third country fulfils the requirements of Art. 5(10) and Art. 5(12) and (13) DGA and, thus, adequate safeguards for the use of the data have been put in place.[100] Before transferring non-personal data of the data categories mentioned in Art. 3(1) DGA to third countries, the re-user must inform the public sector body of this intention to transfer as well as the purpose of the data transfer (Art. 5(9) DGA). If one of the cases of Art. 5(6) DGA applies, the re-user, if necessary, with the help of the public sector body, must inform the legal person whose rights and interests may be affected of the intention to transfer, its purpose and the appropriate safeguards (Art. 5(9) DGA). According to Art. 5(9) DGA, re-use of the data in these cases is only possible if the legal person allows the data transfer to the third country. If a re-user wishes to transfer non-personal confidential data or data protected by intellectual property rights to a third country, it must contractually undertake to fulfil the obligations regarding the protection of intellectual property rights as well as regarding confidentiality set out in Art. 5(7) and (8) DGA also in the third country and to accept the jurisdiction of the courts of the Member State in which the transmitting public sector body is located for all disputes in this context (Art. 5(10) DGA).

73 In order to facilitate the transfer of non-personal data to third countries in the future, Art. 5(11) DGA, in a similar way to the GDPR, provides for the Commission to adopt implementing acts with **model contractual clauses** to fulfil the obligations set out in Art. 5(10) DGA.[101] Analogous to Art. 45 GDPR[102] regarding the transfer of personal data to third countries, the Commission may also determine the adequacy of the protection of non-personal data in third countries in adequacy decisions pursuant to Art. 5(12) DGA.[103] This is the case if a third country offers a level of protection that is to be regarded as essentially equivalent to the level of protection prevailing in the EU.[104]

74 For certain **highly sensitive categories of non-personal data,** the transfer and re-use in third countries can also be made subject to additional conditions or, in exceptional cases, even completely prohibited, for example if public safety or public health appear to be put at risk as a result of such transfer or re-use (Art. 5(13) DGA).

---

96 Rec. 15 DGA.
97 Rec. 20 DGA; Miadzvetskaya European Data Protection Law Review 2023, 13 (14).
98 Spindler CR 2021, 98 (101) mn. 13.
99 Miadzvetskaya European Data Protection Law Review 2023, 13 (14).
100 Rec. 20 DGA.
101 Miadzvetskaya European Data Protection Law Review 2023, 13 (15).
102 Spindler CR 2021, 98 (101) mn. 12.
103 Miadzvetskaya European Data Protection Law Review 2023, 13 (15).
104 Rec. 21 DGA.

75 If a transfer of non-personal data to a third country or access to such data by governmental organisations of a third country is in **conflict with national or Union law,** all parties involved must take all reasonable technical, legal (including contractual agreements) and organisational measures to prevent such transfer or access (Art. 31(1) DGA). According to Art. 31(1) DGA, this obligation applies to both the public body and the natural or legal person who has been granted the right to re-use data, but also to the respective data intermediaries or data altruism organisations. Further restrictions on international access to and transfer of non-personal data are included in Art. 31(2)–(5) DGA.

III. Avoidance of exclusive contracts for re-use

76 In order to promote the freest possible re-use of data held by public sector bodies, Art. 4 DGA provides in principle for a **prohibition of exclusive arrangements** with regard to such data.[105] Any type of agreement or other practice that aims at or brings about such exclusivity or otherwise restricts re-use by parties other than the contracting parties is thus to be prevented. The granting of an exclusive right of re-use is only allowed in cases where this is strictly necessary for the provision of a service or the provision of a product in the general interest (Art. 4(2) DGA). This exclusivity is also limited to a maximum duration of 12 months (Art. 4(4) DGA). If an exclusive right of re-use does not comply with the requirements of this regulation, it shall be invalid.[106] Already existing exclusivity agreements shall not be renewed after their expiry or terminated within 30 months after the entry into force of the DGA, i.e., by 24.12.2024 at the latest (Art. 4(6) DGA).[107]

E. Penalties

77 Art. 34(1) DGA obliges Member States to adopt and apply rules on penalties applicable to infringements of certain DGA requirements[108]. According to Art. 34(1) DGA, these penalties must be **effective, proportionate and dissuasive**. When imposing penalties for violations of the DGA, the Member States shall, according to Art. 34(2)(a)–(e) DGA, take into account, inter alia, the following criteria:

(i) the nature, gravity, extent, and duration of the infringement (lit. a);
(ii) any action taken by the data intermediary to mitigate or remedy the damage caused by the infringement (lit. b);
(iii) any previous infringements by the data intermediary (lit. c);
(iv) the financial benefits gained, or losses avoided by the data intermediary due to the infringement, insofar as these can be reliably established (lit. d); as well as
(v) any other aggravating or mitigating factors applicable to the circumstances of the case (lit. e).

---

[105] Spindler CR 2021, 98 (100) mn. 8.

[106] Rec. 13 DGA.

[107] Rec. 14 DGA.

[108] According to Art. 34(1) DGA, infringements of Art. 5(14) and Art. 31 DGA (obligations regarding the transfer of non-personal data to third countries), Art. 11 (notification obligation for providers of data intermediation services), Art. 12 (conditions for providing data intermediation services) and Art. 18, 20, 21 and 22 (conditions for registration as a 'data altruism organisation recognised in the Union') shall be penalised.

F. Reception and outlook: How effective will the DGA be?

More restrictive requirements for data intermediation services, transparent registers and compliance monitoring by authorities lead to more trust in such services. More trust leads to a greater willingness to share data. The bigger amounts of data, in turn, create an improved basis for innovation and decision-making and facilitate progress in achieving goals such as combating climate change, creating improved mobility solutions or improvements in the health sector. At least that seems to be the Commission's reasoning.[109] In any case, in view of large, established oligopolies in the field of data collection and use, which already have enormous amounts of data at their disposal, achieving these goals will be no easy feat.[110] The establishment of new, secure data intermediaries and data spaces in a 'European' manner is pitched against strong network and lock-in effects of already existing data pools.[111] Neutral data intermediaries could, however, represent an attractive counter-model to such data monopolies for both data providers and users.[112] It remains to be seen whether 'data intermediation services provider recognised in the Union' and 'data altruism organisation recognised in the Union' can gain a foothold in the market as strong, trustworthy labels and generate sufficient interest on the part of data subjects and data holders as well as data users. It is worth noting (and often criticised), that the DGA does not contain any actual incentives to provide consent or permission.[113] Moreover, the (potential) data intermediaries themselves should not be forgotten, whose successful participation under the DGA would require an attractive business model.[114] However, the literature rightly criticises that the DGA does not provide any legal incentives for providers to act as data intermediaries in the sense of the DGA at all, e.g., through easing some restrictions stipulated by the GDPR.[115] On the contrary, the DGA even imposes additional regulatory requirements on data intermediaries in the area of data protection and IT security, which could deter potential providers.[116] In addition, the framework provided by the DGA comes with 'high legal uncertainty'[117] for the data intermediaries, as both scope and rules set out in the DGA are rather vague. 78

Moreover, the Member States are responsible for the further specification of the sanction instruments. A certain patchwork of penalty options is therefore to be expected, which could lead to inconsistent enforcement practices by the authorities and a certain amount of 'forum shopping' in the selection of the Member State in which a legal representative is designated.[118] Therefore, it is still unclear how incisive the penalties 79

---

[109] Similarly, Roßnagel ZRP 2021, 173 (176), who sees the protection of fundamental rights as a 'prerequisite for trust and thus a condition for success for a European-style data economy'.

[110] Hornung/Schomberg CR 2022, 508 (513) mn. 28 et seq.; Schütrumpf/Person RDi 2022, 281 (281); Specht-Riemenschneider et al. MMR-Beil. 2021, 25 (32); Spindler CR 2021, 98 (108) mn. 47.

[111] Cf. Roßnagel ZRP 2021, 173 (173).

[112] Hornung/Schomberg CR 2022, 508 (513) mn. 28.

[113] Hornung/Schomberg CR 2022, 508 (514) mn. 38; Schildbach ZD 2022, 148 (152); Steinrötter ZD 2021, 61 (62).

[114] Specht-Riemenschneider et al. MMR-Beil. 2021, 25 (26).

[115] Hornung/Schomberg CR 2022, 508 (514) mn. 33, 38; Specht-Riemenschneider et al. MMR-Beil. 2021, 25 (32); Steinrötter DuD 2021, 794 (796, 798).

[116] Fanderl/Niclas/von Blumenthal ITRB 2022, 145 (145); Richter GRUR International 2023, 458 (465, 467); Schildbach ZD 2022, 148 (153); Specht-Riemenschneider et al. MMR-Beil. 2021, 25 (32); Spindler CR 2021, 98 (107 et seq.) mn. 45; Steinrötter DuD 2021, 794 (796 et seq.); Veil PinG 2023, 1 (8). Of a different opinion: Roßnagel ZRP 2021, 173 (175 et seq.), who considers these additional requirements inadequate from a data protection perspective.

[117] Richter GRUR International 2023, 458 (465).

[118] Cf. Spindler CR 2021, 98 (104) mn. 30; Richter GRUR International 2023, 458 (465).

under the DGA will really be – and accordingly how effective its enforcement will be in practice. However, effective monitoring of the data intermediaries by the competent authorities is a key prerequisite for the trust of the various data actors,[119] on which the impact of the DGA ultimately depends.

[119] Hornung/Schomberg CR 2022, 508 (513) mn. 29.

§ 20
Platform-specific requirements of the Data Act

Literature: *Armstrong*, 'Competition in two-sided markets', Rand Journal of Economics 2006, 668; *Bakos*, 'Does Anyone Read the Fine Print? Consumer Attention to Standard-Form Contracts', Journal of Legal Studies 2014, 1; *Bar-Gill*, Seduction by Contract: Law, Economics, and Psychology in Consumer Markets, Oxford 2012; *Belleflamme/Peitz*, The Economics of Platforms: Concepts and Strategy, Cambridge 2021; *Ben-Shahar/Schneider*, 'The Failure of Mandated Disclosure', University of Pennsylvania Law Review 2011, 647; *Bomhard/Merkle*, 'Der Entwurf eines EU Data Acts', RDi 2022, 168; *Budzinski/Mendelsohn*, 'Regulating Big Tech: From Competition Policy to Sector Regulation?' ORDO 72/73 (2023) 217–255; *Coase*, 'The Problem of Social Cost', Journal of Law and Economics 1960, 1; *Cooter/Ulen*, Law and Economics, 6th edn Berkeley 2016;; *Eckhardt/Kerber*, 'Property rights theory, bundle of rights on IoT data and the Data Act', Andrássy Working Paper Series in Economics and Business Administration No 51, 2023 (forthcoming in: European Journal of Law & Economics 2024); *Engeler*, 'Der Konflikt zwischen Datenmarkt und Datenschutz', NJW 2022, 3398; *Farrell/Saloner*, 'Standardization, Compatibility, and Innovation', Rand Journal of Economics 1985, 70; *Graef/Husovec/van den Boom*, 'Spill-Overs in Data Governance: Uncovering the Uneasy Relationship Between the GDPR's Right to Data Portability and EU Sector-Specific Data Access Regimes', EuCML 2020, 3; *Greis*, Just Price in Markets, Yale 2023; *Hennemann/Steinrötter*, 'Data Act – Fundament des neuen EU-Datenwirtschaftsrechts?', NJW 2022, 1481; *Hutt*, Economists and the Public: A Study of Competition and Opinion, London 1936; *Jacobides/Lianos*, 'Ecosystems and Competition Law in Theory and Practice', ICC 2021, 1199; *Jones/Tonetti*, 'Nonrivalry and the Economics of Data', AER 2020, 2819; *Katz/Shapiro*, 'Network Externalities, Competition, and Compatibility', AER 1985, 424; *Katz/Shapiro*, 'Systems Competition and Network Effects', 8/2 JEP 1994, Vol 8 No 2, 93–115; *Kerber*, 'Governance of IoT Data: Why the EU Data Act will not Fulfill Its Objectives', GRUR Int., 120–135; *Kerber/Zolna*, 'Konsumentensouveränität und Datensouveränität als ökonomischer Sicht', in: Augsberg/Gehring (eds.), Datensouveränität – Positionen zur Debatte, Frankfurt am Main 2022, p. 43; *Knapp/Kobler/Richter*, 'Was der Bauer (nicht) kennt ... Datengenossenschaften', in Heinze (ed), Tagungsband DSRI-Herbstakademie, Edewecht 2022, p. 443; *Martens*, 'Data access, consumer interests and social welfare – An economic perspective on date', in German Federal Ministry of Justice and Consumer Protection/Max Planck Institute for Innovation and Competition (eds), Data Access, Consumer Interests and Public Welfare, Baden-Baden 2021, p. 69. *McColgan*, Abschied vom Informationsmodell im Recht der Allgemeinen Geschäftsbedingungen, Tübingen 2020; *Mendelsohn/Budzinski*, 'DMA: Background, Objectives and its Relationship to Competition Law', in: Schmidt/Hübener, New Digital Markets Act, Baden Baden/Oxford 2023, p. 5; *Metzger/Schweitzer*, 'Shaping Markets: A Critical Evaluation of the Draft Data Act', ZEuP 2023, 42; *Nullmeier*, 'Dateneigentum', in: Klenk/Nullmeier/Wewer (eds), Handbuch Digitalisierung in Staat und Verwaltung, Wiesbaden 2020, p. 255; *Peitz*, 'Marktplätze und indirekte Netzwerkeffekte', PWP 2006, 317; *Prüffer/Schottmüller*, 'Competing with Big Data', Journal of Industrial Economics 2021, 967; *Robertson*, Antitrust Market Definition for Digital Markets, Concurrences N° 2 2021, 3; *Rochet/Tirole*, 'Two-sided Markets: A Progress Report', Rand Journal of Economics 2006, 645; *Schmidtchen/Kirstein*, Competition as a Discovery Process, German Working Papers in Law and Economics, 2001, 10; *Schweitzer/Metzger*, 'Data Access under the Draft Data Act, Competition Law and the DMA: Opening the Data Treasures for Competition and Innovation', GRUR Int. 2023, 337; *Scott Morton/Crawford/Crémer/* Dinielli/Fletcher/Heidhues/Schnitzer, Equitable Interoperability: The Supertool of Digital Platform Governance, Yale Journal of Regulation Vol. 40, 2023, 1013; *Smith*, 'Markets as Economizers of Information', Economic Inquiry 1982, 165; *Specht-Riemenschneider*, 'Data access rights – A comparative perspective, in German Federal Ministry of Justice and Consumer Protection/Max Planck Institute for Innovation and Competition (eds), Data Access, Consumer Interests and Public Welfare, Baden-Baden 2021, p. 401; *Specht-Riemenschneider*, 'Der Entwurf des Data Act', MMR 2022, 809; *Steinrötter*, 'Verhältnis von Data Act und DSGVO, Zugleich ein Beitrag zur Konkurrenzlehre im Rahmen der EU-Digitalgesetzgebung', GRUR 2023, 216; *von Hayek*, 'Competition as a Discovery Procedure', in: von Hayek, New Studies in Philosophy, Politics, Economics and the History of Ideas, London 1978; *Williamson*, 'Legal Implications of Imperfect Information in Consumer Markets', JITE 1995, 49; *Zuboff*, The Age of Surveillance Capitalism, New York 2018.

A. Introduction and aim of the chapter

1 The business models of all large digital platforms and ecosystems rely on **data-driven value creation mechanisms** as well as **data-driven network effects** and **economies of scale.** This value creation is not limited to personal data, but increasingly includes so-called '**machine data**': data generated, stored and processed through the use of connected devices and IoT systems. In the absence of the explicit legal allocation of this data,[1] it currently falls to the producers and manufacturers of these devices to grant or exclude others from access and use.[2] The newly enacted Data Act[3] is the first piece of EU legislation to address questions of fair access (to data). Alongside the Digital Markets Act (DMA), which addresses market failures in the digital economy, the General Data Protection Regulation (GDPR) and the Data Governance Act (DGA), which regulate the rights to and management of personal and other data, the Data Act aims at a '*fairer*' allocation of data and aims to albeit 'equip and empower citizens and businesses with the ability to benefit from an inclusive and fair data market'[4] and 'to foster the development of new, innovative connected products or related services, stimulate innovation on aftermarkets, (and to develop) entirely novel services making use of the data concerned'.[5]

2 The Data Act is designed as a **horizontal, cross-sectoral regulation.**[6] Apart from the asymmetric excemption from access claims for large platforms – i.e., undertakings designated as gatekeepers by the DMA (Art. 5(3) Data Act) – the Data Act does not contain any regulations specifically related to these companies. However, since the tech giants or

[1] Specht-Riemenschneider MMR 2022, 809 (815); Hennemann/Steinrötter NJW 2022, 1481 mn. 4; Drexl/Banda/Otero/Hoffmann/Kim/Kulhari/Moscon/Richter/Wiedemann, 'Positions Statement of the Max Planck Insitute for Innovation and Competition of 25 May 2022 on Commission's Proposal of 23 February 2022 for a Regulation on harmonised rules on fair access to and use of data (Data Act)' <www.ip.mpg.de/fileadmin/ipmpg/content/stellungnahmen/Position_Statement_MPI_Data_Act_Formal__13.06.2022.pdf> (last accessed: 22.2.2024), mn. 49.

[2] Metzger/Schweitzer ZEuP2023, 42.

[3] Regulation (EU) 2023/2854 of the European Parliament and of the Council of 13 December 2023 on harmonised rules on fair access to and use of data, OJ L 2023/2854.

[4] Rec. 19 Data Act.

[5] Rec. 32 Data Act.

[6] Schweitzer/Metzger GRUR Int. 2023, 337 (338): 'Legislation of this kind no longer limits itself to addressing well-defined market failures (like market power). Rather, it follows a market-shaping approach: it creates a new sort of parallel rights of access and use of data and thereby redefines the legal infrastructure based on which markets evolve.'

so-called GAF(M)A/GAMAM companies (the platforms and ecosystems mentioned in → mn. 1)[7] are leaders in numerous IoT markets,[8] they are all addressees of the Data Act and expect to be significantly impacted by it. The Data Act is thus a **core element of future platform regulation**.

3 This chapter is dedicated to the Data Act in its specific application to these tech platforms, all of which are also considered to have a significant degree of '**data power**'.[9] First, the European Data Strategy and platform-specific data-related features are explained. Next, the concepts and provisions of the Data Act are described briefly. In order to assess the possible effects of these provisions on the distribution of and the creation of value from the data of platform companies, this article then turns to the key instruments and provisions of the Data Act and their effects. This part thus looks at the Data Act's creation of *in situ rights*, its market-related approaches (consent and contractual solutions) and anticipated dynamics, such as the creation of *aftermarkets*. Last, this chapter shows inconsistencies that arise in connection with the overall goals of platform regulation.

B. Basics: Platform-based data benefits and the European data strategy

4 Looking at the Data Act in the context of the EU Data Strategy, this chapter describes the benefits that platforms experience in relation to data and how the Data Act intends to improve **value creation** from this data.

I. Data in IoT ecosystems and the platform economy

5 With respect to large platforms, the Data Act primarily serves to **better create and allocate value** derived from the data in the digital economy. In this context, access to IoT or machine data promises the creation of data-interoperable and consumer-oriented networks or **digital ecosystems** without the relevant data benefiting only one company, which dominates the ecosystem. The objectives of the Data Act are thus not only in line with the general EU Data Strategy, but also reflect the current **interoperability efforts** in competition and regulatory policy.[10] These seek to realise network effects at the market level and not only at platform or company level.[11] In order to show the relevance of data in and for platforms and IoT ecosystems and the above mentioned effects, the next section will first reiterate some of the economic fundaments of these concepts and briefly explain the relevant data benefits in each case.

---

[7] Google – now Alphabet, Facebook – now Meta Platforms, Amazon, Apple and Microsoft.

[8] For the example of voice assistants, see European Commission, 'Preliminary Report – Sector inquiry into Consumer Internet of Things', 9.6.2021, SWD(2021) 144 final, 4, 34, 59, 111.

[9] Metzger/Schweitzer ZEuP2023, 42 (51); Prüfer/Schottmüller Journal of Industrial Economics 2021, 967.

[10] Interoperability is the subject of numerous competition proceedings (e.g. against the Google Android system and now the Apple Pay wallet system). The DMA now contains numerous interoperability provisions, including for number-independent interpersonal communications services in Art. 7 DMA.

[11] Scott Morton/Crawford/Crémer/Dinielli/Fletcher/Heidhues/Schnitzer, Yale Journal of Regulation Vol. 40, 2023, 1013 Scott Morton/Kades, 'Interoperability as a competition remedy for digital networks', 22.02.2021 <ssrn.com/abstract=3808372> (last accessed: 28.08..2024): 'Having a remedy in its toolkit that removes network effects at the level of the company – and instead makes them operate at the level of the market, available to all – will be of tremendous benefit to future consumers'; Kerber/Schweitzer JIPITEC 2017, 39.

6 Although there is no fixed definition of a **digital ecosystem** and existing descriptions are complex and multi-layered,[12] it refers to *'a network of different (online) markets and/or actors that are interconnected or linked by a digital information services market'*.[13] The term **digital ecosystem** can thus refer to a group or firm structure as well as to a market with digital interconnections and interdependencies. Such an information services market quite often takes the form of a central platform – *'an economic intermediary between different market sides or groups/actors'*[14]. According to *Belleflamme* and *Peitz* (digital) platforms are 'facilitators of interaction and trade and managers of network effects'.[15] The economic novelty of both platforms and digital ecosystems relates to direct and indirect network effects and economies of scale.

7 **Direct network effects** describe benefits that individual users experience when a large number of them use the same product or service.[16] A classic example is software (such as Microsoft Word) that has become a standard tool. Numerous platforms, especially communication platforms, are characterised by direct network effects. These account for the size of the platforms (measured in user numbers) and make effective competition or the parallel existence of smaller networks difficult. **Indirect network effects** arise when the benefit on one side of the market (e.g. an advertising market) increases with the number of users on the other side of the market or even depends on it.[17] On many platforms data-driven indirect network effects arise almost naturally and justify the position of single entities or companies as 'gatekeepers' between the market and users.[18] An important further **supply-side economy of scale** experienced by consumers on platforms such as *Amazon* is that they can purchase numerous (related or even diverse) goods from a single source. A natural limit to this advantage, which occurs in the form of supply and information overload or oversaturation of consumers, is increasingly being mitigated through algorithm- and data-driven optimisations and personalisations of offers and services on digital platforms.[19]

II. Data concentration in IoT markets

8 The GAF(M)A/GAMAM platforms also dominate the so-called **IoT markets** – markets for interrelated electronic devices that connect with eachother and exchange data or information. For example, Amazon's Alexa, Alphabet's Google Assistant and Apple's Siri currently share the voice assistant market. Such systems and products that are interconnected via the internet often also form a IoT ecosystem thus *'encompass(-ing) various services, devices and technologies that support the interaction of consumers with*

---

[12] Jacobides/Lianos ICC 2021, 1199; Robertson Concurrences N° 2–2021, 3.

[13] Mendelsohn/Budzinski in Schmidt/Hübener, New Digital Markets Act, § 2 mn. 2.

[14] Mendelsohn/Budzinski in Schmidt/Hübener, New Digital Markets Act, § 2 mn. 2.

[15] Belleflamme/Peitz, The Economics of Platforms: Concepts and Strategy, p.13.

[16] The conventional definition of direct network effects comes from Katz and Shapiro (1985). Thus, the utility that a consumer derives from a good depends on the number of other consumers of the good. The size of the network has a direct impact on the utility of the network participants. See Katz/Shapiro AER 1985, 424; Katz/Shapiro JEP 1994, 93; Farrell/Saloner Rand Journal of Economics 1985, 70.

[17] Rochet/Tirole Rand Journal of Economics 2006, 645; Armstrong Rand Journal of Economics 2006; Mendelsohn/Budzinski in Schmidt/Hübener, § 2 mn. 7.

[18] Crémer/de Montjoye/Schweitzer, 'Competition Policy for the Digita Era' (Report for Commission, 2019) <ec.europa.eu/competition/publications/reports/kd0419345enn.pdf> (last accessed: 22.2.2024), p. 54; Peitz PWP 2006, 317.

[19] Mendelsohn/Budzinski in Schmidt/Hübener, New Digital Markets Act, 2 mn. 7.

connected devices ('things'), which collect and exchange data over the internet'.[20] The European Commission's IoT sector inquiry of 2021[21] shows that the integration of different components of many IoT ecosystems depends one such voice assistant or operating system. These serve as an interface between different devices. The fact that these ecosystems are often identical to or owned by the GAFMA/GAMAM companies means that these IoT ecosystems are largely closed and without integration or interoperability options for smaller competitors. Accordingly, there is no competition and the value creation falls to only one company. Importantly, the manufacturers of IoT devices generate, collect and process a wide range of unique data. The quality of many self-learning and data-driven IoT devices depends on access to large **amounts of data**. Thus strong data-related network effects and economies of scale are also present here. In addition, the monetisation opportunities of data grow exponentially with its volume. Data concentration can therefore lead to innovation and welfare losses in the long term. This also contradicts the idea of competition as a an open and fair process,[22] and hinders thus optimal **data value distribution**. In order to '**open up**' existing IoT ecosystems and ensure the innovation and competitiveness of competing products, the Data Act introduces a far-reaching **data access** solution.

III. Data and EU data strategy

The Data Act aims at improving value creation from data and thus forms part of the **European Data Strategy**. This in turn is embedded in the **European Digital Strategy** and in **Europe's Digital Decade**.[23] All these policies taken together should enable the utilisation of the economic characteristics of data and the resulting potential for value creation in a way that is based on European fundamental rights and puts people at the centre.[24] 9

The economic potential of data lies in its function as a primary resource for data-driven technology (→ mn. 13 et seq.). One economic characteristic of data is their **non-rivalry**.[25] This means that data and data sets can be shared without loss in terms of quality and quantity, duplicated almost free of charge and used indefinitely. EU estimates place the value of the European data economy at 829 billion EUR by 2025.[26] While data is non-rivalrous, it is, however, easily possible to exclude others from their use. Advances in **data access and shared use** are thus needed to lead the way in enabling businesses and the public sector to make data-based decisions and to create value for the economy and society.[27] 10

[20] European Commission, 'Preliminary Report – Sector inquiry into Consumer Internet of Things', 9.6.2021, SWD(2021) 144 final, 13.

[21] European Commission, 'Preliminary Report – Sector inquiry into Consumer Internet of Things', 9.6.2021, SWD(2021) 144 final.

[22] v. Hayek, 1978, p. 179; Smith, p. 165: *'[…] the complete set of rules (or customs) which specify the process through which economic agents communicate, exchange information and negotiate contracts for the exchange of items or services of value'*; Schmidtchen/KirsteinGerman Working Papers in Law and Economics 2001, 10.

[23] European Commission, 'A European strategy for data', 19.2.2020, COM(2020) 66 final, 1 et seq.

[24] European Commission, 'A European strategy for data', 19.2.2020, COM(2020) 66 final, 5.

[25] Jones/Tonetti AER 2020, 2819 (2819).

[26] Compared to 301 billion EUR in 2018; see press release on European Commission, 'A European strategy for data', 24.02.2021 <https://www.europarl.europa.eu/topics/en/article/20210218STO98124/european-strategy-for-data-what-meps-want≥ (last accessed: 22.2.2024).

[27] Cf. rec. 6 Data Act.

11 In addition to sharing and access concerns, the Data Strategy envisions improvements in the following areas: data availability and quality, market power, interoperability, data governance, data infrastructure, data literacy and cybersecurity. In this context, an increase in **data availability** and **data quality** in both the private and public sectors could enable innovative reuse and would be further enhanced by increased interoperability. In addition, the European legislator has indentified market imbalances in cloud services relating to **data access** as well as **data use** and intends to address the resulting data advantages. The underlying ideal of improved **data governance** includes new concepts and instruments for the use of existing data spaces within the existing legal framework.[28] In addition, investment in data and blockchain technologies mitigate deficits in **data infrastructures** and cybersecurity.[29] Investments in skills programmes to increase individual **data literacy** are also needed.[30] All of these goals are to be reached in an energy-efficient, independent and decentralised manner.

12 To address these challenges, the EU's Data Strategy creates four pillars[31] of measures: (1) horizontal governance requirements for data access, sharing and use consisting of the DGA (governance) and the Data Act (access); (2) investments in high-impact projects intend to strengthen European data spaces and their positive impact on interoperability developments (with key actions of cloud regulation EU Cloud Rulebook, European Marketplace for Cloud Services[32]); (3) promotion of individual data literacy and empowering individuals to control their data; (4) promotion of data spaces in strategic sectors and domains of public interest (manufacturing, green developments, health, finance). The Data Act unfolds its effect conceptually as part of the first and third pillars by establishing data access rights and strengthening data subject rights, especially for machine-generated data.

IV. Basic ideas on access and use and their implications

13 The allocative choices underlying the Data Strategy and the Data Act are by no means compelling. On the contrary, the EU legislator was faced with various options for creating incentives for an increased data sharing while taking privacy considerations into account. The alternatives range from indtroducing **exclusive rights**[33] on the one hand to comprehensive **access and exploitation rights** on the other.[34] The starting point is that both an increased generation of data and an increased volume of shared data are seen as fundamentally economically desirable.[35] Reconciling these two objectives,

---

[28] European Commission, 'A European strategy for data', 19.2.2020, COM(2020) 66 final, 8.

[29] European Commission, 'A European strategy for data', 19.2.2020, COM(2020) 66 final, 9.

[30] European Commission, 'A European strategy for data', 19.2.2020, COM(2020) 66 final, 10.

[31] European Commission, 'A European strategy for data', 19.2.2020, COM(2020) 66 final, 12 et seq.

[32] See Member States, 'Declaration. Building the next generation cloud for businesses and the public sector in the EU', 15.10.2020.

[33] On the *bundle of rights* theory, which remains relevant, see Eckhardt/Kerber European Journal of Law & Economics (forthcoming 2024), 4 et seq.; on the wider legal framework Schweitzer/Metzger GRUR 2023, 337.

[34] Building on this, various data governance and intermediary models exist in this area of tension, which either accentuate exclusivity aspects or focus on access rights and can accordingly be implemented differently under the DGA and the Data Act. On data ownership, see Nullmeier in Klenk/Nullmeier/Wewer, p. 255 et seqq. On data cooperative as distinct from data trust, see Knapp/Kobler/Richter in Heinze, p. 451 and on a data omnibus model, Bertschek/Bonin/Kühling/Thüsing/Wenzel, 'Entwicklung eines Konzepts zur Datenallmende' (IZA Research Reports 119, July 2021) <docs.iza.org/report_pdfs/iza_report_119.pdf.> (last accessed: 22.2.2024). Overall see, Mulgan/Straub 'The new ecosystem of trust' (Nesta 2019) <www.nesta.org.uk/blog/new-ecosystem-trust/> (last accessed: 22.2.2024).

[35] Martens in Drexl, Data Access, Consumer Interests and Public Welfare, p. 5 et seq.

has however, proven difficult. Exclusive rights may incentivise data holders to generate data and exclusively exploitate them, but do not promote an increased sharing. Inversely, far-reaching **access rights** generally incentivise the broad use of data, but may not create an incentive for data generation. Thus, the initial situation requires a consideration of which incentive regime appears to be most effective to ensure a functioning data economy. For personal data for instance, the best possible trade-off between individual data protection interests and the value created by sharing and using the data can only be made by the data subject herself.[36] This logic does, however, not naturally extend to machine data since there are more interests and sources of data creation/derivation at stake.[37]

Against the background of these options and interests, the Data Act favours **access rights** for reasons of utility – because 'the same data set may potentially be used and reused for a variety of purposes and to an unlimited degree, without any loss in its quality or quantity'.[38] The extent to which the Data Act succeeds in fulfilling these goals is the subject of the analysis of the individual provisions below (→ mn. 15 et seqq.). In this context it must be taken into account that the legal impact assessment on which the Data Act is based showed a preference for its moderate regulatory approach.[39] 14

C. The Data Act

This section looks at the individual sections of the **Data Act.** 15

I. Objectives and legal nature

The Data Act is designed as a horizontal, fully harmoned EU regulation and is part of the **European Data Strategy** (→ mn. 9 et seqq.). With it the Commission aims to 'ensure fairness in the allocation of value from data among actors in the data economy and fostering access to and use of data in order to contribute to establishing a genuine internal market for data'.[40] 16

The **Data Act** aims to facilitate **data access** – though not for large gatekeepers or platfroms – without, however, foregoing incentives to invest in data-related value creation. To this end, switching between cloud services is to be facilitated, unlawful data transfers by cloud providers prevented, interoperability standards developed and important B2G (*business to government*) data transfers are to be made possible. The implementation of these goals is also to be carried out in coherence with the existing data law regulations.[41] 17

The proposed regulation is intended to complement existing regulations on the processing of personal data. The Data Act thus stands alongside the EU data protection provisions as well as the sector-specific regulations. In particular, there should be no compromise on the level of protection of the GDPR and the Data Act should not be regarded as a *lex specialis* to it. In event of a conflict, the provisions of the GDPR shall prevail.[42] 18

[36] Jones/Tonetti AER 2020, 2819 (2854).
[37] On the relevant idea of co-creation and thus co-ownership of such data see, Metzger/Schweitzer ZEuP2023, 42.
[38] Rec. 1 Data Act.
[39] European Commission, 'Impact Assessment Report', 23.2.2022, SWD(2022) 34 final, 66.
[40] Rec. 119 Data Act.
[41] Rec 7 Data Act.
[42] Rec. 7 Data Act.

II. Chapters and provisions

The 11 chapters of the Data Act contain the following provisions:

19 The **first chapter** contains general and fundamental provisions pertaining to the subject matter and scope of the regulation: Art. 1(1) and (2) Data Act state the subject matter and scope of the regulation. Art. 1(3) describes the regulation's addressees and Art. 2 contains relevant legal definitions.

20 The **second chapter** deals with **data access and data exchange** in B2B and B2C relationships. Art. 3(1) makes direct data access for users obligatory. According to this provision products and related services must be manufactured and designed in a manner that makes the relevant data directly accessible to the user where relevant and technically feasible. Art. 4(1) in turn contains a data access claim in the event that direct access is not possible. The articles of the second chapter also contain pre-contractual information obligations (Art. 3(2) and (3)), specific data processing prohibitions (Art. 4–6), the possibility of a direct transfer of data to third parties, but not to large platform services or ‚gatekeepers' as defined by the DMA (Art. 5(3)) and an exception for micro and small enterprises in Art. 7 (*de minimis rule*). The **third chapter** contains obligations to provide data from data holders to data recipients, including rules on the respective contractual conditions (Art. 8–12). The **fourth chapter** (Art. 13) declares unfair terms used unilaterally against small enterprises invalid. The **fifth chapter** lays down rules for making data available to public bodies (B2G), in particular where there is an exceptional need for the provision of the data (Art. 14–22).

21 The data access provisions in chapters two, three and five are central to achieving the **goals** of the Data Act. In Art. 3(1) and 4(1) the Commission's preference of a **data accessibility by default** and an **in-situ access** solution are evident. Hence, users must be able to access generated data directly, but they are not stored in the user's sphere.[43] The requirements which are placed on this claim to access are laid out in Art. 3(1) and Art. 3(2) which ensure that users are informed about the data generated by the products and related services.[44] In contrast Art. 4(1) governs the right of data to be made available where data cannot be accessed directly. While the objectives of the Data Act, as well as the wording of Art. 3 make a claim for the full transmission of user data is conceivable, the explanations in the recitals speak against this. **In-situ access** (data access on servers of the data owner without actual transmission) should therefore also meet the requirements of Art. 3(1).[45] In accordance with the same principles, Art. 5(1) establishes a **right of access for third parties**. This is, however, limited by the prohibition of data processing for the development of competing products (Art. 4(10).[46] In return, the data holder is required to use non-personal data exclusively within the framework of a contractual agreement with the user (Art. 4(13)).

22 The articles of chapters three and four apply to the relationship between the data holder and third parties. Although default access and access claims (Art. 3, 4) are non-contractual by nature,[47] the conditions for a **data transfer** from the data holder to the

---

[43] Specht-Riemenschneider MMR 2022, 809 (815).

[44] While many are in favour of these information rights, see Metzger/Schweitzer ZEuP2023, 42 (52); others are sceptical, see Hennemann/Steinrötter NJW 2022, 1481 (1483).

[45] Rec. 21 Data Act.

[46] Picht, 'Caught in the Acts: Framing Mandatory Data Access Transactions Under the Data Act, Further EU Digital Regulation Acts, and Competition Law' (Max Planck Institute for Innovation and Competition Research Paper No. 22–12, 6.4.2022) <www.ip.mpg.de/en/publications/details/caught-in-the-acts-framing-mandatory-data-access-transactions-under-the-data-act-further-eu-digital-regulation-acts-and-competition-law.html> (last accessed: 22.2.2024).

[47] See also Metzger/Schweitzer ZEuP 2023, 42.

designated data recipient must be agreed by these two parties, at least in cases of **user request** as defined by Art. 5. The compensation must be fair, reasonable and non-discriminatory – so-called **FRAND conditions** – (Art. 8) and the conditions when making data available B2B must be non-discriminatory and reasonable (Art. 9).[48]

According to Art. 14, the data controller shall (on request) provide data to a **public sector body** or to an institution, body or agency of the Union which demonstrates an exceptional need to use the requested data (Art. 15). 23

The **sixth chapter** concerns **switching** between data processing services. The focus here is on removing user-related obstacles to switching (Art. 23). Art. 24–27 regulate the **contractual terms,** as well as information, good faith and transparency obligations The **seventh chapter** concerns governmental access and transfer of non-personal data (Art. 32). **Chapter eight** is dedicated to interoperability and portability and formulates essential requirements for both data sharing and data processing services, without, however, naming technical specifics itself. **Chapter nine** contains application and enforcement provisions. 24

Chapter ten (Art. 43) is intended to prevent the undermining of access and use rights in the area of databases by standardising an **application exception** for the sui generis specific property right of Art. 7 of Directive 96/6/EC[49]. The **eleventh and last chapters** contain final provisions for the entry into force and further modalities. 25

III. Enforcement

Art. 37 establishes the obligation to designate **competent authorities** in the Member States, whose tasks are also defined by this provision. Natural and legal persons shall have the right to lodge a related complaint to the authorities to be designated (Art. 38). The Data Act does not contain a sanction regime, but standardises requirements for the catalogue of sanctions to be issued by the Member States (Art. 40). Furthermore, breaches of chapters two, three and five are also to be sanctioned by existing data protection supervisory authorities (see Art. 51 GDPR). Finally, Art. 41 recommends non-binding model contract terms for data access and data use to promote balanced contracts. 26

D. Further data access obligations for platforms

The **access regime of** the Data Act must be coordinated with numerous other access regulations that also apply to platforms. These include the following: 27

I. GDPR

The General Data Protection Regulation **(GDPR)** also contains data access obligations that apply to platforms without restriction. These obligations complement and mirror the data subject rights of the third chapter of the GDPR, specifically the right of access (Art. 15 GDPR) and in particular the right to data portability (Art. 20 GDPR). According to these, the data subject has the right to obtain the personal data concerning her or him that she or he has provided to a holder. Art. 20(2) GDPR also permits direct 28

[48] For an extensive discussion of contractual terms and conditions, see Metzger/Schweitzer ZEuP2023, 42.
[49] Commission Directive 96/6/EC of 16 February 1996 amending Council Directive 74/63/EEC on undesirable substances and products in animal nutrition, OJ 1996 L 49, 29.

transfer to another holder.[50] The resulting obligations apply to platforms, insofar as they act as controllers as defined in Art. 4(7),(24) and (26) GDPR.

29 The Data Act supplements the provisions of the GDPR to the extent that it covers data generated by a product or connected service of the user. However, Art. 1(5) Data Act clarifies that the regulation itself does not constitute a legal basis for the processing of personal data. Additionally, in cases of conflict, the GDPR prevails (→ mn. 18).

II. DMA

30 The relationship of the Data Act to the other elementary components of the **data or digital strategy** – the DMA, DSA and DGA – also needs to be explored.

31 The two objectives of the **DMA** are to establish and ensure fairness and contestability in digital markets (→ § 11 mn. 17 et seqq.). In contrast to the Data Act, the DMA is an asymmetric and sector-specific regulation. The latter imposes numerous conduct-related, often self-executing obligations (32 in total) on the tech giants or large digital service providers, which the DMA designates as 'gatekeepers' (→ § 11 mn. 26 et seqq.). Since these gatekeepers all benefit from data-based economies of scale and network effects, many of these obligations also include data access rules. However, the access regimes of the DMA serve a different objective. While the Data Act seeks to promote the equitable distribution of and value creation from data, the DMA is dedicated to the market failures associated with the gatekeeper status and 'data power' of the tech giants. The DMA's access rights are thus intended to open up digital service markets to competition and to prevent the further expansion of existing power positions created by the aggregation, tapping or re-use of data. Overall, the (albeit asymmetric) data access approach of the DMA goes beyond the obligations of the Data Act: access claims that are established under the DMA are, for example, **free of charge and not limited to FRAND conditions.**

32 Art. 5(2)(a) DMA prohibits gatekeepers from processing personal data of their users for online advertising services. Based on the Facebook Case of the German Federal Cartel Office (Bundeskartellamt),[51] gatekeepers are prohibited from:

a) processing the personal data of end-users using third party services for the purpose of operating online advertising services,
b) merging personal data from one service or platform with others,
c) reusing such data in other platform services or
d) logging end users into other services of the gatekeeper without explicit (revocable) consent in order to merge personal data (→ § 10 mn. 45).

Art. 6(2) DMA prohibits platforms or gatekeepers from **competing with their commercial users** on the basis of the data generated by them (→ § 10 mn. 75). According to Art. 6(8) DMA, gatekeepers must grant advertisers on their platforms free access to **performance measurement** tools and data (→ § 10 mn. 77). Art. 6(9) DMA obliges gatekeepers to transfer any data provided or generated through use to users upon request and free of charge and also to provide free tools to facilitate **data portability.** Pursuant to

---

[50] Rec. 68 GDPR.

[51] See BKartA 6.2.2019 – B6–22/16, GRUR-Prax 2019, 266; OLG Düsseldorf 26.8.2019 – Kart 1/19 (V), MMR 2019, 742; BGH 23.6.2020 – KVR 69/19, GRUR 2020, 1318; OLG Düsseldorf 30.11.2020 – Kart 13/20 (V), BeckRS 2020, 33848; AG Rantos 20.9.2022 – case C-252/21, ECLI:EU:C:2022:704 = GRUR-RS 2022, 24109 – Meta Platforms and Others v Bundeskartellamt; ECJ 4.7.2023 – case C-252/21, ECLI:EU:C:2023:537 = GRUR 2023, 1131 – Meta Platforms and Others v Bundeskartellamt.

Art. 6(10) DMA, gatekeepers shall provide their business users with **real-time access** to aggregated and non-aggregated data (including personal data of end-users, provided there is appropriate consent and a direct connection with the use of the business user's product/service) free of charge (→ § 10 mn. 31). According to Art. 6(11) DMA, gatekeepers must provide **search engine data** (on FRAND conditions, Art. 6(12) DMA) to their competitors in the search engine market (→ § 13 mn. 42 et seq.). According to Art. 7(8) DMA, the disclosure of personal data is mandatory if it is necessary for effective **interoperability** of number-independent interpersonal communications services.

III. Relationship to other existing provisions

The Data Act takes its place in an existing system of regulations relating to **personal** 33 **data** (GDPR, ePrivacy Directive[52]) and supplements them with rights in relation to data generated by the user's products.[53] Furthermore, the Data Act builds on the regulation on the free movement of non-personal data with regard to facilitated switching of cloud providers (SWIPO – Switching Cloud Providers and Porting Data).[54] Since self-regulatory approaches with industry-developed codes of conduct (Art. 6 Regulation (EU) 2018/1807) have proven to be ineffective, the Data Act intends to make better use of the rights to switch cloud providers and transfer data that were already in place and provides for a stronger regulatory approach to influence market dynamics.[55]

The Data Governance Act **(DGA)**, which addresses voluntary data sharing, forms an- 34 other elementary component of the data and digital strategy (→ § 19 mn. 2) and is thus supplemented by the Data Act.[56] In addition to content and platform regulating provisions, the Digital Services Act **(DSA)** also contains obligations for data sharing with science and public authorities and complements the Data Act in this respect.

The Data Act is intended to be **coherent** with the other existing regulations in the 35 policy area, but without directly influencing them. This applies in particular to competition law, the Database Directive[57] (with the exception of individual clarifications regarding its scope of application), the P2B Regulation[58] (→ § 16) and the Open Data Directive[59]. In general, the Data Act aims at cross-sectoral harmonisation through convergence, without, however, limiting the scope for vertical sector-specific regulations.[60]

[52] Directive 2002/58/EC of the European Parliament and of the Council of 12 July 2002 concerning the processing of personal data and the protection of privacy in the electronic communications sector (Directive on privacy and electronic communications), OJ 2002 L 201, 37.

[53] Rec. 7 Data Act.

[54] Regulation (EU) 2018/1807 of the European Parliament and of the Council of 14 November 2018 on a framework for the free flow of non-personal data in the European Union, OJ 2018 L 303, 59.

[55] Rec. 79 Data Act.

[56] Rec. 26 Data Act.

[57] Directive 96/9/EC of the European Parliament and of the Council of 11.3.1996 on the legal protection of databases, OJ 1996 L 77, 20.

[58] Regulation (EU) 2019/1150 of the European Parliament and of the Council of 20.6.2019 on promoting fairness and transparency for business users of online intermediary services, OJ 2019 L 186, 57.

[59] Directive (EU) 2019/1024 of the European Parliament and of the Council of 20.6.2019 on open data and the re-use of public sector information, OJ 2019 L 172, 56.

[60] Rec. 6 Data Act.

E. Critical appraisal of the platform-specific provisions in and applications of the Data Act

36 This last chapter looks at the specific application of the Data Act to (large) platforms and what this means for the design and goals of the regulation, the effectiveness of its instruments and its interaction with other laws and regulations.

I. Platforms as addressees

37 In order to be able to assess the platform-specific regulatory content of the Data Act, a closer look at its **addressees** is helpful. According to Art. 1(3) the Data Act applies to (1) manufacturers of connected products and providers of related services that are placed on the market in the Union; (2) users of such products or services; (3) data controllers that provide data to data recipients in the Union; (4) public bodies and institutions, agencies and other bodies of the Union, as well as providers of data processing services that offer such services to customers in the Union. While the Data Act is horizontal in nature and only Art. 5 and 6 contain provisions that specifically address gatekeepers or large platforms and specify exceptions for them, there is a considerable overlap between the companies that fulfil the gatekeeper definition of the DMA and those that are the addressees of the Data Act, i.e. manufacturers of IoT products, providers of connected services or data holders.[61] This results both in a overlap and dual-application of data-related provisions and in a platform-specific relevance of the Data Act. Against this background, it is necessary to examine whether the instruments of the Data Act are suitable for achieving its objectives with regard to large platforms.

II. In situ rights and contractual access conditions

38 The provisions of the Data Act must not only be measured against the objectives of the act and those of the European Data Strategy, but must also be convincing when compared with alternative instruments. Such instruments should also serve **data protection and data economy interests.**[62] This applies both to the decision in favour of a mere data access claim (without a transfer of the data into the users sphere, Art. 3), and to the contract requirement (without more specific requirements) as the basis for data use by the data controller (Art. 4(13)). The relevance of the choice of instruments and the corresponding **initial allocation of rights** becomes all the more important in welfare economic terms the higher the **transaction costs** are in relation to them.[63] Accordingly, the contractual solution as well as the hurdles for a de facto full access to the data provide for an increased economic need to justify this allocation decision. Contrary to the objective of improved individual data sovereignty, this decision favours data holders, since they exercise actual control over the collected data and only have to provide access, but do not owe a transfer to the user sphere by default. Mere **in situ access** not only thwarts interoperability efforts, but also significantly limits the usefulness of the data for the us-

[61] The classification of a company as a gatekeeper is determined in accordance with Art. 3 DMA; the relevant definitions of the Data Act are contained in its Art. 2.

[62] Engeler NJW 2022, 3398 (3399).

[63] Conclusion from the Coase theorem: The higher the transaction costs, the greater the probability that they will outweigh the benefits from the transaction and that the transaction will therefore not take place and the original allocation will be maintained, which is why exclusive rights should be viewed critically in this context on their own merits. See Coase Journal of Law and Economics 1960, 1.

er, since the user is limited in the possibilities of further use to those that the data holder's software allows.[64] This also legally strengthens the de facto superior position of data holders,[65] which contradicts the overarching goals, especially in the context of gatekeeper platforms: while on the one hand data transfer to gatekeepers is excluded (Art. 5(3)), the de facto allocation of data in relation to users remains untouched.[66] Granting straightforward '**data access**' instead of '**data accessibility by design and default**'[67] would have been closer to the goal of creating **data sovereignty** insofar as the necessary effort to obtain the data would not fall to the user. As a further alternative, the idea of introducing a **trustee solution** could also have been favourable.[68] Here a data intermediary, as can be found in the DGA, would be in a position to facilitate data access as a fiduciary instance of an enabling data privacy right and at the same time assume a control function. To this end, data could be stored in the sphere of such an intermediary, which would then confirm existing access rights and subsequently enable use in an interoperable format.

In the platform-specific context, the contractual requirement for the **processing** of non-personal user data (Art. 4(13)), which also applies in the context of transfer to data recipients (Art. 8(1)), may not present enough of a hurdle to ensure a real balance of interests. In this respect, it is doubtful whether the powerful market position of the gatekeeper platforms will allow for **fair, balanced and interest-based agreements** or whether the exploitation of economies of scale will bias agreements from the outset.[69] The so-called 'privacy paradox', which will be explained in more detail below (→ mn. 40), may play a role here as well as it is particularly relevant in the case of asymmetric information.[70] In addition, the Payment Services Directive,[71] the DMA as well as Art. 20 GDPR provide for free access and questions arise regarding their relationship to one another.[72] In this context, the provisions of the Data Act do not prevent the existence of so-called 'buy-out contracts' (contracts that involve a waiver by the user of his or her rights), which inherently contradict the ideas of user-centred data governance.[73] 39

[64] On the practical problems of in situ access, Podzsun/Offergeld, 'The EU Data Act and the Access to Secondary Markets (Study for the Ludwig-Fröhler-Institut für Handwerkswissenschaften, 2022) <www.ssrn.com/abstract=4256882> (last accessed: 22.2.2024), p. 47 et seqq.

[65] Metzger/Schweitzer ZEuP 2023, 42 (54 et seq.) and Schweitzer/Metzger GRUR Int. 2023, 337 (346).

[66] Drexl/Banda/Otero/Hoffmann/Kim/Kulhari/Moscon/Richter/Wiedemann, 'Positions Statement of the Max Planck Insitute for Innovation and Competition of 25 May 2022 on Commission's Proposal of 23 February 2022 for a Regulation on harmonised rules on fair access to and use of data (Data Act)', 13.06.2022 <www.ip.mpg.de/fileadmin/ipmpg/content/stellungnahmen/Position_Statement_MPI_Data_Act_Formal__13.06.2022.pdf> (last accessed: 22.2.2024), mn. 66.

[67] Thus, direct data transmission instead of an enforceable access claim, Specht-Riemenschneider MMR 2022, 809 (818) mutatis mutandis.

[68] Specht-Riemenschneider MMR 2022, 809 (819).

[69] Kerber GRUR-Int 2023, 120 (125 et seq.).

[70] Part of this is also an expected information overload, Hennemann/Steinrötter NJW 2022, 1481 (1483).

[71] Directive (EU) 2015/2366 of the European Parliament and of the Council of 25 November 2015 on payment services in the internal market, amending Directives 2002/65/EC, 2009/110/EC and 2013/36/EU and Regulation (EU) No 1093/2010, and repealing Directive 2007/64/EC, OJ 2015 L 337, 35.

[72] In addition to the priority of access claims, a conflict rule is needed to resolve conflict situations between provisions of the Data Act and the GDPR, see Steinrötter GRUR 2023, 216.

[73] Bomhard/Merkle RDi 2022, 168 (174); Specht-Riemenschneider MMR 2022, 809 (819).

III. Access rights for users and third parties

40 The core provisions of the Data Act contain data-related rights for users and third parties.[74] Data accessibility obligations (Art. 3), data access rights (Art. 4) and data disclosure rights (Art. 5(1)), as well as the associated information obligations (Art. 3(2)), can be seen as improving '**autonomy**' or promoting '**data sovereignty**'. Borrowing from the idea of consumer sovereignty, which – while it does not play as significant a role in economic theory as consumer welfare – describes the power and freedom that consumers have vis-à-vis companies and producers.[75] The concept of data sovereignty has been used by *Kerber* and *Zolna* to explore '*whether and to what extent individuals are or should be able to decide on access to and use of 'their' data*'.[76] The Data Act addresses this sovereignty not only to increase users' autonomy, but also to solve allocation problems and make the use of data fairer. From a competition policy perspective, this means solving problems related to data bottlenecks to increase competition in upstream and downstream markets. In the same way that the instruments of the GDPR rely on consumer consent solutions, the Data Act primarily relies on user choice and action: in order to solve data bottlenecks, the user's ability to act is increased by granting far-reaching data access obligations and and rights.[77]

41 Empowering users corresponds with the general data strategy and resolves the distribution issue in a way that is generally perceived as fair.[78] And yet its effectiveness is by no means evident. As data protection instruments have shown, merely strengthening the rights of users or consumers is often insufficient in practice and can further overwhelm, rather than aid even tech savvy users.The so-called '**privacy paradox**' describes the contradiction between the pressing concerns users experience in relation to their data and privacy and their seemingly carefree behaviour when asked to disclose their data and general unwillingness to make economic sacrifices in order to achieve a higher level or privacy ('*everybody wants it, but nobody actually cares*'[79])[80]. It is important to note, however, that the cause of this privacy paradox is not so much the laziness or unwillingness of users, but rather the complexity and excessive demands of the instruments themselves. User are often overwhelmed, not only by non-transparent market processes, but also by the regulatory instruments. In particular contractual solutions and **consent instruments** that are imbedllded in general terms and conditions are often simply far too complex, intransparent and, above all, too time-consuming to empower

[74] See Eckhardt/Kerber European Journal of Law & Economics 57 2024, 113 (114 et seqq.).

[75] Kerber/Zolna in Augsberg/Gehring, p. 45 et seq. with reference to Hutt, 1936.

[76] Kerber/Zolna in Augsberg/Gehring, p. 45–58.

[77] Podzsun/Offergeld, 'The EU Data Act and the Access to Secondary Markets (Study for the Ludwig-Fröhler-Institut für Handwerkswissenschaften, 2022) <www.ssrn.com/abstract=4256882> (last accessed: 20.2.2024), p. 11 et seq.

[78] Specht-Riemenschneider Study in German Federal Ministry of Justice and Consumer Protection/Max Planck Institute for Innovation and Competition, p. 401; Leistner/Antoine, 'IPR and the use of open data and data sharing initiatives by public and private actors' (Study for the JURI commitee of the European Parliament, May 2022) <www.europarl.europa.eu/RegData/etudes/STUD/2022/732266/IPOL_STU(2022)732266_EN.pdf> (last accessed: 22.2.2024), p. 16 et seqq.; Podzsun/Offergeld, 'The EU Data Act and the Access to Secondary Markets (Study for the Ludwig-Fröhler-Institut für Handwerkswissenschaften, 2022) <www.ssrn.com/abstract=4256882> (last accessed: 22.2.2024), p. 13 et seq.

[79] Andriychuck, 'Moligopoly as the Coexistence of Structural Monopoly with Cognitive Oligopoly or An Inquiry into the Theory of the Apologetic' (Chillin' Competition, 26.11.2020) chillingcompetition.com/moligopoly-as-the-coexistence-of-structural-monopoly-with-cognitive-oligopoly-or-an-inquiry-into-the-theory-of-the-apologetic-competition-by-oles-andriychuk/ (last accessed: 22.2.2024).

[80] Brief description, Engels/Grunewald, 'Das Privacy Paradox: Digitalisation versus Privacy' (Institut der deutschen Wirtschaft, Kurzbericht 57, 2017) <www.iwkoeln.de/fileadmin/publications/2017/356747/IW-Kurzbericht_2017-57_Privacy_ox.pdf> (last accessed: 22.2.2024).

the average consumer and guarantee adequate protection.[81] Consent-driven instruments have thus long been criticised as altogether implausible means of reducing **information asymmetries.**[82]

For the same reason, some authors criticise provisions such as Art. 5(3) DMA and new data-sensitive doctrines in competition policy,[83] which aim at providing users with increased opportunities for consent in order to ultimately control the data power of market-dominant companies. Despite the fairness of these new regulations and their importance for data protection and protection against exploitative practices, it is difficult to see why end users should bear the burden of regulating markets and ensuring their contestability.[84] Here *Shoshana Zuboff* goes one step futher, and in light of the rise of big tech and market concentrations, questions choice and choice architectures altogether: 42

> *We are trapped in an involuntary merger of personal necessity and economic extraction, as the same channels that we rely upon for daily logistics, social interaction, work, education, healthcare, access to products and services, and much more, now double as supply chain operations for surveillance capitalism's surplus flows.*[85]

It is unclear whether users will not face the same hurdles with regards to the Data Act's access rights and whether the instruments can thus realise their intended effects.[86]

IV. Equitable (optimal) distribution of data and creation of aftermarkets

The extent to which the Data Act can be part of an effective, competition-oriented platform regulation depends on its contribution to the creation of competition by means of data. In this regard the Data Act's primary focus is on '**subsequent services**', ie., secondary markets or **aftermarkets**. With regard to large platforms, two questions are relevant here: First, it must be clarified under which conditions 'gatekeepers' (DMA) must grant access. Second, the parameters for the subsequent services (*aftermarkets*) need to be examined more closely. In general this approach also raises the question of whether the creation of a **data market** could be envisaged. In this context, the instruments, but also the exceptions for the development of competing products (Art. 6(10)) and the transfer of data to gatekeepers (Art. 5(3)) will have to be analysed. 43

(1) According to Art. 6(9) and (10) DMA, gatekeepers shall provide end-users or third parties commissioned by them with **effective portability** of data provided by the end-user or generated by the end-user's activity in connection with the use of the rele- 44

---

[81] Cooter/Ulen, p. 276; Bar-Gill, 2012; Williamson LJITE 1995, 49; Ben-Shahar/Schneider University of Pennsylvania Law Review 2011, 647; McColgan, 2020.

[82] Bakos Journal of Legal Studies 2014, 1; Engeler NJW 2022, 3398; Ben-Shahar/Schneider University of Pennsylvania Law Review 2011, 647.

[83] See BKartA 6.2.2019 – B6–22/16, GRUR-Prax 2019, 266; OLG Düsseldorf 26.8.2019 – Kart 1/19 (V), MMR 2019, 742; BGH 23.6.2020 – KVR 69/19, GRUR 2020, 1318; OLG Düsseldorf 30.11.2020 – Kart 13/20 (V), BeckRS 2020, 33848; AG Rantos 20.9.2022 – case C-252/21, ECLI:EU:C:2022:704 = GRUR-RS 2022, 24109 – Meta Platforms and Others v Bundeskartellamt; ECJ 4.7.2023 – case C-252/21, ECLI:EU:C:2023:537 = GRUR 2023, 1131 – Meta Platforms and Others v Bundeskartellamt.

[84] Graef, 'Why End-User Consent Cannot Keep Markets Contestable' (Verfassungsblog 2.9.2021) <verfassungsblog.de/power-dsa-dma-08/> (last accessed: 22.2.2024).

[85] Naughton, '"The goal is to automate us": welcome to the age of surveillance capitalism' (The Guardian, 20.1.2019) < www.theguardian.com/technology/2019/jan/20/shoshana-zuboff-age-of-surveillance-capitalism-google-facebook> (last accessed: 24.2.2024); Zuboff, The Age of Surveillance Capitalism, 2018.

[86] *Kerber* and *Zolna* describe this as a central weakness of the Data Act in Kerber/Zolna in Augsberg/Gehring, p. 45 et seqq.

vant central platform service free of charge and/or provide commercial users with **effective, high-quality and permanent real-time access to aggregated and non-aggregated data free of charge** (cf. → mn. 32). These access rights largely correspond to those in Art. 3–5 Data Act, but in the Data Act the transfer to commissioned third parties does not always have be free of charge, but granted on fair, reasonable and non-discriminatory terms (Art. 8).[87] This discrepancy is due to the fact that the Data Act seeks to **open up the market for subsequent services** overall – and that in principle actors trade on fair terms in markets[88] – whereas the DMA seeks to **overcome the entrenched market position of gatekeepers.** As a lex specialis for gatekeepers, the DMA regulations are likely to take priority over the corresponding provisions of the Data Act. The price rule in Art. 8 Data Act, can, however, also be questioned more fundamentally. The Commission justifies this with the creation of incentives for innovation.[89] IoT devices are, however, usually not made available free of charge and therefore the normal market incentives already exist.[90] Even insofar as IoT devices are partly 'subsidised' via data, it can be argued that the Data Act does not limit the benefit that IoT manufacturers derive from this data. Since the data obtained is either personal data or data belonging to the **public domain** (see → mn. 36 et seqq.),[91] there is little justification on which to base the manufacturers claim for remuneration. In addition, the platforms and device manufacturers already derive a great utility from the data they collect and generate.

45 *(2)* Closely connected to the questions of price (fees) and contractual conditions is the question of what contribution the Data Act as a whole can make to a **fairer distribution of data** and to the mitigation of data concentration. The aims of the act are clearly in favour of market-based solution. Rec. 1 of the 2020 proposal for a data act set the goal of achieving a 'high quality and interoperable data from different domains increase competitiveness and innovation and ensure sustainable economic growth[…]'.[92] This speaks in favour of the creation of an (open) data market, in which users are free to use the data *'for any lawful purpose'* (rec. 30). However, the same rec. 30 is then limited to *'(making the) data available to a third party providing a so-called aftermarket service'*, which is the focus of the Data Act. In the case of these secondary or vertical services (e.g. repairs) and on these *aftermarkets,* the Data Act seeks to foster competition with the data owners. On aftermarkets or secondary markets products or services are traditionally provided that connect to products or services of the so-called primary market.[93] In contrast to the DMA, the Data Act excludes the processing of data for the development of **competing products** (Art. 4(10)): '*The user shall not use data obtained (…) the development of a product that directly competes with the product, from which the data originate*'). It is, however, questionable whether this exception also applies to so-called gatekeepers or whether a uniform interpretation of the DMA and Data Act would be favourable here,

---

[87] Metzger/Schweitzer ZEuP 2023, 42 (60 et seqq.).

[88] Greiss, 2023.

[89] For more details, see Eckhardt/Kerber European Journal of Law & Economics 57 2024, 113 (114 et seqq.).

[90] Kerber GRUR-Int 2023, 120 (130 et seq.).

[91] Drexl/Banda/Otero/Hoffmann/Kim/Kulhari/Moscon/Richter/Wiedemann, 'Positions Statement of the Max Planck Insitute for Innovation and Competition of 25 May 2022 on Commission's Proposal of 23 February 2022 for a Regulation on harmonised rules on fair access to and use of data (Data Act)', 13.06.2022 <www.ip.mpg.de/fileadmin/ipmpg/content/stellungnahmen/Position_Statement_MPI_Data_Act_Formal__13.06.2022.pdf> (last accessed: 22.2.2024), mn. 49.

[92] European Commission, 'Proposal for a Regulation on harmonised rules on fair access to and use of data (Data Act)', 23.2.2022, COM(2022) 68 final, 3.

[93] Podzsun/Offergeld, 'The EU Data Act and the Access to Secondary Markets (Study for the Ludwig-Fröhler-Institut für Handwerkswissenschaften, 2022) <www.ssrn.com/abstract=4256882> (last accessed: 22.2.2024).

since the DMA serves the very purpose of making the position of gatekeepers contestable.[94] The exception of passing on data to gatekeepers follows a similar (asymmetrical) logic. According to Art. 5(2), gatekeepers may not invoke any access rights. However, this exception is fundamentally criticised for possibly limiting **consumers' choices** contrary to their interests: Why should users not be allowed to transfer their data from one smaller provider or gatekeeper to another gatekeeper if this is in their interests in the individual case? This exception is further weakened by the fact that the data owner may allow the gatekeeper to use the data on a voluntary basis.[95] Even though the Data Act aims for a (secondary) opening of the market, there is a fundamental tension regarding the question of how far a **market solution** should reach and how exceptions from remuneration, for gatekeepers or for competing products and services, can then be justified. If this redistribution of or access to data is not to be free of charge, this could, according to *Kerber,* be done through the creation of a '**data market**'. Data trades could then, for example, also take place via **data intermediaries,** as envisaged in the DGA.[96] Even where the first steps towards the creation of such a market are laid out in the Data Act,[97] it is unclear to what extent such a solution is desired. In the overall debate on the future of the data economy there is an inherent tension between proponents of a rights-based 'data protection' approach, shaped by the principles of public and consitutional law, and proponents of market based solutions.[98] The creation of the true 'data market' is thus hardly conceivable without triggering a fundamental debate.

F. Regulatory approach and enforcement

With the **horizontal approach** of the **Data Act,** the Commission is able to create a new regulatory framework for trade in and the creation of value from data that claims general validity. Despite calls for asymmetric or sector-specific approaches,[99] there is little to be said against this goal in principle. However, certain **contradictions** and **inconsistencies** with other regulations are already becoming apparent. For example, gatekeepers will be subject to partly stricter regulations due to the provisions of the DMA, which may also have to be taken into account by the authorities that will be responsible for the implementation of the Data Act. 46

The **exceptions for gatekeepers** in Art. 5(3) Data Act are an explicitly **asymmetrical element.** Here the Commission wants to avoid any further advantages being accrued to gatekeepers whose data power is already entrenched. This exception may, however, contradict the interest of consumers and hamper the creation of a full market solution that guarantees all forms and levels of competition for and with data. Whether the advantages experienced by gatekeepers cannot be compensated in a more specific and interest-oriented way will become clear over time. 47

Another hurdle for an effective implementation of the EU Data Strategy could be the **distribution of competences.** Where the DMA is enforced centrally by the Commission, the DSA and the Data Act take **decentralised** approaches and their enforcement is 48

---

[94] Budzinski/Mendelsohn ORDO 72/73 (2023) 215–255.

[95] Within the limits of Art. 4(6), see Podzsun/Offergeld, 'The EU Data Act and the Access to Secondary Markets (Study for the Ludwig-Fröhler-Institut für Handwerkswissenschaften, 2022) <www.ssrn.com/abstract=4256882> (last accessed: 22.2.2024), p. 17.

[96] Kerber GRUR-Int 2023, 120 (123).

[97] Kerber GRUR-Int 2023, 120 (129).

[98] On these notions, Engeler NJW 2022, 3398 (3400).

[99] Specht-Riemenschneider MMR 2022, 809 (818); on existing regulations Graef/Husovec/van den Boom EuCML 2020, 3.

left to the Member States. Where data access claims are concerned, uniform or at least converging approaches would therefore have to be developed over time. However, the distribution of competences also has clear advantages. Especially in relation to dynamic markets and in dealing with new challenges and hurdles and testing new approaches, competition for good regulatory approaches (so-called **regulatory competition**),[100] which actually also corresponds to the idea of the internal market and the open European economic order, can ensure that the best ideas are pushed forward and can prevail. Decentralised rules thus carry the promise of being as dynamic, flexible and competitive as the markets they regulate.

G. Summary

49 The newly introduced Data Act aims at a **fair allocation** of IoT data in order to '*increase competitiveness and innovation and ensure sustainable economic growth*' (rec. 1). The big data-driven and data-generating platforms are likely to be particularly affected by this act and are crucial for its success and the desired strengthening of users' **data sovereignty** or **data autonomy** and the **opening of data (after-)markets**. The Data Act can thus be considered as a core component of future platform regulation. As such, not only the isolated exceptions for gatekeepers, but above all the numerous overlaps with – in part stricter – **data access provisions** in sector-specific regulations such as the DMA are to be given special attention here. Particularly with regard to the data power of the platforms, the consequential effects of the *in situ claims*, but also the effectiveness of consent instruments and the limited application of the Data Act to so-called *aftermarkets* can only be met with cautioned enthusiasm.

[100] Budzinski/Mendelsohn ORDO 72/73 (2023) 217–255.

§ 21
Platform-specific requirements of the AI Act

Literature: *Bartels*, A Balancing Act: Data Protection Compliance of Artificial Intelligence, GRUR Int. 2024, 526; *Becker/Feuerstack*, 'Der neue Entwurf des EU-Parlaments für eine KI-Verordnung', MMR 2024, 22; *Berz/Engel/Hacker*, 'Generative KI, Datenschutz, Hassrede und Desinformation – Zur Regulierung von KI-Meinungen', ZUM 2023, 586 *Bomhard/Merkle*, 'Europäische KI-Verordnung – Der aktuelle Kommissionsentwurf und praktische Auswirkungen', RDi 2021, 276; *Bomhard/Siglmüller*, 'AI Act – das Trilogergebnis', RDi 2024, 45; *Buchmann/Panfili*, 'ChatGPT und die DSGVO: Freie Fahrt für freie Bürger?', VuR 2023, 161; *Calo*, 'Digital Market Manipulation', 82 George Washington Law Review 2014, 995; *Chibanguza/Steege*, 'Die KI-Verordnung – Überblick über den neuen Rechtsrahmen', NJW 2024, 1769; *Dienes*, 'Anforderungen an die menschliche Aufsicht über Künstliche Intelligenz – Verständnis als Kernelement des Art. 14 KI-VO', MMR 2024, 456; *Dobber et al.*, 'Do (Microtargeted) Deepfakes Have Real Effects on Political Attitudes?', The International Journal of Press/Politics 2021, 69; *Dornis*, 'Lauterkeitsrecht im KI-Zeitalter – Grundlagen, Strukturen und Fallgruppen (Teil 1)', GRUR 2023, 1729; *Dregelies*, 'Der Schutz vor Dark Patterns im DSA – Wie Art. 25 DSA die Entscheidungsprozesse von Internetnutzern schützen kann', MMR 2023, 243; *Ebers*, 'Beeinflussung und Manipulation von Kunden durch Behavioral Microtargeting – Verhaltenssteuerung durch Algorithmen aus der Sicht des Zivilrechts', MMR 2018, 423; *Ebers*, 'Liability for Artificial Intelligence and EU Consumer Law', JIPITEC 2021, 204; *Ebers/Heinze/Krügel/Steinrötter*, Rechtshandbuch Künstliche Intelligenz und Robotik, Munich 2020; *Ebers/Hoch/Rosenkranz/Ruschemeier/Steinrötter*, 'Der Entwurf für eine EU-KI-Verordnung: Richtige Richtung mit Optimierungsbedarf – Eine kritische Bewertung durch Mitglieder der Robotics & AI Law Society (RAILS)', RDi 2021, 528; *Ebert/Spiecker gen. Döhmann*, 'Der Kommissionsentwurf für eine KI-Verordnung der EU – Die EU als Trendsetter weltweiter KI-Regulierung', NVwZ 2021, 1188; *Engelmann/Brunotte/Lütkens*, 'Regulierung von Legal Tech durch die KI-Verordnung', RDi 2021, 317; *Feuerstack/Becker/Hertz*, 'Die Entwürfe des EU-Parlaments und der EU-Kommission für eine KI-Verordnung im Vergleich', ZfDR 2023, 421; *Frisch/Kohpeiß*, 'KI-Verordnung: Aktueller Stand und Vergleich der Änderungsvorschläge des Rates und des Parlaments', ZD-Aktuell 2023, 01318; *Fuhlrott*, 'Regulierung der Plattformarbeit: Der EU-Richtlinienentwurf', ArbRAktuell 2022, 191; *Geminn*, 'Die Regulierung Künstlicher Intelligenz – Anmerkungen zum Entwurf eines Artificial Intelligence Act', ZD 2021, 354; *Genovesi/Kaesling/Robbins*, Recommender Systems: Legal and Ethical Issues, Cham 2023; *Hacker/Berz*, 'Der AI Act der Europäischen Union – Überblick, Kritik und Ausblick', ZRP 2023, 226; *Hacker/Engel/Mauer*, 'Regulating ChatGPT and other Large Generative AI Models', FAccT 23, 1112; *Hilgendorf/Roth-Isigkeit*, Die neue Verordnung der EU zur Künstlichen Intelligenz, Munich 2023; *Hinderks*, 'Die Kennzeichnungspflicht von Deepfakes', ZUM 2022, 110; *Hoffmann*, 'Möglichkeiten und Zulässigkeit von Künstlicher Intelligenz und Algorithmen im Recruiting – Personalsuche 4.0', NZA 2022, 19; *Horstmann*, 'EU-Parlament und Rat: Einigung im Trilog – avisierte Regelungen zu Transparenz und Targeting politischer Werbung', ZD-Aktuell 2024, 01499; *Hufen*, 'Nudging – Rechtsformen, Möglichkeiten und Grenzen der sanften Beeinflussung des Menschen durch den Staat', JuS 2020, 193; *Jaekel*, Die Macht der digitalen Plattformen – Wegweiser im Zeitalter einer expandierenden Digitalsphäre und künstlicher Intelligenz, Wiesbaden 2017; *Jarass*, Charta der Grundrechte der Europäischen Union unter Einbeziehung der sonstigen Grundrechtsregelungen des Primärrechts und der EMRK, Munich 2021; *Kalbhenn*, 'Designvorgaben für Chatbots, Deepfakes und Emotionserkennungssysteme: Der Vorschlag der Europäischen Kommission zu einer KI-VO als Erweiterung der medienrechtlichen Plattformregulierung', ZUM 2021, 663; *Kaulartz/Braegelmann*, Rechtshandbuch Artificial Intelligence und Machine Learning, Munich 2020; *Krause*, 'Auf dem Weg zur unionsrechtlichen Regelung von Plattformtätigkeiten – Die Kommissionsinitiative zur Plattformarbeit', NZA 2022, 521; *Kumkar/Rapp*, 'Deepfakes – Eine Herausforderung für die Rechtsordnung', ZfDR 2022, 199; *Krönke*, 'Das europäische KI-Gesetz: Eine Verordnung mit Licht und Schatten', NVwZ 2024, 529; *Łabuz*, 'Regulating Deep Fakes in the Artificial Intelligence Act', ACIG Vol. 2 no. 1, 2023, 1; *Linardatos*, 'Auf dem Weg zu einer europäischen KI-Verordnung – ein (kritischer) Blick auf den aktuellen Kommissionsentwurf', GPR 2022, 58; *Loy/Baumgartner*, 'Consent-Banner und Nudging – Tracking-Mechanismen: Wie viel 'Anstupsen' ist erlaubt?', ZD 2021, 404; *Luguri/Strahilevitz*, 'Shining a Light on Dark Patterns', Journal of Legal Analysis 2021, 43; *Malorny*, 'Datenschutz als Grenze KI-basierter Auswahlentscheidungen im Arbeitsrecht', RdA 2022, 170; *Mamaar*, 'Social Scoring – Eine europäische Perspektive auf Verbraucher-Scores zwischen Big Data und Big Brother', CR 2018, 820; *Martens*, Methodenlehre des Unionsrechts, Tübingen 2013; *Martini/Drews/Seelinger/Weinzierl*, 'Dark Patterns – Phänomenologie und Antworten der Rechtsordnung', ZfDR 2021, 47; *Martini/Kemper*, 'Clearview AI: das Ende der Anonymität?', CR 2023, 341; *Martini/Kramme/Kamke*, 'Dark Patterns im Scheinwerferlicht des Digital Services Act – Sind Art. 25, 27 und 31 DSA der erhoffte Lichtblick oder nur heller Schein?', MMR 2023, 323; *Mehlhorn*, 'Transparenz und Targeting – Die Pläne der EU zur Regulierung politischer Werbung', NVwZ 2023, 1388; *Molavi Vasse'i/Udoh*, 'In Transparency we Trust? Evaluating the Effectiveness of Watermarking and Labeling AI-Generated Content', Research Report; *O'Neil*,

'Weapons of Math Destruction – How Big Data Increases Inequality and Threatens Democracy', New York 2016; *Orssich*, 'Das europäische Konzept für vertrauenswürdige Künstliche Intelligenz', EuZW 2022, 254; *Pechstein/Nowak/Häde (eds)*, Frankfurter Kommentar zu EUV/GRC/AEUV I, 2nd edn, Tübingen 2023; *Pesch/Böhme*, 'Verarbeitung personenbezogener Daten und Datenrichtigkeit bei großen Sprachmodellen – ChatGPT & Co. unter der DSGVO', MMR 2023, 917; *Peukert*, 'Copyright in the Artificial Intelligence Act – A Primer', GRUR Int. 2024, 497; *Roos/Weitz*, 'Hochrisiko-KI-Systeme im Kommissionsentwurf für eine KI-Verordnung – IT- und produktsicherheitsrechtliche Pflichten von Anbietern, Einführern, Händlern und Nutzern', MMR 2021, 884; *Rostalski/Weiss*, 'Der KI-Verordnungsentwurf der Europäischen Kommission', ZfDR 2021, 329; *Schallbruch*, 'EU-Regulierung der Künstlichen Intelligenz – Informationstechnische Systeme im Fokus neuer rechtlicher Anforderungen', DuD 2021, 438; *Schemmel*, 'KI im HR – Herausforderungen und Chancen für die Praxis', SPA 2024, 12; *Schmid*, 'Digital Services Act – Zahl der 'aktiven Nutzer', 'Dark Patterns' und weitere aktuelle Fragestellungen nach Inkrafttreten des DSA', MMR-Aktuell 2023, 455779; *Schmidt/Engelen*, 'The ethics of nudging: An overview', Philosophy Compass 4/2020; *Schürmann*, 'Datenschutz-Folgeabschätzung beim Einsatz Künstlicher Intelligenz – Bewertung und Minimierung der Risiken', ZD 2022, 316; *Schwartmann/Keber/Zenner*, 'KI-VO – Leitfaden für die Praxis', 2024; *Spies*, 'ChatGPT & Co. – Keine Insellösungen', MMR 2023, 469; *Spindler*, 'Der Vorschlag der EU-Kommission für eine Verordnung zur Regulierung der Künstlichen Intelligenz (KI-VO-E) – Ansatz, Instrumente, Qualität und Kontext', CR 2021, 361; *Steege*, 'Die Definition Künstlicher Intelligenz in Art. 3 Abs. 1 KI-VO-E – Ein Meilenstein auf dem Weg zu einem harmonisierten Rechtsrahmen?', MMR 2022, 926; *Steege/Chibanguza*, Rechtshandbuch Metaverse, Baden-Baden 2023; *Steinrötter/Schauer*, 'Lauterkeitsrechtliche Behandlung von Dark Patterns', WRP 2024, 873; *Thöne*, 'Italien: Datenschutzbehörde hebt ChatGPT-Sperre auf', ZD-Aktuell 2023, 01254; *Valta/Vasel*, 'Kommissionsvorschlag für eine Verordnung über Künstliche Intelligenz – Mit viel Bürokratie und wenig Risiko zum KI-Standort?', ZRP 2021, 142; *Voigt/Bastians*, 'Neue europarechtliche Anforderungen an die IT-Sicherheit – Rat der EU nimmt NIS2-Richtlinie an – ein erster Überblick', CR 2022, 768; *Voigt/Bastians*, 'Pflicht zur Benennung von EU-Vertretern im europäischen Digitalrecht – "Representative" als neues Mittel zur Rechtsdurchsetzung', MMR 2022, 930; *Veale/Zuiderveen Borgesius*, 'Demystifying the Draft EU Artificial Intelligence Act – Analysing the good, the bad and the unclear elements of the proposed approach', CRi 2021, 97; *Waas*, 'Verbesserung der Arbeitsbedingungen von Plattformbeschäftigten', ZRP 2022, 105; *Wendehorst/Nessler/Aufreiter/Aichinger*, Der Begriff des „KI-Systems" unter der neuen KI-VO – Vorschlag eines „Drei-Faktor-Ansatzes" zur Bewältigung technischer und juristischer Ungereimtheiten, MMR 2024, 605; *Werry*, 'Generative KI-Modelle im Visier der Datenschutzbehörden – Technische Entwicklungen im Zusammenhang mit KI-Modellen begegnen einer Vielzahl datenschutzrechtlicher Herausforderungen', MMR 2023, 911; *Wirtz/Baumann*, 'Einsatz von eDiscovery-Tools durch Unternehmen im Rahmen von internen Untersuchungen – Einstufung als Hochrisiko-KI-Systeme iSd KI-Verordnung?', RDi 2024, 27.

A. Introduction

The AI Act – the first (union-wide) **uniform legal framework for artificial intelligence** (AI) – was published in the EU Official Journal on 12 July 2024.[1] It is pursuing 1

[1] Regulation (EU) 2024/1689 of the European Parliament and of the Council of 13 June 2024 laying down harmonised rules on artificial intelligence and amending Regulations (EC) No 300/2008, (EU) No 167/2013, (EU) No 168/2013, (EU) 2018/858, (EU) 2018/1139 and (EU) 2019/2144 and Directives 2014/90/EU, (EU) 2016/797 and (EU) 2020/1828 (Artificial Intelligence Act); however, it is not AI as a technology itself that is to be regulated, but the application of AI in various areas Bomhard/Merkle RDi

a **risk-based horizontal approach**[2] that ranges from complete bans on certain AI practices, over strict requirements in connection with so-called high-risk AI systems to (mere) transparency obligations with regard to AI systems that pose particular risks of impersonation or deception. Furthermore, the AI Act contains regulations for providers of so-called general-purpose AI models. AI systems that only pose a minimal risk are not regulated in principle. However, providers can voluntarily adopt codes of conduct, for which the AI Act also provides a framework. Even if the focus of the regulation is **not originally on platform regulation**, it nevertheless contains a lot of requirements that (operators of) online platforms must comply with when using internal AI on their platform or offering AI via the platform.[3] The most important provisions will be discussed in this contribution.

2 The following **explanations refer** to the **version** of the AI Act **dated 12 July 2024**. In view of the short time between the publication of the aforementioned final version of the AI Act and the editorial deadline for this book, it is inevitable and must be **noted on the outset** that the following comments cannot deliver a fully comprehensive examination of the final AI Act. However, they should provide sufficient information to show which aspects are of particular interest to platforms and provide references to more in-depth publications.

I. Legislative process

3 The AI Act can be traced back to a draft by the European Commission published on 21 April 2021.[4] After the Council of the EU published its general approach[5] at the end of 2022, the EU Parliament published its proposed amendments mid-2023.[6] The following trilogue was characterized by a certain **urgency** regarding the **upcoming elections** to the European Parliament. After the AI Act had even been at risk of derailing temporarily, the negotiators were able to reach a general agreement after a veritable negotiation marathon in early December 2023. In particular, the rise of generative AI has prompted lawmakers to rethink their regulatory proposals and adapt them to the dynamics of

2021, 276 (277); Geminn ZD 2021, 354 (355); Orssich EuZW 2022, 254 (255); crit. on the question of harmonisation competence Krönke NVwZ 2024, 529 (532); Ebers/Hoch/Rosenkranz/Ruschemeier/Steinrötter RDi 2021, 528 (529); Linardatos GPR 2022, 58 (58 et seqq.); Valta/Vasel ZRP 2021, 142 (143 et seq.); for more information on the preparatory work for the AI Act Geminn ZD 2021, 354 (355); Orssich EuZW 2022, 254 (255); Valta/Vasel ZRP 2021, 142 (142); cf. also Zenner in Schwartmann/Keber/Zenner, part 2 chap. 1 mn. 1 et seqq.

[2] In detail on the development of risk-based approaches in EU law in general Martini in Hilgendorf/Roth-Isigkeit § 4 mn. 5 et seqq.

[3] In-depth on these two types of interplay between platforms and AI Berberich/Conrad in Ebers/Heinze/Krügel/Steinrötter § 30 mn. 16 et seqq.

[4] European Commission, Proposal for a Regulation of the European Parliament and of the Council laying down harmonised rules on artificial intelligence (AI Act) and amending certain Union legislative acts, 21.4.2021, COM(2021) 206 final.

[5] Council of the European Union, 'Proposal for a Regulation of the European Parliament and of the Council laying down harmonised rules on artificial intelligence (Artificial Intelligence Act) and amending certain Union legislative acts - General approach', 22.11.2022.

[6] European Parliament, 'Amendments adopted by the European Parliament on 14 June 2023 on the proposal for a regulation of the European Parliament and of the Council on laying down harmonised rules on artificial intelligence (Artificial Intelligence Act) and amending certain Union legislative acts', 14.6.2023, P9_TA(2023)0236; a good overview of the legislative process and all related documents can be found at Future of Life Institute, 'EU Artificial Intelligence Act Documents', <artificialintelligenceact.eu/documents/> (last accessed: 01.07.2024).

current developments. The compromise found seems to be **far from perfect**.[7] However, in view of the possible threat of AI regulation being fragmented by the individual Member States the agreement is still to be welcomed.

II. Platform definition

The following explanations are based on a **broad understanding** of the term platform. In addition to the platform as an intermediary in multi-sided markets, the platform as a provider of standardised technology to a broad user base will also be covered.[8] In this respect, the concept of platform used in this chapter is broader than the concept of 'online platform' as defined in the Digital Services Act (→ § 2 mn. 40 et seqq.). Nevertheless, this chapter primarily **focuses** on the **use of internal AI** on platforms and not on the offering of AI by platforms. 4

B. Commission guidelines

Special mention should first and foremost be made of the fact that the Commission will develop **guidelines** on the **practical implementation** of the AI Act. Some time may certainly pass before such guidelines are actually available.[9] Nevertheless, it is advisable for legal practitioners to first ascertain whether the Commission has already taken action in this respect. Art. 96 explicitly mentions: 5

- 'the application of the requirements and obligations referred to in Articles 8–15 and Article 25;
- the prohibited practices referred to in Article 5;
- the practical implementation of the provisions related to substantial modification;
- the practical implementation of transparency obligations laid down in Article 50;
- detailed information on the relationship of this Regulation with the legislation referred to in Annex II of this Regulation as well as other relevant Union law, including as regards consistency in their enforcement;
- the application of the definition of an AI system as set out in Article 3(1)'

C. Scope of application

In order to ascertain the relevance of the AI Act for platforms and their regulation, it is first necessary to determine its scope. 6

I. Material scope of application

The **material scope** of the AI Act covers AI systems and general-purpose AI systems as well as general-purpose AI models. 7

[7] Hacker, 'Comments on the Final Trilogue Version of the AI Act' (23.1.2024) <www.europeannewschool.eu/images/chairs/hacker/Comments%20on%20the%20AI%20Act.pdf> (last accessed: 01.07.2024), p. 2.
[8] In detail Berberich/Conrad in Ebers/Heinze/Krügel/Steinrötter § 30 mn. 4 et seqq.
[9] Cf. Bomhard/Siglmüller RDi 2024, 45 (54).

1. AI systems

8 The AI Act defines the term AI system in Art. 3 no. 1 as a

> 'machine-based system that is designed to operate with varying levels of autonomy and that may exhibit adaptiveness after deployment and that, for explicit or implicit objectives, infers, from the input it receives, how to generate outputs such as predictions, content, recommendations, or decisions that can influence physical or virtual environments'.

This definition is orientated on the **OECD's revised definition**[10] of the term AI system. The European legislators are trying to achieve legal certainty, international convergence and wide acceptance with doing so.[11]

9 The first requirement for qualification as an AI system would therefore be that the system in question is a **'machine-based system'**. This wording is in sync with the Parliaments proposal while it differs from the proposals of the Council and the Commission. The Commission used the term 'software' – and was widely criticised for the almost incomprehensible breadth of this formulation.[12] The Council on the other hand simply used the term 'system' and omitted the clarification that the system must be machine-based to fall within the material scope of the regulation. According to the recitals, the wording 'machine-based system' – unsurprisingly – serves to clarify that AI systems run on machines.[13] However, this change will probably not help to clarify the precise limits of the material scope.[14] It seems difficult to imagine artificial intelligence that is not machine-based, regardless of what exactly is meant by the term 'machine-based' – the AI Act does not provide any further information on this. The term 'system' may also be understood very broadly without further guidance from the European legislators.

10 Furthermore, the system must be **'designed to operate with varying levels of autonomy'**. According to rec. 12 this means that the system has 'some degree of independence of actions from human involvement and of capabilities to operate without human intervention'. The adjustment, compared to the initial definition of an AI system in the Commission draft, which did not address the autonomy of the system, may be welcomed at first sight. However, it can be criticised that the AI Act does not provide any guidance as to when a sufficient level of independence from human involvement and capability to operate without human intervention is reached.[15] In the broadest possible sense, even simple software that does not appear 'intelligent' at all could be subsumed under this definition. In fact, the recital seems to be describing automation rather than autonomy.[16] At least, a historical argument can be put forward to argue that the threshold of autonomy to be achieved should not be set too low: In contrast to the Council's proposal, which formulated 'designed to operate with elements of autonomy', the AI Act now refers to

---

[10] Russel/Perset/Grobelnik, 'Updates to the OECD's definition of an AI system explained' (29.11.2023) <oecd.ai/en/wonk/ai-system-definition-update> (last accessed: 24.02.2024); in further detail OECD 'Explanatory memorandum on the updated OECD definition of an AI system' (05.03.2024) <https://www.oecd.org/en/publications/explanatory-memorandum-on-the-updated-oecd-definition-of-an-ai-system_623da898-en.html> (last accessed: 01.07.2024).

[11] Rec. 12.

[12] See for example Spindler CR 2021, 361 (362 et seq.); Steege MMR 2022, 926 (928); Ebers/Hoch/Rosenkranz/Ruschemeier/Steinrötter RDi 2021, 528 (529).

[13] Rec. 12.

[14] Bomhard/Siglmüller RDi 2024, 45 (45); Keber/Zenner in Schwartmann/Keber/Zenner, part 2 chap. 1 mn. 14; Wendehorst/Nessler/Aufreiter/Achinger MMR 2024, 605 (606 et seq.).

[15] Similar Chibanguza/Steege NJW 2024, 1769 (1770).

[16] Hacker/Berz ZRP 2023, 226 (227).

'levels' of autonomy.[17] However, this argument is only valid if one assumes that many elements are necessary to reach a certain level of autonomy. Ultimately, this part of the definition is unlikely to be useful for demarcation purposes.[18] The wording can further be criticised as it is misleading insofar as it allows an understanding that a single system must be able to operate with several levels of autonomy. Rather, one 'level of autonomy' should be considered sufficient.[19]

In addition to that ('and') the system **'may exhibit adaptiveness after deployment'**. 11
The European legislators only give one example of adaptiveness but do not define it any further. Rec. 12 states that 'the adaptiveness that an AI system could exhibit after deployment refers to self-learning capabilities, allowing the system to change while in use'. Use cases could be recommender systems that are able adapt to individual preferences.[20] However, as the wording 'may' indicates, adaptiveness is not a mandatory characteristic for classification as an AI system.

The addition, which refers to the fact that AI systems infer **'for explicit or implicit** 12
objectives', is unlikely to provide much certainty to the differentiation between AI systems and other systems either. According to rec. 12 'the reference to explicit or implicit objectives underscores that AI systems can operate according to explicit defined objectives or to implicit objectives'. To illustrate this, one can think of a self-driving system that pursues the explicit objective of observing traffic regulations. The implicit objective of the self-driving system, on the other hand, would be to protect life and health of the people it encounters.[21] However, the implicit goal does not necessarily have to result from explicit goals previously defined but may also be incorporated through training data and system architecture.[22]

---

17 Wendehorst/Nessler/Aufreiter/Achinger MMR 2024, 605 (607) argue that that even a 'level 0' without any autonomy at all represents a 'level of autonomy' and can therefore be considered sufficient; on the consideration of historical arguments in European law Martens, p. 396 et seqq.

18 See also Hacker, 'Comments on the Final Trilogue Version of the AI Act' (23.1.2024) www.europeannewschool.eu/images/chairs/hacker/Comments%20on%20the%20AI%20Act.pdf (last accessed: 01.07.2024), p. 3 et seq.; similar Wendehorst/Nessler/Aufreiter/Achinger MMR 2024, 605 (607).

19 See Russel/Perset/Grobelnik, 'Updates to the OECD's definition of an AI system explained' (29.11.2023) <oecd.ai/en/wonk/ai-system-definition-update> (last accessed: 01.07.2024), 'Also, the previous wording, "operate with varying levels", might be read as describing a single system whose level of autonomy and adaptiveness might change over time, which was not the intended reading.' Accordingly, the OECD changed that part of the definition: 'Different AI systems vary in their levels of autonomy and adaptiveness after deplyoment'.

20 Russel/Perset/Grobelnik, 'Updates to the OECD's definition of an AI system explained' (29.11.2023) <oecd.ai/en/wonk/ai-system-definition-update> (last accessed: 01.07.2024); OECD 'Explanatory memorandum on the updated OECD definition of an AI system' (05.03.2024) <https://www.oecd.org/en/publications/explanatory-memorandum-on-the-updated-oecd-definition-of-an-ai-system_623da898-en.html> (last accessed: 01.07.2024); cf. Wendehorst/Nessler/Aufreiter/Achinger MMR 2024, 605 (608) who argue that there are currently only a few fields of application where AI systems are used that actually allow or require (certain) model optimisations during operation based on the current inputs and outputs of the AI system.

21 Russel/Perset/Grobelnik, 'Updates to the OECD's definition of an AI system explained' (29.11.2023) <oecd.ai/en/wonk/ai-system-definition-update> (last accessed: 01.07.2024); OECD 'Explanatory memorandum on the updated OECD definition of an AI system' (05.03.2024) <https://www.oecd.org/en/publications/explanatory-memorandum-on-the-updated-oecd-definition-of-an-ai-system_623da898-en.html> (last accessed: 01.07.2024).

22 OECD 'Explanatory memorandum on the updated OECD definition of an AI system' (05.03.2024) <https://www.oecd.org/en/publications/explanatory-memorandum-on-the-updated-oecd-definition-of-an-ai-system_623da898-en.html> (last accessed: 01.07.2024).

13 The (only) **decisive criterion** for categorisation as an AI system is that of inference.[23] The system is to be categorised as an AI system if it **'infers from the input it receives, how to generate outputs such as predictions, content, recommendations, or decisions.'** This requirement allows 'simpler traditional software systems or programming approaches' as well as 'systems that are based on the rules defined solely by natural persons to automatically execute operations'[24] to be excluded from the material scope of application. The necessity of having an input and an output is unlikely to be of much help. The actual decisive factors for the distinction between AI systems and other systems can essentially be found in the explanation of the concept of interference in rec. 12. This is unfortunate, as one could have considered adapting the list of techniques and approaches covered in Annex I provided for in the Commission draft[25], so the important distinguishing features could at least be found in the legal text and not just in the recitals. However, the more detailed definition in rec. 12 reads as follows:

> 'This **capability to infer** refers to the process of obtaining the outputs, such as predictions, content, recommendations, or decisions, which can influence physical and virtual environments, and to a capability of AI systems to derive models or algorithms, or both, from inputs or data. The techniques that enable inference while building an AI system include machine learning approaches that learn from data how to achieve certain objectives, and logic- and knowledge-based approaches that infer from encoded knowledge or symbolic representation of the task to be solved. The capacity of an AI system to infer transcends basic data processing by enabling learning, reasoning or modelling.'

14 Unfortunately, it seems that this 'clarification' leaves more questions open than it answers.[26] Nevertheless, it can be concluded that a system lacks sufficient inference capability and, as a result, cannot be considered an AI system if it is only capable of **'basic data processing'**. What exactly 'basic data processing' is supposed to mean, however, remains unclear. The 'narrow procedural tasks' mentioned in Art. 6(3)(a) (→ mn. 92) already seem to go beyond basic data processing when the European legislators speak of them being performed by AI systems. On the other hand, it seems that no 'basic data processing' can be assumed when using machine-learning and/or logic- and knowledge-based approaches. Why the more detailed definitions of **'machine learning approaches'** and **'logic- and knowledge-based approaches'**, which were included in the Council's proposal[27], are not included in the final text remains questionable.[28] In this context it further remains unclear what the legislators mean by 'learning, reasoning or modelling'[29] and whether a specific degree of 'learning, reasoning or modelling' ability is required. The definition of 'learning' from the Council's proposal[30] according to which , 'learning refers to the computational process of optimizing from data the parameters of the model, which is a mathematical construct generating an output based on input data' cannot be used here since it was not adopted in the final text.

---

[23] See also Hacker, 'Comments on the Final Trilogue Version of the AI Act' (23.1.2024) <www.europeannewschool.eu/images/chairs/hacker/Comments%20on%20the%20AI%20Act.pdf> (last accessed: 01.07.2024), p. 3; similar Chibanguza/Steege NJW 2024, 1769 (1770).

[24] Rec. 12.

[25] See also Becker/Feuerstack MMR 2024, 22 (23).

[26] Cf. also Wendehorst/Nessler/Aufreiter/Achinger MMR 2024, 605 (609).

[27] Rec. 6a and 6b Council's proposal.

[28] See however the explanations on the terms 'machine learning' and 'symbolic or knowledge-based AI systems' in OECD 'Explanatory memorandum on the updated OECD definition of an AI system' (05.03.2024) <https://www.oecd.org/en/publications/explanatory-memorandum-on-the-updated-oecd-definition-of-an-ai-system_623da898-en.html> (last accessed: 01.07.2024).

[29] One may even argue that machines cannot 'learn' at all. See for example Solove, 'Artificial Intelligence and Privacy' (George Washington University Law School, 1.2.2024) <papers.ssrn.com/sol3/papers.cfm?abstract_id=4713111> (last accessed: 01.07.2024), p. 13.

[30] Rec. 6a Council's proposal.

However, as the AI Act oriented its definition on the OECD's revised definition, an **example of sufficient inference capability** can probably be extracted from the OECD's explanation of its new definition of an AI system[31]: 'An AI system is said to "infer how to generate outputs" when it receives input from the environment and computes an output by processing the input through one or more models and underlying algorithms. For example, a visual object recognition system implemented by a deep neural network performs "inference", i.e., infers how to generate its output (in this case, a classification of the object in the image) by passing its input (the pixels of the image) through the deep network (a parameterised algebraic expression composed of addition, multiplication, and certain nonlinear operations).' 15

According to the wording ('include'), the mentioned techniques (machine-learning and/or logic- and knowledge-based approaches) are **not exhaustive**. It is therefore possible that (in the future) other techniques are also covered if they are sufficiently capable of inference. Of course, a perfectly clear demarcation has not been reached – and perhaps cannot be reached at all. But at least a certain downward demarcation has been achieved, so that really simple software programs are no longer covered.[32] 16

The fact that the system can only be categorized as an AI system if the output, which the system inferred to generate **'can influence physical or virtual environments'** will be of little help for demarcation purposes.[33] A machine-based system that generates output that cannot have (any) influence on either its physical or digital context seems difficult to imagine. Ultimately, every system that can be perceived by humans also influences its environment.[34] The AI Act does not seem to require a specific threshold of influence here. 17

In the light of the above, the **first step** for platforms and platform operators is to check whether the systems they use have sufficient capacity to infer in the sense of the AI Act or whether they can be classified as systems that only perform 'basic data processing'.[35] In this context, it is irrelevant whether the AI system is used on a stand-alone basis or is integrated into another product.[36] However, the classification of one of the platform's systems as an AI system will not lead to the entire platform being classified as a single AI system.[37] Rec. 6b of the parliamentary draft, which points in this direction was not adopted in the final text.[38] The decisive demarcation criterion here is that of the 'machine-based system'. 18

2. General-purpose AI models

In Art. 3 no. 63 a general-purpose AI model (GPAI model) is defined as an 19

> 'AI model, including where such an AI model is trained with a large amount of data using self-supervision at scale, that displays significant generality and is capable of competently performing a wide

[31] Russel/Perset/Grobelnik, 'Updates to the OECD's definition of an AI system explained' (29.11.2023) <oecd.ai/en/wonk/ai-system-definition-update> (last accessed: 01.07.2024).

[32] See also Hacker, 'Comments on the Final Trilogue Version of the AI Act' (23.1.2024) <www.europeannewschool.eu/images/chairs/hacker/Comments%20on%20the%20AI%20Act.pdf> (last accessed: 01.07.2024), p. 3.

[33] Cf. also Wendehorst/Nessler/Aufreiter/Achinger MMR 2024, 605 (608).

[34] Gless/Janal in Hilgendorf/Roth-Isigkeit § 2 mn. 24.

[35] Wendehorst/Nessler/Aufreiter/Achinger MMR 2024, 605 propose a 'three-factor approach' for classification under Art. 3 no. 1.

[36] Rec. 12.

[37] This question is raised by Bomhard/Merkle RDi 2021, 276 (277) in respect of the Commission draft.

[38] The recital stated that a larger system (not necessarily: AI system) into which an 'AI component' is inserted is only to be regarded as a (single, large) AI system in its entirety if the larger system would not function without the 'AI component'.

range of distinct tasks regardless of the way the model is placed on the market and that can be integrated into a variety of downstream systems or applications, except AI models that are used for research, development or prototyping activities before they are placed on the market.'

20 Reading this definition, the first question that arises is what is meant by a **'model'** and how is it different from a system. Rec. 97 provides further explanation on this as it states that 'AI models are essential components of AI systems' but 'they do not constitute AI systems on their own'. To become AI systems, they therefore 'require the addition of further components, such as for example a user interface'.[39] This also explains why it is a necessary requirement of general-purpose AI models that they **'can be integrated into a variety of downstream systems or applications'**.[40] However, the model cannot be categorised as a general-purpose AI model if it is **'used for research, development or prototyping activities'** before it is placed on the market.

21 The addition 'including where such an AI model is **trained with a large amount of data** using **self-supervision** at scale' seems like a redundant clarification at first glance because rec. 97 shows that neither training with a large amount of data nor the use of self-supervision are necessary characteristics to qualify a model as a GPAI model ('typically'). Even if these features may be characteristic for some GPAI models, they are therefore not relevant for the categorisation. However, the addition becomes relevant when it comes to the generality and the capability of the model (→ mn. 22).

22 The decisive characteristics for categorisation as a GPAI model are the models' **'significant generality'** and its **capability of competently performing a wide range of distinct tasks**. The latter appears to be a sub-case of generality – however, it is explicitly mentioned by the European legislators. What exactly is meant by 'generality' and when the generality of the system is considered 'significant' is not specified in the AI Act. Furthermore, it is unclear as to when a 'wide range of distinct tasks' can be assumed and when exactly it can be postulated that the system 'competently' performs these tasks. The European legislators at least try to provide some guidance in the recitals: Firstly, rec. 99 identifies large generative AI models as a typical example of GPAI models, 'given that they allow for flexible generation of content, such as in the form of text, audio, images or video, that can readily accommodate a wide range of distinctive tasks'. The ability to generate content as the result of a prompt therefore should be sufficient to assume 'significant generality' of the model.[41] Rec. 98 goes on to clarify that the generality of the model can be determined by a variety of criteria – one of those being the models' parameters. Unfortunately, the AI Act does not specify what exactly these other criteria could be and does not give a few other examples. With regard to the parameters of the model, however, rec. 98 provides a presumption, as models 'with at least a billion of parameters and trained with a large amount of data using self-supervision at scale

[39] Cf. Bomhard/Siglmüller RDi 2024, 45 (49 et seq.) with the example of GTP-4 as the model and ChatGPT as an AI system.

[40] Bommasani et al., 'On the Opportunities and Risks of Foundation Models' (Stanford University, 12.7.2022) <arxiv.org/abs/2108.07258> (last accessed: 07.01.2024), p. 7 have, like the Parliaments proposal, favoured the term foundation model. They argue that this better expresses the fact that 'a foundation model is itself incomplete but serves as the common basis from which many task-specific models are built via adaptation'. They further wanted to 'connote the significance of architectural stability, safety, and security: poorly constructed foundations are a recipe for disaster and well-executed foundations are a reliable bedrock for future applications'.

[41] See also Bommasani et al., 'On the Opportunities and Risks of Foundation Models' (Stanford University, 12.7.2022) <arxiv.org/abs/2108.07258> (last accessed: 01.07.2024), p. 5 'GPT-3 [...] permits in-context learning, in which the language model can be adapted to a downstream task simply by providing it with a prompt (a natural language description of the task), an emergent property that was neither specifically trained nor anticipated to arise'.

should be considered to display significant generality and to competently perform a wide range of distinctive tasks'.[42] Of course, the question of when a 'large amount of data' can be assumed still remains open.[43] In addition, placing this presumption in the legal text and not in the recitals could have provided for greater legal certainty.

3. General-purpose AI systems

Art. 3 no. 66 defines the term **general-purpose AI system** as an 'AI system which is based on a general-purpose AI model and which has the capability to serve a variety of purposes, both for direct use as well as for integration in other AI systems'. An AI system is **'based on'** a general-purpose AI model if the model is 'integrated into' it or 'forms a part' of it.[44] 23

II. Personal and territorial scope of application

The **personal scope** of the AI Act can essentially be found in Art. 2(1). 24

1. Providers placing on the market or putting into service in the Union

The personal scope in Art. 2(1)(a) firstly addresses 25

> '**providers** placing on the market or putting into service AI systems or placing on the market general-purpose AI models in the Union, irrespective of whether those providers are established or located within the Union or in a third country'.

Whereas

> '"provider" means a natural or legal person, public authority, agency or other body that **develops** an AI system or a general-purpose AI model **or** that **has** an AI system or a general-purpose AI model **developed** and places it on the market or puts the AI system into service **under its own name or trademark**, whether for payment or free of charge', Art. 3 no. 3.

Unfortunately, there is no definition of **'development'** in the AI Act. The European Data Protection Supervisor (EDPS) criticised this lack of definition in October 2023[45] – however, a definition was not introduced subsequent to the criticism. The EDPS states that 'data processing for training is a fundamental part of the development of machine learning-based AI systems'. In his view, this means that anyone who trains an AI system could also be considered a developer and therefore a provider of the system. Particularly regarding the possibility of retraining AI systems, he called for clarification to the effect that 'AI operators retraining pre-trained AI systems should be qualified as 'providers' in order to guarantee that compliance the requirements of the AI Act remains ensured'. Yet, the European legislators were well aware that retraining is possible and even address this in the recitals in context with the AI value chain.[46] This is supported by the fact that 26

[42] For comparison: GPT3 has 175 billion parameters see Bommasani et al., 'On the Opportunities and Risks of Foundation Models' (Stanford University, 12.7.2022) <arxiv.org/abs/2108.07258> (last accessed: 01.07.2024), p. 3.

[43] Bommasani et al., 'On the Opportunities and Risks of Foundation Models' (Stanford University, 12.7.2022) <arxiv.org/abs/2108.07258> (last accessed: 01.07.2024), upon whose contribution the wording of the provision was probably orientated, do not describe in more detail when training on 'broad data' can be assumed.

[44] Rec. 100.

[45] EDPS, 'Opinion 44/2023 on the Proposal for Artificial Intelligence Act in the light of legislative developments', 23.10.2023, p. 8 mn. 15 et seqq.

[46] Rec. 88.

Art. 25 contains explicit regulations on when modifications to AI systems (after their placing on the market or putting into service) lead to a shift in the provider role (→ mn. 41 et seqq.). An overly broad understanding of the term 'development' would circumvent these regulations.

27 In addition, the **placing on the market** or **putting into service** of an AI system or GPAI model is necessary for categorisation as a provider. Those terms are defined in Art. 3 no. 9 and 11 as follows:

> '"placing on the market" means the first making available of an AI system or a general-purpose AI model on the Union market';
> '"putting into service" means the supply of an AI system for first use directly to the deployer or for own use in the Union for its intended purpose'.

28 It is expressly clarified that it has **no relevance** whether the provider is **established** or **located** within the Union or in a third country. Providers established outside the Union must note that they may be obliged under Art. 22 to appoint an **authorised representative** established in the Union, prior to making their systems available on the Union market, as long as those systems are high-risk AI systems. The same applies, in general, for providers of GPAI models established outside the Union, Art. 54.[47]

2. Deployers established or located within the Union

29 The AI Act further applies to

> '**deployers** of AI systems that have their place of establishment or are located within the Union', Art. 2(1)(b).

A platform will be considered a **deployer** if it is

> '**using** an AI system **under its authority** except where the AI system is used in the course of a personal non-professional activity', Art. 3 no. 4.

30 Given the broad understanding of the term platform used in this chapter, the exception mentioned for personal, non-professional activities will be of little practical relevance. The provision of standardised technology to a broad user base should regularly lead to a classification as a professional activity. In the case of the platform acting as an intermediary, the activity will not be classified as personal.[48] Many platforms will therefore be categorised as deployers if they cannot already be classified as providers. If they do not have their place of establishment within the Union, they may still fall under the personal scope according to Art. 2(1)(c).

3. Providers and deployers established or located in a third country

31 Art. 2(1)(c) states that the AI Act also applies to

> 'providers and deployers of AI systems that have their place of establishment or are located in a third country, where the **output** produced by the system is **used in the Union**'.

This extension of the scope of application is intended to **ensure** that the applicability of the **AI Act cannot** be **circumvented**, for example, by contracting 'certain services to an operator established outside the Union in relation to an activity to be performed by

[47] On the obligation to appoint representatives pursuant to other EU legislation Voigt/Bastians MMR 2022, 930.

[48] Nevertheless, it remains particularly unclear whether a purely internal use, where customers and employees do not come into contact with the AI system, would also be covered cf. Keber/Zenner in Schwartmann/Keber/Zenner, part 2 chap. 1 mn. 20.

an AI system that would qualify as high-risk'.[49] The problem identified by the European legislators is that 'in those circumstances, the AI system used by the operator outside the Union could process data lawfully collected in and transferred from the Union, and provide to the contracting operator in the Union the output of that AI system resulting from that processing, without that AI system being placed on the market, put into service or used in the Union'.

The scope of application is extremely unclear and broad in this respect. It is broad because even AI systems developed outside the Union, located there and furthermore only developed with non-European data may nevertheless be covered.[50] Ambiguities arise from the fact that the European legislators do not further define when the **usage** of an **output** can be assumed. There is no clear limitation in Art. 2(1)(c) to the effect that, for example, only the direct output is covered.[51] If interpreted as broadly as possible, it would therefore be possible for a non-EU-based provider of AI systems to fall within the scope of the AI Act without his knowledge, because a result produced by one of his AI systems is used in the EU – possibly after some time and several processing stages later.[52] Consequently, there could be a risk for EU citizens that many AI systems or their outputs will simply not be offered in the Union due to these uncertainties.[53] To prevent this, it is appropriate to focus on whether the used result was **intended to be used in the Union.**[54] Unfortunately, this restriction does not result from the direct wording of the provision, like the Parliament had proposed. Nevertheless, the wording of rec. 22 is expressly limited to 'outputs intended to be used in the Union'.[55] 32

4. Importers and distributors

According to Art. 2(1)(d) the AI Act is also applicable for '**importers** and **distributors** of AI systems'. Whereas 33

> '"importer" means any natural or legal person located or established in the Union that places on the market an AI system that bears the name or trademark of a natural or legal person established in a third country', Art. 3 no. 6

and

> '"distributor" means any natural or legal person in the supply chain, other than the provider or the importer, that makes an AI system available on the Union market', Art. 3 no. 7.

The obligations of importers and distributors are regulated in more detail in Art. 23 and Art. 24. It should be noted that a single operator can be considered both a distributor and importer of the same AI system, rec. 83. Moreover, if the criteria of Art. 25 are met, it is possible for importers or distributors to switch to the role of a provider of the AI system in question (→ mn. 41 et seqq.). 34

---

[49] Rec. 22.

[50] Crit. Valta/Vasel ZRP 2021, 142 (145).

[51] However, this would probably also lead to Art. 2 (1)(c) being circumvented by technically modifying the output before retransferring into the Union, cf. Bomhard/Merkle RDi 2021, 276 (278).

[52] Cf. Krönke NVwZ 2024, 529 (530); Bomhard/Merkle RDi 2021, 276 (278) and Geminn ZD 2021, 354 (356).

[53] Gless/Janal in Hilgendorf/Roth-Isigkeit § 2 mn. 24; Valta/Vasel ZRP 2021, 142 (145).

[54] Similar Krönke NVwZ 2024, 529 (530); Keber/Zenner in Schwartmann/Keber/Zenner, part 2 chap. 1 mn. 25 point out that, on the contrary, one could understand rec. 22 as clarifying that a mere intention to use an output can be sufficient. This is, however, contradicted by the unambiguous wording of Art. 2(1)(c) ('is used').

[55] However, as the output of AI systems is not physical and does not arrive 'as a container at the docks', the EU authorities may have a difficult time tracking the use of the output within the EU, Bomhard/Siglmüller RDi 2024, 45 (46); similar Keber/Zenner in Schwartmann/Keber/Zenner, part 2 chap. 1 mn. 25.

5. Product manufacturers, authorised representatives and affected persons

35 Also covered by the scope of application according to Art. 2(1)(e), (f) and (g) are 'product manufacturers placing on the market or putting into service an AI system together with their product and under their own name or trademark', 'authorised representatives of providers, which are not established in the Union'[56] as well as 'affected persons that are located in the Union'.

III. Temporal scope

36 The temporal scope of the AI Act is outlined in more detail in Art. 113 and Art. 111, whereby Art. 113(1) first stipulates that the AI Act **enters into force** on the twentieth day following of its publication in the Official Journal of the European Union which was **1 August 2024**. According to Art. 113(2) the AI Act then in general **applies** from **2 August 2026**. However, there are **many deviations** from this and the point of time at which compliance with the AI Act must be established mainly depends on which group of risk the system falls into and whether the system or model was already placed on the market or put into service at the time of applicability of the AI Act.[57] The following regulations are likely to be the most important in the context of platforms:

37 Chapters I (**general provisions**) and II (**prohibited practices** → mn. 47 et seqq.) will apply from **2 February 2025**, Art. 113(3)(a). In contrast to earlier versions of the trilogue result, the final legal text now merely refers to Chapters I and II and no longer contains the addition of '[Prohibitions]' in brackets. Consequently, Art. 4 (**AI literacy**) must also be assumed to be subject to the exception in Art. 113(3)(a). **High-risk AI systems** according to Art. 6(2) in conjunction with Annex III (→ mn. 95 et seqq.) must fulfil the requirements of the AI Act from **2 August 2026** according to the general regulation, while high-risk AI systems pursuant to Art. 6(1) will have another year until 2 August 2027, Art. 113(3)(c). If high-risk AI systems have **already been placed on the market or put into service before 2 August 2026**, they are generally not covered, unless 'from that date, those systems are subject to significant changes in their designs', Art. 111(2).[58] The European legislators justify this approach by stating that they want to ensure legal certainty and avoid disruptions in the market.[59] The concept of 'significant changes', according to rec. 177, 'should be understood as equivalent in substance to the notion of substantial modification'. Chapter III Section 4 (Notifying authorities and notified bodies), Chapter V (**GPAI models**), Chapter VII (Governance), Chapter XII (Penalties) and Article 78 (Confidentiality) will apply from 2 August 2025, Art. 113(3)(b). This however explicitly does not apply to Art. 101, which contains regulations on the fines for providers of GPAI models. If a GPAI model has already been placed on the market before 2 August 2025, providers have to comply by 2 August 2027, Art. 111(3).

---

[56] Cf. Art. 3 no. 5.

[57] Cf. Hacker, 'Comments on the Final Trilogue Version of the AI Act' (23.1.2024) <www.europeannewschool.eu/images/chairs/hacker/Comments%20on%20the%20AI%20Act.pdf> (last accessed: 01.07.2024), p. 13; a great overview of all relevant key dates can be found at Future of Life Institute, 'Implementation Timeline', <artificialintelligenceact.eu/documents/> (last accessed: 01.07.2024).

[58] This is rightly criticised by Hacker 'Comments on the Final Trilogue Version of the AI Act' (23.1.2024) <www.europeannewschool.eu/images/chairs/hacker/Comments%20on%20the%20AI%20Act.pdf> (last accessed: 01.07.2024), p. 13 et seq. because this 'opens a significant loophole and contradicts general legislative practices in the field of product safety. After all, if a risk exists, it is irrelevant if the product was on the market at the time of the applicability of the Act or if it is only introduced after that moment'.

[59] Rec. 177.

IV. Exceptions

Art. 2(3)–(12) contain several exceptions to the scope of application, which cannot all be discussed in detail here.[60] These exceptions concern, **for example**, certain AI systems in the **military**, **defence** or **national security** context or AI systems and models specifically developed and put into service for the sole purpose of **scientific research** and **development**. The following exceptions are of particular **relevance in the platform context**: 38

Firstly, not covered by the AI Act is 'any **research**, **testing** or **development** activity regarding AI systems or models **prior** to being placed on the market or put into service'. Therefore, if platforms develop their own AI systems or models, they are exempt from complying with the AI Act in this respect. Due to a counter-exception, however, any 'testing in real world conditions'[61] is covered. If, on the other hand, platforms want to test in real-world conditions, the use of regulatory sandboxes (Art. 57) can be an option. 39

Secondly, the AI Act does not cover **AI systems** 'released **under free** and **open-source licences,** unless they are placed on the market or put into service as high-risk AI systems or as an AI system that falls under Art. 5 or 50', Art. 2(12). Art. 5 identifies the prohibited AI practices (→ mn. 47 et seqq.) – Art. 50, on the other hand, refers to the transparency obligations for providers and deployers of certain AI systems (→ mn. 116 et seqq.). It should be noted that only AI systems are covered by this exception. For **GPAI models** under free and open-source licences, different provisions exist in the AI Act (→ mn. 141). Rec. 102 and 103 provide some more details on when a release under 'free and open-source licences' can be assumed. These recitals do not directly refer to AI systems, but rather to free and open source GPAI models and 'AI components', including 'tools, services or processes on an AI system'. However, due to the similar purpose of the exemption, the clarification may probably be adopted with caution here. Accordingly, a licence 'should be considered free and open-source also when it allows users to run, copy, distribute, study, change and improve software and data, including models under the condition that the original provider of the model is credited, the identical or comparable terms of distribution are respected'. It will, on the other hand, **not be assumed** if the AI system is **'provided against a price or otherwise monetised'**. Monetisation can, according to rec. 103, already be assumed for the 'provision of services', including 'technical support' or the 'use of personal data' which is not used 'exclusively for improving the security, compatibility or interoperability of the software, with the exception of transactions between micro enterprises'. Regarding the 'provision of services', the wording is somewhat ambiguous. What is meant is probably, as described in the parliamentary proposal, 'charging a price for technical support services' and 'providing a software platform through which the provider monetises other services'.[62] In practice, the exception could therefore be largely ineffective with such a narrow interpretation.[63] 40

[60] For more detailed explanations see Schwartmann/Keber/Zenner, part 2 chap. 1 mn. 26 et seqq.

[61] Cf. Art. 3 no. 57.

[62] Rec. 60b of the Parliaments proposal.

[63] See also Bomhard/Siglmüller RDi 2024, 45 (54) and Keber/Zenner in Schwartmann/Keber/Zenner, part 2 chap. 1 mn. 33.

D. Responsibilities along the AI value chain

41 Platforms not already qualifying as providers should be aware that they can still be subject to provider obligations under certain circumstances.[64] It lays in the very nature of AI systems, and GPAI models in particular, that their life cycle and value chain can be highly complex and may involve numerous operators. Accordingly, it must be clearly defined which involved parties have which responsibilities. With the regulations laid down in Art. 25, the European legislators seek to ensure legal certainty in this regard.[65] Therefore

> 'Any distributor, importer, deployer or other third-party shall be considered to be a provider of a high-risk AI system for the purposes of this Regulation and shall be subject to the obligations of the provider under Article 16, in any of the following circumstances:', Art. 25(1).[66]

42 Firstly, distributors, importers, deployers or other third-parties can be considered as providers is when they 'put their **name** or **trademark** on a **high-risk AI system** already placed on the market or put into service'. However, this applies 'without prejudice to contractual arrangements stipulating that the obligations are otherwise allocated', Art. 25(1)(a).

43 Secondly, and probably much more relevant than the first scenario, the mentioned parties can be considered as providers if they 'make a **substantial modification** to a high-risk AI system that has already been placed on the market or has already been put into service and in a way that it remains a high-risk AI system pursuant to Article 6', Art. 25(1)(b). According to Art. 3 no. 23 the term substantial modification means

> 'a change to the AI system after its placing on the market or putting into service which is not foreseen or planned in the initial conformity assessment carried out by the provider and as a result of which the compliance of the AI system with the [requirements for high-risk AI systems] is affected or results in a modification to the intended purpose for which the AI system has been assessed'.

This question can become viral especially when GPAI systems, which are already classified as high-risk[67], are fine tuned to adapt them to specific circumstances and use cases by platforms.[68] Such an adaption can, for example, be reached by updating the parameters of the underlaying model or through the inclusion of new data.[69] If the fine-tuning is not within the scope of the initial conformity assessment, the complex question of differentiating between a **(mere) fine-tuning** and a **substantial modification** arises. European legislators also differentiate between 'modifications' and 'fine-tuning' in this respect.[70] However, without a legal definition of fine-tuning, this is not helpful for

---

[64] Art. 28(4) also contains some provisions for providers of high-risk AI systems that are being supplied by third parties with, for example, tools or components regarding the written agreement they should enter to enable the provider to comply with the AI Act. However, it remains unclear whether this is a genuine obligation to enter a contract, Bomhard/Siglmüller RDi 2024, 45 (49). The wording 'shall' leaves some room for interpretation.

[65] In great detail on the responsibilities along the AI value chain Zenner/Schwartmann/Hansen in Schwartmann/Keber/Zenner, part 2 chap. 1 mn. 478 et seqq.

[66] Art 28(3) contains similar provisions for high-risk AI systems that are safety components of products to which the legal acts listed in Annex II, Sec. A apply.

[67] See rec. 85 'General-purpose AI systems may be used as high-risk AI systems by themselves or be components of other high risk AI systems'.

[68] Cf. Hacker, 'Comments on the Final Trilogue Version of the AI Act' (23.1.2024) <www.europeannewschool.eu/images/chairs/hacker/Comments%20on%20the%20AI%20Act.pdf> (last accessed: 07.01.2024), p. 9 et seq.

[69] Bommasani et al., 'On the Opportunities and Risks of Foundation Models' (Stanford University, 12.7.2022) <arxiv.org/abs/2108.07258> (last accessed: 01.07.2024) p. 85 et seqq.

[70] Rec. 109 'In case of a modification or fine-tuning of a model'.

the demarcation. Generalised answers cannot be made here, and decisions need to be made on a case-by-case basis. Nonetheless, a substantial modification should at least be assumable 'in cases of fine-tuning on a data set that is known to contain a significant amount of hate speech or of explicit removal of the safety layer of models'.[71] Changes to the system that are due to the fact that it continues to learn after being placed on the market or put into service, on the other hand, should not be categorised as a substantial modification 'provided that those changes have been pre-determined by the provider and assessed at the moment of the conformity assessment', rec. 128. As a result, some uncertainty remains.[72] This is even more a problem as the understanding of the concept of substantial modification can have a significant impact on whether the AI Act is applicable at all to high-risk AI systems already placed on the market or put into service before 2 August 2026 (→ mn. 37).

Thirdly, the mentioned parties can be considered as providers if they 'modify the intended purpose of an AI system, including a general-purpose AI system, which has not been classified as high-risk and has already been placed on the market or put into service in such manner that the AI system **becomes** a **high risk** AI system in accordance with Article 6', Art. 25(3). Therefore, before platforms modify the intended purpose of a system, they should carry out a hypothetical assessment to determine whether the system will subsequently fall into the high-risk category. **44**

If one of the provisions of Art. 25(1) applies, there is a **shift** in the **provider-position.** **45** According to Art. 25(2) 'the provider that initially placed the AI system on the market or put it into service shall no longer be considered a provider of that specific AI system for the purposes of this Regulation'. Art. 25(2) sent. 2 further stipulates that the (then) former provider shall closely cooperate with the new provider. However, this only applies if the former provider has not expressly excluded the change of its system into a high-risk system, Art. 25(2) sent. 3. The cooperation of the former with the new provider must also consider the 'need to respect and protect intellectual property rights and confidential business information or trade secrets in accordance with Union and national law', Art. 28(5).

E. AI literacy

Art. 4 provides special incentives for platforms to **offer professional trainings** in order to **educate employees and other third parties,**[73] stipulating that **46**

> 'providers and deployers of AI systems shall take measures to ensure, to their best extent, a sufficient level of AI literacy of their staff and other persons dealing with the operation and use of AI systems on their behalf, taking into account their technical knowledge, experience, education and training and the context the AI systems are to be used in, and considering the persons or group of persons on whom the AI systems are to be used'.

AI literacy, according to Art. 3 no 56, means

> 'skills, knowledge and understanding that allows providers, users and affected persons, taking into account their respective rights and obligations in the context of this Regulation, to make an informed deployment of AI systems, as well as to gain awareness about the opportunities and risks of AI and possible harm it can cause'.

---

[71] Hacker, 'Comments on the Final Trilogue Version of the AI Act' (23.1.2024) <www.europeannewschool.eu/images/chairs/hacker/Comments%20on%20the%20AI%20Act.pdf> (last accessed: 01.07.2024), p. 10.

[72] Similar Chibanguza/Steege NJW 2024, 1769 (1772 et seq.).

[73] Cf. Bomhard/Siglmüller RDi 2024, 45 (47); see also rec. 20.

F. Prohibited practices

47 Following the risk-based approach, the AI Act in Art. 5 first addresses those practices that are contrary to the values of the Union and therefore prohibited.

I. Subliminal techniques beyond a person's consciousness and purposefully manipulative or deceptive techniques

48 According to Art. 5(1)(a)

> 'the placing on the market, the putting into service or the use of an AI system that deploys **subliminal techniques** beyond a person's consciousness or **purposefully manipulative** or **deceptive techniques**, with the objective, or the effect of materially distorting the behaviour of a person or a group of persons by appreciably impairing their ability to make an informed decision, thereby causing them to take a decision that they would not have otherwise taken in a manner that causes or is reasonably likely to cause that person, another person or group of persons significant harm'

is prohibited.

49 First, it should be noted, that the prohibitions for AI practices mentioned in Art. 5(1)(a) are complementary to the provisions in the **Unfair Commercial Practices Directive** (henceforth UCP-Directive).[74] Practices covered by this Directive in particular unfair commercial practices leading to economic or financial harms to consumers are prohibited under all circumstances, irrespective of whether they are put in place through AI systems or otherwise', rec. 29. Dark patterns, for example, are partially covered by the UCP-Directive.[75] It is further important to note that some use cases in a **medical context** are not covered by the ban in Art. 5(1)(a).[76]

50 The AI Act does not define in detail what is meant by **techniques of subliminal influence** outside a person's consciousness. Rec. 29, however, provides guidance: What is meant is the deploying of components like audio, image or video stimuli that people cannot perceive as such because they are beyond human perception. Probably the most prominent example of this is the display of advertising messages for fractions of a second.[77]

51 Also covered by the prohibition are **purposefully manipulative** or **deceptive techniques**. Included are techniques that persons are not consciously aware of as well as techniques that even if aware they can still be deceived or are not able to control or resist.[78] The latter especially addresses **machine-brain interfaces** and **virtual reality** (VR) 'as they allow for a higher degree of control of what stimuli are presented to persons', rec. 29. This is to be welcomed as simulations can or may in the future be so advanced

---

[74] Directive 2005/29/EC of the European Parliament and of the Council of 11 May 2005 concerning unfair business-to-consumer commercial practices in the internal market and amending Council Directive 84/450/EEC, Directives 97/7/EC, 98/27/EC and 2002/65/EC of the European Parliament and of the Council and Regulation (EC) No 2006/2004 of the European Parliament and of the Council ('Unfair Commercial Practices Directive'), OJ 2005 L 149, 22.

[75] European Commission, 'Commission Notice – Guidance on the interpretation and application of Directive 2005/29/EC of the European Parliament and of the Council concerning unfair business-to-consumer commercial practices in the internal market (2021/C 526/01)', 29.12.2021, OJ 2021 C 526, 99 point 4.2.7.

[76] Rec. 29.

[77] Linardatos GPR 2022, 58 (60).

[78] Rec. 29.

that behaving like they are not real becomes extremely hard.[79] Platforms that utilise VR technology should therefore pay particular attention to the prohibition in Art. 5(1)(a). Rec. 29 further clarifies that 'AI-enabled manipulative techniques can be used to persuade persons to engage in unwanted behaviours, or to deceive them by nudging them into decisions in a way that subverts and impairs their autonomy, decision-making and free choices'. After all, a **universally applicable definition** of manipulative techniques, however, is likely to be **difficult to find**, as there is already no apparent consensus on a uniform concept of manipulation per se.[80]

The placing on the market, putting into service or use of such an AI system further 52
must happen 'with the **objective**, or the **effect** of **materially distorting** the behaviour of a person or a group of persons by appreciably impairing their **ability to make an informed decision**'.

In contrast to the Commission's draft, the prohibition under Art. 5(1)(a) now does 53
not require an **intention** to distort. Accordingly, a distortion can also be the **(mere) consequence** to fall under the prohibition.[81] On the other hand, it seems unfortunate that the provision speaks of **'purposefully'** manipulative or deceptive techniques. This wording suggests that it is the purpose of the use that counts and not solely the ultimately effective outcome. How a purposefully manipulative or deceptive technique is to be used without the objective to materially distort a person's or a group of persons' behaviour seems difficult to imagine. The extension of the prohibition to the mere effect of distorting will therefore probably mainly have an effect around techniques of subliminal influence. It should be noted that according to rec. 29 it may not be possible 'to assume that there is an intention to distort behaviour where the distortion results from factors external to the AI system which are outside the control of the provider or the deployer, namely factors that may not be reasonably foreseeable and therefore not possible for the provider or the deployer of the AI system to mitigate', rec. 29. This raises the question of whether an intention to distort should be presumed in other cases. And if so, what for? Art. 5(1)(a) expressly states that the effect of a distortion is sufficient for an AI system to fall under the prohibition.

It is also not further explained in the AI Act when a **materially distortion** (of a per- 54
son's or a group of persons' behaviour) can be assumed. The AI Act only clarifies that the distortion must be achieved **'by appreciably impairing their ability to make an informed decision'**. This wording seems to be derived from Art. 2(e) UCP-Directive, so that existing literature and judgements may be used as guidance here. According to Art. 2(e) UCP-Directive 'to materially distort the economic behaviour of consumers means using a commercial practice to appreciably impair the consumer's ability to make an informed decision, thereby causing the consumer to take a transactional **decision that he would not have taken otherwise**'.

The decision the affected person(s) took lastly must **cause** or be **reasonably likely to** 55
cause 'that person, another person or group of persons **significant harm**'. In contrast to the Commission's draft, not just physical or psychological harm but every (significant)

---

[79] Cf. Solove, 'Artificial Intelligence and Privacy' (George Washington University Law School, 1.2.2024) <papers.ssrn.com/sol3/papers.cfm?abstract_id=4713111> (last accessed: 01.07.2024), p. 37 et seqq.; Steege/Chibanguza in Steege/Chibanguza § 8 mn. 45.

[80] Boine, 'AI-enabled Manipulation and EU Law' (1.6.2021) <ssrn.com/abstract=4042321> (last accessed: 01.07.2024), p. 23 et seqq.; cf. also Grisse in Genovesi/Kaesling/Robbins, ch. 6.4.

[81] Contrary to this, Schwartmann/Pottkämper in Schwartmann/Keber/Zenner, part 2 chap. 1 mn. 58 et seqq. seem to assume that an intention of manipulation is still required under the final version of Art. 5(1)(a). However, this is in clear contradiction to the wording ('with the objective or the effect').

harm is now covered.[82] The AI Act does not further determine what exactly can be categorised as a harm, when any harm is significant and when such harm is sufficiently likely to occur.[83] In this regard rec. 29 only refers to 'sufficiently important adverse impacts on physical, psychological health or financial interests'.

56 In view of the above, some techniques and practices on platforms appear to be at risk of falling within the scope of the prohibition. Firstly, AI-supported **nudging** as well as **dark patterns** can be mentioned. These decision architectures are usually characterised by trying to steer affected persons in a certain decision direction by differentiating the (often freely selectable) options in the way they are presented.[84] Nudging and dark patterns are similar in nature, but different in purpose. While nudging generally aims to help people to make decisions that (at least in part) correspond to their preferences, dark patterns essentially influence human decisions solely in favour of the user's agenda.[85] The use of nudging and dark patterns may thus be seen as targeting the subconscious[86] and therefore be qualified as the use of a **subliminal technique**. One could also argue that nudging and dark patterns should rather be categorised under the concept of '**purposefully manipulative** or **deceptive techniques**'. Ultimately, it is not necessary to distinguish between the different techniques, as there are no divergent consequences regarding this categorisation.

57 The similarity between the wording in Art. 5(1)(a) and the definition of dark patterns in rec. 67 DSA is difficult to overlook. If one understands dark patterns as defined in rec. 67 DSA, then the use of AI-powered dark patterns will generally be covered as a forbidden technique. For nudging, however, platforms will be able to argue that this is not covered as a prohibited technique. Although rec. 29 explicitly addresses nudging ('nudging them into decisions in a way that subverts and impairs their autonomy, decision-making and free choices') the wording of the prohibition expressly states that the person concerned must take a decision that he or she would not have made otherwise. Nudging, as understood here, however, (at least in parts) helps a person to make a decision that he or she would have made anyway.[87] If nudging were to be categorised as a manipulative technique, it could therefore be argued that it is not materially distorting a person's or a group of persons' behaviour. In both cases, as well as all other mentioned cases in this

---

[82] Contrary to this, Schwartmann/Pottkämper in Schwartmann/Keber/Zenner, part 2 chap. 1 mn. 58 et seqq. seem to assume that (still) only physical or psychological harms are covered.

[83] What can be categorised as a harm ultimately remains unclear. Feuerstack/Becker/Hertz ZfDR 2023, 421 (439) therefore ask, whether the mere manipulation of emotions can be enough to constitute harm or whether the influencing of political opinions constitutes harm to a group of people, in this case the democratic society; Boine, 'AI-enabled Manipulation and EU Law' (1.6.2021) <ssrn.com/abstract=4042321> (last accessed: 01.07.2024), p. 42 argues that manipulation is a harm in itself. In contrast to the AI Act text leaked in early February 2024, the final text now again says that a harm must be reasonably likely and not only likely to occur. This could be used as an argument in favour of not setting the threshold for the likelihood of such harm too low.

[84] Dark Patterns can occur in various forms; cf. Hufen JuS 2020, 193 (193 et seq.); Schmidt/Engelen Philosophy Compass 4/2020; Steinrötter/Schauer WRP 2024, 873.

[85] Martini/Drews/Seelinger/Weinzierl ZfDR 2021, 47 (51); similar Loy/Baumgartner ZD 2021, 404 (404).

[86] Hufen JuS 2020, 193 (193) on nudging; Martini/Drews/Seelinger/Weinzierl ZfDR 2021, 47 (50); Luguri/Strahilevitz, Journal of Legal Analysis 2021, 43 (48 et seqq.) on dark patterns. With a different opinion on nudges in general probably Sunstein, 'Eight Misconceptions About Nudges' (16.2.2023) <ssmn.com/abstract=4357437> (last accessed: 01.07.2024), p. 2 et seq.

[87] Similar Boine, 'AI-enabled Manipulation and EU Law' (1.6.2021) <ssrn.com/abstract=4042321> (last accessed: 01.07.2024), p. 40 et seq. suggests that Art. 5(1)(a) should ban 'AI systems that use techniques or information beyond a person's knowledge likely to cause that person to make a decision they would not have made otherwise and that is in the interest of one of the operators of the AI system'.

subsection, platforms will also be able to argue that harm caused is not significant or that a significant harm is not sufficiently likely to occur.

58 So-called **behavioural microtargeting** on platforms could also be covered.[88] This is the personalized targeting of individuals based on (behavioural and personality-based) user profiles. These are usually likely to be the result of the application of an AI system, which makes it possible to collect, process and analyse enormous amounts of data.[89] As a result platforms can, for example, tailor their advertising, their products and their prices to customer profiles[90] or platform operators can improve the quality of matching between buyers and sellers.[91] However, in contrast to the display of advertising messages for fractions of a second, it seems questionable whether one can speak of subliminal influence here.[92] Certain behavioural microtargeting techniques are more likely to fall under the category of **purposefully manipulative** or **deceptive techniques**. It will be crucial to differentiate between (permitted) highly persuasive and (prohibited) manipulative advertising.[93] As described, platforms must observe the UCP-Directive in addition to the AI Act. The UCP-Directive as well as the corresponding Commissions guidance might therefore provide helpful orientation here.[94] Especially because 'common and legitimate commercial practices, for example in the field of advertising, that comply with the applicable law should not, in themselves, be regarded as constituting harmful manipulative AI-enabled practices', rec. 29. On targeted advertising in the area of job advertisements (→ mn. 107 et seqq.). Certain types of targeting will also be covered by Art. 5(1)(b) (→ mn. 62).

59 **Recommender systems** on platforms may also be considered as prohibited under Art. 5(1)(a), as recommending something can always be seen as an attempt to take influence.[95] However, a prohibition under Art. 5(1)(a) will nevertheless only be considerable in a few special cases. Most of the time, compliance with the transparency obligations for recommender systems (→ § 4 mn. 62) will allow affected persons to take an informed decision so that it cannot be assumed that the recommender system materially distorted the affected persons behaviour.[96] As with behavioural microtargeting in general, it is important to distinguish between highly persuasive and manipulative recommendations. Certain types of recommendations are more likely to be covered by Art. 5(1)(b) (→ mn. 61 et seqq.).[97]

60 The generation of **deep fakes** alone cannot be categorised as a purposefully manipulative or deceptive technique. This is shown by the fact that there are separate transparency rules for deep fakes (→ mn. 128 et seqq.). However, it does not seem impossible that systems are designed in such a way that overall, the deployment of such prohibited techniques can nevertheless be assumed, and they can lead to material distortion, which in turn could lead to significant harm. One could think of AI systems that are specifically used to initiate extreme hatred campaigns and ultimately lead to

---

88 Bomhard/Merkle RDi 2021, 276 (279); Rostalski/Weiss ZfDR 2021, 329 (338).

89 See Ebers MMR 2018, 423 (423) with reference to Calo 82 George Washington Law Review 2014, 995, (1015 et seqq.) and O'Neil, p. 194 et seqq.

90 Ebers MMR 2018, 423 (423).

91 Cf. Berberich/Conrad in Ebers/Heinze/Krügel/Steinrötter, § 30 mn. 16.

92 In this direction Ebers MMR 2018, 423 (423).

93 Similar Boine, 'AI-enabled Manipulation and EU Law' (1.6.2021) <ssrn.com/abstract=4042321> (last accessed: 01.07.2024), p. 34 et seqq.

94 Cf. Boine, 'AI-enabled Manipulation and EU Law' (1.6.2021) <ssrn.com/abstract=4042321> (last accessed: 01.07.2024), p. 35.

95 Grisse in Genovesi/Kaesling/Robbins, ch. 6.5.1.

96 Cf. Grisse in Genovesi/Kaesling/Robbins, ch. 6.5.2.

97 Cf. Grisse in Genovesi/Kaesling/Robbins, ch. 6.5.3.2.2 and 6.5.3.2.3.

violence against (certain) people.[98] Two further examples for deep fakes that may be covered could be microtargeted deep fakes[99] and deep fakes which use mimicry or facial resemblance to increase their trustworthiness among recipients.[100]

II. Techniques to exploit vulnerabilities

61 Art. 5(1)(b) is very similar to Art. 5(1)(a) as it stipulates that

> 'the placing on the market, the putting into service or the use of an AI system that **exploits** any of the **vulnerabilities** of a natural person or a specific group of persons due to their age, disability or a specific social or economic situation, with the objective, or the effect, of materially distorting the behaviour of that person or a person belonging to that group in a manner that causes or is reasonably likely to cause that person or another person significant harm'

is prohibited.

62 The main difference in comparison to Art. 5(1)(a) is that when certain vulnerabilities of a natural person or a specific group of persons are exploited, none of the techniques mentioned under Art. 5(1)(a) needs to be used to be covered by the prohibition.[101] It is further not necessary that the affected person's ability to make an informed decision is impaired for Art. 5(1)(b) to be applicable. It is also irrelevant whether the affected person takes a decision (that he or she would not have taken otherwise). What the European legislators probably wanted to address with this regulation is the fact that the use of AI systems makes it possible to process incredibly large amounts of data and merge data from a variety of sources.[102] As described above (→ mn. 58), this means that platforms may create user profiles and thus address users in a targeted manner. These user profiles can contain information about the user's **age, disabilities**[103] or **social** or **economic situation**. For example, the targeting of a person with **emotion-based advertising** respectively **recommendations** at a specific time when recognising a vulnerable mood due to events in a person's social life ('social situation') should be covered.[104] Here too, however, the **harm requirement** must be considered, so that some techniques may nevertheless fall outside the scope of the prohibition. When emotion-based techniques are being used, the provisions on emotion recognition systems may also need to be observed (→ mn. 71 et seqq., 100, 126 et seqq.).

III. Social scoring

63 Art. 5(1)(c) generally[105] prohibits the placing on the market, putting into service or use of AI systems for so-called **social scoring**. The prohibition covers

---

98 Similar Steege/Chibanguza in Steege/Chibanguza, § 8 mn. 45.

99 Dobber et al. The International Journal of Press/Politics 2021, 69 (69 et seqq).

100 Łabuz ACIG 2023, 1 (15).

101 The AI Act does not further define the terms 'vulnerability' and 'exploitation'.

102 Cf. Dornis GRUR 2023, 1729 (1731).

103 According to rec. 29, this refers to disabilities within the meaning of Directive (EU) 2019/882 of the European Parliament and of the Council of 17 April 2019 on the accessibility requirements for products and services, OJ 2019 L 151, 70.

104 Cf. also Dornis GRUR 2023, 1729 (1731); an example may be showing anti-stress items to a stressed user or showing (overprized) cosmetic items to insecure teenage girls Grisse in Genovesi/Kaesling/Robbins, ch. 6.5.3.2.2.

105 Cf. rec. 31.

> 'AI systems for the evaluation or classification of natural persons or groups of persons over a certain period of time based on their social behaviour or known, inferred or predicted personal or personality characteristics'.

64 If left alone, a wide range of AI-based **reputation mechanisms** would be covered in the platform context. For example, systems on social networking platforms that process comments, shared content, assigned likes or contacts to create a user profile would be prohibited. The same would apply to **platforms of the sharing economy** – for example, bike-sharing companies who identify untrustworthy users by whether they return dirty or damaged bikes.[106] **Trading platforms** that use AI to create a rating of their users based on their response time, the number of complaints and the rating of other users would also be considered prohibited.[107] One-time ratings, on the other hand, seem to remain permitted ('over a certain period of time').[108]

65 While the **private sector** was not covered in the Commissions draft, the prohibition in Art. 5(1)(c) now covers any social scoring.[109] However, the prohibition **only applies if** the social score leads to either a

> 'detrimental or unfavourable treatment of certain natural persons or groups of persons in social contexts that are unrelated to the contexts in which the data was originally generated or collected'

or a

> 'detrimental or unfavourable treatment of certain natural persons or groups of persons that is unjustified or disproportionate to their social behaviour or its gravity'.

66 Therefore, a detrimental or unfavourable treatment due to a scoring would remain permissible in the same social context as long as it is not unjustified or disproportional.[110] Based on the example of the bike-sharing platform mentioned above, Art. 5(1)(c) would not prohibit the charging of a higher fee or even the (temporary) blocking of a customer who has been rated as less reliable.[111] However, the question arises of when a social score **'leading'** to a result can be assumed. Platforms may try to avoid the ban by saying that scoring was not a decisive factor at all.[112] Unfortunately, it also remains unclear up to which point a **related social context** can still be assumed. It will probably often be possible to find some kind of contextual connection.[113] One solution could be to set the threshold to be reached in order to categorise a treatment as unjustified or disproportionately lower, the more distant the (still related) social context is.

---

[106] For more details and an example from China see Maamar CR 2018, 820 (823).

[107] Cf. Jaekel, p. 121 et seq. According to Berberich/Conrad in Ebers/Heinze/Krügel/Steinrötter § 30 mn. 17, reputation mechanisms are a central component of almost every platform.

[108] Linardatos GPR 2022, 58 (61); on the imprecision of this wording Martini in Hilgendorf/Roth-Isigkeit § 4 mn. 31; crit. EDPS, 'Opinion 44/2023 on the Proposal for Artificial Intelligence Act in the light of legislative developments', 23.10.2023, p. 23 mn. 79.

[109] Crit. in view of the fact that GDPR scoring requirements already apply in the private sector Steege/Chibanguza in Steege/Chibanguza, § 8 mn. 53 et seqq.

[110] Crit. Linardatos GPR 2022, 58 (61).

[111] Similar Veale/Zuiderveen Borgesius CRi 2021, 97 (100).

[112] Crit. in this respect Ebers/Hoch/Rosenkranz/Ruschemeier/Steinrötter RDi 2021, 528 (530).

[113] Cf. Veale/Zuiderveen Borgesius CRi 2021, 97 (100) 'A wider view however might consider credit card records and welfare support as the same context, as both involve financial flows'.

IV. Predictive policing

67 Art. 5(1)(d) prohibits

> 'the placing on the market, the putting into service for this specific purpose, or the use of an AI system for making risk assessments of natural persons in order to assess or **predict the risk** of a natural person **commiting a criminal offence**, based solely on the profiling of a natural person or on assessing their personality traits and characteristics'.

68 The prohibition does not apply, however, to 'AI systems used to support the human assessment of the involvement of a person in a criminal activity, which is already based on objective and verifiable facts directly linked to a criminal activity'. The ban will be of minor relevance for platforms at most.

V. Scraping of facial images

69 Art. 5(1)(e) prohibits

> 'the placing on the market, the putting into service for this specific purpose, or the use of AI systems that **create** or **expand facial recognition databases** through the **untargeted scraping** of facial images from the internet or CCTV footage'.

70 Such techniques can increase the feeling of mass surveillance and significantly affect the right to privacy of those concerned.[114] The prohibition seems to be aimed in particular at providers who use AI to read biometric data from social media. One example is the provider Clearview AI[115], which had already collected around three billion portrait photos of people from various sources on the internet by scraping in 2020.[116] Unfortunately, some uncertainty remains as the AI Act does not describe in more detail when scraping is to be classified as **'untargeted'**.

VI. AI systems to infer emotions in the areas of workplace and education

71 Lastly, Art. 5(1)(f) prohibits

> 'the placing on the market, the putting into service for this specific purpose, or the use of AI systems **to infer emotions** of a natural person in the **areas of workplace and education** institutions, except in cases where the use of the AI system is intended to be put in place or into the market for medical or safety reasons'.

72 In the context of platforms, one can think of systems that are used in the context of **distance learning** or **online-conferences** in order to analyse the attention, approval or rejection of those involved.[117] According to various reports, the video call platform Zoom, for example, was once planning to analyse the emotions of call participants.[118]

73 The AI Act does not further define the terms 'workplace' and 'educational institution', so it could be argued that online situations are not covered. However, the dangers of

---

[114] Rec. 43.

[115] Martini/Kemper CR 2023, 341 on data protection aspects under the GDPR.

[116] Hill, 'The Secretive Company That Might End Privacy as We Know It' (The New York Times, 18.1.2023) <www.nytimes.com/2020/01/18/technology/clearview-privacy-facial-recognition.html?smtyp=cur&smid=tw-nytimes> (last accessed: 01.07.2024).

[117] Rostalski/Weiss in Hilgendorf/Roth-Isigkeit § 3 mn. 17.

[118] Linß/Böttcher, 'Emotionserkennung im Videochat' (Deutschlandfunk Kultur, 21.5.2022) <www.deutschlandfunkkultur.de/zoom-videochat-emotionserkennung-100.html> (last accessed: 01.07.2024).

emotion recognition in these situations are independent of the local position of those involved. In the educational context, there is a risk that the recognition of certain emotions, such as disinterest, will have a negative influence on the evaluation and grading of those involved.[119] At the same time, the knowledge of those affected about the use of the technology creates an enormous pressure to adapt and perform, which has a negative effect on the self-determination of the individuals concerned.[120] These dangers arise for those affected regardless of their localisation, so that the **online matters** mentioned are **also covered** by the ban.

Apart from this, the question arises as to **how far the areas** of workplace and education institutions **should be drawn**. In this respect, rec. 44 states that the imbalance of power (in combination with the intrusive nature of these systems) legitimises the prohibition of such systems. If one were to focus only on this imbalance of power, the areas would have to be drawn widely. This would probably even include a job interview as being seen 'in the area of workplace' as an imbalance of power can already be assumed here. Especially in view of the 'serious concerns about the scientific basis' of such systems, which even the EU legislators recognise[121], a broad interpretation seems reasonable. 74

It should also be noted that Article 5(1)(f) does **not refer to the term 'emotion recognition system'** (as legally defined in the AI Act) in the wording of its prohibition, but rather refers to 'AI systems to infer emotions'. This causes unclarity because the classification as an emotion recognition system under Art. 3 no. 39 concerns systems 'for the purpose of identifying or inferring emotions or intentions of natural persons on the basis of their biometric data'. Since the concept of biometric data now seems very broad anyway (→ mn. 80), it is not clear why the ban does not simply refer to the legally defined concept of an emotion recognition system. This must apply even more as the reference to the legally defined term would lead the ban to cover the identification or inference of emotions and intentions, whereas the prohibition under Art. 5(1)(f) expressly only mentions emotions. That is an unconvincing result in view of the imbalance of power in the areas of education and workplace mentioned above. 75

It will be difficult to determine what can be categorised as an **emotion** or **intention**. Rec. 18 attempts to describe in more detail what exactly can be categorised as an emotion or an intention, but causes some confusion in doing so. Firstly, rec. 18 mentions some **examples** for emotions and intentions. Those are 'happiness, sadness, anger, surprise, disgust, embarrassment, excitement, shame, contempt, satisfaction and amusement'. However, **not included** are '**physical states**, such as pain or fatigue'. Keeping in mind that one of the reasons for the creation of the ban is the power imbalance mentioned, it seems to make little sense that pain and fatigue are not covered as they can be exploited in the same way as emotions. It also remains unclear how physical states are to be distinguished from emotions and intentions, especially as pain, for example, could also be categorised as an emotion. As an example for systems inferring physical states rec. 18 mentions 'systems used in detecting the state of fatigue of professional pilots or drivers for the purpose of preventing accidents'. 76

Rec. 18 goes on to say that it does also **not include** 'the mere detection of **readily apparent expressions, gestures or movements**, unless they are used for identifying or inferring emotions. These expressions can be basic facial expressions such as a frown or a smile, or gestures such as the movement of hands, arms or head, or characteristics of a person's voice, such as a raised voice or whispering'. 77

119 Rostalski/Weiss in Hilgendorf/Roth-Isigkeit § 3 mn. 18.
120 In detail Rostalski/Weiss in Hilgendorf/Roth-Isigkeit § 3 mn. 17 et seqq.
121 Rec. 44.

78 Finally, criticism can be voiced against the **exception** to the ban. It remains completely unclear what is meant by 'medical or safety reasons'. According to the wording of the provision, there is also no requirement that the medical or safety reasons predominate, nor that they have any connection to the area of workplace or education. The example of a system to detect tired pilots or drivers mentioned in rec. 18 could indeed fit here and at least provide some guidance. However, in the current wording of rec. 18 it does not refer to the exemption from the ban for medical or safety reasons, but rather completely excludes such systems from the ban, as it only gives an example for a system detecting 'physical states'.[122]

VII. Biometric categorisation

79 Art. 5(1)(g), which was not included in the previous versions of the AI Act in this form, prohibits

> 'the placing on the market, the putting into service for this specific purpose, or the use of **biometric categorisation systems** that categorise individually natural persons based on their biometric data to **deduce or infer** their **race, political opinions, trade union membership, religious or philosophical beliefs, sex life** or **sexual orientation**'.

80 Whereas

> '"biometric categorisation system" means an AI system for the purpose of assigning natural persons to specific categories on the basis of their biometric data, unless it is ancillary to another commercial service and strictly necessary for objective technical reasons', Art. 3 no. 40,

and

> '"biometric data" means personal data resulting from specific technical processing relating to the physical, physiological or behavioural characteristics of a natural person, such as facial images or dactyloscopic data', Art. 3 no. 34.

81 The first thing that stands out is that the **definition of biometric data** has changed compared to the Commission's and the Parliament's draft of the AI Act. Although it is still based on the definition in Art. 4 no. 14 GDPR, the addition that the data 'must allow or confirm the unique identification of that natural person' has been removed in the legislative process.[123] Accordingly, data categorised as biometric data pursuant to Art. 4 no. 14 GDPR are in any case covered. But the removal means that the term biometric data can be understood much more broadly here and thus covers any type of personal data that is based on physical, psychological or even behavioural characteristics. In addition to **facial images** and **dactyloscopic data**, for example, also to be covered and of special relevance in the context of platforms will be the **voice** or **typing behaviour** of the platform's users. **Mouse behaviour** and **touchscreen behaviour** are also covered.[124]

82 However, there is an **exception** for systems that are 'ancillary to another commercial service and strictly necessary for objective technical reasons'. Therefore, AI systems are not covered, if they are 'a **purely ancillary feature intrinsically linked to another commercial service,** meaning that the feature cannot, for objective technical reasons, be used without the principal service and the integration of that feature or functionality

[122] Confusingly enough, European Commission, 'Artificial Intelligence – Questions and Answers' (12.12.2023) <ec.europa.eu/commission/presscorner/detail/en/qanda_21_1683> (last accessed: 01.07.2024), states differently 'Emotion recognition in the workplace and education institutions, unless for medical or safety reasons (i.e. monitoring the tiredness levels of a pilot)'.

[123] Cf. Keber/Schwartmann in Schwartmann/Keber/Zenner, part 2 chap. 1 mn. 94 et seqq.

[124] Some more examples can be found in rec. 15.

is not a means to circumvent the applicability of the rules of this Regulation', rec. 16. Examples for this can be filters that perform categorisations to allow customers to **pre-view** the display of the **product on themselves** as well as **filters in social networks.**[125] The second half-sentence of the prohibition contains a further exception in the area of law enforcement.

VIII. Biometric real-time remote identification

Art. 5(1)(h) generally prohibits[126] 83

> 'the use of **"real-time" remote biometric identification systems** in publicly accessible spaces for the purposes of law enforcement'.

The second half sentence provides some exceptions to this prohibition. The lack of relevance of this provision for platforms results from the fact that 'publicly accessible space' is only understood to mean physical places, cf. Art. 3 no. 44. **Online spaces** are **not covered.**[127]

G. High-risk AI systems

Chapter 3 contains regulations on high-risk AI systems. 84

I. Obligations

The **obligations** regarding high-risk AI systems differ depending on the classification 85 of the respective operator. Since platforms will generally qualify either as a provider or (in most cases) as a deployer of an AI system, the duties regarding providers and deployers of high-risk AI systems will be briefly described here.

1. Providers

Art. 16 lists the **obligations for providers** of high-risk AI systems. The first impor- 86 tant point here is Art. 16(a), which stipulates that providers must ensure that their high-risk AI systems are compliant with the **requirements** set out in chapter 3 section 2 (Art. 8–15). These requirements relate to:

Art. 9	Risk management systems[128]
Art. 10	Data and data governance
Art. 11	Technical documentation
Art. 12	Record-keeping
Art. 13	Transparency and provision of information to deployers

[125] Cf. rec. 16.

[126] Crit. on the classification as a 'prohibited' AI practice and in detail on the exceptions from the prohibition Rostalski/Weiss ZfDR 2021, 329 (342 et seqq.).

[127] Rec. 19; cf. also Veale/Zuiderveen Borgesius CRi 2021, 97 (101); crit. 'EDPS-EDPB Joint Opinion 5/2021 on the Proposal for a Regulation of the European Parliament and of the Council laying down harmonised rules on artificial intelligence (Artificial Intelligence Act) and amending certain acts of the Union', 18.6.2021, p. 14 mn. 32.

[128] Note rec. 118 regarding VLOPs and VLOSEs already subject to the risk-management framework under the DSA.

Art. 14	Human oversight[129]
Art. 15	Accuracy, robustness and cybersecurity

87 Other **requirements** that do not refer to the system itself, but rather **to the provider** relate to:

Art. 16(b)	Indicating the providers name, registered trade name or registered trade mark and the address at which they can be contacted
Art. 16(c)	Having a quality management system in place which complies with Art. 17
Art. 16(d)	Documentation-keeping referred to in Art. 18
Art. 16(e)	Keeping automatically generated logs referred to in Art. 19
Art. 16(f)	Ensuring that the AI system undergoes the relevant conformity assessment referred to in Art. 43 prior to its placing on the market or putting into service
Art. 16(g)	Drawing up an EU declaration of conformity in accordance with Art. 47
Art. 16(h)	Affixing the CE marking on the System to indicate conformity with the AI Act in accordance with Art. 48
Art. 16(i)	Complying with the registration obligations referred to in Art. 59(1)
Art. 16(j)	Taking the necessary corrective actions and providing information as required in Art. 20
Art. 16(k)	Demonstrate the conformity of the AI system with the requirements in Art. 8–15 upon reasoned request of a national authority
Art. 16(l)	Ensuring that the AI system complies with accessibility requirements in accordance with the EAA[130] and the WAD[131]

It should be noted that the **transparency requirements** of Art. 50 (→ mn. 116 et seqq.) may also be applicable in addition.

2. Deployers

88 Platforms will often not develop the AI systems they use themselves or have them developed and are therefore not categorised as providers but rather as deployers. The **obligations for deployers** of high-risk AI systems can be found in Art. 26:

Art. 26(1)	Taking appropriate technical and organisational measures to ensure they use the system in accordance with the instructions for use
Art. 26(2)	Assigning human oversight to natural persons who have the necessary competence, training and authority, as well as the necessary support[132]

[129] In detail Dienes MMR 2024, 456.

[130] Directive (EU) 2019/882 of the European Parliament and of the Council of 17 April 2019 on the accessibility requirements for products and services (European Accessibility Act), OJ 2019 L 151, 70.

[131] Directive (EU) 2016/2102 of the European Parliament and of the Council of 26 October 2016 on the accessibility of the websites and mobile applications of public sector bodies (Web Accessibility Act), OJ 2016 L 327, 1.

[132] Note that Art. 26(3) states that 'the obligations in paragraph 1 and 2, are without prejudice to other deployer obligations under Union or national law and to the deployer's freedom to organise its own resources and activities for the purpose of implementing the human oversight measures indicated by the provider'.

Art. 26(4)	Ensuring that input data is relevant and sufficiently representative in view of the intended purpose of the high-risk AI system[133]
Art. 26(5)	Monitoring the operation of the high-risk AI system based on the instructions for use as well as suspending the use of the high-risk AI system and reporting obligations under certain conditions
Art. 26(6)	Keeping automatically generated logs[134]
Art. 26(7)	Informing workers' representatives and the affected workers that they will be subject to the use of the high-risk AI system before putting into service or using a high-risk AI system at the workplace[135]
Art. 26(8)	Registration obligations for deployers of high-risk AI systems that are public authorities, or Union institutions, bodies, offices or agencies
Art. 26(9)	Using information provided under Art. 13 to comply, where applicable, with the obligation to carry out a data protection impact assessment (DPIA)
Art. 26(10)	Obligations regarding the use of AI systems for post-remote biometric identification
Art. 26(11)	Informing natural persons that they are subject to the use of a high-risk AI system if the system referred to in Annex III makes decisions or assists in making decisions related to natural persons
Art. 26(12)	Cooperating with the relevant national competent authorities

Here, again, the **transparency obligations** pursuant to Art. 50 may apply in addition. **89**
Deployers of high-risk AI systems also must note that Art. 86 provides for a **right to explanation** of individual decision-making in cases where a decision is taken on the basis of the output from an high-risk AI system listed in Annex III[136] 'which produces legal effects or similarly significantly affects that person in a way that they consider to have an adverse impact on their health, safety and fundamental rights'. The deployers explanation must include clear and meaningful explanations on 'the role of the AI system in the decision-making procedure and the main elements of the decision taken'. However, as the right to explanation only applies to the extent that it is not already provided under Union legislation, Art. 86(3), or otherwise restricted under Union or national law, Art. 86(2), it remains to be seen how big of a role Art. 86 will play in practice.[137]

The obligation for deployers to perform a **fundamental rights impact assessment** **90**
under Art. 27 in general only applies to 'deployers that are bodies governed by public law or private entities providing public services', so that this may be of less relevance in the context of platforms. However, operators deploying high-risk AI systems referred to in

[133] This applies only to the extent the deployer exercises control over the input data and without prejudice to Art. 26(1) and Art. 26 (2), see Art. 26(4).

[134] But only 'to the extent such logs are under their control for a period appropriate to the intended purpose of the high-risk AI system, of at least six months, unless provided otherwise in applicable Union or national law, in particular in Union law on the protection of personal data'.

[135] Only for deployers who are employers.

[136] With an exception for systems listed in in Annex III point 2.

[137] See further Hacker, 'Comments on the Final Trilogue Version of the AI Act' (23.1.2024) <www.europeannewschool.eu/images/chairs/hacker/Comments%20on%20the%20AI%20Act.pdf> (last accessed: 01.07.2024), p. 12 who points towards the existing right to explanation under GDPR and the scope of Art. 15(1)(h) GDPR being broadly interpreted in recent court decisions.

Annex III no. 5(b) and no. 5(c) (creditworthiness, life and health insurance) are covered regardless of whether they are private or public in nature.[138]

II. Classification as high-risk AI system

91 When an AI system is to be classified as a **high-risk AI system** first follows from Art. 6(1), which addresses AI systems that are 'intended to be used as a safety component of a product, or the AI system is itself a product, covered by the Union harmonisation legislation listed in Annex I' (lit. a). Also covered are AI systems when 'the product whose safety component pursuant to point (a) is the AI system, or the AI system itself as a product, is required to undergo a third-party conformity assessment with a view to the placing on the market or putting into service of that product pursuant to the Union harmonisation legislation listed in Annex I' (lit. b). Of **greater relevance** in the context of platforms is Art. 6(2), which refers to **Annex III** (→ mn. 95 et seqq.) for the classification of an AI system as high-risk.

1. Additional horizontal layer

92 Art. 6(3) stipulates a derogation from para. 2 in providing an **additional horizontal layer** (except for AI systems that perform profiling on natural persons[139]). The mere classification to an Annex III category is therefore not sufficient to categorise an AI system as high-risk. Rather 'an AI system shall not be considered to be high risk where it does not pose a significant risk of harm to the health, safety or fundamental rights of natural persons, including by not materially influencing the outcome of decision making'. Art. 6(3) mentions four criteria, of which the fulfilment of one is enough for the **exemption** to apply. These are:

- 'the AI system is intended to perform a **narrow procedural task**'. Examples are systems transforming unstructured into structured data, systems classifying incoming documents into categories or systems used to detect duplicates among applications.[140]
- 'the AI system is intended to **improve** the result of a previously **completed human activity**' such as AI systems that are intended to improve the language in drafted documents in relation to professional tone, academic style of language or by aligning a text to a certain brand messaging.
- 'the AI system is intended to detect **decision-making patterns** or deviations from prior decision-making patterns and is not meant to replace or influence the previously completed human assessment, without proper human review'. An example would be an AI system that helps teachers to check whether they have deviated from their grading pattern.
- 'the AI system is intended to perform a **preparatory task** to an assessment relevant for the purpose of the use cases listed in Annex III.' This could cover smart solutions for file handling, which include various functions from indexing, searching, text

[138] Crit. Hacker, 'Comments on the Final Trilogue Version of the AI Act' (23.1.2024) <www.europeannewschool.eu/images/chairs/hacker/Comments%20on%20the%20AI%20Act.pdf> (last accessed: 01.07.2024), p. 11.

[139] As understood 'within the meaning of Article 4, point (4) of Regulation (EU) 2016/679 or Article 3, point (4) of Directive (EU) 2016/680 or Article 3, point (5) of Regulation (EU) 2018/1725', rec. 53.

[140] These and the following examples can be found in rec. 53.

and speech processing or linking data to other data sources, or AI systems used for translation of initial documents.

Even if there is still some room for interpretation, the examples provide plenty of guidance and are to be welcomed. The provision is likely to be of particular importance in practice, as platforms can use it to try to avoid the obligations in relation to high-risk AI systems.[141] However, they must bear in mind that the risk of misclassification is certainly not insignificant.[142] The additional horizontal layer is also quite a **dynamic element** in the AI Act, because Art. 6(6)–(7) empowers the Commission to make wide-ranging changes (modifications, additions, deletions) to the list of criteria mentioned. In the future, further guidance will also result from the fact that, according to Art. 6(5), the Commission will provide **guidelines** specifying the practical implementation of Art. 6 together with a comprehensive list of practical examples of use cases of AI systems that are high risk and not high risk . 93

2. Assessment documentation

According to Art. 6(4), providers who consider their system referred to in Annex III as non-high-risk, for example because in their opinion it is only performing a preparatory task, shall **document** their **assessment** before their system is placed on the market or put into service. The national competent authorities may then request the provider to provide the documentation of the assessment. Such providers are also obliged to **register** themselves and their system in a database, Art. 6(4), 49(2), 71. 94

3. High-risk use cases according to Annex III

The relevant **use cases** in which AI systems are to be regarded as high-risk in principle can be found in Annex III. The Commission is empowered to adopt **delegated acts** to amend the list in Annex III) Art. 7(1), 7(3). 95

a) Biometrics

Annex III no. 1 addresses biometrics, insofar as their use is permitted under relevant Union or national law. The biometrics section firstly covers under lit.a) **'remote biometric identification systems'** except for 'AI systems intended to be used for biometric verification the sole purpose of which is to confirm that a specific natural person is the person he or she claims to be'. 96

Whereas a remote **biometric identification system** is defined in Art. 3 no. 41 as

> 'an AI system for the purpose of identifying natural persons, without their active involvement, typically at a distance through the comparison of a person's biometric data with the biometric data contained in a reference database'

and **biometric verification** is defined in Art. 3 no. 36 as

> 'the automated, one-to-one verification, including authentication, of the identity of natural persons by comparing their biometric data to previously provided biometric data'.

In the platform context, the **exception** for **biometric verification** is highly relevant, as an AI system that uses facial recognition (or recognition based on other biometric 97

---

[141] Cf. Bomhard/Siglmüller RDi 2024, 45 (49).

[142] Hacker, 'Comments on the Final Trilogue Version of the AI Act' (23.1.2024) <www.europeannewschool.eu/images/chairs/hacker/Comments%20on%20the%20AI%20Act.pdf> (last accessed: 01.07.2024), p. 9.

data) for example to verify authorisation to access a service or log in to an account[143] would otherwise be qualified as a biometric identification system and therefore as high-risk. In this context, it is important to note that the exception only refers to **'previously provided'** data. An example for such provision of biometric data may be a user scanning his face from different angles before biometric verification can be used to gain access to a platform account instead of entering a password. In many cases, however, it may not even be the platforms AI system that performs the biometric verification, but rather recourse is taken to the verification mechanism of the mobile phone used. An example for an AI system falling under Annex III no. 1 would be an AI system that can identify (unlinked) users from other people's posts in order to suggest linking that person.

98 Further included under Annex III no. 1 are (lit. b)

> 'AI systems intended to be used for **biometric categorisation**, according to **sensitive** or **protected attributes** or characteristics based on the inference of those attributes or characteristics'.

99 Therefore, as far as an AI system used for biometric categorisation is not already considered prohibited under Art. 5(1)(g) (→ mn. 79), it may still be considered high-risk. With regard to sensitive attributes or characteristics, rec. 54 refers to Art. 9(1) GDPR. What is noteworthy here is that the concept of a biometric categorisation system is not used here, and the provision rather speaks of 'AI systems intended to be used for biometric categorisation'. Accordingly, the exception for systems that are 'ancillary to another commercial service and strictly necessary for objective technical reasons' (→ mn. 82 et seqq.) may not be usable here.

100 Lastly, the biometrics section covers (lit.c)

> 'AI systems intended to be used for **emotion recognition**'.

Again, it seems unclear why the European legislators did not simply refer to the defined concept of emotion recognition systems. Nevertheless, as long as the prohibition according to Art. 5(1)(f) does not apply, especially when an AI system is used for emotion recognition outside the areas of workplace or education, it will most likely be considered high-risk according to this provision. This category is also likely to include systems for emotion recognition that fall outside the scope of the ban due to the exception for medical and safety reasons (→ mn. 78).

b) Critical (digital) infrastructure

101 Annex III no. 2 covers

> 'AI systems intended to be used as **safety components** in the management and operation **of critical digital infrastructure**, road traffic and the supply of water, gas, heating or electricity.'

102 The area of critical digital infrastructures appears to be particularly relevant in the platform context at first sight. Rec. 55 clarifies that the provision refers to critical digital infrastructure as listed in Annex I point 8 of CER-Directive[144], which refers to:

- Providers of internet exchange points as defined in Art. 6 no. 18 NIS2-Directive[145];

---

[143] Cf. rec. 17.

[144] Directive (EU) 2022/2557 of the European Parliament and of the Council of 14 December 2022 on the resilience of critical entities and repealing Council Directive 2008/114/EC (Critical Entities Resilience Directive), OJ 2022 L 333, 164.

[145] Directive (EU) 2022/2555 of the European Parliament and of the Council of 14 December 2022 on measures for a high common level of cybersecurity across the Union, amending Regulation (EU) No 910/2014 and Directive (EU) 2018/1972, and repealing Directive (EU) 2016/1148 (NIS2-Directive), OJ 2022 L 333, 80. A brief introduction to the NIS2-Directive can be found at Voigt/Bastians CR 2022, 768.

- DNS service providers as defined in Art. 6 no. 20 NIS2-Directive, excluding operators of root name servers;
- Top-level-domain name registries as defined in Art. 6 no. 21 NIS2-Directive;
- Providers of cloud computing services as defined in Art. 6 no. 30 NIS2-Directive and
- Providers of data centre services as defined in Art. 6 no. 31 NIS2-Directive.

A common platform will generally not fall under any of these terms. If, in rather exceptional cases, it does, AI systems used by it as a safety component (Art. 3 no. 14) are generally categorised as high-risk.

c) Education and vocational training

Annex III no. 3 addresses several use cases of AI systems in the field of education.[146] These firstly are 103

> 'AI systems intended to be used to determine **access or admission** or to assign natural persons to educational and vocational training institutions at all levels', lit. a).

Unfortunately, the AI Act does not describe in detail what is meant by **'educational'** and **'vocational training'**. However, the wording 'such systems may be particularly intrusive and may violate the right to education' in the corresponding rec. 56 should make it sufficiently clear that the terms are to be understood in accordance with Art. 14 CFR. The term 'educational training' should therefore include pre-school, primary and secondary school education[147], as well as universities and universities of applied sciences.[148] 'Vocational training' includes any form of training which prepares for a qualification or competence for a particular profession or occupation, or which confers a particular qualification for the pursuit of a profession or occupation.[149] Information and **application platforms** could insofar be considered as falling under Annex III no. 3(a). However, this is only the case if none of the exceptions under Art. 6(3) applies, for example because the system only performs a preparatory task. In addition, often such application platforms will only forward and transmit applications but will not make decisions on access and admission themselves. 104

Lit. b) further covers 105

> 'AI systems intended to be used to **evaluate learning outcomes**, including when those outcomes are used to steer the learning process of natural persons in educational and vocational training institutions at all levels'

as well as (lit. c))

> 'AI systems intended to be used for the purpose of assessing the appropriate level of education that an individual will receive or will be able to access, in the context of or within educational and vocational training institutions at all levels'.

However, these should be of less relevance in the platform context. In particular because (private) **learning platforms**, for example for learning foreign languages, will probably not be categorised as falling in the 'education' area of the regulation.

Lit. d) lastly covers 106

> 'AI systems intended to be used for monitoring and detecting prohibited behaviour of students during tests in the context of or within educational and vocational training institutions at all levels'.

---

[146] In depth Schwartmann/Keber/Zenner, part 2 chap. 1 mn. 176 et seqq.
[147] Thiele in Pechstein/Nowak/Häde CFR Art. 14 mn. 10.
[148] Jarass in Jarass, CFR Art. 14 mn. 6.
[149] Thiele in Pechstein/Nowak/Häde CFR Art. 14 mn. 12.

AI-supported **proctoring** offered by platforms can be considered here, for example to monitor students taking exams at home. AI systems may be used in such cases to check that the student's eyes do not stray from the screen to avoid the use of textbooks.[150]

d) Employment, workers management and access to self-employment

107 Annex III no. 4 covers the area of **employment, workers management** and **access to self-employment.**[151] This can be further divided into the areas of recruitment and selection and decisions in work-related relationships. In the area of **recruitment and selection**, Annex III no. 4(a) includes

> 'AI systems intended to be used for recruitment or selection of natural persons, in particular to place targeted job advertisements, to analyse and filter job applications, and to evaluate candidates'.

108 The provision in lit. a) is likely to be relevant especially for **online job exchanges**. Platforms will be covered if they use internal AI to ensure, for example, that only applications from persons who fit the employer's specified profile are received by the employer – i.e. AI systems to **analyse and filter applications**. The mere 'screening or filtering', as covered by the Parliaments proposal, is no longer sufficient. Therefore, a certain threshold should be reached before the 'analysis' of an application can be assumed, especially since classifying incoming documents into categories and detecting duplicates in applications ('narrow procedural task') falls outside the high-risk area anyway. No. 4(a) also covers **targeted job advertisements**, whereby advertisers should especially be aware that under certain circumstances even a prohibition under Art. 5(1)(a) or 5(1)(b) may apply. The **evaluation of candidates** will generally take place in interviews or tests.[152] However, unlike in the Commission's draft, the provision is no longer explicitly limited to such settings. For example, services that collect publicly available information about candidates to use it for evaluation are also to be covered by no. 4(a).[153]

109 **Decisions in work-related relationships** are covered by Annex III no. 4(b) which classifies

> 'AI systems intended to be used to make decisions affecting terms of work-related relationships, the promotion or termination of work-related contractual relationships, to allocate tasks based on individual behaviour or personal traits or characteristics or to monitor and evaluate the performance and behaviour of persons in such relationships'

as high-risk.

110 According to rec. 57, 'relevant work-related contractual relationships should, in a meaningful manner, involve employees and persons **providing services through platforms** as referred to in the Commission Work Programme 2021'. The proposal for a Directive on improving working conditions in platform work[154], which is based on the aforementioned work programme and was adopted by the Parliament on 24.4.2024, thus

---

[150] Martini in Hilgendorf/Roth-Isigkeit § 4 mn. 67; cf. also Schwartmann/Keber/Henning/Köhler in Schwartmann/Keber/Zenner, part 2 chap. 1 mn. 181.

[151] Cf. also Wünschelbaum in Schwartmann/Keber/Zenner, part 2 chap. 1 mn. 202 et seqq.

[152] Cf. Schemmel SPA 2024, 12 (13) referring to JustEat, using AI-driven chatbots to recruit new customer support staff. This chatbot sends potential applicants screening questions and cognitive ability tests.

[153] Hoffmann NZA 2022, 19 (20).

[154] European Commission, 'Proposal for a Directive of the European Parliament and of the Council on improving working conditions in platform work', 9.12.2021, COM(2021) 762 final. For more detailed information on the proposal see Fuhlrott ArbRAktuell 2022, 191; Krause NZA 2022, 521 and Waas ZRP 2022, 105.

provides some guidance. According to the recently adopted version of the proposal, a digital work labour platform refers to

> 'any natural or legal person providing a service which meets all of the following requirements:
>
> - it is provided, at least in part, at a distance through electronic means, such as a website or a mobile application;
> - it is provided at the request of a recipient of the service;
> - it involves, as a necessary and essential component, the organisation of work performed by individuals in return for payment, irrespective of whether that work is performed online or in a certain location;
> - it involves the use of automated monitoring or decision-making systems;'
>
> Art. 2(1) of the proposal.

If digital work platforms use AI systems to manage the processes referred to in lit. b) above, the AI systems used are in principle to be considered high-risk AI systems.[155] It should be noted that the monitoring or the evaluation of performance and behaviour alone should be sufficient in themselves to fall under lit. b) and that both do not necessarily have to occur cumulatively, as the wording of Annex III no. 4(b) ('to monitor and evaluate performance') suggests, cf. rec. 57 ('monitoring or evaluation of persons'). It is also important to note that Parliament's proposal according to which it should be sufficient for the AI system to fall under lit. b) to 'materially influence' a covered decision was not adopted. It is therefore necessary that the AI system really makes the decision to fall under no. 4(b). When this is the case cannot be said with much certainty – especially in view of the ECJ's broad understanding of the term 'decision' under the GDPR.[156] **111**

e) Access to and enjoyment of essential private services and essential public services and benefits

In the platform context, especially Annex III no. 5(b) and 5(d) seem to be of relevance, which include **112**

> 'AI systems intended to be used to evaluate the **creditworthiness** of natural persons or establish their **credit score**, with the exception of AI systems used for the purpose of detecting financial fraud'

and

> 'AI systems intended to be used for risk assessment and pricing in relation to natural persons in the case of **life and health insurance**'.

If such systems are used on or offered by a platform – e.g. a platform that first determines creditworthiness and then acts as an intermediary between lenders and borrowers – such systems are to be considered as high-risk AI systems. The same applies to platforms acting as intermediaries regarding life and health insurance services.

f) Administration of justice and democratic processes

Annex III no. 8(b) stipulates that **113**

> 'AI systems **intended** to be used for **influencing the outcome of an election** or referendum or the voting behaviour of natural persons in the exercise of their vote in elections or referenda'

are to be considered as high-risk in principle.

---

155 In detail on the question of whether eDiscovery tools are covered by the AI Act Wirtz/Baumann RDi 2024, 27; AI systems may also be used to predict employees' intentions to resign cf. Malorny RdA 2022, 170 (171).

156 In detail Wünschelbaum in Schwartmann/Keber/Zenner, part 2 chap. 1 mn. 220.

114 Systems whose output natural persons are not directly exposed to, on the other hand, are expressly not to be covered. As an example, the AI Act mentions 'tools used to organise, optimise and structure political campaigns from an administrative and logistic point of view'. Covered systems will be automated social bots, used to ensure that certain posts gain prominence through the (mass) allocation of likes or comments. In addition, AI systems may often be used to influence voting decisions through microtargeting. Finally, AI systems seem to be on the rise that aim to make it easier for citizens to obtain information about the respective parties by allowing them to ask the system specific questions and not having to rely on reading all the party programmes.[157] However, it seems at least debatable whether systems that merely aim to encourage citizens to exercise their right to vote by providing them with information should be classified as high-risk in principle. According to the wording of the provision, they would be considered high-risk since a (intended) higher turnout also leads to a change in the outcome of the election. In this respect, the additional horizontal layer (→ mn. 92) could provide a corrective. Further requirements to be observed regarding political advertising (will in future) result from the **Regulation on the transparency and targeting of political advertising** (→ § 23 mn. 1 et seqq.) on which an agreement was reached in the trilogue negotiations at the beginning of November.[158]

g) Further high-risk use cases

115 Also to be classified as high-risk AI systems are those AI systems that fall under Annex III no. 6 (Law Enforcement), no. 7 (Migration, asylum and border control management) as well as those not further discussed under Annex III no. 5 and no. 8. These are likely to be of less relevance in the general platform context and are therefore not discussed in detail.[159]

H. Transparency obligations for certain AI systems

116 Art. 50 provides **transparency obligations** for certain AI systems that pose particular risks of impersonation or deception.[160] A classification as an AI system subject to the transparency obligations under Art. 50 does not suspend the requirements and obligations for high-risk AI systems, Art. 50(6). High-risk AI systems may therefore additionally be covered by Art. 50. They must then fulfil the following transparency obligations as well as the requirements for high-risk AI systems.[161] The transparency obligations of Art. 50 can be divided into those that address providers and those that address deployers.

[157] Merholz, 'ChatGpT erklärt Wahlprogramme: Wie KI demnächst Wahlen beeinflussen wird' (Merkur, 27.5.2023) <www.merkur.de/politik/chatgpt-politik-wahlen-bundestagswahlen-zr-92306542.html> (last accessed: 01.07.2024).

[158] Cf. Mehlhorn NVwZ 2023, 1388 and Horstmann ZD-Aktuell 2024, 01499.

[159] It is worth mentioning here that Parliament's proposal to include AI systems intended to be used in recommender systems of social media platforms that have been designated very large online platforms (as defined by the DSA) are to be classified as high-risk in principle, was not adopted. According to the European Commission, 'Artificial Intelligence – Questions and Answers' (12.12.2023)<ec.europa.eu/commission/presscorner/detail/en/qanda_21_1683>, (last accessed: 01.07.2024), this is due to the fact that 'they are already covered in other legislation (DMA/DSA)'.

[160] Rec. 132.

[161] Orssich EuZW 2022, 254 (259 et seq.); in detail on the transparency requirements for high-risk AI systems under the AIA-COM Kumkar in Hilgendorf/Roth-Isigkeit § 6.

I. Providers

The first set of transparency obligations addresses **providers** of certain AI systems. 117

1. Direct interaction with natural persons

AI systems 'intended to **interact directly with natural persons**' are regulated by Art. 50(1). They must be designed and developed in a way that the persons concerned are informed about the fact that they interact with an AI system. The provision seems to be aimed in particular at **chatbots.**[162] Their main field of application in the context of platforms is likely to be **customer advice** or general assistance (help area) regarding the use of the platform.[163] However, the AI Act does not provide a general definition of the term 'interaction' within the meaning of Art. 50(1). In this respect, a definition could be orientated on natural language – according to which a reciprocal and interrelated action would fulfil the constituent element of interaction. Any haptic and acoustic influence on an AI system would then be sufficient, except for merely passive listening and watching.[164] 118

There are **two exemptions** to the provision. Firstly, the provision does not apply to 'AI systems authorised by law to detect, prevent, investigate and prosecute **criminal offences**, subject to appropriate safeguards for the rights and freedoms of third parties, unless those systems are available for the public to report a criminal offence'. This might be of less relevance to platforms. 119

Secondly, the provision does not apply in cases where it is **obvious** for the affected person that they interact with an AI system 'from the point of view of a natural person who is reasonably well-informed, observant and circumspect, taking into account the circumstances and the context of use'. Particular attention in this regard should be given to characteristics of vulnerable groups, insofar as the system is intended to interact with those groups.[165] With regard to the regulation of chatbots, this exemption should be of great importance as providers will probably regularly argue that such obviousness is given. However, the AI Act itself does not specify when the latter should be assumed but at least clarifies that the circumstances and context of use are decisive.[166] The use of the description 'virtual assistant' might already be considered sufficient here.[167] Ultimately, however, this needs to be decided on a case-by-case basis. 120

2. Content generation

The second transparency obligation under Art. 50 for providers aims at '**AI systems**, including general-purpose AI systems, **generating** synthetic audio, image, video or text **content**'. These systems becoming more widely available pose a significant danger on 121

---

[162] European Commission, 'Proposal for a Regulation of the European Parliament and of the Council laying down harmonised rules on artificial intelligence (AI Act) and amending certain Union legislative acts', 21.4.2021, COM(2021) 206 final, 3; Kalbhenn ZUM 2021, 663 (669); Orssich EuZW 2022, 254 (259); Rostalski/Weiss ZfDR 2021, 329 (350).

[163] It should be noted, however, that chatbots may also be used to spread fake news on a large scale. Moreover, the provision does not only cover AI systems on online platforms, see Kalbhenn ZUM 2021, 663 (669).

[164] Bomhard/Merkle RDi 2021, 276 (282).

[165] Rec. 132.

[166] Rostalski/Weiss ZfDR 2021, 329 (351) would welcome some examples in the recitals; cf. Kalbhenn ZUM 2021, 663 (669).

[167] Similar Kremer/Haar in Schwartmann/Keber/Zenner, part 2 chap. 1 mn. 460 who further assume that the obviousness can result from the functionality of an application (such as Microsoft's Copilot).

the integrity and trust in the information ecosystem as well as risks of misinformation and manipulation.[168] Therefore, providers shall ensure that the outputs of such systems are '**marked** in a machine-readable format and detectable as artificially generated or manipulated'.[169] The technical solutions used by the providers shall thereby be '**effective, interoperable, robust** and **reliable**'. This, however, only applies insofar as this is technically feasible and taking into account 'specificities and limitations of different types of content, costs of implementation and the generally acknowledged state-of-the-art, as may be reflected in relevant technical standards'.[170] Examples of such technical solutions may be watermarks, metadata identifications, cryptographic methods, logging methods and fingerprints.[171]

122 Unfortunately, Art. 50(2) nevertheless leaves a lot of room for interpretation. **Watermarking**, for example, in general describes the planting of a statistical signal in an output to verify, by using a detection algorithm, that an output was generated by a specific model.[172] While **strong watermarking** leads to attackers not being able to modify the output to remove the watermark without a significant quality degradation, **weak watermarking** – at a minimum – only flags output that was copied and pasted.[173] Can the latter still be considered effective and robust? Is a modified output still an 'output' in the sense of the regulation or is it only the direct output that is meant?[174]

123 An example for current **state of the art** marking should be the use of **metadata** embedding in combination with **cryptographic watermarking** according to the **C2PA specification**[175] – an open standard that has been implemented by Meta within its platforms and by OpenAI in its DALL-E 3 image AI. Even if this standard also has its weaknesses[176], in view of the big-name companies using the C2PA standard, it can nevertheless be argued that the C2PA standard is the current **state of the art**. It remains to be seen to what extent the labelling obligation can be effectively implemented.[177] Those platforms subject to the regulation should carefully consider all possible marking

---

[168] Cf. rec. 133; Zhang et al., 'Watermarks in the Sand: Impossibility of Strong Watermarking for Generative Models' (15.11.2023)<doi.org/10.48550/arXiv.2311.04378> (last accessed: 01.07.2024), p. 2.

[169] In-depth on possible disclosure methods Molavi Vasse'i/Udoh 'In Transparency we Trust? Evaluating the Effectiveness of Watermarking and Labeling AI-Generated Content',p. 21.

[170] Crit. Kremer/Haar in Schwartmann/Keber/Zenner, part 2 chap. 1 mn. 464 according to which the provision is largely ineffective if effective labelling is simply not possible.

[171] Cf. rec. 133.

[172] Zhang et al., 'Watermarks in the Sand: Impossibility of Strong Watermarking for Generative Models' (15.11.2023) <doi.org/10.48550/arXiv.2311.04378> (last accessed: 24.02.2024), p. 1; cf. also Tambiama Madiega, 'Generative AI and watermarking' (European Parliament Research Service, December 2023) <www.europarl.europa.eu/RegData/etudes/BRIE/2023/757583/EPRS_BRI(2023)757583_EN.pdf> (last accessed: 01.07.2024), p. 2; in detail on different watermarking methods Molavi Vasse'i/Udoh 'In Transparency we Trust? Evaluating the Effectiveness of Watermarking and Labeling AI-Generated Content', p. 27 et seqq.

[173] Zhang et al., 'Watermarks in the Sand: Impossibility of Strong Watermarking for Generative Models' (15.11.2023) <doi.org/10.48550/arXiv.2311.04378> (last accessed: 01.07.2024), p. 2; cf. regarding other limitations and drawbacks Tambiama Madiega, 'Generative AI and watermarking' (European Parliament Research Service, December 2023) <www.europarl.europa.eu/RegData/etudes/BRIE/2023/757583/EPRS_BRI(2023)757583_EN.pdf> (last accessed: 01.07.2024), p. 3.

[174] Bomhard/Siglmüller RDi 2024, 45 (47).

[175] See <c2pa.org/specifications/specifications/1.3/index.html> (last accessed: 01.07.2024).

[176] See <c2pa.org/specifications/specifications/1.0/security/Security_Considerations.html> (last accessed: 24.02.2024).

[177] Bomhard/Siglmüller RDi 2024, 45 (47); cf. Hacker/Engel/Mauer FAccT 23, 1112 (1119).

methods[178], especially taking into account the context, the platform and the risks to be mitigated.[179]

Art. 50(2) **does not apply**, according to its second sentence, 'to the extent the AI systems perform an **assistive function for standard editing** or do **not substantially alter the input** data provided by the deployer or the semantics thereof, or where authorised by law to detect, prevent, investigate and prosecute criminal offences'. In the platform context, especially the first exemption is of special interest. The exemption is likely to be aimed at AI-based image editing programs, for example, which make it possible to remove unwanted objects or automatically adjust colours and contrasts in the best possible way. Functions that insert objects generated based on a prompt into an image or generatively enlarge the edges of the image are also likely to be addressed. First, however, it is likely to be difficult to identify the threshold at which a substantial alteration of the input data can be assumed, as the AI Act does not provide any guidance here. In any case, the threshold should be reached when a deep fake (→ mn. 128 et seqq.) is generated as a result, even it is not always necessary to manipulate many elements of an input to generate a deep fake.[180] Secondly, it can be criticized that even minor changes as well as standard editing can have a major economic impact and can lead to consumers being misled.[181] Take, for example, the replacement of a sponsor on the jersey of a world famous soccer player. As long as no other guidance is available, it will ultimately be necessary to determine the extent to which the editing may realize or increase the risks mentioned in rec. 133. 124

II. Deployers

The second set of transparency obligations addresses **deployers** of certain AI systems. 125

1. Emotion recognition and biometric categorisation systems

Art. 50(3) states that 126

> 'Deployers of an **emotion recognition system** or a **biometric categorisation system** shall **inform** the natural persons exposed thereto of the operation of the system and shall **process** the personal data in accordance with Regulation (EU) 2016/679, Regulation (EU) 2016/1725 and Directive (EU) 2016/280, as applicable'.

Here, platforms should pay particular attention to the fact that emotion recognition systems and biometric categorization systems regularly fall into the high-risk category at the same time and may even be prohibited under certain circumstances. 127

2. Deep fakes and published texts on matters of public interest

Art. 50(4) has two subparagraphs, whereas the first one addresses **deep fakes** while the second one addresses AI-generated or manipulated **texts on matters of public interest**. 128

[178] On the pros and cons of machine-readable methods Molavi Vasse'i/Udoh 'In Transparency we Trust? Evaluating the Effectiveness of Watermarking and Labeling AI-Generated Content, p. 33 et seqq.

[179] Molavi Vasse'i/Udoh 'In Transparency we Trust? Evaluating the Effectiveness of Watermarking and Labeling AI-Generated Content', p. 41 et seqq.

[180] Dobber et al. The International Journal of Press/Politics 2021, 69 et seqq.

[181] Cf. rec. 133.

a) Deep fakes

129 According to the first subparagraph of Art. 50(4)

> 'Deployers of an AI system that generates or manipulates image, audio or video content constituting a deep fake, shall **disclose** that the content has been **artificially generated or manipulated**'.[182]

130 Whereas the term deep fake is defined in Art. 3 no. 60 as

> 'AI generated or manipulated image, audio or video content that resembles existing persons, objects, places, entities or events and would falsely appear to a person to be authentic or truthful'.

131 Unlike in earlier versions of the AI Act not only the resembling of **persons** is covered, but also of **objects**, **places**, **entities** or **events**. This is to be welcomed since even untrue representations that do not contain persons can have significant consequences for our information environment.[183] Some problems may arise in determining when content can **falsely appear to a person to be authentic or truthful**. This will have to be decided on a case-by-case basis and will certainly also have to take into account circumstances such as the context of the presentation, the context of the content as well as the contents quality.

132 Since Art. 50(4) subpara. 1 as well as Art. 50(2) address AI systems that generate content, generated deep fakes should already be marked as artificially generated or manipulated. However, the marking is not equivalent to the **disclosure** required by Art. 50(4) subparagraph 1, as the marking does not necessarily have to be recognizable by the human eye at first glance or at all.[184] However, it is only necessary to (merely) indicate that the content was generated or manipulated.[185] The Parliament's proposal according to which, whenever possible, the name of the natural or legal person that generated or manipulated the content should be disclosed, was not adopted, so that this information cannot be required. More on the implementation of the transparency requirements under → mn. 138.

133 The provision, however, constitutes **two exemptions**. The first one refers to criminal offences and is of less relevance for platforms. The second one, on the other hand, will be of much more relevance. It states that

> 'where the content forms part of an **evidently artistic**, **creative**, **satirical**, **fictional or analogous** work or programme, the transparency obligations set out in this paragraph are limited to disclosure of the existence of such generated or manipulated content in an appropriate manner that does not hamper the display or enjoyment of the work'.

134 This exception relates to the protection of the right to freedom of expression and the right to freedom of the arts and sciences guaranteed in the CFR of the EU[186] and is to be welcomed in principle. Nevertheless, it can cause some interpretation problems, because it may be hard to determine, when an **evidently** artistic, creative, satirical or fictional nature of the content can be assumed.[187] This will, again, have to be assessed

---

182 See also Kumkar/Rapp ZfDR 2022, 190 (212 et seqq.) who discuss the data protection implications of deep fakes.

183 Łabuz ACIG 2023, 1 (6 et seq.).

184 Rather, it is algorithmically detectable Tambiama Madiega, 'Generative AI and watermarking' (European Parliament Research Service, December 2023) (last accessed: 24.02.2024), p. 2; cf. also Bomhard/Siglmüller RDi 2024, 45 (47). A good illustration of the various disclosure methods can be found at Molavi Vasse'i/Udoh 'In Transparency we Trust? Evaluating the Effectiveness of Watermarking and Labeling AI-Generated Content', p. 21.

185 On the pros and cons of huma-facing disclosure methods Molavi Vasse'i/Udoh 'In Transparency we Trust? Evaluating the Effectiveness of Watermarking and Labeling AI-Generated Content', p. 25 et seqq.

186 Rec. 134.

187 Łabuz ACIG 2023, 1 (21 et seqq.).

on a case-by-case basis 'because it might depend on contextualisation as well as the cognitive abilities, media knowledge, or social and political awareness of recipients'.[188] Furthermore there will be a lot of room for interpretation on when an 'an **appropriate manner** that does not hamper the display or enjoyment of the work' can be assumed. According to rec. 134, the exemption expressly only covers such works and programmes which are subject to appropriate **safeguards for the rights and freedoms of third parties**. An addition that is not found in the legal text itself. Ultimately, the exception itself can be criticized for the fact that satirical deep fakes do not necessarily only serve the realization of fundamental rights, but in the worst case may even be misused to propagate ideological beliefs.[189]

Social media platforms in particular are unlikely to be deployers of AI systems that generate deep fakes, so they are less likely to be affected by this regulation. 135

b) Texts on matters of public interest

As the concept of deep fakes does not include textual content, Art. 50(4) subpara. 2 complementary stipulates that 136

> 'deployers of an AI system that generates or manipulates **text** which is published with the purpose of **informing the public on matters of public interest** shall disclose that the text has been artificially generated or manipulated'.

Again, the provision contains **two exemptions**. The first one is the same as in subpara. 1 and refers to criminal offences. The second one is of more importance as it states that the obligation does not apply 'where the AI-generated content has undergone a process of **human review** or **editorial control** and where a natural or legal person holds editorial responsibility for the publication of the content'. 137

III. Implementation of the transparency obligations

Art. 50(5) is to be welcomed insofar as it provides more details on how the aforementioned transparency obligations of Art. 50 are to be implemented. It states that the information must be provided to the concerned natural person 'in a **clear** and **distinguishable manner** at the latest at the time of the **first interaction or exposure**'.[190] The information also must respect the applicable accessibility requirements. The technical solution used may vary here and should consider what form of media is used.[191] 138

I. General-purpose AI models

Chapter V of the AI Act contains a separate section with regulations on GPAI models. This became necessary because GPAI models cannot be easily categorised in 139

---

188 Łabuz ACIG 2023, 1 (24).

189 Łabuz ACIG 2023, 1 (24).

190 According to Kremer/Haar in Schwartmann/Keber/Zenner, part 2 chap. 1 mn. 454, this means that the information must be provided at the latest before the end, but not necessarily before the start of the interaction.

191 Łabuz ACIG 2023, 1 (21 et seqq.); cf. also European Commission, 'Guidelines for Providers of Very Large Online Platforms and Very Large Online Search Engines on the Mitigation of Systemic Risks for Electoral Processes' (26.4.2024) <https://eur-lex.europa.eu/legal-content/EN/TXT/HTML/?uri=OJ:C_202403014> (last accessed: 01.07.2024) 'when labelling generative AI content, the Commission recommends that providers of VLOPs and VLOSEs apply efficient labels, easily recognised by users, taking into account aspects such as graphics, position and timing, drawing on scientific research on the effectiveness of labels'.

the risk-based system of the AI Act due to their wide range of possible applications.[192] The requirements of the AI Act address providers of **GPAI models.** The AI Act further stipulates additional requirements for providers of **GPAI models with systemic risk.**[193]

I. Obligations for providers of GPAI models

140 The **requirements** for providers of GPAI models can mainly be found in Art. 53 and Art. 54. These relate to:

Art. 53(1)(a)	Drawing and keeping up-to-date technical documentation of the model, including its training and testing process and the results of its evaluation[194]
Art. 53(1)(b)	Drawing, keeping up-to-date and making available information and documentation to providers of AI systems who intend[195] to integrate the model into their AI system, enabling them to have a good understanding of the capabilities and limitations of the model and to comply with their obligations under the AI Act[196]
Art. 53(1)(c)	Putting in place a policy to comply with Union law on copyright and related rights, and in particular to identify and comply with, including through state-of-the-art technologies, a reservation of rights expressed pursuant to Article 4(3) of Directive (EU) 2019/790[197]
Art. 53(1)(d)	Drawing up and making publicly available a sufficient detailed summary about the content used for training the model according to a template provided by the AI Office[198]
Art. 53(3)	Cooperating as necessary with the Commission and the national competent authorities
Art. 54(1)	Appointing an authorised representative, if established in a third country[199]

141 However, according to Art. 53(2), the requirements set out in Art. 53(1)(a) and Art. 53(1)(b) **do not apply** to 'providers of AI models that are released under a **free and open-source licence** that allows for the access, usage, modification, and distribution of the model, and whose parameters, including the weights, the information on the model architecture, and the information on model usage, are made publicly available'. A **counter-exception** applies to (free and open licence) models with **systemic risk**

[192] Cf. also Bomhard/Siglmüller RDi 2024, 45 (49).

[193] In detail on both Zenner/Schwartmann/Hansen in Schwartmann/Keber/Zenner, part 2 chap. 1 mn. 485 et seqq.

[194] Minimum elements are set out in Annex XI which can be amended by the Commission, Art. 53(6). See also Art. 53(5).

[195] Crit. and pointing out that such an intention may easily be faked Bomhard/Siglmüller RDi 2024, 45 (50).

[196] The obligation is 'without prejudice to the need to respect and protect intellectual property rights and confidential business information or trade secrets in accordance with Union and national law'; minimum elements are set out in Annex XII which can be amended by the Commission, Art. 53(6).

[197] In much detail and crit. on Art. 53(1)(c) and (d) Peukert GRUR Int. 2024, 497; crit. also Bomhard/Siglmüller RDi 2024, 45 (50 et seq.).

[198] In detail Peukert GRUR Int. 2024, 497.

[199] On the obligation to appoint representatives pursuant to other EU legislation Voigt/Bastians MMR 2022, 930.

(→ mn. 143 et seqq.), Art. 53(2)(2). The same (free and open-source licence exemption and counter-exemption for models with systemic risk) applies for the obligation to appoint an authorised representative, Art. 54(6).

Art. 53(4) stipulates that providers may rely on **codes of practice** according to Art. 56 to demonstrate their compliance with the obligations laid out in Art. 53(1) until a **harmonised standard** is published. Compliance with a harmonised standard grants providers the presumption of conformity.[200] Art. 53(7) stipulates that the **confidentiality** obligations set out in Art. 78 apply to any information and documentation obtained pursuant to the providers obligations from Art. 53. 142

II. Obligations for providers of GPAI models with systemic risk

If GPAI models present a systemic risk, the AI Act places additional requirements on their providers. These obligations are likely to be of **no relevance for most platforms** as they will not qualify as providers of GPAI models with systemic risk. When a GPAI model is to be **categorised** as such with systemic risk is determined by Art. 51 while the **procedure** is determined in Art. 52. According to Art. 51, a GPAI model shall be classified as a GPAI model with systemic risk if 143

> 'it has high impact capabilities evaluated on the basis of appropriate technical tools and methodologies, including indicators and benchmarks'

or

> 'based on a decision of the Commission, ex officio or following a qualified alert by the scientific panel, it has capabilities or impact equivalent to those of point (a)'.

High impact abilities, referred to in lit. a) shall be presumed[201] when the cumulative amount of compute used for the models training measured in **floating point operations** (FLOPs) is **greater than 10^25**, Art. 51(2).[202] This threshold may be amended by the Commission by delegated acts to reflect the state of the art, Art. 51(3).[203] The **obligations** for providers of GPAI models with systemic risk can be found in Art. 53. 144

J. Interplay with DSA and GDPR

The AI Act cannot be assessed in a stand-alone context and will probably raise a lot of questions about the interaction with other regulations, not all of which can be addressed here.[204] However, some of the most important points for platforms regarding 145

---

200 Providers of GPAI models with systemic risk who do not adhere to an approved code of practice shall, according to Art. 53(4), demonstrate alternative adequate means of compliance for approval of the Commission.

201 Cf. Art. 52(2).

202 Crit. Hacker, 'Comments on the Final Trilogue Version of the AI Act' (23.1.2024) <www.europeannewschool.eu/images/chairs/hacker/Comments%20on%20the%20AI%20Act.pdf> (last accessed: 24.02.2024), p. 5 et seq.; cf. also Bomhard/Siglmüller RDi 2024, 45 (51 et seq.); in detail on computing power and AI Sastry/Heim/Belfield et al., 'Computing Power and the Governance of Artificial Intelligence' (13.2.2024) <doi.org/10.48550/arXiv.2402.08797> (last accessed: 01.07.2024).

203 Crit. Bomhard/Siglmüller RDi 2024, 45 (51 et seq.).

204 In detail Schwartmann/Keber/Zenner, part 2 chap. 3 mn. 1 et seqq.; very good explanations of liability, data protection, intellectual property and cybersecurity issues surrounding generative AI can be found at Novelli/Casolari/Hacker/Spedicato/Floridi, 'Generative AI in EU Law: Liability, Privacy, Intellectual Property, and Cybersecurity' (17.1.2024) <papers.ssrn.com/sol3/papers.cfm?abstract_id=4694565> (last accessed: 01.07.2024); a great contribution on the intersection between AI and privacy can be

the interaction with other regulations are indicated below. Apart from the already mentioned interactions with other legal frameworks, the interaction with the Digital Services Act (DSA) and the General Data Protection Regulation (GDPR) are likely to be the most relevant in the context of platforms.[205]

I. Digital Services Act

146 The AI Act does not contain any detailed rules on the interaction with the DSA but at least provides that the application of the provisions on liability of intermediaries set out in Chapter II of the DSA (→ § 3 mn. 93 et seqq.), shall not be affected by the AI Act, Art. 2(5). The AI Act also contains some referrals to the DSA in its recitals.[206] The DSA, on the other side, does not contain any explicit provisions on the relationship with the AI Act. As a result, the obligations of both acts are to be understood **cumulative** in general – platforms must therefore comply with the provisions of the AI Act in addition to those of the DSA.[207] However, as the provisions on the liability of intermediaries are to remain unaffected, the liability privilege for platforms is likely to prevail.[208] The following are the main points where the AI Act and the DSA overlap or interplay.

1. Recommender systems

147 In principle, **AI-based recommender systems** are not regulated by the AI Act. Requirements for them (regarding the relation between AI Act and DSA) therefore only arise from the DSA. The DSA defines a recommender system as

> 'a fully or partially automated system used by an online platform to suggest in its online interface specific information to recipients of the service or prioritise that information, including as a result of a search initiated by the recipient of the service or otherwise determining the relative order or prominence of information displayed'.

148 Regulations on the transparency of recommender systems can be found in Art. 27 DSA (for more details → § 4 mn. 62). However, **regulation under the AI Act** may arise in some **special cases**. A prohibition under Art. 5(1)(a) may be considered – but probably only in some few extremely limited cases (→ mn. 59).[209] Consideration should also be given to the fact that recommender systems used to **influence elections** may also be considered as high-risk AI systems (→ mn. 113 et seqq.).

2. Risk assessment and mitigation of risks

149 Providers of very large online platforms and very large online search engines (→ § 2 mn. 55 et seqq.) must consider, among other things, the design of their recommender systems and other relevant algorithmic systems in the risk analysis they must conduct (in more detail → § 6 mn. 32 et seqq.), Art. 34(1) and (2)(a) DSA.[210] They also have to put in place

found at Solove, 'Artificial Intelligence and Privacy' (George Washington University Law School, 1.2.2024) <papers.ssrn.com/sol3/papers.cfm?abstract_id=4713111> (last accessed: 01.07.2024).

205 On the relationship to other product safety regulations Spindler CR 2021, 361 (364).

206 Cf. rec. 11, 118, 119, 120, and 136.

207 Cf. rec. 118.

208 Ebers/Hoch/Rosenkranz/Ruschemeier/Steinrötter RDi 2021, 528 (537).

209 Cf. also Steege MMR 2022, 926 (929); Kalbhenn ZUM 2021, 663 (665 et seq.).

210 Cf. rec. 118.

'reasonable, proportionate and effective mitigation measures, tailored to the specific systemic risks identified pursuant to Article 34, with particular consideration to the impacts of such measures on fundamental rights', Art. 35(1) DSA.

These measures include **ensuring** that **deep fakes are distinguishable** through prominent markings when presented on their online interfaces and providing an easy-to-use functionality which enables recipients of the service to indicate deep fakes, Art. 35 (1)(k) DSA. This provision is likely to be of particular importance in combating disinformation through deep fakes in the 2024 election year since most sections of the AI Act will not yet be in force for most upcoming elections. The Commission recently also published 'Guidelines for Providers of Very Large Online Platforms and Very Large Online Search Engines on the Mitigation of Systemic Risks for Electoral Processes'[211] which platforms should be aware of. 150

3. Content moderation – generative AI

In the case of **AI-supported content moderation**, the following applies: in principle, it is not regulated by the AI Act either. As already described in → mn. 113 et seqq., in individual cases the intention to influence an election may lead to a qualification as high-risk and therefore regulation by the AI Act. 151

Provisions on AI-supported content moderation can be found in Art. 14, Art. 17 and 34 DSA.[212] Art. 14(1)(2) DSA stipulates that providers of intermediary services must provide information in their general **terms and conditions** on algorithmic decision-making in the moderation of content (for more details → § 4 mn. 58 and § 5 mn. 36). Article 17(1) in conjunction with 17(3)(c) of the DSA stipulates that the content of the **statement** of reasons that hosting service providers must provide to affected users **in the event of content restrictions** also includes information on means of automated decision-making. 152

Even if one might assume at first glance that a breach of the transparency obligations according to Art. 50 must lead to the corresponding content being classified as **illegal content** (→ § 5 mn. 19 et seqq.) within the meaning of the DSA[213], this does not appear to be the case for unlabelled AI generated content. This is because rec. 136 states that 'the requirement to label content generated by AI systems under this Regulation is without prejudice to the obligation in Article 16(6) of Regulation 2022/2065 for providers of hosting services to process notices on illegal content received pursuant to Article 16(1) and should not influence the assessment and the decision on the illegality of the specific content'.[214] That assessment should, according to rec. 136, be performed solely with reference to the rules governing the legality of the content. 153

Lastly, the question arises whether **generative AI systems** or **generative AI models themselves** are **covered** by the scope of the **DSA**. This question becomes virulent because, although content posted by humans or bots on covered services, especially social media platforms (e.g. Twitter) is governed by the DSA, the dissemination of generated content in private messaging services (→ § 2 mn. 41 et seqq.) (e.g. WhatsApp) is not.[215] The material scope of the DSA covers 'intermediary services' (→ § 2 mn. 19 et seqq.), i.e. 'mere conduit, caching or hosting services'. Generative AI systems and models, however, 154

---

[211] European Commission, 'Guidelines for Providers of Very Large Online Platforms and Very Large Online Search Engines on the Mitigation of Systemic Risks for Electoral Processes' (26.1.2024) <https://eur-lex.europa.eu/legal-content/EN/TXT/HTML/?uri=OJ:C_202403014> (last accessed: 01.07.2024).

[212] For more details, see Kalbhenn ZUM 2021, 663 (671).

[213] Kalbhenn ZUM 2021, 663 (669, 671).

[214] It remains unclear why rec. 120 is almost the same as rec. 136, however, without the latter addition.

[215] Hacker/Engel/Mauer FAccT 23, 1112 (1117 et seqq).

are unlikely to fall in any of these categories, so that the **material scope of application** of the DSA remains **closed** and hate speech and disinformation generated by generative AI cannot be combated by the means of the DSA.[216] Some authors therefore argue that some provisions of the DSA (trusted flaggers; notice-and-action mechanism) should be extended to the domain of generative AI.[217]

4. Chat bots

155 A reference to Art. 50 can be found in Art. 12(1) DSA. According to this provision, providers of intermediary services (→ § 2 mn. 19 et seqq.) shall designate a **single point of contact** that enables users to communicate with them directly and rapidly, by electronic means and in a user-friendly manner. In establishing this single point of contact, the providers, according to Art. 12(1) DSA, 'shall not solely rely on automated tools'. However, if users choose to communicate with a chatbot[218], the transparency requirements of Art. 50(1) (→ mn. 118 et seqq.) must be observed. Providers of intermediary services will however not be able to refer to the exemption from the transparency requirement for chatbots (→ mn. 120) because rec. 43 DSA states that it should be expressly indicated when a user is communicating with chatbots.

156 Chatbots may also **qualify as online search engines** under the DSA, if they perform searches 'of, in principle, all websites, then incorporates the results into its existing knowledge and uses the updated knowledge to generate a single output that combines different sources of information'.[219] If the threshold of active users is reached, the applicability of the requirements for VLOSEs (→ § 6 mn. 1 et seqq.) will therefore also be applicable for chatbots.

5. Dark patterns

157 AI-supported dark patterns are likely to be considered prohibited under Art. 5(1)(a) in many cases (→ mn. 56 et seqq.). Classification (at least) as a high-risk AI system is also a possibility, provided that **electoral influence** is intended.

158 The DSA addresses dark patterns in its Art. 25. According to Art. 25(1) DSA, online platforms shall 'not design, organise or operate their online interfaces in a way that deceives or manipulates the recipients of their service or in a way that otherwise materially distorts or impairs the ability of the recipients of their service to make free and informed decisions'. However, according to Art. 25(2) DSA, practices covered by the GDPR,

---

[216] Berz/Engel/Hacker ZUM 2023, 586 (590 et seq.); see also Hacker, 'Comments on the Final Trilogue Version of the AI Act' (23.1.2024) <www.europeannewschool.eu/images/chairs/hacker/Comments%20on%20the%20AI%20Act.pdf> (last accessed: 01.07.2024), p. 4 et seq. and Novelli/Casolari/Hacker/Spedicato/Floridi, 'Generative AI in EU Law: Liability, Privacy, Intellectual Property, and Cybersecurity' (17.1.2024) <papers.ssrn.com/sol3/papers.cfm?abstract_id=4694565> (last accessed: 01.07.2024), p. 25 et seq.; cf. on the other hand rec. 119 which states that 'AI systems subject to this Regulation may be provided as intermediary services or parts thereof'.

[217] Berz/Engel/Hacker ZUM 2023, 586 (590 et seq.); see also Hacker, 'Comments on the Final Trilogue Version of the AI Act' (23.1.2024) <www.europeannewschool.eu/images/chairs/hacker/Comments%20on%20the%20AI%20Act.pdf> (last accessed: 01.07.2024) and Novelli/Casolari/Hacker/Spedicato/Floridi, 'Generative AI in EU Law: Liability, Privacy, Intellectual Property, and Cybersecurity' (17.1.2024) <papers.ssrn.com/sol3/papers.cfm?abstract_id=4694565> (last accessed: 01.07.2024), p. 25 et seq.; cf. also Tambiama Madiega, 'Generative AI and watermarking' (European Parliament Research Service, December 2023) <www.europarl.europa.eu/RegData/etudes/BRIE/2023/757583/EPRS_BRI(2023)757583_EN.pdf> (last accessed: 01.07.2024), p. 5.

[218] Which they can, as Art. 12(1) DSA expressly states that the recipients may choose the means of communication.

[219] Cf. Rec. 119.

among others, are exempt from this prohibition. For more detail on the interplay between DSA and GDPR in the area of dark patterns (→ 9 mn. 82 et seqq.).[220]

II. GDPR

159 The AI Act states in Art. 2(7) that it **'shall not affect'** the GDPR, without prejudice to arrangements provided for in Art. 10(5) and Art. 59. As AI is largely dependent on collecting and processing huge amounts of data, it goes without saying that GDPR-compliance plays a major role in the use of AI systems.

1. Generative AI

160 Especially since the Italian data protection authority issued a decision against ChatGPT[221], the GDPR-compliance of generative AI has been a hotly debated topic.[222] Most recently, the non-governmental organisation noyb lodged complaints with eleven data protection supervisory authorities against Meta for its processing of personal data for AI training purposes[223], leading to Meta delaying its AI plans in the EU.[224]

161 It is neither possible nor the objective of this contribution to provide a comprehensive overview of all the complex and evolving issues in this context. However, some important points regarding the interplay between generative AI and the GDPR that platforms should consider may be the following[225]:

162 Apart from the ever-present question of the applicability of the GDPR[226] platforms should carefully analyse whether they are the **controller** concerning the data processing in question.[227] Platforms should then further analyse on what **legal basis** they can justify

[220] Cf. also Martini/Kramme/Kamke MMR 2023, 399 on the regulation of dark patterns trough Digital Markets Act and Data Act.

[221] Cf. for example Thöne ZD-Aktuell 2023, 01254.

[222] See e.g. recently CNIL, 'AI: CNIL publishes its first recommendations on the development of artificial intelligence systems' (07.06.2024) <https://www.cnil.fr/en/ai-cnil-publishes-its-first-recommendations-development-artificial-intelligence-systems> (last accessed: 01.07.2024); EDPB, 'Report of the work undertaken by the ChatGPT Taskforce' (24.05.2024) <https://www.edpb.europa.eu/our-work-tools/our-documents/other/report-work-undertaken-chatgpt-taskforce_en> (last accessed: 01.07.2024).

[223] 'noyb urges 11 DPAs to immediately stop Meta's abuse of personal data for AI' (06.06.2024) <https://noyb.eu/en/noyb-urges-11-dpas-immediately-stop-metas-abuse-personal-data-ai> (last accessed: 01.07.2024).

[224] Stefano Fratta, 'Building AI Technology for Europeans in a Transparent and Responsible Way' (10.06.2024) <https://about.fb.com/news/2024/06/building-ai-technology-for-europeans-in-a-transparent-and-responsible-way/> (last accessed: 01.07.2024).

[225] A valuable contribution with useful explanations on technical aspects can be found at Bartels GRUR Int. 2024, 526; cf. also the complaints issued by noyb 'noyb urges 11 DPAs to immediately stop Meta's abuse of personal data for AI' (06.06.2024) <https://noyb.eu/en/noyb-urges-11-dpas-immediately-stop-metas-abuse-personal-data-ai> (last accessed: 01.07.2024); in detail Schwartmann/Keber/Zenner, part 2 chap. 3 mn. 1 et seqq.

[226] Cf. for example Landesbeauftragter für Datenschutz und Informationsfreiheit Baden-Württemberg, 'Diskussionspapier: Rechtsgrundlagen im Datenschutz beim Einsatz Künstlicher Intelligenz' (November 2023) <www.baden-wuerttemberg.datenschutz.de/rechtsgrundlagen-datenschutz-ki/> (last accessed: 01.07.2024), p. 6 et seqq. on the question which data can be qualified as personal data in the AI context. One may even argue that an AI model itself can qualify as personal data cf. Novelli/Casolari/Hacker/Spedicato/Floridi, 'Generative AI in EU Law: Liability, Privacy, Intellectual Property, and Cybersecurity' (17.1.2024) <papers.ssrn.com/sol3/papers.cfm?abstract_id=4694565> (last accessed: 01.07.2024), p. 13; Pesch/Böhme MMR 2023, 917 in detail.

[227] Cf. Bartels GRUR Int. 2024, 526 (530 et seq.); Landesbeauftragter für Datenschutz und Informationsfreiheit Baden-Württemberg, 'Diskussionspapier: Rechtsgrundlagen im Datenschutz beim Einsatz Künstlicher Intelligenz' (November 2023) <www.baden-wuerttemberg.datenschutz.de/rechtsgrundlagen-datenschutz-ki/> (last accessed: 01.07.2024), p. 9 et seqq.; cf. also Novelli/Casolari/Hacker/Spedicato/

their data processing with respect to the **training** of their AI system. As gathering consent (Art. 6(1)(a)GDPR) is most of the time impracticable[228] and a contractual relationship with the data subject (Art. 6(1)(b) GDPR) will only rarely exist[229], the focus shifts to Art. 6(1)(f) GDPR – the **balancing test**. Here one may consider if the application in question can be considered 'socially beneficial'[230], the type of data used or the degree of transparency towards data subjects among many other factors.[231] Ultimately, whether Art. 6(1)(f) GDPR can provide a legal basis for the processing of personal data is a matter of case-by-case analysis.[232] Problems may also arise from the fact that Art. 9 GDPR (**sensitive data**) is interpreted very broadly by the CJEU and if Art. 9 is applicable, data processing for training purposes generally[233] cannot be based on a balancing of interests, but only on explicit consent.[234]

163 A separate question is on what basis personal data may be processed that is not used to train the AI system or model, but is **entered during its use**, usually in the form of prompts. If a prompt contains personal data of the user, it is likely that the processing can be justified by consent. However, if a user enters personal data of third parties, similar problems arise as regarding the training of the system or model.[235]

Floridi, 'Generative AI in EU Law: Liability, Privacy, Intellectual Property, and Cybersecurity' (17.1.2024) <papers.ssrn.com/sol3/papers.cfm?abstract_id=4694565> (last accessed: 01.07.2024), p. 11 et seq.

228 Werry MMR 2023, 911 (912); Novelli/Casolari/Hacker/Spedicato/Floridi, 'Generative AI in EU Law: Liability, Privacy, Intellectual Property, and Cybersecurity' (17.1.2024) <papers.ssrn.com/sol3/papers.cfm?abstract_id=4694565> (last accessed: 01.07.2024), p. 10; cf. also CEDPO, 'Generative AI: The Data Protection Implications' (16.10.2023) <cedpo.eu/generative-ai-the-data-protection-implications/> (last accessed: 01.07.2024), p. 10 et seq.; crit. also Landesbeauftragter für Datenschutz und Informationsfreiheit Baden-Württemberg, 'Diskussionspapier: Rechtsgrundlagen im Datenschutz beim Einsatz Künstlicher Intelligenz' (November 2023) <www.baden-wuerttemberg.datenschutz.de/rechtsgrundlagen-datenschutz-ki/> (last accessed: 01.07.2024), p. 11 et seq.

229 Landesbeauftragter für Datenschutz und Informationsfreiheit Baden-Württemberg, 'Diskussionspapier: Rechtsgrundlagen im Datenschutz beim Einsatz Künstlicher Intelligenz' (November 2023) <www.baden-wuerttemberg.datenschutz.de/rechtsgrundlagen-datenschutz-ki/> (last accessed: 01.07.2024), p. 13 et seq.

230 Novelli/Casolari/Hacker/Spedicato/Floridi, 'Generative AI in EU Law: Liability, Privacy, Intellectual Property, and Cybersecurity' (17.1.2024) <papers.ssrn.com/sol3/papers.cfm?abstract_id=4694565> (last accessed: 01.07.2024), p. 10.

231 Novelli/Casolari/Hacker/Spedicato/Floridi, 'Generative AI in EU Law: Liability, Privacy, Intellectual Property, and Cybersecurity' (17.1.2024) <papers.ssrn.com/sol3/papers.cfm?abstract_id=4694565> (last accessed: 01.07.2024), p. 10; Landesbeauftragter für Datenschutz und Informationsfreiheit Baden-Württemberg, 'Diskussionspapier: Rechtsgrundlagen im Datenschutz beim Einsatz Künstlicher Intelligenz' (November 2023) <www.baden-wuerttemberg.datenschutz.de/rechtsgrundlagen-datenschutz-ki/> (last accessed: 01.07.2024), p. 16 et seqq.; in great detail also Bartels GRUR Int. 2024, 526 (532 et seq.).

232 Novelli/Casolari/Hacker/Spedicato/Floridi, 'Generative AI in EU Law: Liability, Privacy, Intellectual Property, and Cybersecurity' (17.1.2024) <papers.ssrn.com/sol3/papers.cfm?abstract_id=4694565> (last accessed: 01.07.2024), p. 10; cf. also CEDPO, 'Generative AI: The Data Protection Implications' (16.10.2023)<cedpo.eu/generative-ai-the-data-protection-implications/> (last accessed: 01.07.2024), p. 8 et seq.

233 See Art. 9(2)(j) GDPR, which, however, cannot be used to exploit generative AI commercially cf. Novelli/Casolari/Hacker/Spedicato/Floridi, 'Generative AI in EU Law: Liability, Privacy, Intellectual Property, and Cybersecurity' (17.1.2024) <papers.ssrn.com/sol3/papers.cfm?abstract_id=4694565> (last accessed: 01.07.2024), p. 11.

234 Novelli/Casolari/Hacker/Spedicato/Floridi, 'Generative AI in EU Law: Liability, Privacy, Intellectual Property, and Cybersecurity' (17.1.2024) <papers.ssrn.com/sol3/papers.cfm?abstract_id=4694565> (last accessed: 01.07.2024), p. 11.

235 Cf. Bartels GRUR Int. 2024, 526 (534 et seq.); Werry MMR 2023, 911 (913); Novelli/Casolari/Hacker/Spedicato/Floridi, 'Generative AI in EU Law: Liability, Privacy, Intellectual Property, and Cybersecurity' (17.1.2024) <papers.ssrn.com/sol3/papers.cfm?abstract_id=4694565> (last accessed: 01.07.2024), p. 12.

Furthermore, the **data protection principles** laid down in Art. 5 GDPR must be observed.[236] For example: According to Art. 5(1)(d) GDPR, personal data 'shall be **accurate**, and where necessary, kept **up to date'**.[237] This entails two problems: First, it is probably inevitable that generative AI will occasionally produce **inaccurate outputs** (containing personal data).[238] Depending on how strictly the requirements of the principle are understood, one may assume a breach of the principle in individual cases.[239] Secondly, it should also be noted that many systems only work with data that has been collected up to a certain point in time. This can cause problems as the personal data contained in the output may not be **'up to date'**.[240] The need for the use of large amounts of data to train generative AI models or systems also raises the question of compliance with the principles of **data minimisation** (Art. 5(1)(c) GDPR) and **purpose limitation** (Art. 5(1)(b) GDPR).[241] **164**

Furthermore, the **rights of data subjects** (Art. 12 et seqq. GDPR), in particular the right to rectification, the **right to erasure**[242], the right to restriction of data processing and the right of data subjects to object must be observed. To this end, data controllers must comply with the **information requirements** of the GDPR, which may vary depending on the type of data collection. As long as personal data is collected from the data subject, Art. 13 GDPR applies. The collection of training data, on the other hand, does not usually involve the data subject directly, so that Art. 14 GDPR becomes applicable. According to this, the processor is obliged to provide information to data subjects where personal data have not been obtained from them. A possible solution for generative AI controllers could lie in Art. 14(5)(b) GDPR in individual cases, if they can demonstrate that the provision of such information would involve a disproportionate effort.[243] **165**

Further aspects which must be taken into account are the requirements on **automated individual decision-making** (Art. 22 GDPR) and the **protection of minors** (cf. Art. 8(2) GDPR; rec. 38 GDPR).[244] **166**

---

[236] Cf. Bartels GRUR Int. 2024, 526 (535 et seq.).

[237] In more detail CEDPO, 'Generative AI: The Data Protection Implications' (16.10.2023) <cedpo.eu/generative-ai-the-data-protection-implications/> (last accessed: 01.07.2024), p. 4 et seq.

[238] Pesch/Böhme MMR 2023, 917 (921); Bartels GRUR Int. 2024, 526 (536); cf. Werry MMR 2023, 911 (913 et seq.) pointing out an example where ChatGPT wrongly accused an Australian major of being a criminal.

[239] Werry MMR 2023, 911 (913 et seq.) argues that it lays in the very nature of AI that it is only trained through errors and therefore not every factually inaccurate personal output constitutes a breach of the data accuracy principle, as long as providers take measures to ensure that personal data which are inaccurate, having regard to the purposes for which they are processed, are erased or rectified without delay; stricter Pesch/Böhme MMR 2023, 917.

[240] CEDPO, 'Generative AI: The Data Protection Implications' (16.10.2023)<cedpo.eu/generative-ai-the-data-protection-implications/> (last accessed: 01.07.2024), p. 5.

[241] Bartels GRUR Int. 2024, 526 (536 et seq.); Novelli/Casolari/Hacker/Spedicato/Floridi, 'Generative AI in EU Law: Liability, Privacy, Intellectual Property, and Cybersecurity' (17.1.2024) <papers.ssrn.com/sol3/papers.cfm?abstract_id=4694565> (last accessed: 01.07.2024), p. 14 et seqq.

[242] Novelli/Casolari/Hacker/Spedicato/Floridi, 'Generative AI in EU Law: Liability, Privacy, Intellectual Property, and Cybersecurity' (17.1.2024)<papers.ssrn.com/sol3/papers.cfm?abstract_id=4694565> (last accessed: 01.07.2024), p. 13 et seq.

[243] Cf. Berz/Engel/Hacker ZUM 2023, 586 (589); CEDPO, 'Generative AI: The Data Protection Implications' (16.10.2023) <cedpo.eu/generative-ai-the-data-protection-implications/> (last accessed: 01.07.2024), p. 28; Bartels GRUR Int. 2024, 526 (535 et seq.).

[244] Werry MMR 2023, 911 (914 et seq.).

2. Other relevant regulations

167 The AI Act itself is limited to a few references to the applicability of certain provisions of the GDPR and to certain exceptions to the provisions of the GDPR.[245] First of all, Art. 10(5) permits the processing of **sensitive data** within the meaning of Art. 9(1) GDPR for the purpose of bias detection and correction in relation to high-risk AI systems under strict conditions. Further, Art. 26(9) stipulates that deployers of high-risk AI systems should use the information provided to them under Art. 13 to comply with their obligation to conduct a **data protection impact assessment** under Art. 35 GDPR, if applicable.[246] In this context, it is also important to note Art. 27(4), which contains a provision regarding the interplay between fundamental rights impact assessments (→ mn. 90) and data protection impact assessments. Besides that, Art. 50(3) states that deployers of emotion recognition systems and biometric categorisation systems shall process personal data in accordance with the GDPR. The AI Act contains **relaxations** regarding the **principle of purpose limitation** for the purpose of developing AI in **regulatory sandboxes.**[247] Lastly, the **EU declaration of conformity** (cf. Art. 47) has to contain a statement that the AI system complies with the GDPR, Annex V(5).

K. Supervision, enforcement, and sanctions

168 The Member States must establish or designate at least one **notifying** and at least one **market surveillance authority** for the purpose of the AI Act as national competent authorities, Art. 70(1). The **AI Office** will also be of particular importance. Its tasks include contributing to standardisation and promoting the development of codes of practice. It is also planned to establish an **AI Board** consisting of one representative per Member State. The Board will mainly act in an advisory role to the Commission and the Member States.[248]

169 Art. 99 provides for **penalties of up to EUR 35 million** or (in the case of companies) **up to 7 % of the total worldwide annual turnover of the preceding financial year.**[249] In detail:

Non-compliance with Art. 5 – **prohibited practices**	Up to 35 million EUR / 7 % of total worldwide annual turnover
Non-compliance with **obligations** of – **providers** (Art. 16), – authorised representatives (Art. 22), – importers (Art. 23), – distributors (Art. 24), – **deployers** (Art. 26); Requirements and obligations of notified bodies (Art. 31, 33(1), 33(3), 33(4), 34); **Transparency obligations** for providers and deployers (Art. 50)	Up to 15 million EUR / 3 % of total worldwide annual turnover

[245] More closely Ebers/Hoch/Rosenkranz/Ruschemeier/Steinrötter RDi 2021, 528 (536 et seq.).
[246] Crit. on this Schallbruch DuD 2021, 438 (443); cf. Schürmann ZD 2022, 316.
[247] More closely Spindler CR 2021, 361 (364 and 371).
[248] In more detail on the AI Office and the AI Board Bomhard/Siglmüller RDi 2024, 45 (52).
[249] Note Art. 99(6) regarding SMEs and start-ups.

Supply of incorrect, incomplete or misleading information to notified bodies and national competent authorities in reply to a request	Up to 7,5 million EUR / 1 % of total worldwide annual turnover

Provisions on **fines for providers of GPAI models** can be found in Art. 101 and can reach up to 15 million EUR or 3 % of the total worldwide annual turnover.

§ 22
Platform-specific requirements of the DSM Directive

Literature: *Barudi*, '§ 1 Urheberrechts-Diensteanbieter-Gesetz' in Barudi (ed), Das neue Urheberrecht, Baden-Baden 2021; *Bridy*, 'The Price of Closing the Value Gap: How the Music Industry Hacked EU Copyright Reform', Vanderbilt Journal of Entertainment and Technology Law 2020, 323; *Dreier/Schulze* (eds), Urheberrechtsgesetz, 7th edn, Munich 2022; *Dreier*, 'Die Schlacht ist geschlagen – ein Überblick', GRUR 2019, 771; *Gielen/Tiessen*, 'Die neue Plattformhaftung nach der Richtlinie über das Urheberrecht im digitalen Binnenmarkt', EuZW 2019, 639; *Janal*, 'Friendly Fire? Das Urheberrechts-Diensteanbieter-Gesetz und sein Verhältnis zum künftigen Digital Services Act', GRUR 2022, 211; *Jani*, 'Das europäische Leistungsschutzrecht für Presseverleger', ZUM 2019, 674; *Kafsack*, Europaparlament billigt Urheberrechtsreform, FAZ of 27.3.2019, 1; *Kahl*, 'Wen betrifft das Leistungsschutzrecht für Presseverleger? – "Kleinste Textausschnitte" vor dem Hintergrund der BGH-Rechtsprechung', MMR 2013, 348; *Metzger/Pravemann*, 'Der Entwurf des UrhDaG als Umsetzung von Art. 17 DSM-RL – Ein gesetzgebungstechnischer Drahtseilakt', ZUM 2021, 288; *Metzger/Senftleben*, 'Comment of the European Copyright Society – Selected Aspects of Implementing Article 17 of the Directive on Copyright in the Digital Single Market into National Law', JIPITEC 2020, 115; *Nolte*, 'Drei Thesen zur aktuellen Debatte über Haftung und Verteilungsgerechtigkeit bei Hosting-Diensten mit nutzergenerierten Inhalten', ZUM 2017, 304; *Ohly*, "Volenti non fit iniuria" – Die Einwilligung im Privatrecht, Tübingen 2002; *Raue*, '»Unberührt« – das Verhältnis von DSA zur DSM-RL und zum UrhDaG', ZUM 2023, 160; *Schack*, 'Das neue Leistungsschutzrecht für Presseverleger – Ein schlechtes Vorbild wird reformiert', ZUM 2020, 165; *Schippan*, 'Der Schutz von kurzen Textwerken im digitalen Zeitalter', ZUM 2013, 358; *Schricker/Loewenheim*, Urheberrecht, 6th edn, Munich 2020; *Spiegel*, '§ 5 Presseverlegerschutzrecht' in Barudi (ed), Das neue Urheberrecht, Baden-Baden 2021; *Spindler*, 'Die neue Urheberrechts-Richtlinie der EU, insbesondere "Upload-Filter" – Bittersweet?', CR 2019, 277; *Stieper*, 'Die Richtlinie über das Urheberrecht im digitalen Binnenmarkt', ZUM 2019, 211; *Suwelack*, 'Leistungsschutzrecht und Upload-Filter aus ökonomischer Perspektive', MMR 2018, 582; *Volkmann*, 'Art. 17 Urh-RL und die Upload-Filter: verschärfte Störerhaftung oder das Ende der Freiheit im Internet?', CR 2019, 376; *Wandtke/Bullinger*, Praxiskommentar zum Urheberrecht, 6th edn, Munich 2022; *Wimmers/Barudi*, 'Zur Mitteilung der Kommission zur Modernisierung des Urheberrechts', IPRB 2016, 16; *Wimmers/Barudi*, 'Der Mythos vom Value Gap', GRUR 2017, 327.

A. Introduction

Digitisation is advancing, and the **law** is following suit. Almost 15 years after the last major EU copyright reform, the Commission published its Communication '**Towards a modern, more European copyright framework**'[1] in December 2015, announcing the Juncker administration's goals for modernising copyright rules at EU level in the coming years. Copyright law was to be adapted to 'new technological realities' and designed to conform to the internal market.[2] **Several projects** were implemented with this goal in mind: in addition to the Portability Regulation,[3] the 'Marrakesh Directive',[4] the Online SatCab Directive[5] and other legal acts, the **DSM Directive**[6] ('DSM Dir') gains particular importance. The DSM Directive updates and supplements the InfoSoc Directive[7] ('InfoSoc Dir') from 2001 and leads to further harmonisation in core areas of copyright. With a total of 32 articles, it contains a colourful bouquet of copyright contract law topics, new or now mandatory exception provisions (e.g. text and data mining, caricature, parody and pastiche, digital teaching, etc.), new exploitation rights (press publisher protection), collecting societies' topics (collective licensing with extended effect) and other aspects. In particular, however, the DSM Directive establishes a **new concept of liability for online content-sharing service providers** (hereinafter also: 'service providers'). These hosting services have certain characteristics for which an independent copyright regime has been created in Art. 17 DSM Dir. The first part of this chapter deals with these platform-specific requirements of Art. 17 DSM Dir. In a brief second part, the new **press publisher protection law** resulting from Art. 15 DSM Dir is presented in overview form. The respective national implementations of Art. 15, 17 DSM Dir are not the subject of this chapter.[8] 1

B. Liability concept for online content-sharing service providers (Art. 17 DSM Dir)

A **controversially discussed project** for the DSM Dir was the realignment of a liability concept of online content-sharing service providers. According to the **previous-** 2

[1] European Commission, 'Towards a modern, more European copyright framework', 9.12.2015, COM(2015) 626 final; on this Wimmers/Barudi IPRB 2016, 16.

[2] European Commission, 'Towards a modern, more European copyright framework', 9.12.2015, COM(2015) 626 final, 3.

[3] Regulation (EU) 2017/1128 of the European Parliament and of the Council of 14.6.2017 on cross-border portability of online content services in the internal market, OJ 2017 L 168, 1.

[4] Directive (EU) 2017/1564 of the European Parliament and of the Council of 13.9.2017 on certain permitted forms of use of certain works and other subject-matter protected by copyright or related rights for the benefit of persons who are blind, visually impaired or otherwise print disabled, and amending Directive 2001/29/EC on the harmonisation of certain aspects of copyright and related rights in the information society, OJ 2017 L 242, 6.

[5] Directive (EU) 2019/789 of the European Parliament and of the Council of 17.4.2019 on rules for the exercise of copyright and related rights concerning certain online broadcasting organisations and retransmission of television and radio programmes and amending Council Directive 93/83/EEC, OJ 2019 L 130, 82.

[6] Directive (EU) 2019/790 of the European Parliament and of the Council of 17.4.2019 on copyright and related rights in the Digital Single Market and amending Directives 96/9/EC and 2001/29/EC, OJ 2019 L 130, 92.

[7] Directive 2001/29/EC of the European Parliament and of the Council of 22.5.2001 on the harmonisation of certain aspects of copyright and related rights in the information society, OJ 2001 L 167, 10.

[8] For the transposition of the DSM Directive into German law including the UrhDaG, see comprehensively Barudi, § 1 et seq.; for the transposition of the press publisher protection law into national law, see Spiegel in Barudi § 5 mn. 1 et seq.

ly applicable legal situation, these service providers did not perform an own **act of communication to the public** and were therefore not liable as perpetrators for copyright infringements committed by users via their services. The CJEU did not depart from this principle in its judgment on the joined cases C-682/18 and C-683/18.[9] According to this ruling, hosting services **do not, in principle, engage in an own communication to the public**; only in narrowly defined categories of exceptions can this principle be deviated from.

3 **The efforts to change the legal situation**, which culminated in the adoption of Art. 17 DSM Dir, were triggered by the efforts of the rightsholders' industry since at least 2015, which described the liability privileges for hosting services as no longer up to date.[10] A 'value gap'[11] was claimed that needed to be closed. The preliminary work on the DSM Dir was already characterised by this term, whose meaning was not very tangible and was understood in different ways. At the EU level, this led to a **discussion about more distributive justice** in the online use of copyright-protected content. In the Commission's Communication 'Towards a modern, more European copyright framework'[12] this discussion was briefly outlined for the first time. The Commission's 2016 Impact Assessment[13] contained more concrete indications of possible changes to the legal framework. At the same time, the Commission published its proposal for the DSM Dir.[14] Several amendments later, the provision – listed as Art. 13 at the draft stage – found its final version in Art. 17 DSM Dir. Depending on the perspective, the provision was classified as a 'victory for democracy', as a 'yes to the digital future of culture and media and to a lively and diverse creative landscape in Europe', as a 'wrong turn', or a 'restriction of freedom'.[15]

4 The **deadline for transposing** Art. 17 DSM Dir into national law was 7.6.2021. Member States chose various ways to implement the provision into national law. Germany, for example, created a separate statute besides the Copyright Act (UrhG) – the Copyright Service Providers Act (UrhDaG).[16] The Commission referred several Member States to the CJEU for failing to notify the Commission of complete transposition measures.[17]

5 The provision has already been the subject of an **action for annulment** before the CJEU.[18] On Poland's initiative, the CJEU examined whether the liability concept as laid down in Art. 17(4) DSM Dir is compatible with the fundamental rights of freedom of expression and information under Art. 11 CFR. The CJEU **declared the provision** to be **effective** and certified that the legislator of the directive had maintained an **appropriate**

---

[9] CJEU 22.6.2021 – joined cases C-682/18 and C-683/18, ECLI:EU:C:2021:503 = GRUR 2021, 1054 – Frank Peterson v Google LLC and Others and Elsevier Inc. v Cyando AG.

[10] See Wimmers/Barudi GRUR 2017, 327; Bridy Vanderbilt Journal of Entertainment and Technology Law 2020, 326.

[11] Wimmers/Barudi GRUR 2017, 327; Nolte ZUM 2017, 304.

[12] European Commission, 'Towards a modern, more European copyright framework', 9.12.2015, COM(2015) 626 final; see also Wimmers/Barudi IPRB 2016, 16.

[13] European Commission, 'Impact Assessment on the modernisation of EU copyright rules', 26.4.2018, SWD(2016) 301 final.

[14] European, Comission, 'Proposal for a Directive of the European Parliament and of the Council on Copyright in the Digital Single Market', 14.9.2016, COM(2016) 593 final.

[15] Cf. Kafsack FAZ of 27.3.2019, 1.

[16] Cf. comprehensively on the UrhDaG: Barudi in Barudi § 1.

[17] European Commission, 'The European Commission decides to refer 11 Member States to the Court of Justice of the European Union for failing to fully transpose EU copyright rules into national law' (Commission Press Release, 15.2.2023), <ec.europa.eu/commission/presscorner/detail/en/ip_23_704> (last accessed: 12.3.2024).

[18] CJEU 26.4.2022 – case C-401/19, ECLI:EU:C:2022:297 = GRUR 2022, 820 – Republic of Poland v European Parliament and Council of the European Union.

balance between the different fundamental rights and interests involved in Art. 17 DSM Dir.

I. Legitimation

Art. 17 DSM Dir largely turns the previous legal situation on its head and establishes a **new 'specific liability mechanism'**.[19] The decisive factor for this is the view of the legislator that the **market for online content** had **'gained in complexity'** and that there had been **legal uncertainty** as to whether service providers were themselves responsible under copyright law for the content uploaded by their users and therefore had to obtain rights of use.[20] When designing the liability rules in Art. 17 DSM Dir, the legislator had audio and video streaming services in mind, which play an important role in the relevant market and compete with content providers.[21] The Commission's Impact Assessment, which forms the basis of the draft DSM Dir, confirms this focus. In it, the Commission explicitly and very extensively referred to representatives of the music and film industry as well as video and audio platforms such as YouTube, SoundCloud, Dailymotion and Vimeo. The Commission described the service providers as competitors to content providers who suffered a competitive disadvantage. In the music sector, consumers would regard the services mentioned as substitutes for Spotify, Deezer, etc. 6

II. Scope of application

Art. 17 DSM Dir refers to **online content-sharing service providers**. Who is to be considered as such a service provider is **defined by Art. 2 no. 6 DSM Dir**. This is any 'provider of an information society service of which the main or one of the main purposes is to store and give the public access to a **large amount** of copyright-protected works or other protected subject matter uploaded by its users, which it **organises** and **promotes for profit-making purposes**'. An information society service is a service normally provided for remuneration, at a distance, by electronic means and at the individual request of a recipient of services.[22] 7

The definition in Art. 2 no. 6 DSM Dir is intended to **limit the scope of** the specific liability mechanism.[23] **Explicitly excluded from the liability concept of Art. 17 DSM Dir** are non-profit online encyclopedias (e.g. Wikipedia), non-profit educational and scientific repositories (e.g. arxiv.org), open source software development and sharing platforms (e.g. GitHub), providers of electronic communications services within the meaning of Directive (EU) 2018/1972[24] (e.g. WhatsApp), online marketplaces (e.g. eBay), cloud services provided between companies (e.g. Amazon Web Services) and 8

[19] Rec. 66 subpara. 1 DSM Dir; CJEU 26.4.2022 – case C-401/19, ECLI:EU:C:2022:297 = GRUR 2022, 820 – Republic of Poland v European Parliament and Council of the European Union.

[20] Rec. 61 DSM Dir.

[21] Rec. 62 DSM Dir; cf. also Gielen/Tiessen EuZW 2019, 639 (641).

[22] Art. 2 no. 5 DSM Dir in conjunction with Art. 1(1)(b) of Directive (EU) 2015/1535 of the European Parliament and of the Council of 9.9.2015 laying down a procedure for the provision of information in the field of technical regulations and of rules on information society services, OJ 2015 L 241, 1 (15).

[23] Cf. CJEU 26.4.2022 – case C-401/19, ECLI:EU:C:2022:297 = GRUR 2022, 820 – Republic of Poland v European Parliament and Council of the European Union; the German legislator assumes in the medium term that 13 service providers fall within the scope of the act; cf. BT-Drs. 19/27426, 61.

[24] Directive (EU) 2018/1972 of the European Parliament and of the Council of 11.12.2018 on the European Electronic Communications Code, OJ 2018 L 321, 36 (214).

cloud services that allow their users to upload content for their own use (cyberlocker such as Dropbox, Magenta Cloud).[25]

9 The large number of services excluded from the scope of application of the liability rules underlines the intention of the directive's legislator to create a **special regime, to be interpreted narrowly,** primarily for the audio content and audiovisual content sector in relation to services which, by virtue of their importance and bargaining power, play an **important role in their market.**[26]

10 In its declaration on Art. 17 DSM Dir, the Federal Republic of Germany emphasises, in line with the directive's issuer, 'that creators should participate in the exploitation of their content through upload platforms'.[27] This recognition is important. On the one hand, it follows that it is **creators and artists** who should benefit from the changes in copyright law. Secondly, Art. 17 DSM Dir should only cover those platforms where there is typically a risk that third parties upload content that they do not create themselves and with which they have no copyright relationship.

11 If a service provider offers different services, it must be **examined separately for each individual service** whether the criteria of the definition in Art. 2 no. 6 DSM Dir are fulfilled.[28] If a company operates both a commercial video platform and an email service or cloud storage space for individual use, the provisions of the DSM Dir only apply to the video platform, but the general legal situation continues to apply to the email service and the cloud storage space.

1. Main purpose; large amount

12 In order to fall within the scope of Art. 17 DSM Dir, the **main purpose** or one of the main purposes of **the service provider** must be to store **a large amount** of copyright works or other subject matter uploaded by its users and to provide public access thereto. If the possibility of uploading content to a platform is only a secondary purpose and not a central element of the service, it is already not covered by the definition in Art. 2 no. 6 DSM Dir.

13 Sometimes it is difficult to determine which of several purposes is the main purpose of a service. This is complicated by the fact that the term 'purpose' can be understood both subjectively and objectively. The purely subjective perception of the service provider is not decisive, as this is regularly not verifiable and is therefore not a practicably suitable distinguishing criterion. Rather, an **evaluative, objectified analysis** should be made, which must have as its goal the identification of the most important purpose[29] of the service. If the main purpose of the service is other than to enable users to upload and share a large amount of copyrighted content in order to make a profit from this activity, Art. 17 DSM Dir does not apply to this service provider.[30] Something else might

[25] Art. 2 no. 6 subpara. 2 DSM Dir. Cf. OLG Nürnberg 1.8.2023 – 3 U 2910/22, GRUR 2023, 1453.

[26] Cf. European Commission, 'Impact Assessment on the modernisation of EU copyright rules', 26.4.2018, SWD(2016) 301 final, 142.

[27] Council of the EU, 'Draft Directive of the European Parliament and of the Council on copyright related rights in the Digital Single Market and amending Directives 96/9/EC and 2001/29/EC (first reading) – adoption of the legislative act – Statements', 15.4.2019, 7986/19 ADD 1 REV 2, 2 (Statement by Germany, point 2).

[28] Cf. European Commission, 'Guidance on Article 17 of Directive 2019/790 on Copyright in the Digital Single Market', 4.6.2021, COM(2021) 288 final, 6.

[29] See also rec. 62 DSM Dir: 'This Directive applies to services the principal purpose of which is exclusively or inter alia […]'.

[30] Cf. rec. 62 DSM Dir: 'Such services should not include services the principal purpose of which is other than to enable users to upload and retransmit a large amount of copyright-protected content for the purpose of profiting from that activity'.

only result if, in addition to this main purpose, the storage and making available to the public of the content uploaded by users can also be identified as another main purpose with equal weight and value. In practice, it is **important to identify the different functions** of a service and to set their importance and purposes in relation to the service.

What is to be understood as a 'large amount' in the sense of the definition in Art. 2 no. 6 DSM Dir may vary depending on the circumstances. Rec. 63 DSM Dir emphasises the **necessary case-by-case consideration.**[31] 14

2. Organising the content

Only those service providers who organise the uploaded content are covered by Art. 2 no. 6, 17 DSM Dir. If a service provider **assigns the content to existing categories and structures** it, this speaks for organising in the sense of the definition.[32] The decisive factor is that the service provider acts with the aim to 'attract a larger audience'.[33] Organising of content by the service provider does not take place if the service **merely provides infrastructure** and leaves it to the users of the service to organise and structure the content by putting it into categories and 'drawers'. Services on the internet must be designed in a user-friendly way and have clear graphical user interfaces. This alone does not lead them to intervene in and organise the content itself. The same applies to search functions, which many services have. Such functions are merely part of the infrastructure. 15

3. Promoting the content for profit

The service provider must also promote the content for the purpose of making a profit. According to the wording of Art. 2 no. 6 DSM Dir, the **content** must be **specifically promoted.** This is to be distinguished from the advertising of the service itself. It is also irrelevant that a service provider operates the service with the intention of making a profit and generally generates advertising revenue. This is because an information society service is, by definition, usually operated for remuneration.[34] Moreover, a profit-oriented activity is present in almost every service and is also necessary because of the financing of the service and its costs. Promoting content for profit must therefore be a **clearly definable additional criterion.** 16

A **recognisable connection** must exist between the content of the service and the revenue generated from its promotion is necessary, e.g. through advertising directly related to the specific content.[35] The legislator considers it crucial that there be 'targeted promotion' within the content.[36] Simple banner advertising without reference to specific content is not covered by this. Art. 17 DSM Dir is linked to the exploitation of content protected by copyright. Such exploitation of content is not yet present if general advertising space is available on a service. 17

---

[31] In detail on this with regard to the UrhDaG Barudi in Barudi § 1 mn. 14 et seq.; a 'large quantity' of works protected by copyright implies at the same time that not every service provider who has functions for uploading content is automatically covered by the scope of Art. 17 DSM Dir, cf. Metzger/Senftleben JIPITEC 2020, 115 (117).

[32] Rec. 62 DSM Dir.

[33] Rec. 62 DSM Dir.

[34] Art. 1(1)(b) of Directive (EU) 2015/1535 of the European Parliament and of the Council of 9.9.2015 laying down a procedure for the provision of information in the field of technical regulations and of rules on information society services, OJ 2015 L 241, 1 (15).

[35] See also European Commission, 'Guidance on Article 17 of Directive 2019/790 on Copyright in the Digital Single Market', 4.6.2021, COM(2021) 288 final, 5.

[36] Rec. 62 DSM Dir.

III. Communication to the public by the service provider

18 Art. 17(1) DSM Dir stipulates that the service provider performs an own communication to the public. This **statutory determination of an act of use is** remarkable and **foreign to the familiar system of copyright law**. Usually, the focus of legislative activities is on exclusive rights of the right holder and provisions on limitations. In contrast, Art. 17 DSM Dir names the person who performs an act of exploitation under copyright law. This represents a **shift in perspective** when examining copyright issues in this area.

19 Now the focus is not on whether the constituent elements of an act of use are present, but whether a service provider fulfils the characteristics which then fictitiously constitute an act of use. Basically, Art. 17(1) DSM Dir is an **attribution standard,** as there is no specific analysis of an act of use.

20 The communication to the public according to **Art. 17(1) DSM Dir substantiates Art. 3 InfoSoc Dir**. In its guidance, the Commission also emphasises that Art. 17 DSM Dir does not constitute a new, independent right of communication to the public, but rather defines Art. 3 InfoSoc Dir in more detail for the purposes laid down in the DSM Dir.[37] Nevertheless, Art. 17(1) DSM Dir does not represent a manifestation of previously applicable law, but a '**paradigm shift**' because of the act of use by a service provider, which was regularly to be denied under the previous legal situation.[38] This is because the CJEU emphasised in its decision on the joined cases C-682/18 and C-683/18 that a **hosting service in principle does not make any communication to the public** and that an act of use can only be considered in narrowly defined exceptional cases.[39]

21 Art. 17(1) DSM Dir only concerns the **communication to the public** and not any associated acts of reproduction. The Commission is rightly of the opinion that service providers do not need permission from the right holder for a technically necessary reproduction.[40] In view of the objectives of Art. 17 DSM Dir, this is appropriate, because the reproduction is initiated by the uploading user, and it is basically to be regarded as his act.[41] Moreover, the regulatory concept of Art. 17 DSM Dir is based on the **economic significance of the communication to the public** of copyright-protected content, not on the technically necessary reproduction for the purpose of communication to the public. The latter has no independent economic significance.[42]

22 Regardless of the service provider's fictitious act of use, it remains the case that the **user** who uploads content to the platform regularly **makes it available to the public.**[43]

[37] European Commission, 'Guidance on Article 17 of Directive 2019/790 on Copyright in the Digital Single Market', 4.6.2021, COM(2021) 288 final, 2.

[38] Dreier GRUR 2019, 771 (775); Volkmann CR 2019, 376, emphasises that the copyright liability created by the DSM Dir turns the liability concept 'on its head'.

[39] See the operative part of the decision in CJEU 22.6.2021 – joined cases C-682/18 and C-683/18, ECLI:EU:C:2021:503 = GRUR 2021, 1054 – Frank Peterson v Google LLC and Others and Elsevier Inc.v Cyando AG: 'there is "no communication to the public […] unless […]"'.

[40] European Commission, 'Guidance on Article 17 of Directive 2019/790 on Copyright in the Digital Single Market', 4.6.2021, COM(2021) 288 final, 7.

[41] Cf. in this respect BGH 10.1.2019 – I ZR 267/15, GRUR 2019, 813 (818) para. 47 et seq. – Cordoba II.

[42] It is true that under German law the reproduction of a work for the subsequent making available to the public constitutes an independent use of the work, cf. BGH 19.1.2017 – I ZR 242/15, GRUR 2017, 390 (392) para. 28 – East Side Gallery; BGH 10.1.2019 – I ZR 267/15, GRUR 2019, 813 (818) para. 51 – Cordoba II. However, this is at most a subordinate preparatory act that does not constitute an independently licensable type of use, cf. v. Ungern-Sternberg in Schricker/Loewenheim UrhG § 19a mn. 64; Bullinger in Wandtke/Bullinger UrhG § 19a mn. 12.

[43] CJEU 22.6.2021 – joined cases C-682/18 and C-683/18, ECLI:EU:C:2021:503 = GRUR 2021, 1054 para. 71 et seq. – Frank Peterson v Google LLC and Others and Elsevier Inc.v Cyando AG; OLG München 28.1.2016 – 29 U 2798/15, GRUR 2016, 612 (613) para. 25 – Allegro Barbaro; OLG Hamburg 1.7.2015 – 5 U 87/12, GRUR-RS 2015, 14370 para. 138; see also BT-Drs. 19/27426, 45.

Art. 17(2) DSM Dir assumes that the conduct of a user is to be measured against Art. 3 InfoSoc Dir. In this respect, in the scope of application of Art. 17 DSM Dir, **two acts of use of equal rank** exist for an action that is to be considered uniformly by virtue of the legal fiction.

IV. Responsibility for communication to the public

With the legally mandated communication to the public of copyright-protected content by the service provider, the question of **copyright liability is of decisive importance**. In order to compensate for the fiction of the act of use, the legislator of the directive has established a **specific liability concept** that enables the service provider not to be responsible for his own communication to the public. In this context, the 'specific liability regime'[44] of Art. 17 DSM Dir first provides that the service provider makes his own communication to the public, for which he needs to have permission (Art. 17(1) DSM Dir). If he cannot rely on rights of use or on limitations, the service provider is liable if he has not made **best efforts** to prevent copyright infringing content on his platform. Limited obligations apply to start-ups (Art. 17(6) DSM Dir). The details of this liability concept in Art. 17(4) DSM Dir are presented in more detail below. 23

1. No liability privilege

Art. 17(3) subpara. 1 DSM Dir declares Art. 14 E-Commerce Directive[45] inapplicable if there is an act of communication to the public by the service provider. However, this **exclusion only applies within the scope of application of Art. 17 DSM Dir**, i.e. only for the purposes of liability due to the communication to the public of content uploaded by users. Art. 17(3) subpara. 2 DSM Dir clarifies that the privilege of liability under Art. 14 E-Commerce Directive continues to apply for purposes outside the scope of Art. 17 DSM Dir.[46] With regard to content that infringes other intellectual property rights or personal rights, for example, the service provider can continue to invoke Art. 14 E-Commerce Directive and Art. 6 DSA respectively.[47] The same applies to copyright issues that do not concern the communication to the public. 24

2. Best efforts for obtaining an authorisation from the rights holder

In accordance with general copyright principles, the service provider's communication to the public is **lawful if it is authorised**. Art. 17(1) subpara. 2 DSM Dir clarifies that the service provider must in principle seek permission from the right holder. 25

a) Types of authorisation

It is in line with the intention of Art. 17 DSM Dir to promote a market for the granting of rights of use.[48] However, the term **'authorization' is to be understood broadly**. 26

---

[44] CJEU 26.4.2022 – C-401/19, ECLI:EU:C:2022:297 = GRUR 2022, 820 para. 34 – Poland v. Parliament.

[45] Directive 2000/31/EC of the European Parliament and of the Council of 8.6.2000 on certain legal aspects of information society services, in particular electronic commerce, in the Internal Market, OJ 2000 L 178, 1 (16).

[46] In a systematic and teleological interpretation, the exclusion of the liability privilege of Art. 17(3) DSM Dir is only limited to communication to the public pursuant to Art. 17(1) DSM Dir. The wording 'for purposes falling outside the scope of this Directive' used in Art. 17(3) DSM Dir is too broad.

[47] Art. 14 E-Commerce Directive is replaced by Art. 6 DSA, without this entailing a change in the liability privilege.

[48] Rec. 61 DSM Dir.

Art. 17 DSM Dir does not define the term, but rec. 64 suggests that a licensing agreement is only one of several possibilities.[49] Art. 17 DSM Dir does not otherwise prescribe what a permission should look like. It is therefore possible to seek authorisations that do not constitute 'genuine' rights of use agreements. In this respect, there is a 'tree of permissions'.[50] Consent or retrospective authorisation by the right holder are also conceivable and make the unlawfulness of an encroachment on copyright cease to exist.

27 It is up to the respective parties whether and what **consideration** is agreed upon for **a permission.** By no means does this always have to involve **money.** For example, the transfer of **data sets** from the service provider, from which the rights holder can draw valuable insights for his own economic development, may in certain cases be far more important to the rights holder than monetary remuneration. It is also conceivable to offer other valuable consideration instead of money, such as an **advertising opportunity** on the platform.[51] Of course, a rights holder can also allow the use of his works **free of charge**, for example on the basis of a Creative Commons licence.[52] The rights holder's permission must also be assumed if he uses the service himself or commissions a third party to place his works there for public access.

28 Insofar as users have permission from the rights holder, this extends to the service provider.[53] According to the meaning and purpose of the liability concept, the service provider is not liable if the user can invoke a relevant limitation provision.[54]

b) No obligation to contract

29 Art. 17 DSM Dir does not provide for any obligation to contract. The rights holder is **not restricted in** his **contractual freedom**; he is not obliged to grant permissions to use his content on online content sharing services.[55] There may be good reasons why rights holders want to keep their content off platforms, for example, in order not to torpedo primary exploitation via other channels. An exception to the contractual freedom of rights holders applies – as elsewhere – to collecting societies insofar as they are subject to an obligation to conclude agreements (cf. § 34 VGG). Similarly, the service provider's obligation to obtain permission cannot be enforced. The efforts of the service provider must therefore be correctly qualified as an **obligation,** not as a statutory duty in the narrow sense that could be enforced.[56] The service provider is free to fulfil this obligation. However, failure to do so can lead to legal disadvantages for the service provider – specifically to possible liability for copyright infringements through uploads by its users.

c) 'Best efforts' in the absence of permission

30 Even if there is no permission from the rights holder for the communication to the public by the service provider, it does not follow that the service provider is liable for this

---

[49] Rec. 64 DSM Dir: 'Consequently, online content-sharing service providers should obtain an authorisation, including via a licensing agreement, from the relevant rightholders'.

[50] The term was coined by Ohly, p. 41 et seq., cf. also Ohly in Schricker/Loewenheim UrhG § 29 mn. 23.

[51] Cf. European Commission, 'Guidance on Article 17 of Directive 2019/790 on Copyright in the Digital Single Market', 4.6.2021, COM(2021) 288 final, 6.

[52] Cf. European Commission, 'Guidance on Article 17 of Directive 2019/790 on Copyright in the Digital Single Market', 4.6.2021, COM(2021) 288 final, 6.

[53] Rec. 69 DSM Dir.

[54] See for the German UrhDaG BT-Drs. 19/27426, 132, 136; rec. 69 DSM Dir does not contain any restriction that the authorisation for the user only works in favour of the service provider if it is a licence agreement.

[55] Clarifying CJEU 26.4.2022 – case C-401/19, ECLI:EU:C:2022:297 = GRUR 2022, 820 – Republic of Poland v European Parliament and Council of the European Union.

[56] Cf. for the UrhDaG BT-Drs. 19/27426, 132.

reason alone. Art. 17(4)(a) DSM Dir provides that the service provider must **only make 'best efforts'**[57] to obtain permission. This is linked to considerations of proportionality. Art. 17 DSM Dir does not define the term 'best efforts' and only gives few indications as to when negotiations between the parties meet this standard. Only rec. 61 offers an outlook on the objectives of such negotiations; they should produce 'just solutions and a fair balance between the two parties' and constitute 'adequate remuneration'.[58] It is always necessary to consider the **individual case.**[59] Both the Commission in its guidance and the German legislator with the national implementation of Art. 17 DSM Dir through the UrhDaG offer various **consideration criteria** worthy of attention. Firstly, it can be taken into account which of the parties should take the first step towards negotiations. This may vary according to the **size and prominence of the respective right holders.**[60] Service providers cannot be expected and it is simply not possible to know or track down all right holders. Furthermore, the **scope and nature of the content** available on the platform should play a decisive role in the negotiations (cf. § 4(2) no. 1 UrhDaG).[61] If a service is designed to reproduce and communicate only **excerpts and not complete works,** this must be taken into account in the negotiations and may have an impact, for example, on the amount of remuneration.[62] Furthermore, service providers must be free to decide that they do not consider certain types of content to be in line with the orientation of the platform and therefore do **not want to license but rather block them.**[63] A 'must-carry' obligation cannot be inferred from the provision.

Especially in view of the sometimes very **complex and complicated design of such agreements,** negotiations can extend over a **long period of time.** Negotiations lasting several months would already be considered speedy. In addition, the parties must also gain an overview of whether and to what extent the content on the platform is used at all. It is immediately obvious that service providers **cannot be obliged to accept permissions on unreasonable terms** (§ 4(2) no. 4 UrhDaG).[64] This, too, is an outgrowth of the **principle of proportionality**, which comprehensively underlies Art. 17 DSM Dir. 31

3. Best efforts to prevent copyright infringements

If, despite 'best efforts', the negotiations of the parties do not result in an agreement 32
allowing the use of the content on the service, and if the user's upload is not lawful either

[57] The term 'all efforts' used in the German version of the DSM Dir is to be interpreted restrictively as 'best possible efforts' in the sense of the intention of the EU legislator and according to the other language versions of the directive, see also BT-Drs. 19/27426, 132.

[58] See also European Commission, 'Guidance on Article 17 of Directive 2019/790 on Copyright in the Digital Single Market', 4.6.2021, COM(2021) 288 final, 10.

[59] European Commission, 'Guidance on Article 17 of Directive 2019/790 on Copyright in the Digital Single Market', 4.6.2021, COM(2021) 288 final, 9 et seq.

[60] Thus, § 4 (1) no. 2, 3 UrhDaG names 'representative rightholders' or collecting societies established in Germany, which the service provider must contact in principle. In this context, the Commission mentions 'easily identifiable rightholders' and 'collective management organisations', cf. European Commission, 'Guidance on Article 17 of Directive 2019/790 on Copyright in the Digital Single Market', 4.6.2021, COM(2021) 288 final, 9.

[61] European Commission, 'Guidance on Article 17 of Directive 2019/790 on Copyright in the Digital Single Market', 4.6.2021, COM(2021) 288 final, 9 et seq.

[62] Cf. for the UrhDaG Raue in Dreier/Schulze UrhDaG § 4 mn. 40; BT-Drs. 19/27426, 132.

[63] For example, a service provider whose platform specialises in texts should not be required to license videos and photos as well. This is the German implementation in § 4(2) UrhDaG, cf. BT-Drs. 19/27426, 133: 'A service provider, on the other hand, is not obliged to put content online if it is unattractive for the service provider. Moreover, there is no obligation for service providers who specialise in content of a certain genre – such as a certain genre of music – to license works of other genres'.

[64] European Commission, 'Guidance on Article 17 of Directive 2019/790 on Copyright in the Digital Single Market', 4.6.2021, COM(2021) 288 final, 10.

through a permission of the rights holder or through a relevant limitation provision, the responsibility of the service provider in the further course depends on whether it has made best efforts 'in accordance with high industry standards of professional diligence' to prevent copyright infringements on the platform. In this respect, Art. 17(4)(a)–(c) DSM Dir provides for a **graduated approach**. Insofar as the right holder provides the service provider with '**relevant and necessary information**', the service provider must prevent the works or protected subject matter from being accessible on the service (Art. 17(4)(b) DSM Dir). However, the **principle of proportionality** also applies in this respect (cf. Art. 17(5) DSM Dir). There is **no liability** in the event that copyright-infringing content is available on the platform despite the service provider having exercised the necessary diligence.[65] If no relevant and necessary information is available or if works have not been found despite 'best efforts', the service provider must act without undue delay after receiving a sufficiently substantiated notice from the right holder and remove or block the reported content from the service or block it (Art. 17(4)(c) DSM Dir).

a) Upload filters and required information

33 Art. 17(4)(b) DSM Dir fills the term 'upload filter' used in the legislative process at EU level[66] with life. For regularly, the prevention of copyright infringements in accordance with this provision will not be possible in any other way than to use **automated procedures** (based on more or less sophisticated technology) **to identify content** – insofar as they exist, e.g. for music and video.[67][68] In the CJEU annulment proceedings,[69] which dealt with this very provision, no party to the proceedings was able to show how Art. 17(4)(b) DSM Directive would work without automated procedures.[70]

34 Service providers are **free to choose the technology they use**.[71] They have the necessary and most far-reaching expertise to be able to assess which procedures are most suitable in relation to their respective service and best meet the requirements of Art. 17(4)(b) DSM Dir against the background of proportionality and in view of the available resources and possibilities.[72] There will be situations for which suitable technology does

[65] Rec. 66 subpara. 2 sent. 4 DSM Dir; cf. for the German implementation BT-Drs. 19/27426, 137.

[66] In a statement on the DSM Dir, Germany announced that it wanted to prevent upload filters in the implementation if possible, cf. Council of the EU, 'Draft Directive of the European Parliament and of the Council on copyright related rights in the Digital Single Market and amending Directives 96/9/EC and 2001/29/EC (first reading) – adoption of the legislative act – Statements', 15.4.2019, 7986/19 ADD 1 REV 2, 2 (Statement by Germany, point 2); see also Metzger/Pravemann ZUM 2021, 288 (289).

[67] European Commission, 'Impact Assessment on the modernisation of EU copyright rules', 26.4.2018, SWD(2016) 301 final, 140 et seq.

[68] CJEU 26.4.2022 – case C-401/19, ECLI:EU:C:2022:297 = GRUR 2022, 820 para. 54 – Republic of Poland v European Parliament and Council of the European Union; for the German transposition cf. BT-Drs. 19/27426, 137.

[69] CJEU 26.4.2022 – case C-401/19, ECLI:EU:C:2022:297 = GRUR 2022, 820 – Republic of Poland v European Parliament and Council of the European Union.

[70] CJEU 26.4.2022 – case C-401/19, ECLI:EU:C:2022:297 = GRUR 2022, 820 = para. 54 – Republic of Poland v European Parliament and Council of the European Union.

[71] CJEU 26.4.2022 – case C-401/19, ECLI:EU:C:2022:297 = GRUR 2022, 820 para. 75 – Republic of Poland v European Parliament and Council of the European Union; European Commission, 'Guidance on Article 17 of Directive 2019/790 on Copyright in the Digital Single Market', 4.6.2021, COM(2021) 288 final, 12.

[72] Thus CJEU 26.4.2022 – case C-401/19, ECLI:EU:C:2022:297 = GRUR 2022, 820 para. 75 – Republic of Poland v European Parliament and Council of the European Union; see also European Commission, 'Guidance on Article 17 of Directive 2019/790 on Copyright in the Digital Single Market', 4.6.2021, COM(2021) 288 final, 12 et seq.

not yet exist.[73] Service providers can monitor and drive technical developments, so that the state of the art may be assessed differently today than in the future.[74] In addition, the **measures** used must be **strictly target-oriented** and must not go beyond what is necessary; in particular, they must not result in lawful content being unavailable.[75] Furthermore, rights holders do not always have the same needs. For example, rights holders may only have certain rights for which certain solutions are particularly suitable, so that **different systems** can be offered.[76] For this balancing act, service providers are to be granted leeway precisely via **proportionality**, within which different technologies can be tried out and refined. Art. 17(5) DSM Dir explicitly provides for this principle of proportionality. In this respect, the **total costs** incurred by service providers due to the filtering technologies used must also be taken into account.[77]

In order to use upload filters, information is needed to search for matching content on a service. This **information depends on the technology used**, so that different service providers may need different information.[78] If systems are used that require **reference files**, for example, the rights holder must provide them.[79] 35

In addition, correct **information about the work and the ownership of the rights** to it is necessary.[80] This includes that rights holders specifically designate the rights on which they rely. This is because rights holders often assert derivative rights. The scope of such derivative rights is determined by the agreements between the author and the rights holder, which the service provider does not know. Accordingly, it is imperative to **specifically set out the rights in terms of space, time and content** and, if the service provider has doubts, to prove them. A simple assertion that one has acquired exclusive rights of use does not suffice. 36

Art. 17(4)(b) DSM Dir depends on the **cooperation of the parties**. If rights holders do not provide the necessary information, service providers cannot take action. Liability is then ruled out from the outset.[81] 37

For small **start-ups**[82], the obligations under Art. 17(4)(b) DSM Dir do not apply in accordance with Art. 17(6) DSM Dir. 38

b) User rights

The use of automated technologies carries the **particular risk of unjustified restriction of users' freedom of expression and information** if lawful content is mistakenly blocked (**'overblocking'**).[83] Art. 17(7) subpara. 1 DSM Dir clarifies that efforts to take action against copyright-infringing content on a service must not result in lawful con- 39

---

[73] Cf. European Commission, 'Guidance on Article 17 of Directive 2019/790 on Copyright in the Digital Single Market', 4.6.2021, COM(2021) 288 final, 13.

[74] Cf. Rec. 66 para. 2 DSM Dir.

[75] CJEU 26.4.2022 – case C-401/19, ECLI:EU:C:2022:297 = GRUR 2022, 820 para. 81 – Republic of Poland v European Parliament and Council of the European Union; Rec. 66 para. 2 DSM Dir.

[76] Cf. European Commission, 'Guidance on Article 17 of Directive 2019/790 on Copyright in the Digital Single Market', 4.6.2021, COM(2021) 288 final, 12 et seq.

[77] European Commission, 'Guidance on Article 17 of Directive 2019/790 on Copyright in the Digital Single Market', 4.6.2021, COM(2021) 288 final, 13 et seq.

[78] European Commission, 'Guidance on Article 17 of Directive 2019/790 on Copyright in the Digital Single Market', 4.6.2021, COM(2021) 288 final, 14.

[79] Cf. Rec. 66 para. 3 DSM Dir.

[80] European Commission, 'Guidance on Article 17 of Directive 2019/790 on Copyright in the Digital Single Market', 4.6.2021, COM(2021) 288 final, 14.

[81] Rec. 66 para. 5 DSM Dir.

[82] See calculation in Art. 17(6) DSM Dir.

[83] See ECJ 26.4.2022 – case C-401/19, ECLI:EU:C:2022:297 = GRUR 2022, 820 para. 68 – Republic of Poland v European Parliament and Council of the European Union.

tent being unavailable. Once again, the **multipolar tension** that Art. 17 DSM Dir seeks to balance becomes apparent. In order to take due account of users' positions, Art. 17(7) subpara. 2 DSM Dir introduces a mandatory EU-wide limitation on quotations, criticism and reviews, as well as on use for the purpose of caricature, parody or pastiche. In this context, the CJEU explicitly speaks of the **rights of users**;[84] also linguistically, the perspective of users in the multipolar environment thus comes more strongly to bear. In this respect, the aim of Art. 17 DSM Dir is to create a **balance** between the right to intellectual property on the one hand and freedom of expression and information on the other.[85] The fact that service providers are obliged to **inform users in their general terms and conditions** that copyright-protected subject matter may be used under exceptions and limitations provided for in EU law (Art. 17(9) subpara. 4 DSM Dir) is a further piece in the mosaic of the legislator's efforts to actually achieve the desired balance.

40 Due to the great importance of freedom of expression and information, the regulations concerning upload filters must be brought into line with the requirements for the protection of users. In this context, the Commission even assumes a duty in favour of users, according to which an inadmissible restriction of user rights must be prevented under all circumstances.[86] Precisely because technology can find so-called 'matches' but cannot recognise whether content is illegal or lawful, **automated filtering technologies** must be used **cautiously.**[87] Moreover, the use of a technology that extensively blocks content without being able to sufficiently distinguish between unlawful and lawful content is not compatible with the fundamental rights of the Union.[88]

41 The Commission suggests that the use of upload filters should be **limited to content that is manifestly infringing copyright.**[89] All other content should first be put online and be subject to a subsequent review of its illegality. Criteria for obviously infringing content could be, for example, the length or size of a work in the uploaded content or the proportion of matching content in relation to the total uploaded content.[90] In contrast, non-manifestly infringing content can be content that only partially matches the required information of the right holders or that only shows a small excerpt of the entire work.[91] With the '**presumptively permitted uses**', the German legislator has created a detailed regulatory system that takes into account the balance of the different fundamental rights and interests involved (§§ 9 et seq. UrhDaG).[92]

42 In order to further strengthen users' rights, Art. 17(9) DSM Dir provides for **procedural safeguards** to enable users to take action against blocking of their content.[93] Ser-

---

[84] ECJ 26.4.2022 – case C-401/19, ECLI:EU:C:2022:297 = GRUR 2022, 820 para. 86 – Republic of Poland v European Parliament and Council of the European Union.

[85] Rec. 70 para. 1 DSM Dir.

[86] European Commission, 'Guidance on Article 17 of Directive 2019/790 on Copyright in the Digital Single Market', 4.6.2021, COM(2021) 288 final, 20.

[87] European Commission, 'Guidance on Article 17 of Directive 2019/790 on Copyright in the Digital Single Market', 4.6.2021, COM(2021) 288 final, 20.

[88] ECJ 26.4.2022 – case C-401/19, ECLI:EU:C:2022:297 = GRUR 2022, 820 para. 86 – Republic of Poland v European Parliament and Council of the European Union.

[89] '[…] automated blocking, i.e. preventing the upload by the use of technology, should in principle be limited to manifestly infringing uploads', European Commission, 'Guidance on Article 17 of Directive 2019/790 on Copyright in the Digital Single Market', 4.6.2021, COM(2021) 288 final, 20.

[90] European Commission, 'Guidance on Article 17 of Directive 2019/790 on Copyright in the Digital Single Market', 4.6.2021, COM(2021) 288 final, 21 et seq., where the Commission gives further examples of how to identify manifestly infringing content.

[91] European Commission, 'Guidance on Article 17 of Directive 2019/790 on Copyright in the Digital Single Market', 4.6.2021, COM(2021) 288 final, 21, with further examples.

[92] In detail Barudi in Barudi § 1 mn. 108 et seq.

[93] See also CJEU 26.4.2022 – case C-401/19, ECLI:EU:C:2022:297 = GRUR 2022, 820 para. 93 – Republic of Poland v European Parliament and Council of the European Union.

vice providers must provide effective and speedy **complaint and redress procedures.** In addition, judicial redress is also possible. The Commission and the German legislator provide for detailed notification and information procedures that include both users and rights holders.[94]

c) Sufficiently substantiated notice

Upload filters are only one element in preventing copyright infringement. Such systems are not perfect and they cannot distinguish lawful uses from unlawful content with absolute accuracy and without error; **technology has limits.**[95] Moreover, there may be situations and areas where appropriate technology does not (yet) exist (→ mn. 34). The DSM Dir emphasises that illegal content may under some circumstances only be blocked if the rights holders have notified the service provider.[96] As rights holders are not obliged to provide the relevant and necessary information required for the use of automated filtering systems, such rights holders can only expect an *ex post* action from the outset. In all these situations, protected subject matter may be found on a service that a rights holder wants removed. 43

In order to undertake 'best efforts', Art. 17(4)(c) DSM Dir therefore provides, as a '**minimum protection**' provision, that a service provider must react if it has received a sufficiently substantiated notice of copyright-infringing content from the rights holder. 44

It follows from this, on the one hand, that a notice from the entitled person is required. According to the clear wording, any **information from third parties is not sufficient.** This is also true according to the meaning and purpose of the provision, because only the rights holder knows what the scope of his rights is and whether content that can be found on the service infringes those rights. A third party may not know whether permission exists for the reported content. 45

Furthermore, a **notice must be sufficiently substantiated.** The standard for this is strict, especially against the background of the **necessary balancing of the fundamental rights involved**. The rights holder has a constitutionally protected interest in having copyright-infringing content removed quickly. However, the service provider is not obliged, on the basis of his entrepreneurial freedom, to carry out elaborate research on the factual and legal situation himself. And users have interests protected by fundamental rights that their lawful content is not blocked as a result of reports of possible copyright infringements. Therefore, the CJEU has stated that the notice 'must contain sufficient information to enable the online content-sharing service provider to satisfy itself, **without a detailed legal examination**, that the communication of the **content at issue is illegal** and that **removing that content is compatible with freedom of expression and information**'.[97] The Commission also stresses that the notice must be 'sufficiently precise and adequately substantiated' and enable the service provider to 'take an informed and diligent decision in respect of the content to which the notice relates, in particular whether or not that content is to be considered illegal content'.[98] This also in- 46

[94] For more details see European Commission, 'Guidance on Article 17 of Directive 2019/790 on Copyright in the Digital Single Market', 4.6.2021, COM(2021) 288 final, 24 et seq.; on the UrhDaG see Barudi in Barudi § 1 mn. 108 et seq.

[95] Cf. European Commission, 'Guidance on Article 17 of Directive 2019/790 on Copyright in the Digital Single Market', 4.6.2021, COM(2021) 288 final, 15.

[96] Rec. 66 para. 2 DSM Dir.

[97] CJEU 26.4.2022 – case C-401/19, ECLI:EU:C:2022:297 = GRUR 2022, 820 para. 91 – Republic of Poland v European Parliament and Council of the European Union.

[98] European Commission, 'Guidance on Article 17 of Directive 2019/790 on Copyright in the Digital Single Market', 4.6.2021, COM(2021) 288 final, 16.

cludes a statement of reasons 'why the notice provider considers that content to be illegal', as well as the exact location of the content.[99] This **standard** follows the principle that **already** applied **before the DSM Dir came into force.**[100] In its judgment on *YouTube* and *Cyando* on Art. 3 InfoSoc Dir and Art. 14 E-Commerce Directive, the CJEU explicitly refers to the opinion of Advocate General *Saugmandsgaard Øe,* who deals in detail with the requirements for a notice. According to this, the notice must be so specific that the illegality is 'apparent' in the sense of being manifest.[101] The service provider should not have to decide complicated legal questions and should **not act as a 'judge of online legality'**.[102] Otherwise, there would be a considerable risk of overblocking.[103] In copyright law in particular, assessing the illegality of content requires a range of **contextual information** to be communicated by the rights holder. This includes that the notice specifically identifies the protected work and describes the infringement complained of in a substantiated manner; furthermore, it must provide sufficiently clear indications of the rights that the notifying party claims to have; and the notice must contain adequate explanations as to why a copyright exception or limitation cannot be considered.[104]

47 If there is a sufficiently substantiated notice, the service provider must act **'expeditiously'** and block or remove the content in question (**'take down'**). Insofar as Art. 17(4)(c) DSM Dir also states that the service provider must make 'best efforts' to prevent the future uploading of the works or subject-matter, this is a reference to the requirements in lit. b. It follows that the service provider can only act if it obtains the relevant and necessary information required under Art. 17(4)(b). Both the CJEU and the Commission clarify that action by the service provider beyond the take-down is only prompted if rights holders have provided him with the 'relevant and necessary information'.[105] The German legislator has implemented this in the UrhDaG in this differentiated manner (cf. § 8(1), (3) UrhDaG).[106]

4. Burden of presentation and proof

48 Art. 17(4) DSM Dir basically requires the service provider to demonstrate and prove that it is not responsible for the communication to the public.[107] However, this **distribution of the burden of proof** must be **assessed in a differentiated manner** on closer ex-

---

[99] European Commission, 'Guidance on Article 17 of Directive 2019/790 on Copyright in the Digital Single Market', 4.6.2021, COM(2021) 288 final, 16.

[100] Cf. CJEU 22.6.2021 – joined cases C-682/18 and C-683/18, ECLI:EU:C:2021:503 = GRUR 2021, 1054 para. 116 – Frank Peterson v Google LLC and Others and Elsevier Inc.v Cyando AG; see for German law BGH 2.6.2022 – I ZR 140/15, GRUR 2022, 1308 (1320) para. 114 et seq. – YouTube II.

[101] AG Saugmandsgaard Øe 16.7.2020 – joined cases C-682/18 and C-683/18, ECLI:EU:C:2020:586 = GRUR-RS 2020, 18772 para. 187 – Frank Peterson v Google LLC and Others and Elsevier Inc.v Cyando AG.

[102] AG Saugmandsgaard Øe 16.7.2020 – joined cases C-682/18 and C-683/18, ECLI:EU:C:2020:586 = GRUR-RS 2020, 18772 para. 187 – Frank Peterson v Google LLC and Others and Elsevier Inc.v Cyando AG.

[103] 'Over-cautionary removal', see AG Saugmandsgaard Øe 16.7.2020 – joined cases C-682/18 and C-683/18, ECLI:EU:C:2020:586 = GRUR-RS 2020, 18772 para. 190 – Frank Peterson v Google LLC and Others and Elsevier Inc.v Cyando AG.

[104] See AG Saugmandsgaard Øe 16.7.2020 – joined cases C-682/18 and C-683/18, ECLI:EU:C:2020:586 = GRUR-RS 2020, 18772 para. 190 – Frank Peterson v Google LLC and Others and Elsevier Inc.v Cyando AG.

[105] CJEU 26.4.2022 – case C-401/19, ECLI:EU:C:2022:297 = GRUR 2022, 820 para. 89 – Republic of Poland v European Parliament and Council of the European Union; European Commission, 'Guidance on Article 17 of Directive 2019/790 on Copyright in the Digital Single Market', 4.6.2021, COM(2021) 288 final, 16.

[106] BT-Drs. 19/27426, 138.

[107] Cf. also Rec. 66 para. 3 DSM Dir.

amination. Many of the aspects mentioned in Art. 17(4) DSM Dir are not within the sphere of perception of the service provider. For example, the service provider cannot know which rights holder has which specific rights. With regard to the negotiations on a licence, it is therefore incumbent on the rights holder to demonstrate his legal status as well as his ability to effectively conclude corresponding agreements. The same applies to the appropriateness of the conditions for offered rights of use. The situation is similar with regard to the requirements for a sufficiently substantiated notice, because in this respect it is also incumbent on the rights holder to present the legal situation as well as any limitations.

V. Relationship between Art. 17 DSM Dir and the DSA

With the Digital Services Act (DSA), copyright regulations concerning hosting services are also updated at EU level and expanded to include new requirements. The scope of the DSA is regulated in its Art. 2. There it is clarified that the **Union provisions in the field of copyright and related rights** remain **unaffected by the DSA** (Art. 2(4)(b) DSA). In addition, the DSA explicitly emphasises in rec. 11 that its provisions do not affect the DSM Dir. Insofar as a service provider falls within the scope of application of Art. 2 no. 6, Art. 17 DSM Dir, these provisions conclusively regulate the responsibility for copyright matters concerning communication to the public.[108] 49

For **hosting services that are not service providers** within the meaning of Art. 2 no. 6, 17 DSM Dir, the previous case law of the CJEU on Art. 3 InfoSoc Dir, i.e. in particular the *YouTube* and *Cyando* judgement[109] as well as the liability privileges stemming from Union law continue to apply. Art. 14 of the E-Commerce Directive is replaced by Art. 6 of the DSA.[110] 50

To the extent that the DSA provides for other rules for hosting services that do not address the specifics of the DSM Directive, those rules shall apply to the services. 51

C. Protection of press publications (Art. 15 DSM Dir)

I. Introduction

Art. 15 DSM Dir provides that press publishers receive an **independent right of exploitation** as a related right. Although there are **no international requirements** for this provision,[111] it is modelled on the **German press publisher protection law,** which was introduced in 2013.[112] Sometimes referred to as the 'Lex Google'[113], the German initiative was overturned by the CJEU in its *VG Media* ruling in 2019 after the Court found that the press publisher protection rules should have been notified.[114] The national regulations were inapplicable because of this ruling. 52

[108] Janal GRUR 2022, 211 (217) speaks of 'clear alternatives'; differentiating Raue ZUM 2023, 160.

[109] CJEU 22.6.2021 – joined cases C-682/18 and C-683/18, ECLI:EU:C:2021:503 = GRUR 2021, 1054 – Frank Peterson v Google LLC and Others and Elsevier Inc.v Cyando AG.

[110] The reference in Art. 17(3) DSM Dir will be to Art. 6 DSA instead of Art. 14 E-Commerce-RL.

[111] Dreier in Dreier/Schulze UrhG § 87 et seq mn. 1.

[112] On the history of the national press publisher protection law see Spiegel in Barudi § 5 mn. 1 et seq.

[113] Kahl MMR 2013, 348 (349).

[114] ECJ 12.9.2019 – case C-299/17, ECLI:EU:C:2019:716 = GRUR 2019, 1188 – VG Media Gesellschaft zur Verwertung der Urheber- und Leistungsschutzrechte von Medienunternehmen mbH v Google LLC.

53 In connection with the efforts to modernise copyright and related rights, the EU legislator took the opportunity to roll out the press publisher protection law at EU level, which had been frequently criticised at German national level and failed in the end.[115] Art. 15 DSM Dir provides for **full harmonisation.**[116]

54 The legislator justifies the idea of extending a press publisher protection right to all Member States – despite the low level of acceptance at national level – with the need to safeguard 'quality journalism' and 'a free and pluralistic press'.[117] There are 'problems in licensing the online use' of press products by online aggregators.[118] Finally, it is also a matter of recognising 'the organisational and financial contribution' of press publishers.[119] However, not everyone is convinced by these **justifications.**[120]

II. Object of protection

55 The previous protection for press publishers consisted mainly of derived rights of their authors. Art. 15 DSM Dir gives them their **own right to remuneration**. This is limited to the **online use of press publications.**

56 The **term 'press publication'** is defined in Art. 2 no. 4 sent. 1 DSM Dir. According to this, a press publication is 'a collection composed mainly of literary works of a journalistic nature, but which can also include other works or other subject matter, and which: (a) constitutes an individual item within a periodical or regularly updated publication under a single title, such as a newspaper or a general or special interest magazine; (b) has the purpose of providing the general public with information related to news or other topics; and (c) is published in any media under the initiative, editorial responsibility and control of a service provider'.

57 **Difficulties of demarcation** exist above all with contributions of a 'journalistic nature' from those that are not covered by the definition.[121] Publications published for scientific or academic purposes are expressly excluded (Art. 2 no. 4 sent. 2 DSM Dir). Scientific publishers generally do not benefit from this related right for the academic journals they publish.[122]

58 Press releases are **protected for** a **period of two years** after publication (Art. 15(4) DSM Dir).[123]

---

[115] Cf. on the lack of necessity of such a property right from an economic perspective Suwelack MMR 2018, 582 (583 et seq.); on the criticism in general cf. Schack ZUM 2020, 165 with further references; Stieper ZUM 2019, 211 (214 et seq.).

[116] Rec. 55 DSM Dir; Spiegel in Barudi § 5 mn. 5; Jani ZUM 2019, 674 (675).

[117] Rec. 54 DSM Dir.

[118] Rec. 54 DSM Dir.

[119] Rec. 55 DSM Dir.

[120] Cf. only Stieper ZUM 2019, 211 (214 et seq.); Schack ZUM 2020, 165 (166).

[121] Cf. Spindler CR 2019, 277 (282); Spiegel in Barudi § 5 mn. 9.

[122] In individual cases, journals which are not only addressed to the professional public but to the general public may fall within the scope of application, cf. Spiegel in Barudi § 5 mn. 13; Spindler CR 2019, 277 (282).

[123] The cut-off date for the beginning of the period shall be 1st January of the year following the date of publication of the press release.

III. Exploitation rights and limitations

The right of press publishers is specifically directed against providers of information society services.[124] **Online news aggregators** and **media monitoring services** are to be covered.[125] 59

Insofar as a press publication exists, the press publisher enjoys the exploitation **rights of reproduction** (Art. 15(1)(1) DSM Dir in conjunction with Art. 2 InfoSoc Dir) and of **making available to the public** (Art. 15(1)(1) DSM Dir in conjunction with Art. 3(2) InfoSoc Dir) within the framework of 'online use'. Compared to the previous national regulation, the right of reproduction constitutes an extension of the right.[126] 60

However, the exploitation rights of the press publisher are **not affected if only individual words or very short extracts** are used (Art. 15(1) subpara. 4 DSM Dir).[127] It was already unclear for the former German statute what still constituted 'very short extracts'.[128] In any case, protection for 'pure facts' cannot be sought.[129] For the delimitation, one will have to check with rec. 58 in each individual case from which length the use of the excerpt impairs the investment interests of the press publisher.[130] It would be unjustifiable to include small word phrases that neither enjoy copyright protection nor reflect the investments of the press publisher in the protection. In this respect, there would be a **danger of monopolising precisely facts that are not protected, at least in part**, if the facts cannot be conveyed in any other way than in just that word phrase. In any case, the scope of protection must be limited to the specifically defined representation.[131] 61

Furthermore, **private or non-commercial use** by individual users is excluded from the exploitation rights (Art. 15(2)(2) DSM Dir). Likewise, the right cannot be asserted with regard to setting a **hyperlink** (Art. 15(1) subpara. 3 DSM Dir). The latter takes into account the idea that hyperlinks are 'necessary for the proper functioning of the Internet'[132]. 62

Furthermore, the other **provisions on limitations** under **copyright law** according to Art. 5 InfoSoc Dir are also applicable to the law on the protection of press publishers (Art. 15(3) DSM Dir). 63

IV. Outlook

Whether the press publisher protection law now introduced at EU level will be successful remains to be seen. The parties struggle to **find reasonable solutions** for 64

---

[124] For delimitation in individual cases, see Spiegel in Barudi § 5 mn. 19 et seq.

[125] Cf. rec. 54 DSM Dir.

[126] Cf. Spiegel in Barudi § 5 mn. 25.

[127] For a comprehensive discussion of the national implementation, see Spiegel in Barudi § 5 mn. 38 et seq.

[128] OLG München 14.7.2016 – 29 U 953/16, GRUR-RR 2017, 89; Spindler CR 2019, 277 (283); Schippan ZUM 2013, 358 (372).

[129] Rec. 57 DSM Dir.

[130] Cf. for the German implementation BT-Drs. 19/27426, 113.

[131] If the press publisher's investment is the foundation of this property right, a comparison with the justification of the phonogram producer's right is obvious. According to this, the phonogram producer enjoys protection for his investment in the initial recording. The phonogram producer's right does not grant protection against the recording being re-created by a third party by re-recording a piece of music and thus creating another sound recording, cf. BVerfG 31.5.2016 – 1 BvR 1585/13, GRUR 2016, 690 (694) para. 97 et seq. – Metall auf Metall; BGH 20.11.2008 – I ZR 112/06, GRUR 2009, 403 (405) para. 17 – Metall auf Metall I; Vogel in Schricker/Loewenheim UrhG § 85 mn. 25; Schulze in Dreier/Schulze UrhG § 85 mn. 34.

[132] CJEU 9.3.2021 – case C-392/19, ECLI:EU:C:2021:181 = GRUR 2021, 706 para. 49 – VG Bild-Kunst v Stiftung Preußischer Kulturbesitz.

appropriate remuneration. At the German level, the Arbitration Board of the German Patent and Trademark Office was called in mid-2022 to mediate in the negotiation conflict between service providers and press publishers.[133] Google announced that as of June 2023 it had entered into more than 1,500 agreements in 15 Member States covering publications on the EU level; and that Corint Media and Google found an interim agreement.[134]

[133] Editorial team of beck-aktuell, 'Urheberrecht: Schiedsstelle in Streit zwischen Corint Media und Google eingeschaltet' (beck-aktuell, 22.7.2022) < becklink 2024093> (last accessed: 12.3.2024) – on the dispute between Corint Media and Google; Gitta Kharraz, 'Urheberrecht: Corint Media schaltet wegen Microsoft Schiedsstelle ein' (beck-aktuell, 8.6.2022) <becklink 2023485> (last accessed: 12.3.2024) – on the dispute between Corint Media and Microsoft.

[134] Rabenstein, 'An update on our implementation of the press ancillary copyright in Germany' (Google Blog, 12.10.2023) <blog.google/intl/de-de/unternehmen/engagement/presseleistungsschutzrecht-google-corint-media-einigung-mehrjaehrige-interimsvereinbarung/> (last accessed: 12.3.2024).

§ 23
The European Regulation on the Transparency and Targeting of Political Advertising

Literature: *Bayer*, 'The Proposal for a Regulation on transparency and targeting of political advertising – The educated citizenry', MMR 2022, 535; *Di Fabio*, 'Transparenz politischer Werbung', MMR 2024, 467; *Egidy*, 'Microtargeting politischer Werbung in der europäischen Demokratie Regulierungsbedarf und Regulierungsansätze', ZG 2022, 334; *Mehlhorn*, 'Transparenz und Targeting – Die Pläne der EU zur Regulierung politischer Werbung', NVwZ 2023, 1388.

A. Introduction

1 Since the revelations about Cambridge Analytica[1], a company that obtained millions of Facebook users' personal data without their consent and used it for targeted **political advertising**[2] with the aim of **influencing voters**, the **potential danger** of political

[1] Cadwalladr/Graham-Harrison, 'Revealed: 50 million Facebook profiles harvested for Cambridge Analytica in major data breach' (The Guardian, 17.03.2018) <https://www.theguardian.com/news/2018/mar/17/cambridge-analytica-facebook-influence-us-election> (last accessed: 14.8.2024); Bump, 'Everything you need to know about the Cambridge Analytica-Facebook debacle' (The Washington Post, 19.03.2018) <https://www.washingtonpost.com/news/politics/wp/2018/03/19/everything-you-need-to-know-about-the-cambridge-analytica-facebook-debacle/> (last accessed: 14.8.2024).

[2] In particular, in the context of the 2016 US election campaign and the UK's Brexit referendum.

advertising combined with **new technical possibilities** for the **democratic process** of an election has become part of the collective consciousness. The same applies to the risk of **interference in elections** by certain third-country entities or third-country nationals[3], including the **(mis)use of disinformation**.

2 However, in the past, **union law** did not provide a comprehensive solution to those risks. As a result, many member states had their own national rules on political advertising, resulting in a high degree of legal fragmentation within the EU.[4] Furthermore, these national regulations tended to focus on traditional media.[5] This situation resulted in **loopholes** that allow political advertising to be disseminated without complying with the relevant national rules. It also led to **legal uncertainty**[6] that may have discouraged especially smaller providers of political advertising services from providing their services across borders.[7]

3 To address those risks and misguided development, on 25 November 2021, the Commission presented a **proposal** for the **Regulation on the Transparency and Targeting of Political Advertising**[8] as part of its **Action Plan for Democracy**[9], which aims to promote **free and fair elections** and **strong democratic participation**.[10] After some amendments during the legislative process, the European Parliament[11] and the Council[12] adopted the Regulation on the Transparency and Targeting of Political Advertising (hereinafter referred to as 'Political Advertising Regulation' or 'PAR'), which is particularly based on Art. 16(2) and 114 TFEU, in March 2024.[13]

4 According to Art. 30(1) PAR, the Political Advertising Regulation **entered into force on 9 April 2024**, following its publication in the Official Journal[14]. However, against the Commission's initial plan[15], due to delays in the legislative process **almost**[16] **all provisions** will **only apply from 10 October 2025**, as stated in Art. 30(2) PAR, and were therefore not applicable to the European elections in 2024.

5 Despite the delayed application, platform providers should already have the PAR under review, as its **scope of application** extends far beyond the European elections

[3] Rec. 19(1)(1) of the Regulation (EU) 2024/900 of the European Parliament and of the Council of 13 March 2024 on the transparency and targeting of political advertising, OJ L 2024/900 ('PAR').

[4] Rec. 7(1)(1) PAR.

[5] Rec. 7(1)(1) PAR.

[6] Rec. 9 PAR.

[7] Rec. 10 PAR.

[8] European Commission, 'Proposal for a regulation of the European Parliament and of the Council on the transparency and targeting of political advertising', 3.12.2020, COM(2021) 731 final.

[9] European Commission, 'Communication from the Commission to the European Parliament, the Council, the European Economic and Social Committee and the Committee of the Regions on the European democracy action plan', 3.12.2020, COM(2020) 790 final.

[10] European Commission, 'Communication from the Commission to the European Parliament, the Council, the European Economic and Social Committee and the Committee of the Regions on the European democracy action plan', 3.12.2020, COM(2020) 790 final, p. 3; see also Mehlhorn NVwZ 2023, 1388 (1389 et seq.) who elaborates on the process of free will formation as a prerequisite for democracy.

[11] European Parliament, 'Parliament adopts new transparency rules for political advertising', press release 20240223IPR18071, 27.02.2024.

[12] Council, 'EU introduces new rules on transparency and targeting of political advertising', press release 203/24, 11.3.2024.

[13] The legality of the recourse to the internal market competence (Art. 114 TFEU) is occasionally called into question: Di Fabio MMR 2024, 467 (467 et seq.) with further references.

[14] Regulation (EU) 2024/900 of the European Parliament and of the Council of 13 March 2024 on the transparency and targeting of political advertising, OJ L 2024/900.

[15] Initially, the Commission aimed for the regulation to be applicable before the European elections in 2024.

[16] According to Art. 30(2)(1) PAR, Art. 3 and 5(1) PAR (→ mn. 28) apply from the date of the regulation's entry into force (i.e. since 9 April 2024).

and **platform providers** are likely to fall within the **personal scope of application** (→ mn. 16 et seqq.). Therefore, this chapter aims to provide an overview of the scope of application (→ mn. 6 et seqq.) and key regulatory content (→ mn. 25 et seqq.) of the Political Advertising Regulation.

B. Scope of application

The scope of application was the crucial point during the **negotiations** between the legislative bodies. In particular, **NGOs** have expressed concerns that the regulation's scope could be too broad and could affect non-commercial political statements, including those made by private individuals, which are essential for public democratic discourse.[17] The final version of the regulation now strikes a balance[18], achieved by weighing the need for **effective regulation** against the importance of **freedom of expression and the press.** 6

I. Substantive scope of application

The PAR applies, pursuant to Art. 2(1) PAR, 'to political advertising where the political advertisement is disseminated in the Union, is brought into the public domain in one or several Member States or is directed to Union citizens, irrespective of the place of establishment of the provider of political advertising services or of the place of residence or establishment of the sponsor, and irrespective of the means used'. Consequently, the **PAR's entry point** is essentially determined by the **definition of 'political advertising'**. 7

According to Art. 3 no. 2 PAR, 'political advertising' is generally defined as 'the preparation, placement, promotion, publication, delivery or dissemination, by any means, of a **message**, normally provided for **remuneration** or through in-house activities or as part of a political advertising campaign', if it is 8

- by, for or on behalf of a **political actor**, unless it is of a purely private or a purely commercial nature (Art. 3 no. 2(a) PAR), or
- liable and **designed to influence** the outcome of an election[19], voting behaviour or a legislative or regulatory process, at **Union, national, regional or local level** (Art. 3 no. 2(b) PAR).

The first part of the definition ensures that **non-commercial messages** are generally not classified as political advertising unless they are disseminated through in-house activities[20] or as part of political campaigns. This approach is mainly dedicated to the 9

[17] Holznagel, 'The EU Draft Regulation on Political Advertising Might De-Amplify Political Everyday-User Tweets – and Become a Blueprint for Stronger Online Platform Regulation' (Verfassungsblog, 23.3.2023) <https://verfassungsblog.de/political-advertising-and-disinformation/> (last accessed: 14.8.2024); ARTICLE 19, 'The implications of the proposed EU Political Advertising Regulation for freedom of expression' (ARTICLE 19, 23.8.2023) <https://www.article19.org/wp-content/uploads/2023/08/A19-The-implications-of-the-Proposed-EU-Political-Advertising-Regulation-A19_clean.pdf> (last accessed: 14.8.2024).

[18] Holznagel KuR 2/2024, Editorial.

[19] According to Rec. 31 PAR the term 'election' means 'elections to the European Parliament, all elections or referendums organised at national, regional and local level in the Member States, and elections to establish political party leadership' and does not include 'other forms of elections such as professional or privately organised ballots'.

[20] According to Rec. 24(1)(2) PAR, 'in-house activities' are 'activities carried out within an entity that comprise or substantially contribute to the preparation, placement, promotion, publication, delivery or

activities of well-resourced entities that can create and disseminate their own political advertising without the need to pay a third party (e.g. political parties doing their own data mining and targeting or advertising companies that place political ads in their own interest).[21]

10 The second part of the definition narrows the scope by requiring the message to be connected ('by, for or on behalf') to a political actor[22] or — if there is no such connection — to be able and designed to influence voters (→ mn. 12). The **connection** to a political actor may be **direct or indirect**. The decisive factor is whether the political actor would ultimately be in a position to determine the political nature, content or publication of the political advertising.[23]

11 However, even if a message is connected to a political actor, there is a counter-exception if the message's nature is **purely private** or **purely commercial**. To determine this, all relevant factors of the individual case must be considered in an overall assessment.[24] **Relevant factors** can be, for example, the message's content and sponsor, the language used to convey the message and its context, including the period of dissemination, the message's objective, and the means by which it is prepared, placed, promoted, published, delivered, or disseminated as well as the targeted audience.[25] Messages concerning a political actor's **family status** or **business activities** are likely to fall under the exception.[26]

12 If a message is not connected to a political actor in the sense described, it can still be classified as political advertising if it is cumulatively **able** (objective) and **designed** to (subjective)[27] influence the outcome of an election or referendum, voting behaviour or a legislative or regulatory process at Union, national, regional or local level. This requires a **clear and substantial link** between the message and its potential to influence[28], which must be assessed by taking into account all relevant factors (e.g. sponsor-identity, form and content, context, dissemination period, spoken or written language, etc.).[29]

13 Even if a message could be categorised as political advertising in accordance with the aforementioned explanations, Art. 1(2)–(3) PAR contains two further exceptions that take particular account of **freedom of expression** and the **editorial freedom of the media**.[30]

14 According to Art. 1(2) PAR, political opinions and other editorial content that are subject to editorial responsibility shall not be considered to be political advertising, unless **specific payment** or **other remuneration** is provided by third parties. However, when such political opinions are subsequently promoted, published, or disseminated by providers of political advertising services, they could constitute political advertising.[31]

---

dissemination, by any means, of a message which is liable and designed to influence the outcome of an election or referendum, voting behaviour or a legislative or regulatory process'.

[21] Allen, 'New EU Rules on Political Advertising Set to Have Limited Impact on Advertising Ecosystem' (Center for Democracy & Technology, 20.3.2024) <https://cdt.org/insights/new-eu-rules-on-political-advertising-set-to-have-limited-impact-on-advertising-ecosystem/> (last accessed: 14.8.2024).

[22] As defined in Art. 3 no. 4 PAR.

[23] Rec. 22(1)(2) PAR.

[24] Rec. 22(1)(5) PAR.

[25] Rec. 22(1)(5) PAR.

[26] Rec. 22(1)(6) PAR.

[27] The subjective element was deliberately incorporated into the definition during the legislative process with the intention of limiting its scope: Council, 'Outcome of proceedings', 13.12.2022, 16013/1/22 REV 1, p. 43.

[28] Rec. 23(1)(3) PAR.

[29] Rec. 23(1)(4) PAR.

[30] Art. 3 no. 2 (b)(i)–(iii) PAR contains further exceptions for messages from official sources (i), public communication that aims to provide official information (ii) and presenting candidates in specified public spaces or media (iii), subject to certain conditions.

[31] Rec. 29(1)(4) PAR.

The same applies, according to Art. 1(3) PAR, to political opinions expressed in a personal capacity. As part of the **freedom of expression**, these are generally not covered by the PAR unless specific renumeration from a third party is provided.[32] The identification of political opinions expressed in a personal capacity should normally result from **individual self-determination**.[33] However, to ensure the effectiveness of the regulation, the **plausibility** of the self-determination should be verified with other contextual elements. Such elements can include whether the opinion is issued on behalf of another entity, whether the message intends to self-promote a candidacy or campaign in an election, whether it is expressed by an individual who is generally active in campaigning or taking action for change on political or social issues, and whether the message is disseminated to an indefinite number of persons.[34] 15

II. Personal scope of application

The PAR aims to establish a **comprehensive legal framework**, with a **broadly** defined **personal scope** which covers the entirety of the political advertising value chain. This reflects the political ambition to set binding rules for all key actors in political advertising in the European Union and to eliminate existing loopholes, particularly for non-traditional media. By ensuring that all participants follow transparent and accountable practices, the PAR aims to establish fair competition in digital political communication and consequently ensure the integrity of elections. 16

Depending on the specific obligation, the PAR mainly addresses 'providers of political advertising services' (→ mn. 18 et seqq.), 'political advertising publishers' (→ mn. 22), 'sponsors' (→ mn. 23) and 'controllers' (→ mn. 24). **Online platforms** may fall under any of these terms (also at the same time), depending on the specific circumstances of each case.[35] 17

1. Provider of political advertising services, Art. 3 no. 6 PAR

Pursuant to Art. 3 no. 6 PAR, a 'provider of political advertising services' is 'a natural or legal person engaging in the provision of political advertising services, with the exception of **purely ancillary services'**. The understanding is thus based on the definition of political advertising services as defined in Art. 3 no. 5 PAR. Accordingly, a 'political advertising service' means a service consisting of political advertising, except for an **online 'intermediary service'** (→ § 2 mn. 19 et seqq.) that is provided without consideration. This excludes, for example, content uploaded by a user of an online intermediary service that is disseminated by the online intermediary service without consideration, unless the user has been remunerated by a third party for the political advertisement.[36] The same applies to the sharing of information through **electronic communication services**, such as **electronic message services** or **telephone calls**, provided that no political advertising service is involved.[37] An **indirect remuneration** of the service, for example through advertising revenue generated from users' personal data and uploads, may not be suffi- 18

---

[32] Rec. 30(1)(5) PAR; see mn. 19 for influencers.

[33] Rec. 30(1)(3) PAR.

[34] Rec. 30(1)(4) PAR.

[35] Holznagel, 'The EU Draft Regulation on Political Advertising Might De-Amplify Political Every-day-User Tweets – and Become a Blueprint for Stronger Online Platform Regulation' (Verfassungsblog, 23.3.2023) <https://verfassungsblog.de/political-advertising-and-disinformation/> (last accessed: 14.8.2024).

[36] Rec. 47(1)(2) PAR.

[37] Rec. 48 PAR.

cient, as this would circumvent the specific exemption for online intermediary services.[38]

19 The definition also covers **influencers** who receive payment for their political activities on social media. Invoking freedom of expression to avoid the obligations of the PAR is not possible.[39]

20 If a political advertising service has been identified, generally (see for the exception → mn. 21) anyone who is **engaged** in this is to be classified as a **provider** of a political advertising service. The term 'engaged' refers to providers that are involved in the preparation, placement, promotion, publication, delivery, or dissemination of political advertisements.[40] This corresponds to the definition of political advertising (→ mn. 8 et seqq.) in that it **starts early** in time, namely **during** the **preparation of political advertising**.

21 However, **'ancillary services'** are excluded and understood as additional services that complement political advertising but do not directly influence its content, presentation, or preparation (e.g. transportation, financing, sales, catering, marketing, computer services, cleaning, maintenance, postal services, printing services, and graphic, sound, or photographic design).[41] **'Mere conduit'** (→ § 2 mn. 26 et seqq.) and **'caching' services** (→ § 2 mn. 32 et seqq.) within the meaning of the DSA are also likely to be categorised as ancillary services, as they were explicitly listed as examples in the Council's draft.[42] However, the final version does not include those examples explicitly.

2. Political advertising publisher, Art. 3 no. 13 PAR

22 According to Art. 3 no. 13 PAR, a 'political advertising publisher' is defined as a 'provider of political advertising service that publishes, delivers or disseminates political advertising through any medium'. Following the logic of the definition, publishers of political advertising are always also a provider of political advertising. The publisher attribute is narrower than the provider attribute and typically occurs at the end of the chain of political advertising. Therefore, the PAR considers **publishers as key actors** with specific, additional requirements.[43] In particular, **online platforms** that offer political advertising services are likely to fall under this definition as they usually serve — at the end of the chain — as the interface with the public.

3. Sponsor, Art. 3 no. 10 PAR

23 A **'sponsor'** within the meaning of the PAR is a 'natural or legal person at whose request or on **whose behalf** a political advertisement is prepared, placed, promoted, published, delivered or disseminated'. Consequently, sponsors are usually at the **beginning of each chain** and are often **political actors**. However, political advertising can also be sponsored by other actors.

---

[38] Di Fabio MMR 2024, 467 (470).

[39] Di Fabio MMR 2024, 467 (470 et seq.).

[40] Rec. 38(1)(1) PAR.

[41] Rec. 39 PAR.

[42] Council, 'Outcome of proceedings', 13.12.2022, 16013/1/22 REV 1, p. 12 rec. 26; Di Fabio MMR 2024, 467 (470).

[43] Rec. 42 PAR.

4. Controller, Art. 3 no. 14 PAR

The PAR adopts the definition of a **'controller'** from the **GDPR**[44] and, where applicable, the GDPR for EU institutions[45]. As **platform operators** typically fall under those definitions, they are also usually subject to the obligations for controllers contained in Chapter III (→ mn. 70 et seqq.). 24

C. General requirements for political advertising services, Art. 5 PAR

As part of the regulation's general provisions, Art. 5 PAR establishes **general requirements** for the provision of political advertising services (→ mn. 18) in the EU, containing a **principle of non-discrimination** (→ mn. 26 et seqq.) and a **temporary ban of foreign-controlled political advertising services** (→ mn. 29 et seqq.). 25

I. Principle of non-discrimination, Art. 5(1) PAR

According to Art. 5(1) PAR, providers of political advertising services (→ mn. 18 et seqq.) are not allowed to make the provision of their services subject to **discriminatory restrictions** solely based on the **place of residence** or **establishment** of the sponsor. In particular, they are not permitted to restrict the provision of their services to a 'European political party'[46] or a political group in the European Parliament, solely on the basis of its place of establishment, except where the difference of treatment is justified and proportionate in accordance with Union law.[47] 26

This considers the fact that the European political parties are playing a **key role** in contributing to forming European political awareness and in expressing the will of citizens of the Union as set out in Art. 10(4) TEU.[48] 27

Unlike the rest of the PAR (→ mn. 4), according to Art. 30(2)(1) PAR, Art. 5(1) PAR applies together with Art. 3 PAR from the date of the **regulation's entry** into force (i.e. since 9 April 2024). 28

[44] Art. 4 no. 7 of Regulation (EU) 2016/679 of the European Parliament and of the Council of 27 April 2016 on the protection of natural persons with regard to the processing of personal data and on the free movement of such data, and repealing Directive 95/46/EC (General Data Protection Act), OJ 2016 L 119, 1 ('GDPR'): "controller' means the natural or legal person, public authority, agency or other body which, alone or jointly with others, determines the purposes and means of the processing of personal data; where the purposes and means of such processing are determined by Union or Member State law, the controller or the specific criteria for its nomination may be provided for by Union or Member State law'.

[45] See Art. 3 no. 8 of Regulation (EU) 2018/1725 of the European Parliament and of the Council of 23 October 2018 on the protection of natural persons with regard to the processing of personal data by the Union institutions, bodies, offices and agencies and on the free movement of such data, and repealing Regulation (EC) No 45/2001 and Decision No 1247/2002/EC, OJ 2018 L 295, 39 ('GDPR for EU institutions').

[46] Refers to 'European political party' as defined in Art. 2 no. 3 of Regulation (EU, Euratom) 1141/2014 of the European Parliament and of the Council of 22 October 2014 on the statute and funding of European political parties and European political foundations, OJ 2016 L 317, 1.

[47] Rec. 18(1)(3) PAR.

[48] Rec. 19(1)(5) PAR.

II. Temporary ban of foreign-controlled political advertising services, Art. 5(2) PAR

29 Furthermore, Art. 5(2) PAR contains a temporary ban of foreign-controlled political advertising in the last **three months** before an election. During this period, the provision of political advertising services pertaining to that election is only permitted to a sponsor or service provider acting on behalf of a sponsor, who declares itself to be:

- a **citizen of the Union** (Art. 5(2)(a) PAR),
- a third-country nationals **permanently residing** in the Union with the **right to vote** in that election (Art. 5(2)(b) PAR), or
- a **legal person established in the Union** which is not controlled by third-country entities (Art. 5(2)(c) PAR).

30 In order to facilitate **compliance** with the **three-month period**, Art. 26(2) PAR provides a **public portal** through which the Member States are required to indicate the dates of their elections immediately following the announcement. If an election is announced less than three months in advance, the time period only applies from the date of the announcement.[49] This ensures that prior political advertising does not constitute a violation of the PAR before the election is announced.

31 The three-month period is only a **minimum European standard**.[50] Member States are free to adopt stricter rules, especially longer time periods, as the risk of foreign influence on elections varies from one Member State to another. Therefore, platform providers should continue to **monitor national laws**. However, many Member States are expected to stick to the three-month period to contribute to the overall objective of establishing a harmonised legal framework for political advertising within the EU.

D. Transparency and due diligence obligations, Art. 6–17 PAR

32 To ensure transparency of political advertising and thus increase **voter maturity**, chapter II (Art. 6 et seqq. PAR) contains several new **transparency** and **due diligence obligations** for providers (→ mn. 18 et seqq.), publishers (→ mn. 22) and sponsors (→ mn. 23) of political advertising.

I. Identification of political advertising services, Art. 7 PAR

33 In the future, the initial challenge for providers of political advertising services will be to determine whether an advertisement must be classified as political advertising. This **classification** is of **significant importance**, as the applicability of the PAR depends on it (→ mn. 7). Thus, the PAR requires a specific procedure for the identification of political advertising services.

34 According to Art. 7(1)(1) PAR, providers of advertising services shall request a **declaration** from sponsors and providers of advertising services acting on behalf of sponsors as to whether the advertising service that they have requested constitutes a political advertising service within the meaning of Art. 3 no. 5 PAR (→ mn. 18) and whether they fulfil any of the requirements under Art. 5(2) (→ mn. 29).

---

[49] Rec. 19(1)(8) PAR.
[50] Rec. 19(1)(7) PAR.

According to Art. 7(2)(1) PAR[51], providers of political advertising services are obliged to ensure that the **contractual arrangements** concluded for the provision of a political advertising service require the sponsors and providers acting on behalf of sponsors to provide the above-mentioned declaration and additionally the relevant information necessary to comply with Art. 9(1) (→ mn. 40), 11(1) (→ mn. 41 et seqq.) and 12(1) PAR (→ mn. 44 et seqq.). These arrangements should ensure the information is transmitted in **good faith**, in a **complete** and **accurate** manner, and without undue delay.[52] 35

In principle, the provider may rely on the information provided in accordance with Art. 7(1) PAR, as the declarants are responsible for the accuracy of their declarations. Providers have **no general obligation** to monitor the truthfulness of declarations concerning the political nature of advertisements or to engage in excessive or costly fact-finding exercises.[53] Only if the declaration or information submitted is **manifestly erroneous**, is the provider obliged to require the sponsor, or provider acting on behalf of a sponsor, to correct that declaration or information (Art. 7(4)(1) PAR). This should always be assumed if the error is apparent from the content of the advertisement, the identity of the sponsor, or the context in which the relevant service is provided.[54] 36

In the event that the provider identifies a manifestly erroneous declaration or information and requests a **correction**, the sponsor, or provider acting on behalf of sponsor, must make such correction complete and accurate without undue delay (Art. 7(4)(2) PAR). In general, all parties are obliged to notify the relevant element in the chain of political advertising if they become aware that any information transmitted has changed, is incomplete, or inaccurate (for details see Art. 6(3) PAR). 37

To efficiently implement the requirement to complement, update, or correct the declaration or information, providers of political advertising services, should adapt their **online interfaces** to facilitate compliance with such obligations (Art. 7(5) PAR).[55] 38

If the publisher of political advertising is also a **very large online platform** or a **very large online search engine** within the meaning of Art. 33(1) DSA (→ § 2 mn. 55 et seqq.), it should, as part of its risk assessments under Art. 34 DSA (→ § 6 mn. 32 et seqq.), diligently identify, analyse, and assess any systemic risks that their political advertising services pose and put in place reasonable, proportionate, and effective mitigation measures in accordance with Art. 35 DSA to address those risks.[56] 39

II. Record-keeping obligations, Art. 9 PAR

Providers of political advertising services must retain the information listed in Art. 9(1) PAR 'to the extent necessary to comply with this Regulation' for **seven years**[57] and make reasonable efforts to ensure completeness and accuracy. This obligation does not apply to **micro-undertakings**[58] provided that the provision of advertising services is purely marginal and ancillary to their main activities (Art. 9(4) PAR). 40

---

[51] See also Art. 6(2) PAR.

[52] Rec. 44(1)(1) PAR.

[53] Rec. 44(1)(3) PAR.

[54] Rec. 45 PAR.

[55] Rec. 44(1)(4) PAR.

[56] Rec. 46 PAR.

[57] According to Art. 9(3) PAR, the period starts with the date of the last preparation, placement, promotion, publication, delivery or dissemination.

[58] As defined in Art. 3(1) of Directive 2013/34/EU of the European Parliament and of the Council of 26 June 2013 on the annual financial statements, consolidated financial statements and related reports of certain types of undertakings, amending Directive 2006/43/EC of the European Parliament and of the Coun-

III. Labelling and transparency requirements for political advertisement, Art. 11 PAR

41 Art. 11 PAR constitutes the heart of the new transparency requirements for political advertising. It requires political advertising publishers (→ mn. 22) to link every advertisement to **specific transparency information**. According to Art. 11(1) PAR, political advertising publishers must ensure that each political advertisement is made available together with the following information:

- a statement that it is a political advertisement (Art. 11(1)(a) PAR),
- the **identity** of the sponsor of the political advertisement and, where applicable, the entity ultimately controlling the sponsor (Art. 11(1)(b) PAR),
- where applicable, the election[59], legislative or regulatory process to which the political advertisement is linked (Art. 11(1)(c) PAR),
- where applicable, a statement to the effect that the political advertisement has been subject to targeting[60] or ad-delivery techniques[61] (Art. 11(1)(d) PAR), and
- a **transparency notice** (→ mn. 44 et seqq.) or a clear indication of where it can be easily and directly retrieved (Art. 11(1)(e) PAR).

42 The **labelling** must be prominent, clearly, saliently, and unambiguously in the form of labels adapted to the medium used and shall remain if the advertisement is further disseminated (e.g. being posted on another platform or is forwarded between individuals)[62]. The Commission will adopt **implementing acts** establishing the **format** and the **template** of the labels for the different media by 10 July 2025.

43 The manner in which the publisher obtains the information mentioned above is specified in Art. 10 PAR. Generally, the providers of political advertising services are obliged to provide the publisher with the necessary information in a **timely**, **complete**, and **accurate manner** and to indicate any changes. When the political advertising publisher is the only provider of political advertising services within the chain, the responsibility lies with the sponsor (Art. 10(1) subpara. 3).

IV. Transparency notice, Art. 12 PAR

44 As mentioned above, the transparency notice is part of the labelling requirements set out in Art. 11 PAR. While the **information named in Art. 11(1)(a)–(d) PAR** must always be **directly available** in the political advertisement itself to ensure that certain basic information is conveyed immediately when perceiving the advertisement, the **transparency notice** does not have to be directly included in the advertisement. According to Art. 11(1)(e) PAR, an indication of where the transparency notice can be found is sufficient, which reflects the fact that the transparency notice provides more detailed infor-

---

cil and repealing Council Directives 78/660/EEC and 83/349/EEC, OJ 2013 L 182, 19 ('Directive 2013/34/EU').

[59] See fn. 19.

[60] According to Art. 3 no. 11 PAR, 'targeting techniques' are 'techniques that are used to address a political advertisement only to a specific person or group of persons, or to exclude them, on the basis of the processing of personal data'.

[61] According to Art. 3 no. 12 PAR, 'ad-delivery techniques' means 'optimisation techniques that are used to increase the circulation, reach or visibility of a political advertisement on the basis of the automated processing of personal data and that can serve to deliver the political advertisement to a specific person or group of persons only'.

[62] Rec. 62(1)(2) PAR.

mation and will therefore generally be so extensive that it is often not useful to include it directly in the advertisement. In the context of online political advertising, a **hyperlink** to a website with the transparency notice appears to be particularly suitable.

The required information is listed in Art. 12(1) PAR and partly corresponds to the information required under Art. 11 PAR (→ mn. 41). However, Art. 12(1) PAR requires more detailed information, in particular: 45

- further contact details (name, e-mail address, if applicable, postal address/place of establishment) of the sponsor, the entity ultimately controlling the sponsor and, if different, the person providing remuneration in exchange for the political advertisement (Art. 12(1)(a)–(b) PAR),
- the dissemination period (Art. 12(1)(c) PAR),
- any **linked election**, legislative or regulatory process (if applicable, together with a link to information from official sources) (Art. 12(1)(g)–(h) PAR),
- the **amount spent** for and the value of other benefits received in part or full exchange for the specific advertisement as well for the entire political advertising campaign and their source (public or private, from inside or outside the Union) as well as the methodology used for the calculation (Art. 12(1)(d)–(f) PAR),
- where applicable and technically feasible, the reach of the political advertisement in terms of the number of views and of engagement with the political advertisement[63] (Art. 12(1)(m) PAR), and
- other information to ensure the fairness of the dissemination of the political advertisement.

According to Art. 12(2) subpara. 2 PAR, transparency notices must be kept **up to date** throughout the period of publication of the political advertisement and be presented in a **machine-readable format** if the advertisement is made available electronically. 46

The **retention period** is seven years (Art. 12(4) PAR), except for micro-undertakings[64] provided that the provision of advertising services is purely marginal and ancillary to their main activities (Art. 12(5) PAR). 47

Since the Commission is empowered to add points to the list of Art. 12(1) PAR, affected parties should regularly check the list for **future additions** and adjustments. In addition, the Commission will adopt **implementing acts** by 10 July 2025 establishing the format of and provide technical specifications for the transparency notice to ensure that it is adapted to the medium used (Art. 12(7) PAR). 48

V. European repository for online political advertisements, Art. 13 PAR

Art. 13(1) PAR provides for the creation of a **European public repository** by the Commission containing all online political advertisements published in the Union or directed to Union citizens or residents in the Union and the information provided by the publishers referred to in Art. 12(1) (→ mn. 45). 49

Publishers of political advertising that are **very large online platforms** or **very large online search engines** (→ § 2 mn. 55 et seqq.) are obliged to make each political advertisement together with the above-mentioned information available in a repository, as re- 50

[63] According to Rec. 58(1)(2) 'the reach of the message' relates to data which enables quantifying geographical distribution and number of individuals who viewed, received or otherwise interacted with the political advertising, including the number of views, impressions and clicks.

[64] As defined in Art. 3(1) of Directive 2013/34/EU.

ferred to in Art. 39 DSA (→ § 4 mn. 52 et seqq.), and enable access to that information through the European repository from the moment of publication until seven years after the advertisement was last presented on their online interfaces (Art. 13(2) PAR).

51 **Other publishers** of political advertising that publish political advertisements through an online service are obliged to make that information available in the European repository no later than **72 hours** after the first publication of the political advertisement (Art. 13(3) PAR). In order to facilitate the sharing of information, the Commission will establish a hosting service through which the information can be uploaded **free of charge** (Art. 13(1)(b) PAR) and, by April 2026, adopt **implementing acts** to set out detailed arrangements for the provision of a common data structure and standardised metadata (Art. 13(6) PAR).

52 By uploading the information, publishers of political advertising are not released from their **responsibility** to ensure that the information is correct and remain up to date.[65]

VI. Periodic reporting on political advertising services, Art. 14 PAR

53 According to Art. 14(1) PAR, publishers of political advertising[66] are obliged to include in their **management report**[67] information on the amounts or the value of other benefits received in part or full exchange for the services provided, including on the use of targeting techniques and ad-delivery techniques, aggregated by campaign, and make the information available to the competent authorities.

VII. Indication of non-compliant political advertisements, Art. 15 PAR

54 Art. 15 PAR contains certain requirements for publishers of political advertising regarding the establishment of a **notification mechanism** for potential non-compliant political advertisements (→ mn. 55 et seqq.) and the handling of such notifications (→ mn. 59 et seqq.).

1. Obligation to set up a notification mechanism, Art. 15(1)–(3) PAR

55 Art. 15(1)–(2) PAR states that publishers of political advertising must provide a **free, user-friendly mechanism** for reporting **potentially non-compliant political advertisements**. This mechanism should be accessible from the transparency notice (→ mn. 44 et seqq.) and, where technically possible, allow indications to be made electronically (Art. 15(2) PAR) with a substantiated explanation, information enabling the identification of the political advertisement, and the name and e-mail address of the submitting person (Art. 15(3) PAR).

56 It is recommended – where necessary – to put in place **technical measures** to ensure minimum information technology security standards, including measures to prevent automated notifications.[68] Otherwise, in individual cases, complying with the obligations regarding the handling of notifications (→ mn. 59 et seqq.) could become difficult.

[65] Rec. 64(1)(5) PAR; cf. Art. 13(5) PAR.

[66] This does not apply to micro, small or medium-sized undertakings qualifying under Art. 3(1), (2) and (3) of Directive 2013/34/EU.

[67] See Art. 19 of Directive 2013/34/EU.

[68] Rec. 69(1)(5) PAR.

If a political advertising publisher is, with regard to the political advertisements hosted at the request of the recipients of their services, also an **online hosting service provider** within the meaning of the DSA (→ § 5 mn. 8 et seqq.), he should be able to rely on the notice and action mechanisms pursuant to that Regulation (→ § 5 mn. 18 et seqq.) for notifications concerning non-compliance of such advertisements with this Regulation.[69] **57**

In the future, the Commission is expected to develop **guidelines** to support the preparation of suitable technical specifications for the mechanisms, adapted for audio-visual and printed media as well as online and offline advertising.[70] This should ensure a consistent **implementation** of notification mechanisms.[71] **58**

2. Handling of notifications, Art. 15(4)–(10) PAR

The **receipt** of a notification must be **confirmed** by the publisher to the submitting person **without undue delay** (Art. 15(4) PAR). **59**

If the publisher is a **very large online platform** or **very large online search engine** (→ § 2 mn. 55 et seqq.), he must examine and address the received notification in a diligent, non-arbitrary and objective manner without undue delay (Art. 15(5)(a) PAR) and inform the submitting person on the follow-up given to it (Art. 15(5)(b) PAR). **60**

Other publishers are only obliged to make best efforts to examine and address the notifications in the manner described (Art. 15(6)(a) PAR) and inform the submitting person at least upon request (Art. 15(6)(b) PAR).[72] **61**

According to Art. 15(9) PAR, all publishers, regardless of their size, must without undue delay **inform** the **sponsor** or **provider** of a political advertising service, of any measures they take following notifications made under this Article, that affect the availability, or the presentation of the political advertisement concerned. **62**

The **requirements** for handling notifications are significantly **stricter** in the **month leading up to** the relevant **election**. According to Art. 15(7) PAR, publishers are then obligated to examine and address such notifications in the above-described manner within **48 hours**. This does not apply to incomplete reports that cannot be fully processed based on the information provided. However, in this situation it appears to be advisable to confirm receipt of this notification within 48 hours and inform the submitting person that information is missing for complete processing. Otherwise, a lack of response within the 48-hour period could be considered a violation of the PAR. **63**

The 48-hour period does not apply to publishers qualifying as **micro, small,** or **medium-sized undertakings** (Art. 3(1), (2) and (3) of Directive 2013/34/EU). They are obliged to make **best efforts** to process any notification that they receive regarding a political advertisement linked to that election referendum without undue delay. **64**

Art. 15(10) PAR allows publishers to respond to **multiple notifications** regarding the same advertisement or advertising campaign collectively, including by making use of automated tools or by making an announcement on their website referring to the notifications concerned. **65**

---

[69] Rec. 69(1)(5) PAR.

[70] Rec. 70 PAR.

[71] Rec. 70 PAR.

[72] However, political advertising publishers qualifying as micro-undertakings under Art. 3(1) of Directive 2013/34/EU are only obliged to make best efforts to ensure their compliance with this point.

VIII. Transmission obligations, Art. 16–17 PAR

66 At the **request** of the **competent national authorities** or other **interested entities** specified in Art. 17(2) PAR (e.g. journalists) providers of political advertising services must transmit the requested information to the extent described in Art. 16(1) PAR (request by national authority) or Art. 17(1) PAR (request by other interested entity).

67 According to Art. 16(3) PAR, in the event of a **request from national authorities**, providers of political advertising services are obliged to **acknowledge receipt** of that request within **two working days**, indicate the steps taken to comply with it, and **provide** the **requested information** within **eight working** days.[73] In the **last month preceding an election**, the requested information, which is in the possession of the provider, must be provided without undue delay and no later than **48 hours** (Art. 16(4)(1) PAR).[74] For the interaction with the authorities, an appropriate **contact point** must be designated, which may also be an external natural person in the case of micro, small or medium-sized undertakings[75].

68 In contrast, the requirements for responding to requests from **other interested parties** are significantly lower. In particular, there is a maximum period of **one month** for the provision of the requested information (Art. 17(3) PAR), which is not reduced within the last month before an election. In addition, an **acknowledgement of receipt** is **not required**. However, the information, in principle, must be provided **free of charge**. Only if the processing of the request entails significant costs, the provider of political advertising services may charge a fee that does not exceed the administrative costs (Art. 17(6) PAR). They are also allowed to aggregate the relevant amounts or place them in a range to the extent necessary to protect their **commercial legitimate interests** (Art. 17(4) PAR).

69 If requests from other interested parties are unclear, excessive or seek information that is no in the provider's possession, the provider has the **right to refuse** the request, providing the requesting party with a reasoned response and with means of redress, including, where applicable, those that exist under Directive (EU) 2020/1828[76] (Art. 17(5) PAR).

E. Targeting and ad-delivery requirements, Art. 18–20 PAR

70 Chapter III (Art. 18 et seq. PAR) deals with **targeting**[77] and **ad-delivery**[78] **techniques** of online political advertising, which makes it highly relevant for platform providers. It contains **specific requirements** for targeting and ad-delivery techniques

[73] The period of eight working days does not apply to providers of political advertising services qualifying as micro, small or medium-sized undertakings under Art. 3(1), (2) and (3) of Directive 2013/34/EU; they are obliged to make reasonable efforts to provide the requested information within 12 working days and thereafter, without undue delay (Art. 16(3)(3) PAR).

[74] This does not apply to providers of political advertising services qualifying as micro or small undertakings under Art. 3(1) and (2) of Directive 2013/34/EU; they are obliged to provide the requested information that is in their possession without undue delay and where possible before the date of the election or referendum (Art. 16(4)(2) PAR).

[75] Within the meaning of Art. 3(1), (2) and (3) of Directive 2013/34/EU.

[76] Directive (EU) 2020/1828 of the European Parliament and of the Council of 25 November 2020 on representative actions for the protection of the collective interests of consumers and repealing Directive 2009/22/EC, OJ 2020 L 409, 1.

[77] See fn. 60; see also Egidy, ZG 2022, 334 on the microtargeting of political advertising in the European democracy.

[78] See fn. 61.

(→ mn. 71 et seqq.) as well as **additional transparency requirements** (→ mn. 82 et seqq.).

I. Specific requirements related to targeting techniques and ad-delivery techniques, Art. 18 PAR

Art. 18 PAR sets out **specific requirements** regarding the use of targeting and ad-delivery techniques in the context of online political advertising. 71

1. General requirements for the use of personal data, Art. 18(1) PAR

Art. 18(1) PAR states that targeting techniques or ad-delivery techniques involving the processing of personal data are only permitted if the following conditions are met: 72

- the controller collected the personal **data from the data subject** (Art. 18(1)(a) PAR),
- the data subject has provided **'explicit consent'**[79] to the processing of personal data separately for the purpose of political advertising (Art. 18(1)(b) PAR), and
- those techniques do not involve **'profiling'**[80] using **'special categories of personal data'**[81] (Art. 18(1)(c) PAR).

It follows from the first condition that **personal data** received by a controller **from third parties** are not allowed to be used for targeting or ad-delivery techniques. 73

In addition, the use of personal data requires **explicit consent, separately** for the purpose of political advertising. According to Art. 18(4)(a) PAR, the controller must ensure that the data subject is not requested to consent if it is already indicated by **automated means** that consent will not be given unless the request is justified by a substantial change of circumstances. This allows users to opt out of personalised political advertising generally via a **browsers default setting** ('do not track'). 74

Controllers are not allowed to make their service dependent on consent. Users, who have not given their consent, must be offered an **equivalent alternative** for using the online service without receiving political advertising (Art. 18(4)(b) PAR). This constitutes a ban of so-called **'tracking walls'**, which require a user to make a **'take-it-or-leave-it choice'** and implements a judgement of the European Court of Justice.[82] 75

Eventual, Art. 18(1) PAR establishes with its third condition an **absolute ban** of the use of techniques based on **profiling** using **special categories** of **personal data**, which encompasses profiling using special categories of personal data evaluated from personal data that are not themselves special categories of personal data.[83] 76

---

[79] As understood within the GDPR and GDPR for EU institutions.

[80] As defined in Art. 4 no. 4 GDPR and in Art. 3 no. 5 GDPR for EU institutions: ''profiling' means any form of automated processing of personal data consisting of the use of personal data to evaluate certain personal aspects relating to a natural person, in particular to analyse or predict aspects concerning that natural person's performance at work, economic situation, health, personal preferences, interests, reliability, behaviour, location or movements'.

[81] As referred to in Art. 9(1) GDPR and in Art. 10(1) GDPR for EU institutions: 'Processing of personal data revealing racial or ethnic origin, political opinions, religious or philosophical beliefs, or trade union membership, and the processing of genetic data, biometric data for the purpose of uniquely identifying a natural person, data concerning health or data concerning a natural person's sex life or sexual orientation shall be prohibited'.

[82] Judgment of the Court of Justice of 4 July 2023, Meta Platforms and Others (Conditions générales d'utilisation d'un réseau social), C-252/21, ECLI:EU:C:2023:537; Rec. 81 PAR.

[83] Rec. 79(1)(1) PAR.

77 This could be the case, for instance, where the user of a **social network** visits a particular page or uses an application that relates to one of the categories referred to in Art. 9(1) GDPR and provides personal data in the course of interacting with the social network.[84] The processing of those personal data constitutes a **'processing of special categories of personal data'** within the meaning of Art. 18(1) PAR and is, therefore, in principle prohibited where that data processing allows information falling within one of those categories to be revealed, irrespective of whether that information concerns a user of that social network or any other natural person, regardless of whether the data subject was made aware of the intention to use such data for the purpose of targeting or ad-delivery of political advertisements at the time that it was collected.[85]

78 The ban also applies to the **exceptional cases** mentioned in Art. 9(2) GDPR and Art. 10(2) GDPR for EU institutions.[86] Therefore, even **explicit consent** (Art. 9(2)(a) GDPR, Art. 10(2)(a) GDPR for EU institutions) **cannot override the ban**, nor can the controller rely on 'legitimate interests' in this context.

2. Ban of targeting and ad-delivery techniques on very young people, Art. 18(2) PAR

79 Notwithstanding compliance with the above requirements, the use of targeting and ad-delivery techniques that involve the processing of personal data of a data subject that is known by the controller with **reasonable certainty** to be at least **one year under the voting age** established by national rules is prohibited (Art. 18(2)(1) PAR). This ban is intended to take account of the fact that **very young people** constitute a particularly **vulnerable group** that can be exploited through the misuse of targeting and ad-delivery techniques.[87]

80 Neither the legal text nor the recitals define more precisely when the controller must assume a certain age with reasonable certainty. Art. 18(2)(2) PAR merely states that the controller is **not obliged** to **process additional personal** data to assess whether the data subject is one year under the voting age. The lack of a more precise definition creates **legal uncertainty** for controllers that will have to be resolved by case law. Until then, it is advisable to assume reasonable certainty at an earlier stage than a later one.

81 The requirement implies that controllers must always **check the voting age** for the election they are advertising for and, if necessary, **adjust** their **algorithms** accordingly.

II. Additional transparency requirements, Art. 19 PAR

82 Controllers must meet **additional transparency requirements** when using targeting or ad-delivery techniques in the context of **online political advertising** involving the processing of **personal data**. According to Art. 19(1) PAR, the following additional requirements must be met:

- the adoption and implementation of an **internal** (publicly available) **policy** describing clearly and in plain language how the techniques are used, and retain such policy for a period of seven years from the last use of those techniques (Art. 19(1)(a) PAR),
- keeping records of their use (Art. 19(1)(b) PAR),

---

[84] Rec. 79(1)(1) PAR.
[85] Rec. 79(1)(4) and (5) PAR.
[86] Rec. 77(1)(2) PAR.
[87] Rec. 82 PAR.

- providing, together with the indication that an advertisement is a political advertisement, any additional information necessary to enable the data subject to understand the logic involved[88] (specified in Art. 19(1)(c) PAR),
- carrying out an **annual risk assessment** of the use of these techniques in relation to fundamental rights and freedoms (Art. 19(1)(d) PAR), and
- provide, together with the political advertisement, unless it is included in the transparency notice (→ mn. 44 et seqq.), a **reference to effective means** of support individuals exercise their rights under the GDPR and the GDPR for EU institutions, which is to include a link to an interface allowing for the exercise of such rights (Art. 19(1)(e) PAR).

The various parties involved (i.e. the controller, the publisher of political advertising and the provider of political advertising) are obliged to **provide information** to the extent necessary (i.e. when there is no personal identity) for a party to comply with those obligations (Art. 19(2) and (3) PAR). **83**

Since the Commission is empowered to add points to the above-mentioned list (Art. 19(5) PAR), affected parties should regularly check the list for **future additions**. **84**

F. Supervision and enforcement, Art. 21–26 PAR

Chapter IV then deals with the **supervision** and **enforcement** (Art. 21 et seqq. PAR). **85**

Art. 21(1) PAR stipulates the obligation of **political advertising service providers** who are **not based in the EU** to designate, in writing, a natural or legal person as its **legal representative** in one of the Member States where that provider offers its services. **86**

In addition, according to Art. 25(1) PAR, the Member States will lay down rules on **sanctions** or **other measures** on sponsors and providers of political advertising services for infringements of the PAR. The **maximum** amount of the financial penalties is generally set at **6 % of the annual income or budget** (whichever is highest) or **6 % of the annual worldwide turnover** (Art. 25(2) PAR). The exact amount of a sanction will depend on the specific circumstances of each case. **Relevant factors** are, for example, the nature, gravity and duration of the infringement, the intentional character of the infringement, actions taken to mitigate damage and the degree of cooperation with the competent authority. **87**

For **infringements** of the obligations laid down in **Art. 18** (→ mn. 71 et seqq.) **and 19** (→ mn. 82 et seqq.) PAR, the supervisory authorities referred to in Art. 51 GDPR may within their competence impose **fines** in line with Art. 83 of GDPR and up to the amount referred to in Art. 83(5) GDPR (Art. 25(6) PAR). **88**

[88] Rec. 83(1)(2) PAR.

Index

Bold numbers refer to articles, normal ones to margin numbers.